FILM NOIR

the encyclopedia

FILM NOIR
THE ENCYCLOPEDIA

◇

edited by
Alain Silver • Elizabeth Ward
James Ursini • Robert Porfirio
Co-editor: Carl Macek

Designed by Bernard Schleifer

OVERLOOK DUCKWORTH
New York • London

ACKNOWLEDGMENTS

For invaluable assistance in viewing additional films which at the time were otherwise unavailable from the classic period, thanks primarily to the late David Bradley, the Mark Haggard Archives of Sherman Oaks, and also to Lee Sanders and Glenn Erickson. For helping define Neo-Noir and offering numerous suggestions, Todd Erickson. Other helpful comments and assistance came from filmmakers, among them directors Walter Hill, Noel Black, Mark Rutland, Carl Colpaert, Kurt Voss, Christopher Coppola, Gary Walkow, and the late directors John Flynn, Budd Boetticher, Andre De Toth and Robert Wise. Producers Zane Levitt, Lawrence Bender, Dan Hassid, Alexander W. Kogan, Jr., and Dan Ireland also merit mention. For putting up with countless hours of noir playback in VHS, DVD, and most recently DVR formats, all of which could fill the room with screams and gunshots late into the night, a special thank you to Linda Brookover.

As before the research on this edition would have been much harder to accomplish without the existence of the Margaret Herrick Library of the Academy of Motion Picture Arts and Science and its most helpful staff. Additional research was done at the Beverly Hills Public Library and on-line mostly using the Internet Movie Database (imdb.com). Unfortunately many of the errors of earlier editions have found there way onto IMDB and other databases, so we hope that the repairs made herein will help to correct those.

Of course, none of these editions would have been possible without the persistence of vision of our publisher Peter Mayer and the support of a long line of editors at Overlook Press from Mark Gompertz on.

Since the First Edition was published scores of persons whose names do not appear here have contributed directly and indirectly to the Editors' ongoing journey through the heart of noir. In some early instances, the mere expression of enthusiasm about this book helped those of us responsible for it to sustain our interest, which has naturally waxed and waned over the decades. More recently from the various producers of our DVD commentaries to a host of e-mail correspondents, many new voices have been added. Since we cannot hope to recall all the names, we must leave it at that.

This Volume is fondly dedicated to the memory of our colleagues: Jonathan Benair, Art Lyons, and Bill McVicar

This edition first published in hardcover in the United States in 2010 by Overlook Duckworth, Peter Mayer Publishers, Inc,

New York:
Overlook
141 Wooster Street
New York, NY 10012
www.overlookpress.com
For bulk and special sales, please contact sales@overlookny.com

London:
Duckworth
90-93 Cowcross Street
London EC1M 6BF
www.ducknet.co.uk
inquiries@duckworth-publishers.co.uk

Cataloging-in-Publication Data is available from the Library of Congress

Book design and typeformatting by Bernard Schleifer
Manufactured in the United States of America
First Edition
10 9 8 7 6 5 4 3 2
ISBN 978-1-59020-144-2 (US)
ISBN 978-0-7156-3880-4 (UK)

CONTENTS

◇

CONTRIBUTORS   6

PREFACE   11

PART ONE: The Classic Period
   INTRODUCTION: The Classic Period   17
   The Films - A to Z   23
   Sidebars
      GERMAN INFLUENCE & PROTO-NOIR   41
      FATAL MEN   164
      WHERE DANGER LIVES   322
   Appendix
      Chronology   343

PART TWO: Neo-Noir
   INTRODUCTION: Neo-Noir   349
   The Films - A to Z   351
   Sidebar
      Neo-Noir/Retro-Noir   365

Bibliography   469

Index   475

CONTRIBUTORS

◇

EDITORS

AS—ALAIN SILVER wrote *The Samurai Film*, a dozen other books with James Ursini or Elizabeth Ward, and co-edited six Readers on noir, horror and gangster films. His articles have appeared in *Film Comment, Movie, Wide Angle*, anthologies on *The Philosophy of Film Noir* and Akira Kurosawa and the on-line magazines *Images* and *Senses of Cinema*. His screenplay adaptations include Dostoevsky's *White Nights* and the Showtime MOW *Time at the Top*. He has also produced a score of independent feature films and forty soundtrack albums. His commentaries may be heard and seen on numerous DVDs discussing the classic period, Raymond Chandler, and the gangster film. His Ph.D. in motion picture critical studies is from UCLA.

BP—ROBERT PORFIRIO received a M.A. in Film from UCLA and completed his doctoral work at Yale University with his seminal dissertation, *The Dark Age of American Film: A Study of American Film Noir (1940-1960)*, in 1979. He is an editor of *Film Noir Reader 3* and contributed articles to the other three volumes in the series. He also contributed to *The Noir Style* and wrote the forward to *The Philosophy of Film Noir*. He was formerly assistant professor of American Studies at California State University, Fullerton, where he taught the first accredited course in film noir beginning in 1973. He currently resides in France where he spends idle moments viewing rare French film noirs.

EW—ELIZABETH WARD co-wrote *Raymond Chandler's Los Angeles, Robert Aldrich*, and *The Film Director's Team* with Alain Silver as well as an essay on Leigh Brackett for *American Screenwriters*, an introduction to noir for the *Los Angeles Times*, and an interview with Walter Hill for *Movie*. She has worked as a production manager and assistant director in feature films and series television and is presently a researcher in Northern California. She has done on-camera commentary on Raymond Chandler, *Double Indemnity*, and for the Warner Bros. Film Noir Collection Vol. 4 which includes audio tracks on *Mystery Street* and *Tension* with Audrey Totter.

JU—JAMES URSINI co-wrote *The Noir Style, L.A. Noir, The Vampire Film, More Things than Are Dreamt Of*, and director studies of David Lean, Robert Aldrich, and Roger Corman with Alain Silver. His other books include *Modern Amazons, Cinema of Obsession, Femme Fatale* and monographs on Bogart, Dietrich, Elizabeth Taylor, Mae West, and De Niro for the Taschen Icon series. His seminal book on Preston Sturges was reprinted by the San Sebastián Film Festival. His film noir DVD commentaries include *Out of the Past, The Dark Corner, Nightmare Alley, Lady in the Lake, Kiss of Death, Brute Force* and *Crossfire*. He has been a producer on features and documentaries, and lectured on filmmaking at UCLA and at other colleges in the Los Angeles area where he works as an educator.

CO-EDITOR

CM—CARL MACEK has written original screenplays for several feature-length animated films, produced the television series *Robotech* for Harmony Gold U.S.A. and formed his own distribution company, Streamline Pictures, which released films such as *Akira* and *Vampire Hunter D*. Previously he was West Coast editor of *MediaScene*, a contributing author for McGill's Survey of the Cinema, and the author of *The Art of Heavy Metal: Animation for the Eighties; Robotech Art 3: The Sentinels*, as well as the novel *War Eagles* based on a story by Merian C. Cooper. He was also the original curator of the Archive of Popular Culture, California State University at Fullerton from which he graduated with a degree in the Theory and Criticism of Visual Media.

CONTRIBUTORS

AJS—AEON SKOBLE is Professor of Philosophy and Chair of the Philosophy Department at Bridgewater State College, in Massachusetts. He is the author of *Deleting the State: An Argument about Government*, and co-editor of *Political Philosophy: Essential Selections, The Simpsons and Philosophy*, and *Woody Allen and Philosophy*. In addition to his work in moral and political philosophy, he writes frequently on philosophical aspects of popular culture, including such subjects as superheroes, science fiction, Tolkien, Hitchcock, Scorsese, classic film noir, and neo-noir, and he has recently co-edited *The Philosophy of TV Noir*.

AL—ART LYONS wrote more than twenty books, mostly mystery novels in Jacob Ashe detective series, such as *The Dead are Discreet, Dead Ringer, Three On a Bullet*, and *Castles Burning* which become the movie-of-the-week *Slow Burn* (1986). Shortly after the publication of *Death On The Cheap: The Lost 'B' Movies of Film Noir*. he founded the annual summer Palm Springs Film Noir Festival. He died in early 2008.

AM—ADRIAN MARTIN is Associate Professor and Head of Film and Television Studies at Monash University (Melbourne Australia); author of *Que es el cine moderno?, Raul Ruiz: obsesiones sublimes, The Mad Max Movies, Once Upon a Time in America* and *Phantasms*; and Co-Editor of the BFI publication *Movie Mutations* and the Internet film journal *Rouge* (www.rouge.com.au). His essay on *Gun Crazy* appears in *Film Noir Reader 4*.

BL—BLAKE LUCAS is a Los Angeles-based writer and film critic. Some of his writing on cinema may be found in the anthologies *The Western Reader, The Film Comedy Reader, The Science Fiction Film Reader*, and *Defining Moments in Movies*. His pieces have also appeared in *The Film Journal* online, in over 100 individual essays on films, filmmakers, film and film theory in *Magill's Survey of Cinema* (English-Language, Silent and Foreign Language) and *Magill's Cinema Annual*s, and in a monograph on John Ford for a retrospective at the Cannes Film Festival.

BMV—BILL MACVICAR was a former journalist and director of public education at Erie County Council for the Prevention of Alcohol and Substance Abuse in Buffalo, New York. He graduated from Brown University and held a Masters degree from the University of Toronto. His past work on noir appears online at the Big Chat and the noir-of-the-week blog. He was in the process of adapting his extensive writing on the Internet Movie Database into entries for this book when he died in 2007.

CD—CHRIS D. is author of *Outlaw Masters of Japanese Film* as well as the upcoming *Gun And Sword: An Encyclopedia of Japanese Gangster Films 1955-1980*. He recently saw DVD release of his first feature film as director, *I Pass For Human,* and also worked as a programmer at The American Cinematheque in Hollywood.

CF—CHRISTOPHER E. FORTH is the Howard Professor in Humanities & Western Civilization at the University of Kansas. He is the author or co-editor of eight books, most recently *Civilization and its Malcontents: Masculinity and the Body in the Modern West* and the co-edited volume *Confronting Modernity in Fin-de-Siècle France.*

CV—CONSTANTINE VEREVIS is senior lecturer in Film and Television in the School of English, Communications and Performance Studies at Monash University, Melbourne. He is author of *Film Remakes* and co-editor of *Second Takes: Critical Approaches to the Film Sequel.* His essay "Through the Past Darkly: Noir Remakes of the 1980s" appears in *Film Noir Reader 4.*

CMCA—COLIN MCARTHUR, formerly Head of the British Film Institute`s Distribution Division, is now a freelance teacher, writer and graphic artist. He has written extensively on Hollywood cinema, British television and Scottish culture. His most recent book is *Brigadoon, Braveheart and the Scots: Distortions of Scotland in Hollywood Cinema.*

DMH—DANIEL HODGES taught a course at the University of California at Berkeley, Extension, "From Center to Sidelines: The Transformation of Women in Alfred Hitchcock and Film Noir." He works as technical writer in the East Bay area of Northern California and is the president of an organization working for single-payer universal health care, Health Care for All-California.

DLW—DENNIS L. WHITE has a degree in film from UCLA and has worked as an Art Diretor and Prop Master. Lives on the Northern California Coast where he deals in collectible books and is completing a biography of W. R. Burnett. He teaches Cinema at the College of the Redwoods.

EK—ELLEN KENESHEA holds Masters Degrees in Journalism and Motion Picture History and Criticism from the University of California at Los Angeles. She is a freelance writer and film editor. As an editor she has cut independent feature films and worked at Walt Disney Feature Animation for fifteen years where she edited *The Hunchback of Notre Dame, Atlantis,* and *Meet the Robinsons* among others.

EM—EILEEN MCGARRY practices entertainment law in Los Angeles, teaches, contributes to California State Bar publications and continues her career as an itinerant intellectual.

GE—GLENN ERICKSON is an Emmy-nominated film editor with a background in special effects. He also reviews films under the web alias DVD Savant, for which he has won a Rondo award. His reviews are collected in *DVD Savant: A Review Source Book.* He has also contributed to two of the *Film Noir Reader*s and *Horror Film Reader.*

GF—GEOFF FORDHAM is a public policy adviser in the field of urban regeneration and neighborhood renewal. He has been a visiting professor in the Faculty of Continuing Education and Community Development at Birkbeck College, University of London. His film interests focus on crime in the movies and on the gangster—his essay on *The Godfather* films appear in *Gangster Film Reader*—and film noir traditions in particular.

GJ—GARY JOHNSON is the publisher of *Images Film Journal* (www.imagesjournal.com). His articles about film have appeared in *Film Noir Reader 4* and *Encyclopedia of U.S. Popular Culture.* He earns a steady paycheck as a technical writer for a software company. On weekends, Gary frequently goes caving in the Ozarks and his articles about caves have appeared in the National Speleological Society's monthly magazine *NSS News* and other caving publications.

GT—GRANT TRACEY teaches at the University of Northern Iowa and edits *North American Review.* He has published three collections of fiction. His most recent, *Lovers and Strangers,* was ranked one of the top 100 books of 2009 by the *Kansas City Star.* His essays appear in *Film Noir Readers 2* and *4.*

JB—JONATHAN BENAIR was a film programmer at the Los Angeles County Museum of Art for eight years in the 1970s and '80s, wrote the screenplays *Beethoven's Tenth, Jagged Edge 2,* and *Trollops,* and contributed to the talk-show spoof *America Tonight.* He was also a voice actor most notably as the black-and-white TV set in *The Brave Little Toaster.* He was often interviewed about film history and appeared on the festival and repertory circuit. A long-time member of the Writers Guild of America, he died in 1998.

JC—JOAN COHEN was Assistant Film Programmer at the Los Angeles County Museum of Art from 1974-1987. Since leaving the museum, she has been a free-lance film researcher for books, scripts, and both documentary and feature films such as *Birth of the Cool, The Celluloid Skyline: New York in Film; Munich; The Good, the Bad and the Beautiful: Images of Women in Film, Visions of Ligh*t; *The Old Gringo, The Aviator.*

JEB—JERRY BARRON is a film curator, writer and graphic designer. He founded the annual noir festival Summer in the Dark in Santa Fe, NM, and is the Artistic Director of the Santa Fe Film Festival. Additionally with his graphics company Mission Control Inc. he produces the annual 3-Minute Film Fest. His graphic design can be found in many publications and websites and at missioncontrolsf.com.

JK—JULIE KIRGO has written television (*One Day At a Time, Dr. Quinn, Medicine Woman, National Geographic's Expeditions to the Edge, L.A. Forensics, Stories From the E.R.*), film criticism, and liner notes for dozens of film music CDs. She was an associate professor of Cinema Studies at Burlington College and recently wrote and co-produced the documentary film *Becoming John Ford.*

JP—JAMES PARIS is a freelance writer, computer information specialist, and administrator for an accounting firm in West Los Angeles. He studied film at Dartmouth College and was in the graduate film history program at UCLA. His essay on *Double Indemnity* appears *Film Noir Reader 4.*

JBW—JANS B. WAGER is a professor of English and Literature and Coordinator of Cinema Studies at Utah Valley University. She is the author of *Dames in the Driver's Seat: Rereading Film Noir* and *Dangerous Dames: Women and Representation in the Weimar Street Film and Film Noir.* Her current book project is tentatively titled *Jazz and Cocktails: Censorship and Representation in Film Noir.*

LB—LINDA BROOKOVER is a researcher and writer who works in the field of multi-cultural education. She has written on a variety of American Indian/ethnographic subjects for *oneWorld,* an on-line magazine which she co-edited. She wrote several essays for *Film Noir Reader*s 1 and 2, a piece on Weegee for *The Noir Style,* and to *Horror Film Reade.* She co-wrote the Showtime family feature *Time at the Top* and was a production executive on the independent feature *Beat.*

LS—LEE SANDERS is a motion picture projectionist, political activist, and film collector. Since 1984 he has been an officer of the Projectionists Local 150 IATSE.

MTC—MARK T. CONARD is Associate Professor of Philosophy and Head of the Philosophy and Religious Studies Program at Marymount Manhattan College in New York City. He's the co-editor of *The Simpsons and Philosophy,* and *Woody Allen and Philosophy* and is editor of *The Philosophy of Film Noir, The Philosophy of Neo-Noir, The Philosophy of Martin Scorsese,* and *The Philosophy of The Coen Brothers.*

MB—MEREDITH BRODY is a journalist who writes about food and restaurants for the *San Francisco Weekly* and has reviewed films for the *Chicago Reader.* She has also contributed pieces to *Film Comment, Variety,* and the Los Angeles and New York *Times.* After graduating from the USC film school she worked in for A-Team Productions and wrtter/director John Milius.

MG—MICHAEL GROST is a computer software analyst-designer. He has a Ph.D. in Mathematics from the University of Michigan. He has written extensively on popular culture and his pieces on film, which are focused primarily on a formal analysis of visual style, can be found on-line at *Classic Film and Television* (http://members.aol.com/MG4273/film.htm). He is also the author of a critical history of mystery fiction from 1830 to 1960, *A Guide to Classic Mystery and Detection* and a detailed critical study of selected American comic books from 1935 to 1966, Classic Comic Books. He is also an abstract painter.

PAD—PAOLO DURAZZO is a graduate of Penn State University and worked in Pennsylvania producing local TV spots, culy shorts such as *Black Fu,* and as a firefighter/paramedic. He presently works as a videographer, assistant director, and has produced independent features and television seies such as *The Aquanauts.* He is a member of the Directors Guild

of America and his production company is Scura Citta or "Dark City."

RA—RON ABRAMS studied phenomenology and film theory under William Earle, Gerald Temaner and James Leahy at Northwestern University and film theory at UCLA (M. A and a C. Phil). His dissertation "Cinema Verite and World-View: The Dialectics of the Representation of the Concrete" has never been read by anybody but himself. He produced and directed a cinema-verité documentary, *Armwrestling in America* and was initiated and consulted on *Family Circle,* a documentary about child abuse. He also co-wrote the feature film *Kiss Daddy Goodbye.* He works as a location manager in the entertainment industry.

RBP—R. BARTON PALMER is Calhoun Lemon Professor of Literature and Director of Film Studies at Clemson University. He is the author, editor, or general editor of more that thirty-five books on film and literature including *Hollywood's Dark Cinema: The American Film Noir, Perspectives on Film Noir,* and *Joel and Ethan Coen.*

RH—REYNOLD HUMPHRIES is Professor of Film Studies at the University of Lille 3 and author of *Fritz Lang: Genre and Representation in His American Films, The American Horror Film. An Introduction,* and *The Hollywood Horror Film, 1931-1941. Madness in a Social Landscape.* He has contributed to *Film Noir Reader 4, Gangster Film Reader, Docufictions, 100 European Horror Films, Monstrous Adaptations, Stanley Kubrick: the Legacy, 501 Directors* and forthcoming volumes on Tod Browning, John Huston, Edgar G. Ulmer and the modern American horror film. Articles on film noir, crime, and the Hollywood witch hunts, as well as aspects of the horror film, have appeared in France, America and the online journal *Kinoeye.* His latest book is *Hollywood's Blacklists. A Political and Cultural History.*

RS—RICHARD SCHICKEL has written, co-written or edited 37 books, mostly about the movies. By a curious coincidence he has directed, written and produced the same number of documentaries about film history and filmmakers, while also writing or producing a number of other titles. He has been a film critic for over forty years, mainly at *Time* magazine, but also at *Life* and, currently at Time.Com. He has as well written essays and introductions for a number of other books and for well over 50 other publications. He has held a Guggenheim Fellowship and was awarded an honorary doctorate by the American Film Institute.

RSW—ROGER WESTCOMBE is the coordinator of the Big House Film Society in Canberra, where he screens and presents educational seminars on film noir. His writings on noir are collected on the crimeculture website at Lancashire University. With Dr. Christopher Forth he jointly curated the "Double Crossing" retrospective on French and American film noir at the Brisbane International Film Festival. He is continuing his post-graduate research on Hollywood's peacetime propaganda films of World War II at Flinders University, Adelaide

RW—ROBIN WOOD is the author of numerous books on motion pictures including seminal English-language auteur studies of Alfred Hitchcock, Howard Hawks, Ingmar Bergman, and Arthur Penn and most recently Hollywood from Vietnam to Reagan as well as contributions to *Film Noir Reader*s *1* and 4,

Horror Film Reader and *Gangster Film Reader*. He is a former Professor of Film Studies at Queen's College and York University and remains a founding member of the collective which edits the film journal *CineAction!*

SCB—SHERI CHINEN BIESEN is associate professor of Radio, Television and Film at Rowan University and author of *Blackout: World War II and the Origins of Film Noir*. She received her Ph.D. at The University of Texas at Austin following an M.A. at The University of Southern California School of Cinema-Television and has taught film at USC, University of California, University of Texas, and in England. She has contributed to *Film Noir Reader 4, Gangster Film Reader, Film and History, Quarterly Review of Film and Video , Literature/Film Quarterly, Popular Culture Review, The Historian, Television and Television History* and edited *The Velvet Light Trap*.

SMS—STEVEN M. SANDERS is Professor Emeritus of Philosophy at Bridgewater State College. He is the author of a monograph on the TV series *Miami Vice* and coeditor of *The Philosophy of TV Noir* to which he contributed an extensive historical and analytic introduction. His recent work includes essays on Alfred Hitchcock's *Strangers on a Train*, Stanley Kubrick's *The Killing*, and Martin Scorsese's *Casino*, as well as the chapter on Television Noir for the forthcoming *Companion to Film Noir*.

SV—STEVE VANCE is a Los Angeles-based film editor whose credits include the independent feature films *Beat, Crashing*, and *White Nights*. He is also an artist, writer, and art director who has been awarded both a Grammy (for "Brain in a Box," an anthology of sci-fi-themed music) and an Eisner (for Simpsons Comics #1).

TE—TODD R. ERICKSON is an entertainment marketing executive with Hill and Knowlton and previously served as creative services director at Rogers & Cowan, Inc. Previous to that he wrote and produced training films for the U.S. Air Force and worked in various production capacities with Tisch/Avnet Productions and WGN Television. While in the Masters program at Brigham Young University, he taught undergraduate film classes and managed the university's film society in order to screen as many noir films as possible. He co-authored an *Introduction to Motion Picture Art & Analysis* and is currently adapting his thesis on neo-noir for publication.

TT—TRACEY THOMPSON worked as cataloguer and researcher for the Museum of Modern Art and on *Motion Pictures, Television and Radio: A Union Catalogue of Manuscript and Special Collections in the Western United States*. After serving as development executive and producer on numerous film and television projects such as *Under Wraps* and *His Bodyguard* in the 1990s, she started PetFriendlyTravel.com in 2000 for people who travel with their animal companions. She holds an M.A. in Cinema Studies from NYU.

TW—TONY WILLIAMS is the co-author of *Italian Western: Opera of Violence*, co-editor of *Vietnam War Films* and *Jack London's The Sea Wolf: A Screenplay by Robert Rossen*. He is the author of *Jack London: the Movies*; *Hearths of Darkness: the Family in the American Horror Film*; *Larry Cohen: Radical Allegories of an American Filmmaker*; *Structures of Desire: British Cinema 1949-1955*; and *John Woo's Bullet in the Head*. His articles have appeared in *Cinema Journal, CineAction, Wide Angle, Jump Cut, Asian Cinema, Creative Filmmaking*, and several *Film Noir Reader*s. He is an Associate Professor and Area Head of Film Studies in the Department of English, Southern Illinois University at Carbondale.

WC—WILLIAM COVEY is Associate Professor of English and Coordinator of the Film and Media Studies minor program at Slippery Rock University of Pennsylvania. His dissertation for Purdue University is entitled *Compromising Positions: Theorizing American Neo-Noir Film)*. His critical essays on neo-noir have been published in *Journal Of Film And Video, Mfs: Modern Fiction Studies, Quarterly Review Of Film And Video*, and *Film Noir Reader 2*.

RESEARCHERS

DEBRA BERGMAN. Freelance writer, researcher, and script supervisor. Research assistant at the Academy of Motion Picture Arts and Sciences. Graduate, Syracuse University Film Department.

RICHARD H. PRINCE is a line producer/production manager working in motion pictures and television. His credits include *CSI-NY, The Invasion, License to Wed, Dukes of Hazzard, Saw, The Animal, The Replacements, Rules of Engagement, Angels in the Outfield, Rocket Man, The Distinguished Gentleman, Only the Lonely, White Fang, The Bedroom Window* and *Personal Best*. He has also worked as assistant director on such films as *Risky Business, Uncommon Valour, Winter People, The Slugger's Wife,*and *My Bodyguard* and was co-producer of several episodes of *That's Hollywood*. He is a graduate of the UCLA Film School and also its Anderson Graduate School of Management.

ROBERTA M. WARD was a freelance writer and researcher who died in 1984.

PREFACE TO THE 4TH EDITION

◇

SINCE THE FIRST EDITION OF THIS ENCYCLOPEDIA AND with contributions from our fellow editors Elizabeth Ward and Robert Porfirio, and scores of others, James Ursini and I have done seven other books about film noir. In the course of those books, some of the assumptions originally made for the first edition of this volume changed, most notably the inclusion of B-titles and non-contemporary narratives in our study of *The Noir Style*. Consequently the starting point for a complete revision of a book that was begun more than three decades ago was the addition of over 100 titles to what is now Part One. Perhaps more distinctly than ever now thoroughly inscribed onto new media, the films of the classic period continue to speak for themselves. That much has become clear to us as we have revisited them not just while writing and editing new books and essays but also while providing audio and video commentary for more than score of DVD releases. Because we have imposed stricter chronological limits on Part One, a few proto-noir have been deleted and early neo-noir pictures have been moved. The result comprises just over 400 detailed entries from *The Stranger on the Third Floor* (1940) to Samuel Fuller's 1964 *The Naked Kiss*.

As for neo-noir, given that it has existed as a derivative genre since before the original volume was published, it was also clear that it now deserved more than just a lengthy essay. So in Part Two with the earliest examples relocated from Part One as a starting point nearly 150 neo-noir movies are individually discussed. Finally as we did with contributions from Bob Porfirio and Linda Brookover in *The Noir Style*, we have added some sidebars that focus on proto-noir and selected specific aspects of noir narrative and style.

From the first edition of this volume the aim has always been to make it an accessible work both as a specific reference and as an overview. The lists of films by year and by studio, which both casual readers and scholars have extensively utilized, remain an essential part of this encyclopedia reference. To keep the volume's size from become unwieldy, we have abridged the filmographic data so that only key creative collaborators are included (more complete details now being readily available via on-line resources) and cut down the lengthier plot summaries. In reconfiguring or expunging all the other Appendices, which had by the 3rd edition expanded to more than a quarter of the pages, we hope to make the book easier to use than ever.

With thirty new contributors bringing new points of view any imposition of an overriding methodology rather than a mere format would still have been quite constraining. This book was originally conceived as a series of essays on aspects of film noir,

and we are pleased that it ultimately inspired the *Film Noir Reader* series, the first two of which include all the seminal articles on the movement. In an "encyclopedic" approach, however, whether they relate to auteurism, genre expectation, sociological context, gender study, dramatic expression through the use of the noir style or anything else, underlying critical assumptions should be transparent. While many of the contributors did and continue to ascribe creative responsibility to the director, the reader may choose to consider any person's name a cipher for the abstract, phenomenological "intentionality" that creates meaning in any collaborative work of art. From the first volume it was obvious that although film noir was not a formal genre, its creators were quick to recognize the viewer expectations that became associated with it and to exploit them. It was equally clear that, although film noir was not particularly conducive to the expression of a "world view" by individual auteurs, it was not antithetical to such expression either. As Paul Schrader suggests in his seminal essay over 35 years ago:

> Film noir seemed to bring out the best in everyone: directors, cameramen, screenwriters, actors. Again and again, a film noir will make the high point on an artist's career graph. Some directors, for example, did their best work in film noir (Stuart Heisler, Robert Siodmak, Gordon Douglas, Edward Dmytryk, John Brahm, John Cromwell, Raoul Walsh, Henry Hathaway); other directors began in film noir and, it seems to me, never regained their original heights (Otto Preminger, Rudolph Maté, Nicholas Ray, Robert Wise, Jules Dassin, Richard Fleischer, John Huston, Andre de Toth, and Robert Aldrich); and other directors who made great films in other molds also made great film noir (Orson Welles, Max Ophuls, Fritz Lang, Elia Kazan, Howard Hawks, Robert Rossen, Anthony Mann, Joseph Losey, Alfred Hitchcock, and Stanley Kubrick).

In 1986 in the British movie *The McGuffin* used the first edition of this book as neo-noir prop: when a film critic portrayed by Charles Dance needed to check on a classic period plot, he pulled it down from his reference shelf. Because of the widespread recognition of this volume, the search for new collaborators was quickly accomplished, and we were gratified that it included several eminent critics whose own writing on film noir ante-dated the first edition. In fact, no less than eight of our new contributors have written or edited their own volumes about noir. Ably assisted by these new voices, we hope that a return to the original design of the Encyclopedia has been accomplished for readers old and new, for those who can now retire their early hardcover in and its frayed dust-jacket and for a new generation of film noir admirers as well.

PART ONE

◇

The Classic Period

INTRODUCTION: THE CLASSIC PERIOD

◇

IT IS AS TRUE NOW AS IT WAS WHEN THIS BOOK WAS FIRST published three decades ago that, with the "Western," film noir shares the distinction of being an indigenous American form. Unlike Westerns, noir films do not spring from precise antecedents in terms of a period in American history or specific literary genre. What may be termed the noir cycle has a singular position in the history of American motion pictures: a body of films that not only presents a cohesive vision of America but that does so in a manner transcending the influences of *auteurism* or genre, studio policy or social context. Film noir is grounded neither in personal creation nor in translation of another tradition into cinematic terms. Rather it is a self-contained reflection of American cultural preoccupations in film form. In short, it is the unique example of a wholly American film style. "Film noir" is literally "black film," not just in the sense of being full of physically dark images, nor of reflecting a dark mood in American society, but equally, almost empirically, as a black slate on which the culture could inscribe its ills and in the process produce a catharsis to help relieve them.

That may seem a substantial claim to make for a group of films whose plots frequently turn on deadly violence or sexual obsession, whose catalogue of characters includes numbers of down-and-out private eyes, desperate women, and petty criminals. Nor does the visceral unease felt by a viewer who watches a shadowy form move across a lonely street or who hears the sound of car tires creeping over wet asphalt automatically translate into sociological assertions about paranoia or guilt. At the same time, it is clear that the emergence of film noir coincides with these and other popular sentiments at large in America during World War II and at the start of a cold war dominated by fear of the atomic bomb.

This is not to claim that film noir is without antecedents of any sort. Although noir as a term has penetrated deeply into colloquial American in the past six decades and could without fear of misunderstanding be used as an adjective to suggest dark variants of any art form from anime to zydeco, "film noir" is a specific creature. Whatever developments, social, historical, aesthetic, or even scientific, that may have helped to shape the rough beast that is film noir, it slouched towards Hollywood to be born. There it lived, one might even say it thrived, for a scant few years. When this introduction originally appeared it was part of the first English-language survey of the noir movement. Scores of books have followed (no less than four more of them using an encyclopedic format) and hundreds of essays

have dissected film noir from just about every perspective imaginable. Despite all this, the history of film noir is simple enough. If there were a road map through the heart of film noir, it might reveal a course full of twists and turns with steep hills, dangerous cross roads, and side streets that dead end without warning. But despite its surface complexity, despite occasional squabbling over specific titles, even over the identity of the first—or the last—noir film, the big picture is clear. More than a half century after its zenith, there is a basic agreement on the key films. And for the time being at least, English-language commentators have also agreed that, after some early prototypes, the "classic period" of film noir transpired over a mere two decades, roughly beginning with *The Maltese Falcon* in 1941 and approximately ending with *Touch of Evil* in 1958.

In the concluding paragraph of this introduction in 1979, I wrote that it could be said that the cycle of noir films never did conclude, as such. Rather, for whatever varied reasons, the noir cycle diminished gradually in scope and impact until it was lost in some vanishing point in film history. The few productions in the 1960's and 1970's are not so much a part of that cycle as individual attempts to resurrect the noir sensibility. One thing is certain: in the "classic" period, the span of years from just before World War II to just after the Korean conflict, the major and minor studios put several hundred noir films into distribution. From a more distant, 21st century perspective, it could now be said that in the early 1960's, the cycle of films that transcended genre and that defined a noir style ended. Within a few years afterwards, a genre of neo-noir films began to appear and accumulate; and several of the movies included in the original encyclopedia from *Point Blank* to *Taxi Driver* are part of that thriving genre. Nonetheless what my co-editors and I thought about film noir in 1979 is essentially unchanged. Consequently, the rest of this introduction with a few brief additions will be essentially unrevised.

To begin with, it may seem strange for a group of films indigenously American to be identified by a French term. This is simply because French critics were the first to discern particular aspects in a number of American productions initially released in France after World War II. They also noticed a thematic resemblance between these motion pictures and certain novels published in France at the time under the generic title of "Serie Noire." This "Serie Noire" and its later publishing competitor, "Fleuve Noire," use the French word for "black" to designate a type of detective fiction. As it hap-

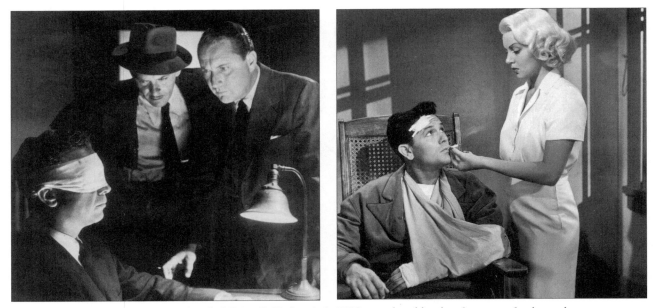

The second adaption of Chandler's Fairwell, My Lovely *by RKO was released less than four years afterthe novel.*
Cain's tale of adulterous killers took a dozen years to reach the screen.

pens, the majority of the "Serie Noire" titles were translations of American novels and featured the work of such authors as Hammett, Chandler, James M. Cain, and Horace McCoy. The association between such films as *Double Indemnity, Murder My Sweet, Mildred Pierce, or The Postman Always Rings Twice* and the "Serie Noire" novels by James M. Cain and Raymond Chandler from which they were adapted was unmistakable. Together they inspired the title of an essay published by Jean-Pierre Chartier in 1946: "Americans Also Make 'Noir' Films." [The entire article by Chartier as well as Nino Frank's earlier survey of 1946 American releases in France are reprinted in *Film Noir Reader 2*–see bibliography.]

Equally obvious was the fact that the narratives of these noir films possessed an economy of expression and a graphic impact substantially different from the hard-boiled novels or the pulp short stories of the "Black Mask" magazine from which they may have been derived. Certainly that genre of writing—as well as the social realism of the American theater in the 1920's and 1930's or the proletarian literature of the same period—reflects many of the stylistic and cultural preoccupations from which film noir ultimately emerged. But film noir is equally if not more significantly a product of other mediating influences, precisely of those social, economic, technical, and aesthetic developments that preceded its inception.

The first two areas are powerful yet indirect in their influence on film noir. Both the social upheaval of World War II and the sociopathy on a smaller scale of American gangsterism in the decade preceding it created a class of individuals that would frequently be depicted in film noir. From the latter came the film stereotype of the ambitious criminal and his corrupt organizations; from the war, in considerably greater number, came the veteran and his burden of readjustment to civilian life. The film industry began its exploitation of the gangster myth in the 1920's and developed it to its fullest extent as a genre in the following decade. By transmuting contemporary figures and events, the gangster films

of the 1930's rapidly defined a genre that was grounded in social verisimilitude but elaborated through such violent icons as machine guns and fast cars. The criminal archetype that emerged was romanticized in response to an undercurrent of social alienation: by ingenuity and daring the individual achieved power and success. Simplistically the cause of such a figure's destruction was usually reduced to a megalomaniac loss of self-control. In short, the gangster most often perished from the consequences of his own excesses.

Such a figure in its initial stages antedates the noir sensibility to some extent. However, whereas the gangster is a chaotic element ultimately eradicated by the forces of social order, the truly noir figure more often represents the perspective of normality assailed by the twists of fate of an irrational universe. The soldier returned from combat falls midway between these categories. In the underlying irony of film noir, the viewer realizes from convention that the war veterans depicted in such diverse films as *Somewhere in the Night, Ride the Pink Horse,*

and *The Blue Dahlia* have undergone physical and emotional changes that alter their perceptions of civilian society. At the same time, the expressive components of film noir compel the viewer—in a manner that the gangster film never could—to participate actively in that character's distorted point-of-view. Various background elements are recruited to mask this effect. In *Ride the Pink Horse* the unfamiliar western locale and the ingenuous denizens of the carousel constantly reinforce the uneasiness of the urban man, Gagin. In *The Blue Dahlia* a severely disturbed supporting character like Buzz, with his shrapnel-damaged skull and psychotic aversion to "monkey music," his somewhat racist euphemism for jazz, makes the sexual estrangement and violence of protagonist Johnny Morrison seem normal in comparison. An even more obvious cipher for the difficulties of readjustment is the amnesiac ex-Marine George Taylor in *Somewhere in the Night*. His loss of memory and identity is an absolute metaphor for the inability of the noir hero to distinguish between the benign and the malignant as he moves through the complex noir underworld.

Foremost in the list of socio-political developments that influenced the post-World War II film industry are McCarthyism and nuclear weapons. The effect of the former has been well documented. The resultant blacklists altered or aborted careers in all phases of motion picture production; but of the prominent actors, producers, writers, and directors associated primarily with film noir, such as Abraham Polonsky, Joseph Losey, John Berry, Cy Enfield, and Edward Dmytryk, a disproportionate number were affected. The potential hazards of the atomic bomb, and after 1949 the threat of nuclear war, may have been depicted most explicitly in the scores of radioactive monsters raised from the ocean depths off Japan or the visions of Armageddon produced in the science fiction genre; but such concepts also altered the narratives of film noir. In fact, McCarthyism and the specter of the Bomb became the unspoken inspirations for a leitmotif of fear or, more specifically, the deep paranoia that resounded through the noir cycle after the war. *Night and the City, The Pretender, Out of the Past, Force of Evil, Nightfall*—all are typical in their depiction of characters once in control but turned fugitives and struggling to survive. While a manifest treatment of McCarthyism was for obvious reasons not possible, the parallels between congressional "Red-Hunts" and the actions of

frenzied lynch mobs in films like *Johnny Guitar* or *Try and Get Me* were none too subtle, even though the latter picture directed by a soon-to-be-blacklisted filmmaker Cy Enfield was based on a real event.

Two motion pictures directed by Robert Aldrich most clearly invoke the portent of nuclear power. In *World for Ransom,* a nuclear physicist is kidnapped so that his knowledge may be sold to the highest bidder among various competing nations. In *Kiss Me Deadly,* forces vie for a hot box of mysterious contents, the "great whatsit," which proves to be radioactive material that triggers a literally explosive conclusion. *Kiss Me Deadly* is unique in its direct identification of the unstable noir underworld with the elemental instability of fissionable matter. Such an association creates a powerful metaphoric statement in that particular film; but the converse is also true: The unstable universe depicted in so many noir films is a continual reflection of those senses of cultural upheaval and apprehension deriving from both the "Red menace" and the chances of nuclear devastation.

Several other mediating forces within the film industry helped to perpetuate and enlarge the noir cycle after the war. The gradual demise of the "B" or "program picture" supported by block-booking compelled the major studios to produce less expensive films that would appeal to exhibitors on their own merits. In such a context, film noir with a record of favorable audience response and a potential for being profitably promoted on the basis of sensational and/or violent content became a preferred stock. A number of technical innovations further supported film noir's growing appeal. More sensitive, fine-grain negatives, higher-speed lenses, smaller camera dollies, and portable power supplies, all perfected during World War II, alleviated many of the logistical problems previously connected with location filming. The location work in such productions as *Thieves' Highway, M, T-Men, Act of Violence,* and *White Heat* demonstrated that noir films could be made not only with greater verisimilitude but also with greater economy. Novel location methods also permitted such striking sequences as the aerial shots that open *They Live by Night* and *Criss Cross,* the meat-packing plant robbery in *Gun Crazy,* or the pursuit through the train yards in *Mystery Street.*

Studio sets were still used, of course, but even within them filmmakers could exploit the new technology for stylistic effect. In discussing the camera movement in *The Blue Gardenia,* Fritz Lang asserted that the film's fluid tracking shots, which relentlessly pursue his guilt-ridden heroine, could not have been executed without the compact crab dolly. The detailed exterior night work in *Kiss Me Deadly,* repeatedly framing its protagonist against dark structures and flashing streetlights, is a conspicuous example of expressive implementation of higher speed lenses and film stock. Handheld camerawork in that same film, or ten years earlier in the fight sequences of *Body and Soul,* underscore at yet another level that sense of instability so central to the noir vision.

Before being blacklisted, writer Abraham Polonsky became a director on the 1948 release Force of Evil *and in the context of film noir reversed character expectations: an ethical bookie Leo Morse (Thomas Gomez, left) spurns the offers of big money from his attorney brother Joe (John Garfield) who represents a gambling syndicate [Note: after his politicaltroubles, Polonsky's next credit as a feature director was more than two decades later.]*

In an industry where economics of wartime and its immediate aftermath dictated recycling of existing sets, exploiting stock film libraries, and generally minimizing shooting times, the flexibility of film noir made it a fiscally sounder proposition than many other types of motion picture. Film noir already had an established emphasis on low-key lighting. The influx of foreign directors and other craftsmen before and during World War II—most notably the German "refugees" Fritz Lang, Robert Siodmak, Max Ophuls, Billy Wilder, Edgar G. Ulmer, William Dieterle, Fred Zinnemann, and Otto Preminger—had previously helped to refine film noir's distinctive visual style. They brought to film a familiarity with not just low-key photography but the full heritage of German Expressionism: moving camera; oddly angled shots; a chiaroscuro frame inscribed with wedges of light or shadowy mazes, truncated by foreground objects or punctuated with glinting highlights bounced off mirrors, wet surfaces, or the polished steel of a gun barrel. The years of production immediately after the war, with production more able to incorporate exterior locales, more mobile cameras, and more filmmakers, both foreign and domestic, ready to test the limits of technical innovations, became the most visually homogeneous of the entire noir cycle.

Here is a list of eight motion pictures released over a period of just 18 months from May, 1947 through November, 1948: *Framed, Brute Force, The Unsuspected, Out of the Past, Pitfall, The Big Clock, Cry of the City,* and *Force of Evil.* It doesn't take much more than the titles to tell these are film noir; but the details of the creative credits for all eight—that is, producer, director, writers, cinematographer, composer, and actors—are what is truly remarkable. Before anything was recorded on film, eight different scripts were written by fourteen different people and six scripts were adapted from novels or original stories by others. Eight different producers oversaw the development of these screenplays into movies working with eight different directors and eight different cinematographers. This octet of films starred twenty different actors and was scored by eight different composers. Finally, each film was released by a different one of the eight major studios.

These are eight ostensibly unrelated motion pictures from completely diverse hands with one cohesive visual style. Such a cohesion is clearly not coincidental; yet there is no express chain of causality leading up to it. Visual experimentation in the gangster and horror genres at Warner Bros. and Universal respectively during the 1930's broadened the number of filmmaking personnel familiar with exterior and low-key photography. At RKO the seminal impact of the Welles/Toland collaboration on *Citizen Kane* in 1941 validated for later directors, cinematographers, and designers many less frequently used but visually striking staging options. Nevertheless, film noir's visual integrity raises a broader question than the vestigial influences of German Expressionism or the earliest manifestations of technological advances, whether by individual filmmakers or studio staffs. At the root of the issue is the simple consideration of what binds film noir together.

Unlike any number of film groups that antedate it and unlike a genre, film noir does not possess a ready catalogue of icons. It has none of the paraphernalia of the cowboy, the soldier, the gangster or the supernatural being. At another level, the expressive conventions of film noir are not used to engender or fulfill a set of key genre expectations analogous to those in the Western, war, gangster or horror film. More specifically there is nothing intrinsic in side-light or a moving camera that connotes such qualities as alienation, obsession, or paranoia in the manner that a tied-down pistol may imply a gunfighter or the drone of planes, an air raid; a cello case, a hidden tommy-gun; or red marks on the neck, a vampire. Film noir does exhibit certain relationships between elements of style, not icons, and narrative events or character sentiments. A side-lit close-up may reveal a face, half in shadow, half in light, at the precise narrative moment of indecision. A sustained moving camera may forge a visual link between characters or events simultaneously with a parallel narrative connection. But such relationships between image and narrative only lead to the same abstractions, which are basically generalizations of protagonists' mental states; and such generalizations do not evoke a generic milieu equivalent to a cattle drive, a tank attack, a shakedown in a speakeasy, or a plague of zombies.

If the relationship of film noir to genre is a tenuous one at best, how then is the cycle to be classified? Film noir is best viewed as a group "movement" like its contemporary, Italian Neo-realism, or its antecedent, German Expressionism, or a succeeding phenomenon, the French New Wave. Those film movements are normally defined as a group of filmmakers who share political and/or aesthetic beliefs and demonstrate a common stylistic approach. The noir cycle evidently possesses the latter quality and, to an arguable extent, the former also. Does it also supersede generic constructs or display a narrative diversity in the manner of these other movements, which may encompass war films as well as psychological melodramas and may range from the horrific to the comic? There are noir Westerns, noir period films, and certainly noir gangster films. One might argue for noir war movies, noir comedy, and/or noir horror as well. But noir does not expunge the iconic identity of a genre picture that crosses over to the dark side.

Pursued is a psychological melodrama, which happens to be set in the post-Civil War West. While the visual style, the flashback narrative structure, and the lead performance by Robert Mitchum are all palpably noir, there is no ignoring the spurs and the six-guns. Are existential motifs, as per Robert Porfirio's seminal essay, more common in film noir? It would seem so. But there are certainly ample illustrations of existential figures in Westerns, war films, horror film, gangster film, etc. which are not noir. In the end, is it not the stylistic tie that preeminently binds a genre picture to the noir movement? No matter one's answer to that question, it is possible to make a case for or against *Pursued* or *Blood on the Moon* or *Devil's Doorway* as noir films based on style, character psychology, or narrative. Despite any deviations from the generic "norm" in terms of style, character psychology, or narrative, they are all unquestionably Westerns. From our perspective, they are all unquestionably noir.

Certainly most noir films, as a list of the motion pictures included in the classic period section of this volume confirms, do not also have clear genre identities. The characteristics of a prototypical film noir are fairly apparent and straightforward. It is contemporaneous, usually urban, and almost always American in setting. Exceptions usually involve either urban men in a rural locale or Americans abroad. There is a narrative

The Big Night: *In the universe of film noir, a typical teenager (John Barrymore, Jr.) can find himself with a gun in his hand.*

assumption that only natural forces are in play: extraordinary occurrences are either logically elucidated or left unexplained and no metaphysical values are adopted. Finally, the noir cycle's consistent visual style is most often keyed specifically to recurrent narrative patterns and character emotions. Because these patterns and emotions are repeatedly suggestive of certain abstractions, such as alienation or obsession, it may seem that film noir is overly dependent on external constructions, such as Existentialism or Freudianism, for its dramatic meanings. Irrefutably, film noir does recruit the ethical and philosophical values of the culture as freely as it recruits visual conventions, iconic notations, or character types from other extrinsic sources. The results of such a process are neither aesthetically invalid nor structurally amorphous. Such a process does,

however, enrich and dislocate the noir cycle as a phenomenon and does so in a way that resists facile explication.

Apart from its visual style the most consistent aspect of film noir is its protagonists. If a usable definition of the "noir hero" is to be formulated, it must encompass two key character motifs. Most intrinsic of the two is alienation. The examples are certainly multiform: from the ostensibly ordinary people in *Side Street* and *The Big Night* to the driven war vets in *Thieves' Highway* and *Ride the Pink Horse* to the explicitly psychotic figures in *The Dark Mirror* and *The Dark Past*. The darkness that fills the mirror or the past, which lurks in a dark corner or obscures a dark passage across dark waters or out of the dark city, is not merely the key adjective of so many film noir titles but the obvious metaphor for the condition of the protagonist's mind. As these figures struggle through their particular dark night of the soul, alienation is the common factor, the narrative constant that binds together the policemen (*The Big Heat, The Big Combo*) and the criminals (*This Gun for Hire, The Burglar*); the psychologist (*Woman in the Window*) and the mental patient (*The Night Runner*); the rich and famous (*Caught, Mr. Arkadin*); the middle class (*Pitfall, The Reckless Moment*) and the poor and desperate (*Try and Get Me*); the doctors (*Where Danger Lives*), lawyers (*Force of Evil, Party Girl*), sideshow performers (*Nightmare Alley, Gun Crazy*), private detectives (*Murder My Sweet, Kiss Me Deadly, Out of the Past*), boxers (*Body and Soul; The Set-Up*), newspapermen (*Scandal Sheet, Call Northside 777*), salesmen (*Double Indemnity*), seers (*Night has a Thousand Eyes*), and even screenwriters (*In a Lonely Place*). While the individual plots must dictate the particular events entrapping the protagonists, the anguished expression of Bradford Galt in *The Dark Corner* is prototypical: "I feel all dead inside. I'm backed up in a dark corner, and I don't know who's hitting me."

With its simple, graphic language, Galt's statement captures the basic emotion of the noir figure. The assailant is not a person but an unseen force. The pain is more often mental than physical: the plunge into spiritual darkness

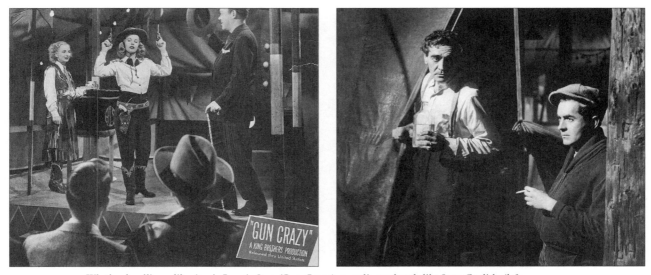

*Whether headliners like Annie Laurie Star (*Gun Crazy*) or ordinary hands like Stan Carlisle (left, Nightmare Alley) film noir carnies dream of escaping the sideshsow.*

evokes the sense of being "dead inside." For Galt in his dark corner the mere fact of being outside the law is neither new nor terrifying. It is the loss of order, the inability either to discover or to control the underlying causes of his distress that is mentally intolerable. The narrative position of Galt, the ex-con, like that of the returning veterans is made all the more ironic because of the scorn and egocentricity with which he initially confronts postwar society. As he senses the ground being cut from beneath him, Galt's cynicism quickly gives way to desperation. As with many, pre- and post-noir figures from Eddie Taylor in *You Only Live Once* (1937) to Phil Gaines in *Hustle* (1975), this protagonist may seem more acutely despondent or alienated because of having once been idealistic or romantic.

Even as fallen idealists or estranged romantics, a classic-period character's response to being thrown into Galt's "dark corner" usually betrays some residue of their initial positive social attitudes. If it also seems that events must conspire to crush these positive inclinations or destroy ethical constraints whether they be lawyers, doctors, detectives, or boxers, their despair only becomes fully as ironic as Galt's when they are compelled to pause and assess their situations. While Galt ultimately penetrates the structure of his trap, others like the hapless Al Roberts in *Detour* are frustrated and finally destroyed by that structure. "Someday fate or some mysterious force can put the finger on you or me for no reason at all." Roberts' sober if somewhat self-pitying reflection does not save him. For him or for characters as radically different as Joe Morse in *Force of Evil* or John Triton in *Night has a Thousand Eyes*, this moment of realization, this resignation to being annihilated by a relentless, deterministic abstraction, is the only bitter solace that the noir vision permits.

Roberts "mysterious force" is to some degree the film noir equivalent of an existential belief in the "benign indifference" of the material world. Camus illustrates his term for the absence of malice in the world's random causality with an observation that is very similar to Roberts: "At any street corner, the absurd may strike a man in the face." As manifestations of the absurd, the quirks of fate that permit the hard-bitten Galt to survive while they slowly kill an equally innocent and more sympathetic figure like Frank Bigelow in *D.O.A.*—a man poisoned because he happened to notarize an incriminating bill of sale—could well exemplify a concept such as "benign indifference" at work in the noir universe. However, while Camus' fictional characters experience an "existential despair" that is based on the consequences of choosing and the operation of free will, the choices of the noir protagonists are often overwhelmed by an underlying determinism that is neither benign nor indifferent. The critical distinction is not between *Detour's* image of a pointed finger and Camus' of a slap in the face, but between that film's dramatization of "fate" and Camus' notion of "the absurd." For absurdity in Camus' philosophy may occasionally prove perilous; but fate in the noir vision almost always becomes fatality. It could easily be said that film noir anticipates fatality. From its very titles, the noir cycle uses boldface and continually points that deadly finger. Its figures are the *Accused, Abandoned, Cornered, Framed, Railroaded, Convicted, Caged,* and *Desperate*. A character menaced by an *Act of Violence* makes a *Journey Into Fear* or lives *Between Midnight and Dawn, Somewhere in the Night, On Dangerous Ground* and

does so in isolation: *I Walk Alone, In a Lonely Place*. Ultimately, the fateful narrative patterns that precipitate the remarks of Bradford Galt and Al Roberts bring forth even simpler generalizations: Nick Blake mouthing the words of the title in *Nobody Lives Forever* or even more directly the Swede in *The Killers* saying, "Everybody dies." However predestined their alienation, and whether or not their awareness of their condition is truly existential, the reaction of its protagonists to these structural elements is the fundamental conflict in film noir.

There are certain characters, like Walter Neff in *Double Indemnity*, whose behavior is more classically existential because he understands from the beginning that he need not have chosen, as is metaphorically explained to him, to get on a "streetcar that only goes one way." Because he is subsequently enmeshed by the undesired aftereffects of his choice, unlike Galt, Neff never escapes from his dark corner. Still as he sits in his darkened office at the film's conclusion finishing the dictation of his bleak narrative, Neff may begin to perceive that his choice was not so free as it seemed. Neff is less a victim of alienation than of the second key emotion in the noir universe: obsession. To a certain extent—the extent of which it is neither rational nor predictable—obsessive behavior transcends such ordinary considerations as morality and causality. "I never cared about the money. All I wanted was you. I walked the streets of strange cities thinking about you." Steve Thompson's avowal of fidelity to his ex-wife in *Criss Cross* is indicative of the forlorn quality of typical noir obsession. In its sexuality, it may appear patently Freudian: Thompson is attached to Anna because she symbolizes not just sexual release but psychological reunion with a happier, less complicated life, a fantasy of escape from the present and its ennui. In his narration and his dialogue, when he speaks of walking alone in strange places while lost in thoughts of her. Thompson reveals his underlying romanticism. Thompson's past with Anna seems neither metaphorically dark nor physically threatening as those of so many other noir figures. Indeed, Thompson recalls it as the best part of his life. Nevertheless, his obsessive attachment literally seals his doom from the narrative's beginning.

Certainly Thompson is not unique in the way he idealizes a particular woman. The same quasi-tragic flaw threatens and destroys other men in films as diverse as *Where Danger Lives, Scarlet Street, Angel Face,* and *The Locket*. What these films do have in common are characters with the fatal inability to perceive the dishonesty of the women, the femmes fatales, with whom they involve themselves. A different, perhaps more extreme, example would be the male protagonists of *Laura* or *Woman in the Window*. For them such qualities as honesty and reciprocation of feeling cannot be important, as they are initially fascinated to the point of distraction not by actual women but by mere paintings of them. Another extreme is the male half of the fugitive couple in *Gun Crazy*, a man whose youthful fascination with firearms eventually leads into a relationship with a woman who not only shares his "gun craziness" but who also completes his initiation into the parallel worlds of eroticism and violence.

Again the overtly Freudian aspects of such relationships function as a foundation on which to construct a sequence of narrative events that typify the noir vision. Obsession like Roberts' "mysterious force" erodes the sense of free will as it undermines the characters ability to make rational decisions. Not all the victims are entrapped by a purely sexual obsession. Unquestionably Neff in *Double Indemnity*, who first considers murder as he drives away from his visit to the Dietrichson house, does so as much out of passion for the married Phyllis Dietrichson (whose interest clearly begins with money) as over the challenge of the crime itself: the possibility of beating the very system in which he works. In the same vein but even more abstracted is a fixation like that of Mike Hammer in *Kiss Me Deadly*, who is caught up in his quest for a "great whatsit" without even knowing what it contains. Like inveterate gamblers, neither Hammer nor Neff can resist the opportunity of "making a play." Like their alienated counterparts, the compulsive behavior of such figures can lead to sardonic, bitter, even existential realizations. Of course, those who perish do not always do so alone. Thompson and his wife slump together in a final lifeless union at the close of *Criss Cross*. Equally lethal is the last embrace of Neff and Phyllis in *Double Indemnity*, where they clasp their bodies together and shoot each other in a deadly parody of sexual climax.

The irony of Neff's position, when he discovers that as predicted he must "ride to the end of the line" resides less in the sexuality than in the self-destructive quality of his actions. To a certain extent all of the figures that act similarly in film noir, whether they are obsessed sexually or otherwise, concurrently know at some level that they restrain themselves if they wish to survive to old age. For a man or woman whom "the absurd may strike in the face," psychological trauma follows from being in a double bind, unable and unwilling to choose between equally bleak alternatives. For those whose illogical attachment to another person or thing imperils them, there is no double-faceted irony. As Neff winces from the pain of his bullet wound at the conclusion of *Double Indemnity*, Keyes, the man who represents the system which Neff tried to defeat, lights a match for him. With that gesture, the subtlest nuance of the *noir* sensibility is invoked: the greatest failure is not in succumbing to the temptation, in falling prey to illicit attraction or being caught in a double bind. The greatest failure is never accepting the possibility of redemption, however small.

If the range of the noir vision is initially defined by such characterizations as Galt and Neff, it is sustained by its distinctive visual style. Influenced as it may be other movements and by technology and by the proclivities of particular filmmakers, that style is an expression of both character emotions and narrative concepts through a pattern of visual usage. It could be asserted that there is considerable preconception involved when someone "detects" alienation lurking beyond the frame line in a panorama of dark, wet city streets or obsession in a point-of-view shot that picks a woman's face out of crowd. On the other hand to resist such a reading is to deny the full potential of figurative values not merely in film noir but in all film. Obviously none of the various elements of visual style—angle, composition, lighting, depth of staging, camera movement or montage—which inform any given shot or sequence are unique to film noir. As with the group of eight films discussed earlier, what sets the noir cycle apart is the unity of its formal approach applied by diverse hands.

This unity goes beyond such bravura effects as the equation of a drug-induced breakdown with visual distortion in *Murder My*

Kiss Me Deadly: *When a sardonic anti-Galahad like Mike Hammer is intent on make a play, neither a greedy morgue attendant nor a sleepy-eyed femme fatal can long deter him.*

Sweet or the unbroken subjective cameras in *Dark Passage* or *Lady in the Lake*. If anything such displays run counter to the emphasis on naturalistic staging in most noir films. Consider instead the film which followed *Lady in the Lake* for director and star Robert Montgomery, *Ride the Pink Horse*, and the remarkable manipulation of plastic reality in an opening created with cinematographer Russell Metty: After crossing a desert highway under the credits, a bus arrives in a fictional southwestern town and a figure with a briefcase emerges. Recognizing Montgomery, the viewer knows from the credits that this is no businessman but "Lucky" Gagin, although the expression suggests that his luck must have been hard. This is an actual daylight exterior, so, as the camera follows the character towards the door of the adobe-walled station, Metty uses the second telephone pole through the foreground to buffer an exposure change needed as the camera moves inside where there is less light.

The set dressing over the door under which Gagin hesitates and glances up is subtly ironic. It reads "Buenas Dias" which reinforces the fact that Gagin has not descended from a bus into Middle America where he might blend in more easily. It also says "Howdy!" the folksiness of which only exacerbates the sneer of a character who already reeks of alienation. There will be no dialogue until the very end of this long take that constitutes an entire sequence. At this point, as he strolls around the interior of the station, the mise-en-scène and Montgomery's performance are relatively neutral on the question of whether Gagin is a shady character. That changes somewhat when he opens the briefcase and the viewer can see the gun inside, while Gagin's expression makes it clear that he is keenly aware of the possibility of prying eyes. The enhancement of the subtle sounds as the briefcase is opened and closed could be taken as a slight subjectification: from Gagin's wary point-of-view these typically innocuous sounds seem louder and likelier to attract attention.

As the shot continues without the cut that typically comes within 15 or 20 seconds, the sequence shot begins to frustrate viewer expectation. After Gagin puts a piece of paper from the briefcase into a locker, he then goes to a gum dispenser, so that a 1947 viewer who wanted more plot information might well have wondered, "What's with the gum?" The answer has

Another long take in Ride the Pink Horse *leads Montgomery as Gagin from a dinner table across a dance floor and out a side entrance with the cut withheld until the protagonist is stabbed with an ice pick.*

to wait until Gagin works it around in his mouth a bit before using it to conceal the key behind a map display. In the strictest sense, all the actions here are direct enough; but the unbroken moving shot in which they are inscribed rivets the audience's attention. The use of a long take instills suspense into the otherwise ordinary acts. From his silent and methodical activity, the concentrated staging also distills for the viewer a sense of the tenacity in Gagin's character. At the same time, the sustained camera "imprisons" the protagonist temporarily within the unattractive limits of the bus depot, while it hints at some unknown or menacing person who might want that key so that it must be hidden before Gagin emerges and takes the dusty road to town. During the extended first-person point-of-view in *Lady in the Lake*, Montgomery sometimes stitched together long takes to create the illusion of sequence, and many are remarkable. Ultimately, however, the conceit in that movie has as many or more distractions as it has stylistic reinforcements of character perspective and narrative suspense. The opening long take in *Ride the Pink Horse* begins that movie with an integration of visual and aural elements, performance, and viewer expectation to create a powerful integration of dramatic tension and stylistic connotations.

Whether through a shot that lasts the entire sequence or just a few seconds, the most familiar or evocative images of the noir universe reverberate just as powerfully. Whether it is a general motif of street lights reflecting unevenly off those damp, urban landscapes or a particular broken sign flashing "kill . . . kill . . . kill" with its remaining neon letters outside a murderer's window in *The Unsuspected,* such uses are arguably also the most naturalistic. A high angle, long shot, cluttered with dark foreground shadows entangles the private detective in a deterministic web in *Kiss Me Deadly*. A traveling camera traces a long, slow arc around an oversized mechanism to reveal a figure concealed behind its threatening bulk in *The Big Clock*. A succession of low, wide angle cuts awkwardly frames a fleeing man as he moves around corners and down steps against an unending array of back streets and narrow alleys in *Night and the City*. All are proto-

typical of the noir style. The key elements of each sequence differ radically, from static shot to moving one to montage, from high angle to low; but the result is the same. The viewer understands from convention that the characters are threatened, alienated, hemmed in. It is through this sort of direct, nonverbal association that film noir's visual substance is created, that relationships or situations established through narrative and characterization are anticipated, refined, or reassessed.

There is no absolute grammar attached to this visual substance because its conventions of expression cannot be analogous to those of language. The side-lit close-up, the long take, the foreground object bisecting the frame may respectively imply a person's indecision, a building tension, a figurative separation; or they may not. The potential meaning is always there. The specific image may or may not participate in it. Again, such an observation holds true for all film. It is the associations that film noir repeatedly elects to make that are telling, so that early in the cycle the audience came to understand that the dark streets were emblems of alienation; that a character's unrelenting gaze was obsessive; that a visual environment full of shafts of light and distorted shadows was deterministic, hostile, and chaotic. Can such diverse, disruptive effects be truly unifying factors in a cycle of films? The ultimate demonstration of this unity resides with those films. The frequent use of flashback and other diffuse narrative techniques may endistance the audience. Leering villains like those in *Kiss of Death* and *The Garment Jungle* or other equally grotesque caricatures may threaten suspension of disbelief. Nevertheless, the underlying texture remains constant. The visualization brings the viewer back again and again into the fixed perspective of film noir.

As difficult as it may be to penetrate the screen of mediating influences that surrounds the inception of film noir, it would be much easier to designate an arbitrary point where the cycle began than a similar point where it ended. Given that the cycle did end and that this occurred sometime around 1960, several factors suggest themselves as causes. A change in exhibition patterns in the film industry that caused a severe reduction in the total number of motion pictures produced began in the early 1950's. In response to competition from free television dramas—where some would assert "TV noir" was born—color film stock and widescreen processes, both of which made low-key lighting difficult, were increasingly used during the 1960's. Perhaps most important of all was a sociological change, a shift in national preoccupations as an extended postwar malaise was replaced by legitimate if less apocalyptic concerns over economic recessions and suburban conformity.

As the individual entries in this volume will detail, the motion pictures that constitute the classic period of film noir vary considerably in many respects from plot to production value; but they reflect a common ethos. They consistently evoke the dark side of the American persona. The central figures in these films, caught in their double binds, filled with existential bitterness, drowning outside the social mainstream, are America's stylized vision of itself, a mirror of the mental dysfunction of a nation in uncertain transition and a distillation of an American style.

ABANDONED (1949)

Director: Joseph M. Newman. **Screenplay**: Irwin Gielgud with additional dialogue by William Bowers from articles published in the *Los Angeles Mirror*. **Producer**: Jerry Bresler. **Director of Photography**: William Daniels. **Music**: Walter Scharf. **Art Directors**: Bernard Herzbrun, Robert Boyle. **Editor**: Edward Curtiss. **Cast**: Dennis O'Keefe (Mark Sitko), Gale Storm (Paula Considine), Jeff Chandler (District Attorney McRae), Meg Randall (Dottie Jensen), Raymond Burr (Kerric), Marjorie Rambeau (Mrs. Donner), Jeanette Nolan (Major Ross), Mike Mazurki (Hoppe), Will Kuluva (Little Guy DeCola), David Clarke (Harry), William Page (Scoop), Sid Tomack (Mr. Humes), Perc Launders (Dowd), Steve Darrell (Brenn), Clifton Young (Eddie), Ruth Sanderson (Mrs. Spence), Narrator (Jeff Chandler). **Location**: Los Angeles, California. **Completed**: May 28, 1949. **Released**: Universal, October 28. 78 minutes.

A young woman, Paula Considine, comes to Los Angeles to find her missing sister. She is befriended and assisted by a newspaperman, Mark Sitko. Unfortunately, they soon discover that the sister died of an apparent suicide shortly after giving birth to a baby. All the evidence points to a baby-brokering racket. Considine and Siko pose as a married couple looking to adopt a baby in order to infiltrate the racket in the hopes of breaking up the operation and finding her dead sister's child. Kerric, a P.I. involved with the phony adoption scheme, decides to double-cross his partners. In the ensuing confusion, the syndicate kidnaps Considine and her sister's baby. Sitko, with the help of the district attorney, raids the hideout and rescues Considine and the child.

Abandoned finds its place securely within the docu-noir movement. In the tradition of films like *House on 92nd Street*, *Call Northside 777*, and *T-Men*, the film employs the elements of location shooting, stories drawn from the headlines, and "voice of God" narration to affect the tone and look of a documentary. In this case the subject is illegal baby-brokering and the setting Los Angeles. The film opens and closes on the iconic art deco monument to municipal government, City Hall, while the narrator (Jeff Chandler, who also plays the crime-fighting district attorney) introduces the "true to life story behind one such headline."

Hoping to recreate the success of Mark Hellinger's *The Naked City* (the studio even uses the same award-winning cinematographer William Daniels), the film effectively utilizes numerous locations including City Hall as mentioned (both as an exterior and an interior), Echo Park, Bunker Hill, and downtown Los Angeles while wearing its social awareness on its sleeve. Dennis O'Keefe, in a role diametrically opposed to his masochistic one in *T-Men*, plays the cynical,

fast-talking newspaperman Sitko who becomes involved with Paula in her quest to find her sister's baby more out of sexual attraction than any altruistic motives. Gale Storm's performance as the disraught Paula pales beside O'Keefe's macho bravura. She is, in fact, the weak element in the film, demonstrating none of the strengths typical of females in noir films.

Noir icon Raymond Burr delivers another striking performance as Kerric, a P.I. who is beginning to have qualms (both moral and emotional) about his involvement with the syndicate. The inheritor of Laird Cregar's mantle (the men were colleagues and friends), the actor manages to infuse the morally flawed Kerric with a sensitivity and vulnerability which keep the character from becoming a flat, one-dimensional heavy like Mike Mazurki's Hoppe, the syndicate's chief thug. His large figure "skulking" (Sitko's words) moodily as he tracks the reporter and Paula through their investigation; the compulsive wringing of his hands when he confronts the "spider woman" character of the piece, Mrs. Donner, who heads the baby-brokering racket; and finally his torture at the hands of the hoods when they discover his betrayal—all help create the type of conflicted and sympathetic characterization with which Burr would soon become associated. JU

THE ACCUSED (1949)

Director: William Dieterle. **Screenplay**: Ketti Frings and [uncredited] Leonard Spigelgass, Barre Lyndon, Jonathan Latimer, Allen Rivkin, Charles Schnee based on the novel, *Be Still, My Love*, by June Truesdell. **Producer**: Hal Wallis. **Director of Photography**: Milton Krasner. **Music**: Victor Young. **Art Directors**: Hans Dreier, Earl Hedrick. **Editor**: Warren Low. **Cast**: Loretta Young (Wilma Tuttle), Robert Cummings (Warren Ford), Wendell Corey (Lt. Ted Dorgan), Sam Jaffe (Dr. Romley), Douglas Dick (Bill Perry), Suzanne Dalbert (Susan Duval), Sara Allgood (Mrs. Conner), Mickey Knox (Jack Hunter). **Location**: Veterans Administration Hospital, Los Angeles. **Completed**: May 28, 1948. **Released**: Paramount, January 12. 101 minutes.

On the pretext of discussing his research on "psychothymia," student Bill Perry takes a professor of psychology, Wilma Tuttle, to a remote stretch of beach where he attempts seduction. Wilma panics after initially responding and fatally hits Bill with a steel bar. She disguises his murder as an accident and then hitches a ride home. In despair, she attempts suicide but is found and hospitalized. During the ensuing routine police investigation, Wilma meets Warren Ford, Perry's lawyer and guardian, and Lt. Ted Dorgan, both of whom are romantically drawn to her. At the news that the

coroner's jury finds Bill's death accidental, Wilma is distraught. This arouses the suspicions of both Ford and Dorgan. Furthermore, Perry's girlfriend suddenly recalls that he was meeting with a "psychothymiac" the night he died. A clinical police scientist helps Dorgan make Wilma incriminate herself. Ford is her defense attorney and wins her acquittal from the murder charge by proving that Wilma's only crime was concealment of the accident.

The Accused is strongly reminiscent of Lang's *Woman in the Window*, but it eliminates the "framing" story of the latter and replaces the older man with a young woman as the shy, retiring professor of psychology. The opening night-for-night exterior sequence, in which the disheveled and frightened Wilma leaves the beach to be picked up by a truck driver on the highway, precedes the revelation of the killing and attempted cover-up through a series of flashbacks via Wilma's nightmares and hallucinations. Visually and thematically the noir style is thoroughly in play. *The Accused* is also a typical example of Hollywood's post-World War II psychologizing and its subsequent stereotypes of frustration: Sam Jaffe's brief but excellent portrayal of the callous scientist whose quest for knowledge demeans his empathy for others, and Loretta Young's portrayal of the prim and proper teacher whose frenetic responses suggest the sexual energies beneath her rigid persona. A good deal of the prevailing American attitude towards women is implicit in the fact that Wilma, in her role as an intellectual and teacher, must repress her sexuality. It is only when she temporarily abandons this role that she is able, literally, to let her hair down and become a "complete" woman or, rather, that aspect of a postwar woman so pointedly mocked a half dozen years later in the opening of *Kiss Me Deadly*: "Ah, woman, the incomplete sex. And what does she need to complete her? One man, wonderful man."

In terms of the "wonderful men" who want to "complete" Wilma, Dorgan is much closer to the prototypical noir hero. His obsession with Wilma, despite her open preference for Ford, creates an emotional conflict with his investigation of her and tempts him to tamper with evidence. Although Dorgan convinces himself that he has done his job in spite of his feelings, he is afflicted by doubts that his ill-concealed desire for her may affect her prosecution. It is, in fact, a source of great relief to Wilma, but of equally great distress to

Dorgan, when his constant questioning finally causes her to break down and reveal her actions. Repeated close-ups isolate Dorgan in the courtroom as he watches Wilma sitting confidently next to Ford. These shots reveal his complex and bitter realization: that his relationship with Wilma, albeit non-physical, will soon be over, that she will be acquitted and marry Ford, thereby becoming that "complete" woman; and that he will have tormented her, gaining only her hatred. **AS & BP**

ACE IN THE HOLE [aka **THE BIG CARNIVAL**] (1951)

Director/Producer: Billy Wilder. **Screenplay**: Wilder, Lesser Samuels, and Walter Newman. **Director of Photography**: Charles B. Lang. **Music**: Hugo Friedhofer. **Art Directors**: Hal Pereira, Earl Hedrick. **Editors**: Doane Harrison, Arthur Schmidt. **Cast**: Kirk Douglas (Charles Tatum), Jan Sterling (Lorraine), Robert Arthur (Herbie Cook), Porter Hall (Jacob Q. Boot), Frank Cady (Mr. Federber), Richard Benedict (Leo Minosa), Ray Teal (Sheriff), Lewis Martin (McCardle), John Berkes (Papa Minosa), Frances Dominguez (Mama Minosa), Gene Evans (Deputy Sheriff), Frank Jacquet (Smollett), Harry Harvey (Dr. Hilton), Bob Bumps (Radio Announcer), Geraldine Hall (Mrs. Federber), Richard Gaines (Nagel), Paul D. Merrill, Stewart Kirk Clawson (Federber Boys). **Location**: Gallup and Albuquerque, New Mexico. **Completed**: September 11, 1950. **Released**: Paramount, as *Ace in the Hole* on June 29, as *The Big Carnival* on July 6. 119 minutes [110 minutes in previews as *Ace in the Hole*.].

Charles Tatum, once an ace journalist, is now an alcoholic has-been who talks his way into a job with the local paper in Albuquerque, New Mexico. Always looking for an angle that can take him back to the big time, Tatum is sent to cover a seemingly minor story of a man trapped by a cave-in. By shoring up the cave's weakened tunnels, rescue workers could reach the entombed Leo Minosa in a matter of hours; but Tatum remembers the national sensation caused by the 1925 Floyd Collins story and has other plans for Leo. He recommends rescue by a lengthy drilling process, pointing out to Leo's faithless wife, Lorraine, the profits to be made selling refreshments to sensation seekers and convincing the local sheriff that his upcoming election campaign can be helped by prolonged publicity. Drilling begins, the story goes out, and hordes of eager onlookers, reporters, and radio and television personalities pour into the dingy little town. Tatum is on top again. But before the rescuers can reach him, Leo dies. Realizing what he has wrought, a wounded Tatum returns to the newspaper office where he collapses and dies.

Ace in the Hole is one of the most grimly cynical motion pictures ever to emerge from Hollywood. It was condemned as a compassionless and contemptuous distortion of human nature, while several newspaper film reviewers complained that American journalists had been slandered. However, although the film was reportedly banned in Malaya for portraying a facet of American life "that might be misunderstood," it received the Venice Film Festival award for the outstanding Hollywood film of that year. The controversy inspired Paramount executives to nickname the film "Ass In the Wringer." None of this can detract from *Ace in the Hole*'s evident strengths. Its cynicism is so unrelenting that it becomes compelling; and the atmosphere in which that cynicism is presented is so painstakingly detailed, so richly realized, that its point of view defies repudiation. Audiences of the postwar, anti-Communist witch-hunt years were forced to turn their backs on such darkness; if *Ace in the Hole* had been made today, in an age that makes a fetish of acknowledging errors, it might very well have been a success.

The film has two determinedly noir performances by Kirk Douglas and Jan Sterling. Douglas is all bluster and calculation; never has he made such significant use of his manic laugh, his egotistical ferocity, and the cheap, slick side of his personality. In contrast to Douglas' "big" performance, Sterling's is quiet and subtle, conveyed by the obsequious look of her saucer-shaped eyes, in the twist of her pouting mouth, and through the brassy tone of her voice. Urged to strike a prayerful pose for publicity photos, she snarls, "I don't pray. Kneeling bags my nylons." The power of Sterling's performance is that she reveals the fear and the emptiness beneath her tough-broad facade. Her emptiness is reflected also in the film's bleak locale: the tawdry roadside cafe and souvenir shop, typical of those that unremittingly punctuate the American landscape.

Familiar, too, is what this emptiness becomes when inundated by gawkers, sensation-seekers, profiteers, and "gentlemen" of the press—all feeding off the misery and ultimately the death of another human being. The enthusiastic attempted rescue of Leo Minosa is presented by the filmmakers as a universally hypocritical and exploitative sideshow. With exaggerated precision and detail, the narrative builds through an interview with the doomed man, crescendos with a topical tune entitled, "We're Coming, Leo," sung by the spectators to cheer him and culminates in a silent visual eulogy as Leo's fans garner grisly souvenirs from around the death site before dispersing, leaving the desert empty except for their wind-swept litter. The major events of the film take place in a glaring desert sunlight that gives a hard edge to every action of the characters and twist of the plot. In contrast to the literally bright and cheerful sympathizers, Leo truly suffers in a dank cave where he ultimately dies of pneumonia. In Wilder's noir vision, the indi-

vidual is figuratively frozen by the neglect of his fellow human beings, even as they imitate concern. Leo, as a film noir figure, dies without realizing that his world is supported by humanitarian ideals made only of sand. **JK & EW**

ACT OF VIOLENCE (1949)

Director: Fred Zinnemann. **Screenplay**: Robert L Richards based on a story by Collier Young. **Producer**: William H. Wright. **Director of Photography**: Robert Surtees. **Music**: Bronislau Kaper. **Art Directors**: Cedric Gibbons, Hans Peters. **Editor**: Conrad A. Nervig. **Cast**: Van Heflin (Frank R. Enley), Robert Ryan (Joe Parkson), Janet Leigh (Edith Enley), Mary Astor (Pat), Phyllis Thaxter (Ann Sturges), Barry Kroeger (Johnny), Nicholas Joy (Mr. Gavery), Harry Antrim (Fred Finney), Connie Gilchrist (Martha Finney), Will Wright (Pop). **Locations**: Downtown Los Angeles & Big Bear Lake, California. **Completed**: July 7, 1948. **Released**: MGM, January 23. 81 minutes.

Limping war veteran Joe Parkson arrives in a Central California town in search of Frank Enley, a respected contractor and civic-minded man. Parkson tracks Enley to a nearby lake but he has already left. Learning that Parkson is in town, Enley panics. Explaining to his wife, Edith, that this man is mentally disturbed, Enley leaves for a convention in Los Angeles. Edith confronts Parkson and hears his story. Later, her husband confess that while a prisoner during WWII he informed on an escape plan because he believed the Germans would spare the men involved. Parkson is the only man who survived the escape attempt. Enley flees into city's streets where he meets Pat, who provides him shelter. Through her, he arranges for a hired assassin. Parkson and Enley confront one another at the train station, but Enley realizes he cannot commit another betrayal and sacrifices himself.

Act of Violence is a film noir with a social theme. It is primarily involved with the torments of Enley's conscience: he cannot forget that his comrades were shot down but his recollection of the events focuses on such marginal questions as the food with which the enemy had rewarded him. Parkson is

Ace in the Hole: Left, Tatum (Kirk Douglas) and Leo (Richard Benedict); right Lorraine (Jan Sterling) and Tatum .

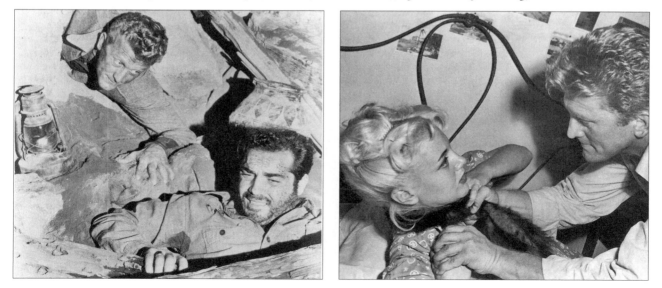

Act of Violence: *Enley (Van Heflin) and wife Edith (Janet Leigh).*

not a complex character, so his desire for revenge could indeed be taken as more the result of his mind being unbalanced by his wounds than by any genuine moral outrage. The entire film moves toward Enley's act of atonement but without suggesting an attitude to the incident that precipitated his guilt. Consequently, as is often true of films directed by Fred Zinnemann, the social theme is not forceful and the whole tone of the film is dispassionate. While Enley and Parkson are not among the more interesting portrayals by Heflin and Ryan in film noir, the presence of these two actors does create a dynamic, iconic context. Ryan's performance in the opening scenes—the methodical and unemotional manner in which Parkson learns that Enley has gone fishing, hires a car, drives to the lake, rents a boat, rows out to an ambush position and pulls out his pistol—all take place before the viewer knows what Enley could possibly have done to incur such hatred. Only in the context of Van Heflin's performance when Enley reacts by fleeing and furtively holing up in his home, shades drawn, lights off, wife and child thrown into a panic without explanation, does the viewer begin to suspect that Parkson may be more than just a ruthless, cold-blooded killer.

In terms of the noir cycle the visual schematization to the film is predictable. It begins in daylight in unthreatening surroundings and proceeds to a seamier environment as Enley wanders the empty urban streets in the hours before dawn desperately seeking a place to hide from Parkson's fury. These later scenes reveal the talent of photographer Robert Surtees, who contributes atmospheric night-for-night exteriors and evocatively lit interiors that are worthy of the best film noir. Enley's confession, which is the emotional center of *Act of Violence*, is a remarkable sequence constructed of a long take that lasts for just over two minutes. Enley and his wife retreat to a stairwell for privacy, and it is a remarkable amalgam of angled set pieces created by the twisting stairs, dark handrails and distorted shadows from some chain link and from their figures cast on the back walls. As the tension of the long take builds, Enley comes to the foreground and, looking away from her, tells Edith he lied about the mental condition of the man who is stalking him. When Enley pivots and tries to justify this by saying he did not want her to "carry it, too," Zinnemann stays on Janet Leigh as Edith, allows her expression to reveal her dark realization that, despite what her hus-

band wanted, she is now fully immersed the world of noir. When she comes into the light, the emotional focus shifts to her. In the context of a tense long take, Zinnemann even permits a four-second pause in the dialogue. In the second half of the scene, Zinnemann intercuts, starting with a significant visual shift to a low angle that puts Enley's continuing confession in foreground and isolates Edith. By switching to performance editing that relies on seeing reactions, Zinnemann completes the scene conventionally. After a pseudo-iris holds the couple together on the stairs, Enley gets up and stands on the platform above. From this point, putting the two actors in separate shots subtly suggests at this decisive point in the story that they may not share the same fate. **AS & BL**

AFFAIR IN HAVANA (1957)

Director: Laszlo Benedek. **Screenplay**: Maurice Zimm, Burton Lane based on a story by Janet Green. **Producer**: Richard Goldstone. **Director of Photography**: Alan Stensvold. **Production Designer**: Gabriel Scognamillo. **Music**: Ernest Gold. **Editor**: Stefan Arnsten. **Cast**: Raymond Burr (Mallabee), John Cassavetes (Nick), Sara Shayne (Lorna), Lilia Lazo (Fina), Sergio Pena (Valdes), Celia Cruz (Singer). **Released**: Allied Artists, October 1. 77 minutes.

At the airport in Havana, sugar-cane tycoon Mallabee, confined to a wheelchair due to an accident he blames his wife for, deplanes with his young wife Lorna. Instead of heading out to Mallabee's baronial estate in the mountains, they dine at a Havana club where the pianist Nick is performing. Nick seems uneasy, as does Lorna, which is understandable, since they have been carrying on a clandestine affair. Mallabee invites Nick to his estate and Nick, somewhat reluctantly, accepts. Mallabee, who has hired a detective to document his wife's infidelities. including her affair with Nick, concocts a plan to force his wife to murder him. The plan works only partially. Instead of Lorna committing the murder, the dog-loyal servant Valdes drowns Mallabee, thinking he is protecting Lorna. Her plot eventually unravels as Nick can no longer handle the guilt he feels and extricates himself from Lorna and her web and returns to his piano.

Affair in Havana showcases an ambiguous femme fatale. Initially, Lorna, the melancholic wife of the crippled industrialist Mallabee, elicits the audience's sympathy with her downcast gaze, neediness, and demure appearance. But as the film progresses her solicitude and kindness towards her husband is compromised by revelations to the audience of her greed and lust. Slowly, Mallabee begins to displace her as the sympathetic center of the film. With his hulking body strapped into a wheelchair, he impotently stares at his wife's half-naked body, forlornly watches 16mm footage taken by a detective of his wife with her new lover and broods over the boating accident that left him paralyzed. Even when he concocts his plan to force his wife to murder him, it is more the despairing act of a man tormented by his fate and his love for his sexually unobtainable wife than an invidious scheme for revenge.

By this point in the film, Lorna has transformed herself into a full-blown femme fatale. The murder scene is particularly relevant: intercut with a Cuban fiesta, where singing star Celia Cruz performs, Mallabee stares into the pool and taunts his wife, hoping she will drown him, thus putting him out of his misery. As he struggles with her, the smitten servant Valdes enters, pushing Mallabee into the pool and drowning him, as if, like a zombie (the trance-like native music reinforces this interpretation), he is acting out the words of hate his beloved mistress had uttered a few seconds earlier. Lorna, now released, runs joyfully to her lover, who reacts with horror.

An admirable example of truth in labeling, *Affair In Havana* is about just that. The film, in fact, resembles nothing so much as a swift, steamy verismo opera, albeit one set to a Cuban-bop score. This is the pre-Castro Cuba whose final days were so vividly summoned in *The Godfather II*: Batista's venal, wide-open playground for wealthy Americans (the movie was filmed entirely on location). The film is also notable for another emotional performance by noir regular Raymond Burr, this time sporting a platinum buzz cut, as the bitter and obsessed industrialist Mallabee and John Cassavetes delivering an early version of his high-strung hipster persona, this time as the jazz pianist lover of Mallabee's wife. **JU & BMV**

AFFAIR IN TRINIDAD (1952)

Director: Vincent Sherman. **Screenplay**: Oscar Saul, James Gunn based on an original story by Bernie Giler, Virginia Van Upp. **Producer**: Vincent Sherman (Beckworth Corporation). **Associate Producer**: Virginia Van Upp. **Director of Photography**: Joseph Walker. **Music**: Morris W. Stoloff, George Duning. **Art Directors**: Walter Holscher. **Editor**: Viola Lawrence. **Cast**: Rita Hayworth (Chris Emery), Glenn Ford (Steve Emery), Alexander Scourby (Max Fabian), Valerie Bettis (Veronica Huebling), Torin Thatcher (Inspector Smythe), Howard Wendell (Anderson), Karel Stepanek (Walters), George Voskovec (Doctor Franz Huebling), Steven Geray (Wittol), Walter Kohler (Peter Bronec), Juanita Moore (Dominique), Gregg Martell (Olaf, Fabian's Chauffeur), Mort Mills (Martin, Wittol's Henchman), Ralph Moody (Coroner). **Released**: Columbia Pictures, July 29. 98 minutes.

After receiving an urgent missive from his brother, American World War II veteran Steve Emery flies to Trinidad to find his brother mysteriously dead and his brother's sultry, voluptuous American nightclub singer wife, Chris, carousing with some dubious, suspicious characters. Sparks fly as widow and brother-in-law clash and the couple spar in a tumultuous love-hate affair. Police inspector Smythe suspects Emery's death may have involved foul play by prominent gangster club owner, Max Fabian, and Smythe asks Chris to go undercover to crack the case, but Steve is livid with jealousy. Fabian is not only a murderer but also engaged in nefarious Cold War activities developing missles in the Caribbean. He meets his demise as Steve and Chris fall in love and fly off to America.

"SHE'S BACK! With that man from GILDA!" heralded this comeback vehicle for Columbia star Rita Hayworth after a four-year absence from the screen. *Affair in Trinidad* recast costar Glenn Ford in a Cold War noir variation on *Gilda*, with a bit of *Notorious* thrown in for good measure. Studio chief Harry Cohn was glad to have Hayworth, Columbia's signature star and 1940s "love goddess," back making films after her long hiatus following *The Loves of Carmen* (1948) and the actress' departure from Hollywood in the wake of her 1949 marriage (and eventual breakup) to Ali Khan. After an extended contract suspension, Columbia had to start paying the star's lucrative

$3,500 a week salary and brought in freelance director Vincent Sherman for her return project, *Affair in Trinidad*.

Veteran (former Warner Bros.) director Sherman would also produce the picture, a Beckworth Corporation production released through Columbia, after original producer Bert Granet walked off the project. Columbia writer-producer and former studio production chief Virginia Van Upp crafted a story for the film that recaptures the spirit of *Gilda* in hopes of repeating its tremendous success. Van Upp also served as associate producer on *Affair in Trinidad*. She had previously mentored and groomed Hayworth for Columbia's *Cover Girl* (1944), *Gilda*, and *The Lady From Shanghai* (1947) all during the period of Van Upp's writing and production supervision at the studio.

Like *Gilda*, *Affair in Trinidad* is filled with intrigue, gender distress, and Hayworth's redeeming femme with great chemistry opposite Ford, plus wonderfully brooding, atmospheric noir cinematography, yet with a new Cold War 1950s spin and cultural context. Valerie Bettis choreographed Hayworth's dances in *Affair in Trinidad* such as "Trinidad Lady," which sought to remind viewers of the salacious excitement of the star's famed "Put the Blame on Mame" coded-striptease number from *Gilda*. While *Affair in Trinidad's* musical numbers, costumes and choreography don't quite capture the magic of *Gilda*, it is a solid, fascinating moody noir melodrama. Hayworth and Ford give wonderful performances as tormented lovers. Hayworth is compelling as a beautiful albeit reluctant undercover spy for the authorities to breakup a dangerous Cold War cartel and save the Western hemisphere from destruction. Although the budget for *Affair in Trinidad* rose above $1 million, the film was incredibly successful, earning $7 million in the US alone, and out-grossing *Gilda*. **SCB**

AMONG THE LIVING (1941)

Director: Stuart Heisler. **Screenplay**: Lester Cole, Garrett Fort based on a story by Brian Marlow and Cole. **Producer**: Sol C. Siegel. **Director of Photography**: Theodor Sparkuhl. **Art Director**: Haldane Douglas. **Editor**: Everett Douglas. **Cast**: Albert Dekker (John Raden/Paul Raden), Susan Hayward (Millie Pickens), Harry Carey (Dr. Ben Saunders), Frances Farmer (Elaine Raden), Gordon Jones (Bill Oakley), Jean Phillips (Peggy Nolan), Ernest Whitman (Pompey), Maude Eburne (Mrs. Pickens). **Completed**: June 6. **Released**: Paramount, December 12. 67 minutes.

John Raden and wife Elaine return home for his father's funeral. John believes he is the sole heir of his proud and prosperous Southern family, until family physician Dr. Saunders informs him that his identical twin brother, Paul, thought to have died as a child, is alive but hopelessly insane, ensconced in the abandoned family manor under the care of faithful servant Pompey. Paul's illness stems from an injury sustained when trying to stop his father's abuse of his mother. To conceal the family scandal, Saunders falsified Paul's death and received the money for a badly needed town medical center. Saunders and John go to the mansion and find that Pompey has been killed. When a bar-girl's body is found, a reward is offered for her killer. John wants to tell the police, but Saunders threatens to accuse John of insanity. Locals who believe the killer is hiding at the old Raden house arrive just as Paul attacks a young woman, Millie, who befriended him. Paul is shot but escapes, knocking down John in the process. No one believes John's story that his twin Paul is responsible, and enraged townspeople prepare to lynch him. But John escapes and finds Paul's body at their mother's grave while Saunders tells the sheriff the truth.

Among the Living was released in the fall of 1941, about the same time as *The Maltese Falcon,* and these films stand at the beginning of the noir cycle, before many of the conventions of film noir had been established. It looks backward to the horror films of the 1930s and was promoted as such at the time of its release. As social commentary this film stands between earlier films like *Fury,* and later film noirs like *Try and Get Me.* But what makes *Among the Living* more than a curio is the near brilliant photography of Theodor Sparkuhl, who had worked on a number of classic German films in the 1920s. His work here is a prime example of film noir's debt to German Expressionism. The scene in which Paul follows the bar-girl down the cluttered streets of the Southern mill town, for example, would not be out of place in any of the "street films" of the German cinema. Additionally, the shot of him killing her within the narrow confines of an alley is an example of extreme depth staging, a stylistic hallmark of film noir. Finally, the montage in the bar which preceded it, where the music, brawls, and suggestive dancing all drive Paul to a state of distraction, foreshadows later film noir like *The Phantom Lady* and *The Killers* in its concatenation of jazz, sex and violence. **BP**

Among the Living: *Dr. Saunders (Harry Carey, left) confronts Paul Baden (Albert Dekker).*

Angel Face: *Frank Jessup (Robert Mitchum) and Diane Tremayne (Jean Simmons).*

ANGEL FACE (1953)

Director and Producer: Otto Preminger (Howard Hughes Productions). **Screenplay**: Frank Nugent and Oscar Millard based on a story by Chester Erskine. **Director of Photography**: Harry Stradling. **Music**: Dimitri Tiomkin. **Art Directors**: Albert S. D'Agostino, Carroll Clark. **Editor**: Frederic Knudtson. **Cast**: Robert Mitchum (Frank Jessup), Jean Simmons (Diane Tremayne), Mona Freeman (Mary), Herbert Marshall (Mr. Tremayne), Leon Ames (Fred Barrett), Barbara O'Neil (Mrs. Tremayne), Kenneth Tobey (Bill), Raymond Greenleaf (Arthur Vance), Griff Barnett (Judge), Robert Gist (Miller), Morgan Farley (juror), Jim Backus (Judson). **Completed**: September 27, 1952. **Released**: RKO, February 2. 91 minutes.

Ambulance driver Frank Jessup is called to a hillside estate and saves the life of Mrs. Tremayne, who was almost asphyxiated by gas in her bedroom. When Frank tells Diane Tremayne that her stepmother has survived, Diane becomes hysterical. Despite this, he is attracted to Diane who encourages her father to hire Frank as the family chauffeur. He soon suspects that Diane plans to murder her stepmother by contriving a car accident. Yet his emotions do not allow him to leave Diane or warn her victim. Mr. Tremayne is also killed when his wife's car careens off a cliff. Both Diane and Frank are indicted for the murder and their lawyer, Fred Barrett, urges them to marry to help their case. Both are acquitted and Frank is ready to abandon this murderess. But he cannot refuse her offer to drive him to the bus station and she succeeds in killing them both.

At its melodramatic extremes in Otto Preminger's work, sexuality may be either therapeutic (*Tell Me That You Love Me, Junie Moon*) or destructive (*Fallen Angel, Carmen Jones; Such Good Friends*). *Angel Face* epitomizes the latter quality. The fascination that Frank, the lower-class ambulance driver, develops for the spoiled but beautiful and wealthy Diane not only evokes the traditional noir motivations of sex and money but the danger of obsessive relationships as well. Although Preminger does not suggest that Frank is a hapless victim, his *mise-en-scène,* which repeatedly frames the figures in obliquely angled medium shots against the depth of field created by the expensive furnishings of the Tremayne mansion, and Mitchum's subdued portrayal engender an atmosphere of fatality that is generally understated. The climactic moments of murder and suicide, however, are not attenuated by the casting against type of Jean Simmons. Her more usually heroic parts belie the barely repressed violence of her character for the viewer as well as for Frank. By encouraging the audience to empathize with Frank's uncontrollable attraction to Diane and by adding visual stability to her insular, mentally unbalanced world, Preminger compels them to co-experience both Frank's hopes for ultimate salvation and also, in the film's fundamental noir statement, the moral resolution of his death. **AS**

APOLOGY FOR MURDER (1945)

Director: Sam Newfield. **Screenplay**: Fred Myton. **Producer**: Sigmund Newfeld. **Director of Photography**: Jack Greenhalgh. **Music**: Leo Erdody. **Art Director**: Edward Jewell. **Editor**: Holbrook Todd. **Cast**: Ann Savage (Toni Kirkland), Hugh Beaumont (Kenny Blake), Russell Hicks (Harvey Kirkland), Charles D. Brown (Ward McGee), Pierre Watkin (Craig Jordan), Sarah Padden (Janitress), Norman Willis (Allen Webb), Eva Novak (Maid). **Released**: PRC, September 27. 67 minutes.

Reporter Kenny Blake is assigned to interview wealthy Harvey Kirkland and is quickly seduced by Kirkland's young, devious wife, Toni. Kenny is not strong enough to resist Toni's wiles and together they concoct a scheme to kill Kirkland so that Toni will inherit his money. Kenny manages to kill Kirkland but the plan goes awry. There is an eyewitness who has seen Kenny but fails to recognize him later. Eventually an innocent party is arrested for the murder and Kenny's editor and best friend, Ward McGee, assigns him to cover the story. McGee has a gut feeling that the police have the wrong man and encourages Kenny to continue probing. In the process Kenny realizes that he has been duped by Toni and replaced by the young lawyer who is representing her in the settlement of the Kirkland estate. When he confronts her she tries to shoot him but he kills her instead. Wounded and bleeding badly, he returns to his empty newspaper office late at night to type up the real story. McGee enters the office just as Kenny finishes the story, lighting his cigarette with the lighter that Kenny had left behind at the scene of Toni's murder.

Prior to its release the producers of *Apology For Murder* claimed that its story was drawn from the actual murder case that was the basis of the Cain novel and Paramount's *Double Indemnity*. From today's perspective it appears that this was little more than a ploy to avoid legal action, as this film displays too many gambits contained in that earlier film to be mere coincidence: the framing of the dying protagonist dictating his story is replaced by him typing it out in a darkened office; the paternal superior is replaced by the paternal editor, even to the point where their roles are reversed at the end when McGee lights Kenny's cigarette with Kenny's lighter; *Double Indemnity's* Walter is at first drawn to Phyllis' anklet just as Kenny is first fixated by Toni's ankle strap . . . and so on.

Apology For Murder was released just prior to *Detour*, a film which would immortalize Ann Savage as a *femme noire*, and her presence here is this film's main asset. Beaumont's protagonist lacks the hard-edged cynicism of MacMurray's Neff (of course Fred Myton was no Chandler or Wilder) and the fatherly Charles Brown lacks the dyspeptic obsessiveness of Robinson's Keyes. Most tragically, this PRC quickie lacks the hand of an Edgar Ulmer to make every foot of film count and to cover budget deficiencies with expressive lighting. Scene transitions are often abrupt and, worse, day-for-night shots are sometimes so bad they look like day-for-day. The most noir scenes, understandably, are those of Kenny in a darkened office under an overhead light telling his story with the help of a typewriter, like the good noir protagonist that he is. **BP**

APPOINTMENT WITH DANGER (1951)

Director: Lewis Allen. **Screenplay**: Richard Breen and Warren Duff. **Producer**: Robert Fellows. **Director of Photography**: John F. Seitz. **Music**: Victor Young. **Art Directors**: Hans Dreier, Albert Nozaki. **Editor**: LeRoy Stone. **Cast**: Alan Ladd (Al Goddard), Phyllis Calvert (Sister Augustine), Paul Stewart (Earl Boettiger), Jan Sterling (Dodie), Jack Webb (Joe Regas), Stacy Harris (Paul Ferrar), Henry Morgan (George Soderquist), David Wolfe (David Goodman), Dan Riss (Maury Ahearn), Harry Antrim (Taylor, Postmaster), Paul Lees (Gene Gunner). **Released**: Paramount, May 9. 89 minutes.

A postal inspector named Al Goddard is sent to investigate the killing of a post office detective in Gary, Indiana. The two killers, Joe Regas and George Soderquist, work for local hoodlum Earl Boettiger, who has a plan to defraud the postal service of a million dollars. Regas knows they were spotted at the murder scene and wants to find and kill the nun, Sister Augustine, who can identify them. Soderquist opposes this, and Boettiger doesn't think she could identify them anyway. On his own, Regas tries unsuccessfully to kill her, which convinces Goddard that he is on the right track in obtaining the nun's help. Goddard goes undercover to infiltrate Boettiger's gang and learns of their plan. Regas is suspicious of Goddard and convinces Boettiger that Soderquist is a weak link. Earl consents to eliminating Soderquist. The criminals discover that Goddard is a government agent when he unsuccessfully attempts to get help from Earl's moll, Dodie. Regas and Boettiger plan to kill both Goddard and the nun, whom they have abducted, but Goddard gains time by pretending to be open to bribery. The gang takes its hostages to a remote industrial section of town, but with the nun's aid Goddard is able to fight it out with

them until the police arrive. Goddard's toughness and cynicism have been mollified through his association with Sister Augustine.

Perhaps the most significant thing about *Appointment With Danger* is that it is the last (and the weakest) Ladd vehicle of the noir cycle. And by the time it was produced, the conventions of the semi-documentary thriller (use of a stentorian narrator, undercover agent trapped inside a gang, last minute rescue, etc.) were losing their originality. Certainly the corrosiveness of such earlier efforts as *The Glass Key* and *Blue Dahlia* is lacking and while a fresh approach to a Ladd vehicle was called for, the writers' insistence on peppering the dialogue with humorous asides and the rather trite "conversion" of Goddard at the film's conclusion was not the direction to take. Conversely, there is a liberal sprinkling of crisp, tough dialogue throughout by writers Warren Duff and Richard Breen (who would become Jack Webb's principal writer on the *Dragnet* series). A case in point: when told he doesn't know what love is, Goddard replies, "Sure I do, it's something that goes on between a man and a .45 that won't jam." Finally, the film contains two scenes which epitomize film noir's uncanny ability to create tension by charging mundane objects with menace: the "testing" of Goddard in a squash match with Regas where the ball becomes a deadly missile; and the killing of Soderquist by his buddy Regas. As Soderquist is packing to leave town, Regas casually picks up the bronzed booties that are a revered memento of Soderquist's departed son and beats him to death with them. **BP**

ARMORED CAR ROBBERY (1950)

Director: Richard Fleischer. **Screenplay**: Earl Felton and Gerald Adams based on a story by Robert Angus and Robert Leeds. **Producer**: Herman Schlom. **Director of Photography**: Guy Roe. **Music**: Roy Webb. **Art Directors**: Albert D'Agostino, Ralph Berger. **Editor**: Desmond Marquette. **Cast**: Charles McGraw (Lt. Cordell), Adele Jergens (Yvonne McBride), William Talman (Dave Purvis), Douglas Fowley (Benny McBride), Steve Brodie (Al Mapes), Don McGuire (Danny Ryan), Don Haggerty (Cuyler), James Flavin (Lt. Phillips), Gene Evans (Ace Foster). **Location**: Los Angeles. **Completed**: January 27, 1950. **Released**: RKO, June 8. 67 minutes.

Dave Purvis is a cruel, intelligent criminal who maintains a clean police record by changing identities, moving frequently and planning robberies carefully. He meets strong-arm men, Al Mapes and Ace Foster, through ex-con Benny, whose wife Yvonne is having an affair with Purvis. Benny convinces Mapes and Foster that Purvis is the best "brain man" in the business, and they agree to help Purvis rob an armored car. During the robbery a police car cruising the area spots them, and in the ensuing confrontation Benny is shot. By disguising themselves as oil-field workers, the thieves get through a roadblock to their hideout near the waterfront, where Purvis finishes off the wounded Benny. When the police, led by Lt. Cordell, surround the hideout, Ace is killed while Mapes and Purvis escape. The police locate Purvis through his phone number, which Benny kept. But the police arrest Mapes first and then learn the identities of Yvonne and Purvis. The fleeing couple is trapped at the airport before they can board a private plane. During a gun battle with the

police, Purvis is run over by an airliner, and the stolen money is scattered about his body.

Armored Car Robbery, an early caper film, did not possess the budget of *The Asphalt Jungle*, which was released at the same time, or the pretensions of *The Killing*, which told essentially the same story. The latter, of course, became a classic by virtue of the way Kubrick restructured the chronological order. But plot similarities abound, most notably the ironic ending in which the loot is blown about over the runway. *Armored Car Robbery* is a modest entry in the RKO noir series, possessing many of the attributes of the thrillers produced at that studio in the post-Welles era: high contrast photography integrating studio and location sequences via expressionistic lighting; marked use of deep focus shots; and a musical score by Roy Webb. This film is another in a string of RKO noirs directed by Richard Fleischer prior to *The Narrow Margin* which allowed Fleischer to graduate to A-budget productions. Until that justly famous film, Fleischer's work in the noir cycle reveals the debt he (and others) owe to Anthony Mann, the scene in which Purvis pops the ears of the badgering Mapes being just one minor example. **BP**

THE ASPHALT JUNGLE (1950)

Director: John Huston. **Screenplay**: Ben Maddow and Huston based on the novel by W.R. Burnett. **Producer**: Arthur Homblow, Jr. **Director of Photography**: Harold Rosson. **Music**: Miklós Rózsa. **Art Directors**: Cedric Gibbons, Randall Duell. **Editor**: George Boemler. **Cast**: Sterling Hayden (Dix Handley), Louis Calhern (Alonzo D. Emmerich), Jean Hagen (Doll Conovan), James Whitmore (Gus Minissi), Sam Jaffe (Doc Riedenschneider), John McIntire (Police Commissioner Hardy), Marc Lawrence (Cobby), Barry Kelley (Lt. Ditrich), Anthony Caruso (Louis Ciavelli), Terese Calli (Maria Ciavelli), Marilyn Monroe (Angela Phinlay), William Davis (Timmons), Dorothy Tree (May Emmerich), Brad Dexter (Bob Brannom), Alex Gerry (Maxwell), Thomas Browne Henry (James X. Connery), James Seay (Janocek), Don Haggerty (Andrews). **Completed**: December 21, 1949. **Released**: MGM, June 8. 112 minutes.

Criminal mastermind, Doc Riedenschneider, devises an elaborate jewel robbery with the financial backing of corrupt lawyer, Alonzo D. Emmerich. Doc carefully assembles a small group of semiprofessional local criminals and proceeds with plans. But Emmerich launches a double-cross. Dix Handley,

The Asphalt Jungle: *Above, Dix Hanley (Sterling Hayden) and Doll (Jean Hagen). Right, Emmerich (Louis Calhern) and his mistress Angela (Marilyn Monroe).*

the "hooligan" of the gang, catches wind of Emmerich's swindle. He is wounded while putting a stop to it and escapes. The police corner Emmerich who commits suicide. Dix gallantly persuades Doc to accept some of the money before insisting they separate into the nearby Kentucky farmland. But it is futile. Doc is captured when he stops to look wistfully at a group of farmhands. Moments later, Dix dies in a field alongside a disinterested horse.

John Huston directed this naturalistic film noir, which is derived from the novel by W.R. Burnett, best known for *Little Caesar*, whose work combined elements of the hardboiled and social realist traditions. Burnett's novels often depicted criminals honoring personal codes in an environment of urban decay. In adapting W.R. Burnett's novel to the screen, Huston and Ben Maddow instilled *The Asphalt Jungle* with a feeling of authenticity unmatched in films of that period. The dialogue is gritty and the attitudes developed by the film point to distinctively sympathetic portraits of the small-time crooks who elevate the ritual of Doc's meticulous robbery to an act of salvation, as they believe there is nothing criminal in what they do. This idealization quickly melts into a slush of wasted ambitions and petty obsessions. Surrounding the very human criminals is a society almost as corrupt as they are. Society's hypocrisy, illustrated by the crooked dealings of

bad cops and the irresponsible judgments given by uninvolved onlookers, is a bitter comment on the brutal realities of the noir world. It is one of Ben Maddow's major concerns, which he explored elsewhere in such films as *Intruder in the Dust* and *The Unforgiven*.

The Asphalt Jungle is a vivid contrast to Huston's other noir films. He has eliminated the claustrophobic quality found in both *The Maltese Falcon* and *Key Largo*, replacing it with a smooth uncluttered style. However, grotesque characters are still present in *The Asphalt* Jungle, although they exist on the periphery of the action rather than residing at the core, like Gutman in *The Maltese Falcon* and the mobsters in *Key Largo*. The failure of Doc and his associates to transcend the common nature of criminals suggests the irony of many of Huston's films. *The Asphalt Jungle* is a classic noir film because of its elements of despair and alienation. It is also the film that serves as the dividing line between the old Huston and the new Huston. After *The Asphalt Jungle*, Huston concerned himself with filmic adaptations of classic literary works such as *The Red Badge of Courage*, *Moby Dick*, and *Night of The Iguana*. He also experimented with color in *Moulin Rouge* and with structure in *Freud*. Following *The Asphalt Jungle*, Huston put aside the noir world and concentrated on other goals. **CM**

BACKFIRE (1950)

Director: Vincent Sherman. **Screenplay**: Ivan Goff, Ben Roberts, Larry Marcus from his story. **Producer**: Anthony Veiller. **Director of Photography**: Carl Guthrie. **Music**: Daniele Amfitheatrof; Max Steiner [uncredited]. **Art Director**: Anton Grot. **Editor**: Thomas Reilly. **Cast**: Virginia Mayo (Julie Benson), Gordon MacRae (Bob Corey), Edmond O'Brien (Steve Connolly), Dane Clark (Ben Arno), Viveca Lindfors (Lysa Randolph), Ed Begley (Capt. Garcia), Frances Robinson (Mrs. Blayne), Richard Rober (Solly Blayne), Sheila Stephens [MacRae] (Bonnie), David Hoffman (Burns), Monte Blue (Det. Sgt. Pluther), Ida Moore (Sybil), Leonard Strong (Quong), John Ridgely (Plainclothesman), Charles Lane (Dr. Nolan). **Released**: Warner Bros., January 26. 91 minutes.

As Bob Corey recuperates from spinal cord injuries in a veterans' hospital, he plans to buy a ranch with army buddy Steve Connolly. While Corey is semi-conscious from pain medication, a visitor tells him that Connolly is hurt and in trouble with the police. Unable to find Connolly after he is released, Corey tracks him down through the labyrinthine underbelly of postwar Los Angeles. Corey is questioned by the police who tell him that Connolly's gambling may have gotten him mixed up with gangsters and that he is suspected of murdering a syndicate kingpin. Corey is aided in his quest by his nurse Julie Benson but thrown off the trail by a mysterious foreigner Lysa Randolph.

    The dislocation felt by returning servicemen was one of the chief topical themes of the noir cycle. After being primed to take risks but no prisoners in the anarchic and violent theaters of World War II, many ex-GIs found it difficult to ratchet back down to normal behavior after their return to a society many of them perceived as jarringly altered. Amnesia was the primary noir metaphor: having to reconstruct an entire past life from scratch has darkly existential implications. Others faced having to cope with disabilities; still others, having spent the "best years of their lives" in hell holes abroad, weren't about to wait for the high life on the installment plan. *Backfire* forgoes amnesia for the latter two categories, but as always in the noir scheme things are rarely what they at first seem, particularly for returning vets drawn into a postwar urban cesspool. While sometimes awkwardly acted and staged, *Backfire* nevertheless keeps up the pace and the suspense, drawing, similarly to *Somewhere in the Night,* on the central concerns of the cycle. **BMV**

BACKLASH (1947)

Director: Eugene Forde. **Screenplay**: Irving Elman. **Producer**: Sol M. Wurtzel. **Director of Photography**: Benjamin Kline. **Music**: Darrell Calker. **Art Director**: Robert Peterson. **Editor**: William F. Claxton. **Cast**: Jean Rogers (Catherine Morland), Richard Travis (Richard Conroy), Larry J. Blake (Det. Jerry McMullen), John Eldredge (John Morland), Leonard Strong (Willis), Robert Shayne (James O'Neil), Louise Currie (Marian Gordon), Douglas Fowley (Red Bailey), Sara Berner (Dorothy), Richard Benedict (Det. Tom Carey), Wynne Larke (Patricia McMullen). **Released**: 20th Century-Fox, March 1. 66 minutes.

When a burned-out car containing remnants of a body is discovered in a ravine, the police presume that the victim is criminal attorney John Morland. The suspects include an accused cop-killer whom the lawyer saved from a murder charge, the law partner who owed Morland big money, the district attorney who may have been seeing his restless younger wife, Catherine, and temptress Marian Gordon who is connected to both the partner and the cop-killer, among others. Ultimately it is revealed that Morland staged his own death in hopes of implicating both his partner, whom he subsequently kills, and his wife.

    While *Backlash* is an ordinary programmer, it is built upon a pointedly noir premise: a jealous husband who so hates his wife that he frames her for his own murder. Morland is a successful lawyer, middle-aged, grey-haired and sporting a Thomas E. Dewey mustache, and seems indistinguishable from just about every other adult male in the cast, which creates both a narrative and a visual confusion. In fact there are a few too many red herrings squeezed into this compact, 66-minute can.

Surprisingly, *Backlash* does boast one fine scene which almost looks as though it was cut from a far superior production and spliced in by mistake. In a railroad yard at night, one of the principals meets up with a drifter who offers to share his bottle and some philosophical musings. It's filmed as an extended, highly shadowed two-shot that grows tighter and more oppressive as the talk turns to the murder case that dominates the headlines. If a single sequence can make a mediocre film worth a look, this is *Backlash*'s qualifier. **BMV**

THE BEAT GENERATION (1959)

Director: Charles Haas. **Screenplay**: Richard Matheson, Lewis Meltzer. **Producer**: Albert Zugsmith. **Director of Photography**: Walter H. Castle (CinemaScope). **Music**: Lewis Meltzer, Albert Glasser. **Art Directors**: William A. Hornin and Addison Hehr. **Editor**: Ben Lewis. **Cast**: Steve Cochran (Dave Culloran), Mamie Van Doren (Georgia Altera), Ray Danton (Stan Hess), Fay Spain (Francee Culloran), Louis Armstrong and his All Stars (Band), Maggie Hayes (Joyce Greenfield), Jackie Coogan (Jake Baron), Jim Mitchum (Art Jester), Cathy Crosby (Singer), Ray Anthony (Harry Altera), Dick Contino (Singing Beatnik), Irish McCalla (Marie Baron), Vampira (Poetess), Billy Daniels (Dr. Elcott), Maxie Rosenbloom (Wrestling Beatnik), Charles Chaplin, Jr. (Lover Boy), Grabowski (Beat Beatnik), Anne Anderson (Meg). **Completed**: November 13, 1958. **Released**: MGM, October 21. 93 minutes. **Television title**: *This Rebel Age*.

Detectives Dave Culloran and Jake Baron are assigned to the case of a rapist-robber known as the Aspirin Kid, because of his modus operandi: asking to use the telephone after a supposed car problem and then distracting the woman by feigning a headache and requesting aspirin. Culloran, an experienced street cop, doubts the story of the first victim and insinuates she may have invited the sexual assault. The prime suspect, Arthur Jester, has an alibi. While Culloran and Baron argue over continuing their investigation, Jester confronts the actual Aspirin Kid, Stan Hess, who has used Jester's name. Supported by a wealthy, dissolute father, Hess knows he can keep Jester quiet by blackmail but is furious that the cops have gotten close to him. Learning that Culloran is newly remarried, Hess targets Culloran's wife, Francee. Outraged at the assault but also alienated because under his puritanical standards his wife has been "soiled," Culloran becomes obsessed in his pursuit of the Aspirin Kid. Concerned that he may have gone too far, Hess persuades Jester to imitate his M.O. on Georgia Altera, and throw the police off the track. While Culloran spends his nights and days on the case, Francee turns to Baron and his wife for counsel, because she is pregnant and fears complete estrangement from her husband. Culloran refuses to give up, even when Francee is hospitalized with premature labor pains. Georgia Altera recognizes Jester, and Culloran follows him to a gathering of beatniks at Hess' beach house. Hess panics and attempts to flee but is caught in the surf and viciously beaten by Culloran, who is prevented from killing him only by Baron's arrival. Purged of his doubts, Culloran is reconciled with Francee and accepts their child.

Promoted at the time of its release as a quasi-satire of the contemporary youth cult, the actual narrative structure of

Underwater battle ends on the beach as the criminal "Beatnik" is hauled from the surf (Steve Cochran, Ray Danton, Mamie Van Doren).

The Beat Generation is a parallel character study of alienated criminal and equally alienated cop. In a noir plot twist, the stressed-out detective becomes almost as sociopathic as those he is paid to bring to justice. Culloran reconciles with his wife at the end, but his compulsive and ruthless behavior following the attack on her, particularly his exploitation of Georgia Altera's sexual attraction to him—which ultimately imperils her life—draws criticism from all his peers and unalterably undercuts his pose of moral righteousness for the audience. Despite the parallels with Dave Bannion in *The Big Heat*, the stakes are not as high for Culloran: although the attack on his wife is an attack on him, she is not blown to pieces in the family car. Unlike Debby Marsh, Georgia Altera is neither disfigured nor killed. Still the emotional engagement for Culloran is much the same as with Bannion. While cop and criminal battle each other through intermediaries, the similarities between the two become all the more apparent. The few glimpses offered into their pasts, such as the scene between Hess and his father and Culloran's bitter remarks about the virtue of his first wife, not only suggest a causality for their brutishness but reinforce the similarity in their disturbed psychologies. Both are abusively misogynistic; Hess obviously so in his sexual assaults but Culloran equally vicious and demeaning in his interaction with women on a verbal level. Both have no qualms about manipulating others for their own aims; Hess in his extortion of Jester, and Culloran with Georgia Altera.

The visual style of *The Beat Generation* is eclectic. Frequent close-ups of Hess and Culloran underscore the narrative focus of parallel protagonists. Also, these shots' slight flattening effect simultaneously emphasize both the physical resemblance and the behavioral contrast between the men, aided by Ray Danton's icily self-assured portrayal of Hess and Steve Cochran's nervous and explosive rendering of Culloran. The *de rigueur* scenes of bearded bongo drummers and recitals of free verse in dimly lit coffee houses are reserved for Culloran and Altera's search for her assailant and, at the level of *mise-en-scène*, provide an almost surreal background for Culloran's growing sense of estrangement. Scenes such as these, or the moment of comic relief when Culloran and Baron, who is dressed as a woman, stake out a lovers' lane in a parked car, give *The Beat Generation* a staccato tempo that matches the senses of both physical and psychological unease, which its protagonist and antagonist share. Typical of these shifts in mood is the fact that the film's only killing, when the lovers' lane bandit is shot, follows immediately after its most comic moment. The more Culloran begins to blame his environment for his difficulties—from the attack on his wife and home to something as simple as burning his hand on a coffee pot—the less he is able to cope with the natural instability of that environment. Ultimately, of course, guided by a less deterministic hand than Fritz Lang's, all ends happily. **AS**

BEHIND LOCKED DOORS (1948)

Director: Oscar [Budd] Boetticher, Jr. **Screenplay**: Eugene Ling, Marvin Wald. **Producer**: Eugene Ling. **Director of Photography**: Guy Roe. **Art Director**: Edward L. Ilou. **Music**: Irving Friedman. **Editor**: Norman Colbert. **Cast**: Lucille Bremer (Kathy Lawrence), Richard Carlson (Ross Stewart), Douglas Fowley (Larson), Ralf Harolde (Fred Hopps), Thomas Browne Henry (Dr. Clifford Porter), Herbert Hayes (Judge Drake), Gwen Donovan (Madge), Ralf Harolde (Fred Hopps) Tor Johnson ("The Champ"), Kathleen Freeman (Nurse), Dickie Moore (Jim, uncredited). **Released**: Eagle-Lion, September 3. 62 minutes.

Proposing that they share the $10,000 reward, investigative reporter Kathy Lawrence solicits the help of detective Ross Stewart to find Judge Drake, who is wanted on corruption charges. Kathy has observed the judge's girlfriend, Madge, sneaking in the side door to Dr. Clifford Porter's La Siesta Sanitarium, but needs proof that Drake is really hiding there. Posing as Kathy's husband, Ross tricks another doctor into signing the commitment papers. Once inside the clinic, he clashes with male nurse Larson, a sadist who routinely brutalizes patients. By encouraging a pyromaniac to start a fire, Ross confirms that the judge is hidden in a locked wing for special cases. However, before he can contact Kathy, he's caught and placed in the cell of a hulking, dangerous patient known as "The Champ," to be "accidentally" killed. Told that Ross has met with an accident, Kathy enters the sanitarium by impersonating Madge. Dr. Porter shoots and kills The Champ, but sympathetic nurse Fred Hopps calls the police, and Porter, Drake and Larson are all arrested.

The storyline of *Behind Locked Doors* was already well worn by dozens of cheap novels and radio shows; Samuel Fuller would use the same idea for his later *Shock Corridor*, adding his own blend of political hysteria. *Behind Locked Doors* has no interest in social comment and instead generates tension by isolating Ross Stewart in a peculiar trap. As a mental case he has no rights, and can do nothing when the sadistic Larson arranges for another patient to be murdered. Cult actor Tor Johnson's menacing monster is underdeveloped, as is Nurse Hopps, who shows a selectively protective attitude toward his patients, especially the attractive, mute teenager Jim. Although Ross's predicament isn't nearly as disorienting as the earlier Joseph H. Lewis noir *My Name Is Julia Ross*, *Behind Locked Doors* is just noir enough to qualify.

Director Boetticher overcomes the low budget by sticking with Ross's subjective POV. The visuals may not be in John Alton's class, but Guy Roe's expressive shadows are definitely within the noir style. The humor in Eugene Ling and Marvin Wald's script veers toward self-parody in the early scenes

Berlin Express: *Lindley (Robert Ryan) and Lucienne (Merle Oberon)*.

before Richard Carlson's spirited detective understands how badly he is trapped. Ex-MGM musical star Lucille Bremer (*Meet Me in St. Louis,* etc.) is the adventuress who charms Ross into walking into a tight spot. Douglas Fowley's thug Larson is an energetic if generic psychopath, while Thomas Browne Henry's crooked medico is almost sympathetic. The result is a modest noir in a classic style contrasting with Boetticher's later docu-inflected *The Killer Is Loose*. **GE**

BERLIN EXPRESS (1948)

Director: Jacques Tourneur. **Screenplay**: Harold Medford based on a story by Curt Siodmak. **Producer**: Bert Granet. **Executive Producer**: Dore Schary. **Director of Photography**: Lucien Ballard. **Music**: Frederick Hollander. **Art Directors**: Albert S. D'Agostino, Alfred Herman. **Editor**: Sherman Todd. **Cast**: Merle Oberon (Lucienne), Robert Ryan (Robert Lindley), Charles Korvin (Perrot), Paul Lukas (Dr. H. Bernhardt), Robert Coote (Sterling), Reinhold Schunzel (Walther), Peter Von Zerneck (Hans Schmidt), Otto Waldis (Kessler), Fritz Kortner (Franzen), Michael Harvey (Sgt. Barnes), Richard Powers (Major). **Location**: The Reich's Chancellery, Reichstag, Brandenburg Gate, and Adlon Hotel, Berlin; Frankfurt, West Germany; Paris, France. **Completed**: November 21, 1947. **Released**: RKO, May 1. 86 minutes.

Just after V-E day, elder statesman, Dr. H. Bernhardt, travels by train from Paris to Berlin with plans for the reunification of Germany. A covert un-pacified Nazi group attempts his assassination, but they fail and kidnap him instead. Foreign colleagues of the statesman join forces and search through war-torn Frankfurt for their missing comrade. Realizing that one or more of the members of their group must be allied with the remnant Nazi faction, suspicion is leveled at everyone involved as they comb the rubble and hollowed office buildings for clues. Bernhardt's secretary, Lucienne, wanders through the nightmarish landscape in the hope of finding him while accompanied by an American scientist, Robert Lindley. After almost all hope is lost, they stumble onto the Nazi hideout. The occupation forces are alerted, the nest of conspirators captured and Bernhardt is freed from his hellish abduction.

Berlin Express is the first non-military film production allowed in post-WWII Germany. Director Jacques Tourner brings an existential bias to the film through images depicting the enormity of Germany's destruction: architectural icons of the Third Reich and ages-old, glorious cities are now only widely scattered mounds of debris with traumatized citizens trying to live amongst pulverized dreams. The futility of waste is echoed in the humanistic sentiments of Bernhardt's Thomas Mann-like character. But all depictions of a ruined and hopeless civilization are contrasted with the pervasive, yet muted, reconstructive ideals of Bernhardt's non-military colleagues. In order to forge a New Germany, they persevere in uncovering and destroying a pernicious remnant of Nazi resistance. Nevertheless, many of the characters populating the film display an ambivalence indicative of the disillusionment that followed World War II, even while the grotesques contained in the plot are conventions of the black thriller and further emphasize the decay and corruption rooted in the film noir sensibility. **CM**

BETWEEN MIDNIGHT AND DAWN (1950)

Director: Gordon Douglas. **Screenplay**: Eugene Ling based on a story by Gerald Adams and Leo Katcher. **Producer**: Hunt Stromberg. **Director of Photography**: George E. Diskant. **Music**: George Duning. **Art Director**: George Brooks. **Editor**: Gene Havlick. **Cast**: Mark Stevens (Rocky Barnes), Edmond O'Brien (Dan Purvis), Gale Storm (Kate Mallory), Donald Buka (Richie Garris), Gale Robbins (Terry Romaine), Anthony Ross (Masterson), Roland Winters (Leo Cusick), Tito Vuolo (Romano), Grazia Narciso (Mrs. Romano), Madge Blake (Mrs. Mallory), Lora Lee Michel (Kathy), Jack Del Rio (Louis Franissi), Phillip Van Zandt (Joe Quist), Cliff Bailey (Sgt. Bailey). **Completed**: March 20, 1950. **Released**: Columbia, October 2. 89 minutes.

Police partners Dan Purvis and Rocky Barnes have been buddies since the war. Barnes is easygoing, while Purvis is intense and disillusioned by his experiences with "scum." Both men have fallen for the voice of dispatcher Kate Mallory over their police radio, but she is more attracted to Rocky. Purvis becomes increasingly frustrated by witnesses who are too frightened to identify despicable local hoodlum Richie Garris, who bombed an Italian grocery. When syndicate figure Leo Cusik moves into town and attempts to force Garris into his organization, the recalcitrant Garris kills him. Dan and Rocky arrest Garris, but he escapes, swears revenge, and later fatally shoots Rocky. Dan is now obsessed with Garris' capture and tries to intimidate Terry Romaine, Garris' girl friend, into providing information. Later a stakeout spots Garris entering Terry's apartment, but Garris uses a little girl as cover. From the apartment fire escape Dan heaves a tear-gas bomb inside. His quick action saves the girl but when Garris is about to shoot Dan, Terry steps in front of the gun and is killed instead. Dan in turn kills Garris and concedes that perhaps Terry wasn't so bad after all.

Posing as a semi-documentary, with opening credits over a nocturnal Los Angeles skyline and an off-screen narrator praising the police, *Between Midnight and Dawn* was written for matinee crowd appeal. It has many weaknesses, but the director, Gordon Douglas, is efficient in handling sequences of action or brutality. He includes two grisly noir scenes: the brutal shooting of Rocky Barnes and the final gunfight where Garris, by grabbing the wall before falling, leaves the bloody imprint of his hand there. Despite the film's simplistic approach, Don Buka's stylish portrayal of Garris is compelling and contrasts effectively with Edmond O'Brien's stolid, embittered Dan. But the story of a disillusioned cop who skirts the law would be handled more sensitively in the classic *On Dangerous Ground*. In the hands of a director like Nicholas Ray, the issues of law, order and individual rights are not subsumed by the action. **BP**

BEWARE, MY LOVELY (1952)

Director: Harry Horner. **Screenplay**: Mel Dinelli based on his play and short story "The Man." **Producer**: Collier Young (The Filmakers). **Director of Photography**: George E. Diskant. **Music**: Leith Stevens. **Art Directors**: Albert S. D'Agostino, Alfred Herman. **Editor**: Paul Weatherwax. **Cast**: Ida Lupino (Mrs. Gordon), Robert Ryan (Howard), Taylor Holmes (Mr. Armstrong), Barbara Whiting (Ruth Williams), James Williams (Mr. Stevens), O. Z. Whitehead (Mr. Franks), Dee Pollack (Grocery Boy). **Completed**: August 3, 1951. **Released**: RKO, August 7. 76 minutes.

Howard, an itinerant handyman, flees in terror when he finds his employer strangled but remains unaware that he has killed her in a moment of rage. He goes to another town, where he finds work at the home of a teacher and war widow, Mrs. Gordon. Howard is a morose and unhappy loner who begins to suspect Mrs. Gordon of secretly spying on him. When a teenager, Ruth Williams, taunts him for doing "women's work," it precipitates another breakdown. After Ruth departs, Howard locks himself in with Mrs. Gordon. All her frantic attempts to escape fail, until, in a moment of frenzy, Howard tries to strangle her, causing her to faint. When she comes to she sees Howard calmly going about his work, as if nothing has happened. He is once again unaware of his insane outburst. When a telephone repairman calls, Howard leaves peaceably with him and is turned over to the police.

Mel Dinelli's earlier success with screenplays grounded in suspenseful situations (*The Spiral Staircase, The Window*) was not repeated in *Beware, My Lovely*. By 1952 the noir cycle was playing out and many elements and devices previously original and emotionally effective had become pre-

dictable through overuse. Despite better than average production values, photography and some excellent performances by the principals (particularly Ryan, who draws pathos from an essentially negative character), much of the narrative is devoted to redeveloping stereotypes of Ida Lupino as a typically lonely and harassed young woman and Robert Ryan as the alienated man teetering between psychosis and normalcy. Cinematically, expressionistic shots such as the superimposition of a corpse in the water bucket into which the psychotic Ryan is staring or his distorted reflection in a Christmas ornament become, in context, a complement of visual clichés. For all of its failings, *Beware, My Lovely* is an interesting film and a good example of how film noir could rapidly develop and exhaust the dramatic impact of its stylistic conventions. **BP**

BEWITCHED (1945)

Director: Arch Oboler. **Producer:** Jerry Bresler. **Screenplay**: Arch Oboler. **Director of Photography**: Charles Salerno, Jr. **Music**: Bronislau Kaper. **Art Directors**: Cedric Gibbons and Malcolm Brown. **Cast**: Edmund Gwenn (Dr. Bergson), Phyllis Thaxter (Joan Alris Ellis), Henry H. Daniels Jr (Bob Arnold), Addison Richards (John Ellis), Kathleen Lockhart (Mrs. Ellis), Francis Pierlot (Dr. George Wilton), Sharon McManus (Small girl), Gladys Blake (Glenda), Will Wright (Mr. Herkheimer), Horace (Stephen) McNally (Eric Russell), Oscar O'Shea (Captain O'Malley), Minor Watson (Governor), Virginia Brissac (Governor's wife), Audrey Totter (Voice of Karen). **Completed**: November-December 1944. **Released**: July 1945. 65 minutes.

Joan Alris Ellis appears to be a "normal," healthy young ingenue, enjoying a high society party, when suddenly she turns to boyfriend Bob and asks, "Do you hear someone talking?" Bob ignores the warning signs, and the competing voice in her head gets louder: "I won't go back in the dark. I'll live, I'll live," the alter-ego promises. Fearful of destroying her family and fiancé, Joan flees home and travels east. Briefly, she finds peace. But when a young suitor and promising lawyer (Eric Russell) awakens her sexual desires, Joan's dark side—who we later find out is named Karen—re-emerges and this time possesses her speaking voice. Again Joan runs, only to find Bob in her apartment, ready to take her home. She wants to return, but Karen orders Joan to kill Bob with a pair of scissors and she does. Eric, unaware of Joan's personality disorder, defends her against murder charges. But in order to protect Eric from the wrath of Karen, Joan admits to killing Bob and she is sentenced to die. Eric, confused by Joan's statement "When I die, she dies too," asks Dr. Bergson for his help. With the aid of hypnosis, Bergson unravels the mystery of "two mind systems occupying the one brain."

In the 1940's, film noir was very much interested in psychoanalysis. From crazed killers with artistic inclinations (*Phantom Lady*) or a love for fire (*Raw Deal*) to lovers with neurotic impulses (*Gun Crazy*) or a domineering desire to possess and destroy (*Leave Her to Heaven*), noir has always been populated with figures who exist outside the boundaries of the rational. In *The Dark Mirror*, the doppelganger was an evil twin sister, but what makes *Bewitched* such an eerie little "B-chiller" is that the doppelganger resides within

a nice, vulnerable woman, or as the film's tagline graphically puts it: "She lived two amazing lives! Darling of society . . . cruel Love-Killer!" Joan Ellis lives within the boundaries of small-town normalcy. But when she starts hearing voices, her family dismisses the warning signs and believes that she just being "nervous" or "high strung." Fearful of hurting those she loves, Joan tries to run from her past but she can't run from herself: her alter ego is always there.

Director and creator of the *Inner Sanctum* radio series, Arch Oboler brilliantly captures this nightmare. Midway through the film, Joan rushes through the night's wet streets. In her head a voice sings, "crazy, crazy," but the road, the row houses, the street lamps, the "Eats" signs, all look the same. Her journey is full of repetition. There is no bright future or sense of change. Eventually, she leaves town. When she falls in love with a young man (lawyer Eric Russell), the dark alter ego possesses her speaking voice and wants to possess Eric too. Eventually, in an act of love, Joan decides to kill herself and her alter-ego (through state execution) to prevent destroying anyone else she loves. Dr. Bergson had believed that "she is responsible for her actions," but upon hearing of Joan's repeated mantra: "When I die, she dies too," he decides to investigate. The hypnosis scene is genuinely creepy as two personalities emerge: the dewy eyed, soft-mannered Joan and the brassy and brittle, deeply eye-shadowed Karen (voiced by noir legend Audrey Totter). The doctor, in a kind of exorcism, succeeds in making Karen disappear, but a residual sadness remains. In later films about personality disorders, such as *Sybil*, the story line builds to a revelation scene in which initial trauma started the illness. In Oboler's *Bewitched* there is no such moment. Madness just is. **GT**

BEYOND A REASONABLE DOUBT (1956)

Director: Fritz Lang. **Screenplay**: Douglas Morrow. **Producer**: Bert Friedlob. **Director of Photography**: William Snyder. **Music**: Herschel Burke Gilbert. **Art Director**: Carroll Clark. **Editor**: Gene Fowler, Jr. **Cast**: Dana Andrews (Tom Garrett), Joan Fontaine (Susan Spencer), Sidney Blackmer (Austin Spencer), Philip Bourneur (Thompson), Shepperd Strudwick (Wilson), Arthur Franz (Hale), Edward Binns (Lt. Kennedy), Robin Raymond (Terry), Barbara Nichols (Sally), William Leicester (Charlie Miller), Dan Seymour (Greco), Rusty Lane (Judge), Joyce Taylor (Joan), Carleton Young (Kirk). **Completed**: August 7, 1956. **Released**: RKO, September 5. 80 minutes.

Tom Garrett, a rising novelist, enters into an agreement with Austin Spencer, a wealthy publisher who is also the father of Tom's fiancée Susan. The two plan a journalistic coup: they will incriminate Tom in a local murder and allow him to be tried and sentenced to death so that they can discredit capital punishment by revealing Tom's innocence. Their plan goes amiss when Tom is convicted and then Spencer is accidentally killed, thereby destroying the evidence needed to exonerate Tom. As the date of the execution approaches, Susan's increasingly frantic maneuvering produces additional evidence to save Tom. But in the critical moments before he is to be pardoned, Tom accidentally reveals to Susan that he is the killer, being the murder victim's long missing husband who took advantage of the scheme to rid himself of a threat to his forthcoming marriage and subsequent social

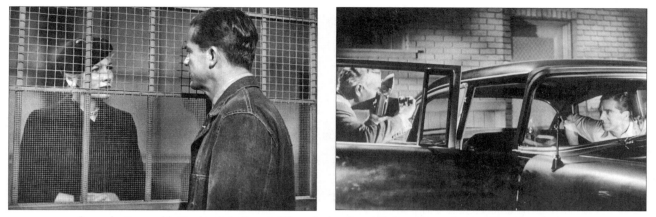

Beyond a Reasonable Doubt: *Left: Garrett (Dana Andrews) and his fiancé Susan Spencer (Joan Fontaine).*
Right: Austin Spencer (Sidney Blackmer) and Garrett (Dana Andrews).

advance. Susan reveals this to the authorities before Tom can be pardoned.

Beyond A Reasonable Doubt is Fritz Lang's last American film, made on a low budget, with poor production values and, on the surface, not strikingly directed. Nevertheless, the film has considerable impact, due not so much to visual style but to the narrative structure, emotional mood and to the expertly devised plot in which the turnabout is both surprising and convincing. A subtle sense of narrative uneasiness, conveyed mainly through the acting and *mise-en-scène*, permeates the entire length of the film and subtly foreshadows the final plot twist. The film poses a social statement about the plight of an innocent man but it is filled with an array of submerged plot elements that belie a far more complex and sinister world than is otherwise suggested by the simple sets and washed-out images.

First, there is the lurking possibility that the entire scheme is a trap engineered by Spencer to frame Tom. When this is suddenly dispelled by Spencer's death, his place is filled by the missing husband whom Susan believes to be the murderer. Both possibilities function to produce the suspicion that the crime is far more complex than the random sex murder it first appears to be. There is also a certain coldness and sterility in Tom himself: he dispassionately witnesses an execution at the film's opening and he jokes with Susan about marrying her for her money. There are a number of small, seemingly irrelevant incidents such as an unexplained phone call to Tom and the fact that, even before he knows of Spencer's scheme, he postpones his marriage to Susan. In addition, at Tom's trial there emerges certain, quite damaging evidence against him that was not planted by Spencer —evidence that, at the time, the viewer assumes to be coincidental.

Finally and most unusually, there is an odd stylistic tendency evident throughout the film. First, Lang cuts repeatedly to seemingly insignificant actions such as picking up a drink or lighting a cigarette; and, second, he inexplicably focuses on such inanimate objects as matchbooks and ashtrays. Although most of these actions and objects turn out to be irrelevant to the plot, they put the viewer on edge with disorienting detail and create a subliminal uncertainty about surface reality. These elements are not particularly intrusive and, until the final revelation, the dominant reality for the viewer is that Tom is innocent. Indeed, the threat of Tom's death

forces the viewer to accept this concept all the more. Yet on the subconscious level, these elements give the film a disturbing quality that prepares us for the final sordid revelation. The plot elements have been cleverly devised so that the surprise ending is not much of a surprise; but it is a shock of insight, in which all the unsettling facts reassemble to create a new reality that is far more emotionally and logically convincing. Consistent with this revelation is Susan's decision to allow the execution of her fiancé to continue. **DLW**

BEYOND THE FOREST (1949)

Director: King Vidor. **Screenplay**: Lenore Coffee based on the novel by Stuart Engstrand. **Producer**: Henry Blanke. **Director of Photography**: Robert Burks. **Music**: Max Steiner. **Art Director**: Robert Haas. **Editor**: Rudi Fehr. **Cast**: Bette Davis (Rosa Moline), Joseph Cotten (Dr. Lewis Moline), David Brian (Neil Latimer), Ruth Roman (Carol), Minor Watson (Moose), Dona Drake (Jenny), Regis Toomey (Sorren), Sarah Selby (Mildred Sorren), Mary Servoss (Mrs. Wetch), Frances Charles (Miss Elliott). **Location**: Lake Tahoe, Truckee River, Angeles Crest, California. **Released**: Warner Bros., October 22. 97 minutes.

Rosa Moline, the dissatisfied wife of a small-town doctor, has an affair with Neil Latimer, a Chicago millionaire vacationing at his cabin near her hometown. After Latimer returns to the city, Rosa collects her husband's past-due bills to pay for a Chicago shopping trip. She confronts Latimer, who admits he is engaged to a wealthy society woman. Rosa returns home and discovers she is pregnant. Dr. Moline feels confident that the baby will solidify their marriage. Attending a party for their friend, Moose, caretaker for Latimer's cabin, Rosa is surprised to find Latimer present too. He tells Rosa his engagement is off. But Moose threatens Rosa that he'll tell Latimer about her pregnancy if she leaves Dr. Moline. The next day at a hunting party, Rosa shoots Moose and claims it accidental. She is absolved of murder. But Dr. Moline intercepts her telephone call from Latimer, in which Rosa agrees to an abortion. Moline confronts her and Rosa leaps into a ravine, causing a miscarriage. She develops blood poisoning but insists on leaving for Chicago. She staggers out of her house but, as she nears the local train station, she falls and dies.

Beyond the Forest: *Rosa Moline (Bette Davis)*.

King Vidor's vision of melodrama in small-town America is never darker than in *Beyond the Forest*. Unlike the rather random violence of *Ruby Gentry* or the aptly titled *Lightning Strikes Twice*, the arrangement of formal elements in *Beyond the Forest* possesses the rigor and occasionally the overstatement of a Euripidean tragedy. Even as a third-person narrator introduces Rosa Moline as an evil person who scandalized the inhabitants of her hometown, isolated shots capture the causes of Rosa's own sense of oppression: the gaunt faces of the townspeople following her as she goes to trial for the shooting of Moose; the glaring white-washed walls of their meager homes; the constant aural assault from the blast furnace of the local mill. Vidor uses the fiery image of the furnace with its constant, barely controlled explosive rumbling as a straightforward metaphor for Rosa's passion. Bette Davis' performance of Rosa conveys the hysteria beneath the pulled-back hair, while her make-up creates a swarthy complexion that makes her eyes seem to flash each time she widens then.

The revelation that Rosa Moline's "evil' is a role forced on her by her repressive environment is what transforms Vidor's passion play from an updated rendering of *Madame Bovary* into film noir. Because, as the narrator notes, she had ambitions beyond marriage and child rearing, because she "put on airs in an unschooled attempt to be somebody," Rosa was ostracized long before her trial for killing Moose. By beginning with the trial and flashing back, Vidor uses a narrative structure typical of noir to delineate the context for Rosa's reputation. The audience knows that Rosa is a murderer. The jury of peers does not fully exculpate Rosa but merely discharges her for lack of evidence. Ultimately Rosa's alienation is personal, not social. The visual scheme of Rosa's last hours as a noir figure, as a debased femme fatale, repeatedly captures her crazed behavior in sharp side-light or an even more unnatural low-light that underscores her fever-induced madness. The climax uses montage for a restatement of the furnace metaphor combined with a traveling shot that moves back from Rosa over the train's departure, and with it the promise of happiness and freedom. When the cars all pull away and the intermittent light from their windows has abated, Rosa's figure is visible, crumpled and alone in the roadway. **AS**

THE BIG CLOCK (1948)

Director: John Farrow. **Screenplay**: Jonathan Latimer, adapted by Harold Goldman based on the novel by Kenneth Fearing. **Producer**: Richard Maibaum. **Director of Photography**: John F. Seitz. **Music**: Victor Young. **Art Directors**: Hans Dreier, Roland Anderson, Albert Nozaki. **Editors**: Eda Warren, Gene Ruggiero. **Cast**: Ray Milland (George Stroud), Charles Laughton (Earl Janoth), Maureen O'Sullivan (Georgette Stroud), George Macreadly (Steve Hagen), Rita Johnson (Pauline Delos), Elsa Lanchester (Louise Patterson), Harold Vermilyea (Don Klausmeyer), Dan Tobin (Roy Cordette), Henry Morgan (Bill Womack), Richard Webb (Nat Sperling), Tad Van Brunt (Tony Watson), Elaine Riley (Lily Gold), Luis Van Rooten (Edwin Orlin), Lloyd Corrigan (McKinley), Margaret Field (Second Secretary), Philip Van Zandt (Sidney Kisiav). **Completed**: April 11, 1947. **Released**: Paramount, April 9. 93 minutes.

George Stroud is the brilliant editor of *Crimeways* magazine, one of the many publications of media mogul, Earl Janoth, who treats his employees like slaves. *Crimeways* is renowned for its staff's ability to track down criminals eluding the police. George is on the eve of departure for his five-year overdue honeymoon, but Janoth insists that he cannot leave the magazine's helm. Sick of it all, George quits and heads for the train station. But he misses the train while distracted by a lovely woman, Pauline, who suggests they have a little fun until the next train leaves. Later, George deposits Pauline at her apartment, unaware that Janoth has arrived because she is the mogul's mistress. Having seen but not recognized "another man," Janoth kills the woman in a jealous rage. Panicked, he plots to implicate the man he saw leaving Pauline's apartment. Meanwhile, George makes the later train, joining his wife at a resort. She accepts his excuses until Janoth calls to demand George's return to New York to solve Pauline's murder. Fearing he will be implicated, George departs, ignoring his wife's claim that their marriage is finished. As the *Crimeways* staff pieces the clues together,

The Big Clock: *Earl Janoth (Charles Laughton) and his assistant Steve Hagen (George Macreadly)*.

George stays barely one step ahead of them and his frame-up. Ultimately, he proves Janoth is the murderer and confesses the whole story to his wife, winning her back.

The opening of *The Big Clock* contains many classic noir elements: a pan across a dark city into a darkened corridor then to a dark figure hiding and running; a voice-over of the character bemoaning his fate; and a flashback to explain the origin of his current trouble. The body of the film, however, reveals fewer stylistic characteristics of film noir and the instances of low-key lighting, asymmetric or dramatic compositions, and radical camera angles are rare.

The only visual device of note is the "slightly-too-wide-angle" lens, which is used for close-ups of Laughton during his vilest moments; it distorts his face just enough to be uglier than real, but not enough to break startlingly with naturalism. The use of this subtle distortion increases quite gradually during the film, until, when the flashback catches up with the opening of the film, the viewer may be convinced of the arch villain's both superhuman and subhuman capabilities. The performances are all adequate to the roles but Laughton and Lanchester are especially noteworthy. Laughton affects a rapid and nearly monotone speech pattern that equates Janoth's mechanical and compulsive behavior with that of his mammoth clock, the focal point of his building's lobby which symbolizes his corporate power and synchronizes all other clocks in Janoth's global empire. When George is chased and momentarily hides within this symbol of Janoth's egomania, he accidentally stops the clock and must start it up again, thus presaging his final victory over Janoth.

To counter the media mogul's insanity with a lighter side of the same dark coin, Elsa Lanchester gives a memorable rendition of an extremely talented but totally zany artist. Her home is filled with the clutter of four or five young children, each of whom, she blithely announces, has a different father and provides a living history of her checkered marital career. The combination of Janoth's madness and the Frankensteinian horror of finding his own machine turned against him is the central darkness of this film's plot. In a more thoroughly noir film, the protagonist generates much of his own miserable fate through misjudgment, stubbornness, or greed. But George's only folly is to dally too long with Pauline. **EM**

THE BIG COMBO (1955)

Director: Joseph Lewis. **Screenplay**: Philip Yordan. **Producer**: Sidney Harmon. **Director of Photography**: John Alton. **Music**: David Raksin. **Production Designer**: Rudi Feld. **Editor**: Robert Eisen. **Cast**: Cornel Wilde (Leonard Diamond), Richard Conte (Mr. Brown), Brian Donlevy (McClure), Jean Wallace (Susan Lowell), Robert Middleton (Peterson), Lee Van Cleef (Fante), Earl Holliman (Mingo), Helen Walker (Alicia), Jay Adler (Sam Hill), John Hoyt (Dreyer), Ted De Corsia (Bettini), Helene Stanton (Rita), Roy Gordon (Audubon), Whit Bissell (Doctor), Steve Mitchell (Bennie), Baynes Barron (Young Detective), James McCallion (Lab Technician), Tony Michaels (Photo Technician), Brian O'Hara (Malloy), Rita Gould (Nurse), Bruce Sharpe (Detective), Michael Mark (Hotel Clerk), Philip Van Zandt (Mr. Jones), Donna Drew (Miss Hartleby). **Completed**: September 21, 1954. **Released**: Allied Artists, February 13. 89 minutes.

The head of a local mob, Mr. Brown, has thoroughly capti-

The Big Combo: *Susan Lowell (Jean Wallace) and Det. Leonard Diamond (Cornel Wilde).*

vated a young society woman, Susan Lowell. In love with Susan, Detective Leonard Diamond is obsessed with exposing Brown as a top mob financier and uses harassing tactics of mass false arrests to pressure the criminals. Pushed too far by the detective, Brown reacts according to the philosophy of "first is first and second is nobody." A contract is put out on Diamond who is then picked up by two hit men, Mingo and Fante. They torture Diamond, using the hearing aid of one-time top mobster, McClure, to amplify sounds past the point of normal tolerance. The detective recovers and links the mobster with the murder of a racket boss. Brown eliminates McClure and his henchmen before they discover his treacheries, but he is betrayed by his ex-wife. Cornered in an isolated airplane hangar, Brown and Diamond shoot it out and the mobster is killed.

There is a sense of fatalism and perverse sexuality found in *The Big Combo* that exists in few other noir films. The relationship between Susan Lowell and Mr. Brown is a blending of fatalistic deference combined with a feeling of raw sexual abandon. Brown adores Susan's body. In one sequence, he brings her to the height of sexual excitement by worshipping her with lewd compliments and lavishing her entire body with kiss after kiss. Despite her sense of guilt, Susan resigns herself to this situation because of her own sexual dependence on Brown. Her eventual suicide attempt and apparent "rebirth" at Diamond's insistence, suggests no more than a weak effort to alter her amoral lifestyle. Beyond this obvious sexual exploitation, this film has a crude sexual bias for brutal, erotic violence. Mingo and Fante's homosexuality is smothered in a ritualistic atmosphere of murder and sadistic torture, while Diamond appears to be compensating for impotence. Much in the same way as Lewis' classic *Gun Crazy*, there is an affinity between sex and violence; and the exploration of futility presents an ambience strangely reminiscent of an earlier period of noir films, such as *Scarlet Street* and *Woman In The Window*. These attitudes combine with John Alton's cinematography to create a film noir of striking contrasts between the black and white images and Lewis' sexual overtones. *The Big Combo's* characters are isolated within a dark universe of unspoken repression and graphic violence. **CM**

The Big Heat: Vince (Lee Marvin) and the boss' moll Debby (Gloria Grahame).

THE BIG HEAT (1953)

Director: Fritz Lang. **Screenplay**: Sydney Boehm based on the novel by William P. McGivern. **Producer**: Robert Arthur. **Director of Photography**: Charles Lang. **Sound**: George Cooper. **Music**: Daniele Amfitheatrof. **Art Director**: Robert Peterson. **Editor**: Charles Nelson. **Cast**: Glenn Ford (Dave Bannion), Gloria Grahame (Debby Marsh), Jocelyn Brando (Katie Bannion), Alexander Scourby (Mike Lagana), Lee Marvin (Vince Stone), Jeanette, Nolan (Bertha Duncan), Peter Whitney (Tierney), Willis Bouchey (Lt. Wilkes), Robert Burton (Gus Burke), Adam Williams (Larry Gordon), Howard Wendell (Commissioner Higgins), Chris Alcaide (George Rose), Michael Granger (Hugo), Dorothy Green (Lucy Chapman), Carolyn Jones (Doris), Ric Roman (Baldy), Dan Seymour (Atkins), Edith Evanson (Selma Parker), John Crawford (Al), John Doucette (Mark Reiner). **Completed**: April 18,1953. **Released**: Columbia, October 14. 90 minutes.

While investigating the supposed suicide of police officer Duncan, Sgt. Dave Bannion is suddenly told by higher-ups to "lay off the case." But Bannion is aware of unsavory implications detailed to him by Duncan's girlfriend, Lucy, who believes that his widow is blackmailing gangster Mike Lagana with the contents of a hidden suicide confession note. When Lucy's tortured body is found, Bannion resumes his now-forbidden investigation and discovers that the town and its police force are in the grip of mob syndicate chief Lagana. Bannion confronts the hoodlum, but Lagana retaliates by planting a bomb in the detective's car, which accidentally kills Bannion's wife instead. After he complains the police are ignoring this murder he loses his job. He hides his threatened child with in-laws and becomes a lone wolf whose single purpose is to wreak vengeance on Lagana. He involves the mobster's girlfriend and devises the downfall of Lagana. Vindicated, Bannion returns to his desk at homicide.

Sgt. Dave Bannion is squarely in the tradition of the crusading detective: honest, tough, unbought and unbuyable; plus with the dogged persistence to confront any situation no matter how complex or dangerous. But something is wrong with this noble character. He must live in the real world where crooks do not fall down when good guys point a finger. Bannion is compulsively upright and thorough in his investigations but works in a city where not only does crime pay, but morality has a very low return. At one level of the film, Bannion is the avenging angel and must be admired: his vendetta puts in motion the elements that finally bring down the title's "big heat" upon the criminal syndicate and its lackeys. The cost of this "heroic" action however is the lives of four women, the loss of Bannion's home, and his daughter traumatized by fear and grief. While women are to be protected like cherished property by normal civilization, this film noir shows how society considers them expendable when power, moral principles, or male egos are at stake.

Further, there are two classes of females in *The Big Heat*. First are the women who have demonstrated legitimate pedigree by marriage, purity, and innocence of youth, i.e. Bannion's wife and daughter, and, to a certain extent, the innocent daughter of the gangster chief Lagana. In the other category fall those women who through age, infirmity, or indications of independent sexuality are "things": Mrs. Duncan, Lucy, the crippled woman from the garage, and Debby. The differentiation of women is unconscious for Bannion who slanders Lucy as a whore for loving Duncan but is enraged when a gangster uses insulting language to his wife. The detective does not mind exposing the crippled woman to possible harm even while his own daughter is guarded from the same group of thugs by armed men. Debby is the most compelling link between the two groups of women, but she is a connection that Bannion does not comprehend clearly, as her faults are numerous and offensive to him. Sophisticated and sexy, Debby is consciously happy despite being involved with the sadistic Vince Stone. But she becomes useful to Bannion and therefore sympathetic. Her deeply buried innocence surfaces with Bannion's ministrations. She is trying to cross the line into decency, but a woman like Debby, once sullied, can never be totally accepted. The only possible "salvation" for Debby is death, by which she approaches the status of Bannion's sainted wife. Her dual nature is illustrated by the pure and disfigured sides of her face. When she dies with her hideous scars hidden in the mink bought by Lagana, she is transformed into a lovable object for the detective. Leaving behind him a wake of death and destruction, Bannion is restored to good standing on the police force and in the community. On the human scale, however, the victory is pyrrhic; and the noir vision of the film is indeed nihilistic. **EM**

THE BIG KNIFE (1955)

Director, Producer: Robert Aldrich (Associates and Aldrich). **Screenplay**: James Poe based on the play by Clifford Odets. **Director of Photography**: Ernest Laszlo. **Music**: Frank DeVol. **Art Director**: William Glasgow. **Editor**: Michael Luciano. **Cast**: Jack Palance (Charlie Castle), Ida Lupino (Marion Castle), Wendell Corey (Smiley Coy), Jean Hagen (Connie Bliss), Rod Steiger (Stanley Hoff), Shelley Winters (Dixie Evans), Ilka Chase (Patty Benedict), Everett Sloane (Nat Danziger), Wesley Addy (Hank Teagle), Paul Langton (Buddy Bliss), Nick Dennis (Mickey Feeney), Bill Walker (Russell), Mike Winkelman (Billy Castle), Mel Welles (Bearded Man), Robert Sherman (Bongo Player), Strother Martin (Stillman), Ralph Volkie (Referee), Michael Fox (Announcer), Richard Boone (Narrator). **Completed**: May 14, 1955. **Released**: United Artists, November 25. 111 minutes.

(continued on page 44)

Many movies anticipate aspects of classic period film noir and certainly the contributions of German-speaking filmmakers who came to Hollywood in the 15 years prior to World War II cannot be overstated. Possibly the earliest influence is a series of unconventional, quasi-proletarian, crime-related films directed at the end of 1920s by Josef von Sternberg, an Austrian émigré who came to New York City as a child. Remarkably both naturalistic and stylized, *Underworld* (1927), *The Docks of New York* and *The Dragnet* (both 1928), *The Case of Lena Smith* and *Thunderbolt* (both 1929), all benefited from realistic scripts by the likes of Ben Hecht and Jules Furthman, shot by such distinguished silent-era cinematographers as Bert Glennon and Harold Rosson. *Underworld* may be regarded as one of the first modern gangster films in which the heroes are actually criminals. There were serious films that dealt with the world of crime and gangsterism prior to *Underworld*, films that were limited by a strong moral code and hampered by a social rationale such as D. W. Griffith *Musketeers of Pig Alley* and *Dream Street* as well as Allan Dwan's *The Perfect Crime* and Raoul Walsh's *The Regeneration*. *Underworld* eliminated most of the causes for crime and focused on the criminals themselves and in this sense anticipates not only the flurry that gangster films released prior to the enforcement of the Production Code in the early 1930s but also the narratives and characters of film noir.

Certainly the exotic visual preoccupations of von Sternberg are best known from his series of pictures he made with Marlene Dietrich at Paramount which helped to define the fatal woman of the noir cycle. In *Underworld* the script written by ex-newspaperman Ben Hecht realistically details the personalities populating the sordid speakeasies and dingy dwellings of the gangsters. As they did in his classic period work, Hecht's characters contain a strange blend of humor and brutality. In all his work and in the noir manner, von Sternberg's romanticized style creates a tension with the non-visual content from cynical dialogue to forlorn or obsessive character. In *Underworld* the overriding implications of claustrophobia, alienation, and corruption combine with the dark ambience of a highly romanticized criminal environment and mark the film as one of the earliest proto-noirs. Von Sternberg's last underworld picture, *Thunderbolt*, also features George Bancroft as a doomed criminal, and the moral nature of the gangster is scrutinized in the constricting environment of a prison. *Thunderbolt* also is filled with strong personalities who transcend their convict status and function substantively as heroes much as would the doomed men in numerous noir cycle caper films or the bleak prison drama *Brute Force*. Again the proto-noir sensibility of the film derives from von Sternberg's shadowy visuals and darkly cynical dialogue of Jules Furthman's screenplay, many years before the writer's classic period adaptations of *The Big Sleep* and *Nightmare Alley*.

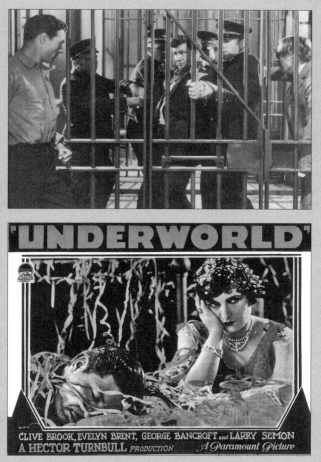

While von Sternberg's direct contributions to the noir cycle are limited, few filmmakers surpass the output of another émigré, Fritz Lang. As a refugee from Nazism, Lang had already established his deterministic outlook in movies as varied as *M* (1931), *Spione* (1928), *Metropolis* (1927), *Die Nibelungen* (1924), and the Dr. Mabuse features starting in 1922. After having excelled in thrillers, crime films, mythic sagas and science fiction, in his first two American pictures, Lang immediately crafted two proto-noirs.

Lang's 1936 *Fury* has a socially conscious, anti-lynching theme; but its portrayal of a Joe Wheeler, a newly-embittered protagonist unrelentingly set on revenge, is what makes it proto-noir. In fact, the "fury" of the title could apply just as strongly to the emotional state of Wheeler in the second half of the film as it does to that of the mob in the first portion. By dividing his picture into two parts and focusing in turn on social and individual anger, Lang suggests the potential for transference between the two, that alienation or angst are both personal

The pointedly expressive performances of actors in Lang's films was carried over from his German work to his first pre-noir feature in the United States: Peter Lorre as the title figure in M *to Sylvia Sydney and Spencer Tracy as the unlucky lovers in* Fury.

and mass ills. Moreover, Lang adapts the fateful visual style of his earlier German expressionism, full of Freudian and crypto-religious symbolism, to the more prosaic reality of the American depression.

The film opens with an alternation of static and moving shots following Joe and his girlfriend Catherine just before her departure for a better-paying job in another state. The couple gaze at a window display of bedroom furniture, consider going to a movie, and finally, not knowing what to do with their last few hours, simply walk in the rain. When they reach out to each other in the station, the train jerks them apart, until Catherine is lost in a haze of lights. From the beginning the staging and editing convey an ominous sense of disquiet. Lang multiplies the details of milieu and the couple's relationship rapidly, establishing a context for his personal notions of destiny that will inform so many of his later noir films. At the same time, the economic necessity of the couple's separation maintains the film's contemporary relevance. Having introduced this background of both personal and social instability, Lang injects a deterministic plot twist in the form of Wheeler's arrest and his possession of an incriminating bill. With noir-like irony his problems continue to be linked to money. After indulging in some sardonic visual metaphors—for instance, the gossiping townswomen spreading word of Joe's arrest are intercut with hens in a barnyard—Lang returns to a direct, if visually diffracted, statement for lynching: Wheeler "meets his fate" in a flurry of flashing torches, shattered glass, and bodies hurled up against windows.

The trial of the lynch party that follows is a sequence that could be described as semi-documentary and yet verges on expressionism. While the prosecutor reads aloud figures about lynching and recapitulates the defendants' various alibis in voice-over, the newsreel footage shows them throwing rocks and breaking up furniture for the fire. Lang cuts between freeze-frames of a mechanic spreading kerosene, a housewife hurling a firebrand, and another man severing a

fire hose and close-ups of the same people on the stand. The final bit of manipulation is reserved for the melodramatic climax of the trial sequence: the verdict. As a sober-voiced clerk reads the jury's decisions, he begins with "not guiltys," at which point all the defendants turn to congratulate each other. He then follows with a chain of "guiltys," and each one named, in ironic parallel to the newsreel, "freezes" in disbelief. Although Wheeler reappears to spare the mob members further punishment, it cannot be assumed that he does so out of forgiveness. Lang does not imply that the people of the town have learned their lesson. He does imply that Wheeler's existence has been permanently altered by his ordeal; and that, like many noir heroes to follow, he may never entirely escape the disturbing specter of his past.

Lang's next picture *You Only Live Once* (1937) is a fugitive couple picture, a sub-set that resonates throughout classic and neo-noir. In his survey of noir, "Paint It Black," Raymond Durgnat gives a thumbnail sketch of the fugitive couples

under the heading "On the Run: Here the criminals, or the framed innocents are essentially passive and fugitive, and, even if tragically or despicably guilty, sufficiently sympathetic for the audience to be caught between, on the one hand, pity, identification and regret, and, on the other, moral condemnation and conformist fatalism." As usual, Durgnat's prose is so densely packed that it masks the shortcomings of his analysis. What permits, even compels, viewer pity or identification with the innocent and guilty is the nature of most fugitive couples' love: obsessive, erotically charged, far beyond simple Romanticism. In that regard, no later film-maker has ever surpassed Lang's seminal couple in *You Only Live Once*.

The narrative focus of *You Only Live Once* is typical of the director's fatalistic world view and like *Fury* is as concerned with the outrage of the unjustly punished as with the fugitive couple. As it did with Spencer Tracy and Sylvia Sidney as Joe and Catherine, the naturalistic staging relies on the conventions of casting and the innate audience sympathy for stars Henry Fonda and Sidney, again, to maintain identification with a fugitive couple irrevocably at odds with the forces of law and order. As Eddie Taylor is released from his third term in prison, he is greeted at the gate by his fiancée Jo Graham. Eddie promises her that he is through with crime; and he marries her, settles down, and takes a job as a truck driver. Yet after a local bank is robbed and an employee killed, Eddie becomes a prime suspect. Although innocent, he is arrested, convicted on circumstantial evidence, and, in view of his past record, sentenced to death. Not only is Eddie Taylor thus rapidly overwhelmed by the fateful forces of the film's narrative, but Lang accents his harsh determinism in *You Only Live Once* with an accumulation of chance encounters and telling images, culminating when the truck used in the robbery, evidence which could prove Taylor's innocence, slips silently beneath the surface of a pool of quicksand. That image becomes a metaphor for the luckless Taylor, slowly and helplessly drowning under the weight of circumstantial events. Ultimately, because Lang is, in Andrew Sarris' words, "obsessed with the structure of the trap," the deadly turn of events is more important than the reasons for Eddie and Jo's devotion to one another.

Henry Fonda's interpretation of Taylor contains residues of hope and idealism which are almost incongruous in a man thrice-imprisoned by society for his past criminal acts. Nonetheless this outlook would become prototypical of later noir figures in the same predicament as Eddie. Whereas *Fury* concentrated on the question of mob psychology and recruited such stereotypes as the gruffly authoritarian sheriff, the politically motivated governor, and even the righteously liberal district attorney to probe that psychology, Lang does not elect to dramatize many of the possible parallel events in *You Only Live Once*. As the title suggests, the individual protagonists, Eddie and Jo, and their "one" life are the major concern. On the date set for his execution, Eddie is sent a message that a gun has been hidden for him in the prison hospital. By the act of slitting his wrists, he has himself admitted to the hospital, finds the gun, and, holding the prison doctor as a hostage, demands his release. Both Eddie and the warden are unaware that the actual robber has been captured and that a pardon is being prepared for Eddie. When this word arrives and the warden announces it to him, Eddie assumes that it is merely a ruse. He refuses to give up and impulsively shoots the chaplain who bars his way.

Being more subjective than Lang's other films, with its

You Only Live Once

direction keyed to the emotions of Eddie and Jo, adds another proto-noir aspect to *You Only Live Once*. In the opening sequences, a series of elegiac details establish Eddie and Jo's romantic dependence on each other, culminating as they stand in the evening by the frog pond of a small motel where Eddie explains to Jo that the frogs mate for life and always die together. Even as they feel secure in themselves, the motel manager is inside searching through his collection of pulp detective magazines under the harsh glare of his desk lamp. When he finds several photos and a story on Eddie's criminal past, Lang underscores the irony first with a shot of a frog jumping into the pond and diffracting Eddie's reflection in the water. Then comes a view of a dark, vaporous swamp where the truck that could prove Eddie innocent of a crime of which he is not yet aware sinks into the quicksand. Although the frog pond scene could have either ridiculed the naivete of Lang's characters or awkwardly stressed their lowly social status, Lang's staging and cutting makes it a simple, evocative metaphor for the entire narrative. This moment is also a stylistic prototype for the treatment of a young and innocent couple on the run that endured throughout the film noir cycle.

When a pregnant Jo joins Eddie after his escape, the audience must expect that, as it would be for numerous later fugitives in film noir, the only way to freedom for this couple is through death. After their baby is born and entrusted to Jo's sister, they drive toward the border to escape. At a roadblock a flurry of gunfire forces them to abandon the car and flee on foot. A few yards from freedom, both are shot, Eddie falling last while he carries the already mortally wounded Jo in his arms. Despite the non-realistic, quasi-religious conceit—reworked from Lang's *Der Müde Tod* (1921)—of having the dead chaplain cry out "Open the Gates" in voice-over, the final shot of his couple through the cross hairs of a police sniper's gun scope is an image that is both characteristically noir and surprisingly modern. **AS, LB & CM**

The Big Knife: *Stanley Hoff (Rod Steiger) excoriates actor Charlie Castle (Jack Palance).*

Charlie Castle, a former Broadway actor and current star of Hoff Federated Pictures, does not want to renew his contract and has told his agent Nat Danziger to inform studio boss Stanley Hoff of his decision. Charlie's insecurity and alcoholism have estranged him from his wife Marion with whom he hopes to be reconciled after breaking with Hoff. But the studio chief comes to see Charlie in person and, after histrionic appeals have failed, resorts to blackmail: he will expose Charlie as the drunken driver of a car which killed a child in an accident for which Buddy Bliss took the blame. Faced with this threat, Charlie agrees to sign; but Marion is disappointed and refuses to return to their home. Smiley Coy, Hoff's aide, confides to Charlie that he is concerned about Dixie Evans, a bit player and former girlfriend who knows the truth about the accident. When Charlie backs out of the deal, Hoff makes good on his threat. Even though Marion has learned the truth and agreed to return to him, Charlie cannot live with himself and commits suicide.

Much of the invective of *The Big Knife* derives from the original Odets play. The film adds a quasi-satirical dimension: Rod Steiger's blubbering, imbalanced Stanley Hoff: "Charlie, Charlie . . . the pain of this moment!"; Wendell Corey's unctuous press agent Smiley Coy; Jack Palance's leering, paranoiac Charlie Castle. The portrayals form an ensemble not only of Hollywood's clichés about itself but also of prototypical Robert Aldrich gargoyles. The unabashed theatrics, the drum rolls, the wildly expressive dialogue— "You came in here and threw this mess of naked pigeons in my face!"— create the vulgarity and hysteria that are fundamental to Aldrich's stylized, personal interpretation of the dark side of Hollywood. For Charlie Castle, in specific, the Hollywood dream resolves itself into an oppressive, imbalanced purgatory largely of his own making. Insulated in the ranch-style home, assaulted by his parasites and demons, Aldrich's extreme angles and short lenses distort the perspectives of Charlie's world and externalize the frenzy of Charlie's own viewpoint. Charlie seeks shelter in the rear ground of his claustrophobic environment, behind lamps, sofas, and other furnishings, and in the romantic conception of himself as "the warrior minstrel with the forlorn hope." Such thoughts and actions are both psychologically telling and futile.

Emotionally, Charlie is trapped in the patriarchal psychology of the old-style studio system which Hoff represents. Visually, the framing shifts so that the foreground and background become constricting rather than concealing elements. The sequence shot of Charlie at the studio with Hank Teagle is most informative. Only there in his element with its connotations of fictional existences and false settings is there any visual or figurative continuity to Charlie's life. Only among the painted flats and artificial daylight is he at ease. The fluid motion that follows him at eye level captures the sense of barriers being removed. Yet even then the underlying tension created by the sustained shot mirrors the imbalance in his life that keeps him on the edge of a mental breakdown.

Presented with two unacceptable alternatives, Charlie steps around both of them by choosing to end his life. As a noir figure and in purely existential terms, it is the ultimate affirmation of control over one's own destiny. The final craning shot of the film after Charlie's suicide, up out of the set and into the heights of the actual sound stage on which *The Big Knife* was filmed, completes the metaphor. The Charlie who has suffered existential anguish and taken his own life is, after all, just a character in a movie. As the camera moves further and further back, piercing the imaginary fourth wall and ceiling of the set, it creates a sardonic afterthought: "Hollywood" life is not, figuratively or literally, a real life. It is not lived but only acted out in an empty search for stage center with darkness surrounding. **AS**

THE BIG NIGHT (1951)

Director: Joseph Losey. **Screenplay**: Stanley Ellin and Joseph Losey based on the novel, *Dreadful Summit,* by Stanley Ellin. **Producer.** Philip A. Waxman. **Director of Photography**: Hal Mohr. **Music**: Lynn Murray. **Art Director**: Nicholas Remisoff. **Editor**: Edward Mann. **Cast**: John Barrymore Jr. (George La Main), Preston Foster (Andy La Main), Joan Lorring (Marion Rostina), Howard St. John (Al Judge), Dorothy Comingore (Julie Rostina), Philip Bourneuf (Dr. Lloyd Cooper), Howland Chamberlin (Flanagan), Emil Meyer (Packingpaugh), Myron Healey (Kennealy), Mauri Lynn (Terry Angeleus), Robert Aldrich (Ringside Fight Fan). **Completed**: August 1951. **Released**: United Artists, December 7. 75 minutes.

George La Main, a teenager often teased for being shy and inarticulate, celebrates his birthday at the bar owned by his widowed father, Andy. When George asks about the absence of his father's longtime girlfriend Frances, Andy does not answer. Al Judge, a local sportswriter and semi-invalid, arrives and forces Andy to remove his shirt, kneel, and submit to a vicious caning. Outraged by his father's lack of resistance, George runs from the bar taking both his father's gun and the prizefight tickets that were a birthday present. Outside the arena, George is asked to sell his extra ticket by Lloyd Cooper but is hustled out of the money by small-time hood Packingpaugh posing as a policeman. The fight ends quickly, but not before George has spotted Judge at ringside. With Cooper, George follows Judge to a bar but his plan to corner him is frustrated by Packingpaugh, whom an enraged George savagely beats. Cooper tries to distract George by taking him to meet the Rostina sisters. Eventually George finds Judge in Frances' apartment, where the man explains that Frances was his sister and her suicide was caused by Andy's refusal

The Big Night: *Georgie (John Barrymore, Jr.) confronts Al Judge (Howard St. John).*

drinking, and finally the deafening roar of the newspaper's presses constitute an unrelieved assault on George's senses, which culminate in his confrontation with Judge. All these scenes are underscored with a visual directness, punctuated by an occasional side-lit close-up of George as his intentions vacillate. After Judge is shot, George suddenly discovers a noir cityscape that was hidden from him earlier by his anger and the night. His dwarfed figure moves past ominous buildings barely outlined by the dawn's light and goes in and out of shadows cast from massive structures such as oil tanks. The final ritual, after the denial of sanctuary at the Rostina apartment, is one of confirmation. In noir terms, that cannot be a simple and painless slap on the cheek but requires the exculpation of his father and surrender to the police. **AS**

THE BIG SLEEP (1946)

Director and Producer: Howard Hawks. **Screenplay**: William Faulkner, Leigh Brackett, Jules Furthman, Philip Epstein [uncredited, reshoot scenes], based on the novel by Raymond Chandler. **Director of Photography**: Sid Hickox. **Music**: Max Steiner. **Art Director**: Carl Jules Weyl. **Editor**: Christian Nyby. **Cast**: Humphrey Bogart (Philip Marlowe), Lauren Bacall (Vivian Stemwood), John Ridgeley (Eddie Mars), Martha Vickers (Carmen Sternwood), Dorothy Malone (Bookstore Proprietress), Patricia Clarke (Mona Mars), Regis Toomey (Bernie Ohls), Charles Waldron (Gen. Sternwood), Charles D. Brown (Norris), Louis Jean Heydt (Joe Brody), Elisha Cook, Jr. (Harry Jones), Sonia Darrin (Agnes), Bob Steele (Canino), James Flavin (Capt. Cronjager), Thomas Jackson (Wilde), Thomas Rafferty (Carol Lundgren), Theodore Von Eltz (Arthur Gwynne Geiger), Dan Wallace (Owen Taylor), Joy Barlowe (Taxi Driver). **Completed**: January 12, 1945 (original shoot). **Released**: Warner Bros., August 31. 118 (1945 version)/114 minutes. NOTE: During the 18 months between its original completion and official release, the original version was released for the armed forces but held back from general release. Then, new scenes were shot and the general release version reedited to add emphasis to the relationship of the Bogart and Bacall characters [for more details see also the relevant essay in *Film Noir Reader 4*, Silver & Ursini, editors].

Private detective Philip Marlowe is asked by wealthy Gen. Sternwood to handle a blackmailer named Geiger who holds compromising photos of Sternwood's younger daughter, Carmen. Marlowe accepts the case and discovers that Geiger's Hollywood bookstore is a front for a large-scale blackmailing racket. But before the detective can intervene, Geiger is murdered. Marlowe becomes entangled in a confusing web of murder and blackmail surrounding not only Carmen, but her older sister, Vivian. Trying to make sense of it all, Marlowe is threatened by Eddie Mars, who is Vivian's missing husband, various other thugs, and later also by a "little guy" who, along with Geiger's secretary, Agnes, now has Geiger's blackmail files. After a double-cross (or is it two?), Marlowe buys information from Agnes that directs him to a ranch house outside the city. Vivian is there planning to pay off the blackmailers who will arrive any minute, but soon realizes that her actions may cost Marlowe his life. With her help, Marlowe ambushes Mars and extracts the man's confession. Then Marlowe forces the racketeer out the front door where his own men gun him down. Safe inside the house, Marlowe and Vivian await the arrival of the police.

to marry her. When Judge threatens to have George arrested as further revenge on Andy, they wrestle over the gun and Judge is shot. When Cooper will not let him return to the Rostina place, George goes back to confront his father. Andy admits that he would not marry Frances because George's mother who deserted them is probably still alive. George initially allows his father to take the blame for the shooting but, seeing Andy handcuffed, confesses, and learns that Judge was only wounded.

Although it is burdened with narrative structure that is at times self-consciously allegorical, at its core *The Big Night* functions as film noir because of the relationship it establishes between the protagonist and his mutable environment. George La Main's half-Odyssey, half-vendetta, which takes him through a series of unfamiliar settings and metaphorically acts as a rite of passage from adolescence to adulthood, is constructed from the same proletarian perspective as *Force of Evil*. Al Judge's cane, as well as his very name, and Andy La Main's gun, which in George's pocket gives him the confidence to beat Packingpaugh, are easily read as symbols of corrupting power. Cooper, the alcoholic college professor, represents intellectual decadence. Unlike *Force of Evil* with its rather theatrical confrontations, *The Big Night* exploits conventions that are more purely noir. Because the figures of Andy Main and Al Judge both play against type— as the burly Main meekly submits to Judge's beating and the older, lame journalist vents his anger with a sadistic frenzy— the audience shares George's disturbance and inability to reconcile this visual anomaly. Already estranged from his peer group, who administer a ritual spanking to him in the first scene after the credits, George retreats into the security of his father's bar, only to have his reassuring birthday celebration viciously disrupted by Judge and his father, the emblem of George's own emerging manhood, humiliated. Without unnecessary psychologizing, the audience can again empathize from the situation, as well as from visual convention, with George's extreme alienation and the fact that he quickly refocuses his total discontent on the figure of Judge.

George's pursuit of Judge takes him out of the familiar locus of the bar into the public arenas of a boxing auditorium, after-hours joint, nightclub, and newspaper office. His humiliation by Packingpaugh followed by the prize fight,

The Big Sleep: *Marlowe (Humphrey Bogart) shoots Canino (Bob Steele) while Vivian Sternwood (Lauren Bacall) looks on.*

Vivian (Luren Bacall) confesses her involvement to Marlowe (Humphrey Bogart).

Los Angeles adds a horizontal dimension to film noir. In place of the looming monoliths and endless urban alleyways of the Eastern cityscape, there is a physical and moral sprawl; a chain of suburbs full of legal and illegal activities linked by wide boulevards and expressways. As a resident of L.A. from 1906 until the mid-1950s, Chandler saw the city evolve from nice town to monster-lopolis. He crafted *The Big Sleep*, like all his other novels set in Los Angeles, into a series of journeys across a mythical, motorized landscape of darkened bungalows, decaying office buildings, and sinister nightspots. As Chandler wrote in "The Simple Art of Murder," his critical essay on the genre of detective fiction, "Down these mean streets a man must go . . . who is not himself mean, who is neither tarnished nor afraid."

What Chandler's prose described as Marlowe drove down those mean streets is something akin to the film noir vision of the world. Unlike many protagonists original to film noir, Chandler's Philip Marlowe enters that world with a number of prescriptive literary qualities that insure his survival. Although Marlowe may seem just a fallen idealist, capable of being physically worn out or romantically duped, he is neither mean, tarnished nor afraid because, as Chandler asserted, "The detective in this kind of story must be such a man . . . the best man in his world." As this "best man," Marlowe investigates a case by examining intricate webs of hidden motivations, disguised as stylistic analogues of dark streets, lonely houses, and tarnished opulence.

The Big Sleep graphically displays the chaotic underworld of the novel through noir setting and visualization rather than plot. The complexities of narrative exist of course, but they do not constitute the main ground against which the noir figure of Marlowe is defined. Instead, *The Big Sleep* stresses expressionistic characterization and visual style, rather than events. This is completely in accord with the novelist's intention, as the story is ultimately reduced and then irretrievably tangled into minor significance as the characters increase their interaction. Instead of "the play's the thing," as Shakespeare taught storytellers, it is the characters who are most important in *The Big Sleep,* as is true in all of Chandler's books. His stories were rapidly made into films, many more than once, but never scripted by him. Of all these, only Hawk's *The Big Sleep,* and Robert Altman's

The Long Goodbye, express Chandler's unique quality fully, but his characters are always indelible. Chandler also added his character-rich talent through his screenplays for the films *The Blue Dahlia, Double Indemnity,* and *Strangers on a Train.*

As a detective, Marlowe is an outsider who requires an invitation before he may enter the world of the rich and powerful Sternwoods. Marlowe searches this different world for the case's facts but also takes note of any fleeting glimpses of compassion, although he is unwilling to be the first to betray such feeling. In fact, Marlowe guards his private ground so tenaciously that he is outraged when Carmen, assuming too much, invites herself into his bed. Marlowe possesses an explicit sense of courtesy as well as privacy. The presence of such amoral people as Carmen, Canino, Eddie Mars, and Agnes casts a heavy pall of pessimism over the film's background characterizations, which is broken only in Marlowe's final scenes with Vivian. In effect, Vivian's high-echelon facade ill conceals a desperate concern about her psychotic sister and sickly father; and Marlowe's hard guy pose is a thin veneer easily pierced by his admiration for the loyal heroism of a "little man" like Harry Jones who lets himself be poisoned rather than reveal his lady's whereabouts.

After the initial inscription of the noir underworld via dark compositions of the opening sequences and via several cynical exchanges of dialogue, such as that between Marlowe and Mars puzzling over the blood stain in Geiger's house: "Got any ideas, soldier?" asks Mars, to which Marlowe replies, "A couple. Somebody gunned Geiger, or somebody got gunned by Geiger who ran away, or Geiger had meat for dinner and likes to do his butchering on the parlor floor," *The Big Sleep* becomes a series of character encounters in which the drama of trust tendered, trust betrayed, and trust restored is played out. For Marlowe, whose world is always associated with such active and violent concepts as "gunning," "running away," and "butchering," trust is a different concept entirely: one that is both difficult and necessary for him. Marlowe needs at least one person upon which to anchor his own shaken code of beliefs. Beaten and unable to overcome Canino alone, Marlowe is forced to the realization that his life is *en prise* and its continuance depends on the sufferance of those he does not fully trust. Vivian frees him; and that act is a consummation of their uncertain relationship established in earlier scenes. The sexual tension between Marlowe and Vivian is suggested by their mannerisms in their first encounter and supported by subsequent dialogue: First, Marlowe: "You've got a touch of class, but I don't know how you'll do over a stretch of ground." Then, Vivian: "A lot depends on who's in the saddle." Against her own better judgment, Vivian cannot rid herself of Marlowe. She goes to his office with that idea in mind but ends by sitting on his desk and helping him throw the police off track. Moreover, the interpretation of Marlowe and Vivian by Bogart and Bacall is full of nonverbal expressions of sympathy that quickly undermine the initial antagonism of the characters. By the time Vivian frees Marlowe at the ranch house, they have realized that mutual trust is essential to their survival. With that understanding established, Marlowe succeeds in killing both Canino and Mars; and Vivian concedes to Marlowe that there is nothing wrong with her that he can't fix.

The novel's Marlowe always begins and ends alone (except when he finally marries, and Chandler left that last story, "Poodle Springs," half-done). But with stars like Bogart/Bacall in 1946, there has to be a big movie-star finale. After the big shoot-out, the stars huddle in a combined extreme close-up within Geiger's shadowy parlor and the sound of police sirens approaching combines with Max Steiner's lush orchestration to signal the resumption of law and order. Nonetheless, *The Big Sleep* is ultimately faithful to the noir vision because that final image has an underlying irony. Visually the couple is surrounded by dark portents: aurally ominous sirens encroach on the romantic score; and they stand all the while near the bloodstain, the emblem of Geiger's death and the beginning of a series of murders and betrayals. Although both Marlowe and Vivian have survived blackmail and its violent chain of events, they have been pushed through a noir hell, and there is no guarantee it will not happen again. **JP**, **JK**, **AS**, & **EW**

THE BIG STEAL (1949)

Director: Don Siegel. **Screenplay**: Gerald Drayson Adams, Geoffrey Homes [Daniel Mainwaring], based on the story, "The Road to Carmichael's," by Richard Wormser. **Producers** Jack J. Gross. **Executive Producer**: Sid Rogell. **Director of Photography**: Harry J. Wild. **Art Director** Ralph Berger. **Music**: Leigh Harline. **Editor**: Samuel E. Beetley. **Cast**: Robert Mitchum (Lt. Duke Halliday), Jane Greer (Joan Graham), William Bendix (Capt. Vincent Blake), Patric Knowles (Jim Fiske), Ramon Novarro (Inspector General Ortega), Don Alvarado (Lt. Ruiz), John Qualen (Julius Seton), Pascual García Peña (Manuel). **Released**: RKO, July 9. 71 minutes.

Army Lieutenant Duke Halliday encounters Joan Graham in Vera Cruz, Mexico, where they soon realize they are both chasing Jim Fiske. Their quarry absconded with a few thousand dollars from Joan, his former fiancée, plus many times that amount from an Army payroll that was Halliday's responsibility. Halliday must not only find Fiske but also avoid apprehension by the perfidious Capt. Blake who wants the money for himself. As Halliday and Graham reluctantly team up, the parameters of the chase change repeatedly, especially after local authorities get embroiled and precipitate a final confrontation just outside Mexico City.

A quick look at the credits list might suggest that RKO devised *The Big Steal* to cash in on the success of *Out of the Past*: a script by Daniel Mainwaring with characters portrayed by Robert Mitchum and Jane Greer. However, the reality was a bit different. Mitchum was waiting to serve a jail sentence for a marijuana conviction; a secretly pregnant Greer was a last minute replacement for Lizabeth Scott; and as Mainwaring said (in *Film Noir Reader 3*), "The only way Don Siegel would agree to direct was if I would go to Mexico with him. A paid vacation sounded good, so I did it. I thought the script was terrible, just awful."

In fact, the filmmakers took the complex narrative and injected a considerable amount of parody from William Bendix reprising his menacing white-suited character in *The Dark Corner* in the context of physical gags and racist jokes about the pidgin English spoken by the Mexican authorities. At the core of this is a quasi-Hawksian antagonism between Halliday and Graham. In that context, *The Big Steal* certainly plays with the expectations of viewers, as it segues from an action opening to a proto-"meet cute" between male and female protagonists much in the way *His Kind of Woman* would two years later. Some might argue that in doing this *The Big Steal* relocates itself outside the traditional confines of a classic period film; but the iconic counterbalance of the cast and the other creative elements tip the scale back, if ever so slightly, into noir. **AS**

THE BIGAMIST (1953)

Director: Ida Lupino. **Screenplay**: Collier Young based on a story by Larry Marcus and Lou Schor. **Producer**: Collier Young. **Director of Photography**: George Diskant. **Art Director**: James Sullivan. **Music**: Leith Stevens. **Editor**: Stanford Tischler. **Cast**: Edmond O'Brien (Harry Graham), Ida Lupino (Phyllis), Joan Fontaine (Eve Graham), Edmund Gwenn (Mr. Jordan), Kenneth Tobey (Tom Morgan), Jane Darwell (Mrs. Connelley), Lillian Fontaine (Landlady). **Released**: Filmakers, December 3. 80 minutes.

Salesman Harry Graham and his wife, Eve, are building their family business. He travels repeatedly to Los Angeles to see clients. When he is there, he begins to see a waitress he meets on a bus, Phyllis, who is unaware he is married. They soon fall in love and eventually she becomes pregnant.

Harry Graham's visits to Los Angeles (shot on actual locations, such as Bunker Hill, MacArthur Park, Beverly Hills, etc.) away from his home with high-powered career woman wife Eve in San Francisco, are narrated by Harry himself in classic noir style. He talks of his loneliness: calling his busy but loving wife for reassurance, sleeping in shadowy hotel rooms lit by neon, walking alone through downtown, taking tour bus rides to fill the void. On one of these buses, he meets the guarded and cynical waitress Phyllis (played by Lupino in a reprise of her "tough dame" roles of the classic period: *The Hard Way*, *Road House*, etc.) with whom he first forms a liaison and then, after she becomes pregnant, marries. Although Harry intends to ask his San Francisco wife for a divorce, he can never seem to summon the courage to break with her or with Phyllis, although he resolves to do so, several times. For on a very deep level, Harry is a fatally weak man, a needy (a word traditionally reserved for females) man who uses these very different women to fulfill his desires.

This lack of courage and almost child-like need for a mother-wife to assuage his alienation eventually causes both women great grief and dislocation once the bigamy is revealed. The final images of the movie are of Harry, in tears, screaming to the judge that he should be punished while the two women whose lives he has ravaged watch him in a combination of disappointment, anger, and sympathy. As he is being led away and Phyllis has left the courtroom, Lupino dwells on the weeping Eve, who turns her back on the camera (audience) and looks towards her exiting husband, visually hinting that she may even accept him back. The ambiguity of her feelings possibly reflects the audience's; and are best expressed by the adoption agency investigator when he tells Harry: "I can't figure out my feelings towards you. I despise you. And I pity you. I don't even want to shake your hand. And yet I almost wish you luck." In the final analysis, Harry remains a supremely complex character. which Lupino refuses to stereotype but, like a true noir artist, chooses instead to analyze. JU

BLACK ANGEL (1946)

Director: Roy William Neill. **Screenplay**: Roy Chanslor based on the novel by Cornell Woolrich. **Producers**: Tom McKnight, Roy William Neill. **Director of Photography**: Paul Ivano. **Music**: Frank Skinner. **Art Directors**: Jack Otterson, Martin Obzina. **Editor**: Saul A. Goodkind. **Cast**: Dan Duryea (Martin Blair), June Vincent (Catherine), Peter Lorre (Marko), Broderick Crawford (Capt. Flood), Constance Dowling (Marvis Marlowe), Wallace Ford (Joe), Hobart Cavanaugh (Jake), Freddie Steele (Lucky), Ben Bard (Bartender), John Phillips (Kirk Bennett), Junius Matthews (Dr. Courtney), Maurice St. Clair, Vilova (Dance Team), Pat Starling (Tap Dancer), June Vincent (singer). **Completed**: May 17, 1946. **Released**: Universal, August 2. 83 minutes.

After his treacherous wife, Marvis, leaves him, composer Marty Blair becomes an alcoholic. Marvis lives in a luxurious apartment and Marty goes there one night to see her but is refused admittance on Marvis' instructions. Later, Marvis is found murdered. Marty is the logical suspect but he was sleeping in his room at the time of the murder. Kirk Bennett, who went to her apartment to retrieve incriminating letters before they were sent to his wife, Catherine, is convicted of

Unable to break with Eve, he sets up Phyllis as his second wife. When Eve and Harry apply to adopt a baby, the agency's investigator, Mr. Jordan, discovers Harry's deception. The law intervenes and the bigamist is soon convicted.

In 1953, director Ida Lupino and writer Collier Young paired their mainstream noir film *The Hitch-Hiker* with a more unusual noir melodrama called *The Bigamist*. Like many of Lupino's directed films, including *The Hitch-Hiker*, the director dwells sympathetically on vulnerable males, allowing them to exhibit emotions usually reserved for female characters in films. With *The Bigamist*, she once again casts noir mainstay Edmond O'Brien as a man consumed by loneliness and alienation, who can only find fulfillment in the arms of a woman. Therefore, he sets up two families for his two centers of business: San Francisco and Los Angeles. In most American films this situation would be either treated as a satirical comedy or as a violation of the nuclear family by a "monster." But Lupino, who became a star in the noir movement, takes a much more existential view of the subject, choosing instead to investigate with great sympathy the psychology of such a conflicted and morally ambiguous man.

the crime. In spite of her husband's involvement with Marvis, Catherine believes him innocent and enlists the aid of Marty, who remembers a stranger leaving her apartment the night of the murder. This was Marko, a shady nightclub operator, who hires Marty and Catherine to play and sing in his club. They work for Marko, hoping to find a jeweled, heart-shaped brooch that Marty had given to Marvis. The brooch, which disappeared the night of the murder, can incriminate Marko. But Marko is innocent of the murder and was in fact being watched by the police at the time of her death. Marty is convinced that Bennett did the killing and he asks Catherine to start a new life with him, but she rejects Marty, declaring that she still loves her husband. Despondent and in an alcoholic haze, Marty sees Marvis' jeweled heart on a woman in a bar and realizes that he indeed murdered his wife, subsequently blocking it from his mind. Marty calls the police just in time to save Bennett's life.

The Black Angel is a modest but imaginative film, with an ingenious script. Dan Duryea, a very interesting actor unfortunately too often typed for his successful portraits of pathological villains and insidious pimps, not only has the leading role but is allowed to play an affectingly romantic character. This unusual casting of Duryea (also a distinguishing feature of *World for Ransom* and *The Burglar* in the 1950's) makes the dramatic thrust of the story even more intriguing. While Duryea is the murderer, he remains the most sympathetic character in the film and far worthier of the heroine than her weak and disloyal husband, the "innocent" Bennett. Certainly, the opening sequence with its complex boom shot from the street to the interior of Marvis' penthouse apartment and the expressionistic re-creation of the murder through Marty's drunken consciousness effectively realize the potential of the material. Likewise, the Duryea character is so carefully drawn that the climax of the story has a feeling of genuine tragedy.

Also, it is interesting to note that the encouragement given to art directors and photographers in "B films" is very much in evidence in *The Black Angel*. The design of Marko's nightclub, in particular, belies the limitations of a modest budget. **BL**

BLACKMAIL (1947)

Director: Lesley Selander. **Screenplay**: Royal K. Cole, Albert DeMond based on a story by Robert Leslie Bellem. **Director of Photography**: Reggie Lanning. **Art Director**: Frank Arrigo. **Music**: Mort Glickman. **Editor**: Tony Martinelli. **Cast**: William Marshall (Daniel Turner), Adele Mara (Sylvia Duane), Ricardo Cortez (Ziggy Cranston), Grant Withers (Inspector Donaldson), Stephanie Bachelor (Carla), Richard Fraser (Antoine le Blanc). **Released**: Republic, July 24. 67 minutes.

Private eye Dan Turner is hired by Ziggy Cranston, an entertainment tycoon, to put a stop to a blackmail plot against him. It seems that a few nights before, at a gambling club called the Silver Swan, Cranston ran into the club singer, an old flame who expressed some animosity about being dumped for a new singer and proceeded to drug Cranston's drink. When he awakened, Cranston found himself alone in the singer's apartment. After incriminating photos arrived, the singer made contact and demanded $50,000 for the negatives but was soon after murdered. While Turner is contemplating whether to take the case, the singer's gigolo boyfriend, who also worked at

the Silver Swan, shows up at Cranston's house and demands $100,000 for the same incriminating photos. He and Turner get into a fist fight, and during the scuffle, the gigolo is shot and falls into the swimming pool. Sylvia, Cranston's new girlfriend and protégée singer, shows up to witness the event, but when the cops show up, the body is missing and she denies she ever saw it. Turner's investigation eventually leads to Cranston's chauffeur and Sylvia, who are lovers and in cahoots to shake down Cranston. In a showdown, Sylvia accidentally shoots her boyfriend and is taken away by the cops.

Blackmail, directed by veteran low-budget director Lesley Selander*,* is one of Republic's entries into the world of the hardboiled. Republic cast William Marshall, who had been a singer in the Fred Waring band in the 1930's, presumably trying to repeat the coup staged by RKO in casting crooner Dick Powell against type as hardboiled Philip Marlowe in *Murder, My Sweet*. Dan Turner himself was one of the longest running of all the private eye characters from the pulps. Humorist S.J. Perlman once called Turner "the apotheosis of all private investigators out of Ma Barker by Sam Spade." Robert Leslie Bellem, Turner's creator, was the ultimate pulpster, publishing over three thousand stories in his lifetime under various pen names and in various genres. **AL**

BLAST OF SILENCE (1961)

Director: Allen Baron. **Screenplay**: Allen Baron, Waldo Salt (narration). **Producer**, **Director of Photography**, **Editor**: Merrill Brody **Music**: Meyer Kupferman. **Art Director**: Charles Rosen. **Cast**: Allen Baron (Frank Bono), Molly McCarthy (Lorrie), Larry Tucker (Big Ralph), Peter Clume (Troiano), Canny Meehan (Petey), Milda Memonas (Troiano's Girl), Dean Sheldon (Nightclub Singer), Charles Creasap (Contact Man), Joe Bubbico (Gangster), Bill DePrato (Sailor), Erich Kollmar (Bellhop), Ruth Kaner (Building Supervisor), Gil Rogers, Jerry Douglas (Gangsters), Don Saroyan (Lorrie's Boyfriend), Jeri Sopanen (Waiter), Mel Sponder (Drummer), Betty Kovac (Troiano's wife), Narrator: Lionel Stander. **Location**: Manhattan, Brooklyn, Staten Island, New York. **Released**: Universal, August 1961. 77 minutes.

A train hurtles out of a tunnel toward Manhattan, bringing with it Frank Bono, a hired killer. A cautious professional brought to town by the syndicate to eliminate one of their own members, Bono insists on taking the time to chart the movements of his intended victim. In the course of his work, he re-encounters a former girlfriend. He is disturbed to discover that he is still attracted to her, as that might interfere with his assignment. A misunderstanding over the "clean" gun to be used in the job leads Bono to kill Big Ralph, a grossly overweight, minor criminal. Despite lingering doubts about the problems he has had, Bono fulfills his contract. However, when he goes to a prearranged spot to collect the remainder of his fee, he is ambushed, chased and shot down.

Coming as it does after the close of the 1950s, certain elements of *Blast of Silence* already seem to be caricatures of classic noir motifs. The fact that almost the entire cast of this low-budget New York-based production were non-professionals before its release does not mitigate the occasional sense of "Hollywood" types playing against each other. The bulky Big Ralph, Troiano's moll, and an odd assortment of other street people glimpsed briefly as Bono walks around

Manhattan, add both a real-life feel and some local color to Bono's unrelentingly grim odyssey. Short on resources, filmmakers Allen Baron and Merrill Brody use the sights and sometimes sounds (as much of the movie appears to have been shot "wild" without production sound being recorded) as filler with narration (written by blacklisted scenarist Waldo Salt) and a jazzy score as a substitute for dialogue and/or sound effects. Still the anonymous, gray background fused from a succession of location exteriors effectively counteracts the probing asides of an unseen narrator: a nasal, cynical voice that speaks to Bono in the second person like a hardboiled superego. Thus, the running commentary by this unnamed and unseen "character" restrains the viewer from fuller empathy with Bono, as it filters his physical and emotional isolation.

While both the theme and the visual treatment conform to the docu-noir standards set by *The Naked City*, it is Allen Baron's portrayal of the stolid, compulsive Bono, rather than his direction, that most fully informs the noir mood of *Blast Of Silence*. After the explosive opening of the film, in which a sustained shot of a train takes several minutes to traverse a tunnel before finally roaring out, Baron is content to situate his dark figure simply and effectively in the various urban settings. This contrasts graphically with, but is figuratively analogous to, the aspect of the cautious assassin, White Suit, in *The Dark Corner*: a man playing out a role and quietly awaiting his inexorable betrayal. **AS**

BLIND SPOT (1947)

Director: Robert Gordon. **Screenplay**: Martin Goldsmith from a story by Harry Perowne. **Producer**: Ted Richmond. **Director of Photography**: George Meehan. **Music**: Paul Sawtell, Mischa Bakaleinkoff. **Art Directors**: Ben Hayne and Cary Odell. **Editor**: Henry Batista. **Cast**: Chester Morris (Jeff Andrews), Constance Dowling (Evelyn Green), Steven Geray (Lloyd Harrison), James Bell (Dt. Lt. Fred Applegate), Forrest (Henry Small), Sid Tomak (Mike, bartender), Paul Burns (Night Watchman). **Released**: Columbia, Feb. 6. 73 minutes.

Jeff Andrews, an accomplished but unsuccessful mystery writer, gets drunk and then goes to his publisher Henry Small demanding release from his extortionate contract. Barely coherent, Andrews brags that he can come up with a good story even while drunk and begins to pitch his "locked-room plot" to Small and Lloyd Harrison, a successful client of Small's, before he is shown the door. Downstairs in the bar, Andrews continues recounting his story to the bartender, Mike, and they are soon joined by Small's secretary, Evelyn, who quickly becomes fascinated with the story. Next morning, the police arrest Andrews for the murder of Small who was found dead in his locked office. Unfortunately Andrews cannot remember much of the previous evening nor even the ending of his new plot. To complicate matters, both Mike and Evelyn have disappeared. Harrison convinces Lt. Applegate to release Andrews into his custody and takes him to his apartment. Unable to sleep, Andrews escapes to search for Mike, finally locating his dead body in the bartender's home. Next to the body is one of Evelyn's earrings. Returning to his own apartment, Jeff finds Evelyn hiding there and then discovers a check for $500 in his pocket.

Realizing that he must have sold his story to Small and that Harrison might have killed Small to steal the story, Andrews enlists the aid of the police. Confronted by the evidence, Harrison confesses that he killed Small believing that Jeff's locked-room idea would cast suspicion on Jeff. When Harrison realized that Mike knew about the murder, he killed him too and left Evelyn's earring, which he had found in Small's office, next to the body.

Blind Spot was one of many "B-movie" mysteries released by Columbia during the 1940s. Ted Richmond produced a number of these, including *Night Editor* and *So Dark the Night*, both of which were superior to this as film noir. In a departure from his starring role in the 1940s *Boston Blackie* movie-series, also produced at Columbia, Chester Morris plays the writer on the skids, traversing a nocturnal New York that borrows heavily from Woolrich's universe of hackwriters, blackouts, people disappearing, and strings of murders, etc. A hoary locked-room murder mystery retooled in full noir trim for the post-war era, *Blind Spot* sports the grungy, wrong-side-of-the-tracks look of early low-budget entries like *Suspense*, *Fall Guy* and *The Guilty*. It compensates, perhaps even over-compensates, with hopped-up performances and some particularly gaudy patter, such as the descriptive statement "a 45-caliber toothache." **BMV & BP**

BLONDE ICE (1948)

Director: Jack Bernhard. **Screenplay**: Kenneth Gamet, Dick Irving Hyland, Raymond L. Schrock based on the novel *Once Too Often* by Whitman Chambers. **Producer**: Martin Mooney. **Director of Photography**: George Robinson. **Art Director**: Joseph Kish. **Music**: Irving Gertz. **Editor**: W.L. Bagier, Jason H. Bernie. **Cast**: Leslie Brooks (Claire Cummings), Robert Paige (Les Burns), Michael Whalen (Stanley Mason), James Griffith (Al), Emory Parnell (Police Captain), John Holland (Carl Hanneman), Walter Sande (Hack Doyle, Editor), Russ Vincent (Blackie Talon, Pilot), Mildred

Coles (June Taylor), Selmer Jackson (District Attorney), David Leonard (Dr. Kippinger), Jack Del Rio (The Butler), Julie Gibson (Mimi Doyle). **Released**: Film Classics/Martin Mooney Productions, July 24. 73 minutes.

Claire Cummings is a journalist with a lust for men, wealth, and power. To achieve her ends she marries wealthy Carl Hanneman. But when he threatens to divorce her because of her continuing love affair with her fellow journalist Les Burns, she murders him. Burns comes to her defense as does her smitten editor. However, Claire cannot remain faithful or control her desire for power. She seduces a lawyer with political ambitions—Stanley Mason. He proposes to her. Meanwhile the pilot who had flown Claire from Los Angeles to San Francisco so she might murder her husband begins to blackmail her. Claire eliminates him. A psychiatrist friend of Mason convinces him that Claire is mentally unbalanced. When Mason tries to break off the engagement, Claire stabs him and frames Les. Finally trapped by the psychiatrist, she confesses. As the men around her wrestle her for the gun, it goes off and Claire dies.

Blonde Ice is a minor gem in the "deadly female" subset of film noir. Utilizing veteran character actors like James Griffith, Emory Parnell, Walter Sande, and Robert Paige, this independently produced noir delights in the psychotic antics of its cool and gorgeous blonde as she turns a bevy of men into her dim-witted love slaves. Leslie Brooks as Claire Cummings projects a lethal quality rivaling that of Barbara Stanwyck in *Double Indemnity* or Peggy Cummins in *Gun Crazy*. When we first see her she is marrying a rich man for security while eyeing her "true love" (her own words), fellow journalist Les Burns. Only minutes after the minister pronounces the final vows, Claire is on the balcony with Les amorously violating her legal commitments while telling her lover, with more than a slight touch of sadism, "I'll be thinking of you on my honeymoon."

Les, like a typical noir "chump" (witness Steve Thompson in *Criss Cross* or The Swede in *The Killers*, to name but two) keeps returning to Claire, no matter how dire or absurd the circumstances. He picks her up at the airport when she returns early from her honeymoon, after murdering her husband. He deflects the police investigation away from her and on to him. When she decides she wants to "trade up" and add a politically powerful lawyer to her "stable," he stands by and watches her go to work on her newest victim. As a reflection of noir's love affair with psychoanalysis, it takes a psychiatrist to finally penetrate the icy facade of this woman. Trapped and vulnerable, Claire exhibits her first moment of weakness, confessing to her crimes while she strikes out one more time, wildly shooting at the doctor. It finally takes a room full of men to literally and figuratively bring down this perverse woman warrior, who now lies on the floor of the chiaroscuro office as the men around her exit the stage. **JU**

BLOOD ON THE MOON (1948)

Director: Robert Wise. **Screenplay**: Lillie Hayward, Luke Short, Harold Shumate, based on the novel *Gunman's Chance* by Luke Short. **Producer**: Theron Warth. **Director of Photography**: Nicholas Musuraca. **Art Director**: Albert S. D'Agostino, Walter E.

Keller. **Music**: Rob Webb. **Editor**: Samuel E. Beetley. **Cast**: Robert Mitchum (Jim Garry), Barbara Bel Geddes (Amy Lufton), Robert Preston (Tate Riling), Walter Brennan (Kris Barden), Phyllis Thaxter (Carol Lufton), Frank Faylen (Jake), Tom Tully (John Lufton), Charles McGraw (Milo Sweet), Clifton Young (Joe Shotten). **Released**: RKO, November 9. 88 minutes.

Jim Garry is an uninvolved drifter and gun-for-hire who finds himself enmeshed in a range war over beef and land between the Luftons and Tate Riling, Garry's friend. Initially, Jim goes to work for Tate partially because he needs the money and partially out of a sense of loyalty, even though Tate has told him about his plans to cheat the Luftons. Jim participates in several of Tate's nefarious acts, including the stampeding of the Luftons' herd which causes two deaths. The deaths plus a growing romantic involvement with Amy, Lufton's daughter, become a moral turning point for Jim. By film's end, he is both psychologically and physically damaged: knifed by one of Tate's henchmen and forced to kill his once close friend, Tate.

Blood on the Moon, directed by Robert Wise and photographed by Nicholas Musuraca, both important figures in noir, presents another noir icon, Robert Mitchum, as Jim Garry, an uninvolved drifter and gun-for-hire who finds redemption in the form of a woman and in a struggle between the powerful and the dispossessed in the Old West. What is most striking about the film is its almost self-conscious noir visual look. *Blood on the Moon* opens on the protagonist riding across the plains at evening with stormy skies in the background and ends in the woods at night, as a wounded Jim is forced to kill his friend Tate in order to protect himself and his newfound love. In the final scene the camera follows Jim through the shadowy woods, creating even more suspense by limiting the view of the audience as well as the characters. After Jim has shot his friend, he bends down close to him for an exchange of grief-stricken expressions in shadowy close-up which summarizes the pain of both men whose affection for each other was never the issue, only the paths they had chosen. **JU**

Blood on the Moon: *Milo Sweet (Charles McGraw) and Jim Garry (Robert Mitchum) listen to Tate Riling (Preston Foster).*

THE BLUE DAHLIA (1946)

Director: George Marshall. **Screenplay**: Raymond Chandler. **Producer**: John Houseman. **Director of Photography**: Lionel Lindon. **Music**: Victor Young. **Art Directors**: Hans Dreier, Walter Tyler. **Editor**: Arthur Schmidt. **Cast**: Alan Ladd (Johnny Morrison), Veronica Lake (Joyce Harwood), William Bendix (Buzz Wanchek), Howard da Silva (Eddie Harwood), Doris Dowling (Helen Morrison), Tom Powers (Capt. Hendrickson), Hugh Beaumont (George Copeland), Howard Freeman (Corelli), Don Costello (Leo), Will Wright (Dad Newell), Frank Faylen (the Man), Walter Sande (Heath, Gangster). **Locations**: Miramar Hotel, Santa Monica; Encino, Malibu, Hollywood. **Completed**: May 22, 1945. **Released**: Paramount, April 19. 98 minutes.

War veteran Johnny Morrison returns to the residence hotel he calls home to discover that his wife Helen has been unfaithful. He leaves her and soon afterward becomes the prime suspect when she is found murdered. As Morrison evades the police, a mysterious woman attempts to befriend him, but he mistrusts her. Later he discovers that she is Joyce, the wife of Eddie Harwood, a nightclub owner who played a prominent role in his wife's infidelity. In the meantime, Morrison's Navy buddies, Buzz and George, try to clear him of the murder charges. The evidence suggests that Buzz may actually have committed the murder while suffering a blackout caused by a war wound. A series of brutal beatings and private sleuthing carried out by Morrison and Joyce lead to a final confrontation in which Harwood is accidentally shot by his own henchmen. Dad Newell, the hotel detective, is tricked by the police investigator and is shot after confessing to the killing of Johnny's wife after his blackmail scheme involving Harwood fell apart.

Because of its original screenplay by Raymond Chandler, *The Blue Dahlia* is an important postwar released film noir, although it was filmed before the war's end and under the constraints of the limited availability of its star, Alan Ladd, due to armed services commitments. Chandler originally devised Buzz as the murderer, to personify the brutalizing effects of war. The studio met with objections from the Navy and forced Chandler to rewrite the film with Newell as the murderer. The ambience of Chandler's hardboiled novels found mixed equivalents in Ladd's laconic characterization and Bendix's frenzied amnesia. With its overriding sense of corruption hidden below the surfaces and tainting many of the characters, *The Blue Dahlia* sets the tone for the developing postwar sensibility of the classic period. With the use of the unfaithful lover/wife as the key to its noir narrative, *The Blue Dahlia* is in the same element as such mainstream dramas as William Wyler's *The Best Years of Our Lives*. While none of Wyler's characters face murder charges or must flee the police, the same sense of painful reintegration into society underlies both narratives. Ironically Chandler's fictionalized Buzz, susceptible to derangement when "monkey-music" reverberates against the steel plate in his skull, is a more frenzied and at some level empathetic figure than the armless but brave Homer Parrish (portrayed by actual veteran, Harold Russell). Since Chandler was prevented from making Buzz a killer driven by a disabling compulsion not of his own making, the ultimate production moved *The Blue Dahlia* away from probing the psychologies of disturbed and betrayed veterans as well as quintessential film noir towards the clichés of a stylish but somewhat routine mystery. **CM & AS**

THE BLUE GARDENIA (1953)

Director: Fritz Lang. **Screenplay**: Charles Hoffman based on the short story "Gardenia" by Vera Caspary. **Producer**: Alex Gottlieb. **Director of Photography**: Nicholas Musuraca. **Music**: Raoul Kraushaar. **Art Director**: Daniel Hall. **Editor**: Edward Mann. **Cast**: Anne Baxter (Norah Larkin), Richard Conte (Casey Mayo), Ann Sothern (Crystal Carpenter), Raymond Burr (Harry Prebble), Jeff Donnell (Sally Ellis), Richard Erdman (Al), George Reeves (Police Capt. Haynes), Ruth Storey (Rose Miller), Ray Walker (Homer), Nat "King" Cole (Himself), Celia Lovsky (Blind Woman). **Completed**: December 24, 1952. **Released**: Warner Bros., March 28. 90 minutes.

After she gets a "Dear Jane" letter from her fiancé in Korea, Norah Larkin impulsively accepts a blind date with Harry Prebble who phones for her absent roommate Crystal. They meet at the Blue Gardenia restaurant where the beautiful but naive Norah is easy prey for painter/playboy Prebble, who plies her with liquor then takes her to his apartment. When he gropes at her, she panics, strikes Prebble with a poker and then passes out. The next day she cannot remember the previous evening—

The Blue Gardenia: *Norah (Anne Baxter) and her friend Crystal (Ann Sothern).*

until reading that Prebble has been clubbed to death. She recalls her encounter and becomes convinced that she has killed him. Reporter Casey Mayo writes a story captioned "Letter to An Unknown Murderess" urging the killer to give herself up. Norah calls him and poses as a "friend" of the murderess. After a few meetings, Casey promises that his newspaper will support Norah's "friend" if she comes forward. When Norah finally confesses to Casey that she is the guilty party, police Capt. Haines arrests her. Casey convinces Haines to investigate another suspect. This suspect attempts suicide with a piece of broken glass, but the police arrest her and discover that she is Prebble's pregnant girlfriend, Rose. The night of the murder, she arrived at Prebble's house shortly after Norah had fled. She killed him when he refused to marry her. Norah is freed and prepared to forgive Casey for his part in her arrest. Sensing this, Casey gives his "little black book" to his partner, Al.

Fritz Lang is one of the few major directors whose name is repeatedly associated with the noir cycle during the 1950's through such films as *Clash By Night*, *The Blue Gardenia*, *The Big Heat*, *Human Desire* and *Beyond a Reasonable Doubt*. This film's unimaginative narrative makes it the weakest of the lot, despite such contemporary "touches" as some LA location photography and the presence of Nat Cole singing the title song. More significantly, it reunited Fritz Lang with Nick Musuraca, this time however at Warner studios—which may account for the fact that its look is flatter and less expressionistic than their earlier effort at RKO, *Clash By Night* (of course the economies of overhead lighting had already been demonstrated in the production of TV films). Yet even *Clash By Night*, with its use of authentic Monterey locales, was more naturalistic than the RKO noir style which Musuraca helped to define in the 1940s. This, in turn, testifies to the diminished influence of a particular studio or visual style as the 1950s progressed.

But if the noir cycle was already in decline by 1953, it was not dead, as Lang and Musuraca here demonstrate. Two cases in point: the image of Prebble screaming in the broken mirror as Norah is about to strike him; and, especially, the extreme deep focus shot from inside the darkened press room, across the desks, through the press room entrance and across the vestibule to show Norah emerging from the elevator and slowly entering the room while the word "Chronicle" is silhouetted on the walls, presumably motivated by an exterior light blinking through the lettered windows of the building! Finally, Lang makes adept use of the heightened realism afforded by the crab dolly which follows Norah on her nocturnal forays, often circling around the unfortunate girl to enhance her sense of entrapment. **BP**

BLUEBEARD (1944)

Director: Edgar G. Ulmer. **Screenplay**: Pierre Gendron. **Producer**: Leon Fromkess. **Director of Photography**: Jockey A. Feindel, Eugen Schufftan (uncredited). **Music**: Leo Erdody. **Art Director**: Paul Palmentola. **Cast**: John Carradine (Gaston Morrell), Jean Parker (Lucille), Nils Asther (Insp. Lefevre), Ludwig Stossel (Jean Lamarte), George Pembroke (Insp. Renard), Teala Loring (Francine), Sonia Sorel (Renee), Henry Kolker (Deschamps), Emmett Lynn (Le Soldat), Iris Adrian (Mimi), Patti McCarty (Babette), Carrie Devan (Constance), Anne Sterling (Jeanette). **Released**: PRC, November 11. 72 minutes.

Lucille and two friends make the acquaintance of Morrell, a portraitist and puppeteer, who invites them to a puppet opera of *Faust*. After the show, he meets alone with Lucille. Later, a previous employee, Renee, arrives. She is jealous and asks to have her job back. Morrell agrees but when she asks too many questions, he paints her portrait and then strangles her. Usually, his paintings are only sold abroad. However, when one portrait stays in Paris for public exhibition, the police recognize the woman as the fourth victim of an unknown murderer they have nicknamed "Bluebeard." All of the city's models are questioned by the police, but the murders remain unsolved. Lamarte, Morell's art dealer, is offered money to arrange for a portrait of Francine, an undercover agent. Unfortunately the police spring their trap too late and Morrell escapes, leaving behind Francine and Lamarte dead. Unintentionally, Lucille reveals to Inspector Lefevre that she's suspicious Morrell is Bluebeard. When she goes to Morrell's home, the police secretly follow. The police break in and chase Morrell to the rooftop. Losing his footing, Morrell falls to his death in the Seine, the river from which the police have fished out his victims.

Although *Bluebeard* is set in nineteenth century Paris, it relates to wartime America by depicting a large population of single women, holding jobs and enjoying nightlife. Two of these women, the sisters Lucille and Francine, are responsible for ending Morrell's murder spree. When the men in the police department cannot discover the identity of Bluebeard, they call in Francine to lead the investigation. She comes up with a plan that lures the killer into the open. Lucille, a seamstress, recognizes the cravat she mended for Morrell as a murder weapon. Because Morrell is attracted to Lucille as a lovely yet modest woman, he opens up to her about what made him start killing. He says he saw a woman, Jeanette, collapse in the street. He took care of her in his house. He painted her as the "Maid d'Orleans" (Joan of Arc, a virgin). After she got well, she disappeared. He searched for her and when he found her, he saw she was a woman with sexuality and money. Outraged at the "real" Jeanette, he strangled her. Morrell's confession reveals that, while Jeanette was bedridden and dependent on him, he developed an idealization of her. When he discovers his image of female purity doesn't match reality, he kills Jeanette for "defiling" that image. Afterwards, in a city filled with independent women, Morrell murders one more "Jeanette" after another.

Morrell's other reason for killing women, which he doesn't tell Lucille, is to make ends meet. Lamarte, Morrell's landlord and art dealer, procures the victims. After Morrell paints a woman, he strangles her and gives the painting to Lamarte, who sells it and pockets most of the money. With the leftover he gets from Lamarte, Morrell pays his rent and has the leisure to create puppets. After the Faust opera, Morrell tells Lucille that each puppet resembles someone he knows. He refers to Mephistopheles as "the evil one" and his "business manager." The face of Mephistopheles, with its outwardly pointing beard, is a dead-ringer for Lamarte. However, it's Lamarte who pulls Morrell's strings. Morrell is unable to refuse any of Lamarte's demands for another painting, though both of them know it means another murder. Manipulated by Lamarte to keep painting for blood money and powerless to stop strangling the women he paints, Morrell can only control the little wooden people that he carves. **DMH**

Body and Soul: *Charlie (John Garfield) and Alice (Hazel Brooks)*.

BODY AND SOUL (1947)

Director: Robert Rossen. **Screenplay**: Abraham Polonsky. **Producer**: Bob Roberts (Enterprise Productions). **Director of Photography**: James Wong Howe. **Music**: Hugo Friedhofer. **Art Director**: Nathan Juran. **Editors**: Francis Lyons, Robert Parrish. **Cast**: John Garfield (Charlie Davis), Lilli Palmer (Peg Bom), Hazel Brooks (Alice), Anne Revere (Anna Davis), William Conrad (Quinn), Joseph Pevney (Shorty Polaski), Canada Lee (Ben Chaplin), Lloyd Goff (Roberts), Art Smith (David Davis), James Burke (Arnold), Virginia Gregg (Inna), Peter Virgo (Drummer), Joe Devlin (Prince), Shimen Rushkin (Grocer), Mary Currier (Miss Tedder), Milton Kibbie (Dan), Tim Ryan (Shelton), Artie Dorrell (Jack Marlowe). **Completed**: April 1947. **Released**: United Artists, August 22. 105 minutes.

Charlie Davis enters into a partnership with Roberts, a gambling promoter, and tries to use his skill as a boxer to escape poverty. However, the money and glory alienate Charlie from those closest to him. He grows distant from his mother and rejects Peg, the woman who loves him, for Alice, one of the girls hanging about Roberts and his cohorts. Heeding neither his best friend, Shorty Pulaski, nor his faithful trainer and sparring partner, Ben Chaplin, Charlie does nothing when Roberts eventually causes Shorty's death. However, Charlie reaches a pivotal moment after agreeing to throw the next fight to fix the odds for Roberts. When Ben dies, Charlie begins to question his values and decides to try and win the fight instead, despite what consequences may occur.

Body and Soul contains many elements of the social-realist dramas made in the 1930s and, as allegory, it can be seen as one of the last cries of liberalism before the House Un-American Activities Committee's investigations were to crush many of its principals. Pitting the classic conflicts between truth and corruption, selfish profit and virtue, Charlie has to choose whether to be a pawn or a hero. All along the way, Charlie rejects the virtuous choices of his mother, his girlfriend and his longtime friend, Shorty. Finally, it is the death of the last remaining "good" person in his life,

the aging Ben, that leads him to perform the positive act that sets him free from the gangsters. This shift to affirmation and growth at the end of the film is partly a reflection of director Robert Rossen's own idealism and partly that of writer Abraham Polonsky's social conscience.

The visualization has few expressionistic devices but does include techniques that reinforce Davis' sense of entrapment. For instance, the long craning shot in the training camp moves slowly over the ring and other boxing paraphernalia, then in through a window, where it reveals Davis lying awake on his bed. This third-person camera relentlessly tracking the protagonist acquires a subjective quality in the actual fight sequences, when the hand-held camera alternately lunges at Davis and his opponent, accentuating the alienating violence of his profession with a graphic naturalism. **JC & AS**

BODYGUARD (1948)

Director: Richard Fleischer. **Screenplay**: Fred Niblo, Jr. and Harry Essex from story by Geo. W. George and Robert Altman. **Producer**: Sid Rogell. **Director of Photography**: Robert De Grasse. **Music**: Paul Sawtell. **Art Director**: Albert D'Agostino and Field M. Gray. **Editor**: Elmo Williams. **Cast**: Lawrence Tierney (Mike Carter), Priscilla Lane (Doris Brewster), Philip Reed (Freddie Dysen), June Clayworth (Connie Fenton), Elizabeth Risdon (Gene Dyson), Steve Brodie (Fenton), Frank Fenton (Lt. Borden), Chas. Cane (Capt. Wayne). **Location**: Los Angeles. **Released**: RKO, September 4. 62 minutes; 75 minutes (Director's cut).

Hot tempered homicide detective Mike Carter quits the LA police force after getting into a fight with his immediate superior, Lt. Borden. Temporarily unemployed, he is offered a job by Freddie Dyson to act as a bodyguard for his wealthy aunt, Gene Dyson, who owns a local meat factory. Mike refuses at first until someone takes a shot at Gene in her house while Mike is present. Taking the case, Mike later follows Gene and her butler to the packing house, where he is waylaid and knocked unconscious. He awakens to find himself in his car, stalled on the railroad tracks with a train barreling down and Lt. Borden's dead body next to him. He escapes in time but realizes he will be wanted for Borden's murder. Mike gets his girlfriend, Doris, a secretary in homicide, to provide him with a summary of Borden's most recent cases. Mike ultimately discovers that Borden helped to cover up the murder of a government inspector at the meatpacking plant by confirming his death as an accident in return for hush money. Mike gets Gene to confess that Fenton, the plant foreman, was behind the inspector's death because Fenton had been injecting the meat with water to increase its weight and that Freddie was in on the scheme. Meanwhile Doris, who had gone to the plant to interrogate the night watchman, secretly witnesses Freddie shoot Fenton after admitting to Fenton that he himself had killed Borden for "being too greedy." Doris accidentally reveals herself before Freddie can dispose of the body, and he pursues her through the plant but Mike arrives in time to stop him, followed by the police. Mike is reinstated to the force and prepares to take a long honeymoon with Doris.

A consensus seems to be developing among commentators on *Bodyguard* that the film fails to satisfy precisely because 13 minutes were cut from the director's original version. Certainly Fleischer's later film noirs were superior to this entry but that could also be due to his growing mastery of the application of documentary techniques to the thriller. Fleischer, after all, had directed segments of the RKO documentary series "This is America" and after the release of *T-Men* it was not too difficult for him to follow in the wake of his mentor, Anthony Mann. In any case, by 1948 the RKO noir style was well enough established for him to capitalize upon as even the 62 minute version demonstrates his ability to maintain a brisk pace while smoothly combining location and studio shots. The excised footage would doubtless have patched up some holes in the leaky plot. Additionally, a fuller version would probably make, as has been remarked, for a more grisly finale instead of fizzling out as it does in the current print. What with the meat saws whining and the meat grinders rumbling, surely Fleischer did not intend to conclude the story with Freddie just hurling an empty pistol at Mike which is almost instantly followed with Mike and Doris leaving on their honeymoon! **BMV & BP**

BOOMERANG (1947)

Director: Elia Kazan. **Screenplay**: Richard Murphy based on an article by Anthony Abbot [Fulton Oursler]. **Producer**: Louis De Rochemont. **Director of Photography**: Norbert Brodine. **Music**: David Buttolph. **Art Directors**: Richard Day, Chester Gore. **Editor**: Harmon Jones. **Cast**: Dana Andrews (Henry Harvey), Jane Wyatt (Madge Harvey), Lee J. Cobb (Chief Harold Robinson), Cara Williams (Irene Nelson), Arthur Kennedy (John Waldron), Sam Levene (Dave Woods), Taylor Holmes (T.M. Wade), Robert Keith (Mac McCreery), Ed Begley (Paul Harris), Karl Malden (Det. White), Barry Kelley (Sgt. Dugan), Lewis Leverett (Harvey's assistant), Philip Coolidge (Crossman), Bert Freed (Herron), Walter Greaza (Mayor Swayze), Arthur Miller (Suspect). **Released**: 20th Century-Fox, March 5. 88 minutes.

Father George Lambert is shot and killed on the streets of small Connecticut city whose populace is outraged by the crime. Fearing repercussions in an election year, the mayor pressures prosecutor Henry Harvey and Police Chief Harold Robinson to find the murderer and bring him to justice. The police track down John Waldron, a down-and-out veteran with a handgun who left for Ohio after arguing with the priest. Although Waldron proclaims his innocence, several bystanders identify him and three days of police interrogation break down his resistance. As Harvey prepares for the trial, he discovers inconsistencies in his own case that give him a reasonable doubt as to Waldron's guilt. In a surprising reversal of procedure, Harvey impugns the police case and undermines the testimony of his own eye-witnesses. Waldron is acquitted and, although a suspicious character is in the courtroom, the case remains unsolved.

Boomerang is, perhaps, more of a Louis De Rochemont movie than it is an Elia Kazan film. That is to say, it partakes more of the "semi-documentary" manner of the producer's influential *House on 92nd Street*—true story, authentic locations, non-professional actors in many of the small roles, narration voiced not by a character in the story, but by an anonymously authoritarian speaker—than it does of the intimate emotional intensity of the director's more famous films. Despite the fact that it contains a great deal of night shooting,

it is not a film noir in the fullest sense of the word. Yes, it is about an innocent man accused of a crime—a noir trope if ever there was one—but there is no dark and doomed romance in the film and little of the highly stylized lighting and photography that are so important to noir. It is more a combined police procedural and courtroom melodrama.

Nevertheless, it was an important film for Kazan, whose two previous films (*A Tree Grows in Brooklyn* and *Sea of Grass*) had been studio bound and therefore frustrated his drive for realism that motivated most of his movie work. "The important thing," he said many years later, "was that I caught something in the background, in the life of a city like that [Stamford, Conn., where every shot in the picture was made]. And I enjoyed that a lot. It gave me confidence. It made me feel, 'I can go anywhere and make a film.'" It led on, he firmly believed, to *Panic in the Streets* and, most important, to *On the Waterfront*.

The film is also significant in the Kazan canon because, aside from its two leads, Dana Andrews and Jane Wyatt, it features many of the actors who would become almost a stock company for him in his later stage and screen work—Lee J. Cobb, Karl Malden, Arthur Kennedy, Ed Begley. He even found small roles in the production for Arthur Miller, the playwright, whose *All My Sons* Kazan would begin directing on Broadway immediately after *Boomerang* wrapped, and for his raffish uncle, whose immigrant story would form the basis of his novel and film, *America America*, as well as a couple of other Kazan novels.

All of which says nothing about the intrinsic melodramatic power of *Boomerang*'s story, which involves Andrews' prosecutor coming to doubt his own case against the presumptive murderer and risking his life—not to mention the opprobrium of the community, which is in a lynch mob mood—to free the suspect. Dana Andrews was a rather stiff actor with a stentorian voice, but those qualities are put to excellent use in this film; so-so performers can be good in courtroom dramas, since lawyering often encourages the display of false emotions and moralistic posturing, which are well within their range. Kazan would later say that making this movie, was something of a political turning point for him. As a devoted leftist he had in the 1930s and early 1940s intrinsically believed "that the good in American society will finally win out." Working on this film Kazan began to think that our basic institutions, exemplified in *Boomerang* by the legal system, were not just occasionally led astray by corrupt individuals, but were inherently rotted, insusceptible to reform. It was a notion more often given full range in his theatrical productions than on the screen, though in both realms his general contempt for bourgeois values did come more and more to the fore. But this is perhaps of small consequence; *Boomerang* remains a well-made movie that deserves more attention than it has received in recent decades, both as a marker in a major directorial career and as an intrinsically entertaining contribution to a socially conscientious moment in American movie history. **RS**

BORDER INCIDENT (1949)

Director: Anthony Mann. **Screenplay**: John C. Higgins based on a story by Higgins and George Zuckerman. **Producer**. Nicholas Nayfack. **Director of Photography**: John Alton. **Music Director**: André Previn. **Art Directors**: Cedric Gibbons, Hans Peters. **Editor**:

Conrad A. Nervig. **Cast**: Ricardo Montalban (Pablo Rodriguez), George Murphy (Jack Beames), Howard Da Silva (Owen Parkson), James Mitchell (Juan Garcia), Arnold Moss (Zopilote), Alfonso Bedoya (Cuchillo), Teresa Celli (Maria), Charles McGraw (Jeff Amboy), Jose Torvay (Pocoloco), John Ridgely (Mr. Neley), Arthur Hunnicutt (Clayton Nordell), Sig Ruman (Hugo Wolfgang Ulrich), Otto Waldis (Fritz), Harry Antrim (John Boyd). **Location**: Mexicali, Mexico. **Completed**: May 24, 1949. **Released**: MGM, November 19. 96 minutes.

A crooked rancher, Owen Parkson, smuggles Mexicans with phony work permits into the California valleys, where the Mexicans are exploited. The criminal operation leads to murder. Immigration officials on both sides of the border join forces to investigate. A U.S. agent, Jack Beames, and a Mexican agent Pablo Rodriguez, infiltrate. The former poses as a petty crook in Parkson's gang while the latter is disguised as a *bracero* delivered to Parkson's ranch. Pablo and Jack witness the inhuman treatment of the Mexicans by the psychopathic Parkson and his sadistic henchman. Jack's true identity is discovered, and he dies horribly as the helpless Pablo watches. Finally, Pablo and the immigration authorities destroy Parkson and smash his gang.

The reputation made by Anthony Mann and John Alton with *T-Men* and their other Eagle-Union pictures rapidly earned them work at MGM. It is no surprise that Mann directed a film modeled closely on *T-Men*. Thus, *Border Incident* features two undercover men who are immigration officials rather than Treasury agents, and in an egalitarian spirit, one is WASP while the other is Mexican while both are equally sympathetic protagonists. The scene in *T-Men* in which O'Brien must watch Genaro be killed, is matched in *Border Incident* by the scene of Jack run down by a tractor as Pablo looks on. The latter scene is more visually impressive as a close, wide-angle shot that vividly captures Jack's terror as he desperately claws at dirt to save himself. Certainly, this death scene is one of the most grisly in this period of film history. It was later copied by the makers of *Prime Cut*. However, the comparable scene in T-Men includes a more complex emotional exchange between O'Brien and the heroic Genaro.

Border Incident's photography by John Alton consists primarily of deep focus compositions with high contrast. In the Mexican sequences, chiaroscuro lighting enhances the visual

impression. Additionally, the landscape of Californian farmland is used for the first time by Mann to enhance dramatically the moral and emotional thrust of the action, prefiguring the Westerns he would begin making the following year. **BL**

BORN TO KILL (1947)

Director: Robert Wise. **Screenplay**: Eve Greene and Richard Macaulay based on the novel *Deadlier than the Male* by James Gunn. **Producer**: Herman Schlom. **Executive Producer**: Sid Rogell. **Director of Photography**: Robert de Grasse. **Music**: Paul Sawtell. **Art Directors**: Albert S. D'Agostino, Walter E. Keller. **Editor**: Les Millbrook. **Cast**: Claire Trevor (Helen Trent), Lawrence Tierney (Sam Wild), Walter Slezak (Arnold Arnett), Philip Terry (Fred Grover), Audrey Long (Georgia Staples), Elisha Cook, Jr. (Marty Waterman), Isabel Jewell (Laury Palmer), Esther Howard (Mrs. Kraft), Tony Barrett (Danny), Grandon Rhodes (Inspector Wilson). **Completed**: June 21, 1946. **Released**: RKO, May 3. 92 minutes.

Former boxer and rancher Sam Wild is in Reno gambling with his friend, Marty Waterman, who often has to restrain Sam's quick temper. Later, Sam sees his girl friend, Laury Palmer, out with another man, and kills them both in a jealous rage. The bodies are discovered by Helen Trent, who has been living next door. The just divorced Helen decides not to report the murders, so that she can leave Reno that night and return to San Francisco without becoming involved. On Marty's advice Sam flees to San Francisco while Marty keeps track of the murder investigation in Reno. Helen, who is the adopted sister of newspaper heiress Georgia Staples and is engaged to young steel heir Fred Grover, meets and flirts lightly with Sam on the train. Sam visits Helen at the Staples mansion but learns of her engagement and courts Georgia instead. They marry after a brief romance. Marty attends the wedding and is followed by Arnold Arnett, a dishonest private detective hired by Laury's neighbor, Mrs. Kraft. When Arnett blackmails Sam, Helen strings Arnett along. Marty plans to kill Mrs. Kraft to protect Sam and tries to warn Helen away. Sam sees Marty leave Helen's room, follows Marty to a lonely stretch of beach where he is to meet Mrs. Kraft, and murders Marty instead. Despite everything,

Born to Kill: *A porter (Napolean Whiting) watches Sam Wild (Lawrence Tierney) and Helen (Claire Trevor) detrain.*

Helen is unable to overcome her fascination with Sam. She meets with Mrs. Kraft and "persuades" her to drop her investigation. Finally Helen calls the police, makes Georgia witness Sam's adulterous behavior and then tries to convince Sam to shoot Georgia. The police arrive but Helen's plan is foiled. When Sam learns who sent for them, he shoots Helen and is then killed by the police.

Born To Kill is a grim and complicated melodrama, most intriguing as the first of a number of noir films directed by Robert Wise, who had previously been associated with Orson Welles and then with Val Lewton at RKO. This could lead us to the interesting speculation that the RKO noir style, certainly the most distinctive of the classic period, was born of the marriage of the baroque, expressionistic style of Welles and the moody, Gothic atmosphere of Lewton. Whatever the case, this film contains the two least likeable leads in the cycle, Lawrence Tierney (who drew iconic value from his earlier *Dillinger* and *The Devil Thumbs a Ride*) and Claire Trevor (e.g., *Murder, My Sweet*), as two characters equally pathological in their own unique ways. Their most memorable scene together is when their lust is aroused by recalling the circumstances of the double murder. But arguably the film's best performance belongs to Walter Slezak as a seedy, somewhat shady private eye who peppers the action with bits of wisdom stolen from the classics. **BP**

THE BRASHER DOUBLOON (1947)

Director: John Brahm. **Screenplay**: Dorothy Hannah; adapted by Dorothy Bennett and Leonard Praskins from the novel *The High Window* by Raymond Chandler. **Producer**: Robert Bassler. **Director of Photography**: Lloyd Ahern. **Music**: David Buttolph. **Art Directors**: James Basevi, Richard Irvine. **Editor**: Harry Reynolds. **Cast**: George Montgomery (Philip Marlowe), Nancy Guild (Merle Davis), Conrad Janis (Leslie Murdock), Roy Roberts (Lt. Breeze), Fritz Kortner (Vannier), Florence Bates (Mrs. Murdock), Marvin Miller (Blaire), Houseley Stevenson (Morningstar), Bob Adler (Sgt. Spangler), Jack Conrad (George Anson), Alfred Linder (Eddie Prue), Jack Overman (Manager), Jack Stoney (Mike), Ray Spiker (Figaro), Paul Maxey (Coroner), Reed Hadley (Dr. Moss). Edward Gargan (Truck Driver). **Completed**: September 13, 1946. **Released**: 20th Century-Fox, February 6. 72 minutes. Note: Original release title was to be *The High Window*.

A stolen gold coin brings Philip Marlowe into the employ of a rich and eccentric widow, Mrs. Murdock. Her motives for discovering the whereabouts of her rare doubloon become moot as soon as Marlowe realizes that there is more to this case than a simple robbery. The trail leads from robbery and blackmail to murder, with Marlowe in the middle. When Marlowe feels he finally has a clear picture of the events surrounding the brasher doubloon, he suffers a savage beating at the hands of the grotesque Vannier. Then, while attempting to straighten out a blackmail scheme involving Mrs. Murdock's mentally disturbed secretary, Merle Davis, Marlowe finally puts the pieces of this bizarre puzzle together. His investigation comes full circle as his original client, Mrs. Murdock, is revealed as a murderess and the perpetrator of the entire affair.

In transferring the ambience and hardboiled character of Raymond Chandler's novel *The High Window* to the screen,

The Brasher Doubloon may not succeed in carrying over the complexity of the novel but it definitely succeeds as a film noir. Visually, the film is filled with moody, low-key images supported by a dense and occasionally threatening background. The script is bland and director John Brahm gives *The Brasher Doubloon* a comparatively understated style. There is little out of the ordinary or flamboyant in Brahm's hardboiled world. The environment is a far cry from his classic period noir films like *The Lodger* and *Hangover Square*. Even the music, usually so important in film noir, is strangely absent in most of the film. Still, *The Brasher Doubloon* functions as a film noir because of the power of Chandler's world and the creatures populating it. Most of the acting in the film is undistinguished with the exception of Fritz Kortner, a veteran actor molded in the expressionist cinema of Germany in the 1920s. His depiction of Vannier brings a sense of aberrant vitality to Chandler's truncated story. **CM**

THE BREAKING POINT (1950)

Director: Michael Curtiz. **Screenplay**: Ranald MacDougall based on the novel, *To Have and Have Not,* by Ernest Hemingway. **Director of Photography**: Ted McCord. **Music**: Ray Heindorf. **Art Director**: Edward Carrere. **Editor**: Alan Crosland, Jr. **Cast**: John Garfield (Harry Morgan), Patricia Neal (Leona Charles), Phyllis Thaxter (Lucy Morgan), Juano Hernandez (Wesley Park), Wallace Ford (Duncan), Edmond Ryan (Rogers), Ralph Dumke (Hannagan), Guy Thomajan (Danny), William Campbell (Concho), Sherry Jackson (Amelia), Donna Jo Boyce (Connie), Victor Sen Yung (Sing), Peter Brocco (Macho), John Doucette (Gotch), James Griffith (Charlie). **Location**: Newport Bay, California. **Completed**: May 10, 1950. Warner Bros., September 30. 97 minutes.

Harry Morgan is the owner of the *Sea Queen*, a Newport, California, charter boat business which barely supports his wife, Lucy, and their two daughters. A flashy sports fisherman, Hannagan, and his mistress, Leona Charles, charter Harry's boat to Mexico. But then Hannagan goes ashore without paying his bill and Harry is stranded in Mexico without funds. A disreputable lawyer, Duncan, makes Harry a money offer, which he accepts, to smuggle Chinese nationals into the country. The leader of the Chinese, Sing, double-crosses Harry and is killed. Then Harry makes the other Chinese jump in shallow Mexican waters. But the Coast Guard hears of the smuggling attempt and impounds Harry's ship. Despondent, Harry returns home and has a brief affair with Leona. When Duncan secures a court order to release Harry's boat, he then blackmails him to accept another illegal charter party. Together with his alcoholic first mate, Wesley Park, Harry motors a group of hoodlums to Catalina Island to deliver stolen racetrack receipts. En route, the criminals kill Wesley and Harry realizes they intend to kill him also. One by one, Harry kills each of the thieves and is severely wounded by them. A Coast Guard cutter finds Harry and brings him to homeport. Lucy persuades Harry that she still loves him and that he must let the doctors amputate his wounded arm or die. Harry agrees and lives to start a new life with Lucy.

As its story indicates, *The Breaking Point* has many of the fatalistic tendencies associated with film noir although, strictly speaking, it is equally a romantic melodrama, ranging from California to Mexico and exploiting its coastal locations. *The Breaking Point* is a remake of *To Have And Have Not*, but is altogether more faithful to the Hemingway novel than Howard Hawks' film. A pervasive feeling of hopelessness and futility surrounds the protagonist and, although he displays the characteristic toughness of the action hero, his vulnerability and capacity for suffering make him an archetypically defeated noir figure. John Garfield gives one of his best performances in the role, which is matched by that of Juano Hernandez as the first mate. Photographically, the work is in deep focus, which allows for a rewardingly detailed *mise-en-scène*. **BL**

THE BRIBE (1949)

Director: Robert Z. Leonard. **Screenplay**: Marguerite Roberts based on the short story by Frederick Nebel. **Producer**: Pandro S. Berman. **Director of Photography**: Joseph Ruttenberg. **Music**: Miklós Rózsa . **Art Directors**: Cedric Gibbons, Malcolm Brown. **Editor**: Gene Ruggiero. **Cast**: Robert Taylor (Rigby), Ava Gardner (Elizabeth Hintten), Charles Laughton (Bealer), Vincent Price (Carwood), John Hodiak (Tug Hintten), Samuel S. Hinds (Dr. Warren), John Hoyt (Gibbs), Tito Renaldo (Emilio Gomez), Martin Garralaga (Pablo Gomez). **Completed**: August 2, 1948. **Released**: MGM, February 3. 98 minutes.

Federal Agent Rigby is sent to a small South American island to break up a ring dealing in contraband war surplus materials. The organization is headed by Carwood, an apparently naive American playboy/sportsman. Carwood is assisted by the cynical and slovenly J.S. Bealer and by Tug Hintten, who smuggles the goods out on his ship. When Tug becomes ill with a heart ailment and is totally dependent upon his wife, Elizabeth, Carwood makes new arrangements. Carwood realizes Rigby is an agent and plots his "accidental" death on a fishing trip, but Emilio Gomez, a young native guide, is killed by the sharks instead. Rigby enlists the aid of Emilio's father to break up the ring but in the meantime Carwood kills Tug, making his death look like a heart attack. Rigby and Elizabeth are romantically involved and Bealer blackmails her to drug the agent so that the contraband can be transported while he is unconscious. Rigby recovers in time

An undercover man meets the strangest suspects in his strange business.

to foil their plans and then forces Bealer to turn against Carwood. The playboy-smuggler fights with Rigby during a spectacular fireworks display and in the ensuing gunfight Carwood is killed. Rigby by now has sworn to quit his job as government agent and is free to return with Elizabeth who, he realizes, has been no more than an innocent pawn in the hands of corrupt men.

The Bribe is a minor MGM noir in which the studio used a contemporary story of post-war intrigue as an excuse to pair two of its major stars romantically. But such plot elements as smuggling are rather tangential to the noir tradition. As far as the post-war setting is concerned, there are scattered references to the fallen nature of this "brave new world" in dialogue: "What's a little graft . . . everybody does it," a theme that would be better developed in *The Third Man* (1949), which, while produced in Europe, places its intrigue squarely within the noir universe. What this film does have is an "A" budget which provided for a good cast and some brilliant low-key photography by Joseph Ruttenberg, whose expressionistic talents had been honed earlier in *Dr. Jekyll and Mr. Hyde* (1941) and *Gaslight*. Ava Gardner's persona here capitalizes on the moral ambivalence of her earlier role in *The Killers*. Once again she looks beautiful enough to tempt anybody, so that when the stalwart Rigby is ready to give up his integrity for her, it resonates with the audience. Taylor, as well, has iconic values of both hero and anti-hero (see, e.g., *Undercurrent*) and since a fair amount of the film's action reflects Rigby's retrospective viewpoint, his voice-over narration carries some of the angst of such earlier anti-heroes protagonists as Walter Neff and Jeff Bailey. Vincent Price and Charles Laughton, as might be expected, almost steal the film, especially Laughton as the sweating, alternately threatening and pathetic "Pie-shaped" Bealer, who only wants to make enough money for a foot operation so that he can walk without pain. **BP**

THE BROTHERS RICO (1957)

Director: Phil Karlson. **Screenplay**: Lewis Meltzer and Ben Perry based on the novelette *Les Freres Rico* by Georges Simenon. **Producer**: Lewis J. Rachmil (William Goetz Productions). **Director of Photography**: Burnett Guffey. **Music**: George Duning. **Art**

Director: Robert Boyle. **Editor**: Charles Nelson. **Cast**: Richard Conte (Eddie Rico), Dianne Foster (Alice Rico), Kathryn Grant (Norah), Larry Gates (Sid Kubik), James Darren (Johnny Rico), Argentina Brunetti (Mrs. Rico), Lamont Johnson (Peter Malaks), Harry Bellaver (Mike Lamotta), Paul Picerni (Gino Rico), Paul Dubov (Phil), Rudy Bond (Gonzales), Richard Bakalyn (Vic Tucci), William Phipps (Joe Wesson), Mimi Aguglia (Julia Rico), Maggie O'Byrne (Mrs. Felici), George Cisar (Dude Cowboy), Peggy Maley (Jean), Jane Easton (Nellie). **Completed**: December 27, 1956. **Released**: Columbia, September 4. 92 minutes.

The syndicate asks Eddie Rico, an ex-mobster turned successful businessman, to locate his younger brothers who have apparently double-crossed their gangland associates. He feels obliged to search for his brothers not only to protect their lives but the lives of his family as well. As he tracks his brothers down, the elder Rico begins to suspect ulterior motives for the frenzied manhunt. Finding his brother Johnny secluded in a rundown resort house, the entire puzzle unravels itself. The power play of the mob was merely a way of seeking revenge for a crime committed against the mob by the Rico brothers. Unable to save his brothers, the elder Rico extricates himself from all connection to the treachery and returns to his wife and family scarred by the deadly affair.

Utilizing material adapted from the writing of mystery writer Georges Simenon, director Phil Karlson creates in *The Brothers Rico* a thriller deeply rooted in the style of police thrillers like *The Lineup* and *Phenix City Story*. In these films the subtly ritualized violence and dark ambience of film noir was replaced by an overt emphasis on crude violence and a dull, almost flat, visual style. This type of thriller became the heir apparent to the rapidly declining noir output of the 1950's. Throughout *The Brothers Rico*, Richard Conte provides the only physical link to the noir pattern set during the 1940's. In this film, he characterizes a personality out of step with the rest of society. His meaningless quest and inability to control his surroundings was not the prevalent mood of the late 1950's. These feelings of hopelessness and impotence lead *The Brothers Rico* onto a noir plane. However, the conventions of true noir film making, which emphasized a world devoid of sentiment and which strongly rejected compassion and sensitivity, had long since wasted away. *The Brothers Rico* is a simple thriller that displays very little in the way of noir ambience, a film constructed from archaic conventions and petty obstacles that strongly points to the decline of the noir series during the 1950's. **CM**

BRUTE FORCE (1947)

Director: Jules Dassin. **Screenplay**: Richard Brooks based on a story by Robert Patterson. **Producer:** Mark Hellinger. **Director of Photography**: William Daniels. **Music**: Miklós Rózsa . **Art Directors**: Bernard Herzbrun, John F. DeCuir. **Editor**: Edward Curtiss. **Cast**: Burt Lancaster (Joe Collins), Hume Cronyn (Capt. Munsey), Charles Bickford (Gallagher), Yvonne De Carlo (Gina), Ann Blyth (Ruth), Ella Raines (Cora), Anita Colby (Flossie), Sam Levene (Louie), Howard Duff (Soldier), Art Smith (Dr. Walters), Roman Bohnen (Warden Barnes), John Hoyt (Spencer), Richard Gaines (McCollum), Frank Puglia (Ferrara), Jeff Corey (Freshman), Vince Barnett (Muggsy),

Brute Force: *Tom Lister (Whit Bissell) gives an illicit fur coat to Cora (Ellen Raines).*

James Bell (Crenshaw), Jack Overman (Kid Coy), Whit Bissell (Tom Lister), Sir Lancelot (Calypso), Ray Teal (Jackson), Jay C. Flippen (Hodges), James O'Rear (Wilson), Howland Chamberlain (Gaines), Kenneth Patterson (Bronski). **Completed**: April 19, 1947. **Released**: Universal, June 6. 95 minutes.

Behind the walls of an isolated prison, the sadistic Capt. Munsey dehumanizes convicts in his charge. Not being able to stand idly by as inmates are tortured and exploited by the captain of the guards, Joe Collins and his comrades make escape plans. Their plot includes the help of the "big man," Gallagher, whose influence with the rest of the convicts is essential for their success. After Munsey's informer falls into a huge punch press, the Captain resorts to acts of uncontrollable brutality in order to get information regarding the planned breakout, but is unsuccessful. At the designated moment, Gallagher stages a protest in the prison yard as a diversion for Collins and his men on the mine detail. The subsequent breakout turns into a savage eruption of fatal violence that destroys the escaping convicts and Munsey.

The essence of the Jules Dassin/Mark Hellinger *Brute Force* is violence. Functioning as a blatant allegory for an existential vision of the world (Sartre's *No Exit* is its theatrical counterpart), the prison of *Brute Force* becomes a living hell from which escape is impossible. This hopeless situation is echoed by the remarks of the prison doctor who constantly reminds anyone willing to listen, "Nobody escapes, nobody ever escapes." It remains for the violent action found throughout the film to serve as a liberating force for the inmates, as well as indicating a way of life adopted by the sadistic, Nazi-like Munsey.

Dassin's film constructs a microcosm of the world in which a perverse sense of order surrounds the activities of Munsey and his henchmen. Their treatment of the prisoners is taken to the point of absurdity. The outrageously brutal attitude of Munsey is the catalyst, which solidifies the wide variety of inmates in cell R17 into comrades who fight without hope of their own liberation in order that a few may escape. Written by Richard Brooks, whose noir scripts include *Crossfire* and *Key Largo, Brute Force* is concerned with existential meaninglessness transcended only by an act of violence, because "outside" life becomes valueless in the confines of the prison. The overtly romantic flashbacks detailing the various reasons for some of the inmates' imprisonments lack the vitality needed to make their previous lives attractive. The only goal that matters is the destruction of Munsey. With this single purpose in mind, the inmates play out a strange ritualized existence. Dassin's direction, fleshed with a taut urgency, makes the stylized tortures conceived by Munsey a striking counterpoint to the magnificent brutality of the abortive prison breakout. There are aspects of despair, corruption and displacement at the core of every element of *Brute Force*. These aspects, essential to films of a noir character, transform the film into an indictment of a contemporary society that tolerates a brutal, desensitized, and insular world beyond its control. **CM**

THE BURGLAR (1957)

Director: Paul Wendkos. **Screenplay**: David Goodis based on his novel. **Producer**. Louis W. Kellman (Samson Productions). **Director of Photography**: Don Malkames. **Music**: Sol Kaplan. **Art Director**: Jim Leonard. **Editor**. Herta Horn. **Cast**: Dan Duryea (Nat Harbin), Jayne Mansfield (Gladden), Martha Vickers (Della), Peter Capell (Baylock), Mickey Shaughnessy (Dohmer), Wendell Phillips (Police Captain), Phoebe Mackay (Sister Sara), Stewart Bradley (Charlie), John Facenda (News Commentator), Frank Hall (News Reporter), Bob Wilson (Newsreel Narrator), Steve Allison (State Trooper), Richard Emery (Harbin as a Child), Andrea McLaughlin (Gladden as a Child), Vince Carson (singer). **Locations**: Philadelphia, and Atlantic City. **Completed**: 1956. **Released**: Columbia, June 12. 90 minutes.

Gladden helps Nat Harbin and his two henchmen, Baylock and Dohmer, successfully steal a diamond necklace from a spiritualist's mansion. But the gang was spotted by the police and must carefully plan their next move. Nat is an orphan who was raised by Gladden's father, whose will made him the

young woman's guardian. When Dohmer makes a pass at Gladden, Nat sends her to Atlantic City. One night Nat meets Della and later overhears her plotting with a dishonest policeman Charlie, to steal the necklace from Nat's gang by kidnapping Gladden. Taking Dohmer and Baylock, Nat drives to Atlantic City to rescue Gladden but Dohmer is killed en route. When Nat arrives at Gladden's hotel, she is talking to Charlie, innocent of his real intentions. Nat hides the necklace under her pillow and cannot convince her to leave town. Charlie discovers Baylock's hiding place and kills him, also confronting Nat, forcing him to reveal where the necklace is hidden. Della stays with Nat while Charlie hurries to Gladden's hotel. Nat escapes from Della and meets Gladden on the boardwalk where she has slipped past Charlie and carries the necklace. Chased, Gladden and Nat are cornered on the Steel Pier. Nat gives the necklace to Charlie in return for Gladden's freedom and Charlie kills Nat. When the police arrive, Charlie swears that the necklace was thrown into the ocean and that he killed Nat in self-defense. But Della arrives, reveals their plot and Charlie is arrested for murder and theft.

Like other works by David Goodis, *The Burglar* is more concerned with the often perverse feelings of its characters than with its melodramatic pulp story. Some of this feeling is expressed by the direction of Paul Wendkos; but in the main, he is concerned in this film, his first directorial effort, with ostentatious imagery in the manner of Orson Welles. Affinities between the Steel Pier sequence and the fun house sequence of *The Lady From Shanghai*, as well as the burglary that begins the story with a visual tour de force of tense close-ups and startling cuts, demonstrates Wendkos' artistic intentions. Like many late 1950s noir films, *The Burglar* suffers from a self-consciousness, which makes its artistry less impressive than that of earlier works having a subtler ambience. **BL**

CAGED (1950)

Director: John Cromwell. **Screenplay**: Virginia Kellogg and Bernard C. Schoenfeld. **Producer**: Jerry Wald. **Director of Photography**: Carl Guthrie. **Music**: Max Steiner. **Art Director**: Charles H. Clarke. **Editor**: Owen Marks. **Cast**: Eleanor Parker (Marie Allen), Agnes Moorehead (Ruth Benton), Ellen Corby (Emma), Hope Emerson (Evelyn Harper), Betty Garde (Kitty Stark), Jan Sterling (Smoochie), Lee Patrick (Elvira Powell), Olive Deering (June), Jane Darwell (Isolation Matron), Gertrude Michael (Georgia), Sheila Stevens (Helen), Joan Miller (Claire), Marjorie Crossland (Cassie), Gertrude Hoffman (Millie), Lynn Sherman (Ann), Queenie Smith (Mrs. Warren), Naomi Robison (Hattie), Esther Howard (Grace), Marlo Dwyer (Julie). **Completed**: September 10, 1949. **Released**: Warner Bros., May 19. 97 minutes.

Sentenced to a term in prison for having helped her husband in a small robbery, Marie Allen changes from a naive and fundamentally innocent young woman to a hardened and knowing adult. The warden of the prison, Ruth Benton, is a sympathetic and well-meaning woman who means to rehabilitate the prisoners; but the prison is actually run by a sadistic matron, Evelyn Harper, who holds her job because of crooked political influence. Marie is already a woman of tragic circumstances as her husband was shot in the robbery and she suffered a miscarriage. As she witnesses the corrupting influence of Evelyn Harper on her fellow inmates and suffers the cruelties of prison life, Marie is disillusioned but determined to go straight. Kitty, the leader of a shoplifting ring, wants to recruit her for work on the outside when she is paroled. Marie resists her advances and also those of Elvira Powell, who is the influential head of a lucrative prostitution organization. Later, Kitty kills Evelyn Harper and another inmate goes "stir crazy" when denied parole. For the chance of an early parole, Marie capitulates and is released from prison to become a prostitute. The Warden observes sadly that Marie will be back.

The best woman's prison film ever made, not necessarily high praise in itself, *Caged* represents a union between the semi-realistic and socially conscious dramas made by Warner Bros. in the 1930s and the more stylized world of film noir. With this film, Warner Bros. extends the potential of its powerful but often simplistic social dramas while retaining the virtues of the earlier films. *Caged* is totally unsentimental, damning the society that could corrupt the soul of a Marie Allen but refusing to absolve the character herself and depict her as a complete victim. It is equally clear that her fellow inmates, many of them cynical and apparently insensitive, have followed the same route as Marie.

Caged: *Eleanor Parker as Marie.*

The film's conclusion is universally pessimistic; the implication is that all humans, if punished long enough and cruelly enough, will look for an easy way out and willingly turn their back on the positive values they once cherished. Marie exits from the prison to her criminal life with a hard smile on her face. John Cromwell reaches his peak in the direction of this gritty Warner's film, controlling every element of the work. Eleanor Parker gives the best performance of her career under Cromwell and creates a convincing metamorphosis from a shy and innocent young girl to a woman of the world. She performs with a multiplicity of nuance, in scenes which are both low-key and emotionally charged. As the sadistic and presumably lesbian matron, the physically imposing Hope Emerson adds to the list of her portrayals of female villains of film noir. Equally impressive is Cromwell's visual realization of the claustrophobia of prison life, aided by the low key and high contrast photography of Carl Guthrie. Each shot is complexly composed and lit, while many images provide nightmarish tableaux. **BL**

CALCUTTA (1947)

Director: John Farrow. **Screenplay/Producer**: Seton I. Miller. **Director of Photography**: John F. Seitz. **Music**: Victor Young. **Art Directors**: Hans Dreier, Franz Bachelin. **Editor**: Archie Marshek. **Cast**: Alan Ladd (Neale Gordon), Gail Russell (Virginia Moore), William Bendix (Pedro Blake), June Duprez (Marina Tanev), Lowell Gilmore (Eric Lasser), Edith King (Mrs. Smith), Paul Singh (Mul Raj Malik), Gavin Muir (Inspector Kendricks), John Whitney (Bill Cunningham), Benson Fong (Young Chinese Clerk). **Completed**: August 9, 1945. **Released**: Paramount, May 30. 83 minutes.

A trio of commercial pilots based in India, Neale, Pedro, and Bill are also close friends. Bill becomes engaged to be married but is mysteriously killed. Neale, suspicious by nature and especially distrustful of women, brutally questions Bill's fiancée, Virginia Moore. But once Virginia's innocence is ascertained, Neale is friendly. He "borrows" a scarab diamond given to Virginia by Bill, and traces it to a sinister Indian smuggler, Mr. Malik. When a star sapphire and a cache of diamonds are discovered hidden aboard one of his company's planes, Neale realizes that they are being used to transport illegal jewelry. Neale is threatened by Malik with a knife but subdues him. Malik is shot before he can reveal any information. Again suspicious of Virginia, Neale questions the hotel clerk who refutes her alibi. When she continues to deny her guilt, Neale slaps a confession out of her. He is stopped by Mr. Lasser, a sophisticated owner of a local club and part of the smuggling ring. In the ensuing melee, Lasser is shot by Neale, who is impervious to Virginia's pleas not to turn her over to the authorities.

At first glance, *Calcutta* appears to be a typical action-adventurer geared to appeal to Alan Ladd's fans. Closer inspection reveals the strong influence of the hardboiled fictional tradition, not only in the glacial performance of Ladd but especially in his attitude toward women. Later, Ladd and Paramount would become more aware of his popularity with youngsters, so *Calcutta* is unusual because of his sexual involvement with women. Paramount alternated Veronica Lake and Gail Russell as romantic "damsels in distress" in Ladd's films, but in a shrewd bit of reverse casting Russell is allowed to play the femme fatale in *Calutta*, and a nasty one at that as Virginia Russell's exotic features, warm manner, and soft voice invariably gave her a connotation of innocence and vulnerability, capitalized on in most of her films. By contrast, when Ladd as Neale Gordon rips a pendant from Virginia's neck or slaps her around, it makes him appear all the more cruelly imperious to women. Their interaction holds this film together while demonstrating the misogynistic strain of hardboiled fiction, a strain which was quite implicit in much of post-war popular American culture and would reach a crescendo in the fiction of Mickey Spillane. It is Neale's resistance to feminine wiles that allows him to survive, as indicated in a number of classic exchanges between him and Virginia. He quotes for her an old Gurkha saying, "Man who trust woman walk on duckweed over pond."

When she tells him he had nothing in common with his dead pal, that he's "cold, sadistic, egotistical," he replies, "Maybe, but I'm still alive." Finally, paraphrasing Sam Spade's ultimate rejection of Brigid in *The Maltese Falcon,* Neale tells Virginia, "You counted on your beauty with guys, even ones you were going to kill." **BP**

CALL NORTHSIDE 777 (1948)

Director: Henry Hathaway. **Screenplay**: Jerome Cady and Jay Dratler, adapted by Leonard Hoffman and Quentin Reynolds based on "Chicago Times" articles by James P. McGuire. **Producer**: Otto Lang. **Director of Photography**: Joe MacDonald. **Music**: Alfred Newman. **Art Directors**: Lyle Wheeler, Mark-Lee Kirk. **Editor**: J. Watson Webb Jr. **Cast**: James Stewart (McNeal), Richard Conte (Frank Wiecek), Lee J. Cobb (Brian Kelly), Helen Walker (Laura McNeal), Betty Garde (Wanda Skutnik), Kasia Orzazewski (Tillie Wiecek), Joanne de Bergh (Helen WiecekRayska), Howard Smith (Palmer), Moroni Olsen (Parole Board Chairman), John McIntire (Sam Faxon), Paul Harvey (Martin Burns), George Tyne (Tomek Zaleska), Richard Bishop (Warden), Otto Waidis (Boris), Michael Chapin (Frank Jr.), E.G. Marshall (Rayska), Truman Bradley (Narrator). **Location**: Chicago and the Illinois State Prison. **Completed**: November 15, 1947. **Released**: 20th Century-Fox, February 18. 111 minutes.

A woman inserts a classified advertisement in a Chicago newspaper, offering a reward of $5,000 for information that may lead to her son's release from prison. A newspaper editor sees the ad and sends McNeal, a skeptical reporter, out to investigate. He discovers that the woman, Tillie Wiecek, has been scrubbing floors for eleven years, saving nickels and dimes until able to offer the $5,000. The advertisement thus becomes a human-interest story and the newspaper involves itself in a crusade for her son's liberation. McNeal goes to the state prison to talk to Frank Wiecek, sentenced to life imprisonment for killing a policeman during a grocery store robbery. Wiecek insists that he was framed and was at home with his wife during the robbery. His conviction was based on his being named in a lineup by Wanda Skutnik who claimed to have seen him at the scene of the crime. McNeal has Wiecek submit to a lie detector test which comes out in the prisoner's favor. Next, the paper interviews Wiecek's ex-

wife and child and their picture is featured on the front page. This upsets Wiecek terribly; he insists that the paper drop the investigation, fearing his son's future will be jeopardized. But McNeal is convinced of the man's innocence and seeks out Wanda Skutnik. She refuses to change her story and the police withhold information from McNeal. The paper decides to drop the proposed hearing for Wiecek due to lack of evidence. But McNeal finds a newspaper photograph of Wanda Skutnik and Wiecek walking in the police station together. He reschedules the hearing, has the picture enlarged, and convinces the hearing board that the date on the photo proves that Wanda first saw Wiecek at the time he was booked, not at the time of the crime. McNeal watches as the freed Wiecek reunites with his son.

Shot in a realistic, almost documentary style, *Call Northside 777* is a fine example of what might be called "newspaper noir." The hardboiled world of a big city daily newpaper is examined, with James Stewart portraying the reporter to whom the story is everything. His cynical veneer gradually cracks as he becomes convinced of Wiecek's innocence. But it does not matter what the newspaperman believes. The legal system controls Wiecek's future. The police department's role is particularly interesting. Not exactly corrupt, the police do not like to be proven wrong, especially since Wiecek was accused of shooting a patrolman. Instead of helping McNeal on his search for evidence, the police continually throw obstacles in his path. As McNeal gets deeper and deeper into the case, he sees that justice and the law are not always the same. When the woman who convicted Wiecek will not change her story, the newspaper is unwilling to continue what appears to be a losing battle and wants to drop the case. But it is McNeal's personal quest. He continues to look for the one piece of evidence that will free Wiecek, who has become not only his story, but also his conscience. Thus, the reporter's victory in freeing the prisoner becomes a triumph not only for the forces of justice, but also for a man who pitted himself against the apparatus of the state. But, in typical noir fashion, all is still not sewn up neatly. Wanda Skutnik, who obviously committed perjury, never changes her story and remains at large. Wiecek's wife remarried long ago, leaving him alone in his newly found freedom except for occasional weekends with his son. His eleven years in prison cannot be given back to him; but at least his mother did not waste her $5,000. **JC**

CALLING DR. DEATH (1943)

Director: Reginald Le Borg. **Screenplay**: Edward Dein. **Producer**: Ben Pivar. **Director of Photography**: Virgil Miller. **Art Director**: Ralph M. DeLacy, John Goodman. **Music**: Paul Sawtell. **Editor**: Norman A. Cerf. **Cast**: Lon Chaney, Jr. (Dr. Mark Steel), Patricia Morison (Stella Madden), J. Carrol Naish (Inspector Glegg), David Bruce (Robert Duval), Ramsay Ames (Maria Steel), Fay Helm (Mrs. Duval), Holmes Herbert (The Butler), Mary Hale (Marion), Alec Craig (The Watchman). **Released**: Universal, December 17. 63 minutes.

Dr. Mark Steel is a psychiatrist who wakes up in his office unable to remember if he killed his unfaithful wife Maria or not. With the help of his assistant Stella and through the prodding of the persistent police inspector Gregg, he tries to regain his memory of that "lost weekend." Suspecting, at least on the surface, Maria's lover Duval, Gregg arrests

A UNIVERSAL PICTURE

Duval. He is convicted of the murder and sentenced to death. Both Gregg and Steel have doubts about Duval's guilt. Steel even uses hypnosis on himself to determine his guilt or innocence. In the end Steel turns the hypnosis on Stella and she reveals that she is the murderer.

Director Reginald Le Borg, much like his noir cohort and fellow émigré Edgar G. Ulmer, labored in the thankless fields of the ultra low budget film for decades. *Calling Dr. Death* is probably Le Borg's most typically noir film. The director brings his expressionistic mindset, so common to the émigré directors (like many Le Borg studied at the feet of German stage director Max Reinhardt), and turns a programmer into an engaging noir mystery. Packaged as part of a Universal series which drew inspiration from the successful radio show "Inner Sanctum," *Dr. Death* gave Le Borg numerous opportunities to subjectify the material beyond the obvious one: the film is narrated in an internal monologue by the protagonist Dr. Steel, which Lon Chaney, Jr. plays acceptably but with trademark stiffness.

Dr. Steel is a famous psychiatrist who can cure others of their neuroses (we see him hypnotizing a young patient at the beginning of the film) but who cannot deal with his own angst over a cheating wife. Drawn to his supportive assistant Stella and with mounting evidence of his wife's affairs (he watches his wife's lover drop her off at their apartment late at night in one scene), he still is unable to act, even though he does half-heartedly try to strangle her after she taunts him. Not only do we witness Steel's noirish angst over his cuckolding but his narration further amplifies the audience's sense of identification with his tortured soul. When Maria is finally murdered, Steel blames himself (having blocked out the entire weekend of the murder) and in the classic noir style of such films as *Scandal Sheet* and *Female Jungle* seeks evidence which may lead to his own conviction for the murder.

Le Borg further enhances the subjectification of the film by incorporating expressionistic sequences which are half-dream, half-memory, particularly in the final scene in which a suspicious Steel hypnotizes Stella as they await the execution of the innocent Duval. As the camera tracks into a tight close up of her face, we see her thoughts and memories intermixed: buildings close in on her as she runs, Duval transforms into Stella as he is being led to the execution chamber, shadows move across the cityscape threateningly. With Stella's arrest by Gregg, Steel, we are led to assume, has resolved his angst over his wife and her death but is left bereft of another woman he loved. **JU**

CANON CITY (1948)

Director and Screenplay. Crane Wilbur. **Producer**. Robert T. Kane for Bryan Foy Productions. **Director of Photography**: John Alton. **Music Director**: Irving Friedman. **Art Director**: Frank Durlauf. **Editor**: Louis H. Sackin. **Cast**: Scott Brady (Jim Sherbondy), Jeff Corey (Schwartzmiller), Whit Bissell (Heilman), Stanley Clements (New), Charles Russell (Tolley), De Forest Kelley (Smalley), Ralph Byrd (Officer Gray), Warden Roy Best (Warden), Henry Brandon (Freeman), Alfred Linder (Lavergne), Ray Bennett (Klinger), Bob Bice (Turley), Mabel Paige (Mrs. Oliver), John Doucette (Mr. Bauer), Reed Hadley (Narrator). **Location**: Canon City, Colorado. **Released**: Eagle-Lion, June 30. 82 minutes.

A group of convicts successfully escape from the Colorado Penitentiary in Canon City. Forcing another inmate, Jim Sherbondy, to go along against his will, they flee over the desolate, snow-covered countryside terrorizing local citizens along the way. Ultimately, all but Sherbondy are killed, and he takes refuge in Mr. Bauer's farmhouse. When Bauer's son has an appendicitis attack, Sherbondy allows Mrs. Bauer to leave to get help and then tries to escape on foot. A grateful Mr. Bauer, realizing Sherbondy is not a hardened criminal, picks him up in his car and tries to help him, but the convict is recaptured at a police roadblock.

Canon City is a prison semi-documentary, which was shot on location at the very penitentiary where the event occurred. After a conventional text introduction guaranteeing its authenticity, it goes a step further than most films of this sort by opening with interviews with the warden and some of the actual convicts there. The director, Crane Wilbur, began as a screenwriter in the silent era and became something of a specialist in gangster and prison films throughout the 1930's and 1940's. Subsequent to this, he scripted *He Walked By Night* as well as *Outside The Wall*, which he also directed. Neither the semi-documentary approach enhanced by Reed Hadley's narration nor John Alton's photography gives this film the noir ambience of productions like *T-Men* or *He Walked By Night,* which indicates that Anthony Mann's contribution to this variety of film noir was rather substantial. **BP**

CAPE FEAR (1962)

Director: J. Lee Thompson. **Screenplay**: James R. Webb based on the novel, *The Executioners*, by John D. MacDonald. **Producer**: Sy Bartlett. **Director of Photography**: Samuel Leavitt. **Music**: Bernard Herrmann. **Art Directors**: Alexander Golitzem, Robert Boyle. **Editor**: George Tomasini. **Cast**: Gregory Peck (Sam Bowden), Robert Mitchum (Max Cady), Polly Bergen (Peggy), Lori Martin (Nancy), Martin Balsam (Chief Dutton), Jack Kruschen (Grafton), Telly Savalas (Sievers), Barrie Chase (Diane), Paul Comi (Garner), Page Slattery (Deputy Kersek), Ward Ramsey (Officer Brown), Thomas Newman (Lt. Gervasi), Edward Platt (Judge), Will Wright (Dr. Pearsall). **Location**: Savannah, Georgia. **Released**: Universal, April 12. 105 minutes.

Violent psychopath Max Cady seeks revenge against a lawyer Sam Bowden, whom he holds responsible for sending him to prison. The psychopath terrorizes Bowden's wife, Peggy, and teen-age daughter, Nancy, until the entire family is in torment, but Cady does so without breaking any laws. Realizing he must trap the psychopath, Bowden hides Peggy and Nancy in a houseboat on the Cape Fear River, where he expects Cady will find them. As Max attacks the two women, Bowden overpowers him in the river and has the evidence needed to send Cady back to a life term in prison.

Many films use the subject of a secure family threatened by dark and violent outside forces. Usually, however, there is a dramatic meaning to the portrayal of this situation. At its most bourgeois and uninteresting, it is the affirmation of the family unit, as in *The Desperate Hours*, where tensions extant in the family are resolved by the crisis. At its most complex and moving, it is the qualification of the family's values by the persuasiveness of the intruder's values, especially if the dark intruder is himself a member of the complacent family. Hitchcock's *Shadow Of A Doubt* is the supreme example of the latter, made even more compelling because of the character of young Charlie, poised between the family and the intruder whom Charlie alone comprehends. *Cape Fear* does not exploit the possibilities of such a situation, and the family is fundamentally unchanged at film's end. The sole point of the motion picture seems to be that the evil character circumvents the law and causes the lawyer, the personification of rationality, into rejecting civilized law and plunging into the primal world of brute force so he may safeguard his family.

However simplistic the thrust of this film it does possess distinction in the very effective score of Bernard Herrmann, which is a further reminder of the film's sub-Hitchcock quality, and the performance of Robert Mitchum as the psychopath. Although Mitchum's twisted preacher in *The Night of the Hunter* is a more complex and subtly created character, his swaggering presence in *Cape Fear* has a menacing authority. His ability to appear reptilian as he crawls up the riverbank seems totally antithetical to the sensitive emotional responses that distinguish his more archetypal characterizations. **BL**

THE CAPTIVE CITY (1952)

Director: Robert Wise. **Screenplay**: Karl Kamb and Alvin M. Josephy, Jr. based on a story by Alvin M. Josephy, Jr. **Producer**: Theron Warth (Aspen Productions). **Director of Photography**: Lee Garmes. **Music**: Jerome Moross. **Production Designer**: Maurice Zuberano. **Editor**: Ralph Swink. **Cast**: John Forsythe (Jim Austin), Joan Camden (Marge Austin), Harold J. Kennedy (Don Carey), Ray Teal (Chief Gillette), Marjorie Crossland (Mrs. Sirak), Victor Sutherland (Murray Sirak), Hal K. Dawson (Clyde Nelson), Geraldine Hall (Mrs. Nelson), Martin Milner (Phil Harding), Gladys Hurlbut (Linda Percy), Ian Wolfe (Reverend Nash), Jess Kirkpatrick (Anderson), Sen. Estes Kefauver (Himself in Prologue/Epilogue). **Released**: United Artists, March 26. 90 minutes.

Jim Austin and his wife Marge flee from their home in Kennington, a "nice town" of 300,000, to appear before Senator Kefauver's Committee on Organized Crime. As they stop in a smalltown. Austin tape records his story as a precaution against an "accident." As the editor of the *Kennington Journal*, Austin recalls how he first learned of organized crime in his town when a private detective, Nelson, informed Austin that he was investigating a local bookie, Murray Sirak. Nelson was harassed by the local police and eventually his license was revoked by the state. Austin is dubious of Nelson and is reassured by Kennington Police Chief Gillette that there are no rackets in his town. But when Nelson is killed and the police seem uninterested in finding the murderer, Austin becomes suspicious. Investigating on his own, Austin discovers the Kennington police are controlled by the mob. After Murray Sirak threatens Austin, he leaves town quietly with his wife, in hopes that an appearance before Senator Kefauver's committee will help. A crime syndicate representative offers him money at the hearing if Austin will forget the whole thing. Of course, Austin turns him down.

Captive City is an important transitional film, for it represents an uneasy synthesis of the noir style with the exposé format. The exposé film represents one of a handful of film genres, such as the police semi- documentary, the caper film, and the "social problem" film, that grew out of the noir tradition as it fragmented along new lines before disappearing in the 1960s. Through skillful use of *mise-en-scène* and photography, Wise and Garmes almost completely recapture the romanticized style of the earlier noir films with lonely cars prowling the night, muffled footsteps in an alley, and frightened faces emerging from the shadows.

It is also apparent that the film was designed to capitalize on the public's renewed interest in organized crime, due in part to the fame of the Kefauver Committee's investigations which began in 1950. However, the public's preoccupation with a nationwide criminal organization such as the Mafia was not strong enough in the 1950s to displace the Communist paranoia, and thus the films that illustrated efforts to contain the Communist menace were much more successful than those describing organized crime. Perhaps, as well, Communism was an easier (and safer) target for the film industry than the Mafia. **BP**

CAUGHT (1949)

Directors: Max Ophuls [and John Berry]. **Screenplay**: Arthur Laurents based on the novel *Wild Calendar* by Libbie Block. **Producer**: Wolfgang Reinhardt (Enterprise Productions). **Director of Photography**: Lee Garmes. **Music**: Frederick Hollander. **Art Director**: P. Frank Sylos. **Editor**: Robert Parrish. **Cast**: James Mason (Larry Quinada), Barbara Bel Geddes (Leonora Eames), Robert Ryan (Smith Ohlrig), Ruth Brady (Maxine), Curt Bois (Franzi), Frank Ferguson (Dr. Hoffman), Natalie Schaefer (Dorothy Dale), Art Smith (Psychiatrist), Sonia Darrin (Miss Chambers), Bernadene Hayes (Mrs. Rudecki), Ann Morrison (Miss Murray), Wilton Graff (Gentry), Jim Hawkins (Kevin), Vicki Raw Stiener (Lorraine). **Released**: MGM, February 17. 88 minutes.

Department store model Leonora Eames believes that the way to happiness is to marry a rich man. She gets her chance when she meets Smith Ohlrig, a millionaire known for his reclusiveness, who takes her as his wife to spite his psychiatrist. Leonora is alternately neglected and vilified by the paranoid Ohlrig, while her only allowed companion is Ohlrig's parasitical assistant Franzi. Leonora finally leaves Ohlrig and takes a job as a receptionist for the dedicated young Dr. Quinada. Ohlrig finds Leonora and entices her back by promising that he is willing to change, but he immediately schedules a business trip and she returns to Quinada's office. The young Doctor proposes marriage to her, yet soon she discovers she is pregnant by Ohlrig and returns to the millionaire's "prison" for financial security. Quinada comes to the mansion and implores her to leave with him, but Leonora refuses because she assumes Ohlrig

Caught: *Dr. Quinada (James Mason) and Leonora (Barbara Bel Geddes).*

would never divorce her. Ohlrig tortures her through the remaining months of her pregnancy by waking her at odd hours of the night and giving her no peace. Ultimately she rebels but has a miscarriage. Although she loses her baby, Leonora is now free to start life over with Quinada.

From its opening scene, Max Ophuls' *Caught* concentrates on the sharp and often tragic difference between dream and reality. Opening on a shot of a woman's hands languidly turning the pages of a slick fashion magazine while a disdainful voice declares that "mink is so everyday," Ophuls' mobile camera swiftly pulls back to reveal a shabby flat peopled by two ordinary showgirls with dreams of marrying "a handsome young millionaire." However, with graphic strength, Ophuls and scenarist Arthur Laurents demonstrate through this film what might happen if that dream came true.

Ophuls develops Ohlrig's character in a terrifying session with his helpless psychiatrist. When Robert Ryan's Ohlrig, his face a closed, tight mask, says through clenched teeth, "I have these attacks because I have a bad heart," the cut to Leonora underscores its ominous implications. Soon she is ensconced in jeweled splendor in Ohlrig's gloomy mansion and is a prisoner of her own fantasies. In a dazzling set piece, Leonora, her face a smear of misery, waits for her errant husband while his lackey, the egregious Franzi, torments her. Pounding out Viennese schmaltz on the piano and taunting "Tough, tough, darling" as Leonora begs him to stop, Franzi takes it all as just part of the ritual when she finally slaps him across the face. "That's all right," he says. "It saves him [Ohlrig] from getting it . . . that's what I'm paid for." In fact, Franzi, Leonora, and his business associates are all Ohlrig's paid objects, trapped as much by their own desire for some ill-defined "security" as by the millionaire's coercive methods. Even when she discovers love and fulfillment with the blessedly sane and charming Dr. Quinada, Leonora is relentlessly drawn back to Ohlrig, unable to shake her ingrained need for all the things that she thinks money can buy. She is willing to stay with a man who tells her, "All I care about is breaking you," because she has been taught since birth that money and power are the supreme objects of desire and worship.

In a switch of primary film noir elements, *Caught* reveals a psychotic *homme fatale*. Olhrig's trap of seduction through materialism disguises this obsessive tyrant as the answer to a poor girl's dreams. Unable to remove herself from a fairy tale gone wrong, Leonora's ultimate exhaustion causes her to accept her fate as his victim. She does not escape from Ohlrig due to any personal strength but is bodily borne away by her true humble love-hero, the Doctor. This recasting of such a fairy tale is given contemporary interest by the depth of Robert Ryan's obsessive strength as the *homme fatale*, Barbara Bel Geddes' increasing descent into paranoia and Franzi's ominous Germanic mannerisms. Under Ophul's taut direction, with Lee Garmes' lush film noir cinematography and Sylos' complementary art direction, this script is propelled into film noir and transformed beyond a simple potboiling morality fable into a powerful stew of dark motives threatening the luminous qualities of healthy normalcy. **JK & EW**

CAUSE FOR ALARM (1951)

Director: Tay Garnett. **Screenplay**: Mel Dinelli and Tom Lewis based on a story by Larry Marcus. **Producer**: Tom Lewis. **Director of Photography**: Joseph Ruttenberg. **Music**: André Previn. **Art Directors**:

Cedric Gibbons, Arthur Lonergan. **Editor**: James E. Newcom. **Cast**: Loretta Young (Ellen Jones), Barry Sullivan (George Z. Jones), Bruce Cowling (Dr. Ranney Grahame), Margalo Gillmore (Mrs. Edwards), Bradley Mora (Hoppy Billy), Irving Bacon (Mr. Carstori, Postman), Georgia Backus (Mrs. Warren), Don Haggerty (Mr. Russell), Art Baker (Superintendent), Richard Anderson (Lonesome Sailor). **Completed**: May 11, 1950. **Released**: MGM, January 29. 74 minutes.

An insanely jealous husband, George Z. Jones, who is recuperating from a lingering heart disease, begins to fantasize that his wife, Ellen, is having an affair with the family doctor. He informs her that he is about to kill himself after he watches her mail a letter for him that denounces both Ellen and the doctor as his murderers. Frantic, Ellen tries to recover the incriminating letter before it is too late. Stopped at every turn, Ellen's life becomes a nightmare as her normal suburban routine takes on a menacing attitude, and she is at her wit's end by the cruel torture perpetrated on her. When all hope has left her, the letter is returned unopened due to a routine post office problem. Ellen is freed from the jealous plotting of her psychotic husband.

A melodrama with a noir flair, *Cause for Alarm* is an exercise in paranoia and claustrophobia. Directed by Tay Garnett, the film presents the Jones house as a threatening maze filled with hidden evil. The film takes every opportunity to subvert normal everyday situations into perverse visions of madness. The true noir flavor comes in the total dehumanization experienced by Ellen Jones. She might survive the ordeal brought about by her warped husband, but her life will never be the same. Stylistically, the film owes more to television staging than it does to film noir. *Cause For Alarm* falls into a group of melodramas like *The Trial* and *Autumn Leaves*, where the world perceived by the camera may be normal, and yet seen through the eyes of the characters, it becomes distinctly bleak and hopeless. **CM**

CHAMPION (1949)

Director: Mark Robson. **Screenplay**: Carl Foreman based on a short story by Ring Lardner. **Producer**: Stanley Kramer. **Director Photography**: Franz Planer. **Music**: Dimitri Tiomkin. **Production Designer**: Rudolph Sternad. **Editor**: Harry Gerstad. **Cast**: Kirk Douglas (Midge Kelly), Marilyn Maxwell (Grace Diamond), Arthur Kennedy (Connie Kelly), Paul Stewart (Tommy Haley), Ruth Roman

Champion: *Kirk Douglas as Midge Kelly.*

(Emma Bryce), Lola Albright (Palmer Harris), Luis Van Rooten (Jerry Harris). **Released**: United Artists, April 9. 99 minutes.

Midge Kelly and his brother Connie are penniless drifters, looking for an opportunity to make a living. It seems a lucky break when, thrown off a boxcar, Midge agrees to participate in a boxing match to make a few dollars. He does well enough to attract the attention of promoter/trainer Tommy Haley, but the brothers decide to move on to Los Angeles. There they get a job working in a hash house, and Midge romances the owner's daughter, Emma. A shotgun wedding follows, but Midge soon departs to try his luck elsewhere. In a gym, he meets up again with Tommy, who trains him in the fight game. Despite Connie's objections, he keeps boxing after initial successes, but crosses the mob when he fails to throw a fight with Johnny Dunne and receives a beating instead from mob thugs. Hooking up with femme fatale Grace Maxwell, Midge fires Tommy and signs on with the shadier Jerry Harris. Romancing Grace, Midge gets involved with yet another woman, Palmer Harris, who agrees to sculpt him. This affair ends when Jerry buys Midge off with the promise of extra money for the title fight. Tommy joins their team. After the death of their mother, Connie tells Midge that Emma is getting a divorce to marry him. Midge asks Emma to wait until after the title fight, and it seems that they then might get back together. Connie and Midge get into a fight over Emma before the title bout, in which he knocks out Johnny Dunne to win the championship. After the fight, Midge seems disoriented and soon collapses, dying of a brain hemorrhage.

Like other noir boxing movies, most notably *The Set-Up* and *Body and Soul*, *Champion* uses the sport as a metaphor for the pursuit of the American dream, in particular indicting the ruthlessness toward others (and the indifference to the damage inflicted upon oneself) which it requires for success. Screenwriter Carl Foreman, noted for his leftist antipathy to the individualism of the capitalist ethos, does nothing to mute the critique of American society contained in the original story by Ring Lardner. Seduced by the prospect of a quick path to riches, Midge finds himself increasingly indifferent to his relations with others, all of which deteriorate as

he moves closer to the pinnacle of success. The film preserves intact Lardner's melodramatic ending—the ironic conjunction of victory with premature death and the dashing of hopes for a life that could have accommodated something of a spiritual regeneration. With its setting in the transient world of cheap hotels, hash houses, and run-down gyms, the film never provides an image of what material success might bring. Despite his energies and talent, Midge remains the typical noir protagonist, trapped by circumstances he never manages to control, tempted by two femmes fatales to abandon those relationships that nurture him most. He wins his two fights with Dunne, but is beaten senseless after the first and dies soon after the second, his triumph in each case deprived of meaning and reward. **RBP**

THE CHASE (1946)

Director: Arthur Ripley. **Screenplay**: Philip Yordan based on the novel *The Black Path of Fear*, by Cornell Woolrich. **Producer**: Seymour Nebenzal (Nero Producers). **Director of Photography**: Franz F. Planer. **Music**: Michel Michelet. **Art Director**: Robert Usher. **Editor**: Edward Mann. **Cast**: Michele Morgan (Lorna), Robert Cummings (Chuck Scott), Steve Cochran (Eddie Roman), Peter Lorre (Gino), Lloyd Corrigan (Emmerrich Johnson), Jack Holt (Commander Davidson), Don Wilson (Fats), Alexis Minotis (Acosta), Nina Koschetz (Madame Chin), Yolanda Lacca (Midnight), James Westerfield (Job), Jimmy Ames (the Killer), Shirley O'Hara (Manicurist). **Released**: United Artists, November 22. 86 minutes.

As a reward for returning a lost wallet, down-on-his-luck veteran Chuck Scott is hired as chauffeur by wealthy Miami businessman Eddie Roman, his wife, Lorna, and his aide, Gino. Scott learns that Roman is cruel and a questionable businessman when Roman has Gino eliminate business rival Emmerrich Johnson, while making his death seem a suicide. Lorna asks Chuck to help her escape to Havana. Before they can leave, Chuck suffers a recurrence of malarial fever and lies down to sleep it off. He dreams that after arriving in Havana with Lorna, she is stabbed to death and he is arrested for murder. Escaping from the police, Scott encounters Gino who kills him. Scott awakens from the nightmare and does not remember his plans to leave with Lorna until after he speaks with his doctor, Commander Davidson. Roman discovers Lorna's plans and rushes with Gino to make the late

boat to Havana but both men are killed attempting to overtake a train. Chuck and Loma arrive safely in Havana where the coachman from Chuck's dream drops them off at the same nightclub as in his dream.

The Chase fails to capture the morbid ambiance of Woolrich's novel, in which the story is told through the eyes of the protagonist, Scott, and the stabbing of Lorna at a Havana nightclub is no dream, but real, and where Scott ultimately strangles Roman before returning to Havana. However, as a film noir it deserves to be rescued from obscurity. For one thing, Arthur Ripley and Michel Michelet had earlier teamed on *A Voice in the Wind*, among the darkest of film noirs (though its score here leaves something to be desired). For another, it was photographed by Franz Planer whose background in German Expressionism makes him a major player in the noir cycle and who, in the Havana sequence at least, presents us with a visual correlative of Woolrich's dark verbal power. Most saliently *The Chase* contains almost equal proportions of those qualities that Borde and Chaumeton consider to be quintessentially noir: its onerism or dream-like atmosphere (e.g., the whole first segment in Havana); its sadistic eroticism (e.g., the scene where Roman sexually badgers and then abuses his female barber and manicurist); its use of "insolite" or unprecedented plot devices (e.g., killing off the two leads, which first-time audiences of that era would not have foreseen as a dream); finally, the ambivalence of its cruel actions (e.g., the semi-comic sequence with Emmerrich Johnson which culminates in his being led to the wine cellar only to be killed by Roman's dog). **BP**

CHICAGO DEADLINE (1949)

Director: Lewis Allen. **Screenplay**: Warren Duff, based on the novel *One Woman*, by Tiffany Thayer. **Producer**. Robert Fellows. **Director of Photography**: John F. Seitz. **Music**: Victor Young. **Art Directors**: Hans Dreier, Franz Bachelin. **Editor**: LeRoy Stone. **Cast**: Alan Ladd (Ed Adams), Donna Reed (Rosita Jean d'Ur/Ellen Rainer), June Havoc (Leona), Irene Hervey (Belle Dorset), Arthur Kennedy (Tommy Ditman), Berry Kroeger (Solly Wellman), Harold Vermilyea (Anstruder), Shepperd Strudwick (Blacky Franchot), John Beal (Paul Jean d'Ur), Tom Powers (Howard), Gavin Muir (G.G. Temple), Dave Willock (Pig), Paul Lees (Bat). **Completed**: September 18, 1948. **Released**: Paramount, November 2. 87 minutes.

A journalist, Ed Adams, discovers the body of a young girl, Ellen Rainer, dead of tuberculosis in a cheap hotel room. He is immediately drawn to this emaciated but exquisite corpse and wants to know more about her, so he steals her address book before the police arrive and commits himself to the rehabilitation of her memory. Using her book as a guide in his investigation, he meets a diverse group of individuals, some of whom are at first reluctant to acknowledge her, which makes Ed press on all the more steadfastly. As each person tells his/her story in flashback, a variety of differing images of the girl, whose real name was Rosita Jean d'Ur, is presented. Ultimately, Ed uncovers two murders and several blackmail attempts connected with Rosita's friends. His life is threatened, but Ed tricks the killer, Solly, who dies instead. At the girl's funeral Ed burns her address book, and her brother, Tommy, tells him that he probably knew Rosita better than anybody.

As Borde and Chaumeton point out in *Panorama du Film Noir Américain, Chicago Deadline* could have been a classic film noir in the manner of *Laura* had a more mordant sensibility prevailed: "If the film-makers had insisted on the bizarre nature of the investigation and the morbid character of Adams' devotion to the dead girl; . . . if the hero, exhausted but victorious, had died of his wounds after hearing an entire mass said for this purified martyr; if Alan Ladd had not played a superman whose gaze controlled every situation; if, finally, a director of talent had handled the *mise-en-scène*, we'd undoubtedly be in the presence of a major work . . ." While these faults might well be placed at the doorstep of the director, it is more likely that the noir sensibility demanded by Borde and Chaumeton would not have been allowed in a Ladd vehicle by the executives at Paramount, since his one film about romantic defeat, *The Great Gatsby*, had done poorly at the box office earlier in the year. **BP**

CHRISTMAS HOLIDAY (1944)

Director: Robert Siodmak. **Screenplay**: Herman J. Mankiewicz based on the novel by W. Somerset Maugham. **Producers**: Felix Jackson and Frank Shaw. **Director of Photography**: Woody Bredell. **Music**: Hans J. Salter. **Art Directors**: John B. Goodmam, Robert Clatworthy. **Editor**: Ted Kent. **Cast**: Deanna Durbin (Jackie Lamont/Abigail Manette), Gene Kelly (Robert Manette), Richard Whorf (Simon Fenimore), Dean Harens (Charles Mason), Gladys George (Valerie de Merode), Gale Sondergaard (Mrs. Manette), David Bruce (Gerald Tyler). **Completed**: February 12, 1944. **Released**: Universal, June 30. 93 minutes.

While on Christmas furlough, Lt. Charles Mason is delayed in New Orleans by a rainstorm. At a roadhouse, he meets local chanteuse Jackie Lamont and escorts her to midnight mass. When Lamont learns that Mason has received a "Dear John" telegram from his fiancée, she tells him that her real name is Abigail Manette and her husband Robert is serving a life sentence for murder. After they were married, Abby refused to recognize that Robert was a wastrel whose surface charm belied his violent temper. When Robert kills his bookie, he and his mother conspire to cover up the crime while Abby goes along against her better judgement. Nonetheless, Robert is arrested, convicted and sentenced to prison and Mrs. Manette turned on her. Her story finished, Abby says good-

Chrismas Holiday: *Menette (Gene Kelly, right foreground) confronts Abigail (Deanna Durbin).*

bye. Meanwhile, Robert has escaped from jail and lures Abby into a back room at the roadhouse where she explains that she took this degrading job so that she might empathize with Robert in prison. Unable to accept what she has become, Robert threatens her with a gun but a pursuing policeman shoots him first. As Robert lies dying in her arms, he tells her, "You can let go now, Abigail."

Christmas Holiday remains as Robert Siodmak's most exotic, if not successful, film noir. Even its title is the most unusual and misleading one in the entire noir canon. Its central theme of *l'amour fou* is given a strong twist in the direction of the oedipal so that the film has more the feel of a French film noir than an American, and therefore it is quite fitting to have New Orleans as its setting. Perhaps this is what drew Siodmak to the story in the first place, as he would explore quasi-incestuous relationships again in *Uncle Harry*. In any case, though he had at his disposal the talents of Woody Bredell, he mutes visual expressionism (except in the very last sequence) in favor of compositions that contextualize the relationships of the central characters. So it is that the Rockwellian scene of husband and wife playing and singing at the piano while mother knits in a nearby chair is undermined by the action of the story which, appropriately, is told in a series of flashbacks initiated by the morose Abby.

Siodmak and Salter use classical music to good effect here, especially in their choice of "Liebestod" from Wagner's *Tristan and Isolde*, to frame the lovers' story. More ingenious is their choice of popular music. By allowing Abby to reprise Irving Berlin's bromide "Always" in such a slow, syncopated manner, the whole nature of her obsessive love is ironically revealed. Though Siodmak complained that Deanna Durbin balked at playing a prostitute (so instead she is a singer/"hostess") and increasingly demanded a more "wholesome" look, her garish makeup in the roadhouse scenes leaves little doubt as to what Abby had become. In fact, it recalls the synthetic sexuality of Ella Raines' impersonation of a floozy in *The Phantom Lady*. Finally, the reverse casting of Gene Kelly as Robert Manette is near-perfect. The sinister side of his persona, first apparent in his performance in Broadway's *Pal Joey* which capitalized on his forced smile, his quick retorts and phony charm, would never again be so fully exploited. **BP**

CITY FOR CONQUEST (1940)

Director: Anatole Litvak. **Executive Producer**: Hal B. Wallis. **Associate Producer**: William Cagney; **Screenplay**: John Wexley based on a novel by Aben Kandel. **Directors of Photography**: James Wong Howe and Sol Polito. **Music**: Max Steiner. **Art Director**: Robert Haas. **Cast**: James Cagney (Danny Kenny), Ann Sheridan (Peggy Nash), Frank Craven ("Old Timer"), Arthur Kennedy (Eddie Kenny), Donald Crisp (Scotty MacPherson), Frank McHugh ("Mutt"), George Tobias ("Pinky"), Elia Kazan ("Googi"), Anthony Quinn (Murray Burns), Jerome Cowan ("Dutch"), Lee Patrick (Gladys), Blanche Yurka (Mrs. Nash), George Lloyd ("Goldie"), Joyce Compton (Lilly), Thurston Hall (Max Leonard), Ben Welden (Cobb), John Arledge (Salesman), Ed Keane (Gaul), Selmer Jackson (Doctor), Joseph Crehan (Doctor), Kit Guard (Mickey Miller). **Released**: September 21. 103 minutes.

Danny Kenny, a Lower East Side truck driver, enters the world of boxing to win the affections of his girl Peggy and help finance his brother's music education. As "Young Sampson," Danny is a dynamo in the ring, quickly rising to the championship bout. But there he is victim of cheating, as his opponent and his handlers put rosin on the boxer's gloves, blinding Danny. Young Sampson's career is over and Danny's reduced to eking out a living on a corner newsstand. Meanwhile, boyhood pal and now ganglord Googi seeks vengeance on the mobsters who cheated Danny and fellow prizefight fans. Googi kills Dutch for rigging the fight, but in a mishap gets gunned down nearby the Hudson River. Peggy too fails in her quest to attain high-class dancing fame and finds herself a lonely burlesque dancer on the Westside. But Eddie succeeds in climbing the ladder of success when his "Symphony for the City" debuts at Carnegie Hall. He dedicates his night to Danny, with the words, "In his heart and soul there was such wealth and music, music of the city. The music that led him on to glory, to conquest, to tragedy, and defeat. But in that very defeat, he conquered."

City for Conquest was a prestige picture with a big budget that attempted, in its sprawling grandeur, to tell the story of the immigrant struggle in New York City. More of a crime film and Manhattan melodrama than noir, *City For Conquest* strives for documentary authenticity. Frank Craven, who played the "Stage Manager" in *Our Town* (1940), is once again a humanistic commentator, a poet of the Bowery,

telling how the city "smells of ambition." And much like the later de Rochemont noirs, stark, canted documentary images are used to provide a context: this story concerns the fight to climb the ladder of success. Similar to the gangster films of the 1930s, a sense of social determinism overrides the narrative. In an early sequence from Forsythe and Delancey (a street out of the same back lot that *Angels With Dirty Faces* was photographed on), we see younger selves of the principals: Peggy dances in the street while Danny fights to protect her honor, Eddie hangs back with an accordion, Googi is warned, "Don't get caught," by the Old Timer for stealing a piece of bread off a pushcart. But these youngsters are caught, already trapped in a web of social determinism.

Cagney's portrayal, unlike his more pugnacious gangster counterparts, is quieter in this film, soft-spoken and low-key: "I just want to be happy," he tells Peggy. But her desire for success forces him into the boxing ring. While sparring in a club, Danny has a stark moment of prescience when he points out a punch drunk pug who is now just a janitor, claiming he never wants to be like him. But like Mickey, Danny's future is predetermined and he too will pay dearly for participating in the fight game. He doesn't wind up punch drunk but is blinded by a boxing injury and so reduced to selling newspapers. The other principals from the East Side also find their ambitions thwarted. The film's ideology suggests that people should just be contented with their lot in life, but *City for Conquest* allows success for the classical musician Eddie. In noir, high-art aficionados are usually scorned and ridiculed, i.e., Clifton Webb in *Laura* and *The Dark Corner*, or presented as a psychotic such as Franchot Tone in *Phantom Lady*. However, in *City For Conquest,* only the artist Eddie conquers the city through his powerfully transcendent music, possibly because his symphony pays adoring tribute to the megalopolis. **GT**

CITY OF FEAR (1959)

Director: Irving Lerner. **Screenplay**: Steven Ritch and Robert Dillon. **Producer**: Leon Chooluck. **Director of Photography**: Lucien Ballard. **Music**: Jerry Goldsmith. **Art Director**: Jack Poplin. **Editor**: Robert Lawrence. **Cast**: Vince Edwards (Vince Ryker), John Archer (Lt. Mark Richards), Steven Ritch (Dr. Wallace), Patricia Blair (June), Kelly Thordsen (Sgt. Johnson), Lyle Talbot (Chief Jensen), Sherwood Price (Hallon), Joseph Mell (Crown). **Released**: Columbia, February. 81 minutes.

Escaped convict Vince evades roadblocks to reach a motel where he briefly reunites with his girlfriend. Police are told Vince stole a canister of radioactive cobalt 60 from the prison hospital in powder form, thinking it was medicinal heroin. A government scientist warns police of the extreme nuclear threat this poses if Vince remains free. Police agonize over the risks of a public panic. They plan to apprehend Vince using squad cars with geiger counters, plus delay alerting the governor until the last minute. Vince meanwhile suffers from worsening nausea, cramps and cold sweats but continues to evades capture. The senior detective overrides his subordinate and tells the governor, who agrees on a deadline for a public announcement. A taxi tracked by a geiger counter car leads police to Vince's room just ahead of the deadline while Vince carries the canister to a café whose radio announces the governor's warning. As customers leave in alarm, Vince—

now nearly blind—staggers out to the street where he dies and is covered by a shroud bearing a radioactive symbol.

Lerner uses a parallel structure of twin threats that steadily grow to locate the real criminality in the institutions—police, science and politics—that enable the nuclear threat. That bogey is explicitly described early in one of those editorializing asides Hollywood relied upon to separate reality from fiction, but the blame for how this happened is laid on the trio of establishment representatives—a pragmatic cop, his politically-attuned boss and the government's scientific expert who are repeatedly triangulated through overhead shots and camera movement into one monolithic force. That they are institutional symbols, not idiosyncratic individuals, is reinforced by their constant depersonalization through visual strategies that cut them off at the waist, shooting them linked from behind or from below in expressive displays not unlike those deployed for Nazis in pre-war Hollywood.

The establishment's scientific apparatus is forcefully legitimized by their fleet of siren-mounted black-and-white squad cars and this fusion is criminalized further: a geiger counter is aimed like a gun by a Fed bursting into a room, and Vince's symptoms of radioactive poisoning take on the effects of a junkie going cold turkey. Vince may be a hoodlum, but he's an individual with feelings and notably a sexuality, "not an animal,"as society sees him. Constantly using close framing and point of view shots, Lerner creates an intimacy that means we relate to this recognizable human, even though he is a criminal. The result is a portrait of a highly alienated individual hunted by a state that is skilled at containment, large and small. That its social institutions are distanced is indicated deftly through Vince's dialogue with authority figures occurring only when he talks back to the radio. Such objectification is not just of Vince but also his girlfriend June, whom we are introduced to as a sexualized, understandably conflicted human, but one who is seen first by the bureaucrats as a sex object—shot from the ankles up, like Stanwyck in *Double Indemnity* and Lana Turner in *The Postman Always Rings Twice*. Another institution, the media, is not similarly criminalized; a reporter who is mystified by the presence of agents with instruments at a crime scene shows the fourth estate situated outside the narrative's small conspiracy—and the subtext's larger one.

Vince, notwithstanding his criminality, which is barely glimpsed in the film, is a classic noir protagonist who experiences excessive retribution for a small error of judgment. Punishment is enacted not by the logic of the law but by nature as Lerner indicates with customary visual efficiency in a truly expressionistic shot when the shadow of the heavily-irradiated fugitive blows out like a grotesque balloon. Vince's reaction to this society may be excessive, making him vermin needing to be exterminated, as a billboard he blends into indicates, but as the government's radiological expert says of the horrific effects of nuclear exposure, "I doubt if anyone could explain it calmly." **RSW**

CITY THAT NEVER SLEEPS (1953)

Director/Associate Producer: John H. Auer. **Screenplay**: Steve Fisher. **Executive Producer**: Herbert J. Yates. **Director of Photography**: John Russell, Jr. **Music**: R. Dale Butts. **Art Director**: James Sullivan. **Editor**: Fred Allen. **Cast**: Gig Young (Johnny Kelly), Mala Powers (Sally Connors), William Talman (Hayes Stewart), Edward Arnold (Penrod Biddel), Chill Wills (Sgt. Joe, the "Voice of Chicago"), Marie Windsor (Lydia Biddel), Paula Raymond (Kathy Kelly), Otto Hulett (Sgt. John Kelly Sr.), Wally Cassell (Gregg Warren), Ron Hagerthy (Stubby), James Andelin (Lt. Parker), Thomas Poston (Detective). **Location**: Chicago, Illinois. **Completed**: January 5, 1953. **Released**: Republic, August 8. 90 minutes.

Married police officer Johnny Kelly stops by a nightclub where his girlfriend Sally Connors is a stripper. She tells him that if he won't leave town with her, she will depart with her ex-boyfriend Gregg Warren. Johnny agrees and plans on quitting the police force, a job he only took to appease his father, Sgt. John Kelly, Sr. Later that night, Kelly meets Penrod Biddel, an affluent lawyer who wants to trap his wife Lydia with Johnny's friend, Hayes Stewart, and promises the officer enough money to "give your life dignity." When Biddel confronts the lovers first, Stewart shoots him. Discovered by Sergeant Kelly at the nightclub, Stewart kills both Kelly Sr. and Lydia, unaware that the "mechanical man," Gregg Warren, has witnessed the murders and plans to tell the police. As Warren does his routine, Sally, hidden in the wings, warns him about risking his life. When she promises to start a new life with him, Gregg begins to cry. Seeing the tears,

Stewart realizes the "mechanical man" is a real person and takes a shot at Gregg but misses. Pursued by Johnny to the elevated streetcar tracks, Stewart falls to his death. At dawn, Johnny reconciles with his wife Kathy, and "Sgt. Joe," the "Voice of Chicago," opines that Johnny has been born again.

City That Never Sleeps attempts to do for Chicago what *He Walked by Night* (and its successor, *Dragnet*) did for Los Angeles and *The Naked City* did for New York, but it lacks the impact of those films. Instead of a stentorian narrator and a preoccupation with police procedure, it substitutes the voice of the fanciful "Sgt. Joe" and concentrates instead on the lives of the people whom Johnny encounters in the course of one evening. By abandoning the pretense of semi-documentary authority, this film had the potential to be more noir than *The Naked City* and certainly the elements existed. Veteran pulp writer and noir contributor Steve Fisher was responsible for the screenplay and cameraman Russell was given the chore of location work done virtually all at night. The iconic William Talman brings a good deal of menace to the figure of a stage magician gone bad. Finally, Wally Cassell moves beyond pathos in his portrayal of Gregg, the "mechanical man," who fantasized a new life with the stripper, Sally. The sight of tears streaming down his face speaks directly to those motifs of self-debasement, alienation and dehumanization so dear to the film noir. Unfortunately, writer Fisher never allows the lives of the characters to move beyond vignettes, perhaps due to the distraction of police procedures. From the standpoint of the noir critic, this film's major impediment is the moralizing voice of "Sgt. Joe" which replaces the sardonic tone of the true film noir with a sentimentality that is hard to overcome. Nowhere is this more evident that when he assures the audience that Johnny has been redeemed at the film's conclusion. **BP**

CLASH BY NIGHT (1952)

Director: Fritz Lang. **Screenplay**: Alfred Hayes with contributions by David Dortort based on the play by Clifford Odets. **Producer**: Harriet Parsons. **Executive Producer**: Jerry Wald (Wald-Krasna Productions.). **Director of Photography**: Nicholas Musuraca. **Music**: Roy Webb. **Art Directors**: Albert S. D'Agostino, Carroll Clark. **Editor**: George J. Amy. **Cast**: Barbara Stanwyck (Mae Doyle D'Amato), Paul Douglas (Jerry D'Amato), Robert Ryan (Earl Pfeiffer), Marilyn Monroe (Peggy), J. Carroll Naish (Uncle Vince),

Clash by Night: *Marilyn Monroe as Peggy.*

Keith Andes (Joe Doyle), Silvio Minciotti (Papa D'Amato).
Location: Monterey, California. **Completed**: February 20, 1952.
Released: RKO, June 18. 104 minutes.

Disillusioned by big city high-life, Mae Doyle returns to her hometown of Monterey after a long absence. Her sophisticated air attracts the attention of Jerry D'Amato, a good-natured fisherman she knew in her youth and his movie projectionist friend, the cynical Earl Pfeiffer. Mae's brother Joe is engaged to a young woman Peggy, who longs to live with the freedom she believes Mae represents. Although Mae and Earl are immediately drawn to each other, their mutual cynicism prevents a relationship from developing. Mae decides to marry the kind but unexciting Jerry, who genuinely loves her. They have a child and live uneventfully but happily together for a short time. Soon, however, Mae wearies of her life with Jerry and embarks on an affair with Earl. When Jerry learns of her infidelity, Mae decides to go off with Earl. But she discovers that his cynicism disgusts her and she returns to Jerry, asking him to take her back and they are reunited.

Clash By Night is a film with a modest scenario, but its characters—subtly graded, complex creations that are never wholly one thing or another—transform the plot's eternal triangle. Stanwyck's portrayal of Mae, a free-living woman of dubious past who cuckolds her husband, is also a character of liberated imagination and one who can ultimately see the flaws in a situation of her own creation. Robert Ryan's caustic cynic, Earl Pfeiffer, is capable of coldly informing Mae that in every decisive circumstance, "somebody's throat has to be cut" but he is the same person who cries, "Help me, Mae, I'm dying of loneliness!"

As in many noir films, Ryan delivers *Clash By Night's* most anguished performance. As the model of the alienated man, pain constantly flickers beneath the sardonic mask of his face, although he holds his mouth tightly in check and his powerful body in a useless rigidity. Ryan sketches a complex portrayal of an unhappy personality whose desires are expressed in acts of cruelty but who is accepted with some degree of audience understanding. The extraordinary opening of *Clash By Night*, which details the day-to-day work of fishermen and cannery laborers, reinforces Earl Pfeiffer's imprisonment in his milieu. Fritz Lang referred to this documentary sequence as a "three hundred foot introduction" and it situates the film firmly in a naturalistic, working class reality that supports the alienation of its characters. **JK**

CLAY PIGEON (1949)

Director: Richard Fleischer. **Screenplay**: Carl Foreman. **Producer**: Herman Schlom. **Director of Photography**: Robert DeGrasse. **Music**: Paul Sawtell. **Art Director**: Albert D'Agostino and Walter Keller. **Editor**: Samuel Beetley. **Cast**: Bill Williams (Jim Fletcher), Barbara Hale (Martha Gregory), Richard Quine (Ted Niles), Richard Loo (Ken Tokoyama aka The Weasel), Frank Fenton (Lt. Cmdr. Prentice), Frank Wilcox (Navy Doctor), Marya Marco (Mrs. Minoto), Martha Hyer (Miss Harwick), James Craven (John Wheeler), Grandon Rhodes (Naval Intel. Agent Clark). **Released**: RKO, June 29. 63 minutes.

When Jim Fletcher comes out of a coma at a Long Beach naval hospital, he is suffering from amnesia. He knows who he is but not why he's there. When he overhears the staff talking about

his impending court-martial (apparently he snitched on some of his comrades in a Japanese prison camp, leading some to die) he grabs some clothes and escapes, headed for San Diego and the widow of one of his dead buddies, Martha Gregory. She is understandably hostile so he is forced to kidnap her and head north in her car. Then pursuers almost run their car off the road, so Martha starts to believe his story about being innocent. In L.A., Fletcher seeks the aid of another war buddy, Ted Niles, who warns him to lay low because navy agents are watching him. One evening at a restaurant in Chinatown, oddly run by Japanese, he spots among them the most sadistic of former captors, nicknamed "The Weasel." He soon finds himself the fall guy, or "clay pigeon", in a trans-pacific scheme to launder millions in counterfeit currency printed in anticipation of a Japanese victory. It turns out that his old buddy was the real informant and the one who hit Fletcher over the head when he discovered Niles' guilt, a blow which caused Fletcher's memory loss. Now pretending to help Fletcher, Niles is actually in collusion with "The Weasel" to peddle the money. Together they set Fletcher up to be killed on a train, but he is saved when the police arrive in time to catch the perpetrators.

Fleischer's first feature film, *Clay Pigeon*, is one of several trim and stripped-down film noirs that the director churned out in the immediate post-war years. While not as deftly worked out as *Armored Car Robbery* or *The Narrow Margin*, it clocks in at just over an hour and delivers the goods. The plot, of course, interweaves many elements familiar enough to devotees of the film noir: the amnesiac veteran; the innocent fall-guy; breathless chases in a menacing (often nocturnal) urban setting; unsettling flashbacks. Bill Williams recaptures a good deal of the naïveté of a confused sailor that had previously served him well in *Deadline at Dawn*. And his wife, a pre-*Della Street* Barbara Hale, does equally well as Martha. Fleischer benefits from the skills of his RKO crew, imparting that glistening noir look to everything—both studio and L.A. locales. And the finale, taking place in the cramped quarters of a railroad car, is, for Fleischer, a precursor of things to come. **BMV & BP**

CONFLICT (1945)

Director: Curtis Bernhardt. **Screenplay**: Arthur T. Horman and Dwight Taylor based on an original story by Robert Siodmak and Alfred Neumann. **Producer**: William Jacobs. **Director of Photography**: Merritt Gerstad. **Music**: Frederick Hollander. **Art Director**: Ted Smith. **Editor**: David Weisbart. **Cast**: Humphrey Bogart (Richard Mason),

Alexis Smith (Evelyn Turner), Sydney Greenstreet (Dr. Mark Hamilton), Rose Hobart (Katherine Mason), Charles Drake (Prof. Norman Holdsworth), Grant Mitchell (Dr. Grant), Patrick O'Moore (Detective Lt. Egan), Ann Shoemaker (Nora Grant), Frank Wilcox (Robert Freston), James Flavin (Detective Lt. Workman). **Completed**: August 25, 1943. **Released**: Warner Bros., June 15. 86 minutes.

Richard and Katherine Mason are not as happily married as they appear; but when Richard admits that he loves her sister, Evelyn, his wife refuses to give him up. One night driving home from a dinner party given by their friend, psychiatrist Mark Hamilton, Richard injures his leg in an auto accident. He later conceals that it has healed and declines Katherine's invitation to join her for a stay at a mountain resort. Instead he intercepts her car on a lonely mountain road, strangles her and then pushes her car into a log-filled ravine. Shortly after reporting her missing, a series of strange incidents occur causing Richard to doubt Katherine's death: the odor of her perfume in a room; the reappearance of a piece of her jewelry and her handkerchief, and finally a letter in her handwriting. These occurrences, when reinforced by anonymous phone calls and the glimpse of a woman dressed in her clothes, lead Richard to doubt his sanity. Richard returns to the scene of the crime to prove to himself that Katherine is really dead. Once there, however, Hamilton and the police arrive. Richard discovers that the entire series of incidents were part of an ingenious plan contrived by Hamilton who had spotted a flaw in Richard's initial description of Katherine's last appearance.

What might have been little more than a trite mystery is given a noir ambience by the effective performances of Warner Bros.' stock players. More importantly, the romantic fatalism so prevalent in mid-1940s film noir is present in *Conflict,* contrived by the heavy Germanic influence of author Robert Siodmak and director Curtis Bernhardt with this as his first noir film. Though its overly-melodramatic structure attenuates its noir atmosphere, *Conflict* does have some memorable moments: the use of the song "Tango of Love" as leitmotif to indicate the putative presence of Katherine, background strings providing an auditory link to the scent of her perfume; the opening trucking shot through the rain-soaked night up to the window of the Mason house, which allows the audience to eavesdrop on the dinner party; and the sinister appearance of Mason as he emerges from the fog and shadows to murder his wife. **BP**

Conflict: *Evelyn (Alexis Smith) and Mason (Humphrey Bogart).*

CONVICTED (1950)

Director: Henry Levin. **Screenplay**: William Bowers, Fred Niblo Jr., and Seton I. Miller based on the play *Criminal Code,* by Martin Flavin. **Producer**. Jerry Bresler. **Director of Photography**: Burnett Guffey. **Music**: George Duning. **Art Director**: Carl Anderson. **Editor**: Al Clark. **Cast**: Glenn Ford (Joe Hufford), Broderick Crawford (George Knowland), Millard Mitchell (Malloby), Dorothy Malone (Kay Knowland), Carl Benton Reid (Capt. Douglas), Frank Faylen (Ponti), Will Geer (Mapes), Martha Stewart (Bertie Williams), Henry O'Neill (Detective Dorn), Douglas Kennedy (Detective Baley), Roland Winters (Vernon Bradley), Ed Begley (Mackay), Frank Cady (Eddie), John Doucette (Tex), Ilka Gruning (Martha Lorry), John A. Butler (Curly), Peter Virgo (Luigi), Whit Bissell (Owens). **Completed**: January 19, 1950. **Released**: Columbia, August 9. 91 minutes.

An innocent man, Joe Hufford, is convicted of murdering a member of an important family. The district attorney, George Knowland, feels that Joe is innocent, but he is helpless because the lawyer assigned to defend Hufford totally mishandles the case. Given a lighter sentence at the district attorney's prompting, Joe becomes a model prisoner. A concentrated effort on both sides of the prison's walls finally reveals the real killer and frees Hufford. Although now innocent of any crime, Hufford's experience has soured his personality, making chances of resuming his previous normal life problematic.

Prison pictures rarely become noir films. The inherent claustrophobic atmosphere allows fewer opportunities to express the hopelessness and feelings of alienation, which convey a dark cynical noir attitude; and there can be little anticipation of redemption. *Convicted* is a film that lacks originality. Its overworked themes and obvious amelioration are opposed to the noir framework, but there is a noir quality in the film due primarily to the presence of Glenn Ford. Ford's presence in many of the noir films of Columbia Pictures during the post-war period (*Framed, The Undercover Man*, and the superb *Gilda*), established a screen personality that, of itself, articulated a close affinity to the noir world. The ironies of the plot, playing off Ford's assumed persona, imbue *Convicted* with a noir sensibility that would have been unattainable without him. **CM**

CORNERED (1945)

Director: Edward Dmytryk. **Screenplay**: John Paxton based on a story by John Wexley. **Producer**: Adrian Scott. **Director of Photography**: Harry J. Wild. **Music**: Roy Webb. **Art Director**: Albert D'Agostino, Carroll Clark. **Editor**: Joseph Noriega. **Cast**: Dick Powell (Gerard), Walter Slezak (Incza), Micheline Cheirel (Mme. Jarnac), Nina Vale (Señora Camargo), Morris Carnovsky (Santana), Edgar Barrier (DuBois), Steven Geray (Señor Camargo), Jack La Rue (Diego), Luther Adler (Marcel Jarnac), Gregory Gay (Perchon). **Completed**: August 17, 1945. **Released**: RKO, December 25. 102 minutes.

Laurence Gerard, a Canadian pilot recently released from a POW camp, begins a quest to avenge the death of his young French war bride, who was betrayed by Marcel Jarnac, a Vichy official. Jarnac is a man of mystery. Few people can recall his appearance, and Gerard, skeptical of the official report of Jarnac's death, follows his trail. It leads to Switzerland and ultimately to Buenos Aires. There, Mme. Jarnac is part of a set of wealthy expatriates and local gentry, including Mr. DuBois, Señor Santana and Mr. and Mrs. Thomas Camargo. Gerard is suspicious of the whole group, unaware that DuBois, Santana, and the servant Diego belong to an organization dedicated to ferreting out former Nazis and collaborators. Gerard's brusque manner and headstrong actions inadvertently bring about the death of Diego and force Santana to reveal the existence of the anti-Fascist group to Gerard, who refuses an offer to join them. Gerard learns that Mme. Jarnac has never seen Jarnac but married him by proxy to escape France, since she and her sister were the daughters of collaborators. Keeping close tabs on collaborator Thomas Camargo and his wife, Gerard discovers that a mysterious figure he assumes is Jarnac has meetings at the Bar Fortunato. Going there alone, Gerard finds Incza, a petty informant, and Camarago in a back room. Jarnac steps out of the shadows with a gun, kills the unreliable Incza, and instructs the weak-willed Camargo to kill Gerard. A scuffle ensues, disabling Camarago, and Jarnac attacks Gerard with a knife. During the fight Gerard goes into a momentary "trance," an affliction plaguing him since his release from the POW camp. Regaining his senses he finds that he has beaten Jarnac to death, but Santana and DuBois, having followed Gerard, promise to help him with the authorities.

Director Dmytryk, star Powell, photographer Wild, and the writer-producer team of Paxton and Scott had previously been involved with *Murder, My Sweet*, a film that more clearly defined the characteristics of the noir private eye series than

the excellent *Maltese Falcon*, which still looked backward to the classic studio film of the 1930s. Although Dmytryk does not embellish *Cornered* with all the expressionistic devices of *Murder, My Sweet*, the film has more graphic ingenuity than the average postwar thriller, no doubt because by 1945 the nucleus of the RKO noir style had been established. Moreover, Dick Powell here achieves his finest delineation of the tough guy, adept enough at quick action and cynical dialogue but romantic enough to cry at the memory of his lost wife. And the character of Laurence Gerard carries a good deal of the moral ambiguity of a Sam Spade: he is ruthless in his pursuit of Jarnac; does not hesitate to use others to get to his goal; his reckless actions lead to the death of Diego and, lest we forget, he does beat Jarnac to death. Finally, *Cornered* contains a now-dated attack on Fascism which is not surprising given the ideological proclivities of many of the filmmakers, some of whom were soon to suffer later at the hands of the Hollywood blacklisters. **BP**

CRACK-UP (1946)

Director: Irving Reis. **Screenplay**: John Paxton, Ben Bengal and Ray Spencer based on the short story "Madman's Holiday" by Fredric Brown. **Executive Producer**: Jack J. Gross. **Director of Photography**: Robert de Grasse. **Music**: Leigh Harline. **Art Directors**: Albert D'Agostino, Jack Okey. **Editor**: Frederick Knudtson. **Cast**: Pat O'Brien (George Steele), Claire Trevor (Terry Cordeau), Herbert Marshall (Traybin), Ray Collins (Dr. Lowell), Wallace Ford (Cochrane), Dean Harens (Reynolds), Damian O'Flynn (Stevenson), Erskine Sanford (Mr. Barton), Mary Ware (Mary Ware). **Completed**: February 16, 1946. **Released**: RKO, October 6. 93 minutes.

George Steele, who had been an expert on art forgeries for the army during the war, is suspended from his position as lecturer and tour guide at the New York Metropolitan Museum due to his erratic behavior there one night. He appears to have been drunk, but Steele claims his condition was the result of his involvement in a train wreck. However, he has no recollection of what happened between the time of the wreck and his appearance at the museum and the police find there is no record of the train accident. Under suspicion, Steele retraces his movements and uncovers a devious plot for substituting forgeries for several of the masterpieces on loan at the museum.

Steele begins to suspect several substantial dealers and collectors but then discovers that the museum's director, Mr. Barton, is being forced to go along with the scheme. Steele is assisted by his girl friend, newspaper columnist Terry Cordeau, who, unknown to Steele, is also assisting an undercover Scotland Yard agent, Traybin, to discover the source of the forgeries. To get information, Lowell, a psychiatrist, puts Steele under the influence of sodium pentothal, the same drug the doctor used on him to simulate the train wreck. Lowell plans to kill both Steele and Terry, but they are rescued in the nick of time by Traybin, who had been waiting outside to gain the necessary evidence against Lowell.

Though not among the best of the RKO noir series due to its plot contrivances and lackluster direction, *Crack-Up*'s treatment of art, psychiatry, and technology says much about American attitudes at the close of WWII. The use and abuse of art in such films as *The Big Sleep, Laura,* and *The Dark Corner* has already garnered a good deal of critical attention. Here, however, the role of art—its "meaning," its value, and its very place in our society—is made central to the action of the film. Protagonist ex-army Capt. Steele is a spokesman for "art for the masses" who has an aesthetic bias strongly in favor of personal taste. He compares knowing what one likes in a piece of art with knowing what one likes in a mate or a house while deprecating those "who know everything about art except what they like and can only tell good painting from bad by its price tag."

Opposed to him are those officials, critics, collectors and wealthy snobs who lack his democratic sensibility and often use art merely as a means of social climbing. That Steele turned up Nazi forgeries during the war not only parallels the Nazi desire to hoard art with that of the villain but helps to explain the association of high art with villainy, a common motif in many postwar films. Lowell, in rationalizing his theft of the paintings, becomes the spokesman for the elitist bias: "Did you ever want to possess something that was unattainable? Museums have a habit of wasting great art on dolts who can't differentiate between it and trash. These masterpieces . . . mean everything in life to me." Like art, technology can be used or misused: in the hands of a Steele it can be used to expose falsehood (forgery); in the hands of a Dr. Lowell it can be used to control others. Ironically, both the X-ray and pentothal are means of discovering "truth." When Lowell reminds us that narcosynthesis was a by-product of the war, American concern with the abuse of technology is linked again to the war that culminated in using an atomic bomb. Finally, the film's bias against surrealism, an art style amusingly dismissed by Steele, says much about America's wariness of anything too foreign, too Freudian, too radical. Ironically, *Crack-Up*'s most arresting visual—the simulated train wreck in which the camera tilts down from Steele's face in the train window to the car's wheels, superimposing the face of his wrist-watch over the wheels—is itself surreal, perhaps subconsciously so. **BP**

CRIME OF PASSION (1957)

Director: Gerd Oswald. **Screenplay**: Jo Eisinger. **Executive Producer**: Bob Goldstein. **Producer**: Herman Cohen. **Director of Photography**: Joseph LaShelle. **Music**: Paul Dunlap. **Art Director**: Leslie Thomas. **Editor**: Marjorie Fowler. **Cast**: Barbara Stanwyck (Kathy Ferguson), Sterling Hayden (Bill Doyle), Raymond Burr (Inspector Tony Pope), Fay Wray (Alice Pope), Royal Dano (Capt. Alidos), Virginia Grey, (Sara

Alidos), Dennis Cross (Detective Jules), Robert Griffin (Detective James), Jay Adler (Nalence), Malcolm Atterbury (Officer Spitz), Brad Trumbull (Detective Johns). **Completed**: July, 1956. **Released**: United Artists, January 9. 85 minutes.

Kathy Ferguson is a lovelorn columnist in San Francisco who gets her big break when she convinces a murderess to give herself up. On her way to a better job in New York City, Kathy stops off in Los Angeles to have dinner with her new friend, Detective Lt. Bill Doyle of the L.A.P.D. The dinner leads to deeper involvement, and she forsakes her newspaper career to marry Doyle and settle down in a tract home in suburban L.A. Bored with her husband's circle of friends and with suburban life in general, she decides her marriage has become a prison and that Bill must enhance his status on the force. With this in mind, she "arranges" for them to become sociable with Doyle's boss, Inspector Tony Pope, and his wife, Alice. Kathy influences Pope to favor her husband over Bill's chief rival and good friend, Capt. Alidos. She destroys this friendship through a series of poison pen letters which convince Bill that the Alidos, husband and wife, have it in for them. When Bill and Alidos are called before Pope for fighting in one of the precinct rooms, Pope transfers Alidos and promotes Bill to Captain. Kathy uses her affair with Pope to extract his promise to appoint Doyle his successor on retirement, which is hastened by Alice's ill health. When he remains oblivious to her entreaties, she fatally shoots him with a gun she has stolen from the police station. Bill heads the investigation into Pope's death and eventually discovers the murder weapon and how it disappeared from the precinct. Good cop that he is, he must arrest his wife for the murder.

Crime of Passion capitalizes on the iconography and motifs of classic film noir, but it is very much a film of the 1950s. For one thing, except for a few scenes (a darkened interior here, a night-for-night exterior there) this film eschews the chiaroscuro visuals of the noir style for the heightened realism of a greater latitude of grays made possible by innovations in film stocks and lighting techniques. Moreover, it was shot in a wide screen format (1.66:1) which emphasizes width as opposed to depth-staging. Most importantly, perhaps, is the way it articulates a preoccupation of 1950s America with the problems associated with the "massification" of American society (e.g., social conformity, middle-class malaise, suburbanization). It does so in a manner that earlier film noirs like *Pitfall*, *Mildred Pierce*, and *Too Late for Tears* could only hint at and thus points the way to such later exposés as *Rebel Without a Cause* and *No Down Payment*. Of course the iconic values of casting Barbara Stanwyck as a highly intelligent, scheming and driven woman to counter Sterling Haden as the stalwart cop were givens even back in 1956. More nuanced, perhaps, is the performance of Raymond Burr who, shedding his earlier image as a "heavy" (both figuratively and literally), makes the character of Tony Pope come alive as a man who walks a fine line between despicable opportunism and integrity. Finally, the fact that author Eisinger gives Kathy few options between being a "happy housewife" (as Capt. Alidos would have her) or one of Pope's "hysterical female criminal cases" would appear rather questionable in today's post-feminist world. **BP**

CRIME WAVE (1954)

Director: Andre De Toth. **Screenplay**: Crane Wilbur, adapted by Bernard Gordon and Richard Wormser, from the story, "Criminals Mark," by John and Ward Hawkins, published in *Saturday Evening Post*. **Producer**: Bryan Foy. **Director of Photography**: Bert Glennon. **Music**: David Buttolph. **Art Director**: Stanley Fleischer. **Editor**: Thomas Reilly. **Cast**: Gene Nelson (Steve Lacey), Phyllis Kirk, (Ellen), Sterling Hayden (Detective Sgt. Sims), James Bell (Daniel), Ted De Corsia (Doc Penny), Charles [Bronson] Buchinsky (Ben Hastings), Ned Young (Gat Morgan), Jay Novello (Otto Hessler), Walter Dub Taylor (Gus Snider), Richard Benjamin (Mark), Mack Chandler (Sully), Gayle Kellogg (Detective), James Hayward (Zenner), Timothy Carey (Johnny Haslett). **Location**: Glendale, California. **Completed**: December 3, 1952. **Released**: Warner Bros., January 12. 73 minutes.

Two former inmates of the same prison implicate Steve Lacey, an ex-convict, in a holdup. Steve, who has gone straight since his release, is forced to cooperate with the two thugs in order to protect his wife, Ellen, and their family. But a hardened detective, Sims, harasses Steve, apparently convinced of the young man's guilt in the crime. Steve finally foils the two crooks but is not off the hook until Sims reverses his position and helps Steve to clear himself.

Crime Wave is an engaging low-budget film that maintains visual excitement throughout its 73-minute running time by imaginative compositions in the noir tradition and vivid photography in the city exteriors, as well as offbeat touches of character. Although the premise is familiar, considerable sympathy is established for the hero, Steve, who does not have the tiresome moral righteousness of many wronged protagonists. Curiously, Andre De Toth directed few film noirs. *Crime Wave* and *Pitfall* are the only two examples of his work in the cycle, although the influence of film noir is felt strongly in his Westerns, *Ramrod*, *Man in the Saddle*, and *Day of the Outlaw*. De Toth's treatment of the characters' betrayals and reversals of character in *Crime Wave* is direct and free of moral posturing. As Sims, Sterling Hayden gives full throttle to impulsive behavior and wild tempers. The final image, in which Sims, who chews toothpicks throughout the film because he is attempting to quit smoking cigarettes, finally lights up, takes just one drag before throwing the cigarette away and walks off chewing a match, is memorable for its offhand and semi-comic paraphrasing of the noir archetype of alienated ambivalence. **BL**

THE CRIMSON KIMONO (1959)

Director, Producer, and Screenplay: Samuel Fuller (Globe Enterprises). **Director of Photography**: Sam Leavitt. **Music**: Harry Sukman. **Art Directors**: William E. Flannery, Robert Boyle. **Editor**: Jerome Thoms. **Cast**: Victoria Shaw (Christine Downs), Glenn Corbett (Detective Sgt. Charlie Bancroft), James Shigeta (Detective Joe Kojaku), Anna Lee (Mac), Paul Dubov (Casale), Jaclynne Greene (Roma), Neyle Morrow (Hansel), Gloria Pall (Sugar Torch), Barbara Hayden (Mother), George Yoshinaga (Willy Hidaka), Kaye Elhardt (Nun), Aya Oyama (Sister Gertrude), George Okamura (Karate), the Reverend Ryosho S. Sogabe (Priest), Robert Okazaki (Yoshinaga), Fuji (Shuto). **Location**: Little Tokyo, Los Angeles, California. **Completed**: March 10, 1959. **Released**: Columbia, October 1. 82 minutes.

Detectives Charlie Bancroft and Joe Kojaku are best friends who live and work together in Los Angeles. When a stripper, Sugar Torch, is murdered, they are assigned to the case. Searching for clues, they meet a beautiful artist, Christine. Both men fall in love with her and she, a Caucasian, reciprocates the feelings of Joe, a Nisei. Charlie is jealous but Joe mistakes his friend's reaction for racism against Joe and

Crime Wave: *Det. Sims (Sterling Hayden) and Steve Lacey (Gene Nelson)*.

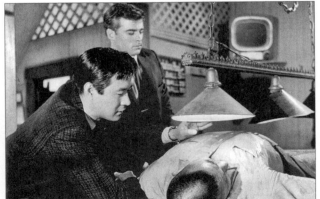

The Crimson Kimono: *Detectives Kojaku (James Shigeta) and Bancroft (Glenn Corbett) overcome martal artist Shuto (Fuji)*.

Christine as an integrated couple. In a traditional Kendo match, Joe loses control and beats Charlie senseless. Back at work, Joe chases and shoots Roma, who confesses that she killed Sugar Torch out of jealousy that her lover preferred Sugar. The killer's situation forces Joe to see his problems clearly and he and Christine are united.

Many of Fuller's films shockingly juxtapose moments of sensitivity and gentleness with others of vulgarity and violence. *The Crimson Kimono* is his one film most consistent in revealing character emotions and runs counter to the view that Fuller is abrasive and unsubtle. There is nothing primitive or naive about the unusual love triangle in which the heroine prefers an Asian over a Caucasian, especially as both men are likable and attractive. The love story is well integrated into the central narrative's pursuit of a killer. Joe's neurosis over his racial identity is challenged by the self-understanding he gains in discovering the cause of the murder. Similarly, the use of actual locations in Little Tokyo and metropolitan Los Angeles reinforce the personal, cultural, and racial considerations of the narrative.

As usual in a Fuller film, there are numerous imaginative elements of characterization, action and style. The alcoholic artist, Mac, played by Anna Lee, is another offbeat mother figure in the tradition of Thelma Ritter in *Pickup on South Street* and anticipates Beatrice Kay in *Underworld U.S.A.* The violence in the film, notably Charlie and Joe's fight with a huge Korean and the chase down Little Tokyo's streets amidst the masked figures of the Japanese festival, reflects on the film's themes of celebratory racial unity countered by Joe's ambivalence toward his culture. Some sequences, such as Joe playing the piano for Christine, are directed in an unobtrusive manner while at other times, as during the Kendo match, Fuller appropriately accelerates the pace of his cutting. His close-ups maintain their expressiveness, particularly in the striking moment of Joe's changing look as he holds Roma and listens to her dying words. The final shot of Joe and Christine in a feverish kiss is erotically charged. **BL**

CRISS CROSS (1949)

Director: Robert Siodmak. **Screenplay**: Daniel Fuchs based on the novel by Don Tracy. **Producer**: Michel Kraike. **Director of Photography**: Franz Planer. **Art Directors**: Bernard Herzbrun and Boris Leven. **Music**: Miklós Rózsa. **Editor**: Ted J. Kent. **Cast**: Burt Lancaster (Steve Thompson), Yvonne De Carlo (Anna), Dan Duryea (Slim Dundee),

Criss Cross: *Anna (Yvonne De Carlo) and her ex-husband Steve Thompson (Burt Lancaster).*

Stephen McNally (Pete Ramirez), Richard Long (Slade Thompson), Esy Morales (Orchestra Leader), Tom Pedi (Vincent), Percy Helton (Frank), Alan Napier (Finchley), Griff Barnett (Pop), Meg Randall (Helen), Joan Miller (Lush), Edna M. Holland (Mrs. Thompson), John Doucette (Walt), Marc Krath (Mort). **Completed**: July 28, 1948. **Released**: Universal, January 12. 88 minutes.

Some months after his divorce, Steve Thompson returns home to Bunker Hill in Los Angeles. Still haunted by the image of his ex-wife, Anna, Thompson frequents a nightclub where they spent time together and sees Anna on the dance floor. She tells him of plans to marry Slim Dundee, a gambler with syndicate connections. But although Dundee spends money lavishly, Anna makes it clear that the physical intensity of her marriage is lacking. Despite warnings from her family and his detective friend Pete Ramirez, Thompson sees Anna while Dundee is out of town. When Dundee catches them together, Thompson hastily improvises an explanation: he has plans to rob the armored car company for which he works and needs Dundee's help. Anna promises Dundee that she'll return to him once Thompson has money. Still suspicious, Dundee plans to double-cross Thompson. During the robbery, Dundee's men murder Thompson's partner and wound Thompson, who retaliates and brings several of them down. Although Thompson is hospitalized and praised for his heroics, Ramirez suspects his complicity. Because Anna has disappeared with the money, Dundee has Thompson kidnapped as he suspects he and Anna plan a double-cross. However, Thompson bribes his abductor into taking him to Anna's hideout instead. Terrified by Thompson's arrival and the knowledge that Dundee will soon be tipped off, Anna prepares to abandon the wounded man. However, before she can leave, Dundee arrives with the police in pursuit. Killing Thompson and Anna, Dundee then runs toward the sound of approaching sirens.

From the opening aerial shot across the darkened city and into the parking lot of a small nightclub, *Criss Cross* invokes several indicators of fatality in film noir: a distanced view of an anonymous urban landscape, the frenetic chords of Miklós Rózsa's music gradually ceding to the dance rhythms emanating from a nightclub, and the camera's movement

inward to it, drawn by an unknown object or person. As the image dissolves from an omniscient perspective to a particularized one, the headlights of a car sweep across the club's parking lot and illuminates two figures embracing. The deterministic quality of the narrative is effectively anticipated. This introduction of the lovers, Steve and Anna, exploits the noir conventions of plunging the viewer abruptly into the characters' point of view and also isolates a moment that mixes fear of discovery with sexual excitement. Only through subsequent flashbacks is the true nature of Thompson's relationship to Anna detailed. His narration is almost a lament and explicitly deterministic: "From the start, it all went one way. It was in the cards or it was fate or a jinx or whatever you want to call it."

The fear and excitement so obvious in that first scene are components of Thompson's fatal obsession which he details when he recalls his reencounter with Anna. Alone at the bar, not dissolute but seeking escape, the viewer intrudes into his reverie. As Thompson tries to dispel his ill-defined disquiet, a point-of-view shot abruptly compels the audience to co-experience what he sees. Through the hazy room, a long lens isolates one couple dancing. As Thompson strains for a better look, the woman turns. For a moment, her face is visible then lost again in the crowd. The woman is Anna, Thompson's former wife, with whom he is obviously continues to be emotionally and physically obsessed. Not only do the formal elements of the shot idealize Anna's appearance, but the use of point-of-view makes an economic, nonverbal connection between her appearance and Thompson's opinion of her. Anna is suddenly there, oneirically before him as if sprung from the depths of that initial reverie. In fact, Thompson might at first suspect that he is hallucinating since there is no reason, other than his overwhelming desire, for her to be in the nightclub. Because this articulation of their relationship is purely visual, it cannot be misconstrued. The audience is not given a perspective that is literally what Thompson sees, the long lens and slow motion belie that. Rather the shot is remarkably subjective: it is what Thompson sees as distorted by the powerful emotion that he feels.

This sequence is the key to *Criss Cross* and to the ultimate destruction of its protagonist. The day-lit exteriors of Angel's Flight, where Thompson lives, those of his visits to Anna at Dundee's spacious home, or the full-lit shots of him at work are all naturalistic in their lighting and composition. As informed by the subjective viewpoint and voiceover of first scenes, they become functionally if not stylistically noir, for they reflect Thompson's rekindled dissatisfaction with his drab environment. The expressionistic staging of the robbery with its violence, its dark, masked figures moving apprehensively through smoke-filled frames, and its deadly excitement becomes a nightmarish variant, again from Thompson's point of view, of the sexual promise of the initial sequence. This carries over into the claustrophobic paranoia of Thompson in the hospital, where, in a new series of anxious close shots echoing the introductory ones of him, he hopes simultaneously for and against Anna's arrival. Finally, the slow pan down to Thompson's and Anna's bodies fallen together in a mortal repose undisturbed by the rising blare of sirens, reverses the inward sweep of the film's first shot while Rózsa's same ominous score forms a dirge-like coda.

By beginning with the dynamics of the relationship between Thompson and Anna and by establishing it precisely and particularly through the *mise-en-scène*, Siodmak irrevocably ties all the events that follow to that first fatal moment in the nightclub, a moment that will govern Thompson's destiny. Would it be "in the cards" without Anna's false promises? "All those things that happened to us, everything that went before, we'll forget it," she tells Steve. "You'll see. I'll make you forget it. After it's done, after it's all over and we're safe, it'll be just you and me. You and me. The way it should've been all along from the start." In using the flashback structure and narration, Siodmak makes it clear, "from the start," that Anna's vision of "you and me" is doomed.

After the sudden death of Mark Hellinger, the producer on *The Killers*, reworking the complex narrative of *Criss Cross* was left to Siodmak and writer Daniel Fuchs. The novel's setting of a racetrack robbery was changed to an armored car hold-up. Siodmak and his collaborators combine the elements of obsessive love, heist gone wrong, and emotional duplicity even more powerfully than in *The Killers* and makes *Criss Cross* one of the most tragic and compelling of film noir. **AS**

CROOKED WAY (1949)

Director: Robert Florey. **Screenplay**: Richard H. Landau based on the radio play "No Blade Too Sharp" by Robert Monroe. **Producer**: Bendict Bogeaus (La Brea Productions). **Director of Photography**: John Alton. **Music Score**: Louis Forbes. **Production Design**: Van Nest Polglase. **Editor**: Frank Sullivan. **Cast**: John Payne (Eddie Rice), Sonny Tufts (Vince Alexander), Ellen Drew (Nina), Rhys Williams (Lt. Williams), Percy Helton (Petey), John Doucette (Sgt. Barrett), Charles Evans (Capt. Anderson), Greta Granstedt (Hazel), Harry Bronson (Danny), Hal Fieberling (Coke), Crane Whitley (Dr. Kemble), John Harmon (Kelly), Snub Pollard (News Vendor). **Completed**: December 1948. **Released**: United Artists, April 22. 87 minutes.

Eddie Rice, awarded the Silver Star, is finally released from a veterans' rehabilitation ward, victim of a war wound that has left him a permanent amnesiac. The only information he has concerning himself is that he comes from Los Angeles, so he returns there to try and recover his past. Arriving at Union Station, he runs into Lt. Williams and some other police detective who all know him as Eddie Ricardi. Williams is skeptical of Eddie's memory loss, and informs him that prior to the war Ricardi had been the partner of a local racketeer named Vince Alexander. Eddie meets Nina Martin, his ex-wife, and she takes him to the hotel where he used to live and secretly informs her boss, Vince Alexander, of his whereabouts. Later, Vince has Eddie escorted to his office and beaten up because Vince believes that Eddie enlisted in the armed forces under a phony name, leaving Vince to take the blame for a crime. Vince warns Eddie to leave town quickly but changes his mind later when he realizes he can frame Eddie for some of his own crimes. He then forces Nina to seduce Eddie so that the man will remain in town. When Lt. Williams confronts Vince with evidence linking him to a thug's murder, Vince shoots the policeman and has Eddie set up to take the blame. But Eddie escapes

Crooked Way: *Eddie Rice (John Payne) and police Lt. William (Rhys Williams).*

Crossfire: *Det. Finley (Robert Young) speaks with Leroy (William Phipps) and Sgt. Kelley (Robert Mitchum).*

and convinces Nina that he is a new man, no longer the old Eddie Ricardi. Although wounded by Vince's henchmen, she instructs Eddie to find an old friend, Petey, who is hiding in a waterfront warehouse. Petey informs Vince of Eddie's visit and when Vince arrives at the warehouse a gun battle ensues between the two men. When the police arrive, Vince uses Eddie as a shield but is shot at by Petey. Losing his cover, Vince turns on the cops and is shot to death. Nina and Eddie are finally reunited, and Eddie assures her that his old personality will never return.

The Crooked Way is a minor film noir, though John Payne does a credible job as the morally ambiguous hero so typical of the cycle. The use of voice-over narration—first from an unseen narrator, then of the psychologist examining Eddie and then of Eddie himself sporadically throughout the film—disrupts the flow of the action and betrays the film's origin as a radio drama. The theme of an amnesiac veteran who must function as a detective in an effort to uncover his own sordid past was done better in the earlier *Somewhere in the Night.* But once again a minor film is rescued by the brilliant photography of John Alton, who perhaps better than any other cinematographer imbued authentic locations with a noir style that invariably heightens the tension. Robert Florey, who began his career as an assistant to Louis de Feuillade and ended it as a director of American B-films, draws upon his acquaintance with both expressionism and surrealism to capitalize on Alton's talents. The final sequence of the shootout at the warehouse, amidst the clutter of war-surplus materials and punctuated by the coughing of the rodent-like Petey, accompanied by his beloved cat, is particularly baroque. **BP**

CROSSFIRE (1947)

Director: Edward Dmytryk. **Screenplay**: John Paxton based on the novel, *The Brick Foxhole*, by Richard Brooks. **Producer**: Adrian Scott. **Executive Producer**: Dore Schary. **Director of Photography**: J. Roy Hunt. **Music**: Roy Webb. **Art Directors**: Albert S. D'Agostino, Alfred Herman. **Editor**: Harry Gerstad. **Cast**: Robert Young (Det. Finlay), Robert Mitchum (Sgt. Keeley), Robert Ryan (Montgomery), Gloria Grahame (Ginny), Paul Kelly (the Man), Sam Levene (Joseph Samuels), Jacqueline White (Mary Mitchell), Steve Brodie (Floyd Bowers), George Cooper (Cpl. Mitchell), Richard Benedict (Bill Williams), Tom Keene (Detective Dick Powers), William Phipps (Leroy), Lex Barker (Harry), Marlo Dwyer (Miss Lewis). **Completed**: March 28, 1947. **Released**: RKO, July 22. 85 minutes.

Four army buddies, Leroy, Montgomery, Floyd, and Mitchell go on leave. They meet Joseph Samuels and his girlfriend, Miss Lewis, in a nightclub. Mitchell is invited to Samuels' apartment and Floyd Bowers follows them. Later, while Montgomery and Mitchell are arguing with Samuels, a Jew, Montgomery beats him to death. The police suspect Mitchell who hides in an all-night movie house, but Sgt. Keeley helps Detective Finlay discover the real killer. Montgomery then murders Bowers to avoid capture as Samuels' murderer. The police suspect Montgomery and use Leroy to set a trap for the killer, who tells Montgomery that Bowers wants to see him. Confused, Montgomery returns to the killing place to see how the man could still be alive, and the waiting police arrest him.

Authentic film noir or message picture? *Crossfire* is probably both, but leans strongly toward the latter and in doing so vitiates the force inherent in the Richard Brooks novel on which the film is based. Director Edward Dmytryk does little to alleviate the visually static nature of many scenes, such as that in which Finlay delivers his sermon to the hapless Southern boy, Leroy. Then he pretentiously stages the subsequent sequence between Montgomery and Leroy with a tricky use of mirrors. In other words, *Crossfire* is a film of stylistic flourishes but lacking a meaningful style. On the whole, the characters have little individual depth. Actors such as Robert Mitchum, Robert Ryan, and Gloria Grahame bring noir iconography to any film by their collective presence. Ryan's performance, in particular, has a certain reputation; but he had played and would play psychopaths again in many noir films. His comparable role as a bigot in *Odds Against Tomorrow* possesses more fascinating twists and turns of character. The one truly unusual characterization is of Ginny's boyfriend, briefly portrayed by Paul Kelly. A predictable structure dominates the story except for Montgomery's flashback lie. Racial prejudice is an apt theme for a movie with noir overtones. The subject is more compelling however when engaged in the conflict between accomplices in *Odds Against Tomorrow* or in Fuller's *Crimson Kimono,* where the intimate personal relationship between the police partners adds an ironic layer not present in *Crossfire.* **BL**

CRY DANGER (1951)

Director: Robert Parrish. **Screenplay**: William Bowers based on a story by Jerome Cady. **Producers**: Sam Wiesenthal and W.R. Frank (Olympic Productions). **Director of Photography**: Joseph F. Biroc. **Music**: Emil Newman, Paul Dunlap. **Art Director**: Richard Day. **Editor**: Bernard W. Burton. **Cast**: Dick Powell (Rocky), Rhonda Fleming (Nancy), Richard Erdman (Delong), William Conrad (Castro), Regis Toomey (Cobb), Jean Porter (Darlene), Jay Adler (Williams), Joan Banks (Alice Fletcher), Gloria Saunders (Cigarette Girl), Hy Averbach (Bookie), Renny McEvoy (Taxi Driver), Lou Lubin (Hank), Benny Burt (Bartender). **Released**: RKO, February 21. 79 minutes.

Rocky, framed for a murder and robbery of $100,000, has his case reviewed and is released after five years of his jail sentence. However, his best friend, Danny, also framed, remains in prison. Rocky sets out to clear Danny and seeks revenge on the man responsible, a racketeer named Castro. Complicating matters is the renewed affection between Rocky and Nancy, who was his girl but then married Danny. Rocky finally pins the crime on Castro after finding out that Danny really was Castro's accomplice and that Nancy has known it all along. She has kept half of the stolen money as payment for remaining silent.

Familiar as the plot is, with its characteristically devious woman, betrayals, and infringement of the past upon the present, the emotional tone of *Cry Danger* is dissimilar to other noir films of its type. Rather than a pessimistic and harsh view of human nature as in *Out of the Past* and *Criss Cross*, it emphasizes the essential health of its hero, who is deeply disappointed in his friend and the girl he loves, but looks forward to a better life without them. In this respect, this modest picture thematically anticipates director Robert Parrish's work in other genres, such as *The Purple Plain* and *The Wonderful Country*. These as well as *Cry Danger* portray

a hero in the last, therapeutic stages of abandoning the vestiges of a neurotic and crippling past. **BL**

A CRY IN THE NIGHT (1956)

Director: Frank Tuttle. **Screenplay**: David Dortort based on the novel *All through the Night* by Whit Masterson. **Producer**: Alan Ladd (Jaguar Productions), George C. Bertholon. **Director of Photography**: John F. Seitz. **Art Director**: Malcolm C. Bert. **Music**: David Buttolph. **Editor**: Folmar Blangsted. **Cast**: Raymond Burr (Harold Loftus), Edmond O'Brien (Taggart), Natalie Wood (Liz Taggart), Brian Donlevy (Captain Ed Bates), Richard Anderson (Owen Clark), Irene Hervey (Helen Taggart), Carol Veazie (Mabel Loftus), Mary Lawrence (Madge Taggart), Anthony Caruso (Tony, a cop), George J. Lewis (George, a cop), Peter Hansen (Dr. Frazee), Tina Carver (Marie Holzapple), Herb Vigran (Sgt. Jensen), Alan Ladd (Narrator). **Released**: Warner Bros., August 17. 75 minutes.

While necking in "lover's loop" above the city, Liz Taggart is kidnapped by a mentally handicapped Harold Loftus, who also knocks out her boyfriend. Loftus takes Liz to a hideout in a downtown brickyard while the police in conjunction with her rogue cop father and wounded boyfriend search frantically to identify the kidnapper and find Liz. A call from Loftus' mother to the station looking for her son, leads the pursuers to her and an identification of the kidnapper. After Loftus' car is found in the brickyard, the police surround the hideout and capture the frightened Loftus, rescuing Liz in the process.

A Cry in the Night is a low-budget film produced by Alan Ladd's company Jaguar for Warner Bros. It utilizes various noir luminaries at the tail end of the classic period: most notably, veteran cinematographer John F. Seitz and actors Raymond Burr and Edmond O'Brien. By the mid-1950s noir had fallen on hard times as fewer and fewer films in the style were produced. For one, the anti-Communist "witch hunts" had decimated noir's talent while the conformism and enforced optimism of the Eisenhower years made the production of gloomy and critical films the exception rather than the rule.

A Cry in the Night confronts male patriarchy as well as the stifling nuclear family with a bravery typical of films of the previous decade, most notably Andre de Toth's *Pitfall*. Edmond O'Brien plays Taggart, an abusive rogue cop who treats his family in the same manner as his suspects. He interrogates his female household, sets down arbitrary rules, and frightens away suitors who wish to date his daughter. When Liz is kidnapped while necking with her boyfriend, he blames his wife for being permissive. In a rage which even his colleagues cannot control, he threatens to kill the kidnapper as well as roughing up the boyfriend. In a remarkable scene, for the late 1950s that is, towards the end of the movie, the filmmakers turn the popular television show of the period, *Father Knows Best*, on its head as the women in his household revolt. They tell the patriarch exactly what they think of him, ending with a slap delivered to him by his sister.

Concurrent with this exploration of the nuclear family, the filmmakers also develop the character of the kidnapper, Loftus. Chalking up yet another deft performance, Raymond Burr turns the sexually confused "Baby," his overbearing

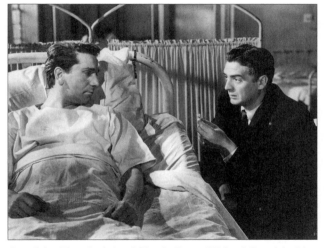

Cry of the City: *An injured Martin Rome (Richard Conte) is visited by Lt. Candella (Victor Mature).*

mother's nickname for him, into a sympathetic figure much like Lenny in Steinbeck's *Of Mice and Men.* Holed up in a brick yard with his *belle captive,* he tells Liz over and over how "pretty" she is, lying next to her on the floor as she sleeps on a cot. He brings her a sexy dress to wear and even gives her a piece of pie intended for his mother, though he admits his mother will be "mad." Liz alternates between placating this virginal man, who has never kissed a girl, and making futile attempts at escape. When he is finally caught by Taggart, who begins to beat him mercilessly, Loftus calls for his mother to help him which even shames the out-of-control Taggart into relenting, as the brutal cop shares for a moment the sympathy the audience must now feel for the confused "Baby." **JU**

CRY OF THE CITY (1948)

Director: Robert Siodmak. **Screenplay**: Richard Murphy based on the novel *The Chair for Martin Rome,* by Henry Edward Helseth. **Producer**: Sol Siegel. **Director of Photography**: Lloyd Ahern. **Music**: Alfred Newman. **Art Directors**: Lyle Wheeler, Albert Hogsett. **Editor**: Harmon Jones. **Cast**: Victor Mature (Lt. Candella), Richard Conte (Martin Rome), Fred Clark (Lt. Collins), Shelley Winters (Brenda), Betty Garde (Mrs. Pruett), Barry Kroeger (Niles), Tommy Cook (Tony), Debra Paget (Teena Riconti), Hope Emerson (Rose Given), Roland Winters (Ledbetter), Walter Baldwin (Orvy), June Storey (Miss Boone), Tito Vuolo (Papa Roma), Mimi Aguglia (Mama Roma), Konstantin Shayne (Dr. Veroff), Howard Freeman (Sullivan). **Location**: New York City. **Completed**: February 24, 1948. **Released**: 20th Century-Fox, September 29. 96 minutes.

Wounded while killing a cop, tough, young Martin Rome refuses to reveal to homicide officer Lt. Candella the identity of the girl who secretly visited him the previous night in the hospital. Candella grew up with Martin in New York's Little Italy and is a friend of his family, but Candella believes the mystery girl is implicated in the "de Grazia case" jewel robbery. Martin uses his charm and persuades Nurse Pruett to find and then hide the young, innocent girl, Teena. Transferred to a prison ward, Martin escapes and murders Niles, a crooked lawyer who balked at financing his escape. Candella almost traps Martin in Teena's apartment, but the gangster is tipped off by his young brother, Tony. Later Candella stumbles onto Martin at the home of his parents, but he again escapes. Suffering from his wounds, Martin asks his former girlfriend, Brenda, to find a doctor who will treat him in a car. Martin offers Rose Given, a masseuse, the key to a subway locker containing the de Grazia jewels in exchange for $5,000 and steamship tickets to South America. When the deal is made, Martin tells Candella where to pick Rose up. Suspicious, Rose forces Martin to accompany her to the subway locker. When she sees the police, she aims to shoot Martin, but hits Candella instead and Martin escapes once more. Wounded, Candella visits Nurse Pruett, who reveals that Teena is meeting Martin in a neighborhood church. Meanwhile, Martin persuades Tony to help him "borrow" money for a getaway from their parents. In the church, Martin convinces Teena that he has only killed in self-defense. Just as she is about to go off with him, Candella arrives and persuades Teena to leave before challenging Martin to shoot it out. Gunless, Candella bluffs Martin into turning his gun over to him and walking outside. Once there, Candella sinks to the sidewalk, weak from loss of blood. Martin makes a break for it. Candella warns him to stop, and when Martin refuses, he kills him.

Cry of the City was Fox's attempt to repeat the success of its earlier *Kiss of Death,* shot almost entirely on location in New York. It is a key film insofar as it represents an effort on the part of Robert Siodmak, most closely associated with the highly artificial, expressionistic style of the studio film noir, to exploit a semi-documentary style that was purportedly incompatible with the former production method. Siodmak himself stated that he was not completely satisfied working on location. However, he was able to extract from the discordant elements of this film's pseudo-realism—with its extraneous sights and sounds; its brief, incisive, character studies; and its stunning jailbreak scene—a cohesive, thoroughly stylized film noir without sacrificing the sociological implications of a naturalistic Italian ghetto.

The location touches in *Cry of the City* may have implied that Siodmak was Americanizing his style, but surely the noir aspects of the film—its cruel eroticism in the person of Rose Given; its insistence on urban corruption and finally its use of interiors with enclosed spaces and expressionistic lighting—give it as much of an oppressive atmosphere as any of Siodmak's earlier studio films. It also confirms that the studio films were not stylistically at odds with the later semidocumentary ones. Looking at the latter from the perspective of today's naturalistic techniques, it is evident that their audience's own sense of reality was conditioned by these films. The *mise-en-scène* of films like *T-Men, Kiss of Death,* or *Street with No Name* (eventually even TV shows like *Dragnet* or *Naked City*) is highly controlled, its realism an artificial one that, location work and all, could be manipulated by adept photographers and directors to produce a world as hermetic and stylized as the best studio films. In fact, an element such as Alfred Newman's musical "Street Scene" theme, a trademark of the Fox noirs, only becomes a veritable cry of the city when it is superimposed with its manifest stylization over the naturalistic images of New York. The real cry of the city must come from those Italians, and countless ethnic groups after them, trapped in the ghetto. **BP**

CRY OF THE HUNTED (1953)

Director: Joseph H. Lewis. **Screenplay**: Jack Leonard, based on a story by Jack Leonard, Marion Wolf. **Producer**: William Grady, Jr. **Director of Photography**: Harold Lipstein. **Music**: Rudolph G. Kopp. **Art Directors**: Cedric Gibbons, Malcolm Brown. **Editor**: Conrad A. Nervig. **Cast**: Vittorio Gassman (Jory), Barry Sullivan (Lieutenant Tunner), Polly Bergen (Janet Tunner), William Conrad (Goodwin), Mary Zavian (Ella), Robert Burton (Warden Keeley), Harry Shannon (Sheriff Brown), Jonathan Cott (Deputy Davis). **Released**: Metro-Goldwyn-Mayer, May 8. 80 minutes.

Released from prison solitary, a young Creole, Jory, is questioned by Lieutenant Tunner about his accomplices in a robbery in which the prisoner claims he was duped into participation. While being moved to another prison, Jory escapes and Tunner travels to a Southern bayou hometown to find him. When Jory later arrives at his shack, Tunner is waiting to arrest him but uncuffs Jory so he can reunite with his wife and the son. Jory manages to escape back into the swamp. Chasing the escapee, Tunner drinks swamp water which causes him to hallucinate. After hospitalization, he returns to the swamp with his deputy Goodwin. While camping, they are frightened by an emaciated old woman calling out to a bird's spirit. Abandoned by Goodwin, Tunner finds Jory but gets trapped in quicksand from which Jory rescues him, although injuries now make Jory delirious and he unwittingly reveals the truth of the robbery, which exonerates him. Tunner returns Jory to prison to complete a light sentence.

Cry of the Hunted provides an exotic point of departure for the noir fundamentals of the repressed Everyman protagonist adrift in an unfamiliar, threatening underworld. Feeling trapped professionally, Lieutenant Tunner is a freedom-loving suburbanite who forges a mirror identity with a not-quite bad guy whom he must pursue through swamps, where police encounter resentful Creoles and later the more elemental threat of alligators. Hunter and hunted are relentlessly conjoined, through dialogue, visuals and structure, both equally prisoners of their circumstances. The pattern is set in the opening scene, where the two men are shown commonly trapped behind bars both actual and shadowy, in a fight which ends with them sitting side by side, smoking. Before the pursuit begins, "home" is the description given by Tunner for the two men's very different—geographically, if not spiritually—destinations. We are introduced to Jory in an extraordinarily noir visual of a pillbox slit of light on his eyes in otherwise deep shadow. Aesthetically this is an anomaly in this bright film, but director Lewis maintains pacing by always finding fresh visual angles. He explicitly problematizes the South for its inhumanity in a filmic manner that draws successfully on the legacy of the 1930s chain gang movie cycle.

Despite its overall lack of noir visuals, tensions are heightened by an extraordinary dream sequence which firmly ties this film to the noir canon, as in *The Lady from Shanghai*, whose famous mirror-shooting it reprises when Tunner explodes a series of expanding shadows of Jory in a similarly fruitless fashion. This sequence is fogbound in gauzy white mist, a motif of almost heavenly purity which Lewis used similarly in the climax of *Gun Crazy*.

Overlooked in the director's oeuvre, its mix of otherworldly and personal issues merits wider recognition for *Cry of the Hunted*. **RSW**

CRY VENGEANCE (1954)

Director: Mark Stevens. **Screenplay**: Warren Douglas and George Bricker. **Producer**: Lindsley Parsons. **Director of Photography**: William A. Sickner. **Art Director**: Dave Milton. **Music**: Paul Dunlap. **Editor**: Elmo Veron. **Cast**: Mark Stevens (Vic Barron), Martha Hyer (Peggy Harding), Skip Homeier (Roxey), Joan Vohs (Lily Arnold), Douglas Kennedy (Tino Morelli), Cheryl Callaway (Marie Morelli), Mort Mills (Johnny Blue-Eyes), Warren Douglas (Mike Walters), Lewis Martin (Dick Buda), Don Haggerty (Lt. Pat Ryan), John Doucette (Red Miller), Dorothy Kennedy (Emily Miller). **Released**: Allied Artists, November 21. 82 minutes.

Ex-cop Vic Barron is released from prison. Framed by local San Francisco mobsters and his family murdered in a car bomb explosion, Vic is filled with hatred and vengeance. He heads for Alaska when he discovers that the mobster he considers responsible, Tino Morelli, is living in Ketchikan, Alaska with his young daughter Marie. There he stalks Tino and his daughter. With the help of Peggy Harding, a local bar owner, he discovers that Tino did not order the murder of his family and that the true murderer was the hitman, Roxey. However, Roxey has followed Vic and murders Tino. But before Roxey can murder Vic too, he wounds him in a shoot-out and then tries to save him as he falls from a bridge. Vic returns to San Francisco after a farewell to Peggy and Tino's orphaned daughter. The film ends with a hint that he may return.

This protagonist's desire for vengeance has the fearful symmetry of an Old Testament story, especially since Vic's signature line in the film is "I never forget." In many ways *Cry Vengeance* is a sequel to *The Dark Corner,* in which Stevens played the "all dead inside" detective Bradford Galt. However, as both director and star in *Cry Vengeance,* Stevens adds further levels of psychic and physical suffering. Vic Barron is literally and figuratively "eating himself up inside." He compulsively chews on his nails and lips; walks stoop-shouldered as if racked by body pains and is propelled by an inner fury with outbursts of violence shaking his wiry frame. Even sympathetic bar owner Peggy notices immediately that he has "hate behind [his] eyes."

Cry Vengeance: *Mark Stevens as Vic Barron.*

Compounding the moral ambiguity and irony of Vic Barron's mission (which includes the murder of not only mobster Tino Morelli but his young daughter as well), the audience learns that single father Tino has reformed his life in the wilds of Ketchikan, Alaska (the film is shot partially on location there) and is now a devoted father to his child. And to add even more to the irony, the filmmakers reveal that Tino was not the one who ordered the murder of Stevens family. A particularly unsettling scene filled with this moral ambiguity and irony is the one in which Vic approaches Tino's innocent daughter and gives her a bullet for her father. As the film progresses the bucolic environment coupled with the sympathetic ministrations of the level-headed Peggy have a calming effect on the furious Vic. So when he next approaches Tino's daughter, she shakes his resolve by her loving acceptance of him, externalized by her act of kissing his scarred face. Forced to realize that he has been reduced to Roxey's level and no better than this maniac who murdered his own family, Vic abandons his mission and returns to San Francisco, more balanced but still haunted by his past. **JU**

D.O.A. (1950)

Director: Rudolph Maté. **Screenplay**: Russell Rouse and Clarence Greene. **Producers**: Leo C. Popkin, Harry M. Popkin. **Director of Photography**: Ernest Laszlo. **Music**: Dimitri Tiomkin. **Art Director**: Duncan Cramer. **Editor**: Arthur H. Nadel. **Cast**: Edmond O'Brien (Frank Bigelow), Pamela Britton (Paula Gibson), Luther Adler (Majak), Beverly Campbell (Miss Foster), Lynn Baggett (Mrs. Philips), William Ching (Halliday), Henry Hart (Stanley Philips), Neville Brand (Chester), Laurette Luez (Marla Rakubian), Jess Kirkpatrick (Sam), Cay Forrester (Sue), Virginia Lee (Jeanie), Michael Ross (Dave). **Location**: Los Angeles and San Francisco, California. **Completed**: November 1949. **Released**: United Artists, April 30. 83 minutes.

Frank Bigelow, a certified public accountant, leaves his hometown of Banning, California, for a vacation in San Francisco. After enjoying a night on the town, he feels ill the next day and undergoes a medical examination. The doctor informs him that he has suffered radiation poisoning and has only a few days to live. While preparations are made to admit him to a hospital, Bigelow escapes and is determined to find his killers. Calling his fiancée and secretary, Paula, Bigelow traces a shipment of iridium, which he notarized, and learns it later fell into criminal hands. At the Los Angeles firm that handled the shipment's transportation, he discovers that the company's boss at the time of the iridium shipment has also mysteriously died of radioactivity exposure. Suspecting the same people are responsible for his poisoning, Bigelow is confronted by the actual killer. After a frenetic chase through Los Angeles, Bigelow kills his assassin and explains his story to the police just before his death.

D.O.A is an unusually cynical noir film. The concept of a murder victim who functions as his own detective combined with the coincidental nature of the murder motive and entire incident, gives *D.O.A.* a unique point of view. Directed by Rudolph Maté, the film is fast-paced and designed as a thriller. *D.O.A.* becomes noir through certain key sequences. After a conventional beginning, the basic atmosphere of the film is significantly reversed during a scene in a sleazy, water-front nightclub. The intense use of jazz music, interpreted through the tight close-ups of sweating musicians caught up in the fury of their music combines with images of patrons lost in the pounding jazz rhythms and approaches a chaotic climax. This chaos is compromised when an unseen assassin exploits the exotic locale as a screen and poisons an unsuspecting witness to an earlier crime. As the doomed Frank Bigelow, Edmond O'Brien is transformed from an ordinary man into an obsessed avenger bent on discovering the reason behind his imminent death. His quest leads him into an ever-darkening nightmare world filled with grotesque and crazed

D.O.A.: *Chester (Neville Brand) threatens Frank Bigelow (Edmond O'Brien).*

people. Chester, played by Neville Brand, is the archetypal noir killer, who is a caricature of psychosis.

The inspiration for *D.O.A.* comes from a 1931 German film entitled *Der Mann, Der Seinen Morder Sucht*, directed by Robert Siodmak, which deals with a dying man's attempt to discover the cause of his approaching unnatural demise. Utilizing this basic story, *D.O.A.* is a prime example of a thriller accentuated by factors of cynicism, alienation, chaos, and the corrupt nature of society to convey a dark vision of post-atom bomb America. This noir vision remains solid throughout the film except for the strangely humorous quality provided by Dimitri Tiomkin's music. His intent in offering inappropriate musical reinforcements to Bigelow's wolfish womanizing combined with a pretentious classical score, works to vitiate the chaotic atmosphere created in the jazz sequence. However, the portrait of Bigelow and the nightmarish world into which he stumbles transcend Tiomkin's score to evoke the sordid underworld of film noir. *D.O.A.* may not be a perfect film noir, yet it typifies the hopeless plight of people manipulated by forces they are unable to control or comprehend; and it is through this existential outlook that *D.O.A.* contributes to the noir canon. **CM**

THE DAMNED DON'T CRY (1950)

Director: Vincent Sherman. **Screenplay**: Harold Medford and Jerome Weidman based on a story by Gertrude Walker. **Producer**: Jerry Wald. **Director of Photography**: Ted McCord. **Music**: Daniele Amfitheatrof. **Art Director**: Robert Haas. **Editor**: Rudi Fehr. **Cast**: Joan Crawford (Ethel Whitehead/Loma Hansen Forbes), David Brian (George Castleman), Steve Cochran (Nick Prenta), Kent Smith

Warner Bros. flaming stars of 'Flamingo Road' meet in another scarlet alley!

JOAN CRAWFORD · DAVID BRIAN
The Damned Don't Cry!

(Martin Blackford), Hugh Sanders (Grady), Selena Royle (Patricia Longworth), Jacqueline de Wit (Sandra), Morris Ankrum (Mr. Whitehead), Sara Perry (Mrs. Whitehead), Richard Egan (Roy), Jimmy Moss (Tommy), Edith Evanson (Mrs. Castleman), Eddie Marr (Walter Talbot). **Released**: Warner Bros., May 13. 103 minutes.

After her young son Tommy dies, Ethel Whitehead leaves her husband Roy and moves to New York City. Capitalizing upon her beauty, Ethel soon advances from cigar store clerk to a modeling job. Advised to accept "paid dates" with rich men of sinister backgrounds, Ethel soon enters the inner circle of George Castleman, a refined but ruthless gangster. He finances her transformation into a socially prominent Texas heiress dubbed "Lorna Hansen Forbes. " She becomes his mistress as well as one of his lackeys and is soon directed to trap Nick Prenta, a rebellious member of Castleman's gang. But Lorna falls in love with Nick and attempts to sabotage Castleman's plans. She is warned against this by Blackford, an accountant she recommended to the syndicate. Castleman arrives and kills Nick despite Lorna's attempt to save him. Blackford persuades Castleman that Lorna is still a useful tool while she escapes to her parents' home. Following her, Castleman wounds Lorna but he is then killed by the pursuing Blackford. Although freed of criminal ties, Lorna's future is uncertain and she is beyond caring.

The problems of the protagonist, Ethel, in The *Damned Don't Cry* are those of survival in face of class oppression and economic misery. The opening scene's giant oil rigs appear as carnivorous dragons hovering over the squalid home of Ethel's parents and clearly express the family's situation. Later, Castleman's dirty money is equated with further oppression and exploitation, yet that offers comfort. Like many film noir, this film takes a view of circumstance that is at once darkly romantic and deterministic. From the universe presented in the film, it would appear that there are only two choices in life: honest but grinding poverty or ill-gotten opulence. Although Ethel's willful decision to follow the high life and damn the consequences is represented as hers alone throughout the film, it is reinforced by the identical behavior of her new friends Sandra and Patricia.

Joan Crawford's portrayal of the unsophisticated but ambitious young woman who undergoes a metamorphosis into an elegant society lady is striking. At first modest and unpreten-tious, Ethel soon achieves a higher status than any of the girl-friends who helped her new career get started. She learns to hide her disgust so well that she eventually believes herself above any passion except selfishness, and equally impervious to disaster. Becoming Lorna, and sunning herself luxuriously at poolside, her serenity is disrupted when Blackford appears. The shot is a noir classic as the man's shadow cast over Lorna's gracious form externalizes the pall over her soul. Then, in a dynamic close-up, she looks up and the sunlight's glare brilliantly bounces off her sunglasses. Lorna cannot just ignore this messenger's presence and must take off her blinders to confront the ugly reality of consequences. The noir plot takes a twist and suddenly, she realizes her emotions are not dead and that she must stop the threat to Nick's life. When she fails, Lorna is merely an empty shell. Returning to her parents' home and confronting Castleman, she appears not to care what occurs. Most noir protagonists are disillusioned with life, and many are misanthropic; but few noir characters trace Ethel/Lorna's development from disillusionment with the romantic notions of love and family to an ultimate and complete disillusionment with oneself. In *The Damned Don't Cry,* the noir protagonist realizes she has destroyed herself because, thinking it irrelevant, she knowingly bartered her soul for trinkets. **EM & EW**

DANGER SIGNAL (1945)

Director: Robert Florey. **Screenplay**: Adele Comandini and Graham Baker based on the novel by Phyllis Bottome. **Producer**: William Jacobs. **Director of Photography**: James Wong Howe. **Music**: Adolph Deutsch. **Art Director**: Stanley Fleischer. **Editor**: Frank Magee. **Cast**: Faye Emerson (Hilda Fenchurch), Zachary Scott (Ronnie Mason/Marsh), Dick Erdman (Bunkie Taylor), Rosemary DeCamp (Dr. Silla), Bruce Bennett (Dr. Andrew Lang), Mona Freeman (Anne Fenchurch), John Ridgely (Thomas Turner), Mary Servoss (Mrs. Fenchurch), Joyce Compton (Katie), Virginia Sale (Mrs. Crockett). **Completed**: May 22, 1945. **Released**: Warner Bros., November 14. 78 minutes.

Ronnie Mason is a smooth scoundrel who makes his living by preying on unhappy women. He steals the wedding ring and money from a young woman who is lying dead in an Eastern hotel room, leaves a suicide note and then escapes with his loot through the window. The newspapers report the death as a suicide but the woman's husband, Thomas Turner, is suspicious of her boyfriend, a mysterious artist known as Mason. Mason takes a bus to Los Angeles, steals a service pin from a sleeping passenger, and disguises himself as an injured veteran named Ron Marsh. He rents a room in the Fenchurch house occupied by Hilda, a former stenographer, Anne, her spirited teen-age sister and their mother. Although Hilda has an established courtship with Dr. Andrew Lang, a typical absent-minded professor, she succumbs easily to Ronnie's persuasive charms. But when Ronnie learns that Anne will soon receive a large inheritance, he romances her which leaves Hilda broken-hearted and suspicious. She confides her, troubles to her friend, Dr. Silla, a psychoanalyst who quickly discerns Ronnie's personality type. Anne refuses to heed Hilda's warnings, so Hilda and Dr. Silla scheme to get Ronnie alone at Silla's beach house where they can break him down. Hilda decides at the last moment to poison Ronnie while they are both alone at the beach house. Her

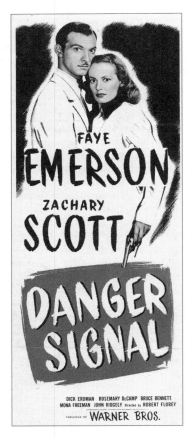

plan is discovered by Dr. Silla and, with Dr. Lang, she rushes to stop Hilda. Meanwhile Hilda discovers she cannot commit a murder. Ronnie leaves, only to encounter Mr. Turner, the husband of the dead woman. Attempting to flee, Ronnie falls to his death from a cliff.

Danger Signal seems little more than an attempt to rework the essential ingredients of Hitchcock's *Shadow of a Doubt* in an urban setting. Regrettably, it contains little of its predecessor's suspense and develops so slowly that even the abrupt increase in its tempo by using the wheel-screeching race against time at the conclusion is largely ineffective. Scott can always be relied on to play a cad, as can Bennett as a stalwart if somewhat stiff hero. An experienced director of French origins, Robert Florey was well positioned to take advantage of the talents of James Wong Howe, and it is its visuals (especially its opening sequence) more than anything else that gives *Danger Signal* its noir flavor. **BP**

DANGEROUS PASSAGE (1944)

Director: William A. Berke. **Screenplay**: Geoffrey Holmes [Daniel Mainwaring]. **Producer**: William H. Pine, William C. Thomas [both uncredited]. **Director of Photography**: Fred Jackman Jr.. **Music**: Alexander Laszlo. **Production Designer**: Frank Paul Sylos. **Editor**: Henry Adams. **Cast**: Robert Lowery (Joe Beck), Phyllis Brooks (Nita Paxton), Charles Arnt (Daniel Bergstrom), Jack La Rue (Mike Zomano), John Eldredge (Vaughn), Victor Kilian (Buck Harris, 1st Mate), Alec Craig (Dawson, the Steward), William Edmunds (Captain Saul). **Released**: Paramount, December 18. 60 minutes.

Joe Beck, a young fortune-hunter working in Central America, receives news that his grandfather has died. After displaying his identity papers to a sleazy lawyer named Bergstrom he is informed that his grandfather has left him a fortune but he must get up to Galveston with his papers in order to collect. Leaving Bergstrom's office, he is attacked by a swarthy individual later identified as Mike Zomano who intends to knife him and steal his papers. They tussle and both fall off the pier into the ocean, but Joe alone is helped back onto land by Dawson, a steward on a cargo ship departing for points north that very evening. Joe is brought to the captain and manages to book passage on the ship. Among the tiny venue of passengers is Anita, a night club performer who has attracted Joe's attention and Vaughn, a middle-aged businessman with whom she is entangled and who resents Joe's presence on the ship. Anita reveals that she has been helping her friend Dawson, an insurance investigator, to gain evidence against Vaughn and Capt. Saul, who were part of an insurance scam leading to the destruction of several cargo ships. When Bergstrom and Zomano (who is posing as Joe Beck) attempt to steal his papers, Joe tells them that he has mailed them to himself in Galveston. Meanwhile Saul successfully grounds the ship on some rocks and manages to escape with the crew on the one good lifeboat, leaving Bergstrom, Zomano, Joe and Anita behind on the slowly sinking ship. Joe survives and traces Anita to her apartment, where she is being held captive by the two men, and in the ensuing melee Joe shoots Zomano and Bergstrom, under gunpoint, and calls the police. Joe, in turn, realizes that Anita only had his best interests at heart.

Dangerous Passage is a rather trite, low budget thriller whose main interest is in the fact that it was written by Daniel Mainwaring, a one-finger exercise for his later novel and screenplay of *Out of the Past*. As a writer, Mainwaring was a major contributor to the film noir and his professed admiration for Dashiell Hammett is evidenced here in the way his screenplay borrows liberally from *The Maltese Falcon*. Anita's music box, like the falcon itself, ultimately hides the very documents whose possession promises great wealth. Anita herself, like Brigid O'Shaughnessy before her, is a woman of mystery and ambiguous morality, though she ends up finally on the right side of the scales. And in Bergstrom and Zomano we have an interesting variation on Gutman and Wilmer. As the "gunsel" Jack LaRue as Zomano literally towers over the rest of the cast, unlike the diminutive Elisha Cook, Jr. And yet, in each and every encounter with Beck, Zomano is undone. On the other hand, Charles Arnt (veteran of many a film noir) as Bergstrom is much smaller than the portentous Sydney Greenstreet, yet his laughter is equally distinctive, his pomposity equally appealing, his flattery equally disarming. Indeed, this film only really comes to life during his scenes. Finally, the scene in which Joe and Anita are serenaded by a group of Mexican musicians on the beach contains the seeds of those wonderful moments that Kathy and Jeff spend in Mexico in *Out of the Past*. It is unfortunate that this film fails to live up to the promise of that early scene in which Beck walks through the fog-ridden night, danger lurking around every corner—a potential for violence that is implicit in any film that can accurately be described as a film noir. **BP**

DARK CITY (1950)

Director: William Dieterle. **Screenplay**: John Meredyth Lucas and Larry Marcus, with contributions from Leonardo Bercovici and adapted by Ketti Frings based on the story "No Escape" by Marcus. **Producer**. Hal Wallis. **Director of Photography**: Victor Milner. **Music**: Franz Waxman. **Art Directors**: Hans Dreier, Franz Bachelin. **Editor**: Warren Low. **Cast**: Charlton Heston (Danny Haley), Lizabeth Scott (Fran), Viveca Lindfors (Victoria Winant), Dean Jagger (Capt. Garvey), Don DeFore (Arthur Winant), Jack Webb (Augie), Ed Begley (Barney), Henry Morgan (Soldier), Walter Sande (Swede), Mark Keuning (Billy Winant), Mike Mazurki (Sidney Winant), Stanley Prager (Sammy), Walter Burke (Bartender). **Locations**: Los Angeles and Las Vegas. **Completed**: May 10, 1950. **Released**: Paramount, October 18. 98 minutes.

After losing a considerable sum of money to Danny Haley in a somewhat questionable poker game, Arthur Winant commits suicide. This situation forces the gambling racketeers to hesitate before cashing a check signed over to them by the now dead Winant. Tension begins to mount when another gambler is found murdered, his limp body dangling grotesquely from a thin cord. Eventually Haley goes to visit Winant's widow. Once there, he confirms suspicions that Winant's brother, Sidney, is a homicidal maniac. Haley's tough exterior is penetrated by Victoria Winant's dedication to her family and struggle to make a home for her fatherless son. Haley travels to Las Vegas in an attempt to win some money to ease her problems. Ultimately, Sidney is apprehended and the nightmare of terror is finally put to an end.

The basic premise of *Dark City* is certainly noir. Also, the characteristic grotesques are present: Ed Begley's snarling gambler, Barney; Jack Webb's gutless small-time hood, Augie; and Mazurki's diabolical killer, Sidney. There is a cinematic tension and atmosphere that recalls the crisp, dark streets and unsavory elements of films like *Street with No Name*, *Where the Sidewalk Ends* and even *T-Men*. Actor Charlton Heston rejects the potent nature of his physical presence to personify the classy, but ultimately punk gambler, Danny Haley. All the basic noir elements are there. Nonetheless, this film has an overriding sense of hope and compassion, which leads *Dark City* away from the noir world. While Lizabeth Scott, as Haley's girl friend, spends most of her time singing dull and raspy torch songs for a living, there is no surrendering to the noir angst and aura of helplessness. And Haley's transformation into a hero as the

film moves toward its climax displaces much of the noir feeling which has been injected by Director William Dieterle and cameraman Victor Milner. *Dark City* is just a peek into the noir world because it lacks the fatal emphasis of the noir ethos. **CM**

THE DARK CORNER (1946)

Director: Henry Hathaway. **Screenplay**: Jay Dratler and Bernard Schoenfeld based on the short story by Leo Rosten. **Producer**: Fred Kohlmar. **Director of Photography**: Joe MacDonald. **Music**: Cyril Mockridge. **Art Directors**. James Basevi, Leland Fuller. **Editor**: J. Watson Webb. **Cast**: Mark Stevens (Bradford Galt), Lucille Ball (Kathleen), Clifton Webb (Hardy Cathcart), William Bendix (White Suit), Kurt Kreuger (Tony Jardine), Cathy Downs (Mari Cathcart), Reed Hadley (Lt. Frank Reeves), Constance Collier (Mrs. Kingsley), Eddie Heywood and His Orchestra (Themselves), Molly Lamont (Lucy Wilding), John Russell (Policeman). **Released**: 20th Century-Fox, April 9. 99 minutes.

Bradford Galt, a private detective released from jail after being framed for a crime by his ex-partner Tony Jardine, finds himself followed by a man in a white suit for unknown reasons, but suspects Jardine is behind it. Actually, a vicious and cultured art dealer, Hardy Cathcart, has hired "White Suit" to tail Galt in the hopes that this will provoke him into murdering Jardine, who is having an affair with Cathcart's beautiful wife, Mari. But Galt does not act against Jardine, so Cathcart has "White Suit" kill his wife's lover. The body is taken into Galt's apartment where a maid finds it. While Galt dodges the police, Cathcart double crosses "White Suit" and pushes him out of a skyscraper window. Yet, with the help of his secretary, Kathleen, Galt ties Cathcart into the crime and confronts him at his art gallery. Mari walks in and after listening to Galt's accusations is convinced that her husband is the murderer. Meanwhile, Cathcart prepares to kill Galt himself and report him as a robber, but Mari intervenes and shoots her husband first.

Released in 1946, *The Dark Corner,* is in many ways the prototypical reflection of postwar malaise in film noir and, albeit metaphorically, a more effective statement about the price of social readjustment than such a self-conscious film as *The Best Years of Our Lives.* Like the protagonists of *Nobody Lives Forever* and *Somewhere In The Night,* Bradford Galt is discharged before the film begins. Unlike them, his release is not from the Army but from prison. Initially, Galt, portrayed with terse sullenness by Mark Stevens, attempts to reassume his role as a tough private detective. Harassed by the police and bitterly unable to reconcile himself to his incarceration after betrayal by a partner, Galt suddenly finds himself framed again, this time by unknown enemies. The immediate result is a cry of existential anguish, captured in the remark to his secretary: "I feel all dead inside. I'm backed up in a dark corner and I don't know who's hitting me."

The extreme nature of Galt's alienation must be partially attributed by the viewer to events that occurred before the film began. By invoking the dark past as the fundamental cause of Galt's afflictions, the narrative acquires deterministic overtones that reinforce the hopelessness of Galt's position in his "dark corner." Darkness becomes the pervasive motif of Galt's world. Although the streets he walks are frequently daylit and Galt's nemesis dresses in a white suit, his office and apartment are filled with ominous shadows. They leave isolated wedges of light on the back walls and bisect figures and faces. This visual instability, conveyed by cinematographer MacDonald's broken shafts of crosslight, is incorporated by director Hathaway into a pattern of narrative irony that balances Galt's uncertainty against Cathcart's intellectual arrogance and amoral self-assurance. Although he cannot know of its intensity, Cathcart assumes the existence of Galt's anguish. In fact, he regards and even relishes it with the self-satisfaction of an author who has created a convincing portrait of a tormented character. Cathcart himself is more fully ensnared by the narrative of *The Dark Corner* than he realizes. Despite his ruthless murder of "White Suit," his obsession with the melodrama he has scripted causes him to take too much time with Galt. Mari's subsequent intrusion and Cathcart's destruction are not part of a victory of proletarianism over decadent intellectualism, as much as actuality and emotion represented by Gait's desperation and Mari's hatred of the theatricality and effete mannerism of Cathcart. As Mari pitilessly empties her gun into Cathcart's body, Galt is stripped of any sense of triumph over those dark forces afflicting him and is allowed only relief that they have of their own abated. **AS**

THE DARK MIRROR (1946)

Director: Robert Siodmak. **Producer and Screenplay**: Nunnally Johnson based on a story by Vladimir Pozner. **Director of Photography**: Milton Krasner. **Music**: Dimitri Tiomkin. **Production Designer**: Duncan Cramer. **Editor**: Ernest Nims. **Cast**: Olivia De Havilland (Terry Collins/Ruth Collins), Lew Ayres (Dr. Scott Elliott), Thomas Mitchell (Detective Stevenson), Dick Long (Rusty), Charles Evans (District Attorney Girard), Garry Owen (Franklin), Lester Allen (George Benson), Lela Bliss (Mrs. Didriksen), Marta Nfitrovich (Miss Beade), Amelita Ward (Photo Double). **Completed**: March 29, 1946. **Released**: Univeral October 18. 85 minutes

Dark Mirror: *Det. Stevenson (Thomas Mitchell) questions the twin sixters, Terry and Ruth (Olivia de Havilland).*

The police scrutinize a set of mature identical twins, Terry and Ruth Collins, when one of the ladies' gentleman admirers is found dead. Although the twins are physically identical, they have complete opposite personalities. Ruth is a kind, passive, and loving person, but Terry is a ruthless, aggressive, and spiteful human being. A psychologist, Dr. Elliott, begins talking to the women in the hopes of discovering if either twin was responsible for the murder. Finding the pressures of this scrutiny too great, the evil sister plans to do away with her sweeter counterpart and take her place. The plan almost succeeds. Fortunately, the psychologist is able to detect slight differences in their characters, the police close in, and Terry is revealed as the murderess.

The Dark Mirror reflects noir attitudes and style mainly through Robert Siodmak's capable direction. His particular interest in the aberrant behavior of disturbed minds, as explored in his earlier *Spiral Staircase,* is underscored to a much greater extent in *The Dark Mirror's* contemporary, urban setting. There is none of the visual objectifications that made the *Spiral Staircase* a fine example of American gothic filmmaking. Rather, Siodmak deals with the subject of the doppelganger. The defining noir motif in this film is the juxtaposition of twisted implications arising when two people who are seemingly identical have completely different psychological attitudes. This use of the double had been a classic film motif since the 1913 film *The Student of Prague.* However, this expressionistic device of revealing the dark side of people's personalities found little exposure in the films of that period. For the most part American noir films substitute mirror images and reflections for the actual doppelganger. In *The Dark Mirror,* with its title hinting at the perverse imagery, Siodmak returned to the simple double image. The Collins twins are characterized through a facile interpretation of Freudianism, which is prevalent in many noir films. Lost and confused in a world of alienation and depression, the twins spin through a macabre dance of rejection and isolation. **CM**

DARK PASSAGE (1947)

Director: Delmer Daves. **Screenplay**: Delmer Daves based on the novel by David Goodis. **Producer**: Jerry Wald. **Director of Photography**: Sid Hickox. **Music**: Franz Waxman. **Art Director**: Charles H. Clarke. **Editor**: David Weisbart. **Cast**: Humphrey Bogart (Vincent Parry), Lauren Bacall (Irene Jansen), Bruce Bennett (Bob), Agnes Moorehead (Madge Rapo), Tom D'Andrea (Taxi Driver), Clifton Young (Baker), Douglas Kennedy (Detective), Rory Mallinson (George Fellsinger), Houseley Stevenson (Dr. Walter Coley). **Location**: San Francisco. **Completed**: January 30, 1947. **Released**: Warner Bros., September 27. 106 minutes.

Vincent Parry, wrongly convicted of his wife's murder, escapes from San Quentin prison. Irene, a beautiful and wealthy San Francisco artist, finds him and offers refuge. However, while Irene is out, her friend Madge drops by, knocking on the door and calling out for Irene. Vincent recognizes the woman's voice because she was coincidentally his wife's friend. It was Madge's false testimony that helped to convict him. Vincent tells Madge to go away, and she, puzzled, obeys. Soon Vincent undergoes plastic surgery to construct a "new face." A blackmailing punk contacts Vincent and is accidentally killed. Vincent then confronts Madge with his knowledge that she is the murderer of his wife. Madge commits suicide rather than confess to the police. Preparing to leave the country alone, Vincent reconsiders and calls Irene. They rendezvous in Peru and celebrate beginning a new life.

Dark Passage is an interesting film that carries its basic visual premise too far. The exclusive use of the first person point-of-view camera for the first half of the film is unusual, but also somewhat unsuccessful at invoking the physical existence of a protagonist. The film is thirty minutes old before even a shadowed glimpse of Bogart's figure, as Vincent Parry, is seen; and it is a full sixty-two minutes before his "new" face appears on the screen. However, the subjective camera is an interesting device and more integral to this film's plot than that of *Lady in the Lake*, which used this camera p.o.v. technique the previous year. Thirty-two pages of production notes were originally appended to the script of *Dark Passage* tackling special problems such as achieving "natural" effects for the first person point-of-view shots, concerning the postures of sitting, getting up and lying down. Suggestions were made to accommodate set construction and enhance camera

effects, including a lens mask (not used in the final film) to simulate eyelids and lashes. The initial effect of this point-of-view device actually does involve the viewer emotionally and forces identification with Vincent while he rolls down a hill and escapes. However, the device diminishes in impact as it continues far beyond novelty value.

Audience identification is also weakened by the fact that Vincent's voice and narration is so easily recognizable as Bogart's. The viewer knows what Vincent looks like all along. A less-well known actor or less identifiable voice might have been better suited to this visual premise. Some low-key lighting and San Francisco's fog and rain add to the noir atmosphere created by the point-of-view camera; but this film is not fully immersed in the noir style. Vincent is an innocent man framed not by a seductive femme but by a spider-woman type, stalked not only by a vulturous punk but also by the police, whose net draws close. However, unlike the central figure in many noir films, Vincent is not entangled in this net through his own weakness or stubbornness; all of the causality is external. The more characteristic noir figures generate much of their own misery through misconceptions or dogged persistence, and efforts of extrication only entangle them more hopelessly into dangerous circumstances. These external pressures are further mitigated in *Dark Passage* by Irene, who generously provides Vincent with the means to escape and with whom he is reunited at the end of the film. Vincent's union with his female rescuer in the South American resort might seem both unearned and undeserved, because he was at least the catalyst, if not the cause, of the two semi-accidental deaths of Madge and Baker, and the reason for another murder. It is more typical for the noir protagonist to suffer some less delightful consequences of fear, guilt, and legal retribution. In spite of the attempt to exploit noir stylistic devices, this film ultimately lacks much of the internal structure of human weakness and fatalism central to a complete film noir. **EM**

THE DARK PAST (1948)

Director: Rudolph Maté. **Screenplay**: Philip MacDonald, Michael Blankfort and Albert Duffy adapted by Malvin Wald and Oscar Saul based on the play *Blind Alley* by James Warwick. **Producer**: Buddy Adler. **Director of Photography**: Joseph Walker. **Music**: George Duning. **Art Director**: Cary Odell. **Editor**: Viola Lawrence. **Cast**: William Holden (Al Walker), Nina Foch (Betty), Lee J. Cobb (Dr.

Andrew Collins), Adele Jergens (Laura Stevens), Stephen Dunne (Owen Talbot), Lois Maxwell (Ruth Collins), Barry Kroeger (Mike), Steven Geray (Professor Fred Linder), Wilton Graff (Frank Stevens), Robert Osterloh (Pete), Kathryn Card (Nora), Bobby Hyatt (Bobby), Ellen Corby (Agnes), Charles Cane (Sheriff), Robert B. Williams (Williams). **Completed**: June 21, 1948. **Released**: Columbia, December 22. 74 minutes.

Andrew Collins explains to the police why criminals should be rehabilitated through careful psychiatric treatment by relating a personal experience. Dr. Collins and his wife Ruth are spending a weekend at their lakeside cabin with their son Bobby, and their friends, Frank and Laura Stevens. They are awaiting the arrival of Fred Linder when a radio news bulletin announces that a notorious killer, Al Walker, has escaped from jail. Suddenly the criminal and his girl friend, Betty, and two henchmen, Mike and Pete, intrude on the vacationers and hold them hostage while awaiting transportation to freedom. Through the course of their terror, Dr. Collins gradually unravels the motivation behind Al's behavior. The realization that he was responsible for his father's death, when he betrayed the man to the police, changes Al and he cannot fire the trigger of his gun when confronted by the police. He and his gang are captured and the vacationers are safe.

A remake of the 1939 film *Blind Alley*, *The Dark Past* is a prime example of Hollywood's simplification of Freudian psychology. Using a pop analysis of dreams to serve as the basis for criminal and aberrant psychological problems, *The Dark Past* follows in the tradition of Alfred Hitchcock's morose *Spellbound*. Dream sequences in *The Dark Past* borrow from avant-garde surrealist films by projecting the sequence in its negative form. William Holden is atypically crude in his performance of the tough-guy criminal, Al. **CM**

DARK WATERS (1944)

Director: Andre De Toth. **Screenplay**: Frank Cockrell, Marian Cockrell, Joan Harrison. **Producer**: Benedict Bogeaus. **Executive Producer**: James Nasser. **Director of Photography**: John Mescall, Archie Stout. **Music**: Miklós Rózsa. **Art Director**: Charles Olds. **Editor**: James Smith. **Cast**: Merle Oberon (Leslie Calvin), Franchot Tone (Dr. George Grover), Thomas Mitchell (Mr. Sydney), Fay Bainter (Aunt Emily), Elisha Cook Jr. (Cleeve), John Qualen (Uncle Norbert), Rex Ingram (Pearson Jackson), Nina Mae McKinney (Florella), Odette Myrtil (Mama Boudreaux), Eugene Borden (Papa Boudreaux). **Released**: United Artists, November 21. 90 minutes.

Leslie is traumatized and alone after surviving a submarine attack while on a cruise with her parents. They are killed and she has no friends who can help her. Although she has never met her only relatives, Aunt Emily and Uncle Norbert, she writes to them from her New Orleans hospital bed. They invite her to live with them on a defunct plantation in the Louisiana backwoods. George, a local doctor, meets her and immediately lets her know he is attracted to her. At the estate, the slimy Cleeve and the malevolent Sydney keep unnerving her with reminders of her tragedy at sea. Because strange incidents at night make her think she is losing her mind, she turns down George's marriage proposal. She learns the incidents are all part of an elaborate hoax from a day laborer, Pearson, who is then murdered. She discovers

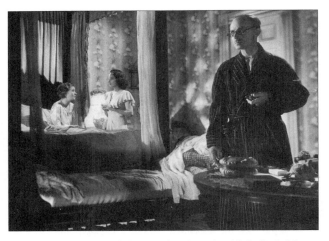

Dark Waters: *Aunt Emily (Faye Bainter) speaks with Leslie Calvin (Merle Oberon) while Uncle Norbert (John Qualen) listens..*

Emily and Norbert are imposters, and that Cleeve killed her true relatives. It is not her sanity that is at risk, but her life. Sydney has led a plot to kill her and sell her estate. Cleeve and Sydney take Leslie and George out on a boat to kill them. However, the young lovers escape into the bayou. After Cleeve dies horribly in quicksand, Sydney gives himself up to George who leads Leslie to safety.

Typically, before a woman-in-distress doubts her sanity, she feels fine. Later she believes she is losing her mind. Suspense is built on her growing fear of going mad. For example, this happens to Anna in *Gaslight*. In *Dark Waters*, however, Leslie's story has the reverse trajectory. At first, she is suffering from actual mental trauma. The plot is not about her decline, but her recovery. The film indicates the prescription for her cure is socializing. George takes Leslie to meet the Boudreaux, a happy Cajun family with six children, and she brightens up. Next, he takes her to a "fais do do" (a Cajun community square dance). Although Emily and Sydney protest against her going, George insists. When Leslie arrives, she scowls and mutters, "I'm not going to have a good time." He asks her what she said and she speaks up, "I said I was going to have a good time!" Moreover, she really does. These scenes may seem out of place. In fact, they are critical because they show Leslie's recovery requires her to enjoy living again, which happens through social interaction such as dancing.

Although the rise and fall of mental health for the woman-in-distress is mirrored in *Gaslight* and *Dark Waters*, these films take the opposite approach to suspense. Tension in *Gaslight* increases the longer Anna thinks she is cracking up. In contrast, Leslie finds out relatively fast she is not going crazy. Following some minor incidents that disturb her, Leslie's worst experience is hearing her name called from the bayou. She goes outside and runs into Pearson, who says he heard it, too. Suspense is sacrificed in *Dark Waters* in favor of having Leslie know she is not delusional. Furthermore, the noir style is associated with Leslie's actual predicament, which is her physical well being, not psychological plight. The style is insignificant in scenes where mind games are played on her. Instead, the strongest visual style occurs the night she finds herself a prisoner in the dark house. In an outstanding deep focus shot, she looks over the second floor banister and sees Sydney sitting under a lamp on the ground floor. Large shadows of the staircase supports rake across her like cell bars. She steps onto the veranda and finds Cleeve and Norbert each guarding one end of it. Shadows of vines entangle her. In the climax, George tells her to jump off the boat into the bayou. Recovered from the horror of the lifeboat, she jumps. Instead of water terrifying her with memories of death, it saves her. Contrary to the conclusion of *Gaslight,* Leslie does not learn she has been sane all along in *Dark Waters.* Instead, George asks her if she's "all right." She softly says she is. Behind her, he smiles, aware of what it means. Realizing they can be married, she beams and firmly says it again, "I'm all right!" Her recovery is complete. **DMH**

THE DAY THE EARTH STOOD STILL (1951)

Director: Robert Wise. **Screenplay**: Edmund North from short story "Farewell to the Master" by Harry Bates. **Producer**: Julian Blaustein. **Director of Photography**: Leo Tover. **Music**: Bernard Herrmann. **Art Director**: Addison Hehr, Lyle Wheeler. **Editor**: William Reynolds. **Cast**: Michael Rennie (Klaatu, a.k.a. Mr. Carpenter), Patricia Neal (Helen Benson), Hugh Marlowe (Tom Stevens), Sam Jaffe (Prof. Barnhardt), Billy Gray (Bobby Benson), Frances Bavier (Mrs. Barley), Lock Martin (Gort). **Released**: 20th Century-Fox, September. 28. 92 minutes.

When a saucer-shaped spaceship lands on a baseball field in D.C. one afternoon, it is quickly surrounded by curious spectators, the police, and the national guard. Eventually a humanoid alien in a spacesuit speaking perfect English emerges, followed by a giant robot. But when Klaatu, the alien, pulls a telescope out of his suit as a gift for the president, an overly-zealous GI wounds him and destroys the gift. Gort, the robot, immediately unvisors an eye-level disintegrating ray and eliminates all the army's weapons but is quickly frozen into immobility at a word from the wounded Klaatu. He is taken to Walter Reade hospital and there convinces a White House aide to have the president request a meeting of the world's leaders. When political divisions vitiate such a meeting, Klaatu escapes in civilian clothes, adopts the alias Carpenter, and seeks to learn more about humans. He takes up residence in a boarding house and is quickly befriended by Helen Benson, a war widow, and her young son, Bobby. With Bobby's help Klaatu meets with Prof. Barnhardt, a mathematician of Einsteinian stature, who states that he can use his influence to gather together many of the world's top scientists, philosophers and religious leaders once Klaatu has demonstrated to the world the power he has at his command. That evening Klaatu enters the guarded ship with Gort's help and communicates with his home planet but Bobby has secretly followed him and reports the incident to his mother and her fiancé, Tom Stevens. Realizing that his identity has been compromised, Klaatu calls on Helen the next day at her office where the two are trapped alone together in an elevator. Klaatu explains that he has arranged for a global cutoff of electric power, except in critical areas, for a period of one-half hour. She agrees to help him get his message out to the world, but Tom, despite Helen's entreaties, insists on informing the army of Klaatu's whereabouts. As Helen and Klaatu attempt to get to Bernhardt's house in a cab, Klaatu has Helen mem-

orize an alien phrase that will stop Gort from destroying the earth in the event Klaatu is killed. Klaatu is indeed killed but Helen, though terrified, is able to get out the requisite phrase in the nick of time. Gort locks Helen on the spaceship, rescues Klaatu's cadaver from the jailhouse, and is able to reanimate him aboard the spaceship. Klaatu emerges from the impenetrable spaceship with Gort and Helen just as the world's leading personalities are assembling and is finally able to impart his message of peace.

The Day the Earth Stood Still has become a classic science fiction film and thus has evoked a good deal of explication, especially as regarding its potential as allegory (political, social, religious). Our purpose here is not to engage those controversies but rather to justify its inclusion in the noir cycle. A glance at the credits provides a good enough start, bearing in mind that in 1951 there still existed a distinct studio style and that Fox, together with RKO, betrays the mark of the most recognizable noir style. Composer Bernard Herrmann, of course, is a major contributor to film noir and much has already been written about this score and its use of the theremin to enhance its minatory aspect. By 1951 the theremin was already a stable of noir scores, thanks, in part, to Rózsa. Unfortunately, its overuse in science fiction films would soon make it a cliché (if it wasn't already, having been used in *Rocketship X-M* [1950] and *The Thing* [1951] previously).

But the key figure here is director Robert Wise, former member of the Welles and Lewton units at RKO and a veteran of both the noir style and the semi-documentary—the latter enhancing the tension here in its use of stock footage and the inclusion of authentic radio/television news commentators. Wise himself had a good deal of influence on Tover's low-key visual style, which prevails through much of the exteriors (including a good deal of night-for-night), the boarding house interiors and even those on the spaceship. Since the science fiction film genre was virtually born in 1950-51, something should be said regarding its cultural context. The success of *The Thing* and *The Day the Earth Stood Still* (both adapted from stories first found in the pulps) in 1951 helped establish science fiction as a commercial film genre. Since each was produced at a major studio (RKO and Fox respectively) and each associated with a major film maker (Hawks and Wise respectively), the two films have become major antipodes in discussions regarding

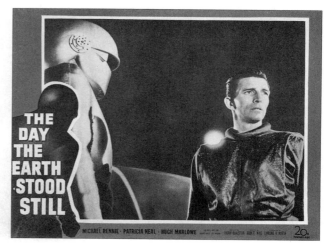

THE DAY THE EARTH STOOD STILL

MICHAEL RENNIE · PATRICIA NEAL · HUGH MARLOWE

the role of science fiction film as political allegory during the cold war (conservative vs. liberal, etc.). But whether or not Klaatu was the seminal sympathetic alien, his remark to an increasingly disinterested newsman—"I am fearful when I see people substituting fear for reason"—can still give us food for thought. **BP**

DEAD RECKONING (1947)

Director: John Cromwell. **Screenplay**: Oliver H.P. Garrett and Steve Fisher, adapted by Allen Rivkin, from a story by Gerald Adams and Sidney Biddell. **Producer**: Sidney Biddell. **Director of Photography**: Leo Tover. **Music**: Marlin Skiles. **Art Directors**: Stephen Goosson, Rudolph Stemad. **Editor**: Gene Havlick. **Cast**: Humphrey Bogart (Rip Murdock), Lizabeth Scott (Coral Chandler), Morris Camovsky (Martinelli), Charles Cane (Lt. Kincaid), William Prince (Johnny Drake), Marvin Miller (Krause), Wallace Ford (McGee), James Bell (Father Logan), George Chandler (Louis Ord), William Forrest (Lt. Col. Simpson), Ruby Dandridge (Hyacinth). **Completed**: September 4, 1946. **Released**: Columbia, January 22. 100 minutes.

The disappearance of an army buddy piques Rip Murdock's curiosity. His subsequent investigation leads him to Coral Chandler, his friend's old girlfriend. From Coral, Rip receives a confusing series of clues. His conclusions are brought into focus when Rip discovers that Coral actually "belongs to Martinelli," a local gangster who operates a gambling joint and to whom she is secretly married. Coral and Martinelli are responsible for the death of Rip's friend. Dredging up these facts makes Rip the target for Martinelli's sadistic henchmen. After being beaten and hunted, Rip succeeds in smashing their operation and killing Martinelli. When he confronts duplicitous Coral, Rip is almost drawn into her seductive trap but is jolted back to reality by a car crash that kills Coral.

In something of a departure from his straightforward tough-guy roles, Bogart portrays Rip Murdock as a thoughtful man caught in a web of threatening circumstances, a prototypical position for a noir figure. While Rip may ultimately resort to violence of his own, he never surrenders to it. As both hunter and hunted, Rip walks a noir tightrope. The film

is structured as a guilty confession, which Rip feels compelled to redraw as a doomed romance.

Having used aspects of the noir style in his early talkie underworld films such as *The Mighty* (1929), *Scandal Sheet*, and *Vice Squad* (both 1931), director John Cromwell used postwar milieu to develop a vision of the femme fatale that is mainstream noir. In shots filled with oblique angles and low-key lighting effects, Cromwell evokes Coral's entrapped world and visually reinforces the doomed nature of her emotional manipulations. Her death, accompanied by the metaphorical image of a parachute drifting into a black void, is a graphically powerful variant on the ending of *Maltese Falcon* in which a much tougher Bogart as Spade merely throws over Bridgid O'Shaughnessy but does not precipitate her demise. Because of Coral's misguided belief that she can use her sexuality to overcome any obstacle, she suffers the deadly fate of many classic period femme fatales. **CM**

DEADLINE AT DAWN (1946)

Director: Harold Clurman. **Screenplay**: Clifford Odets from the novel by William Irish [Cornell Woolrich]. **Producer**: Adrian Scott. **Director of Photography**: Nicholas Musuraca. **Music**: Hanns Eisler. **Art Directors**: Albert D'Agostino, Jack Okey. **Editor**: Roland Gross. **Cast**: Susan Hayward (June Goth), Paul Lukas (Gus Hoffman), Bill Williams (Alex Winkley), Joseph Calleia (Val Bartelli), Osa Masson (Helen Robinson), Lola Lane (Edna Bartelli), Jerome Cowan (Lester Brady), Marvin Miller (Sleepy Parsons), Steven Geray (Edward Hornick, Gloved Man), Constance Worth (Mrs. Raymond), Joe Sawyer (Babe Dooley), Joseph Crehan (Lt. Kane), Phil Warren (Jerry Robinson). **Completed**: July 3, 1945. **Released**: RKO, April 3. 83 minutes.

Alex Winkley, a young sailor on 24-hours leave, discovers that he inadvertently took some money from a nightclub "hostess," Edna Bartelli, when he was drunk. Enlisting the aid of a taxi dancer, June Goth, he goes to return the money and finds Edna dead in her apartment. Winkley can't remember all that happened when he was with Edna, but June believes he is innocent of her murder and agrees to help him try to discover the truth. They have but a few short hours, for Winkley is due to be on a bus for Norfolk in the morning. A kindly, philosophical taxi driver agrees to take them wherever they wish to go free of charge and they meet a number of possible suspects: Sleepy Parsons, a blind pianist and Edna's estranged husband who had argued with the dead girl over money; the girl's brother, Val, a mean, small-time hood; and a few people from whom she was extorting money. By dawn, they discover the real murderer is actually the taxi driver, who killed Edna to prevent her from hurting any more people, including his daughter, Helen Robinson. Alex and June also discover that they are in love and plan to start a life together.

Like its predecessor, *The Phantom Lady*, *Deadline at Dawn* captures the essence of the Woolrichian world if very little of that writer's original novel—all from the vantage of the studio lot. Here again are the dark, menacing streets of New York filled with desperate people on a hot, muggy night where the life of one sympathetic character hangs in the balance. This film, however, boasts that behind the scenes were some major figures of the defunct Group Theater (Clurman, Odets) and their progressive friends (Adrian Scott, Hanns

Eisler). Whether or not the above were all Marxists, they imbued this film with very little of Marx's spirit (which in any case was incompatible with the *Weltschmerz* of either Woolrich or the film noir) other than a patronizing concern with the proletariat.

Odets did fill the air, though, with some rather portentous dialogue that seems out of place in the film noir and even more in the mouths of the "common folk" so beloved by him (e.g., at one point in his desperate search for clues Winkley blurts out, "Time takes so long and goes so fast"!!!). Fortunately for today's audiences, the film is rescued by the RKO noir style, already well refined by the time of its production. It is also rescued by some very competent acting, in both major and minor roles. In a change of pace, Marvin Miller draws a good deal of sympathy out of the character of Sleepy Parsons whose only "crime" was to love his ex-wife too deeply, despite her despicable treatment of him, and who deserved better than to have a fatal heart attack while being beaten by her malicious brother. As does Steven Geray, as the pathetic Hornick, with his fixation on white gloves and his platonic obsession with June. He is unable to draw even a wink of approval from her despite his pride in his newly acquired U.S. citizenship. Even better is Paul Lukas' portrayal of Gus Hoffman, the philosophical taxi driver who loves to quote statistics; who waited unsuccessfully for six years for his wife to return to him, but who, in the end, betrayed by his love for his daughter and humanity in general, is forced to admit that it matters little what statistics tell us. Musing on the prospects of an untimely execution, he whimsically remarks, "Imagine, at my age, having to learn to play the harp." It is of such characters and situations that the noir world is constructed. **BP**

DECOY (1946)

Director: Jack Bernhard. **Screenplay**: Ned Young from a story by Stanley Rubin. **Producers**: Jack Bernhard, Bernard Brandt. **Director of Photography**: L.W. O'Connell. **Music**: Edward J. Kay. **Art Director**: Dave Milton. **Editor**: Jason Bernie. **Cast**: Jean Gillie (Margot Shelby), Edward Norris (Jim Vincent), Herbert Rudley (Dr. Lloyd Craig), Robert Armstrong (Frank Olins), Sheldon Leonard (Sgt. Joseph Portugal), Marjorie Woodworth (Nurse), Philip Van Zandt (Tommy), John Shay (Al). **Completed**: May 11, 1946. **Released**: Monogram, September 14. 76 minutes.

Dazed and weakened, Dr. Lloyd Craig enters the apartment of Margot Shelby, the pretty but vicious brain of a gang of thieves, and shots ring out. Detective Sgt. Joseph Portugal arrives to find the doctor dead and Margot dying of a gunshot wound. He gently sets her on a couch and she demands that he hand her a small wooden box. However, she is too weak and in too much pain to open it. To take her mind off her troubles, Portugal lets her fill in the details that brought her to this predicament. Margot admits she loves money and that is why she became an associate of Frankie Olins, who hid a stolen $400,000 before being sentenced to die in the gas chamber for killing a bystander. Frankie would not reveal where the money was hidden but Margot devised an intricate plan to rescue Frankie's body immediately after the execution so that he could be given an antidote to cyanide gas. Moreover, as this requires the cooperation of a doctor, Margot cleverly seduces Dr. Lloyd Craig who certifies the prison deaths. The plan succeeds without a hitch. Frankie's body is brought to Craig's office and revived. He draws a map of the money's hiding place and gives half of the map to Margot. When he tries to kiss her, Jim Vincent, Frankie's associate who has secretly been conspiring with Margot, shoots Frankie and takes his half of the map. Vincent and Margot force the doctor to help them search for the money. Driving to the spot where the money is buried, Margot simulates a flat tire, which Vincent gets out to repair. As Vincent finishes, she ruthlessly runs him over, takes his half of the map and then continues driving on to the hiding place. Margot becomes increasingly frenzied as the doctor digs up the money-box, and then, overcome with paroxysms of laughter, she shoots him and returns home with the box intact. But the doctor recovers and returns to her apartment for revenge.

Decoy's opening shot of hands being washed in a filthy service station sink followed by the camera tilting up into a mirror fragment which reveals the disheveled face of Dr. Lloyd Craig sets the tone for the entire film. One must look beyond the absurdities of the plot and the inconsistencies of some poorly done day-for-night shots to the exciting performance of British actress Jean Gillie as Margot Shelby, the most vicious *femme fatale* of the noir cycle prior to Annie Laurie Starr in *Gun Crazy*. Margot uses men without qualm and admits receiving particular pleasure from seducing Dr. Craig, particularly because she thereby smashed the fortress of his ideals. Her sadism is revealed when she runs her car over Jim Vincent, after which she calmly gets out of the car, takes his portion of the treasure map off of his body and replaces the car's jack in the trunk before resuming her journey. Unregenerate to the very end, Margot even attempts to degrade Sgt. Portugal by using the diminutive "Jojo" and asking him to "come down to my level just this once." When he bends close to her, instead of kissing him she laughs in his face. **BP**

DESPERATE (1947)

Director: Anthony Mann. **Screenplay**: Harry Essex, with additional dialogue by Martin Rackin based on a story by Dorothy Atlas and Anthony Mann. **Producer**: Michel Kraike. **Director of Photography**: George E. Diskant. **Music**: Paul Sawtell. **Art Directors**: Albert S. D'Agostino, Walter E. Keller. **Editor**: Marston Fay. **Cast**: Steve Brodie (Steve Randall), Audrey Long (Anne Randall), Raymond Burr (Walt Radak), Douglas Fowley (Pete), William Challee (Reynolds), Jason

Robards, Sr. (Ferrari), Freddie Steele (Shorty), Lee Frederick (Joe), Paul E. Burns (Uncle Jan), Ilka Gruning (Aunt Klara). **Completed**: December 26, 1946. **Released**: RKO, May 20. 73 minutes.

A young newlywed, Steve Randall, is the innocent dupe in a warehouse racketeering scheme. The plans of several small-time gangsters fail, resulting in the death of a policeman and the capture of one of the gang members. The captured criminal, who is the brother of the gang's headman, Walt Radak, is found guilty of murder and is sentenced to die in the electric chair. In a move designed to clear their condemned associate, the remaining fugitives attempt to blackmail Randall into confessing to be the sole party responsible for the murder and apparent robbery or else his wife, Anne, will become the gang's next target. Thinking there is no way out of this frustrating dilemma, the young man and his bride run away to the questionable safety of an isolated farm owned by relatives. However, the gangsters soon track them down. The innocent couple are saved mere seconds before the criminals carry out their plan of retribution.

As the first in a series of noir films directed by Anthony Mann, *Desperate* is a perversion of middle-class values and structure. The paranoia of the young married couple is derived not out of fear of the law, but rather from fear of the criminals' vengeance. There is a sense of hopelessness in this situation, which brings the film fully within the noir sphere; and a tone of cynicism and brutality that impugns American social life as well. Violence exists as a "real" entity in Mann's films, as there is no distortion of brutality through innuendo or subtlety, and *Desperate* has a raw impact unmatched in most noir films of the period. Even in an early Mann film like *Desperate*, the visual quality of the violence is well defined. The brutal beating of Randall in a dank basement hideout is a startling example of American expressionist filmmaking. The scene is illuminated by a single unshaded electric light bulb, which flashes on a variety of images as the bulb is wildly batted about from the vigorous movement of the blows hitting Randall. **CM**

THE DESPERATE HOURS (1955)

Director: William Wyler. **Screenplay**: Joseph Hayes based on his novel and play. **Producer**: William Wyler. **Director of Photography**: Lee Garmes. **Music**: Gail Kubik. **Art Directors**: Joseph McMillan Johnson.

Editor: Robert Swink. **Cast**: Humphrey Bogart (Glenn Griffith), Fredric March (Dan C. Hilliard), Arthur Kennedy (Deputy Sheriff Jesse Bard), Martha Scott (Eleanor Hilliard), Dewey Martin (Hal Griffith), Gig Young (Chuck Wright), Mary Murphy (Cindy Hilliard), Richard Eyer (Ralphie Hilliard), Robert Middleton (Sam Kobish), Alan Reed (Detective), Bert Freed (Tom Winston), Ray Collins (Sheriff Masters), Whit Bissell (FBI Agent Carson), Ray Teal (State Police Lt. Fredericks). **Released**: Paramount, October 5. 112 minutes.

Three escaped convicts take over a middle-class home where Dan and Ellie Hilliard live with their teenage children, Cindy and Ralph. The captors do not find their task easy. They soon fall out amongst themselves. Hal, the younger brother of the trio's leader, Glenn, leaves the group while Kobish, a simple minded psychopath, refuses to return the gun lent to him by Glenn. Outside, Hal is soon tracked and killed by the police. Finding the gun registered to Dan Hilliard, the police soon arrive outside the home. Meanwhile, a woman bringing the captors some essential cash money changes the plan and mails it instead. Glenn sends Dan out to pick it up. The police have surrounded his house and give him a gun, which Dan unloads and allows Glenn to discover. Kobish, never loyal to Glenn, unsuccessfully makes a play for the money. Then, Dan tricks Kobish and gets his pistol. Kobish runs outside into police fire. Glenn tries to shoot Dan's gun, but nothing happens. Dan, holding the only loaded pistol, tells Glenn that Hal is "full of police bullets, and you did it!" Glenn steps outside and hurls the empty gun at the cops to provoke them to finish him off.

In noir kidnapping plots, the criminal invades a place, takes hostages, and then must wait for someone or some cash to arrive. When he waits for a person, the woman or man never arrives; whether to the diner in the desert, as in *The Petrified Forest*, the lakeshore cottage in *Blind Alley* and *The Dark Past*, the train station in *Suddenly*, or the Hilliard's home in *The Desperate Hours*. While the noir homme waits for money, the police locate him, as in *The Night Holds Terror* and *The Desperate Hours*. Right after the invasion, the killer is in complete control over everyone else. His commitment to waiting, however, leads to his loss of control and his capture or death. As a rule, the police defeat the killer, either attacking him from the outside or tricking him from the inside, as in *Suddenly*, in which two of the hostages are the town sheriff and a retired secret service agent.

The Desperate Hours is however different in several ways. Not only does each member of the Hilliard family resist Glenn from the outset, but Hal and Kobish also turn against him. Furthermore, Dan, not the police, takes Glenn down. Twenty years before, in *The Petrified Forest*, Humphrey Bogart began his film career as Duke Mantee, who keeps everyone in line. In *The Desperate Hours*, Bogart's penultimate screen character cannot keep anyone in line. Glenn's downfall is even dramatized visually, via deep focus shots in three phone calls to the house. The first shot is low from the first floor looking up toward the second floor hallway. Cindy, with the phone, and Glenn, with a gun, are in the foreground to the left. Ellie is mid-distance at the bottom of the stairs. Hal, Dan and Ralph are small figures standing behind the second floor banister. This is after the invasion when Glenn has control over the Hilliard family. The second shot is almost the reverse of the first. It is above Dan on the second floor looking down to the first floor. He is holding the phone. Cindy and Ellie stand nearby at the end of the railing. Glenn is now the small figure, downstairs in the left corner of the frame. This is after Hal has been killed. Glenn's time is running out. The third shot is head high on the second floor. On the right, Cindy holds the phone and Ellie stands in front of her. On the left, Kobish points a gun at them. Glenn, a tiny figure downstairs, is in the middle at the bottom of the frame. After the police surround the Hilliard house, Glenn is shown inside two pickets of the upstairs railing. His time is up.

Glenn and Dan are doppelgangers in three ways. First, they are similar in age. (This is specific to the film. Bogart and March were in their late fifties. In the novel and the play, Dan's character was written to be in his forties, while Glenn is in his twenties.) Second, Glenn makes Dan become like himself, a man willing to kill. When Dan points a loaded gun at him, Glenn says, "You ain't got it in you, Pop." Dan retorts, "I got it in me! You put it there." Third, each confronts opposition to his authority from the younger generation. Glenn assumes Hal wants Cindy for her body. In fact, Hal wants her respect. He protests whenever Glenn treats "the Spitfire" as a sex object. But Hal gets nowhere with Cindy, and it hurts. When he asks her in a friendly way, "What time's the next news," she looks at him with contempt. She walks away and he looks down, humiliated. After observing the middle class world of the Hilliard family, as well as, through the living room curtain, a group of well-dressed teenagers across the street singing in a convertible, Hal recognizes his alienation from them as a class difference. Glenn brags about all that he has "learned" from his brother, but Hal complains, "You taught me everything, except how to live in a house like this." That remark cuts Glenn to the quick because he disdains people like Dan. In one of several outbursts in which he smears Dan and his class, Glenn shouts, "Guys like you. Smart-eyed, respectable! Suckers! We seen 'em, ain't we, Kobish? Sittin' on parole boards. 'Throw 'em back in the cell! They ain't fit to live with decent folk!'" Hal, however, doesn't share Glenn's class anger. He infuriates Glenn by calling Dan, "Mr. Hilliard." Also, Hal, like Kobish, refuses to give up his gun when Glenn asks him for it.

It is the conflict amongst the gangsters, and Glenn's failure to overcome them, that make *The Desperate Hours* more truly noir, not the plot's struggle between criminals and a wholesome family. Furthermore, tensions within the family dilute the noir in the film because Dan's confrontation with the younger generation is the stuff of melodrama. In the first scene Dan and Ellie get an earful. Their son wants to be called Ralph instead of "Ralphy," and he wants to shake his father's hand good-bye instead of kissing his cheek. Dan does not want Cindy to marry her boyfriend, Chuck, because "she's still a child." Showing off her breasts in front of a mirror, she counters, "Even though she doesn't look like a child!"

After the invasion, Ralph thinks his father is afraid of the gangsters. Dan must prove to Ralph he knows what he is doing; i.e. that father knows best. His triumph comes when he commands Ralph to run to him and the boy does, even though Glenn has a gun against Ralph's head. As Hal is a rebel to Glenn, so is Chuck to Dan. Chuck drives a sports car, but to Dan it is a "hot-rod." Dan sees Chuck, an attorney in a black overcoat, as if he is a JD or Hal in a black leather jacket. Concomitant with 1950s anti-communist paranoia, all kinds of Hollywood invaders—gangsters, juve-

nile delinquents, "redskins," and red planet monsters—are vanquished and "decent folk" regain their security. With Glenn and Kobish lying bullet-ridden on the Hilliard's front lawn, the final scene can be associated with a rollback of evil by the middle class. Ellie, Cindy and Ralph hug Dan outside their home. Ralph even kisses Dad's cheek as they walk together through the front door. Chuck, seemingly the outsider if not the outcast, is left alone in the yard, facing the closed door with his back to the camera. However, the final shot shows that completing the family melodrama means bridging the generation gap. Dan steps back through the doorway and, with a broad smile, waves Chuck to come join them. Chuck romps up the brick steps into the house. Glenn starts as the unrivaled authority over his henchmen and hostages; he ends unable to dominate anyone. Dan starts as a declining patriarch to his children; he ends with their admiration and obedience. As with the best noir in the classic period, Glenn suffers a nightmare of everything going wrong. Consistent with a 1950's family melodrama, Dan masters a crisis, one that is exacerbated by the external complications from the invasion. The final scene appropriately ends the film noir with corpses, and the family melodrama with reconciliation. **DMH**

DESTINATION MURDER (1950)

Director: Edward L Cahn. **Screenplay**: Don Martin. **Producers**: Edward L. Cahn, Maurie M. Suess (Prominent Pictures). **Director of Photography**: Jackson J. Rose. **Music**: Irving Gertz. **Art Director**: Boris Leven. **Editor**: Philip Cahn. **Cast**: Joyce MacKenzie (Laura Mansfield), Stanley Clements (Jackie Wales), Hurd Hatfield (Stretch Norton), Albert Dekker (Armitage), Myrna Dell (Alice Wentworth), James Flavin (Lt. Brewster), John Dehner (Frank Niles), Richard Emory (Sgt. Mulcahy). **Released**: RKO, June 8. 72 minutes.

Laura Mansfield witnesses the murder of her father, a local racketeer, by a young man dressed in a messenger suit who has been driven to the Mansfield house by a man known only as Armitage. Later during a police lineup, she thinks she recognizes Jackie Wales as the messenger boy and decides to date him to find out the truth. Jackie brings her to the Vogue Nightclub, ostensibly owned by Armitage and run by his first lieutenant, Stretch Norton, who, unknown to all but Armitage, is actually in command. Romantic intrigues complicated by blackmail end with Jackie's death and Laura's romantic involvement with Stretch. She prevails upon Stretch to help her get proof that Armitage was responsible for her father's murder and Stretch pretends to go along with the idea. Stretch, after gaining possession of a letter written by Jackie naming Armitage as the responsible party and believing his position as kingpin of the city's rackets secure, turns the Vogue over to Armitage. Stretch then invites Armitage over to his apartment to celebrate, drugs Armitage's champagne, places the Mansfield murder weapon in Armitage's hand, and then tricks Laura into shooting the groggy Armitage whom she believes is about to kill Stretch. The police find Jackie's incriminating letter in the nightclub safe but the whole case appears too convenient to satisfy Lt. Brewster who is heading the investigation. Attempting to determine the true nature of Stretch's relationship with Armitage, Brewster releases Frank Niles, a racketeer who had been framed for Mansfield's murder. Niles, carrying a police wire, confronts Stretch and tells him he is taking over the rackets. Niles refuses the man's offer to take Armitage's role. Brewster intrudes, there is a scuffle and in the ensuing melee Stretch is shot and killed. Knowing that Stretch was the person behind the series of murders starting with her father's, Laura is now free to go on with her life.

Destination Murder is only one in a long list of B-noirs produced at RKO, better than some but worse than many others. It can boast of a plot almost as convoluted as *The Big Sleep*, and a good deal more muddled. In addition, it shares that earlier film's flirtation with the homoerotic as well as its bias against phony aestheticism and class privilege. The exact nature of Armitage's relationship with Stretch is never made clear but his "girl," Alice, deprecates his manhood and when she tries to seduce Stretch, he tells her he doesn't mix girls and business. Indeed, the character of Armitage—with his mansion filled with books and art works, his insistence on referring to himself in the third person, and his penchant for beating or killing people while Beethoven's *Moonlight Sonata* blares from a player-piano—is the most interesting aspect of this film. Moreover, Albert Dekker plays him as if he were warming up for his role as Dr. Soberin in *Kiss Me Deadly*. The fact that his aestheticism disappears when he is alone with Stretch and that he then assumes the position of an underling indicates that "Armitage" may be merely a persona, a creation perhaps of Stretch Norton. Hurd Hatfield, as well, must shift acting gears when he moves from the stoic first officer to the wily commandant. Both actors do a credible job, which is more than can be said of Joyce MacKenzie as the female lead. **BP**

DETECTIVE STORY (1951)

Producer and Director: William Wyler. **Screenplay**: Philip Yordan and Robert Wyler based on the play by Sidney Kingsley. **Director of Photography**: Lee Garmes. **Art Directors**: Hal Pereira, Earl Hedrick. **Editor**: Robert Swink. **Cast**: Kirk Douglas (Jim McLeod), Eleanor Parker (Mary McLeod), William Bendix (Lou Brody), Cathy O'Donnell (Susan), George Macready (Karl Schneider), Horace McMahon (Lt. Monahan), Gladys George (Miss Hatch), Joseph Wiseman (First Burglar), Lee Grant (Shoplifter), Gerald Mohr (Tami Giacoppetti), Frank Faylen (Gallagher), Craig Hill (Arthur), Michael

Strong (Lewis Abbott), Luis Van Rooten (Joe Feinson). **Completed**: March 24, 1951. **Released**: Paramount, November 6. 103 minutes.

Jim McLeod, a New York detective, believes that people's tendencies toward lawbreaking should be stamped out before they begin a career of crime. His prosecution verges on persecution, as he metes out justice to a variety of characters that come into the police station on one particular day. His superior officer becomes suspicious when McLeod is particularly ruthless to an abortionist. The suspect's lawyer accuses McLeod of having personal reasons for his unprofessional behavior toward the doctor, and it is revealed that McLeod's wife had an abortion early in her life, performed by the same doctor whom her husband now holds in the station. McLeod cannot bring himself to forgive his wife, even though she is the one person he loves; his confusion becomes so great that he deliberately steps into the line of fire from a desperate hoodlum who pulls a gun attempting to escape from the station. As he dies in his wife's arms, McLeod recites the Act of Contrition.

Dashiell Hammett was contracted to write the screenplay of Sidney Kingsley's Broadway play, and one wonders what qualities the sadistic McLeod would have acquired in Hammett's hands. Instead this modern morality play set in a New York police station was transposed from stage to screenplay by director Wyler and screenwriter Yordan. Furthermore, William Wyler was proud to be very popular among actors as an "Actor's Director." More so than most other directors of his generation, he collaborated with each actor in developing their unique meaningful character whose interactions propelled the film's action, gave it intensity and conveyed the film's theme. Thus, Kirk Douglas, as Detective McLeod, is even more explosive than in *Ace in the Hole* and the ensemble cast all have their moment to shine.

Douglas' Detective McLeod represents virtue driven mad by the evil around him. McLeod is self-righteous and shows no mercy toward anyone. He single-handedly attempts to equalize "blind justice" with "law of the streets." Outside the precinct station, crimes against society are perpetrated, while inside the station McLeod commits crimes against individuals. Using the events in just one day of his harried life, *Detective Story* exposes McLeod's breaking point: he collapses when his harsh judgmental stance toward sin and

Detour: *Vera (Ann Savage) and the hapless Al Roberts (Tom Neal).*

mankind clashes with, and then destroys, his faith in the one person he loves. By becoming a target for the escaping criminal's bullet, McLeod finds his own escape from a world in which he cannot accept human sin.

Director William Wyler begins the film in a naturalistic style, but the claustrophobia of the one-room police station presses in relentlessly, increasing the pace and ultimately illustrating the panic created by McLeod's hysteria. The uselessness of McLeod's death is not redeemed by his final prayers. He is an alienated noir figure, stubbornly set apart by his righteousness and simply overwhelmed by the modern world's clash of values. **JC & EW**

DETOUR (1945)

Director: Edgar G. Ulmer. **Screenplay**: Martin Goldsmith. **Producer**: Leon Fromkess. **Director of Photography**: Benjamin H. Kline. **Music**: Leo Erdody. **Art Director**: Edward C. Jewell. **Editor**: George McGuire. **Cast**: Tom Neal (Al Roberts), Ann Savage (Vera), Claudia Drake (Sue), Edmund MacDonald (Charles Haskell Jr.), Tim Ryan (Diner Proprietor), Roger Clark (Policeman) Pat Gleason (Joe, trucker). **Completed**: June 30, 1945. **Released**: PRC, November 30. 68 minutes

Al Roberts is a pianist in a New York nightclub where his girlfriend, Sue, is a singer. They plan to marry, but Sue is ambitious and leaves for "stardom" in Hollywood. Left alone, Roberts calls her one night and Sue tells him that she works as a waitress. He decides to join her by hitchhiking. Eventually, he is picked up by Haskell who is carrying a lot of cash and driving all the way to Los Angeles. Haskell talks about a female hitchhiker who scratched him viciously when he made a sexual advance. Later, Roberts drives so Haskell can sleep. When it begins to rain, Roberts attempts rousing Haskell to put up the convertible top, but Haskell is mysteriously dead. Roberts stops the car and opens the passenger door to check the man more throughly. Haskell slips through Roberts arms and his head hits a rock. Panicked, Roberts believes the police will never accept his innocence. He hides the body and drives on alone. The next day Roberts picks up Vera, initially unaware that she is the same woman who scratched Haskell. She recognizes the car and asks what happened to its real owner. Roberts' story doesn't convince her that he's innocent, but she agrees to remain silent if he will

follow her plans. Arriving in Los Angeles, they rent a room and Vera plans that Roberts will sell the car using Haskell's identity. But when she discovers that Haskell was the heir of a dying millionaire and that his family has not seen him for years, she plans to pass Roberts off as Haskell. That night they argue about her scheme. Vera runs into the other room threatening to call the police, slams the door but collapses drunkenly upon the bed with the telephone cord entwined about her neck. Roberts pulls on the cord from the other side of the locked door, inadvertently strangling her. Without ever seeing his fiancée, Robert flees to Reno, where he sits in a diner and reflects on the strange circumstances that have him in such a hopeless situation and then leaves to be apprehended by the police.

A "poverty row quickie," *Detour* is a film that does not need to affirm conventional values and thus can embrace the bizarre implications of film noir more completely than any more obviously distinguished productions. Edgar G. Ulmer is paradoxically a director who thrives at this level of production, which is usually scorned by accomplished filmmakers. The story of *Detour*, fraught with outrageous coincidence, would be ridiculous in most hands, but Ulmer possesses the temperament to make it convincing. He persuades the audience to reflect on the film's premise that, in the protagonist's final words, "Fate or some mysterious force can put the finger on you or me for no good reason at all." Bitter at his fiancée, Roberts would certainly like to punish her for abandoning him, as demonstrated in his punishment of the piano during his crazed interpretation of a Brahms waltz; but Roberts deludes himself that he desires joining her. In fact, he has a need for Haskell and Vera, as they provide him with the opportunity to redirect his repressed emotions. His struggle against fate is self-defeating, for in spite of his protestations to the contrary, the "detour" is really the road he wants to travel. How appropriate that Haskell and Vera are both predatory and dying of fatal diseases. Roberts must always encounter the same projection of his own sense of pessimism and doom in rebellion against his soft and accommodating nature. Vera is his true female complement, however intolerable and false she seems to him. It is not just Vera's bizarre schemes for their behavior that keeps them together as a couple in the cheap Los Angeles motel room; the claustrophobic visuals seem to affirm that they belong together. The tawdry complexity of Vera is complete with strange classical allusions: Vera is compared to both Camille and Caesar in dialogue that is well up to the riotous standards set by other portions of the script and well-handled by actress Ann Savage.

In his mind, Roberts restructures his journey with Vera; it is both externalized in his memory as images and internalized by the incessant confessional tone of his narration. Ulmer's camera, shackled by a modest production budget, obviously never really moves from New York to Los Angeles. If the journey is made, it is because Roberts voyages metaphorically to an understanding of his immediate present through images and the sound of his own voice, through the process of reviewing his arrival and imagining the closed door of his future. Such an understanding precludes the self-awareness that could reveal to him that his own character has determined the twists of the road. **BL**

THE DEVIL THUMBS A RIDE (1947)

Director: Felix Feist. **Screenplay**: Felix Feist based on the novel by Robert C. DuSoe. **Producer**: Herbert Schlom. **Director of Photography**: J. Roy Hunt. **Music**: Paul Sawtell. **Musical Director**: C. Bakaleinikoff. **Art Directors**: Albert S. D'Agostino, Charles F. Pyke. **Editor**: Robert Swink. **Cast**: Lawrence Tierney (Steve Morgan), Ted North (James "Fergie" Ferguson), Nan Leslie (Carol Demming), Betty Lawford (Agnes), Andrew Tombes (Joe Braden), Harry Shannon (Detective Owens), Glenn Vernon (Jack Kenny), Marian Carr (Diane Ferguson), William Gould (Captain Martin). **Released**: RKO Radio Pictures, February 20. 62 minutes.

Jim "Fergie" Ferguson is driving home to Los Angeles after a party in San Diego. He's young, happily married, and anxious to see his wife again. At a street corner, a man thumbs a ride, and Fergie eagerly agrees to provide a lift. It's after midnight and a rider might help him stay awake. However, the rider, Steve Morgan, has just robbed and killed a theater manager who was making a night deposit at a bank. Morgan's eyes frequently narrow to slits as he constantly assesses everything he sees. At a service station, Morgan agrees to give a ride to two women, without first consulting Fergie. The night then spirals downward for Fergie as Morgan continues to take control—even backing the car over a motorcycle patrolman who stops them on a deserted backroad. They end up at a beach house, where Morgan plans to party and hide until police remove the highway checkpoints/roadblocks. However, Morgan's predatory sexual appetite—and his anger when spurned—leads to further violence. Meanwhile, a tip from a gas station attendant puts police on Morgan's trail.

In a collection of his essays titled *The Devil Thumbs a Ride and Other Unforgettable Films*, novelist Barry Gifford (writer of *Wild at Heart*) says actor Lawrence Tierney invests *The Devil Thumbs a Ride* "with such genuine virulence that *Devil* must be ranked in the upper echelon of indelibly American noir." While there is certainly some hyperbole in this claim, Gifford is not far off the mark. Tierney stalks this movie with an intensity that is unnerving. As Gifford says, "Evil doesn't lurk in his face, it gloats." However, this movie isn't just a one-trick pony: rarely does a movie provide such a consistently fascinating crew of supporting characters—from the poker-loving detective hot on

Morgan's trail to a sleepy woman awakened by Fergie. Each character is lovingly developed with a minimum of on-screen time, so the character vignettes never get in the way of the crime drama. To the contrary, they provide a solid background that makes Fergie's desperate situation all the more poignant.

Working from his own screenplay and based on a book by Robert C. DuSoe, director Felix Feist delivers a hard-nosed crime drama drenched in shadows. It's a surprisingly brutal movie delivered with bad-boy delight. In terms of content, *The Devil Thumbs a Ride* is archetypal noir, in which the protagonist, Fergie, makes one mistake—to give Morgan a ride—and this mistake threatens to destroy him. However, the movie departs from archetypal noir in the underlying comedic tone that occasionally surfaces, providing brief respites from Morgan's caustic presence. Ultimately, instead of heading for utter destruction, Fergie finds redemption. The mix of tones, from brutal crime drama to light character comedy, works throughout most of the movie, with Fergie's slightly tipsy and generally genial businessman contrasted with the brick-jawed, amoral Steve Morgan.

The women who catch a ride in Fergie's car—Carol and Agnes—are female versions of Fergie and Morgan. Carol is young, demure, and attractive while Agnes is cynical and wisecracking. While Carol turns down Morgan's offer of liquor, Agnes readily drinks from the bottle. The movie allows Fergie a route to safety from Morgan, but Carol gets the full brunt of Morgan's brutality. Agnes is blind to Morgan's threatening manner. As Morgan threatens Carol with rape at the beach house, Agnes tells them to "close the door" for privacy. Later, Agnes will be seduced by money from Morgan into eagerly lying to the police. As he gives her a C-note, she says, "Stevie, you're really a right guy." The dichotomy of Carol and Agnes provides no alternative for survival in Morgan's presence. The only way to survive is to avoid Morgan, which is almost impossible. Near the end, the movie's balancing act of brutality and comedy shifts toward the latter, and this shift weakens the movie's ending with some unintentional laughs, but otherwise this is an astonishing movie that will shock viewers with its blunt cynicism and brutality, while charming them with the well-crafted characterizations that emerge in the movie's quieter scenes. Director Felix Feist directed numerous B movies and *The Devil Thumbs a Ride* is arguably the best. However, for contemporary audiences, his most famous movie is the science fiction drama *Donovan's Brain*. The directorial skill displayed by *The Devil Thumbs a Ride* suggests Feist's résumé warrants further attention. **GJ**

DEVIL'S DOORWAY (1950)

Director: Anthony Mann. **Screenplay**: Guy Trosper. **Producer**: Nicholas Nayfack. **Director of Photography**: John Alton. **Art Director**: Cedric Gibbons, Leonid Vasian. **Music**: Daniele Amfitheatrof. **Editor**: Conrad Nervig. **Cast**: Robert Taylor (Lance Poole), Louis Calhern (Verne Coolan), Paula Raymond (Orrie Masters), Marshall Thompson (Rod MacDougall), James Mitchell (Red Rock), Edgar Buchanan (Sheriff Zeke Carmody), Rhys Williams (Scotty MacDougall), Spring Byington (Mrs. Masters), Fritz Leiber (Mr. Poole), Chief John Big Tree (Thundercloud). **Released**: MGM, September 15. 84 minutes.

Lance Poole comes back from the war fighting side by side with Whites in the Union forces and winning the Congressional Medal of Honor. He returns to Sweet Meadows, the land of his father, and wants to build a cattle ranch. He does so successfully until the White settlers come to his homestead. They inform him that because he is an Indian, he is not entitled to his own land. He hires a lawyer, Orrie Masters, but she is also unable to change the laws which lead to bloody battles over the land, headed by the racist lawyer Verne Coolan. Coolan instigates the sheepherders, settlers, and the townspeople to attack Lance's ranch. When the Army arrives and his people are decimated, Lance surrenders to the troops and dies.

Devil's Doorway, directed by noir innovator Anthony Mann and photographed by John Alton—Mann's favorite cinematographer during his noir period—mixes the socially aware theme of American racism with the core noir theme of determinism. Broken Lance returns from the Civil War with the Congressional Medal of Honor and a faith in the country and people for whom he bled. "Why should anyone want to bother me?" Broken Lance tells his father who replies ominously and prophetically, "You are home. You are again an Indian." Over the years Broken Lance acquires land, cattle and wealth while Wyoming becomes a territory and begins enforcing anti-Indian laws. This begins the downward spiral of Broken Lance's fortunes along with his sense of optimism. He is shot at and humiliated in a bar where he now cannot drink alcohol. His land is divided up by incoming sheepmen.

Broken Lance tries legal methods at first, hiring a lawyer–Orrie Masters–but all to no avail. "You are a ward of the government," she tells the distraught but stoic war hero. Egged on by a bitter, racist lawyer Verne Coolan, the town turns further against him. Broken Lance's friend, Sheriff Carmody, is killed in a series of battles in which Lance shoots one of the sheepmen. Coolan organizes a posse to go after Broken Lance and his people. They are surrounded and decimated. Orrie, who is now infatuated with him, appeals to Broken Lance to surrender once the army arrives but he is now so filled with so much anger and pain that he cannot see beyond it. He bends to kiss her but cannot even allow himself that; "A hundred years from now it might have worked." He has accepted his fate, a common theme in noir films. In a telling touch of irony, he puts on his army uniform and congressional medal and walks out shooting, knowing he will be killed by the soldiers of a government he once fought for but that no longer considers him one of its citizens. **JU**

DOUBLE INDEMNITY (1944)

Director: Billy Wilder. **Screenplay**: Wilder and Raymond Chandler based on the novella by James M. Cain. **Producer**: Joseph Sistrom [uncredited]. **Director of Photography**: John F. Seitz. **Music**: Miklos Rózsa with excerpts from Symphony in D Minor by César Franck. **Art Director**: Hal Pereira. **Editor**: Doane Harrison. **Cast**: Fred MacMurray (Walter Neff), Barbara Stanwyck (Phyllis Dietrichson), Edward G. Robinson (Barton Keyes), Porter Hall (Mr. Jackson), Jean Heather (Lola Dietrichson), Tom Powers (Mr. Dietrichson), Byron Barr (Nino Zachetti), Richard Gaines (Mr. Norton), Fortunio Bonanova (Sam Gorlopis), John Philliber (Joe Peters), Betty Farrington (Nettie the Maid). **Completed**: November 24, 1943. **Released**: Paramount, September 7. 106 minutes.

A stricken Walter Neff arrives at his insurance office in the middle of the night and records his story on a Dictaphone. He has been seduced by Phyllis Dietrichson into helping to murder her husband and collect on an accident insurance policy. After the crime is committed, Neff is worried that his mentor Barton Keyes, claims manager for Pacific All Risk, will become suspicious of the timing on the policy issuance and the unlikely "double indemnity" accident on a train. Initially Keyes scoffs at the possibility of suicide raised by the company owner but soon thereafter does suspect foul play. Not wanting to risk seeing Phyllis, Neff learns she may be involved the boyfriend of her step-daughter Lola, who soon visits Neff herself at his office and claims that Phyllis was responsible for her father's death. After spending time with Lola to assuage her, Neff goes to confront Phyllis who is expecting him and shoots him. Suddenly professing her love, Phyllis embraces the wounded Neff, who takes the gun and kills her. Summoned by the elevator operator, Keyes arrives and overhears the last of Neff's confession. Believing he can still escape to Mexico, Neff tries to leave but, as Keyes predicted, collapses at the door.

Conspiracy and betrayal, love and sex, murder and the perfect crime—all linchpins of noir are integral to *Double Indemnity*. Certainly murder for profit or murder for love are conceits much older than the noir cycle; but as a tale of murder that combines the two, *Double Indemnity* is for many the quintessential film noir. Like nature and a vacuum, the noir cycle abhors a perfect crime and seldom paints any picture of perfection. Even for those not familiar with the original novella, the failure of would-be "perfect criminals" Walter Neff and Phyllis Dietrichson is not likely to surprise the viewer. Or as *Double Indemnity*'s protagonist, Walter Neff, puts it when he begins his narration: "Yes, I killed him. I killed him for money and for a woman. I didn't get the money and I didn't get the woman. Pretty, isn't it?"

Pretty it's not. In fact, the sordidness of *Double Indemnity* is counter-balanced only by the serendipitous elements that came together and permitted it to be made. *Double Indemnity* is based on a very short novel by the quasi-hardboiled author James M. Cain, and its script is coauthored by fully hardboiled Raymond Chandler; but, in spite of their strong personalities, the nature of the film

Double Indemnity: *Barton Keyes (Edward G. Robinson) and a wounded Walter Neff (Fred MacMurray).*

seems to have been determined more by co-scenarist and director Billy Wilder than by either Cain or Chandler. On the surface, the film's origins go back to Cain's story which first appeared serialized over eight issues of *Liberty* magazine in 1935-36. Of course, there is also Cain's first novel, *The Postman Always Rings Twice* (1934), to be considered, as it is a remarkably similar tale of murder for money and for a woman. But before that, Cain was a reporter for the *New York World* and one of many such to attend the sensational 1927 trial of Ruth Snyder and Judd Grey, a pair of real-life, would-be perfect criminals who turned on each other and both ended up in the electric chair.

From that real event, Cain fashioned two stories which were soon optioned by Hollywood. But neither Paramount, which owned the novella, nor M.G.M., which had purchased the rights to *Postman*, could get a script past Joe Breen, the head of the Hays Office and enforcer of the motion picture code, until World War II put such things in perspective. Even then, *Double Indemnity* might have turned out quite differently had Billy Wilder's regular collaborator, Charles Brackett, not loathed the material; had Cain himself not been under contract to a rival studio; had Joe Sistrom not just read a novel by Raymond Chandler. In the end, with Fred MacMurray being cast after George Raft and Alan Ladd had passed, with Barbara Stanwyck in a hand-me-down blonde wig from Marlene Dietrich, with Edward G. Robinson as the canny Keyes, Wilder and his collaborators fashioned from an imperfect process applied to a plot about an imperfect crime what might well be the perfect film noir. Beyond the influences of Cain as novelist, Chandler as the co-scenarist, and Billy Wilder—whose work in the USA came after directing films in Germany and France—there is the superb cinematography by John Seitz, including extensive night location work, a score by Miklos Rózsa; and, of course, Stanwyck, MacMurray, and Robinson, all cast somewhat against type.

This was Wilder's first and truest film noir, for *Sunset Boulevard* is flawed by sentimentality in the hero's relationship with the nice girl and the harsh cynicism of *The Big Carnival (Ace In The Hole)* smacks of over-protestation.

A perverse sense of humor informs *Double Indemnity's* grim story, in the exchanges between Neff and Phyllis, and tellingly, between Neff and Keyes in the final scene. The apparent "throwaway" of having Neff continually light the cigars of the "matchless" Keyes has an extraordinary payoff in the final moments of the film, when Keyes tenderly lights the cigarette of the bleeding Neff. Night-for-night exteriors and moodily lit interiors (notably the meeting at Neff's apartment between Neff and Phyllis) coupled with the rhythmic flow of MacMurray's narration and the transposition of the story to flashback, anticipate other important film noir such as *Out of the Past, The Killers,* and *Criss Cross.* In *Double Indemnity,* Wilder found an ambience and narrative closely akin to his own sensibilities. Abetted but not overshadowed by Chandler's contributions, Wilder used the noir structure to color and restrict the romanticism of Neff's character and emphasize instead the doomed and obsessive qualities of his entanglement in Phyllis' web.

There are few women in film noir who would rival Phyllis. Jane Palmer in *Too Late for Tears,* who kills a corrupt private detective and her own husband (and probably killed her first husband as well); the cool, aristocratic exploiter Lisa Bannister in *Lady from Shanghai*; even the repeatedly duplicitous Kathie Moffat in *Out of the Past* are all distant seconds. The black widow played by Stanwyck is the classic period archetype. In fact, *Double Indemnity* has a panoply of prototypes beyond a perfect plan that goes awry and a femme fatale. In terms of content there is the ironic, first-person narration; extensive flashbacks; greed and lust that leads to murder; as forthright a portrayal of adultery as the Production Code Office would permit; several other "pairings," not just the old/young attractions of Neff and Lola and Phyllis and Sachetti but also Neff and Keyes; a savvy investigator; and finally, of course, betrayal and death (actual and implied) for the illicit lovers.

From the first, the tone is far different from Cain, as stylistically *Double Indemnity* also sets several standards. It opens with an unusual title sequence: while Rózsa's minor chords portend some vague doom, the silhouette of a man on crutches moves towards the camera. In the first sequence, a car speeds through a downtown area at night and stops in front of a large office building. There is bizarre comic relief as the elevator operator jokes about his purported heart condition but soon the wounded Neff has the Dictaphone in hand and the voiceover flashbacks can begin. Cain reveals the situation more directly and traditionally, with the first hint of something abnormal only coming halfway through opening chapter: "All of a sudden she looked at me and I felt a chill creep up my back and into the roots of my hair. 'Do you sell accident insurance?'" For all its notoriety, Cain's novella was actually fairly tame. His Walter Huff is described as having a "vividness of speech" but it consists of some occasional argot and misuse of some third person plural and singular. From the earliest images of him, overcoat draped awkwardly over his shoulder and answering the elevator man with a clipped, "Let's ride," the viewer can see that Neff is someone entirely different. Cain's ending in which Huff and "Mrs. Nirdlinger" execute a suicide pact on the high seas is more soap opera than noir, so Wilder and Chandler had to do a lot more than just change their names. Their construction of Neff's voiceover narration is repeatedly more chilling than any moment in the book. Wilder's deft use of selected longer takes and fluid two shots in the scenes between Neff and his mentor Keyes sharply focus that relationship. For Neff much more than for Huff, the desires for a woman and for money are confounded with the desire to beat Keyes, to overcome a powerful father figure. But most significantly, the narration, the performance, plus Wilder's staging and cutting, all underscore the inescapable fatality of the plot. As Neff says in voiceover after everything has gone as planned, "Suddenly it came over me that everything would go wrong. It sounds crazy, Keyes, but it's true so help me: I couldn't hear my own footsteps. It was the walk of a dead man."

The fatalistic tone of *Double Indemnity*, the subtle sense of malaise, is sustained as much by its naturalistic and hardbitten performances as by its visual style. Certainly Seitz's work here and with several other Paramount noir from the earlier *This Gun for Hire,* to the later *The Big Clock* and *Night Has a Thousand Eyes* for John Farrow, would help define approaches to interior lighting and location shooting perfected by John Alton later in the decade. The flashbacks begin with a familiar image of Hollywood from the 1930s or '40s, a Spanish-style house in the Hollywood Hills. Inside the house Neff recounts "sunshine coming in through the Venetian blinds showed up the dust in the air." Outside as he drives away he notices the "smell of honeysuckle all along that street. How could I have known that murder can sometimes smell like honeysuckle?" Although the drive-away is a process shot and the house interior a stage reconstruction, the essentially realistic composite geography of the movie fully underscores the narrative tone. This house and its surroundings are a core metaphor of the film. To Neff it contains all the possibilities of the American dream: wealth, love, and beating the system. When the blonde-haired Phyllis first appears on the second floor landing, wrapped in only a towel, Neff is awestruck. When she comes down later to indulge in a bit of classic double entendre, Neff cannot keep his eyes off her dangling foot and its "honey of an anklet," symbolizing not only her sexual power over him but also the wealth for which he yearns. On the second visit, denser shadows and shallower light show less dust and become a visual equivalent of the web in which Phyllis is about to enmesh Neff.

Neff's apartment, where a key love scene is played out, was modeled after Wilder's dingy apartment at the Chateau Marmont where he first lived after arriving in Los Angeles. In contrast to the Dietrichson home, it's cramped, shadowy, and spare, much like its bitter, world-weary tenant. After the crime, when the couple furtively meets in the aisles of Jerry's Market, the flat lighting and stacks of canned goods reinforce the lovers' sense of still being trapped in the mundane and everyday, the very thing they killed to escape. In Keyes' impromptu visit to Neff, who is waiting for Phyllis at his apartment, Seitz and Wilder distill all the peril of the noir universe into one sequence. Although the front door must be hung so that it uncharacteristically opens out into the corridor, on the brink of being discovered Phyllis manages to hide behind the door as Keyes departs.

The final deadly embrace of Neff and Phyllis in the parlor lit only by the thin shafts of light that manage to pierce the closed Venetian blinds is a tour-de-force of noir light-

Double Indemnity: *Phyllis Dietrichson (Barbara Stanwyck) and Walter Neff (Fred MacMurray) dump her husband's body.*

ing. Lit otherwise, the scene's impact would certainly be altered, but in the final analysis, it is the screen presence of the actors that sells the moment. The perfect crime having eluded them, Neff and Phyllis suffer the fate predicted by his mentor Keyes: "Murder is never perfect. When two people are involved . . . it's not like taking a trolley ride together where they can get off at different stops. They're stuck with each other and they've got to ride all the way to the end of the line. It's a one-way trip and the last stop is the cemetery." **AS & BL**

A DOUBLE LIFE (1947)

Director: George Cukor. **Screenplay**: Ruth Gordon and Garson Kanin. **Producer**: Michael Kanin. **Director of Photography**: Milton Krasner. **Music**: Miklós Rózsa. **Production Design**: Harry Horner. **Editor**: Robert Parrish. **Cast**: Ronald Colman (Anthony John), Signe Hasso (Brita), Edmond O'Brien (Bill Friend), Shelley Winters (Pat Kroll), Ray Collins (Victor Donlan), Philip Loeb (Max Lasker), Millard Mitchell (Al Cooley), Joe Sawyer (Pete Bonner), Charles La Torre (Stellini), Whit Bissell (Dr. Stauffer), John Drew Colt (Stage Manager), Peter Thompson (Assistant Stage Manager), Elizabeth Dunne (Gladys), Alan Edmiston (Rex), Wilton Graff (Dr. Mervin), Harlan Briggs (Oscar Bernard). **Location**: The Empire Theatre, New York City. **Completed**: August 18, 1947. **Released**: Universal, December 25. 103 minutes.

Anthony John, an actor who is so obsessed with his stage roles that he cannot leave them in the theater, is cast as Othello in a production for the Broadway stage. His former but still friendly wife, Brita, is the actress playing Desdemona. Anthony begins to act strangely toward Pat Kroll, a pathetically lonely waitress, who invites him to her apartment and ultimately to her bed. By opening night, Anthony is feeling the jealous madness of Othello in real life. He suspects the play's press agent, Bill Friend, of having an affair with Brita. When she quarrels with Anthony about this, he drifts inexorably to Pat's place. As he recites lines from the play, he chokes the helpless woman to death and smothers her with a kiss. Bill learns of Pat's death and devises a publicity scheme linking it with the play. Anthony goes into a rage, arousing

Bill's suspicion. Aided by a homicide detective, Bill arranges for a girl disguised as Pat to confront Anthony. The actor's horrified surprise confirms the detective's suspicions. However, before Anthony can be arrested after that night's performance of *Othello*, the actor realizes he has been exposed. He plunges a dagger into his heart and dies in the theater's wings.

George Cukor's only excursion into the noir genre, *A Double Life* is an appropriate vehicle for this director's special talents. Unlike most noir films, it boasts the "high-toned" background of theater, and, excepting Shelley Winters' pathetic proletarian waif, equally high-toned characters. The film's recreation of the theatrical world is meticulous, with the theater-bred director and writers Ruth Gordon and Garson Kanin drawing on their firsthand knowledge of that special world to lend verisimilitude to an unusual story. Milton Krasner's chiaroscuro cinematography aids in creating a landscape of glittery shifting surfaces beneath which lurk the black depths of psychological disturbance. With Ronald Colman on stage, the viewer must squint out past the glare of the footlights into a void haunted by bodiless voices. With him, we walk rain washed streets gleaming under the streetlights and stretching away into empty night. Virtually every shot in this film is a visual metaphor for Colman's state of mind, sparkling with lucidity and wit one moment before plunging into bizarre and haunted depths the next.

Although it has been suggested that Colman was not sufficiently demonic for the part of Anthony John/Othello, he gives a powerful, highly original performance, which provides a portrait of disintegration, if not of evil. The least vain of actors despite his matinee-idol looks, Colman allows his character's mental anguish to emerge from within and distort his perfect features in appropriate Jekyll-and-Hyde fashion. As its title suggests, *A Double Life* is truly a picture of opposing forces, mirror images and deadly doubles. Anthony John is at war with Othello, the elegant world of the theater is opposed to the squalid existence of Shelley Winters' Pat Kroll, and illusion versus reality are all conveyed in the opposing lights and darks of Krasner's luminous photography. **JK**

DRIVE A CROOKED ROAD (1954)

Director: Richard Quine. **Screenplay**: Blake Edwards adapted by Richard Quine based on a story by James Benson. **Producer**: Jonie Taps. **Director of Photography**: Charles Lawton, Jr. **Music**: Ross DiMaggio. **Art Director**: Walter Holscher. **Editor**: Jerome Thoms. **Cast**: Mickey Rooney (Eddie Shannon), Dianne Foster (Barbara Mathews), Kevin McCarthy (Steve Norris), Jack Kelly (Harold Baker), Harry Landers (Ralph), Jerry Paris (Phil), Paul Picerni (Carl), Dick Crockett (Don), Mort Mills (Garage Foreman), Peggy Maley (Marge). **Completed**: November 3, 1953. **Released**: Columbia Pictures, April 2. 83 minutes.

Eddie Shannon is a mechanic and amateur-racing driver who leads a lonely existence until he meets Barbara Mathews. However, she is the mistress of Steve Norris, who insists Barbara romance Eddie so he will be involved in a Palm Springs bank robbery Norris is planning. The plan requires a driver of Eddie's caliber to cover a difficult backload in a matter of minutes, thereby eluding any police roadblocks on the main highway. Eddie hesitates to participate but Barbara convinces him. The robbery is a success; but Eddie discovers he has been duped. Over the protestations of the guilty Barbara, Steve and his other partner, Harold, decide to kill Eddie. At gunpoint, Harold forces Eddie to drive to a secluded spot, but Eddie purposefully crashes the car and kills Harold. Seriously injured, Eddie returns to Steve's house and finds him beating Barbara. After killing Steve, Eddie consoles Barbara as the police arrive.

The expressionistic lighting and camera angles associated with film noir of the 1940s gave way to a streamlined, or at least more modest, "fifties" style, as typified here by Lawton's cinematography. Director Quine moves the story in a straightforward fashion while taking full advantage of readily available locations, such as Los Angeles' streets and nearby beaches. The film's interiors have sparse and functional décor except that

Eddie's apartment displays racing trophies that express his hopes and dreams, but it emphasizes his anonymity in virtually every other way. The moderation of style extends to the characterizations. Dianne Foster and Kevin McCarthy portray treacherous villains who seem more down-to-earth and coolly rational than their 1940s counterparts do. As Barbara, Foster's remorse over destroying Eddie seems genuine but she accepts it as necessary to the crime's success.

The lack of pretentiousness in a film like *Drive a Crooked Road* could be mistaken for a lack of artistic zeal; but such films take the cycle's motifs out from the dark corners of a noir underworld and bring them into a flood of sunlight, to show that human nature remains just as corrupt. The victimized noir protagonist of Eddie, played by ex-ingenue Mickey Rooney (who was intent, like many aging actors of the period—e.g., Jimmy Stewart, Dick Powell—on "noiring" his image), is all the more poignant because his character is a wholesome, ordinary human being who suffers from the simplest of alienated emotional states: heterosexual loneliness. The most striking shot in the film shows Eddie tossing and turning on his bed when Barbara refuses to see him, a brief but evocative scene. **BL**

DUEL IN THE SUN (1946)

Director: King Vidor, Josef von Sternberg, Otto Brower, William Dieterle, William Cameron Menzies, David O. Selznick. **Screenplay**: Oliver H.P. Garrett, David O. Selznick, Ben Hecht based on the novel by Niven Busch. **Producer**: David O. Selznick. **Director of Photography**: Lee Garmes, Ray Rennahan, Harold Rosson. **Production Designer**: J. McMillan Johnson. **Music**: Dimitri Tiomkin. **Editor**: John Faure, William H. Ziegler. **Cast**: Jennifer Jones (Pearl Chavez), Gregory Peck (Lewt McCanles), Joseph Cotten (Jesse McCanles), Lionel Barrymore (Senator McCanles), Lillian Gish (Laura Belle McCanles), Walter Huston (Preacher), Charles Bickford (Sam Pierce), Tilly Losch (Mrs. Chavez), Joan Tetzel (Helen Langford), Butterfly McQueen (Vashti). **Released**: Selznick Releasing Organization, December 31. 144 minutes [Roadshow engagements]; 129 minutes [general release].

Pearl Chavez is the daughter of an upper class Southern aristocrat and a Native American dancer. After her father shoots her mother in a fit of jealousy and is executed for murder, Pearl moves to live with a relative, Laura McCanles, and her racist, overbearing husband. While staying there she is courted by three men: Lewt, the n'er-do-well McCanles son; Jesse, Lewt's righteous brother; and Sam Pierce, an aging rancher. Meanwhile, in a battle between ranchers and the railroad, Lewt takes his father's side and initiates a violent terror campaign against the railroad while Jesse becomes the railroad's representative. Pearl and Lewt are irresistibly drawn together, but Lewt refuses to marry her. This pushes her into the arms of Sam, whom the jealous Lewt kills. In another fit of jealousy, Lewt shoots his own brother. Pearl decides to end her lover's reign of terror and tracks him up into the mountains where they kill each other in a gunfight.

After a brief prologue (narrated by Orson Welles in his typical "Voice-of-God" tone) sets a mythic tone ("And this is what the legend says: a flower, known nowhere else, grows from out of the desperate crags where Pearl vanished, Pearl who was herself a wild flower sprung from the hard clay, quick to blossom and early to die"), this David O. Selznick

Duel in the Sun: *Lewt (Gregory Peck) backs Pearl (Jennifer Jones) into a dark corner.*

noir epic opens in a brawling border town where teenage half-breed, Pearl, waits outside a dance hall. Inside, her Native American mother entertains a rowdy audience of men with a salacious dance. Pearl watches in a mixture of fascination and shock. As her mother finishes her dance, her lover sweeps her away. Pearl follows and then witnesses the murder of her mother and her lover by her cuckolded father. After he is executed, Pearl follows her father's wishes. She is determined to be a "lady" as she says ("I'll be a good girl. I promise I will) and resists what she considers the lure of her mother's sensuality as well as the taint of "dark blood" (the racism of the movie should not be overlooked). However, even with her well-to-do relatives, Pearl cannot escape the fact that her "dark beauty," combined with a childlike innocence, attracts men inexorably. She soon becomes the object of desire of the two McCanles brothers (the "bad boy" Lewt and the upstanding Jesse) as well as an older cowhand—Sam—who wants to be her protector.

The central conflict of the movie is Pearl's fluctuation between the world of sensuality and that of moral responsibility. She is drawn to Lewt because he radiates danger and sex. Her dance for him after he finds her naked at the swimming hole (cut from the wide release version of the movie) and a particularly passionate and violent bit of lovemaking in her room during a fierce storm illustrate their attraction. Yet, her defense of Jesse and her attraction to the fatherly Sam denote her conflicting desire to conform to the conventions of family and society.

Although she continues to waver between these various men and the options they present, she ultimately aligns herself with the moralistic Jesse. No longer able to abide Lewt's careless attitude towards her or his possessiveness that leads him to threaten his own brother's life, she decides on a course of action. The climax of the movie is one of the prime examples of noir amour fou as Pearl mounts her horse, takes her rifle and heads out to kill Lewt before he can do any further harm. In a battle in the mountains, the lovers exchange shots and fatally wound each other. But even amidst this holocaust, the couple cannot hide their savage passion as Pearl crawls through the rocks to join her lover who calls out to her plaintively. The tormented lovers are finally united peacefully in death. **JU**

EDGE OF DOOM (1950)

Director: Mark Robson [uncredited additional scenes, Charles Vidor]. **Screenplay**: Philip Yordan, Charles Brackett [uncredited] with additional scenes by Ben Hecht based on the novel by Leo Brady. **Producer**. Samuel Goldwyn. **Director of Photography**: Harry Stradling. **Music**: Hugo Friedhofer. **Art Director**: Richard Day. **Editor**: Daniel Mandell. **Cast**: Dana Andrews (Father Roth), Farley Granger (Martin Lynn), Joan Evans (Rita Conroy), Robert Keith (Detective Lt. Mandel), Paul Stewart (Craig), Mala Powers (Julie), Adele Jergens (Irene), Harold Vermilyea (Father Kirkman), John Ridgely, Douglas Fowley (Detectives), Mabel Paige (Mrs. Pearson), Howland Chamberlain (Mr. Murray), Frances Morris (Mrs. Lynn). **Completed**: January 10, 1950; additional sequences shot August, 1950. **Released**: August 3. 99 minutes.

Martin Lynn, a floral delivery clerk, is a frustrated young member of New York's poverty row because he cannot save enough money to marry his girl, Julie, or to send his mother, dying of consumption, to a healthier climate. Although a hard worker, Martin's boss procrastinates over giving him a raise. When his mother dies, Mr. Craig, a neighbor and small-time grifter, encourages Martin to ask the local Catholic parish for a proper funeral. That evening, alone in the rectory and distracted by personal problems, Father Kirkland sees Martin and agrees to help with the funeral expenses. However, Martin demands a fancy funeral and Kirkman explains that is impossible. Obsessed with his mother's funeral, Martin loses control and kills Kirkman, bludgeoning him with a crucifix. The young man attempts to rush home, but a nearby box office theft leads police to arrest him as a suspect for that crime. The next day Father Roth, who becomes pastor at Kirkman's death, hears of Martin's arrest and persuades Lt. Mandel to release him into his custody. Mandel later arrests Craig for the murder based on an eyewitness' identification. After demanding an expensive floral arrangement from his boss, Martin is fired. Meanwhile, Father Roth discovers that Martin is guilty. Grief-stricken and thwarted at every turn, Martin prays before his mother's body and finally confesses to Father Roth, explaining that he will turn himself in providing he is allowed to attend his mother's funeral.

   Given that the characteristic existential and pessimistic bias of film noir runs counter to the essential optimism of Christianity, it is surprising to find even one entry in the cycle that might easily be labeled "Catholic noir." What is not surprising is that the film flopped when it premiered in N.Y.C., prompting Goldwyn to have Ben Hecht write the framing scenes that are now part of this film. Without them, this film is pure noir, but even with them it is pretty bleak.

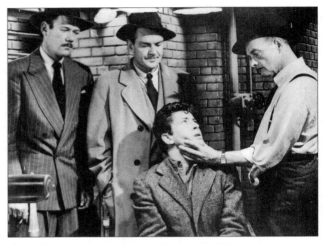

Edge of Doom: *Det. Lt. Mandel (Robert Keith) interrogates Martin Lynn (Farley Granger) while two detectives (John Ridgely, left, and Douglas Fowley) look on.*

For even though Father Roth tells the younger priest that he saw God in Martin Lynn, it is difficult to believe audiences would have, especially when the external world that so oppresses Martin is weighted so heavily against redemption. It is, as well, rendered strikingly in RKO noir style by Harry Stradling. **BP**

THE ENFORCER (1951)

Director: Bretaigne Windust [and Raoul Walsh]. **Screenplay**: Martin Rackin. **Producer**: Milton Sperling (United States Pictures). **Director of Photography**: Robert Burks. **Music**: David Buttolph. **Art Director**: Charles H. Clarke. **Editor**: Fred Allen. **Cast**: Humphrey Bogart (Martin Ferguson), Zero Mostel (Big Babe Lazich), Ted de Corsia (Joseph Rico), Everett Sloane (Albert Mendoza), Roy Roberts (Capt. Frank Nelson), Lawrence Tolan (Duke Malloy), King Donovan (Sgt Whitlow), Robert Steele (Herman), Patricia Joiner (Teresa Davis/Angela Vetto), Don Beddoe (Thomas O'Hara), Tito Vuolo (Tony Vetto), John Kellogg (Vince), Jack Lambert (Zaca), Adelaide Klein (Olga Kirshen), Susan Cabot (Nina Lombardo), Mario Siletti (Louis). **Completed**: August 31, 1950. **Released**: Warner Bros., February 24. 88 minutes.

Assistant District Attorney Martin Ferguson is ready to prosecute Albert Mendoza for a number of seemingly unrelated and unsolved homicides when his only witness, Joseph Rico, is killed on the eve of the trial. Ferguson and Police Capt. Frank Nelson spend the night going through the collected

The Enforcer: *Capt. Nelson (Roy Roberts), "Big Babe Lazich" (Zero Mostel), and D.A. Martin Ferguson (Humphrey Bogart).*

prosecution files and tape recordings, putting together a grisly picture of Mendoza's scheme to sell murder by hiring gunmen to kill for a fee, thereby eliminating all chance of detection through motive. At the last moment, Ferguson finds a clue that leads to the discovery of another witness and secures his case against Mendoza.

The Enforcer is one of the first films to deal realistically with the criminal business of killing as represented by Murder, Inc. (also known as the Syndicate or the Mob). *The Enforcer* borrows the semi-documentary flavor of earlier film noir such as *The House on 92nd Street* and *Naked City*, but is also a topical film, produced about the same time that Senator Estes Kefauver's committee was investigating organized crime. Bogart plays Martin Ferguson, the assistant district attorney. He is determined to put Albert Mendoza in prison for his part in creating the murder organization that embodies the perfect murder method for the paranoid noir psychology, dealing as it does in motiveless, unexplainable, nightmare crime. Everett Sloane as Mendoza is only one of a cast of familiar noir faces, including Jeff Corey, King Donovan, Ted de Corsia, and, in a brief but unusual role, Zero Mostel. *The Enforcer* is briskly paced, for the story, told primarily in flashback, is of an urgent job that must be completed in twelve hours. The harsh photography by Robert Burks complements the relentless tone of the film; but it is principally Raoul Walsh's (uncredited) direction that plays Ferguson's barely repressed outrage against Mendoza's lethal self-assurance that he can deal with any threat.

The finale of *The Enforcer* is positive but curiously ambiguous. The witness that Ferguson needed to ensure his case's success has been found; but there are no scenes of the trial, and the film has already suggested that justice is often blind when dealing with the cold-blooded killers of Murder, Inc. In this world of shifting values and uncertain motivation where anything may happen, the viewer is left to speculate on whether justice will triumph and, if so, for how long. **MB & AS**

ESCAPE IN THE FOG (1945)

Director: Budd Boetticher. **Screenplay**: Aubrey Wisberg. **Producer**: Wallace MacDonald. **Director of Photography**: George Meehan. **Music**: Mario Castelnuovo-Tedesco, Sidney Cutner, Louis Gruenberg, Ernst Toch [uncredited excerpts]. **Art Director**: Jerome Pycha Jr. **Editor**: Jerome Thoms. **Cast**: Otto Kruger (Paul Devon), Nina Foch (Eileen Carr), William Wright (Barry Malcolm), Konstantin Shayne (Schiller), Ivan Triesault (Hausmer), Ernie Adams (George Smith), Elmo Lincoln (Cop), Shelley Winters (Taxi Driver). **Released**: Columbia, April 5. 65 minutes.

As Nurse Eileen Carr is walking one fog-bound night on the Golden Gate Bridge, she sees three men piling out of a taxi trying to kill a fourth. She awakens screaming in bed at the hospice where she is recovering from mental fatigue. There she meets Barry Malcolm, the victim in her dream, whom she has never before laid eyes upon. They hit it off, and he persuades her to join him for a few days in San Francisco. However, government agent Malcolm receives orders from his operator Paul Devon to courier top-secret documents to Hong Kong. Agents of the Axis powers led by Schiller waylay Malcolm. Luckily, Carr believes that her nightmare was in fact a premonition, and rushes off to the Golden Gate Bridge to save Malcolm.

While not an especially memorable noir, *Escape in the Fog* is clever and atmospheric. Its ingenuity is at times a bit stretched in the manner of the Saturday matinee serials of the era. Of course, there is also the obligatory dose of wartime rhetoric, with much derision of "Japs" and all the Germans speaking in the most guttural tones they can reach without doing irreparable damage to the larynx. Still, director Boetticher keeps those fog machines churning to mask the cheap sets on which skullduggery in Chinatown at midnight actually takes place.

Dutch-born actress Nina Foch had the good fortune to segue from one economically made Boetticher/Columbia noir and reprise her damsel in distress for Joseph H. Lewis in *My Name Is Julia Ross*, for whom she worked again in *Undercover Man*. Like many minor noir icons, she left the cycle for television work as the 1940s ended. **BMV**

EXPERIMENT IN TERROR (1962)

Director and Producer: Blake Edwards (Geoffrey-Kate Productions). **Screenplay**: Gordon Gordon and Mildred Gordon based on their novel *Operation Terror*. **Director of Photography**: Philip Lathrop. **Music**: Henry Mancini. **Art Director**: Robert Peterson. **Editor**: Patrick McCormack. **Cast**: Glenn Ford (John "Rip" Ripley), Lee Remick (Kelly Sherwood), Stefanie Powers (Toby), Roy Poole (Brad), Ned Glass (Popcorn), Anita Loo (Lisa), Patricia Huston (Nancy), Gilbert Green (Special Agent), Clifton James (Capt. Moreno). **Location**: Oakland Bay Bridge, Candlestick Park, San Francisco. **Completed**: November 11, 1961. **Released**: Columbia, April 13. 123 minutes.

Kelly Sherwood, a young, single bank teller, is approached in her garage late one night by a man who seems to know a great deal about her life. Invisible in the darkness and with an asthmatic voice, he threatens her and her younger sister with harm if she will not comply with his demand to give him $100,000 from the bank where she works. Against her assailant's instructions, Kelly calls the F.B.I. Agent John Ripley handles the case, posting guards round Kelly and her sister, and informing the president of the bank. Informants are murdered after identifying the perp Lynch to the F.B.I. But when Kelly's sister is kidnapped to ensure the plan's success, the F.B.I. advises her to steal the money as stipulated. Kelly does so, and Lynch tells her to meet him at Candlestick Park during a ball game. F.B.I. agents infiltrate the crowd and Lynch is killed in a shoot-out as he attempts to escape.

Film noir is associated with urban settings, and for his locale, Edwards effectively utilizes the graceful bridges and leisurely cable cars of San Francisco. By placing his menace in a sophisticated milieu, Edwards heightens the threat, expressing the noir concern that the city is outwardly respectable but inwardly seething with nameless terrors that spring to life when least expected. His use of the Bay Area as a location is rivaled only by Don Siegel in *The Lineup* and *Dirty Harry*. In all of these films, leaving your heart in San Francisco is not only a lyric's fancy but also a grim possibility.

The heroine is surrounded by people but is still very alone, defenseless, and vulnerable to attack from the criminal who has singled her out as his prey. She is most susceptible in the place that people normally feel most secure: her home. Additionally, although her dangerous position is known by the F.B.I., their plans leave her unprotected. In film noir's urban landscapes, one is safe nowhere.

The killer is a rarely seen shadowy presence, with an asthmatic wheeze that hints of whispery evil. Heavies in film noir often have distinct physical deformities, such as Everett Sloane's limp in *The Lady from Shanghai*, or vivid mannerisms, such as Richard Widmark's high-pitched giggle in *Kiss of Death*, to correspond to their tainted souls. In *Experiment in Terror*, Ross Martin's throaty susurrations give the heroine and the audience a sense of quiet but deadly menace. Henry Mancini scored the film with a slow autoharp that echoes the slithery sounds of the villain's voice. Throughout, there is effective manipulation of sound and image. The end of one scene is punctuated by the piercing scream of a young woman; the cut shows us the yelp of fear emanating from a girl about to be tossed off the diving board of a public swimming pool. Tension slackens momentarily as the scream is revealed as a cry of pleasure, only to be tightened seconds later when the first girl is kidnapped. The murder of one informant takes place in the auditorium of a silent movie theater during a frenetic slapstick comedy accompanied by a raucous piano.

The climax of the film is at Candlestick Park during a crowded Giants baseball game. The killer, like an unreal figure from the subconscious, bursts out of the mob against the background of this great American pastime. Wearing a hooded parka and sunglasses, he is cornered and makes his last move on the pitchers mound, all under the glaring lights with thousands of eyewitnesses. Like the Dodger pitcher in the bottom of the ninth, he faces "sudden death." Like an insect, he is ground down by something larger: the whirring helicopter overhead. In a large sense, the whole of America is an arena for the nightmare conflicts epitomized by film noir. Therefore, whether it is the deserted Kezar Stadium where the protagonist of *Dirty Harry* apprehends the sniper or a teeming Candlestick Park in *Experiment in Terror*, it is appropriate that such epic, symbolic confrontations in American life take place in stadiums. **JB**

FALL GUY (1947)

Director: Reginald Le Borg. **Screenplay**: Jerry Warner with additional dialogue by John O'Dea based on the short story "Cocaine" by Cornell Woolrich. **Producer**: Walter Mirisch. **Director of Photography**: Mack Stenger. **Music Director**: Edward J. Kay. **Art Director**: Dave Milton. **Editor**: William Austin. **Cast**: Clifford Penn (Tom Cochrane), Teala Loring (Lois Walter), Robert Armstrong (Mac McLaine), Virginia Dale (Marie), Elisha Cook Jr. (Joe), Douglas Fowley (Shannon), Charles Arnt (Uncle Jim Grossett), Harry Strang (Taylor), Iris Adrian (Mrs. Sindell), John Harmon (Mr. Sindell). **Completed**: November 22, 1946. **Released**: Monogram, March 15. 64 minutes.

Tom Cochran passes out on a New York street one evening and because his clothes are bloodied and he has a bloody knife, the police suspect foul play. He has no memory of what has happened, and when the police doctor informs Shannon, the lead detective, that he is under the influence of alcohol and a powerful narcotic that has robbed him of his memory, Shannon decides to hold him as a suspect while the police investigate. Tom escapes from the hospital ward and manages to get to the apartment of his friend, Mac McLaine, also a police detective. Under intense questioning by Mac, Tom remembers bits and pieces of the previous evening: he went to a bar after a quarrel with his girlfriend, Lois Walters, and met a guy named Joe who took him to a party; he engaged the attention there of a comely singer named Marie, but after finishing his drink he passed out; when he awoke, alone, he discovered the body of a young woman in a closet and somehow picked up the bloody knife before passing out in the street. Mac believes Tom and with his and Lois' help manages to elude the pursuing police. They find the party's location and the closet, but there is no body inside. However, Tom sees a neon sign outside spelling "ACE" instead of "PAL" as on the night of the murder and realizes that the body was in the upstairs apartment. The body is found, but the police arrest Mac. Tom escapes, finds Marie and ultimately discovers that she was hired by Lois' guardian, the disapproving "Uncle" Jim, to lure Tom to the party and drug him.

Fall Guy, a cheaply made Monogram release, is slightly better than *The Guilty* as far as film versions of Woolrich's fiction are concerned. Its visuals are uneven and eclectic but significant in one respect: the use of the familiar noir icon of a neon sign outside of a window, while not flashing in typical fashion, is here fully integrated into the plot (and not figuratively as in *The Unsuspected*). The screenwriters also took great liberties with Woolrich's original story, but managed to use enough of his motifs for this to qualify as a film noir. Woolrich himself had some strange ideas regarding the use of narcotics to indicate one's loss of self-determination. His characters often commit crimes (or think they have) and suffer from amnesia, recurrent nightmares and entrapment while in drug or alcohol-induced states. In fact, the party scene in *The Guilty* is somewhat reminiscent of the jazz sequence in *The Phantom Lady* in its confluence of drugs, alcohol, sex and jazz. **BP**

FALLEN ANGEL (1946)

Director and Producer: Otto Preminger. **Screenplay**: Harry Kleiner based on the novel by Marty Holland. **Director of Photography**: Joseph LaShelle. **Music**: David Raksin. **Art Directors**: Lyle Wheeler, Leland Fuller. **Editor**: Harry Reynolds. **Cast**: Alice Faye (June Mills), Dana Andrews (Eric Stanton), Linda Darnell (Stella), Charles Bickford (Mark Judd), Anne Revere (Clara Mills), Bruce Cabot (Dave Atkins), John Carradine (Madley), Percy McBride (Pop), Olin Howlin (Joe Ellis). **Location**: Orange, California. **Released**: 20th Century-Fox, February 6. 98 minutes.

Down to his last dollar, Eric Stanton arrives by bus in a little northern California town where he immediately becomes interested in Stella, a waitress, and pretends to be a medium. He succeeds in impressing one of the town's most respectable women, June Mills, although her sister Clara is skeptical of his intentions. Eric plans to romance June to acquire her money and then marry Stella, who remains aloof. Several other men are also interested in Stella, including Pop, proprietor of the café where she works, and slick Dave Atkins. A former New York detective, Mark Judd, comes into the cafe regularly and drinks

Fallen Angel: *Stella (Linda Darnell) and Eric Stanton (Dana Andrews).*

coffee. Eric tries but is unable to get hold of June's money without marrying her. When Stella is murdered, Eric is the main suspect. The relentless Judd investigates, and Eric flees to Francisco with June, discovering that he loves her. He returns to the town and proves that Judd is actually the murderer.

Made as a follow-up to the highly successful *Laura*, this less celebrated film boasts many of the same qualities, including Joseph LaShelle's imaginative lighting, a romantic David Raksin melody that complements the action, and the ideal Preminger actor, Dana Andrews, whose presence encourages a moral uncertainty. Preminger's mise-en-scène and subtle development of ambiguous characters belie his films' resolutions, which are often disappointing simplifications of complex moral and visual structures. *Fallen Angel* avoids this because of the two women with whom the protagonist is involved: one light and the other dark. June is guileless in her attractiveness, while Stella exploits her sexuality blatantly. Preminger forces contemplation of the meaning behind the sensual and behavioral qualities of the two women by cross-cutting close-ups between them at key moments, and in the dance sequence, connecting them with an ostentatious, sustained shot. There is a possible interpretation that the protagonist stands between an angel and a devil, heaven and hell; or the title can support the implication that he is a cipher figure, particularly since his past is mysterious and his attachments suspect. The real emotional pull in the film is away from Stella and toward June. Eric's apparent desire to possess Stella seems more willed than felt. He quickly forgets her once she is dead. Thus, it makes metaphorical sense that the complementary Lucifer figure, Judd, is Stella's killer because an "angel" such as June did not stop his descent into hell.

Another notable aspect of *Fallen Angel* is Preminger's direction of the scenes in the cafe. The counter's shape facilitates arresting and graceful moves of the camera. Eric and Judd are always situated on opposite sides of the cash register. When they drink their coffee, they become mirror images of each other, as Pop and Stella work. Although Stella, Pop, and Eric apparently dominate these scenes, the dramatic core is characteristically provided by the actions of Judd, the nonparticipant. Ritualistically, he comes in, sips his coffee, and plays the same song on the jukebox, "Slowly I Open My Eyes," and then he leaves. This is the extent of his involvement in the story before Stella's murder; but it is remarkably sufficient. The ritual actions become retrospectively dramatic when Judd repeats them as a central character accused of murder. **BL**

THE FALLEN SPARROW (1943)

Director: Richard Wallace. **Screenplay**: Warren Duff based on a novel by Dorothy B. Hughes. **Producer**: Robert Fellows. **Director of Photography**: Nicholas Musuraca. **Art Director**: Van Nest Polglase. **Music**: Rob Webb. **Editor**: Robert Wise. **Cast**: John Garfield (John "Kit" McKittrick), Maureen O'Hara (Toni Donne), Walter Slezak (Dr. Skaas), Patricia Morison (Barbi Taviton), Martha O'Driscoll (Whitney Parker), Bruce Edwards (Ab Parker), John Banner (Anton), John Miljan (Inspector Tobin), Hugh Beaumont (Otto Skaas). **Released**: RKO, August 19. 94 minutes.

After escaping from a prison in Franco's Spain, Kit McKittrick returns home to New York to discover the mystery behind the death of his friend Louie, a New York cop. While

The Fallen Sparrow: *John Garfield as John "Kit" McKittrick.*

home he becomes involved with a circle of upper class friends and new acquaintances, all of whom have some connection with the death of Louie. Tormented by his torture while incarcerated, Kit still pursues the solution to the mystery. He falls for Toni Donne who seems tied to this group of refugees by Dr. Skaas, a shadowy figure. After the death of another friend, Ab, Kit discovers that the group around Skaas is a ring of Nazi spies and that Skaas himself was the man who tortured Kit in Spain and ordered the death of Louie. Skaas is obsessed with retrieving the battle standard of Kit's brigade and delivering it to Hitler. Skaas injects Kit with a truth serum but is shot by Kit. Learning Toni is part of the conspiracy, Kit delivers her over to the authorities.

John Garfield, in such noir films as *Body and Soul* and *Force of Evil*, always had a knack for combining a proletarian savvy with an intellectual's sense of existential angst. His performance in *The Fallen Sparrow* is no exception. Kit McKittrick, the protagonist of the film, refers to himself as a combination of a "mug" (he has a background with shady mobster types) and a "gentleman" (his family comes from the upper echelons of New York). But most importantly Kit is an idealist. He fought in the Spanish Civil War against Franco and his fascist allies. After escaping from prison in Spain, he returns home a victim of post-traumatic stress disorder. In the first shot of him on the train traveling from an Arizonan sanitarium back to New York, Kit stares out into the darkness and questions himself as to whether he has the courage and "guts" to avenge the death of his cop friend, Louie, who has died under mysterious circumstances.

Once back, Kit is subject to periodic breakdowns: hearing the sound of the dragging foot of the Nazi who tortured him in prison; tormented by the sound of a faucet dripping, or noisy cars outside his penthouse window. In response, he drowns out the sound by banging frantically on the piano or self-medicating himself with liquor. But, of course, Kit's perceptions are not totally paranoid. He *is* being pursued by the same man who was his torturer—Dr. Skaas, who on behest of Adolph Hitler wants the battle standard of Kit's massacred regiment (the references to *The Maltese Falcon* are numerous.). Although his love interest, Toni, tells him that the banner is not worth dying for, Kit cannot betray his dead comrades and give Hitler what he wants. His idealism pushes him further into darkened rooms where friends are murdered and where he cringes in the darkness in anguish.

Even his final victory over Skaas, whom he shoots while partially immobilized by a truth serum, only temporarily relieves his angst. For now he must reveal to the authorities that Toni has been lying to him all along and that she is in cahoots with the other Nazis in this ring of espionage. Again, as in *The Maltese Falcon*, the protagonist turns in his betraying lover and returns to the isolation engendered by his own sense of honor. **JU**

FEAR (1946)

Director: Alfred Zeisler. **Screenplay**: Zeisler and Dennis Cooper based on the novel *Crime and Punishment* by Fyodor Dostoevsky. **Producer**: Lindsley Parsons. **Director of Photography**: Jackson Rose. **Art Directors**: F. Paul Sylos, Dave Milton. **Editor**: Ace Herman. **Cast**: Warren William (Capt. Burke), Anne Gwynne (Eileen/Cathy), Peter Cookson (Larry Crain), James Cardwell (Ben), Nestor Paiva (Schaefer), Francis Pierlot (Professor Stanley), Johnny Strong (John), William Moss (Al), Darren McGavin (Chuck), Henry Clay (Steve), Almira Sessions (Mrs. Williams). **Completed**: July 26, 1945. **Released**: Monogram, March 2. 68 minutes.

His scholarship discontinued, medical student Larry Crane is forced to pawn his few possessions with Professor Stanley. Still lacking sufficient funds, Larry convinces himself that Stanley has exploited him and kills the professor. Panicking when he hears someone coming, Larry leaves the money and some clues behind. However, his situation improves when a romance blossoms with a recent acquaintance, Eileen, and his article is published in the *Periodical Review,* which pays him $1,000 and motivates the faculty to renew his scholarship. The premise of the article, that exceptional people are above the law, arouses the suspicions of police Capt. Burke who is investigating the murder of Professor Stanley. Larry accuses the police of persecuting him while simultaneously dropping "hints" that implicate him. Distraught, Larry attempts suicide but is saved by a stranger. He finally confesses his crime to Eileen but shortly thereafter Burke apologizes to him and explains that another suspect has confessed. Larry gets tickets to leave town but is hit by a car. At this point, Larry wakes up and realizes that he has been dreaming.

This low budget film is hardly pure Dostoevsky, but it has a visual style superior to and more cohesive than the typical Monogram product. The framing device of the dream, trite from a literary viewpoint, actually reinforces the noir quality of *Fear* by virtue of its oneirism. This is further supported by a visual style full of oblique angles, depth staging, and expressionistic lighting. **BP**

FEAR IN THE NIGHT (1947)

Director: Maxwell Shane. **Screenplay**: Maxwell Shane based on the short story *Nightmare* by Cornell Woolrich. **Producers**: William H. Pine, William C. Thomas. **Director of Photography**: Jack Greenhalgh. **Music**: Rudy Schrager. **Art Director**: F. Paul Sylos. **Editor**: Howard Smith. **Cast**: Paul Kelly (Cliff Herlihy), De Forest Kelley (Vince Grayson), Ann Doran (Lil Herlihy), Kay Scott (Betty Winters), Robert Emmett Keane (Lewis Belnap), Jeff York (Deputy Torrence), Charles Victor (Capt. Warner), Janet Warren (Mrs. Belnap). **Released**: Paramount, April 18. 71 minutes.

In a small, octagonal room composed entirely of mirrored doors, a woman stands over a man who cuts into a safe with a torch. Somnambulistically, Vince Grayson enters through one of the doors and the men struggle. Vince grabs an awl from the woman's hand and thrusts it into the man's heart. The woman disappears through one of the doors and Vince, stuffing the body into a closet, runs through another door, clutching a button from the victim's jacket and the key to the closet door. Waking the next morning, Vince finds the key and the button, indicating that he was not simply dreaming. Upset, Vince seeks the aid of his brother-in-law, homicide detective Cliff Herlihy, who insists it was just a nightmare. A few days later, Cliff and his wife Lil have a picnic with Vince and his girlfriend, Betty. A sudden storm forces them to take cover and Vince leads them to a large, empty mansion. Furthermore, Vince seems familiar with the house and discovers a mirrored room. This convinces Cliff that his brother is indeed guilty of murder. Cliff delays arresting Vince for the sake of his wife, and his sympathies are aroused when he saves Vince from suicide. Cliff learns that the middle-aged roomer next door visited Vince the night of the murder carrying a candle. He is wealthy Dr. Belnap, the mansion's owner and husband of the woman in Vince's "dream," who was killed in an auto accident after leaving the mansion the night of the murder. Cliff suspects Belnap hypnotized Vince. After Mrs. Belnap's funeral, Vince confronts Belnap in the mirrored room, which has been wired to a recording device nearby. The doctor confirms all of Vince's suspicions. To further exonerate himself, Vince allows Belnap to hypnotize him again and, in a trance, writes a confession of the killings, preparatory to drowning himself in a lake. However, Cliff and the police arrive to save Vince, and Belnap, fleeing the police in his car, loses control and is killed.

Of all the low-budget thrillers taken from Woolrich's fiction, *Fear In The Night* comes closest to capturing both the spirit and the plot of the original, demonstrating again the capabilities of a good B-movie which makes the most of its low budget and short screening time. Like the novelette, the film's action moves through the protagonist's first-person narration, although it is sporadic. But with lines like— "There was danger there…I wanted to turn and run, but I couldn't. It seemed as if my brain was handcuffed and I had to do what I'd come to do"—the presence of Woolrich is felt throughout. Greenhalgh's photography is sufficiently effective (except for the poor day-for-night at the film's conclusion), especially the scenes in the mirrored room and the darkened interior of Vince's hotel room (where a flashing light announces again that this is a film noir). More impressive are the process shots, which, as in *Murder, My Sweet*, herald the protagonist's descent into his particular dark nightmare. At the precise moment when Vince is reminded of the murder, the event is superimposed over a close-up of his irises before he passes out—a shot which defines the oneiric element of film noir as well as any other moment. **BP**

FEMALE JUNGLE (1955)

Director: Bruno VeSota. **Screenplay**: Bruno VeSota, Burt Kaiser. **Producer**: Burt Kaiser. **Director of Photography**: Elwood Bredell. **Art Director**: Ben Roseman. **Music**: Nicholas Carras. **Editor**: Carl Pingitore. **Cast**: Lawrence Tierney (Det. Sgt. Jack Stevens), Burt Kaiser (Alex Voe), John Carradine (Claude Almstead), Kathleen Crowley (Peggy Voe), Jayne Mansfield (Candy Price),

Female Jungle: Det. Sgt. Stevens (Lawrence Tierney) menaces Claude Almstead (John Carradine).

Duane Grey aka Rex Thorsen (Det. Sgt. Duane), James Kodl (Bar owner), Davis Roberts aka Robert Davis (Janitor), Eve Brent aka Jean Lewis (Monica Madison), Connie Cezan (Connie), Bruno VeSota (Connie's husband), Cornelius Keefe aka Jack Hill (Detective Captain). **Released**: Kaiser Productions, January 12. 73 minutes.

A famous actress, Monica Madison, is murdered in the streets as she exits a sleazy club. Alcoholic cop Jack Stevens, recovering from one of his blackouts, suspects that he may be the killer. In order to redeem himself he sets out to find the murderer. The first suspect is Claude Almstead, the actress' ex-lover. Although he seems the most likely, the death of a second woman, the B-girl Candy Price, leads Stevens to the caricaturist Alex Voe. In a chase through a warehouse, Voe is killed and the case solved.

Lawrence Tierney has become a minor icon of film noir as much for his personal life as his performances. Fallen into obscurity by the mid-1960s, he was pulled back into the limelight by a younger generation of filmmakers, most notably Quentin Tarantino with *Reservoir Dogs*. Tierney in *Female Jungle* brings the violent, alcoholic cop Jack Stevens to life with a credibility drawn from personal experience (Tierney was arrested several times for drunkenness and brawling). Stevens is a direct descendant of private detectives like Galt in *The Dark Corner*. Having been disgraced and "chewed out" by his own captain after another alcoholic blackout in which he may or may not have killed Monica Madison, he pulls himself together in order to solve the case and in the process find personal redemption.

Director/writer Bruno VeSota (who worked extensively with low-budget master Roger Corman) sets his film within the perimeter of a few darkened streets of an unnamed urban center (much like his silent horror classic *Daughter of Horror*, 1955) and within the real time of the movie—the case is solved in a little over an hour. Adhering to these Aristotelian unities, the filmmaker mixes several noir archetypes in this tale of violence and passion. John Carradine is the obsessive columnist who has been dumped by the actress and a prime suspect (shades of *Laura*, of course).

Co-writer and producer Burt Kaiser is the tormented artist who takes his anger out on his wife as well as several other women, including the actress. Jayne Mansfield, in one of her first roles, plays the femme fatale, Candy, replete with form fitting leopard-print capris and pointelle knit sweater. She strings along several men, including Stevens and Voe, while trying to maintain her independence and marginal lifestyle. **JU**

THE FILE ON THELMA JORDON (1950)

Director: Robert Siodmak. **Screenplay**: Ketti Frings based on a story by Marty Holland. **Producer**: Hal B. Wallis. **Director of Photography**: George Barnes. **Music**: Victor Young. **Art Director**: Hans Dreier, Earl Hedrick. **Editor**: Warren Low. **Cast**: Barbara Stanwyck (Thelma Jordon), Wendell Corey (Cleve Marshall), Paul Kelly (Miles Scott), Joan Tetzel (Pamela Marshall), Stanley Ridges (Kingsley Willis), Richard Rober (Tony Laredo), Minor Watson (Judge Calvin Blackwell), Barry Kelley (District Attorney Pierce), Laura Elliott (Dolly), Basil Ruysdael (Judge Hancock), Jane Novak (Mrs. Blackwell), Gertrude W. Hoffman (Aunt Vera Edwards), Harry Antrim (Sidney), Kate Lawson (Clara), Theresa Harris (Esther), Byron Barr (McCary), Geraldine Wall (Matron), Jonathan Corey (Timmy Marshall), Robin Corey (Joan Marshall). **Completed**: April 2, 1949. **Released**: Paramount, January 18. 100 minutes.

Late one evening, Thelma Jordon visits a small town's district attorney to discuss attempted burglaries at her elderly aunt's mansion, where Thelma also resides. However, only the assistant district attorney, Cleve Marshall, is there. A clandestine love affair begins between them despite his marriage and social status. However, Thelma appears confused when she encounters Tony Laredo, a sinister man who apparently knows her quite well. Later, Thelma tells Cleve she is unhappily married to Tony who has followed her. Subsequently, Thelma's aunt is killed and her emerald necklace stolen. An intricate series of events compels Cleve to the scene of the crime before the police have discovered it but after Thelma has cleaned up evidence that she fears implicates Tony. Advising Thelma to feign sleep, Cleve is seen escaping but is not recognized by the butler, who discovers Aunt Vera's body. Thelma, protesting innocence, is arrested for murder the following day. Tony Laredo is established as being in Chicago at the time of the crime. Slowly, Cleve learns of Thelma's corrupted past, and nevertheless anonymously pays for her lawyer, Kingsley Willis, and plans her case, although he is the prosecuting attorney. Meanwhile, the police cannot find "Mr. X," the unidentified man seen by the butler, and Thelma's guilt cannot be proven. Acquitted, Thelma and Tony arrange to leave town, but Cleve confronts her. Bitterly, she confesses that their affair was all a plot. Tony beats Cleve unconscious and departs with Thelma. On a mountain road, Thelma's remorse overwhelms her and she causes their car to plunge over a cliff. Tony is killed, but Thelma survives long enough to confess her crimes to the police with Cleve in attendance. She still refuses to reveal "Mr. X" however, explaining that she truly loves him. Cleve admits to his partner, Miles, that he is "Mr. X," but Miles has deduced that fact. Knowing his life and career are ruined, Cleve walks off into the shadows.

The File on Thelma Jordon: *Thelma Jordon (Barbara Stanwyck) and Cleve Marshall (Wendell Corey).*

As Thelma Jordon, Barbara Stanwyck portrays a different type of femme fatale than Phyllis Dietrichson in *Double Indemnity,* although the two characters have a similar method and motivation. Similar to Phyllis, Thelma ensnares the innocent Cleve Marshall to ensure the success of her criminal plan. However, Thelma falls truly in love with her victim. Phyllis was emotionally frozen and only admitted to loving Walter Neff as she shot him in a futile attempt to save herself. Additionally, Cleve is a truly innocent victim rather than an accomplice as was Walter Neff, who admittedly considered many illicit methods of collecting insurance money before he met Phyllis.

The lovers of *Double Indemnity* were chillingly logical, timing every moment of their joint crime. But Cleve and Thelma are romantics and each impulsively acts to rescue the other. He heroically decides to cover-up her crime while she suddenly kills Tony as well as herself in order to clear her true love's name. The crucial moment that determines Thelma's fate is not when she murders her aunt but when Cleve confronts her at the mansion after her acquittal. Cleve faces her squarely, but his presence in the room is shadowed by Tony Laredo. Literally a man of darkness with an animalistic sexuality, Tony is irresistible to Thelma. As she realizes that she does have one last option, Thelma attempts redemption through a flaming car crash and confession, hoping that her death will salvage Cleve's shattered life. However, Cleve, the noir hero unwittingly pulled into a nightmare, cannot be redeemed. He is not completely ostracized from society, but he is scarred immeasurably. An emotional Sisyphus, Cleve must from then on bear the weight of his tragic mistake "because of his children and because of the years." **EW**

FIVE MINUTES TO LIVE (1960)

Director: Bill Karn. **Producer**: James Ellsworth. **Executive Producer**: Ludlow Flower. **Screenplay**: Cay Forester from a story by Palmer Thompson and an adaptation by Robert L. Joseph. **Director of Photography**: Carl Guthrie. **Music**: Gene Kauer, Johnny Cash. **Art Director**: Edwin Shields. **Cast**: Johnny Cash (Johnny Cabot), Donald Woods (Ken Wilson), Cay Forester (Nancy Wilson), Pamela Mason (Ellen), Midge Ware (Doris), Victor Tayback (Fred Dorella), Ronnie Howard (Bobbie Wilson), Merle Travis (Max), Howard Wright (Pop), Norma Varden (Priscilla); **Release Date**: Sutton Pictures, January. 74 minutes.

Low-level wiseguy Fred Dorella thinks he has come up with the perfect crime. With the help of gunman Johnny Cabot, Dorella plots to walk into a small town bank and ask banker Ken Wilson for $70,000. The heist should work because Cabot, just ten minutes away by car, has a gun trained on the banker's wife, Nancy. Mr. Wilson has five minutes to give Dorella the money. If he doesn't comply his wife will be executed. But what Dorella's caper does not consider is the strength of the relationship between the Wilsons. Ken is not sure he still loves his wife and hesitates to hand over the money. Tension ripples at the Wilson home, as Cabot croons to Nancy, "There ain't no alternative / you've got forty seconds to live." Eventually Mr. Wilson relents, but he delays long enough so that Dorella is apprehended and Cabot is killed by the police.

Before he kicked out the floor lights at the Grand Old Opry and gave a cameraman the finger, before he sported an outlaw look and six-guns on his albums *Ride This Train* and *Johnny Cash Sings the Ballads of the True West*, the "Man in Black" played a vicious gangster in this indie noir. His Johnny Cabot embodies aspects of the embittered speaker of "Folsom Prison Blues." Cabot truly is someone who would shoot a man "just to watch him die." With his high pompadour and rockabilly angst, Cabot exudes danger and enjoys terrorizing Mrs. Wilson in her neat, suburban-style home. Strumming his Gibson guitar, Cabot serenades her with the film's menacing title song, and then smashes Mrs. Wilson's collectibles on her mantle piece, orders her to wear a negligee, and even attempts to rape her. Before horrifying Mrs. Wilson, Cabot had machine-gunned a cop in a low-lit garage. The gangster's face ripples with ecstasy. Violence gives him sexual release.

Along with portraying an intense evil incarnate, *Five Minutes to Live* peels back the sheen of country life's innocence and happiness. While sitting in a car, casing the Wilson's home, Fred Dorella says to Cabot that this is a neighborhood where "nothing ever happens." At 7:35 every morning, Mrs. Wilson picks up the milk and newspaper. Here people "live the lives magazine ads talk about." However, Dorella misreads the small town. Inside the Wilson home percolates bitterness. They squabble and neglect one another. Mr. Wilson is busy at the bank and she is busy with the woman's club. Bobbie, their son, wants a baseball uniform and neither has time to get it. Mr. Wilson's unhappiness leads to an affair with Ellen and they are planning an escape to Las Vegas. Later when Dorella makes his ransom demands, the banker hesitates. "Suppose I told you I didn't care what happened to my wife," Mr. Wilson says, and he is not bluffing. Director Bill Karn cuts to medium close-up and Donald Woods smiles creepily. Of course the chill doesn't last long: Mr. Wilson turns contrite, and through the terror of Johnny Cabot, the Wilson's recommit to one another while driving off to Vegas for a second honeymoon. But despite the status-quo happy ending, the film's questioning of small-town contentment shades the proceedings in a long black veil of doubt and darkness. **GT**

FOLLOW ME QUIETLY (1949)

Director: Richard Fleischer and [uncredited] Anthony Mann. **Screenplay**: Lillie Hayward from a story by Francis Rosenwald and Anthony Mann. **Producer**: Herman Schlom. **Director of Photography**: Robert de Grasse. **Music**: Leonid Raab, Paul Sawtell. **Art Directors**: Albert S. D'Agostino, Walter E. Keller. **Editor**: Elmo Williams. **Cast**: William Lundigan (Grant), Dorothy Patrick (Ann), Jeff Corey (Collins), Nestor Paiva (Benny), Charles D. Brown (Mulvaney), Paul Guilfoyle (Overbeck), Edwin Max (The Judge), Frank Ferguson (McGill), Marlo Dwyer (Waitress), Michael Brandon (Dixon). **Completed**: September 4, 1948. **Released**: RKO, July 7. 59 minutes.

A serial killer, known only as the Judge, commits a series of brutal murders to rid the world of "evil." The police cannot get a complete description of the killer. Utilizing what little eyewitness evidence they obtain, obsessed detective Grant has constructed a mannequin that approximates the criminal's physical characteristics, minus a face. An ambitious scandal sheet reporter named Ann joins Grant in his search. After putting together several clues, Grant and his partner Collins stake out the area where they believe the Judge lives. He walks into the trap and a chase through a refinery begins. Grant traps the Judge but the murderer falls to his death before he can be apprehended.

Follow Me Quietly is one of the earliest examples of a subgenre of neo-noir so popular today: the serial killer film (*Zodiac*, etc.). In this film co-writer and co-director Anthony Mann, as in most of his noir films, draws heavily on German expressionism—one of the main sources of film noir—for his style. The Judge himself is a shadowy figure with almost supernatural powers. Resembling in physical appearance and action Murnau's character of Nosferatu (from the 1922 German film of that name) more than any modern serial killer, his powers seems to be beyond the norm. In one particularly eerie scene, the obsessed detective Grant is in his office, thinking aloud before a mannequin of Judge constructed from clues. The rain pours down against the office's window while stray lights silhouette the mannequin. Collins interrupts Grant's reverie and they exit. However, the camera then returns to the mannequin as it suddenly rises and leaves the room. Obviously, on a literal level, the Judge has slipped

into the detective's office and replaced the mannequin with himself but the effect is quite different. It is as if some Golem has come to life and is leaving to re-unite with its master.

The filmmakers' use of setting and mood is also quite striking. The film opens on the first of several rainstorms, as the puritanical Judge only kills victims he has deemed "evil" during intense nighttime showers. Neon from the surrounding buildings light a pool of water, as the female protagonist of the piece, the reporter Ann, paces back and forth nervously, her high-heel shoes splashing through this puddle as the ominous score fills the soundtrack. After several murders in the rain, these city storms take on a true ominous quality. In an interesting switch, the final chase is during daylight and the filmmakers add a Gothic dimension when police bullets burst water pipes above the captured killer. Water begins to pour down on the frantic Judge, seeming to impart to him superhuman power to escape from his handcuffs and the burly detective holding him. **JU**

FORCE OF EVIL (1948)

Director: Abraham Polonsky. **Screenplay**: Abraham Polonsky and Ira Wolfert based on the novel *Tucker's People* by Wolfert. **Producer**: Bob Roberts (Enterprise Studios). **Director of Photography**: George Barnes. **Music**: David Raksin. **Art Director**: Richard Day. **Editors**: Walter Thompson, Art Seid. **Cast**: John Garfield (Joe Morse), Beatrice Pearson (Doris Lowry), Thomas Gomez (Leo Morse), Howland Chamberlain (Freddy Bauer), Roy Roberts (Ben Tucker), Marie Windsor (Edna Tucker), Paul McVey (Hobe Wheelock), Tim Ryan (Johnson), Sid Tomack (Two & Two Taylor), Georgia Backus (Sylvia Morse), Sheldon Leonard (Ficco), Jan Dennis (Mrs. Bauer), Stanley Prager (Wally). **Location**: New York City. **Completed**: August 10, 1948. **Released**: MGM, December 26. 88 minutes.

Gambling-syndicate lawyer Joe Morse is bound by a set of ethics that he does not fully understand. He uses his own fear of failure and the ability to make easy money to justify his role in "legalizing" a large-scale numbers racket. The only obstacle is his brother, Leo, who runs a small bookie joint and who will not relinquish his independence to join the syndicate. Eventually the situation is taken out of Joe's hands and the larger syndicate moves in and destroys Leo. The corrupt lawyer is forced to realize the true nature of his busi-

Force of Evil: *John Garfield as Attorney Joe Morse.*

ness. Joe battles to break free from the syndicate with the help of a young woman who worked for his brother. Involved beyond the point of salvation, Leo perishes but Joe succeeds in exposing the syndicate.

Adapted and directed by Abraham Polonsky, after his association with Robert Rossen and John Garfield in *Body and Soul, Force of Evil* reflects the same context of societal ills as that earlier movie. Besides Garfield, Polonsky uses the iconography and other personalities of the noir series, effectively masking his social criticism under the melodramatic veneer of gangsterism and corruption. For example, Marie Windsor co-stars in a pivotal role as a femme fatale who is used to manipulate Joe into accepting the brutal destruction of his brother's organization and maintaining the artificial legality of the syndicate's racket. What emerges is an extraordinarily existential vision; Polonsky transcends the quasi-mythical aspects of gangsterism and delineates the rackets realistically by using extensive location shooting and a semi-documentary treatment of the government reformers. *Force of Evil* portrays racketeering generally as a purely capitalistic enterprise and Garfield's character in particular as a key stooge of the enterprise, a position he embraces in the face of perceived social injustice—his own past impecuniousness—that clouds his individual moral sense.

When Joe Morse is finally radicalized by his brother's death and the sudden self-image of his own corruption, his revolt is driven as much by existential anguish as by any newfound political awareness. Joe makes a revelation of his betrayal to the mobsters at a rendezvous by the East River, fully realizing and even anticipating that it may precipitate his own murder. In contrast to the claustrophobic reality of his parting with Doris in the back seat of a taxi (photographed by Polonsky in a long-take two shot), a bridge with its span of steel girders looms over the final sequence on the riverbank like a piece of expressionistic stage dressing. Not only does Joe play out his personal drama dwarfed by this manifestation of society and its overweening structures; but also the scene acquires a theatrical aura that is entirely appropriate. Although there is clearly more than just one life at stake in the climax of *Force of Evil*, Joe's choice is more overtly philosophical and political that the similar, impromptu self-immolation of Harry Fabian for the sake of his girlfriend in *Night and the City*. **CM** & **AS**

FRAMED (1947)

Director: Richard Wallace. **Screenplay**: Ben Maddow based on a story by Jack Patrick. **Producer**: Jules Schermer. **Director of Photography**: Burnett Guffey. **Music**: Marlin Skiles. **Art Director**: Stephen Gooson. **Editor**: Richard Fanti. **Cast**: Glenn Ford (Mike Lambert), Janis Carter (Paula Craig), Barry Sullivan (Stephen Price), Edgar Buchanan (Jeff Cunningham), Karen Morley (Mrs. Price), Jim Bannon (Jack Woodworth), Sid Tomack (Bartender), Barbara Woodell (Jane Woodworth), Paul Burns (Assay Clerk). **Completed**: October 30, 1946. **Released**: Columbia, May 25. 82 minutes.

Mike Lambert, an unemployed mining engineer, takes work as a truck driver. He is seduced by Paula Craig, a waitress, who wants to use him as part of a plan she has concocted with her lover, Stephen Price. Price has married into a prominent family and is vice-president of the local bank. He and Paula have been planning to embezzle $250,000 and run

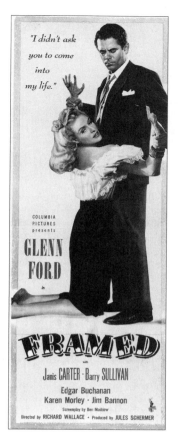

off together as soon as they found someone who looked sufficiently like Stephen that could be framed for the crime. Mike had been chosen, but Paula realizes she loves him. After the robbery, she double-crosses and kills her former lover, Stephen. She tells Mike he killed Stephen in a drunken rage. However, Mike's friend Jeff is arrested for the murder and Mike wants to confess to the police. He finally realizes that Paula is guilty and traps her into incriminating herself, so that she is arrested.

Framed is photographed by Burnett Guffey in a rather "flat" style without the expressionistic flourishes of a film like *So Dark the Night*, which says something about the role of the director in determining a film's visual style, especially at Columbia. The plot line owes much to James M. Cain who helped bring crime out of the underworld and into a middle-class milieu. Glenn Ford, as usual, does a good job playing an honest man who succumbs to the wiles of a femme fatale. But *Framed* benefits most from the presence of Janis Carter, who, had she not remained in low budget films, might have rivaled Barbara Stanwyck as a major icon of the noir cycle. Carter was quite adept at adding sexual overtones to sadistic acts. As Paula, she displays a marked degree of sexual fervor when Stephen's car goes off the cliff, rivaling a sequence in the earlier *Night Editor* where she becomes increasingly aroused while watching a girl being beaten to death. In a singular example of the perfidious nature of the fatal woman, she poisons Mike's coffee when he seems averse to her plans, only to withdraw the coffee at the last moment when his conversation takes on a more reassuring tone. **BP**

GAMBLING HOUSE (1951)

Director: Ted Tetzlaff. **Screenplay**: Marvin Borowsky from story by Erwin Gelsey. **Producer**: Warren Duff. **Executive Producer**: Sid Rogell. **Director of Photography**: Harry J. Wild. **Music**: Roy Webb. **Art Director**: Albert D'Agostino and Alfred Herman. **Editor**: Roland Gross. **Cast**: Victor Mature (Marcus Furioni, aka Mark Fury), Terry Moore (Lynn Warren), William Bendix (Joe Farrow), Zachary Charles (Willie), Basil Ruysdael (Judge Ravinek), Donald Rudolph (Lloyd Crane), Cleo Moore (Sally), Ann Doran (Mrs. Lucas), Don Haggerty (Sharky), Jack Kruschen (Burly Italian immigrant). **Released**: RKO, March 18. 80 minutes.

Mark Fury, a small-time gambler and drifter, is injured in a shooting at a gambling casino in which a man is killed. Under suspicion by the police, he agrees to take the rap for Joe Farrow, owner of a chain of casinos in the New York area, in exchange for $50,000 and Farrow's promise to "get him out" if things do not go well at the trial. Mark is acquitted, but after the trial he is ordered to be deported by immigration authorities because he was born in Italy and his father had never become a U.S. citizen. Mark's only chance at avoiding deportation is to convince a skeptical judge to allow him to become a citizen under a special provision for GI's (he had served during WWII) before the order takes effect. Along the way, Mark enlists the aid of Lynn Warren, a social worker in whose coat pocket he had secreted the little book to keep it away from Farrow's thugs. He gifts his $50,000 to Lynn's immigrant aid agency to keep a Polish family from being deported and even convinces the judge to let him stay. But when Mark ventures out of his apartment one night, Farrow and some of his men confront him. Farrow orders one of his thugs, Sharkey, to shoot Mark but Mark's fast talking has convinced Farrow's men that Farrow will set up one of them as the "fall guy" just as he had done to Mark. Instead of killing Mark, Sharkey shoots Farrow, only to be arrested by the police who have been tipped off by Willie.

Gambling House attempts to combine the conventions of the noir cycle with those of the "social problem" film that began to displace the film noir in the 1950s and 1960s. Measured against the yardstick of *No Way Out*, which tackled the problem of racism in America without vitiating either the noir style or sensibility, this film, released a few months later, is largely unsuccessful. The image of Victor Mature in overcoat prowling the streets of New York (cf. *Kiss of Death* and *Cry of the City*) while trying to outsmart William Bendix, back to portraying a tough hood, promises more than this film delivers. Perhaps this is so because the "problem" of post-war immigration is so overladen with patriotic evangelism that the "message" consumes the film. Nor does it help

that its major spokesperson is Terry Moore, who is too much the ingénue to be anybody's foil.

The presence of Cleo Moore might have provided some balance had she been cast as a tough, cynical blonde but she is wasted as Willie's dutiful wife. Actually the best parts of the film, certainly the most noir, are the beginning and ending sequences. The film opens with the camera dogging Mark's lower torso as he progresses down a darkened street and up the stairs to his apartment, trailing blood all the way. It closes with the final confrontation between Mark and Farrow on a darkened New York street, with Farrow outside the car and his men inside, all with guns drawn—clearly stolen from the closing sequence of *Kiss of Death*. Indeed, as Mark walks slowly down the street and into the darkness of the film's final seconds, the music segues into a watered down version of Alfred Newman's "city theme" (cf. *I Wake Up Screaming, Dark Corner, Cry of the City*, etc.) as if the very presence of Victor Mature had somehow tainted RKO's distinctive noir style with an inferior imitation of that of Fox. **BP**

THE GANGSTER (1947)

Director: Gordon Wiles. **Screenplay**: Daniel Fuchs from his story. **Producers**: Maurice and Frank King. **Director of Photography**: Paul Ivano. **Music**: Louis Gruenberg. **Art Director**: F. Paul Sylos. **Editor**: Walter Thompson. **Cast**: Barry Sullivan (Shubunka), Belita (Nancy Starr), Akim Tamiroff (Jammey), Joan Lorring (Dorothy, the cashier), Henry Morgan (Shorty, the waiter), John Ireland (Karty), Sheldon Leonard (Cornell), Virginia Christine (Mrs. Karty), Fifi D'Orsay (Olga), Leif Erickson (Beaumont), Charles McGraw (Dugas), John Kellogg (Sterling), Elisha Cook Jr. (Oval), Ted Hecht (Swain). **Completed**: March 12. **Released**: Allied Artists, October 6. 84 minutes.

Shubunka runs a protection racket in a seaside town on the East Coast. He is more interested in his girlfriend Nancy than in the racket and counts on his associate Jammey, who owns an ice-cream parlor, to see things run smoothly. A crime syndicate moves in to take over and starts buying out Shubunka's employees until only Jammey is left. The leader of the syndicate, Cornell, unsuccessfully exerts pressure on Jammey to get him to betray Shubunka. Jammey is also being pestered for money by Karty who is in debt to his wife's brothers as a result of gambling. When Jammey is confronted by the desperate Karty at the precise moment when he is counting his week's takings, Karty knocks him down and kills him. As Cornell had warned Shubunka that he would kill him if anything happened to Jammey, the gangster goes into hiding. Abandoned by everyone, he confronts Cornell's men in the street and is shot down. The film ends

The Gangster: *Belita as Nancy Starr.*

with an off-screen voice telling how the police rounded up Cornell and his men.

The Gangster turns on money and its place in society. The film's originality stems from the way money is a form of exchange, a mediator between characters who are determined by its power before being defined as individuals. Indeed, the film makes it clear that Shubunka's notion of individuality and what constitutes success is part of pre-history in the new world represented by Cornell.

Both Shubunka and Cornell are entrepreneurs but, for the former, society has evolved smoothly from Prohibition to the present, as if WWII had not taken place and brought new business methods with it. For Cornell is the signifier of modern corporate capitalism, where a business has a nominal head who himself works, not for an absent boss or "godfather" but for the ideological big Other: profits, mergers and investments. Although the film is less politically committed in its analyses than *I Walk Alone* (1948), the parallels are striking, Shubunka looking ahead to the Lancaster character and Cornell to the Douglas character of that film. The difference lies in the absence of the role of banks, although the so-called invisible hand of the market can be read between the lines in everything Cornell says and does.

Shubunka and Jammey worship money but in diametrically opposed ways. For Shubunka, money comes from his control of the rackets and he spends it on Nancy in an obsessive attempt to get her to succeed in show business, the better to control her. Jammey deplores the way his wife squanders his hard-earned dollars on beauty treatments, another version of Nancy's desire to be a showgirl. He is an ideal associate for Shubunka: he wants to accumulate capital and tries to prevent Shubunka from wasting his. Because Jammey is a figure from the past and believes in the Protestant work ethic, he takes seriously his association with Shubunka and his murder by Karty is deeply ironic: Karty squanders his money on horses and must either rob Jammey or suffer torture and murder at the hands of his wife's brothers.

Wiles (with the help of novelist and noir writer Daniel Fuchs) succeeds in creating a powerful atmosphere of constriction, solitude and social decay, aided and abetted by a lack of money: the film's modest budget forces Wiles, a trained art director, to be economical. Whether it be Shubunka's luxury apartment, Jammey's ice-cream parlor or the scene on the beach where Cornell's hoods try to lean on the hero when he is enjoying himself (for once) with Nancy, the lack of decor is cleverly exploited by Wiles to communicate the notion of being alone, hemmed in or trapped. The most striking example is where Jammey is literally squeezed between two of Cornell's hoods in a restaurant. The decor is minimalist, allowing the shots' framing and acting to admirably reinforce each other. Thus informing the spectator that a new era has dawned, one where Cornell's love of good food comes to condense money, brutality and the new neo-liberal consensus. **RH**

THE GARMENT JUNGLE (1957)

Directors: Vincent Sherman and Robert Aldrich [uncredited]. **Screenplay**: Harry Kleiner from a series of articles "Gangsters In the Dress Business" by Lester Velie. **Producer**: Harry Kleiner. **Photography**: Joseph Biroc. **Music**: Leith Stevens. **Art Director**: Robert A. Peterson. **Editor**: William Lyon. **Cast**: Lee J. Cobb (Walter Mitchell), Kerwin Matthews (Alan Mitchell), Gia Scala (Theresa Renata), Richard Boone (Artie Ravidge), Valerie French (Lee Hackett), Robert Loggia (Tulio Renata), Joseph Wiseman (Kovan), Adam Williams (the Ox), Harold J. Stone (Tony), Wesley Addy (Mr. Paul), Willis Bouchey (Dave Bronson), Robert Ellenstein (Fred Kenner), Celia Lovsky (Tulio's Mother). **Completed**: December 20, 1956. **Released**: Columbia, May 22. 88 minutes.

Alan Mitchell returns from the Korean War to join his widowed father Walter's dress manufacturing business. The garment industry itself is under pressure from local unions to sign shop contracts and Alan suspects that the death of his father's partner in a fall down an elevator shaft may not have been accidental. Already alienated by his father's anti-union stance and his affair with young buyer Lee Hackett, Alan further learns that his father has been paying a union-busting syndicate run by Artie Ravidge. Alan meets and confides in union organizer Tulio Renata and his wife Theresa. When Tulio is brutally murdered by Ravidge, Walter attempts to disconnect

The Garment Jungle: *Alan Mitchell (Kerwin Matthews) speaks with his father Walter (Lee J. Cobb).*

himself from the mobster and is himself killed by Ravidge's men. Alan, who is looking after Theresa and her child, seeks evidence against Ravidge and gets some from Lee. While that material is taken to the district attorney, Alan goes to confront Ravidge. Their fight is broken up by the arrival of Theresa and the police who arrest the beaten Ravidge.

Made near the end of the noir cycle, *The Garment Jungle* combines the traditional character of the weary veteran with Robert Aldrich's precise visualization of the noir viewpoint. At the beginning of the film, Alan Mitchell is an uncertain and ineffective figure, bullied in turn by his father, his father's hired thug, and union organizer Renata. Renata also draws Mitchell out of the semi-insular world of Roxton Fashions—where sustained camera and full-light create an aura of stability—into the world of darkness and corruption which Aldrich evoked so effectively two years earlier in *Kiss Me Deadly*. When Mitchell is both fascinated and repelled by Renata's revelations, Aldrich alters his composition to include more low angles punctuated by top-light and side-light that cast irresolute shadows on the protagonist's faces. Talking to Renata also brings down on Mitchell the ire of Artie Ravidge, who with his even white teeth flashing from a pock-marked face personifies the menace of the noir under-world. With this clichéd, quasi-satirical characterization, Aldrich satisfies the genre expectations of the viewer and the character expectations of Mitchell's liberal sensibilities while retaining the possibility that Ravidge, who keeps peo-ple at a distance with the tip of a burning cigarette, may be more effete and assailable than he appears.

The conflicting forces at work in the narrative are under-scored by a variety of stylistic devices, including Aldrich's often-used metaphor for sub-surface chaos: the ceiling fan. As Ravidge's hoods close in on a victim, a low angle medium shot reveals a web of twisting shadows from such a fan thrown on all the surrounding walls. These distracting shad-ows and odd angles inject a visual instability, which matches that of the narrative's violence. The murders of Renata and Walter Mitchell, like the image of the black elevator shaft down which Walter's partner plummets at the film's begin-ning, evoke the ever-present threat of annihilation with a shuddering simplicity. The final sequence in which Alan Mitchell physically defeats Ravidge offers some reduction of that threat. But Mitchell himself is quickly swept up by the undertow of business demands and, in existential terms, is constrained by them as thoroughly as he might have been by Ravidge. The film ends sardonically on a shot of a Roxton Fashions operator as she mechanically switches lines and informs Alan's callers, just as she did with his father, that "Mr. Mitchell is busy." **AS**

GASLIGHT (1944)

Director: George Cukor. **Screenplay**: John Van Druten, Walter Reisch, and John L. Balderston based on the play *Gas Light* by Patrick Hamilton. **Producer**: Arthur Hornblow, Jr. **Director of Photography**: Joseph Ruttenberg. **Music**: Bronislau Kaper. **Art Director**: Cedric Gibbons. **Editor**: Ralph E. Winters. **Cast**: Charles Boyer (Gregory Anton), Ingrid Bergman (Paula Alquist Anton), Joseph Cotten (Brian Cameron), Dame May Whitty (Bessie Thwaites), Angela Lansbury (Nancy Oliver), Barbara Everest (Elizabeth Tompkins), Emil Rameau (Maestro Mario Guardi), Edmund Breon (Gen. Huddleston),

Gaslight: *Charles Boyer as Gregory Anton*

Halliwell Hobbes (Mr. Muffin), Tom Stevenson (Williams), Heather Thatcher (Lady Dalroy), Lawrence Grossmith (Lord Dalroy), Jakob Gimpel (Pianist). **Completed**: November, 1943. **Released**: MGM, May 4. 113 minutes.

After her famous opera singer aunt-guardian is strangled in their London home, traumatized niece Paula leaves the country, heading to Italy for a decade to heal her demons. She meets and marries mysterious stranger-pianist, Gregory, who encourages her to return to London and reside in her aunt's home. Paula struggles with terrifying memories as a series of strange occurrences makes her believe she is going crazy. She hears footsteps, sees the gaslights dim and spirals into an increasingly fragile psychological and emotional state. Eventually suspicious events begin to reveal that her husband may have been her aunt's killer and now is perhaps trying to kill her, as misogynist killer Gregory engages in a sadistic game of psychological abuse to push her to the brink of hysteria. Scotland Yard detective Brian becomes interested in the situation and learns that the opera singer had valuable jewels, which were never found. Brian and Paula learn that Gregory worked with her aunt, and has been the cause of the footsteps and lights as he secretly searches the house for the jewels. In the final confrontation, Gregory discovers the jew-els but is caught.

A classic British gothic thriller in the roman noir tradition, *Gaslight* is rife with gender distress, and female hysteria. The film received an Oscar for art direction because of its macabre atmosphere, baroque claustrophobic clutter and its shadowy cinematography. The movie was filmed entirely on studio backlots and shrouded enclosed soundstages during World War II. Cukor directed notable performances from émigré actors Charles Boyer and Ingrid Bergman, who won the Best Actress Oscar for her paranoid lead which she researched by visiting insane asylum patients. MGM spent over $2 million on this lavish production and its impressive cast—borrowing Bergman and Joseph Cotten from producer David O. Selznick, opposite French star Boyer and 17-year-old Angela Lansbury in her debut.

Based on a British play from early 1939, *Gaslight* was first adapted as an excellent leaner-budgeted British National film in 1940 with a stunning performance by Anton Walbrook. (This impressive 1940 British version is now available on DVD; some even prefer this fine earlier version to Cukor's later more famous version.) The next year Columbia acquired the American screen rights to release the British film version of *Gaslight* in the US (as *A Strange Case of Murder*), but were prevented from releasing the film by Traube, who owned the American dramatic rights and produced *Gaslight* on the New York stage, opening two days before Pearl Harbor in early December 1941 under the title *Angel Street*. MGM cut a deal and paid $150,000 for the screen rights to produce its hefty-budgeted Hollywood screen version of *Gaslight*. By 1944, trades even reported MGM was rumored to have destroyed all copies and negatives of the original 1940 British film, but it was finally released in the US as *Angel Street* in April 1953. Cukor's acclaimed 1944 version was nominated for best actor, best picture, cinematography, writing and supporting actress, and grossed over $4 million. Is it film noir? *Gaslight* is more female gothic thriller-melodrama with elements of psychological horror than other more typical gritty hardboiled contemporary story fare, but it has the classic period's noir ingredients of an amply dark, low-key noir visual style, violent crime, entrapment of its protagonist and was incredibly successful. Cukor's 1944 version was released in Britain as *Murder in Thornton Square*. **SCB**

GILDA (1946)

Director: Charles Vidor. **Producer**: Virginia Van Upp. **Screenplay**: Marion Parsonnet adapted by Jo Eisinger and Ben Hecht from an original story by E.A. Ellington. **Director of Photography**: Rudolph Maté. **Music**: Morris Stoloff. **Art Directors**: Stephen Goosson, Van Nest Polglase. **Editor**: Charles Nelson. **Cast**: Rita Hayworth (Gilda), Glenn Ford (Johnny Farrell), George Macready (Ballin Mundson), Joseph Calleia (Obregon), Steven Geray (Uncle Pio), Joe Sawyer (Casey), Gerald Mohr (Capt. Delgado), Robert Scott (Gabe Evans), Lionel Royce (German Agent), S.Z. Martel (Little Man). **Released**: Columbia, May 15. 110 minutes.

Johnny Farrell is a down-on-his-luck gambler who is rescued by businessman Ballin Mundson from a thug attempting to rob Johnny of his winnings. Ballin then hires Johnny as manager of his casino. All is well until Mundson returns from a trip with his beautiful new wife, Gilda. There is tension between Gilda and Johnny because they were once lovers. Mundson gives Johnny the unpleasant responsibility of spying on the reckless Gilda, who resents both Mundson and Johnny's treatment. Johnny, although tempted, refuses to betray his friend/boss by having an affair with Gilda. Mundson, now fronting for an international Nazi-controlled cartel, gets into a fight and kills a man. He rushes home and, finding Johnny struggling with a drunken Gilda, assumes they have renewed their affair. Mundson boards an escape plane, which crashes in the ocean immediately after takeoff. Believing Mundson dead, Johnny marries Gilda, planning to punish her. Gilda flees this horrible relationship and finds a job singing but Johnny uses his money and resources to have her brought back to him. Ballin reappears and is shot by an aging janitor. Johnny and Gilda re-unite.

Gilda's triangle of obsession is so entangled in layers of repressed sexuality, divided loyalties, latent homoerotic

Gilda: *Rita Hayworth as Gilda*

desire, and sadomasochism as to make it singular and unique. The film has become iconic due to the performance of Rita Hayworth in the title role and the image of her in that black silk sheath dress by Jean Louis is among the most reproduced photos of the classic Hollywood period. However, in recent decades more perceptive critics, particularly in feminist studies of film noir like the BFI's *Women in Film Noir*, have re-examined the movie with a more psychoanalytical eye.

The love triad of the movie consists of Ballin, his wife Gilda, and Johnny, Ballin's right hand man and also Gilda's ex-lover. Ballin is the patriarch of the trio, referring to both Gilda and Johnny as his "little friends"—a term he also uses when referencing his overtly phallic sword-tipped cane. Ballin sees the two as his possessions, very much like his cane, to be used as defenses against the hostile world of political intrigue and violence in which he is mired, as the film is set in post-World War II Argentina.

Although Ballin claims to be "mad" about his trophy wife, the glamorous Gilda, he seems equally fond of Johnny, both of whom he picked up out of "the gutter." Although his meaningful looks imply that he suspects that they were lovers, he never attempts to act upon his suspicions until the final scene. On the contrary, he pushes them together, ordering Johnny to be her caretaker as she continues to see other men (Gilda: "I'm going to do exactly what I want when I want") while Ballin stays at home or at the office with this third "little friend" (a none too thinly veiled reference to masturbation). In this subtle manner the film lets 1940s audiences know that Ballin cannot satisfy his wife and so she turns to other men (although in a cop-out ending, typical of Production Code-bound Hollywood, the Argentinian police captain tells Johnny that Gilda never had sex with these men, even though the evidence of our eyes contradicts his words).

Whatever the truth, Ballin's inability or unwillingness to satisfy his overtly sensual wife puts Johnny into the position of masochist to Gilda's sadist. Both are bitter towards each other but still deeply in love, or as the captain tells Johnny earlier, "It's the most curious love-hate pattern I've witnessed." But it is a role Johnny seems born for. It is the role he has rehearsed as Ballin's devoted assistant, carefully protecting his mysterious boss, even saving his life on several occasions.

With Gilda, of course, there is more history, and with that more anger. But still Johnny submits—picking her up from dates, watching her strip in front of an audience during her famous "Put the Blame on Mame" number, and sullenly dancing with her during carnival as she dons the garb of a gaucho, her whip placed tellingly at the nape of his neck; Ballin: "I see you are going to carry a whip. Did you warn Johnny?" She did not. And even though he attempts to score a little payback, after Ballin's supposed suicide, by marrying her and keeping her prisoner in a gilded apartment, it is still he who suffers as she goes on with her "cuckolding" activities. It is Johnny who now wallows in sexual repression while she freely expresses her desires and needs (even if one believes the coda's slant on the events).

In the final scene it is Johnny who, like a child frightened of losing his mother, caves in and begs Gilda to let him go away with her: "I want to go with you. Please take me." And she of course, like any classic Hollywood movie diva, graciously grants his wish. JU

THE GLASS KEY (1942)

Director: Stuart Heisler. **Screenplay**: Jonathan Latimer from the novel by Dashiell Hammett. **Producer**: Fred Kohlmar. **Director of Photography**: Theodor Sparkuhl. **Music**: Victor Young. **Art Directors**: Hans Dreier, Haldane Douglas. **Editor**: Archie Marshek. **Cast**: Brian Donlevy (Paul Madvig), Veronica Lake (Janet Henry), Alan Ladd (Ed Beaumont), Bonita Granville (Opal Madvig), Joseph Calleia (Nick Varna), Richard Denning (Taylor Henry), Moroni Olsen (Senator Henry), William Bendix (Jeff), Margaret Hayes (Eloise Matthews), Arthur Loft (Clyde Matthews), George Meader (Tuttle), Donald MacBride (District Attorney Farr), Eddie Maff (Rusty). **Completed**: March 30. **Released**: Paramount, October 15. 85 minutes.

Ed Beaumont, whom political boss Paul Madvig took from the gutter and eventually made chief aide, is quite loyal to his boss but is opposed to Madvig's decision to support Senator Henry's "reform" ticket in the upcoming election. Ed believes that the senator and his beautiful daughter Janet, to whom Paul is engaged, are simply using Madvig. Moreover, the reform platform calls for the elimination of vice and gambling, which will arouse the enmity of local racketeer Nick Varna. Senator Henry's wastrel son Taylor, who has been having an affair with Opal Madvig, Paul's sister, is killed. Paul is implicated but refuses to do anything to clear his name despite a series of accusatory letters sent to District Attorney Farr. Parting company from Paul, Ed pretends to work for Varna to foil the gangster's plans to set Paul up for murder. Janet is romantically drawn to Ed, but he rejects her because of his loyalty to Paul. Ed uncovers another of Varna's plans, this one to have newspaper publisher Matthews print

Opal's accusations that her brother is Taylor's murderer. Matthews commits suicide and Ed destroys the man's holographic will which appoints Varna executor. Ed then discovers that it is Janet who is writing the letters and who believes that Paul is guilty. Guessing the identity of the real killer, Ed has the D.A. arrest Janet for murder. The arrest leads Senator Henry to confess that he accidentally killed his son when they fought outside the Henry mansion and that Paul, a witness, covered up for the senator.

Except for *The Maltese Falcon* of 1941, this adaptation of *The Glass Key* remains the best screen version of a Hammett story, although the film lacks the powerful ending of the original novel. Alan Ladd's stoic portrayal makes Beaumont even more of a cipher than in the novel and aside from the film's insistence on his inherent loyalty to Madvig, Beaumont's character in the film is considerably more amoral than in the novel. He encourages Mrs. Matthews to respond to him sexually, which leads directly to her husband's suicide; and then he callously steals Matthews' will. He stands idly by while Jeff strangles Varna, whereas in the book he tells Jeff he wants no part of a killing. Finally, he is even willing to sacrifice Janet to get a confession, proclaiming to the police, "I was getting worried—afraid we'd have to hang the girl to make the old man crack."

Most memorable, however, are the scenes between Bendix and Ladd. Bendix emphasizes the character Jeff's vulgarity by spitting on the floor and stuffing his mouth with food, and his relationship with Beaumont has more than just a tinge of the homoerotic: he fondles Beaumont, calls him "sweetheart" and "baby" and enjoys beating him almost literally to death. Although Beaumont's masochism is deemphasized from the novel by eliminating his suicide attempt and alcoholism, there exists a brutal, almost symbiotic link between the two men. Sparkuhl's low-key photography is an evocative change from the traditionally lit 1935 film version of *The Glass Key*, as is former pulp writer Latimer's catalogue of "tough" lines like "He trow'd another Joe," "We got to give him the works," or the oft-repeated "Gimme da roscoe." Indeed, much could be learned about the dynamics of the film noir by comparing that earlier version with this film, where a darker visual style is complimented by the further amoralization of Beaumount's character. Moreover, by choosing the diminutive Alan Ladd (coming off his success as the cold-blooded killer in *This Gun*

For Hire) to portray Beaumont, this visual "reverse English" of often found in noir iconography comes into play. As Borde and Chaumeton point out: "Only his expressionless features in situations of great tension reveal a fearsome, inhuman frigidity in this fallen angel." **BP**

THE GLASS WALL (1953)

Director: Maxwell Shane. **Screenplay**: Ivan Tors, Maxwell Shane. **Producer**: Ivan Tors. **Director of Photography**: Joseph F. Biroc. **Music**: Leith Stevens. **Art Director**: Serge Krizman. **Editor**: Stanley Frazen. **Cast**: Vittorio Gassman (Peter Kaban), Gloria Grahame (Maggie Suthand), Ann Robinson (Nancy), Douglas Spencer (Inspector Bailey), Robin Raymond (Tanya Zakoyla), Jerry Paris (Tom), Elizabeth Slifer (Landlady, Mrs Hinckley), Richard Reeves (Eddie), Joe Turkel (Freddie Zakoyla), Michael Fox (Inspector Toomey). **Released**: Columbia, April. 82 minutes.

A European war refugee, Peter, arrives as an illegal stowaway in New York Harbor where authorities reject his asylum request. His claim that during the war he rescued a GI named Tom, a former New York clarinet player, cannot be substantiated. However, Peter escapes into Manhattan closely pursued by officers. He seeks out clarinetists in the hope of validating his story. While eating in a diner, he observes Maggie flee with a stranger's coat and helps her evade the police. Across town, Tom's wife secures him a prestigious audition and he discovers Peter's predicament in newspaper headlines. Maggie joins Peter's hunt, but injuries sustained while escaping force them to separate. She is captured by the authorities who have been joined by Tom. Peter reaches the United Nations Building alone, unaware that he is now safe and nearly jumps to his death before Tom arrives to cry out that he is saved.

That particular quality of urban isolation in which one is alone while within a crowd, has rarely been expressed visually as strongly as it is in *The Glass Wall*. Peter's disconnectedness runs deeper than mere circumstance or personality. It endures because of the complacency of the everyday people in the undifferentiated masses who surround him, often as a roiling current that carries him along. While Broadway's "Great White Way" has never seemed brighter, director Shane is careful to align his lighting with the turns of the narrative, so that when Peter first reaches out to the city, it's the night skyline that greets him. Peter's first moments of mobility, stowed away in the back of a flatbed truck, are sunk in an encompassing well of blackness broken only by horizontal bars framing him—with unfortunate accuracy—as the trapped figure he is. This classically noir visual strategy sees the lighting's intensity rise and fade according to Peter's optimism, subtly reinforcing our identification with him as the unjustly denied protagonist.

The great incidental pleasure of *The Glass Wall* is its constantly recurring Gotham street scenes. The abundant location shots are the pivot around which the story swings. With a deadline looming, darkness becomes Peter's friend and ordinary people the enemy. In numerous key transitional moments, these tensions are combined in collisions that yield extraordinary intensity. One such places Peter in a scene that shows the city as an unsympathetic, mocking and barren environment from which he seeks escape behind the curtain of a coin-operated photo booth. A group of rubes enjoying the town's cheap pleasures startle him by setting off a blinding flashbulb—thematically aligning them with earlier official interrogations—and send him spinning, with their faces seen in a grotesque kaleidoscope effect, into an alley of classic noir shadows. After another very noir chase scene, he and Maggie are linked as two aliens united by exclusion, evading the faceless authority of police shown in shadow like a cameo profile. Although several opportunities for cinematic suspense throughout the film are not taken, these scenes of being hounded work well.

One of those missed dramatic opportunities says much about the film's agenda. When it appears the whole of Manhattan is looking for Peter, the camera focuses on a radio but rather than the expected alert, it goes to jazz, while the more paranoia-inducing medium of television is used to prosecute the manhunt. That is just one aspect of *The Glass Wall*'s unusually leftist polemic, a prescient thrust in which a large range of social and industrial issues, spanning gender, race, class and privilege are efficiently canvassed. Building on the foundation of urban isolation endemic to classic noir, this ideological element is not jarring but rather strengthened, and in fact through enmeshing these concerns extends the genre politically much further than usual. Although the eponymous glass wall (also a pun on society's invisible barriers) of the United Nations Building is first seen by its inverted reflection in a puddle that makes it look like a snow bubble, subsequent shots repeatedly stress its awe-inspiring qualities to reveal the promise held by the filmmakers for this socio-political experiment. Letting their guard down, the production surrenders to polemic as Peter delivers an impassioned "one world" speech to an empty chamber. This breakout is mercifully brief before *The Glass Wall* resumes its thriller discourse for a climactic scene that packs an undeniable punch, especially if you are scared of heights! Peter is a noir protagonist, not through his own mistakes that trigger moral panic but through society's, but it is the noir environment that enables the resulting polemic to fully deliver. **RSW**

THE GREAT FLAMARION (1945)

Director: Anthony Mann. **Screenplay**: Heinz Herald, Richard Weil, Anne Wigton based on a story by Wigton and Vicki Baum. **Producer**: W. Lee Wilder. **Director of Photography**: James S. Brown, Jr. **Art Director**: Frank Paul Sylos. **Music**: Alexander Laszlo. **Editor**: John F. Link. **Cast**: Erich von Stroheim (Flamarion), Mary Beth Hughes (Connie Wallace), Dan Duryea (Al Wallace), Steve Barclay (Eddie Wheeler), Lester Allen (Tony), Esther Howard (Cleo), Michael Mark (Night watchman), Jack Chefe (Hotel Desk Clerk). **Released**: Republic, January 14. 78 minutes.

The Great Flamarion is a sharpshooter whose only obsession is his act. He employs a seductive assistant, Connie Wallace, and her drunken husband Al as assistants. Although initially resistant, Flamarion is seduced by Connie who convinces him to murder her husband onstage so they can be together. Flamarion shoots Al, making it look like an accident. Although Connie promises to join him in a few months, she instead marries her lover Eddie and heads out on a tour of Central America. A broken Flamarion pursues her to Mexico

The Great Flamarion: *Eric von Stroheim as the*
"Great" Flamarion.

City and there as she shoots him, he strangles her. He tells his story to the stage clown as he dies.

The Great Flamarion is veteran noir director Anthony Mann's entry into the obsessive love subset of film noir. Like classics *The Killers* and *Criss Cross*, Mann twists and bends the conventions of the film of obsession to fit his own perverse ends. Rather than a triangle (a convention of obsessive love stories all the way back to the Arthur-Guinevere-Lancelot triad) Mann constructs a shifting quadrangle with the femme fatale of the piece, Connie Wallace (played with a zaftig intelligence by Mary Beth Hughes—*The Ox-Bow Incident, Inner Sanctum*, etc.), stringing along as many as three men at any given time (a husband, "sugar daddy," and lover) who can change their respective positions at a whim (her lover Eddie becomes her husband and then is replaced by yet another lover) in this chess game of power and sex.

The one constant in this tale of amour fou is of course the narrator of the piece, Flamarion, who tells his story while dying. Mann uses the Teutonic persona of director-actor Erich von Stroheim (much as Billy Wilder will do a few years later in *Sunset Boulevard*) in developing the image of this initially cold and disciplined sharpshooter. While Connie usually has very little trouble manipulating men, including her drunken husband Al (played by Dan Duryea, in another stellar rendering of a weak noir male), Flamarion is unusually resistant, rebuffing her initial advances. However, even this "immovable object" is ultimately no match for the power of Connie. During a train ride to San Francisco, where she and her husband will perform in Flamarion's act, she ensconces herself in Flamarion's apartment and amps up the seduction, telling him he is metaphorically "asleep" and kissing him, like some gender-bending fairy tale prince, to awaken his emotions. By the next scene, the work-obsessed Flamarion

has changed the object of his desire. At a plush restaurant, he showers Connie with oysters, champagne, and dresses while bowing repeatedly in devotion to kiss her hand. By the end of the film he has killed her bothersome husband for her, spent all his money, and descended into the depths of degradation as he hitchhikes to Mexico City to confront his "destroyer." **JU**

GUEST IN THE HOUSE (1944)

Director: John Brahm, Andre De Toth [uncredited], Lewis Milestone [uncredited]. **Screenplay**: Ketti Frings from the play by Hagar Wilde, Dale Eunson. **Producer**: Hunt Stomberg. **Director of Photography**: Lee Garmes. **Music**: Werner Janssen. **Art Director**: Nikolai Remisoff. **Editors**: Walter Hannemann, James E. Newcom. **Cast**: Anne Baxter (Evelyn Heath), Ralph Bellamy (Douglas Proctor), Aline MacMahon (Aunt Martha), Ruth Warrick (Ann Proctor), Scott McKay (Dr. Dan Proctor), Marie McDonald (Miriam), Jerome Cowan (Mr. Hackett), Margaret Hamilton (Hilda, the Maid), Percy Kilbride (John, the Butler), Connie Laird (Lee Proctor). **Released**: United Artists, December 8. 121 minutes.

Evelyn is brought by Dan, who loves her, to the home of his brother's family so she can recuperate from an unspecified illness. The members of the household are generous, gregarious and gullible. No one suspects that Evelyn, one by one, is causing them to move out. She convinces Dan to finish his medical studies. She gets Lee and Ann to think Douglas, a commercial artist, is having an affair with Miriam, his model. Insulted by the accusation, Miriam leaves. Lee, whose pet bird terrifies Evelyn, starts to imitate Evelyn's manipulative manner. Finally, Ann learns what Evelyn's up to. But because Douglas won't believe her, Ann goes away with Lee. Alone together, Evelyn tells Douglas she loves him, and he is appalled. Douglas reconciles with Ann and brings her and Lee back home. He plans to place Evelyn in a sanatorium. To prevent that, Evelyn calls Dan, and he comes for her. Before they go, she sees Lee's birdcage is empty. Thinking the bird is loose in the house, she panics. Aunt Martha, to protect Dan, stirs up Evelyn's bird phobia. Hysterical, Evelyn runs from the house and disappears over a nearby cliff into the sea.

Whatever the different contributions of three directors to this film, a very strong noir style pervades *Guest in the House*. At the start, as the credits roll, different rooms in the Proctor's home are shown. In each one, a huge shadow passes across the rear wall, blotting out sunlight on the wall. The interior architecture of the house is used to excellent effect. The screen image is incessantly crisscrossed by ceiling beams, hallways, doorframes, window panes, and the banister and pickets of the staircase. There are riveting shots, as when Evelyn looks through her rain-swept bedroom window at Ann's departure. Entire scenes are over-the-top. When the scales are lifted from Douglas' eyes about Evelyn, they are in darkness in the living room, with only the slightest illumination from an unseen fireplace. As Evelyn frantically scurries around looking for Lee's bird, the camera is similarly active, cutting back and forth between her and Aunt Martha, looking up at Evelyn's legs, then down at her upturned anguished face. The soundtrack renders Evelyn's phobia through the noise of fluttering wings.

Guest in the House is a *rara avis* in film noir: it is not a crime story, but it features a femme fatale. Evelyn is destructive to Ann and Douglas materially as well as emotionally. The night Douglas draws a sketch of Evelyn on a lamp shade, they get under each other's skin. Evelyn wants to make him (and the house) hers. Douglas wants her to model for a church mural. The subject is St. Cecilia, patron saint of the blind, which is fitting since the Proctor household cannot see what Evelyn is really like. Without Miriam and obsessed with the mural, Douglas stops earning money. Soon the family budget is in dire straights. Ann's rationalization for their troubles is to believe Evelyn's innuendoes about Douglas and Miriam.

At a time when so many women were entering the labor force, a wife at home could easily fret about her husband carrying on with an attractive co-worker. Until Evelyn's arrival, Douglas is amorous with Ann at night, and Ann is not bothered about what Douglas and Miriam do together in the day. Although Evelyn insinuates otherwise, the film shows Douglas and Miriam are just professionals and friends. Neither Douglas nor Miriam makes a play for the other, even when he draws her nude, swims with her, squeezes her from behind to loosen up her back, or is drunk with her in his car. Furious that Ann did not have faith in him and frustrated that he cannot finish the mural, Douglas hits the bottle. According to *Guest in the House*, a wife needs to trust her husband and the women he works with. Ann and Douglas narrowly get through this test of their marriage. The film implies that with Evelyn's sinister presence removed, fun will return to the House of Proctor. Supposedly Douglas will like life again, will enjoy being with Ann at night and stop drinking himself into a stupor, resume working with Miriam and the family finances will recover. **DMH**

THE GUILTY (1947)

Director: John Reinhardt. **Screenplay**: Robert R. Presnell, Sr. from the short story "Two Men in a Furnished Room" by Cornell Woolrich. **Producer**: Jack Wrather. **Director of Photography**: Henry Sharp. **Music**: Rudy Schrager. **Art Director**: Oscar Yerge. **Editor**: Jodie Caplan. **Cast**: Bonita Granville (Estelle Mitchell/Linda Mitchell), Don Castle (Mike Carr), Wally Cassell (Johnny Dixon), Regis Toomey (Detective Heller), John Litel (Alex Tremholt), Netta Packer (Mrs. Mitchell), Thomas Jackson (Tim McGinnis), Oliver Blake (Jake), Caroline Andrews (Leonola Waters, the whistler). **Completed**: November 27, 1946. **Released**: Monogram, March 22. 71 minutes.

Mike Carr returns to his old neighborhood, attracted by Estelle Mitchell whom he has been trying to forget. While waiting for her, he tells the bartender the story of why he left the area six months ago. It all started when Linda, Estelle's twin sister, disappeared after leaving the apartment he shared with Johnny Dixon, a mentally unstable war buddy. The girl's mother called the police, and Detective Heller found Linda's body stuffed into a barrel of gravel on the roof of Mike's apartment building. Evidence indicated that her neck was broken when the murderer had first tried to stuff her in the incinerator shaft. The police pursued Dixon and when he felt he had nowhere to turn, he tried to hang himself. But Mike thwarted Dixon's suicide attempt

The Guilty: *Don Castle as Mike Carr.*

and uncovered new facts, which led the police to arrest Alex Tremholt, an avuncular man who lived with the Mitchells. Tremholt had apparently killed Linda because he believed she was the perfidious Estelle who had been leading him on. Finishing his story, Mike greets Estelle and, kissing her, he discovers she no longer exerts the same charm. Leaving the bar, Mike goes to the scene of the crime, where he is arrested by Heller on newly discovered evidence that he killed Linda, mistaking her for the faithless Estelle. Though Estelle remains alive, Mike knows that he has finally freed himself from her.

Of all the poverty-row productions of Woolrich's fiction, *The Guilty* may well be the shoddiest. One would like to attribute its claustrophobic feel to the Germanic sensibilities of Austrian-born John Reinhardt but it is more likely due to a budget and a shooting schedule which dictated a reliance on little more than four sets: three interiors and one exterior of an ubiquitous, nocturnal city street. However, photographer Sharp displayed his talents in one startling shot: Carr is on the phone in the living room of his darkened flat and there is an ingenious use of depth-staging which silhouettes him with the wind blowing the window curtains in both the living room and the bedroom at the far side of the screen. Unfortunately, the tension generated by the use of chiaroscuro in scenes like this was not matched by any other production values. Consequently, the film's 71 minutes go by rather slowly. Perhaps as well the writers made a mistake by adding too many noir conventions to an already complicated original. Woolrich's story has the Tremholt character turn out to be the killer and the ingénue is only one character, not twins. Still, there is something of a challenge in giving the "hero" triple functions. The character of Mike plays amateur detective (wearing a trenchcoat in virtually every scene in which he is "investigating" the murder) as well as the narrator and finally as the guilty party. Indeed, his final line at the close of the film is one quite worthy of Woolrich: "Who'd want to look at a girl the rest of his life and always be reminded of murder." **BP**

HOW INNOCENT CAN A BYSTANDER BE?

LAUREL FILMS
in association with
EDMUND L. DORFMANN
productions present

ZACHARY SCOTT
FAYE EMERSON

with MARY BOLAND
Sam Levene · J. Edward Bromberg
Kay Medford · Jed Prouty
EDMUND L. DORFMANN, Executive Producer

in "Guilty Bystander"

Directed and Co-produced by JOSEPH LERNER · Produced by REX CARLTON
Screenplay by Don Ettlinger · From the novel by Wade Miller
Released by FILM CLASSICS, INC.

GUILTY BYSTANDER (1950)

Director: Joseph Lerner. **Screenplay**: Don Ettlinger, from the novel by Wade Miller. **Producer**: Rex Carlton. **Director of Photography**: Gerald Hirschfeld. **Music**: Dimitri Tiomkin. **Production Designer**: Leo Kerz. **Editor**: Geraldine Lerner. **Cast**: Zachary Scott (Max Thursday), Faye Emerson (Georgia), Mary Boland (Smitty), Sam Levene (Capt. Tonetti), J. Edward Bromberg (Varkas), Kay Medford (Angel), Jed Prouty (Dr. Elder), Harry Landers (Bert), Dennis Harrison (Mace), Elliot Sullivan (Stitch), Gamey Wilson (Harvey), Ray Julian (Johnny). **Location**: New York City. **Completed**: October 10, 1949. **Released**: Film Classics, April 21. 92 minutes.

Max Thursday is a former police detective who was discharged for alcoholism, after repeated newspaper criticisms of him during a tough case. He is now the house detective for the tawdry Bridgeport Hotel. His lovely ex-wife Georgia enters his bare, unkempt room and wakes him from a drunken stupor to ask his help in finding their son, who has been kidnapped. The boy was taken by her brother, Fred Mace, while on an errand for Dr. Elder to whom Mace was financially indebted. Thursday, shaky but sober, decides to visit Elder's office. Elder and a mysterious person known as St. Paul greet Thursday and ply him with liquor until he passes out. Then Thursday awakens in the police station to learn from his old friend, Capt. Tonetti, that Elder has been murdered and that Max could easily be charged with the crime, but Georgia has provided Max's alibi. He returns to his hotel

and asks the proprietress, Smitty, a woman who is intimate with underworld circles, if she knows a man named Varkas, who is associated with Elder. Varkas is a smuggler with offices in a Brooklyn warehouse. Thursday is surprised when he meets Varkas to learn that he is also seeking St. Paul. Stopping at a bar frequented by Mace's sadistic girlfriend, Angel, Thursday is told by her that Mace was supposed to pick up smuggled jewelry for Elder but that he kept the contraband for himself and she is hiding him. On the way to Angel's apartment, Thursday is waylaid by Varkas' henchmen and Mace disappears. Thursday is wounded and ready to admit defeat but, finding Varkas and his hoodlums dead, he discovers a clue. Returning to the Bridgeport Hotel, Thursday realizes that the mysterious St. Paul is actually Smitty, and he forces her to lead him to Mace, who reveals where Thursday's son is hidden. Ignoring Smitty's offers to share her ill-gotten gains with him, Thursday turns her over to the police. He finds his son and, together with Georgia, walks away from his corrupt surroundings to start his life over.

Guilty Bystander is marred by budget limitations and an over-reliance on verbal exposition, a device that fails to mask its extremely contrived plot and a great deal of uninteresting photography despite the use of New York locations. Its redeeming aspect is that, heightened by the use of locale, *Guilty Bystander* is able to portray a world populated by losers. Scott's Max Thursday is the bottom-of-the-line private detective, an alcoholic who is forced into action but keeps returning to the bottle. The hypochondriac Varkas is portrayed by heavy-lidded Bromberg in properly oblique fashion. Finally, Mary Boland brings pathos to her portrayal of the principal villain, Smitty, who double-crossed the smugglers so that she might live out her old age in comfort. **BP**

GUN CRAZY
[aka DEADLY IS THE FEMALE] (1950)

Director: Joseph H. Lewis. **Screenplay**: Dalton Trumbo [uncredited], MacKinlay Kantor and Millard Kaufman [fronting for Trumbo] from the *Saturday Evening Post* story "Gun Crazy" by Kantor. **Producers**: Frank and Maurice King (King Brothers). **Director of Photography**: Russell Harlan. **Music**: Victor Young. **Production Designer**: Gordon Wiles. **Editor**: Harry Gerstad. **Cast**: Peggy Cummins (Annie Laurie Starr), John Dall (Bart Tare), Barry Kroeger (Packett), Morris Carnovsky (Judge Willoughby), Anabel Shaw (Ruby Tare), Harry Lewis (Clyde Boston), Nedrick Young (Dave Allister), Trevor Bardette (Sheriff Boston), Mickey Little (Bart Tare, Age 7), Rusty Tamblyn (Bart Tare, Age 14), Paul Frison (Clyde Boston, Age 14), Dave Bair (Dave Allister, Age 14). **Completed**: July, 1949. **Released**: United Artists, as *Deadly Is the Female*, January 26. Re-released as *Gun Crazy* on August 24. 87 minutes.

Bart Tare's fascination with weapons gets him into trouble as a boy. Back in his hometown after a term in juvenile correction and a tour of duty in the army, Bart accompanies two old friends to a carny sideshow where he is fascinated by trickshooter Annie Laurie Starr. Bart accepts her challenge and outshoots her. Seeing this impromptu contest, the sideshow manager Packett invites Bart to join the act but fires them both when Laurie's affections stray from the manager to Bart. The couple marry but as their money runs out, Laurie threatens to leave him. So, Bart agrees to a holdup and they quickly graduate from filling stations and liquor stores to banks. While Bart abhors the thought of murder, Annie Laurie thrives on violence. Ultimately the couple arrive in California where they plan a last, big score followed by a flight across the border to Mexico. They take jobs in a meat-packing plant and plan to steal the payroll, but their attempt is marred when Annie Laurie kills two employees. Prevented by police vigilance from crossing the border but unwilling to go underground separately, the couple returns to Bart's home town and his sister's place. When one of Bart's boyhood friends, now a deputy sheriff, comes to arrest the couple, they flee on foot. As night falls and their pursuers close in, Bart realizes that Laurie should not be taken alive and shoots her before he is cut down by police bullets. Their bodies fall together in a final, lifeless embrace.

The noir style, grim narrative, and pervasive aura of eroticism in *Gun Crazy* make it one of the key films of the classic period. Although not the only low-budget independent to attain that status, *Gun Crazy* has certainly had more influence on neo-noir than pictures like *Detour* or *Raw Deal*. From *Bonnie and Clyde* to the present, four decades of neo-noir fugitive couples have echoed the *Gun Crazy*'s protagonists. The lovers in *Breathless* (1983*)* even take refuge in a movie theater where Lewis' film is being projected on screen and the couple in the quasi-remake *Guncrazy* are similarly enraptured with firearms. The narrative core of *Gun Crazy*—the fugitive couple—is a concept grounded in such proto-noir as *You Only Live Once* and *City Streets* and elaborated in *They Live By Night*, whose Bowie and Keechie have an asexual serenity that almost permits their salvation.

The atavistic, precipitous amour fou of Annie Laurie Starr and Bart Tare in *Gun Crazy* is the root cause of their destruction. While earlier productions underplayed both the sexuality and the violence of their lovers, *Gun Crazy* contains no scenes of domesticity to belie the couple's fundamental lawlessness. In *Gun Crazy,* sex and violence are the major motifs of the noir universe. This attitude, also in Lewis' later *The Big Combo,* not only contrasts with the perspectives of earlier directors but also anticipates and, to some degree, goes beyond similar aspects in Penn's *Bonnie and Clyde.* While the literal violence may pale compared with that of newer, exaggerated pastiches such as *Natural*

Born Killers (1994) or *Wild at Heart* (1990), the performances in *Gun Crazy* have a sexual directness seldom seen before or after its release in classic period noir.

When Clyde first shows Bonnie his gun in Penn's film, she expresses her arousal by fondling the barrel. Such an action seems understated next to Bart's initial encounter with Annie Laurie in the sideshow. Lewis' introductory shot is taken from an emphatic low angle as she strides into frame wearing a cowgirl costume and firing two pistols above her head. Bart accepts the challenge to his shooting skill and, figuratively, to his masculinity, and the two square off onstage. The winner of the exhibition will be the one who can light the most matches worn in a crown on the opponent's head by grazing them with .45 caliber bullets. Lewis ends the sequence with an exchange of glances between the two: Annie Laurie smiling encouragingly; Bart, the victor with his potency amply established, grinning from ear to ear. At this point, the relationship of Annie Laurie and Bart evolves into an amour as fou as any in film noir. He abandons his friends and family to join her in the sideshow. She denies further sexual favors to Packett, which ultimately leads to their being fired and financial dire straits. Despite Bart's fascination with guns, it is Annie Laurie who must initiate their criminal activity. When they have run out of money, she sexually blackmails him from pawning his collection of sidearms. She also argues that they could earn more by staging their shooting exhibitions in banks rather than carnival tents. When he hesitates, she sits down on the edge of a broken-down motel bed, seductively slips on her stockings, and threatens to leave him unless he agrees.

Lewis' choice of rural rather than an urban locales for most of the action supports the narrative concept of obsessive and destructive sexuality waiting to explode from beneath the surface of everyday America. Isolated in small towns or hiding out in country motels, Annie and Bart have nothing to distract them from themselves and their lack of prospects. Alternately, Lewis uses diverse icons besides guns—automobiles, clothes (Annie favors berets and tight sweaters when not in her cowgirl regalia), and in the early sequences the sights and sounds of the carnival—to create an underlying sense of ostracism and decay. When they drive into Hampton to rob the local bank during a Western festival, they dress in Western shirts and Stetsons to make them-

Gun Crazy: *Annie Laurie Starr (Peggy Cummins) and Bart Tare (John Dall).*

selves seem a part of it; but the inescapable visual metaphor is that their primitive amour fou is as anachronistic as their garb, part of an earlier, lawless era.

In that same sequence, Lewis uses a single long take to underscore the equation of sex and violence at a stylistic level. The camera mounted in the back seat of their car begins by recording their nervousness and anxiety, like teenagers on their first date, on the outskirts of town. Their excitement mounts as they approach the savings and loan building: they fret over whether things will go as planned, over the detail of whether there will even be a place to park in front of the building. During the actual robbery, the camera remains in the car with Annie and only pans over to the sidewalk when she must slip out to distract a passing policeman by admiring his revolver. When Bart emerges, she clubs the policeman with her gun. Even after this climactic moment, the unbroken shot is maintained as their vehicle races out of town. Annie Laurie glances back at the camera, while leaning toward Bart as if to embrace him, and sees that they are not being followed. Lewis ends the sequence and the shot by fading out on her look: secure, gratified, breathless as if after sex, and now smiling lasciviously as she did when Bart won the shooting contest.

Lewis' staging of a violent crime as if it were a sexual act is not unique in film noir; but his consistent stylization of *Gun Crazy* in those terms imbues the erotic and criminal acts of Annie Laurie and Bart with a desperation and fatality that defines the noir vision. By 21st century standards, the mere innuendo of sexual pleasure from a criminal act may seem rather tame. But the staging of the scene in *Gun Crazy*, the tightly controlled perspective from the back of the car and the use of a sequence-shot, creates a tension for the viewer that is subtly analogous to the couple's. The release of the tension as the sequence ends is keyed to Laurie's expression. What is building, to use more contemporary terminology, is an addiction. Laurie's addiction to violence, initially

motivated by the desire for "money and all the things it will buy," is now also the need for an adrenaline rush. In feeding her habit, Bart is a typical co-dependent. Unlike other fugitive couples of the classic period, who flee to save themselves from unjust or exaggerated accusations, Bart and Laurie choose to become criminals. As they come to depend more and more on each other, the inversion of *They Live by Night* is complete: rather than being innocents whose platonic interdependence becomes a sexual one, Bart and Laurie's purely physical attraction evolves into an emotional and neurotic connection.

Moreover, Lewis gives his characters a greater self-consciousness of their "mad love" than the fugitive couples of *You Only Live Once, They Drive By Night,* and even *Bonnie and Clyde.* It is already there just beneath the surface when, as Packett observes to Annie Laurie, they first look at each other "like wild animals." Bart in particular, once he has been initiated into the sexual thrill of violence by Annie Laurie, seems existentially aware of his position and the consequences of his choice. He replies fatalistically to her suggestion, at one point, that they split up because she is destroying him by observing with a most appropriate simile that they cannot separate because "we go together ... like guns and ammunition." That statement characterizes both the explosive and fateful qualities of their relationship: they are made for each other but only in the context of violence and death. That awareness also leads Lewis' couple—very unlike Ray's Bowie and Keechie, innocents who move slowly from platonic interdependence to sexual experience—from an initial, chance encounter and simple sexual attraction to a final position of self-destructive romanticism.

Perhaps the most telling sequence is the wordless one after Annie Laurie has convinced Bart to take a separate route for a while and rejoin her later. After he drives her to where a second car is waiting, they start off in opposite directions. Abruptly and at the same instant, the cars veer around as if irresistibly drawn back together and almost collide. In that sequence, the machines express what their drivers have understood but never fully verbalized. The expressionistic conclusion of *Gun Crazy* with the couple pursued across country by Bart's former friends recapitulates the irrational noir quality of amour fou. Bart's return to the locus of his childhood and the nascence of his "guncraziness" may be either a search for the causes of his impending annihilation or a flagrant display to his childhood friends of his sociopathic freedom (or both). In any case, the stylized setting and the ritual of the fugitive couple's death, fallen together in the foggy marshland, add an unusual, quasi-operatic final note to their fate. Both the "gun-craziness" and the "mad love" of the protagonists are typical of the noir world, yet no other film integrates these concepts as fully on a variety of levels as *Gun Crazy*. The viewer would have understood from convention the inevitable result of Annie Laurie and Bart's passion even if Lewis had left them standing in each other's arms between their idling cars in the middle of the highway. After that, the inevitability of their downfall is a given. They die together, he shooting her in a last, perverse act of love and a detached affirmation of necessary demise. **AS & CM**

HANGOVER SQUARE (1945)

Director: John Brahm. **Screenplay**: Barré Lyndon from the novel by Patrick Hamilton. **Producer**: Robert Bassler. **Director of Photography**: Joseph LaShelle. **Music**: Bernard Herrmann. **Art Directors**: Maurice Ransford, Lyle Wheeler. **Editor**: Harry Reynolds. **Cast**: Laird Cregar (George Harvey Bone), Linda Darnell (Netta Longdon), George Sanders (Dr. Allan Middleton), Glenn Langan (Eddie Carstairs), Faye Marlowe (Barbara Chapman), Alan Napier (Sir Henry Chapman), J.W. Austin (Det. Insp. King), Charles Coleman (Man at bonfire), Francis Ford (Ogilby), J. Farrell MacDonald (Street Vendor), Frederick Worlock (Supt. Clay). **Released**: 20th Century-Fox, February 27. 77 minutes.

In late Victorian London, composer George Harvey Bone is working to complete a piano concerto commissioned by Sir Henry Chapman, his mentor and the father of his fiancée Barbara. Bone suffers seizures when he hears cacophonous sounds. After one such episode, he suddenly finds himself in an unfamiliar part of the city and later reads a newspaper report of a murder in that neighborhood of an antique dealer with whom Bone had a dispute. Bone is questioned by a Scotland Yard consulting psychiatrist Allan Middleton, who recommends that Bone take some time off from his work. At a local music hall, Bone is smitten with Netta, for whom he writes a song. When Bone realizes that Netta is professing to love him only to get more songs, he strangles her and throws her body as if it were a Guy Fawkes effigy onto a bonfire. As he completes the concerto, Bone realizes that the police are on to him. Bone performs his concerto for the first and last time, perishing in a fire he sets.

It is uncanny: Almost everyone connected with *Hangover Square* came to a bad (often untimely) end. The novel on which it was very loosely based was by Patrick Hamilton, who had known vast popular success with his plays, *Rope* and *Gas Light,* both adapted into famous movies; he died at age 58 of alcoholism. The director, John Brahm, was a rising star at Fox (see also his terrific *I Wake Up Screaming*) when he made this film, but ended his career grinding out dozens of episodic television shows, not to mention that ultimate B movie, *Hot Rods to Hell.* Laird Cregar, his star, died of a heart attack shortly after making this movie at age 29. Linda Darnell, who played the tarty music hall singer, Netta, loved to murderous distraction by Cregar's George Henry Bone, died in a fire at her home (while watching one of her old films on TV) at age 44. George Sanders, who plays Allan Middleton, the film's pioneering forensic scientist, lived to be 66, growing ever more sardonic with the passing years (and cast in ever lousier roles) before committing suicide,

Hangover Square: *A Street Vendor (J. Farrell MacDonald) and George Harvey Bone (Laird Cregar).*

leaving a note saying he was—quite literally—bored to death.

Yet, despite all these sad endings, *Hangover Square* is a movie to conjure with—if only as a non-stop compendium of film noir imagery. It is, of course, of the Victorian noir sub-species, set at the turn of the 20th century, where the lack of electrical lighting and the amount of heavy drapery commonly used in interior design naturally require low light levels (if memory serves, there are not more than two or three quite inconsequential day-lit sequences in the movie). It is a deep focus film, as so many movies of its day (in particular period pieces) were, and it is hard to think of another film so relentlessly shadowed, or so deeply fog-enshrouded (it even creeps into the interiors). This quality is richly and radically enhanced by the alternation of radically high and low angles which Brahm and his cameraman Joseph LaShelle— coming off his Oscar-winning work on *Laura*—brilliantly employ.

And that says nothing about Bernard Herrmann's score. He was not far removed from *Kane* and *Ambersons*, and this was the second movie to which he contributed lengthy pieces to be played on camera (the operatic fragment for *Kane* was the first, the Albert Hall symphony in *The Man Who Knew Too Much* was the third—with Herrmann himself on Hitchcock's podium). Here he gives us the piano concerto over which Cregar's composer-protagonist ceaselessly toils and dies playing at the film's end—a piece that is full of half-suppressed shrieks, an atonal madness struggling to find expression in the still tonal world of upper-class London over a hundred years ago.

This, it should be observed, is not the world of Hamilton's novel. His George Henry Bone was not a composer at all; he was a common (and poverty-stricken) drunk, who could not recall the crimes he committed for the simple reason that he was always lost in an alcoholic haze when he struck. There are serious literary people who believe that Hamilton ranked with the likes of Malcolm Lowry in portraying the condition to which he was himself prey, but that was of small concern to 20th Century-Fox, looking for a sequel to the successful 1944 Brahm-Cregar collaboration, *The Lodger,* which was similarly situated. So poor Bone is driven "round the bend by discord—the screech of a cat, say, or a load of pipes being overturned in the street." It is the Sanders character, a sort of Sigmund as Sherlock, who at first suspects and eventually explains Bone's aberration.

But he's pretty much a sop to the literal minded. This is a movie that depends upon style triumphing over believable substance, and it is important to note that fire is the hallmark of that style. In the opening sequence Bone is seen killing an antique dealer (his motive is unspecified) and setting his shop ablaze to cover his tracks. Later, after killing Netta, he wraps her in a cloak, covers her face with a mask, and pretending that she is just another effigy of the kind kids regularly used to ritually incinerate on these occasions, totes her body up a ladder at a towering Guy Fawkes night bonfire. There is something hellishly inhuman in this sequence, a kind of frenzy in its staging that is not at all common—or at least as beautifully realized—in movies of its era.

Finally, there is the long, gorgeously staged climax to consider: Bone is at last playing his concerto at a society concert when he sees the police, led by Middleton, closing in. He turns the piano over to his faithful, clueless girlfriend, confronts the cops, then sets fire to the place with a hurled gas lamp. He then returns to the piano to play the last chords of his music (solo, of course, orchestra and audience having fled). This is one of the more spectacular movie conflagrations, directed by Brahm with an energy and a heightened realism that matches his Guy Fawkes sequence, and it forms a delirious climax to the film.

You can argue that *Hangover Square* is a hopelessly preposterous piece of work—especially in its protagonist's absurd psychological profile, which is not made any more persuasive by Cregar's pop-eyed playing when the madness is upon him. But there is also something touching about him, a shambling politeness, a nerdy eagerness to please, when he is in a normal phase. As Middleton keeps reminding him (and us) he is not responsible for his insanity; he is, instead, its hapless victim. Couple this characterization with the elegance of Brahm's manner and the power he brings to his major sequences, and you have a studio picture that clings to memory with surprising intensity. **RS**

THE HARDER THEY FALL (1956)

Director: Mark Robson. **Screenplay**: Philip Yordan; from the novel by Budd Schulberg. **Producer**: Philip Yordan. **Director of Photography**: Burnett Guffey. **Music**: Hugo Friedhofer. **Art Director**: William Flannery. **Editor**: Jerome Thoms. **Cast**:

The Harder They Fall: *Promoter Nick Benko (Rod Steiger, left) listens to a conversation between Eddie Willis (Humphrey Bogart) and Leo (Nehemiah Persoff).*

Humphrey Bogart (Eddie Willis), Rod Steiger (Nick Benko), Jan Sterling (Beth Willis), Mike Lane (Toro Moreno), Max Baer, Sr. (Buddy Brannen), Jersey Joe Walcott (George), Edward Andrews (Jim Weyerhause), Harold J. Stone (Art Leavitt), Carlos Montalban (Luis Agrandi), Nehemiah Persoff (Leo), Felice Orlandi (Vince Fawcett), Herbie Faye (Max), Rusty Lane (Danny McKeogh), Jack Albertson (Pop). **Completed**: December 29, 1955. **Released**: Columbia, May 9. 108 minutes.

Eddie Willis, once a well-known sports columnist, is now down on his luck. He is hired for his abilities and contacts in the sports world by Nick Benko, the head of a fight promotion syndicate. His job is to promote the syndicate's latest acquisition, a blundering Argentinian boxer, Toro Moreno. Formidable looking and gigantic, Moreno is an inept fighter with a glass jaw. Nevertheless, Moreno wins a series of fixed bouts, arranged to give him a shot at the championship fight. Moreno is matched against the ex-champ, Gus Dundee. Dundee loses and subsequently dies of a brain hemorrhage. Thinking himself to blame, Moreno suffers great guilt. Willis informs him that all of his fights have been fixed and that the cause of Dundee's death was a beating he had taken from champ Buddy Brannen in a previous fight. Determined to fight Brannen anyway and take the prize money back home to his family in South America, Moreno is severely beaten in the ring. When Willis goes to collect Moreno's winnings from Benko, he is told that the total profit is a mere $49.07. Giving in to the disgust he has felt all along, Willis gives his $26,000 share of the profits to Moreno and puts him on a plane to Argentina. Willis then sits down to write a series of articles exposing Benko and his syndicate. Although threatened with harm, Willis is determined to outlaw boxing in the United States "if it takes an act of Congress to do it."

The Harder They Fall is an expose of organized crime's influence in the world of professional boxing and based on Budd Schulberg's novelization of the career of Primo Canera. The film's treatment of the topic and the general tone of outrage are reminiscent of the Warner Bros' style of socially realistic motion pictures of the 1930s with their sense of immediacy. Humphrey Bogart's presence particularly links *The Harder They Fall* with the WB pictures of the 1930s.

Bogart is a key iconographic figure in all of film noir, since the roles he played throughout his lengthy career touched on all of the cycle's major thematic concerns. Whether as a gangster, detective, or an initially aloof figure straddling the fence, Bogart's characters were often beyond the law. One of his early WB appearances, in *Kid Galahad,* was as a fight-fixing mobster. In *The Harder They Fall,* he is an ex-sports columnist turned boxing promoter; and Bogart plays the cynical loner for the last time. It was his most popular on-screen persona and a key noir character. A cynic is a reformed idealist who has experienced too much pain and disillusionment to risk sticking his neck out for anyone because of the fear of reactivating the old hurt. But if action defines character then the character must act, finally, when something crucial is at stake. The name may be Rick as in *Casablanca,* or Harry Morgan as in *To Have and Have Not,* but Bogart's characters eventually shed their hard shells and respond to a moral code that has been hibernating. The strong cynical edge of this film, rooted in the script by Philip Yordan, is supported by the harsh black-and-white photography and unsentimental direction and editing. **JB**

HE RAN ALL THE WAY (1951)

Director: John Berry. **Screenplay**: Guy Endore (front for Hugo Butler and Dalton Trumbo) from the novel by Sam Ross. **Producer**: Bob Roberts, John Garfield. **Director of Photography**: James Wong Howe. **Music**: Franz Waxman. **Art Director**: Harry Horner. **Editor**: Francis D. Lyon. **Cast**: John Garfield (Nick Robey), Shelley Winters (Peg Dobbs), Wallace Ford (Mr. Dobbs), Selena Royle (Mrs. Dobbs), Bobby Hyatt (Tommy Dobbs), Gladys George (Mrs. Robey), Norman Lloyd (Al Molin). **Completed**: March 13, 1951. **Released**: United Artists, July 13. 77 minutes.

Nick Robey, a small-time thief, joins his friend Al in a payroll robbery. The thieves panic and Al and a guard are wounded. Nick runs with the money to a nearby public swimming pool where he meets Peg Dobbs. When the pool closes, he escorts Peg to her home and is introduced to her parents and younger brother. The family goes to a movie, leaving Nick and Peg at home. When the parents return, Nick thinks they have found out about him and holds them at gunpoint. The morning paper reveals that the guard which he shot died and Nick is now wanted for murder. He holds the family hostage, alternately befriending and terrorizing them. Nick trusts only Peg and gives her money to buy a car so that they can escape together. When the car fails to arrive, Nick panics and turns on Peg, forcing her out of the apartment where her father stands ready to kill him. Choosing between her father and Nick, she shoots Nick just as the car he wanted pulls up.

He Ran All the Way was one of the first films to use the noir theme of a "normal" family trapped in their own home by outside "subversive" forces. It is similar in mood to William Wyler's *The Desperate Hours* in which a middle-class family is held hostage by a trio of inarticulate and violent escaped convicts. However, in *He Ran All The Way,* the killer and the hostaged family share the same background, which adds an interesting ambivalence to their relationship. John Garfield as Nick conveys the feeling of a wounded animal rather than a cold-blooded killer. As a man rejected by his own family, he

He Ran All the Way: *A wounded Nick Robey (John Garfield, right), Peggy Dobbs (Shelley Winters) and her father (Wallace Ford).*

tries to become part of his new "adopted" family. The film continually points out how much alike the killer and his hostages are; they view society similarly because they are members of the same proletarian class. In other circumstances, they might well be on the same side. Written, directed, and produced by victims of McCarthyism —John Berry, Dalton Trumbo, Hugo Butler, and John Garfield himself— Nick's paranoia is matched throughout the film by references to a larger, more repressive society. The father hesitates to call the police, because, like firemen at a fire, "they chop, chop, chop," again reinforcing a kind of proletarian solidarity. The connection between the killer and his prey makes the relationship of Nick and Peg believable. However, in the final explosive sequence when Peg must choose between her father and her lover, her moral sense leaves her no choice. She shoots the intruder to the accompaniment of Franz Waxman's cacophony, and the camera pans away to an image of desolation: the rain-splashed streets. **JC**

HE WALKED BY NIGHT (1949)

Director: Alfred Werker and Anthony Mann [uncredited]. **Screenplay**: John C. Higgins and Crane Wilbur, with additional dialogue by Harry Essex from an unpublished story by Crane Wilbur. **Producer**: Robert Kane (Byran Foy Productions). **Director of Photography**: John Alton. **Music**: Leonid Raab. **Art Director**: Edward Ilou. **Editor**: Alfred DeGaetano. **Cast**: Richard Basehart (Morgan/Martin), Scott Brady (Sgt. Marty Brennan), Roy Roberts (Capt. Breen), Whit Bissell (Reeves), Jimmy Cardwell (Chuck Jones), Jack Webb (Lee), Bob Bice (Detective Steno), Reed Hadley (Narrator), Los Angeles Police Chief Bradley (Himself), Jack Bailey (Pajama Top), Mike Dugan, Garrett Craig (Patrolmen). **Completed**: October 8, 1948. **Released**: Eagle-Lion. February 6. 79 minutes.

Ray Martin is a brilliant, technically adept young man and a skilled thief. He also becomes a murderer when he kills a police officer who observed him attempting an electronics store burglary. Martin's skills at intercepting police calls, altering his appearance and changing his *modus operandi* to escape detection are considerable but police are determined to capture this unique criminal who has killed one of their own and maimed another. Through a piece of abandoned equipment, they are able to trace him to an electronics firm owned by Paul Reeves, to whom Martin consigns stolen and modified equipment. With Reeves' cooperation, the police set a trap to capture him there at night, but Ray proves too wary. A gun battle ensues and Ray flees via flood control channels that lie beneath the streets of Los Angeles. With a great deal of patience and skills enhanced by modern technology, the L.A. police are able to create an accurate composite drawing of Martin which leads to the discovery of his true identity: Ray Morgan, a veteran who had been a civilian radio technician for the Pasadena Police Department. Following another lead, police detective Sgt. Brennen, disguised as a milkman, locates Martin's hideout in a Hollywood bungalow apartment. Under the cover of night, the police surround him again but Roy manages to escape through a roof hatch. He once again heads for the nearest curbside entrance to the subterranean channels, but Capt. Breen is prepared with police cars blocking all manholes and other openings. Cornered by the police in one of the tunnels, Roy attempts to shoot his way out in a hopeless maneuver that leads to his death.

He Walked by Night may not be among the most distinguished of the semi-documentary thrillers that became part of the noir cycle in the 1940s and 1950s, but in some ways it is a seminal film. For one thing, the subterranean tracking and killing of Roy Martin is a sequence whose visual and auditory style anticipates the more famous sequence in the British production of *The Third Man (1949)*, released seven months later the same year, in which villain Harry Lime is trapped and killed in the sewers of post-war Vienna. More significantly, this is the film from which Jack Webb drew the inspiration for his popular radio show (1949) and later television series *Dragnet* (which debuted in 1951). Clearly it stands as a major source for future media excursions into the police semi-documentary: a written introduction which guarantees the "authenticity" of the story (borrowed from the earlier *T-Men*) warning that "only the names have been changed to protect the innocent"; an opening visual montage that places the action within the contemporary setting of the real city of Los Angeles; finally, a stentorian narrator (Reed Hadley) whose voice lends credence to the accuracy of the proceedings.

Together with the earlier *Naked City*—whose plein-air photography was closer in style to the true documentary than the darker expressionism of *He Walked by Night*—this film proved to be a major ancestor of a class of popular films and of television shows whose descent leads directly to the contemporary media, as evidenced by the proliferation of series such as *Law and Order* and *CSI*. This film also reunited its uncredited director Anthony Mann with photographer John Alton. Their teamwork on *T-Men* helped to establish many of the conventions of the police thriller. While that earlier film was superior in terms of its execution (plot deficiencies and the lack of character development mar this latter work), *He Walked by Night* is a more representative film noir precisely insofar as it eschews giving the audience a privileged position from which to view police procedures and the often heroic daily activities of the individual police officer because it focuses attention instead on the mostly nocturnal activities of the criminal. It is Roy Martin, not the police officers who track him down, who is the film's real protagonist and Richard Basehart's deft performance in that role transforms

a shallow character into an intriguing cipher. Misanthropic and isolated, with only a small dog for friend, Basehart's Martin becomes the epitome of the "underground man," whose willful alienation is perhaps nowhere better reflected than in the mirrored image of him removing a bullet from the flesh of his torso with the skilled precision and detachment of a surgeon—all the while grimacing in pain. Though Martin's death at the hands of the police satisfied the demands of that era's motion picture code, it was perfectly consistent with a character who could find meaning only by making the mode of his death his own existential choice. **BP**

HELL'S HALF ACRE (1954)

Director: John H. Auer. **Screenplay**: Steve Fisher. **Producer**: Herbert J. Yates. **Director of Photography**: John L. Russell. **Music**: R. Dale Butts. **Editor**: Fred Allen. **Cast**: Wendell Corey (Chet Chester alias Randy Williams), Evelyn Keyes (Donna Williams), Elsa Lanchester (Lida O'Reilly), Nancy Gates (Sally Lee), Jesse White (Tubby Otis), Marie Windsor (Rose), Keye Luke (Police Chief Dan), Philip Ahn (Roger Kong), Leonard Strong (Ippy). **Locations**: Honolulu, Hawaii. **Completed**: Mid-September 1953. **Released**: Republic, June 1. 91 minutes.

Donna Williams hears a new song, whose lyrics are identical to an old love note from her late husband Randy Williams— who she always believed died ten years before in the attack on Pearl Harbor. She tracks down the author of the song, who turns out to be a stylish ex-racketeer in Honolulu who calls himself Chet Chester. Photos of Chester reveal he looks strikingly similar to Randy Williams. Chester has recently been arrested because his current girlfriend, Sally

Lee, was murdered. But he escapes from the police and Donna Williams helps him search through Honolulu's seedy vice district, known as "Hell's Half Acre." They meet up with the real killer, mobster Roger Kong. Chester eventually confesses to his wife that he is really Randy Williams, but dies so that his girlfriend's killer can be brought to justice.

Hell's Half Acre is a decent if lurid crime thriller that is notable for several things. Firstly, it is a noir with elements of the "woman's picture." The heroine is as much trying to resolve her romantic situation as she is dealing with crime. The film is loaded with roles for actresses. Elsa Lanchester shines in her zany comedy relief role as a spirited taxicab driver who aids the heroine. The film also has a juicy role for Wendell Corey, who specialized in playing good-natured but weak-willed WASPs, whose generations of refined breeding left them easily overwhelmed by the romantic lures of femme fatales. Here Corey plays another man who is willing to overturn his life in favor of an irresistible woman. In some ways, Corey can be seen as a chump who violates the male code of toughness. In other ways, he is a rare Hollywood example of a man willing to sacrifice all for love. Quite a few women must have found this secretly attractive, and a welcome change of pace from he-man tough guys who can always shrug off dames.

The title refers to a seedy district of Honolulu, the closest that this "paradise city" had to a slum in 1954. Lots of film noirs were shot in the low rent districts of Los Angeles, such as downtown and the Angel's Flight neighborhood. *Hell's Half Acre* offers the Hawaiian equivalent, a neighborhood full of back alleys with outdoor staircases and jerry-rigged multi-story dwellings. The film is unique in preserving a visual record of this picturesque part of American architecture and history. The hidden subtexts of these films present these areas as urban locales infinitely more colorful than suburbia. **MG**

HELL'S ISLAND (1955)

Director: Phil Karlson. **Screenplay**: Maxwell Shane, Phil Karlson, John Payne from an unpublished story by Jack Leonard and Martin M. Goldsmith. **Producers**: William H. Pine, William C. Thomas. **Director of Photography**: Lionel Lindon. **Music**: Irvin Talbot. **Art Director**: Hal Pereira. **Editor**: Archie Marshek. **Cast**: John Payne (Mike Cormack), Mary Murphy (Janet Martin), Francis L Sullivan (Barzland), Arnold Moss (Paul Armand), Paul Picerni (Eduardo Martin), Eduardo Noriega (Inspector Pena), Walter Reed (Lawrence), Sandor Szabo (Torbig), Robert Cabal (Miguel). **Released**: Paramount, May 6. 83 minutes.

Mike Cormack is a former district attorney who, after losing his job because of alcoholism, finds work as a bouncer in a Las Vegas casino. He is approached by Barzland, a wheel chair-bound "financier" of questionable reputation, who offers a $5,000 reward for a ruby possibly lost in a plane that crashed en route from the Caribbean. Cormack soon learns that he was solicited because his former fianceé Janet Martin is now married to the man suspected of sabotaging the plane carrying the ruby. Although she had left him, Janet greets Cormack warmly and asks for his

help in clearing her husband of murder charges. Cormack agrees; but after being beaten by Barzland's henchmen and detained by the local police he learns that Janet has been abducted and taken to Hell's Island. Despite the warnings of a police inspector, Cormack rescues her only to discover that Janet was responsible for the plane crash in an attempt to kill her husband for his insurance and that she stole the ruby. When Barzland and his men realize this, Cormack kills them in self-defense and then turns Janet over to the authorities.

Hell's Island comes near the end of the noir cycle, after the release of several other noir films featuring its star John Payne and directed by Phil Karlson, including *99 River Street* and *Kansas City Confidential*. By the time of *Hell's Island*, Payne's world-weariness has become symptomatic of the movement's protagonists. Still Payne's unsmiling and fatigued expression was something of a particular noir icon. His portrayal of Cormack, like that of Ernie Driscoll the fallen prizefighter in *99 River Street*, develops from that of a defeated and hopeless figure to someone tenaciously clinging to a second chance. As he moves, shoulders slumped, first out of place in a tuxedo among the casino patrons and then framed alone against the visually idyllic tropical backgrounds, Cormack carries with him the resilience of one who knows he cannot be beaten down any further. Because Janet Martin represents not merely a lost woman but, in the sexual transference of the film noir, lost self-esteem, Cormack willingly endures both bodily injury and emotional humiliation to win her back. By developing the narrative as a flashback from Cormack on an operating table, the writers permit Karlson to mold a first-person narration that is both subjective and heavily ironic. As Cormack dispassionately recalls the events leading to Janet's arrest, he is also chronicling his own blindness to her true nature, which caused him to be deceived a second time. As such, the entire narrative becomes a compelling confession of human weakness. His record of mental suffering and the graphic depiction of physical punishment become purgative rituals by which Cormack ultimately restores his own being. **AS**

High Sierra: *Roy Earle (Humphrey Bogart) and Marie (Ida Lupino)*.

HIGH SIERRA (1941)

Director: Raoul Walsh. **Screenplay**: John Huston and W.R. Burnett from his novel. **Producer**: Hal B. Wallis. **Associate Producer**: Mark Hellinger. **Director of Photography**: Tony Gaudio. **Music**: Adolph Deutsch. **Art Director**: Ted Smith. **Editor**: Jack Killifer. **Cast**: Humphrey Bogart (Roy Earle), Ida Lupino (Marie), Alan Curtis (Babe), Arthur Kennedy (Red), Joan Leslie (Velma), Henry Hull (Doc Banton), Barton MacLane (Jake Kranmer), Henry Travers (Pa), Elisabeth Risdon (Ma), Cornel Wilde (Louis Mendoza), Minna Gombell (Mrs. Baugham), Paul Harvey (Mr. Baugham), Donald MacBride (Big Mac), Jerome Cowan (Healy), John Eldredge (Lou Preiser). **Location**: Inyo County, California. **Completed**: September 16, 1940. **Released**: Warner Bros., January 4. 100 minutes.

Notorious criminal "Mad Dog" Roy Earle is helped to escape from prison by Big Mac, an old gangland associate who wants him to go to California to engineer the holdup of a resort hotel. On the way, Roy meets the Goodhues and their granddaughter, Velma, a clubfooted girl for whom he feels a sympathetic attraction. Arriving at a mountain hideout, Roy finds that Red and Babe, the henchmen assigned to him, have brought along a dance-hall girl, Marie. At first opposed to her presence, Roy soon comes to trust her, while she quickly falls in love with him. But his mind is on Velma; after planning the holdup with the inside help of Mendoza, a corrupt clerk at the hotel, he goes to visit the girl, giving her money for an operation to correct her clubfoot. The holdup takes place, and Roy makes his getaway with Marie; but Babe and Red are killed in a car crash. Mendoza talks, setting the police after Roy, who has gone to Big Mac for help, only to find him dead. Roy then goes to a now-cured Velma, but she has thrown him over for another man. He gives the ring intended for Velma to Marie, and the two misfits go on the run together. But the police are closing in; Roy puts Marie on a bus before heading for a mountain pass in the High Sierras, but he is trapped. Hearing about her love's last stand Marie halts her flight and comes after him, arriving just in time to see him killed.

The reputation of Raoul Walsh is based largely on his talents as an action-adventure director. But such films as *They Died with Their Boots On, White Heat, The Roaring Twenties, They Drive by Night* and *High Sierra,* while indeed boasting action sequences, also offer affecting character studies of strongly defined individuals operating both in and out of society. Walsh's protagonists are people struggling, in the words of *High Sierra's* Roy Earle, "to crash out" to an unfettered, free life of which they are both maker and master. *High Sierra* may well be Walsh's most powerful expression of the individual's quest for freedom, a fact that in some ways seems to divorce it from the noir cycle. The sun shines generously; the characters are freed from the stricture of bleak little rooms and are led out into grassy parks and lush mountain pathways where the night skies are filled with stars rather than fogged with neon. But Walsh's lavish display of the glories of the natural world reinforce, by contrast, his grim view of human existence. Surrounded by magnificence, man is miserable. The superbly soaring peaks of the Sierras mock his insignificance and are monuments to his unreachable desires.

Walsh's sense of a cruel, inexorable fate viewed in *High Sierra* with a mordant humor is also a noir conception. Velma's defection after Roy has literally turned her life around, Big Mac's badly timed death, and the wind's disposal of Roy's note absolving Marie of collaboration in his crimes —all seem like hideous practical jokes perpetrated against the film's helpless protagonists. Still, Walsh's characters are far more than pathetic victims. Doomed from the start (Roy's face seems stamped with death and Marie has the bruised look of a fallen angel), they nevertheless struggle toward freedom. Roy looks up at a starry sky and observes to an untouched Velma that the earth seems to him like "a little ball turning through the night with us hanging on to it." In fact, Roy does hang on, with what can only be called a noble tenacity. His last flight is straight up, to a mountains peak, to the last clear patch of sky and finally, to death. The conclusion of *High Sierra* is unusually exultant, even mystical. With Roy shot down from his mountaintop, a stricken Marie turns to a policeman and asks him the meaning of Roy's reiterated desire "to crash out." The man tells her that it means to be free. She raises her tear-stained face to the sky and murmurs "free" repeatedly to herself, like an incantation. Then, in tight closeup, her tears are gone and she wears an expression of joyful exaltation. Roy is free, and soon, perhaps, Marie will join him. **JK**

HIGH TIDE (1947)

Director: John Reinhardt. **Screenplay**: Robert Presnell, Sr. based on the story "Inside Job" by Raoul Whitfield, with additional dialogue by Peter Milne. **Producer**: Jack Wrather. **Director of Photography**: Henry Sharp. **Music**: Rudy Schrager. **Art Director**: Lewis C. Creber. **Editor**: Stewart S. Frye, William H. Ziegler. **Cast**: Lee Tracy (Hugh Fresney), Don Castle (Tim Slade), Julie Bishop (Julie Vaughn), Anabel Shaw (Dana Jones), Douglas Walton (Clinton Vaughn), Regis Toomey (Inspector O'Haffey), Francis Ford (Pop Garrow), Anthony Wade (Nick Dyke), Argentina Brunetti (Mrs. Cresser), Wilson Wood (Cleve Collins), George H. Ryland (Doctor at Shooting Scene). **Released**: Monogram, September 13. 72 minutes.

Fresney, an unscrupulous newspaper editor, has a broken back and cannot get out of his car. Slade, a private detective, has a leg caught under it. The car is stuck on a beach at the waterline, and the tide is coming in. Fade to flashback. Fresney hires Slade under the pretext of finding out who wants to kill him. In fact, Fresney intends to use Slade as "an alibi and a fall guy." Vaughn, the paper's publisher, has Garrow secretly investigating Fresney and Dyke, the local crime boss. Dyke's men kill Garrow, but only Slade knows where Garrow hid the information he gathered. Fresney first murders Vaughn and then betrays his silent partner, Dyke. As Fresney speeds along a coastal highway, Slade tells him that Garrow discovered Fresney planned to "get control of the paper" so he and Dyke could "run the town and all the rackets." He also reveals that Inspector O'Haffey has Garrow's information. Fresney is beaten but not yet finished. He drives his car over a cliff above the beach to try to kill Slade as well as himself. The flashback ends. In the last scene, Slade climbs up the cliff to resume his life.

Nearly every book or article about film noir treats the private detective as one of the icons and character prototypes of the classic period. In fact, the private investigator is rarely the main man in any film noir. In contrast, for example, the woman-in-distress is rarely mentioned in most published work, although she is the key character in many film noirs. Discussions of detective film noirs focus on the private eye character—challenged by a femme fatale, a corrupt world and a convoluted plot – and relate him to issues such as masculine identity and possession of or lack of control (over his client, the case or even language). As a rule, these discussions do not address the extent to which a detective film is inherently limited as noir because the protagonist's attributes are heroism, moral integrity and so on. Moreover, these discussions ignore a critical recurring character, i.e. the "criminal client." He or she hires the private detective as a cover-up for murders committed or ordered and meanwhile imperils the shamus. Brigid O'Shaughnessy is the criminal client in the first detective film noir, *The Maltese Falcon*. Other examples include not only Hugh Fresney in this film but also the characters Velma/Mrs. Grayle in *Murder, My Sweet*, Murdock in *The Brasher Doubloon*, Whit Sterling in *Out of the Past*, and Cathcart in *The Dark Corner,* in which the aristocratic villain hires two "private eyes." Cathcart orders one, known as "White Suit" Stauffer, to commit murder and frame private detective Bradford Gault for it. Then, Cathcart kills Stauffer and Galt must discover the mastermind behind it all. In such films, the criminal client's

motives for retaining and then turning against the gumshoe are the raison d'être for making the story noir.

Additionally, *High Tide* has two especially strong points. First, it is nocturnal. Apart from a couple of scenes on the morning when Vaughn's corpse is found, every other scene occurs after dark. Second, Fresney and Vaughn's wife Julie are characters straight out of the best pages of hard-boiled crime fiction, some of which were written by Raoul Whitfield, the author of the story on which *High Tide* is based. Fresney is as scheming and venal as they come while Julie, cracking wise between sips of anything-on-the-rocks, is obsessed with the man she did not marry. However, these filmic strengths are associated with notable weaknesses. Except for the brief scene of Vaughn's murder, a strong noir visual style is missing. Julie and Fresney, furthermore, begin tough but finish soft. Early on, Julie tries to arouse Slade, her ex-boyfriend, and she could care less that her husband is watching. She only married Vaughn for his money. When he worries that someone wants to kill him, she quips, "I'm rather looking forward to being a rich widow." Yet, by nightfall after his death, Julie is "pretty broken up" about it. At the start of the film, Fresney wants Slade to drown with him. Nevertheless, by the film's finale, Fresney saves Slade's life. Meanwhile, both Julie's and Fresney's personalities become watered down for the same reason: so that Dana and Slade can become a romantic couple. No matter how much a

PI is drugged and slugged, he survives and solves the mystery. Then, at least in hard-boiled fiction, he finds himself alone. But in the typical detective film noir, like *High Tide*, he and a beautiful young woman find love. **DMH**

THE HIGH WALL (1947)

Director: Curtis Bernhardt. **Screenplay**: Sydney Boehm and Lester Cole from the novel and play by Alan R. Clark and Bradbury Foote. **Producer**: Robert Lord. **Director of Photography**: Paul Vogel. **Music**: Bronislau Kaper. **Art Directors**: Cedric Gibbons, Leonid Vasian. **Editor**: Conrad A. Nervig. **Cast**: Robert Taylor (Steven Kenet), Audrey Totter (Dr. Ann Lorrison), Herbert Marshall (Willard Whitcombe), Dorothy Patrick (Helen Kenet), H.B. Warner (Mr. Slocum), Warner Anderson (Dr. George Poward), Moroni Olsen (Dr. Philip Dunlap), John Ridgely (David Wallace), Morris Ankrum (Dr. Stanley Griffin), Elisabeth Risdon (Mrs. Kenet), Vince Barnett (Henry Cronner), Jonathan Hale (Emory Garrison), Charles Arnt (Sidney X Hackle), Ray Mayer (Tom Delaney). **Completed**: August 26, 1947. **Released**: MGM, December 25. 100 minutes

Steven Kenet, an ex-army pilot, is found unconscious behind the wheel of a wrecked car next to his wife, Helen, who has been strangled, and he is arrested for murder. Steven has headaches and blackouts, which are the result of a hematoma from a wartime brain injury. Steven refuses the required operation as he realizes that he will not be executed for murder if he cannot be judged legally sane. Subsequently, he is committed to a veterans' mental institution that is surrounded by a high wall. He arouses the interest and sympathy of Dr. Ann Lorrison, who persuades him to undergo the necessary operation. After the operation, he still cannot recall the events leading to Helen's death and agrees to undergo narcosynthesis. Under its influence, he relates to Dr. Lorrison that his wife was bored at home and became a

secretary to Willard Whitcombe, an executive with a religious book publishing company. Steven found her one night at Whitcombe's apartment with her overnight bag. In a burst of temper, Steven began to strangle her and then blacked out. Revisiting the Whitcombe apartment with Dr. Lorrison, Steven realizes that his wife's overnight bag was missing following her death. A few days later, Steven is visited at the sanatorium by Whitcombe who desires to permanently unbalance Steven by confessing privately that he killed Helen. Losing control of himself at this news, Steven escapes from the institution. However, later Dr. Lorrison joins him and together they return to Whitcombe's apartment. When Whitcombe arrives they scuffle and Steven knocks Whitcombe out. Dr. Lorrison administers sodium pentothal to Whitcombe, who confesses to the murder under the drug's influence.

German emigré Curtis Bernhardt, apparently drawn to thrillers with psychological overtones such as *Conflict* and *The Possessed*, embellishes the straightforward plot of this otherwise ordinary melodrama with a noir *mise-en-scène*, supported by Vogel's fine camerawork and MGM production values. The occasional use of Taylor's voice-over narration, especially when reinforced by images of lonely cars on rain-soaked streets, creates an atmosphere (or *stimmung*, as Bernhardt would have called it) quite appropriate to film noir. Bernhardt was wise in using Vogel's proficiency with subjective camerawork judiciously in the murder flashback where it supports Steven's mental process in the act of trying to recall each detail of that fatal evening. It is interesting to compare the effect of this camera technique to Robert Montgomery and Vogel's ill-advised "experiment" using a "purely" subjective camera for the earlier *Lady In The Lake*. Herbert Marshall, equally adept as villain or victim, lends ambiguity to his portrayal of the stodgy Whitcombe, whose sexual passion betrays his desire to succeed in that most conservative of businesses, religious book publishing. The manner in which he kills Cronner, a witness to his crime, is one of those chilling noir scenes in which killing is reduced to an offhand gesture. Cronner is on a stool repairing an elevator as Whitcombe casually slips the handle of his umbrella around the stool's leg, pulling it out from under Cronner and sending the hapless man plummeting down the open elevator shaft to his death. **BP**

HIGHWAY DRAGNET (1954)

Director: Nathan Juran. **Screenplay**: Fred Eggers, Tom Hubbard, Herb Meadow, Jerome Odlum from a story by U.S. Anderson and Roger Corman. **Producer**: Jack Jungmeyer Jr., Roger Corman, William F. Broidy, A. Robert Nunes. **Director of Photography**: John J. Martin. **Art Director**: Dave Milton. **Music**: Edward J. Kay. **Editor**: Ace Herman. **Cast**: Richard Conte (James Henry), Joan Bennett (Mrs. Cummings), Mary Beth Hughes (Terri Smith), Wanda Hendrix (Susan), Reed Hadley (Detective Lt. Joe White Eagle), Iris Adrian (Waitress), Tom Hubbard (Det. Sgt. Ben Barnett). **Released**: Allied Artists, February 7. 71 minutes.

James Henry, a Marine discharged from a stint in Korea, is in Vegas, where he picks up a seductive blonde, Terri Smith, in a bar. While hitchhiking the next day, he is arrested by the police for Terri's murder. He escapes from custody and ends up getting a ride from professional photographer Mrs.

Cummings and her model, Susan. When Cummings and Susan hear motorcycle cops talking about the escaped murderer, they try to decide what to do. Susan wants to notify the police, but she is stopped by Cummings who reminds her that the dead woman was having an affair with Cummings' husband. Cummings is afraid she will become a suspect in the case. Meanwhile, Henry now steals another car. With the two women as hostages, he makes his way across the desert in a desperate attempt to rendezvous with a Marine buddy who can provide him with an alibi for the night of the murder. They end up at the Salton Sea only to find that Henry's friend left the day before. Detective White Eagle catches up to Henry, and Susan is about to reveal the truth about Cummings when the photographer grabs Henry's gun and shoots White Eagle. Cummings tries to get away but when she gets stuck in a pool of sand and water, she confesses to having killed Terri.

The redoubtable Roger Corman wrote the original story and co-produced this noir road picture. The film is also notable for the presence of three noir icons: Richard Conte plays the maladjusted war veteran Henry, falsely accused of a murder but fully capable of it; Mary Beth Hughes plays the tough-talking and sensual platinum blonde Terri who is looking for a good time but ends up dead with a dog leash around her neck; and of course Joan Bennett, whose films with Fritz Lang in the 1940s helped develop the noir style, plays the true femme fatale, Mrs. Cummings, a successful career woman consumed by jealousy and grief over her husband's affair with a younger woman, Terri, and guilty of his subsequent death.

The final sequence in the film, set in the Salton Sea near Palm Springs, like much of the film, is photographed in glaring desert light, an example of the naturalistic 1950s style of noir. Its white sands, salt plains, abandoned houses, and murky pools of water create an eerie atmosphere appropriate for a noir climax. Towards the end, Cummings finds herself stuck in one of those pools of sand, salt, and water. Her struggles to extricate herself symbolize her desire to escape from her own murky pool of deception, murder, and grief.

The film is also notable as an object lesson of what happened to film noir by the middle 1950s. Once its talent was decimated by the Blacklist and corporations redefined the zeitgeist in terms of conformism and the American Dream,

there was little space for dystopic and "gloomy" films like *Pitfall, Double Indemnity* or *Criss Cross*. Noir's best actors, like the ones in this film, were forced to the margins as were noir films themselves, waiting to be reborn some decades down the cinematic road. **JU**

HIS KIND OF WOMAN (1951)

Director: John Farrow and [uncredited] Richard Fleischer. **Screenplay**: Frank Fenton, Jack Leonard and Earl Felton [uncredited] from the unpublished story "Star Sapphire" by Gerald Drayson Adams. **Producer**: Robert Sparks. **Executive Producer**: Howard Hughes. **Director of Photography**: Harry J. Wild. **Music**: Leigh Harline. **Production Designers**: J. McMillan Johnson, Albert S. D'Agostino. **Editors**: Eda Warren, Frederic Knudtson. **Cast**: Robert Mitchum (Dan Milner), Jane Russell (Lenore Brent), Vincent Price (Mark Cardigan), Tim Holt (Bill Lusk), Charles McGraw (Thompson), Marjorie Reynolds (Helen Cardigan), Raymond Burr (Nick Ferraro), Leslie Banning (Jennie Stone), Jim Backus (Myron Winton), Philip Van Zandt (Moffo). **Completed**: May 23, 1950. **Released**: RKO, August 1. 120 minutes.

Deported syndicate boss Nick Ferraro wants to return to the United States to oversee his troubled criminal holdings. His plan is to assume the identity of a U.S. citizen. One member of Ferraro's gang sets up Dan Milner for a beating by a bookmaker's strong-arm man then hires him for a $50,000 job in Mexico. En route, Milner meets Lenore Brent, a singer posing as an heiress and traveling south to pursue an affair with film star Mark Cardigan. At Morro's Lodge, a resort in Baja Califomia that is also Lenore's destination, Milner is to await instructions. He passes the time with Lenore and Cardigan and even assists a young couple who have run up a large gambling debt. Finally, American immigration official Bill Lusk reveals that Ferraro plans to undergo plastic surgery by the former Nazi surgeon Krafft and assume Milner's identity. When Lenore tells Cardigan, he assembles a rescue party. His initial assault on the boat fails because their boat sinks. Milner is savagely beaten by Ferraro's men. As Cardigan and his men approach in a second boat, Krafft convinces Ferraro to let him give Milner a mind-destroying injection that will cause death within a year. Cardigan storms the yacht and captures Ferraro's men.

His Kind of Woman: *Robert Mitchum as Dan Milner*

Milner shoots Ferraro when he tries to come up behind Cardigan. Back at Morro's, Cardigan holds a triumphant press conference, and Milner is reunited with Lenore.

On a literal level, because it is set almost entirely at night, *His Kind of Woman* is among the most oppressively dark of film noir. Narratively, however, it balances comedy that verges on slapstick as Cardigan leads his unlikely band of rescuers against Ferraro's ship, with the graphic violence of Milner's prolonged beating and torture: first he is whipped with the buckle end of a belt and thrown into the steam-filled engine room; then Ferraro revives him, points a gun between his eyes and mutters, "Wake up, little boy, I want you to see it coming;" and finally Krafft has him held down for a fatal injection. The effect of such abrupt shifts in narrative tone and content is both grisly and chaotic. In Mitchum, Burr, and even Price, reprising his effete role of *Laura*, familiar icons of film noir are isolated and exaggerated. Ultimately Ferraro and his minions become less and less real, not so much characters as the embodiment of the vague, impersonal peril that has threatened Milner throughout the film. Each cutaway to inept Cardigan reemphasizes the illogical chaos of Milner's situation and prolongs his ordeal in a manner suggestive of the hazards and incongruities of the noir universe.

In this sense, *His Kind Of Woman* deals almost self-consciously and exclusively in archetypes of the noir world. Milner, as portrayed by Mitchum, is an equally exaggerated characterization: weary, sardonic, unexcited but critically unaware that the components of a fateful plot, which will ensnare him and compel him into action, are already in motion. In a core *mise en scène* that combines long takes with compositions in which wedges of light and bizarre shadows clutter the frame and distract the viewer, Milner is the only predictable element, he is the only emblem of stability, however uncertain. Milner's introduction in the late night diner is fully as stylized as Ferraro's as he explains to an acquaintance behind the counter that he is out of money and has just spent thirty days on a county road gang for an implicit vagrancy. The counterman gives Milner a free meal but his stance with his back to the gambler betray his working stiff's inability to understand a gambler's life-style. The suggestion that Milner inhabits the noir underworld is reinforced in the next sequence. First, a long shot isolates Milner on a dark street, where he climbs a set of wooden steps to a cheap second-floor apartment. Inside Milner finds three men waiting. In the course of a long take, Milner shrugs off their accusations of reneging on a bet and finally, after telling them it would "be nice if you guys cleaned up this mess before you got out of here," snubs out a cigarette in the palm of one of the men. The sustained shot is broken as Milner falls out of frame under the fists of the other two. Milner's self-destructive defiance is symptomatic of his world-weariness. After this first of many beatings he will endure during the course of the film, Ferraro's man calls with his proposition and Milner offhandedly tells him, "I was just getting ready to take my tie off . . . wondering whether I should hang myself with it."

For Milner, who understands the complexities of odds, the offer of something for nothing is a puzzle. He moves through Mexico almost like a somnambulist in search of a waking reality. In typically noir values, there is some degree of that reality to be found, but only in money and in sexuality as represented by Lenore. At that, Milner's relationship with sex and money is somewhat eccentric. He jokingly remarks to the vacationing financier that he buries his money in the ground. When Lenore drops by his room late at night, she finds him ironing currency: "When I have nothing to do and can't think I always iron my money." Clearly, Milner is not avaricious; nor is he as likely to inflict violence as to endure it. In terms of film noir conventions, because Lenore *is* his kind of woman, Milner's relationship with her and its sexual tension is crucial to his survival. He survives; and the tensions of both exaggerated violence and comedy are finally combined and dissipated in the movie's last shot and last sexual metaphor: an iron burning Milner's pants while he and Lenore embrace. **AS**

HIT AND RUN (1957)

Director: Hugo Haas. **Screenplay**: Hugo Haas based on a story by Herbert O. Phillips. **Producer**: Hugo Haas. **Director of Photography**: Walter Strenge. **Art Director**: Rudi Feld. **Music**: Franz Steininger. **Editor**: Stefan Arnsten. **Cast**: Cleo Moore (Julie), Hugo Haas (Gus/Dave), Vince Edwards (Frank), Dolores Reed (Miranda), Mara Lea (Anita), Pat Goldin (Undertaker), Carl Milletaire (Lawyer), Robert Cassidy (Sheriff). **Released**: United Artists, March. 87 minutes.

Gus is the owner of a gas station/junk yard who finds himself attracted to a struggling actress named Julie. Gus falls hard and asks Julie to marry him. Initially she is hesitant but agrees after realizing he can supply security and money. Soon Julie finds herself attracted to Frank, Gus' hunky mechanic, and they begin an affair. Frank proposes a scheme to get rid of Gus and puts it into action, running over a man he believes to be Gus. However, it turns out the individual is instead Gus' twin brother Dave, who had just been released from prison. Discovering their scheme, Gus pretends to be Dave, informs his lawyer of their plot, and proceeds to torment the couple into confession.

Hit and Run is a virtual remake of Hugo Haas' first noir *Pickup*. The triad of older cuckolded man, young vibrant wife, and muscular romantic younger man, as old as the Arthurian myths, is here played with a few more outrageous twists: Frank, the lover, runs over Gus' twin brother by mistake; Gus then pretends to be his brother in order to torture the lovers, etc.; but the mood and effect is much the same as the original film, with one major change—the presence of actress Cleo Moore.

Cleo Moore, as opposed to Beverly Michaels in the earlier film, is a much more sympathetic femme fatale. Her tone, manner, and physical appearance is much softer than the hard-edged Michaels. Consequently, the audience's sympathy for her is increased. She seems genuinely depressed over her lack of success as an actress and genuine in seeing Gus as a "safe harbor" in the storm of her life. In addition, she initially resists Frank's murderous scheme to get rid of her husband, even though she finds it hard to resist his sexual allure, especially considering the clearly implied sexual inadequacies of her aging husband. **JU**

THE HITCH-HIKER (1953)

Director: Ida Lupino. **Screenplay**: Collier Young and Ida Lupino, adapted by Robert Joseph from an unpublished story by Daniel Mainwaring [uncredited]. **Producer**: Collier Young. **Director of Photography**: Nicholas Musuraca. **Music**: Leith Stevens. **Music Director**: Constantin Bakaleinikoff. **Art Directors**: Albert S. D'Agostino, Walter E. Keller. **Editor**: Douglas Stewart. **Cast**:

Edmond O'Brien (Ray Collins), Frank Lovejoy (Gilbert Bowen), William Talman (Emmett Myers), José Torvay (Capt. Alvarado), Sam Hayes (Sam), Wendell Niles (Wendell), Jean Del Val (Inspector General), Clark Howat (Government Agent), Natividad Vacio (José). **Location**: Lone Pine, California. **Completed**: December, 1952. **Released**: RKO, April 29. 71 minutes.

Emmett Myers is a psychotic killer who hitch-hikes with, then robs and murders his benefactors. He is wanted and on the run, so when he is picked up by Ray Collins and Gil Bowen, two men on a fishing trip, he holds them hostage while they drive him to Baja California. Myers' curious personality may be the result of parental hatred compounded by the physical deformity of a right eye that cannot close, even when he is asleep. The two vacationers try to formulate an escape plan but are literally always in his sight. Along the way, Myers toys with them by deprecating their softness and proclaiming the superiority of those strong enough to take what they want. They arrive at a small Mexican village and wait to ferry across to the Mexican mainland where Myers believes he will be safe. But Bowen had secretly left his wedding ring on a service station gas pump. This tips off local police and they catch up in time to capture Myers before he is able to kill the two men.

Director Ida Lupino brings a special sensibility that underscores the movie's exploitation of a particular noir theme: the sudden intrusion of the noir underworld into normal lives. Under her direction, the performances of Edmond O'Brien and Frank Lovejoy evolve from simple shock at their abduction through despair of being rescued to gritty resolve to save themselves. Yet the film probably owes much of its noir sensibility to Daniel Mainwaring's original story, which went uncredited because Mainwaring's "radical" reputation made him *persona non grata* at RKO, then controlled by Howard

Hughes. Although the film is purportedly based on a true story, it is less a public-service warning about hitch-hikers than the product of an American paranoia in the 1950s that was prompted by imaginary and real fears of the "red menace," nuclear holocaust, and government-enforced conformity.

It was up to popular culture to transform these fears into commercially viable vehicles where they were often personified as an all-too-ordinary intrusion into our daily lives, such as the "pod people" in Mainwaring's script for *Invasion of the Body Snatchers*. *The Hitch-Hiker's* desert locales, though not so graphically dark as a cityscape at night, isolate the protagonists in a milieu as uninviting and potentially deadly as any in film noir. That is exacerbated when they arrive in Baja and become literal strangers in a strange land. As with Bigelow in *D.O.A.*, the upheaval of Collins' and Bowen's lives is sudden, ill-chanced, and impersonal. Their perilous trip becomes a typical noir reflection of the lack of security or stability in everyday living, no matter how commonplace. It is telling that Collins suffers more than Bowen—probably because his family ties are not as firm (Bowen resists the temptation of the Mexicali bars, much to the chagrin of Collins). But at least Collins, unlike his predecessor Frank Bigelow, survives. **BP & AS**.

HOLLOW TRIUMPH (1948)

Director: Steve Sekely. **Screenplay**: Daniel Fuchs from the novel by Murray Forbes. **Producers**: Paul Henreid, Bryan Foy. **Director of Photography**: John Alton. **Music**: Sol Kaplan. **Art Directors**: Edward Ilou, Frank Durlauf. **Editor**: Fred Allen. **Cast**: Paul Henreid (John Muller/Dr. Bartok) Joan Bennett (Evelyn Nash), Eduard Franz (Frederick Muller), Leslie Brooks (Virginia Taylor), John Qualen (Dr. Swangron), Mabel Paige (Charwoman), Herbert Rudley (Marcy). **Completed**: March 1948. **Released**: Eagle Lion: October 28. 82 minutes.

When Johnny Muller, a former medical student, con-man and phony psychologist is convicted of payroll theft and later released from jail, his brother Fred suggests a low-paying but safe job with a medical supply firm. However Johnny soon takes up with his old mob and persuades them to rob a club owned by a racketeer. The robbery does not go off as planned and only Johnny and his friend Marcy get out alive. After they split the stolen $60,000, Johnny returns to his job.

Discovering that a psychiatrist, Dr. Victor Bartok, is his exact look-alike except for a scar that Bartok carries on his cheek, Johnny romances Bartok's secretary, Evelyn Nash. Through her he learns about the doctor's practice and obtains a copy of his signature. Johnny quits his job and becomes a parking attendant in the garage where Bartok keeps his car. A photographer makes an enlargement of Bartok's picture for Johnny and, using a scalpel, he makes a duplicate incision on his own face. What Johnny does not know is that the photographer "flopped" the negative and printed the scar on the wrong cheek. Only after he kills the unsuspecting Bartok does Johnny realize that the scar is wrong. But no one, except for an elderly charwoman, notices the change in the location of the scar, and his patients prefer his new bedside manner. "Bartok" even fools Fred, who comes to tell Johnny that he is now safe. Evelyn discovers the impersonation and, bitter at being used, decides to leave town. Johnny refuses to let her go and arranges for them to travel by ship to Honolulu the next evening. As he is rushing to join Evelyn on the ship, he is stopped by two hoods who inform him that Bartok owed a gambler $90,000. Johnny explains that he is not Bartok but the hoods pay no attention. Realizing he may miss the boat, he attempts to escape and they shoot him. Johnny dies while crawling towards the ship as people around him pass unheedingly by.

The Hollow Triumph's fine use of Los Angeles exteriors demonstrates again that John Alton was a master at photographing authentic locales in the noir style. As in many of these B-noirs, the plot is heavy with contrived coincidences although the movie's conclusion is as downbeat as any noir film since *Scarlet Street*. Its quality is further enhanced by the performances of its actors—especially that of the two leads. Joan Bennett, as the cynical Evelyn, gets the film's most sardonic line: "You can't go back and start again. The older you get, the worse things get!" But it is Paul Henreid who dominates the film with his deft realization of both the distracted Bartok and the unmitigatedly villainous Muller and who, by delineating Muller's unfailing confidence in his own criminal guise, greatly adds to the film's central irony: Muller dies because he has finally outsmarted himself. **BP**

HOLLYWOOD STORY (1951)

Director: William Castle. **Screenplay**: Frederick Kohner, Fred Brady. **Producer**: Leonard Goldstein. **Director of Photography**: Carl Guthrie. **Art Director**: Bernard Herzbrun, Richard H. Riedel. **Music**: Frank Skinner. **Editor**: Virgil Vogel. **Cast**: Richard Conte (Larry O'Brien), Julie Adams (Sally/Amanda), Richard Egan (Lt. Bud Lennox), Henry Hull (Philip Ferrara aka Vincent St. Clair), Fred Clark (Sam Collyer), Jim Backus (Mitch Davis), Francis X. Bushman (Himself), Betty Blythe (Herself), William Farnum (Himself), Paul Cavanagh (Roland Paul). **Released**: Universal, June 1. 76 minutes.

Larry O'Brien is a stage director who comes to Hollywood to try his hand at pictures. Mitch Davis, his agent, has rented a studio for him and O'Brien becomes obsessed with a bungalow on the lot where the unsolved murder of a silent movie director took place twenty years earlier. He decides to write a screenplay about it and begins interviewing the dead director's contemporaries, many of whom try to discourage him from delving into the matter. A series of events force O'Brien

to try to solve the murder and find the killer. Prime suspects are bit player Roland Paul, the director's partner, Sam Collyer, and Philip Ferrara, the director's screenwriter. In the end the culprit turns out to be Ferrara, who was in reality the brother of the dead man. He had been jealous of his brother's fame and resentful of the fact that the director had stolen Hull's work and put his own name on it.

Hollywood Story was an apparent attempt by Universal to cash in on the success of Paramount's *Sunset Boulevard*, released a year before. Loosely based on the unsolved murder of silent movie director William Desmond Taylor, the film would have been more interesting if it had stuck to the facts of the real case. Upon the release of *Hollywood Story*, Universal promoted the appearance of several formerly famous silent screen stars in the film. Francis X. Bushman and Helen Gibson, who had speaking parts, received $55 a day for their roles in the film. Others, such as Elmo Lincoln, the first screen Tarzan, were used as extras and did not talk. At the time, Lincoln complained bitterly to the press about being exploited, saying that the studio paid him $15 for one day's work and got $15,000 worth of free publicity out of it. Said Lincoln, "Every time they want to exploit something like *Hollywood Story* they call on us. . . . The motion picture business is the most unappreciative, selfish business in America today." **AL**

THE HOODLUM (1951)

Director: Max Nosseck. **Screenplay**: Sam Neuman, Nat Tanchuck. **Producer**: Maurice Kosloff. **Director of Photography**: Clark Ramsey. **Art Director**: Fred Preble. **Music**: Darrell Calker. **Editor**: Jack Killifer. **Cast**: Lawrence Tierney (Vincent Lubeck), Allene Roberts (Rosa), Marjorie Riordan (Eileen), Lisa Golm (Mrs. Lubeck), Edward Tierney (Johnny Lubeck), Stuart Randall (Lt. Burdick), Angela Stevens aka Ann Zika (Christie Lang), Tom Hubbard (Police Sgt. Schmidt), John De Simone (Marty). **Released**: United Artists, July 5. 61 minutes.

Hard-case Vincent Lubeck, in jail for armed robbery, is paroled into his mother's custody. He starts to work at his brother's gas station but immediately gathers a gang together and plans an armored car robbery. To get information from the bank, he starts to date a secretary who works there. At the same time he seduces Rosa, his brother's longtime fiancée. When Rosa tells Lubeck she wants to break up with his brother and marry him, he rebuffs her and she commits suicide by throwing herself off the roof. When an autopsy reveals the girl had been pregnant, Mrs. Lubeck realizes who did the deed. Lubeck's brother catches on to the armored car robbery scheme and tries to stop Vincent, who knocks him out. During the robbery, two guards are killed, and the gang gets away with the money. Lubeck is double-crossed by the rest of the gang, who knock him out and abscond with the loot. Desperate and hiding from the cops, Lubeck goes to the bank secretary and threatens to tell the cops she was in on it unless she hides him out, but she refuses. He goes to his mother, who also turns him away, telling him he's rotten before she dies. Vincent's brother, knowing the truth about his fiancée, enters the house and at gunpoint takes Vincent to the dump, where he intends to kill him. He can't bring himself to do it, but the cops show up and take care of the job, shooting Vincent down on the heap of garbage, the smell of which had been his life-long complaint.

The Hoodlum is considered by some to be not noir but simply a gangster film. Some elements do, however, clearly put it in the noir category—the Lawrence Tierney character's sociopathy, his isolation resulting from his willingness to betray everyone, including his own brother, and the underlying tone of sexual perversity. The difference between the old-style Cagney-Bogart-Robinson gangster film and the noir gangster film is pivotally summed up in the beginning of *The Hoodlum* when a member of the parole board, vehemently protesting Lubeck's release, intones that Lubeck's type is "not like the old style gangsters anymore. These people are committing crimes against *people*." Cheaply made in the extreme, *The Hoodlum* suffers from poor production values. Tierney's role was probably the only kind he could get at the time, as his career was in serous decline. His performance, however, was appropriately menacing, and he apparently still had enough clout to manage the acting debut of his brother Edward Tierney, whose career essentially began and ended with this film. **AL**

HOODLUM EMPIRE (1952)

Director: Joseph Kane. **Screenplay**: Bruce Manning and Bob Considine from Considine's story. **Producer**: Herbert J. Yates. **Director of Photography**: Reggie Lanning. **Music**: Nathan Scott. **Art Director**: Frank Arrigo. **Editor**: Richard L. Van Enger. **Cast**: Brian Donlevy (Sen. William J. Stephens), Claire Trevor (Connie Williams), Forrest Tucker (Charley Pignatalli), Vera Ralston (Marte Dufour), Luther Adler (Nick Mansani), John Russell (Joe Gray), Gene Lockhart (Sen. Tower), Grant Withers (Rev. Simon Andrews), Taylor Holmes (Benjamin Lawton, Attorney), Roy Barcroft (Morris Draper), William Murphy (Pete Dailey), Richard Jaeckel (Ted Dawson), Don Beddoe (Sen. Blake). **Released**: Republic, April 15. 98 minutes.

The start of a Senate hearing into organized crime is covered by television and watched from his penthouse by a key witness, Nick Mansani, who when called to appear is claimed to be unreachable. At the hearings, a blind man recalls combat experiences in WWII France of an army unit that included him, the hearing's chair, Senator Stephens, and the alleged mobster Joe Gray. A female associate of Mansani recalls Joe's return stateside, when he tells both her and Nick that he is leaving the Mob to lead an honest life away from the city. Joe is tricked into meeting a mobster in Mansani's suite who attempts to kill Joe but is foiled by Nick. Back in his small town gas station, Joe and several army buddies who work for him fight off hoodlums trying to force slot machines on them. Meanwhile, Joe learns the Mob is using his name locally as their silent partner, backed up by a forged paper trail that convinces Senator Stephens that Joe is still corrupt. In a showdown, Mansani is killed while Joe's innocence is recorded on tape, which leads to Senator Stephens publicly apologizing and exonerating Joe at the hearings.

The Kefauver hearings of the early 1950s were as revelatory of the new medium of television as they were of the organized crime they sought to expose. From the outset of *Hoodlum Empire*, television cameras are introduced as central participants in the Senate hearings that form its narrative spine. Their mediated point of view, through the hearings' live broadcasts, is a constantly recurring perspective throughout. However, this provides a springboard not for any media analysis but rather a constant series of lectures for the audi-

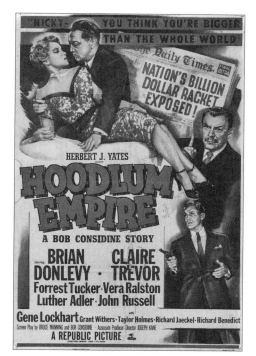

ence, which is subjected to what in effect is one long civics lesson. Those lectures, like the plot in which they are intertwined, empower ordinary citizens as agents of change, a positioning reinforced by repeated illustrations of corruption in high places and mobsters in corporate settings.

But these citizens, and the film, are living in the past if the narrative's domination by flashbacks is any guide. Unlike noir's postwar amnesiac cycle, which focused on returning GI's and the reconstruction of an absent memory, here memory *is* narrative. However, unlike amnesiac noir, neither memory's lapses, nor its subjectivity, show it being undermined here. Similarly, the real-time TV broadcasts are, like one old-fashioned newspaper headline, presented as objective, unmediated reality. While the constant time shifts created by the flashbacks place the problems of racketeering in the past, the film's "present" optimistically shows the Senate hearings as that problem's solution.

With the film's final shot indicating not closure but rather the ongoing nature of the hearings, *Hoodlum Empire* provides its audience with a panacea: these concerns are behind us and are being dealt with now. That is just as well because the past, in the persistent form of the war, overshadows the consciousness of the film's players throughout. Cinematically it intrudes completely, as the first flashback takes the audience into the different, albeit equally familiar, genre of the war film. Here an efficient conversion narrative is completed, essaying *Hoodlum Empire*'s only attempt at analysis, as we see how the fraternal values of the small town "apple-knockers" who are his fellow GI's transform the young New York racketeer Joe (who by film's end has taken on the righteous cast of a Gregory Peck) into preferring the simple verities of the life of a wage-earning "chump." The rural/city divide of good and evil is validated though not explained, and tellingly re-articulated in a context meaningful for the more affluent 1950s, as Joe's European war refugee wife says she would be happy with a small car and a modest house. Noir's visual strategies only emerge once, late in the film. Just such a domestic setting as the wife desires is shown and reflects how, despite leaving urban traumas behind, the suburban home was still a site of anxiety in early 1950s noir. **RSW**

HOUSE BY THE RIVER (1950)

Director: Fritz Lang. **Screenplay**: Mel Dinelli from the novel *The House by the River* by A.P. Herbert. **Producer**: Howard Welsch. **Director of Photography**: Edward Cronjager. **Production Designer**: Boris Leven. **Music**: George Antheil. **Editor**: Arthur Hilton. **Cast**: Louis Hayward (Stephen Byrne), Jane Wyatt (Marjorie Byrne), Lee Bowman (John Byrne), Dorothy Patrick (Emily Gaunt), Ann Shoemaker (Mrs. Ambrose). **Released**: Fidelity Pictures, March 25. 88 minutes.

In a Southern suburb at the end of the Victorian era, novelist Stephen Byrne lives in a villa next to a turbulent river. Suffering writer's block after manuscript rejections, Stephen indulges in morbid neuroses. One night, when his wife Marjorie is away, Stephen forces himself upon their maid, Emily, and inadvertently strangles her to death. Stephen convinces his brother John to keep the murder a secret and help dispose of the corpse, which they drop into the river, wrapped in a sack bearing John's name. At a local party, Stephen is exuberant while John is increasingly guilt-ridden. Stephen becomes famous writing about Emily's disappearance; he begins a novel, *The River*, which is virtually a confession of his crime. Neighbor Mrs. Ambrose notices a sack floating in the water; Stephen fails to recover it, and appeals again to John for help. Policeman Sarten investigates the case; suspicion falls on John and Stephen supports this view, implying that he is Marjorie's lover and planting evidence to this effect. During their confrontation on a pier, Stephen pushes John into the water. Returning home, he finds Marjorie reading *The River*, and begins strangling her—but, frightened by what seem to be ghostly apparitions as John arrives, Stephen falls to his death.

For many decades overlooked by critics and scholars, *House by the River* has only recently received the re-evaluation it richly deserves. Made as a B-film in the wake of the commercial failure of *Secret Beyond the Door*—and ushering in Lang's highly austere, severe works of the 1950s – it lays bare the perverse underpinnings of the director's imagination. Thomas Elsaesser once described Lang's overriding obsession as "the creation and uncreation of those who appear on the screen . . . Lang is on the 'demonic' side, the side of power and pessimism." Of all his films, *House by the River* is most intensely, unsettlingly fixed on the demonic or vampiric aspects of the creative process: Stephen the writer (a perverse alter ego of Lang the artist) can only "unblock" himself once he has killed.

The thematic logic of the piece is as precise as it is bleak: the generalized abjectness of the world presented is clinched by images of the dirty river (offering up its repressed secrets), draining sink water, and a crawling spider whose only destiny is to be splattered. No one is innocent, all are complicit in this claustrophobic social circle where transgression is endlessly inviting, desire inevitably strays, and even the most ordinary citizen enjoys the "trashy" culture of popular crime literature. Lang's investment in this vision is conveyed by the loving meticulousness with which he stages the murder scene: a high point of his career, it is structured upon what critic Jacques Lourcelles describes as "an eroticism of frustration, a morbid élan," a drawn-out tension that inexorably draws the viewer into a disturbing kind of sympathy with the deranged Stephen—who registers as the Everyman version of Peter Lorre's grand criminal in Lang's *M* (1931).

The film also marks (here the low budget proved fortuitous) a return by Lang to a certain deliberate, silent-era primitivism in his *mise en scène*: a rigorously minimalist use of repeated compositions (of successive women on the stairway, for instance), married to a suitably histrionic mode of acting, and, for its time, a quite advanced sense of the possibilities of sound design (particularly the use of silence and contrapuntal noise effects). As much as it intersects with Hitchcock's noirish tales of the transference of guilt between characters, *House by the River* is also an intriguing precursor to Laughton's *The Night of the Hunter* (1955) in its haunted, dreamlike lyricism—especially evident in the spookily poetic underwater imagery. **AM**

HOUSE OF BAMBOO (1955)

Director: Samuel Fuller. **Screenplay**: Harry Kleiner based on his screenplay for *Street with No Name*, with additional dialogue by Samuel Fuller. **Producer**: Buddy Adler. **Director of Photography**: Joe MacDonald. **Music**: Leigh Harline. **Art Directors**: Lyle R. Wheeler, Addison Hehr. **Editor**: James B. Clark. **Cast**: Robert Ryan (Sandy Dawson), Robert Stack (Eddie Kenner/Spanier), Shirley Yamaguchi (Mariko), Cameron Mitchell (Griff), Brad Dexter (Capt. Hanson), Sessue Hayakawa (Inspector Ito), Biff Elliot (Webber), Sandro Giglio (Ceram), Elko Hanabusa (Japanese Screaming Woman), Harry Carey Jr. (John), Peter Gray (Willy), Robert Quarry (Phil), De Forrest Kelley (Charlie), John Doucette (Skipper). **Location**: Tokyo, Japan. **Completed**: March 28, 1955. **Released**: 20th Century-Fox, July 1. 105 minutes.

Sandy Dawson has organized a criminal ring of former G.I.'s in Tokyo after the war. The Army sends Eddie Kenner, under the assumed identity of Spanier, to infiltrate this gang. In order to cover himself after joining Sandy's group, Kenner must live with Mariko, the widow of one of Sandy's men, who has become a "kimono girl." During a robbery, Sandy violates his own rule and saves Kenner's life. Kenner becomes Sandy's right-hand man, replacing Griff, whom Sandy brutally kills when he believes the man has betrayed the gang to authorities. However, later Sandy discovers that Kenner/Spanier is the real betrayer and tries to set him up to be shot by the army, but fails. Kenner pursues him to a rooftop amusement park where the two engage in a gunfight. Sandy is fatally shot, his body left spinning lifelessly aboard a ride as Kenner is reunited with Mariko.

House of Bamboo, shot in color and CinemaScope, is a direct remake of *Street with No Name*, made just a few years earlier, itself a semi-sequel to *House on 92nd Street*, and a typical undercover-man film noir. The Samuel Fuller production of Harry Kleiner's script is a totally rethought work, transposing certain generic elements into a setting that renders them unconventional by virtue of cultural contrasts. The pachinko parlors, Kabuki troupe, Great Buddha, whirling-globe ride, and cherry blossoms have an almost surreal relationship to the criminal activities of Sandy's gang.

Director of Photography: George J. Folsey. **Music**: André Previn. **Editor**: John McSweeney Jr. **Cast**: Jack Palance (Arnie and Bill Judlow), Harold J. Stone (Henry Nova), Edward Platt (Warden), Barbara Lang (Ruth Judlow), Joe Turkel (Convict), Timothy Carey (Arnie's Cell Mate). **Released**: MGM, September 12. 90 minutes.

Arnie Judlow is doing life in San Quentin for killing a man in a fight: he was a boxer so his hands are "lethal weapons." His wife Ruth and twin brother Bill move to San Francisco as part of a plan to spring Arnie. The scheme is far from simple and involves Bill's smuggling himself into prison and posing as Arnie; but things go wrong, such as Bill and Ruth happening to rent a house next to that of a prison guard who knows Arnie, and then falling in love with one another.

Though *House of Numbers* may be the least violent Big-House story ever produced, director Russell Rouse does not let the reins go slack. He twists the plot along to its surprisingly sedate conclusion, and brings it off. As director and screenwriter, Rouse usually had something a little different up his sleeve, at least when he was toiling in film noir. His (as screenwriter) *D.O.A.* remains one of the best-remembered films of the cycle, and he also contributed to *The Thief, Wicked Woman*, and *New York Confidential*, each of them at least some distance off the beaten track. His films tended to be less ostentatious than their rivals, none quieter, of course, than *The Thief*, that dialogue-free experiment. *House of Numbers* was Rouse's last urban crime drama; he would go on to helm a few westerns and in 1966 garner much opprobrium for *The Oscar*.

Even more memorable than the presence of minor noir icon Jack Palance in the dual role is Barbara Lang's subdued and touching performance. It is a puzzle and a shame that this blonde femme fatale had almost no noir credits before moving on to a career in 1950s television. André Previn's score is also noteworthy. Previn's years in Hollywood, before he left to become a "serious" conductor and composer, were spent on a large number of lower budgeted MGM productions, many of them noir. **BMV**

HOUSE OF STRANGERS (1949)

Director: Joseph L Mankiewicz. **Screenplay**: Philip Yordan, Joseph L. Mankiewicz from the novel *I'll Never Go There Again* by Jerome Weidman. **Producer**: Sol C. Siegel. **Director of Photography**: Milton Krasner. **Music**: Daniele Amfitheatrof. **Art Directors**: Lyle Wheeler, George W. Davis. **Editor**: Harmon Jones. **Cast**: Edward G. Robinson (Gino Monetti), Susan Hayward (Irene Bennett), Richard Conte (Max Monetti), Luther Adler (Joe Monetti), Paul Valentine (Pietro Monetti), Efrem Zimbalist, Jr. (Tony), Debra Paget (Maria Domenico), Hope Emerson (Helena Domenico), Esther Minciotti (Theresa Monetti), Diana Douglas (Elaine Monetti), Tito Vuolo (Lucca), Albert Morin (Victoro), Sid Tomack (Waiter), Thomas Henry Brown (Judge). **Completed**: February 23, 1949. **Released**: 20th Century-Fox, July 1. 101 minutes.

Gino Monetti, patriarch of an Italian-American family, rules his sons with an iron hand except for his favorite, Max, who is a lawyer. All the sons work at their father's bank and suffer in silence as he alternately berates them and listens to opera recordings every night during dinner. Although already engaged to a girl approved by his father, Max falls in love with

Rather than appearing to be an incidental background, these aspects of the mise-en-scène express the subject of the film: that one culture may absorb and contain another, even if the alien culture expresses itself in a violent and disruptive way.

The American occupation of Japan had never before been presented, even metaphorically, as rife with criminal elements and underground enterprise before Fuller, whose revision of Kleiner's plot relies on this concept. The idea of American exploitation of Japan and its people is particularly ironic in his construction of the sympathetic interracial romance between Kenner and Mariko. As he did with the grifter and B-girl in *Pickup on South Street*, Fuller puts heavy spin on their love story. Using the widescreen format to separate the couple symbolically yet hold them in the same frame at night visually reinforces their sense of psychological estrangement. Fuller's feel for the specific visuals to add irony and nuance to his narrative is evident in the palette and dynamic composition of Joe MacDonald's photography. The violent scenes have particular power. The tracking shot of the factory robbery with black-coated, hunched and running figures has a compelling visual sweep; and the climactic battle between Sandy and Kenner on the whirling globe is choreographed with a precision analogous to a *Noh* drama.

Sandy's homosexual inclinations are revealed in his treatment of Mariko and his blind trust of Kenner. Despite his villainy and lack of compunction over murder, this makes him a particularly vulnerable figure. Kenner is forced to assume the unexpected role of *ichi-ban* or "number one man" after Sandy has saved his life. Although he does so reluctantly, as his army duty compels him to take advantage of Sandy's sexual attraction and good will, Kenner's deception is not altogether sympathetic. In these perverse circumstances, Kenner is like the character Thelma Jordon or any other sexual exploiter in film noir. Fuller evokes a performance from Robert Stack that makes it clear Kenner feels as uncomfortable in his role as betrayer of Sandy's affection as he does being forced into a relationship with Mariko. **BL & AS**

HOUSE OF NUMBERS (1957)

Director: Russell Rouse. **Screenplay**: Don Mankiewicz, Russell Rouse from the novel by Jack Finney. **Producer**: Charles Schnee.

House of Strangers: *Gino Monetti (Edward G. Robinson) and his son Pietro (Paul Valentine).*

Irene Bennett, a chic woman from the other side of town. Gino maintains his affection for Max. After Gino is arrested for violating banking laws and regulators oversee the bank, he turns the assets over to his wife. She gives them to his vindictive sons. Max cannot get his brothers to help defend their father; and the eldest son, Joe, has Max arrested for attempting to bribe a juror. Gino is exonerated, but Max is sentenced to seven years. He returns home to find that his father has died and his brothers have reopened the bank. Afraid of Max's animosity, Joe tries to kill him; but another brothers kills Joe instead. Max is reunited with Irene and begins a new life.

House of Strangers exploits the traditional concept of the immigrant family in order to develop a corrosive story of a patriarchal domination that is destroyed from within. Typically movies about large families emphasize the loyalty of the family members to each other against outside forces. *House of Strangers* is exceptional in illustrating the familial hatred generated when a man insists on being the master of his sons in the tradition of older generations and foreign cultures. Paradoxically while the other sons have bitter dreams of freedom from their father's rule, Max is both the most independent and the most loyal. As a result, the relationship between Max and Irene, a conventional romance, acquires a distinctive tension because she is an outsider relative to his family's cultural bias.

Director Mankiewicz generates theatrical expansiveness in the sequences involving large gatherings. As the narrative is in flashback with Max recalling the story's events on the day of his release from jail, the introduction of his father descending a staircase to the strains of Rossini and joining his family gathered below is stylized like a personal memoir. The side-light and detailing in the Monetti home evoke both the milieu and the suffocating monomania of Gino. Conte's performance as Max, in particular, exploits the fact that he had not been iconically associated with educated and heroic characters. The positive image that might carry over with viewers from portrayals in *Thieves' Highway* or *Call Northside 777* are decidedly working class and very different from the Italian mobster in *Cry of the City.* As with Nick Garcos in *Thieves' Highway*, the

paternal devotion of Conte's character is key to his portrayal and any moral ambiguity is resolved during his father's crisis. That Max is ultimately punished by his brothers and society for his father's crimes is doubly ironic. This situation reflects on the traditions of older cultures that held the sons responsible for the sins of their fathers. It also makes Max the prototypical noir victim of a cataclysmic turn of events from which his otherwise normal life cannot protect him. **BL & AS**

HOUSE ON 92ND STREET (1945)

Director: Henry Hathaway. **Screenplay**: Barre Lyndon, Charles G. Booth, and John Monks, Jr. from Booth's unpublished story. **Producer**: Louis De Rochemont. **Director of Photography**: Norbert Brodine. **Music**: David Buttolph. **Art Directors**: Lyle Wheeler, Lewis Creber. **Editor**: Harmon Jones. **Cast**: William Eythe (Bill Dietrich), Lloyd Nolan (Inspector Briggs), Signe Hasso (Elsa Gebhardt), Gene Lockhart (Charles Ogden Roper), Leo G. Carroll (Hammershon), Lydia St. Clair (Johanna Schwartz), William Post, Jr. (Walker), Harry Bellaver (Max Coburg), Bruno Wick (Adolphe Lange), Harro Meller (Conrad Amulo), Charles Wagenheim (Gus Huzmann), Alfred Linder (Emil Kline), Reed Hadley (Narrator). **Locations**: Washington, D.C.; New York City. **Completed**: August 29, 1945. **Released**: 20th Century-Fox, September 26. 89 minutes.

Brilliant student Bill Dietrich is approached by the Nazis and asked to join the German cause. When he informs the F.B.I. of this attempted recruitment, agents ask him to go undercover and report the activities of German spies and subversives. As the United States enters World War II, Dietrich proves to be a most valuable asset. Discovering that the Germans have been stealing information about the Manhattan Project, Dietrich is determined to uncover the identity of a high-level traitor. The Germans learn that Dietrich is a spy but not before he gets the information he wants. Led by Inspector Briggs, agents arrive in time to rescue Dietrich and rout the Germans. As the Nazis flee, one of them shoots Elsa Gebhart, the leader of the espionage ring, in the mistaken belief that she is Dietrich.

Produced by Louis De Rochemont, whose *March of Time* newsreel series begun in the 1930s became a major source of news for moviegoers during World War II, *House on 92nd*

House on 92nd Street: *William Eythe (right) as Agent Bill Dietrich.*

Street is the first of several features in which De Rochement adopted elements of the visual style and narrative conventions of these earlier newsreels and applied them to fiction filmmaking. Utilizing location photography and a stentorian narrator, the film possesses a surface but nonetheless artificial realism common to few movies of that period. The film makes a point of indicating that it is based on actual F.B.I. cases with only the names being changed; and director Hathaway was allowed to shoot portions of the film in the actual locales of the original incidents.

Many of the actors in the film were nonprofessionals and some were actual F.B.I. personnel. Although these concepts were outside the sensibilities of film noir at that time, other filmmakers of the post-War classic period like Anthony Mann and Mark Hellinger adopted this "docu-noir" approach in films such as *T-Men, He Walked by Night* and *The Naked City*. De Rochement himself followed up at Fox on *13 Rue Madeleine* (with Hathaway) and *Boomerang!* In addition, Hathaway used the style again, most notably on *Call Northside 777*. In this early example of that noir style variant, the flat characterizations and the naturalistic atmosphere are counterposed with the menacing, stereotyped Nazis, sometimes using full, semi-documentary lighting but also with some low-key interiors. The threatening aura typical of noir and most apt in a narrative about an imperiled undercover agent binds these visual styles together and established the methodology for most subsequent "docu-noirs." **AS & CM**

THE HOUSE ON TELEGRAPH HILL (1951)

Director: Robert Wise. **Screenplay**: Elick Moll and Frank Partos from the novel *The Frightened Child* by Dana Lyon. **Producer**: Robert Bassler. **Director of Photography**: Lucien Ballard. **Music**: Sol Kaplan. **Art Directors**: Lyle Wheeler, John DeCuir. **Editor**: Nick DeMaggio. **Cast**: Richard Basehart (Alan Spender), Valentina Cortese (Victoria Kowelska/Karen de Nakova), William Lundigan (Maj. Marc Anders), Fay Baker (Margaret), Gordon Gebert (Chris). **Location**: San Francisco, California. **Completed**: October 12, 1950. **Released**: 20th Century-Fox, May 13. 92 minutes.

Victoria Kowelska assumes the identity of Karin de Nakova, a woman who died in a German concentration camp, in order to gain entry to the United States. De Nakova's young son, Chris, has lived since birth with her wealthy aunt in San Francisco, so Victoria travels there. But before she arrives the aunt dies, so Victoria uses Karin's identity to inherit the aunt's estate, which includes a mansion atop Telegraph Hill. Victoria falls in love with the estate's trustee, Alan Spender, and they marry. Soon unexplainable accidents cause Victoria to fear that Alan and the child's governess, Margaret, are not only plotting her death but may have murdered the aunt to gain control of the estate. Alan attempts to poison Victoria but she tricks him and Alan gets the poisoned orange juice instead. Margaret had been promised a share in the estate by Alan if she became his accomplice, but ultimately her desire to protect Chris' life leads her to refrain from calling a doctor as agreed and Alan dies. When the police arrive and decide to arrest Margaret, Victoria tells her that she will testify in her defense but Margaret retorts, "I'll let my conscience be my witness."

The House on Telegraph Hill finds itself in the film noir canon primarily because of the atmospheric photography of

Lucien Ballard and the mannered use of authentic locales that enhances the immediacy of a threatening milieu. Furthermore, there is romantic narration by Valentina Cortese telling Victoria's story in flashback, the devious characterization of Alan Spender by Richard Basehart, and the glacial performance of Fay Baker as the governess, Margaret. These elements together with hints of sexual aberration, the intrusion of an enigmatic past, the isolation and ultimate entrapment of the heroine in the old mansion all exploit certain conventions of noir period films such as *Gaslight* and *The Spiral Staircase*. Like these earlier films, *The House on Telegraph Hill* has a climactic scene revealing that the victim's peril is not imaginary—specifically where Alan and Victoria confront each other in the child's playhouse and it appears momentarily that Alan is going to let his wife fall through a hole in the wall and down the steep embankment. The shooting and staging of this scene make it much more direct and menacing than similar confrontations in *Suspicion* or *Phantom Lady*. **BP**

HUMAN DESIRE (1954)

Director: Fritz Lang. **Screenplay**: Alfred Hayes from the novel *La Bête Humaine* by Emile Zola. **Producer**: Lewis J. Rachmil. **Director of Photography**: Burnett Guffey. **Music**: Daniele Amfitheatrof. **Art Director**: Robert Peterson. **Editor**: William A. Lyon. **Cast**: Glenn Ford (Jeff Warren), Gloria Grahame (Vicki Buckley), Broderick Crawford (Carl Buckley), Edgar Buchanan (Alec Simmons), Kathleen Case (Ellen Simmons), Diane DeLaire (Vera Simmons), Grandon Rhodes (John Owens), Dan Seymour (Bartender), John Pickard (Matt Henley), Paul Brinegar (Brakeman). **Location**: Rock Island Railroad lines, Oklahoma. **Completed**: January 25, 1954. **Released**: Columbia, August 6. 90 minutes.

Carl Buckley's uncontrollable temper has jeopardized his railroad job. He asks his wife Vicki to use her influence with Mr. Owens, a wealthy shipper, to save his position and she reluctantly agrees. But then her husband suspects adultery. Haunted by jealousy, he forces his wife to rendezvous again with the shipping magnate onboard a train. Carl confronts them in a compartment and kills Owens. Unfortunately, Vicki was seen near Owen's compartment by Jeff Warren, an off-duty railroad engineer. At the coroner's inquest, Jeff lies

Human Desire: *Lovers Jeff (Glenn Ford) and Vicki (Gloria Grahame) hide from a watchman.*

to protect Vicki and eventually they engage in an adulterous liaison. Meanwhile Carl is obsessed with the idea that Vicki was "somebody's leftover" and starts drinking heavily. Carl still loves Vicki and maintains a hold on her with an incriminating letter. When he pressures her to leave town with him, Vicki persuades Jeff to waylay her drunken husband and make his murder appear an accident. Jeff cannot kill Carl but does retrieve the letter and return it to Vicki. Disgusted, Vicki leaves town with Carl. On the train, she taunts her hapless husband by telling him of her plan to kill him and of her sexual exploits. Carl loses control of himself and kills her. The film closes as it opened, with Jeff and his colleague, Alec, in a locomotive's cab.

Most of the explicit sexuality of Jean Renoir's earlier adaptation of *La Bête Humaine* (1938) had to be bowdlerized for this contemporary American version. The same was true of Lang's previous "remake" of Renoir, *Scarlet Street*, in which the prostitute heroine and her pimp euphemistically became a model and her boyfriend. Still, Gloria Grahame's portrayal of Vicki is as sexually charged as Simone Simon's in the French original. Her final confrontation with Carl, when she details her sexual adventures, is more perverse than any aspect of Simon's lighter rendering of the same character moment.

Visually, *Human Desire* is constructed with a graphic determinism that is more relentless than any usage in Renoir's film and brings it a bit closer in spirit to Zola's naturalistic novel. The metaphorically ominous sequence of a churning dark sea under the titles of Lang's *Clash By Night* are echoed in *Human Desire* by opening and closing shots of a myriad of railroad tracks randomly interweaving and separating in a switching yard. This obvious metaphor for human paths crossing and affecting each other under the pull of some unseen relentlessly moving fate is linked directly to Jeff Warren, since the image is revealed as his point-of-view from the cab of an engine. As the narrative develops, every line and bar shadow added as a background detail recalls those fateful vectors of the first sequence, vectors that mock the ineffectual attempts by the film's characters to redeem their desolate lives with desperate pleasures. Unlike the Zola original, the protagonist here is no longer a "human beast" but simply a victim of his own "human desire," one who finally retreats into his own solitude. Like "Charlie" in Truffaut's *Shoot the Piano Player* (1960), Jeff settles for the role of observer rather than player in the drama of life. **BP**

THE HUNTED (1948)

Director: Jack Bernhard. **Screenplay**: Steve Fisher. **Producer**: Scott R. Dunlap. **Director of Photography**: Harry Neumann. **Art Director**: F. Paul Sylos. **Music**: Edward J. Kay. **Editor**: Richard Heermance. **Cast**: Preston Foster (Detective Johnny Saxon), Larry Blake (Hollis Smith), Pierre Watkin (Simon Rand), Russell Hicks (Detective Dan Meredith), Frank Ferguson (Paul Harrison), Cathy Carter (Sally Winters), Belita (Laura Mead), Charles McGraw (Detective). **Released**: Allied Artists, April 7. 88 minutes.

Laura Mead gets out of prison on parole, having been sent up by her police detective boyfriend, Johnny Saxon, for a jewel robbery. She claimed she was framed, but the evidence was too overwhelming for Saxon to ignore. She visits Saxon after her release and toys with his emotions. He is torn, not knowing whether to believe in her innocence, and his emotions are complicated by the fact that she threatened to kill him. In the end, he can't keep away and forces himself to believe her even though her own attorney, Simon Rand, claims she was guilty. Saxon wangles her a job in an ice-skating show, and she is a sensation. When Rand is murdered, the finger of guilt once more points to Laura, and she bolts. Saxon catches up with her and is about to arrest her, but she shoots him. In the hospital, Saxon decides in spite of it all to help her and resigns from the force. At the same time, a thief is arrested for killing a stoolie and confesses to the murder of Rand, who had been the brains behind a gang of jewel thieves and who framed Laura. The thief had murdered the man after being double-crossed. In the end, Saxon and Laura finally get their honeymoon.

This was the second noir released under the Allied Artists banner to differentiate Monogram's cheap from upscale product, the first being *The Gangster* (1947), a far superior picture. Belita, an ice-skater Monogram hoped would be its answer to Sonja Henie, achieved "stardom" only in a handful of Monogram films. Hard-boiled writer Steve Fisher was responsible for the screenplay for *The Hunted*, which is not up to his usual hard-boiled par because of the story's implausibility and everybody's sappy willingness to forgive and forget. **AL**

I CONFESS (1953)

Director: Alfred Hitchcock. **Screenplay**: George Tabori, William Archibald from a play by Paul Anthelme. **Producer**: Alfred Hitchcock. **Director of Photography**: Robert Burks. **Music**: Dimitri Tiomkin. **Art Director**: Ted Haworth. **Editor**: Rudi Fehr. **Cast**: Montgomery Clift (Fr. Michael William Logan), Anne Baxter (Ruth Grandfort), Karl Malden (Inspector Larrue), Brian Aherne (Willy Robertson), Roger Dann (Pierre Grandfort), Dolly Haas (Alma Keller), Charles Andre (Fr. Millars), O.E. Hasse (Otto Keller), Judson Pratt (Det. Murphy), Ovila Légaré (Villette). Location: Quebec, Canada. **Released**: Warner Bros., March 22. 95 minutes.

Father Logan hears the confession of the rectory handyman Otto Keller, who has murdered lawyer Villette to earn money for his long-suffering wife, Alma. Inspector Larrue suspects that Logan may be the killer, as Villette was blackmailing Ruth Grandfort, the wife of a prominent politician, for an alleged adulterous relationship with Logan. Because he cannot divulge what he has learned in confession, Logan refuses to cooperate with Larrue. Although Logan and Ruth's relationship ended before he took his priestly vows, Ruth also assumes that Logan is guilty. Public hostility toward Logan mounts at the trial. Declared innocent but presumed guilty even by the judge, Logan is assailed by a mob outside the courtroom. Alma comes to his aid and is shot by her now deranged husband. Larrue's detectives pursue Keller into a hotel. Keller tries to shoot Logan, and when mortally wounded, begs for Logan's ministrations.

I Confess is a courtroom melodrama animated by a superficial plot mechanism: accused of a murder, a priest cannot defend himself without violating the Seal of the Confessional. Alfred Hitchcock dramatized a Catholic miracle in *The Wrong Man* but here makes the seeming moral contradiction of the Confessional into yet another of the thematic gimmicks he explored in the early 1950s. Perhaps responding to Robert Bresson's *Diary of a Country Priest*, Hitchcock elevates Father Logan's moral dilemma. Montgomery Clift's delicate performance illuminates a man forced to take Christ's role, and Hitchcock's insistent visuals of judgmental skies above church spires are capped by a pretentious image comparing Logan to a statue of Jesus bearing the cross.

Hitchcock's "devout noir" manipulates characters and narrative to maintain the theme of a priest humbling himself before a heavenly law higher than man's. Larrue's unimaginative policeman never wonders what circumstances might compel a priest to refuse to tell what he knows; the prosecutor is one of Hitchcock's frivolous legal bureaucrats. Subverting the entire romantic mystery subgenre, Ruth

I Confess: *Father Logan (Montgomery Clift) and his murderous housekeeper Otto Keller (O. E. Hasse).*

Grandfort's leading lady is a reckless fool clinging to idealized memories visualized in a series of delirious "lying" flashbacks. Ruth's unreliable flashback memories gloss over Michael Logan's decision to become a priest and other details that might clear up the mystery, leaving Logan isolated with his conscience. The insufferably selfish Ruth supports Logan when she thinks he has killed for her but abandons him the moment she realizes that he is still committed to his vows. Compared to Logan's higher devotion, worldly love is but a sham.

I Confess struggles against its rigid premise. Logan wishes to take the sins of others onto his shoulders, yet his principles contribute to several deaths that include the murder of the idealized Alma. Her martyrdom is unfairly forgotten in the rush to glorify Logan's ethical stand. Further confusing the issue, Otto Keller's unbalanced German refugee behaves like a stereotyped Nazi, making mad threats and brandishing a Luger pistol. The chaotic ending forces us to ask if Logan's stoic commitment held back the noir forces of havoc, or encouraged them. **GE**

I DIED A THOUSAND TIMES` (1955)

Director: Stuart Heisler. **Screenplay**: W.R. Burnett from his novel *High Sierra*. **Producer**: Willis Goldbeck. **Director of Photography**: Ted McCord. **Music**: David Buttolph. **Art Director**: Edward Carrere. **Editor**: Clarence Kolster. **Cast**: Jack Palance (Roy Earle), Shelley Winters (Marie Gibson), Lori Nelson (Velma), Lee Marvin (Babe), Earl Holliman (Red), Perry Lopez (Louis Mendoza),

'I died a thousand times' JACK PALANCE · SHELLEY WINTERS
WARNER BROS. CinemaScope WarnerColor

Gonzalez Gonzalez (Chico), Lon Chaney, Jr. (Big Mac), Howard St. John (Doc Banton), Ralph Moody (Pa), Olive Carey (Ma). **Location**: Mount Whitney, California. **Completed**: April 4, 1955. **Released**: Warner Bros., November 9. 109 minutes.

Roy Earle, a pardoned ex-convict, plans to lead a robbery at a resort hotel. While setting up the raid, Roy begins an affair with a member of the gang, Marie, and also befriends a mongrel dog. Meanwhile, Roy meets Velma, a "good" girl. Velma is crippled; but after Roy pays for an operation that cures her, she rejects him. The robbery goes wrong, and Roy ends up on the run with Marie. Later, Roy drives alone into Los Angeles to fence the gems and is wounded in a double-cross. Then police chase him into the California Sierras where he is cornered. A crowd gathers to witness the police action. Marie stands among them watching helplessly as Roy is gunned down.

Although *High Sierra* may be aesthetically more satisfying and historically more significant as early film noir, *I Died A Thousand Times* is in some respects a more cohesive film, possibly because novelist W.R. Burnett worked alone on this screenplay. There are large sections of this film that duplicate *High Sierra* but there are also significant narrative differences. While it is slightly longer than *High Sierra*, Burnett has, in fact, cut material from the original and brought *I Died A Thousand Times* closer to the novel as well as closer to creating a first person point of view. The openings of the respective versions illustrate this difference.

High Sierra begins with a series of vignettes about Roy's rural childhood, his membership in a gang, and his arranged pardon. *I Died A Thousand Times* opens with Jack Palance as Roy Earle already driving through the desert, with the Sierras and his ambiguous destiny looming ahead of him. Throughout his chance meetings, first with Velma and her family and then his fatalistic conversation with a gas station attendant, he is noticeably affected by the landscape around him. It is not until the arrival at Shaw's camp that Earle's name and his past are revealed. What was exposition and sentimentality in *High Sierra* becomes an ironic sequence in the later film. Not only does it set a mood, it establishes a unity of place and time by beginning Earle's story in geographical proximity to where it will end. Additionally, by making Earle a more mysterious figure it

produces a stronger sense of his existential isolation; and because considerable action occurs before Roy is identified as a criminal on a job, the film is structured as a character study and not as a genre piece. **DLW**

I SHOT JESSE JAMES (1949)

Director and Screenplay: Samuel Fuller. **Executive Producer**: Robert L. Lippert. **Producer:** Carl K. Hittleman. **Director of Photography**: Ernest Miller. **Music**: Albert Glasser. **Production Designer**: Frank Hotaling. **Editor**: Paul Landres. **Cast**: Preston Foster (John Kelley), Barbara Britton (Cynthy Waters), John Ireland (Bob Ford), Reed Hadley (Jesse James), J. Edward Bromberg (Harry Kane), Victor Killian (Soapy), Tom Tyler (Frank James), Tommy Noonan (Charles Ford), Barbara Woodell (Mrs. Zee James). **Location**: Iverson Ranch, Chatsworth, Los Angeles, California. **Released**: Film Classics, February 26. 81 minutes.

Jesse and his infamous gang of thieves are in the process of robbing a bank when the manager sets off an alarm and Jesse is forced to shoot him. The gang escapes but one of its members, Bob Ford, is wounded and drops the money bag in front of the bank. Realizing the gang members need time to recuperate, Jesse decides to return to their home in Missouri, and takes in Bob and his brother Charlie while Bob recovers from his wound. Later, Bob goes into town and renews his longtime relationship with Cynthy Waters, a local music hall entertainer. There he discovers that she is also pursued by John Kelley, a wealthy prospector. Bob wants to marry her, but Cynthy makes it clear that the only way to win her is for him to quit the gang and settle down on a farm. When Bob discovers that the governor is offering amnesty and a $10,000 reward to the person responsible for Jesse's death, he begins to believe that such an act may be his best chance. Bob shoots his friend in the back while Jesse is straightening a painting. But Bob's life now takes a turn for the worse when the government only pays $500. In desperation, Bob decides to head to Creed, Colorado in search of silver. He finds that his old nemesis, Kelley, is also prospecting there but Bob gets lucky and finds enough silver to afford to send for Cynthy. Once she arrives, however, Bob realizes she can no longer love him as in the past. He sets out after his rival, Kelley. In the ensuing nighttime shoot-out, Bob is killed by Kelley.

It is an ostensible love triangle that propels the action of this film. Bob Ford and John Kelley vie for the love of Cynthy Waters, leading Bob to kill his friend Jesse for money enough to win the woman, and moving the action still further forward until Kelley kills his rival. As his directorial debut and with his own script, Sam Fuller brings a psychological dimension that belies the geometrical simplicity of the plot. Love and betrayal are the essential ingredients of the action but if there is a triangle it is one composed of Jesse, Bob and Cynthy. Jesse quite obviously functions as Bob's father figure, taking him in even though it is against the better judgment of his wife Zee. Nor do we have to veer too far in a Freudian direction to detect the homoerotic nature of their relationship: Jesse, lying naked in a water trough, gives Bob an expensive pearl-handed revolver as a gift, and then asks him to wash his back.

Later, when Jesse slowly and ritualistically removes his coat and his revolvers in his living room, he states that the removal of his guns makes him "feel naked" and once again presents his back to Bob, who seizes the moment and shoots him. Appropriately enough, Ford's rival Kelley is portrayed by Preston Foster, an actor who was quite a bit older than either John Ireland or Barbara Britton. Ironically, it is Kelley who befriends Ford when he comes to Colorado, sharing a room, and even a bed, with him and ultimately saving his life when Frank James arrives for a revenge killing. Once again, the "son" goes after the "father," only this time the "father" survives to replace the "son" as the putative mate in the film's most noir sequence: a typical western gunfight with the two rivals coming at each other on a lonely street, but shot at night with close-ups emphasizing the sweat on the two men's faces (rather reminiscent of Bill Shell's death in *Ramrod*). Ford's pearl-handed revolver is no match for Kelley's double-barreled shotgun, and as Ford dies in Cynthy's arms, his final words are an admission of his love for Jesse, rather than for Cynthy. **BP**

I, THE JURY (1953)

Director: Harry Essex. **Screenplay**: Harry Essex; from the novel by Mickey Spillane. **Producer:** Victor Saville (Parklane Productions). **Director of Photography**: John Alton. **Music**: Franz Waxman. **Art Director**: Wiard Ihnen. **Editor**: Fredrick Y. Smith. **Cast**: Biff Elliot (Mike Hammer), Preston Foster (Capt. Pat Chambers), Peggie Castle (Charlotte Manning), Margaret Sheridan (Velda), Alan Reed (George Kalecki), Frances Osborne (Myrna), Robert Cunningham (Hal Kines), Elisha Cook, Jr. (Bobo), Paul Dubov (Marty), Mary Anderson (Eileen Vickers), Tani Seitz (Mary Bellamy/Esther Bellamy), Robert Swanger (Jack Williams), John Qualen (Dr. Vickers). **Completed**: April 30, 1953. **Released**: United Artists, August 14. 88 minutes.

Jack Williams, an amputee, is shot several times by a mysterious intruder as he attempts to crawl to his gun. His best friend, private detective Mike Hammer, swears vengeance even though he has been warned against illegal methods by his friend, Pat Chambers of the NYPD. As he checks out guests at a party that Jack gave before he was killed, Hammer focuses on five people: Myrna, a former heroin addict and Jack's fiancée; psychiatrist Charlotte Manning; the apparently love-starved but beautiful Bellamy twins; and George Kalecki, a fight promoter turned art collector. As Hammer investigates further, his path becomes strewn with corpses. Finally, the detective discovers that Kalecki is the head of a narcotics racket and kills him, but Kalecki's organization keeps going. More clues lead Hammer to confront his own fiancée Charlotte with the fact that she wanted to take over Kalecki's racket and is responsible for several murders. As Hammer continues with his accusations, the woman stops denying the charges and partially disrobes. Embracing Hammer, she reaches for a hidden gun but before she can use it the detective shoots her.

I, The Jury was the first of the Saville-produced Spillane adaptations and is probably the only film noir to be shot in 3D. John Alton's photography is as always brilliant although budget limitations forced the use of stock footage and other short cuts. Another liability is Biff Elliott's portrayal of Hammer. Dramatic impact is lessened by Elliott's limited expressive ability and lack of an iconic persona. It is left to supporting actors like Elisha Cook, Jr. to make the necessary iconic connection to previous detective films in the noir cycle. Most of the sadism of the Spillane novels is missing here, except for the startling opening and closing sequences. In the first, a faceless assassin toys with the victim by letting the amputee crawl slowly to his gun before killing him, while "Hark, The Herald Angels Sing" plays in the background. This contrapuntal use of Christmas music throughout the film is reminiscent of Robert Montgomery's *Lady In The Lake* (though the film might be better served by Franz Waxman's atonal jazz score). In the closing scene, a more explicit version of the *Double Indemnity* climax, Hammer shoots the disrobing Charlotte in the stomach as they embrace. When she asks, "How could you?" he replies simply, "It was easy." At the time this film was released it promised more than it delivered, playing up the sensationalistic aspects of Spillane's controversial fiction. Yet despite the fact that much of the novel's sex and violence are here eliminated, the tone of its *machismo* sexuality remains, including Spillane's basic misogyny and distaste for homosexuals. **BP**

I WAKE UP SCREAMING [aka HOT SPOT] (1942)

Director: H. Bruce Humberstone. **Screenplay**: Dwight Taylor from the novel by Steve Fisher. **Producer**: Milton Sperling. **Director of Photography**: Edward Cronjager. **Music**: Cyril J. Mockridge. **Art Directors**: Richard Day, Nathan Juran. **Editor**: Robert Simpson. **Cast**: Betty Grable (Jill Lynn), Victor Mature (Frankie Christopher), Carole Landis (Vicky Lynn), Laird Cregar (Ed Cornell), William Gargan (McDonald), Alan Mowbray (Robin Ray), Allyn Joslyn (Larry Evans), Elisha Cook, Jr. (Harry Williams), Chick Chandler (Reporter), Morris Ankrum (Assistant District Attorney), May Beatty (Mrs. Handel). **Completed**: August 26, 1941. **Released**: 20th Century-Fox, January 16. 82 minutes.

Promoter Frankie Christopher is accused of the murder of Vicky Lynn, a young actress he "discovered"' as a waitress with the aid of ex-actor Robin Ray and gossip columnist Larry Evans. Frankie hides out with Vicky's sister Jill with whom he has fallen in love but is captured. The relentless and obsessive investigating officer, Ed Cornell, decides to make sure Frankie is indicted and convicted. Frankie realizes he must find Vicky's murderer himself, so he escapes and searches for

I Wake Up Screaming: *Jill Lynn (Betty Grable) and Frankie Christopher (Victor Mature).*

evidence. Ultimately he traps Vicky's neighbor, Harry Williams, and the lonely elevator operator confesses that he murdered Vicky. Harry also relates that he confessed to Cornell but was told to keep silent because both men were jealous of Frankie and agreed to see him executed for the murder. Frankie turns in his evidence to Cornell's superiors and is now free to enjoy his romance with Jill.

I Wake Up Screaming exemplifies various aspects of the developing film noir style in the early stages of the cycle. The locations, casting, and lighting use low-key and dark shadows to create a quasi-naturalistic and threatening ambience. In the original novel, hardboiled writer Steve Fisher uses his insider's view of Hollywood to evoke that milieu; but studio chief Zanuck had declared "Hollywood" pictures taboo and compelled the filmmakers to switch the story's location to New York City with its equally atmospheric haunts of nightclubs, ritzy apartments, local police precincts, and neighborhood movie houses. Director H. Bruce "Lucky" Humberstone was not known for his work in melodrama, but his mise-en-scène easily meshes with the Fox-style lighting of cinematographer Edward Cronjager, consisting of high contrast and interesting details, particularly the slanting shadows of venetian blinds.

This visual contrast is complemented by the film's casting which pairs the dark-haired Victor Mature with the blondes Carole Landis and Betty Grable (in her first non-musical role) and the physically imposing Laird Cregar against the nervous, birdlike Elisha Cook, Jr. In minor roles, character actors like Alan Mowbray as a conceited ham actor and Allyn Joslyn as the ruthless gossip columnist contribute to the sardonic and brutal undercurrents of the film. As with many noirs, *I Wake Up Screaming* contains suggestions of sexual perversity. Jill finds herself irresistibly attracted to the man who possibly murdered her sister. The scene in which Frankie wakes to find Cornell seated beside his bed and obsessed with proving Frankie's guilt also hints at Cornell's repressed homosexual passion. *I Wake Up Screaming* is exemplary of what the developing noir style could do for a movie. The plastic beauty inherent in such a style creates a mood and resonance that are often beyond the implications of the script. As Paul Schrader has suggested, adopting its icons and style, many unremarkable directors did their best work in film noir. **MB & AS**

I WALK ALONE (1948)

Director: Byron Haskin. **Screenplay**: Charles Schnee adapted by Robert Smith and John Bright from the play *Beggars Are Coming to Town* by Theodore Reeves. **Producer**: Hal B. Wallis. **Director of Photography**: Leo Tover. **Music**: Victor Young. **Art Directors**: Hans Dreier, Franz Bachelin. **Editor**: Arthur Schmidt. **Cast**: Burt Lancaster (Frankie Madison), Lizabeth Scott (Kay Lawrence), Kirk Douglas (Noll Turner), Wendell Corey (Dave), Kristine Miller (Mrs. Richardson), George Rigaud (Maurice), Marc Lawrence (Nick Palestro), Mike Mazurki (Dan), Mickey Knox (Skinner), Roger Neury (Felix). **Completed**: March, 1947. **Released**: Paramount, January 22. 98 minutes.

During the days of bootlegging Frankie Madison and Noll Turner were partners. Chased by the cops on a night run, they struck a deal whereby Turner would attempt to escape on foot while Madison would stick with the truck so that if

I Walk Alone: *Noll Turner (Kirk Douglas) and Frankie Madison (Burt Lancaster).*

either was caught, the other could keep their nightclub operating and save half the profits for the unlucky partner to collect when free. Madison is released from prison some years later and returns to claim his share. His brother Dave now works as an accountant for Turner who owns a new club; singer Kay Lawrence works at the club and is Turner's girlfriend although she develops feelings for Madison. Turner makes it clear that he will not split profits evenly with Madison. Madison is particularly enraged that his own brother has helped Turner. Madison is even more enraged when his brother, who finally stands up to Turner, is murdered. Determined to sabotage Turner's operations and get revenge as well as the money owed him, Madison tricks Turner into confessing in front of the police.

I Walk Alone features the noir duo of Burt Lancaster and Kirk Douglas. Douglas in films like *Out of the Past* and this one had found his niche as a suave villain while Lancaster in *The Killers* and *Brute Force* epitomized the masochistic male in noir. In his early films, Lancaster suffers endlessly. His use of his body as a tool to express his emotions, rooted in his background as an acrobat, links him to the great expressionistic actors of the past—Emil Jannings, Conrad Veidt, and of course Lon Chaney Jr.—for whom Lancaster expressed great admiration. In this film, Lancaster's Frankie Madison expressively carries the burden of bitterness and anger rooted in betrayal by not only his old friend and gangster cohort Turner but by his own brother, the weak-willed Dave, who now works for the perfidious Turner.

In addition, *I Walk Alone*, like Daniel Fuchs' script for *The Gangster*, deals with an anachronism, a man of another era—the era of Al Capone and bootlegging—who emerges from prison in a period of monumental change, including the transformation of the mob into "legitimate" businessmen. The oily Turner, of course, symbolizes this change, using his nightclub as a money laundering business for less savory operations while ordering murders and beatings to protect his "new world." Madison, however, is old school. He is willing to suffer without complaint until he can reach his goals—the destruction of Turner's operations and the loot Turner owes him. By the end of the film, he has accomplished both objectives with techniques drawn more from the gangster past than from this new, slicker present. **BL**

I WAS A COMMUNIST FOR THE FBI (1951)

Director: Gordon Douglas. **Screenplay**: Crane Wilbur from the *Saturday Evening Post* article "I Posed As a Communist for the FBI" by Matt Cvetic as told to Pete Martin. **Producer**: Bryan Foy. **Director of Photography**: Edwin DuPar. **Music**: Max Steiner. **Art Director**: Leo K. Kuter. **Editor**: Folmar Blangsted. **Cast**: Frank Lovejoy (Matt Cvetic), Dorothy Hart (Eve Merrick), Philip Carey (Mason), Dick Webb (Crowley), James Millican (Jim Blandon), Ron Hagerthy (Dick Cvetic), Paul Picerni (Joe Cvetic), Frank Gerstle (Tom Cvetic), Russ Conway (Frank Cvetic), Hope Kramer (Ruth Cvetic), Kasia Orzazekski (Mrs. Cvetic), Eddie Norris (Harmon), Ann Morrison (Miss Nova), Konstantin Shayne (Gerhardt Eisler), Roy Roberts (Father Novac). **Completed**: February 22, 1951. **Released**: Warner Bros., May 2. 84 minutes

Matt Cvetic, a Pittsburgh steel company worker, has joined the Communist Party but, unknown to anyone including his family, he is an undercover agent for the FBI. His family is embarrassed and hostile to him because he is a "slimy red." Matt's immediate superiors in the party, Blandon and Harmon, are part of a large-scale plan to disrupt the nation by making sure Communists hold key positions in industry and unions. When Matt becomes the chief party organizer, he is spied on by other Communists as part of their strategy for ferreting out traitors. Matt's politics cause his son to be involved in a school fight which later causes the boy to turn away from his father. Matt foolishly writes a letter to his son explaining that he is working for the FBI, but accidentally loses it. Later, Eve Merrick, who is his son's teacher and a Communist Party member, discovers it. However, she is upset with Communist Party tactics and does not use the letter against him. But Matt is forced to report her unhappiness to his superiors and they plan to get rid of her. Rescuing Eve, Matt is followed by a Communist agent. They fight in a train tunnel and he is shot. A federal probe of Communist activities takes place and Matt testifies. His true role is revealed, which redeems him in the eyes of family and friends.

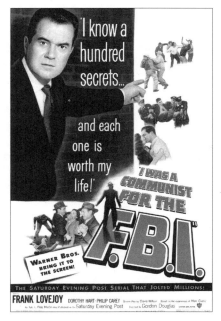

I Was a Communist for the FBI, a quite obvious product of 1950s red hysteria, demonstrates how easily the conventions of noir thrillers could be used for these propaganda pieces, which were produced by the motion picture studios more for political reasons than for commercial value. Of all of them, including *The Red Menace, Iron Curtain, I Married a Communist,* and *The Whip Hand,* the most visually noir is *I Was a Communist for the FBI*. Its popular success is indicated by the famous spin-off TV series *I Led Three Lives* (1953), based on the memoirs of undercover agent Herb Philbrick. *I Was a Communist* also recruits the conventions of the police documentary, most noticeably in its use of a stentorian narrator testifying to the story's veracity. Here, however, the criminals have been replaced by "Commies," and the undercover cop or G-Man by an "average" citizen, Matt Cvetic (evidently a quite sanitized version of the real Cvetic). **BP**

I WOULDN'T BE IN YOUR SHOES (1948)

Director: William Nigh. **Screenplay**: Steve Fisher from the novel by Cornell Woolrich. **Producer**: Walter Mirisch. **Director of Photography**: Mack Stengler. **Music**: Edward Kay. **Art Director**: Dave Milton. **Editor**: Roy Livingston. **Cast**: Don Castle (Tom), Elyse Knox (Ann), Regis Toomey (Judd), Charles D. Brown (Insp. Stevens), Rory Mallinson (1st Detective), Robert Lowell (Kosloff), Bill Kennedy (2nd Detective). **Completed**: February 6, 1948. **Released**: Monogram, May 23. 70 minutes.

Tom and Ann Quinn are a dance team down on their luck and subsisting on Ann's income as an instructor for a nearby dance academy. Late one night Tom inadvertently throws his good dance shoes out the window to scare off a howling cat. When he goes outside to retrieve them, he is unable to find them. Surprisingly, they show up outside his apartment the next day. Though Tom is unable to find work for the couple as dance team, their depression is momentarily relieved when he discovers a wallet filled with $2000 worth of old-fashioned $20 bills but no I.D. Tom wants to turn the wallet over to the police, but Ann persuades him to wait and see if anyone advertises its loss in the local papers. Coincidentally a reclusive miser in their neighborhood has been murdered and over $10,000 in old bills has been stolen from his place. Police detective Judd discovers the ostensible culprit's footprints outside the victim's house and since they are specially made shoes they are traced to Tom. The police cleverly delay arresting Tom until the couple begins to spend the money. Tom is unable to explain his footprints nor can he account for the rest of the money. Though he continues to plead his innocence, Tom is peremptorily tried, convicted and sentenced to death. Ann recognizes Judd as one of her former dance students and when he confesses his feelings for her, she uses her feminine wiles to get Judd to reopen the case. In so doing, Judd finds evidence that points to a man named Kosloff whom he arrests for murder. Just when it appears that Kosloff is the guilty party he comes up with an ironclad alibi. To cheer up Ann, Judd goes to the dance studio and tries to persuade her to see the luxury apartment he has rented for her. Distraught, Ann insults him and in a moment of pique, Judd leaves her with a $20 tip. Recognizing the old currency, Ann catches up with Judd and gets him to show her the apartment. Once there, she entices him into confessing to the murder and frame-up. Having been tipped off by Ann, the police arrive and when Judd resists arrest, they shoot him.

This film is a low-budget thriller in the tradition of *Detour* but without the guiding hand of an Edgar Ulmer to rescue it. However, *Shoes* escapes being ordinary only insofar as it is able to capture the peculiar atmosphere of the Woolrichian universe (reworked here by Steve Fisher), which is a universe so filled with ironies, accidents and absurdities that its inhabitants have very little control over their lives. Despite budget limitations and the obvious use of lackluster sets, Mack Stengler has nonetheless managed to recreate the oppressive nature of Woolrich's New York at night (though not as well as Woody Bredell in *Phantom Lady*). And by structuring the action so that much of it (except for the film's final segment) proceeds as a series of flashbacks initiated by the doomed man on the eve of his execution, the fatalism of the film noir remains quite intact.

More telling is the way screenwriter Fisher has changed the ending of Woolrich's novella, in which Tom is left on death row with his fate undetermined. By Fisher's own account, he pointed out this plot deficiency to Woolrich while he was writing the screenplay and asked him to suggest an ending. Woolrich then advised him to use the ending of Fisher's own pulp novel, *I Wake Up Screaming*, which had been filmed in 1941. That novel's "heavy" was Ed Cornell (whose physical description bore an uncanny resemblance to Woolrich), a police detective who manipulates evidence to frame the protagonist for murder and, when discovered, commits suicide. Here Judd, like Cornell, is a police detective whose obsession with a woman causes him to lose his integrity and ultimately his life. While Cornell's obsession with feminine beauty culminates in the altar to Vicky's memory that he places in his apartment, Judd's is no less unhealthy: he furnishes the apartment he rents as a surprise for Ann with many of her favorite things, a knowledge gained from his rigorous investigation of her past. And, despite appearances, Ann proves to be even more devious than the Vicky Lynn of Fisher's novel. In this film's most memorable low-key scene, Ann arranges to meet Judd in the murdered man's home. Dousing the flashlight, she displays her loneliness and vulnerability to Judd, allowing him to kiss her with the promise of much more to come. But after Kosloff is freed, she treats him with the utmost disdain, telling him that her affection was nothing more than a ruse. **BP**

ILLEGAL (1955)

Director: Lewis Allen. **Screenplay**: W. R. Burnett, James R. Webb, based on the play "The Mouthpiece" by Frank J. Collins. **Producer**: Frank Rosenberg. **Director of Photography**: J. Peverell Marley. **Art Director**: Stanley Fleischer. **Music**: Max Steiner. **Editor**: Thomas Reilly. **Cast**: Edward G. Robinson (Victor Scott), Nina Foch (Ellen Miles), Hugh Marlowe (Ray Borden), Robert Ellenstein (Joe Knight), DeForest Kelley (Edward Clary), Albert Dekker (Garland), Jayne Mansfield (Angel O'Hara), Edward Platt (Ralph Ford), Jay Adler (Joseph Carter), James McCallion (Allen Parker), Ellen Corby (Miss Hinkel). **Released**: Warner Bros., October 28, 88 minutes.

A tenacious district attorney, Victor Scott, on his way to the governor's mansion resigns when a man he had sent to the electric chair proves innocent. But when the civil practice he hopes to undertake goes bust, he takes to the bottle . Down and out, in a drunk tank, Scott meets a man there, defends him in court and decides to apply his legal acumen to becoming a sharp, high-priced criminal attorney. He's such a brilliant mouthpiece he comes to the attention of civic crime boss Garland, for whom he begins to work. Meanwhile back at the D.A.'s office, he's left behind his protégé Ellen Miles. Though he harbors romantic feelings for her, he gives his blessing when she announces her marriage to a young, ambitious lawyer, Ray Borden. But a series of leaks from the office concerning Garland's activities brings suspicion on all three. Ultimately, Robinson finds himself defending Ellen for murder after she shoots Borden, the actual "leaker," in self-defense. He wins his case after being shot by his gangster cronies.

The fast and too complicated plot takes a few pointless and baffling turns. Although on the talky side, there's a high quotient of gunplay. Still, it's absorbing to watch the character of Scott portrayed by Edward G. Robinson. In the midst of a string of B-pictures owing to his guilt-by-association in the wake of the anti-Communist crusade, Robinson holds everything together with a professionalism and subtlety he is rarely given credit for. Not only did he leave his mark on the gangster film in the 1930s (*Illegal*'s co-writer W.R. Burnett was also responsible for the novel used in Robinson's breakthrough movie *Little Caesar*), he also extended his influence to noir through a series of masochistic portrayals in the 1940s, namely *Scarlet Street*, *The Woman in the Window*, and *Night Has a Thousand Eyes*. **BMV**

Impact: *Irene Williams (Helen Walker) discusses her missing husband with Lt. Quincey (Charles Coburn).*

IMPACT (1947)

Director: Arthur Lubin. **Screenplay**: Dorothy Reid (Davenport) and Jay Dratler from his story. **Producer**: Leo C. Popkin (Cardinal Pictures). **Executive Producer**: Harry M. Popkin. **Director of Photography**: Ernest Laszlo. **Music**: Michel Michelet. **Art Director**: Rudi Feld. **Editor**: Arthur H. Nadel. **Cast**: Brian Donlevy (Walter Williams), Ella Raines (Marsha Peters), Charles Coburn (Lt. Tom Quincy), Helen Walker (Irene Williams), Anna May Wong (Su Lin), Robert Warwick (Capt. Callahan), Clarence Kolb (Darcy), Art Baker (Eldridge), William Wright (District Attorney), Mae Marsh (Mrs. King), Sheilah Graham (Herself), Tony Barrett (Jim Torrance), Philip Ahn (Ah Sing), Glen Vernon (Ed). **Released**: United Artists, March 20. 111 minutes.

Walter Williams is a millionaire industrialist with a young wife who would prefer him dead. During a botched murder attempt, Walter is beaten with a lug wrench and left for dead. His would-be assassin is killed and unrecognizably burned in a car accident while driving Walter's car. Amnesiac and mistaken for dead, Walter winds up in a small Idaho town where he finds work as a gas station mechanic and falls in love with the station owner, Marsha Peters. Marsha convinces Walter to return to his previous life in order to clear his wife of murder charges. However, he is then charged with the murder himself and forced to defend himself in court.

Amnesia proves once again to be an excellent vehicle for a noir, with a man forced to face his past and his past proving just as violent a force on his life as a murder attempt. Donlevy brings his trademark stiff-as-a-board acting to a setting and narrative that seems to suit it, throwing in an unexpected crying jag for good effect. Ella Raines brightens up the picture considerably and this performance adds to her previous ones in *Brute Force* and *Phantom Lady*, creating an impressive noir oeuvre considering her short movie career. *Impact* fits in neatly with other B-noir, with Lubin providing simple, straightforward direction while Laszlo shoots with an unimposing grayscale palette. A true and convincing noir film, *Impact* has all the classic and most enjoyable noir elements: femme fatale, a past that would best be forgotten, a conflicted hero, an innocent girl, and, of course, an opportunity for redemption, in this case, fulfilled. **JEB**

IN A LONELY PLACE (1950)

Director: Nicholas Ray. **Screenplay**: Andrew Solt, adapted by Edmund H. North from the novel by Dorothy B. Hughes. **Producer**: Robert Lord (Santana Productions). **Director of Photography**: Burnett Guffey. **Music**: George Antheil. **Art Director**: Robert Peterson. **Editor**: Viola Lawrence. **Cast**: Humphrey Bogart (Dixon Steele), Gloria Grahame (Laurel Gray), Frank Lovejoy (Brub Nicolai), Carl Benton Reid (Capt. Lochner), Art Smith (Mel Lippman), Jeff Donnell (Sylvia Nicolai), Martha Stewart (Mildred Atkinson), Robert Warwick (Charlie Waterman), Morris Ankrum (Lloyd Barnes), William Ching (Ted Barton), Steven Geray (Paul), Hadda Brooks (Singer), Alice Talton (Frances Randolph), Jack Reynolds (Henry Kesler), Ruth Warren (Effie). **Completed**: December 1, 1949. **Released**: Columbia, May 17. 94 minutes.

Screenwriter Dixon Steele, out of work because of his alcoholism and belligerency, invites the hatcheck girl at a local bar to his apartment, so she can tell him the story of a book he may turn into a movie. She flirts with him; but he gives her a kindly brush-off and sends her home in a taxi. The next morning her brutally battered body is discovered and Steele is questioned by the police on suspicion of murder. However, his new neighbor, Laurel Gray, tells the police that she saw the hatcheck girl enter Steele's apartment and leave alone later. Although he is still a suspect, Steele is released. After becoming acquainted, Steele and Laurel fall in love. Under Laurel's influence, Steele returns to writing and the work goes well. But his violent temper and jealousy, along with the continuing suspicion of the police, unnerve Laurel; and she begins to suspect that he may have been involved in the murder. Sensing her distrust, Steele's violence increases in a series of incidents. Although she promises to marry him, Laurel is afraid of him and tries to leave town. Steele stops her in a murderous rage, tries to strangle Laurel; just then, the phone rings. It is the police; the real murderer is the hatcheck girl's jealous boyfriend, who has just confessed. But the confession comes too late for Steele and Laurel; her distrust and his rage have torn them apart forever.

Like its title, *In A Lonely Place* is strange, sad, and hauntingly romantic. A peculiar kind of film noir, it combines a harsh murder mystery in a somewhat sleazy milieu with a

In A Lonely Place: *Laurel Gray (Gloria Grahame) and Dixon Steele (Humphrey Bogart).*

colorful semi-hard-boiled cast of characters. Like almost all of Nicholas Ray's films, *In a Lonely Place* concerns alienation, effort, failure, and loss. It seems hardly to matter that the characters of Dixon Steele and Laurel Grey love each other genuinely and passionately; nor does it make any difference that in many ways, they are good for one another, each lifting the other briefly from a common morass of cynicism and depression. Their inherent goodness and their efforts to relate are all in vain.

Ray sees the world as dark with distrust; it is a disease that eats its way even into the bones of those who resist it most by doing that hardest thing of all: opening themselves to others. This candor renders Steele, in particular, vulnerable to suspicion. When he reveals his dark side to Laurel, her distrust of him becomes inevitable. That Laurel's distrust and brutal betrayal is a grievous, albeit understandable, failing is largely due to the structuring of the film. Until the end, the viewer cannot be absolutely certain of Steele's innocence and comes to share Laurel's suspicions and bewilderment at how this man who is kind and loving in some instances can be abruptly brutal in others. Steele's life guilt and angst become sinister qualities that make the film's love scenes, by contrast, reverberate with a tenuous sexuality.

In spite of the violence and hardness of much of the film, *In a Lonely Place* is understated and naturalistic in its portrayal of a love affair between two people who left their innocence behind long ago. It is no moonlit and misty-eyed Hollywood version of romance; in fact, Steele is almost proletarian when he tells Laurel that his idea of two people in love is two people like them: a guy cutting grapefruit and a girl with sleep in her eyes. Still, Steele is basically a fallen romantic, as his coda-like remarks quoted by Laurel at the film's end reveal: "I was born when you kissed me. I died when you left me. I lived a few weeks while you loved me." Steele's inability to reconcile the worthlessness of his past successes adds to the obsessive burden of his current failure at the movie's beginning. If Laurel redeems him momentarily, it is only because she distracts him from the concentrated existential anguish of his position. The violence that expresses his malaise is ultimately suicidal; but that, too, fails. In Ray's vision of the noir universe, destructive impulses such as Steele's must eventually short-circuit the sexual and creative potency that Laurel temporarily inspires. Like the forced melodrama of his screenplays and of his final remarks, Steele is a noir hero trapped in a compulsive role—caught, almost frozen, between the dark past and a bleak future. He is unable to see a continuum that valorizes the present except through Laurel. Hence, Steele is literally and figuratively in a lonely place. The final images, which frame Steele and Laurel together but not facing each other, renders them alien and alone once again. **JK & AS**

INNER SANCTUM (1948)

Director: Lew Landers. **Screenplay**: Jerome T. Gollard. **Producer**: Richard B. Morros. **Director of Photography**: Allen G. Siegler. **Art Director**: William Ferrari. **Music**: Leo Klatzkin. **Editor**: Fred Feitshans Jr. **Cast**: Mary Beth Hughes (Jean Maxwell), Charles Russell (Harold Dunlap), Dale Belding (Mike Bennett), Billy House (McFee), Fritz Leiber (Psychic), Nana Bryant (Thelma Mitchell), Lee Patrick (Ruth Bennett), Eve Miller (Marie Kembar), Roscoe Ates (Willy), Eddie Parks (Barney). **Released**: Film Classics, October 15. 62 minutes.

A psychic tells a woman, Marie Kembar, a story on a train. A man, Harold Dunlap, while defending himself, kills his unfaithful lover and escapes during a flood to a small town in the Northwest. There he hides out with the family of a boy, Mike Bennett, who had witnessed him throwing the body of the woman onto the train. Alternately trying to befriend and threaten the boy he hopes to stay long enough to escape when the bridge is repaired. While there, a bitter Jean Maxwell falls for him and tries to convince him to take her away to the city. His identity is revealed by Mike and the police close in. Meanwhile, on the train, the woman ignores the psychic's story, rushes from the train and repeats the first scene of the story.

Inner Sanctum (taking its name from the successful mystery radio show of the period) draws themes and motifs from two major noirs: *The Night Has a Thousand Eyes* and Alfred Hitchcock's *Shadow of a Doubt* while it foreshadows another: *The Window* (1949), Cornell Woolrich's tale of a young boy under threat from murderers whose crime he witnessed. Its opening has a psychic (played by supernatural/sci-fi writer Fritz Leiber's father) telling the impetuous Marie a story of passion and murder as a cautionary tale. As with John Triton in *The Night Has a Thousand Eyes*, the Cassandra-like psychic is not believed. And so the woman rushes from the train and recreates the same scene as in the beginning of the story (she attacks her lover with a nail file and is in turn stabbed in the heart with it by him), this time shot from a different angle, reaffirming the inexorability so inextricable from the core of noir.

As the murderer, Harold, hides out in a small town during a flood, the film begins to draw on Hitchcock's classic for its menace. Harold rents a room in a boarding house where he broods and skulks his way through the remainder of the movie, attempting to kill and/or threaten the befuddled boy, Mike, who has witnessed his deed while fighting off the advances of the disillusioned femme fatale Jean (played seductively by noir icon Mary Beth Hughes). Jean has set her sights on Harold from his first appearance at the boarding house. To her he represents a one-way ticket out of the stifling small-town life in which she is suffocating. Her pursuit of him is sassy and unrelenting (typical of many of Hughes's characterizations). She even takes a blow to the jaw when she interrupts him attempting to silence Mike, and still she comes back. In many ways they are a perfect couple, both wrapped in a pall of gloom and cynicism about life and past relationships, all of which have been destructive in one way or another (as revealed in a flirtatious dish washing scene earlier). As they sit on the porch, side by side, in the final scene of the psychic's story, waiting for the police to arrive, they are already psychologically joined as one, if not yet romantically. Jean says, "The road's open." Harold replies, "Not for me . . . I'm tired of running." Both doomed romantics stare out into the night as the sirens grow louder on the film's soundtrack. **JU**

INVADERS FROM MARS (1953)

Director: William Cameron Menzies. **Screenplay**: Richard Blake from a story by John Tucker Battle. **Producer**: Edward L. Alperson (National Pictures Corporation). **Director of Photography**: John F. Seitz. **Music**: Raoul Kraushaar. **Production Designer**: William

Cameron Menzies. **Editor**: Arthur Roberts. **Cast**: Helena Carter (Dr. Pat Blake), Arthur Franz (Dr. Stuart Kelston), Jimmy Hunt (David Maclean), Leif Erickson (George Maclean), Hillary Brooke (Mary Maclean), Morris Ankrum (Col. Fielding), Janine Perreau (Kathy Wilson). **Released**: 20th Century-Fox, April 22. 78 minutes.

Soon after he witnesses a flying saucer landing behind his house, young David Maclean discovers that hostile creatures from outer space have possessed his father George, mother Mary and the little girl next door. David seeks help in town, only to find that the police chief is under alien control as well. Health services doctor Pat Blake alone believes David's story. She shields him from his parents and helps him convince astronomer Stuart Kelston that a Martian invasion is underway. David and Pat are pulled into the Martian's underground lair, but Army Colonel Fielding and his troops follow and place explosives on the spaceship. Kelston saves Pat before the "Alien Intelligence," a tentacled creature in a glass ball, can implant a control device in her brain. David uses a Martian ray gun to burn an escape route to the surface, and all flee as the saucer attempts to take off. David awakens and discovers that the entire experience was a dream. However, later that night he re-awakes and sees a flying saucer landing, perhaps this time for real.

An adolescent science fiction tale about outlandish alien invaders perhaps seems unrelated to film noir, yet *Invaders from Mars* exhibits strong thematic ties to the style. As in Ted Tetzlaff's *The Window,* a young innocent is traumatized when adults will not believe his reports of strange phenomena. In Andre de Toth's *Pitfall,* a tot (also played by Jimmy Hunt) suffers nightmares stemming from tensions between his parents, but his upset is blamed on lurid comic books about monsters from space. *Invaders* is exactly the nightmare this boy might experience, like a space age *Alice through the Looking Glass.* The film also features some chiaroscuro photography by noir veteran John F. Seitz and subjectified *mise en scène* courtesy of prestigious production designer and director Cameron Menzies.

Instead of a Buck Rogers empowerment fantasy, the boy protagonist of *Invaders* encounters a paranoid dilemma, a subjective maze even more intense than the *Dark Corners* and *Detours* that torment adult noir protagonists. The subjective distortions of reality felt by overwrought noir figures

become the entire visual text of *Invaders from Mars.* Loved and respected adults are perceived as menacing zombies. Obsessive details signify terrible secrets: staring eyes, scars on the backs of necks; and some settings, such as the distorted perspective of the alien-infested sand pit, all bear similarities with the 1920 avant-garde German expressionist film *Cabinet of Dr. Caligari.* Moreover, absurd character behavior and non-sequitur dialogue make sense only if *Invader from Mars* is indeed the nightmare of a twelve-year-old child. David Maclean's dream of Martians with death rays is an expression of the anxieties in his daily life—family stresses, the Cold War atomic standoff—and as such makes him a noir protagonist, junior grade. The image of David running without moving, trapped in a nightmare that refuses to end, is a key expression of noir angst. **GE**

INVASION OF THE BODY SNATCHERS (1956)

Director: Don Siegel. **Screenplay**: Daniel Mainwaring, Richard Collins (uncredited) based on a 1954 serial in *Collier's* magazine and the novel *The Body Snatchers* by Jack Finney. **Producer**: Walter Wanger. **Director of Photography**: Ellsworth Fredericks. **Music**: Carmen Dragon. **Production Designer**: Ted Haworth. **Editor**: Robert S. Eisen. **Cast**: Kevin McCarthy (Dr. Miles J. Bennell), Dana Wynter (Becky Driscoll), Larry Gates (Dr. Dan "Danny" Kaufman), King Donovan (Jack Belicec), Carolyn Jones (Teddy Belicec), Jean Willes (Nurse Sally Withers), Ralph Dumke (Police Chief Nick Grivett), Virginia Christine (Wilma Lentz), Tom Fadden (Uncle Ira Lentz), Kenneth Patterson (Stanley Driscoll). **Locations**: Beechwood Canyon, Bronson Canyon, Cahuenga Pass in Los Angeles; Sierra Madre, California. **Completed**: July 1955. **Released**: Allied Artists, February 5. 80 minutes.

Inside a hospital emergency room a psychiatrist listens as his patient, himself a doctor, tells his story: in Santa Mira several of Dr. Miles Bennell's patients report that their relatives are impostors, or "not themselves." As Miles rekindles his romance with college girlfriend Becky Driscoll, his writer friend Jack Belicec discovers a "blank" body slowly taking on his physical characteristics. A fantastic biological conspiracy has seized the town: giant seed pods from outer space are replacing human beings with passive duplicates, simulacra devoid of emotion. Furthermore, local farmers are growing more pods to spread the menace to other communities. After Jack and his wife Teddy become replicants, Miles and Becky run to the hills, but Becky succumbs to the replacement process. Miles refuses to give up and attempts to warn travelers on the interstate by shouting "You're next! You're next!" Psychiatrists presume him mad until an accident report mentions a truck filled with odd seed pods and the FBI is alerted.

1950s science fiction often visualized Cold War anxieties as giant monsters and mechanized invasions from space. A more insidious post-nuclear disquiet informs *Pitfall* and especially *Kiss Me Deadly,* but the strongest paranoid fifties film is *Invasion of the Body Snatchers,* which utilizes the familiar noir fear of an unseen menace prowling nighttime streets. In place of a noir underworld of crime and corruption, *Invasion* fashions a political allegory about infiltration and possession: exposure to dangerous ideas will transform a person into an agent of a conformist alien ideology. The conspiracy spreads until the pod contagion is disseminated at

Invasion of the Body Snatchers: *Becky Driscoll (Dana Wynter) and Miles Bennell (Keven McCarthy) flee the alien townspeople.*

open street rallies and possessed lawmen forcibly victimize citizens in broad daylight. Behind the political threat is the personal fear of losing one's identity, one's human essence. Awareness brings no comfort, for Miles and Becky become a hunted minority in a new order of conformity to a collective will. The "traditional value" Miles fights to retain is his essential individuality.

Miles was aware of an erosion of human emotions before the pods came. Both he and Becky feel like personal failures and alienated from normal society because of their recent divorces. Their jaundiced view of society's norms parallels the key noir themes of emotional displacement and disillusion. Family ties vanish. Miles observes an unnaturally tranquil pod family placing a fresh pod next to a baby's crib: after the duplication, there will be "no more tears." Miles' and Becky's struggle against the ideological/biological invasion forces them to bond, much like the fugitive lovers of *Gun Crazy* or *They Live By Night*. But love is powerless against the totalitarian onslaught of the pods.

Invasion of the Body Snatchers satisfies on both the commercial and critical level. The film has substantially the same plot as Finney's *Collier's* magazine serial but Siegel and Mainwaring make significant changes to its structure and ending. They eliminate virtually all of Finney's pseudoscientific theorizing about the pods. By jettisoning this metaphysical baggage, they allow the film to develop psychological tension with its focus on a central character drawn increasingly toward paranoia. Screenwriter Mainwaring (*Out of the Past, The Phenix City Story*) references the small-town ambience of *Shadow of a Doubt* as a model for Santa Mira. Siegel uses location shooting rather than studio sets to recreate Finney's Santa Mira, sustaining the film's ostensible psychological realism by projecting Miles' fears against the backdrop of a small town with its roadside vegetable stands, shady residential streets, central square and other remnants of mid-century America in which almost incomprehensible evil is taking form. With its bewildered protagonist in jeopardy and his ultimate betrayal by a femme fatale, *Invasion*

reflects the deceptive appearances and unstable reality of the noir universe itself.

Past commentary on *Invasion of the Body Snatchers* often focuses on the imposition of the "frame story" by studio executives, though written by Mainwaring and directed by Siegel, and on the question of whether the film's themes of the loss of individuality and perils of conformity reflect the anti-communist hysteria of the 1950s, a critique of American Cold War ideology, or an attack on the Hollywood power structure itself. Siegel, an individualist and ironist, may well have been commenting on all of these. Siegel's first cut had no flashback structure and ended with a close-up of Miles Bennell shouting, "You're next!" followed by an abrupt cut to black. Allied Artists insisted that the ending be lightened with a "story frame," but *Invasion* does its job too well and the pods still seem well on their way to victory.

Siegel emphasizes a gradual shift toward claustrophobia and Ellsworth Frederick's photographic style alternates between ordinary daylight and hallucinatory night scenes, as with the unnerving deep focus view of the fresh pod on Jack Belicec's pool table. While the addition of the frame story in postproduction has been widely criticized, it should be noted that the frame and voice-over narration along with depth of field, canted and low-angle shots, chiaroscuro, and claustrophobic framing contribute to the film's noir style and are especially appropriate if *Invasion of the Body Snatchers* is read as a reflection not of political fears associated with postwar communist infiltration or the aftermath of McCarthyism and House Un-American Activities Committee investigative zeal but of a more general anxiety. It seems clear that for Miles, the threat is moral and existential: to submit to the pods is to relinquish the most fundamental aspects of his identity as a person, his freedom and autonomy. His defiance of the pods is his way of affirming what it means to be human.

Siegel internalizes Miles' struggle and confusion by having him frequently advert to his fear in his voice-over narration. Additionally, this fear is externalized through claustrophobic imagery such as dark closets, narrow hallways, tunnels, and other enclosures. Believing that he is pursued by a relentless peril that threatens his very identity as a person, Miles' only hope is to take action before it is too late. Several emblematic scenes convey the nightmare aspect of the story in which everything conspires against Miles. First, the greenhouse sequence, in which seed pods burst open to reveal duplicates before the terrified eyes of Miles, Becky, Jack, and Teddy. As Miles plunges a pitchfork into the chest of his duplicate, Siegel quickly cuts to the hallway telephone. This fast cut to the ringing telephone gathers the tension of the greenhouse scene and discharges it into the next scene as Miles takes Becky by the hand and says, "We're getting out of here right now."

In the tunnel scene, Becky is exhausted after running from the mob and falls asleep while Miles is momentarily absent. In the process she, too, becomes a pod person. Miles' realization that a moment's sleep had transformed the woman he loved into an inhuman enemy dedicated to his annihilation as a person leads him to say, in voice-over, "I didn't know the real meaning of fear until I kissed Becky." Her "pod-scream" alerts their pursuers as he takes flight. In what is perhaps the film's signature scene, Miles attempt to escape from Santa Mira takes him to a busy highway at night. The frantic pace of the scene, with its cars, trucks, headlights, horns, and angry motorists shouting insults and coming perilously close to hitting him become an objective correlate of Miles's confused and disordered consciousness as he shouts "You're next! You're next!" Such is the ambiguity of the film's subtext that watching it suspends the viewer between two alternative and conflicting possibilities: one promises hope as Miles feels relief when Dr. Hill calls in the F.B.I. But the other possibility, i.e. Mile's warning of "We're next," confirms our worst nightmares. More than fifty years after its release, *Invasion of the Body Snatchers* maintains its reputation as one of the greatest science fiction films even as it transcends its era and genre as the ultimate, futuristic expression of noir alienation. It has become both a persistent source of inspiration and a touchstone of American popular culture. *Invasion of the Body Snatchers* has been remade by Phillip Kaufman (1978), Abel Ferrara (*Body Snatchers*, 1993), and Oliver Hirschbiegel (*The Invasion*, 2007), but it is unlikely that any of these will achieve the iconic status of their illustrious predecessor. **SMS & GE**

IVY (1947)

Director: Sam Wood. **Screenplay**: Charles Bennett based on the novel *The Story of Ivy* by Marie Belloc Lowndes. **Producer**: William Cameron Menzies. **Executive Producer**: Sam Wood (Interwood Productions, Universal International Pictures). **Director of Photography**: Russell Metty. **Music**: Daniele Amfitheatrof. **Art Director**: Richard H. Riedel. **Editor**: Ralph Dawson. **Cast**: Joan Fontaine (Ivy Lexton), Patric Knowles (Roger Gretorex), Herbert Marshall (Miles Rushworth), Richard Ney (Jervis Lexton), Cedric Hardwicke (Insp. Orpington), Lucile Watson (Mrs. Gretorex), Sara Allgood (Martha Huntley), Henry Stephenson (Judge), Rosalind Ivan (Emily), Lilian Fontaine (Lady Flora), Molly Lamont (Bella Crail), Una O'Connor (Mrs. Thrawn), Isobel Elsom (Miss Chattle), Alan Napier (Sir Jonathan Wright). **Released**: Universal, June 26. 99 minutes.

Ivy hates "being poor." When she meets millionaire Miles Rushworth she takes advantage of the opportunity and makes him fall for her. However, before they can marry, she must obtain a divorce and end a love affair. It looks like Miles and his money are lost when her husband and lover both refuse to be provoked. However, alone with Roger's medicines, she puts a spoonful of poison into her handbag's secret compartment. After slowly killing Jervis, she hides the handbag. Circumstantial evidence implicates her lover, Roger, not her. At his trial, her testimony incriminates him. Realizing she set him up, Roger changes his plea to guilty. Orpington observes this pleases Ivy, and he looks into the case more closely. Roger's servant, who has been afraid to come forward, tells Orpington about Ivy's handbag and the jar of poison. He discovers Ivy's motive was Miles. Before Ivy can dispose of the handbag, he finds it. Roger is reprieved, and Miles tells Ivy they are through. As Orpington is about to arrest her, she accidentally falls into an empty elevator shaft.

In the gripping first scene, Ivy is delighted by a fortune-teller's predictions that "an abundance of money" and "another man" will soon come her way. When she meets Miles that afternoon, it seems the prediction has come true. However, Ivy and Miles are not foreordained to run into each other. People are not the playthings of fate in *Ivy*. What they do is by choice for which they must bear responsibility and suffer consequences. For example, Roger's obsessive pursuit of Ivy almost gets him executed. In contrast, Miles believes, "The most despicable thing a man can do is make love to another man's wife." Therefore, after Miles kisses the married Ivy, he feels ashamed and stays away from her. In fact, the fortune-teller gets it wrong. She counsels Ivy to break up with Roger. She says nothing about Jervis. This implies Ivy's new lover will be as in favor of adultery as her current lover. But Miles is not like Roger. Ivy's hopes for lucrative romance with Miles are doomed because she can neither get a divorce nor get away with murder. Ivy is caught in the era of a social trap that believed a woman's finances depended entirely upon the status of her husband, and her only option to get ahead is to marry a rich man. It is no wonder Ivy seeks advice from someone who supposedly has supernatural powers and is eager to act out that prediction.

The most significant year of the femme fatale in film noir is 1947, as shown not only in the frequency but also by the variety of ways the archetype appears. The character is principally associated with hard-boiled film noir. In this year, *Out of the Past* was released and, of all hard-boiled film noirs, it has perhaps the most celebrated femme fatale, Jane Greer's Kathy Moffat. Although Alfred Hitchcock may be an exemplar of the auteur, nonetheless the same changes occur to the important female characters in his films, from 1942-1947, as in those of other directors. During the early war years, a woman with a job often helps a hunted man prove his innocence. In 1942, Hitchcock made *Saboteur*. By the end of the war and in postwar years, the woman who can take charge changes to the woman-in-distress. In 1946, he made *Notorious*. In addition, he made *The Paradine Case*, with Alida Valli as the femme fatale, in 1947. Gaslight melodramas often have a women-in-distress or even a homme fatale. The first femme fatale in a gaslight film noir is Joan Fontaine's Ivy in 1947. The original *New York Times* review of *Ivy* suggests a shorter running time would have improved the film. But tightening the narrative would come at the expense of reducing what is best in *Ivy*, a noir visual style that is compelling from first scene to last. **DMH**

JEOPARDY (1953)

Director: John Sturges. **Screenplay**: Mel Dinelli from a story by Maurice Zimm. **Producer**: Sol B. Fielding. **Director of Photography**: Victor Milner. **Music**: Dimitri Tiomkin. **Art Director**: William Ferrari, Cedric Gibbons. **Editor**: Newell Kimlin. **Cast**: Barbara Stanwyck (Helen Stilwin), Barry Sullivan (Doug Stilwin), Ralph Meeker (Lawson, the fugitive), Lee Aaker (Bobby Stilwin), Rico Alaniz (1st Roadblock Officer), Salvador Baguez (2nd Roadblock Officer), Paul Fierro (Police Lt.). **Released**: MGM, March 30. 69 minutes.

The Stilwins, Doug, Helen and young Bobby, are on a family vacation in Baja California. Doug drives them to a remote beach where he went fishing with his army buddies some years ago. Before long, Bobby wanders out to the end of a dilapidated pier and gets his foot stuck under a plank on his way back. With the help of Doug, Bobby gets back safely but a portion of the pier collapses under Doug's weight. Doug appears unhurt but a piling has pinned his leg on the rocks at shoreline. Regaining her composure, Helen sets out in the car for a garage they had passed along the way to get a tow rope to pull the piling off Doug's leg before the tide comes in. Bobby stays behind to support Doug. Forced to break into the garage to get the rope, Helen suddenly sees an American standing near her car and begs him for help. She lets him jump behind the wheel only to discover that Lawson is an escaped convict and murderer. He abducts Helen and the car in order to get past the roadblocks of the police who are combing the countryside for him. When Lawson seeks refuge at an abandoned ranch, Helen realizes the only way she can rescue Doug is to seduce Lawson into helping them. She promises to run off with him once Lawson has rescued Doug to obtain his civilian clothing and identification. Eventually they return to the beach and by ingeniously using a pier plank tied to the car as a lever, Lawson is able to lift the piling just enough for Doug to free his leg. After Helen admits to Lawson that she can only have feelings for her husband, he takes Doug's clothes but he releases her of her promise, shakes her hand and disappears on foot into the twilight, hotly pursued by the police.

Jeopardy was one of a series of noir films released by MGM during the aegis of Dore Schary. It was directed by John Sturges who had also directed *Mystery Street* and *The People Against O'Hara*. Unlike those earlier films, *Jeopardy's* milieu is virtually all plein-air (there is only one rather negligible night-time scene). Though it lacks the expressionistic touches of *The Hitch-Hiker* or the gut-wrenching suspense of *Wages of Fear*, both released in 1953, it might well have been termed a "sturdy little thriller" by contemporary critics.

In any case, it is a film whose structure is built upon a series of ironies: a pleasant vacation becomes a day in hell for the Stilwins; "Bienvenidos," Mexico's sign of welcome, is transformed into an invitation to disaster; Helen's inability to ask for a rope in proper Spanish from some peasants leads her into the clutches of Lawson; the gun Doug brings along to protect his family is used by Lawson to threaten his wife; and, finally, a hardened killer sets aside his selfishness in rescuing Doug and allowing Helen to remain with her husband. However, the film's central irony is that Helen is willing to commit adultery to save the life of the husband she loves. The fact that this ostensible moral conundrum was played up heavily in the advertising of the time ("How far will a woman go . . .") tells us as much about the mores of 1950s America as it does about America of today. **BP**

JOHNNY ANGEL (1945)

Director: Edwin L. Marin. **Screenplay**: Steve Fisher adapted by Frank Gruber from the novel *Mr. Angel Comes Aboard* by Charles G. Booth. **Producer**: Jack Gross. **Director of Photography**: Harry J. Wild. **Music**: Leigh Harline. **Art Directors**: Albert S. D'Agostino, Jack Okey. **Editor**: Les Millbrook. **Cast**: George Raft (Johnny Angel), Claire Trevor (Lilah), Signe Hasso (Paulette), Lowell Gilmore (Sam Jewell), Hoagy Carmichael (Celestial O'Brien), Marvin Miller (Gustafson), Margaret Wycherly (Miss Drumm), J. Farrell MacDonald (Capt. Angel), Mack Gray (Bartender). **Completed**: January 16. **Released**: RKO, December 27. 76 minutes.

Captain Johnny Angel discovers his father's ship abandoned and his father killed. He returns to his homeport of New Orleans to find the killer. The owner of Angel's ship, Gusty Gustafson, pampered since childhood by his nurse, Miss Drumm, does not take any interest in the murder mystery. However, Angel's friend, taxi driver Celestial O'Brien, helps him find a witness to the crime named Paulette. Celestial hides Paulette who reveals the true story: Capt. Angel had been forced by Gusty to carry contraband gold and was the victim of a mutiny led by his first mate and an unknown assailant who then killed the first mate, double-crossed the other mutineers, and escaped with the gold. By flattering Lilah, Gusty's wife who is infatuated with him, Johnny discovers that Gusty masterminded the crime. Johnny eventually confronts Gusty, who has survived being stabbed by Lilah and confesses to the killings, claiming that his wife badgered him into stealing the gold. Then Gusty prepares to shoot Johnny, but Miss Drumm kills him and is just about to shoot Lilah also when Johnny stops her and turns the two women over to the police.

The story and screenplay for this film were written by

Johnny Angel: *George Raft (center) as Johnny Angel.*

Steve Fisher and Frank Gruber, veterans of pulp fiction with close ties to film noir. Also, *Johnny Angel* was photographed by Harry Wild, following in the wake of Nick Musuraca who pioneered the RKO noir style with *Stranger on the Third Floor.* That style is most notable here in the threatening ambience of Raft's nighttime foray into his father's abandoned ship and down the back streets of New Orleans. Claire Trevor, drawing upon the iconic value of previous roles, epitomizes the lethal black widow, while Marvin Miller, ruthless in a petulant way in *Brasher Doubloon* and *Dead Reckoning*, is reduced here to the role of a infantile adult, manipulated by a sensual, avaricious wife and spoiled by an overbearing mother-figure who appropriately kills the monster she helped to create. **BP**

JOHNNY COOL (1963)

Director: William Asher. **Screenplay**: Joseph Landon based on the novel *The Kingdom of Johnny Cool* by John McPartland. **Producer**: William Asher. **Executive Producer**: Peter Lawford (Chrislaw Productions). **Director of Photography**: Sam Leavitt. **Music**: Billy May, Les Vandyke [John Worsley]. **Art Director**: Frank T. Smith. **Editor**: Otto Ludwig. **Cast**: Henry Silva (Johnny Cool/Salvatore Giordano), Elizabeth Montgomery (Darien "Dare" Guiness), Richard Anderson (Correspondent), Jim Backus (Louis Murphy), Joey Bishop (Homes), Brad Dexter (Lennart Crandall), Wanda Hendrix (Miss Connolly), Marc Lawrence (Johnny Colini), John McGiver (Oscar B. "Oby" Hinds), Mort Sahl (Ben Morrow), Sammy Davis, Jr. ("Educated"), Telly Savalas (Vincenzo Santangelo), Joan Staley (Suzy), Frank Albertson (Bill Blakely), Elisha Cook, Jr. (Undertaker). **Released**: United Artists, October 2. 103 minutes.

Ex-WW II-partisan Salvatore Giordano grew up an orphan in Sicily. By the 1960s, he is a wanted man and is kidnapped by a corrupt Italian military. A look-alike is killed, and Giordano is spirited to Rome where deported American Mafia don, Colini, coerces him to be an assassin who will return to America to dispatch mob boss Santangelo, real estate developer Murphy, casino owners Hinds and Morrow and oil magnate Crandall who ratted him out to the crime commission. Giordano ends up in New York City as the new incarnation of Colini aka "Johnny Cool." Meeting fast-living socialite

"Dare" Guiness, who falls for him, he takes her under his wing. Cool kills Murphy, then jets to Vegas to eliminate Hinds and Morrow—but not before Morrow warns that boss Colini will have the same fate in store for him once he has completed his mission. Cool heads to Los Angeles to meet Guiness and bomb Crandall into oblivion. He arranges to rendezvous with Guiness in New York. However, after Cool machine-guns to death Santangelo in his Big Apple office, the still-in-California Guiness becomes rattled and tips off the remaining bosses. Captured, Cool has nothing to look forward to except slow death by torture, and, in the last scene, Guiness is picked up by the Feds for questioning.

A production tangential to the Sinatra Rat Pack, with various cronies involved both behind and in front of the camera (producer Lawford, actors Silva, Davis, Bishop, et. al.), *Johnny Cool* can't seem to decide if it wants to be a hard-boiled action noir or a goof on the genre. To be fair, it leans toward the former, only to be broken up by enjoyable yet pointless cameos by stars like Davis and Bishop. The script is too episodic as a whole, and, although the film captures a hard driving, pitiless verisimilitude, the piecemeal narrative serves to diffuse tension at key moments.

Director William Asher was the veteran of scads of disposable Frankie and Annette beach pictures as well as the *Bewitched* TV series starring then-spouse Elizabeth Montgomery. Later, he helmed the uncompromisingly perverse psycho-sexual thriller *Night Warning* (1983) with Susan Tyrell and Bo Svenson. However, in *Johnny Cool* Asher uses a surprisingly straightforward, no-nonsense style that is complemented by the generally good cast only to be sabotaged by a mediocre script. Characters begin to develop, then are hamstrung by too little back story, too much superficial dialogue or having to move arbitrarily onto the next set piece. Cool/ Giordano never quite cuts it as a tragic noir figure because his fall-from-grace is too ill defined and ambiguous. There is no transition illustrating how his common sense instinct for survival when he first comes to the USA mutates into egocentric megalomania by the climax. On the plus side, the picture has an effectively Spartan look with many on-location exteriors blending fairly well with stripped-to-the-bone studio interiors. The film deserves credit for its refreshingly fast-moving, violent *mise-en-scène*, with gritty, unsentimental echoes of some of the French

noir crime thrillers from the 1950s and early 1960s, not to mention homegrown noirs. It also seems a good guess that this was the archetypal film that inspired Italian producers to cast actor Silva in lead roles in numerous ultra-violent Italian crime pictures released during the late 1960s through the 1970s. **CD**

JOHNNY EAGER (1942)

Director: Mervyn LeRoy. **Screenplay**: John Lee Mahin and James Edward Grant, from his unpublished story. **Producer**: John W. Considine, Jr. **Director of Photography**: Harold Rosson. **Music**: Bronislau Kaper, Daniele Amfitheatrof. **Art Directors**: Cedric Gibbons, Stan Rogers. **Editor**: Albert Akst. **Cast**: Robert Taylor (Johnny Eager), Lana Turner (Lisbeth Bard), Edward Arnold (John Benson Farrell), Van Heflin (Jeff Hartnett), Robert Sterling (Jimmy Lanthrop), Patricia Dane (Garnet), Glenda Farrell (Mae Blythe), Barry Nelson (Lew Rankin), Henry O'Neill (A.J. Verne), Charles Dingle (A. Frazier Marco), Cy Kendall (Bill Halligan), Don Costello (Billiken), Paul Stewart (Julio). **Completed**: October 28, 1941. **Released**: February 19. 102 minutes.

In a taxi driver's uniform, Johnny Eager reports on his success in the legitimate world to parole officer A.I. Verne, who introduces to him two sociology students, Lisbeth Bard and Judy Sanford. Johnny returns to his cab and drives to his office at a new dog-racing track, which he plans to open soon with the help of bribed politicians. After taking care of the day's business with nightclub owner Lew Rankin and his associate Marco, he is then visited by his alcoholic lawyer, Jeff Hartnett, who baffles everyone with constant literary allusions. That night, Johnny threatens nightclub owner Rankin and finds Lisbeth at Rankin's club. He escorts her home and learns that she is the daughter of John Benson Farrell, the district attorney whose case against Eager sent him to the penitentiary. Farrell threatens to reimprison Johnny if he sees Lisbeth again. Insulted and hoping to blackmail Farrell, the gangster invites Lisbeth to his apartment. He stages a brutal fight between himself and Julio, calling out for her to shoot his assailant. Lisbeth complies and is shocked to discover she is capable of committing mur-

der. Meanwhile, Rankin struggles for control of the city's rackets. Johnny kills the renegade and hides from Rankin's associates and the police. Lisbeth suffers a mental breakdown over her alleged crime and Farrell begs Johnny to tell her the truth. But it is Jeff Hartnett who convinces Johnny to meet with Lisbeth and convince her that she is innocent of any crime. As Rankin's men close in, Lisbeth refuses to leave Johnny. Knocking her unconscious so that she will be safe, Johnny exposes himself to the police and is killed by a policeman he had once befriended.

In this early film noir, the supporting characters of Jeff Hartnett and Lisbeth Bard display more overt noir characteristics of disillusion and weakness than the protagonist, Johnny Eager. Hartnett is a wounded soul; a gangster's lawyer who realizes that he has betrayed himself by perverting his profession to serve the purposes of crime. He hides his self-hate behind an alcoholic haze and cryptic quotations, which the remorseless gangster, Johnny Eager, finds amusing but unintelligible. Lisbeth Bard is literally an innocent schoolgirl attracted to the underworld's excitement. Rich and secure, she complacently believes herself to be in control of her destiny. When she discovers herself capable of murder, she breaks with reality rather than cope. Even Lisbeth's powerful father, the district attorney, realizes that he does not control fate either as the gangster forces him to sacrifice his ideals to save his daughter. The charming and brash Johnny Eager is transformed when Jeff makes the racketeer realize that his power has corrupted him beyond what is necessary to survive and achieve his criminal goals. Significantly, however, Johnny's attempts to reverse the damage he caused Lisbeth is futile. She does not even hear his confession that Julio's "murder" was staged, and he must inflict more damage on her to save her life. As a surviving noir heroine, Lisbeth is permanently scarred. In a moment of existential self-immolation Johnny demands a more tangible punishment and proof that he is mortal. Yelling "Come and get me," he dies in the dark, wet street, killed by a policeman who was his friend but now fails to recognize him. **EW**

JOHNNY GUITAR (1954)

Director: Nicholas Ray. **Screenplay**: Philip Yordan from a novel by Roy Chanslor. **Executive Producer**: Herbert J. Yates. **Director of Photography**: Harry Stradling, Sr. **Music**: Victor Young. **Art Director**: James W. Sullivan. **Editor**: Richard L. Van Enger. **Cast**: Joan Crawford (Vienna), Sterling Hayden (Johnny "Guitar" Logan), Mercedes McCambridge (Emma Small), Scott Brady (Dancing Kid), Ward Bond (McIvers), Ben Cooper (Turkey Ralston), Ernest Borgnine (Bart Lonergan), John Carradine (Tom), Royal Dano (Corey), Frank Ferguson (Marshal Williams), Paul Fix (Eddie), Rhys Williams (Mr. Andrews), Ian MacDonald (Pete), Robert Osterloh (Sam the dealer) Trevor Bardette (Jenks), Will Wright (Ned the bank clerk), Dennis Hopper, Denver Pyle, Clem Harvey, Sheb Wooley (Posse). **Location**: Sedona, Arizona. **Completed**: December 14, 1953. **Released**: Republic Pictures, May 27. 110 minutes.

Saying he was promised a job, a drifter who calls himself Johnny Guitar rides into Vienna's gambling establishment during a windstorm. Vienna's supper with railroad man Andrews is next interrupted by a posse led by rancher

Johnny Eager: *Johnny Eager (Robert Taylor) and Lisbeth (Lana Turner).*

Johnny Guitar: *Emma Small (Mercedes McCambridge, center) looking for stage robbers.*

Johnny Guitar: *Johnny Guitar (Sterling Hayden) and Vienna (Joan Crawford).*

McIvers and egged on by Emma Small looking for stage robbers and finally by their prime suspects, the "Dancing Kid" and his colorful cohorts. Although having no proof, McIvers gives them all twenty-four hours to leave the territory. Since their mine is played out, a resentful Dancing Kid suggests they rob a bank on the way out of town. As it happens, Vienna is there getting money to pay off her men so that she can wait alone for the railroad. Unable to escape because of blasting for the rail construction. the robbers head back to their claim but a wounded young Ralston falls behind and ends up at Vienna's. After she hides him, the posse returns and finds him. They lynch Ralston but Johnny saves Vienna, and they make their way to the hideout. The Dancing Kid is told that the guitarist is actually notorious gunslinger Johnny Logan, Vienna's old flame. When the posse surrounds them, Lonergan betrays the others. Emma shoots the Dancing Kid before Vienna kills her. The disheartened posse permits Vienna and Johnny to leave.

The reputation of Nicholas Ray's *Johnny Guitar* depends largely on its purported anti-blacklist sub-text. Certainly scenarist Philip Yordan had a long association with blacklisted colleagues, for whom he sometimes ghosted; but he often farmed out early drafts of scripts to others without regard to anything but their ability to write quickly and to specification. On this movie because of Joan Crawford, its highly paid and highly demanding star, Yordan actually spent a lot of time on location helping Ray to alter the script on a day-to-day basis. Certainly one could read some of the dialogue between Johnny and Vienna—"A posse isn't people . . . a posse is an animal; it moves like one and thinks like one." "They're men looking for somebody to hang"—as a thinly veiled discussion of the Congressional red hunts. One could also imagine that the scene in which the posse cajoles Turkey into "naming names" by promising leniency, until he says Vienna was part of the robbery plan although he knows she was not, is meant to mirror the methodology of HUAC.

Since Herbert Yates' main concern as Republic ventured cautiously into the realm of multi-million dollar budgets was to keep a lid on costs, Ray had more creative latitude than at RKO or on loan to Columbia and was more concerned with drama than political allegory. Crawford wanted to portray Vienna mannishly—as Sam the dealer says, "I've never seen a woman who was more a man: she thinks like one, acts like one"—so Ray created a minor gender reversal between her and Sterling Hayden as Johnny Guitar/Logan. The result is at once quasi-noir and quasi-operatic. Many commentators have remarked on Yordan's borrowing of motifs from *Casablanca* (Vienna as a gun-toting Rick) and *To Have and Have Not*, but there is no foreign intrigue in *Johnny Guitar*. With Crawford's demand as a springboard, Ray puts a spin on genre conventions. There is certain redundancy in the simple exchange where Emma tells Vienna, "I'm going to kill you" and gets the laconic response, "I know—if I don't kill you first," because that much is clear to the viewer from the first. When Ray dresses the posse all in black and Vienna in white, it is not for any facile or symbolic reason, as it is a visual reminder of the inevitable gunfight at the film's conclusion.

Ultimately there is a much clearer line to the motifs that Ray had explored in his earlier pictures and that are typical of the noir vision. Like Nick Romano in *Knock on Any Door*, young Turkey seems determined to live fast, die young, and leave a good-looking corpse. It is Johnny Guitar who sounds Ray's familiar refrain: "I'm a stranger here myself." While Chanslor's novel (and first draft script) may have been a pastiche Western, Ray changes emphasis and turns the disdainful "I'm not the fastest gun west of the Pecos" into a deconstruction of genre expectations. In a noir Western, Ray can use the tough guy persona established by Hayden in both earlier noir and earlier Westerns and let such a line play self-consciously. Once expectations are undercut, the revelation that Logan, who is lurking beneath Guitar's troubadour persona, could well be the fastest gun west of the Pecos turns the disclaimer into irony, which is deepened when Vienna remarks that Logan is not just fast but "gun crazy." By emotionally transposing a troubled character type that closely resembles Jim Wilson in his earlier noir *On Dangerous Ground,* and by putting him in a milieu where violent behavior and gun-craziness go with the territory, Ray seamlessly blends noir style and Western iconography. Finally, as with many noir figures, few of Ray's characters can ever shed the deterministic burden of the past. Unlike Bowie and Keechie, Vienna and Logan survive their brief interlude as a fugitive couple. Still, as the protagonist in François Truffaut's fugitive couple movie *La Sirène du Mississippi* (1969) observes, *Johnny Guitar* is noir because it's a Western focused not on horses and six-shooters but on characters and emotion. **AS**

JOHNNY O'CLOCK (1947)

Director: Robert Rossen. **Screenplay**: Robert Rossen from an unpublished story by Milton Holmes. **Producer**. Edward G. Nealis (J.E.M. Productions). **Director of Photography**: Burnett Guffey. **Music**: George Duning. **Art Directors**: Stephen Goossom, Cary Odell. **Editors**: Warren Low, Al Clark. **Cast**: Dick Powell (Johnny (O'Clock), Evelyn Keyes (Nancy Hobbs), Lee J. Cobb (Inspector Koch), Ellen Drew (Nelle Marchettis), Nina Foch (Harriet Hobbs), Thomas Gomez (Pete Marchettis), John Kellogg (Charlie), Jim Bannon (Chuck Blayden). **Completed**: September 6, 1946. **Released**: Columbia, March 27. 95 minutes.

Johnny O'Clock is a junior partner in a New York gambling casino owned by Pete Marchettis. A bribed policeman, Chuck Blayden, decides to replace Johnny in the organization and also breaks off with his girlfriend, Harriet, who works in the gambling club. Blayden disappears after Harriet's body is found in her apartment, an apparent suicide. The woman's sister, Nancy, arrives in town to investigate and is attracted to Johnny O' Clock. Marchettis' wife, Nelle, also loves Johnny and presents him with a diamond watch that is identical to her husband's. Inspector Koch suspects both Johnny and Marchettis of murder when Blayden's body is found in the river and the coroner discovers that Harriet was poisoned. Marchettis learns of Johnny's diamond watch and orders his thugs to eliminate his partner. But Johnny escapes and confronts Marchettis to dissolve their business arrangement. Marchettis shoots Johnny, who retaliates and kills the senior partner. When Johnny rejects Nelle, she informs the police that Johnny murdered her husband in cold blood. Surrounded outside the office by the police, Johnny takes Inspector Koch hostage and plans to escape. But when he sees that Nancy is also outside, he realizes that their love is too important to waste by spending the rest of their lives as fugitives and gives himself up.

After writing a series of gangster thrillers in the 1930s and one particularly noir film in the mid-1940s, *The Strange Love of Martha Ivers,* Robert Rossen turned his attention to the possibility of serving as director as well and *Johnny O'Clock* was his first directorial effort. He utilized many of the standard conventions of the noir period including the characteristic photographic style, the use of the tough guy, and the contemporary underworld setting. Even the choice of Dick Powell to portray the slick gambler who had fallen on bad times referenced Powell's noteworthy turn as Philip Marlowe in *Murder, My Sweet*. However, the film is emotionally detached and the character portrayed by Powell was not obviously vulnerable. It is through a sense of the protagonist's weakness that most films approach the noir classification. But *Johnny O'Clock* is not privy to this important attitude. Although the motivations are correct

Johnny O'Clock: *Nelle (Ellen Drew) and husband Pete Marchettis (Thomas Gomez).*

and the settings are particularly corrupt and ambiguous, the elements lack a sense of fear and powerlessness that Rossen managed to capture in some of his later films, particularly *Body and Soul.* **CM**

JOHNNY STOOL PIGEON (1949)

Director: William Castle. **Screenplay**: Robert L. Richards from a story by Henry Jordan. **Producer**: Aaron Rosenberg. **Director of Photography**: Maury Gertsman. **Music**: Milton Schwarzwald. **Art Director**: Bernard Herzbrun, Emrich Nicholson. **Editor**: Ted J. Kent. **Cast**: Howard Duff (George Morton), Shelley Winters (Terry Stewart), Dan Duryea (Johnny Evans), Tony Curtis (Joey Hyatt), John McIntire (Nick Avery), Leif Erickson (Pringle), Barry Kelley (William McCandles), Wally Maher (T.H. Benson), Hugh Reilly (Charlie). **Released**: Universal, September 22. 76 minutes.

Narcotics agent George Morton knows his only chance to crack an international drug ring is by springing former dealer Johnny Evans (the stool pigeon of the title), whom he helped to put in Alcatraz. The cop-and-convict team of unwilling partners travels first from San Francisco to Vancouver then with gang moll Terry Stewart in tow to a dude ranch near Tucson run by the mob. Although young Joey Hyatt suspects something is not right, Morton and Evans maintain their cover until a final reckoning during a dangerous drug buy at the Nogales border crossing.

Federal agents risking mortal danger to infiltrate criminal syndicates supply one of the basic templates for film noir. The crooks can variously be counterfeiters as in the Anthony Mann/John Alton *T-Men* or traffickers in illegal laborers as in *Border Incident* or here in *Johnny Stool Pigeon* heroin smugglers. *Johnny Stool Pigeon* was shot by Maury Gerstman, veteran of Universal B-Westerns, and directed by William Castle, who went on to become the king of cheapie horror flicks and produce *Rosemary's Baby* after an apprenticeship in film noir. His *When Strangers Marry* may be the best of his noir efforts.

Johnny Stool Pigeon is a creditable if not especially memorable effort, thanks mostly to a cast headed by Dan Duryea,

Howard Duff, Shelley Winters and even a young Tony Curtis, billed as "Anthony" but not as anonymous as he was in the same year's *Criss Cross* where his manic rhumba with Yvonne De Carlo went uncredited. The plot's tension depends on the possibility of Morton being sold out by Evans or one of them being recognized by Hyatt—Curtis spends much the movie knitting his brows in an effort to remember where he'd seen Morton before. As a straight arrow, Duff's performance is straightforward and effective, much like his debut in *Brute Force* but not as not complex as his more ambivalent roles in movies like *Shakedown* or *The Naked City*, where his character was a slithery chameleon. The reliable Duryea relies on the sneering and cynical persona perfected working for Fritz Lang, and Winters adds a dash of femme fatale. It all adds up to a fairly routine but efficient 75 minutes of noir. **BMV**

JOURNEY INTO FEAR (1943)

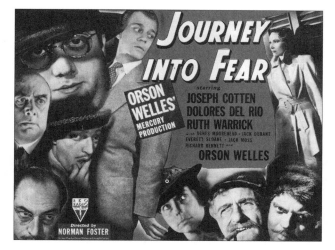

Director: Norman Foster and [uncredited] Orson Welles. **Screenplay**: Joseph Cotten, Orson Welles, Richard Collins, Ben Hecht from the novel by Eric Ambler. **Producer**: Orson Welles. **Executive Producer**: George J. Schaefer (Mercury Productions). **Director of Photography**: Karl Struss. **Music**: Roy Webb, Rex Dunn. **Art Directors**: Albert S. D'Agostino, Mark-Lee Yirk. **Editor**: Mark Robson. **Cast**: Joseph Cotten (Howard Graham), Dolores Del Rio (Josette Martel), Orson Welles (Col. Haki), Ruth Warrick (Stephanie Graham), Agnes Moorehead (Mrs. Mathews), Everett Sloane (Kopeikin), Jack Moss (Banat), Jack Dutant (Gogo), Eustace Wyatt (Dr. Haller), Frank Readick (Matthews), Edgar Barrier (Kuvetli), Stefan Schnabel (Purser), Hans Conreid (Oo Lang San, the Magician). **Released**: RKO, March 18. 68 minutes.

The attempted assassination of Howard Graham, a naval engineer, is the first hint of a dangerous Nazi conspiracy. Warned by Col. Haki, a Turkish military official, that he has information vital to the Nazi war effort, Graham is hastily ushered out of Turkey and befriended by the evasive Kopeikin and an exotic dancer named Josette. Graham's escape route takes him aboard a sinister steamship populated by a host of suspicious characters. Banat, a grotesque Nazi assassim silently watches Graham throughout the trip, and a variety of agents and double agents are promptly disposed of until Graham is unsure of everyone he meets.

Finally captured by Nazi agents, Graham makes a desperate escape and rejoins his wife, who is unaware of the intrigue surrounding her husband. Banat follows Graham and chases him onto the rain-drenched ledge of a hotel three stories above the street. Graham is saved thanks to the efforts of Col. Haki and the rain which obscures Banat's vision during a barrage of gunfire, causes him to fall to his death.

Deeply rooted in a tradition of international intrigue, *Journey into Fear* is a marginal film noir. The whimsical flavor of Graham's narration is a deflating counterpoint to the threatening noir atmosphere and sardonic characterization exhibited by Banat. Orson Welles' Mercury company produced the film, with Welles contributing to the direction and ultimate visual quality of the film. It is an early noir film, but *Journey into Fear* presents interesting flashes of a sensibility that Welles would develop more fully in *The Stranger* and *The Lady from Shanghai*. The overriding sense of dread that permeates *Journey into Fear* combines with a visual style that uses contrasts between light and shade as a metaphor for the instability and futility typical of the noir universe. However, few films dealing with this type of intrigue are fully realized film noir because they require a broad base of action and a more socialized hero, which forces the film to reject the alienated attitudes found in noir films of the 1940s for a more conventional bias. **CM**

KANSAS CITY CONFIDENTIAL (1952)

Director: Phil Karlson. **Screenplay**: George Bruce, Harry Essex, Phil Karlson, John Payne from an unpublished story by Harold R. Greene and Rowland Brown. **Producer**. Edward Small (Associated Players and Producers). **Director of Photography**: George E. Diskant. **Music**: Paul Sawtell. **Art Director**: Edward L. Ilou. **Editor**: Buddy Small. **Cast**: John Payne (Joe Rolfe), Coleen Gray (Helen), Preston Foster (Timothy Foster), Dona Drake (Teresa), Jack Elam (Harris), Neville Brand (Kane), Lee Van Cleef (Tony), Mario Seletti (Timaso), Howard Negley (Andrews), Ted Ryan (Morelli), George Wallace (Olson), Carleton Young (Assistant District Attorney Martin). **Completed**: August, 1952. **Released**: United Artists, November 28. 98 minutes.

Timothy Foster is a retired Kansas City police captain embittered by his meager pension. He uses incriminating evidence to blackmail three felons into robbing an armored car. Foster remains anonymous and brings the men together wearing masks to conceal their identities. They use a facsimile florist's van as a getaway vehicle. The police arrest the driver of the real van, an ex-convict named Joe Rolfe, question him brutally about the robbery, but eventually release him for lack of evidence. Still under suspicion, Rolfe uses his former underworld contacts to track one of the robbers to Tijuana. When that man is killed by local police, Rolfe assumes his identity. At a rendezvous point in a resort town further south Rolfe makes the acquaintance of Foster's daughter Helen. Rolfe discovers that Foster is planning to turn in the men and collect the insurance company's reward, as well as embarrass the Kansas City police force. A gun battle breaks out in which the two accomplices are killed and Foster is mortally wounded. When Helen arrives with the police, Rolfe lies and credits Foster with helping find the robbers and clear his name.

Independent producer Edward Small, perhaps best known for a series of comedies starring Dennis O'Keefe and directed by Allan Dwan in the mid-1940s, crossed over to film noir with *Raw Deal* (also with O'Keefe and directed by Anthony Mann). *Kansas City Confidential* is the first of two noirs that Small produced with actor John Payne and director Phil Karlson, who followed this film with *99 River Street*. Both features combine elements of the docu-noir style developed by Louis De Rochemont and Mark Hellinger. The narrative scheme, which brings a bitter ex-cop and a bitter ex-con by chance into direct conflict, not only reverses their previous roles as criminal and policeman but ironically keeps them unaware of the other's true identity and purpose until the film's conclusion. As in his other noirs with Payne, *99 River Street* and *Hell's Island,* Karlson uses physical violence and

Kansas City Confidental: *The incognito robbers.*

Payne's hard-bitten screen persona to evoke the conflicting forces of menace and endurance at work in the noir underworld. In *Kansas City Confidential* the use of character actors Jack Elam, Lee Van Cleef, and Neville Brand— all frequently on view in the gallery of noir criminals—as the actual robbers provide daunting antagonists for Payne.

Like Galt in *The Dark Corner*, Rolfe is made a suspect and nearly destroyed by unknown forces, forces which he will discover bore him no personal malice. His unrelenting and brutal search is both a moral vindication and a simple assertion of existential outrage. Because Rolfe's disruption of Foster's plans can be seen as unwitting, the ultimate irony of *Kansas City Confidential* is that Rolfe brings down the same type of mischance—albeit more deadly—that Foster had visited on him from the same "unknowing" position. Thus each man in turn becomes the deterministic key to the other's destiny with Foster, the ultimate antagonist in this noir melodrama, appropriately becoming the final victim of the fatal mechanism that he set in motion. **AS**

KEY LARGO (1948)

Director: John Huston. **Screenplay**: Richard Brooks and John Huston from the play by Maxwell Anderson. **Producer**: Jerry Wald. **Director of Photography**: Karl Freund. **Music**: Max Steiner. **Art Director**: Leo K. Kuter. **Editor**: Rudi Fehr. **Cast**: Humphrey Bogart (Frank McCloud), Edward G. Robinson (Johnny Rocco), Lauren Bacall (Nora Temple), Lionel Barrymore (James Temple), Claire Trevor (Gaye Dawn), Thomas Gomez (Curley), Harry Lewis (Toots), John Rodney (Deputy Sawyer), Marc Lawrence (Ziggy), Dan Seymour (Angel), Monte Blue (Ben Wade), Jay Silver Heels,

Key Largo: Frank McCloud (Humphrey Bogart), Gaye Dawn (Claire Trevor), and Nora Temple (Lauren Bacall).

Rodric Redwing (Osceola Brothers). **Completed**: March 13, 1948. **Released**: Warner Bros., July 16. 100 minutes.

Frank McCloud, an ex-army officer, comes to Key Largo and stays at a run-down hotel owned by invalid James Temple. Living with Temple is his widowed daughter-in-law, Nora, whose husband had served under McCloud. Frank is present when the hotel is taken over by gangster Johnny Rocco and his henchmen. Although he has the chance to kill Rocco, McCloud is too disillusioned by his war experience to act. A hurricane hits the island, which panics Rocco. Frank is outraged by Rocco's treatment of his alcoholic mistress Gaye Dawn and gets beaten when he tries to help her. To protect Temple and Nora, Frank agrees to pilot a boat to Cuba for Rocco and his henchmen. Once at sea, Frank arms himself and kills Rocco. Slightly wounded, Frank heads back to Key Largo and Nora.

In *Key Largo* Edward G. Robinson returns to the gangster persona he created in *Little Caesar* almost two decades earlier. Robinson brings to Johnny Rocco all the swagger and propensity for violence of Rico Bandello. However, Rocco and his gang are not young anymore but clearly relics of an old order that has passed. Based on a Maxwell Anderson's blank-verse play, *Key Largo* is updated from the original's 1930s time frame into gangster-gothic. Director John Huston retains some of Anderson's poetic touches and Robinson as Rocco is evil incarnate. With its unusual setting, the gangsters are not in a dark city but in an isolated, shabby hotel on one of the Florida keys. The exotic scenery, the storm, and the claustrophobic feel as the characters ride out the hurricane in the hotel lounge create a heavy atmosphere which combines with the compressed time frame to sustain considerable tension. Using Humphrey Bogart and Lauren Bacall in the equally alienated roles of a disillusioned veteran and an embittered widow provides a short-cut for their romantic attraction, which the audience of the era immediately presumed from their real-life relationship and former roles in noir films like *The Big Sleep* and *Dark Passage*.

As individual character and stereotype, the gangster is typically a complete anti-romantic, often both sadist and a misogynist. Hating women was part of Robinson's gangster image from the first—in fact *Little Caesar* had a homoerotic subplot—but at no other time is he as cruel to females as in *Key Largo* when he forces Gaye into her pathetic rendition of "Moaning Low" and then refuses to give her a drink. During the storm scene, when he suffers uncontrollable shakes, Robinson uses broad physical acting to reveal the emotional state of a character. His performance reflects the desperate nostalgia of one who has been "a somebody." JC.

KEY WITNESS (1960)

Director: Phil Karlson. **Producer**: Kathryn Hereford. **Screenplay**: Alfred Brenner and Sidney Michaels based on a novel by Frank Kane. **Director of Photography**: Harold E. Wellman. **Music**: Charles Wolcott. **Art Directors**: George W. Davis and Malcolm Brown. **Cast**: Jeffrey Hunter (Fred Morrow), Pat Crowley (Ann Morrow), Dennis Hopper ("Cowboy" William L. Tompkins), Joby Baker ("Muggles"), Susan Harrison (Ruby), Johnny Nash (Apple), Corey Allen ("Magician"), Frank Silvera (Detective Rafael Torno), Bruce Gordon (Arthur Robbins), Terry Burnham (Gloria Morrow) Dennis Holmes (Phil Morrow), Harry Lauter (Hurley), Eugene Iglesias (Emelio Sanchez), Will J. Wright (Deputy Wright). **Release Date**: October 6. 81 minutes.

A real-estate agent, Fred Morrow, stops in an East LA diner and witnesses the switchblade killing of Emilio Sanchez by Cowboy and his gang (Muggles, Magician, and Apple). When no one else volunteers, Morrow becomes the state's key witness. Although the state gives Morrow anonymity, Cowboy's gang gets Morrow's name and address from a police officer they beat up. They give Morrow "the needle," demanding that he "tear up" his witness statements. They call him while he's shopping at Safeway, ram his rear bumper, threaten his wife at gun point, and luridly suggest raping his seven-year-old daughter. When that fails they toss a wrench through his window, slash car tires, attack his wife at Cowboy's arraignment, and try to kidnap his son. The law-abiding Morrow eventually perjures himself and refuses to identify Cowboy. After visiting his son at the hospital (who was wounded in a botched kidnapping), Morrow returns home to find Apple who now wants to testify for the state. The two argue, and Cowboy's gang arrives to kill them both. Morrow and Apple stand back to back and break "the circle," defeating Cowboy's gang just as detective Torno arrives to make the arrest.

Key Witness (1960) is a marginal noir, owing more to crime thrillers and the juvenile delinquent films of the 1950s. *Rebel without a Cause* bad-boys Corey Allen and Dennis Hopper have grown up but they haven't graduated: they're still menacing and threatening violence. Charles Wolcott's score pulses with a jazz undercurrent, and the opening-credit sequence borrows the pop-art presence of Saul Bass, imbuing the film with a bright ebullience that runs contrary to noir. Moreover, the gang's dialogue ripples with smatterings of forced bebop and Beat musings. Cowboy prattles, "I just came from a bop, I just came from a battle, huh? I don't want my hair messed up." Muggles snaps his fingers as if he were at a bongo jamboree before throwing riddles Fred Morrow's way: "This is the watch bird, watch a boo-boo. Don't make a boo boo because this is the watch bird watching you." "Magician" doesn't say much; he just broods in the background.

Despite these fanciful ruptures to the noir aesthetic, the film succeeds as noir because of the characterization of Morrow and Phil Karlson's direction. Morrow is resilient, strong, and endures. He's an innocent man caught up in a violent web and tries to do the right thing. He witnesses a heinous crime, steps forward, even though his family, his very home, is threatened. Midway through the film, in a poetic moment, Karlson has Morrow walk outside his house and in the dark-lit night look upon the peaceful, quiet street of his suburb. He's achieved the American Dream, but there's menace in the air. Moments later, a wrench is tossed through the window of his house; he flees to the garage and finds his car tires slashed and "Key Witness" sprayed on the hood. His flight to the suburbs does not guarantee safety. The dangers of East LA gang violence can pursue anyone to any neighborhood, so a man has to take action. Perhaps because he's a veteran, Morrow has the strength to persevere. He may have perjured himself, but in the final showdown he finds personal redemption in protecting his home and his sense of self. Karlson's direction also builds on the menace, creating rhythmic suspense through several key scenes, including a high-speed chase on the Harbor Freeway, Ruby's attack on Mrs. Morrow in a phone booth at the municipal courthouse, and the final showdown as Apple and Morrow, back to back, take on the dangerous "circle" of Cowboy and his posse. **GT**

THE KILLER IS LOOSE (1956)

Director: Budd Boetticher. **Screenplay**. Harold Medford from the story by John and Ward Hawkins published in the *Saturday Evening Post*. **Producer**. Robert L. Jacks (Crown Productions). **Director of Photography**: Lucien Ballard. **Music**: Lionel Newman. **Art Director**: Leslie Thomas. **Editor**: George Gittens. **Cast**: Joseph Cotten (Sam Wagner), Rhonda Fleming (Lila Wagner), Wendell Corey (Leon "Foggy" Poole), Alan Hale, Jr. (Denny), Michael Pate (Chris Gillespie), Virginia Christine (Mary Gillespie), John Larch (Otto Flanders), John Beradino (Mac), Paul Bryar (Greg), Dee J. Thompson (Grace Flanders). **Completed**: August 27, 1955. **Released**: United Artists, March 2. 73 minutes.

Foggy Poole, so named because of his extreme myopia, is a bank clerk who acts as the inside man in a holdup. When the other robbers are caught, Poole is identified and the police arrest him. Poole's wife is accidentally shot and killed, and a devastated Poole blames the arresting officer, Sam Wagner. At his trial Poole's vengeful plan to kill Lila, the officer's wife, is revealed. Poole is a model prisoner and is soon sent to a prison farm from which he escapes. As he heads back to the city, it is obvious that his psyche has become dangerously deranged and he menaces several hostages. Meanwhile, Sam Wagner is worried and tries to marshal the forces of the police to protect Lila and capture Poole at the same time. Wagner reluctantly agrees to let Lila be used as bait, and Poole almost succeeds in killing her before he is shot down.

A Killer Is Loose is a characteristic thriller of the 1950s, possessing relatively naturalistic decor and lighting as compared to the preceding decade of film noir. Its tautness is the result of a concise screenplay, unmannered compositions, and effective crosscutting, The action is situated largely in unpoeticized suburban settings; and the only character given

The Killer Is Loose: *Leon "Foggy" Poole (Wendell Corey) and Grace (Dee J. Thompson).*

any distinctive treatment is Poole. Director Budd Boetticher is best known for his Randolph Scott Westerns, especifically those written by Burt Kennedy. They are consistently distinctive, but many of his other films are impersonal and routine. *The Killer Is Loose* immediately precedes the cycle of Westerns, which are followed by the director's only other significant contribution to the urban crime genre, *The Rise and Fall of Legs Diamond*. Both of the modern subjects confirm Boetticher's way with violence and relate to the Westerns in interesting ways. The charmingly pathological Legs Diamond is a logical and imaginative extension of the gregarious, colorful antagonists of the Westerns. Poole, on the other hand, is a thematic forerunner of the Randolph Scott hero, who typically seeks revenge for his wife's death. This coincidence is noteworthy because the characterization of Poole is the most outstanding quality of *The Killer Is Loose*. The thick glasses required by his myopia, immediately striking when associated with a villain, are a visual manifestation of helplessness; and actor Wendell Corey seizes on this trait as an opportunity to project a subtle pathos. **BL**

THE KILLER THAT STALKED NEW YORK (1951)

Director: Earl McEvoy. **Screenplay**: Harry Essex from a *Cosmopolitan* magazine article "Smallpox: The Killer That Stalked New York" by Milton Lehman. **Producer**: Robert Cohn. **Director of Photography**: Joseph Biroc. **Music**: Hans Salter. **Art Director**: Walter Holscher. **Editor**: Jerome Thoms. **Cast**: Evelyn Keyes (Sheila Bennet), Charles Korvin (Matt Krane), William Bishop (Dr. Ben Wood), Dorothy Malone (Alice Lorie), Lola Albright (Francie Bennet), Barry Kelley (Johnson), Carl Benton Reid (Commissioner Ellis), Ludwig Donath (Dr. Cooper), Art Smith (Moss), Whit Bissell (Sid Bennet), Roy Roberts (Mayor). **Released**: Columbia, January 4. 79 minutes.

Sheila Bennet returns to New York City from Cuba, where she has carefully followed her husband Matt's plan to obtain stolen diamonds and mail them back to him in the United States. She realizes that she is being followed by a federal agent but is not aware that she has contracted smallpox and is a carrier. Matt, who is having an affair with his wife's sister, Francie, instructs Sheila to stay at a hotel. Feeling ill, she sneaks out and, after losing the federal agent, visits the

The Killer That Stalked New York: *Matt Krane (Charles Korvin)
and Sheila Bennett (Evelyn Keyes).*

The Killers: *Kitty (Ava Gardner) and Swede (Burt Lancaster).*

office of Dr. Wood where she infects a young girl. The doctor treats Sheila's symptoms as a cold but later, when the young girl dies of smallpox, medical authorities realize that Sheila is a carrier and try to locate her. Sheila is staying with Matt but he does not inform her that the diamonds have arrived because he intends to double cross both Sheila and Francie. Dr. Woods and the federal agents realize they are searching for the same woman and trace her to her brother's flophouse. By now Sheila has discovered Matt's affair and his plans to leave town once he fences the diamonds. Though she realizes she is fatally ill, she perseveres in her decision to kill him, blaming him for her sister's suicide. Gun in hand, she confronts him in the darkened office of the fence, Moss, whom Matt has killed. She falters but Matt dies anyway when he falls from the ledge of the office building trying to escape from the police. Sheila then gives the doctor a full list of all the people she contacted before she succumbs to the disease.

The Killer That Stalked New York is one of the semi-documentary film noirs, complete with narration by Reed Hadley and location photography by the talented Joseph Biroc (who worked with a number of contributors to the noir cycle, including Robert Aldrich). As in *Kiss of Death*, the use of actual locales does not really detract from the noir style and Biroc adroitly captures the oppressive atmosphere of New York City, especially in the night scenes. By concentrating more on the criminal who becomes progressively sicker and alienated rather than on the efforts of the young doctor to combat the plague, *The Killer That Stalked New York* is considerably more noir than *Panic in the Streets*, an earlier film with a similar theme. At the time of this film's completion the conventions of the semi-documentary had become so well established that audiences came to expect a generous amount of location work. Unfortunately, the use of a stentorian narrator was becoming more and more a device for filmmakers to patch narrative gaps, as they do here. Of course, this film was based on an actual incident that resulted in the vaccination of most of New York City's inhabitants, but in extolling the rapid response of city, state and federal authorities to the "threat" of smallpox, *The Killer That Stalked New York* may well have played into the growing paranoia of the cold-war audience. **BP**

THE KILLERS (1946)

Director: Robert Siodmak. **Screenplay**: Anthony Veiller, Richard Brooks, John Huston based on the short story by Ernest Hemingway. **Producer**: Mark Hellinger. **Director of Photography**: Woody Bredell. **Music**: Miklós Rózsa. **Art Directors**: Jack Otterson, Martin Obzina. **Editor**: Arthur Hilton. **Cast**: Edmond O'Brien (Riordan), Ava Gardner (Kitty Collins), Albert Dekker (Colfax), Sam Levene (Lubinsky), John Miljan (Jake), Virginia Christine (Lilly), Vince Barnett (Charleston), Burt Lancaster (Swede), Charles D. Brown (Packy), Donald MacBride (Kenyon), Phil Brown (Nick), Charles McGraw (Al), William Conrad (Max), Queenie Smith (Queenie). **Completed**: June 28, 1946. **Released**: Universal, August 28. 105 minutes.

A pair of hired killers, Max and Al, walk into a small town diner expecting to see the Swede. When he doesn't show up, they go to his darkened room where despite having been warned, he waits to be shot. An insurance investigator Riordan learns of the murder's circumstances while following up a routine claim for a very minor amount of money and becomes obsessed with finding out why Swede would allow two men to murder him. He learns that the victim had been involved in a gang, headed by Colfax, which robbed a factory payroll. Riordan also learns that Swede double-crossed the others for a woman, Kitty Collins—Colfax's girlfriend—who in turn betrayed him. Depressed and broken the Swede buries himself in a small town. Out of sympathy for the dead man, Riordan devises a scheme to trap the gang leader Colfax along with Kitty Collins. In a shoot-out Colfax dies and Kitty is arrested.

Often cited as a quintessential 1940s noir, *The Killers* derives its inspiration from a purely literary—as opposed to hardboiled—source, a Hemingway short story. From the first, the film brings noir elements to bear as it visualizes the author's objective, realistic prose. The actors who portray the killers, William Conrad and Charles McGraw, completely typify the personae of the noir world. However, Heminway's story ends shortly after Swedes death. The remainder of the film uses this sequence to serve as a prologue in order to deal with the real story of why someone would lose the desire to live. Given somewhat free rein once

FATAL MEN

The archetypal female characters, the seductive femme fatale and bland but safe femme attrapée (often identified as the woman as redeemer), delineate the gendered landscape of classic film noir, a landscape consistently read as focused on unstable or threatened masculinity. But that focus on masculinity has somehow obscured that the same archetypal male characters are also present in these narratives. Just as the femme fatale, with her glamour, sexuality and seemingly outrageous desires, overwhelms her more subdued counterpart on screen, the homme fatal, played by enticing actors such as Robert Mitchum, Burt Lancaster or Humphrey Bogart, also renders his counterpart invisible. Like the femmes, the hommes fatals and attrapés of classic film noir have a choice in whether or not to participate in society. The futility of resisting the dominant social order during the noir years was reinforced by the film industry's own censorship organization, the Production Code Administration (PCA), which insisted that no crime or illicit sex could go unpunished. At the same time, industrial and social changes brought about by U.S. involvement in World War II caused a relaxation of Code enforcement, a situation that benefited the often violent and criminal narratives of film noir and perhaps allowed more ambiguity into the choices the hommes and femmes make. Burt Lancaster plays the homme fatal to Sam Levene's homme attrapé in *The Killers*. Robert Mitchum plays the homme fatal in the RKO productions *Out of the Past* and *Angel Face*, with the hommes attrapés portrayed by virtually unknown character actors, Richard Webb and Kenneth Tobey respectively.

The femme fatale may be fatal to the male protagonist in film noir, but her desires, her refusal to play the girl next door or doting wife, doom her to death, torture, jail, or if she eventually acquiesces, to marriage. Similarly, the homme fatal is most often identified as fatal to a woman; examples include roles played by Dennis O'Keefe in *Raw Deal* (1948), Jack Palance in *Sudden Fear* (1952), and Burt Lancaster in *Sorry, Wrong Number* (1948). But the homme fatal dooms himself as well. He usually wants more than legal forms of capitalism provide; he ensures his destruction by desiring a sexually dominant and demanding woman— "dynamite of the female sort." In this taxonomy, Humphrey Bogart's character Roy Earle in *High Sierra* (1941), Fred Mac Murray's Walter Neff in *Double Indemnity* (1944), Burt Lancaster's Swede in *The Killers*, and Steve in *Criss Cross* (1949), William Holden's Joe in *Sunset Boulevard* (1950), John Dall's Bart Tare in *Gun Crazy* (1950), and Mitchum's characters in *Out of the Past* and *Angel Face* are all hommes fatals, eventually destroyed by an industry standard that insisted, "[no] picture shall be produced which will lower the moral standards of those who see it. Hence the sympathy of the audience should never be thrown to the side of crime, wrong-doing, evil or sin." Part of what makes film noir so vibrant in the cultural imagination is the fact that these characters do garner the sympathy of the audience. Film noir presents the risks of resistance and submission to society's demands quite clearly. Those who resist are wildly alluring on screen; they live sexy and violent but short lives, sometimes narrating from the grave as the film begins, always dead by the final reel. Those who participate live grey and quietly devoted or desperate lives that extend beyond the plot that drives the film. The disjuncture between the alluring hommes and femmes fatals and the bland hommes and femmes attrapés produced meaning beyond the bounds of acceptable Code-imposed morality and values. They allow spectators to revel in resistance before reigning in desire in the final reel and help account for film noir's near mythic appeal. **JBW**

Burt Lancaster

Robert Mitchum

Dennis O'Keefe

Jack Palance

The Killers: *The Killers Al and Max (Charles McGraw, left, and William Conrad) question George (Harry Hayden).*

he went to Universal, Mark Hellinger brought to the development and casting process an attention to detail which made him a successful columnist in New York. Hellinger also discovered noir icon Burt Lancaster, to whom he gave his first role in this picture.

The sensibilities of Siodmak and Veiller and the hardboiled realism of Hellinger combine to exemplify the most interesting aspects of noir film making. Initially the structure of the film isolates *The Killers* from more conventional noir films. Utilizing a convoluted time structure, the story of Swede is unfolded in a series of disconnected flashbacks much in the same way as *Citizen Kane*. This use of time, disjointed and at times overlapping, creates an unusual texture for the film. The alienating disjunction felt by Swede and his subsequent surrender to the femme fatale Kitty Collins is selectively high-lighted by the flashback structure of the film.

The overwhelmingly corrupt universe into which the young boxer-turned-criminal is immersed is simply the noir world. The undercurrent of violence that runs through most noir films is paired here with existential anger which serves to create a chaotic environment, dark motives, and hopeless situations. No vindication or amelioration exists in *The Killers*. Rather, the entire structure of good and evil has been pared down to melodramatic essentials. Investigator Riordan uses the situation of Swede to move beyond the boring routine of his job and enter a world of corruption and chaos. His efforts produce the required results, yet nobody really triumphs. Riordan's outrage over Kitty's corruption and Swede's hopelessness is a personal not a social response. By the time *The Killers* was remade in 1964 with the same basic elements, the femme fatale and her heartless exploitation of a man's infatuation had lost most of its novely. After a score of films, this particularly noir characterization was degraded from archetype to cliché. **CM**

KILLER'S KISS (1955)

Director/Director of Photography/Editor: Stanley Kubrick. **Screenplay**: Kubrick, Howard Sackler. **Producers**: Kubrick and

Morris Bousel (Minotaur). **Music**: Gerald Fried. **Cast**: Frank Silvera (Vincent Rapallo), Jamie Smith (Davy Gordon), Irene Kane (Gloria Price), Jerry Jarret (Albert, the Fight Manager), Mike Dana, Felice Orlandi, Ralph Roberts, Phil Stevenson (Hoodlums), Julius Adelman (Owner of Mannequin Factory), David Vaughn, Alec Rubin (Conventioneers). **Released**: United Artists, November 2. 67 minutes.

Gloria, a dancer in a sinister nightclub, is ultimately befriended by Davy, a young boxer, when he rescues her from an apparent assault by her boss and lover, Vincent. They make plans to leave the city and begin a new life but the coziness of their newfound relationship is short-lived. Vincent, the owner of the nightclub where Gloria works, has "plans" for Gloria and does not like interference from outsiders, especially from a down-on-his-luck boxer. At every opportunity Vincent attempts to seduce his unwilling employee. Frustrated by Gloria's teasing but ultimate rejection of him for Davy, Vincent becomes violent. He has Davy's friend Jerry killed, thinking he is Davy. Vincent then kidnaps Gloria and takes her to a warehouse used to store dismantled mannequins and waits for Davy. The boxer and the grim nightclub owner engage in a brutal and deadly fight. Davey walks away alone and decides to leave the city and return home. At the last moment on the train platform, he is joined by Gloria and they leave together.

Killer's Kiss is Kubrick's second feature, and it displays a visual unity unusual in a low-budget, independently produced film. The atmosphere Kubrick creates in the film is dark and unwholesome; an overwhelming sense of violence lurks below the surface of the people populating the New York of *Killer's Kiss*. Much of the film, however, is an experiment. Kubrick's use of obtuse flashbacks and surreal nightmare sequences, presented on negative film stock, give the film an alienating visual quality. Yet the most striking element of *Killer's Kiss* is its tendency to associate sex and violence, as illustrated by the attempted seduction of Gloria, which is accelerated by the brutal prizefight on television and in the finale in which disjointed parts of female mannequins and a fire axe are used as weapons in a fistfight. **CM**

THE KILLING (1956)

Director. Stanley Kubrick. **Screenplay**: Stanley Kubrick with additional dialogue by Jim Thompson from the novel The *Clean Break* by Lionel White. **Producer**: James B. Harris. **Director of Photography**: Lucien Ballard. **Art Director**: Ruth Sobotka Kubrick. **Editor**: Betty Steinberg. **Cast**: Sterling Hayden (Johnny Clay), Coleen Gray (Fay), Vince Edwards (Val Cannon), Jay C. Flippen (Marvin Unger), Marie Windsor (Sherry Peatty), Ted de Corsia (Randy Kennan), Elisha Cook, Jr. (George Peatty), Joe Sawyer (Mike O'Reilly), Timothy Carey (Nikki Arane), Jay Adler (Leo), Kola Kwarian (Maurice Oboukhoft), Joseph Turkell (Tiny), James Edwards (Parking Attendant). **Completed**: November, 1955. **Released**: United Artists, May 20. 84 minutes.

Ex-convict Johnny Clay, a small-time criminal, plots a daring race-track robbery with the assistance of a corrupt cop, Randy Kerman; the track bartender, Mike O'Reilly; the betting window teller, George Peatty; a chess-playing wrestler; and a sharpshooter, Nikki Arane. With the shooting of a race horse as a diversion, the heist goes off as planned. During the getaway the sharpshooter is killed. Sherry, the avaricious wife of the timid teller, has learned of the plan and tipped off her boyfriend. He and a crony attempt to rob the gang members when they meet to divide the loot. All die in a shoot-out except for the mortally wounded teller who staggers home and murders his unfaithful wife. Clay arrives late at the scene of the slaughter and takes the money. He is apprehended at the airport, when the money-laden suitcase falls off a baggage cart and scatters the bills in the wind.

The Killing presents what has become a familiar Stanley Kubrick theme: the fallibility of man and his plans. As they do in non-noir films that brought him fame, from *Dr. Strangelove* to *2001: A Space Odyssey*, the perfect enterprise, complete with contingency plans, falls to pieces. Whether brought down by greed or simple human error, the consequences are usually fatal, although *The Killing* does reduce a disproportionate number of its protagonists to bullet-ridden corpses.

Detailing a robbery through the eyes of the participants or an investigator is a device popularized by 1940s film noir. The flashback is a standard narrative ploy in many noir films, such as *The Killers, Dead Reckoning,* and *Out of the Past.* Where *The Killing* differs most strikingly from such predecessors is in its manipulation of time in bits and pieces. As the viewer is introduced to the various members of the gang and the roles they will play in the holdup, elements of the narrative are revealed. Once a character is established, the film leaps backwards, and picks up another character until all the component parts come together like the pieces of a jigsaw puzzle. This motif is again used for the robbery itself. Using a shot of dray horses pulling the starting gate into position for the race as a time reference, we see how each gang member fulfills his function until the robbery is completed. It was a unique structure at the time and effectively solved the problem of showing several actions occurring simultaneously.

Staging, lighting, and cutting create and sustain a raw, nervous style that may sometimes seem forcedly hardboiled but yields many memorable touches, such as the grotesquely grinning rubber clown mask Clay uses to hide his face, the offbeat puppy-loving sharpshooter played by Timothy Carey, whose permanent death rictus of a smile foreshadows his own demise; or simply the shrieking parrot that accompanies the marital squabbles of the Peattys. **JB**

A KISS BEFORE DYING (1956)

Director: Gerd Oswald. **Screenplay**: Lawrence Roman based on the novel *A Kiss Before Dying* by Ira Levin. **Producer**: Robert L. Jacks (Crown Productions). **Director of Photography**: Lucian Ballard. **Music**: Lionel Newman. **Art Director**: Addison Hehr. **Editor**: George Gittens. **Cast**: Robert Wagner (Bud Corliss), Jeffrey Hunter (Gordon Grant), Virginia Leith (Ellen Kingship), Joanne Woodward (Dorothy Kingship), Mary Astor (Mrs. Corliss), George Macready (Leo Kingship), Robert Quarry (Dwight Powell), Howard Petrie (Howard Chesser, Chief of Police), Bill Walker (Bill, the Butler), Molly McCart (Annabelle Koch), Marlene Felton (Medical Student). **Locations**: Downtown; Tucson, Arizona; Inspiration Consolidated Copper Company, Miami; Arizona; Tucson Mountain Park, Arizona; University of Arizona, Tucson, Arizona; Valley National Bank Building, Tucson, Arizona (Lufton municipal building). **Released**: United Artists, June 12. 94 minutes.

Bud and Dorie are having a secret affair. With a legitimate marriage, he will fulfill his dream of becoming wealthy at her father's copper mining company. However, she gets pregnant and doesn't care that her father, Leo, will disown her. Bud asks her to meet him at the marriage license bureau. He takes her to the building's rooftop and pushes her off. He makes her death look like suicide. Next he gets engaged to Ellen, Dorie's sister. Ellen figures out Dorie thought she was going to marry someone, and he killed her. She tracks down Dwight, an ex-boyfriend of Dorie's, and accuses him of the murder. He denies it. Dwight goes to his dorm room to get the address of Dorie's next boyfriend. Bud, who has been following Ellen, is waiting there. He shoots Dwight, making it look like Dwight committed suicide in remorse for killing Dorie. Gordon, the police chief's nephew and once Dorie's tutor, discovers Dwight couldn't have killed Dorie, so he had no reason kill himself. Evidence against Bud mounts. Desperate to avoid arrest, he tries to murder Ellen, but he is accidentally killed instead. Gordon has longed for Ellen since they met, but it is unclear what their future holds in store.

The Killing: *George Peaty (Elisha Cook, Jr.) and his wife Sherry (Marie Windsor).*

A Kiss Before Dying: Gordon Grant *(Jeffrey Hunter), Dorothy Kingship (Joanne Woodward), and Bud Corliss (Robert Wagner).*

Although *A Kiss Before Dying* recalls *A Place in the Sun*, a significant difference is that in *A Place* there's no question that men love women (as mothers, girlfriends, wives, or daughters), whereas in *A Kiss* a key question is whether Bud or Leo is capable of sincere affection for women. Unlike George Eastman, Bud doesn't have a benevolent rich uncle to help him get ahead. He only has will power, signified each time he hunches his shoulders (he'll do whatever it takes, including murder) and by a framed newspaper article that says in school he was voted the most ambitious and the most likely to succeed. In the opening scene the camera pans through his bedroom until it's above Bud, who's looking down at the back of Dorie's head. She's not important enough to be seen; she's only a means for him to get a place in the Kingship copper company. Bud's working class mother embarrasses him. He recoils at her tastelessness in clothes and unsophisticated conversation. Although *A Kiss Before Dying* brims with bright colors—especially orange, yellow and light blue—Dorie's sports car and his mother's hair are the color of copper. Since this color associates the women with Bud's goal, it objectifies them, reinforcing that they serve to help him realize his ambition. Because Dorie is a means to an end, if Bud has to get rid of her, he'll use Ellen instead. If Bud has to murder Ellen, too, then he'll advance himself without marrying any of Leo's daughters. (In Ira Levin's novel, Bud murders two sisters and tries to kill a third.) Just before Bud attacks Ellen, he tells her, "Your father and I will grieve together. We'll have that to share between us." However, Bud not only fails to kill Ellen, but also at the conclusion of the film he and Leo no longer share a clump of ore where there should be a heart.

Bud may not change during the movie, but the transformation of Leo from a heartless to a sensitive father is central to the second half of the film. Dorie and Ellen disdain him because he divorced their mother, "sick and all," after she'd made "one little slip." Since the police believe Dorie committed suicide, Leo accepts Gordon's advice not to look for the man she has been dating, to avoid stimulating "talk" about her death. Adding insult to injury in Ellen's view, Leo refuses to take with him the "valuables" found in Dorie's purse. He tells the police chief, "Dispose of them as you see fit. I'd consider it a personal favor." Leaving the police station, he reaches to touch Ellen, but she moves away. When Ellen gives reasons Dorie didn't kill herself, Leo thinks she's "distorting the facts," and Gordon says her ideas are "farfetched." So she hunts the killer on her own.

The night scene where Ellen confronts Dwight shows the most noir style in the film. She's shot high overhead as she walks toward a bar and then crosses a wet street to an alley. There she is framed close up against a brick wall — her head's shadow looms behind her and another shadow angles across her chest. Presumably, the imagery presages her death because, if Dwight killed Dorie and he sees Ellen, he will kill her, too. Dwight does see her and chases her to the end of the alley, where a huge diagonal shadow runs down the wall and over her entire body. Dwight grabs her arms, as Bud later does when he tries to kill her. The noir style misleadingly suggests Ellen is in peril because, in fact, she fights back, shouting, "Let me go! Take your hands off me!" Ellen's resistance to Dwight is as strong as her insistence to Leo and Gordon that Dorie was murdered. When Ellen comes home, there's a volte-face in Leo's behavior toward her. Although she won't let him touch her, he shares her relief that Dorie didn't commit suicide. "If you're better, I'm fine," he smiles. After Ellen survives Bud's attack, Leo approaches her but doesn't touch her. She bumps into him as she walks past him. Neither says a word. They turn and face each other. Ellen puts her hand on Leo's arm. Completing their rapprochement, Leo gently holds hers. The finale isn't about Ellen and Bud or Ellen and Gordon. The conclusion of *A Kiss Before Dying* is that Leo at last has a heart and Ellen knows it. **DMH**

KISS ME DEADLY (1955)

Director/Producer: Robert Aldrich. **Screenplay**: A.I. Bezzerides from the novel by Mickey Spillane. **Executive Producer**: Victor Saville (Parklane Productions). **Director of Photography**: Ernest Laszlo. **Art Director**: William Glasgow. **Music**: Frank DeVol. **Editor**: Michael Luciano. **Cast**: Ralph Meeker (Mike Hammer), Albert Dekker (Dr. Soberin), Paul Stewart (Carl Evello), Maxine Cooper (Velda), Gaby Rodgers (Gabrielle/Lily Carver), Wesley Addy (Pat), Juano Hernandez (Eddie Yeager), Nick Dennis (Nick), Cloris

Kiss Me Deadly: *Velda (Maxine Cooper) embraces* homme fatal *Mike Hammer (Ralph Meeker)*.

Leachman (Christina), Marian Carr (Friday), Jack Lambert (Sugar), Jack Elam (Charlie Max), Jerry Zinneman (Sammy), Percy Helton (Morgue Doctor), Fortunio Bonanova (Carmen Trivago), Silvio Minciotti (Mover). **Completed**: December 23, 1954. **Released**: United Artists, May 18, 105 minutes.

Private investigator Mike Hammer picks up a woman named Christina who tells him, should anything happen to, "Remember me." Hammer's car is run off the road. Christina is killed by unseen assailants; but Hammer survives. After his friend Nick sets him up with a new car, Hammer drives around after disconnected leads. He ends up at the home of small-time hood Carl Evello where he turns down a pay-off to drop the case. He finds Christina's roommate Lily Carver but after he hides her in his apartment, he is abducted by Evello's men. At the gangster's beach house he encounters Dr. Soberin, whose voice Hammer recognizes as that of Christina's killer. Despite being given sodium pentothal, Hammer kills Evello and escapes. Interpreting the poem "Remember Me" by Christina Rossetti leads Hammer to the morgue and a key Christina had swallowed. That leads to a locker containing what his secretary Velda dubs "the great what's it," a box full of some white hot, growling element. With Velda and Carver both missing, Hammer heads back to the beach house, where he discovers Lily Carver has killed Soberin to gain control of the box. After Carver shoots Hammer and opens the container, the radioactive contents set her on fire and begin a chain reaction. A wounded Hammer finds and frees Velda and together they stumble into the surf as the house explodes. [**Note**: At some point in the 1960s the negative of *Kiss Me Deadly* was damaged and several shots from its ending were lost so that in new prints and the original video release it appeared that Hammer and Velda never got out of the house. As the script indicates and Aldrich confirmed on several occasions, the scenes in the surf were always meant to be in the movie. In 1997 a duplicate European negative was used to restore the ending.]

At the core of *Kiss Me Deadly* are speed and violence. The adaptation of Mickey Spillane's novel takes Mike Hammer from New York to Los Angeles, where it situates him in a landscape of somber streets and decaying houses even less inviting than those stalked by Spade and Marlowe in the preceding decades of Depression and War years. Much like Hammer's fast cars, the movie swerves frenziedly through a series of disconnected and cataclysmic scenes. As such, it typifies the frenetic, post-A-bomb L.A. and an era full of malignant undercurrents. It records the degenerative half-life of an unstable universe as it moves towards critical mass. When it reaches the fission point, the graphic threat of machine-gun bullets cutting through the front door of a house on Laurel Canyon in *The Big Sleep* in the 1940s is explosively superseded in the 1950s as a beach cottage in Malibu becomes ground zero.

From the beginning, *Kiss Me Deadly* is a true sensory explosion. In the pre-credit sequence, as Christina stumbles out of the pitch darkness her breathing fills the soundtrack with amplified, staccato gasps. Blurred metallic shapes flash by without stopping. She positions herself in the center of the roadway, until oncoming headlights blind her with the harsh glare of their high beams. Brakes grab, tires scream across the asphalt, and a Jaguar spins off the highway in a swirl of dust. A close shot reveals Hammer behind the wheel: over the sounds of her panting and a jazz piano on the car radio, the ignition grinds repeatedly as he tries to restart the engine. Finally, he snarls at the woman, "You almost wrecked my car! Well? Get in!"

As in Aldrich's first noir, *World For Ransom*, the shot selection and lighting immediately invoke the noir world. But the dark highway of the opening is a kind of narrative limbo: the elements of the plot have not yet been brought into line, let alone focused. Certainly, contemporary viewers brought with them expectations about character and plot both from the underlying novel and from the conventions of film noir. *Kiss Me Deadly* has no clearly defined landscape at this point to use as a textural reinforcement. The countryside and the rural gas station are all unidentified settings. They are open, shadowy, and, even within the fringes of the station's neon lights, menacing. Generically this last trait primes the viewer for Christina's murder under torture and Hammer's near death.

In terms of subject/object tension, the Aldrich/Bezzerides conception of Hammer is both more objective and "anti-Spillane." Spillane's use of first-person prose is certainly in the hardboiled tradition. For Spillane, Hammer's very name revealed all: a hard, heavy, unrelenting object pounding away mindlessly at social outcasts like two-penny nails. The filmmakers pointedly refine this archetype: Hammer does think, mostly about how to turn a buck. As Ralph Meeker's interpretation propels Hammer beyond the smugness and self-satisfaction of the novel into a blacker, more sardonic disdain for the world in general, the character becomes a cipher for all the unsavory denizens of the noir underworld. But a dichotomy between the audience's and the "hero's" viewpoints is building, creating a subject/object split which runs counter to the first person elements of the novel. Hammer first asks, "What's in it for me?" as he speaks to Pat Murphy in the corridor after the inquiry. That utterance completes the character composite: Hammer is certainly not like Callahan, not another selfless "Galahad" as he begins a quest for "something big," for the private eye's grail.

Hammer certainly is a quester. He is not an outsider in the noir underworld or any equivalent of a mythic "other world." If this is a foreign or alien milieu, Hammer is at home there. For Hammer, the dark streets and ramshackle buildings are a questing ground which is conspicuously detached from the commonplace material world. Deception is the key to this world. Deception not detection is Hammer's trade. His livelihood depends on the divorce frame-up and the generally shady deal. Deception is Lily Carver's game also, from the false name she assumes to the vulnerable pitch of her voice to the pathetic way she brings her hand up against her face like a wing of Christina's dead canary. Failure to deceive is what costs Christina and others their lives.

This deception and uncertainty, as in most noir films, lay the groundwork for *Kiss Me Deadly*'s melodramatic tension. The plot-line has all the stability of one of Nick the Mechanic's "Va-va-voom's," so inversion becomes a constant; and subsurface values become central concerns. In this milieu, the first "torpedo" set to go off when a car key is turned necessarily posits a second rigged to explode at a higher speed. From the viewer's objective vantage, the shift from one level of appearances to another is occasionally discernible. An early example is the transformation of the sensual Carver, first framed behind a bed post and swinging a hip up to expose more of her leg through the fold of the terry cloth robe, then becoming shrill and waif-like for Hammer's benefit. Usually, though, the viewer is also deceived.

For those on a quest in the noir underworld, instability is the overriding factor and disjunction is the rule. The sensational elements in *Kiss Me Deadly* follow this rule. The craning down and the hiss of the hydraulic jack as the screaming Nick is crushed under the weight of a car; the pillar of fire that consumes Lily Carver; the eerie growl of the black box; even a simple "Pretty pow!" as Nick jams a fist into his open palm—these random acts have no organizing principles. They transcend context to deliver a shock that is purely sensory. Still they fit homogeneously into the generic fabric and the subversive whole of the narrative. Most of *Kiss Me Deadly*'s visual devices are standard noir style: high and low angles, depth of field, constriction of the frame through foreground clutter. Like John Farrow, Siodmak, and Ophuls, Aldrich adds the long take or sequence shot. There are four examples of it in *Kiss Me Deadly*, all of which might be classed as interrogation scenes: Pat Murphy's first visit to Hammer's apartment, and Hammer's questionings of Harvey Wallace, Carmen Trivago, and Eddie Yeager. The specifics of the shots vary, from the slow traveling into close shot during the brief discussion with the truck driver, Wallace, to the elaborate tracking and panning in Hammer's apartment, shifting characters front to back and left to right in an uneasy search for equilibrium. In no sequence shot does Hammer get answers to everything he asks; yet each takes him to the brink of some discovery. As in *World for Ransom, The Big Knife*, and many non-noir Aldrich films, the trap is a key part of *Kiss Me Deadly*'s figurative scheme. Again, its constructs are primarily visual. For example, in the high angle long shot of Hammer outside Lily Carver's room, the dark foreground of stairway and balustrades are arrayed concentrically about Hammer's figure and seem to enclose him. Usages such as this contribute to *Kiss Me Deadly*'s figurative continuity of instability or inversion and the lurking menace, all set up in the opening sequences.

Kiss Me Deadly's dark metaphors also rely on explicit, aural fabric to complete the play of myth and anti-myth. The Christina Rossetti poem "Remember Me" is an explicit and recurrent example. Other background sounds are keyed to character. The Caruso recording with which Carmen Trivago sings is the Flotow opera, *Martha*. More classical music plays on the radio in Christina's room as the manager remarks, "She was

Kiss Me Deadly: *Lily Carver is incinerated.*

always listening to that station." A prize fight is being broadcast in the background when Evello and Sugar Smallhouse are killed at the beach house. While such sounds may not be as fully incorporated into the narrative structure as the poem is, all provide immediate textural contrast if not subsidiary meaning. The sibilant tone of Evello's gasp as he is killed echoes the hiss of the car jack in Nick's murder. Both tropes recall the statement of the old Italian mover who equated vitality with a "deep-a breath." The play of sounds and meaning can create other anomalies. At one point Velda approaches Mike asking, "But under any other name, would you be as sweet?" and he, not paying attention to her, says, "Kowalski." On one level, all these can be appreciated as textural noise or non sequiturs. On another, they are conscious metaphors and puns.

Velda's statements about the "great what's it" and "the nameless ones who kill people" reinforce the sense that the vagaries of chance or destiny, a word which the mythically-minded Dr. Soberin would likely have preferred, are an underlying constant. Soberin himself is one of the most consciously allusive characters in film noir. He brings up the notion of rising from the dead after Christina expires: "Do you know what that would be? That would be resurrection." He mentions Lazarus again during a conversation with Hammer. The old moving man also speaks of "the house of my body" that can only be left once. These concepts run parallel to Hammer's own search for meaning in the cryptic pentameter of the Rossetti poem: "But when the darkness and corruption leave/A vestige of the thoughts that once we had." Myth becomes a surface value entirely in the case of the "great what's it." What police detective Pat Murphy calls a "few, harmless words . . . .just a bunch of letters scrambled together, but their meaning is very important. . . . Manhattan Project. Los Alamos. Trinity." are as much words to conjure with as Soberin's pedantic analogies. Soberin's references to Lot's wife and "cerberus barking with all his heads" are too archaic and unfrightening to keep Gabrielle/Lily Carver from opening her own Pandora's box. In the final analysis, the "great what's it" contains pure phlogiston. The quest for it becomes the quest for the cleansing, combustible element, for the spark of the purifying fire that reduces the nether world of *Kiss Me Deadly* to radioactive ash.

As modern myth, as anti-myth, and/or as film noir, *Kiss Me*

Deadly's narrative outlook is equally somber. "A savage lyricism hurls us into a decomposing world ruled by perversity and brutality," wrote Borde and Chaumeton, after which "Aldrich brings to bear the most radical of solutions: nuclear apocalypse." The choice of setting and the use of real locations reinforce this sense of apocalyse. The general decay of the city coupled with specific usages such as the flashing street lights and isolated gas station create the tone of lingering menace mentioned earlier. Other usages comment metaphorically on the confusion of identities. The mirrors and panning movement when Hammer visits Velda in her exercise room create a complex of confusing doppelgängers. As the shot opens, the viewer sees two sets of figures as Hammer steps into the room. The pan reveals that neither set was "real" and displaces them with the actual people reflected in still another mirror. Even as Velda elaborates figuratively on the possible consequences of his investigation and speaks of a "thread" leading to a "rope" by which he might well "hang," she spins around on the pole. Her action and the reflections actively undercut the surrounding reality.

Certainly *Kiss Me Deadly* ranks with the most important examples of film noir by any director. It has the menace of *Night and the City*, the grim determinism of *Out of the Past*, the cynicism of *Double Indemnity*, the reckless energy of *Gun Crazy*, and the visual flourish of *Touch of Evil*. *Kiss Me Deadly* also reflects such contemporary issues as McCarthyism and moral decline and the nuclear peril that haunted the end of the noir period. These, too, are part of the fabric of film noir. Aldrich's early career coincides with the beginning and end of the classic period of film noir; and he would revisit many of the noir cycle's themes in later films, most notably *Hustle*. But as a symbol of what film noir epitomized or of the powerful, malevolent forces lurking in its vision of the modern world, nothing would ever loom larger than a mushroom cloud over Malibu. **AS**

KISS OF DEATH (1947)

Director: Henry Hathaway. **Screenplay**: Ben Hecht and Charles Lederer from an unpublished story by Eleazar Lipsky. **Producer**: Fred Kohlmar. **Director of Photography**: Norbert Brodine. **Music**: David Buttolph. **Art Directors**: Lyle Wheeler, Leland Fuller. **Editor**: J. Watson Webb, Jr. **Cast**: Victor Mature (Nick Bianco), Brian Donlevy (Asst. District Attorney Louis D'Angelo), Coleen Gray (Nettie), Richard Widmark (Tom Udo), Karl Malden (Sgt. William Cullen), Taylor Holmes (Earl Howser), Howard Smith (Warden), Anthony Ross (Williams), Mildred Dunnock (Ma Rizzo), Millard Mitchell (Max Schulte), Temple Texas (Blondie), J. Scott Smart (Skeets). **Locations**: Chrysler Building, Tombs Prison, Criminal Courts Building, Hotel Marguery, New York City; Sing Sing Penitentiary, Ossining, New York; The Academy of the Holy Angels, Fort Lee, New Jersey. **Completed**: May 17, 1947. **Released**: 20th Century-Fox, August 27. Running Time: 98 minutes. **Note**: While a title claims the picture was shot entirely on location, the concluding scenes were re-shot on the Fox back lot.

Everyone in New York City is enjoying Christmas but Nick Bianco, a man with a criminal record and no job. He goes Christmas shopping for his children by robbing a jewelry store. The jeweler trips the alarm, however, and Nick is wounded in a battle with the police. After Nick recovers, he is taken to Assistant District Attorney D'Angelo, who offers Nick a reduced sentence if he informs on other criminals. Nick

Kiss of Death: *D.A. D'Angelo (Brian Donlevy) questions Tommy Udo (Richard Widmark) and Nick Bianco (Victor Mature).*

refuses and is sent to prison. He worries about his family when his letters are returned unopened; and he soon learns that his wife has committed suicide and his children are in an orphanage. Nettie, who used to baby-sit Nick's kids, visits him in prison and relates good news of his children, but sad tales of his wife's affair with a gangster named Rizzo. Nick contacts D'Angelo and offers information even though it will not free him. D'Angelo conceals Nick's cooperation from other criminals by implicating Rizzo as a police informant. Nick, out on parole, visits Nettie and falls in love. They marry, but D'Angelo constantly demands information from Nick about criminal activities, thereby endangering his family's safety. The district attorney forces Nick to testify against a sadistic killer, Tommy Udo. When Udo is acquitted, Nick lives in fear of the killer's revenge. Sending his family away, Nick seeks out Udo but is ambushed and shot repeatedly. Udo is killed by the police. Although he is seriously wounded, Nick is taken from the scene in an ambulance. The viewer is led to believe that he will survive and begin a new life reunited with his family.

Although praised in 1947 for its realism, *Kiss of Death* displays an uncomfortable alliance of documentary-like locations and stylized script and characterizations. Norbert Brodine's photography contributes to the stylization by making a row house in Queens look like a soundstage set. The cast and crew were transported both to Sing Sing prison and the Tombs in New York City and, in "method" acting spirit, were processed through these institutions as though they were convicts. None of this dissipates the melodramatic atmosphere of the script. Nick's wife, Nettie, narrates the story in voice-over; and the use of a female narrator is somewhat unusual in film noir. However, the exploration of actual social inequities, of the jobless turning to crime because of lack of alternatives, which is introduced by her narration, is never substantially developed. Rather the contradictions in this narrative's content suggest either an attempt to approximate Nettie's biased viewpoint or a weak social commentary to bolster the ambience of realism initiated by the location work.

The narrator introduces Nick Bianco to the viewer as an unlucky individual who steals only to purchase Christmas presents for his children; yet it is soon revealed that his criminal record dates back to his adolescence. Aside from the mention in passing of the fact that Nick's father was also a felon, there is no probing of the economic or environmental causes of Nick Bianco's misspent life. The result is the naive suggestion that criminal inclinations are inherited like a family business. Victor Mature's interpretation of Nick—although, like Widmark's celebrated, leering portrayal of Udo, overly dramatized in context—suggests a character trapped by his compulsive behavior and elicits viewer sympathy despite his criminal past. The overt theme of a "reformed" man inevitably sucked back into the criminal world is less innovative than the brief scenes of illegal deals made by corrupt district attorneys or the intrigues of the script's truest villain, the lawyer who protects the criminal and betrays both the law and the reformed convict. That character and Widmark's psychotic rendering of the sadistic Udo, who pushes old women in wheelchairs down stairs for kicks or gleefully empties his automatic into Nick's body, are also undeveloped. Ultimately, a figure like Udo becomes an incongruous gargoyle of a truly noir world trapped in a narrative of facile social consciousness. **EM**

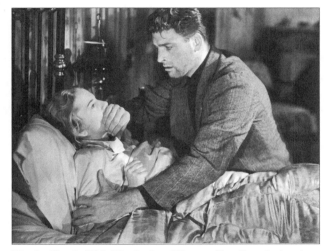

Kiss the Blood off My Hands: *Jane Wharton (Joan Fontaine) and Bill Saunders (Burt Lancaster).*

KISS THE BLOOD OFF MY HANDS (1948)

Director: Norman Foster. **Screenplay**: Leonardo Bercovici, with additional dialogue by Hugh Gray, adapted by Ben Maddow and Walter Bernstein from the novel by Gerald Butler. **Producer**: Richard Vernon. **Executive Producer**: Harold Hecht. **Director of Photography**: Russell Metty. **Music**: Miklós Rózsa. **Art Directors**: Bernard Herzbrun, Nathan Juran. **Editor**: Milton Carruth. **Cast**: Joan Fontaine (Jane Wharton), Burt Lancaster (Bill Saunders), Robert Newton (Harry Carter), Lewis L. Russell (Tom Widgery), Aminta Dyne (Landlady), Grizelda Harvey (Mrs. Paton), Jay Novello (Sea Captain), Colin Keith-Johnston (Judge), Reginald Sheffield (Superintendent). **Completed**: May 8, 1948. **Released**: Univeral October 29. 79 minutes.

Bill Saunders, an embittered war veteran, goes into a rage in an English pub and kills the proprietor. Running from the police, he takes refuge in the room of a shy nurse, Jane, and a sympathetic relationship develops. But he is recognized by the insidious Harry, who witnessed the killing and wants to draw Bill into criminal activities. Bill shuns Harry but, because of his violent temper, he is sentenced to six months in prison. More bitter and lonely than before, Bill finds Jane after his release from prison, and she gets him a job as truck driver at the clinic where she works. But Harry blackmails Bill into stealing medicine for him to sell on the black market. When Jane becomes an unexpected passenger in his truck on the designated assignment, Bill does not go through with the plan. Harry comes to Jane's flat later and attempts to gain her cooperation by playing on her feelings of love and protectiveness toward Bill. In self-defense, Jane kills the menacing Harry, and Bill plans to flee the country with her. At the last minute Bill changes his mind, knowing that if he tells the whole truth, he will be punished for the killing of the innkeeper but Jane will go free for the justifiable killing of Harry.

Conjuring up images of murder, anguish and love, *Kiss the Blood off My Hands* is one of the most evocative titles of any film noir. However, the film itself is simply another entry in the Burt Lancaster cycle of masochistic melodramas, in which a tormented Lancaster journeys through a treacher-

ous world accompanied by the dissonant strains of Miklós Rózsa's music. Joan Fontaine's sincere heroine is in contrast to the destructive women played by Ava Gardner and Yvonne De Carlo in *The Killers* and *Criss Cross* and even to the ambiguous, but ultimately sympathetic, Lizabeth Scott character of *I Walk Alone*. The material itself is inconsistent and the lack of pacing in Robert Newton's performance causes the well-written character of Harry to lapse from an initially strong impression into monotony. The whipping of Lancaster, however, is staged for maximum effectiveness; and Bill and Jane's visit to a zoo, where he is disturbed by his kinship to the animals, is well presented. Taking full advantage of the cinematography of Russell Metty, the director makes the most of the nocturnal flights from the police. Admittedly, it is not entirely clear why the story is set in London in contrast to *Night and the City*, which offers a pointed relationship between the hustling American, Harry, and the city of his curious self-exile. **BL**

KISS TOMORROW GOODBYE (1950)

Director: Gordon Douglas. **Screenplay**: Harry Brown from the novel by Horace McCoy. **Producer**: William Cagney. **Director of Photography**: J. Peverell Marley. **Music**: Carmen Dragon. **Production Design**: Wiard Ihnen. **Editors**: Truman K. Wood, Walter Hannemann. **Cast**: James Cagney (Ralph Cotter), Barbara Payton (Holiday Carleton), Helena Carter (Margaret Dobson), Ward Bond (Inspector Weber), Luther Adler (Cherokee Mandon), Barton MacLane (Reece), Steve Brodie (Jinx Raynor), Rhys Williams (Vic Mason), Herbert Heyes (Ezra Dobson), John Litel (Chief of Police Tolgate), William Frawley (Byers), Robert Karnes (Gray), Kenneth Tobey (Fowler), Dan Riss (District Attorney), Frank Reicher (Doc Green), John Halloran (Cobbett), Neville Brand (Carleton). **Completed**: May 16, 1950. **Released**: Warner Bros., August 4. 102 minutes.

After escaping from a prison farm, Ralph Cotter and a fellow inmate, Jinx Raynor, find refuge in a corrupt, out-of-the-way small town. It takes a shrewd criminal like Cotter little time to discover which police can be bribed; and he plans to blackmail a couple of dishonest cops, Weber and Reece, while stealing money from the mob. Cotter's flamboyant road to the top is paved with the bodies of those inessential to his plans. Even his mistress, Holiday, is sidestepped to allow Cotter the freedom to soil the reputation of a local politician's daughter. He leaves after receiving a large payoff and information that gives him considerable political leverage. The vile schemes of Ralph Cotter come to a cruel and violent end when Holiday kills him rather than give him up to someone else.

A tough and relentless film from the novel by noir novelist Horace McCoy (*They Shoot Horses, Don't They?*), *Kiss Tomorrow Goodbye* is one of the most brutal and cynical noir films. The presence of Cagney as a totally corrupt individual begins where *White Heat* ends. As Cody Jarrett, there was some sympathy developed for Cagney. The role of Ralph Cotter is not burdened by this soft shell. His evil nature completely overshadows the rest of the cast, painting a vivid portrait of the complete noir villain. Like the original novel, *Kiss Tomorrow Goodbye* emphasizes violence and sadistic brutality. There is never a hint of compassion in the nature of Cotter. On the other hand, his crony, Jinx, is weak and filled with the anxieties common to most noir characters. His uncertainty forms a sharp contrast to Cotter and his push for the top. There is no glamour in Cotter's death at the hands of his spurned girlfriend Holiday, killed unexpectedly just as he was about to celebrate his latest triumph; yet Cotter, who trusts only his automatic, summons the grim strength to mock Holiday when the revolver she is using to kill him misfires once. *Kiss Tomorrow Goodbye* is one of the noir films that leaves a bitter aftertaste; order is restored at the expense of suffering. **CM**

KNOCK ON ANY DOOR (1949)

Director: Nicholas Ray. **Screenplay**: Daniel Taradash and John Monks, Jr. from the novel by Willard Motley. **Producer**: Robert Lord (Santana Productions). **Director of Photography**: Burnett Guffey. **Music**: George Antheil. **Art Director**: Robert Peterson. **Editor**: Viola Lawrence. **Cast**: Humphrey Bogart (Andrew Morton), John Derek (Nick Romano), George Macready (District Attorney Kerman), Allene Roberts (Emma), Susan Perry (Adele), Mickey Knox (Vito), Barry Kelley (Judge Drake), Dooley Wilson (Piano Player), Cara Williams (Nelly), Jimmy Conlin (Kid Fingers), Sid Melton (Squint). **Completed**: September 17, 1948. **Released**: Columbia, February 22. 100 minutes.

When a policeman is killed during a robbery, Nick Romano, a rebellious youth with a record as a hoodlum, is put on trial for the crime. Andrew Morton, an attorney who understands Romano well because of their mutual slum background, defends him and believes in his innocence. As the trial proceeds, Romano's history is revealed. Morton tried to help Nick many times, but after seeming to reform, he backslided. The influence of Emma finally reformed Nick, and the two married. But Nick could not keep a job and he gambled in

Knock on Any Door: *Emma (Allene Roberts) and Nick Romano (John Derek).*

attempts to improve things for Emma. When she became pregnant, Nick became more dissolute; and his desperate young wife finally killed herself. Insane with grief and anger, Nick committed the robbery that resulted in the policeman's death. Morton seems to be winning Nick's case when the district attorney pressures Nick about Emma's death, and he confesses to killing the policeman. Stunned by Nick's guilt, Morton speaks passionately about environment and circumstances combining to make Nick what he is. Nevertheless, Nick is sentenced to die in the electric chair, and Morton visits him only moments before the young man goes to his death.

Knock On Any Door is a film that suffers from the explicitness of its social consciousness. All of Nicholas Ray's films have a strong sense of social and moral issues. Usually, however, this social and moral sense is implicit in Ray's treatment and the viewer accepts Ray's attitudes because the director has generated a deep emotional response. Further, there is a complexity in most of his work that is denied in *Knock on Any Door* by the simplification of Nick Romano's character. He is the only Ray protagonist who is solely the victim of his environment. No such assumption is made about the similar characters of Bowie in *They Live by Night* and of Jim in *Rebel without a Cause*. Despite this, however, the character of Nick Romano, as realized in individual scenes, is compelling. John Derek (making his film debut here) played a very similar role as Davey Bishop in Ray's Western *Run For Cover*. One of the reasons that film is so much more successful than *Knock on Any Door* is that the relationship between the misguided youth and the older man, Mat Dow, who tries to help him is a neurotic one. Mat Dow betrays psychological flaws by his continuing faith in the Davey Bishop character, while the comparable Bogart character, Andrew Morton, in *Knock on Any Door* never seems essential to the plot. **BL**

THE LADY CONFESSES (1945)

Director: Sam Newfield. **Screenplay**: Helen Martin based on a story by Irwin Franklyn. **Producer**: Alfred Stern. **Director of Photography**: Jack Greenhalgh. **Art Director**: Paul Palmentola. **Editor**: Holbrook Todd. **Cast**: Mary Beth Hughes (Vicki McGuire), Hugh Beaumont (Larry Craig), Edmund MacDonald (Lucky Brandon), Claudia Drake (Lucile Compton), Emmett Vogan (Police Captain), Barbara Slater (Norma Craig), Edward Howard (Detective), Dewey Robinson (Bartender), Carol Andrews (Marge). **Released**: PRC, May 16. 64 minutes.

Larry Craig's wife returns after a seven-year absence to stop his proposed marriage to Vicki McGuire. That same night she is murdered. The police suspect Craig but his plucky fiancée Vicki refuses to believe them and goes undercover as a nightclub photographer to find the truth. In the process another woman, Lucile Compton—a nightclub chanteuse—is murdered and the blame then shifts to the nightclub owner Lucky Brandon, who owed Craig's wife money. Vicki, however, finds a letter from Lucile which names Larry as the murderer. As Larry tries to strangle his wife, as he did the other two women, he is shot by the police.

The Lady Confesses is another sixty-minute-plus programmer from Producers Releasing Corporation, one of the poverty row studios (e.g., Republic, Allied Artists, etc.) which were approaching noir from the low end in both budget and star power. PRC had found success with Edgar G. Ulmer's noir classics Bluebeard and Detour and so were intent on milking the noir mystery film for whatever it was worth. Utilizing the talents and relative success of noir femme fatale Mary Beth Hughes (her name appears on a separate title card), The Lady Confesses references Cornell Woolrich's Phantom Lady in its story of a devoted Vicki who goes undercover to clear the name of her love Larry Craig. The role is a change of pace for Hughes, known at this point for playing tough platinum blonde femme fatales. Reverting to her normal hair color and swathed in furs, she is a glamorous sleuth hot on the trail of the killer and exhibits very little of the seductive deviousness seen in films like The Great Flamarion.

The lighting in the film, like much of PRC's noir product, is extremely low key, with lights often directed up from below, giving the film an eerie quality as well as hiding the cheapness of the sets (always a consideration in "Z-budget" filmmaking). The marginal status of the film in terms of mainstream cinema, however, also has its advantages. It is able to get away with more than a highly publicized A-film might. Although Vicki at first ignores the Sybil-like wife, who returns "from the grave" in the very first scene to warn Vicki

The Lady from Shanghai: *Rita Hayworth as Elsa Bannister.*

about her husband and sabotage her engagement ("I'm doing you a favor."), she later discovers that the woman was prescient on so many levels. Larry turns out not only to be a sloppy alcoholic but a serial killer who even attempts to strangle his one defender, Vicki. Vicki, however, is a noir heroine and so in the final scene with hardly a look back at her fiance's dead body on the floor, she goes off with the darkly handsome nightclub owner to a brighter future, hopefully one with a few less noir shadows. **JU**

THE LADY FROM SHANGHAI (1948)

Director/Producer: Orson Welles. **Screenplay**: Orson Welles from the novel Before I Die by Sherwood King. **Associate Producers**: Richard Wilson, William Castle. **Director of Photography**: Charles Lawton, Jr. **Music**: Heinz Roemheld. **Art Directors**: Stephen Goosson, Sturges Carne. **Editor**: Viola Lawrence. **Cast**: Rita Hayworth (Elsa Bannister), Orson Welles (Michael O'Hara), Everett Sloane (Arthur Bannister), Glenn Anders (George Grisby), Ted de Corsia (Sidney Broome), Erskine Sanford (Judge), Gus Schilling (Goldie), Carl Frank (District Attorney), **Completed**: February 27, 1947. **Released**: Columbia, June 10. 86 minutes.

Michael O'Hara comes to the aid of a mysterious and beautiful woman who is being mugged. Soon afterward Michael is hired as a crew member for a pleasure cruise south of the border on a yacht owned by Arthur Bannister, who is the husband of his mystery lady, Elsa Bannister. Arthur is a brilliant trial lawyer but is severely crippled. Husband and wife seem to have their own hidden reasons for wanting Michael aboard ship. O'Hara is introduced to Bannister's associate,

Grisby, and is slowly implicated in a bizarre and constantly changing program of murder and fraud. The resulting death of Grisby is blamed on the ill-fated Michael. He is defended in court by Bannister who, although he has never lost a case, is determined to see Michael convicted. O'Hara escapes before the verdict is decided and hides out in a Chinatown theater, where he is followed by Elsa. Several of her oriental associates drug O'Hara and bring him to an abandoned amusement park, where he confronts Elsa for the last time. However, Bannister forces his wife into a final showdown in a hall of mirrors. Amid shattering images of Elsa and the crippled lawyer, both husband and wife are shot. Michael walks away from the dying Elsa.

Orson Welles' *The Lady from Shanghai* carries on the noir tradition of the male "chump." Although in his first-person narration sailor Michael O'Hara has other colorful synonyms for himself like "fool" (a term the femme fatale Elsa takes up when she calls him "my beloved fool"), a "boob," and "stupid," he is still just one more in a long line of masochistic noir males in search of a "cruel" femme fatale to punish him for offenses both personal and existential.

Welles, in his typically baroque style, enhances the victim dimensions of his male protagonist by surrounding him with imagery both dreamlike and mythological, thereby robbing his character of any real will or self-actuating force. After his first meeting in Central Park with the blonde-haired Elsa Bannister, where he saves her from a group of muggers, O'Hara almost immediately begins to act like a zombie, unable to stick by any decision and led along on a metaphorical leash by the seductive Elsa. Although at first he rejects her offer to join her on a cruise ("Would you like to work for me? I'll make it worth your while," she tells him teasingly) when he finds out she is married to an unscrupulous and rich defense attorney, he cannot hold to his resolve for long. Once he sees her dressed in tight shorts, captain's hat and coat (symbolizing the traditional male and female character-

istics Elsa incorporates in her dominant personality) standing aboard her luxurious yacht (named appropriately *Circe,* after the sorceress in *The Odyssey*), he is hooked: "From then on I did not use my head much except to think about her."

As the voyage through the Panama Canal and then up the Mexican coast to San Francisco progresses, Michael, like the other males on the voyage (including her bitter, crippled husband), spends a good deal of his time staring at Elsa as she bathes on the rocks like that mythical siren or lies out at night on her lounge chair. And even though Michael lectures them on their wasted lifestyle, comparing them to sharks who feed off each other in a frenzy (a metaphor reinforced by an image of Elsa before a shark tank in the aquarium), he still follows his lover's lead like a wooden puppet. He becomes involved in a convoluted scheme with Bannister's law partner and then in a murder trial where he is prosecuted for a scheme concocted to obtain the means to take Elsa away in the style she is accustomed to.

A scene which clearly illustrates Elsa's almost telepathic control of Michael takes place in the courtroom where on a nod from Elsa to her husband's pills, Michael swallows the pills and effects an escape when he is transported from the court room. Awaking later in a carnival "crazy house," Michael wanders through a maze of expressionistically distorted rooms to a hall of mirrors where Elsa and her husband, reflected multiple times (symbolizing the duplicities of their characters as well as the labyrinthine complexities of the story), shoot it out with Michael acting as a helpless bystander.

Although Elsa finally frees herself of her oppressive husband, she is fatally wounded in the act. Only then can Michael break her psychic and emotional hold on him. As she once more tries to pull him back in line by ordering him to return to her ("Michael, come back here!"), the sailor disobeys his "boss" for the first time and staggers out into the dawn. While gazing out at the ocean despondently O'Hara's voice is heard: "Maybe if I live long enough I will forget her. Maybe I'll die trying," as he admits Elsa's hold on him is still in place. **JU**

LADY IN THE LAKE (1947)

Director: Robert Montgomery. **Screenplay**: Steve Fisher and [uncredited] Raymond Chandler from Chandler's novel. **Producer**: George Haight. **Director of Photography**: Paul C. Vogel. **Music**: David Snell. **Art Directors**: Cedric Gibbons, Preston Ames. **Editor**: Gene Ruggiero. **Cast**: Robert Montgomery (Philip Marlowe), Lloyd Nolan (Lt. DeGarmo), Audrey Totter (Adrienne Fromsett), Tom Tully (Capt. Kane), Leon Ames (Derace Kingsby), Jayne Meadows (Mildred Haveland), Morris Ankrum (Eugene Grayson), Lila Leeds (Receptionist), Richard Simmons (Chris Lavery), Ellen Ross (Elevator Girl), William Roberts (Artist), Kathleen Lockhart (Mrs. Grayson). **Completed**: July 5, 1946. **Released**: MGM, January 23. 105 minutes.

Private investigator Philip Marlowe meets Adrienne Fromsett, editor of a series of crime magazines published by Derace Kingsby, ostensibly to discuss a story he has submitted. Adrienne actually wants Marlowe to find Kingsby's missing wife, Crystal, so that Kingsby can divorce her. Disdainful of her motives, Marlowe takes the case for a fee. A body is discovered in the lake near Kingsby's vacation cabin but it turns out to Muriel Chess, the wife of the caretaker. When he goes to question Chris Lavery, who might have been

involved with Mrs. Kingby, Marlowe is met by a scatter-brained landlady holding a gun she has found on the premises. After she leaves, Marlowe finds Lavery's body. Although police Lt. DeGarmo is particularly incensed, there is no evidence to hold Marlowe. DeGarmo then runs Marlowe off the road and tries to frame him for drunk driving. Although he manages to escape that set-up, the relentless DeGarmo follows Marlowe when Kingsby sends him to give money to his missing wife. DeGarmo reveals that Mrs. Kingsby was drowned by Muriel Chess aka Mildred Haveland aka Lavery's landlady, who also betrayed DeGarmo's love for her. His plan to kill both her and Marlowe and make it seem they shot each other is only half accomplished when police Captain Kane intevenes. DeGarmo joins the lady in death, and Adrienne and Marlowe are reunited.

One of the most unusual of Hollywood film experiments—along with the first act of *Dark Passage*— *Lady in the Lake* is almost entirely photographed from a subjective point-of-view, with the camera serving as the eyes of detective Marlowe. The only break from the subjective set-up is when Marlowe sits behind his desk in the first scene and interrupts the movie at other moments to speak directly to the audience and clean up some narrative confusion. By restricting the field of vision to a subjective viewpoint, the tension and effectiveness of any surprise violence foisted upon Marlowe is heightened as the scenes where he is punched, run off the road, doused with liquor, or otherwise menaced by the antagonists wreak havoc on the camera as well. When Marlowe crawls across the street and struggles to reach a phone, the camera crawls across the street and struggles to reach a phone. And although Montgomery often had to mask cuts and overlap set-ups to give the sense of unbroken scenes, many are actually shot in real time using long takes. Particularly interesting is the use of mirrors to complement the action. When Marlowe visits Lavery, he turns to look at a clock situated near a mirror. Although Marlowe seems not to notice, the audience can see Lavery's fleeting reflection as he prepares to hit the detective, just before the actual blow lands and the screen fills with blackness.

Additionally, the subjective camera records Marlowe's impressions while he listens to a character speak. For example, as he is interviewed by Adrienne Fromsett, her alluring receptionist enters the room and Marlowe follows her every move while she answers his "stare" with seductive expressions. Not only does this technique increase visual interest, it also contrasts Adrienne's pretentiousness with Marlowe's more honest, albeit coarse, personality. In *Dark Passage* the use of subjective camera in the opening is abandoned once the character undergoes plastic surgery and "becomes" Humphrey Bogart. This is entirely different from the effect of the "you will see what I see" context Montgomery sets up when he first addresses the audience as Marlowe. Having set up this consistent personalization in *Lady in the Lake*, Montgomery refuses to compromise. Sometimes the camera does not wander tellingly about a room or examine a person inch by inch. At other moments as when Marlowe/the Camera encounters the gun-toting landlady then searches through the house until it finds the occupant dead in the shower, Montgomery exploits the device, heavily underscored with David Snell's music, to enhance suspense. Alternately the staging may seem awkward and slow. Unable to intercut his reaction shots to the statements or behavior of other characters—except in those moments when Marlowe/the Camera approaches a mirror—Montgomery deprives himself of what many if not most viewers came to see: his stylish and appropriately laconic acting style. Although Audrey Totter and Jayne Meadows are very effective in playing to the camera and carrying the burdern of providing all the visual performance in many scenes, Lloyd Nolan and Leon Ames are less effective.

Lady in the Lake is the only adaptation of his prose on which Raymond Chandler worked as a screenwriter. As with every Hollywood job from *Double Indemnity* on, Chandler did not enjoy the experience, although he did compel producer Haight to violate Louis B. Mayer's rule for writers' offices and give him a sofa on which he could recline. After Chandler's departure, Steve Fisher brought his own firsthand experience with pulp fiction to the project and gave Chandler's version a new cinematic beginning. Among the self-conscious changes from the novel was the substitution of *Lurid Detective and True Horror* magazine (to which Marlowe has submitted a story entitled, "If I Should Die Before I Wake") for "Gillerlain Regal, the Champagne of Perfumes" and effectively transformation of Chandler's "normal" corrupt enterprise into a commercial literary business run by hypocrites. The dialogue is tough and grifty, as the final screenplay retained much of Chandler's cynical "Marlowe" quips, as when Adrienne says, "I don't like your manner," and Marlowe replies, "I'm not selling it." The movie's Adrienne Fromsett is a more complete character and, initially, Marlowe's chief antagonist, while Chandler kept her in the background as her boss's devoted mistress. When the film's Marlowe breaks up Adrienne's mercenary wedding plans, she bitterly asks him, "On what corner do you want me to beat my tambourine?" Marlowe has little idea that it should be on his corner; and their verbal rivalry is active until the mystery is almost at a close. When Marlowe and Adrienne admit their attraction to each other, it is a sentimental surprise dependent on the filmmaker's presumption that the audience demanded a romantic, happy ending.

Ultimately, what happens in *Lady In The Lake* is immaterial because the visual discipline and suspension of conventional perception required the viewer to eliminate the necessity for complete dramatic development, much in the same way that

A Lady without Passport: *Pallinov (George Macready, left) and Marianne Lorress (Hedy Lamarr).*

the narrative confusion of *The Big Sleep* is functionally irrelevant. Although Montgomery adds a lot of comic relief and humorous bits in support of Marlowe's irreverent attitude (even dropping a pun into the credits which list "Ellay Mort" as the never seen Mrs. Kingsby), touches like this cannot restore equilibrium to the film's somewhat odd style. It wasn't until Montgomery's next directorial effort, *Ride the Pink Horse,* that he found a character and a style fully evocative of the social constriction and existential anguish of film noir. **EW & CM**

A LADY WITHOUT PASSPORT (1950)

Director: Joseph H. Lewis. **Screenplay**: Howard Dimsdale, adapted by Cyril Hume from a story by Lawrence Taylor. **Producer**: Samuel Marx. **Director of Photography**: Paul C. Vogel. **Music**: David Raksin. **Art Directors**: Cedric Gibbons, Edward Carfagno. **Editor**: Frederick Y. Smith. **Cast**: Hedy Lamarr (Marianne Lorress), John Hodiak (Pete Karczag), James Craig (Frank Westlake), George Macready (Palinov), Steven Geray (Frenchman), Bruce Cowling (Archer Delby James), Nedrick Young (Harry Nordell), Steven Hill (Jack), Robert Osterloh (Lt. Lannahan), Trevor Bardefte (Lt. Carfagno), Charles Wagenheim (Ramon Santez). **Released**: MGM, August 3, 1950. 72 minutes.

A government plot to break up an illegal alien smuggling racket headed by Palinov involves undercover work by special agent Pete Karczag. Impersonating a Hungarian immigrant stranded in Cuba who wishes to enter the United States without a passport Karczag gets involved with a beautiful refugee, Marianne Lorress, also seeking asylum in America. However, Karczag blows his cover and is almost killed by the smugglers. Panicked by the discovery of an infiltrator, Palinov takes the still unsuspected Marianne and attempts to escape to America in a small plane. Unable to control the craft, the smuggler crashes the plane in the Florida everglades. A final shootout in the misty swampland results in Palinov's defeat and the rescue of Marianne.

There is a quaint, almost juvenile, noir quality to Joseph H. Lewis' *A Lady without Passport.* Utilizing a number of noir conventions, ranging from the exotic femme fatale to deca-

dent villainy and hardboiled heroes, without any real noir insight, this production falls into that category of films made during the noir period that reproduce the look but without the compex ethos of true film noir. Most of what is noir in *A Lady without Passport* stems from Lewis' particular brand of exoticism, which is sometimes expressionistic and decidedly surreal. Unlike Henry Hathaway and Anthony Mann who treated similar "authentic police dramatizations" with a sense of documentary realism, Lewis instilled his films with an atmosphere of unreality. His more interesting noir films, such as *My Name Is Julia Ross* and *Gun Crazy,* possess an ambience that rejects normal sensibilities while substituting surrealism. *A Lady without Passport,* although not one of Lewis' most interesting films, still draws on this stylistic preoccupation to give a strange and occasionally fascinating treatment to a stereotypical narrative. **CM**

THE LAS VEGAS STORY (1952)

Director: Robert Stevenson. **Screenplay**: Paul Jarrico [uncredited], Earl Felton, Harry Essex, based on a story by Jay Dratler. **Producers**: Howard Hughes, Robert Sparks. **Executive Producer**: Samuel Bischoff. **Director of Photography**: Harry J. Wild. **Music**: Leigh Harline. **Art Directors**: Albert S. D'Agostino, Feild Gray. **Editors**: George Shrader, Frederic Knudtson. **Cast**: Jane Russell (Linda Rollins), Victor Mature (Lt. Dave Andrews), Vincent Price (Lloyd Rollins), Hoagy Carmichael (Happy), Brad Dexter (Tom Hubler), Gordon Oliver (Mr. Drucker), Jay C. Flippen (Capt. H.A. Harris), Will Wright (Mike Fogarty), Bill Welsh (Mr. Martin), Ray Montgomery (Desk Clerk), Colleen Miller (Mary), Robert Wilke (Clayton). **Completed**: June 1951. **Released**: RKO, February 16. 88 minutes.

Desperate for cash to cover a shady business deal, Lloyd Rollins takes his wife Linda to Las Vegas and gambles away her diamond necklace to Clayton, the new owner of the casino where she once sang. Linda, meanwhile, has a tuneful reunion with her former pianist, Happy, and her old boss, Mike, who lost the casino to Clayton. When Clayton is murdered and the necklace stolen, the cop on the case is Dave Andrews, Linda's bitter ex-lover. Tom Hubler, an insurance investigator who's been shadowing Lloyd, places him at the scene of the crime and Lloyd is arrested. But Hubler also saw Linda there. Wanting both her and the diamonds, he tries to pressure her. Happy overhears and tells Dave, who realizes Hubler has revealed details only the killer would know. Before Dave can arrest him, Hubler kidnaps Linda and heads across the desert in a stolen car. Dave pursues in a helicopter, finally rescuing Linda, killing Hubler, and recovering the diamonds. Lloyd is cleared of murder but is arrested for embezzlement. Mike gets his casino back and rehires Linda, who divorces Lloyd and reunites with Dave.

Given its cast and crew of noir veterans and the Hughes bankroll with which to shoot (or recreate) Vegas, this piece would seem to possess the requisite elements for a satisfying noir thriller, but the whole is less than the sum of its parts. Hughes, already wheeling and dealing for Vegas real estate, later wrote of his intention "to represent all that is glamourous and exciting about Las Vegas" in the film, and this boosterish tone dulls whatever edge it otherwise might have possessed. Though the setup, with its love triangle plus piano player in a gambling joint, transparently mimics

Casablanca, Linda isn't given a noble motive for having left Dave and married the wealthy Rollins, and Dave makes no selfless sacrifice to atone for his bitter misogyny. These darker elements are left unexplored, however, and the lovers' conflict is dismissed as an unspecified misunderstanding, forgotten by film's end.

Vegas itself is a carefree playground patrolled by a comic-relief sheriff, and the bad guys are opportunists from out of town. Crime pays off handsomely, albeit not for the criminals: Linda is conveniently rid of her no-good husband and reunited with Dave, kindly old Mike regains the casino he had lost, and Happy can once again freely ogle Linda's cleavage, stationed at his eye level during their closing song. Though the key sets evoke the kitsch-modern elegance of 1950s Vegas—especially the Rollins' suite, with its circular glass shower in which Russell's assets are strategically deployed—the film is visually unremarkable until the climactic chase, first by helicopter and then on foot. This far more dynamic final sequence, moving wordlessly in and out of the shadowy buildings of a wind-swept abandoned airfield, suggests what might have been. After their next feature, *Macao*, Russell and Wild, now essentially her personal DP, were done with anything hinting of noir, moving on to such projects as the Technicolor romp *Gentlemen Prefer Blondes*, while Stevenson subsequently worked primarily for Walt Disney, directing dozens of features and TV episodes and garnering an Oscar nomination for *Mary Poppins*.

The film was a box-office disappointment. Perhaps the script, with its plot holes and motivational loose ends, was responsible. If so, Hughes apparently had no one to blame but himself. During pre-production, screenwriter Paul Jarrico was summoned by HUAC; when he refused to name names, Hughes fired him and left other writers to sort out the tale. Calling it a first step in ridding RKO of subversives, Hughes then removed Jarrico's name from the credits. After initially protesting, the Writers Guild, faced with Hughes' deep pockets and the politics of the time, yielded and allowed producers to deny credit for political reasons, tacitly establishing the system of "fronts" for blacklisted writers—surely the most enduring cultural legacy of this film. **SV**

LAURA (1944)

Director/Producer: Otto Preminger. **Screenplay**: Jay Dratler, Samuel Hoffenstein, Ring Lardner, Jr., and Betty Reinhardt from the novel by Vera Caspary. **Director of Photography**: Joseph La Shelle. **Music Score**: David Raksin. **Art Directors**: Lyle Wheeler, Leland Fuller. **Editor**: Louis Loeffler. **Cast**: Gene Tierney (Laura Hunt), Dana Andrews (Mark McPherson), Clifton Webb (Waldo Lydecker), Vincent Price (Shelby Carpenter), Judith Anderson (Ann Treadwell), Dorothy Adams (Bessie Clary), James Flavin (McAvity), Clyde Fillmore (Bullitt), Ralph Dunn (Fred Callahan), Grant Mitchell (Corey), Kathleen Howard (Louise). **Completed**: June 29, 1944. **Released**: 20th Century-Fox, October 11. 88 minutes.

Investigating the murder of career girl Laura Hunt, Detective Mark McPherson questions her mentor, noted radio personality Waldo Lydecker. It becomes clear that the caustic Lydecker regarded Laura not only as his finest creation but also as his personal property, using his biting wit to stave off her many suitors—all except one. The single exception is

Laura: *Laura (Gene Tierney) and Det. Mark McPherson (Dana Andrews).*

Shelby Carpenter, to whom Laura was engaged at the time of her death, much to the chagrin of Lydecker and Ann Treadwell, an older woman in love with Shelby. As Mark continues his investigation, he, too, falls under Laura's spell. As he is going over her apartment for evidence, he falls into a daze, staring at a stunning portrait of the dead woman. Suddenly, the door opens and in walks Laura. She explains that she's been in the country to decide whether or not to marry Shelby. The detective gets a call informing him that the disfigured body believed to be Laura's is actually that of a model Diane Redfern. Although Mark has several suspects in the murder, Mark is initially most suspicious of Laura. Ultimately, however, he discovers the murder weapon hidden in a clock given to Laura by Lydecker, whom he goes to arrest while leaving Laura alone. As Laura listens to Lydecker's pre-recorded radio broadcast, Lydecker sneaks into her apartment to finish the job he bungled earlier. Vowing that if he can't have her, no one can, Lydecker attacks Laura; but Mark bursts in just in time to save her.

Laura posits a world in which everyone is implicated, in which everyone not only has a motive for, but is seemingly capable of, committing a heinous crime. Given such a premise, the ostensibly happy ending of the film, with the implication that Laura and Mark will embark on a new life together, seems strangely overshadowed. The ambiguity that distinguishes the film is further emphasized by the puzzling spectacle of Mark and Lydecker, entirely different in temperament and personality, yet both enthralled by a woman who reveals little of herself to either of them. Mark is the "hero" and Lydecker the "villain," but both are driven by the same obsession: the Laura that each creates in his own mind. Preminger's gliding, probing camera is the perfect visual analogue to both Lydecker's and Mark's obsession.

Following Mark as he moves around Laura's apartment, peering into her closets, examining her possessions, poring over her letters and diary, makes the audience a party to Mark's insatiable curiosity, conveyed in subtle yet intense terms by Dana Andrews. Overshadowed by Clifton Webb's marvelously idiosyncratic performance as Lydecker, Andrews' quieter portrayal deserves more attention. With his haunted eyes, taut yet sensitive mouth, and softly insinuating voice, Andrews is a highly evocative screen presence, conveying more with a look than many actors do with a soliloquy. As the pragmatic, unromantic cop who, when asked by Lydecker if he's ever been in love, replies, "A doll in Washington Heights got a fox fur out of me once," he is only able to really love the perfumed ghost of a woman he believes is dead, and who becomes a dream expressed in a work of art. **JK**

LEAVE HER TO HEAVEN (1945)

Director: John M. Stahl. **Screenplay**: Jo Swerling from the novel by Ben Ames Williams. **Producer**: William A. Bacher. **Director of Photography**: Leon Shamroy. **Music**: Alfred Newman. **Art Directors**: Lyle Wheeler, Maurice Ransford. **Editor**: James B. Clark. **Cast**: Gene Tierney (Ellen Berent), Cornel Wilde (Richard Harland), Jeanne Crain (Ruth Berent), Vincent Price (Russell Quinton), Mary Phillips (Mrs. Berent), Ray Collins (Glen Robie), Gene Lockhart (Dr. Saunders), Reed Hadley (Dr. Mason), Darryl Hickman (Danny Harland), Chill Wills (Leick Thorne). **Locations**: Bass Lake, Monterey; Busch Gardens, Pasadena; Sedona Basin and Granite Dells, Arizona. **Released**: 20th Century-Fox, December 25. 110 minutes.

Ellen Berent is jealous and possessive of her husband, writer Richard Harland, who resembles her dead father to whom she was also completely devoted. In order to be Richard's sole companion and object of affection, Ellen lets his crippled brother Danny drown, and then murders their unborn child by throwing herself down a staircase. Ellen continues to fear Richard's growing alienation and feels threatened by the presence of her adopted sister, Ruth. Ellen admits to Richard that the recent accidents were planned by her to maintain their love, and he prepares to leave her. Ellen kills herself with poison in such a way as to suggest that she was murdered by Ruth. Ruth is acquitted of Ellen's murder, although Richard is convicted as an accessory to Ellen's crimes because he did not reveal her criminal negligence. When Richard is released from prison, Ruth is waiting for him at the lodge.

Leave Her to Heaven is noir femme fatale Gene Tierney's apotheosis film. As in *The Shanghai Gesture* and *Laura*, Tierney dominates every scene she is in both physically, with her exotic beauty, and psychologically, with her emotional intensity. While in *The Shanghai Gesture* she utilized a consciously stylized hysteria to project the image of a

Leave Her to Heaven: *Gene Tierney as Ellen Berent.*

spoiled teenage decadent bent on shocking and then punishing both her repressive father and her libertine mother, in *Leave Her to Heaven* she opts for a more controlled performance which at time veers into the realm of the supernatural. It is no accident that several of the characters, including her husband Richard, when speaking of Ellen refer to her psychic abilities or make semi-humorous allusions to the "witches of Salem." For there is definitely an otherworldly quality to this controlling woman who "loves too much" (her mother's words). The audience first gets a glimpse of this remarkable imperious woman in a club car on a train heading for New Mexico. There she meets the writer Richard Harland. As soon as she spies him she proceeds to disconcert him completely by staring at him without blinking for almost a minute of real time, as if she is trying to bore into his soul. After he squirms sufficiently, Ellen tells him he resembles her father, a man on whom, we later find out, she has an oedipal fixation.

This mesmerizing scene is followed shortly by another revealing and almost mythical one. Richard finds himself staying at the same resort as Ellen and her family. They are there to spread the ashes of her dead father. Early in the morning, as Alfred Newman's melodramatic and almost hysterical music score (replete with the cadence-like rhythm of timpani) rises on the soundtrack, Ellen sits ramrod straight on her horse like an Amazon warrior and throws the ashes about her, covering both herself and the desert around her, while Richard looks on in awe. After these two key scenes, it is little wonder Richard is left without a will of his own. Ellen proceeds to dump her lawyer fiancée (who by the way declares he will always love her anyway—which Ellen calls a "tribute"—and out of devotion is the one who prosecutes Ruth for her murder) and announce her marriage to Richard without his knowledge. As a doctor later on comments, Ellen seems to be able "to will" events.

Intent on possessing Richard as she possessed her father, she gradually begins to whittle away all of Richard's emotional connections so he can be hers totally: "I'll never let you go. . . never . . . never . . . never." In a scene rather daring for Production Code Hollywood, we see Ellen get up from her twin bed and enter her husband's and play with him, blowing on his face, cuddling up to him, exciting him sexually, until he is distracted by the voice of his crippled brother Danny in the next room. Although she tries initially to bend Danny to her will, he does not respond to her urgings that he attend a boarding school and so in another eerie scene she takes him out to the lake for some physical therapy. Putting on her heartshaped sunglasses and assuming a mask-like expression, she watches as he goes out too far and drowns. Of course, the most shocking moment for an audience of the period is self-induced miscarriage, in which she stages a fall from the stairs, again in order to have no one between her and Richard.

After Ellen realizes she has lost Richard to her foster sister Ruth, she commits suicide in order to separate Richard from his loved ones, even from the grave. She leaves a letter which implicates her foster cousin Ruth in her "murder." With Ellen's death, however, the movie is over. And even though the filmmakers do not have the courage of their convictions to end the movie there (as opposed to Ulmer's *The Strange Woman*—a similar story based on a novel by the same author as *Leave Her to Heaven*) and instead stage a trial which labels Ellen a "monster" and delivers Richard into the arms of the safe "good" girl Ruth, it all seems anti-climactic. For Ellen is such a transgressive, powerful figure that all the other characters seem little more than silhouettes in Ellen's shadow play, unable to command the audience's attention like Ellen had. **JU**

THE LINEUP (1958)

Director: Don Siegel. **Screenplay**: Stirling Silliphant based on characters created by Lawrence L. Klee in the CBS television series *The Lineup*. **Producer**: Jaime Del Valle. **Director of Photography**: Hal Mohr. **Music**: Mischa Bakaleinikoff. **Art Director**: Ross Bellah. **Editor**: Al Clark. **Cast**: Eli Wallach (Dancer), Robert Keith (Julian), Warner Anderson (Inspector Guthrie), Richard Jaeckel (Sandy McLain), Mary La Roche (Dorothy Bradshaw), William Leslie (Larry Warner), Emile Meyer (Inspector Al Quine), Marshall Reed (Inspector Fred Asher), Raymond Bailey (Philip Dressler), Vaughn Taylor (The Man), Cheryl Callaway (Cindy), Bert Holland (Porter), George Eldredge (Dr. Turkel), Robert Bailey (Staples). **Completed**: October 29, 1957. **Released**: Columbia, June 11. 85 minutes

A ship's porter throws a bag into a taxicab. The taxicab hits a cop and a chase ensues, which ends when the cabbie is shot by the police. The bag contains heroin, and detectives Guthrie and Quine must find the source of the heroin shipments. Later, the professional killer, Dancer, and his associate, Julian, arrive by plane. Their assignment is to retrieve parcels of heroin that were unwittingly smuggled into San Francisco by three groups of travelers. The first packet is held by a merchant seaman who knows what is in it, and Dancer kills him. The second packet was brought in by a married couple, who are not at home. Their servant hesitates to accept Dancer's story about switched suitcases and is also killed. The final packet is concealed in a Japanese doll belonging to a little girl. Dancer befriends her mother, and he and Julian are invited to her apartment; but the little girl has discovered the packet and used it to powder her doll's face. He and Julian take the mother and daughter with them to explain to The Man, who is waiting for their heroin deliv-

The Lineup: *Eli Wallach as Dancer.*

ery in an arcade. The Man, a pitiless individual in a wheelchair, will not accept Dancer's explanations and coldly declares they will be killed. Dancer pushes The Man over a railing onto the skating rink, and they all run to escape. The police pursue the criminals in a dizzying chase until their driver makes a wrong turn onto a half-built freeway and has nowhere to go. Julian, Dancer, and the driver die while shooting it out with the cops.

The characters of Julian, McLain, The Man, and especially the Dancer are the core of *The Lineup*. Don Siegel has a flair for developing ostracized characters and Dancer is a good example of what Andrew Sarris refers to as Siegel's "anti-social outcasts." Julian's efforts to give Dancer social polish are both humorous relief and chilling indications of Dancer's imbalance. Whatever Dancer appears to be learning, any crisis causes him to revert to his true role of the psychopathic killer.

Thrillers like *The Lineup* do not possess the poetic iconography of their predecessors. While 1940s noir films follow their characters again and again down dark rain-soaked streets in an endless night, late 1950s thrillers are often enacted in glaring sunshine. The *Lineup* is very much of this latter type but uses imaginative locales like the skating arcade, props such as the Japanese doll, and absurdist twists in the action occurring on a half-built freeway to make the film distinctively fatalistic. The final chase, although half of it takes place before a back-projection screen, is more visually precise than many spectacular chases in recent films. McLain's turn onto the unfinished freeway is a subtly ill-fated moment in which the very cityscape thwarts Dancer. **BL**

LOAN SHARK (1952)

Director: Seymour Friedman. **Screenplay**: Martin Rackin and Eugene Ting from an unpublished story by Martin Rackin. **Producer**: Bernard Luber. **Director of Photography**: Joseph Biroc. **Music**: Heinz Roemheld. **Art Director**: Feild Gray. **Editor**: Al Joseph. **Cast**: George Raft (Joe Gargen), Dorothy Hart (Ann Nelson), Paul Stewart (Lou Donelli), Helen Westcott (Martha Gargan Haines), John Hoyt (Vince Phillips), Henry Slate (Paul

Nelson), William Phipps (Ed Haines), Russell Johnson (Thompson), Benny Baker (Tubby), Larry Dobkin (Walter Kerr). **Completed**: January, 1952. **Released**: Lippert, May 23. 79 minutes.

Released from prison, Joe Gargen goes to live with his sister, Martha, and her husband, Ed. When his hard-working brother-in-law becomes the murder victim of a loan-shark racket, Joe promises the manager of the tire factory where Ed worked to infiltrate the gang and avenge Ed's death in the process. The racket ensnares factory employees who need cash by encouraging them to borrow from Lou Donelli, a "money man," at tremendous interest rates. If the borrowers delay too long in their repayments, they are beaten up or worse. Once inside, Joe manages to ingratiate himself with Donelli's boss, Vince Phillips, and ultimately discovers that the real "Mr. Big" is Walter Kerr, the racket's apparently timid accountant. Joe manages to shoot both Phillips and Kerr during a gunfight in a darkened theater owned by Kerr, and so redeem himself with both his sister and his girlfriend, Ann.

As far as the Raft vehicles of the noir cycle are concerned, this entry is not on a par with either *Johnny Angel* or *Nocturne*, perhaps because it lacked the accoutrements of the RKO noir style. And as a gangland exposé, it is inferior to such earlier entries as *The Enforcer*. Nevertheless, the actors perform well and Joseph Biroc does some good location work at the Goodyear tire factory and the surrounding South Central Los Angeles locales. Surprisingly, *Loan Shark*'s best scene is the pre-credit sequence: a man carrying a suitcase exits an urban brownstone; as he walks down the dark, wet city streets he becomes aware of footsteps coming from behind, but the audience can only see the lower torsos of two men; frightened, the man walks faster, then dashes down a side street only to be trapped in a blind alley where he is pummeled by the two thugs; over his unconscious body, discarded like a piece of waste among the trash cans, the credit titles are superimposed. Auspicious beginning to a film which fails to live up to its promise. **BP**

THE LOCKET (1947)

Director: John Brahm. **Screenplay**: Sheridan Gibney. **Producer**: Bert Granet. **Director of Photography**: Nicholas Musuraca. **Music**: Roy Webb. **Art Directors**: Albert D'Agostino, Alfred Herman. **Editor**: J.R.

Whittredge. **Cast**: Laraine Day (Nancy Blair), Brian Aherne (Dr. Blair), Robert Mitchum (Norman Clyde), Gene Raymond (John Willis), Sharyn Moffett (Nancy, age 10), Ricardo Cortez (Mr. Bonner), Henry Stephenson (Lord Wyndham), Katherine Emery (Mrs. Willis), Reginald Denny (Mr. Wendall), Fay Helm (Mrs. Bonner), Helene Thimig (Mrs. Monks), Nella Walker (Mrs. Wendall). **Completed**: May 11, 1946. **Released**: RKO, March 19. 85 minutes.

John Willis and Nancy Blair are to be married; but on their wedding day, Dr. Blair, Nancy's former husband, comes to Willis and reveals Nancy's history of kleptomania. Blair was ignorant of her illness until Nancy's previous lover, a painter named Norman Clyde, informed him of the unhappiness her kleptomania had caused him. As a child, Nancy coveted a locket that she was denied. Later, she was accused of stealing it. Although Clyde killed himself in anguish, Dr. Blair persistently doubted Clyde's story until an incident in London during the war confirmed Nancy's criminal tendencies. Now Willis refuses to believe Blair, and the marriage goes on as planned. Just prior to the ceremony, however, the locket is given to Nancy and her entire past flashes across her mind. Collapsing, she suffers a mental breakdown and is institutionalized.

The Locket is an unusual psychological melodrama in the visual style of RKO. It is distinctive in its flashbacks within flashbacks, with the story often being told by a third or fourth person removed. This device is handled effectively in preparation for the climactic flashback, which reveals the truth. Also, given the psychological nature of the subject, the complex time structure is much more appropriate and evocative than in the similarly structured *Passage to Marseilles* made at Warner Bros. a few years earlier. The character of Nancy is well realized by the performance of Laraine Day, with less visible affectation than a similar character in Hitchcock's *Marnie*. Although there is a suggestion that Nancy's illness infects her various relationships with men, the sexual content of *The Locket* is much less pronounced than that of *Marnie*, a film that gains a great deal of its emotional tension from the leading character's frigidity. **BL**

THE LODGER (1944)

Director: John Brahm. **Screenplay**: Barre Lyndon based on the novel by Marie Belloc Lowndes. **Producer**: Robert Bassler. **Director of Photography**: Lucien Ballard. **Art Director**: James Basevi, John Ewing. **Music**: Hugo Friedhofer. **Editor**: J. Watson Webb Jr. **Cast**: Laird Cregar (Slade/Killer), Merle Oberon (Kitty Langley), George Sanders (John Warwick), Cedric Hardwicke (Robert Burton), Sara Allgood (Ellen), Aubrey Mather (Supt. Sutherland), Queenie Leonard (Daisy), Doris Lloyd (Jennie), Helena Pickard (Annie), Anita Sharp-Bolster (Wiggy), David Clyde (Sgt. Bates). **Released**: 20th Century-Fox, January 19. 84 minutes.

A mentally disturbed serial killer, who takes the name Slade, finds lodging in the house of a middle-class London family down on their luck. While there he continues his depredations in the Whitechapel district. Soon, however, a clever Scotland Yard detective named Warwick begins to put various clues together which lead him to Slade and the family he is lodging with. Both Warwick and Slade find themselves attracted to the same woman, the cabaret performer Kitty who shares lodgings with Slade. Slade's attraction-repulsion toward Kitty compels him to attend her performance and then attempt to abduct her backstage. He is, however, discovered by Warwick and the police, but before he can be apprehended he jumps to his death in the river below.

Actor Laird Cregar in collaboration with director John Brahm (another of the German refugees who helped shape film noir) and writer Barre Lyndon forged with *The Lodger* and its companion piece *Hangover Square* two classics of the noir period piece. The opening scenes set the tone and mood appropriate for a tale of Jack the Ripper (the source is the same novel used by Hitchcock to tell the story in a very different manner seventeen years earlier) as well as a film noir. The camera ranges through the foggy streets of Whitechapel (the area where most of the Ripper murders occurred). We are introduced to the denizens of the city: entertainers, prostitutes, beggars, and working class stiffs as they go about seeking money and entertainment. Bobbies patrol on horse and foot searching out an elusive serial killer who kills and then disembowels women.

After this moody opening, Laird Cregar as the killer, who has once again escaped the police patrols, emerges from the fog and dark. He looms over the camera, both his height and bulk adding to his sense of menace. But when the camera finally moves into a close-up, the audience sees in his soulful eyes a gentleness and melancholy which helps give dimension to this "monster." Cregar, as he did in most of the performances of his sadly abbreviated career, conveyed the alienation and despair of a noir protagonist with a style reminiscent of the great expressionistic actors of the 1920s, especially Emil Jannings and Lon Chaney. The camera most often shoots him from below, exaggerating his dimensions, in scenes such as the one in which he clutches the bible of the family he has taken up lodgings with, the key light focused on his large eyes, as he tells the lady of the house in his soft voice, "Mine too are the problems of life and death."

The filmmakers spend a great deal of their capital in the film drawing the audience into the mind of the killer: his obsession with his dead brother (he blames women for his brother's early death), which verges on incestuous homo-

The Lodger: *Robert Burton (Cedric Hardwicke), Daisy (Queenie Leonard), Slade (Laird Cregar), Kitty Langley (Merle Oberon), and Ellen (Sara Allgood).*

eroticism; his attraction to the flirtatious yet sympathetic cabaret performer Kitty, the femme fatale of the piece, who simultaneously stimulates and repulses him—intensifying his desire, as he says, to "cut the evil" out of her beauty.

One of the most remarkable scenes of the movie and a tribute to John Brahm's talent as well as Cregar's acting abilities is the final chase through the galleries of the theater. The killer is shot several times and finally cornered by the police in the top tier of the theater. As the killer cringes in a corner like a wounded animal, Brahm drops out everything on the soundtrack except Cregar's labored breathing. And then as the camera moves in, the killer suddenly turns and leaps to his death through a window into the Thames River below, the waters of which he had earlier described as "full of peace." Kitty pronounces his eulogy over the river, expressing empathy for this man who had not only murdered a string of innocent women but threatened her own life, revealing for a final time the filmmakers' mission—to humanize the seemingly "inhuman." **JU**

THE LONG NIGHT (1947)

Director: Anatole Litvak. **Screenplay**: Jacques Viot, John Wexley. **Producers**: Raymond Hakim, Robert Hakim, Anatole Litvak (Select Pictures Inc.). **Director of Photography**: Sol Polito. **Music**: Dimitri Tiomkin. **Editor**: Robert Swink. **Cast**: Henry Fonda (Joe Adams), Barbara Bel Geddes (Jo Ann), Vincent Price (Maximilian), Ann Dvorak (Charlene), Howard Freeman (Sheriff Ned Meade), Moroni Olsen (Chief of Police), Elisha Cook, Jr. (Frank Dunlap), Queenie Smith (Mrs. Tully), David Clark (Bill Pulanski), Charles McGraw (Policeman Stevens), Patty King (Peggy), Robert A. Davis [Davis Roberts] (Freddie). **Released**: RKO, May 28. 101 minutes.

In his cheap hotel room, Joe kills Max with Max's gun. He locks himself in and shoots when cops tell him to come out. State troopers and city police fire fusillades through the room's window and door. People fill up the street. Many are workers from Joe's plant and WW II veterans like him. Joe smokes and has flashbacks about Jo Ann, a young florist he

The Long Night: *Joe Adams (Henry Fonda) and Jo Ann (Barbara Bel Geddes).*

poetic realism were related to the rise and fall of the French government of the Popular Front. At first, they were optimistic. Then they became pessimistic, like *Le Jour se lève*, released in 1939, after the Popular Front had dissolved. Economic crisis continued, and bloodshed with Germany seemed inevitable. François pulls the trigger at a bleak time for France. In contrast, the future of postwar United States looked positive. The "long night" of the Great Depression, fascism and war was over. Crowds voice their support for François as well as Joe. However, only in *The Long Night* do they tell the accused man to give up because he'll get "a fair trial." At the beginning of the film a narrator says this is "a story about average human beings living in an average American town." As Joe is led away by the police, Freddie, a Black man, lights Joe's cigarette. Joe asks Freddie whether they'll "make it." He ends the film by answering his own question, "Think we'll just about make it." There will be a new day for every American, of every race. The conclusion with a Black man recalls the start of the film, which shows a monument put up by the Grand Army of the Potomac to "the GIs of 1865." The U.S. Civil War ended slavery. Joe and his town's other much appreciated "servicemen and servicewomen" defeated the Axis. Joe's earned a future with Jo Ann in a better America. In this context, he deserves to stay alive. **DMH**

THE LONG WAIT (1954)

Director: Victor Saville. **Screenplay**: Alan Green and Lesser Samuels from the novel by Mickey Spillane. **Producer**: Lesser Samuels (Parklane Productions). **Director of Photography**: Franz Planer. **Music**: Mario Castlenuova-Tedesco. **Art Director**: Boris Leven. **Editor**: Ronald Sinclair. **Cast**: Anthony Quinn (Johnny McBride), Charles Coburn (Gardiner), Gene Evans (Servo), Peggie Castle (Venus), Mary Ellen Kay (Wendy), Shirley Patterson aka Shawn Smith (Carol), Dolores Donlon (Troy), Barry Kelley (Tucker), James Millican (Lindsey), Bruno Ve Sota (Packman). **Completed**: November 30, 1953. **Released**: United Artists, July 2. 94 minutes.

Johnny McBride, an amnesia victim who lost his memory in a car accident, is arrested as a murder suspect. He returns to his old hometown in order to clear his name of the presumed murder charges. He literally tears the town apart in

loves. Her past romance with Max, a much older man, torments him. Max, a traveling magician, kept trying to get Joe to give her up. When Joe asked Jo Ann about her relationship with Max, she explained how she got to know him and promised not to see him again. Charlene, who used to be Max's assistant and lover, lets Joe know that Max and Jo Ann had sex. Joe lost his head and murdered Max when Max threatened to reveal "details" of his affair with Jo Ann. As the police prepare to fire tear gas, Jo Ann cuts through the crowd to get to Joe. She implores him to give up and save himself. He does. When he's free again, she'll be waiting.

In *The Long Night*, the main characters, most events and even numerous lines are taken from *Le Jour se lève*, a classic of French poetic realism. Nonetheless, there are significant differences between the films. After knowing each other for three weeks, Joe and Jo Ann talk about kissing, whereas François asks Françoise to sleep with him. When François learns Françoise is a "conquest" of Valentin, he's disappointed, not devastated. But Joe is anguished to find out Jo Ann isn't a virgin ("untouched, unspoiled"). At the beginning of the film he bemoans, "A guy figures if a girl loves him, she'll tell him everything, no matter what." Later he wishes for "someone to have faith in." Maximilian goads Joe about his "naïve conceptions concerning women," which is impossible for Valentin to do to François. The more conservative outlook on sex in the U.S. results in greater despair in Joe than François. At the climax of the film, the noir style peaks as Jo Ann makes her way to Joe's building to save his life. There she pleads for him to "believe in" her. Unlike François, Joe suffers from a crisis of trust. He had a dream-image of Jo Ann, which she didn't live up to. His feeling of betrayal is unfair, and she wants to help him get over it.

François kills himself, but Joe lives. These endings are associated with different historical contexts. The films of

his zeal to get to the bottom of a contradictory set of circumstances. Henchmen working for the local mob leader, Servo, try to end McBride's meddling. McBride is double-crossed when he visits a woman named Venus. After a savage beating, he regains consciousness but finds himself tied up. Venus crawls to Johnny's side. She pulls a gun and, in the ensuing bloodbath, kills Servo, and frees Johnny McBride. He makes his way to the house of Mr. Gardiner, his ex-employer, who is the financier behind the activities of Servo's mob, including the murder blamed on McBride. Johnny exposes the corrupt set-up and in the process regains his self-respect.

Turning Mickey Spillane's novel into a depressing excursion through small-town corruption, *The Long Wait* displays a cynicism and milieu strongly influenced by the noir films of the late 1940s and early 1950s. The inclusion of amnesia, giving the hero a sense of hopelessness compounded by the frustration of his loss of identity, instills a distinct existential bias into McBride's search. This attitude combines with a pervading sense of corruption and dehumanization to give *The Long Wait* a fatalistic noir ethos. There is a quality of violence and brutality, as exhibited by Johnny McBride and Venus, which lies below the surface of many characters populating the fictional town of Lyncastle. *The Long Wait* presents the most low-key vision of Mickey Spillane's hardboiled universe without the discipline provided by his detective Mike Hammer. This allows the film to exhibit an angst found in very few of Spillane's filmed works. **CM**

LOOPHOLE (1954)

Director: Harold Schuster. **Screenplay**: Warren Douglas from an unpublished story by George Bricker and Dwight V. Babcock. **Producer**: Lindsley Parsons. **Director of Photography**: William Sickner. **Music**: Paul Dunlap. **Art Director**: David Milton. **Editor**: Ace Herman. **Cast**: Barry Sullivan (Mike Donovan), Charles McGraw (Gus Slavin), Dorothy Malone (Ruthie Donovan), Don Haggerty (Neil Sanford), Mary Beth Hughes (Vera), Don Beddoe (Herman Tate), Dayton Lummis (Mr. Starling). **Completed**: October 28, 1953. **Released**: Allied Artists, March 12. 79 minutes.

Teller Herman Tate enters a Hollywood bank on inspection day and, pretending to be one of a group of examiners, absconds with $50,000 from the drawer of teller Mike Donovan. Donovan is under suspicion, and the fact that he waits until Monday morning to report the loss further implicates him. However, the bank manager, police detective Neil Sanford, and even the FBI are eventually willing to accept Mike's plea of innocence. But Gus Slavin, special investigator for the bonding company that insured the loss, is convinced of Mike's guilt, and hounds him to turn over the money. The bonding company refuses to underwrite Mike, so he must give up his bank position and look for new work. Every time Mike gets another job Gus informs his new employer of Mike's purported guilt. One day Mike, now a taxi driver, joins his wife while she is depositing money in their meager account and recognizes Tate who is one of the tellers. Mike forces Tate to take him back to Tate's apartment on the pretense of demanding a share of the loot. Tate hands him part of the money, but they are interrupted by the Tate's girlfriend, Vera, who threatens to kill Mike. She and Tate, however, are frightened away by the sudden arrival of Gus who refuses to believe Mike's claim that he was on the track of the real guilty parties. Escaping from Gus, Mike follows the criminals to a remote beach house, unaware that it is a trap. Before entering the house Mike calls Neil, who dispatches the police. Vera confronts Mike and demands he hand over the money previously given him; she also insists that Tate shoot Mike. When Tate refuses, Vera shoots both men. But Mike is only wounded and subdues Vera until the police arrive.

Loophole has too much the look and texture of a 1950s film to be anything more than marginal film noir and even its abundant use of LA exteriors lacks the stylization typical of the classic period. Its inclusion here is demanded more by virtue of its plot and characterization than anything else. In Mike Donovan we have once again the figure of a decent, somewhat naïve individual whose life is all but ruined by a chance occurrence—an event almost as random as the falling beam of the Flitcraft parable in Hammett's novel, *The Maltese Falcon*. Here, however, the succession of events that continues to beleaguer Mike is not evidence of the workings of a blind fate. It is, rather, the result of his persecution by Gus Slavin, a former cop who, like a modern-day Javert, refuses to accept Mike's innocence and relentlessly pursues him in an effort to prove his guilt. In the process Mike's and Ruthie's pursuit of the "American Dream" in a fashionable part of Los Angeles is disrupted and they are forced to live in progressively seedier circumstances. In the end they are returned to their former state and while the off-screen narrator (carry-over from the semi-documentary style) attempts to assure us that order has been restored, the presence of Slavin lurking outside the bank makes all such assurances problematic. Although this is an Allied Artists production it bears the "cheap" imprint of its corporate predecessor, Monogram, and the presence of Mary Beth Hughes as a virago-like character named Vera (cf. *Detour*) seems almost too coincidental. **BP**

M

M (1951)

Director: Joseph Losey. **Screenplay**: Norman Reilly Raine and Leo Katcher with additional dialogue by Waldo Salt based on the 1931 screenplay by Thea von Harbou with Paul Falkenberg, Adolf Jansen and Karl Vash from an article by Egon Jacobson. **Producer**: Seymour Nebenzal (Superior Films). **Director of Photography**: Ernest Laszlo. **Music**: Michel Michelet. **Art Director**: Martin Obzina. **Editor**: Edward Mann. **Cast**: David Wayne (Martin Harrow), Howard Da Silva (Carney), Martin Gabel (Marshall), Luther Adler (Langley), Steve Brodie (Lt. Becker), Glenn Anders (Riggert), Norman Lloyd (Sutro), Walter Burke (McMahan), Raymond Burr (Pottsy), Roy Engel (Chief Regan), Jim Backus (the Mayor). **Released**: Columbia, June 10. 87 minutes.

A child murderer is terrorizing Los Angeles. He has killed little girls and the police's only clue is that he always takes the shoes of his victims. The killer claims his fifth victim, Elsie Coster, after entertaining her by playing his tin flute and buying her a balloon from a blind vendor. The head of the investigation, Inspector Carney, gives a list of newly released mental asylum inmates to his assistant, Lt. Becker, to check out. On the list is Martin Harrow. In the solitude of his urban apartment Martin plays his flute, fondles the shoelaces from his victims' shoes, and then uses a shoelace to "strangle" the clay figure of a child until he is left totally enervated. The operations of the Los Angeles underworld, however, have been disturbed by the police search for the killer. The local syndicate chieftain, Charles Marshall, plans that the underworld will capture the killer themselves and "take the heat off." Eventually Harrow is drawn toward a sixth victim. He buys her a balloon from the same blind vendor, who recognizes the tune Harrow is playing on the flute and informs a pool hustler who plants the chalk letter "M" as an identification mark on the killer's back. Later, the little girl points out the letter and Harrow, frightened, runs away. Marshall's men converge and pursue him to the Bradbury building; there they capture Harrow and take him to the garage of a cab company run by one of Marshall's lieutenants, Pottsy. A kangaroo court composed of the underbelly of society assembles and Marshall appoints Langley, a drunken ex-lawyer, as Harrow's defense. Harrow pleads his own case and begs to be punished. Langley, emphasizing Harrow's sickness, makes an eloquent plea for understanding but is forced to turn him over to the crowd. When Langley, in Harrow's defense, accuses Marshall of criminal acts, Marshall shoots Langley. The police arrive in time to rescue Harrow and, presumably, hold Marshall and his associates for the death of Langley.

M: *Martin Harrow, "M" (David Wayne) and his prospective victim (Janine Perreau).*

Losey's *M* follows Lang's original quite closely (they shared the same producer), but by focusing more attention on the killer and transplanting the action to authentic Los Angeles locales, it does quite well as a film noir. This overlooked (and difficult to come by) film deserves a major place in the noir canon. For one thing, it makes excellent use of such LA icons as Angel's Flight and the Bradbury Building, hardly surprising since the photographer was Ernest Laszlo (no stranger to the noir style). In fact Laszlo had capitalized on the rococo décor of the Bradbury Building in *D.O.A.*, and while *M* is not as dark visually as that film Laszlo matches his earlier work in his expressive use of location photography.

Notable is the opening sequence (over which are the credit titles): a group of passengers (including Harrow) walk past a bundle of newspapers (bearing the headline of Harrow's most recent murder, revealed by an insert) to board the trolley and after Harrow is seated, the camera shoots over his back shoulder to reveal the lights of a noctural downtown LA in deep focus. Notable also is that the assistant director on this film is Robert Aldrich, who would later make even better use of Bunker Hill as a locus of urban decay in *Kiss Me Deadly*. Most striking of all, however, is the scene of the miserable Harrow, alone and restless in his darkened room, able to achieve sexual release only by "strangling" his clay figurine, under the watchful eyes of a photograph of his mother (the film makes explicit the fact that Harrow does not sexually violate his victims). Such a display of alienation and loneliness has seldom been equaled within the noir cycle. The film is also remarkable for Harrow's impassioned plea before the court of thugs at the end of the movie (written tellingly by blacklistee Waldo Salt). **BP**

MACAO (1952)

Director: Josef von Sternberg and [uncredited] Nicholas Ray. **Screenplay**: Bernard C. Schoenfeld and Stanley Rubin from an unpublished story by Bob Williams. **Producer**: Alex Gottlieb. **Director of Photography**: Harry J. Wild. **Music**: Anthony Collins. **Art Directors**: Albert S. D'Agostino, Ralph Berger. **Editors**: Samuel E. Beetley, Robert Golden. **Cast**: Robert Mitchum (Nick Cochran), Jane Russell (Julie Benson), William Bendix (Lawrence Trumble), Thomas Gomez (Lt. Sebastian), Gloria Grahame (Margie), Brad Dexter (Halloran), Edward Ashley (Martin Stewart), Philip Ahn (Itzumi), Vladimir Sokoloff (Kwan Sum Tang), Don Zelaya (Gimpy). **Completed**: October 19, 1950. **Released**: RKO, April 30. 81 minutes

Three Americans enter Macao, the Portuguese colony south of Hong Kong. They are Nick Cochran, an ex-G.I. escaping from a minor criminal charge in the United States, chanteuse Julie Benson, and a detective posing as a salesman named Lawrence Trumble. Trumble intends to capture Vincent Halloran, Macao's leading gambling club owner, because he is wanted for committing murder in New York. Cochran's and Trumble's identities are switched when Julie lifts Cochran's wallet while kissing him. Meanwhile, Julie is hired to sing in Halloran's club and causes his girlfriend, Margie, to be jealous. Trumble exploits Cochran's mistaken identity by offering him a chance to dispose of a large diamond, which is bait to lure Halloran beyond Macao's borders. When Halloran recognizes the gem as one of his own from a bungled smuggling scheme, he plans to murder the ex-G.I.; but the assassin mistakes the authentic Trumble for Cochran thereby mortally wounding the true detective. Before dying Trumble promises that Cochran's criminal offense will be forgotten in the United States if he can deliver Halloran to the waiting authorities outside Macao's three-mile limit. After a vicious battle, Cochran succeeds in capturing Halloran.

As was typical of RKO while controlled by Howard Hughes this project was shot shortly after the other Robert Mitchum/Jane Russell vehicle in 1950, *His Kind of Woman*, but not released until 18 months later. Initially directed by Josef von Sternberg at RKO, *Macao* was almost totally reshot after its completion by director Nicholas Ray. Von Sternberg managed to instill his own brand of exotic, sometimes vulgar pictorialism into *Macao* even though very few of his sequences remain intact in the film. Neither Ray nor vor Sternberg professed much interest in the making of this film, considering it just another assignment for Howard Hughes at RKO. What is interesting about *Macao* is the way in which Robert Mitchum and William Bendix are set against one another. Bendix, who portrayed typical villain roles in earlier noir films like *The Glass Key* and *Dark Corner,* has a slightly mellower role as Trumble in *Macao* while as Cochran, Mitchum maintains a persona that rejects the typical trench-coated, tough-guy sentimentality, replacing it with a sleepy ambivalence that seems to blend with the dreamlike imagery created by von Sternberg and maintained by Nicholas Ray. Furthermore, the noir dilemma of mistaken identity and shifting allegiances is enhanced by Cochran's ignorance.

Mistaken for Trumble, Cochran does not bother to protest the indignities irrationally visited upon his head; the world is irrational, so he just puts up his fists and slugs his way out.

Macao's female characters, Julie and Margie, are each typical noir examples of the good-bad girl dichotomy. But von Sternberg deifies these two women as he had Marlene Dietrich in their collaborations and Gene Tierney in his noir masterpiece *The Shanghai Gesture*. Encasing Jane Russell and Gloria Grahame in metallic gowns, von Sternberg thematically contrasts the women who are kept separated by beaded curtains and surrounded by much of the same exotic paraphernalia that von Sternberg used earlier in *The Shanghai Gesture*. Considering the problems of completing a film directed separately by two different artists, *Macao* may not reflect the full potential of its contributors; but it nevertheless functions as a brutal and competent noir thriller. **MB & CM**

MAKE HASTE TO LIVE (1954)

Producer/Director: William A. Seiter. **Screenplay**: Warren Duff from a novel by Mildred and Gordon Gordon. **Director of Photography**: John L. Russell. **Music**: Elmer Bernstein. **Art Director**: Frank Hotaling. **Editor**: Fred Allen. **Cast**: Dorothy McGuire (Crystal Benson), Stephen McNally (Steve Blackford), Mary Murphy (Randy Benson), Edgar Buchanan (Sheriff Lafe), John Howard (Josh Blake), Ron Hagerthy (Hackenthal), Pepe Hern (Gonzáles), Eddy Waller ("Spud" Kelly), Carolyn Jones (Mary Rose), Rosa Turich (Juana), Julian Rivero (Carlos), Celia Lovsky (Mother), William Bailey (Ed Jenkins). **Released**: Republic, March 25. 90 minutes.

Crystal "Chris" Benson is the editor of a small-town newspaper in New Mexico. Her husband Steve Blackford, a gangster just released from the pen for murder, her murder, is stalking her. Years earlier in Chicago, a woman was killed in a rigged explosion and when the body was identified as hers, Mrs. Blackford packed up and started a new life as someone else. When Blackford shows up at her door, Benson passes him off to their daughter Randy as her black-sheep brother. Realizing her peril she buys a gun and in case of her death leaves a tape-recording for Randy in which she explains her tortured relationship with the man who is actually her father.

The spooky opening sequence of *Make Haste to Live* is prototypically noir: a sinister stranger looms in the bedroom where Benson tosses in restive sleep. But having set up an intriguing situation *Make Haste to Live* loses its way so that an interesting noir narrative becomes a muddled mess. Credulity is strained well past the snapping point, as Benson flip-flops between resourceful adversary for Blackford and the most feckless of battered wives. At times the two roil with hatred for one another but at others a light flirtatiousness colors their interactions. The dark and twisted psychology of this, however, isn't worked out in dramatic terms. There is no sense of the hold Blackford has over his wife, only that he wants to kill her and that she may be willing to die.

A bottomless pit at an old Indian pueblo makes an early appearance but doesn't end up playing the role that the audience might expect that it will. The final resolution comes not out of character but is just another unexpected and ineffective plot twist. As the narrative meanders from one thing to another, *Make Haste to Live* has no urgent destination in mind. **BMV**

THE MALTESE FALCON (1941)

Director: John Huston. **Screenplay**: John Huston from the novel by Dashiell Hammett. **Producer**. Hal B. Wallis. **Director of Photography**: Arthur Edeson. **Music**: Adolph Deutsch. **Music**: Leo F. Frobstein. **Art Director**: Robert Haas. **Editor**: Thomas Richards. **Cast**: Humphrey Bogart (Samuel Spade), Mary Astor (Brigid O'Shaughnessy/Miss Wonderly), Gladys George (Iva Archer), Peter Lorre (Joel Cairo), Barton MacLane (Lt. Detective Dundy), Sydney Greenstreet (Kasper Gutman), Ward Bond (Detective Tom Polhaus), Jerome Cowan (Miles Archer), Elisha Cook Jr. (Wilmer Cook), James Burke (Luke), Murray Alper (Frank Richman), John Hamilton (Bryan). **Completed**: July 22, 1941. **Released**: Warner Bros., October 3. 100 minutes.

After his partner Miles Archer is killed while shadowing a man named Thursby for a mysterious Miss Wonderly, private detective Sam Spade looks for some answers. He first confronts Miss Wonderly, who confesses that her real name is Brigid O'Shaughnessy and that the same person who killed Miles—and, it turns out, Thursby—is also threatening her. Attracted to her, Spade agrees to help her. His investigation leads him to the strange trio of the foppish Joel Cairo, Kasper "Fat Man" Gutman, and Wilmer. All are on the trail of the Maltese Falcon, a bird figurine whose encrustation of priceless gems has been coated with black enamel. Eventually, Spade discovers that Brigid, a psychopathic liar, is as deeply involved in pursuit of the falcon as the others; ancl when the bird falls into his hands via a murdered ship's captain, Spade cleverly draws the cutthroat group together to find out the true story. Learning that Wilmer, working for Gutman, was responsible for the deaths of Thursby and the captain, Spade produces the bird, which turns out to be a fake. The bitterly disappointed Gutman, Wilmer, and Cairo flee. Spade sends the cops after them, and then forces a confession out of Brigid. She killed Miles, hoping to rid herself of her partner, Thursby, by pinning the murder on him. Although she pleads with Spade, professing her love, he turns her over to the police.

Often cited as the movie that began the classic period of film noir, Hammett's jazz age novel had been adapted twice before in 1930 with silent stars Ricardo Cortez as Spade and Bebe Daniels as Brigid and in 1936 as a serio-comic Bette Davis vehicle under the title *Satan Met a Lady*. As an artifact of popular culture the 1941 *Maltese Falcon* seems peculiarly invulnerable to criticism. Its reputation tends to make one forget that it is more like a caricature than a motion picture, because its characters are so one-dimensional that they are scarcely characters at all. Bogart is the tough guy; Mary Astor, the lying bitch of innocent demeanor; Sidney Greenstreet the threatening, chortling Fat Man; Peter Lorre, the mincing menace; Elisha Cook, Jr., the twitchy, stupid little punk. It is difficult to summon up more than such brief phrases to describe the shadowy, undeveloped figures that populate *The Maltese Falcon*.

The film's chief assets are its crisp dialogue and the bravura performances of the principals. That these performances are overloaded with mannerisms is inconsequential in a film that depends on emphasis of the superficial for its effect. More distressing here is the textbook camerawork (e.g,, shooting Greenstreet from low angles to emphasize his bulk) and the general attitude of contemptuous misanthropy, which is common to most of director John Huston's film.

While it is certainly true that most films in the noir genre

The Maltese Falcon: *Sam Spade (Humphrey Bogart) and Wilmer (Elisha Cook, Jr.).*

are despairing in nature, the best are realized in such a way that even the most neurotic characters are endowed with a human dimension and allowed a fascinating ambiguity. But there are no shades of gray in Huston's *The Maltese Falcon*. Sam Spade himself while spouting the obligatory "When your partner gets killed, you gotta do something about it" speech is brushing off that same partner's frantic wife, with whom he has been conducting a casual affair. Only lip service is given here to the private codes of honor that motivate other noir characters. In the end *The Maltese Falcon* itself suffers from its own contempt. As Spade deliberately lays out the pros and cons of letting Brigid "take the fall," he balances her murderous, lying nature against the notion that "Maybe you love me and maybe I love you." Ostensibly, we should feel sympathy for Spade at such a crossroads, forced to make a painful decision between justice and love. But it all rings false as there have been no intimations of anything like love between Spade and Brigid, who are two manipulators par excellence. The thrill felt at the end of *The Maltese Falcon is* not a poignant one; it is something a little uglier. With Huston's Spade, the viewer is getting a thrill out of sending Brigid over. **JK**

THE MAN I LOVE (1947)

Director: Raoul Walsh. **Screenplay**: Jo Pagano, Catherine Turney from the novel *Night Shift* by Maritta M. Wolff. **Producer**: Arnold Albert. **Director of Photography**: Sid Hickox. **Production Designer**: Stanley Fleischer. **Music**: Max Steiner. **Editor**: Owen Marks. **Cast**: Ida Lupino (Petey Brown), Robert Alda (Nicky Toresca), Andrea King (Sally Otis), Martha Vickers (Virginia Brown), Bruce Bennett (San Thomas), Dolores Moran (Gloria O'Connor), John Ridgely (Roy Otis), Don McGuire (Johnny O'Connor). **Released**: Warner Bros. Pictures, January 11. 96 minutes.

Petey, a singer, visits her brother Joe and sisters Virginia and Sally in California for Christmas. She stays to sort out family problems. Sally struggles to make ends meet while her war hero husband Roy recuperates in hospital from a nervous breakdown. Fending off the advances of nightclub owner Nicky, she negotiates Roy's paranoiac jealousy. Virginia has a crush on Johnny, husband of the flighty Gloria, who lives in the apartment across the hall. Petey dates Nicky and gains a singing spot at the club, but soon meets San Thomas, who was once a famous jazz pianist. They begin a relationship, but San has troubles forgetting his ex-wife. Nicky takes up with Gloria, while Johnny remains oblivious. After Nicky asks Joe to take Gloria home from the club, an argument develops and she is killed by a passing car. San announces that he will return to his ship work. Nicky tries to pin Gloria's death on Joe, but Petey intervenes. Roy returns home cured. Virginia is free to pursue Johnny. Petey returns to singing and touring.

The Man I Love's main connection to the noir genre is through its depiction of the jazz music milieu. This is more than simply a novel item of content, breaking somewhat with the glossy Hollywood artifice of previous showbiz musicals, and anticipating the looser, more experimental forms of John Cassavetes' jazz films, *Shadows* (1959) and *Too Late Blues* (1961). *The Man I Love* exhibits a truly genial looseness, a hipness that is more casual than occasional descriptions of

The Man I Love: *Petey Brown (Ida Lupino) and San Thomas (Bruce Bennett).*

its "crackling hardboiled wit" recognize. This tone is set by the disarming opening scene, a relaxed after-hours performance by Petey and her pals of the Gershwin-penned theme tune. Walsh is a director celebrated for his (frequently virile) ethos of action, comedy, and romance, but this film offers a rare expression of melancholy in his career, largely from the women's point of view (largely due to the presence of Catherine Turney—*Mildred Pierce*—as screenwriter) and, alongside the films soon to come from Nicholas Ray or Lupino herself as a director in the 1950s, it explores a more supple and complex model of character psychology than American cinema had hitherto permitted.

Although the story touches on the problems of post-war masculine trauma (especially via the character of the invalid Roy), its portrait of the difficulty of intimate relationships in the modern world seems more rooted in general societal changes: the first stirrings of a Beat era counter-culture (alcohol here gingerly standing in for other intoxicating substances), and a massive shift in the way women consider themselves. As Jean-Pierre Coursodon has observed, every woman in this tale is defined in terms either of her independence from or understandable difficulty with the traditional wife-and-mother role: where Petey is the wisecracking outsider to such convention, her sisters and their friends struggle with often oppressive obligations and restrictions. In its focus on women's freedom—lived, glimpsed, or thwarted—the film also resonates with the de Beauvoir-style existential feminism of its era.

Yet what makes the movie so poignant, ultimately, is the heartache it locates in the gap between this dream of freedom, or the Utopian ideal of a truly reciprocal relation between men and women (such as we intuit in the exchanges between Petey and San), and the old, entrenched attitudes, responses, and behavioral patterns—a gap caught in the subtle contradiction between Petey's avowed tough attitudes and the abject, masochistic yearning encapsulated in the classic lyrics she sings. Everything in this story is deliberately rather tentative, de-dramatized, incomplete, unfulfilled—an ambience immortalized in Walsh's beautiful *mise en scène* of New Year street celebrations, Petey's traditional expectation of a kiss, even from a stranger, met by a brisk and deflating rejection. At once a muted "woman's melodrama" and an unusual film noir whose center of interest is cannily displaced from external action to internal feeling, *The Man I Love* is an under-appreciated, little-discussed, historically transitional work. **AM**

MAN IN THE ATTIC (1953)

Director: Hugo Fregonese. **Screenplay**: Barré Lyndon based on the novel *The Lodger* by Marie Belloc Lowndes. **Producer**: Robert L. Jacks (Panoramic Productions). **Director of Photography**: Leo Tover. **Music**: Hugo Friedhofer. **Art Directors**: Leland Fuller, Lyle Wheeler. **Editor**: Marjorie Fowler. **Cast**: Jack Palance (Slade), Constance Smith (Lily Bonner), Byron Palmer (Insp. Paul Warwick), Frances Bavier (Helen Harley), Rhys Williams (William Harley), Sean McClory (Constable #1), Leslie Bradley (Constable #2), Tita Phillips (Daisy), Lester Matthews (Chief Insp. Melville), Harry Cording (Sgt. Bates), Lisa Daniels (Mary Renihan), Lilian Bond (Annie Rowley), Isabel Jewell (Katy). **Released**: 20th Century-Fox, December. 82 minutes.

Slade, a reclusive and mysterious pathologist takes lodgings with the Harleys, in 1888, at the height of the Jack the Ripper killings, strangely renting the house's isolated attic in addition to the well furnished spare room. This apparently offers Slade the privacy his experiments require. The Harleys' beautiful showgirl niece Lily, who is also staying with them, finds Slade strangely attractive, a development of which her aunt disapproves, since, at least in this version of the saga, the Ripper targets showgirls, and Slade's occupation keeps him out till late at night. When a fourth Ripper victim dies the night Lily introduces a new show to London, witnesses report someone resembling Slade nearby, which brings Inspector Melville to the Harleys to interview the pathologist. After witnessing her can-can, Slade threatens Lily with a knife in the manner of the Ripper, but Melville arrives in the nick of time. A variety of powerful circumstantial evidence emerges during the film (including the fact that one of the earlier victims is Slade's mother), but is Slade really Jack the Ripper? . . .

Fregonese's movie was the third version of the Lowndes story (the first a Hitchcock silent from 1926), and yet another is scheduled for release in 2008, testimony to the power of the Jack the Ripper legend which has spawned as many movies as there are theories about the killer's identity. (Interestingly one of Lily's shows attracts the Prince of Wales, who has been identified as the Ripper in one of the more fanciful theories.) *Man in the Attic* adds little to the Ripper cinema collection; there are many of the ingredients of the noir canon (nighttime settings, dark shadows and stark contrasts, with light reflecting off rain-soaked streets), but it nevertheless rarely rises above B-movie melodrama.

Palance's soft voice and deadpan features lend mystery to the character, and generally his performance is appropriately menacing, assisted by some Delphic lines that he seldom had to cope with in subsequent roles (". . . the river is like liquid night flowing out to infinity"). The rest of the cast however generally fail to rise above stereotypes, and few cope well with British accents, Tita Phillips' maid Daisy in particular, who affects a Cockney accent of which Dick Van

Dyke would be proud. Lyndon's screenplay injects a psychological dimension absent from the original story: Slade professes a hatred for love that derives from his Oedipal ambivalence towards his mother (who had ". . . the face of heaven and the wretched heart of Jezebel.") This leads to a particular mistrust for other beautiful women ("using your beauty to corrupt and deprave"), revealed through the intercutting during a can-can sequence (owing a greater debt to Busby Berkeley than nineteenth-century English music hall), between the dance and Slade's anguished face. On a historical note, Slade disappears at the end of the film, apparently committing suicide in the Thames; only four Ripper victims are described in the movie, whereas at least five are generally attributed to the real Ripper. **GF**

MAN IN THE DARK (1953)

Director: Lew Landers. **Screenplay**: George Bricker, Jack Leonard, William Sackheim from a story by Tom Van Dycke and Henry Altimus. **Producer**: Wallace MacDonald. **Director of Photography**: Floyd Crosby. **Art Director**: John Meehan. **Music**: Russ di Maggio. **Editor**: Viola Lawrence. **Cast**: Edmond O'Brien (Steve Rawley), Audrey Totter (Peg Benedict), Ted de Corsia (Lefty), Horace McMahon (Arnie), Nick Dennis (Cookie), Dayton Lummis (Dr. Marston), Dan Riss (Jawald), Ruth Warren (Mayme). **Released**: Columbia, April 9. 70 minutes.

Steve Rawley is a convicted bank robber who submits to a brain operation to correct his criminal tendencies in exchange for his release from prison. The operation is successful but erases his memory as well as his antisocial behavior. He is abducted by his old gang members, who want to know the whereabouts of the $130,000 Rawley stole. They beat him half to death, but Rawley can't remember where he stashed the loot. With the help of his old girlfriend, Peg, he interprets a recurring dream and finds the money at an amusement park. Realizing that Rawley has regressed to his old greedy self, Peg leaves him. Chasing him on a rollercoaster ride, bad guy Lefty is killed. Although he has a chance to get away, Rawley turns himself and the money in and wins back Peg.

A remake of the 1936 film *The Man Who Lived Twice* with Ralph Bellamy, *Man in the Dark*, although not bad, is an

unremarkable film noir. It is primarily notable because it was directed by king of Poverty Row cheapies Lew Landers; starred noir icons Edmond O'Brien, hardboiled femme fatale Audrey Totter, and bad guy Ted de Corsia; was shot in part at the no longer existent LA Ocean Park Pier; and was one of the two films noirs to be filmed in 3-D (the other being the terrible adaptation of Mickey Spillane's *I, the Jury*)—an expensive process for such a low-budget film. **AL**

THE MAN WHO CHEATED HIMSELF (1951)

Director: Felix E. Feist. **Screenplay**: Seton I. Miller and Philip MacDonald from an unpublished story by Miller. **Producer**: Jack M. Warner. **Director of Photography**: Russell Harlan. **Music**: Louis Forbes. **Art Director**: Van Nest Polglase. **Editor**: David Weisbart. **Cast**: Lee J. Cobb (Ed Cullen), John Dall (Andy Cullen), Jane Wyatt (Lois Frazer), Lisa Howard (Janet Cullen), Alan Wells (Nito Capa), Harlan Warde (Howard Frazer), Tito Vuolo (Pietro Capa), Mimi Aguglia (Mrs. Capa), Charles Arnt (Mr. Quimby), Marjorie Bennett (Mrs. Quimby). **Completed**: July 25, 1950. **Released**: 20th Century-Fox, February 8. 81 minutes.

The Cullen brothers work together as policemen in San Francisco. Lt. Ed Cullen, a tough old pro, is a bachelor and something of a playboy. His younger brother Andy is about to be married and has been given his first plainclothes assignment as Ed's partner. Ed is having an affair with Lois Frazer, a wealthy socialite who is divorcing and disinheriting her husband, Howard. Howard fakes leaving his home for good. Instead of flying out of town, he returns home to rob the house, having set up an alibi of being at the airport during the time of the robbery. Lois, however, has discovered his gun and, fearing for her life, has called Ed to come over immediately. When Howard breaks into his own bedroom Lois is startled and shoots him with his own gun. To calm the distraut Lois, Ed decides to cover up the killing. He puts the body in his car and drives back to the airport, so that it will look as if Howard was killed there. Unfortunately Ed leaves clues: the toll bridge officer recognizes him, and two airport witnesses can identify the car he was driving. Ironically, Ed leads the murder investigation and is assisted by Andy, who eventually suspects his brother. After confronting Ed with the evidence, Andy is knocked unconscious. Ed and Lois attempt to escape in his car but the police, informed by Andy, set up a series of roadblocks. The couple is forced to hide out till nightfall and Ed chooses the abandoned Fort Point at the base of the Golden Gate Bridge where he and Andy played as kids. Andy guesses this might be Ed's hide-out and goes there, not realizing that he is followed by other police who arrest Ed and Lois. Waiting outside the courtroom for the trial to begin, Ed notices that a successful lawyer has replaced him in Lois' affections.

The Man Who Cheated Himself adeptly interweaves several familiar noir elements: a scheming wife, a cop gone bad, police procedures and a concluding chase sequence. The film is enhanced by Russell Harlan's skillful use of San Francisco locales (particularly Ft. Point, which Hitchcock would later use to great effect in *Vertigo*) and credible performances, especially that of Lee J. Cobb. Jane Wyatt, however, is too "sweet" to be a convincing femme fatale. Rather, she is too much the "damsel in distress" to evoke our antipa-

The Man Who Cheated Himself: *Ed Cullen (Lee J. Cobb) and Lois (Jane Wyatt).*

thy and the only real evidence of her treachery is when she switches her affections to her lawyer at the end. Apropos to 1950s America, where conformity was often regarded as a bulwark against "un-American" influences (especially Communism), this film reaffirms the tenet that a conventional married life is preferable to the recklessness of prolonged bachelorhood. Indeed, the idealization of the American family which began with such 1940s radio programs as *The Adventures of Ozzie and Harriet* and *Father Knows Best* became iconic through the TV shows which followed in their wake (Jane Wyatt would play the mom in TV's *Father Knows Best*). In an irony-filled film the central irony—like that of *The Scandal Sheet* in which a man is compelled to investigate a crime that he committed—reinforces the social judgment favoring marriage since the root causes of Ed Cullen's predicament are his lack of permanent sexual ties and Lois' offhanded dissolution of her marriage. **BP**

MAN WITH MY FACE (1951)

Director: Edward Montagne. **Screenplay**: Vin Bogert, T.J. McGowan, Edward Montagne, and Samuel W. Taylor from his novel. **Producer**: Ed Gardner. **Director of Photography**: Fred Jackman, Jr. **Music**: Robert McBride. **Editor**: Gene Milford. **Cast**: Barry Nelson (Charles "Chick" Graham/Albert Rand), Carole Mathews (Mary Davis), Lynn Ainley (Cora Cox Graham), John Harvey (Buster Cox), Jim Boles (Meadows), Jack Warden (Walt Davis), Henry Lascoe (Police Sergeant), Johnny Kane (Al Grant), Chinita Marin (Juanita), Hazel Sherman (Girl at Nightclub Bar). **Released**: United Artists, June 14. 79 minutes.

After the war, Charles "Chick" Graham settles in Puerto Rico and runs a little business with his old army buddy, now his brother-in-law, Buster Cox. One evening he returns home to find his wife Cora staring at him as if he had suddenly grown a second head. In a sense he has, because there in his living room is his exact double, having drinks and playing cards. And as far as Cora and Buster are concerned, this newcomer is the real husband and business partner, respectively. Even his little pooch bites Graham on the hand. Turned out into the warm Caribbean night, Graham enlists the help of an old girlfriend Mary Davis, whom he had thrown over for the blonde if shopworn Cora. Mary's' protective brother Walt is wary but soon joins in trying to figure out the puzzle. It doesn't take long, because Graham's face is on the front page as a Miami bank robber who got away with half a million. This robber is his double and has been in league with the wife and brother-in-law since long before the marriage.

Director Edward Montagne had made the year before *The Tattooed Stranger*, a Z-budget police procedural shot on location in New York City. As in that strange and seedy movie, other than Barry Nelson, the cast of *The Man with My Face* had few credits behind them (or ahead for most of them). Shot entirely in flat subtropical sunshine—*The Man with My Face* has the distinction of being one of the very noir films in the Commonwealth of Puerto Rico—there is little visual style either. But the doppelganger theme holds attention, despite the fact that its ironies and perversities are never pursued to their full noir potential. There are certain quirky characters, not the least of which is King the Doberman who portrays another war veteran, a member of K-9 corps trained to kill and with a slavering maw that chews up several hapless victims. Turning mostly on its wildly improbable plot, *Man with My Face* is a modest and marginally effective film noir. **BMV**

MANHANDLED (1949)

Director: Lewis R. Foster. **Screenplay**: Lewis R. Foster and Whitman Chambers from the short story "The Man Who Stole a Dream" by L.S. Goldsmith. **Producers**: William H. Pine, William C. Thomas (Pine-Thomas). **Director of Photography**: Ernest Laszlo. **Music**: Darryl Calker. **Art Director**: Lewis H. Creber. **Editor**: Howard Smith. **Cast**: Dorothy Lamour (Merl Kramer), Dan Duryea (Karl Benson), Sterling Hayden (Joe Cooper), Irene Hervey (Ruth Bennett), Philip Reed (Guy Bayard), Harold Vermilyea (Dr. Redman), Alan Napier (Alton Bennett), Art Smith (Lt. Dawson), Irving Bacon (Sgt. Fayle). **Completed**: December, 1948. Paramount, May 25. **Time**: 97 minutes.

Alton Bennett recounts to psychiatrist Dr. Redman a dream he had in which he kills his wife Ruth on learning she has been seeing another man. When Mrs. Bennett is found dead with some of her jewels missing, Bennett is suspected by police Lt. Dawson and insurance investigator Joe Cooper. Actually, Dr. Redman's innocent secretary-transcriptionist, Merl Kramer, had been duped by her boyfriend, Karl Benson, an unscrupulous private detective. Benson learned about the Bennett dream and jewelry from Merl, had a duplicate key made to the Bennett apartment, and was following Mrs. Bennett the night of the murder. The real killer, however, is Dr. Redman, who also wanted the jewels and killed Mrs. Bennett for them. However, he was in turn robbed by Benson who ended up with the jewelry. Redman knows that it was Karl who subdued him, so Karl attempts to persuade him to help frame Merl for the murder because the jewels are too hot to fence. Dr. Redman disagrees and, locking Karl in a closet, escapes with the jewels. Karl breaks out quickly and traps Redman in a blind alley where he runs over the doctor with his car. Returning to Merl's apartment to proceed with his plans, Karl learns that

Manhandled: *Joe Cooper (Sterling Hayden) and Merl Kramer (Dorothy Lamour).*

she will implicate him. He attempts to throw Merl off the building's roof but is stopped in time by the police.

With Dan Duryea in the main role of Karl Benson, a crooked private eye, *Manhandled* might have been a classic in that series of thrillers dealing with the degraded cop or investigator. As it is, due to the extremely convoluted plot and slack direction, the film lacks suspense and it never develops the potential of its cast or locales. Moreover, the comic bits between Dawson and his partner Fayle fall flat and disrupt the flow of the action. The film promises much, with credit titles over a rain-soaked window followed by a pan across the room to the back of a figure in a chair, part of what we later learn is a dream sequence. Unfortunately, except for the sequence in which Benson crushes Redman with his car, *Manhandled* fails to live up to its promise as a film noir. **BP**

THE MASK OF DIMITRIOS (1944)

Director: Jean Negulesco. **Screenplay**: Frank Gruber; from the novel *A Coffin for Dimitrios* by Eric Ambler. **Producer**: Henry Blanke. **Director of Photography**: Arthur Edeson. **Music**: Adolph Deutsch and Leo F. Forbstein. **Art Director**: Ted Smith. **Editor**: Frederick Richards. **Cast**: Sydney Greenstreet (Mr. Peters), Zachary Scott (Dimitrios), Faye Emerson (Irana Preveza), Peter Lorre (Cornelius Leyden), George Tobias (Fedor Muishkin), Victor Francen (Wladislaw Grodek), Steve Geray (Bulic), Florence Bates (Madame Chavez), Eduardo Ciannelli (Marukakis), Kurt Katch (Col. Haki). **Completed**: January 27, 1944. **Released**: Warner Bros., June 23. 95 minutes.

Cornelius Leyden, a mystery writer, is intrigued when the Istanbul police chief shows him the murdered body of Dimitrios, an internationally known criminal. Out of professional and personal curiosity Leyden decides to reconstruct Dimitrios' life and death. He meets people from Dimitrios' past who recount the man's career of murder, political assassination, betrayal, and espionage. In his mission, Leyden is helped by Mr. Peters, one of Dimitrios' previous victims, who

The Mask of Dimitrios: *At center, Irana (Faye Emerson) and Dimitrios (Zachary Scott).*

eventually reveals that Dimitrios is not dead but has faked his own murder in order to live a safe and prosperous life. Peters uses Leyden to blackmail Dimitrios, who retaliates by attempting to murder the extortionists. After a struggle, Peters and Dimitrios kill each other.

Although noir film makers have done relatively well when adapting American crime fiction, they have consistently overlooked the potential of the British thriller. Hollywood's three attempts in the 1940s to film Eric Ambler's novels are a case in point: *Background to Danger* is reduced to a secret agent programmer and *Journey into Fear,* although the most literal and appropriately cast Ambler, dissipates its suspense by concentrating more on the mechanics of the central character's mission than on the psychological implications of his plight. *The Mask of Dimitrios* is the most ambitious of the three. The novel's great strengths are its approach to character and structure. Leyden, for instance, is an ordinary man; we can identify with him and, as a result, share his curiousity and then his fear. The book is constructed in a series of flashbacks as Leyden resurrects Dimitrios' career. Each flashback functions on its own; each also carries forward the plot and its sense of sinister inevitability by posing but only partially answering the questions "Who is Dimitrios?","Why did he die?" and "Is he dead?"

Both of these virtues are undercut in the film. Zachary Scott makes a remarkable Dimitrios, but Greenstreet is a predictable Peters and Lorre is completely at odds with Leyden's common-man role. Even more problematic are the low-key lighting effects, stylized sets, and sententious dialogue. They do not support the characters, plot, and structure as effectively as a simple, straightforward style might have; instead, they seem like superficial atmospherics. *The Mask of Dimitrios* has both the visual style and narrative content associated with noir; yet it lacks the emotional effect of a noir film. It is possible that Ambler's characters are not cynical enough for American noir or that his point of view is more radical than existential. **DLW**

MILDRED PIERCE (1945)

Director: Michael Curtiz. **Screenplay**: Ranald MacDougall, William Faulkner, Catherine Turney from the novel by James M. Cain. **Producer**: Jerry Wald. **Director of Photography**: Ernest Haller. **Music**: Max Steiner. **Art Director**: Anton Grot. **Editor**: David Weisbart. **Cast**: Joan Crawford (Mildred Pierce), Jack Carson (Wally Fay), Zachary Scott (Monte Beragon), Eve Arden (Ida), Ann Blyth (Veda Pierce), Bruce Bennett (Bert Pierce), George Tobias (Mr. Chris), Lee Patrick (Maggie Binderhof), Moroni Olsen (Inspector Peterson), Jo Ann Marlowe (Kay Pierce), Barbara Brown (Mrs. Forrester), Butterfly McQueen (Lottie). **Completed**: February 28, 1945. **Released**: Warner Bros., September 28. 113 minutes.

The murder of wealthy Monte Beragon unveils the past of Mildred Pierce. A bored, middle-class housewife, married to real estate broker Bert Pierce, Mildred is obsessed with giving luxuries her daughter Veda, that Bert cannot afford, so she separates from him. Mildred takes a job as a waitress to support her two daughters; but Veda discovers her mother's position and is humiliated. Mildred's plan to open a restaurant placates Veda's snobbery. With the help of Wally Fay, Bert's old partner, Mildred obtains land for a restaurant sponsored by Monte Beragon, an indolent heir who is looking for a little excitement. Veda is attracted to Monte and breaks her engagement to a wealthy man in order to seduce him. Wanting to be even closer to Veda since the death of Kay, her younger daughter, Mildred divorces Bert and marries Monte who quickly bankrupts Mildred's business. Mildred suffers a final humiliation when she sees Monte embrace Veda. In defense, Monte describes Veda as a "rotten little tramp;" and the girl kills him. Shocked, Mildred vows to protect Veda and tries to convince the police that she is the murderess. But Veda is arrested; and Mildred is left to piece together her life, reunited in sorrow with her first husband, Bert.

Like Dashiell Hammett and Raymond Chandler, James M. Cain feels the need for a tough guy hero. Unlike those two, Cain cannot imagine one. The toughest character he develops

Mildred Pierce: *Mildred (Joan Crawford) surprises her daughter Veda (Ann Blyth) with Monte Beragon (Zachary Scott).*

in his novels is Keyes in *Double Indemnity*. But by the time *Mildred Pierce* reached the screen in 1945, filmic conventions of violence and ill-fated love affairs existed, and they altered the form of Cain's original novel so that Mildred Pierce became the "tough guy," albeit an unwilling one. The film *Mildred Pierce* uses the act of murder to develop a dramatic focus and force that eludes the book. Thus Monte's death at the hands of Veda, which does not even take place in the original novel, is the film's focal point. The entire film flashes back from the moment of Beragon's death and each flashback is arranged so that violence informs and dominates it.

Although Mildred is not a detective, she is perhaps the hardboiled detective's counterpart in the only way suited to a 1940s heroine. Mildred has opted out of her patriarchal socially well-defined milieu to become a free agent and successful businesswoman; she makes or breaks herself, acting without the benefit of the community's moral support. Like a Marlowe or a Spade, she is subjected to beatings in the course of her work, which are appropriately financial and emotional rather than physical. Significantly, Mildred misplaces her love and trust not in an evil man but in her daughter Veda, who is the same type of femme fatale that wreaks havoc throughout film noir. Veda demands obsessive passion and Mildred sacrifices herself. When she is finally freed from Veda's clutches, Mildred, like the tough guy, does not triumph but merely survives.

In the opening sequence of the film (which is in fact the end of the story in linear time and the framing device for the movie), Mildred finds herself on the pier. She is wrapped in a luxurious fur which belies the despair she feels inside. Her fur represents the class she has worked so diligently to become part of, only to find her life blighted by murder and betrayal. In this sordid tale of quasi-incest and overweening mother love, Mildred tries to take the blame for her daughter's crime as a form of ultimate sacrifice. The fact that by the end of her story she is not allowed this act of self-sacrifice gives this woman little pleasure. Even her "reconciliation" with her weak-willed husband seems to offer little hope for this ambitious woman who has been thrown back into a life of dependence and alienation. **EK, CM**

MR. ARKADIN (1955)

Director/Screenplay/Art Director: Orson Welles. **Producers**: Welles, Louis Dolivet. **Director of Photography**: Jean Bourgoin. **Music**: Paul Misraki. **Editor**: Renzo Lucidi. **Cast**: Orson Welles (Gregory Arkadin), Paola Mori (Raina Arkadin), Robert Arden (Guy Van Stratten), Akim Tamiroff (Jacob Zouk), Michael Redgrave (Burgomil Trebitsch), Patricia Medina (Mily), Mischa Auer (The Professor), Katina Paxinou (Sophie), Jack Watling (Marquis of Rutleigh), Gregoire Aslan (Bracco), Peter Van Eyck (Thaddeus), Suzanne Flon (Baroness Nagel). **Locations**: France, Spain, Germany, Italy. **Completed**: August, 1954. **Released**: Warner Bros., August 11 in the U.K.; October 11, 1962 in the U.S. 100 minutes.

A bizarre shoot-out near the waterfront involves Guy Van Stratten in a complex web of mystery and double cross. Coming to the aid of a dying man, he hears about the mysterious Arkadin. Knowing that Arkadin is one of the richest men in the world, Van Stratten believes the dying man's words could mean money. He trails Arkadin to a resort area

Mr. Arkadin: *Orson Welles as Arkadin*

in Spain and approaches Arkadin through his daughter, Raina. Shortly afterward, however, he is hired by Arkadin to investigate the tycoon's past because Arkadin claims to have amnesia. Guy accepts the job. As Van Stratten traces the past of this rich and powerful man, he uncovers the history of a white slaver who used the flesh of innocent women to build a fortune. Mysteriously, everyone Van Stratten comes in contact with is soon killed. Van Stratten finally realizes that he is merely a tool helping to destroy all traces of Arkadin's sordid past. To save himself, Guy persuades Raina to tell her father that she knows everything about him. Arkadin, flying home, calls on the radio and is informed of Raina's knowledge. Destroyed emotionally, he jumps to his death from the plane.

Probably one of the most elliptical films directed by Orson Welles, *Mr. Arkadin* remains an unusually haunting portrait of a man obsessed with the past. Drawing from the "pulp" traditions of the 1930s and 1940s in the formation of his screenplay, Welles complements his plot with a totally baroque visual style filled with obtuse camera angles and wildly cluttered environments causing total disorientation. Although reminiscent of *Citizen Kane's* investigation into the past of a powerful and wealthy man, *Mr. Arkadin* becomes a more personalized and highly romanticized vision of power and corruption. The film is hampered by a limited budget, which forced Welles to abandon his original screenplay, entitled *Masquerade*, for the less poetic version finally released. Robert Arden's portrayal of Guy Van Stratten also mars the film because of his inability to sustain audience identification; but the cameo appearances by Michael Redgrave, Akim Tamiroff, and Katina Paxinou offer diverse performances that compensate for Arden's weak screen presence. It seems that initially Welles may have desired Michel Simon to play Arkadin, as the cosmetic makeup for the role suggests. The film's association with the noir sensibility comes less from characterization than from its exotic visual style and from its attempt to deglamorize the wealthy by placing them at the root of corruption. Ultimately, that corruption, like the nature of the scorpion who, Arkadin explains, cannot keep himself from stinging the frog that carries it across the river, is the deterministic force which destroys Arkadin and his cohorts. **CM**

MOONRISE (1948)

Director: Frank Borzage. **Screenplay**: Charles Haas from the novel by Theodore Strauss. **Producer**: Charles Haas. **Director of Photography**: John L. Russell. **Music**: William Lava. **Production Designer**: Lionel Banks. **Editor**: Harry Keller. **Cast**: Dane Clark (Danny Hawkins), Gail Russell (Gilly Johnson), Ethel Barrymore (Grandma), Allyn Joslyn (Clem Otis), Rex Ingram (Mose), Henry Morgan (Billy Scripture), David Street (Ken Williams), Selena Royle (Aunt Jessie), Harry Carey Jr. (Jimmy Biff), Irving Bacon (Judd Jenkins), Lloyd Bridges (Jerry Sykes). **Completed**: February 5, 1948. **Released**: Republic, October 2. 90 minutes

Danny, a young man whose father was hanged as a murderer, is constantly reminded of his "unsavory" heritage as he grows up. His struggle to become a part of his small Southern community meets with constant rejection and harassment. Eventually, his preoccupation with the past leads him to kill Jimmy, one of his arch-tormentors, in self-defense. He is plagued with the fears that he might be discovered and becomes obsessed with the notion that he might have "bad blood." His fears of becoming a criminal ultimately force him to leave his sympathetic girlfriend and schoolteacher, Gilly, and live in the swamps. It is here that Danny ultimately confronts his past through talking to Grandma and is able to see that he is what he makes of himself. Wending his way back from the swamps, Danny rejoins society and surrenders to the authorities with relief.

It is interesting to see how an overtly romantic director like Frank Borzage develops a story with the noir overtones found in *Moonrise*. Rather than take an expressionistic approach, which might have left the film cold and ruthless, Borzage maintained his relatively impressionistic style and gave *Moonrise* a close association with the works of the French poetic realists. The opening sequence of Danny's father being led to the gallows is a stunning vision, which becomes a central image of the film. It is an image that Borzage returns to in the process of establishing the patterns of existence for Danny and the others. Danny is constantly trapped, threatened, and walled in by the *mise-en-scène*. His escape through the swamp up the hill to his grandmother's cabin and his parents' graves becomes increasingly lighter and liberating, like a mythical journey from his own private hell to the heaven of freedom from guilt and pain. The element of redemption is a factor that has potency in many noir films. However, it is completely necessary in Borzage's treatment of the world. Danny's return to civilization—much in the same way as Robert Ryan's reestablishment of personal relationships in Nicholas Ray's *On Dangerous Ground*—fulfills the film. **MB & CM**

MOSS ROSE (1947)

Director: Gregory Ratoff. **Screenplay**: Niven Busch, Jules Furthman, Tom Reed based on the novel *The Crime of Laura Saurelle* by Joseph Shearing. **Producer**: Gene Markey. **Director of Photography**: Joseph MacDonald. **Music**: David Buttolph. **Art Directors**: Richard Day, Mark-Lee Kirk. **Editor**: James B. Clark. **Cast**: Peggy Cummins (Belle/Rose Adair), Victor Mature (Michael Drego), Ethel Barrymore (Lady Margaret), Vincent Price (Insp. Clinner), Margo Woode (Daisy Arrow), George Zucco (Craxton), Patricia Medina (Audrey Ashton), Rhys Williams (Evans). **Released**: 20th Century-Fox, May 30, 1947. 82 minutes.

Belle, born poor and now a music hall dancer, wants to be "a lady." She is also curious about the identity of the "gentleman" who is secretly dating her friend, Daisy. After she sees him rushing from Daisy's room, she finds Daisy dead, next to an open bible with a moss rose on it. She tracks down the man, Michael, and makes an unusual proposal. She won't help the police investigation if she can live like a lady for two weeks at his mansion. As part of her effort to change herself, she drops her stage name, Belle, and returns to her given name, Rose. At Charnleigh Manor, Rose makes Audrey, Michael's fiancée, jealous. Audrey is killed (bible and moss rose nearby), and Michael is detained. When his mother, Lady Margaret, discovers he has fallen for Rose, she tries to murder her. She is so embittered he grew up apart from her in Canada that she won't let another woman come between them. Michael gets home in time to save Rose, and they move to Toronto.

The longstanding view of film noir as having a male subject, with the female relegated to being an object (obstacle

Moonrise: *Danny Hawkins (Dane Clark) and Gilly Johnson (Gail Russell).*

Moss Rose: *Michael Drego (Victor Mature) and Belle Adair (Peggy Cummins).*

or enigma) in relation to the male, is unlikely to remain dominant. New perspectives about women in film noir have already emerged, if for no other reason than to assess leading female characters in movies that are now acknowledged as film noirs but once were defined as *not* film noir. For example, film noir has been contrasted with "female gothic" (and related but not identical terms like "period film" and "gaslight melodrama"). The prime reason female gothic has been called different from film noir is its focus on a woman instead of a man. *Moss Rose* suggests one way the inclusion of women's film noirs (whether set in the gas lit past or the atomic present) should lead to changes in the traditional description of film noir. From the start and throughout the film until the end, Rose narrates her story. Although the voice-over may generally be male, *Moss Rose* shows film noir doesn't preclude, due to any inherent conventions, female control of the story.

Yet Rose's narrative power doesn't mitigate the overall critique of strong women in *Moss Rose*. Lady Margaret represents the "momism" that Philip Wylie excoriated in his *Generation of Vipers*. Michael's father took him away from her when he was a child and raised him in Canada. She can neither forget nor forgive this. Every day she visits his room, which she's kept just as it was when he left, filled with his boyhood toys. To keep Michael for herself, Lady Margaret smothers Daisy and tries to smother Rose. Lady Margaret's outcome is death. Belle's outcome is Rose. The change in her name is part and parcel of her transformation from a working woman to a wife. Shorn of the displacements in the story (Edwardian poor girl who wants to learn how to be a lady), *Moss Rose* is in line with U.S. postwar current events: women exiting jobs they held for the duration and learning the ways of domesticity. Belle is feisty, clever and ambitious. But in realizing her dream of becoming ladylike, her strength in London shifts to weakness at Charnleigh Manor. When Audrey stops by a village shop, Rose complains, "We'd better be getting back. Lady Margaret said, 'Not to be late.'" Rose wants to go call the servants for help after a tree's shadow on the windowpane frightens her. Of course she significantly tones down her accent and demeanor. The noir style in *Moss Rose* parallels what happens to Belle/Rose. The strongest scenes in the style take place on London streets; and the weakest are at the mansion. After Belle becomes Rose, the noir style, like her luminescent personality, tends to vanish. **DMH**

MURDER BY CONTRACT (1958)

Director: Irving Lerner. **Screenplay**: Ben Simcoe, Ben Maddow (uncredited). **Producer**: Leon Chooluck (Orbit Films). **Director of Photography**: Lucien Ballard. **Music**: Perry Botkin. **Art Director**: Jack Poplin. **Editor**: Carlo Lodato. **Cast**: Vince Edwards (Claude), Philip Pine (Marc), Herschel Bernardi (George), Caprice Toriel (Billie Williams), Michael Granger (Mr. Moon). **Released**: Columbia, December 10. 81 minutes.

Claude, a polite and well turned-out young man, calls on Mr Moon asking to become one of his "contractors." Initially denying involvement in business of any kind, Moon takes Claude's telephone number. Calling Brink, the head of the organization, Moon agrees to test Claude by letting him sweat by his telephone for two weeks. Successfully executing two contracts, Claude, on Brink's orders, kills Moon. Sent to Los Angeles to kill a witness about to testify against Brink, Claude is met by Brink's men, Marc and George. Marc is irritated and George intrigued by Claude's delay in making the hit and by his philosophising. Learning that the target is a woman, Billie Williams, Claude renegotiates the contract with Brink. Failing to electrocute Billie with a TV set wired up to a pylon, Claude acquires a high-velocity rifle with which he shoots the female who comes to the door of Billie's house. When it emerges that the dead woman is a police officer, Marc and George are ordered to kill Claude. Disposing of them, Claude gains entry to Billie's house, but psychologically unable to kill a woman close-up, is himself killed by the police.

Murder by Contract enjoys a considerable underground reputation as, to quote James Agee, "a film that knows its own height and weight perfectly." It certainly does not *look* like a classic film noir, being suffused with light and exterior west coast locations in the manner of late 1950s crime films such as *The Lineup*. What is manifestly noirish, however, is the character of Claude, icily rational on the surface but a tangled mass of Freudian repressions underneath. These emerge obliquely: in his response to Moon's raised eyebrow over his apparent chastity ("I don't like pigs"); in his disproportionate tirade against a hotel waiter over lipstick on a cup; and in his lack of interest in the party girl George sends to his hotel room.

Much of the film's reputation hangs on the literary quality of Claude's discourse and on the sophisticated irony of its take on "civilized society" and the parallels between capitalism and contract killing ("instead of price-cutting, throat-cutting"). It is speculated that this derives less from its workaday director or (if, indeed, he exists at all) its one credited screenwriter than from its uncredited writer Ben Maddow, the blacklisted, Oscar-nominated writer of *The Asphalt Jungle* with a left-wing track record going back to the 1930s and a distinctly literary bent before his transition to Hollywood. This is not to say that the film is stylistically uninteresting. Shot in seven days for a one-off production company, its very lack of resources forces on it a kind of Bressonian or Melvillian austerity. The credit sequence of Claude washing and shaving in preparation for his meeting with Moon looks like a dry run for the much more attenuated credit sequence of *Le Samourai* and the interplay between Marc and George echoes other manic/depressive couples from *The Killers* through Laurel and Hardy and Abbott and Costello to Beckett and Pinter. **CMcA**

MURDER IS MY BEAT (1955)

Director: Edgar G. Ulmer. **Screenplay**: Aubrey Wisberg from an unpublished story by Wisberg and Martin Field. **Producer**: Aubrey Wisberg. **Director of Photography**: Harold E. Wellman. **Music**: Al Glasser. **Art Director**: James Sullivan. **Editor**: Fred Feitshans, Jr. **Cast**: Paul Langton (Ray Patrick), Barbara Payton (Eden Lane), Robert Shayne (Capt. Bert Rawley), Selena Royle (Mrs. Abbott), Roy Gordon (Abbott aka Frank Dean), Tracey Roberts (Patsy Flint), Kate McKenna (Mrs. Sparrow, landlady). **Completed**: November, 1954. **Released**: Allied Artists, February 27. 77 minutes.

The body of a Mr. Deane is found with his head in a fireplace, his features burned beyond recognition. Police detective Ray

Patrick arrests a nightclub singer, Eden Lane, for the crime, and she is convicted. While Ray and a police matron travel with her to prison, Eden sees a man through the train window that she identifies as Deane. Ray believes her and he and Eden leap from the train when it slows for a grade. They walk back to town where Ray checks into a motel and rents a car from the owner. Days pass while they search in vain. Ray discovers that Patsy Flint, Eden's old roommate, has registered at a local hotel under an assumed name and, entering with his skeleton key, discovers a large sum of money in her suitcase. Upon returning to his hotel room one evening, he finds Eden gone. The next morning his friend and superior, Capt. Rawley, shows up to arrest him. Ray pleads for twenty-four more hours, and Rawley agrees to help. Following the trail of Patsy Flint, they discover her murdered in her hotel room. They locate Deane in a ceramics factory he owns under his real name, Abbott. Using the alias of Deane on his trips to LA, Abbott had fallen in love with Eden and had hired a private eye to keep track of her; but he murdered the detective when the man threatened blackmail and left his charred body to be identified as Deane. Patsy Flint, however, knew who Deane was and was also blackmailing him until she was slain by Mrs. Abbott. When Patrick and Rawley discover all this, Mrs. Abbott commits suicide rather than face arrest. Eden, who had given herself up to the warden at the state prison, is freed through the efforts of Rawley. Rawley then arranges for her and Ray to be married.

Murder Is My Beat's plot is so contrivance-filled as to be almost ludicrous and it is only as a measure of Ulmer's facility with shoe-string budgets that it warrants serious viewing. Ulmer's name, of course, evokes memories of *Detour*, a comparison to which is inevitable. Both films are centered on a rather impetuous protagonist on the lam with a cheap blonde (in this case, it turns out, an innocent victim) and living out of seedy motels. And, like *Detour*, this film, for the most part, is narrated by that protagonist as he looks back upon the events which have brought him to his sorry

state. It is only at the film's conclusion, when Patrick and Rawley together discover the truth, that the action returns to real time. Unlike *Detour*, however, this film has the prescribed happy "Hollywood" ending. And instead of Ann Savage we have the unfortunate Barbara Payton, at the end of her film career and visibly showing it (she was coming off a long, abusive relationship with the violence-prone Tom Neal at the time she made this film). Fortunately, she was not called upon to do much acting and her phlegmatic demeanor simply enhanced the enigmatic nature of her character. The visual flair that Ulmer had demonstrated in the past is less in evidence here (perhaps because he was less involved with the story) and even the musical score, by the talented Albert Glasser, is less evocative than that of Erdody's in *Detour*. **BP**

MURDER, MY SWEET (1944)

Director: Edward Dmytryk. **Screenplay**: John Paxton from the novel *Farewell, My Lovely* by Raymond Chandler. **Producer**: Adrian Scott. **Director of Photography**: Harry J. Wild. **Music**: Roy Webb. **Art Directors**: Albert S. D'Agostino, Carroll Clark. **Editor**: Joseph Noreiga. **Cast**: Dick Powell (Philip Marlowe), Claire Trevor (Velma/Mrs. Grayle), Anne Shirley (Ann), Otto Kruger (Amthor),

Murder, My Sweet: *Top, Philip Marlow (Dick Powell) and the wealthy, blonde Mrs. Grayle (Claire Trevor). Below, with the unassuming brunette Ann (Anne Shirley).*

Mike Mazurki (Moose Malloy), Miles Mander (Mr. Grayle), Douglas Walton (Marriott), Don Douglas (Lt. Randall), Raff Harolde (Dr. Sonderborg), Esther Howard (Mrs. Florian). **Completed**: July 1, 1944. **Released**: RKO, as *Farewell, My Lovely* in Minneapolis, Minnesota on December 18; as *Murder, My Sweet* in New York City on March 8, 1945. 95 minutes.

As he waits to learn if he has been permanently blinded, private investigator Philip Marlowe tells the cops his story. First he was hired by ex-con Moose Malloy to find his missing girlfriend Velma. As Marlowe hits a dead end in his search for Velma, he was asked to accompany a man as he ransoms some stolen jewels for a lady friend. At the rendezvous the man is killed, and Marlowe is knocked out. When the owner of the jewels, the attractive Mrs. Grayle, learns that her friend has been murdered, she asks Marlowe to find the murderers. At the Grayle mansion Marlowe also meets Ann, who is suspicious of her step-mother. As he makes inquiries, Marlowe is beaten and drugged until the facts surrounding his investigation become confused. Finally the two cases come together, as Marlowe realizes that Velma and Mrs. Grayle are the same person. He contrives a meeting between all the interested parties at a beach house. Moose, Mrs. Grayle, and her husband shoot each other and blind Marlowe. Ann is romantically reunited with Marlowe whose eyesight is not permanently affected.

One of the earliest noir films which drew critical attention for its chiaroscuro and expressionistic style, *Murder, My Sweet* opens with a disorienting shot of a glaring ceiling light as voices level accusations of murder at someone. The camera tilts down and comes to rest on Dick Powell as Philip Marlowe, sitting jacketless and with bandaged eyes at a small table. Marlowe begins to tell his story, prompted by a policeman, and the camera cuts to city lights at night. Pulling in through a window, the camera reveals Marlowe watching the evening and the flashing lights outside. Suddenly, each flash of light reflects a brooding face in the windowpane and a huge presence hulks in the darkness behind Marlowe.

The disorienting angles, high-contrast lighting, even reflection towering over Marlowe as he deals with his blindness in the first scene point to a disordered and ominous world beyond control. *Murder, My Sweet* is a fascinating blend of the hardboiled tradition and a hybrid form of muted expressionism. Taking Raymond Chandler's *Farewell, My Lovely* and transforming it into a film with a dark ambience unknown in most films of this period, director Edward Dmytryk succeeded in transcending the conventions of tough dialogue and mystery films by creating a singularly cynical vision of society. Dmytryk and screenwriter John Paxton were especially careful in evoking this vision through Marlowe's character. They molded the previously uninspired, juvenile crooner persona of Dick Powell into a model of hardboiled toughness that became a classic icon of the noir period.

Novelist Chandler who by this time had been hired to co-adapt *Double Indemnity* but was still resentful of what Hollywood had intially done to his novels *The High Window* and *Farewell, My Lovely*—turn them into programmers with Mike Shayne and Gay "the Falcon" Lawrence substitued for Marlowe—preferred Powell over Bogart and others despite the fact that or perhaps because Powell's smooth features,

aging baby face and perpetual hang-dog expression make him a vulnerable hero who sometimes lashes out at other characters in the film like a spoiled child who hasn't got his way. *Murder, My Sweet* develops within a closed system as Marlowe narrates the flashback and knows the unhappy end. Thus the entire text of the film becomes one of reflection and pause; both because it occurs in flashback and because Marlowe continually interrupts his tale with wry comments on the action: "I gave her a drink. She was a gal who would take a drink if she had to knock you over to get it."

But the dialogue sequences are less important than the narrative. It is not his repartee but his search through the nightmarish landscape devoid of order and ripe with chaotic images that governs the mood of the film. Filled with shadows and half-fit realities, *Murder, My Sweet* has a visual quality that became characteristic of the period. Contrast is all-important. The inclusion of dream images when Marlowe is drugged, complete with threatening symbols and a surreal sense of perversion, create an atmosphere of fear and dislocation. *Murder, My Sweet* is also filled with a succession of grotesque characters that have little relation to the real world. They exist as icons or images of the twilight world of film noir. Ultimately *Murder, My Sweet* is the archetype for a number of films made later. The use of the femme fatale, an atmosphere of paranoia, the vulnerability of the hero, the motivation of violence, the predominance of grotesque characters, and the threatening environment all contribute to this noir ambience. There is nothing sweet in *Murder, My Sweet,* a film that remains not only a highly stylized and complex detective thriller but also an uncompromising vision of corruption and decay. **EK & CM**

MY NAME IS JULIA ROSS (1945)

Director: Joseph H. Lewis. **Screenplay**: Muriel Roy Bolton from the novel *The Woman In Red* by Anthony Gilbert (Lucy Malleson). **Producer**: Wallace MacDonald. **Director of Photography**: Burnett Guffey. **Music**: Mischa Bakaleinikoff. **Art Director**: Jerome Pycha, Jr. **Editor**: Henry Batista. **Cast**: Nina Foch (Julia Ross), Dame May

My Name Is Julia Ross: *Julia Ross (Nina Foch), Ralph Hughes (George Macready) and Alice (Queenie Leonard).*

Whitty (Mrs. Hughes), George Macready (Ralph Hughes), Roland Varno (Dennis Bruce), Anita Bolster (Sparkes), Doris Lloyd (Mrs. Mackie), Leonard Mudie (Peters), Joy Harrington (Bertha), Queenie Leonard (Alice), Harry Hays Morgan (Robinson), Ottola Nesmith (Mrs. Robinson), Olaf Hytten (Reverend Lewis), Evan Thomas (Dr. Keller). **Completed**: August 4, 1945. **Released**: Columbia, November 8. 65 minutes.

Julia Ross, badly in need of a job, is offered the position of resident secretary to Mrs. Hughes, a wealthy matron, and her son, Ralph. Greeted by Ralph, she is taken to her room and given a meal. Julia awakens from a drugged sleep to find herself in different night clothes and in a room that overlooks the Cornwall seacoast far below. She is informed that she is Ralph's wife, Marian, and that she has just come home from being treated for a mental illness. Escaping from the house, she finds the grounds are surrounded by a wall with a locked and guarded gate. One day, however, Ralph takes her into the village and she mails a note to her boyfriend, Dennis, for help. Later, Julia overhears Ralph and his mother plotting to fake her suicide to cover up the fact that Ralph had previously murdered the real Marian Hughes in a fit of temper and disposed of her body in the ocean. Julia pretends to take poison so that a doctor will be called but Mrs. Hughes has the butler, Peters, pose as the doctor and Julia tells him of the note she mailed. Peters goes to London to intercept the letter and is caught trying to steal it. Dennis and the police rush to Cornwall and arrive just as Ralph prepares to kill Julia. Mrs. Hughes is arrested, Ralph is killed trying to escape, and Dennis and Julia return to London to plan their future life together.

Joseph H. Lewis considers *My Name Is Julia Ross* to be his breakthrough film. In any case, it started him on a series of remarkable low-budget film noirs that did not end until *The Big Combo* in the mid-1950s. Lewis and his cameraman Guffey begin to develop a visual style here (heavy use of chiaroscuro; use of 200+° pans with subjective POV; exterior/interior reverses through windows) that would mature shortly with *So Dark the Night* and would serve both well in their future contributions to the noir cycle. This film's plot veers toward the gothic, especially its setting in a creepy mansion at the edge of the Cornwall cliffs. But the situation of a young woman in the clutches of a matriarch and her sociopathic son, robbed of her identity and made to appear to others as mentally unstable and unable to leave the grounds of the estate alone, is a device quite worthy of Woolrich. Lewis moves the film along so briskly it almost gets us past the story's implausibilities as do the sincere performances of most of the actors. But it is George Macready who shines as he seems to relish the role of the suave but unbalanced son of a doting mother. His scarred face was fast beoming an icon of evil and Ralph's knife fetish in this film (at one point he is seen shredding Julia's underwear) would seem to serve Macready well for his later role in *Gilda*. **BP**

MYSTERIOUS INTRUDER (1946)

Director: William Castle. **Screenplay**: Eric Taylor. **Producer**: Rudolph Flotow. **Director of Photography**: Philip Tannura. **Music**: Mischa Bakaleinikoff, Wilbur Hatch (Whistler's Theme). **Art Director**: Hans Radon. **Editor**: Dwight Caldwell. **Cast**: Richard Dix

If you breathe a word of this, I'll . . ."

(Don Gale), Nina Vale (Joan, Gale's Secretary), Barton MacLane (Det. Taggart), Regis Toomey (James Summers), Helen Mowery (Freda Hanson), Mike Mazurki (Harry Pontos), Pamela Blake (Elora Lund), Charles Lane (Det. Burns), Paul Burns (Mr. Stillwell), Arthur Space (Davis, Summer's henchman). **Released**: Columbia, April 11. 61 minutes.

A kindly old music store owner named Stillwell hires Don Gale, an avaricious private detective, to locate Elora Lund, a woman he has not seen since she was a teenager. The shady Gale hires an accomplice, Freda Hanson, to visit Stillwell posing as Elora. Freda learns that Elora has inherited a fortune in rare recordings left with Stillwell by her mother. However Harry Pontos, a menacing thug, enters Stillwell's apartment through the store front, killing Stillwell and running off with Freda and some recordings he mistakenly thinks valuable. Gale lets it be known that Freda is an imposter so that Pontos will release her. Meanwhile Gale has figured out that Freda was actually using Pontos to double-cross him. Gale tells the real Elora, who has now reappeared, about the recordings and, hoping to cut himself in, puts Elora "on ice." Unfortunately, Gale is now the object of a police dragnet for the death of Freda, though she was actually killed by her landlord, James Summers, who had found out about the recordings. In disguise, Gale returns to the music store but once in the basement finds that Summers and an accomplice, Davis, have already found the recordings. Gale retrieves the box with the cylinders but a gunfight ensues in which Summers is shot but Davis escapes. Gale intends to give the recordings to the police and calls them, not realizing that they are already in the building. Mistaking them for Davis, he shoots at them. They return fire, killing Gale and destroying the recordings he was carrying.

Mysterious Intruder is an entry in *The Whistler* film series starring Richard Dix, this time as one of the most morally ambiguous private eyes in the noir cycle. Unlike Sam Spade, Don Gale possesses not even a vestige of that personal code exhibited by Spade though he is not villainous enough to be the "heavy." Indeed, part of this film's appeal is in waiting to discover where Gale's allegiances lie. From the start he is willing to con the naïve Stillwell (had he not done so, Stillwell might not have been killed), under the judgmental eye of his secretary Joan. When he asks Joan "Whenever did I rob a client?" she replies "Whenever you had a chance!" and warns him not to hurt Elora. Even the sweet Elora, upon first meeting him, refuses to shake his hand. Yet in the end Joan remains loyal to Gale and Gale in turn repays that loyalty by retrieving the recordings with the intention of returning them to the police. In that most ironic of conclusions, he is inadvertently killed and the recordings are destroyed. *Mysterious Intruder* is visually the darkest of *The Whistler* series and Dix, always an asset to that series, performs well as the morally weak hero. In the excellent opening segments, Mike Mazurki virtually reprises his Moose Malloy figure, a menacing hulk standing in the shadows outside the music store, then pausing for some moments in front of the store window in a moment quite reminiscent of his introduction in *Murder, My Sweet*. **BP**

MYSTERY STREET (1950)

Director: John Sturges. **Screenplay**: Sydney Boehm and Richard Brooks from an unpublished story by Leonard Spigelgass. **Producer**: Frank E. Taylor. **Director of Photography**: John Alton. **Music**: Rudolph G. Kopp. **Art Directors**: Cedric Gibbons, Gabriel Scognamillo. **Editor**: Ferris Webster. **Cast**: Ricardo Montalban (Lt. Peter Morales), Sally Forrest (Grace Shanway), Bruce Bennett (Dr. McAdoo), Elsa Lanchester (Mrs. Smerrling), Marshall Thompson (Henry Shanway), Jan Sterling (Vivian Heldon), Edmon Ryan (James Joshua Harkley), Betsy Blair (Jackie Elcott), Wally Maher (Tim Sharkey). **Locations**: Cape Cod, Boston, Cambridge, and Harvard University, Massachusetts. **Completed**: December 9, 1949. **Released**: MGM, July 27. 94 minutes

B-girl Vivian Heldon has been having an affair with a wealthy and respected married man and is pregnant. Vivian arranges a meeting with the man but needs a car to get there. She meets a drunk Henry Shanway at the bar where she works and talks him into letting her drive his car. When she drives to Cape Cod he protests so she dumps him, steals his car and proceeds to rendezvous with her lover. When she demands his help, he shoots her, throws her naked body into the sea and sinks the car in a nearby pond. Eventually Vivian's skeleton is found on the beach and local cop Peter Morales investigates. Dr. McAdoo, a forensic scientist at Harvard, helps creates a composite of the victim from the skull, which matches a missing person photo and leads them to Shanway. Moved by the devotion of Shanway's wife, Grace, Morales is not satisfied with Shanway's guilt and uncovers a link between Vivian and James Hartley. Hartley is already being blackmailed by Mrs. Smerrling, the dead girl's avaricious landlady, who found his phone number on the wall by the rooming house phone. Hartley brushed her off but she managed to steal the murder weapon from his desk. During Morales' visit, Hartley realizes the gun is gone and agrees to bring Smerrling a pay-off. When Smerrling asks him for an inordinate sum, he attacks her and after learning that she has secreted the gun at the baggage room of the railroad depot, he strikes her with a candlestick just as Grace arrives, followed in turn by the police. Hartley manages to flee and Smerrling dies of her injuries, but then Morales discovers the baggage claim check. When Hartley goes to pick up the suitcase the next morning, Morales is there to arrest him after a chase across the railroad yard.

Mystery Street is one of a noir mini-series released by MGM during the tenure of Dore Schary as production chief (1948-1956). Familiar enough with the noir style from his days at RKO, it was Schary who provided a favorable atmosphere at MGM for the likes of Anthony Mann, John Alton, Sidney Boehm and others who had been associated with low-budget thrillers. Louis B. Mayer and some of his cronies, with MGM's stars still in their eyes, resisted this change but Schary won out in his fight with Mayer and was allowed to produce "socially relevant" A-films (like *Bad Day at Black Rock*) as well as the B-thrillers that usually made money for the studio.

In any case, Alton was thoroughly conversant with a photographic style that could enhance the detailed scientific investigation in this film and become the bizarre background for a crime as illustrated in the reconstruction of skeletal remains, the dredging of a pond for a car, etc. Alton's lighting of the darkened lab where McAdoo and Morales use a slide projector to superimpose the victim's skull over pictures of missing women until they match it to Vivian combines low-key noir style with newer semi-documentary content, much as Alton had done before in a similar scene in *He Walked By Night*. And Alton once again brings noir style to authentic locales: especially noteworthy here is the final chase sequence at the Boston railroad station with the use of bizarre camera angles and depth of field. In addition, Sturges' proficiency in staging action sequences heightens the tension.

And if *Mystery Street*'s detailing of the new science of forensic investigation looks backward to earlier semi-documentaries, it also points the way to more contemporary productions, such as television's *CSI*. Finally, some mention should be made of this film's social consciousness (a subject no doubt dear to the heart of both Schary and writer Richard Brooks). Hartley's elitism (he contrasts his "American" lineage to Morales' "foreignness") helps to explain his disregard for the lives of those he considers his inferiors. At the same time Morales' willingness to push for Shanway's guilt even when he has certain misgivings is motivated by his desire escape the petty crimes of the Portuguese barrio where he has been mired and advance himself in the eyes of his condescending superiors—a stalwart though slightly flawed hero but one whose actions are readily understandable even in today's America. **BP & AS**

NAKED ALIBI (1954)

Director: Jerry Hopper. **Screenplay**: Lawrence Roman, Gladys Atwater and J. Robert Bren from their story "Cry Copper." **Producer**: Ross Hunter. **Director of Photography**: Russell Metty. **Music**: Herman Stein. **Art Directors**: Alexander Golitzen, Emrich Nicholson. **Editor**: Al Clark. **Cast**: Sterling Hayden (Joe Conroy), Gloria Grahame (Marianna), Gene Barry (Al Willis), Marcia Henderson (Helen Willis), Max Showalter (Det. Lt. Fred Parks), Billy Chapin (Petey), Chuck Connors (Capt. Owen Kincaide), Don Haggerty (Matt Matthews), Stuart Randall (Chief A. S. Babcock), Don Garrett (Tony), Richard Beach (Felix), Tol Avery (Bartender), Paul Levitt (Gerald Frazier), Fay Roope (Commissioner F.J. O'Day), Joseph Mell (Otto Stoltz). **Released**: Universal, October 1. 86 minutes.

A drunken Al Willis is interrogated by local police who suspect him of robbery. When he resists, he is roughed up, even though cop Joe Conroy has exonerating information. Willis, a church-going local baker, promises to get even for being abused. When Lt. Parks, one of Willis' attackers, is killed, Conroy arrests Willis despite evidence that local mobsters may be responsible. When two more officers die in a bombing, Conroy confront Willis at his bakery and violently tries to compel a confession. Conroy is seen and gets thrown off the force. Now obsessed, Conroy follows Willis to a wide-open border town and discovers Willis leads a double life with Marianna, a local singer. Conroy offers to help her and her son Petey if she will implicate Willis, who has revealed his own brutal underside.

The Naked Alibi never capitalizes on the presence of noir icons Sterling Hayden and Gloria Grahame. Hayden, a Nordic giant, was never easy to cast and listlessly reprises the role of the angry cop from *Crime Wave*. Gloria Grahame's kittenish victim had become by this time a staple of the noir cycle; but coming on the heels of her portrayal of hapless moll Debby Marsh in Fritz Lang's *The Big Heat* her role in *The Naked Alibi* seems very much a pallid knock-off. Hayden's performance as he cajoles Grahame's Marianna shows flashes of Glenn Ford's relentless Dan Bannion in *The Big Heat* but never captures the undertone of fury in Lang's film. Ultimately Gene Barry's performance as Willis has the most nuance, as brutal and fixated as Conroy and yet perversely capable of sentiment and outrage when others treat him as ill as he does Marianna. **BMV**

THE NAKED CITY (1948)

Director: Jules Dassin. **Screenplay**: Albert Maltz and Malvin Wald from an unpublished story by Malvin Wald. **Producer**: Mark Hellinger. **Director of Photography**: William Daniels. **Music**: Miklós Rózsa, Frank Skinner. **Art Director**: John F. DeCuir. **Editor**: Paul Weatherwax. **Cast**: Barry Fitzgerald (Lt. Dan Muldoon), Howard Duff (Frank Niles), Dorothy Hart (Ruth Morrison), Don Taylor (Jimmy Halloran), Ted de Corsia (Garzah), House Jameson (Dr. Stoneman), Anne Sargent (Mrs. Halloran), Adelaide Klein (Mrs. Batory), Grover Burgess (Mr. Batory), Tom Pedi (Detective Perelli), Enid Markey (Mrs. Hylton), Frank Conroy (Capt. Donahue), Mark Hellinger (Narrator). **Locations**: Stillman's Gym, Roxy Theater, Whitehall Building, The City Morgue, Roosevelt Hospital, Universal Building, and Williamsburg Bridge, New York City. **Released**: Universal, March 4. 96 minutes.

The seemingly unexplained murder of a beautiful young woman sets off a police investigation headed by veteran detective Dan Muldoon. Working with a younger assistant, Jimmy Halloran, the two detectives begin by tracing down a number of unsubstantial leads. The investigators eventually narrow the search down to two suspects: one, Frank Niles, is the pampered son of a wealthy family who is filled with a passion for high living; the other, Garzah, serves as the strong arm of the pair and is an aberrant muscle boy. Satisfied that Niles and Garzah are responsible for killing the young woman, the police begin to close in. Niles is taken without much difficulty, but Garzah panics and takes off on a frantic race for freedom through the slums and tenement section of New York City. Finally cornered on the girders of the Brooklyn Bridge, the murderer is gunned down by the police below.

Existing as a sort of amalgamation of Broadway columnist-turned-producer Mark Hellinger's beloved New York landscapes, *The Naked City* remains a prime example of

THE STORY OF A LOVE WITH THE LAW AT ITS HEELS!

THE COP   THE KILLER
and the BORDER TOWN WOMAN!

Naked Alibi

STERLING HAYDEN   **GLORIA GRAHAME**
co-starring **GENE BARRY**   **MARCIA HENDERSON**

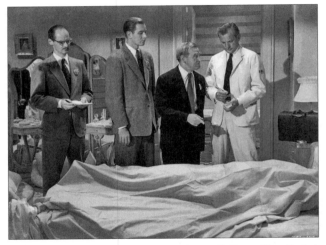

The Naked City: *At center, Detectives Jimmy Halloran (Don Taylor) and Dan Muldoon (Barry Fitzgerald).*

Hollywood's assimilation of documentary style film making. There is not much to associate *The Naked City* and film noir. Rather, functioning as a *film policier, The Naked City* moves on the periphery of the noir sensibilities. Using on-location photography, which won William Daniels an Academy Award, *The Naked City* tells the story of a typical police investigation embellished by the proletarian sympathies of Albert Maltz's screenplay and the crisp assurance of Jules Dassin's direction. The real star of the film becomes the city, which can take on a variety of personalities and moods depending on the situation. *The Naked City* is unlike most of Dassin's other films as it is a vision of the world that forsakes subtlety and deals almost exclusively with black and white absolute truths. **CM**

THE NAKED KISS (1964)

Director/Screenplay/Producer: Samuel Fuller. **Director of Photography**: Stanley Cortez. **Music**: Paul Dunlap. **Art Director**: Eugene Lourie. **Editor**: Jerome Thoms. **Cast**: Constance Towers (Kelly), Anthony Eisley (Griff), Michael Dante (Grant), Virginia Grey (Candy), Patsy Kelly (Mac), Betty Bronson (Miss Josephine), Marie Devereux (Buff), Karen Conrad (Dusty), Linda Francis (Rembrandt), Barbara Perry (Edna), Walter Mathews (Mike), Betty Robinson (Bunny), Gerald Michenaud (Kip), Christopher Barry (Peanuts), George Spell (Tim), Patty Robinson (Angel Face), Edy Williams (B-girl). **Released**: Allied Artists, October 28. 92 minutes.

After beating up her pimp, prostitute Kelly goes on the lam in a small middle-American town. She gets a job nursing handicapped children, establishes a sexual relationship with Griff, a local cop who knows about her past, and meets Grant, a wealthy war hero who regales her with tales of Venice. Gaining self-respect from her highly successful work with the children and from the affection of the townspeople, Kelly tells Grant about her compromised past. To her relief, he "forgives" her and asks her to marry him. Overjoyed, she agrees, although there is something about his kiss that disturbs her. Just before they are to be married, she witnesses him in the act of molesting a little girl.

When he tells her that they belong together because of their mutual "perversions," she kills him. The whole town turns against her, not believing that a respected citizen like Grant could actually be a pedophile. But she convinces Griff to help her find the little girl who ran out of Grant's house as Kelly confronted him. The child is found, tells the truth, and Kelly is acclaimed as a heroine by the town; but she is so disgusted by this experience that she leaves the community.

Samuel Fuller could be described as a primitive talent never introduced to the restraint of polite society. *The Naked Kiss* is, above all, an impolite film, lingering over the uncomfortable subjects of prostitution, perversion, and physical handicaps. From its opening sequence of Kelly's brutal battle with her pimp, during which her wig is snatched off and her shaved head is revealed, *The Naked Kiss* presents a series of increasingly bizarre images: children with withered limbs and sunken eyes are incongruously clad in pirate hats; Kelly stuffs money down the throat of a madam who attempts to lure a young nurse into her shady business; a child skips blithely from the room where she has narrowly escaped the "attentions" of a pedophile; and Kelly bludgeons her lover to death with a telephone receiver. This is a nightmarish vision of Middle America, but it is Fuller's reality, unflinchingly captured by Stanley Cortez's hard, sharply delineated black-and-white photography. That such a bizarre vision proves convincing is due largely to Constance Towers' performance as Kelly. Tough, cynical, and violent, she fulfills the role of the traditionally male film noir protagonist better than many men could; and, like them, she follows a certain code of honor. Her violence, while excessive, is never without motive. It stems from a sense of moral outrage against the pimp who cheats her, the whore who would corrupt innocence, and the lover whose cultured veneer deceives her and hides his unnatural lusts.

If Kelly's presence is anarchic, it is because Fuller considers anarchy a healthy antidote to the strictures of modern society. The handicapped children, sunk in hopelessness prior to Kelly's arrival, are briefly liberated by the workings of her unbridled imagination. Herself a misfit, Kelly appeals to the little band of outsiders by releasing the wilder aspects of their natures, which have been stifled by the reality of their handicaps and by a constrained society that prefers to ignore them. Kelly arrays the children in pirate hats and encourages the outlaw in them, telling them that if they pretend hard enough, they will be free. Through cinematic fantasy, one of the most pathetic of the children actually runs, leaps, and gambols in joyful abandon. Like the other moment of pure fantasy in the film, in which Kelly and Grant float together in a Venetian gondola while enveloped in a fog of dreams, this happy vision cannot be sustained. Reality prevails in *The Naked Kiss*. The children can run and play only in their newly freed imaginations; Kelly can only dream of romantic love; and the "bluebird of happiness," which the children sing about in the haunting little melody taught them by Kelly, is forever out of reach. **JK**

THE NAKED SPUR (1953)

Director: Anthony Mann. **Screenplay**: Sam Rolfe and Harold Jack Bloom. **Producer**: William H. Wright. **Music**: Bronislau Kaper. **Director of Photography**: William Mellor. **Art Directors**: Malcolm Brown, Cedric Gibbons. **Editor**: George White. **Cast**: James Stewart (Howard Kemp), Janet Leigh (Lina Patch), Robert Ryan (Ben Vandergroat), Ralph Meeker (Roy Anderson), Millard Mitchell (Jesse Tate). **Locations**: Lone Pine, California; Durango, Colorado. **Released**: MGM, February 1. 91 minutes.

Having lost his ranch to a duplicitous woman while away at war, Howard Kemp is tracking Ben Vandergroat in the Rockies and happens upon prospector Jesse Tate, whom he hires to help. They corner Vandergroat below a mesa but are held off by rockslides. Roy Anderson, a former cavalryman, hears shooting and rides up. When Kemp is unable to scale the backside of the mesa, Anderson does and, although Vandergroat is accompanied by a young woman named Lina, the three men take him prisoner. When Vandergroat reveals that Kemp is not a law officer and that the missing portion of the wanted poster in Kemp's pocket indicates a $5000 reward, Anderson and Tate want an equal share. As the five of them journey back to Abilene, Vandergroat tries to turn the impromptu partners against each other. Wounded while fighting some Indians pursuing Anderson, a feverish Kemp reveals his past. After a failed escape attempt during which Lina distracts an infatuated Kemp, Vandergroat's stories of buried gold get the best of Tate. After killing Tate, Vandergroat plans to ambush the others, but Lina intervenes. Vandergroat is shot, falls into a river, and Anderson is killed retrieving the body. At Lina's behest, Kemp buries the corpse and gives up the reward.

While this Technicolor Western is not a stylistic match for Mann's standard noir or his black-and-white period pictures, the characters are caught in a dilemma that is prototypically noir. In fact, the moral distance from the venal motives of the ostensibly heroic Kemp to the smiling treachery of

The Naked Spur: *Lina Patch (Janet Leigh) and Howard Kemp (James Stewart).*

Vandergroat is a short one. Certainly Kemp is no criminal, nor is Tate. Even the dishonorably discharged and lecherous Anderson is not clearly a killer; but Vandergroat murdered a peace officer.

In the series of Westerns which James Stewart made with Mann, mostly at Universal, all of his portrayals had anti-heroic aspects. Unlike Ryan who had already established an iconic identity in standard film noir or Meeker, whose performance anticipates the self-serving Mike Hammer in *Kiss Me Deadly* or even Janet Leigh who co-starred with Ryan and caught the unexpected brunt of the noir underworld in *Act of Violence*, other than the cynical reporter in *Call Northside 777* Stewart had no noir credentials. Nonetheless the troubled Kemp, struggling to reverse the effects of betrayal by a woman he loved, is a noir figure. As with his traditional noir films, Mann uses performance to reveal the existential anguish of his protagonists and style to reinforce that. Rather than the shadowy and angular compositions created with John Alton, the color vistas form a brighter but equally menacing background to a narrative focused on personal conflicts. While Tate and Anderson are as transparent as Vandergroat in their motives, only Kemp and Lina grapple with moral issues. As with many classic period figures, Kemp's burden is not his lack of resources but his dark past. Whether the struggle takes place in the shadowy streets of the city at night as in Mann's *T-Men* or *He Walked by Night* or across a bright snow-lit landscape such as the pursuits in *Nightfall, Storm Fear,* or *On Dangerous Ground,* the dilemma is the same. Whether the milieu is contemporary or Western, those who cannot change their perspective usually perish. Digging Vandergroat's grave allows Kemp to survive. **AS**

THE NARROW MARGIN (1952)

Director: Richard Fleischer. **Screenplay**: Earl Felton from the unpublished story by Martin Goldsmith and Jack Leonard. **Producer**: Stanley Rubin. **Director of Photography**: George E. Diskant. **Art Directors**: Albert S. D'Agostino, Jack Okey. **Editor**: Robert Swink. **Cast**: Charles McGraw (Walter Brown), Marie Windsor (Mrs. Neil), Jacqueline White (Ann Sinclair), Gordon Gebert (Tommy Sinclair),

Queenie Leonard (Mrs. Troll), David Clarke (Kemp), Peter Virgo (Densel), Don Beddoe (Gus Forbes), Paul Maxey (Jennings), Harry Harvey (Train Conductor). **Completed**: December 20, 1951 **Released**: RKO, May 4. 71 minutes.

Detective Walter Brown and his partner, Gus Forbes, are assigned to escort Mrs. Neil, a racketeer's widow, by train to appear as a witness against organized crime. Forbes is immediately killed by gangsters; and, although Brown must protect a woman of dubious character so that she will live to give testimony, he feels nothing but contempt for her, believing that his partner's life was of greater value. During the train journey, Brown befriends the refined Ann Sinclair, who is traveling with her son. The gangsters attempt to bribe and intimidate Brown without success, so they kill Mrs. Neil, who turns out to be a policewoman posing as the witness in order to protect the real gangster's widow, Ann Sinclair. Brown is shocked by the death of his colleague. He learns that the reason he was not informed of Mrs. Neil's true identity was that his superiors were not confident that he would not succumb to bribery. The authentic Mrs. Neil arrives safely at her destination, protected by the chastened cop.

The Narrow Margin is a modest, unaffected, and direct but not particularly powerful in its noir statement. The film benefits from the surprises in its story and the good roles afforded to Windsor and McGraw. It is probable that its excellent use of the confined space in the train is the distinguishing quality for which it is critically valued; but other films have made better use of trains, although not always for so much of their length: notably certain works of Hitchcock as well as *The Tall Target* and *Human Desire*. Cinematographer George Diskant, remembered for his films with Nicholas Ray, achieves fine effects in the glistening corridors. Richard Fleischer's direction is sometimes imaginative and supple, more so than in certain of his later, more expansive films. Although the final impression of *The Narrow Margin* might not qualify it as a minor classic, it is possible to respect an honest work in which the moral stature of the characters is relative and which reflects the noir view of an unstable and deceiving surface reality. **BL**

NEW YORK CONFIDENTIAL (1955)

Director: Russell Rouse. **Screenplay**: Clarence Greene and Russell Rouse suggested by the book by Jack Lait and Lee Mortimer. **Producer**: Clarence Greene, Edward Small. **Director of Photography**: Edward Fitzgerald. **Music**: Joseph Mullendore. **Art Director**: Fernando Carrere. **Editor**: Grant Whytock. **Cast**: Broderick Crawford (Charlie Lupo), Richard Conte (Nick Magellan), Marilyn Maxwell (Iris Palmer), Anne Bancroft (Kathy Lupo), J. Carrol Naish (Ben Dagajanian), Onslow Stevens (Johnny Achilles), Barry Kelley (Robert Frawley), Mike Mazurki (Arnie Wendler), Celia Lovsky (Mama Lupo), Herbert Heyes (James Marshall), Steven Geray (Morris Franklin). **Released**: Warner Bros., February 18. 87 minutes.

The New York syndicate is headed by Charlie Lupo, one of a handful of men who control a nationwide crime cartel run like a large corporation. At a "board meeting" it is decided to liquidate one of the minions who made an unauthorized hit, so Lupo arranges for Chicago chief Johnny Achilles to send out Nick Magellan, a professional hit man. He completes his assignment masterfully, and Lupo borrows Nick from Achilles to act as his bodyguard. Lupo is a widower and has a daughter, Kathy, who hates his gangland involvement and would like to leave home. She is attracted to Nick, but he is wary of any relationship with her. The syndicate's plans for an oil-shipping contract with foreign countries under federal subsidy go awry when the lobbyist who is to set this up sells out the syndicate. Board members then decide to kill the lobbyist despite Lupo's protest. Since New York is the target spot, Lupo must make the arrangements. Three "torpedoes" kill the lobbyist but they leave clues, so Lupo dispatches Nick to get rid of them. He eliminates two, but the third, Arnie, escapes and turns to the police, exposing Lupo. Lupo decides to hide out but the syndicate chieftains vote that he must take the rap to protect the organization. Meanwhile Kathy Lupo gets drunk and kills herself in an auto accident. This leads Lupo to decide to disclose syndicate activities to the authorities. Before he can do so, the syndicate instructs Nick, now Lupo's closest friend, to kill him. Although averse to this, Nick obeys orders and, welcomed by a smiling Lupo, eliminates both Lupo and his mistress, Iris. Nick in turn is eliminated by an old foe, thus ensuring the continuance of the system.

New York Confidential is one of a number of films produced in the 1950s and early 1060s that were spawned by the Kefauver Committee's hearings into organized crime beginning in 1950. Most of these films masqueraded as exposés but they tended to pander to the public's taste for the lurid and reinforced a growing fear of a nationwide criminal organization, often termed the Mafia, that eventually rivaled the Communist conspiracy as an object of national concern. It would not be until the 1970s, with Coppola's *Godfather* trilogy, that the activities of the underworld would reach epic proportions and the Mafia would take its place in the American mythos. As far as the noir cycle is concerned, the best of these remains *The Enforcer* although *New York Confidential* (based on the book of the same name by reporters Jack Lait and Lee Mortimer) does have its moments, dominated as it is by the presence of actors like Broderick Crawford and Richard Conte. The narrative entanglement of the characters and the series of double crosses coordinated by the criminal corporate structure anticipates the nihilism of many gangster films of the 1960s. And Conte, as Nick Magellan, gives the character a moral ambivalence based on his earlier roles and a fatalism that anticipates his own destruction with almost existential stoicism. **BP**

NIAGARA (1953)

Director: Henry Hathaway. **Screenplay**: Charles Brackett, Walter Reisch, and Richard Breen. **Producer**: Charles Brackett. **Director of Photography**: Joe MacDonald. **Music**: Sol Kaplan. **Art Directors**: Lyle Wheeler, Maurice Ransford. **Editor**: Barbara McLean. **Cast**: Marilyn Monroe (Rose Loomis), Joseph Cotten (George Loomis), Jean Peters (Polly Cutler), Casey Adams (Ray Cutler), Dennis O'Dea (Inspector Sharkey), Richard Allan (Patrick), Don Wilson (Mr. Kettering), Lurene Tuttle (Mrs. Kettering), Russell Collins (Mr. Qua), Will Wright (Boatman). **Completed**: July 24, 1952. **Released**: 20th Century-Fox, January 21. 92 minutes.

Arriving in Niagara Falls on a belated honeymoon, Polly and Ray Cutler encounter Rose and George Loomis, a newly married couple in the motel room next door. They seem oddly matched; Rose openly flaunts her sexuality while explaining that George, her much older husband, has recently been released from a veterans' mental hospital. Sightseeing, Polly witnesses Rose kissing a younger man, Patrick, by the falls. The illicit couple are planning to murder George and make it appear that he committed suicide. When George is reported missing, Rose is called to the morgue and discovers that Patrick is dead. Not revealing the man's true identity, she faints and is taken to the hospital. Later, Polly sees George, but Ray convinces her that she is mistaken. Fearing George's vengeance, Rose leaves the hospital but is pursued by her husband and strangled. When George tries to escape from the Ontario police by stealing a motorboat, Polly is inadvertently aboard. The boat runs out of gas and is caught by the water flowing toward the falls. George pushes Polly off on a ledge as the boat is slowed temporarily by a rock, but he is unable to save himself and is hurled over the falls to his death on the rocks below.

On the surface *Niagara* may seem less a film noir than a melodramatic showcase designed by 20th Century-Fox to

exploit its contract star, Marilyn Monroe, after establishing her through small roles in *The Asphalt Jungle* and *Clash by Night*. Despite her beginnings in such films, Marilyn Monroe was not to become a conventional film noir actress such as Gloria Grahame, Jane Greer, or even Joan Bennett. Although the sexual domination of Rose over George Loomis may be roughly analogous in character terms to the part played by Joan Bennett in *Scarlet Street,* there is no invocation in Monroe's performance of the stereotypical femme fatale, at once scornful and seductive. Clearly, Rose Loomis is treated initially in *Niagara* as little more than a sexual object; her tight dresses and adolescent mannerisms are meant to titillate the viewer as much as George Loomis.

The abnormality of Rose's relationship with her much older husband is contrasted and filtered through the presence of the bourgeois Cutlers. That the Cutlers' marriage has other aspects than the purely sexual is made clear in their introduction at a customs station: while they explain that they are visiting Canada on a honeymoon delayed for practical reasons, the agent checking the luggage is amused by his discovery of books in the husband's suitcase. Although Ray Cutler is not so taken up with reading that he fails to notice Rose's appearance, Polly seems to typify conventional mores. That both are basically conventional in their attitudes is clear from their reaction to an encounter with Rose and George after the latter couple have obviously just enjoyed a sexual interlude. Ray is somewhat taken aback to find the normally jittery and suspicious George suddenly calm, witty, and terribly pleased with himself, and Polly's sense of sexual intimidation is directly expressed when she replies to Ray's suggestion that she might try wearing a dress like Rose's: "You have to start laying your plans at thirteen for a dress like that."

Nonetheless, Polly is fascinated by the very existence of Rose and George as a couple; and, as mentioned, her perceptions become a meaningful filter both for the viewer and for the film's underlying noir vision. The core of that conception is the character of George Loomis. Although he is tem-

porally removed from the disturbed veterans of earlier film noir, George is as insecure and unable to readjust to society after nearly a decade as many vets were when newly returned from the war. Like the viewer, George's interest in Rose must initially be as an object; but soon she becomes in his disturbed psyche an emblem of the youth he lost to his post-traumatic stress disorder rooted in the war. Therefore, his paranoia over the possibility of her sexual betrayal is as much a fear for the loss of his delicate mental balance as it is over her faithlessness. Ultimately, all the literal and meta-phoric sexuality of *Niagara*—even such oversized examples as the bell tower where George strangles Rose to the orgasmic accompaniment of the bells on the sound track—does prove destructive. In that sense, *Niagara* recruits the symbolism of the falls themselves—the sexual symbolism of which has been appreciated by thousands of actual honeymooners who preceded George and Rose. It is at the foot of the falls that a high-angle long shot reveals Rose's body floating in a now incongruous bright red dress; and it is over the falls that George follows her to his own death. **AS & MB**

NIGHT AND THE CITY (1950)

Director: Jules Dassin. **Screenplay**: Jo Eisinger, Austin Dempster from the novel by Gerald Kersh. **Producer**: Samuel G. Engel. **Director of Photography**: Max Greene. **Music**: Franz Waxman, Benjamin Frankel. **Art Director**: C. P. Norman. **Editors**: Nick DeMaggio, Sidney Stone. **Cast**: Richard Widmark (Harry Fabian), Gene Tierney (Mary Bristol), Googie Withers (Helen Nosseross), Hugh Marlowe (Adam Dunn), Francis L. Sullivan (Phil Nosseross), Herbert Lom (Kristo), Stanislaus Zbyszko (Gregorius), Mike Mazurki (Strangler), Charles Farrell (Beer), Ada Reeve (Molly), Ken Richmond (Nikolas). **Location**: Silver Fox Café, St. Martin's Lane, London. **Completed**: October 11, 1949. **Released**: 20th Century-Fox, June 9. 95 minutes.

Harry Fabian touts for Phil Nosseross' London clip joint where his girlfriend Mary is a singer. Fabian overhears a conversation between wrestling promoter Kristo and his father Gregorius, a legendary Greco-Roman wrestler. By feigning aesthetic outrage Fabian cons Gregorius into helping promote Greco-Roman contests to compete with Kristo's exhibitions. Although he knows his father has been duped, Kristo tells Fabian he will be allowed to stage Greco-Roman contests. Fabian cannot convince Nosseross to loan him money, but the owner's wife Helen will if Fabian can obtain her a

Night and the City: *Mary Bristol (Gene Tierney) and Harry Fabian (Richard Widmark).*

nightclub license. Fabian gives her a forged license, and she leaves Nosseross, who goes to Kristo and offers to entrap Fabian. Nosseross tells Fabian he'll back the enterprise only if the Strangler, a thug despised by Gregorius, is featured. Fabian goads the Strangler into challenging Nicolas, Gregorius' protégé, but Gregorius and the Strangler square off. Gregorius wins but suffers a stroke and dies. Fabian flees in terror as Kristo mobilizes the London underworld with a large reward. Convinced that he will never escape, Fabian pretends Mary has betrayed him so she will get the money. He is killed by the Strangler, and his body thrown into the Thames.

In its opening scenes *Night and the City* recruits the formal conventions of film noir to convey an unmistakable presentiment of fatality. Harry Fabian, the "hero," returns home pursued, anxious, physically out of breath. The mise-enscène first reveals him moving diagonally past dark buildings and stumbling down alleyways then reduces him to a black outline, constricted and redirected by an impersonal cityscape. The wedges of light glistening off the walls and gutters, the angularity and tension of the framing, supported by the insistent, frenetic chords of Franz Waxman's score, enclose him until he reaches an apartment house. There a long shadow spreads out and stops at the foot of the stairs, as does Fabian, exhausted and leaning against an interior wall. At that moment and metaphorically for the remainder of the film, Fabian is caught halfway, transfixed between top and bottom trying to catch his breath.

Stylistically the beginning of *Night and the City* is depersonalized. The urban setting—reinforced by the third-person narration that dispassionately announces, "This is London"—is not photographed in a naturalistic manner; but the viewpoint that affects and distorts the images is not Fabian's. Rather, the connotations are of the exterior, deterministic forces of the noir universe. Other elements of visual usage are keyed to characters and relationships. The extensive use of top-light and side-light, even at the moment of Fabian's triumph, cast shadows under his eyes to suggest fatigue—accentuated by Widmark's gaunt features—or obscure half his face to underscore his indecisiveness. Nosseross, Fabian's corpulent employer, is photographed with a wide-angle lens that artificially enhances his girth and when he smiles at Fabian makes him seem like a malovelent cherub. Another wide-angle lens, as Fabian challenges the Strangler, links the characters within the depth of a single frame and anticipates the transference in which Harry, not the Strangler, will be blamed by Kristo for his father's death. This also distorts Fabian's features grotesquely to match his behavior. Ultimately both exterior and interior connotations may be present in a single sequence. For instance, when Nosseross reveals his treachery to Fabian, as he jeeringly tells him, "You're a dead man, Harry Fabian, a dead man," his large figure constricts Fabian's in the two-shot that encloses them both. At the same time, textured, bar-shaped shadows all about the room externalize the tangled web in which Fabian has enmeshed himself; and mirrored reflections from the rotating ballroom globe flash by at increasing speed, as if foreshadowing the blur of street lights that will streak past in the background of Fabian's flight.

For all its visual diversity *Night and the City* is an extremely concentrated work. If Harry Fabian's frantic greed is endemic of a certain type of figure, then his prolonged and ultimately futile flight across the typically noir landscape of foggy streets, derelict buildings, construction sites, and wharves is an easily read metaphor for the world's antipathy to both his plight and his ordinariness. In his overriding need to "be someone," Fabian overlooks the needs of others, of whom Gregorius is the fatal example. A long take of Harry and the old black-marketeer Anna as he hides on her barge is a summation of Harry's meaningless life. Within the tension and enclosure of the shot, Harry sits with his back to her speaking about "How close I came" and "The things I did." There is no real exchange between them. Fabian doesn't even look at her. She is just a convenient audience for his lament. Footsteps, which he does not know to be Mary's, bring Fabian to his feet. This ruptures the shot and leads to a final side-lit close-up. Mary's presence breaks his indecision and inspires his one selfless gesture. It is, of course, not nearly enough to alter the course of his destruction predestined from the opening frame.

Jules Dassin's remarkable use of London locations creates an irony outside the film, of course, in that after Mark Hellinger's death, Dassin moved to Fox and was soon enmeshed himself in the congressional investigations into Communists in Hollywood. As a cloud formed over the director, studio chief Darryl Zanuck protected him temporarily by assigning this project and sending him outside the United States to make it. Zanuck purportedly warning Dassin that this could be his last American film and urged him to shoot the most expensive scenes first so that the studio couldn't pull the plug on it without serious financial consequences. Like many directors of the classic period, Dassin was indeed compelled to remain in Europe, and it was five years before his next feature—the French-made caper film, the French noir *Rififi*. **AS**

NIGHT EDITOR (1946)

Director: Henry Levin. **Screenplay**: Hal Smith from the radio program "Night Editor" by Hal Burdick and the short story "Inside Story" by Scott Littleton. **Producer**: Ted Richmond. **Directors of Photography**: Burnett Guffey, Philip Tannura. **Music**: Mario Castelnuovo-Tedesco.

Art Director: Robert Peterson. **Editor**: Richard Fantl. **Cast**: William Gargan (Tony Cochrane), Janis Carter (Jill Merrill), Jeff Donnell (Martha Cochrane), Coulter Irwin (Johnny), Charles D. Brown (Crane Stewart), Paul L. Burns (Ole Strom), Harry Shannon (Capt. Lawrence), Frank Wilcox (Douglas Loring), Robert Stevens (Doc Cochrane), Roy Gordon (Benjamin Merrill), Michael Chapin (Doc, as a Boy), Robert Emmett Keane (Max), Anthony Caruso (Tusco), Edward Keane (Chief of Police Barnes). **Completed**: January 12, 1946. **Released**: Columbia, March 29. 66 minutes.

Married police detective, Tony Cochrane, is having an affair with Jill Merrill. Their rendezvous is the site of a brutal murder, which they witness in complete silence. Unable to report the killing due to fear of the scandal that might arise, Cochrane resigns himself to silence. Jill is not so inactive. She discovers the killer and attempts to blackmail him while an innocent man is held for the crime. Rejecting Cochrane, Jill enjoys the social power afforded by her blackmail scheme. In a final attempt to allow Jill to come forth with the truth, Cochrane meets her at a lavish party. His pleas fall on deaf ears as Jill grabs an ice pick and stabs the detective in the stomach. She is taken to jail and Tony Cochrane leaves the police force, only to surface as the narrator of this bizarre story.

Night Editor is a definite B product linked to the noir cycle in its depiction of sadistic brutality and violence. As Tony and Jill are kissing in a secluded spot, the murder they witness seems to function as a sexual stimulus for her. She insists on seeing the body that has been battered by repeated blows from a tire iron. There is little pity in the film, which uses every opportunity to describe people as "rotten through and through," or as "something they serve at the Ritz that has been laying out in the sun too long." The cruelty and lack of compassion found in Jill gives her the quality of a traditionally noir femme fatale, as she uses sex to get what she wants. *Night Editor* even uses the convention of the doomed or romantic narrator to tell its story. Conceived as a pilot film for a series of movies introduced by a "night editor," the film failed in that respect but succeeds as a perverse example of the affinity between sex and violence in the noir universe. **CM**

NIGHT HAS A THOUSAND EYES (1948)

Director: John Farrow. **Screenplay**: Barré Lyndon, Jonathan Latimer from a novel by Cornell Woolrich. **Producer**: Endre Bohem. **Director of Photography**: John F. Seitz. **Music**: Victor Young. **Art Directors**: Franz Bachelin, Hans Dreier. **Editor**: Eda Warren. **Cast**: Edward G. Robinson (John Triton), Gail Russell (Jean Courtland), John Lund (Elliott Carson), Virginia Bruce (Jenny Courtland), William Demarest (Lt. Shawn), Richard Webb (Peter Vinson), Jerome Cowan (Whitney Courtland), Onslow Stevenson (Dr. Walters), John Alexander (Mr. Gilman), Roman Bohnen (Melville Weston, Special Prosecutor), Luis Van Rooten (Mr. Myers). **Released**: Paramount, October 13. 81 minutes.

Elliott Carson stops his fiancee Jean Courtland from suicide one starry night. They go to a cafe and meet with John Triton, who tells them his life story. Triton had a mind reading act twenty years ago in which he was assisted by Jenny, his fiancee, and Whitney Courtland. During one of his acts, Triton received a true premonition and sent a woman in the audience home to save her small son from burning in a fire.

Night Has a Thousand Eyes: *Edward G. Robinson as John Triton.*

During the next few weeks, Triton received many premonitions, including one of Jenny's death in childbirth. Leaving the act, he lived in a deserted gold mine and communicated with no one for five years. Hearing that Jenny married Whitney Courtland and died giving birth to a baby girl, Triton moves to Los Angeles to be near Courtland, now a wealthy industrialist, and his daughter, Jean. He does not reveal himself to them until he receives a premonition of Courtland's death, and then contacts Jean. Elliott Carson thinks that Triton is a fake; but Jean is convinced of his powers when her father is killed in a plane crash. Jean attempted suicide because Triton had a vision of her lying under the stars, which she took as a portent of her death. Elliott contacts the police, and Triton is taken into custody to investigate possible sabotage of Courtland's plane. When Triton makes a correct prediction concerning a prisoner's suicide, the police let him go to Jean, whom he believes is still in a great deal of danger. Reaching her side just in time to stop her from being killed by one of her father's crooked business associates, Triton rushes to her defense and the police accidentally shoot him. In his pocket they find a note predicting his own death that night.

Supported by an appropriately eerie score composed by Victor Young, *Night Has a Thousand Eyes* is a psychological thriller with its seer hero poised on the brink of doom. It is precisely the feeling of doom throughout the film that separates it from most mysteries. John Triton is a man with a gift he never asked for; his power to see flashes of future events could be beneficent, but everything he sees is tragic. Death is usually the subject of his vision. Even his seemingly harmless race track predictions or stock market tips add up to death for Whitney Courtland, who became wealthy because of these tips. For Triton, there is no way out. Despite living as a recluse for twenty years, events pointed him toward his inevitable end.

Farrow's direction of Lyndon and Latimer's script, which is based on Cornell Woolrich's darkly romantic novel, is entirely realistic. The audience must believe that such things happen in an otherwise normal world. Although reasonable explanations are given by the skeptical police inspector of Triton's

predictions, there is never any doubt that Triton is authentic. In a noir sense, man cannot control or rationalize the future. Life is pathetic for the seer, who is helpless and useless despite his efforts to avoid tragedy. Triton's dilemma is epitomized when he tells his best friend's daughter, "I had become a reverse zombie, the world was dead and I was living." *Night Has a Thousand Eyes* depicts the noir universe at its darkest. The night itself is the enemy, and the stars fatally oversee every misadventure. JC

THE NIGHT HOLDS TERROR (1955)

Director/Producer/Screenplay: Andrew Stone. **Director of Photography**: Fred Jackman, Jr. **Music**: Lucien Cailliet. **Editor**: Virginia Stone. **Cast**: Jack Kelly (Gene Courtier), Hildy Parks (Doris Courtier), Vince Edwards (Victor Gosset), John Cassavetes (Robert Batsford), David Cross (Luther Logan), Edward Marr (Capt. Cole), Jack Kruschen (Detective Pope), Joyce McCluskey (Phyllis Harrison), Jonathan Hale (Bob Henderson), Barney Phillips (Stranske), Charles Herbert (Steven), Nancy Dee Zane (Deborah). **Completed**: December 20, 1954. **Released**: Columbia, September 14. 85 minutes.

Returning to his desert home in Lancaster, Gene Courtier picks up a young hitchhiker, Victor Gosset, who pulls a gun on him and is soon joined by two other criminals: the psychopathic leader of the bunch, Robert Batsford, and the gentler Luther Logan. The three men hold Courtier, his wife Doris, and their two small children hostage. The family spends a terrified night but believes that the nightmare will end in the morning when Courtier sells his car for the cash the men seek. But in the morning, Batsford announces a new plan and holds Courtier for ransom as he has learned that Courtier's father is rich. The F.B.I., in cooperation with the telephone company, attempts to trace the source of the criminals' telephone calls and Courtier attempts to escape several times, almost succeeding when the weak Logan becomes frightened at the immensity of the crime. Finally, the efforts of the phone company and the law, as well as Courtier's own resourcefulness, results in the death of the three kidnappers and Courtier is safely returned to his family.

Based on a true story, *The Night Holds Terror* is one of a series of suspense motion pictures written and directed by Andrew Stone in the 1950s, in which the contribution of his wife, editor Virginia Stone, is of paramount importance. Complex cross-cutting between the activities of the law and the phone company, and the drama of the captives and the criminals, effectively creates tension and gives an impression of unusual density for a film of 85-minute duration. Of even more interest than this display of technique, however, is the more genuine noir vision of this film compared to *The Desperate Hours,* a higher-budgeted and considerably more prestigious production on the same subject. *The Desperate Hours* betrays not only its theatrical source but also the complacency of William Wyler when presented with a middle-class family of the 1950s; and it appears that Wyler's reason for making the film is to indulge his predilection for staging scenes in deep focus, especially on staircases.

The Night Holds Terror also uses deep focus compositions but with more fluidity and less self-consciousness. Stone does not use his terrorized family to confirm the virtues of the middle-class lifestyle as does Wyler, but as a reflection of the unforeseen perils of the noir underworld. Stone's family is simply terrorized and needs to summon a little more courage and cunning than is their custom to survive the ordeal. Similarly, Wyler's melodramatic heavies are considerably less frightening than the more realistically presented trio of the Stone film. All in all, Stone's cast of newcomers is superior to the seasoned actors of the Wyler cast. John Cassavetes, always effective in pathological roles, is especially subtle and compelling in the Stone film. **BL**

NIGHT OF THE HUNTER (1955)

Director: Charles Laughton. **Screenplay**: James Agee, Charles Laughton (uncredited), based on the novel by Davis Grubb. **Producer**: Paul Gregory. **Director of Photography**: Stanley Cortez. **Music**: Walter Schumann. **Art Director**: Hildyard Brown. **Editor**: Robert Golden. **Cast**: Robert Mitchum (Harry Powell), Shelley Winters (Willa Harper), Lillian Gish (Rachel Cooper), James Gleason (Uncle Birdie Steptoe), Evelyn Varden (Icey Spoon), Peter Graves (Ben Harper), Don Beddoe (Walt Spoon), Billy Chapin (John Harper), Sally Jane Bruce (Pearl Harper), Gloria Castillo (Ruby). **Locations**: Moundsville, West Virginia; Canoga Park, Los Angeles. **Released**: United Artists, September 29. 93 minutes.

Awaiting execution for murder during a robbery, unemployed Ben Harper shares a jail cell with the psychotic Harry Powell, a slayer of widows posing as a country preacher. Upon his release, Powell romances Harper's widow Willa, hoping that she or her children John and Pearl can lead him to Ben's stolen money. Dazzled by the handsome preacher, Willa ignores John's suspicions and marries Powell. When psychological manipulation and threats fail, Powell murders Willa and prepares to torture John to give up the money. John and Pearl flee downriver in a skiff, where they join the "flock" of Rachel Cooper, a religious woman committed to taking in orphans of the Depression. Powell locates John and Pearl by flirting with Rachel's ward Ruby. When Powell arrives to claim his children, Rachel intuits that he's "a wolf in sheep's clothing" and holds him at bay with a shotgun. Rachel stands guard until the police arrive to arrest Powell for Willa's murder. Curiously, John is traumatized by Powell's arrest. At Christmas, Rachel gives thanks and wonders at the strength of children in a cruel world.

Charles Laughton's sole film directing effort has defied simple categorization despite often being claimed as both a film noir and a horror film. The revivalist hysteria and twisted Americana of Davis Grubb's novel is presented with severe, often frightening expressionistic visuals.

James Agee's script (heavily rewritten by Laughton) sets up a Manichean conflict between Rachel Cooper's god-fearing mother hen and Harry Powell's deranged preacher. The film's dark agenda has only superficial similarities to the themes of film noir. The greedy Powell claims that his murders serve a religion "that God and I have worked out betwixt us," but Icey Spoon also uses faith to mask hypocrisy and suppress sexuality. Young John is too young to oppose Powell yet faces his ordeal with an inner resolve incompatible with the noir ethos. *Night of the Hunter* functions on a different thematic plane, as represented by Harry Powell's battle "between left-hand and right-hand."

But *Hunter's* disturbing expressionistic visuals are decid-

Night of the Hunter: *Robert Mitchum as Harry Powell.*

edly noir. A threatening train announces Powell's arrival with blasts of music and billows of black smoke. Distorted sets flatten perspective as in a primitive painting—the Harper house, a nighttime farm exterior. Willa's bedroom becomes a steepled church interior surrounded by black, and her basement a pit for profane sacrifices. Stylized special effects emphasize the animals that seem to protect the children in their Moses-like river escape. Silhouetted riding a mule against a starry night, Harry Powell is a rude beast slouching toward his next murder. Camera angles evoke the pictorially direct style of D.W. Griffith, while the jarring editing patterns are outside normal Hollywood convention.

Night of the Hunter's terrors do not align with classic noir aims, but its sense of subversive dislocation does. A bucolic fishing scene is interrupted by a vision of a shocking Cocteau-like murder tableau in the water below. John Harper relives the capture of his father at the arrest of the feared Harry Powell. The misery of the Depression, the dreams of an executioner and the joy of Christmas blend into an affirmation of life as both horrible and divine. **GE**

THE NIGHT RUNNER (1957)

Director: Abner Biberman. **Screenplay**: Gene Levitt from a *Cosmopolitan* magazine story by Owen Cameron. **Producer**: Albert J. Cohen. **Director of Photography**: George Robinson. **Music**: Joseph Gershenson. **Art Directors**: Alexander Golitzen, Robert Boyle. **Editor**: Al Joseph. **Cast**: Ray Danton (Roy Turner), Colleen Miller (Susan Mayes), Willis Bouchey (Loren Mayes), Merry Anders (Amy Hansen), Harry Jackson (Hank Hansen), Eddy C. Waller (Vernon), Robert Anderson (Ed Wallace), Jean Inness (Miss Dodd), Jane Howard (Typist), John Stephenson (Dr. Crawford), Richard Cutting (Man Interviewer), Alexander Campbell (Dr. Royce), Steve Pendleton (Capt. Reynolds), John Pickard (Dr. Fisher), Paul Weber (Dr. Rayburn). **Completed**: September 5, 1956. **Released**: Universal, February 9. 79 minutes.

Roy Turner is an inmate at a state mental hospital under treatment for schizophrenia. Because of overcrowding at the hospital Turner is made an outpatient. As he is given his freedom by his psychiatric overseer, Turner is warned to avoid emotionally charged situations. After taking a bus south, Turner finds a motel and decides to remain there indefinitely because he is attracted to the nearby beach. He is also attracted to Susan Mayes, the daughter of the motel owner. When she reciprocates his interest, her father looks into Turner's past and discovers his history of mental illness. After ridiculing him, Mayes threatens to have Turner recommitted unless he leaves his daughter alone. The sudden stress imbalances Turner, and he kills Mayes. He begins to flee with Susan down the beach and considers killing her and himself. After he pushes her into the sea, the shock restores his equilibrium. He rescues her and then turns himself in to the authorities.

Many of *The Night Runner's* story elements are strikingly similar of Hitchcock's *Psycho,* a film it antedates by three years. In fact, the narrative particulars of a schizophrenic young man coming to a secluded motel and capturing the sympathy of the owner's daughter seem almost a planned inversion of the roles in the later film. What makes *The Night Runner* truly noir, rather than a neo-Gothic or psychological melodrama, is the characterization of the "hero," Roy Turner. While Hitchcock regards his psychopath somewhat sardonically, *The Night Runner's* portrayal is sympathetic. The very title suggests what the introductory sequences at the mental hospital confirm expositionally: that the main character is acting under the dark compulsion of an aberration for which he is not morally responsible and of which he is only partially aware. Ray Danton's interpretation is lacking in nervous tics, darting eyes, or other clichéd mannerisms and does not alienate the viewer from the character's quasi-normality.

The Night Runner's imagery is equally restrained. Roy Turner's fascination with birds is, unlike Norman Bates' in *Psycho,* based not on their rapacious traits but their freedom to fly wherever they choose. Mainly, the film draws on the contrasting aspects of the rundown motel and the expansive beach nearby to externalize the conflicting sides of Turner's psyche as he attempts to readjust to society. It does contain moments such as the tracking shot and abrupt subjective tilting when Turner goes mentally "over the brink" that are visually striking. This shot, like those of Turner rapturously watching the seabirds or gloomily side-lit in his room, is a sensorily direct and fairly effective moment of stylistic irony. The central irony of *The Night Runner,* however, is thematic and most typically noir: Turner is undone not by his illness but because his semblance of normality leads to the beginnings of a relationship with Susan Mayes and, in turn, to his unintended murder of her possessive father. **AS**

NIGHT WITHOUT SLEEP (1943)

Director: Roy Ward Baker. **Screenplay**: Frank Partos, Elick Moll based on a story by Elick Moll. **Producer**: Robert Bassler. **Director of Photography**: Lucien Ballard. **Music**: Cyril J. Mockridge, Alfred Newman. **Art Directors**: Addison Hehr, Lyle R. Wheeler. **Editor**: Nick DeMaggio. **Cast**: Linda Darnell (Julie Bannon), Gary Merrill (Richard Morton), Hildegarde Neff (Lisa Muller), Joyce MacKenzie (Laura Harkness), June Vincent (Emily Morton), Donald Randolph (Dr. Clarke), Hugh Beaumont (John Harkness), Louise Lorimer (Mrs. Carter), William Forrest (Mr. Carter), Steven Geray (George, Maitre D'), Mauri Lynn (Singer), Bill Walker (Henry), Mae Marsh

(Mald), Ben Carter (Benny), Harry Seymour (Ned), Sam Pierce (Sam). **Released**: 20th Century-Fox, September 26. 77 minutes.

Composer Richard Morton wakes fully dressed on his lounge room floor from a nightmare with a woman's screams echoing in his head, and thinks back to the first conversation he ever had with his wife. The last time they were together he alluded to dating another woman. Realizing he blacked out for thirteen hours he recalls his psychiatrist warning him against drinking to the point of blacking out because it risks him committing violence against women. Concerned at what he may have done he visits his friend Johnny, at whose apartment he meets movie star Julie. Morton arrives nearly two hours late to his date with Lisa where they quarrel and he threatens her. After Lisa storms out, he takes Julie out and she describes to him how she secretly fell in love with him years ago. Rejecting Julie's advances he visits Lisa's apartment and approaches her threateningly, then blacks out. Waking at home, he phones Lisa, who is unharmed, as is Julie when he phones her. Relieved, he retires to his bedroom where he finds his wife's body and remembers strangling her.

Apart from the blackly ironic ending which seems a long time coming, it is the richly chiaroscuro lighting of *Night without Sleep* and its gradually building mystery elements that satisfy noir expectations. That the mystery grows through a succession of flashbacks adds another layer of genre familiarity. While there is also a flashback within a flashback, the risks of that strategy seem to be underlined later in the story when the heroine, movie actress Julie Bannon, acts out all the parts of a dramatic fantasy as if she was presenting a flashback herself, maintaining the film's temporal integrity at the risk of satirizing its recourse to such stock devices. While its protagonist's dipsomania anticipates *The Lost Weekend* (1945), a film that's always been on the margins of the noir canon, for contemporary viewers Merrill's looks and role of showbiz decline strongly evoke comparisons with James Mason in *A Star Is Born* (1954). That's more like it because, notwithstanding its noir structure and visuals, most of the content here is melodrama, of the bittersweet romantic variety. As befits that genre, its milieu is thoroughly upper middle class; even a Harlem nightclub is a bourgeois, jazz-free zone, although noteworthy in its racial proportions of roughly one aging white couple to every two who are black.

Night without Sleep is overly talky and static, with the flashbacks providing most of its movement, and Merrill's lugubrious and enervating persona as Broadway composer Morton doesn't help. Morton's insistence on regretting memory, punishing himself with its record of lost opportunity, promises the noir payoff of discovering, and hence reconciling, his public and private identities, as in the amnesia noir *Somewhere in the Night.* But *Night without Sleep* doesn't deliver, achieving nothing more than a sour backward glance. So when the final, undeniably noir reversal arrives, the fact that its foundation rests, not on any revelation but on Morton's inability to remember, seems the blackest twist of all. **RSW**

NIGHTFALL (1957)

Director: Jacques Tourneur. **Screenplay**: Stirling Silliphant from the novel by David Goodis. **Producer**: Ted Richmond. **Director of Photography**: Burnett Guffey. **Music**: George Duning. **Art Director**: Ross Bellah. **Editor**: William A. Lyon. **Cast**: Aldo Ray (James Vanning), Brian Keith (John), Anne Bancroft (Marie Gardner), Jocelyn Brando (Laura Fraser), James Gregory (Ben Fraser), Frank Albertson (Dr. Edward Gurston), Rudy Bond (Red), George Cisar (Bus Driver), Eddie McLean (Taxi Driver). **Completed**: April 9, 1956. **Released**: Columbia, January 23. 80 minutes.

Believing he is being followed, Jim Vanning takes refuge in a restaurant where he meets Marie Gardner. When they leave Vanning is abducted at gunpoint by two thugs named John and Red who take him to a deserted oil derrick by the ocean to torture him for information. Vanning escapes and goes to confront Marie for betraying him. He learns that she is innocent and now also in danger. Vanning explains the cause of his dilemma. While on a hunting trip in Wyoming with a doctor friend, they witnessed a car accident and went to aid the occupants, John and Red, who were escaping after a robbery. They shot Vanning and the doctor, whose bag they mistook for the one containing their loot. A wounded Vanning concealed the bag in a snow bank and went into hiding until he recovered. Now both John and Red and an insurance investigator named Fraser are after him. Marie agrees to help him retrieve the money to prove his innocence. They are confronted by Fraser, whom they convince to join their search; but the bag is gone. Nearby they see Red kill John over the money. After Vanning wrestles his gun away, Red climbs into a snowplow and drives towards Fraser and Marie. Vanning pulls him from the cab, and Red falls to his death under the mechanism.

Although made near the end of the cycle, the dilemma of *Nightfall*'s protagonist is archetypically noir due largely to its source—noir novelist David Goodis' novel. A victim of several mischances, Vanning's paranoia compounds these problems significantly. Director Tourneur's editing scheme relegates these causal incidents to a flashback halfway through the film; but he does not allow them to be distorted by Vanning's point-of-view. Rather they reflect Vanning's struggle to comprehend how such violent but basically simple past occurrences have put him in such a dangerous and complicated present predicament. This certainly recalls the narrative structure of Tourneur's earlier *Out of the Past.* But even more than with Jeff Bailey in that earlier film, the likely chain of events is revealed to the viewer after their visible effects,

thereby adding credibility and existential tinge to Vanning's conspiracy theories. In fact, when Vanning is first seen skulking in the shadows of a back street, the visual inscription could easily be that of a culpable figure trying to avoid detection. This contrasts markedly with the introduction of Bailey in *Out of the Past,* who is out by a lake fishing. As such it does not recruit but extends the ironies of that earlier film.

Vanning is basically innocent of any wrongdoing and Bailey clearly was not, so the trap into which Vanning has fallen can and must be interpreted as impersonal or deterministic not retributive. Vanning has a socially motivated paranoia. Physically and temporally removed from the violent events that threatened him before, Bailey seems to expect that his new life will not be disrupted by something out of his past. When Vanning is misjudged and incriminated in the doctor's death, he is unable to restore equilibrium to his life, as Bailey did for a considerable amount of time. Vanning's initial belief that Marie, whose ultimate influence on him is as beneficent as Kathie Moffat's was malign for Bailey, has betrayed him to John and Red is symptomatic of how Vanning's trauma has distorted his outlook. Since Vanning is not haunted by a particularly dark or distant past but driven by an unsettled and immediate one, perhaps the subtlest ironies that Tourneur attaches to this situation are visual rather than narrative. Contrary to common noir usage, for Vanning the black streets promise some measure of safety while the bright snow-covered landscape recalls pain and near death. Low angles and side-light around the oil derrick turn the mechanism into a huge, nightmarish mantis waiting to devour Vanning. In the climactic sequence, the snowplow lumbering after him like a gigantic beast becomes the final metaphor for the larger-than-life terrors that have plagued him. **AS**

NIGHTMARE (1956)

Director: Maxwell Shane. **Screenplay**: Maxwell Shane from the short story by Cornell Woolrich. **Producers**: William H. Pine, William C. Thomas. **Director of Photography**: Joe Biroc. **Music**: Herschel Burke Gilbert. **Art Director**: Frank Sylos. **Editor**: George Gittens.

Nightmare: *Keven McCarthy as Sam Grayson.*

Cast: Edward G. Robinson (René Bressard), Kevin McCarthy (Stan Grayson), Connie Russell (Gina), Virginia Christine (Sue Bressard), Rhys Williams (Deputy Torrence), Gage Clark (Belnap), Barry Atwater (Sheriff Warner), Marian Carr (Madge), Billy May (Louie Simes). **Location**: New Orleans. **Completed**: December, 1955. **Released**: United Artists, May 11. 89 minutes.

New Orleans jazz musician Stan Grayson dreams that he stabs a man to death in a mirrored room and wakes to find scratches, bruises, and other indications that it was not a dream. He relates the incident to his brother-in-law, police detective René Bressard, who assures him that it was a dream. The thought that he may be a killer haunts him, as does an exotic tune that runs through his mind. He prowls the jazz bars on Bourbon Street, trying to find someone familiar with the song but with no success. Hoping to cure Stan's melancholia, René invites him to picnic with his sister and girlfriend, Gina. A sudden rainstorm forces them into the car, but its windshield wipers are broken and, seeking shelter, Stan directs them to a large, empty mansion which turns out to be the house in his dream. He discovers the strange song was nothing more than a popular tune, played on the record player at slow speed. Then he and René find the mirrored room. Later, when René is informed by the local police that a murder did take place there, he believes Stan tried to dupe him. He takes Stan back to Stan's hotel room, informing him that he should leave town or he will turn him in the next day. When Stan attempts to jump from the building's ledge, René saves him and begins to believe his story. Stan then tells about Mr. Britton, his next door neighbor, who, on the night of the murder, came into Stan's room with a lighted candle. René suspects Stan was hypnotized and discovers that the mansion is owned by Mr. Belnap, whose wife was run over the evening of the murder. By doctoring a photograph of Belnap, René has Stan identify it as Mr. Britton and decides to set a trap for Belnap. After Mrs. Belnap's funeral, Stan is outfitted with a microphone to record his conversations.

Then he confronts Belnap in the mirrored room with the information that he was never under hypnosis but had only pretended, so that he could blackmail Belnap later. Belnap hypnotizes Stan again, escapes with him through one of the mirrored doors and instructs Stan to walk into the bayou. However, the police arrive quickly and, as they shoot Belnap, René rescues Stan from a watery death.

Nightmare is a close remake of Shane's earlier adaptation of Woolrich's story, *Fear in the Night*. This time around Shane has a bigger budget, a bigger cast, and a better photographer to capitalize on the New Orleans locations, but somehow this version lacks the B-movie charm of the original (it is also shot in 1.85:1 aperture which slightly changes the noir style). Biroc, however, gives it a more expressionistic look, aided here by a locale which presents him with jazz bars, dark streets and overgrown bayous to work with. Herschel Gilbert's bluesy jazz score is also a benefit and while the use of a jazz tune played at slow speed is little more than a "MacGuffin," its attenuated sound enhances the film's oneiristic atmosphere. Stan's nocturnal odyssey down Bourbon Street evokes memories of a similar interlude in *D.O.A.*, just as the ominous tone of Kevin McCarthy's narration carries with it the same foreboding it had earlier in *Invasion of the Body Snatchers*. **BP**

NIGHTMARE ALLEY (1947)

Director: Edmund Goulding. **Screenplay**: Jules Furthman from the novel by William Lindsay Gresham. **Producer**: George Jessel. **Director of Photography**: Lee Garmes. **Music**: Cyril Mockridge. **Art Directors**: Lyle Wheeler, J. Russell Spencer. **Editor**: Barbara McLean. **Cast**: Tyrone Power (Stanton Carlisle), Joan Blondell (Zeena), Colleen Gray (Molly), Helen Walker (Dr. Lilith Ritter), Taylor Holmes (Grindle), Mike Mazurki (Bruno), Ian Keith (Pete), Julia Dean (Mrs. Peabody), James Flavin (Hoatley), Roy Roberts (McGraw), James Burke (Town Marshal). **Completed**: July 31, 1947. **Released**: 20th Century-Fox, October 9. 110 minutes.

Stanton Carlisle, a small-time carnie, obtains the secrets of a fake mind reader Pete who dies of alcoholism. Joining with Pete's widow Zeena, he beomes a hit in the carnival as a mentalist. Forced into marrying the innocent Molly, he leaves the carnival with her and sets himself up as a spiritualist in Chicago. Joining forces with a corrupt psychologist, Dr. Lilith Ritter, they begin exploiting the rich. Molly inadvertently exposes him during an exhibition where she is supposed to act as the spirit of a rich man's love. Stan's fall is as swift as his success. He is betrayed by Lilith, who steals much of his money, and he drifts from one tavern to another, until he must return to the shoddy carnival as a "geek," a freak-show attraction who eats live chickens to earn his living. In the final scene Molly returns to find him.

Nightmare Alley ranks as one of the bleakest of film noirs in the classic period. Part of the reason is its source material — William Lindsay Gresham's nihilistic novel of the same name and Jules Furthman's (*The Shanghai Gesture*) perverse script. But equally important is the commitment of matinee idol Tyrone Power, who was intent on playing the part even over the objections of studio head Darryl Zanuck. Longing to demonstrate his acting abilities in playing against type, Power incarnated Gresham's amoral, manipulative Stanton Carlisle with

Nightmare Alley: *Molly (Colleen Gray) and Stanton Carlisle (Tyrone Power).*

an authenticity which reinforces the character's almost classically tragic dimensions. Carlisle's rise to fame from carnie mentalist to "The Great Stanton," spiritualist to Chicago's rich and famous, occurs over the bodies and feelings of others: Pete, the man who gives him the code and then dies from a bad batch of liquor Stan gave him; Zeena, his older mentor and lover whom he dumps after bedding the nubile teenager Molly; and even Molly herself, whom he exploits in his act even though she expresses moral qualms about his deceptions.

Being a film noir, the only character who can equal Carlisle in his ruthlessness and hubris is, of course, the femme fatale of the piece: Dr. Lilith Ritter (her first name evokes the rebellious first wife of Adam according to Talmudic folklore). Her androgyny (she dresses in both men's suits as well as glamorous gowns and speaks in a husky voice) and dominating personality (she convinces a momentarily vulnerable Carlisle to submit to therapy) causes him to stumble, trusting her in their schemes to fleece the rich, and eventually to fall as she betrays him for the money.

But in many ways, Carlisle has always sensed his end. The film opens on a performance of a carnie "geek"—a man who rips the heads off of live chickens with his teeth. Carlisle watches mesmerized: "The guy fascinates me." Later in the film he sees the man again, running and screaming through the night. By the final frames of the movie, the alcoholic Carlisle has taken the place of that geek (in a characteristic of old-time bravado the dissolute Carlisle tells the carnie boss "I was made for it"), in the throes of delirium tremens, being chased by his boss, the manager of the carnival. Although Power insisted on respecting the integrity of the novel in every aspect, Zanuck overruled the original nihilistic ending and demanded that Carlisle be presented with a ray of hope. So Molly finds Carlisle in the midst of his fit and holds his hands, promising him love and a brighter future, thereby reaffirming, somewhat incongruously considering the rest of the movie, a more reassuring view of life. **JU**

99 RIVER STREET (1953)

Director: Phil Karlson. **Screenplay**: Robert Smith, John Payne, Phil Karlson from an unpublished story by George Zuckerman.

Producer: Edward Small. **Director of Photography**: Franz Planer. **Music**: Emil Newman, Arthur Lange. **Art Director**: Frank Sylos. **Editor**: Buddy Small. **Cast**: John Payne (Ernie Driscoll), Evelyn Keyes (Linda James), Brad Dexter (Victor Rawlins), Frank Faylen (Stan Hogan), Peggie Castle (Pauline Driscoll), Jay Adler (Christopher), Jack Lambert (Mickey), Eddy Waller (Pop Dudkee), Glen Langan (Lloyd Morgan), John Day (Bud), Ian Wolfe (Walde Daggett), Peter Leeds (Nat Finley), William Tannen (Director), Gene Reynolds (Chuck). **Completed**: July 12, 1953. **Released**: United Artists, October 3. 83 minutes.

Bitter over an eye injury that halted his career as a professional prizefighter, Ernie Driscoll drives a taxi for a living and becomes increasingly estranged from his wife Pauline, who constantly berates him for his failure to earn as much money as he had previously made by fighting. Ernie is consoled only by his friend Stan, a taxi dispatcher, and by Linda James, an aspiring actress with whom he drinks coffee at a drug store. When Pauline threatens to leave Ernie, Stan suggests that having a child might help his rocky marriage. Ernie takes a box of candy to the shop where Pauline works and when he sees her kissing another man he angrily confronts them before driving off in his car. Pauline is not greatly concerned, and she plans to run off with the man, Victor Rawlins, who has just executed a jewel robbery. Rawlins is unable to fence the jewels with a man named Christopher, who objects to Pauline's involvement. Meanwhile, Linda James asks Ernie for help. She claims to have murdered a man and takes Driscoll to the theater where it happened. Driscoll offers to help her conceal evidence of the crime, but it is revealed that Linda's problem is a hoax; the producer's idea of an acting test. Ernie is humiliated and strikes the producer. The same night, Rawlins kills Pauline to appease Christopher. Ernie is sought by the police as the leading murder suspect. The actual murderer forces Christopher to give him money for the jewels and then prepares to depart the country but is followed by Christopher. Also following the murderer are Ernie and a remorseful Linda. She detains Rawlins in a tavern while Ernie waits for the police to find them. At the last minute, Rawlins escapes. A chase ensues in which Christopher crashes his car and Ernie fights with Rawlins—during which time the fighter relives in his mind the fight that finished his boxing career. Rawlins is finally captured by the police.

A compelling and unusual film, *99 River Street* contains ideas not often found in a film noir. Although the squalid marriage of Ernie and Pauline and the criminal activities of Rawlins and Christopher are standard elements, the script's structure gives weight to contrasts between life and theater, as well as between violence as a spectacle and as private destiny. In the opening scene, Ernie is severely beaten. The camera then draws back to reveal that he is watching a television film of his last fight and that he has joined the film's audience as a spectator. Later, audience expectations are cheated again in the theater scene when Linda gives her very effective performance in one long claustrophobic take, with the camera holding on Linda as she moves about the stage. The boxing ring is also a kind of theater but the fight contrasts with Linda's performance because it is an honest spectacle rather than a lie. Additionally, violence actually occurred in the fight film while Linda's violence, although backed up by a "corpse," is not real. These ideas are still further developed when Ernie uses actual violence—beating the producer—on the stage, allowing the revelation of the charade. Additionally, Linda's "act" as a seductress in the tavern with her captive audience is more convincing than her overplayed confession of murder (which was successful only because Ernie believed it). Finally, Ernie's beating of Rawlins in the finale, a private act of revenge for his wife's murder, is transformed and becomes in Ernie's mind the spectacle in the ring that was witnessed at the opening of the film, a fight he had lost but that he now "wins."

The reality of artifice and the sometimes unreal flow of actual events in a person's life are provocative concepts. One expects to see these concepts explored in films about imaginative characters—dreamers and artists—not in a film dealing with desperate men and women looking for a fast buck, a sordid embrace, and a hard punch to the jaw from a thug. But these ideas work very effectively in a film noir context. For film noir, with its unreal atmosphere and extremes of passion and violence, is itself a style conscious of both mocking life and stylizing it. **BL**

NO MAN OF HER OWN (1950)

Director: Mitchell Leisen. **Screenplay**: Sally Benson, Catherine Turney based on the novel *I Married a Dead Man* by William Irish [Cornell Woolrich]. **Producer**: Richard Maibaum. **Director of Photography**: Daniel L. Fapp. **Music**: Hugo Friedhofer. **Art Directors**: Henry Bumstead, Hans Drier. **Editor**: Alma Macrorie. **Cast**: Barbara Stanwyck (Helen Ferguson/Patrice Harkness), John Lund (Bill Harkness), Jane Cowl (Mrs. Harkness), Phyllis Thaxter (Patrice Harkness), Lyle Bettger (Stephen Morley), Henry O'Neill (Mr. Harkness), Richard Denning (Hugh Harkness), Carole Mathews (Blonde), Harry Antrim (Ty Winthrop), Catherine Craig (Rosalie Baker), Esther Dale (Josie), Milburn Stone (Plainclothesman), Griff Barnett (Dr. Parker). **Released**: Paramount, February 21. 98 minutes.

Helen, broke and pregnant, stands outside Stephen's cheap apartment and begs him to take her back. Instead, he pushes a railroad ticket under the door. Inside, his girlfriend warns him never to brush her off like that. Helen takes the train and meets Patrice and Hugh. Patrice is also pregnant, and Hugh's parents have never seen her. As a favor, Helen puts on Patrice's ring. The train suddenly crashes, and Patrice and Hugh die. Because Helen's identified as Patrice by the ring, Hugh's family pays for the best hospital care for Helen and her baby. Desperate to give her child a better life, Helen goes to live with Hugh's parents and his brother, Bill. Helen and Bill fall in love. Stephen, discovering Helen's alive, locates her and blackmails her into marrying him. Her parents-in-law will soon die, and Stephen wants a share of Helen's inheritance. Before Helen fires a gun at Stephen, he looks lifeless. Bill helps her get rid of the corpse. Afterwards, Helen and Bill are tormented by the murder. When the police come to their house, Helen confesses. However, her bullet missed and Stephen was already dead, killed by his girlfriend.

Stephen dumped Helen, and Hugh, whose ring she wears, wasn't her husband. So until Bill says he loves her, Helen hasn't had a man of her own. In the scene after they kiss, Helen's atop a ladder decorating a Christmas tree. It's halfway through the film, and it brings to a head both a romantic storyline and the classic visual style. The classic style reinforces

No Man of Her Own: *Bill Harkness (John Lund) and Helen Ferguson (Barbara Stanwyck).*

Helen's "perfect peace and security" in the Harkness home. For example, although Bill doesn't believe Helen is his sister-in-law, when she commits telltale errors, the visual style remains classic. Were Bill going to expose Helen as an imposter, the style would turn noir. While Helen's up on the ladder, she finds out someone (Stephen) knows who she really is, and she falls to the floor. Thereafter, a crime story (blackmail and murder) supersedes the love story, and the noir style eclipses the classic style.

When Helen's cleared of killing Stephen, her blissful suburban life is restored. In contrast, the original novel ends with Helen and Bill's romance ruined because each suspects the other murdered Stephen. *No Man of Her Own* is a film noir although it doesn't have the bleak conclusion of *I Married a Dead Man*. The difference in their endings derives from the mutually exclusive ways noir and melodrama deal with Helen's social origins and opportunities. Since Stephen personifies noir's inescapable dark past, he must also personify the wrong side of the tracks, where he and Helen come from. Because of noir's determinism (and, therefore, its conservatism), Stephen/her past/her background will topple Helen from her accidental lift up the social ladder. In melodrama, Stephen is simply an invader into an idyllic suburb. The past—Helen's class—won't stop her climb. In melodrama, whether seen as naïve or progressive, unexpected upward social mobility, rags to riches, is conventional. Both the film and novel depict a nightmarish way for a penniless, pregnant, unmarried woman to achieve a postwar American dream—a loving family in a large "warm and friendly" home. Let her survive a freak train wreck that takes scores of innocent lives. In melodrama, Helen's fine character redeems such a deus ex machina. Her replacement of Patrice shows the ease with which class differences can be effaced. In noir, Helen's qualities are irrelevant. The final scene underscores how melodrama, as opposed to noir, doesn't circumscribe people's fates to the cards they were dealt. Helen's voice-over, lauding the charms of her home, speaks for her kind of woman, who deserves to have the good life as much as a woman born to it, like the real Patrice.

[A final note: It might not be altogether by accident that the film was titled *No Man of Her Own*, and Barbara Stanwyck played Helen Ferguson, who has a secret identity (she isn't Patrice Harkness) that is related to her sex life (she is pregnant and single). At the top of the list of Stanwyck's rumored lesbian relationships was her press agent, also named Helen Ferguson.] **DMH**

NO QUESTIONS ASKED (1951)

Director: Harold F. Kress. **Screenplay**: Berne Giler, Sidney Sheldon. **Producer**: Nicholas Nayfack. **Director of Photography**: Harold Lipstein. **Music**: Leith Stevens. **Production Designer**: Cedric Gibbons, Paul Groesse. **Editor**: Joseph Dervin. **Cast**: Barry Sullivan (Steve Keiver), Arlene Dahl (Ellen Sayburn Jessman), George Murphy (Insp. Matt Duggan), Jean Hagen (Joan Brenson), Richard Anderson (Det. Walter O'Bannion), Moroni Olsen (Henry Manston), Danny Dayton (Harry Dycker), Dick Simmons (Gordon N. Jessman), Howard Petrie (Franko), William Phipps (Roger). **Released**: MGM, June. 80 minutes.

Steve Keiver is a young up and coming lawyer who works for a prestigious New York insurance company. He decides to act as a middleman between his firm and a group of thieves in order to secure some stolen furs "no questions asked," thereby earning a large enough "commission" to marry his girlfriend, Ellen Sayburn. When he discovers that Ellen has married someone apparently more affluent than himself, he decides to continue to act as a middleman and go for the quick bucks. Just as his romance with co-worker Joan is looking up, Ellen returns to town with her husband Gordon Jessman and she informs Steve that her marriage is on the rocks. Convinced that he can now afford to keep Ellen, he brings her in on his scheme to do one more really big deal: securing the return of jewelry stolen from some matrons at a social function by two mobsters dressed in drag. In the process he is double-crossed by the Jessmans when Gordon Jessman intervenes, steals the jewelry himself and kills police detective O'Bannion, who has been brought in by Steve. Now Steve is hunted by both the police and Franko, a mob boss looking for the jewels. Kidnapped by Franko's men, Steve manages to grab Franko and use him as a shield. The police arrive in time to arrest Franko and his men and save Steve's life.

This film, like most of the film noirs produced at MGM under the aegis of Dore Schary, favors good production values, sometimes at the expense of those very qualities which make some "lesser" entries in the cycle stand out. Here, for instance, is an opening worth its salt as a film noir: a police car comes screaming down the dark, wet streets of a big city as the camera reveals a man running down side streets and alleys in an effort to evade it. Then the readily identifiable voice of actor Barry Sullivan, who plays the protagonist, begins to describe to the audience how he got into this predicament, so that much of the remainder of the film is done as flashback. Of course this convention was already a bit tired by 1951 but actor Sullivan, by virtue of his vocal qualities and the connotations associated with him from many of his past roles, is able to convey the fear of a man who, hunted by police and criminals alike, is beginning to accept the inevitability of his imminent death.

But unlike the narration of the doomed insurance agent in *Double Indemnity* or the sardonic Shubunka played by Barry Sullivan in *The Gangster*, what follows here fails to engage us in any meaningful way insofar as we never feel the tension we should as the noir world begins to collapse on the protagonist (a motif, coincidentally, that was better developed in an MGM thriller appropriately titled *Tension*, also starring Barry Sullivan, this time as the police detective who saves the day). Perhaps, as suggested, this was because even film noirs were becoming conventionalized at this late date. More likely it had something to do with the fact that the bitter taste left by the true film noir went against the grain of a studio "with more stars than there are in heaven." In any case, at the end of the film we are left with a few memorable moments: a wonderful performance (again) by the gifted Jean Hagen; an odyssey into a New York of cheap bars, disreputable nightclubs, even a seedy theatrical school where young men and women are practicing ballet; the irony implicit in the fact that the film's two toughest killers, Roger and Floyd, are also female impersonators who use their talents to remain undetected when performing criminal acts. **BP**

NOBODY LIVES FOREVER (1946)

Director: Jean Negulesco. **Screenplay**: W. R. Burnett. **Producer**: Robert Buckner. **Director of Photography**: Arthur Edeson. **Music**: Adolph Deutsch. **Art Director**: Hugh Reticker. **Editor**: Rudi Fehr. **Cast**: John Garfield (Nick Blake), Geraldine Fitzgerald (Gladys Halvorsen), Walter Brennan (Pop Gruber), Faye Emerson (Toni), George Coulouris (Doc Ganson), George Tobias (Al Doyle), Robert Shayne (Chet King), Richard Gaines (Charles Manning), Dick Erdman (Bellboy), James Flavin (Shake Thomas), Ralph Peters (Windy Mather). **Completed**: November 10, 1944. **Released**: Warner Bros., November 1. 100 minutes.

New York gambler Nick Blake returns from the service to find that both his girlfriend, Toni, and his gambling operation have been taken over. After extorting a substantial pay-off for his investment, he and henchman Al Doyle leave for California, where Blake wants only to take a vacation from both war and larceny. A former mentor, Pop Gruber, is enlisted by some broken-down sharpsters led by Doc Ganson to con-

vince Blake to assist them in a scheme that involves Gladys Halvorsen, a lonesome widow with a considerable fortune. Ganson's gang merely wants Blake to finance the venture; but after seeing the "mark" Blake decides to handle the job himself and give Ganson a split later. As he puts the plan into operation, Blake finds himself falling for the attractive widow and decides to pull out. When he offers to pay off Ganson with his own money, a recently arrived Toni convinces Ganson that Blake is trying to double-cross him. Ganson and his men kidnap Gladys and hold her for ransom on a deserted pier. Alerted by Pop, Blake rescues her; but in the process Pop and Ganson are killed.

Although shot before the war's end, *Nobody Lives Forever* confronts the question of postwar reassimilation through the noir conventions. Protagonist Nick Blake is not merely an ex-serviceman but also an ex-gambler, stripped of his girl and his status by a stay-at-home associate in a manner that must have been familiar to many veterans. Unlike the ordinary G.I., Blake can afford the luxury of a retreat from society to nurse his psychological wounds. Money, however, does not mitigate his dissatisfaction; nor does his R&R fulfill the need for activity. His encounter with Pop Gruber, former big-time operator reduced to selling views through a telescope, only sharpens Blake's sense of estrangement and the fear that he may have lost his edge.

The visuals associated with Blake's uneasy condition in *Nobody Lives Forever* are not so unrelentingly dark as they are for Bradford Galt in *The Dark Corner* or the amnesiac George Taylor in *Somewhere in the Night* or the vindictive Gagin in *Ride the Pink Horse.* Ironically Blake's beach house and the sun-lit stretch of sand where he takes solitary walks become the locus for his moments of readjustment anxiety. Garfield's nuanced performance suggests that Blake must grapple with the experience of fighting for a just cause and reconciling that with his own shady past. While Blake's attraction to Helen is likely sincere, part of his unease is due to the ignoble characters and motives with whom he is reassociated. Equally ironic, the unused pier with its uninviting expanse of creaking, sea-sprayed timbers surrounded by a black ocean is the unlikely setting in which Blake recommits himself to social interaction. In a typical noir transference, the used-up Pop Gruber dies under Ganson's gun in Blake's stead. His dying comment is at once existential and grimly

reminiscent of the larger holocaust from which Blake has recently returned—as Pop gives voice to the words of the title: "Nobody lives forever." **AS**

NOCTURNE (1946)

Director: Edwin L. Marin. **Screenplay**: Jonathan Latimer, Joan Harrison from an unpublished story by Frank Fenton and Rowland Brown. **Producer**: Joan Harrison. **Director of Photography**: Harry J. Wild. **Music**: Leigh Harline. **Production Designer**: Robert Boyle, Albert S. D'Agostino, Robert Boyle. **Editor**: Elmo Williams. **Cast**: George Raft (Joe Warner), Lynn Bari (Frances Ransom), Virginia Huston (Carol Page), Joseph Pevney (Fingers), Myrna Dell (Susan), Edward Ashley (Vincent), Walter Sande (Halberson), Mabel Paige (Mrs. Warne), Bernard Hoffman (Torp), Queenie Smith (Queenie), Mack Gray (Gratz). **Completed**: June 14, 1946. **Released**: RKO, November 9. 87 minutes.

A composer is shot while working at his piano and detective Joe Warner is assigned to the case. Despite Warner's suspicions that one of the cast-off women from the composer's many and notorious affairs may have murdered him, the official conclusion is that he committed suicide. Warner remains unconvinced; and he continues to make inquiries and search for a woman referred to in one of the victim's songs as "Dolores." His persistence irritates several "suspects," and their complaints lead to Warner's suspension from the police force. Unabashed, Warner interprets this as a sign that he is getting close to the truth. He concentrates his efforts on Frances Ransom to whom he is reluctantly attracted. Ultimately Warner discovers that Ransom has lied to him to protect not herself but her sister, Carol Page, a singer who is also "Dolores." After hours in the nightclub where Page works, Warner confronts her and Ransom. As Page is about to confess her involvement, her accompanist, Fingers, appears and discloses that he is the killer.

Nocturne opens with a long traveling shot across a landscaped model of the Hollywood Hills and into the window of an isolated house. An optically matched dissolve continues the movement through the window, into the room, and toward a man sitting at a piano. As the camera comes up close behind him, a gun fires point-blank at his head. As with the equally elaborate opening of *The Big Clock,* this opening shot is a long take. In this instance the third-person camera seems to be drawn over the dark terrain by the sound of the piano, builds visual tension, and surprises the viewer with the explosion from the gun just before the cutaway. It also initiates a complex irony that will be maintained throughout the film: just as the audience cannot anticipate from the visual treatment the presence of another person in the composer's house or the sudden intrusion into the frame of the flash and smoke from the gun's discharge, Joe Warner will possess information they do not have throughout the entire narrative. Conversely while Warner is confident that the death is not suicide, only the viewer can be certain of that from having witnessed the murder. By endistancing the audience from the protagonist in this way they are compelled to regard Joe Warner's investigation as less a quest for the facts of the murder than for its motives. But what inspires his obsessive behavior, undeterred by the physical punishment he suffers in the course of his search, is never clarified.

Nocturne: *Det. Joe Warne (George Raft) and Frances Ranson (Lynn Bari).*

Nora Prentiss: *Ann Sheridan as Nora Prentiss.*

Nocturne's noir statement resides in the possibility that in a variant of the situation of Det. McPherson in *Laura,* Warner is most fascinated by the life-style of the victim, whose photographs of numerous amorous conquests hang on the walls of an expensive home which the audience will soon see is in marked contrast to the modest interior of the small house Warner shares with his mother. Warner's fascination may be roughly analogous to that of McPherson, but his attraction to Frances Ransom is certainly not as compulsive. To some extent Warner, particularly as underplayed by George Raft, is a cipher, a figure exploring nightclubs, back rooms, and even movie lots to find an answer for the audience while never revealing his own motives. Actually it is the act of investigation rather than any result that interests Warner. For if the composer is the real focus of his obsession, the investigation compels Warner to listen to his songs and follow his former women. The visual tension of the opening sequence may be diminished after Warner's appearance; but its irony never is, becoming instead the foundation for an existential melodrama in which Warner is defined only in terms of his quest. When that quest is resolved and the killer found, Warner's vicarious existence is terminated. **AS**

NORA PRENTISS (1947)

Director: Vincent Sherman. **Screenplay**: Richard Nash and [uncredited] Philip MacDonald from an unpublished story by Paul Webster and Jack Sobell. **Producer**: William Jacobs. **Director of Photography**: James Wong Howe. **Music**: Franz Waxman, Paul Dessau [uncredited]. **Art Director**: Anton Grot. **Editor**: Owen Marks. **Cast**: Ann Sheridan (Nora Prentiss), Kent Smith (Dr. Richard Talbot a.k.a. Robert Thompson), Bruce Bennett (Dr. Joel Merriam), Robert Alda (Phil Dinardo), Rosemary DeCamp (Lucy Talbot), John Ridgely (Walter Bailey), Robert Arthur (Gregory Talbot), Wanda Hendrix (Bonita Talbot), Helen Brown (Miss Judson). **Completed**: April 20, 1946. **Released**: Warner Bros., February 22. 111 minutes.

A successful San Francisco doctor, Richard Talbot, leads an unsatisfying and ordinary life with his wife and two children. He and nightclub singer Nora Prentiss begin an affair that seems hopeless because Talbot cannot summon the courage to ask for a divorce. Nora moves to New York to work in a new nightclub. Desolate, Talbot takes advantage of a patient's sudden demise to fake his own death and leaves home to join Nora in New York. Later he reads that police are investigating his death as a possible murder. Talbot is frightened to leave Nora's apartment and becomes alcoholic while her career proceeds well. Talbot imagines Nora is romancing her boss, Phil, and starts a drunken brawl with the man. Believing he has murdered Phil, Talbot flees from the nightclub and has a serious automobile accident. Undergoing plastic surgery to repair his badly burned face, Talbot no longer looks like himself. He considers the new appearance a blessing and is surprised when he is arrested for the death he faked in California. None of his family or friends recognize him at the trial and Talbot forces Nora to remain silent so that his family will be spared any further shame. Talbot is convicted of his own murder and Nora says goodbye to him in death row.

Nora Prentiss most certainly ranks near the top of female-oriented noirs. Unlike such other Ann Sheridan or Joan Crawford entries as *The Unfaithful, Flamingo Road,* and *The Damned Don't Cry, Nora Prentiss* maintains a sense of hopelessness that does not allow it to lapse into romantic melodrama. Ace cinematographer James Wong Howe moves beyond simple expressionistic touches here, maintaining a closed composition throughout the film which in turn reinforces the entrapment of the two principals. Two scenes in particular elucidate this. In one, Talbot is in prison, his scarred face barely visible in the darkness as his story is told in flashback. In the other, Nora and Talbot are forced to spend long hours together in their New York apartment because the pathetic Talbot is too frightened to go outside and risk being recognized. Kent Smith does a fine job capturing Talbot's rather rapid personality degeneration. But this film is really Ann Sheridan's and she mollifies that hard edge gained over countless Warner programmers just enough to make Nora's predicament believable. **BP**

NOTORIOUS (1946)

Director/Producer: Alfred Hitchcock. **Screenplay**: Ben Hecht, Clifford Odets based on a story by John Taintor Foote. **Director of Photography**: Ted Tetzlaff. **Music**: Roy Webb. **Art Directors**: Albert S. D'Agostino, Carroll Clark. **Editor**: Theron Warth. **Cast**: Cary Grant (Devlin), Ingrid Bergman (Alicia Huberman), Claude Rains (Alexander Sebastian), Louis Calhern (Paul Prescott), Madame Konstantin (Mme. Sebastian), Reinhold Schunzel (Dr. Anderson), Moroni Olsen (Walter Beardsley), Ivan Triesault (Eric Mathis), Alex Minotis (Joseph), Wally Brown (Mr. Hopkins), Gavin Gordon (Ernest Weylin), Sir Charles Mendl (Commodore), Ricardo Costa (Dr. Barbosa), Eberhard Krumschmidt (Hupka), Fay Baker (Ethel). **Completed**: January 17, 1946. **Released**: RKO, August 22. 101 minutes.

As World War II ends Alicia Huberman is a sophisticated playgirl living in Florida while her father—a Nazi spy—is imprisoned elsewhere in the United States. Alicia is persuaded by Devlin, a federal agent, to assist him in a Rio de Janeiro undercover operation to ensnare a Nazi friend of her father's, Alexander Sebastian. Alicia and Devlin are attracted to each other, but Devlin cannot accept her amorous past. Sebastian welcomes Alicia into his home and soon proposes marriage. Believing that Devlin is only interested in the success of their enterprise and not in her happiness, Alicia accepts. Sebastian's mother is highly suspicious of Alicia. During a party at her new home, Alicia and Devlin discover a cache of uranium hidden in the wine cellar. Sebastian realizes that Alicia is a spy but is convinced by his mother to keep the truth concealed from his Nazi colleagues. They begin to poison Alicia slowly. Concerned by Alicia's failure to contact him, Devlin brazens his way into the Sebastian mansion and finds Alicia deathly ill. Assuring her of his love, Devlin carries her boldly out of the house and into his waiting car while Sebastian is surrounded by colleagues who are now aware of his deception.

Although it is ostensibly a romantic thriller, Hitchcock incorporates familiar film noir themes into *Notorious*. The seeds of suspicion and betrayal are sown in various ways but the most interesting is Hitchcock's treatment of the noir staple "bad woman/femme fatale." Ingrid Bergman portrays Alicia initially as a woman who is cynical, promiscuous, and alcoholic. Cary Grant's Devlin is apparently correct in distrusting her. Gradually Hitchcock reveals that misery and self-pity over her father's actions and her alienated position in the United States are the demons that have driven this

Notorious: *Alicia (Ingrid Bergman), Devlin (Cary Grant), and Alexander Sebastian (Claude Rains).*

sensitive woman to various excesses. Moreover, although she denies accepting Devlin's proposal out of a sense of patriotism, the truth is revealed when Devlin plays a recording of her violent argument with her father concerning his Nazi activities. Her deeply romantic nature is revealed by the tremulous, pathetically eager-to-please response to Devlin's reluctant but sincere attention and is a clear indication of Alicia's fundamental innocence.

In a noir manner Devlin is neurotically obsessed with Alicia's past and represses his profound attraction to her, contemptuously comparing her to a leopard that "can't change its spots." Perversely, he pushes her back into the very kind of life for which he condemned her. As a final irony Hitchcock generates audience sympathy for the duped Sebastian by plainly indicating that he loves Alicia unreservedly, something that the strait-laced, unimaginative Devlin cannot do. Hitchcock exploits the noir style while inverting several of the noir conventions. Alicia, his "bad woman," like the later examples of his anti-heroines, Eve Kendall in *North by Northwest* and Madeleine/Judy in *Vertigo*, is bad not by nature nor by design but as a result of circumstances. At first glance, Alicia may seem akin to the predatory Kathie of *Out of the Past,* the deceptive Kitty of *The Killers,* or the traitorous Anna of *Criss Cross;* but Alicia is revealed as a woman inured to misery while still ready to risk herself for emotional fulfillment. Devlin, although similar to other noir heroes in his inability to see beyond a woman's facade, is flawed not by trusting too much but rather by not trusting enough. **JK**

ODDS AGAINST TOMORROW (1959)

Director/Producer: Robert Wise (Harbel Productions).
Screenplay: Nelson Gidding and [uncredited] Abraham Polonsky
(his front was John O. Killens) from the novel by William P.
McGivern. **Director of Photography**: Joseph Brun. **Music**: John
Lewis. **Art Director**: Leo Kerz. **Editor**: Dede Allen. **Cast**: Harry
Belafonte (Johnny Ingram), Robert Ryan (Earl Slater), Gloria
Grahame (Helen), Shelley Winters (Lorry), Ed Begley (Dave
Burke), Will Kuluva (Bacco), Kim Hamilton (Ruth Ingram), Mae
Barnes (Annie), Carmen DeLavallade (Kitty), Richard Bright
(Coco), Lou Gallo (Moriarity), Fred J. Scollay (Cannoy), Lois
Thorne (Edie). **Locations**: N.Y.C.; Hudson, New York.
Completed: May, 1959. **Released**: United Artists, October 15.
96 minutes.

Earl Slater, a racially prejudiced ex-con, is asked by Dave
Burke, an ex-police captain who was disgracefully dismissed from the force, to join in his plan to rob a small-
town bank in upstate New York. Johnny Ingram, an
African-American singer, reluctantly joins Burke and
Slater because a hoodlum named Bacco has threatened
Johnny's ex-wife and small daughter with harm if he does
not repay a debt soon. Everything goes wrong during the
robbery. A cop wounds Burke, who cannot pass the getaway car's keys to his partners, and he kills himself rather
than be arrested. Racial antagonisms come to the fore as
Earl and Johnny fight, and Johnny chases Earl while both
are pursued by the police to the top of some oil storage
tanks. The two criminals take aim and fire at each other,
igniting the tanks. As authorities are sorting through the
wreckage the next day, they find the charred remains of
both men, who cannot be told apart.

Odds Against Tomorrow, produced at the close of the
noir cycle, is a film of many contrasts. It looks backwards
to the classic era in terms of its action (e.g. *White Heat*;
Asphalt Jungle) and its visual style (venetian blinds; dark,
wet streets; lowered ceilings; deep focus, etc.). But it also
looks forward to the contemporary era in terms of its subject matter (racism; homosexuality), its cool jazz score; its
ingenious use of the wide-screen (1.85:1 aperture) and,
most significantly for an A-budget film, the absence of a
definable studio look. Other contrasts abound: the normalcy of the Central Park playground (momentarily
destroyed by the intrusion of the duo of homosexual
hoods) can be measured against the industrial sites and
the dark streets of a small, not-very-picturesque upstate
New York town and Ruth Ingram's very middle-class apartment against the confines of Earl's apartment (again, the
lowered ceilings), where he roams like a caged animal.

Odds Against Tomorrow: *Reluctant partners in crim Earl Slater
(Robert Ryan, left) and Johnny Ingram (Harry Belafonte).*

Film noir is a style based on contrasts: visual, psychological,
societal, etc. Robert Wise's *Odds Against Tomorrow*, co-written
by blacklistee Abraham Polonsky (*Force of Evil*) and co-produced by star Harry Belafonte, effectively expounds these
contrasts with dynamic results. On a visual level, the filmmakers, near the end of the black and white era in movies, paint
canvases, both urban and rural, filled with light and shadow:
Central Park where Ingram plays with his daughter and confronts the hoods who are sent to harass him for his gambling
debts; the picturesque upstate New York river at sunset as a
desperate Ingram and his ex-cop friend Burke wait to execute
the bank heist; the wet, dark streets of the small town where
Burke commits suicide after the heist goes wrong; the oil
refinery in which the two racial antagonists (Ingram and
Slater) blow themselves up (in a reference to the ending of
White Heat). The most obvious contrast, of course, is between
the two main protagonists: one black, one white; one sympathetic, one repellent. Yet their differences are only skin deep
(as the film's ending so facilely demonstrates). Beneath these
visual contrasts are the psychological and political contrasts of
the film. The two main protagonists/antagonists—the African-
American Ingram and the White racist Slater (played by
Robert Ryan in an extension of his performance in *Crossfire*)
—are in many ways doubles, a common motif in noir. The
filmmakers spend much of the first three-quarters of the
movie intercutting Slater's life with Ingram's. Both are veterans who have not been able to capture the American dream
promised to those "heroes" who came back from fighting fascism in Europe and Asia. Both have fallen into debt (Ingram
because of his compulsive gambling; Slater because of his status as an ex-con and his violent personality). Both are estranged

emotionally from their significant others: in Ingram's case his wife and daughter; in Slater's his devoted girlfriend on whom he cheats. And both are willing to take this one last gamble to secure the future they were promised.

The plan is of course doomed from the first. As other heist films have taught audiences (notably *The Asphalt Jungle*, *Criss Cross*, etc.), trust among the participants is crucial. Ingram and Slater's antagonism at first sight, instigated by Slater's racist jibes, continues through the whole process of planning and execution. So it is no surprise to the viewer when the operation fails and the antagonists take off on a personal vendetta. In the famous coda to the movie, two firefighters stand over the burnt bodies of Ingram and Slater. After lifting the shroud, the first says, "Which is which?" The second responds: "Take your pick." In a final irony the antagonists are finally united as one, with all their physical differences erased, both victims of political system rotten, in Polonsky's view, with racism and unfulfilled promises. **BP**

ON DANGEROUS GROUND (1952)

Director: Nicholas Ray. **Screenplay**: A. 1. Bezzerides, adapted by Bezzerides and Nicholas Ray from the novel *Mad With Much Heart* by Gerald Butler. **Producer**: John Houseman. **Director of Photography**: George E. Diskant. **Music**: Bernard Herrmann. **Art Directors**: Albert S. D'Agostino, Ralph Berger. **Editor**: Roland Gross. **Cast**: Ida Lupino (Mary), Robert Ryan (Jim Wilson), Ward Bond (Walter Brent), Charles Kemper (Bill Daly), Anthony Ross (Pete Santos), Ed Begley (Capt. Brawley), Ian Wolfe (Carrey), Sumner Williams (Danny), Gus Schilling (Lucky), Frank Ferguson (Willows), Cleo Moore (Myrna), Olive Carey (Mrs. Brent), Richard Irving (Bernie), Pat Prest (Julie). **Completed**: May 10, 1950. **Released**: February 12. 82 minutes.

Jim Wilson, a New York City policeman, is on the verge of a nervous breakdown. He lives alone in a cheerless apartment and knows no one except his partners and the assortment of criminals he encounters as part of his job. This life has made Wilson bitter and violent. His partners try to help him, but he rejects their reasoning. Finally, as punishment for his most recent display of brutality, Wilson is sent out of town on a case. A disturbed teenager, Danny Malden, has molested and killed a girl. Wilson must initially calm the girl's irate father who wants to kill the youth. Danny's blind sister, Mary, pleads with Wilson to bring her brother in unharmed; but Brent's interference prompts the murderer to flee in panic across the snow-covered countryside. Losing his grip as he tries to scale some rocks, Danny falls to his death. Wilson consoles Mary, and their emotional rapport promises a new beginning for each of them; but a rupture occurs and he heads back to the city. Realizing that desolation is all that awaits him in New York, he returns to Mary.

Nicholas Ray's visual treatment of despair and salvation is one of the most moving in film noir. Although the elements of the plot are somewhat arbitrary and contrived, the central character of Wilson is conceived and delineated with great impact. The structural division of the film is in two parts, city and country. It creates a narrative framework of a journey that is literally from city to country and, subtextually, an inner journey of self-realization. Beginning as an archetypal film noir in its violent and brooding city "overture" (defining the probable "dangerous ground" of the title), the film becomes more profound as the setting changes and Mary is introduced to alter the entire tone of the work. High contrast lighting pervades the city sequences, and the action is harsh and quick with each scene concisely staged. The country sequences are relatively slower and photographed more naturally as the visual style emphasizes the snowy landscape's beauty or the light from Mary's fireplace as it casts strange shadows about her living room. However, the intensity and imbalance of the protagonist's emotional state is expressed also through subjective shots of the road as Wilson drives. That emotion carries over to and from other moments (rendered subjectively with a hand-held camera),

On Dangerous Ground: *Walter Brent (Ward Bond) and Mary Malden (Ida Lupino).*

219 / ONE WAY STREET

such as the chase of a suspect in the city sequence or his subduing of the brutal Brent.

The special qualities of *On Dangerous Ground* are primarily attributable to Nicholas Ray. Strangely, he regards it as a failure, perhaps because of the "miracle" ending in which a series of dissolves of the anguished face of Wilson driving, the country in daylight, and the city street at night, abruptly brings Wilson back into Mary's house and the warmth of her embrace. "I don't believe in miracles," Ray has said. And yet he has suggested in the film that Wilson's violence results from a spiritual crisis precipitated by the dehumanizing nature of his occupation clashing with his innate sensitivity—an internal conflict that cannot withstand the pressure placed on him by a violent environment and that only begins to dissipate in his very first moments with Mary. The film is both psychologically realistic and spiritually mysterious; and, if Ray would not concede this, he could not deny specific virtues found in the creative responses of certain of the film's participants. George E. Diskant (also photographer of Ray's first film, *They Live By Night)* captures exactly the contrasting moods of the city and country locales. Bernard Herrmann contributes one of his most beautiful scores, unusual in its use of horns during the chase and in its viola d'amore theme for Mary. Above all, there is the mesmerizing presence of Ida Lupino and Robert Ryan. Ryan's face expresses the motif of alienation that pervades Ray's work better than any dialogue could. As played by Ryan, Wilson's violent interrogation of a suspect, asking "Why do you punks make me do it?" is one of the most neurotic and self-destructive actions in film noir, so that the character's return to his apartment later that night becomes a gripping vision of loneliness. Wilson looks for a moment at his sports trophies, which are the only positive symbols left in his life, and bitterly asks, "Who cares?" Few actors could give this simple line as evocative a reading. **BL**

ONE WAY STREET (1950)

Director: Hugo Fregonese. **Screenplay**: Lawrence Kimble. **Producer**: Leonard Goldstein. **Director of Photography**: Maury Gertsman. **Music**: Frank Skinner. **Art Directors**: Bernard Herzbrun, Alfred Ybarra. **Editor**: Milton Carruth. **Cast**: James Mason (Dr. Frank Matson), Marta Toren (Laura Thorsen), Dan Duryea (John Wheeler), Basil Ruysdael (Father Moreno), William Conrad (Ollie), Rodolfo Acosta (Francisco Morales), King Donovan (Grieder), Robert Espinoza (Santiago), Tito Renaldo (Hank Torres), Margarito Luna (Antonio Morales), Emma Roldán (Catalina), George Lewis (Captain Rodriguez). **Released**: Univeral, April 1. 79 minutes.

Just as gangster Wheeler and henchmen are about to split the take from their latest haul, Wheeler's physician Matson tells him that a headache pill he has given him is a slow-acting poison. If Wheeler doesn't let him leave with the money, he will die. Wheeler agrees, and Matson promises to call later with the antidote's location. To both men's surprise, Wheeler's girlfriend Laura asks to go along. Unbeknownst to Matson and Laura, hood Arnie has eavesdropped and is hiding in their car. Matson kills Arnie in a struggle, causing a wreck. The couple charter a plane to Mexico City, but a fuel pump forces a landing outside a coastal village where a priest shelters the two.

Once the plane is air-worthy, Laura announces she wants to stay in the peaceful town. Matson acquiesces and soon finds himself village doctor. However, Wheeler sending word he knows their whereabouts causes the couple to return to Los Angeles to settle things. Once there, Laura waits in a café. When Matson arrives at Wheeler's, he finds the gangster dying, shot by previously loyal Ollie. Having hidden a gun in the returned money bag, Matson kills the henchman. Matson meets Laura outside, but goes back to the café for cigarettes and is killed by a car on the rain-slick street.

It's a shame *One Way Street* has such a low profile today because it is one of the better noirs from the early 1950s. Director Hugo Fregonese, along with cast and crew, conjures a sense of life's ongoing flow both before the first shot and after the end credits, the mark of a memorable film. However, the viewer might wish that Lawrence Kimble's script didn't seem more than just a good first draft, that it delved deeper into the lead characters. There is no sense of the impressive tapestry of detail that one finds in noirs like *Out of the Past* and *Criss Cross*, films with which it shares some faint similarities. Indeed, Duryea plays the same kind of obsessive, cuckolded gang boss he did in the earlier *Criss Cross*. But, to be fair, *One Way Street* seems as if it was shot on a lower budget and a much faster schedule than those earlier benchmark pictures. Even though he had just started his American career, Mason already had his tragic-fugitive-on-the-run persona down pat. From Carol Reed's *Odd Man Out* (made in 1947 and one of his last UK films before immigrating to America) through Max Ophuls' *The Reckless Moment*, with the lift of an eyebrow, a slight gesture or a barely perceptible change in voice inflection, Mason could convey a whole history of loneliness, alienation and emotional pain hidden behind a cultured, dignified front. He brings that to his disillusioned doctor, a man who has felt responsible for the death of his sick wife and has lost faith in himself to the extent he feels he can only patch up wounded criminals.

Toren, though previously Duryea's kept woman, manages to finally touch Mason through her ability to ward off crippling cynicism and to follow her decent instincts wherever they may lead. Toren is evenly matched with Mason and is able to convey the same kind of decency, intelligence and passion hiding right below the surface. Along with Mason and old priest Ruysdael, she gives a breathing soul to the film. Duryea is fine as usual as is the supporting cast, especially hoods King Donovan, William Conrad and Jack Elam. I've heard it said that the Mexican sequence, the middle third of the movie, slows the story and takes away some of its "noir credentials." On the contrary, at first, the Mexican village seems like an idyllic counterpoint to the sinister streets of nocturnal Los Angeles. But it turns out to have its own set of problems represented by poverty, ignorance and marauding bandits. Although still a Hollywood creation, perhaps because of Fregonese's Argentine roots the village has some recognizably realistic traits (unlike the deliriously utopian commune where Walter Huston luxuriates after healing a nearly-drowned boy in *The Treasure of the Sierra Madre*). It convincingly serves, along with Toren's love, as the impetus for Mason's redemption, as well as the conduit through which he will keep his date with destiny in the film's almost ridiculously gratuitous—but entirely appropriate—downbeat ending. **CD**

THE OTHER WOMAN (1954)

Director/Screenplay/Producer: Hugo Haas. **Associate Producer**: Robert Erlick. **Director of Photography**: Eddie Fitzgerald. **Music**: Ernest Gold. **Art Director**: Rudi Feld. **Editor**: Robert S. Eisen. **Cast**: Hugo Haas (Darmen), Cleo Moore (Sherry), Lance Fuller (Ronnie), Lucille Barkley (Mrs. Darmen), Jack Macy (Lester), John Qualen (Papasha), Jan Arvan (Collins), Carolee Kelly (First Assistant Director), Mark Lowell (Second Assistant Director), Melinda Markey (Actress). **Released**: 20th Century-Fox, December 21. 81 minutes

Darmen is an émigré director whose Hollywood career is helped because his wife is the daughter of the production chief for a large motion picture company. One day he refuses to use an aspiring actress—Sherry. Sherry resents his decision and schemes to blackmail him, persuading him to take her home to her apartment one evening after work. Once there, she serves him a drugged drink that makes him sleep. When he awakens, she pretends they have had sexual relations. Sherry later announces her pregnancy to Darmen and demands he obtain $50,000 from his father-in-law to avoid a scandal. The director, realizing his career is in jeopardy if he goes to his father-in-law, plans to murder the woman. For an alibi he engineers a sound loop on his editing room's moviola so that it appears to his secretary that he is busy working while he is actually committing the crime. When a police detective sees through Darmen's alibi, the film director confesses.

It is interesting to speculate whether Hugo Haas was working out one of his own worst fantasies in *The Other Woman*. The film is one of a series of low-budget films, such as *Pickup, Bait,* and *Strange Fascination,* that Haas made as director, writer, and star opposite 1950s B-movie, "sexpot" actresses like Beverly Michaels and Cleo Moore. However, *The Other Woman* comes closer in style and substance to true film noir than any other of Haas' efforts, due to the Fox production values of dark, glistening sets and an expressionistic visual style, which is characterized by the enclosed space of small rooms. Additionally, the film collapses the distinction between victim and artist because Haas, as director, speaks directly of his entrapment: first, in the film's opening, when Haas as Darmen tells an actor how to perform a scene in a jail set; and secondly, at the film's close, when Darmen is confined in prison and relates to the audience that in real life there are no happy endings. **BP**

OUT OF THE PAST (1947)

Director: Jacques Tourneur. **Screenplay**: Geoffrey Homes [Daniel Mainwaring], Frank Fenton, and James M. Cain from Mainwaring's novel *Build My Gallows High*. **Producer**: Warren Duff. **Director of Photography**: Nicholas Musuraca. **Music**: Roy Webb. **Art Directors**: Albert S. D'Agostino, Jack Okey. **Editor**: Samuel E. Beetley. **Cast**: Robert Mitchum (Jeff Bailey/Jeff Markham), Jane Greer (Kathie Moffett), Kirk Douglas (Whit Sterling), Rhonda Fleming (Meta Carson), Richard Webb (Jim), Steve Brodie (Fisher), Virginia Huston (Ann), Paul Valentine (Joe), Dickie Moore (The Kid), Ken Niles (Eels). **Location**: Reno, Nevada; Lake Tahoe; San Francisco, California; Mexico City, Acapulco, Mexico. **Completed**: January 9, 1947. **Released**: RKO, November 25. 96 minutes.

In the little town of Bridgeport, California, Jeff Bailey runs a gas station with the assistance of a mute boy, Jimmy. Joe Stefanos drives into town and informs Jeff that Whit Sterling, a racketeer, wants to see him. Jeff relates his life's story to Ann, his present love, as they drive to Sterling's Lake Tahoe mansion. As a private detective named Jeff Markham, he was hired to find Sterling's mistress, Kathie Moffett, who had shot Sterling and escaped with $40,000. Jeff found Kathie in Mexico but fell in love with her and believed her claim that she did not steal any money. They moved to San Francisco and lived anonymously until Jeff's former partner, Fisher, found them. Kathie killed Fisher and Jeff discovered evidence that proved she lied about the money. Disillusioned, Jeff moved to his new life in Bridgeport. Arriving at Sterling's, Jeff assures Ann before she departs that he no longer loves Kathie. Meeting with Sterling, Jeff is surprised to see Kathie. She secretly tells him that Sterling is blackmailing her about Fisher's murder to stay with him. The racketeer blackmails Jeff to obtain tax records from Eels, a renegade accountant of Sterling's gang, but Jeff is being used as a patsy. When Jeff discovers the plot, he unsuccessfully tries to prevent the crime and realizes that Sterling has false evidence that also implicates him as Fisher's murderer. Jeff confronts Sterling, but Sterling is killed by her. Kathie tells Jeff

Out of the Past: *Kathie Moffett (Jane Greer), Whit Sterling (Kirk Douglas), and Jeff Bailey (Robert Mitchum).*

Out of the Past: *Kathie Moffett (Jane Greer) and Jeff Bailey (Robert Mitchum).*

that they belong together and should escape the country. He appears to agree but alerts the police and the two are both killed as she attempts to drive through a roadblock.

Out of the Past is a title evocative of the noir cycle as well as descriptive of this particular film. The existential figure of the ill-fated noir protagonist Jeff, incarnated by Robert Mitchum, is restrained, joyless, and with a look of doom in his sad eyes. The erotic and lethal female Kathie is vividly portrayed by Jane Greer. Co-writer Daniel Mainwaring's complex screenplay uses narration like the voice of fate over a flashback into Jeff's past, which inescapably determines the present and future. The shadowy lighting of a cinematographer attuned to noir, Nicholas Musuraca, combines with the tragic sensibility of the director, Jacques Tourneur, and is well-suited to the downbeat nature of the genre.

However, to say that this is one of the key works of film noir is not necessarily to accept it as unflawed. It can be faulted both for its excessively complex plotting, notably in the San Francisco section, and for a solemnity that almost becomes tedious. Its best section is the flashback sequence that follows an ominous opening sequence reminiscent in mood of Hemingway's "The Killers" and the faithful recreation of that story in Siodmak's film. In the flashback sequence, the combination of Mitchum's mesmerizing narration as Jeff waits for Kathie and eventually sees her walking out of the sunlight into the Mexican cafe, the romantic interlude on the beach, and their desperate flight conspires to give the film the perfect noir mood. Elsewhere, in the film's second half, the screenplay seems protracted and overly emphatic of Jeff's capitulation to his fate and Kathie's duplicity. One melodramatic climax of the film, and one of the strongest visual moments, occurs when Kathie shoots Fisher and Jeff turns, registering shock at seeing Kathie's true nature revealed.

Its many other merits aside and its faults taken into account, *Out of the Past* is, with *Criss Cross,* one of the two films that best evoke a subject central to the genre: the destruction of a basically good man by a morally ambiguous woman he loves. In both films the heroine vacillates between the hero and another man, which results in the destruction of all three, and a flashback traces the hero's "fall." But the two films are quite different, even in the nature of their flashbacks. In the *Criss Cross* flashback,

Steve Thompson is already haunted by Anna, his former wife, and his first view of her in the nightclub recreates his former desire. In the *Out of the Past* flashback, Bailey encounters Kathie for the first time when she walks into the Mexican cafe, so the turning point of his life seems more immediate and placed within the film. The most interesting difference, however, is that Bailey knows before the flashback is over that Kathie is destroying him. The film traces the course in which he gradually accepts this fate and even embraces it, spiritually if not physically. Thompson, on the other hand, in spite of bad experiences with Anna in the past, convinces himself that he trusts her and only fully understands her and her betrayal of him in the very last scene.

But in these two fundamentally different visions of male-female relationships, there is one constant: the woman herself. Film noir is filled with such women as these and the instances in which the woman who is loved represents the best part of the hero rather than the worst, such as Keechie in *They Live by Night,* are the exceptions. This vision of women is resonant in many noir films, such as *Criss Cross, Angel Face, Hell's Island,* and *Double Indemnity* and the noir milieu powerfully underscores it. Alternately, such films as *Pitfall, Nightfall, The Big Sleep, Notorious* suggest the other side of this theme. In each, the hero presumes at some point the heroine's betrayal but is found to be wrong. Still, this presumption never threatens their lives as forcefully as the true betrayal of *Out of the Past.* **BL**

THE OX-BOW INCIDENT (1943)

Director: William Wellman. **Screenplay**: Lamar Trotti based on the novel by Walter Van Tilburg Clark. **Producer**: Lamar Trotti. **Director of Photography**: Arthur Miller. **Art Director**: James Basevi, Richard Day. **Music**: Cyril J. Mockridge. **Editor**: Allen McNeil. **Cast**: Henry Fonda (Gil Carter), Henry Morgan (Al), Dana Andrews (Donald Martin), Mary Beth Hughes (Rose), Anthony Quinn (Juan Martinez/Francisco Morez), William Eythe (Gerald Tetley), Jane Darwell (Jenny Grier), Frank Conroy (Major Tetley), Francis Ford (Old Man), Leigh Whipper (Sparks), Willard Robertson (Sheriff). **Released**: 20th Century-Fox, May 21. 75 minutes.

The Ox-Bow Incident: *Sparks (Leigh Whipper) and Gil Carter (Henry Fonda)*.

Two drifters, Gil and Art, are passing through a Western town, when news comes in that local rancher Kincaid has been murdered and his cattle stolen. The townspeople, joined by the drifters, form a posse to catch the perpetrators. They find three men—an emotionally overwrought Donald Martin, the bandit Juan Martinez, and a senile old man—in possession of the cattle and some circumstantial evidence. Although the men claim they purchased the cattle, the posse, spurred on by the blood thirsty Major Tetley, are intent on lynching the three without a trial. Although several of the posse eventually object to the lynching, including Gil and Art, they cannot stop the execution. After the hanging, they meet the Sheriff and discover that Kincaid is not dead after all. The guilty posse returns to town. Major Tetley shoots himself. In the bar Gil reads aloud the letter Martin gave him to deliver to his wife.

Director William Wellman's *The Ox-Bow Incident* is an early example of the Fox cycle of social realist noirs (*House on 92nd Street, Call Northside 777, Crossfire*, etc). The film introduces its protagonist, Gil, in a dimly lit saloon drinking himself into oblivion while staring longingly at a painting of a reclining, semi-nude woman. The audience learns from the dialogue that he and his friend Art are drifters and that Gil has been jilted by the town "prostitute," Rose, who has recently left town with a wealthy, older husband. In his despair he picks a fight with another customer and has to be knocked out and restrained by the bartender with the aid of Art. Although the tone is somewhat comic and ironic, the pain the character feels is no less real. This is no traditional western hero. He is unshaven, dirty, drunk, and alienated. In short a classic noir anti-hero.

But what is even more disturbing is his lack of interest in "doing the right thing," a necessary characteristic for a classic western hero, but a common failing among noir protagonists from *Double Indemnity* on. Throughout most of this tale of mob "justice" and the necessity of moral commitment, Gil goes along with the majority. He rides with the posse on its pursuit of the individuals they believe to be murderers and cattle rustlers. He never speaks out during the initial deliberations within the posse itself about the legality of their plan. When the African-American minister, Sparks, tries to convince him of the immorality of this rapid pursuit of justice without legal proceedings, Gil replies by spitting and saying, "It's a way of spending time."

Gil finally has his *metanoia* after it becomes clear that the evidence against the three men they eventually capture is just too flimsy and that the posse has simply become a bloodthirsty mob, symbolized by the raucous and cackling laugh of Jenny, the posse's own Greek fury. When the martinet Major Tetley finally calls for a vote, Gil is one of the seven who steps across the line and votes against the lynching. He even physically tries to stop the illegal execution but is restrained by the others. Finally, in the resolution of the movie, it is Gil who reads the poignant letter of one of the victims to a row of shame-faced cowboys who are lined up, heads down, against the shadowy bar. By the end of the movie this alienated drifter has found a purpose and heads off to deliver the letter to the dead man's wife. **JU**

PANIC IN THE STREETS (1950)

Director: Elia Kazan. **Screenplay**: Richard Murphy, adapted by Daniel Fuchs from an unpublished story by Edna and Edward Anhalt. **Producer**: Sol C. Siegel. **Director of Photography**: Joe MacDonald. **Music**: Alfred Newman. **Art Directors**: Lyle Wheeler, Maurice Ransford. **Editor**: Harmon Jones. **Cast**: Richard Widmark (Dr. Clinton Reed), Paul Douglas (Police Capt. Warren), Barbara Bel Geddes (Nancy Reed), Walter [Jack] Palance (Blackie), Zero Mostel (Fitch), Dan Riss (Nefo), Alexis Minotis (John Mefaris), Guy Thomajan (Poldi), Tommy Cook (Vince). **Location**: New Orleans, Louisiana. **Released**: 20th Century-Fox, August 4. 96 minutes.

The unidentified body of a murder victim is discovered to be carrying a deadly communicable disease. Dr. Clinton Reed of the Public Health Service realizes he has 48 hours to track down the murderers who have been exposed to the disease. If he is too late, the disease will become virulent and a large-scale epidemic will result. Meeting resistance from police Capt. Warren, who is assigned to the murder case, Reed decides to take matters into his own hands and investigate on his own. He searches the dilapidated dockside section of New Orleans and faces suspicion and distrust from the people he meets. Eventually he finds the killers, and they are captured after a chase through the New Orleans dock area.

For years, gangsters and criminals have been referred to in films as rats and scum, as a menace to society. *Panic in the Streets* takes this thought to its logical conclusion, making it literally as well as figuratively true. The murderous thugs have been exposed to a deadly plague, brought into the country by the illegal alien whom they killed over a card game. Their arrest becomes a race to avert an epidemic of huge proportions. The film gains its suspense from the fact that the viewer knows the narrative essentials from the beginning. The film continually cuts back and forth between the efforts of the Public Health official to find the murderers; and the culprits themselves, who become increasingly baffled at what seems an undue interest on the part of the police to track them down. It is emphasized that, although a man has been murdered, the police would normally not go out of their way to find the killers of an illegal alien. This gives the film an ironic edge, as the killers are initially smug because they assume nothing will be done about the murder. It is not the criminals alone, however, who are suspicious and xenophobic. The lower class community is wary of the outside world. When Reed begins prowling the cafes, houseboats, and union halls of the district, he is regarded with distrust. A cafe owner with an important lead is dissuaded from telling what he knows by his wife, who does not wish to get involved. Her reluctance is doubly distressing because she already has symptoms of the disease.

The ordinary attitudes of the criminal and lower-class segment of society are thrown into relief by an extraordinary situation. The protagonist in many noir films is the man who walks alone, who is forced to travel a path beyond the limits of the law. Reed, as portrayed by Widmark, is forced to take the law into his own hands for the sake of the society at large. Faced with stubborn official resistance, personified by Paul Douglas as the police captain who, like the criminals, does not realize the enormity of the danger, Reed is required to hunt the guilty by immersing himself in the noir underworld. *Panic in the Streets* evokes that particular underworld through an apt choice of locations. The actual use of the New Orleans wharf district adds graphic reality to the danger and disease. Adding to this unhealthy aura are the characterizations of the criminals. Zero Mostel as Fitch is sweaty, wormy, and obsequious in his devotion to Blackie, played by Jack Palance. Their archetypical performances underscore their symbolic value to the film as human malignancies. The most memorable visual simile comes at the film's climax, when the symbolic and literal actions merge in one telling image. Cornered in the dockside area, Blackie attempts to escape by crawling up the mooring of a ship. The obstacle he encounters is a hawser designed to prevent rats from climbing aboard. It works: like a rat, Blackie falls into the ocean and is caught. **JB**

PARTY GIRL (1958)

Director: Nicholas Ray. **Screenplay**: George Wells from an unpublished story by Leo Katcher. **Producer**: Joe Pasternak. **Director of Photography**: Robert Bronner. **Music**: Jeff Alexander, Andre Previn. **Art Directors**: William A. Horning, Randall Duell. **Editor**: John McSweeney, Jr. **Cast**: Robert Taylor (Thomas Farrell), Cyd Charisse (Vicki Gaye), Lee J. Cobb (Rico Angelo), John Ireland (Louis Canetto), Kent Smith (Jeffrey Stewart), Claire Kelly (Genevieve), Corey Allen (Cookie), Lewis Charles (Danny Rimett), David Opatoshu (Lou Forbes). **Completed**: July 22, 1958. **Released**: MGM, October 28. 99 minutes.

Thomas Farrell, a crippled lawyer who represents members of Rico Angelo's gang in 1930s Chicago, meets nightclub dancer Vicki Gaye at Rico's party celebrating Farrell's latest courtroom victory. Vicki asks Farrell to take her home and they discover that her roommate, Joy Hampton, has committed suicide. Farrell consoles Vicki; and a romance begins, which brings hope into both of their lonely lives. Rico assigns Farrell to defend the hoodlum Cookie from an indictment. Cookie jumps bail and the prosecutor arrests Farrell for bribing a juror. When Farrell won't reveal anything about Rico's activities, the prosecutor sends the word out that Farrell has talked and then releases him. Realizing that Rico will kill him or, worse, harm Vicki, Farrell cooperates with the prosecutor and reveals all he knows. Farrell confronts Rico; Rico has kidnapped Vicki and threatens to disfigure her in revenge for Farrell's betrayal. The police arrive, and Rico is killed. Farrell and Vicki leave Chicago behind and start a new life together.

Party Girl stands out as Nicholas Ray's most antisocial, self-indulgent film. While most of his other works try, no matter how feebly, to set a "realistic" social context—such as Miami of the early 1900s in *Wind Across the Everglades,* North Africa of World War II in *Bitter Victory,* and the urban jungle in *Knock on Any Door*—or to deal with social problems—such as drugs in *Bigger Than Life,* war in *Bitter Victory,* police brutality in *On Dangerous Ground,* ecology in *Wind Across the Everglades,* and the generation gap in *Rebel Without a Cause, Party Girl* makes no such pretense. Even *They Live by Night,* which shares with *Party Girl* the primary theme of two lovers in conflict with society, fails to approach the surreal, fantastical quality of the latter film. At no point in *They Live by Night* is the oppressive social atmosphere that drove these two young people to loneliness and despair forgotten, whereas *Party Girl* makes ample use of exotic dance sequences, costumes, and sets to create its surreal atmosphere. With the ambiguous opening title—"Chicago in the early '30s"—superimposed over a chiaroscuro backdrop of the city, the "unreal" tone of the entire film is set.

Although the film is filled with easily recognizable Hollywood archetypes—brutal yet childlike gangster czar, drooling henchmen, ambitious young punks, loose women with pure hearts, and self-righteous government investigators—*Party Girl* is far from the typical gangster product. Rather it restates one of the most insistent dualities in Ray's work. There is a personal division between Ray's self-acknowledged

Party Girl: *Vicky Gaye (Cyd Charise) and Thomas Farrell (Robert Taylor).*

duty to be involved as a social critic with civilization and his yearning to regress to a more primitive and emotionally pure existence. The final scene of *Party Girl* illustrates this fascination with the hallucinatory, erotic, and violent moment.

After turning in evidence on the mob in fear for Vicki's life (as only this danger can spur him to societal action), Farrell goes to Rico's hideout to confront the gangster. The room is filled with colored lights, decorations, and broken glass, which are the remnants of an all-night celebration. Rico sits on his wooden throne with his coat draped over him like a royal cape and calmly pours acid over a red, papier-mâché bell, thereby draining it of all color and "life." After this demonstration of Rico's power, the kidnapped Vicki is brought in with her face wrapped in bandages. Farrell stares at her in dread that she has already been disfigured. With excruciating slowness, the bandages are removed until her unscathed face is revealed. Farrell breathes easier but now Rico calls for their death. Farrell stalls for time by using a cynical trick he often used to draw sympathy from jurors. Rico almost falls for the ruse, when police sirens are heard and searchlights fill the festive room, followed by a spray of bullets and bursting glass. The acid intended for Vicki is splashed in Rico's face and he frantically, but with a stylized grace, falls through a window to his death. With Rico's death Farrell's and Vicki's connection with society is severed completely, and they walk away from the police and crowd of spectators into the deserted streets. Their action visually sums up the central theme of the movie and of noir sexuality: it can either destroy them or allow them to transcend the boundaries of society.

Compounding the theme of mad love are the dual natures of the hero and heroine and of society's underworld and legitimate "upper world." Vicki and Farrell have both suffered spiritually while Farrell is also physically handicapped. In consequence, as required in film noir, they have adopted cynicism to bandage their wounds. Vicki relates her philosophy very early in the film, when she tells another call girl to "Never get crowded into a corner. Never let them get too close." Farrell expresses his bitterness when he explains, "That's my business—mouthpiece for the mob, guardian angel for punks and gunmen . . . I'm a great believer in the easiest way."

Within this duality, Ray also constructs a complex relationship among Rico, Farrell, and Vicki. Rico Angelo (note the irony of the name) is the incarnation of evil, tempting Farrell with money and, later, threatening violence. Vicki is Farrell's redemption: curiously, this is revealed by Rico who has nicknamed her "Angel." Ray's society, also typical of film noir, divides into two distinct yet overlapping worlds. The underworld is violent, chaotic, and decadent; but it is always oriented to success, as is the "upper world" which imposes order and stability. "Harmful" passions are suppressed, although controlled coercion against the two lovers is accepted. As in the underworld—consider Fabian in *Night and the City*—success is the overriding concern: it legitimizes questionable activity. Farrell, while in jail, asks the prosecutor Stewart, "Incidentally, when do they start pushing you for Senator?" and Stewart replies, "The day you start talking." The difference between Stewart's world and Rico's is in the former's repression of base instincts, and yet his success hinges on the destruction and revelation of the latter's activities. **JU**

THE PEOPLE AGAINST O'HARA (1951)

Director: John Sturges. **Screenplay**: John Monks, Jr. from the novel by Eleazar Lipsky. **Producer**: William H. Wright. **Direct of Photography**: John Alton. **Music:** Carmen Dragon. **Art Directors**: Cedric Gibbons, James Basevi. **Editor:** Gene Ruggiero. **Cast:** Spencer Tracy (James Curtayne), Pat O'Brien (Det.Vincent Ricks), Diana Lynn (Ginny Curtayne), John Hodiak (Louis Barra), Eduardo Ciannelli (Knuckles Lanzetta), James Arness (Johnny O'Hara), Yvette Duguay (Mrs. Lanzetta), Jay C. Flippen (Sven Norson), William Campbell (Frank Korvac), Richard Anderson (Jeff Chapman), Henry O'Neill (Judge Keating), Arthur Shields (Mr. O'Hara), Louise Lorimer (Mrs. O'Hara), Ann Doran (Betty Clark), Emile Meyer (Capt. Tom Mulvaney), Regis Toomey (Fred Colton), Katherine Warren (Mrs. Sheffield). **Completed**: April 20, 1951. **Released**: MGM, September 1. 102 minutes

James Curtayne is an ex-district attorney and criminal lawyer whose alcoholism forced his early retirement. Now on the wagon, Curtayne is making a comeback as a civil lawyer. His daughter, Ginny, who has been postponing marriage to take care of him, is worried lest the pressures of another criminal case drive him back to drink. However, Curtayne takes the case of a young man, Johnny O'Hara, as a favor to his parents who do not have the money for a good lawyer. Johnny is accused of gunning a man down in the streets but he swears to Curtayne that he is innocent, although he will not say where he was at the time of the murder. On the basis of evidence offered by Frankie Korvac, purportedly a friend of Johnny's, the district attorney, Barra, feels he has a strong case. Curtayne's old friend, homicide detective Vince Ricks, helps him discover that Johnny was out with his former girlfriend that fatal night but refused to make this known for fear of getting her in trouble with her husband, gangster Knuckles Lanzetta. Also, Frankie Korvac and his brothers are no real friends of Johnny's, and it is possible that Frankie is the guilty party. Curtayne finds a seaman who witnessed the shooting from across the street, but the man refuses to testify in Johnny's favor unless he is paid. Curtayne reluctantly gives the man money, fearing he cannot win the case without his testimony. During the summation Curtayne's physical condi-

tion weakens his presentation. Barra discovers the bribe and wins the case. Curtayne decides to redeem himself by wearing a mike which will broadcast to a hidden police van. Since he is meeting with the Korvacs to ostensibly return to them a suitcase in which a cache of narcotics is hidden—the lost booty which led to the murder—Barra realizes that Curtayne is setting himself up as a clay pigeon. When the Korvacs attempt to abduct Curtayne, the police descend on them but not in time to prevent Curtayne's death.

John Alton's photography evokes a cluttered and chaotic environment in his use of the New York locations. His night shots, particularly the opening shooting scene and the long odyssey of Curtayne at the film's climax, are as dark and uninviting as any in *T-Men* and build tension in much the same way. *People Against O'Hara* is another film noir produced at MGM during the tenure of Dore Schary and, like *Mystery Street*, it was directed by John Sturges and photographed by John Alton. Although film noirs could be found at virtually every studio during the classic period, they found a most comfortable "home" at RKO, Schary's former studio. Their presence at MGM appears today a bit incongruous and no more so than here where one of that studio's biggest stars, Spencer Tracy, plays a loser. **BP**

PHANTOM LADY (1944)

Director: Robert Siodmak. **Screenplay**: Bernard C. Schoenfeld from the novel by William Irish [Cornell Woolrich]. **Executive Producer**: Milton Feld. **Associate Producer**: Joan Harrison. **Director of Photography**: Woody Bredell. **Music**: Hans J. Salter. **Art Directors**: John B. Goodman, Robert Clatworthy. **Editor**: Arthur Hilton. **Cast**: Franchot Tone (Jack Marlow), Ella Raines (Carol "Kansas" Richman), Alan Curtis (Scott Henderson), Aurora Miranda (Estela Monteiro), Thomas Gomez (Inspector Burgess), Fay Helm (Ann Terry), Elisha Cook, Jr. (Cliff Milburn), Andrew Tombes, Jr. (Bartender), Regis Toomey (Detective), Joseph Crehan (Detective), Doris Lloyd (Kettisha), Virginia Brissac (Dr. Chase), Milburn Stone (Voice of District Attorney). **Completed**: October 28, 1943. **Released**: Universal, February 17. 87 minutes

Scott Henderson, a successful civil engineer, is arrested for the murder of his wife who was strangled in their apartment with his tie. On the night of the murder he met a young lady

Phantom Lady: *Carol "Kansas" Richman (Ella Raines) and Inspector Burgess (Thomas Gomez).*

in a bar and persuaded her to join him in attending a musical show. Part of their arrangement was that they would withhold each other's names, so all he knows about her is that she was wearing a flamboyant hat that was identical to the one that the lead Latin American singer in the show was wearing. Since neither the cabdriver, the bartender, nor the singer can (or will) confirm his story, Scott is tried, convicted, and sentenced to death. Scott's faithful assistant, Carol Richman, believes his story and decides to find the real murderer with assistance from police Inspector Burgess, who is also convinced of Scott's innocence. She haunts the bar where Scott first met the "phantom lady," but when she pressures the bartender to tell the truth, he runs away and is hit by a car and killed. Disguising herself as a "hep kitten," Carol seduces Cliff Milburn, a trap drummer in the musical show who had given the "phantom lady" the eye. Liquored up, Cliff admits that he had been paid off to "forget" the woman. When Carol drops her purse in his apartment, Cliff sees that she had been carrying his police sheet and begins to act in a threatening manner. She escapes to call Burgess but while she is waiting for him to arrive Cliff is strangled with a scarf by Jack Marlow, who takes Carol's purse. Marlow, Scott's best friend, is a schizophrenic artist who was having an affair with Scott's wife and killed her when she refused to run away with him. Jack runs into Carol at the prison when both are visiting Scott, and he agrees to help her try to find the murderer. Through a cooperative milliner, they trace the hat to Ann Terry, who gives Carol the hat. Overjoyed, she accompanies Jack back to his studio apartment where she believes Burgess is to meet them. When she accidentally discovers her stolen purse she realizes Jack is the murderer. As Jack unties his scarf to strangle her, Burgess arrives and Jack jumps through the apartment window to his death. Scott is free to return to his office where he informs Carol, via dictaphone, that he is now able to return her love.

Phantom Lady not only boosted the American career of director Robert Siodmak, but also gave him a métier through which his special Germanic temperament would best express itself—film noir. For all of its silly dialogue and its deviations from one of Woolrich's more implausible plots (unlike the novel, the film reveals early on that Marlow is the killer), it, as much as any other film, defines the studio noir.

Siodmak and his brilliant cinematographer, Woody Bredell, provided *Phantom Lady* with the essential ingredients of Woolrich's world: the desperate innocent at loose at night in New York City, a city of hot, rain-drenched streets and threatening shadows where the sound of footsteps on the pavement could mean trouble; of jazz emanating from low-class bars; of lonely subway platforms; and, most importantly, the suspense engendered by a sense of time running out.

By defining this world almost entirely by *mise en scène* Siodmak and his associates created a virtual template for the studio period of the noir cycle. The second half of the film, in which Franchot Tone predominates as a domestic version of the crazed artist—whose preoccupation with his hands is a throwback to the German classic *The Hands of Orlac*—is certainly the weaker part and the denouement does strain verisimilitude. But these defects can be easily overlooked because of the film's tour de force jazz sequence. Intercutting shots of Elisha Cook, Jr., reaching orgiastic fervor as he climaxes his drum solo, with shots of the sexual innuendoes of Ella Raines as her fervor matches his, Siodmak brilliantly interweaves expressionistic decor with American idiom. If watched without sound, the scene could easily be from one of the classic German films of the twenties. **BP**

THE PHENIX CITY STORY (1955)

Director: Phil Karlson. **Screenplay**: Daniel Mainwaring, Crane Wilbur. **Producer**: Samuel Bischoff, David Diamond. **Director of Photography**: Harry Neumann. **Music**: Harry Sukman. **Art Director**: Stanley Fleischer. **Editor**: George White. **Cast**: John McIntire (Albert "Pat" Patterson), Richard Kiley (John Patterson), Kathryn Grant (Ellie Rhodes), Edward Andrews (Rhett Tanner), Lenka Peterson (Mary Jo Patterson), Biff McGuire (Fred Gage), Truman Smith (Ed Gage), Jean Carson (Cassie), Katherine Marlowe (Mamie), John Larch (Clem Wilson), Ma Beachie (herself), James Edwards (Zeke Ward), Clete Roberts (himself). **Locations**: Phenix City, Alabama. **Released**: Allied Artists, August 14. 100 minutes.

Army prosecutor John Patterson returns from Germany with his family and convinces his father Pat to take a stand against Rhett Tanner and the vice-ridden Phenix City 14th Street mob, which fleeces the soldiers from nearby Ft. Benning.

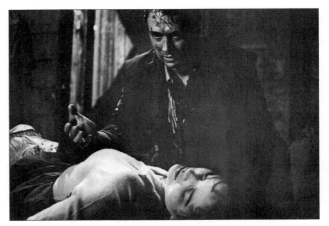

The Phenix City Story: *John Patterson (Richard Kiley) and the murdered Ellie Rhodes (Kathryn Grant).*

Tanner's associates retaliate by strangling black janitor Zeke Ward's little girl and dumping her body on Patterson's front yard. To combat the corruption Pat becomes a candidate for State Attorney General. He relies on inside information from Tanner's card dealer Ellie Rhodes, whose fiancé has been murdered as well. When Patterson wins the primary, Tanner has him assassinated and then personally kills Ellie, a witness to the crime. John restrains his father's supporters from taking vigilante action and calls the capitol to demand that Phenix City be put under martial law.

Filmed where the events occurred and promoted by photo essays in *Life* magazine, *The Phenix City Story* is the prime example of the tabloid-like "exposé" noirs, which in the spirit of the Kefauver crime commission promises to uncover topical corruption. Entrenched organized crime is acknowledged as an existing reality, although the film implies that it may be limited to "Sin Towns" like Phenix City. Although an occasional menacing shadow survives from 1940s expressionism, Phil Karlson's hard-hitting style exemplifies the naturalistic, documentary surface of 1950s noir punctuated by flashes of brutal violence that terrorize the audience. Voters are beaten bloody on Election Day, and small children are confronted by the corpse of another child thrown at their feet. The army lawyer has returned from Germany to find hometown America in the grip of Nazi-like oppression.

At the conclusion, the father of the murdered child restrains John Patterson from taking personal revenge. This nod to the Civil Rights movement places the film as a socially conscious drama at the edge of the noir style. Whereas later exposés (such as Karlson's own *Walking Tall*) would irresponsibly condone southern vigilantism, *The Phenix City Story* instead prescribes lawful political action. The film was originally augmented with a prologue and epilogue featuring the actual John Patterson and man-on-the-street news interviews, and was used several times in Alabama election campaigns. **GE**

PICKUP (1951)

Director: Hugo Haas. **Screenplay**: Hugo Haas, Arnold Philips based on the novel *Watchman 47* by Josef Kopta. **Producer**: Hugo Haas, Edgar E. Walden. **Director of Photography**: Paul Ivano. **Art Director**: Rudi Feld. **Music**: Harold Byrns. **Editor**: W.L. Bagier. **Cast**: Hugo Haas (Jan Horak), Beverly Michaels (Betty Horak), Allan Nixon (Steve Kowalski), Howland Chamberlain (The Professor, hobo), Jo-Carroll Dennison (Irma), Bernard Gorcey (Peddler with Dog), Mark Lowell (Counter-man), Jack Daly (Company Doctor). **Released**: Columbia, July 24. 78 minutes.

Jan is an aging railway station employee in an isolated depot. His only friends are his dog, which has recently died, and an erudite hobo. He goes to town to attend a carnival and buy a replacement for his old canine friend. Instead he meets the alluring, if sluttish Betty, who is attracted to his money. Betty seduces and marries Jan in short order and then moves out to the depot with him. Rapidly disenchanted with her less than virile husband and lonely surroundings, she takes up with the youthful Steve, another employee of the railroad. After Jan's hysterical attack of deafness, Betty tries to convince Steve to murder her husband and run away with his money. But Jan, who has regained his hearing, foils the plot and Betty deserts both husband and lover in the final scene.

Czech expatriate filmmaker-actor Hugo Haas has often been referred to as the "low-rent von Sternberg." Convincing Columbia to distribute his ultra low-budget meditations on cuckolded older men, young femme fatales, and muscular lovers, Haas in the 1950s wrote, directed, and starred in a series of filmic meditations on the pleasures of masochism which, like von Sternberg's movies, compulsively repeated themes, characters, and plot points. The first in the series is *Pickup* starring Beverly Michaels as the embittered, hardened Betty, whom he first spots sitting sidesaddle on a carousel horse, displaying her fishnet-covered legs for a group of salivating local yokels. While the lonely Jan had originally come to the carnival to bring back a loving, obedient puppy, he instead picks up a much less compliant "pet." Within record time the seductive Betty has scoped out the lonely man's bank account and married him to escape what she calls the "sharks" of the world. Soon Jan is serving her breakfast in bed and tiptoeing around the house in order not to disturb her.

Pickup draws heavily from Emile Zola via Jean Renoir's *La Bête Humaine* for its inspiration, as do many film noirs. Veteran noir cinematographer Paul Ivano (*Shanghai Gesture, The Suspect,* etc.), who would shoot a number of Haas's other films, frames the adulterous lovers (Betty and Steve) against the moonlit sky during their trysts in the train depot yards while Jan sits in agony with images of speeding trains intercut, acting—as they did in Zola's work—as symbols of determinism and fate. Haas also introduces several scenes of effective subjectification to the film. After Jan loses his hearing, Haas drops out the normal sound and replaces it with a low-pitched whining, allowing the audience to identify with the afflicted man. The irony of the ending is that even though Jan finally demonstrates his dominance by unraveling Betty's plot to kill him and "casting out" this troublesome siren, the price he pays is a life bereft of any type of excitement, sexual or otherwise. **JU**

PICKUP ON SOUTH STREET (1953)

Director/Screenplay: Samuel Fuller from an unpublished story by Dwight Taylor. **Producer**: Jules Schermer. **Director of Photography**: Joe MacDonald. **Music**: Leigh Harline. **Art Directors**: Lyle Wheeler, George Patrick. **Editor**: Nick De Maggio. **Cast**: Richard Widmark (Skip McCoy), Jean Peters (Candy),

Pickup on South Street: *Skip McCoy (Richard Widmark) and Candy (Jean Peters).*

Thelma Ritter (Moe), Murvyn Vye (Capt. Dan Tiger), Richard Kiley (Joey), Willis B. Bouchey (Zara), Milburn Stone (Winoki), Henry Slate (MacGregor), Jerry O'Sullivan (Enyart). **Completed**: October 16, 1952. **Released**: 20th Century-Fox, June 17. 83 minutes.

A New York City pickpocket and "three-time loser" named Skip McCoy inadvertently lifts some microfilm from the purse of Candy, the former mistress of a Communist spy, Joey. McCoy's nemesis on the police force, Capt. Tiger, cooperates with the federal agent who maintained surveillance over Candy. Skip denies that the film exists and does not yield to the federal agent's patriotic appeal or Tiger's promise to overlook the crime. Moe sells Skip's waterfront address to Candy because she must retrieve the microfilm by any means possible. She and Skip are sexually attracted to one another; but this does not affect his price for the microfilm. Candy refuses to cooperate with Joey when she learns he is a Communist, and she confides in Moe. Joey tries to buy Skip's address from Moe; but he kills her when she refuses to reveal it to a Communist at any price. He then savagely beats and shoots Candy, who had acquired the film but was cooperating with the federal agents. A piece is missing from the film; and Joey, who has obtained Skip's address, goes to meet the pickpocket. Skip avoids the spy and follows him on the subway, where he lifts both the microfilm and Joey's gun. After breaking up Joey's rendezvous, Skip pursues Joey and beats him mercilessly to avenge Candy's shooting and Moe's death.

Much has been written about the contradictions in Fuller's politics. *Pickup on South Street* is anti-Communist, but the sympathetic Americans of the film are not members of respectable society. A pickpocket, a prostitute, and a stool pigeon fight for their country even though they will remain in its gutter. Fuller laughs in the face of righteous patriotic sentiment. When the pious federal man asks solemnly, "Do you know what Communism is?" Skip breezily replies, "Who cares?" In spite of the provocative nature of these themes, the real distinction of Fuller's film is his visual realization.

Pickup benefits from Joe MacDonald's high-contrast black-and-white photography and from the vividly created settings of subways, the waterfront, and Moe's shabby room. Fuller is never stylistically redundant. Long takes, such as the moving shot that stalks Candy as Joey assaults her, alternate with rhythmically cut sequences. Intense close-ups often dominate, but at other times the camera glides over the action, coming to rest and resuming movement at unexpected intervals. Contrast is characteristically a part of the action and Fuller's violent love scenes are the best example. The eroticism of Skip and Candy's encounter is heightened by Skip's readiness to punch Candy in the mouth and then caress the bruise he has created. Equally, she will unhesitatingly knock him unconscious after making love in order to get what she wants. *Pickup* features what is perhaps the most compelling example in all of Fuller's films of his mingling of violence and tenderness. Most of the action is hard, tough, and brutal; but the scene of Moe's death is unexpectedly sensitive and touching. Thelma Ritter's Moe is one of the most embellished supporting characters in film noir. Exhausted by life, her romantic phonograph record accompanies her last moments, when she heroically repulses Joey's threats. The camera holds tellingly on Moe's face as the shabby woman becomes proudly beautiful. **BL**

Pitfall: *John Forbes (Dick Powell) and Mona Stevens (Lizabeth Scott) are menaced by MacDonald (Raymond Burr).*

PITFALL (1948)

Director: André De Toth. **Screenplay**: Karl Kamb, William and André De Toth [uncredited] from the novel by Jay Dratler. **Producer**: Samuel Bischoff (Regal Films). **Director of Photography**: Harry Wild. **Music**: Louis Forbes. **Art Director**: Arthur Lonergan. **Editor**: Walter Thompson. **Cast**: Dick Powell (John Forbes), Lizabeth Scott (Mona Stevens), Jane Wyatt (Sue Forbes), Raymond Burr (MacDonald), John Litel (District Attorney), Byron Barr (Bill Smiley), Jimmy Hunt (Tommy Forbes), Ann Doran (Maggie), Selmer Jackson (Ed Brawley), Margaret Wells (Terry), Dick Wassel (Desk Sergeant). **Completed**: March 18, 1948. **Released**: United Artists, August 24. 86 minutes.

John Forbes, a successful insurance agent married to his high school sweetheart, Sue, lives with her and their young son, Tommy, in a suburb of Los Angeles. John, suffering a mid-life crisis, is bored with his daily routine and believes his youthful dreams have failed to materialize. His firm has paid off on a robbery committed by Bill Smiley and now John is to recover some of the goods that Smiley had bought with the stolen money. With the aid of Mack MacDonald, a private eye who occasionally works for his company, John traces the items to Mona Stevens, Smiley's beautiful girlfriend. A model, Mona lives next to a marina so she can easily take her motorboat out for pleasure rides. Mona is disappointed that she must give up Smiley's gifts and sees through John, calling him "a little man with a briefcase." John is understandably attracted to her, and what starts out as an innocent adventure becomes a love affair. Mack warns John to stay away from Mona, since he also desires her despite her obvious dislike of him. When Mona discovers that John is married she gets John to agree to end the affair. Mack, skeptical that the affair is over, arranges for Smiley's bail and plies him with liquor to arouse his jealousy and hostility towards John. Mona warns John, who puts his family to bed and waits downstairs with a gun. Smiley breaks into the house and is fatally shot. John reveals the entire affair to his wife, who is unsure of her emotions. Meanwhile, Mack tries to force Mona to run off with him but she kills him. After confessing to the authorities, John is exonerated though Mona is arrested. As John and Sue drive home from the courthouse, Sue explains that she will remain his wife although their relationship may never be the same.

Pitfall is one of the earliest films of the noir cycle to move crime from the urban jungle to the suburbs of contemporary America. In describing the fall and later reinstatement of the errant husband from bourgeois respectability it would appear to reinforce the values of middle-class America. At the same time, by scratching below the surface of suburban life it begins to expose the middle class malaise that would become fodder for sociologists a decade later and work its way into such films as *Crime of Passion* and *Rebel without a Cause*. For if Forbes' family status makes his fall from grace less severe than that of his fellow insurance agent, Walter Neff, it is equally true that, unlike Walter, he deludes himself about his motivations and even conceals his marital status from Mona. And Scott's Mona, unlike Stanwyck's Phyllis, is no femme fatale but a woman whose greatest sin is her beauty and her willingness to let men use her.

Dick Powell was a good choice for Forbes because by this time his screen image was both tough and vulnerable and his dour sarcasm a telling mark of the boredom afflicting a husband whose life has fallen into a rut. And Lizabeth Scott seems quite comfortable here working against the image of the hardened blonde. But it is Raymond Burr, stealing some thunder from the late Laird Cregar, who is able to bring a degree of pathos to what would otherwise be a reprehensible character. Finally, Jane Wyatt plays the well-scrubbed, simplistic housewife as only she can and would, in fact, capitalize on that image a few years later in television's *Father Knows Best*, where, ironically, she would be married to that most famous insurance agent/father, Jim Anderson. **BP**

A PLACE IN THE SUN (1951)

Director: George Stevens. **Screenplay**: Michael Wilson, Harry Brown based on the novel *An American Tragedy* by Theodore Dreiser and play *An American Tragedy* by Patrick Kearney. **Producer**: George Stevens. **Director of Photography**: William C. Mellor. **Music**: Franz Waxman. **Art Director**: Hans Dreier, Walter Tyler. **Editor**: William Hornbeck. **Cast**: Montgomery Clift (George Eastman), Elizabeth Taylor (Angela Vickers), Shelley Winters (Alice Tripp), Anne Revere (Hannah Eastman), Keefe Brasselle (Earl Eastman), Fred Clark (Bellows, defense attorney), Raymond Burr (Dist. Atty. R. Frank Marlowe), Herbert Heyes (Charles Eastman), Sheppard Strudwick (Anthony). **Released**: Paramount, August 14. 122 minutes.

With postwar increases in education, incomes and career opportunities, especially for young white male veterans such as George Eastman, director Stevens' decision to portray America as an open class system (signaled in the film's title, *A Place in the Sun*), eschewing Dreiser's view in *An American Tragedy* that it was closed, should be placed in historical context. George, both low-skilled and low-educated, accepts an offer to work in his uncle's swimsuit plant. From afar, he's attracted to Angela, the belle of the young and rich. Since his relatives don't include him in their elite social life, he starts dating Alice, who packs swimsuits at the factory. He gets her pregnant. Unexpectedly, his uncle promotes him and invites him to his next party, where George and Angela fall in love.

A Place in the Sun: *Alice Tripp (Shelley Winters) and George Eastman (Montgomery Clift)*.

The scene that represents the film's strongest endorsement of class mobility takes place at her family's lodge. Angela's father asks George about his background. George replies he grew up poor and left home at thirteen "to do something about it," taking any job he could get. This frankness wins her father's approval for Angela to marry George. Spoiling everything, however, Alice shows up with her own demands for marriage. Alice can't swim, so George takes her out in a rowboat on a deserted lake. Although he changes his mind about drowning her, the boat capsizes and she dies. George is arrested, tried and convicted on circumstantial evidence. Because he deliberately didn't rescue Alice, a priest tells him, "In your heart was murder." Just before George is executed, Angela tells him she'll love him for the rest of her life.

Janus (from which January is derived) was the mythical Roman god of doorways, beginnings and endings. He had two faces, which looked in opposite directions. They symbolized not only the moon and the sun but also time, since one face looked to the past and the other to the future. He represented such dichotomies as barbarity and civilization, rural and urban living, and youth and adulthood. In multiple ways, *A Place in the Sun* is the Janus-film of its time. The original theatrical trailer says, "One love grew in the shadows of night. The other love flamed in the bright light of gaiety and laughter." Not only does each of these love stories have a distinct visual style but each style is associated with a different time. Their affinity with Janus is that the style for love in the shadows looks backward toward film noir of the 1940s, whereas the style for love in bright light looks forward to the romantic melodramas of the 1950s. Indeed, each of these kinds of cinema, film noir and melodrama, is represented by a different face, that of Alice and Angela, respectively. In fact, to face in different directions is how the film begins. As the credits roll, George stands by the side of a highway, his back to the camera. While trying to hitch a ride, he looks at where he's already been. The music swells as he walks backward nearer to the camera. Once the credits end, he turns around and the camera moves in close. He is smiling at his destination, signified by a billboard for Eastman swimsuits. A car horn honks behind him, and he turns with his thumb out. Angela drives by in a white convertible, ignoring him.

The camera and then George's eyes pan after her, as she drives on. Now he faces the direction of his future.

The locations for George's two romances are polarized in class terms, between proletariat and bourgeoisie, the Eastman factory and Alice's city apartment vs. the Eastman suburban mansion and Angela's lakeshore lodge. The romances are also associated with time, which mark the different class situations of George's life. Alice is part of his working class past. He and she immediately catch each other's eye and easily hit it off. Angela is the potential in his future. Since they come from very different worlds, on the first couple of occasions when they cross paths, she literally doesn't see him. Above all, however, the most striking contrast in *A Place in the Sun* is the different visual style that is used, on the one hand, for George's relationship with Alice and, on the other, with Angela. Each style is appropriate to its associated narrative, as well as the dichotomies of time and social class in George's life.

On George's first day at work, his cousin, Earl, takes him on a tour of the plant. As they walk out of a room where lovely women are modeling Eastman bathing suits, George turns his head to look back. Earl notices it and immediately warns him, "There's a company rule against any of us employees mixing with the girls who work here. My father asked me to particularly call this to your attention. That is a must!" This incident contradicts the theatrical trailer's assertion that "fate weaves the strange fabric of his life." George's life isn't destined to end tragically. He chooses to disobey an explicit rule imposed by those who run the factory as well as the community. It's his fault, and not fate, that his place will be in the electric chair instead of in the sun. He should have always looked ahead and complied with new class obligations, never looking back to the working class (swimsuit models or packers) that he should renounce. However, since George does disobey, he and Alice have to hide their affair. In the style of film noir (*A Place in the Sun* is in black and white), the key incidents of George and Alice's affair are set in shadows: their first kiss; the night they sleep together; their conversation in his car after a doctor refuses to perform an abortion; when George hears a radio report about people drowning and gets the idea to murder Alice; and the final six minutes of the scene when Alice drowns and George survives. The shadows that conceal George are also the shades of time and class in his life. As he moves up the corporate ladder, his origins in the working class are supposed to disappear into the past. Time fading is also emphasized via frequent prolonged dissolves, as one scene slowly transforms into another. Because the old scene is as visible as the new, the overlapping creates a Janus-effect by simultaneously showing past and future.

In contrast, and anticipating the lush color cinematography of the remarkable melodramas soon to come, George and Angela's romance is shown in bright light and, most famously, tight close-ups. Angela's association with brightness extends to her clothing. She's often dressed all in white, in a dress, or a full-length coat with a white scarf around her head. In the first half of the movie if she is wearing black, it's under a striking white accessory (a mink stole, a jacket or a Hawaiian lei). George's future — upper management at the plant, marriage to Angela and membership in the community's high society — is associated with a bright visual style. His passion for Angela, as opposed to his alienation from Alice, is evidenced through close-ups. Alice's only close-up with George (which

is medium, not tight) occurs in the rowboat when she asks him if he wishes she were dead. Moments later she plunges into the lake. Angela, on the other hand, may be one of the characters in Hollywood history most identified with close-ups. When she has her first conversation with George in the poolroom at his uncle's house, she is photographed close up and in soft focus. Afterwards, as they dance, the camera moves in even nearer to her face. The huge close-ups continue while Alice is alive. However, Alice's death finishes the film's two separate yet intertwined stories.

In the single narrative that concludes the film (George's trial and punishment) the film noir of *A Place in the Sun* eclipses the romantic melodrama. Prefiguring this, the visual style for the love that began in bright light turns dark. At the lake where Alice will drown, Angela sits on shore in a strapless black swimsuit (no cap) looking outward with her back to the camera as she tells George about a woman who drowned there and whose male companion was never found. When George and Angela kiss the day before Alice dies, Angela's face is unseen in shadows. Prior to his arrest, they kiss in front of her lodge, and then Angela steps through the doorway into darkness. They aren't together again until she comes to his cell. Her appearance is the opposite of their first meeting in the poolroom, when she wore a strapless white dress over petticoats. At the prison she wears a conservative, full-length black dress appropriate for a funeral, with only a small white collar and a black cap covering her hair. The film ends with George facing the camera as he walks toward the execution room. At this moment the film noir and the melodrama converge. Superimposed over a screen-filling close-up of George's face is Angela's, as she's being kissed in his memory. In the film's last shot, their two faces, like Janus, are embodied in one. **DMH**

PLEASE MURDER ME (1956)

Director: Peter Godfrey. **Screenplay**: David C. Chantler, E.A. Dupont, Donald Hyde, A. C. Ward. **Producer**: Donald Hyde. **Executive Producers**: Jack J. Gross, Philip N. Krasne (Gross-Krasne Productions). **Director of Photography**: Alan Stensvold. **Music**: Albert Glasser. **Art Director**: Nicolai Remisoff. **Editor**: Kenneth Crane. **Cast**: Angela Lansbury (Myra Leeds), Raymond Burr (Craig Carlson), Dick Foran (Joe Leeds), John Dehner (District Attorney Ray Willis), Lamont Johnson (Carl Holt), Robert Griffin (Lou Kazarian), Denver Pyle (Detective Lt. Bradley), Alex Sharp (Sergeant Hill). **Released**: Distributors Corporation of America [DCA], March 4. 75 minutes.

With a narrative managed through flashback in standard noir style, lawyer Craig Carlson tells the story of his affair with Myra, wife of his old army buddy, Joe Leeds. Craig helps Myra sue Joe for divorce. After days of brooding tries to persuade Myra to stay; but instead she shoots him. Craig shifts from divorce to defense lawyer and after a courtroom drama, persuades the jury of her innocence, and they plan their new life together. However it transpires that Myra did not act in self-defense, and is also betraying Craig with another lover. He plots his revenge by inducing her to shoot him, recording it all as evidence for the district attorney, thus securing his revenge and justice for Joe.

This was among director Peter Godfrey's last works in features—from the mid-1950s he concentrated on television—and most of his previous films were B-movie melodramas. *Please Murder Me,* despite an implausibly convoluted plot, stops just short of crass B-movie melodrama because of its two powerful central performances. Angela Lansbury portrays a femme fatale who is revealed as an adulterous, gold-digging, cold-blooded killer with a venality that will surprise those only familiar with her later TV roles. Burr played the lawyer Craig Carlson tormented by guilt because of the pain he has inflicted on his best friend, just a year before taking on the persona of the distinctly un-noir attorney Perry Mason, a role he was still playing at the time of his death in 1993. *Please Murder Me* represents an important milestone on Burr's shift from victim and villain (he had co-starred as the white-haired wife murderer observed by Jimmy Stewart in Hitchcock's *Rear Window*) to crusader for justice.

The movie was made during the closing years of the classic film noir era but nevertheless carries the hallmarks. The opening sequence shows Burr walking the streets at night and buying a gun he notices displayed in a store window. We see the gun being loaded under the opening credits. Before dissolving to flashback, as had Walter Neff ten years earlier with a Dictaphone, Carlson dictates his story to a tape recorder, the same one that will eventually be left for the DA to discover at the end. The lighting and shadows get darker as the plot moves to its denouement. As with many of the films of the period, the moral tone of *Please Murder Me,* even a decade later, reflects wartime sacrifices and postwar disillusionment. The strength of Craig's friendship with Joe, and therefore the measure of Craig's treachery, draws on the time they served together in the Iwo Jima campaign during which Joe saved Craig's life. With that sacrifice as the benchmark, Myra's obsession with wealth and materialism—we discover she only married Joe to secure a slice of his successful business—is thrown into sharp contrast. As the dialogue notes: "She isn't a woman. Myra's a disease." Given the family-centered morality of the mid-1950s, Burr's defense of Myra on the grounds that she sought a divorce because she loved another man appears perhaps reckless but, of course, in the context of a noir narrative it works. **GF**

PLUNDER ROAD (1957)

Director: Hubert Cornfield. **Screenplay**: Steven Ritch from an unpublished story by Ritch and Jack Charney. **Producers**: Leon Chooluck, Laurence Stewart. **Director of Photography**: Ernest Haller. **Music**: Irving Gertz. **Art Director**: Robert Gill. **Editors**: Warren Adams, Jerry S. Young. **Cast**: Gene Raymond (Eddie Harris), Jeanne Cooper (Fran Werner), Wayne Morris (Commando

Munson), Elisha Cook, Jr. (Skeets Jonas), Stafford Repp (Roly Adams), Steven Ritch (Frankie Chardo), Nora Hayden (Hazel), Michael Fox (Smog Officer/Narrator), Douglas Bank (Guard #1/Narrator), Stacy Graham (Narrator). **Completed**: July 26, 1957. **Released**: 20th Century-Fox, December 5. 82 minutes.

A gang robs a train of the gold bound for the San Francisco mint. The gang members are: Eddie, a college man who planned the theft; Commando, a widowed ex-con who plans to retire to Rio with his son; Frankie, an ex-race car driver; Skeets, a good-natured former stunt man; and Roly, a gum-chewing truck driver. After the robbery the gold ingots are divided into three lots and hidden on three different vehicles: a moving van, a freight truck supposedly hauling coffee, and a tanker supposedly filled with chemicals. Roly leaves first in the moving van. When he forgets to turn off the police radio on his truck and arouses suspicion at a roadblock, he panics and is killed. Next to depart are Commando and Skeets in the freight truck. At a weighing station, their load gives them away and they are captured. Eddie and Frankie, in the tanker, manage to make it to Los Angeles. They unload the gold at an iron foundry where arrangements have been made by Eddie's girlfriend, Fran. They melt down and cast the gold into bumpers and hub caps, which they chrome and place on a Cadillac. The next day as they drive to board a ship out of the country, an accident backs up traffic on the freeway, and a gawking woman locks bumpers with their car. When the police attempt to help uncouple the cars, the chrome is scraped off. Frankie draws his gun and is shot; Eddie tells Fran to run and heads for the freeway overpass. With the police in pursuit, he jumps off the overpass, trying to land on the top of a truck on the freeway below. He is unable to secure himself, rolls off the truck's top, and is crushed by the oncoming traffic.

Plunder Road makes the most of a very limited budget by dividing its narrative into three major segments and following its characters through a variety of locations atmospherically photographed by Ernest Haller. A sign of the times, Haller shot this in 2.35:1 aspect ratio, a screen width which places humans at the disposition of their surroundings and displaces depth staging. But it is the presence of actors such as Elisha Cook, Jr., and Stafford Repp, archetypal losers from numerous noir films of the 1940s, that anticipates the most noir aspect of this film, the overriding determinism of its narrative. Unlike Kubrick's *The Killing* of a year earlier, *Plunder Road* eschews overlapping scenes or any pointedly analytical devices in favor of a basic irony in which the criminals are defeated by their own elaborate safeguards. Perhaps Eddie has an instant of anguished realization, as he plummets off the overpass, that if only he had simply put the ingots in the trunk of the car rather than doing as he did, he might have succeeded. However, that is less significant than the totality of the actions leading up to that moment. The final shot, pulling back from the freeway clogged with vehicles, underscores the fatally noir statement of the film even as it abandons its characters to existential oblivion. **BP & AS**

PORT OF NEW YORK (1949)

Director: Laszlo Benedek. **Screenplay**: Eugene Ling, Leo Townsend based on a story by Bert Murray and Arthur A. Ross. **Producer**: Aubrey Schenck. **Director of Photography**: George K. Diskant. **Art Director**: Edward Ilou. **Music**: Sol Kaplan. **Editor**: Norman Colbert. **Cast**: Scott Brady (Mickey Waters), Richard Rober (Jim Flannery), K.T. Stevens (Toni Cardell), Yul Brynner (Paul Vicola), Arthur Blake (Dolly Carney), Lynne Carter (Lili Long), John Kellogg (Lenny), William Challee (Leo). **Released**: Eagle-Lion, November 28. 82 minutes.

As a passenger ship arrives in New York, a female passenger witnesses the ship's purser go over the side in a raft. The purser is picked up by a launch, stabbed to death, and dumped into the harbor. The female witness is part of a gang of smugglers headed by Paul Vicola. The purser was killed because he helped the gang steal a shipment of morphine headed from a medical lab. Discovering the narcotics missing, federal agents Waters and Flannery are called into the

case. Vicola's girlfriend, nervous about being part of the murder, contacts the agents and tells them about part of the shipment that she has stored in a locker. Vicola finds out that she is cooperating with the police and kills her. Waters and Flannery stake out the locker and tail the messenger who picks it up to a nightclub, where he delivers the package to the club comedian. They arrest the comedian, and the comic's girlfriend goes to Vicola to see if he can help. The comedian tells the agents about Vicola's yacht, and the pair sneaks aboard to find incriminating evidence. Waters is caught and murdered by the gang. To get inside the operation, Flannery assumes the identity of a Canadian drug dealer. The comedian is inadvertently released by the police and is killed by Vicola's people. Flannery meets Vicola aboard his yacht and arranges for a dope purchase, but while he is there, the comedian's girlfriend shows up and reveals Flannery as a cop. Before they can kill him, the feds show up and arrest Vicola and his cohorts.

Done in voice-over documentary style, this hard-edged, violent film generates a sinister, brooding atmosphere through its use of New York locations and some nice photography and good direction. The film industry must have noticed the latter, as director Laszlo Benedek was soon hired to direct some top-notch A-films, such as *Death of a Salesman* and *The Wild One*. *Port of New York* was Yul Brynner's film debut and one of the few movies in which he appeared with hair. **AL**

POSSESSED (1947)

Director: Curtis Bernhardt. **Screenplay**: Sylvia Richards and Ranald MacDougall from the magazine novelette *One Man's Secret* by Rita Weiman. **Producer**: Jerry Wald. **Director of Photography**: Joseph Valentine. **Music**: Franz Waxman. **Art Director**: Anton Grot. **Editor**: Rudi Fehr. **Cast**: Joan Crawford (Louise Howell Graham), Van Heflin (David Sutton), Raymond Massey (Dean Graham), Geraldine Brooks (Carol Graham), Stanley Ridges (Dr. Harvey Williard), John Ridgely (Lt. Harker), Moroni Olsen (Dr. Ames), Erskine Sanford (Dr. Max Sherman), Gerald Perreau (Wynn Graham), Isabel Withers (Nurse Rosen), Lisa Golm (Elsie), Gerald Perreau (Wynn Graham). **Completed**: November 12, 1946. **Released**: Warner Bros., May 29. 108 minutes.

Wealthy Mrs. Louise Graham is found at dawn, wandering downtown Los Angeles and asking for "David" as if in a trance. Taken to the hospital, doctors learn her story through narcosynthesis. As Louise Howell, she was employed by industrialist Dean Graham as a nurse to his wife, Pauline, an invalid with symptoms of mental illness. Louise is in love with a young engineer, David Sutton, who rejects her and takes a job on one of Graham's projects in Canada. Meanwhile, Pauline Graham imagines a liaison between her husband and Louise and drowns herself. Some time later Mr. Graham proposes marriage to Louise and she accepts. Unexpectedly, David attends the wedding reception and begins to court Carol, Graham's daughter. Louise's mind begins to falter. She comes to believe that she is responsible for Pauline's suicide and she imagines killing Carol. After seeing a psychiatrist under an assumed name, Louise refuses to heed his warnings about her potential mental breakdown. She confronts David and attempts to arouse his pity and

Possessed: *Louise Graham (Joan Crawford) and her husband Dean (Raymond Massey).*

cause him to break with Carol but he refuses and Louise kills him. This act precipitates her catatonic state. The psychiatrist, Dr. Williard, tells her husband that with proper treatment she may recover her sanity in time.

Curtis Bernhardt is one of a number of Germanic directors who display a penchant for films with psychological themes (e.g., *Conflict* and *The High Wall*), especially those of the Freudian school. Though a bit over laden with psychojargon, this film is arguably the strongest of the three. The plot is structured from the point of view of the deranged protagonist (most of it in a series of flashbacks initiated by Louise as she is interrogated by Williard) and Bernhardt, by skillfully presenting flashbacks and fantasies in a straightforward manner, blurs the distinction between reality and Louise's imagination. In Bernhardt's hands, *Possessed* thus becomes a prime example of the oneiric tonality of the noir cycle, an attribute much beloved by Borde and Chaumeton.

Being German, it is not surprising that Bernhardt was also a master at the creation of *stimmung* (atmosphere) and in the opening sequence of Louise wandering, dazed, down the streets of downtown Los Angeles he (assisted by photographer Valentine) displays the uncanny ability to infuse authentic locales with the proper "mood," a mark of those directors and photographers who were masters of the noir style. Other marks of such an expressive style are the subjective point of view, from Louise's position on the gurney as she is wheeled from the ambulance into her hospital room; the slow associative dissolve from the water pitcher to the nocturnal lake where Pauline commits suicide; the use of rain-streaked windows to frame Louise's face; and the use of Schumann's *Carnival* as a leitmotif of Louise's mental instability (rather akin to Bernhardt's use of "Tango of Love" in *Conflict*). Joan Crawford moves smoothly from submissive lover/house-nurse to dominant virago. And Van Heflin, as the devilishly charming but fickle David Sutton, gives authenticity to what is an unusual role for the noir cycle, that of a *homme fatale*. **BP**

THE POSTMAN ALWAYS RINGS TWICE (1946)

Director: Tay Garnett. **Screenplay**: Harry Ruskin and Niven Busch from the novel by James M. Cain. **Producer**: Carey Wilson. **Director of Photography**: Sidney Wagner. **Music**: George Bassman. **Art Directors**: Cedric Gibbons, Randall Duell. **Editor**: George

White. **Cast**: Lana Turner (Cora Smith), John Garfield (Frank Chambers), Cecil Kellaway (Nick Smith), Hume Cronyn (Arthur Keats), Leon Ames (Kyle Sackett), Audrey Totter (Madge Gorland), Alan Reed (Ezra Liam Kennedy), Jeff York (Blair), Charles Williams (Jimmie White), Cameron Grant (Willie), Wally Cassell (Ben), William Halligan, Morris Ankrum (judges). **Completed**: October 26, 1945. **Released**: MGM, May 2. 113 minutes.

A drifter, Frank Chambers, arrives at a small California roadside cafe and is immediately attracted to Cora Smith, a beautiful young woman married to the elderly proprietor of the restaurant. Staying on as an employee, Frank falls hopelessly in love with Cora. They plan to leave together, but after quickly discovering the harsh realities of life on the road they return to the cafe before her husband discovers them missing. Cora convinces Frank that the only way to stay together is to kill her husband and make it appear an accident. Their initial attempts fail. Finally, on a trip to Santa Barbara, the murder is committed. But Frank cannot get out of the car fast enough, and he plunges over the cliff with the doomed husband. While recuperating in the hospital, Frank is placed in a compromising situation. The district attorney is bent on pinning the murder on Cora, and Frank is hustled into signing a complaint against her. Frank's betrayal outrages Cora. The trial is inconclusive and the couple returns to the café. Their relationship is complicated by an affair on the part of Frank and various attempts at blackmail by an unscrupulous court assistant. Finally, believing all their problems to be behind them, Cora and Frank resolve to begin a new life. But they have another automobile accident and Cora is killed. Frank is falsely convicted of her murder and is condemned to die in the electric chair.

Evil and corruption lie just below the surface of the mundane in *The Postman Always Rings Twice*. Virtually the entire film takes place in a bright, rather shabby roadside cafe, one that is, as the narrator informs us at the opening of the film, just like thousands of other roadside restaurants. James M. Cain's novel of treachery and murder, as well as Tay Garnett's adaptation of it, is a classic vision of the noir film's ability to depict *amour fou*, a love which goes beyond the bounds of normal relationships. As a femme fatale, Cora Smith is a far cry from Cain's cold-blooded Phyllis Dietrichson, portrayed

The Postman Always Rings Twice: *Cora Smith (Lana Turner) and Frank Chambers (John Garfield)*.

by Barbara Stanwyck in *Double Indemnity*. Cora is more of a victim, trapped in a world of abundant ironies. Her marriage to the older and financially secure Nick, in order to "get away," leaves her bored and restless. The love affair with Frank ends with both parties dead. She offered Frank a world removed from the ordinary, but in doing so, Cora condemned each of them to a nightmarish existence. Phyllis, on the other hand, constructs her plots with calculating precision, and she manipulates her cast of characters to her whims. Her death at the hands of Walter Neff completes the bizarre ritual of love and death she embraced; and she dies without love or pity.

Cora, however, remains a sympathetic character throughout *The Postman Always Rings Twice*, as she is caught in a situation from which there is no real escape and moves inevitably toward her doom. Tay Garnett's direction highlights this paradox, lending it a surreal quality, as in the sequence in which Frank and Cora swim far out into the deep ocean at night to cleanse themselves of suspicion and reaffirm their love to one another. The dark ocean suggests the surrounding doom and danger that has become a part of their lives and threatens to drown them. Many of Garnett's scenes also consist of two or three simple shots with little tracking or moving of the camera. The claustrophobia of these static shots, which the lovers share with Cora's unwanted husband, seems to compel the lovers toward murderous action as the only way to force her husband to give them breathing room. This link between sex and violence is explicit throughout the film, as Frank tells Cora, "Give me a kiss or I'll sock ya," early in the story. And when she tells him, after the murder, that she wants "kisses that come from life, not death," their fate has already been sealed by their own actions. She is killed in a car wreck caused by giving Frank that kiss from life. As the car door opens after the crash, her arm falls, and her hand releases a tube of lipstick, which drops to the ground. This symbolically reverses the events of their first meeting, when Frank stoops to pick up a lipstick tube rolling toward him; he then looks up to see Cora standing over him with a waiting hand outstretched to receive her possession. **EK & CM**

PRETENDER (1947)

Director/Producer: W. Lee Wilder. **Screenplay**: Don Martin with additional dialogue by Doris Miller. **Director of Photography**: John Alton. **Music**: Paul Dessau. **Art Director**: F. Paul Sylos. **Editors**: Asa Boyd Clark, John F. Link. **Cast**: Albert Dekker (Kenneth Holden/Foster), Catherine Craig (Claire Worthington), Charles Drake (Dr. Leonard Koster), Alan Carney (Victor Korrin), Linda Stirling (Flo Ronson), Tom Kennedy (Fingers Murdock), Selmer Jackson (Charles Lennox), Charles Middleton (William, the butler), Ernie Adams (Thomas, the butler). **Completed**: April 2, 1947. **Released**: Republic, August 13. 69 minutes.

Kenneth Holden, a handsome, middle-aged investment broker, embezzles from a client's estate and then plans to marry his client, Claire Worthington, to cover up his crime. But Claire rejects Ken's proposal because she is already engaged. He then arranges with Vic Korrin, a nightclub owner, to have Claire's fiancé killed, informing him that the victim's photograph will soon appear in the newspaper's society section as a means of identification. When Claire suddenly breaks her engagement with young Dr. Koster and marries Ken, a photo of the newlyweds is published in the paper. Realizing his life is in danger Ken, acting under the alias of a Mr. Foster, calls off the deal with Korrin but Korrin is killed shortly after their meeting. When Ken tries to contact Fingers Murdock, Korrin's successor, he refuses to see a "Mr. Foster" while Ken, becoming increasingly paranoid, avoids a "Mr. Murdock" when Fingers tries to phone him. Ken begins to spend long hours locked in his room, subsisting on canned goods and crackers for fear of being poisoned. Claire tries to help, but Ken does not respond. One evening, Ken sees a man's figure lurking in the street beneath his window and shoots at him. Then he flees from the house in his car, followed by his wife and two other cars. Claire and Dr. Koster catch up with Ken and try to pacify his fears, but when he sees the other vehicles approaching he drives off in a panic over a washed-out bridge and is killed. As fate would have it, one of the pursuing vehicles was driven by the bodyguard Claire had hired to protect her husband and the other by Fingers Murdock, who was attempting to return Holden's money because he knew all along that the murder contract had been called off!

Despite some stilted dialogue and static direction, *The Pretender* is a penetrating example of how the noir style can carry a film—best realized here through John Alton's brashly expressionistic photography and Albert Dekker's stylized performance as Ken. Sets were built with forced perspective to permit depth-staging, as in the scene where Ken is on the phone, lost in pools of darkness, while a brightly-lit party is going on in the background. Rooms are filled with grotesque personalities (such as Charles Middleton's butler) and equally bizarre bric-a-brac. The scene of Holden seated on the floor of his locked room, eating crackers and cold canned food, is the ultimate illustration of entrapment and paranoia. And it is followed by what has come to be a quintessential noir scene—an objective shot of a man, peeking out at night through the Venetian blinds of his darkened room followed by a cut to his point-of-view of a menacing, trench-coated figure standing below beneath a streetlight. Of course the story plays upon the irony of the name confusion that goes on between Holden and Murdock which ultimately leads to Holden's death. And it is an irony which is heightened by the odd, sporadic voice-over narration of Dekker, an interior monologue which, like a dirge, is almost as if Ken were telling the audience his story from beyond the grave. **BP**

PRIVATE HELL 36 (1954)

Director: Don Siegel. **Screenplay**: Collier Young and Ida Lupino. **Producer**: Collier Young, Ida Lupino. **Director of Photography**: Burnett Guffey. **Music**: Leith Stevens. **Art Director**: Walter Keller. **Editor**: Stanford Tischler. **Cast**: Ida Lupino (Lilli Marlowe), Steve Cochran (Detective Cal Bruner), Howard Duff (Detective Jack Farnham), Dean Jagger (Capt. Michaels), Dorothy Malone (Francey Farnham), Bridget Duff (Baby Farnham). **Released**: Filmakers, September 3. 81 minutes.

Bruner and Farnham, two Los Angeles cops, are assigned by their chief Michaels to find the criminal who is passing marked bills from a New York robbery. The search for the money leads to Lilli Marlowe, a nightclub singer. Farnham and Bruner accompany her each day to the race track hoping that she can spot the man who gave the money to her as a tip. Bruner and Lilli begin seeing each other in the evenings as well; but, although their mutual attraction is intense, Lilli sees no future in the relationship as he lacks the wealth she desires. Finally, the crook is spotted leaving the track. Bruner and Farnham chase his car, but the crook drives off the road and dies. Bruner pockets a considerable amount of the remaining money, and a reluctant Farnham goes along with him when Bruner reminds him about his wife and his child. Seemingly, a partner of the dead criminal blackmails Farnham and Bruner by telephone. They arrange to meet him at the trailer park where the money is stashed; but Farnham has already made up his mind that he wants to return the money and take the consequences. In a final gun battle, Farnham is wounded by Bruner, who in turn is killed by the police who have set them up.

Private Hell 36—directed by Don Siegel and co-written by, co-produced by, and starring Ida Lupino—is, like so much of political noir, a mordant critique of the American dream. Both of the male protagonists—the amoral Bruner and the scrupulous Farnham—are working class "stiffs" who just happen to be cops. Bruner likes fines suits and finer women while Farnham is struggling to keep his head above water—paying a mortgage on a suburban house in the Hollywood Hills and supporting his child and unemployed wife (the ideal *Leave It to Beaver* nuclear family). Apropos of this is a particularly revealing sequence of scenes at the Hollywood Park race track. There, with the help of the cynical Lilli (who has now become the "fine" woman Bruner wants to impress), they spend a series of days looking for the criminal from the New York robbery while watching rich people all around them place fistfuls of money on the horses. Even the uptight Farnham succumbs to the temptation, placing a small bet, and of course losing.

The moment of decision comes after a car chase through the hills in which the cops overtake the criminal they are looking for. As the perp's car careens over the side of the mountain, his briefcase flies from the car releasing bills of various denominations throughout the hillside. The cops then rush frantically to collect the cash. Finally, the temptation

Private Hell 36: *Lilli Marlow (Ida Lupino) and Cal Bruner (Steve Cochran).*

becomes too much—as if some sadistic fate is rubbing their financial woes in their faces. Seeing the look of longing on Farnham's face, Bruner convinces him to take part of the money and only return the remaining loot to the police while hiding the rest in a trailer he has rented. The upright Farnham, however, turns out to be the weak link in this plan. He does not have the same ability to rationalize his actions as Bruner. From the first scenes in the movie he is established as a moral and caring individual, lamenting over a dead cop, an emotion the more callous Bruner tells him he cannot understand. And so Farnham begins to drink heavily and slip into depression. The climax of the movie occurs at the trailer (#36)—the symbol of Farnham's own private hell. When Farnham tells his partner he is going to turn the money in and take his punishment, Bruner cannot accept this betrayal of his dream and so shoots him, only to be shot by the waiting police who have already discovered the pair's misdeeds. **JU**

THE PROWLER (1951)

Director: Joseph Losey. **Screenplay**: Hugo Butler, Dalton Trumbo from an unpublished story by Robert Thoeren and Hans Wilhelm. **Producer**: S. P. Eagle [Sam Spiegel] (Horizon Pictures). **Director of Photography**: Arthur Miller. **Music**: Lyn Murray. **Editor**: Paul Weatherwax. **Cast**: Van Heflin (Webb Garwood), Evelyn Keyes (Susan Gilvray), John Maxwell (Bud Crocker), Katherine Warren (Mrs. Crocker), Emerson Tracy (William Gilvray), Madge Blake (Martha Gilvray), Wheaton Chambers (Doctor James), Louise Lorimer (Motel Manager), Robert Osterloh (Coroner), Sherry Hall (John Gilvray). **Completed**: May 1, 1950. **Released**: United Artists, July 2. 92 minutes.

Patrolmen Webb Garwood and Bud Crocker respond to a report of a prowler at the Los Angeles home of Susan Gilvray, wife of a late night radio disc jockey, but they fail to find anyone. Webb returns later "to check up on things." Learning that her husband's will provides Susan with a small fortune and knowing she feels trapped in her marriage, Webb seduces her. One night, Webb pretends to be a prowler outside the Gilvray house and then responds to their police call for help. Mr. Gilvray is outside with a gun, looking for the prowler, and Webb orders him to "Halt!" Mr. Gilvray begs the

The Prowler: *Webb Garwood (Van Heflin) and Susan Gilvray (Evelyn Keyes)*.

policeman not to shoot but Webb kills him and then shoots himself with Gilvray's gun so that it appears Gilvray shot him first. Although suspicious of Webb, Susan does not reveal their affair and a coroner's jury rules her husband's death accidental. Ultimately convinced of Webb's innocence, Susan marries him and they use her money to buy a motel in Las Vegas. But they soon move to a deserted ghost town because Susan is pregnant and Webb fears the baby may be incriminating evidence that he killed Gilvray, who was sterile. Preparing to deliver the baby himself, Webb is forced to call a doctor when Susan's labor proves difficult. The doctor safely delivers the child, but when Webb frantically confesses to Susan that he murdered Gilvray she realizes he is planning to kill the doctor. She helps the doctor escape and he calls the police. When they arrive, Webb attempts to flee. When he doesn't halt after their warning, the police shoot him.

Like most of Losey's American films *The Prowler* is concerned with complex social issues. Losey had a clear influence on Robert Aldrich, who assisted on this picture, *M*, and *The Big Night* and with whom Losey was developing new projects when the Blacklist forced him into exile in England. One could call both Webb Garwood and the anti-heroic Mike Hammer in the Aldrich/Bezzerides adaptation of *Kiss Me Deadly* as examples of a *homme fatal* in film noir (Van Heflin here rekindling memories of his role in *Possessed*). Garwood sees himself as normal and ambitious, almost the All-American guy: the high school star who never quite makes it in college, drinks nothing but milk, who reads *Muscle Power* magazine, and who hopes to improve himself so that one day he can own a motel and "make money while he sleeps." Consequently *The Prowler* is a film that reveals the dark underside of the American dream of status and success.

Like Webb, Susan also desires status and security, the reason she married Gilvray; but she is willing to give that up for Webb. The policeman, who in his own way loves Susan, never sees the shallowness of his desires and, in the first scene following their wedding, he lecherously eyes a young woman who is checking into their motel. At this level, Webb

is as dysfunctional and lacking in self-control as certain noir psychopaths. In many ways he is most reminiscent of Roy Martin in *He Walked by Night*. Losey's most telling indictment of social values is the fact that both Webb and those around him base their judgments on appearances. Webb is successful in his career because his good looks and assured manner support his image as a model policeman. Ironically, Webb is too enmeshed in those values to survive. His paranoia over Susan's pregnancy is based on his own suspicions and hypocrisy rather than any real threat. The final irony is that his lapse into sentimentality in summoning the doctor precipitates his destruction. **BP & AS**

PURSUED (1947)

Director: Raoul Walsh. **Screenplay**: Niven Busch. **Producer**: Milton Sperling. **Director of Photography**: James Wong Howe. **Music**: Max Steiner. **Production Designer**: Ted Smith. **Editor**: Christian Nyby. **Cast**: Teresa Wright (Thorley Callum), Robert Mitchum (Jeb Rand), Judith Anderson (Mrs. Medora Callum), Dean Jagger (Grant Callum), Alan Hale (Jake Dingle), John Rodney (Adam Callum), Harry Carey Jr. (Prentice McComber), Clifton Young (Army Sergeant), Ernest Severn (Jeb, age 11), Charles Bates (Adam, age 11), Peggy Miller (Thorley, age 10). **Location**: Gallup, New Mexico. **Released**: Warner Bros, March 2. 101 minutes.

Jeb Rand, a young rancher/gambler in New Mexico Territory at the turn of the century, returns to the remains of an old ranch on the morning after his wedding. He is being pursued by a group of men intent on killing him and he has chosen this place to rendezvous with his stepsister and, for the past few hours, his bride, Thorley Callum. Despite the fact that Thorley wants them to leave before the men arrive, he needs to recount to her the major events of his life, starting from that eventful evening when Ma Callum made him one of her own, together with her other children, Adam and Thorley. He remembers that at the age of ten he had his horse shot out from under him and mistakenly accused Adam, though the real culprit was Grant Callum, Ma's brother-in-law who had vowed to see Jeb dead no matter how long it took (though Ma kept this a secret from Jeb). When Jeb is old enough, Grant tries to persuade him to join the army fighting against the Spanish, but Jeb demurs, preferring instead to rely on the toss of a coin to decide whether he or Adam will be his family's contribution to the war. Jeb loses the toss, but after being wounded in the leg, he returns home a hero. Grant uses the adulation accorded Jeb to fan the fires of jealously in Adam, encouraging Adam to go to the neighboring township to find out more about the Rand family. When Jeb returns to the family, he and Thorley realize that their feelings for one another are more romantic than familial. Needing little more motivation, Adam demands that either he or Jeb buy out the other and leave the ranch. Jeb settles the dispute again with a toss of a coin, and again he loses. He leaves the ranch, but vows to return the next day to pick up Thorley so they can be married. When Jeb returns on horseback the next day, Adam tries to bushwhack him, and Jeb, not knowing who the assailant is, returns fire and kills Adam. A coroner's jury exonerates Jeb, but Ma and Thorley banish him from the ranch. When a local swain, Prentice McComber, begins to

Pursued: *Thorley Callum (Teresa Wright) and Jeb Rand (Robert Mitchum)*.

court Thorley, Grant intervenes and shames Prentice into going after Jeb with a gun. Jeb tries to avoid the fight, but is unsuccessful and ends up killing Prentice too. Now Jeb initiates a very formal and polite courtship of Thorley and she, with an equal degree of formality, accepts his proposal, intending to kill him once they are married. But Jeb reads her mind and on their wedding night brings her a tray with a glass of wine and a pistol. She shoots at him and misses and, with Jeb's help, realizes that her love for him is greater than her hate. But their wedding night is interrupted when Grant and a group of Callum men that he has collected show up at Jeb's house. Jeb of course escapes, arranging to meet Thorley at the old Rand house. Just as Jeb finishes his recollection, the Callums show up and Grant attempts to kill Jeb but this very act frees Jeb to remember the details of his childhood trauma: from his hiding place beneath the ranch-house floor the young Jeb could see the dead bodies of his brothers and sister, the flashes of light of the guns firing, and the spurs, which belonged to his mortally wounded father. Realizing that the demise of his family was the result of a feud with the Callums prompted by a liaison between Ma Callum and his father, Jeb surrenders to Grant. But just as Grant is about to lynch Jeb, Ma arrives and, with Thorley's encouragement, shoots and kills Grant. Jeb and Thorley are now free to pursue their lives together.

Pursued is a very complex film, too complex to do justice to it in the space afforded here. So let us confine our focus on those attributes which make it an excellent example of the film noir as well as a western. We need look no further than *Citizen Kane* (perhaps the single greatest influence on the noir cycle) to distinguish those characteristics which help to define the film noir: an expressionistic visual style; a convoluted time structure; a morally ambiguous hero; a psychological substructure (which Welles termed "dollar book Freud"); and the use of flashback and first person narration. With the exception of its temporal structure, *Pursued* could be regarded as a primer for a study of film noir. Most obvious is the photography of James Wong Howe, who, despite the limitations of shooting on location (near Gallup, New Mexico), here raises chiaroscuro to new heights. This is evident throughout but is most effective in the gunfight sequence between Prentice and Jeb in which Jeb, trapped in an alley at night, moves in and out of shadows and around a carriage in an effort to avoid the bullets of the neophyte gunfighter. To his credit, Raoul Walsh chose to film many of the outdoor sequences as night-for-night, but even those photographed in daylight favor the striking over the picturesque so that the huge rocks and narrow canyons function as a locus of menace. And the choice of a hollowed-out cabin as the key site of Jeb's flashbacks is a good example of how the naturalism of a real setting can be used to reinforce psychological states.

As far as the psychological dimension is concerned, *Pursued* is *the* seminal psychological western—a veritable Freudian delight with its classic dream symbolism and the specters of incest, sibling rivalry, love-hate relationships and oedipal complications lurking in every nuance. To simplify matters, let us focus on the Rand/Cullum dichotomy and its relationship to the film's principal objects of desire: Ma and Thorley. It is the possession of Medora (appropriately called "Ma" throughout the film) as a (forbidden) sexual object by Mr. Rand that precipitates the feud between the two families and the ensuing carnage. But the violence is actually propelled by Grant whose concern for rectifying the honor of his dead brother by eliminating all the Rands is more than an obsession. It is, in fact, motivated by his own need to keep the object of sexual desire within the Callum family (we never hear of Jeb's mother—presumably she is dead before the feud begins). Appropriately, Ma never remarries after the deaths of her husband and her lover, but she does welcome Jeb into the circle of her love and it is this that incites Grant (indeed he tells Ma that Jeb can never return her love, though the film never really makes a case for this).

Grant's own sexual frustration is symbolized in the loss of his arm as a result of the feud. His position as a local prosecutor is emblematic of his role in enforcing the "law" against sexual transgression and his preoccupation with Jeb's death becomes for him both punishment for such transgressions and the elimination of a sexual rival named Rand (much is made of the fact that young Jeb refuses the Callum family name). Grant plays upon Adam's rivalry with Jeb to make him an instrument of his plans, but it is only when Jeb announces his intention to marry Thorley that Adam acts quickly to kill him—for such a marriage would move Thorley from the Callum to the Rand camp as a sexual object! Remember Jeb comes home limping from a leg injury, a limp that disappears immediately once he and Thorley acknowledge that their love is sexual rather than platonic. And the courtship game that the two later engage in is a charade that allows Thorley to play out her hatred of Jeb by virtue of the bullet she shoots at him, a bullet that in turn frees her to transgress the "law" as embodied in Grant. But Grant intrudes at the very moment of the consummation of their love to reclaim Thorley for the Callums. Given the Freudian momentum of this action, it can only be Ma Callum who can eliminate Grant as Jeb's (impotent) sexual rival, thereby freeing Jeb to reclaim Thorley as the object of his desire. Finally, *Pursued* is a transgressive western precisely in so far as it valorizes the female right to pleasure and happiness over the male prerogative of possession and property. **BP**

Pushover: *Ann (Dorothy Malone), Paul Sheridan (Fred MacMurray), and Leona McLane (Kim Novak).*

PUSHOVER (1954)

Director: Richard Quine. **Screenplay:** Roy Huggins from the serialized story "The Killer Wore a Badge" by Thomas Walsh, the novel *The Night Watch* by Thomas Walsh, and the novel *Rafferty* by William S. Ballinger. **Producer:** Jules Schermer. **Director of Photography:** Lester H. White. **Music:** Arthur Morton. **Art Director:** Walter Holscher. **Editor:** Jerome Thoms. **Cast:** Fred MacMurray (Detective Paul Sheridan), Kim Novak (Leona McLane), Phil Carey (Rick McAllister), Dorothy Malone (Ann), E. G. Marshall (Lt. Carl Eckstrom), Allen Mourse (Paddy Dolan), Phil Chambers (Briggs), Alan Dexter (Fine), Robert Forrest (Billings), Don Harvey (Peters), Paul Richards (Harry Wheeler), Ann Morris (Ellen Burnett). **Completed:** February 13, 1954. **Released:** Columbia, July 30. 88 minutes.

Harry Wheeler's gang robs a bank and kills a guard. Leona meets Detective Paul Sheridan and a romance begins. Sheridan reports to his superior, Lt. Eckstrom, of his success with Leona who is Wheeler's girl. With other detectives, Sheridan is assigned to watch Leona's place. That evening Sheridan follows Leona, who goes to his apartment. She knows he is a cop but admits loving him anyway. So why not kill Wheeler in the line of duty and then leave with her and the stolen money? Initially Sheridan rejects her. Meanwhile his partner is enraptured by Leona's neighbor Ann. After a few days' separation, Sheridan's sexual attraction to Leona causes him to change his mind. The scheme goes wrong. Sheridan kills Wheeler but is seen by another cop, Paddy Dolan, and Ann spots him leaving Leona's apartment after delivering their all-clear signal. Sheridan kills Dolan to conceal his crime and then kidnaps Ann to use as a shield. But Eckstrom and Rick have realized what is going. Sheridan is shot in the ensuing chase, while Ann is unharmed.

Pushover resonates back to *Double Indemnity*: it involves murder for money and a cool, beautiful blonde who seduces a man into betraying his profession and his colleagues. In portraying Detective Paul Sheridan, Fred MacMurray reprises key aspects of Neff. Both characters are similarly vulnerable, superficially clever but unwise, concealing romantic disillusionment behind a mask of cynicism. While the use of MacMurray inevitably recalls Neff, ten years have passed and the evidence of that decade on MacMurray's face has a telling effect. Neff was an ambitious young man in a

well-cut suit, glib, attractive, and on the make. Paul Sheridan is slower in movement and less prone to snappy patter, with a puffy face that betrays an inactive and unrewarding life as palpably as a rumpled rain coat. For Neff, it was not just Phyllis but the challenge of the cheat, outwitting his mentor Barton Keyes, a guy who knew all the angles. For Sheridan, the temptation is all Leona McLane. Again the intricacies of noir narrative create the essential irony: Sheridan is assigned to approach and sweet talk Leona as part of his stake-out, for she is the girlfriend of fugitive bank robber Harry Wheeler. Although Sheridan's con is part of his police work, the role playing alters the reality. The final factor, as it was for Neff and his brief time with Lola in *Double Indemnity*, is the age difference between the vibrant young Leona and the veteran detective, so for Sheridan the chance at having the missing money is a chance to buffer the years between them.

In the police interrogation room early in *Pushover*, Sheridan's younger partner Rick sits pensively by the window and remarks, "Money's nice but it doesn't make the world go 'round." Paul's retort: "Don't it? . . . I promised myself as a kid that I'd have plenty of dough." Sheridan's snort confirms that he knows that the dream is just about over. In this context Leona and the missing $200,000 are a last chance that he cannot pass up. Like Walter and Phyllis in *Double Indemnity* the sexual attraction between Sheridan and Leona helps to sustain viewer identification with the criminal protagonists. While on stake-out Sheridan is forced to watch Rick pine platonically over Leona's neighbor, Ann, a wholesome brunette. Once he has succumbed to Leona's overtures and betrays his badge, Sheridan is both disdainful and jealous of Rick's innocent infatuation. As a middle-aged man MacMurray uses the same facial expressions he did as Neff to convey markedly different meanings. The physical surroundings during Sheridan and Leona's moments together in his apartment are remarkably similar to those of the Neff/Dietrichson rendezvous in *Double Indemnity*. The staging in *Pushover* is almost a mirror reverse of the former but significantly less glamorous, despite or perhaps because Leona's naive, breathless sexuality has replaced Phyllis' sophisticated, throaty lust. Unlike their knowing and unknowing counterparts in *Double Indemnity*, this couple does not redirect the tension of their secret and only partially consummated liaison into a betrayal of the other. It is only Sheridan who believes the money is critical to sustaining their emotional attachment. When confronted by the police, Leona actually urges Sheridan to forget about the money. It is not until he is lying the street grievously wounded that Sheridan realizes and says "We really didn't need the money, did we?"

Since *Pushover* is a film noir. Leona is a femme fatale by default (she actually does bring doom both to Harry Wheeler, whom Sheridan kills, and then Sheridan who is shot by his own partner), but she is far removed from the predatory Phyllis Dietrichson or Kathie Moffat. As a young actress, Kim Novak easily imbues Leona with inexperience and captures the confusion of the character's mixed ambitions. Although he initially accuses her of manipulating him and although Leona's physical youth and beauty give her the power to do that, she is too guileless. Having been manipulated herself by Harry Wheeler, she now becomes as much Sheridan's victim as he is hers. While it may be her suggestion, he, in fact, controls all the elements of their criminal scheme and only gives her simple directions which she follows unhesitatingly. One of Leona's few moments of defiance occurs early on when Sheridan reproaches her for accepting Wheeler's favors. Vehemently refusing to settle for squalor, she turns abruptly from Sheridan and in a rim-lit medium close shot pointedly affirms that "Money isn't dirty. Just people." Sheridan's face is visible behind, as it registers weary understanding of what made her compromise between disgust with her prospects and disgust with Wheeler. His expression also foreshadows the self-immolation to which his own lack of prospects will lead as he contemplates destroying his connection with the law and society.

In his noir-defining essay Jean-Pierre Chartier alluded to the "pure young girls" in film noir who constitute "some hope about future generations." That effect is negligible in *Double Indemnity*. While it is well exemplified in the relationship between Rick and Ann in *Pushover*, it is not without some irony of its own. The gradual and reasonable (they are of like age and appearance) development of the attraction between Rick and Ann strongly contrasts with the impulsive connection between Sheridan and Leona; and the conventional behavior of the career woman and the dedicated police detective reinforces the safety of social values as Sheridan and Leona are driven to desperation and destruction. But the high moral tone is severely undercut by the aspect of voyeurism in Rick, as he literally window shops for the right woman. Sheridan and Leona are brought together on orders from his police superior. Rick's intentions may be honorable, but watching Ann without her knowledge is stalking.

Ann, though, unquestionably fulfills the purpose to which Chartier alludes. Although Sheridan has taken her hostage in his attempt to escape and although her lover Rick saves her, she immediately runs not into Rick's arms but to aid her now-wounded captor. If there is a fundamental aspect of women in film noir and their relationship to social values, a conclusion like this embodies it. Ann understands the emotions which Sheridan has experienced even as he holds a gun on her, even as Rick shoots him down. Rick's view of the patriarchal structures that empower him is inflexible and, even if he were not a police officer, he would be likelier to resort to violence and confrontation to resolve crises. He places his loyalty on those values over his partner's life. Although she is unable to dissuade him and suffers herself as a result, Ann's first allegiance is to the value of human life. Leona and even Thelma share that inclination. Even Phyllis, whom male observers call a "calculating bitch," understands human impulse and empowers herself by exploiting it. Ultimately, what the unintended femme fatale reveals about noir and its deadly underworld is that the doomed male is brought down as much by his own ego and his inability to understand the emotional truth—"We really didn't need the money, did we?"—as by any fatal woman's schemes. **EW**

QUICKSAND (1950)

Director: Irving Pichel. **Screenplay**: Robert Smith. **Producer**: Mort Briskin. **Director of Photography**: Lionel Lindon. **Production Designer**: Boris Leven. **Music**: Louis Gruenberg. **Editor**: Walter Thompson. **Cast**: Mickey Rooney (Daniel Brady), Jeanne Cagney (Vera Novak), Barbara Bates (Helen Calder), Peter Lorre (Nick Dramoshag), Taylor Holmes (Harvey), Art Smith (Oren Mackey), Wally Cassell (Chuck), Richard Lane (Detective Lt. Nelson). **Released**: United Artists, March 24. 79 minutes.

Daniel Brady works in a garage in Santa Monica. He steals money from his boss to take Vera, a blonde temptress with a desire for the "good life," out on a date. Theft eventually leads to mugging as Brady begins a brief "life of crime." Through Vera he meets Nick, an arcade owner who blackmails Brady into further crimes, including the theft of a car from the garage Brady works at. When Brady's boss discovers the theft, he threatens to turn Brady into the police and a fight ensues in which Brady apparently kills his boss. On the lam with his faithful ex-girlfriend Helen, they hijack a car and order the owner to drive them to Mexico. The owner of the car is a lawyer who tells the couple he will help them if they turn themselves in. They return to the Santa Monica Pier. But Brady panics and runs. The police shoot and apprehend him. He learns, however, that his boss is not dead and the lawyer promises to help get him a lighter sentence.

With *Quicksand*, actor Mickey Rooney continued his postwar campaign "to noir" his image and abandon the juvenile roles he was famous for (the *Andy Hardy* series, etc.). Shot largely in Santa Monica, California, the film reverses the focus of noir films like *Gun Crazy* and becomes almost entirely about money rather than lust. There is ordinary lust, of course, as Brady, the Rooney character, falls for the femme fatale of the piece, Vera. There is even a "wholesome" love interest as the faithful ex-girlfriend/good girl Helen stands by her man and eventually aids in his final redemption. But ultimately this film is about the post-war consumer society and what it did to those on the fringes of it.

As with Mildred Pierce, whose fur cannot insulate her from the chill of murder committed by her own child, and like Mona in *Pitfall*, modeling clothes beyond her means, a garment becomes a metaphor. On their first date Vera shows Brady a fur coat in the window of a department store. As Vera sensually rhapsodizes about it, the camera remains on the image of the couple reflected in the window counterposed with a larger-than-life mannequin dressed in the garment. Vera's desire for the coat and Brady's desire to have enough money to take her out on an expensive date drives the noir narrative down a deterministic road and through a series of events, aided and abetted by Nick, an arcade owner on the pier, who blackmails Brady into committing even more crimes. The film culminates as Brady is hunted for assault and robbery. The final chase through and under the Santa Monica Pier is classic noir, as the protagonist-turned-victim-of-events spirals out of control and tries to escape out to the sea and the "freedom" of Mexico beyond, a location seen again and again in noir films as an idyllic refuge from the repressive United States. **JU**

R

THE RACKET (1951)

Director: John Cromwell [uncredited—Nicholas Ray, Tay Garnett, Mel Ferrer, Sherman Todd]. **Screenplay**: William Wister Haines and W.R. Burnett, based on the play by Bartlett Cormack. **Producer**: Edmund Grainger. **Director of Photography**: George E. Diskant. **Music**: Constantin Bakaleinikoff. **Art Directors**: Albert S. D'Agostino, Jack Okey. **Editor**: Sherman Todd. **Cast**: Robert Mitchum (Capt. McQuigg), Lizabeth Scott (Irene), Robert Ryan (Scanlon), William Talman (Johnson), Ray Collins (Welch), Joyce MacKenzie (Mary McQuigg), Robert Hutton (Ames), Virginia Huston (Lucy Johnson), William Conrad (Inspector Turck), Walter Sande (Delaney), Les Tremayne (Chief Craig), Don Porter (Connolly), Walter Baldwin (Sullivan), Brett King (Joe Scanlon), Richard Karlan (Enright), Tito Vuolo (Tony). **Completed**: May 14, 1951. **Released**: RKO, December 12. 88 minutes.

Police Capt. McQuigg and mobster Nick Scanlon struggle against the backdrop of a corrupt Midwestern city during the final days of a municipal election. McQuigg, an honest cop, is infuriated by the crime and graft he sees about him and directs his anger at Scanlon, who is just a middle-level member of the underworld but who symbolizes everything McQuigg hates. The policeman's superiors, Inspector Turck and City Prosecutor Welch, are controlled by the organization and warn him to take it easy. Meanwhile, Scanlon struggles with his superiors, who want him to become a more modern, less violent, and more businesslike gangster, and with a rival hoodlum whom he finally must arrange to have murdered. This assassination leads directly to his own death, as it becomes convenient for the city's political and criminal "Big Boys" to let McQuigg destroy Scanlon. The city's reformers are defeated in the election, the rackets continue as usual. Scanlon is replaced by a more sinister lieutenant. McQuigg remains powerless, and it is hinted that the city's real crime lord is the state governor.

Corruption in *The Racket* is not some kind of abstract force or entity. It is the aggregate of all the desires, ambitions, and compromises of a city; and the film makes no moralistic, good-bad distinctions. Even the worst characters are not evil, sadistic, or very dangerous. Turck, for instance, is shown to be far more intelligent and sensitive than McQuigg. Welch has a streak of honesty counterbalanced by one of pragmatism. When he is asked why he sold out, he answers because he was promised a judgeship. Scanlon, in fact, is the film's most fully drawn and sympathetic character. He is alone, alienated, and doomed by the evolution of one form of gangsterism into another, and by his existential refusal to lose his identity by changing with it.

The Racket: *Ames (Robert Hutton) and Irene (Lizabeth Scott)*.

McQuigg's role is as least as ambiguous. If Scanlon is an old-style mobster, McQuigg is an equally conservative cop who sees his job not as providing justice but maintaining law and order. Welch says that for McQuigg honesty is a kind of disease; and the film offers a great deal of evidence that this is the case. His extreme honesty is as destructive and violent as Scanlon's brute force approach to graft. McQuigg is not a mobster, but he is similar because his methods are outside the law. He tears up writs of habeas corpus, frames suspects, and, finally, allows Scanlon to be killed. His goal is not reform; he does these things to bring down Scanlon, not the corruption.

Howard Hughes was always sensitive to the commercial and aesthetic potentials of underworld material. Bartlett Cormack's play *The Racket* was the second property Hughes filmed in 1927 (it was released in 1928) when he turned his attention to motion pictures. A remake of *The Racket* was one of the first projects announced by the newly Hughes controlled RKO in 1948. Samuel Fuller was the first writer to work on the project, and he envisioned a film grounded in post-World War II society, not the Prohibition era. When he delivered an essentially original script, writer William Haines and director John Cromwell replaced him. They developed a more faithful adaptation of the play, nominally set in the late 1940s but drawing its conflicts and plot from Chicago in the 1920s. Halfway through production, Howard Hughes personally hired writer W.R. Burnett to rewrite the film. Even with Burnett's expertise (he had written the novels and/or scripts on which *Little Caesar*, *Scarface*, *High Sierra*, and *The Asphalt Jungle* are based), $500,000 worth of retakes (some shot by directors other than Cromwell) and the work of a half dozen fine actors, the film is little more than a competent commercial picture; and its situations and characters are somehow out of date and unreal. *The Racket's* problem may be that because it is not really rooted in a specific time or place, its legitimate claim to being the most complex treatment of political, police, and criminal forces in equilibrium is obscured. **DLW**

THE RAGING TIDE (1951)

Director: George Sherman. **Screenplay**: Ernest K. Gann based on his novel. **Producer**: Aaron Rosenberg. **Director of Photography**: Russell Metty. **Art Directors**: Hilyard Brown, Bernard Herzbrun. **Music**: Frank Skinner. **Editor**: Ted J. Kent. **Cast**: Richard Conte (Bruno Felkin), Shelley Winters (Connie), Stephen McNally (Lt. Kelsey), Charles Bickford (Hamil Linder), Alex Nicol (Carl Linder), John McIntire (Corky), Minerva Urecal (Johnnie Mae), Tito Vuolo (Barney). **Released**: Universal International, November. 93 minutes.

A San Francisco hood is rubbed out by rival Bruno Felkin, who himself reports the crime to homicide Lieutenant Kelsey in an alibi scheme which fails. To escape, he stows away on a fishing boat. At sea, skipper Hamil Linder receives Bruno kindly, teaching him fishing; Bruno enlists Hamil's wayward son Carl to deliver messages and act as a liaison to Connie. Then Carl takes an interest in Bruno's girl Connie. Bruno plans to frame Carl. A storm at sea ensues and Bruno finds redemption.

An odd fish of a movie, *The Raging Tide* spins a yarn of crime and redemption, of the city and the sea. It opens as though it's going to be another installment in the urban noir cycle, with mobster Bruno (played by Richard Conte, who made a career playing Italianate noir criminal types in B-films) gunning down a rival in cold blood, phoning in a tip to the police, and fleeing to his meticulously planned alibi. Well, maybe not so meticulously, as his girlfriend Connie (played by Shelley Winters with typically sleazy panache) isn't where he expected her to be. So he stows away on a boat moored at Fisherman's Wharf and is well out to sea when he's discovered by the skipper Hamil and his son Carl. The bounding main proves a convenient hideout, so he signs on and comes to relish the freedom and purity of the seafaring life.

Meanwhile, back in San Francisco, police detective Kelsey grills Connie about Bruno's whereabouts. (He's one tough cop, telling her "You're an old-looking 23.") But she keeps mum, while a go-between, Hamil's son Carl, brings her messages from Bruno, who won't set foot on land. Relationships among the principals intertwine: Hamil, having problems with his unruly son, takes a shine to Bruno, while Carl falls for Connie. Then Bruno hatches a scheme to frame Carl for the murder he's wanted for, using Connie as his cat's paw.

The Raging Tide boasts solid, if slightly hammy, performances; even Charles Bickford as Hamil manages to crawl out from under the heaviest Swedish accent since Anna Christie. The picture's all but stolen by John McIntire as a penniless old salt trying to escape the attentions of Minerva Urecal as the equally salty Johnnie Mae. But the story, sentimental and a bit old-fashioned, stays strong enough to compel interest. What makes the film particularly noir is the climax and resolution where both Connie and Bruno are redeemed by the proletarian honesty of the Linders. **BMV**

RAILROADED (1947)

Director: Anthony Mann. **Screenplay**: John C. Higgins from a story by Gertrude Walker. **Producer**: Charles F. Riesner. **Director of Photography**: Guy Roe. **Music**: Alvin Levin. **Art Director**: Perry Smith. **Editors**: Alfred DeGaetano, Louis H. Sackin. **Cast**: John Ireland (Duke Martin), Sheila Ryan (Rosa Ryan), Hugh Beaumont (Mickey Ferguson), Jane Randolph (Clara Calhoun), Ed Kelly (Steve Ryan), Charles D. Brown (Capt. MacTaggart), Clancy Cooper (Chubb), Peggy Converse (Marie), Hermine Sterler (Mrs. Ryan), Keefe Brasselle (Cowie), Roy Gordon (Ainsworth). **Completed**: August 9, 1947. **Released**: PRC, October 30. 71 minutes.

The robbery of a beauty shop that served as a front for a gambling racket results in the death of a policeman and the apprehension of one of the robbers, Cowie, whose face was badly disfigured. Interrogated by the police at his bedside, the fatally wounded criminal implicates an innocent friend, Steve Ryan, as his accomplice. Not believing that her brother is capable of such heinous crimes, his sister, Rosa, convinces police investigator Ferguson to reopen the case. Their suspicions center on Duke Martin, a gunman who double crossed the gambling racket that hired him by stealing the booty. As Ferguson and Rosa hunt down witnesses who might link Duke to the robbery, the trigger-happy gunman stays ahead of them and leaves a number of corpses in his wake. He ritualizes each murder by perfuming his bullets and polishing his gun before he commits his crime, and this affectation finally gives him away. In a final shoot-out in a deserted bar, Ferguson kills the sadistic Duke.

Railroaded is another low-budget noir gem directed by Anthony Mann and, like the earlier *Desperate*, it is a crisp, well-made thriller. The real tone of the noir sensibility is revealed by John Ireland's grotesque portrayal of Duke Martin. There is an erotic quality to his ritualizing anointment of the bullets and the self-satisfying response to the massaging of his gun barrel. The almost ludicrous Freudian association between sex and violence is carried off so convincingly that Duke's obsession is never questioned or laughed at. In *Railroaded*, Mann is more concerned with the dealings of the noir antagonist, Duke, than in the vindication of the wrongly accused fall guy. The retribution for the crimes committed by Duke is inconsequential. All that matters in

Railroaded: *At center, Duke Martin (John Ireland) and Rosa Ryan (Sheila Ryan).*

Railroaded is that the aberrant nature of Duke's character was not compromised. The screenplay by John C. Higgins (who also wrote *T-Men, Raw Deal, He Walked by Night,* and *Border Incident* for Anthony Mann) is strongly rooted in the hard-boiled tradition of pulp magazines of the period. **CM**

RAMROD (1947)

Director: Andre De Toth. **Screenplay**: Cecile Kramer, Graham Baker, Jack Moffitt based on a story by Luke Short. **Producer**: Harry Sherman. **Director of Photography**: Russell Harlan. **Production Designer**: Lionel Banks. **Music**: Adolph Deutsch. **Editor**: Sherman A. Rose. **Cast**: Joel McCrea (Dave Nash), Veronica Lake (Connie Dickason), Don DeFore (Bill Schell), Donald Crisp (Sheriff Jim Crew), Preston Foster (Frank Ivey), Arleen Whelan (Rose Leland), Charles Ruggles (Mr. Dickason), Lloyd Bridges (Red Cates), Ray Teal (Ed Burma). **Released**: United Artists, May 2. 95 minutes.

The death of his wife and children leaves Dave Nash a shell of a man, an alcoholic with very little will of his own who is humiliated and initially discounted by the antagonists of the piece, especially the villain, Frank Ivey. In fact Dave spends most of the film bounced back and forth between the two female pillars of strength: the angelic Rose and the driven yet sympathetic femme fatale of the story, Connie. Both tend to his psychological and physical wounds in several scenes and protect him from the land-grabbing, ruthless Ivey and his henchmen. His best friend, Bill Schell, loses his own life protecting Dave. Even though Nash shows his potential for strength on several occasions, most notably in taking over the henchman's line camp as a residence for Connie when her ranch house burns or killing Virgil whom he believes murdered his friend Sheriff Jim Crew, his true redemptive act comes at the end when Nash decides to stop running and face Ivey. Nash confronts Ivey in the street and kills him in a shootout.

Next to *Duel in the Sun, Ramrod* presents probably one of the most complex and sympathetic femmes fatales among noir films in general. Connie Dickason is a woman in the old West surrounded by weak men. Her fiancé leaves town in the first scene, afraid to fight for her ranch against the villain Ivey, the only strong male in the film. Her attitude is summarized visually in one shot as she throws herself on the bed in anger and clenches her fists in foreground. Her father calls her "hard" and "headstrong" (words often used to describe women who take on traditional male roles in classic American movies) for refusing to compromise with the greedy Ivey who desperately wants Connie as his wife. In fact, in the early parts of the movie, she is the only one who stands up to the villain of the piece. When Connie convinces the alcoholic Dave Nash to be her foreman, she implies that she is "strong enough" for both of them.

Connie is also, like any true femme fatale, not above using her sexuality to obtain her ends. She seduces a young cowpoke into silence with just a touch of her hand. She manipulates Schell into stampeding her own herd in order to shift the blame to Ivey. She serves Ivey and her father cookies and drinks like a submissive daugher/fiancée while plotting their ruin. In one particularly memorable scene Ivey shows up at the ranch and beats up one of her workers for helping her take over his line camp. In response she slaps him repeatedly and forcefully, an act no one else in the film had dared to do at this point. Connie again and again defies the patriarchal

Ramrod: *Frank Ivey (Preston Foster), Connie Dickason (Veronica Lake), and Dave Nash (Joel McCrea).*

structure and ultimately wins, though as the "good girl" Rose says, "[her battle] is costing too many lives." And even when she is left alone in the town street after Nash shoots Ivey and puts an end to the conflict over her land, an audience cannot help but feel admiration for the strength and subversive power of this woman in a man's world. **JU**

RANCHO NOTORIOUS (1952)

Director: Fritz Lang. **Screenplay**: Daniel Taradash based on the story "Gunsight Whitman" by Silvia Richards. **Producer**: Howard Welsch (Fidelity Pictures Corporation). **Director of Photography**: Hal Mohr. **Art Director**: Wiard Ihnen. **Music**: Emil Newman, Hugo Friedhofer, Arthur Lange. **Editor**: Otto Ludwig. **Cast**: Marlene Dietrich (Altar Keane), Arthur Kennedy (Vern Haskell), Mel Ferrer (Frenchy Fairmont), Gloria Henry (Beth Forbes), William Frawley (Baldy Gunder), Jack Elam (Geary), John Doucette (Whitey), Lane Chandler (Sheriff Hardy), Frank Ferguson (Preacher), Lisa Ferraday (Maxine), Lloyd Gough (Kinch), William Haade (Sheriff Bullock), Francis McDonald (Harbin), John Raven (Dealer), George Reeves (Wilson), Dan Seymour (Comanche Paul), Fuzzy Knight (Barber), Fred Graham (Ace Maguire). **Released**: RKO, March 1. 89 minutes.

After his fiancée Beth is raped and murdered during the course of a robbery, ranch hand Vern Haskell rides out for revenge. Haskell overtakes one of killers, Whitey, whose partner Kinch has left him for dead. Whitey's last words are "Chuck-a-Luck." Before gunning down Ace Maguire, Haskell learns that "Chuck-a-Luck" is a ranch near the Mexican border owned and operated by former saloon-girl Altar Keane. In Virginia City, Altar's former boss Baldy provides another lead: Altar's boyfriend Frenchy Stewart has just been apprehended in the town of Gunsight. Arriving there, Haskell disturbs the peace to get tossed into jail and escapes with Frenchy, who takes him to Chuck-a-Luck, where Altar warns Haskell that there is only one rule: "Don't ask questions." Altar fails for Haskell, who to keep up the outlaw charade is obliged to take part in a bank hold-up. When Haskell sees Altar wearing a brooch that belonged to Beth, Altar violates her own rule and tells him it came from Kinch. Altar is shot and dies in the arms of Haskell and Frenchy after they kill Kinch and all his cronies.

The relationship between *Rancho Notorious* and *The Big Heat* proves the intricate interrelatedness of the Hollywood genres, a further proof of the foolishness of regarding them as discrete and fully autonomous on the grounds of their defining iconography. *Rancho Notorious* and *The Big Heat* are marked off, however, by a complex of specific inflections. In *Rancho Notorious*, the "bad" woman moves to the center of the narrative. Both Marlene Dietrich as Altar and Gloria Grahame as Debby are involved in criminality (the former centrally, the latter marginally—for her "complicit" might be a better word than "involved"); but both differ markedly from the archetypal femme fatale of film noir, an archetype whose range one might define by reference to the Rita Hayworth of *The Lady From Shanghai*, the Joan Bennett of *Scarlet Street* and the Jane Greer of *Out of the Past*, all three characters being crucially revealed as betrayers, as consistently unreliable and when necessary for their own ends treacherous. Altar shares one major characteristic with the typical noir woman: the acquisition (whether attempted or realized, but in either case central to her motivation) of power in the form of money. In the course of the film, each woman falls (genuinely) in love with the hero, commits herself to him, and is morally redeemed by this. The "redemption" is not without its bitter irony, and its function is not to convert her into her opposite, the "good woman," or make her a possible marriage partner for the hero. We might say that she reverses the typical trajectory of the noir woman who initially commits herself to the male protagonist, but this proves to be ambiguous (in *Scarlet Street*, not even that): she is constantly ready to manipulate and betray him, and her death is a punishment for her duplicity. Altar and Debbie begin in the criminal world, gradually learn to commit themselves to the male protagonists (whom they perceive as figures of superior morality and purity) and their deaths are the direct consequence of that commitment.

There are numerous period films with noir elements (a phenomenon made possible by the ambiguous nature of film noir, occupying an indeterminate space between a style and a genre); the typical film noir—those fully embodying what we think of as the noir world—is strictly contemporary. A western, on the other hand, is by definition a period film. But it is also, potentially, more than that: despite the costumes, it can become in some hands virtually *period-less*. I would distinguish roughly here between the historical western and the stylized western—while acknowledging that most examples of the genre contain elements of both. The former (one thinks at once of Ford) is (while not necessarily committed to historical "fact") deeply involved in a sense of the American past which may of course be largely mythical. But the genre, as it evolved, developed an iconography and set of conventions and stereotypes that can be used as more or less neutralized "counters" through which a filmmaker can express a personal thematic that has little or nothing to do with "period" or "history."

"Hate, murder and revenge"—the refrain of the "Ballad of Chuck-a-Luck" that runs through *Rancho Notorious* as Brechtian commentary—has been taken as a kind of motto for Lang's work. The theme and its most obvious message (that revenge, however apparently justified by moral outrage, eventually destroys the soul

of the avenger) is by no means unique to Lang: the western offers dozens of examples and there are many more within film noir, the gangster genre, and the horror film. One specifically Langian inflection is suggested by the ballad itself: its association of "Hate, murder and revenge" with "the gambler's wheel," "the Wheel of Fate." "Fate" is taken to be a common theme of Lang's cinema, and what finally links his American films to German Expressionism. The concept of Fate in Expressionist cinema (and in the American noir films it influenced) is not monolithic, but it can often appear as a metaphysical principle, a pessimistic apprehension of an inescapable and inexplicable doom before which the protagonist can only prostrate him/herself: and this situation is prototypically noir. Already in his later German films (*M*, for instance), Fate for Lang is becoming more a matter of social mechanism than of metaphysical principle: the individual is still trapped and ultimately helpless, but the entrapment can be subjected to analysis and explained. If the protagonist is trapped, the spectator is set free: a central principle of Lang's American films, where "Fate" is the end result of a set of interacting social conditions/ideological assumptions and the men whose actions are determined by them (women are, by and large, its victims rather than its agents). The "Ballad of Chuck-a-Luck," over the opening credits, identifies the "gambler's wheel" as "the Wheel of Fate." Lang comments on this in one of the early flashbacks, when he reveals that the Chuck-a-Luck wheel in the saloon is controlled, not by metaphysical principle, but by the foot of the owner's henchmen. "Fate" in *Rancho Notorious*—the Fate that destroys all the significant characters, without exception—is constructed by the ideological assumptions of patriarchal capitalist society: idealized romantic love, the revenge drive, the greed for money: in short, by the whole dichotomy of illusory purity and dirt that characterizes our culture.

The ending of *Rancho Notorious* fully confirms our sense of the film's ruthless, almost schematic logic and its position as noir Western. It is an extreme example of closure (certainly closure has never been so complete), but not the kind to which the Hollywood cinema has accustomed us: no happy ending, no formation or restoration of the heterosexual couple. In fact, no survivors: the mechanisms of "Fate" that Lang has analyzed culminate in the deaths of all the principal characters. Many people miss this (perhaps because they are reaching for their coats, perhaps because they can't believe their ears), but the final verse of the ballad is quite unambiguous about it: the two men who ride away from Chuck-a-Luck die under a hail of bullets before the day is over. **RW**

RAW DEAL (1948)

Director: Anthony Mann. **Screenplay**: Leopold Atlas and John C. Higgins from a story by Arnold B. Armstrong and Audrey Ashley. **Producer**: Edward Small. **Director of Photography**: John Alton. **Music**: Paul Sawtell. **Art Director**: Edward L. Ilou. **Editor**: Alfred De Gaetano. **Cast**: Dennis O'Keefe (Joe Sullivan), Claire Trevor (Pat), Marsha Hunt (Ann Martin), John Ireland (Fantail), Raymond Burr (Rick Coyle), Curt Conway (Spider), Chili Williams (Marcy). Regis Toomey (Captain Fields). **Released**: Eagle-Lion, July 8. 79 minutes.

Gangster Joe Sullivan is framed by his associates and vows revenge when he is released from prison. Unable to wait, he breaks jail with the help of his girl, Pat. But his old gang kidnaps Ann Martin, a stranger who sympathetically corresponded with Joe while he was in jail. As his plans to exact revenge are complicated by Ann's presence, Joe finds a way to work her into his plans. He decides to seduce her into his world of violence and murder. A fight with the thug Fantail ends with Ann shooting his attacker in the back. After this act of murder, Ann decides she is in love with Joe. He goes to kill Rick, the man who was a key factor in Joe's initial frame-up. Surprised by Joe's sudden intrusion, Rick shoots him and inadvertently starts a fire. Trapped, Rick crashes through the upper-story window to his death. Ann nestles the dying Joe in her arms as Pat resigns herself to a lonely future.

Anthony Mann transcended the typically brutal environment in the gangster film and created an interesting paradox of sex and violence in *Raw Deal*. Joe Sullivan exists as a *homme fatal*, seducing Ann Martin into a world filled with violent action and murder, enticing her with a promise of sexual fulfillment that goes beyond the realm of normal relationships. She surrenders completely to Joe, committing murder as the ultimate expression of her love. Along with this apparent twist of classic noir archetypes, *Raw Deal* creates an atmosphere in grotesquerie and fetishism that reveals the sordid nature of the noir world. Complementing the mood and tone inherent in the film, John Alton's photography suggests a half-lit world magnified by the strong use of shadows and cluttered composition. The ironic narration provided by Pat develops the romantic undercurrent evident in many noir films. **CM**

EDWARD SMALL presents
DENNIS O'KEEFE · CLAIRE TREVOR · MARSHA HUNT
A Reliance Picture · An EAGLE LION FILMS Release

RAWHIDE (1951)

Director: Henry Hathaway. **Screenplay**: Dudley Nichols. **Producer**: Samuel G. Engel. **Director of Photography**: Milton R. Krasner. **Music**: Sol Kaplan. **Production Designer**: George W. Davis, Lyle R. Wheeler. **Editor**: Robert L. Simpson. **Cast**: Tyrone Power (Tom Owens), Susan Hayward (Vinnie Holt), Hugh Marlowe (Zimmerman/Deputy Sheriff Ben Miles), Dean Jagger (Yancy), Edgar Buchanan (Sam Todd/Rawhide stationmaster), Jack Elam (Tevis), George Tobias (Gratz), Jeff Corey (Luke Davis), James Millican (Tex Squires), Louis Jean Heydt (Fickert), William Haade (Gil Scott/stagecoach driver), Milton R. Corey Sr. (Dr. Tucker), Kenneth Tobey (Lt. Wingate). **Location**: Lone Pine, CA. **Released**: 20th Century-Fox, March 25. 89 minutes.

Tom Owens, the son of the manager of the new overland stage from San Francisco to St. Louis, has been sent west to a lonely way station to gain experience under the tutelage of Sam Todd, the gruff station-master, before returning east to a more dignified administrative position. He earns his spurs in spades when an incoming stagehand informs the two men that four escaped convicts have held up a stage, murdered the driver and are now out for the gold that will be coming east the next day. Because of this threat the stage driver orders his female passenger, Vinnie Holt, to disembark at the way station together with her niece, a toddler nicknamed Callie. The convicts' leader, an intelligent but stoic killer named Zimmerman, gets the drop on Tom and Sam by pretending to be the dead deputy sheriff Miles and, together with the other three criminals, Tevis, Yancy and Gratz, takes control of the station but in the process Sam is killed. Since Zimmerman plans to rob the morning stage he needs Tom alive to insure that the evening stage will pass through without incident and then, the next morning, to sound the "all clear" on his horn so that the stage will be lured into Zimmerman's trap. Vinnie agrees to pretend to be Tom's wife so that his mantle of protection will fall on her and the child and together the two try to plan some type of escape despite being locked in Tom's bedroom much of the time. Tom is unsuccessful in trying to pass a note to the men who stop by from the evening stage, but he is able to steal a knife from the kitchen and with it he and Vinnie attempt to tunnel through the shallow adobe bedroom wall. But the next morning things fall apart: Callie escapes through the small hole in the wall, Vinnie tries to rescue her but is thwarted by the sexually obsessed Tevis and when Zimmerman attempts to reassert control, Tevis shoots him in the back and kills Gratz as well. Using Callie as a bargaining chip, Tevis forces Tom to disarm himself, but before he is able to kill Tom, Vinnie shoots him with Gratz's rifle. Meanwhile, the good-natured Yancy has prepared the morning stage for trouble, but it arrives at the station house to find that Tom, Vinnie and Callie have survived to face a future of some promise.

While lacking the dark expressionism of such pure noir westerns as *Blood on the Moon*, *Rawhide* remains the most claustrophobic western of the classic period. Most of the action occurs within the way station and much of that within the tight confines of Tom's bedroom. And when characters do manage to venture outside, their mobility is constrained by a variety of objects—wood piles, bushes, branches, horses and water trough—which are paradoxically both menacing (e.g.,

Callie wandering amidst the horses) and protective (e.g., Tom using the water trough to avoid Tevis' bullets). The long night of the film's midsection in turn stands out in stark contrast to the rest of film which takes place in bright daylight. Milton Krasner's photography is straightforward, devoid of the disjunctive shots so typical of the noir style, but he uses the darkness of these nighttime shots well, so that even when Tom and Vinnie are outside, in the open, the blackness which envelopes them proves more threatening than the well-lit interiors of the station house which ironically is their prison.

One interior nighttime shot, however, is fully within the noir canon: a brooding Tevis is seated at a table at the far side of the screen, his distorted features sufficiently defined by the depth of field, while the rest of the room falls away into darkness. Indeed, not enough can be said of the way Krasner and director Hathaway utilize Jack Elam's peculiar physiognomy, making the actor an embodiment of evil. Of course Hathaway had earlier employed an actor (Richard Widmark) in just such a way in *Kiss of Death*, but here the sexual implications of Tevis' twisted persona are much more precise. In *Kiss of Death* Tommy Udo's misogynism was revealed in one telling phrase: "Girls is no good for having fun." In *Rawhide* Tevis contrasts his obsession with women to Zimmerman's phlegmatic demeanor, explaining "I haven't been cured of women yet . . . I haven't had your medicine, Zim" (surprisingly, the audience is kept in the dark as to what Zimmerman's "medicine" was, until later in the film when we discover that he had killed his unfaithful mistress and her lover). We know Tevis' character is irredeemable when, in order to gain the upper hand with Tom, he shoots at Callie's feet as the toddler tries to make her way back to the station house. It is all too fitting in a Freudian sense that Tevis dies at the end at the hands of Vinnie, the object of his desire, when she shoots him with Gratz's long rifle. **BP**

THE RECKLESS MOMENT (1949)

Director: Max Ophuls. **Screenplay**: Henry Garson and Robert W. Soderberg adapted by Mel Dinelli and Robert E. Kent from the story "The Blank Wall" by Elisabeth Sanxay Holding. **Producer**: Walter Wanger. **Director of Photography**: Burnett Guffey. **Music**: Hans Salter. **Art Director**: Cary Odell. **Editor**: Gene Havlick. **Cast**: James Mason (Martin Donnelly), Joan Bennett (Lucia Harper), Geraldine Brooks (Bea Harper), Henry O'Neil (Mr. Harper), Shepperd Strudwick (Ted Darby), David Bair (David Harper), Roy Roberts (Nagle), Frances Williams (Sybil). **Completed**: April 15, 1949. **Released**: Columbia, December 29. 81 minutes

As she drives with Sybil, Lucia Harper tells her story. While her husband is traveling on business, she discovers that her daughter Bea has fallen in love with an unscrupulous older man named Darby. Bea confronts Darby in the Harper boathouse and hits him with a flashlight, after which he falls into the water and drowns. Lucia hides the body to protect Bea but Darby had confided in Nagle, a loan shark, who sends his partner Martin Donnelly to up the ante on the blackmail initiated by Darby. Donnelly is drawn to Lucia and tells her that one of Darby's shady associates has been arrested for the murder. When Nagle come to Balboa to confront Lucia himself, Donnelly kills him but is wounded. He drives off with Nagle's corpse before Lucia can bandage his cuts. She follows but dis-

The Reckless Moment: *Martin Donnelly (James Mason) and Lucia Harper (Joan Bennett).*

covers that Donnelly has crashed his car. He tells Lucia to leave then confesses to both murders to save Lucia before he dies. Not realizing what Lucia has undergone for their sake, the Harper family eagerly awaits the return of their father.

While there are many female protagonists in film noir, most of them exist in tandem with a male figure. From *Double Indemnity* to *Gun Crazy*, no matter how dominating the woman may be, without a male figure of equal prominence there is no story, without a man to destroy there is no femme fatale. *Nora Prentiss* and *Gilda* are title characters and performers. In the patriarchal construction of film noir it could be said that their "talent" can charm a man into self-destructive behavior. In fact, Nora and Gilda are also victims of a society which both empowers and enslaves a sexually potent woman.

Unlike Nora Prentiss or Gilda, Lucia Harper in *The Reckless Moment* does not perform in nightclubs. She has no shady past. She lives in a comfortable home in upscale Balboa, California with her husband, children, father-in-law, housekeeper, and pets, until a large problem lands on her doorstep: a body of a blackmailer killed by her daughter.

As distinct as its narrative may be in the noir cycle, *The Reckless Moment* does have some analogs. The story is similar to *Woman in the Window* and *Detour* in that there is an attempt to conceal a death results in blackmail. The crucial difference, of course, is that while its protagonist is as morally innocent as the male characters in those earlier films, the person enmeshed by circumstances in *The Reckless Moment* is a woman, a woman whose husband is away on travel and who must deal with a catastrophe alone. An interesting sidenote: while these elements are in the original story by a female author, Elizabeth Holding, that work was part of a series featuring a male hero, a police detective named Levy. As Lucia Harper, Joan Bennett, who happens to be the femme fatale of both *Woman in the Window* and *Scarlet Street*, is an ordinary woman, neither glamorous nor cunning. Somewhat like the women in *Mildred Pierce* or *The Accused*, the irony of her situation is not her innocence but that her middle-class values give her no pause before deciding to conceal a death by misadventure. Unlike Mildred Pierce, who protects her daughter Veda despite knowing that she has become a merciless and murderous schemer, Bea is an ostensibly normal if impressionable teenager and her involvement with Darby is a youthful error. Lucia's decision to try to shield her own family is parental instinct and perfectly "normal." As compared to the ruthless ambition of Mildred Pierce who sacrifices her marriage for the sake of business success and the social advancement of her daughters, or the sexual paranoia of Wilma Tuttle in *The Accused* who lives an inculcated life as a prim academic, Lucia is entirely ordinary.

The visualization of director Max Ophuls stresses the commonplace aspects of Lucia's milieu. Unlike his earlier *Caught* in which the dark corners of her wealthy husband's mansion seemed to swallow the hapless Leonora Eames, the Harper house is well-lit, compact, tidy, and filled with lived-in furnishings. Lucia's outfits, light-colored suits and dresses, are fashionable but quite different from Alice Reed's elegant evening gown and dark shawl when she suddenly appears to Dr. Wanley reflected as *The Woman in the Window*. With short hair, simple make-up, and lighting that leaves her face free of shadows, Bennett is neither mysterious nor ominous. Unlike the tartish, self-centered yet ingenuous Kitty March in *Scarlet Street* Lucia is a mature and thoughtful wife and mother. Yet as mundane as her life surroundings may be, they fail to insulate Lucia from the encroachment of the noir underworld. Since the entire narrative is presented as a long flashback from Lucia's point of view, there is an implicit filter over the events in that the viewer only sees what she remembers. Ophuls' long takes and fluid camera stylistically reinforce this and, as Lucia must venture into the noir universe, create a hybrid vision of what it is literally and what a woman such as Lucia might imagine it to be.

The actions of grifter Martin Donnelly, the would-be blackmailer whose infatuation with Lucia leads him to betray his cronies and die for her, may suggest that there are redeemable persons in the noir underworld. In fact, Donnelly's fascination with Lucia is not "realistic" behavior for a small-time crook. By casting against type and using suave British actor James Mason, Ophuls creates another anomaly. Donnelly becomes an introspective loner, as much out of place with his accomplices in blackmail as he is with Lucia but perfectly suited to her needs. When Ophul's camera follows Donnelly through a smoke-filled barroom, he is like a pilot guiding her through unfamiliar waters. No matter how much Donnelly may aspire to Lucia's goodwill, it is a hopeless dream. Instinctively, unconsciously Lucia uses Donnelly. Aghast at the death and violence that have intruded into her placid life, Lucia fails to understand that the key to her salvation and that of her family is in her values, for that is what binds Donnelly to her and compels his sacrifice. On one level, Donnelly's death is useless. Since neither she nor Bea is really guilty of murder, he dies to save them from little more than embarrassment. On another level, the shock of his death makes clear to Lucia that the world will never be the same, that nothing should ever be taken for granted. Even as the momentarily disrupted facets of her life realign themselves, even as her world falls easily back into place, life will never be commonplace or ordinary again. **AS & BP**

THE RED HOUSE (1947)

Director: Delmer Daves. **Screenplay**: Delmer Daves and Albert Maltz based on a novel by George Agnew Chamberlain. **Producer**: Sol Lesser. **Director of Photography**: Bert Glennon. **Art Direction**:

McClure Capps. **Music**: Miklós Rózsa. **Editor**: Merrill G. White. **Cast**: Edward G. Robinson (Pete Morgan), Lon McCallister (Nath), Judith Anderson (Ellen Morgan), Allene Roberts (Meg), Rory Calhoun (Teller), Julie London (Tibby), Ona Munson (Mrs. Storm), Harry Shannon (Dr. Byrne), Arthur Space (Sheriff). **Released**: Sol Lesser Productions/Thalia, March 16. 100 minutes.

Pete Morgan, along with his sister Ellen, is raising Meg as a foster child. There are rumors about her origins and her connections with the woods and a mysterious red house there. As Meg grows up Morgan becomes more and more fixated on her and the forests around his farm. Forbidding her or anyone else to enter the woods, he hires Teller to guard the area. Meg ventures into the woods repeatedly, at times accompanied by the boy she has fallen for—Nath. After several mishaps she finds the red house. The house she finds out later is the site where her parents were killed by the jealous Morgan, who loved Meg's mother. After the death of his sister who also ventures into the woods, Morgan becomes delusional and takes Meg to the red house. But before he can harm her, Nath and the sheriff arrive. After being shot, Morgan drives his truck into the ice house nearby and drowns.

Delmer Daves, who co-wrote with blacklistee Albert Maltz (*The Naked City*) and directed the landmark noir film *Dark Passage* the same year as this film, crafted in *The Red House* a noir movie that reads very much like a dark fairy tale. After a brief opening which underlines the bucolic nature of the rural landscape and the vagaries of teen love, the film changes trajectory with the introduction of the character of Peter Morgan, played by Edward G. Robinson—who brings to this role a great deal of the angst and compulsiveness he will display the next year in another quasi-supernatural noir *Night Has a Thousand Eyes*. Morgan's ominous limp, his pathological fear of the woods around his isolated farm, his periodic hysterical fits ("screams . . . will follow you all your life."), and most significantly his quasi-incestuous obsession with his ward Meg whom he conflates with her mother Jeannie, the woman he loved and murdered—all mark him as a noir protagonist haunted by a past he is unable to escape.

The many scenes in the woods recall fairy tales, from which characters can only return damaged emotionally or physically in some way: Meg breaks her leg, Morgan's sister dies there, and of course it is the graveyard of both Jeannie and her husband—victims of Morgan's obsession, etc. It is the nexus of mystery and experience. Consequently Daves shoots the forest for the most part at night creating an atmosphere of supernatural horror not unlike Val Lewton's horror films (*Cat People*, *Seventh Victim*, etc.). In addition, composer Miklós Rózsa constructs one of his most compelling noir scores—utilizing everything at hand, including his trademark theremin (first used by Rózsa in Hitchcock's *Spellbound*), to give the woods an unearthly quality—even recreating the screams that Morgan claims any visitor will hear.

The eponymous red house itself is of course right out of a fairy tale. It has a dark magical quality, especially when Meg stumbles upon and stands there frozen, unable to turn away from the place where as a child she must have witnessed the murder of her parents by Morgan. And finally like any good fairy tale, the film rights wrongs and supplies the young lovers (Meg and Nath) a happy ending. Morgan tries to repeat the past by taking Meg to the red house. But as Nath and the sheriff arrive and interrupt his recreation of the past, Morgan takes his obsession one step further and drives his truck into the ice house next to the red house. In close up the audience watches his expressionless face sinking into the water as he chooses to join the bodies of his victims in that muddy well of water. JU

RED LIGHT (1949)

Director/Producer: Roy Del Ruth. **Screenplay**: George Callahan from a story by Donald Barry. **Director of Photography**: Bert Glennon. **Music**: Dimitri Tiomkin. **Art Director**: F. Paul Sylos. **Editor**: Richard Heermance. **Cast**: George Raft (John Torno), Virginia Mayo (Carla North), Gene Lockhart (Warni Hazard), Raymond Burr (Nick Cherney), Barton MacLane (Det. Sarecker), Henry Morgan (Rocky), Arthur Franz (Jess Torno), Arthur Shields (Father Redmond), Frank Orth (Stoner). **Location**: San Francisco. **Completed**: March 30, 1949. **Released**: United Artists, September 30. 84 minutes.

Johnny Torno, the aggressive owner of the Los Angeles based Torno Freight Company, welcomes his brother Jess, a Roman Catholic chaplain, back from the war. Unknown to Johnny, Nick Cherney, an ex-employee who was convicted of embezzlement, is plotting to get even with Johnny by killing Jess. One evening, Johnny visits his brother's hotel room and finds him dying of a bullet wound. Johnny asks him who did it, but Jess can only answer, "In the Bible," before dying. Later Johnny reasons that his brother was referring to the hotel room's Gideon Bible, which is now missing. Johnny hunts for the missing Bible with the help of Carla North and leaves Warni Hazard in charge of the freight company. The Bible is found with the passage "Vengeance is mine saith the Lord" clearly marked. Ultimately, Johnny learns Nick is responsible and chases him to the rooftop, next to the Torno Freight Company sign. Ready to shoot, Johnny remembers his brother's message and drops his gun. But Nick accidentally breaks the neon sign and is electrocuted. Another sign, stating "24 Hour Service," blazes in the background.

Red Light is a strange film since the conventions of film noir do not readily accommodate its religious message. Nor is it helped any by Tiomkin's rather banal score, explicating, as it does, the religious motif by moving back and forth between *Dies Irae* and *Ave Maria*. The film does, however, contain one classic noir scene: Warni, in a state of abject fear, goes down to the darkened truck garage and discovers the distributor wires of his car have been cut. Becoming more fearful, he runs, stumbles, and then climbs under a truck trailer. We see only the pair of legs of his pursuer from Warni's point of view walking up to the trailer and casually kicking out one of the jacks while Warni screams. Then the camera pans up to a shot of the sinister Raymond Burr as Cherney, smoking and smiling. Robert Aldrich was one of the assistant directors on this film, so this scene may have been the inspiration for a similar one in *Kiss Me Deadly*. **BP**

REIGN OF TERROR
[aka **THE BLACK BOOK**] (1949)

Director: Anthony Mann. **Screenplay**: Aeneas MacKenzie and Philip Yordan. **Producer**: W. Cameron Menzies. **Executive Producer**: Walter Wanger. **Director of Photography**: John Alton. **Music**: Sol Kaplan and Irving Friedman. **Art Director**: Edward Ilou. **Editor**: Fred Allen. **Cast**: Robert Cummings (Charles D'Aubigny), Richard Basehart (Robespierre), Arlene Dahl (Madelon), Richard Hart (François Barras), Arnold Moss (Fouché), Norman Lloyd (Tallien), Charles McGraw (Sergeant), Beulah Bondi (Grandma Blanchard), Jess Barker (Saint Just). **Released**: Eagle-Lion, October 15. 89 minutes.

It is 1794 and in Paris Maximilian Robespierre is attempting to consolidate his position as the most powerful member of the Committee of Public Safety. He is supported on the Committee by the handsome Saint Just but opposed by the stalwart Barras, who is against any notion of dictatorship. Assisting him in eliminating his enemies is the head of the secret police, Fouché, a treacherous opportunist willing to switch sides to further himself. Robespierre sends for the notorious executioner Duval, the "Butcher of Strasbourg," who he commissions with the task of finding his lost "black book," a book containing his handwritten list of those he intends to execute and which, in the wrong hands, would destroy him. He does not realize that Duval has been assassinated and replaced by Charles D'Aubigny, an agent of the exiled Lafayette, whose real purpose is to get the black book to Barras, the only leader strong enough and honest enough to thwart Robespierre's plans. Against his better judgment Charles must rely on the good graces of Madelon, an ex-lover and member of a coterie of patriots who support Barras in opposing Robespierre. Charles comes to realize that the "lost" book was no more than a ruse of Robespierre to have Barras arrested and Charles rifles Robespierre's quarters until he finds the book. Charles and Madelon are forced to flee to the countryside where they are pursued by Saint Just and a group of soldiers. Madelon is arrested but Charles is able to get back to Paris under the cover of darkness. Charles gets the book to Tallien, another patriot, just as Robespierre is assembling the convention to "try" Barras. After members of the Committee have read the book they give vocal support to Barras and Robespierre is defeated.

Reign of Terror.

Reign of Terror is one of a number of period films that deserve a place in the noir cycle. The film was made by Anthony Mann and photographer John Alton who together and separately had perfected many noir visual elements—depth of field; tight backward tracking close-ups; low-key, complex lighting patterns. The problem here was to make something interesting out of a routine, low-budget costumer and Mann does so by pulling out all the stops: the action moves even faster than in his previous films (interrupted only by the obligatory love scene); the camera angles are more oblique; there are more high angle/low angle reverse shots; the streets are darker; the sets more expressive; the ceilings lower. Even the remoteness of a period setting did not prevent Mann from building tension, notably in the scene where the old guard is fumbling with the gate key while Charles is trying desperately to get out of Paris or the scene where Grandma Blanchard is trying to retrieve the black book from the cot on which Saint Just is sleeping—somewhat reminiscent of the scene in *T-Men* where the agent is trying to get to the plates he has taped under the sink, in both instances under the watchful eye of actor Charles McGraw. Nor was Mann's unique way of staging violence at all restricted here (one particularly remembers the off-handed way Fouché has Robespierre shot and Robespierre's subsequent attempts to defend himself after his jaw has been shattered). Finally, *Reign of Terror* creates a paradigm of the noir world, a place so filled with suspicion that not even a former lover can be trusted. **BP**

REPEAT PERFORMANCE (1947)

Director: Alfred Werker. **Screenplay**: Walter Bullock from a novel by William O'Farrell. **Producer**: Aubrey Schenck. **Director of Photography**: William O'Connell. **Music**: George Antheil. **Art Director**: Edward Jewell. **Editor**: Al DeGaetano and Louis Sacker. **Cast**: Louis Hayward (Barney Page), Joan Leslie (Sheila Page), Richard Basehart (William Williams), Virginia Field (Paula Costello), Tom Conway (John Friday), Natalie Schafer (Eloise Shaw), Benay Venuta (Mattie), John Ireland (Narrator, uncredited). **Released**: Eagle-Lion, May 22. 91 minutes.

Broadway star Sheila Page wanders into a crowded New Year's Eve party. Visibly shaken, she seeks out her friend, poet William Williams, and confesses that she has just murdered her husband, Barney. Williams indicates that Barney deserved it but tells Sheila to seek the advice of her producer, the good-natured John Friday, before doing anything else. Williams accompanies her and on the way there she tells the poet that she would like to be able to relive the past year. Turning to speak to Williams as they are climbing the stairs to Friday's flat, she discovers he has mysteriously disappeared. Before she is able to confess her crime to Friday she begins to realize that the she has gone back exactly one year in time. She rushes back to her apartment, only to find Barney alive and welcoming her home. Sharing her strange secret with a skeptical Williams, she vows to do everything in her power to make the year turn out differently. She warns Williams not to become the protégé of the rich socialite Mrs. Shaw for otherwise he will spend some time in an asylum. She tries to prevent her husband Barney from having an affair with the successful British playwright Paula Costello and from descending into alcoholism. But despite her best efforts the trajectory of her life seems to follow the same course. Circumstances, however, are a bit different this time. Barney becomes temporarily invalided due to a drunken fall and when Paula ends their affair to return to England, Barney blames all his troubles on Sheila. Able again to walk, Barney comes after Sheila with his cane, but before he is able to strike her he is shot and killed by Williams, who has come to believe Sheila's story and has escaped from the sanitarium.

Repeat Performance is an uneasy mix of several elements—part fantasy, part soap opera, part film noir. At first blush it would seem that the whimsical nature of the fantasy film would make it rather impervious to the thrust of the noir universe, although there are some exceptions (*The Night Has a Thousand Eyes*, also starring Robinson, comes to mind). Some films permit the hermetic nature of the noir universe to be compromised (as here with too much melodrama) but what typically returns them to the noir cycle are strong opening and closing segments. Such is the case here. After John Ireland's unnecessary opening narration over a New York skyline, the camera comes to rest outside of a high-rise apartment. When the wind suddenly blows open the French doors we hear several shots and then the camera tracks inside to reveal a distraught woman standing over a man's body. The camera then follows her as she wanders into the party.

The final segment—Barney's odyssey from the docks through the city streets and into his apartment to confront Sheila—is pure noir, with Barney's growing frenzy matched by Antheil's increasingly minatory score. Their scuffle in the living room, after Sheila knocks over a lamp, is shot in an expressive style that is none too consistent with the rest of the film: extreme low and oblique angle shots; figures silhouetted in the light or moving in and out of the light (most effectively done when Williams enters the room), motivated of course by the fact that the fallen lamp is the only source of light. The acting is a plus too. As the despicable husband, Louis Hayward equals his performance in *House by the River*. Joan Leslie does quite well in the stereotypical role of the long-suffering wife. But Richard Basehart, in his first film, stands out as the high-spirited poet who is willing to sacrifice his future for the sake of the woman with whom he should have been paired. As far as Basehart's future in the noir cycle is concerned, his performance here was a taste of better things to come. **BP**

RETURN OF THE WHISTLER (1948)

Director: D. Ross Lederman. **Screenplay**: Edward Bock and Maurice Tombragel from "All At Once No Alice" by Cornell Woolrich. **Producer**: Rudolph Flotow. **Director of Photography**: Philip Tannura. **Music**: Mischa Bakaleinikoff. **Art Director**: George Brooks. **Editor**: Dwight Caldwell. **Cast**: Michael Duane (Ted Nichols), Lénore Aubert (Alice Dupres Barkley), Richard Lane (Gaylord Traynor), James Cardwell (Charlie aka John Barkley), Ann Shoemaker (Mrs. Barkley), Sarah Padden (Mrs. Hulskamp), Otto Forest (voice of The Whistler). **Released**: Columbia, March 18. 60 minutes.

On a dark, rainy night Ted Nichols, a successful young engineer, and his fiancée, Alice Dupres Barkley, pull up in front of the house of a justice of the peace. They are told that the justice is out of town and won't be able to marry them until the next day, but that they should be able to find lodgings in an adjacent town. The night clerk will not allow Ted to share a room with Alice because they aren't married, so he agrees to spend the night in the garage where he has taken his ailing car. When he goes to pick up Alice the next morning, the night clerk tells him that Alice checked out shortly after he left the previous evening. The skeptical Ted creates a scene but is frustrated in his efforts to get at the truth. A private investigator, Gaylord Traynor, has eavesdropped and offers to help Ted. Together they return to Ted's apartment in the city to see if Alice has "skipped" as Traynor suspects. During their journey Ted tells Traynor that he has only known Alice a few weeks; that she had been briefly married to an American pilot, John Barkley, who had been killed in France during the war; that she came to America to be with John's father but that when she arrived she found that his wealthy father had died and that his mansion was filled with relatives with whom she did not get along. She had been planning to return to France when she met Ted. Alice's clothing is still in Ted's apartment but when Ted shows Traynor pictures of Alice and her marriage license, Traynor knocks Ted out and absconds with the papers. It turns out that Traynor has been working for the Barkleys and that Charlie, John's cousin, had convinced the detective that he is John and that Alice is delusional and sometimes thinks she is a widow. When Ted confronts Charlie in the Barkley mansion, Charlie gives him that same story. Ted remains skeptical and eventually traces Alice to a sanitarium where the Barkleys have committed her so that they can control the family fortune. Charlie attempts to prevent Ted from rescuing Alice but Traynor, having discovered the ruse, arrives with the police in time to have all the guilty parties arrested.

Return of the Whistler was the last of eight features produced at Columbia between 1944 and 1948 (others were *The Whistler, Mark of the Whistler, Power of the Whistler, Voice of the Whistler, Mysterious Intruder, Secret of the Whistler, The 13th Hour*) based on the popular radio show. The narrator of that radio series was the omniscient, disembodied voice of the Whistler (whose theme is the famous 13 notes written by Wilbur Hatch) which acted like a Greek Chorus, sometimes progressing the action, sometimes conscience-like, commenting on it as if in a dialogue with the protagonist, but

always making sure that the protagonist was punished for his/her evil deeds in a final "twist" ending. Like *Suspense*, another extremely popular CBS radio series of the 1940s and early 1950s, *The Whistler* used materials drawn from the pulps, molded to fit its particular format. The two radio series arguably represent radio's best equivalent of the film noir, with *The Whistler* coming closest to the spirit of B-films like *Detour* (and Woolrich) in its emphasis on the inexorable role of fate. In any case, the confluence of pulp fiction, radio, and the film noir remains a good topic for future study.

The Columbia films all starred veteran actor Richard Dix, in a variety of roles both good and evil, until a heart attack forced him to retire in 1947. In this entry the producers decided to replace "star power" with the established appeal of Woolrich's fiction, "All At Once No Alice" being one of his more popular short stories. Unfortunately they drained the tale of much of its suspense, allowing the night clerk to be bribed by the nefarious Charlie (in the original all the characters the protagonist encounters on the fateful evening deny that he was with anybody) and changing the ending so that Alice is no longer rescued from being buried alive at the last moment. In the film series the figure of the Whistler was represented visually (as well as by his distinctive voice) only as the shadow of man in trench coat and hat, perfect opportunity, it would seem, to rely on those chiaroscuro effects so beloved of the noir style. Unfortunately, except for this entry and *The Mysterious Intruder*, the series was shot in a rather pedestrian manner (high key, lots of fill light), seldom evidencing those expressive tics we have come to expect from a film noir. **BP**

RIDE THE PINK HORSE (1947)

Director: Robert Montgomery. **Screenplay**: Ben Hecht and Charles Lederer from the novel by Dorothy B. Hughes. **Producer**: Joan Harrison. **Director of Photography**: Russell Metty. **Music**: Frank Skinner. **Art Directors**: Bernard Herzbrun, Robert Boyle. **Editor**: Ralph Dawson. **Cast**: Robert Montgomery (Gagin), Thomas Gomez (Pancho), Rita Conde (Carla), Iris Flores (Maria), Wanda Hendrix (Pila), Grandon Rhodes (Mr. Edison), Tito Renaldo (Bellboy), Richard Gaines (Jonathan), Andrea King (Marjorie), Art Smith (Bill Retz), Martin Garralaga (Barkeeper), Edward Earle (Locke), Harold Goodwin (Red), Maria Cortez (Elevator Girl), Fred Clark (Frank Hugo). **Completed**: July 3, 1947. **Released**: Universal, October 8. 101 minutes.

An ex-G.I. known only as Gagin comes to a small New Mexico town during its annual fiesta. Gagin's intention is to confront and blackmail a mobster named Frank Hugo. While he waits for Hugo's arrival at the local hotel, Gagin is approached by Bill Retz, an F.B.I. agent, who suspects that Gagin possesses incriminating material on Hugo and asks him to turn it over. Gagin claims to be in town merely as a tourist and denies having any information. Followed by Retz, Gagin does tour the town, spending a good portion of the day near an old carousel operated by Pancho and frequented by Pila, a Native American girl who attaches herself to Gagin. Despite Gagin's efforts to discourage her, she follows him around town and, after his initial meeting with Hugo, witnesses an attempt to kill him. She and Pancho nurse the badly beaten Gagin but cannot dissuade him from approaching Hugo again with predictably poor results. As Hugo men-

Ride the Pink Horse: *Lucky Gagin (Robert Montgomery) and Pila (Wanda Hendrix)*.

aces Pila, Gagin is all but defeated when Retz intervenes and Hugo is arrested. The following morning, Gagin expects Pila to be distraught at his leaving. Instead, she calmly says goodbye and starts to recount the tale of the past two days to the others gathered around the merry-go-round.

Besides *In A Lonely Place*, Dorothy B. Hughes wrote two other novels which were adapted into noir films. In *The Fallen Sparrow* John Garfield is a Spanish Civil War veteran who returns to New York and is pursued by Fascist agents. In the novel *Ride the Pink Horse* Hughes' main character, known only as Sailor, is another urban man on a quest outside the city. Arriving in "San Pablo," a fictionalized Santa Fe, New Mexico, during a fiesta week, Sailor finds "no one who even looked as if he came from the city. A hick town. He didn't like hick towns." In the film of the same name, Robert Montgomery stars (and directs) as Gagin, the man from "no place." As the thoroughly venal Sailor of the novel is transformed into Gagin, a war veteran with somewhat ambiguous motives for extortion and whose cynical attitude is almost proletarian, the film's characters become prototypically noir. Robert Montgomery had just completed an idiosyncratic adaptation of Raymond Chandler's novel, *Lady in the Lake*, with its "first person" camera. To accomplish that, it was necessary that almost all of that film be shot in a studio environment which permitted the control needed for elaborate dolly shots and long takes. While much of *Ride the Pink Horse* was shot on the Universal back lot, and much of that action centered around an authentic Tio Vivo or carousel which the studio rented from the town of Taos, New Mexico, several scenes were filmed on locations in and around the plaza of Santa Fe.

Among the various portraits of weary veterans contained in film noir, Gagin is perhaps most literally devoid of identity. He has no first name—no one uses the ironic nickname "Lucky" that appears only in the titles—just Gagin, clipped, guttural, the perfect epithet for Robert Montgomery's taciturn portrayal. The sobriquet that the villagers give him as he wanders through San Pablo is "the man with no place," an appropriate choice for someone who comes from nowhere in particular and lacks any ultimate destination. As to Gagin's personal connections, he describes them succinctly: "I'm nobody's friend." The elaborate long take at the opening of the film, which is discussed in the Introduction, is not found in the Hughes' novel. As a plot event, it is the creation of preeminent noir screenwriters Ben Hecht and Charles Lederer. As the film developed the influence of Joan Harrison, one of

the few women to produce features in the classic period, may have softened the racist and misogynistic undertones and the criminality of the protagonist in the novel. The opening and other long takes in *Ride the Pink Horse* are more appropriately integrated and hence add more dramatic impact to the narrative and never reduce its protagonist to a cipher for the camera, which, although he may be a "man with no place," detached and disaffected, Gagin never becomes. The typical qualities of the embittered loner in film noir, which the figure immediately evokes through this specific visual introduction, combine with the narrative development of his hatred for Frank Hugo to create a more complex character. The initial assertion of Gagin's generic identity is grounded in understated conflict with the environment, in which he is a stranger. San Pablo itself offers nothing other than the promise of finding Hugo within its confines, nothing to mollify the alienation that Gagin sports so visibly, no alternate reality to the naturalistic images of the terminal, the town, or the crowded hotel lobby. Only after Gagin's quest to even the score for his dead pal, Shorty, is suspended because of Hugo's absence does he discover the denizens of San Pablo, Pancho and Pila, and the Tio Vivo.

Although the first encounter between Gagin and Pila is in a "false" exterior—the soundstage containing the carousel set—the next sequence takes them into the actual Santa Fe plaza, just outside the genuine La Fonda hotel. By using location here and in the night exteriors when the effigy of Zozobra is paraded to his pyre, Montgomery seamlessly imbues the studio sets with a portion of their reality. Within this noir landscape, under the pull of some predetermined inclination, Montgomery/Gagin wanders the town like a lost soul. A last long take is used when Gagin goes to a restaurant to exchange the letter for Hugo's money. En route, Gagin weaves through the crowd of onlookers gathered for the parade and the burning of Zozobra, and a dissolve momentarily superimposes the effigy of Zozobra with a close up of Hugo revealing the true face of Gagin's god of bad luck.

"Tio Vivo" is the central image of *Ride the Pink Horse*. Like other havens in film noir, like Rica's apartment in *Thieves' Highway* or Doll Conovan's place in *The Asphalt Jungle*, it offers refuge to the spiritually and physically wounded hero. But in *Ride the Pink Horse*, Gagin is never fully at ease around the carousel, never understands the emotional relationship between it and its patrons. Perhaps the most telling action at the carousel in terms noir stylistics is the beating of Pancho. Moments after he conceals a wounded Gagin next to Pila in one of the Tio Vivo chairs, two of Hugo's thugs arrive. Pancho keeps several children aboard the carousel by offering a free ride. In several angles the camera is mounted on the carousel, focused on a young boy and girl, another boy alone, and Pila wearing a blanket over her head like a mantilla with a covered Gagin beside her. While the children's heads turn to watch the men walk up in the background, Pila does not move. As the shadows of horses fly across their bodies, the men stand on each side of Pancho, hemming him in. Their verbal interrogation about the man Pancho met in the bar, the man whose name he does not know, quickly gives way to a more severe approach. As they beat him, Pancho's cries and groans and the dull thud of a clenched fist are mixed with the repetitive carillon sound of the carousel. The cutaways to the moving camera reveal closer shots of the now terrified children, trapped on the merry-go-round and unable to run away, grimacing and whimpering as the relentless motion of the mechanism takes them past the wall where the men beat the prostrate Pancho over and over. Finally, as Pancho moans, "Oh, my, you hurt, Panchito," the thugs relent, convinced he knows nothing. The carousel is at once one of the most stylized and one of the most naturalistic objects in the movie. By its very artifice, by the aspects of ritual which its patrons attach to circling a finite space on the small wooden horses, Tio Vivo becomes a quintessentially noir set piece. Gagin, who comes to it burdened by the complex codes of behavior imposed by the noir universe, focused on the belief that he must even the score, cannot see its broader dimensions. **AS**

RIOT IN CELL BLOCK 11 (1954)

Director: Don Siegel. **Screenplay**: Richard Collins. **Producer**: Walter Wanger. **Director of Photography**: Russell Harlan. **Music**: Herschel Burke Gilbert. **Art Director**: Dave Milton. **Editor**: Bruce B. Pierce. **Cast**: Neville Brand (Dunn), Emile Meyer (The Warden), Frank Faylen (Haskell), Leo Gordon (Carnie), Robert Osterloh (The Colonel), Paul Frees (Monroe), Don Keefer (Reporter), Whit Bissell (Snader), Dabbs Greer (Schuyler), William Schallert (Reporter). **Released**: Allied Artists, February 28. 80 minutes.

A Congressional committee hears testimony that the nation's prisons are in a deplorable state of neglect that has led to a series of riots. The scene shifts to Folsom Prison's notorious Cell Block 11, where what the "screws" term "animals" are held in isolation. Led by career criminal Dunn, the inmates overpower the guards and seize control of the area, with a view to negotiating with the warden. They demand better food, work training, and more humane guards—exactly the requests that penny-pinching legislators had denied the warden. Initially refusing to negotiate, prison commissioner Haskell eventually accedes to the convicts' reasonable demands after the rioting takes over the whole facility. But the government might not act on his recommendations. Dunn is blamed for the uprising and has thirty years added to his sentence.

With its documentary stylizations, use of non-professional or little-known actors, realistic settings, and collective narrative, Siegel's film shows the deep impress of Italian neorealism, making it a part of the post war noir documentary

cycle. With its sophisticated, ambiguous treatment of political questions and its refusal to offer the customary emotional satisfactions of Hollywood filmmaking, however, *Riot in Cell Block 11* distinguishes itself from both the more sensational noir documentaries such as *He Walked By Night* and noir prison films in general such as *Brute Force*, with their thematization of sadism and the will to power, showing a closer affinity with the neo-realist social problems films of the era such as *The Men*. In Neville Brand's affecting performance, Dunn is in part the psychopathic criminal mastermind made familiar by noir films like *White Heat*, but, at the same time, he is also opposed to unnecessary violence, conducts the negotiations with officials in good faith, and seems genuinely committed to the welfare of his fellows. Unlike the typical social problem film, *Riot in Cell Block 11*, it must be said, is definitively noir in portraying the political system as irremediably corrupt. **RBP**

ROADBLOCK (1951)

Director: Harold Daniels. **Screenplay**: Steve Fisher and George Bricker from a story by Richard Landau and Geoffrey Homes [Daniel Mainwaring]. **Producer**: Lewis Rachmil. **Director of Photography**: Nicholas Musuraca. **Music**: Paul Sawtell. **Art Directors**: Albert D'Agostino, Walter Keller. **Editor**: Robert Golden. **Cast**: Charles McGraw (Joe Peters), Joan Dixon (Diane Marley), Lowell Gilmore (Kendall Webb), Louis Jean Heydt (Harry Miller), Milburn Stone (Egan), Joseph Crehan (Thompson). **Completed**: October 19, 1950. **Released**: RKO, September 17. 73 minutes.

Joe Peters and Harry Miller are insurance investigators who have completed an important case. On the plane back to Los Angeles, Joe meets Diane Marley and allows her to pose as his wife to fly half-fare. Due to bad weather, they spend an innocent night together in a hotel. Diane calls him "Honest Joe" and explains that they could never be happy together because she cares too much about money while he's more concerned with integrity. Shortly after, Harry and Joe investigate a fur robbery. They suspect Kendall Webb, a wily racketeer who owns the building housing the fur company. In the process Joe discovers that Diane has become Webb's mistress. Joe continues to make moves in Diane's direction but although she is falling for Joe, she tells him she cannot live on his small salary. Joe offers Webb information regarding a rail shipment of used money in exchange for part of the booty. Diane marries Joe regardless of his lack of money, but Joe believes it is too late to extricate him-

self from the robbery attempt. According to plan, the newly-weds go to a mountain cabin for their honeymoon, where Joe will receive his share of the money. But the robbery goes badly and a postal clerk is killed. Joe tries to frame Webb by murdering him and leaving the body in a burning car with part of the stolen money. Harry, Joe's friend, confronts him with knowledge of Joe's complicity but Joe avoids arrest. He tries to escape to Mexico with Diane, but the police have blocked all escape routes. In desperation, Joe drives into the dry Los Angeles riverbed where he is followed by the police. Trapped between two police cordons, Joe pushes Diane out of the vehicle to prevent her arrest. Forced to abandon the car, Joe ignores Harry's entreaties to give himself up. Instead, he scrambles up the concrete embankment where he is killed by a uniformed officer.

Like the corruptible policemen in *The Prowler* and *Pushover*, Joe Peters' destruction is tied to money and sex. Co-author Mainwaring and co-screenwriter Fisher, no strangers to the noir tradition, have infused their pulpy plot with the taint of middle-class malaise that underlies the fallen world to which Peters succumbs. This helps to explain how tough an icon as Charles McGraw (unlike Heflin or MacMurray) could fall prey to such temptations. It makes one wish as well that Hollywood would have made better use of McGraw's talents, for not once in the noir cycle did the actor ever portray the character of the hardboiled private eye (though he came close as the policemen in *Armored Car Robbery* and *The Narrow Margin* and even closer as the undercover agent in the short-lived TV series, *The Falcon*). Like *Pushover*'s Paul Sheridan, Peters learns too late that the impossible object, Diane, could be possessed without recourse to crime. At the same time, there is much wisdom in Webb's warning to Peters that despite Diane's best intentions she would eventually miss "the feel of mink." *Roadblock* does not display much evidence of the RKO noir style, perhaps because the pedestrian direction of Harold Daniels did not allow photographer Musuraca to perform his usual magic. **BP**

ROAD HOUSE (1948)

Director: Jean Negulesco. **Screenplay**: Edward Chodorov from an unpublished story by Margaret Gruen and Oscar Saul. **Producer**: Edward Chodorov. **Director of Photography**: Joseph La Shelle. **Music**: Cyril Mockridge. **Art Directors**: Lyle Wheeler, Maurice Ransford. **Editor**: James B. Clark. **Cast**: Ida Lupino (Lily), Cornel Wilde (Pete), Celeste Holm (Susie), Richard Widmark (Jefty), O.Z. Whitehead (Arthur), Robert Karnes (Mike), George Beranger

(Lefty), Ian MacDonald (Sheriff), Grandon Rhodes (judge), Jack G. Lee (Sam). **Completed**: May 11, 1948. **Released**: 20th Century-Fox, November 7. 95 minutes.

Jefty owns a roadhouse in a town near the Canadian border, and his best friend Pete is the manager. He hires a singer and pianist, Lily, and she becomes an immensely popular entertainer. Jefty falls in love with her while Pete remains aloof. Meanwhile, Susie, the cashier, keeps her feelings for Pete to herself. But when Jefty goes on a hunting trip, Pete and Lily fall in love. Jefty returns with plans to marry Lily but when Pete tells him of their love, the psychotic side of Jefty is revealed. He frames Pete for criminal charges by stealing money from the roadhouse profits and making his employee appear guilty. When Pete is charged, Jefty pretends a change of heart and persuades the judge to release Pete in his custody. Pete and Lily must live in the roadhouse, subject to constant psychological harassment by Jefty. Finally, Jefty takes Pete, Lily, and Susie to a cabin near the border where he plans to torment Pete to the point where the man will attempt to escape across the order at which time Jefty will shoot him. Pete and Lily do make a run for it when they feel they have a chance. Susie obtains evidence of Jefty's machinations and follows them. But Jefty wounds Susie as she tries to warn the fugitives. Pete and Jefty fight, and Lily shoots and kills Jefty.

Road House impresses first of all with its sharp dialogue exchanges between the characters and the bizarre look of the interiors. The roadhouse itself is designed in such a way as to conjure up a synthetic vision of the postwar period, seeming at once modern and rustic. The ambience of the scenes in these interiors is strongly supported by the characteristically moody noir lighting of La Shelle. This usual setting is the background for scenes in which Ida Lupino as Lily sits at the piano, burning grooves into the top of the instrument with her forgotten cigarettes as she sings torch songs in her inimitable voice, prompting the line, "She does more without a voice than anyone I ever heard." When the story moves to

a new setting in the final reels and Jefty becomes totally berserk, the artificial milieu becomes a sound-stage forest in which the characters file towards an unreal lake that rests beneath a painted sky. The artificiality of the noir style was seldom so severe; yet the look of these scenes arguably complements the flamboyant behavior of the characters.

Road House does contain a reasonably subtle and effective contrast between the two characters suffering from unrequited love. Jefty's crazed actions are mostly attributable to the demands of the noir style. On the other hand, Susie, suffering in good-natured silence over Pete's attraction to Lily, demonstrates in a very credible way the reaction most normal individuals would have. Ironically, such a reaction is made to seem almost perverse in the context of the film, especially as it ends in her self-destructive heroism. **BL**

ROGUE COP (1954)

Director: Roy Rowland. **Screenplay**: Sydney Boehm from the novel by William P. McGivern. **Producer**: Nicholas Nayfack. **Director of Photography**: John Seitz. **Music**: Jeff Alexander. **Art Directors**: Cedric Gibbons, Hans Peters. **Editor**: James E. Newcom. **Cast**: Robert Taylor (Christopher Kelvaney), Janet Leigh (Karen Stephanson), George Raft (Dan Beaumonte), Steve Forrest (Eddie Kelvaney), Anne Francis (Nancy Corlane), Robert Ellenstein (Sidney Myers), Robert F. Simon (Ackerman), Anthony Ross (Father Ahearn), Alan Hale Jr. (Johnny Stark), Peter Brocco (Wrinkles Fallon), Vince Edwards (Langley), Olive Carey (Selma). **Completed**: May 14, 1954. **Released**: MGM, September 17. 87 minutes.

Christopher Kelvaney is notorious among his fellow policemen as a rogue cop who finances his expensive life style through payoffs from criminals. His brother Eddie, a rookie patrolman, is determined to restore family honor by his integrity. Eddie witnesses a knife murder by Wrinkles Fallon who asks for help from a syndicate boss, Dan Beaumonte, who in turn tells Kelvaney to buy off his brother. Kelvaney tries to reason with Eddie and Karen Stephanson, Eddie's girlfriend. When that fails, a furious Beaumonte rails against Kelvaney until the cop beats both the mobster and his bodyguard and vows to kill Beaumonte if his brother is harmed. Beaumonte brings in an out-of-town killer named Langley to dispose of both Kelvaney brothers. Eddie is ambushed and killed, and Kelvaney is completely ostracized by his fellow policemen. After Kelvaney gets information from Beaumonte's moll Nancy Corlane, Langley finds her in Karen's apartment and kills her too; but Kelvaney captures him. A desperate Beaumonte sets a trap. In the ensuing gun battle both policemen are wounded.

With *Rogue Cop* and *Scene of the Crime,* Roy Rowland joins Anthony Mann as one of the few directors to make more than a single film noir at MGM. Five years after *Scene of the Crime,* the intricacies of the criminal activities in that earlier production are abandoned in *Rogue Cop.* The focus instead is on the corrupt Chris Kelvaney and his inability to cope with the dissolution of his carefully constructed life-style. Kelvaney's self-justification for being on the syndicate payroll is a personal distaste for the brutality of everyday police work. Accordingly, he uses his money to insulate himself from what he sees as sordid and demeaning. Unlike the earnest and athletic Webb Garwood in *The Prowler,* Kelvaney is a sophisticate. His sense of superiority causes him to pity all those around him: his fel-

Rogue Cop: *George Raft as Dan Beaumonte.*

low officers including his own brother for their poorly paid integrity; Karen Stephanson for her physical impediment; Nancy Corlane for her inanity; and even Beaumonte for being unable to remove the stench of cheap criminality with any amount of expensive cologne. Kelvaney's "business" relationship with Beaumonte has become so routine that he is unprepared to respond when Beaumonte resorts to force. Although he beats the mobster physically, he lacks the ability to prevent his brother's assassination. The final portion of the film concerns a vendetta, but Kelvaney carries it out as much to restore his own sense of identity as to avenge his brother. When Beaumonte takes out the contract on Kelvaney, the corrupt cop is suddenly immersed in a chaotic underworld he thought he had left behind. He stalks the streets for information and captures Langley with a rediscovered authority. Then like Joe Morse in *Force of Evil,* Kelvaney purposely falls for the mobster's trap in expectation that he might have to sacrifice his own life to destroy Beaumonte.

Rowland visually reinforces the dichotomy between Kelvaney's world and that of the streets, and, to some extent, subjectifies the film according to Kelvaney's viewpoint. Initially Kelvaney is seen only in well-lit rooms, relaxed and well groomed as he goes through a charade of police work. His brother Eddie, however, is photographed on his nightly beat, cautiously patrolling neighborhoods of cheap bars and flophouses, walking past dark alleyways in bad parts of town. Kelvaney's fight with Beaumonte is his first brush with physical violence. Ironically it takes place in the mobster's luxurious apartment, so that as Kelvaney breaks up his expensive furnishings, he is also destroying the basis of his own insular mentality. The graphic brutality of that scene, so seemingly out of place, also initiates a predictable transference between the two brothers. When Beaumonte's fury cannot reach Kelvaney, it kills Eddie; and suddenly Chris Kelvaney reverts to depending on a shadowy world of informants and back rooms for survival. Whether he survives or not is never made clear, as the film ends with the ambulance ride through the very streets Kelvaney despised. But that follows a final confrontation that is both an existential catharsis and a moral expiation in which Kelvaney and Beaumonte mindlessly blast away at each other until their revolver hammers fall on empty chambers and their bodies crumple to the ground. **AS**

SCANDAL SHEET (1952)

Director: Phil Karlson. **Screenplay**: Ted Sherdeman, Eugene Ling, and James Poe from the novel *The Dark Page* by Samuel Fuller. **Producer**: Edward Small. **Director of Photography**: Burnett Guffey. **Music**: George Duning. **Art Director**: Robert Peterson. **Editor**: Jerome Thoms. **Cast**: John Derek (Steve McCleary), Donna Reed (Julie Allison), Broderick Crawford (Mark Chapman), Rosemary DeCamp (Charlotte Grant), Henry O'Neill (Charlie Barnes), Henry Morgan (Biddle), James Millican (Lt. Davis). **Completed**: May 18, 1951. **Released**: Columbia, January 16. 82 minutes.

Mark Chapman becomes editor of an almost defunct newspaper, the *New York Express,* and successfully increases its circulation by a series of brash stunts. Steve McCleary is Chapman's protégé, and in love with feature writer Julie Allison, who objects to Chapman's unethical tactics. Chapman organizes a Lonely Hearts Club and sponsors a huge ball to publicize the paper. But Charlotte Grant, his poverty-stricken wife whom Chapman deserted years ago, appears at the ball and later, at her apartment, threatens to expose her ruthless husband. Chapman is furious and strikes her down, killing her. He places her in her bathtub and tries to make it appear that she drowned. Escaping unseen, Chapman removes all traces of her identity. Concussion is determined as the cause of Charlotte's death and McCleary investigates the murder for the newspaper. He finds a pawn ticket belonging to the dead woman, which is accidentally given to his friend, ex-reporter Charley Barnes. Redeeming the ticket, Barnes discovers a photograph of Charlotte with Mark Chapman, who kills him before he can inform McCleary. But Julie and McCleary track down the judge who married Charlotte and Chapman, and he identifies the victim's husband. Mark threatens the group with a gun, but the police arrive and kill him. Disillusioned and sorrowful, Steve writes Chapman's front page obituary.

The real presence behind *Scandal Sheet* is Samuel Fuller. Based on his award-winning novel *The Dark Page*, the screenplay explores the noir world of yellow journalism. Drawn from Fuller's experience in the newspaper world, the film deals with the transformation of a respectable, conservative newspaper into a sensationalist tabloid—all accomplished by the heavy hand of Mark Chapman. As played by Broderick Crawford, Chapman is a bullish, overbearing editor who employs every technique from browbeating "stuffed shirt" stockholders to sensationalizing the news in order to make his periodical "number one." The carefully established surrogate father-son relationship between Chapman and McCleary is the central irony of this film. Chapman has so effectively imparted his brand of

Scandal Sheet: *Mark Chapman (Broderick Crawford) and Steve McCleary (John Derek).*

journalistic skill to McCleary that the protégé becomes the instrument of Chapman's own undoing. Because the "father" murdered in a moment of rashness, the "son" becomes the avenger reporter and the story takes a classical turn. The elder newspaperman can only watch with fear and trepidation as the machinery he has created is manipulated by McCleary and turned against him. As his tragic flaws are finally revealed to his protégé and to the world, it is obvious that Chapman has, in many ways, engineered his own downfall. **JU**

THE SCARF (1951)

Director: E.A. Dupont. **Screenplay**: E.A. Dupont based on a story by I.G. Goldsmith and E.A. Rolfe. **Producer**: I.G. Goldsmith. **Director of Photography**: Franz (Frank) Planer. **Music**: Herschel Burke Gilbert. **Art Director**: Rudolph Sternad. **Editor**: Joseph Gluck. **Cast**: John Ireland (John Barrington), Mercedes McCambridge (Connie Carter), James Barton (Ezra Thompson), Emlyn Williams (Dr. David Dunbar), Lloyd Gough (Dr. Gordon), Basil Ruysdael (Cyrus Barrington), Harry Shannon (Warden Anderson), David Wolfe (Level Louie), Celia Lovsky (Mrs. Barrington). **Released**: United Artists, April 6. 93 minutes.

John Barrington escapes from an asylum for the criminally insane and finds refuge on the ranch of turkey-raiser Ezra Thompson. Barrington, who has suffered from amnesia, finds his memory returning slightly and he sets out on his mission of learning the truth about whether or not he really murdered his sweetheart and is actually insane. He goes to Los Angeles to visit his friend, psychiatrist David Dunbar, who was a witness to Barrington's crime. Dunbar repeats his story to Barrington, convinces Barrington that he did commit the crime, and then betrays him to the police. However,

Thompson, and romantic interest Connie Carter, are not totally convinced of Barrington's guilt and aid him in exonerating himself and finding the true murderer—Dunbar.

Two years after appearing in *All The King's Men*, John Ireland and Mercedes McCambridge reunite in *The Scarf*. Talented actors both, neither of them would enjoy, in number or in quality, movie roles commensurate with their gifts. A obscure find today, *The Scarf* could hardly have been much less so in 1951; under the "Gloria Productions" imprint, it was directed by German Expressionist director E.A. Dupont (*Variety*) who had fallen on hard times.

But while not every emigrant from middle Europe was a Fritz Lang or Robert Siodmak or Billy Wilder, most had tradition behind them and a touch of inspiration, like John Brahm and Edgar G. Ulmer—and Dupont. Though *The Scarf* starts off dead slow—a long, quasi-philosophical dialogue between the turkey-ranching hermit Thompson in the California desert and an escapee from an asylum for the criminally insane who has sought refuge with him, the protagonist Barrington (Ireland)—soon enough the movie picks up its pace and shows flashes of originality and style. The cinematography is by Franz Planer, another refugee steeped in Expressionism who had behind and ahead of him several noirs.

Not coincidentally, the quickened pace comes with McCambridge's arrival, as a singing bar waitress who hitches a ride with Ireland. With her distinctive organ-pipe voice and her instinct for biting off her lines clean, she brings both quirkiness and force to this standard role (tough gal, good heart). Though some of her best known roles showed noir influences (*All The King's Men, Johnny Guitar*) she only appeared in a few noirs. The cycle is poorer for her rarity.

The Scarf's plot, alas, falls under the rubric "far-fetched." It involves Ireland's not quite remembering the crime for which he was committed—strangling a girl with her scarf— and a sinister psychologist, Dunbar (Emlyn Williams), somehow in the employ of Ireland's powerful father. Dupont can't do much with the bulk of it (who could?), but along the way sneaks in some arresting sequences. The best occurs when McCambridge has been ordered to leave town on the 11 P.M. bus for Los Angeles; as she vacillates, looking down the dark road at the sign reading "sheriff's station," it turns into a lure for her to sell out Ireland for the reward on his head, with "$5000" spelled out in beckoning neon. **BMV**

SCARLET STREET (1945)

Director/Producer: Fritz Lang. **Screenplay**: Dudley Nichols from the novel and play *La Chienne* by Georges de la Fouchardiere in collaboration with Mouezy-Eon. **Executive Producer**: Walter Wanger. **Director of Photography**: Milton Krasner. **Music Score**: Hans J. Salter. **Art Director**: Alexander Golitzen. **Paintings**: John Decker. **Editor**: Arthur Hilton. **Cast**: Edward G. Robinson (Christopher Cross), Joan Bennett (Kitty March), Dan Duryea (Johnny Prince), Jess Barker (Janeway), Margaret Lindsay (Millie), Rosalind Ivan (Adele), Samuel S. Hinds (Charles Pringle), Arthur Loft (Dellarowe), Vladimir Sokoloff (Pop Lejon), Charles Kemper (Patcheye). **Completed**: October 8, 1945. **Released**: Universal, December 28. 102 minutes

Christopher Cross is a lonely man tied to a shrewish wife and a dreary cashier's job. All that sustains him is his hobby, painting. When he meets Kitty March, he becomes infatuated

Scarlet Street: *Kitty March (Joan Bennett) and Johnny Prince (Dan Duryea).*

and she encourages his attentions, believing that he is wealthy. Egged on by her con man lover, Johnny Prince, Kitty persuades Chris to establish her in a lavish apartment where he can paint her portrait. Although he must embezzle company funds to pay for Kitty's luxuries, Chris is happy for the first time in his life. Johnny then passes Kitty off as the painter of Chris' canvases, which enjoy sudden critical acclaim. Chris discovers the deception; but Kitty charms him and he forgives her. His wife's first husband is discovered still alive, and Chris runs to tell Kitty that they can marry. But he discovers her in the arms of Johnny and realizes he has been manipulated. When Johnny leaves, Chris stabs Kitty to death and then escapes. Johnny is convicted of her murder and executed. Meanwhile, Chris loses his job when his embezzlement is discovered. Unable to go to the police and unable to paint because his name has been usurped, he suffers a mental breakdown and is haunted by the taunting voices of Kitty and Johnny.

In typical Fritz Lang fashion, *Scarlet Street* is a bleak film in which a common man, under the influence of the corrupting forces of evil, succumbs first to vice and then to murder. Kitty March and Johnny Prince are certainly two of film noir's most casual villains, amoral and reeking of a heady kind of sin. Kitty is the ultimate sex object wrapped in her see-through plastic raincoat like a bonbon in cellophane, ready and waiting for consumption. Johnny is strutting and sexy with his butterscotch-slick hair and straw boater, drawling an insinuating, "Hello, Lazy Legs" to a reclining Kitty. Unsympathetic as these two are, Lang cynically invests them with an irresistible allure and an energy that makes Christopher Cross's fall seem not only believable but inevitable. Additionally, Cross has an incredibly dreary job and an unremittingly shrewish wife who verges on caricature. Nothing could be more pathetic than his testimonial dinner, a brilliant set piece that opens the film. But Fritz Lang seems to imply that this is all that Chris could hope for and when he desperately reaches for the scented warmth and understanding that he thinks Kitty represents, he is doomed.

Christopher Cross' disintegration relies heavily on Milton Krasner's dramatic cinematography to convey precise psychological states. The stark white light of passion illuminates the luxurious boudoir in which Chris murders Kitty by stabbing at her ice-cold heart with the most appropriate of weapons, an ice pick. This white-hot light reveals a look of furious lust on his face as he finally penetrates her long-withheld body. As the shadows encroach on Chris' mind, they also creep into the film's frame; their shapes and origins are strange and unexplained. At the film's end, with his sensibility clouded and his life in ashes, Chris moves through a vague, befogged landscape devoid of significant detail or meaning. Christopher Cross is an artist who is undeniably talented but pathetically weak and vulnerable, a patsy in the hands of those who would use him for their own mercenary ends. There is some pity in Lang's noir vision of this character, but a touch of contempt as well. *Scarlet Street* conveys the attitude that those who live by the imagination can become helpless victims in a cruelly realistic world. **JK**

SCENE OF THE CRIME (1949)

Director: Roy Rowland. **Screenplay**: Charles Schnee from the short story "Smashing The Bookie Gang Marauders" by John Bartlow Martin. **Producer**: Harry Rapf. **Director of Photography**: Paul C. Vogel. **Music**: André Previn. **Art Directors**: Cedric Gibbons, Leonid Vasian. **Editor**: Robert J. Kern. **Cast**: Van Johnson (Det. Mike Conovan), Gloria De Haven (Lili), Tom Drake (Det. C. C. Gordon), Arlene Dahl (Gloria Conovan), Leon Ames (Capt. Forster), John McIntire (Det. Fred Piper), Norman Lloyd (Sleeper), Donald Woods (Bob Herkimer), Richard Benedict (Turk Kingby), Anthony Caruso (Tony Rutzo). **Completed**: March 12, 1949. **Released**: MGM, July 28. 94 minutes.

When Officer Monigan is killed and $1,000 is discovered on his person, it appears he was protecting bookie joints. Monigan's son blames Mike Conovan for his father's death because Mike had recently dropped Monigan and taken on a new partner, young C. C. Gordon. Mike wants to clear Monigan's name, but the only clues are that the murderer was reported to have a mottled face and a twisted hand. Mike decides to locate the two men suspected of robbing the bookie joints, Turk and Lafe. He persuades Lili, a stripper and Turk's ex-mistress, to cooperate with him. They find Lafe in a run-down hotel asleep, with the radio playing. While Mike searches the room, Lafe awakens, and after a vicious fight Mike subdues him. As Lafe is taken to headquarters, shots ring out. Lafe is killed and Mike lies wounded. The murder weapon is found and traced to a man with a twisted hand. Mike's young wife, Gloria, is frightened because of his injury and urges him to take a better job. Frustrated over the Monigan case and worried about his marriage, Mike quits the force. Meanwhile, Lili leaves a tip for Mike to meet with an informant, but an older officer, Fred Piper, takes Mike's place and is killed. Realizing Lili has been helping Turk, Mike returns to the force despite his wife's threat to leave him. The police are tipped to a robbery and discover the crooks are led by Turk in an armored car. Mike commandeers a truck and rams the robbers' car, which bursts into flames. A dying Turk confesses to the mur-

ders and to the deformed disguise. Gloria reconsiders and remains with Mike.

It seems a bit incongruous to have an actor like Van Johnson in a film noir, although this sort of anomaly was typical of the short-lived noir series produced at MGM during the Dore Schary years. And yet MGM provided a smooth transition from the 1930s gangland films to the film noir with its "Crime Does Not Pay" series of shorts and such mysteries as *Kid Glove Killer, Grand Central Murder,* and *Rage in Heaven. Scene of the Crime* contains several elements that are brutally naturalistic, from McIntire's portrayal of the martyred policeman Fred Piper to the savage fight sequence between Lafe and Mike, and, finally, Turk's dying epithet to this faithful moll Lili: "I hate a tramp . . . ya always gotta tell 'em, 'I love you, baby,' . . . a waste of time."

Like his later *Rogue Cop,* Rowland's *Scene of the Crime* exploits the traditional noir locales (in this case LA) through Paul Vogel's stylish photography of the dark streets and the back rooms of old warehouses that are so uncharacteristic of the MGM look. Moreover, Rowland exploits the conventional personae of such actors as Johnson and McIntire to partially play against type and extend his naturalistic treatment to the police force. Gordon, the brash rookie, and Piper, the resigned veteran, contrast with Conovan's laconic competence; and yet Conovan is duped by Lili, even as he feels guilty for exploiting her. Conovan's awareness of the monolithic nature of crime—underscored by the early sequence in which he is allowed to witness the syndicate policing itself—compounds his disillusionment with his "career goals" and causes him to acquiesce to his wife's pressure and to accept a job from her former suitor. The violent climax, like that of *Rogue Cop,* is a spiritual catharsis but only a partial re-affirmation of Conovan's sense of his own ability, which must be permanently overshadowed by his failure with Lili and his temporary withdrawal from the police force. **BP & AS**

SCREAMING MIMI (1958)

Director: Gerd Oswald. **Screenplay**: Robert Blees from the novel by Fredric Brown. **Producer**: Harry Joe Brown and Robert Fellows. **Director of Photography**: Burnett Guffey. **Music**: Mischa Bakaleinikoff. **Art Director**: Carey Odell. **Editor**: Gene Havlick. **Cast**: Anita Ekberg (Virginia Wilson/Yolanda Lange), Philip Carey (Bill Sweeney), Gypsy Rose Lee (Joann), Harry Townes (Dr. Greenwood/Mr. Green), Linda Cherney (Ketti), Romney Brent (Charlie Weston), Alan Gifford (Capt. Bline), Oliver McGowan (Walter Krieg), Red Norvo Trio (Themselves). **Released**: Columbia, August 8. 79 minutes.

Virginia Wilson, an exotic dancer, is visiting with her artist stepbrother at his beachside house. While showering at an outdoor facility she is attacked by an escapee from a nearby mental institution wielding a knife. The incident has so disturbed Virginia that she is soon institutionalized. There she is treated by Dr. Greenwood, a Svengali-like psychologist who develops a morbid attachment to her. Securing her release, he adopts the identify of Mr. Green, her "manager," and gets her a job at a nightclub, "El Madhouse,"as an exotic dancer named Yolanda Lange. There she meets night-beat reporter Bill Sweeney, a friend of the club's owner, Joann. He becomes fascinated with her but is fended off by her possessive manager Green. When Sweeney discovers Yolanda wounded on the streets one night, an apparent victim of a local serial killer nicknamed "the Ripper," he recalls that one of the Ripper's previous victims, another dancer named Lola Lane, had a grotesque statue of a naked screaming woman called "the Screaming Mimi" in her possession at the time of her death. Since he had previously seen a duplicate statue in Yolanda's dressing room, Sweeney believes that Yolanda's possession of the statue had marked her for death and that only the presence of her perennial companion, a vicious Great Dane named Devil, had saved her from the Ripper. Sweeney traces the source of the statues to Charlie Wilson, who confesses that he created them as a means of exorcising the memory of his sister, Virginia. After confronting Yolanda/Virginia with the facts, Sweeney gets her to acknowledge her love for him and agree to reject Greenwood in favor of him. But Greenwood confronts her in her apartment as she is preparing to depart and, in an attempt to reassert his control, threatens to destroy her statue, claiming it is a fetish linked to her mental instability. At this point he is attacked by Devil and falls through the window to the street two floors below. Before dying, Greenwood confesses to the police and Sweeney that he is the killer and that the statue was indeed a fetish. When Virginia disappears shortly after this incident, Sweeney traces her and her dog to a cheap hotel. Observing her disturbed mental state, Sweeney begins to realize that the statue is a fetish for Virginia, not Greenwood, and that she herself is the killer.

Screaming Mimi is really a transitional film between the noir cycle and the more violent and sensationalistic films of the 1960s and 1970s—films which were often filled with as much psycho-babble and perversities as this one (the sado-masochistic implications of Anita Ekberg's bondage dance can hardly be denied). In any case, they would be given a degree of respectability in 1960 with the release of Hitchcock's *Psycho* (the attack on Yolanda in the shower by a knife-wielding maniac predates the more famous scene in Hitchcock's classic) and Michael Powell's *Peeping Tom*.

Directed by Gerd Oswald (*A Kiss Before Dying*, *Crime of Passion*, etc.) who learned his Expressionistic licks at the knees of his father, the prestigious German director Richard Oswald (*Alraune*,1930, the tale of another traumatized blonde femme fatale, is clearly a source for this film), the film is part of a three-film collaboration with actress Anita Ekberg (the brutal sadistic and noirish Western *Valerie*—1957—and the comedy *Paris Holiday*—1958—were the other two) which changed her image from a stereotypical 1950s Hollywood blonde bombshell (a la Monroe and Mansfield) to a femme fatale and in the process brought her to the attention of Italian director Federico Fellini.

In many ways *Screaming Mimi*, like *Valerie*, is a meditation on the ambiguities of the femme fatale as epitomized by Ekberg. The traumatized, murderous, and sexually irresistible Virginia/Yolanda sleepwalks through the movie like the somnambulist Cesar in the German Expressionistic classic *The Cabinet of Dr. Caligari*—1920. She is a femme fatale without even trying, a semi-conscious Gilda. Dr. Greenwood, her psychiatrist, is mesmerized the minute he sees her, peeping in on her at night through the window of her hospital room, even taking her to his house to see her perform one of the two blatantly erotic dances in the movie (the other is the bondage number in the club). Violating his ethics and tossing away his career, he takes on the menial job of her manager when she becomes an exotic dancer. The reporter Sweeney is her second "victim," who becomes emotionally enmeshed when he gazes at her performing at the club and then visits her in her dressing room, dropping his tough guy façade as she displays her legs, almost unconsciously, to him. The final and most perverse obsessive male is Virginia/Yolanda's stepbrother, who kills the man who attacks Yolanda in the shower and then obsessively works on statues of her nude and screaming (the "Screaming Mimi" sculptures of the title), hinting at his quasi-incestuous desire for her. All three men revolve around the semi-catatonic Mimi, trying alternately to save her and control her. But like the chains she breaks during her performance onstage, Virginia/Yolanda is an uncontrollable force. She leaves Greenwood dead on the sidewalk, her stepbrother in despair as he destroys one of his "Screaming Mimi" statues, and Sweeney distraught as he watches his lover being transported back to the mental hospital. **JU**

SECOND CHANCE (1953)

Director: Rudolph Maté. **Screenplay**: Sydney Boehm, D.M. Marshman Jr., Oscar Millard, Robert Presnell Sr. **Producer**: Sam Wiesenthal, Howard Hughes (uncredited). **Executive Producer**: Edmund Grainger. **Director of Photography**: William E. Snyder. **Music**: Roy Webb. **Art Directors**: Carroll Clark, Albert S. D'Agostino. **Editors**: Robert Ford, Albrecht Joseph. **Cast**: Robert Mitchum (Russ Lambert), Linda Darnell (Clare Sheppard, alias Clare Sinclair), Jack Palance (Cappy Gordon), Roy Roberts (Charley Malloy), Dan Seymour (Felipe), Fortunio Bonanova (Mandy, hotel owner), Sandro Giglio (Cable Car Conductor), Reginald Sheffield (Mr. Woburn, English tourist). **Locations**: Cuernavaca, Morelos, Mexico, Taxco, Guerrero, Mexico. **Released**: RKO, July 18. 82 minutes.

Clare was once the girlfriend of a gangster, Vic Spoleto. Now she is willing to turn state's evidence against him before a Senate "Crime Commission." To prevent her from testifying, Vic has sent Cappy to find her and kill her. Clare flees to a Mexican village, where she meets Russ, a prize-fighter who is trying to revive his career. Russ and Clare take an aerial cable car up to the peak of a mountain. They arrive at night as strangers; by the next morning they are lovers. But Cappy is there, too. The three of them and other passengers are on the return ride when a cable snaps. The car's stuck, and the remaining cable is going to break soon. Russ manages to jump to a nearby cliff and climb up to the tram station. He comes back to the rescue in a small freight car. Cappy tries to hijack the freight car for just Clare and him. Russ fights Cappy on top of the cable car and knocks him off it. Russ, Clare and the other passengers get away in the small car just before the cable car follows Cappy in a free-fall down to earth.

In the 1950s a new kind woman-in-distress appears in film noir. Her life's endangered because she can testify against a mobster. The historical context was the Special Committee on Organized Crime in Interstate Commerce, known as the Kefauver Committee, after its original chair, Tennessee Democratic Senator Estes Kefauver. The hearings lasted from May 1950 until September 1951. Although they weren't the first to be televised, they were the first to have a large TV audience. Other film noirs, which are about exposés of racketeering and crack-downs on crime syndicates, are also drawn from the repercussions of the Kefauver Committee. In *The Enforcer* and *The Narrow Margin*, for example, the woman-in-distress is a target of assassination to keep her off the witness stand.

Second Chance goes against the grain because the hit man, Cappy, is madly in love with Clare. He promises not to kill her or Russ if she runs away with him. On top of the mountain, she agrees so that she can save Russ. But the bargain is nothing more than a different kind of contract on her life. In a scene without speech or voice-over, Clare is by herself on the platform of a cable car station. Apparently, she decides living with Cappy would be a fate worse than death. She opens a gate on the platform. She is about to step out into the abyss when Cappy suddenly appears, thwarting her suicide. However, unlike other woman-in-distress films, Clare isn't the most noir character. Instead, it's Cappy.

At the beginning of the film, Cappy talks with Edward, someone else Vic wants shot. Edward has recently seen Clare in the village where she is hiding. Cappy asks him how she looked. Edward replies, "She's a pretty girl." Cappy explodes, "Any man who thinks she's just a pretty girl hasn't got eyes in his head." After Cappy tracks Clare down, he chases her through the village streets. When he catches up to her, she thinks he's going to kill her. But he holds her tightly and says, "Why didn't you come to me when you ran away from Vic? You never even knew I was around. Vic Spoleto's bodyguard. Vic's stooge. That's all I ever meant to you!" Clare's appalled. The plot in *Second Chance* might be stronger if the tension between Cappy and Clare played out more. The cable car crisis is no substitute for the lack of suspense within the romantic triangle. Perhaps the noir style might be in the film if it hadn't been released in 3-D and color. In any event, there's neither expressionist camerawork nor chiaroscuro, which are in other color film noirs. **DMH**

THE SECOND WOMAN (1950)

Director: James V. Kern. **Screenplay/Producers**: Mort Briskin, Robert Smith. **Executive Producer**: Harry Popkin. **Director of Photography**: Hal Mohr. **Music**: Joseph Nussbaum and Nat W. Finston based on themes by Tchaikovsky. **Art Director**: Boris Leven. **Editor**: Walter Thompson. **Cast**: Robert Young (Jeff Cohalan), Betsy Drake (Ellen Foster), John Sutton (Keith Ferris), Florence Bates (Amelia Foster), Morris Carnovsky (Dr. Hartley), Henry O'Neill (Ben Sheppard), Jean Rogers (Dodo Ferris), Raymond Largay (Maj. Badger), Shirley Ballard (Vivian Sheppard), Vici Raaf (Secretary), John Galludet (Mac). **Location**: Monterey and Carmel, California. **Released**: United Artists, July 7. 91 minutes.

Jeff Cohalan, a guest at his neighbor Amelia Foster's house, attempts suicide by carbon monoxide poisoning. His problems are explained by his girlfriend, Ellen, beginning with their first meeting on a train a short time before. An established and talented architect, Jeff's main client is Ben Sheppard, a wealthy landowner whose family's holdings on the Monterey peninsula go back to the Spanish era. Jeff is designing homes for Pinecliff, an exclusive development on a portion of Ben's property. Ben has been a father-figure to Jeff who had been engaged to Ben's daughter, Vivian. Unfortunately, Vivian was killed in an automobile accident on the eve of their wedding with Jeff ostensibly at the wheel. Now for the past year he has been suffering bouts of depression and his behavior appears increasingly erratic. His faith in himself is shaken when he becomes the subject of a series of accidents. Since Jeff lives alone in a beautiful "house with wings" that he designed for his future bride, all indications are that he himself is the source of the mishaps. When this house mysteriously burns down, Jeff moves in temporarily with Ellen and her aunt in Amelia's large mansion. At this point Jeff's friend, Dr. Hartley, warns Ellen against allowing Jeff to stay since he believes Jeff is suffering from "paranoia" and that Jeff caused the accidents to placate his guilt over Vivian's death. Ellen, however, refuses to lose faith in Jeff and pursues a series of clues, ultimately discovering that Keith Ferris, another of Sheppard's employees, resents Jeff because Keith and Vivian were lovers and were running off together when the fatal car accident occurred. Jeff then admits that he was following them and when he discovered Vivian dead took the blame for the accident to cover up the scandal. Believing Jeff responsible, Ben then avenged his daughter's death by having his minions create the series of "accidents." Confronted with the true story, Ben loses control

The Second Woman: *Ellen Foster (Betsy Drake), Jeff Cohalan (Robert Young), and Ben Sheppard (Henry O'Neill).*

and threatens Jeff and Ellen with a gun. Dr. Hartley takes Ben to a hospital, explaining that he may eventually recover from the shock of the truth behind Vivian's death and his subsequent psychosis.

It would appear that the driving force behind this film was producer Harry M. Popkin, whose previous low-budget thrillers had included *Impact* and *D.O.A.* With *The Second Woman* and such subsequent films as *The Well* and *The Thief*, Popkin strove for a greater degree of respectability than was afforded him by his past "potboilers." From today's perspective it is ironic that it is *D.O.A.* and not the others that will remain a classic of the noir cycle. As in so many noir films, the majority of this film's action is presented as *temps perdu* with Betsy Drake's voice-over as Ellen. In this case, however, the narration is not laden with existential angst or some sense of loss, but much more in the style of the "had I but known" school of mystery fiction. Hal Mohr's photography (especially the low-key exteriors) keeps this film visually exciting despite Robert Young's subdued performance as the impotent architect. Of course, Jeff Cohalan is no Ayn Rand character like Howard Roark (if he were the might have tried to stop the devastation of the Monterey landscape by developers) and as a result *The Second Woman* makes no broad statements about creative genius and tyranny as does *The Fountainhead*. **BP**

SECRET BEYOND THE DOOR (1948)

Director: Fritz Lang. **Screenplay**: Silvia Richards from a story by Rufus King. **Producer**: Fritz Lang (Diana Production Company). **Executive Producer**: Walter Wanger. **Director of Photography**: Stanley Cortez. **Production Designer**: Max Parker. **Music**: Miklós Rózsa. **Editor**: Arthur Hilton. **Cast**: Joan Bennett (Celia Lamphere), Michael Redgrave (Mark Lamphere), Anne Revere (Caroline Lamphere), Barbara O'Neil (Miss Robey), Natalie Schafer (Edith Potter), Mark Dennis (David). **Released**: Universal Pictures, January 1. 99 minutes.

Celia encounters architect Mark during a Mexican holiday; he stirs her hitherto hidden passions. However, hurtling into marriage, Celia wonders who this "stranger" really is. After their honeymoon, he begins to act oddly, disappearing for days on end before calling her to join him in Levender Falls near New York. She learns disquieting facts: Mark has a teenage son, David, and his first wife died in mysterious circumstances. She meets Robey, Mark's disfigured secretary, who harbors intense feelings for him. Celia considers leaving Mark, but decides to stay. At a party, Mark takes guests through his meticulously constructed "felicitous rooms"—sites where men murdered women close to them—but leaves one room closed. Celia makes a copy of the room's key; inside, she discovers a room seemingly destined for her. Mark has a dream in which he is both prosecutor and accused; his crime is to have caused his wife's death through his coldness. Celia waits in the secret room; confronting Mark's murderous desire, she releases his traumatic childhood memories. Robey sets fire to the house, and Mark saves Celia. They are happily reunited as a couple, Mark declaring that he is on the path to recovery.

Fritz Lang was not shy in avowing that *Secret Beyond the Door* was conceived and elaborated in response to Hitchcock's successes of the 1940s: aspects of *Rebecca* (a female Gothic romance set in an imposing mansion), *Spellbound* (a man's murderous psychic trauma that must be relived in order to be cured), and also of *Notorious* and the more strictly noir *Shadow of a Doubt* (the woman as a masochistic slave to love, a potential-victim-turned-amateur-detective) are fully evident. Yet, however derivative it may seem at the outset, the film is pure Lang—right from the striking opening passage in Mexico, where Celia is transfixed by the sight and sound of ritual violence that defines the relations between local men and women. All of the drama's ambiguities are announced there: what is a man really, sensitive partner or rapacious beast? And what does a woman really want from him, life-long love or voluptuous death?

The film is also remarkable (particularly from the viewpoint of contemporary architectural philosophy) for its central conceit of Mark's elaborate reconstructions of rooms (a psychosexual complex suggested by Rufus King's original story). As Tom Gunning has suggested, the baroque interiors in Lang (rendered in Cortez's superb cinematography) are not discovered, by the characters and spectators, in the act of seeing and entering them (the Hitchcock way); rather, they pre-exist the characters, in an indomitable and often sinister fashion, like the markers of an eternal, inevitable fate (Preminger's *Whirlpool* offers a related vision). And, given Lang's own youthful connection to the architectural profession, the film also suggests (like *House by the River*) a rather perverse allegory of the artistic/creative process, inherently disturbed and fatal in its consequences.

Like Renoir's *The Woman on the Beach*, with which it shares key elements (including Bennett, and the mix of noir and melodrama), *Secret Beyond the Door* is a film that was, for a long time, dismissed as incoherent and incomplete because of extensive cuts forced on the production. And yet, as in the Renoir, this compression (however rued by Lang) actually ended up heightening the dreamlike atmosphere and logic of the piece (this dreamlike sense is reinforced by Rózsa's daring score that utilizes backwards tape playback). If *Secret Beyond the Door* is fragmented and piecemeal, that is because the identities and subjective experiences of its characters are internally contradictory, lurching from one extreme to another: love-hate, attraction-repulsion, sadism-masochism, passivity-aggression. This sense of fragmentation also adds to the spatial-architectural phantasmagoria of the project: the "felicitous rooms" add up not to a plausible, coherent house, but rather a discontinuous series of imaginary projections, which lodge like barnacles in the memory of the viewer. Finally, the film's special place in the evolution of Lang's career and sensibility should be noted, especially with regards to its upbeat ending: in the words of Jacques Lourcelles, "it is the final film in which the auteur allows his characters a margin—however slender—for happiness." **AM**

THE SECRET FURY (1950)

Director: Mel Ferrer. **Screenplay**: Lionel Houser from a story by Jack Leonard and James O'Hanlon. **Producer**: Jack H. Skirball. **Director of Photography**: Leo Tover. **Music**: Roy Webb. **Art Directors**: Carroll Clark, Albert S. D'Agostino. **Editor**: Harry Marker. **Cast**: Claudette Colbert (Ellen R. Ewing), Robert Ryan (David McLean), Jane Cowl (Aunt Clara Ewing), Paul Kelly (D.A. Eric Lowell), Philip Ober (Gregory Kent), Elisabeth Risdon (Dr. Twining), Doris Dudley (Pearl Collins), Dave Barbour (Lucian Randall), Vivian Vance (Leah), José Ferrer (José), Percy Helton (Justice of the Peace), Burt Kennedy (fisherman), Paul Picerni (Dr. Roth). **Released**: RKO, February 21. 85 minutes.

The marriage of Ellen Ewing and David McLean is interrupted by a man who claims that Ellen already has a husband named Lucian Randall. A telephone call to the town of Riverview confirms this. Ellen and David travel there and stay at a hotel where she is recognized by the staff, particularly a maid named Leah. At a local club, the couple meets Randall, who takes Ellen in a back room, where a shot rings out and he ends up lying dead at her feet. With Ellen is arrested and placed under psychiatric observation by district attorney Eric Lowell, David returns to the hotel to try and find the truth.

The Secret Fury, whose odd title holds a key to its final plot twist, puts a romantic suspense spin on the unknown double-life tale epitomized in Woolrich's *Black Curtain*. Director/actor Mel Ferrer elicits solid performances from his high-profile leads Claudette Colbert and Robert Ryan but cannot overcome an inconsistent and puzzling plot, so that in the end implausibility conquers suspension of disbelief, as it so often does in a noir manqué. The movie's unexpected

highlight is the portrayal of blowsy Leah by Vivian Vance who became Ethel Mertz on the "I Love Lucy" TV series. Before television fame, Vance had very few film roles and was mostly a Broadway performer. In *The Secret Fury*, as a chambermaid suborned to play a minor part in a nefarious scheme, she echoes other hapless supporting characters in noir like those often incarnated by Elisha Cook, Jr. Moments like her half-heartedly trying to wave away the smoke while she puffs a furtive cigarette in the hotel's linen-storage room become darkly ironic when she ultimately pays the supreme penalty for her large and small moral transgressions. **BMV**

THE SET-UP (1949)

Director: Robert Wise. **Screenplay**: Art Cohn from the poem by Joseph Moncure March. **Producer**: Richard Goldstone. **Director of Photography**: Milton Krasner. **Music**: Constantin Bakaleinikoff. **Art Directors**: Albert S. D'Agostino, Jack Okey. **Editor**: Roland Gross. **Cast**: Robert Ryan (Stoker Thompson), Audrey Totter (Julie), George Tobias (Tiny), Alan Baxter (Little Boy), Wallace Ford (Gus), Percy Helton (Red), Hal Fieberling (Tiger Nelson), Darryl Hickman (Shanley), Kenny O'Morrison (Moore), James Edwards (Luther Hawkins), David Clarke (Gunboat Johnson), Phillip Pine (Souza), Edwin Max (Danny). **Completed**: November 11, 1948. **Released**: RKO, March 29. 72 minutes.

While his wife Julie waits in a shabby hotel room, Stoker Thompson, a fighter past his prime, goes to fight the last bout on a night's card, which follows the main event. Although Stoker knows he is no longer at his best and has been losing most of his recent fights, he believes that he might defeat his younger opponent. But his manager, Tiny, has arranged with the opposition for him to lose and is so

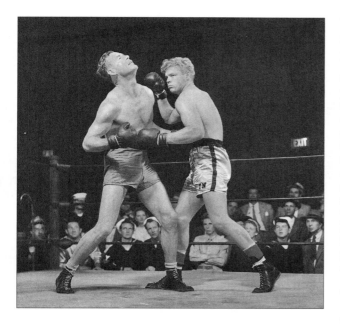

confident that Stoker will be beaten that he does not tell the fighter to "take a dive." In the early rounds, Stoker receives a lot of punishment. However, Stoker endures and gets the advantage of his less experienced opponent. Tiny finally tells him of the deal; but Stoker refuses to cooperate and, dismayed at being sold out by his manager, he goes on to win the fight. Afterward, the crooks who made the deal with Tiny give Stoker a vicious beating. With a broken hand but unbroken spirit, Stoker returns to Julie.

Drawing on his experience working for Orson Welles on *Citizen Kane* and *The Magnificent Ambersons* and his apprenticeship under Gothic horror producer Val Lewton, Robert Wise established his reputation as a director in 1948 and 1949 respectively with two film noirs: the Western *Blood on the Moon* and the boxing classic—*The Set-Up*. *The Set-Up* is a tight, moody film which plays out like an existential Greek tragedy. Following the Aristotelian unities of time (the film takes place in real time), place (the downtown of a small New York town), and action (tracing the events around the last fight of an over-the-hill boxer who refuses to compromise), it paints the portrait of a noble warrior (played with a combination of gentleness and strength by Robert Ryan) who cannot abandon his dream. Although Stoker's face registers scores of beatings and his faithful and loving wife Julie is threatening to leave him unless he quits, it is clear that he only finds meaning in his moments in the ring, no matter how violent and humiliating. Even in the final scenes of the movies when he is brutally beaten by Little Boy's thugs for refusing to throw the fight and his hand is mashed beyond repair, he can only bemoan the fact that he will no longer be able to box. Lying in his wife's arms with the neon from a dance hall called "Dreamland" flashing ironically behind him, all Stoker can see is that the meaning has been drained from his pathetic existence.

The Set-Up also acts as one of the most hard-hitting critiques of professional boxing. Stoker's final fight which occupies the last third of the film is as graphic as anything seen since, including Martin Scorsese's masterpiece *Raging Bull*. Wise does not hold his punches when drawing parallels between Roman gladiator matches and modern-day boxing matches. These modern gladiators wait for their time in cramped, dirty locker rooms where fighter after fighter is brought back, either victorious or on their backs. During the fight itself Wise cuts back and forth between the fighters pounding away at each other (Robert Ryan's background as a boxer adds even more realism to these scenes) and the sadistic and bloodthirsty audience instigating them: a blind man with a sighted interpreter delights in the closing of Stoker's eye by his opponent; a sexually stimulated middle-aged woman calls for more blood; a fat man stuffs his face excitedly with food and drinks as he watches in delight; an anonymous face yells out repeatedly "Kill him." Wise and his screenwriter reaffirm this critique of boxing in the resolution when Julie cradles her husband in her arms. When she learns that his hand has been destroyed and he will never fight again, she can barely hide her joy (her reaction is the polar opposite of her husband) as she turns towards the camera and declares: "We both won tonight." **JU**

711 OCEAN DRIVE (1950)

Director: Joseph M. Newman. **Screenplay**: Richard English and Francis Swan. **Producer**: Frank N. Seltzer. **Director of Photography**: Franz F. Planer. **Music**: Sol Kaplan. **Art Director**: Perry Ferguson. **Editor**: Bert Jordan. **Cast**: Edmond O'Brien (Mal Granger), Joanne Dru (Gail Mason), Donald Porter (Larry Mason), Sammy White (Chippie Evans), Dorothy Patrick (Trudy Maxwell), Barry Kelley (Vince Walters), Otto Kruger (Carl Stephans), Howard St. John (Lt. Pete Wright), Robert Osterloh (Gizzi), Bert Freed (Marshak), Carl Milletaire (Joe Gish). **Location**: Palm Springs, California; Lake Mead and Hoover Dam, Nevada. **Released**: Columbia, July 1. 102 minutes.

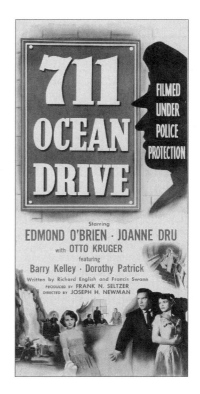

Mal Granger is a hard-working and ingenious telephone repair-man. One day he makes a repair call to a bookie joint, run by two distinguished-looking businessmen, Larry Mason and Vince Walters. Impressed with Mal's technical acumen, they persuade him to engineer a telephone wire service connecting the racing results of all the West Coast tracks. Mal is success-ful and desirous of money and power so when Walters is killed by a disgruntled bookie Mal uses his skills to replace him. Eventually Mal has Mason killed so that he can take over his position in the operation and with Mason's wife, Gail, as well. When the hit man tries to blackmail Mal he runs him over which puts police Lt. Wright on his trail. Mal is forced to join the national syndicate, headed by Carl Stephens, for protection, but when they begin to siphon off the largest share of the prof-its Mal, in turn, steals from them. With both the police and the mob boys after him, Mal is forced to flee to Las Vegas with Gail. Trapped near Hoover Dam, he attempts to escape by crossing the dam on foot but is shot and falls to his death below.

In *711 Ocean Drive* Edmond O'Brien assumes a role quite similar to that of the skilled master of technology he played in *White Heat*. In this case, however, he switches to the other side of the law. Granger's rapid rise to success makes him a variation of the Horatio Alger hero but the perverse path his drive takes him leads to his defeat. His death at the base of Hoover Dam, a major source of electricity, is ironically appropriate given his genius in electronics. Unlike the situa-tion in *Force of Evil*, however, the syndicate is not wiped out after his death. At the film's disquieting conclusion, Carl Stephens (well underplayed by the suave Otto Kruger) returns home to Ohio, quietly but firmly in control. Nor does the film's moralistic narration (hallmark of the semi-docu-mentary) do much to allay our fears. **BP**

SHADOW OF A DOUBT (1943)

Director: Alfred Hitchcock. **Screenplay**: Thornton Wilder, Sally Benson, and Alma Reville from a story by Gordon McDonell. **Producer**: Jack H. Skirball. **Director of Photography**: Joseph Valentine. **Music**: Dimitri Tiomkin. **Art Director**: John B. Goodman, Robert Boyle. **Editor**: Milton Carruth. **Cast**: Teresa Wright (Young Charlie), Joseph Cotten (Uncle Charlie Oakley), Macdonald Carey (Jack Graham), Henry Travers (Joseph Newton), Patricia Collinge (Emma Newton), Hume Cronyn (Herbie Hawkins), Edna Mae Wonacott (Ann Newton), Wallace Ford (Fred Saunders), Irving Bacon (Station Master), Charles Bates (Roger Newton). **Completed**: October 28, 1942. **Released**: Universal, January 12. 108 minutes.

The mysterious but charming Charlie Oakley arrives in Santa Rosa ostensibly to visit his family, but he actually is eluding two investigators. He is welcomed by his adoring niece and namesake, Charlie. However, she gradually sus-pects that her beloved uncle may be wanted by the police for the murder of several wealthy widows. Her suspicions are shared by detective Jack Graham, who meets the family by pretending to be a pollster. At the same time, another sus-pect in the case is accidentally killed and the inquiry is offi-cially closed. But Uncle Charlie becomes aware of his niece's suspicions and decides to kill her. After two unsuc-cessful attempts, he tries to push her off a train into the path of an oncoming engine. In the ensuing scuffle, he falls off and is killed. At his funeral, Uncle Charlie is honored by the townspeople, while the secret knowledge of his guilt draws his niece and the detective together.

Like many of Hitchcock's films, *Shadow of a Doubt* focuses on the character of a psychopath. Charlie's evil is defined ini-tially through contrasts with the normal behavior of his rela-tives in the small California town. His violent verbal outbursts against mankind in general—"Do you know the world is a foul sty? Do you know if you ripped the fronts off houses you'd find swine?"—and the women he has murdered in particular—"Useless women, drinking the money, eating the money, smelling of money"—shatter his niece's security and illusions about life. Hitchcock makes his points about Charlie's charac-ter with a variety of effects; the most celebrated and cinemat-ic is the ominous cloud of black smoke that hangs over the train station as Charlie arrives in Santa Rosa, giving the impression, as François Truffaut remarks, that "the devil was coming to town." Charlie is very like a devil, self-endowed with all the power of a fallen god, passing judgment on the world. He is a killer with a mission, bent on the destruction of what he sees as ugly, his crazed eye fixed on a vision of a lost time when, as he tells his beloved niece, "Everybody was sweet and pretty, the whole world—not like today."

After reading a newspaper article, Gordon McDonell based his original story on a real 1938 incident—about a man from New York who visits family in the small town of Hanford, California and is arrested for murdering a number of affluent females on the east coast—and sold Hitchcock on a six-page idea. McDonell's story "Uncle Charlie" initially called for a "John Garfield type" and "Fontaine type," a less sophisticated killer and more sophisticated "young" girl. Wanting a different spin of the characters and impressed with the classic play about small town life, *Our Town*, Hitchcock hired famed playwright Thornton Wilder to write the screenplay. Shot from early August to November 1942, *Shadow of a Doubt* was written and pro-duced at the height of World War II amid myriad wartime lim-itations, and Hitchcock—known for his huge sets—actually left Hollywood to film on location in Santa Rosa, CA and Newark, NJ to avoid production constraints such as government-man-dated set restrictions, rationing and Los Angeles blackouts; the director also reportedly rode a train to Florida with Wilder to fin-ish the script after the writer joined the Army's psychological warfare unit (writers Benson and Hitchcock's wife, Reville, col-laborated on dialog). After producing *Saboteur*, Skirball signed a one-picture deal with Universal to make the film with Hitchcock directing. *Shadow of a Doubt* is a variation of the female gothic thriller, a noir prelude where a small town family member ends up being a serial-killing criminal city slicker who brings murder to Main Street, USA.

It is just off this prototypical Main Street, that Charlie makes most of the declarations of his strange philosophy to his niece, who is, quite literally, his better half. The bond between them is telepathic: they share the same name and the same thoughts. She tells him, "We're sort of like twins;" and he tells her, "The same blood runs in our veins." The crucial difference between them is that of right and wrong. But Hitchcock is not content with such a neat, black-and-white schematization. The title, *Shadow of a Doubt*, refers not only to young Charlie's suspicions about her uncle, but also to the shadows that impinge upon her goodness. The will to destroy is the motivat-ing force of Uncle Charlie's life; shockingly it turns out that this is yet another thing that young Charlie shares with him, if

Shadow of a Doubt: *Joseph Cotten as Charlie Oakley.*

only momentarily, by accident and by necessity. For in the end, Uncle Charlie is brought down by his better half and young Charlie is driven to destroy the thing she loves.

Although it does involve crime and murder, Hitchcock's gothic suspense thriller is stylistically very bright using an abundance of daytime, outdoors and high-key lighting rather than the darker, low-key shadows more typical of the brooding visually "black" style that made film noir so distinctive. Hitchcock achieves so much light in the picture because he filmed in daylight on location and ended daily shooting before the blackouts began each night in Santa Rosa. If it had been filmed on a Hollywood soundstage during this time, there's a good chance Hitchcock's picture would have been much more visually shrouded; at any rate, considerable effort was made to avoid the strictures of filming in wartime LA. Is it film noir? It's not shadowy. It's not urban. But *Shadow of a Doubt* is a Hitchcock classic, an important prelude to the height of the noir classic period. **SCB & JK**

SHAKEDOWN (1950)

Director: Joe Pevney. **Screenplay**: Alfred Lewis Levitt and Martin Goldsmith from a story by Nat Dallinger and Don Martin. **Producer**: Ted Richmond. **Director of Photography**: Irving Glassberg. **Music Director**: Joseph Gershenson. **Art Directors**: Bernard Herzbrun, Robert Clatworthy. **Editor**: Milton Carruth. **Cast**: Howard Duff (Jack Early), Brian Donlevy (Nick Palmer), Peggy Dow (Ellen Bennett), Lawrence Tierney (Harry Coulton), Bruce Bennett (David Glover), Anne Vernon (Nita Palmer), Stapleton Kent (City Editor), Peter Virgo (Roy), Charles Sherlock (Sam). **Completed**: April 27, 1950. **Released**: Universal, September 1. 80 minutes.

Jack Early is an opportunistic photographer who parlays a probationary job with a major San Francisco newspaper into an important assignment by romancing his boss, Ellen Bennett, and delivering two sensational photos. His next assignment is to photograph Nick Palmer, a camera-shy hoodlum. Jack persuades Palmer that complimentary pictures are in his best interest and Palmer offers him a job photographing one of his unruly henchmen, Harry Coulton, robbing a store. Jack takes the incriminating picture and then blackmails Coulton to prevent the photo from being published. After informing Coulton

that Palmer attempted to frame him, Jack follows Coulton and takes photographs while the hoodlum places a bomb in Palmer's car. Jack gets a perfect picture of Palmer's death as the bomb goes off. This photograph makes Jack famous. He becomes photographer for a national magazine and hides the incriminating pictures of Coulton in Ellen's apartment for future use. She breaks off their relationship when she realizes Jack is unscrupulous and is also seducing Palmer's widow. Some time later, Jack is assigned to photograph a high society party and arranges to have Coulton's gang rob the guests of their jewelry and split the profits with him. But Coulton convinces Nita Palmer that her new lover killed her husband and she threatens to kill Jack. He begs Ellen to bring the incriminating photographs of Coulton to Nita, but Ellen does not believe the pictures exist. Nita is accidentally shot, and Jack attempts to escape but is shot by Coulton. As he dies, Jack squeezes the shutter on his camera and takes a picture of his murderer. This photograph is published by Jack's old newspaper alongside his complimentary obituary.

Shakedown is not a pejorative depiction of the newspaper business as was the 1930 classic, *Five Star Final,* or any of the versions of *The Front Page.* It is an indictment of the American drive for success and the extent to which ambition leads Jack Early to misuse the tremendous power given to him by the press. The complex narrative of ironic counter-purposes would be simplified in later film noirs such as *Scandal Sheet.* In *Shakedown,* Howard Duff, radio's "Sam Spade," again displays his ability to personify a sympathetic heel, a role he had played earlier in *The Naked City.* Lawrence Tierney brings to the role of the villain an iconic identity which the actor had by then forged. **BP**

THE SHANGHAI GESTURE (1941)

Director: Josef von Stemberg. **Screenplay**: Josef von Stemberg, Karl Voilmoeller, Geza Herczeg, Jules Furthman from the play by John Colton. **Producer**: Arnold Pressburger. **Director of Photography**: Paul Ivano. **Music**: Richard Hageman. **Art Director**: Boris Leven. **Editor**: Sam Winston. **Cast**: Gene Tierney (Poppy), Walter Huston (Sir Guy Charteris), Victor Mature (Dr. Omar), Ona Munson (Mother Gin Sling), Phyllis Brooks (Dixie Pomeroy), Albert Basserman (Commissioner), Maria Ouspenskaya (Amah), Eric Blore (Bookkeeper), Ivan Lebedeff (Gambler), Mike Mazurki (Coolie), Clyde Fillmore (Cornprador), Rex Evans (Counselor Brooks), Grayce Hampton (Social Leader), Michael Delmatoff (Bartender). **Released**: United Artists, December 26. 106 minutes.

Mother Gin Sling owns a Shanghai casino which will soon be closed. Despite her bribes, the local authorities are under pressure from British financier Sir Guy Charteris, who has plans for the property and refuses to accept any of Gin Sling's calls to discuss it. Charteris' daughter, Poppy, is a habitué of the casino, so through Dr. Omar, Mother Gin Sling encourages Poppy's gambling. Although furious at Gin Sling's contemptuous treatment of her and suspicious of Omar's fidelity, Poppy continues to patronize the casino. Wanting to intervene Charteris accepts an invitation to Gin Sling's New Year's dinner where she reveals to the incredulous Charteris that she is the wife whom he presumed dead and whose money he appropriated. Shaken, Charteris explains that he thought she had died after betraying him;

The Shanghai Gesture: *Victoria Charteris (Gene Tierney) and Mother Gin Sling (Ona Munson)*.

but Poppy is unable to accept under any circumstances that Gin Sling could be her mother and hysterically denounces the woman. Infuriated by her own daughter's vilification, Gin Sling loses control and shoots her.

The nightmarish, almost baroque environment that von Sternberg creates in *The Shanghai Gesture* contains much of what was to become a standard expression of the noir vision. Numerous changes to the sensational 1925 Broadway play about murder and miscegenation were mandated by the Production Code Office which rejected nearly three dozen earlier treatments until Jules Furthman's screen version, where Mother Goddamn becomes Mother Gin Sling and her brothel becomes a gambling house. Nonetheless von Sternberg evokes an underworld more tangible and more threatening than anything in his proto-noir pictures *Underworld* and *Thunderbolt*. The true nature of Gin Sling's establishment is clearly revealed in such early scenes as her "purchase" of Dixie, a blond playgirl, from the police and culminates in the New Year's auction of women suspended in cages outside the casino. Despite such exotic embellishments or the title disclaimer that "Our story has nothing to do with the present," *Shanghai Gesture* obviously anticipates the postwar noir vision with its fatality and inexplicable malaise.

As both the physical and psychological child of the youthful liaison between Gin Sling and Charteris, Poppy (as played with calculated abandon by soon-to-be noir icon Gene Tierney) is enmeshed in that fatality before her birth. She embodies and must bear the burden of the emotional estrangement that her parents suffered in assuming betrayal by the other. Von Sternberg equates Poppy's fascination with vice and her degeneration with the process by which her parents have alienated themselves from normal relationships. Gin Sling, whose mask-like makeup and exotic head dress outwardly suggest a lifeless doll, and Charteris, who takes satisfaction in frustrating his sycophants by lighting his own cigarette, live in a world of artifice. Poppy initially reacts to Gin Sling's gambling house with an open and natural disdain, "What a witches' sabbath . . . so incredibly evil. I didn't think such a place existed except in my own imagination like a half-remembered dream. Anything could hap-

pen here, at any moment." In the narrative convention of film noir, Poppy's words are prophetic ones. The effects of her surrender to the dark side of her "own imagination" are apparent: her gambling, drinking, drug use, and infatuation with Omar lead to her disheveled appearance, her slow movements, and her frequently slurred words. Her drug addiction is not explicit but abundantly suggested by her own name, her mercurial behavior, and her increasing dependence on Omar.

Von Sternberg visually underscores the concept of Poppy's "evil half-remembered dream" with numerous diffused close-ups, many of them on the half-familiar faces of well-known character actors that portray Gin Sling's minions: Maria Ouspenskaya as the Amah, Gin Sling's attendant; Eric Blore as the bookkeeper; Marcel Dalio as the croupier who controls the gamblers' fates; and Mike Mazurki as the hulking coolie who banters with Charteris in Pidgin English. From cuts of intent faces watching the spinning of the roulette wheel, Sternberg pulls back to overhead long shots of the smoke-filled hall in which its cramped figures are arranged into tiers around the wheel like a rendering of Dante's Inferno in evening dress. In a world where normal relationships are impossible, von Sternberg isolates moments of either detachment or fury.

In contrast to the increasingly frenzied Poppy, who senses herself being slowly crushed just like the wax figurine that Gin Sling rends with her polished nails, there is the imperturbable Omar, laconic and icily unreachable as the Dietrich figures in von Sternberg's earlier films. Omar's dark skin, slicked-back hair, and hooded eyes complement the moment when before kissing Poppy, he spreads his cape around her like a vampire or an incubus who personifies the destructive emotions of the noir underworld. It is the staid Charteris' final appearance in this underworld that precipitates the violent denouement and a return to the darker vision of von Sternberg's earlier films, a much bleaker vision than that found in the fates of the quixotic figures of the later *Macao*. Poppy's death not only verifies her observation that "anything could happen here at any moment" but also denies any possibility of regeneration. The irony of Gin Sling's earlier remark that occasionally "Shanghai decides to clean itself like a swan in a muddy lake" is that the characters have no such option but are trapped in a miasma of their own dissolution. For the murdered Poppy, the question of "paying" for her sins is moot. For Gin Sling and for Charteris, who stumbles out of the casino to suffer a final taunt from the coolie ("You likee Chinee New Year?"), the question is left openended. **AS** & **MB**

SHIELD FOR MURDER (1954)

Directors: Edmond O'Brien and Howard W. Koch. **Screenplay**: Richard Alan Simmons and John C. Higgins adapted by Richard Alan Simmons from the novel by William P. McGivern. **Producer**: Aubrey Schenck (Camden Productions). **Director of Photography**: Gordon Avil. **Music**: Paul Dunlap. **Production Designer**: Charles D. Hall. **Editor**: John F. Schreyer. **Cast**: Edmond O'Brien (Barney Nolan), Marla English (Patty Winters), John Agar (Mark Brewster), Emile Meyer (Capt. Gunnarson), Carolyn Jones (Girl At Bar), Claude Akins (Fat Michaels), Larry Ryle (Laddie O'Neil), Herbert Butterfield (Cabot), Hugh Sanders (Packy Reed), William Schallert

(Assistant District Attorney), David Hughes (Ernest Stemmueller), Richard Cutting (Manning). **Completed**: May 25, 1954. **Released**: United Artists, August 27. 80 minutes.

Barney Nolan, a corrupt policeman, murders a small-time hood who tried to hold back a payoff and steals $25,000 from the corpse. His justification—that the murder was in the line of duty—convinces his superiors. Unfortunately, the entire affair was witnessed by an elderly gentleman who reports it to the police. As no connection is made with the earlier killing, Nolan is assigned to investigate the case. He eventually eliminates the old man and plans to establish himself in suburbia with his fiancée, Patty, in a newly built model home. But Nolan is pursued by a gangster, Packy Reed, and becomes a target for revenge. Mark Brewster, another detective, has meanwhile learned of Nolan's killings and the rogue cop becomes a fugitive hunted by both the police and the gangster. Nolan finds temporary sanctuary at the site of his new home but the police surround the area and gun him down on the lawn.

Starring and co-directed by Edmond O'Brien, a familiar noir actor, *Shield for Murder* was produced late in the cycle and explodes the myth of suburbia. The corruption found in the police officer is carried over into his cozy environment of built-in dishwashers and two-car garages. O'Brien transcends his characterization of the policeman on the take and becomes a symbol of decaying middle-class values. The film is explicit in its violence and brutal in its depiction of greed and lust warped by the false sense of power present behind the police badge. The destruction of the bad cop, Nolan, is inevitable. He follows a course that leads to death, because the redemption he seeks in the shelter of his new home is as insubstantial as the house's stucco facade. Nolan dies, crumpled up on his unplanted front lawn, nothing more than a piece of debris cluttering up the outline of sameness found in the tract of houses. **CM**

SHOCK (1946)

Director: Alfred Werker. **Screenplay**: Eugene Ling from a story by Albert DeMond with additional dialogue by Martin Berkeley. **Producer**: Aubrey Schenck. **Director of Photography**: Joe MacDonald. **Music**: Emil Newman. **Art Director**: Boris Leven, Lyle Wheeler. **Editor**: Harmon Jones. **Cast**: Vincent Price (Dr. Richard Cross), Lynn Bari (Elaine Jordan), Frank Latimore (Lt. Paul Stewart), Anabel Shaw (Janet Stewart), Stephen Dunne (Dr. Stevens), Reed Hadley (D.A. Investigator O'Neill), Charles Trowbridge (Dr. Harvey), John Davidson (Mr. Edwards). **Released**: 20th Century-Fox, Feb. 1. 70 minutes.

Janet is anxiously waiting in a hotel room for her husband, Paul, an ex-P.O.W. whom she hasn't seen for two years. After awakening from a nightmare about Paul, she witnesses Richard Cross bludgeon his wife to death. The next day Paul arrives and finds Janet catatonic. Richard, a psychiatrist staying at the hotel, is asked to evaluate Janet's condition. Realizing she must have seen the murder and gone into shock, Richard takes her to his sanatorium. To prevent her from recovering, Richard and his mistress, Elaine, secretly try to drive Janet insane. Paul asks Dr. Harvey for a second opinion, but he sees nothing wrong. Richard makes his wife's

death look like a fall onto rocks near his lodge. O'Neill, investigating another crime near the lodge, has the wife's body exhumed for autopsy and discovers how she was killed. With O'Neill closing in, Richard and Elaine start to poison Janet with an overdose of insulin. Richard can't go through with it, and he kills Elaine when she tries to make him complete the fatal injection. Paul convinces Dr. Harvey that Janet is in grave danger, and they get to the sanatorium in time.

By 1946, the woman-in-distress and the femme fatale were frequently appearing in film noirs. *Shock*, however, is distinctive for having both together. In an unusual triangle, Elaine, the femme fatale, is not only responsible for Richard's downfall but also for making Janet the woman-in-distress. In both scenes where Richard and Elaine are at his house, he regrets "listening" to her and not calling the police after he killed his wife. In the first scene, he resists when she urges him not to allow Janet's shock "to wear off." He wants "to think" about it. But when she takes his arms and comes close to him, it is understood she'll get her way. In the second scene, Elaine says they should "take care of" Janet so she can't be interviewed by the police. Richard is unwilling to give Janet a lethal injection, and Elaine criticizes him for being weak. Then, with the gentlest of manner, she tries seduction.

In other scenes Richard and Elaine spar over which of them correctly "sees" what's going on. Their relationship is less about romance than the extent to which he's under her sway. That Elaine, a nurse, has such power over Richard, a specialist, shows there are factors, like sexual attraction, other than expertise or a position of authority that determine which of two people is in charge. There are other instances in *Shock*, however, when the person with higher rank has the advantage, for good and ill. Janet arrives at the hotel, and the clerk tells her no room is available. The hotel manager comes out and arranges a room for her. The hotel doctor can only give a non-specialist's evaluation of Janet, so she's turned over to Richard. Due to his position at the sanatorium, Richard can get away with administering an overdose to Janet. Dr. Harvey, under whom Richard studied, has the prestige and confidence to barge into the sanatorium to save Janet. Notably, the film doesn't end with Janet's rescue and, at long last, her reunion with Paul. Instead, the final scene is of Richard being led away by O'Neill. Psychiatry and criminology represent other types of expertise and authority. Dr. Harvey tells Paul, "You realize it's hard to make generalizations," because psychiatry is not an exact science. The police, in contrast, use scientific methods and instruments. For O'Neill, determining the murder weapon is a silver candlestick is, "Just routine." In *Shock*, criminology is counterposed to psychiatry and outclasses it.

The layout of Janet's hotel room foreshadows Richard's sanatorium. The room has two small classical columns, set some distance apart from each other in front of the door to the hallway. In the common area on one floor of the sanatorium, there are two large classical columns, set similarly apart and in front of a door. Also, Janet's nightmare at the hotel, in which she and Paul cannot find one another, foreshadows her confinement in the sanatorium, with its empty white hallways and Paul struggling to be with her. The abuses of hypnotists, psychologists and other manipulators of the human mind are a literary staple and have been fodder for films at least since *The Cabinet of Dr. Caligari*, where the archetype of the evil doctor descends by way of German Expressionism into the horror genre.

In post-war America a growing public awareness of all forms of psychotherapy was tainted with revelations of Nazi scientists using drugs like the "truth serums" as a means of "brainwashing." This in turn helped to create the figure of the psychotherapist as a popular icon with great powers over the human psyche. Such an icon was quickly absorbed by the noir cycle where the figure could be used for good (*Whirlpool*), evil (*The Scarf*) or both (*The Accused*). With time, a more realistic portrayal would develop, especially in films outside of the cycle (e.g., *The Snake Pit*, *Three Faces of Eve*). *Shock* starts out well, with Janet's nightmare done in a semi-surrealistic manner, but it degenerates into a rather static potboiler generating very little suspense. Ironically, most of the visual pyrotechnics and excitement are contained in a scene towards the end of the film where Mr. Edwards, a patient disturbed by a nocturnal storm, gets out of his room and threatens Janet. Vincent Price's subdued performance, however, helps the film. Restricting our focus to Dr. Cross as the film's protagonist we see a relatively sensitive man solidly in the clutches of a real femme fatale (and Lynn Bari turns in a quite credible performance here) whose one thoughtless, violent act leads him down the path of ruin. And in so doing we validate its inclusion here as a film noir. **DMH & BP**

SHOCKPROOF (1949)

Director: Douglas Sirk. **Screenplay**: Samuel Fuller, Helen Deutsch. **Producer**: Helen Deutsch. **Director of Photography**: Charles Lawton Jr. **Art Director**: Carl Anderson. **Music**: George Duning. **Editor**: Gene Havlick. **Cast**: Cornel Wilde (Griff Marat), Patricia Knight (Jenny Marsh), John Baragrey (Harry Wesson), Esther Minciotti (Mrs. Marat), Howard St. John (Sam Brooks), Russell Collins (Fred Bauer), Charles Bates (Tommy). **Released**: Columbia, January 25. 79 minutes.

Jenny Marsh, still dangerously attractive after five years in prison for killing a man in defense of her lover Harry Wesson, clashes at first with parole officer Griff Marat, who is determined to make Jenny go straight. For lack of other prospects Griff finds Jenny a job in his own home, and his objectivity about her wavers, while Jenny continues to meet Harry secretly. However, Jenny transfers her affections from Harry to Griff and marries him. She then shoots her miffed ex-lover in a struggle. Griff and Jenny become a fugitive couple, finding work as migrants. When Jenny finds that Harry was only wounded in the struggle, she decides to turn herself in, with the aid of Griff.

In *Shockproof*, written by Samuel Fuller, Los Angeles county parole officer Griff Marat becomes involved with one of his charges, convicted murderer Jenny Marsh. Although depicted as a man of high ethics and morals, Griff becomes totally obsessed with this seductive and petulant "bad girl" as soon as he first interviews her for her case file. Like so many males in noir, Griff has a sexually tinged messiah complex which compels him to rescue and then possess this "fallen woman." Although she is unrepentant and continues to meet her lover, Griff coerces/persuades Jenny to move into his middle-class house on Bunker Hill and take care of his ailing mother.

Eventually, Griff's sincerity wins Jenny's affections. They marry secretly, again violating the ethics of his profession.

The film soon becomes yet another example in the noir canon of a fugitive couple movie after Jenny shoots her ex-lover accidentally and Griff abandons his middle-class values and ambitions to escape with her.

On the lam they eke out a living as day laborers, much like the couple in *Tomorrow Is Another Day*, until they find out that the man Jenny shot is only wounded and decide to return and face their fate together. The movie, like much of Fuller's noir work as a director, has a strong sense of irony revolving around its portrait of the moralistic and preachy Griff who casts his ethics aside to pursue his sexual obsession. **JU**

SHOOT TO KILL [aka POLICE REPORTER] (1947)

Director: William Berke. **Screenplay**: Edwin V. Westrate. **Producer**: William Berke. **Director of Photography**: Benjamin Kline. **Art Director**: William Glasgow. **Music**: Gene Rodgers, Darrell Calker. **Editor**: Arthur Brooks. **Cast**: Russell Wade (Mitchell), Edmund MacDonald (Lawrence Dale), Vince Barnett (Charlie Gill), Luana Walters aka Susan Walters (Marian Langdon), Robert Kent aka Douglas Blackley (Dixie Logan), Nestor Paiva (Gus), Charles Trowbridge (District Attorney Forsythe), Harry Brown (Jim Forman), Ted Hecht (Al Collins). **Released**: Screen Guild/Lippert, March 15. 64 minutes.

Gangster Dixie Logan is framed by crooked assistant district attorney Lawrence Dale. His wife, Marian, secures a job as Dale's assistant and even pretends to marry him, the better to find proof of Dale's dishonesty. She gets help from reporter Mitchell, who falls in love with her. The district attorney's ties to organized crime are revealed but both Logan and Dale die in a car crash while being pursued. Surviving the same car crash, Marian tells her story to Mitchell while recovering in the hospital.

Aficionados of film noir find very few movies in the cycle without some interest—even the poverty-row programmers that come in just under or over an hour tend to have something to sustain interest. *Shoot To Kill*, alas, is not among them. Though the script contains many, often incomprehensible, twists, the director handles the narrative structure so clumsily that they come not as surprises but as irritations. And the largely unknown cast (and crew) goes through their paces without a spark of originality or inspiration. It's hard to leave a

movie without a positive note to be sounded, but *Shoot To Kill* serves as a reminder of just how depressing bottom-of-the-barrel filmmaking in the postwar years could be. **BMcV**

SHORT CUT TO HELL (1957)

Director: James Cagney. **Screenplay**: Ted Berkman and Raphael Blau based on the 1942 screenplay by Albert Maltz and W.R. Burnett from the novel *A Gun for Sale* by Graham Greene. **Producer**: A.C. Lyles. **Director of Photography**: Haskell B. Boggs. **Music**: Irvin Colbert [Talbot] using excerpts from scores by Harry Sukman, Victor Young, and Miklós Rósza. **Art Directors**: Roland Anderson, Hal Pereira. **Editor**: Ken McAdo. **Cast**: William Bishop (Stan), Robert Ivers (Kyle), Georgann Johnson (Glory Hamilton), Yvette Vickers (Daisy), Murvyn Vye (Nichols), Jacques Aubuchon (Bahrwell), Peter Baldwin (Adams), Richard Hale. **Released**: Paramount, September 19. 89 minutes.

In this remake of *This Gun for Hire*, the hitman and his obese employer are named Kyle and Bahrwell rather than Raven and Gates. When, like Raven, Kyle discovers he had been paid with counterfeit notes, Kyle abducts singer Glory Hamilton, whose fiancé is the detective investigating the murders, and sets off to even the score.

Towards the end of *Short Cut to Hell*, with the two principal characters holed up in an abandoned underground storage bunker and the police cars massed outside, there's a long quotation from the doom-laden score Miklós Rósza wrote for *Double Indemnity*. It's one of several arresting moments in this B-budgeted remake of one of the earliest noir films, *This Gun for Hire*. Whatever its limitations as noir, *Short Cut to Hell* is noteworthy as the only movie James Cagney ever directed. With limited resources from Paramount, Cagney's remake used unknown actors—such as Georgeann Johnson who had already labored anonymously in more that a score of television programs—who for the most part managed to remain that way for the rest of their careers. In the Ladd role of the icy, isolated killer-for-hire, Robert Ivers is little more

than a trench coat and a topper, skin and bones who brings to mind an unlikely amalgam of Elisha Cook, Jr. and James Dean. Pallidly reprising the Laird Cregar role as the pompous fat man is Jacques Aubuchon, who like Cregar before him seems more interested in peppermint patties than pretty young things. Johnson tries gamely but in the wrong way. She has a way with a wisecrack, but it's not in the flirtatious Veronica Lake way—nor that of Lauren Bacall or Gloria Grahame. The spin she puts on the role of sympathetic captive is Eve Ardenish, less seductive than matey, even matronly. So the chemistry between captor and captive never approaches that created by Ladd and Lake. **BMV**

SIDE STREET (1950)

Director: Anthony Mann. **Screenplay**: Sydney Boehm. **Producer**: Sam Zimbalist. **Director of Photography**: Joseph Ruttenberg. **Music**: Lennie Hayton. **Directors**: Cedric Gibbons, Daniel B. Cathcart. **Editor**: Conrad A. Nervig. **Cast**: Farley Granger (Joe Norson), Cathy O'Donnell (Ellen Norson), James Craig (George Garsell), Paul Kelly (Capt. Walter Anderson), Edmond Ryan (Victor Backett), Paul Harvey (Emil Lorrison), Jean Hagen (Harriet Sinton), Charles McGraw (Stanley Simon), Ed Max (Nick Drummon), Adele Jergens (Lucille "Lucky" Coiner), Harry Bellaver (Larry Giff), Whit Bissell (Harold Simpsen), John Gallaudet (Gus Heldon), Esther Somers (Mrs. Malby), Harry Antrim (Mr. Malby), George Tyne (Detective Roffman). **Location**: New York City. **Completed**: June 8, 1949. **Released**: MGM, March 23. 83 minutes.

Wanting a little money so his pregnant wife can have a private hospital room, part-time mailman Joe Norson steals a file folder from the office of shady lawyer Victor Backett. He thinks it contains $200 but he is terrified to discover $30,000 inside, which is money from a blackmail/murder scheme. After pretending he has a job out of town and leaving the cash with local bar owner Nick Drummon, Norson hides out then tries to return the money. Knowing Capt. Anderson and his homicide detectives are investigating, Backett feigns ignorance. He sends his cronies George Garsell and cabbie Larry Giff after Norson, who escapes but finds that Drummon has sold the bar and taken the money. When Drummon is found dead, Norson is accused of murder and hunted by the police. Norson retrieves the folder, finds a picture of Harriet Sinton marked "To Georgie," and tracks her down. She takes them to Garsell, who kills her and plans to do likewise with Norson. Norson is forced to drive the cab during a chase through the streets of New York, until he crashes and the police finally shoot Garsell. Norson's wife arrives at the scene as he is put into an ambulance.

Farley Granger had often portrayed ill-fated characters in films such as *Rope, Edge of Doom* and *They Live by Night*, the fugitive couple saga in which he also costarred with Cathy O'Donnell. In *Side Street*, unlike earlier veteran characters who have problems readjusting, Norson is an ordinary guy who marries and opens a gas station. The narrative opens after that business has failed and Norson is reduced to part-time work and living with his pregnant wife's parents. Sydney Boehm's script uses a narration by Capt. Anderson and director Anthony Mann uses the real streets of New York to give the opening's brief expository scenes a documentary feel, as when Norson sees a fur coat in a window then talks to a beat cop about getting back on his feet

and buying one for his wife. But even in this scene, Mann stages most of the dialogue in a two shot with the patrolman's face much larger on the left hemming in Granger and subtly anticipating Norson's fateful, upcoming difficulties with the law.

Although O'Donnell is a co-star, Granger has much more screen time, and Mann continues to underscore plot and narration alternately between day-lit and night exteriors effectively. The rooftop location, for example, where Norson goes to stash the folder on the morning of the theft is revisited at night, with his features rim-lit and barely visible. After he searches through the folder using a lighter to illuminate the contents, the desperate Norson enters a more palpable noir underworld. Metamorphosed into a grim private investigator, with himself as a falsely accused client, Norson is remarkably efficient as he visits an apartment house, the establishment next door, and canvases through various dingy nightclubs in search of Harriet Sinton. When he stumbles onto her in the middle of a torch song, the scene is almost a parody of P.I. noir as Norson stands and watches her. Then like Spade or Marlowe but without their professional *sang froid*, Norson must steel himself and approach Sinton while pretending to be a friend of "Georgie's." With Jean Hagen whose speaking voice is idiosyncratic and far different from the timbre of her singing, Mann creates a remarkable portrait of a victim mired in the noir underworld. Minutes later clinging to new found hope she is grimly strangled by Garsell.

With all these somewhat exaggerated noir types around him, Granger's naturalistic and uneasy performance as Norson is unrelentingly ironic. Like other somewhat socially conscious noir films, *Side Street* deflates the American dream by confounding it with the darkness and corruption of an underworld more comfortably inhabited by *Kiss Me Deadly's* ruthless Mike Hammer or the hard-bitten cops in this movie and dozens of others. The violence that rests below the surface of American culture is chillingly captured in *Side Street*. Initially Boehm's script provides the opening statistics in the style of *Naked City* or Mann's own *He Walked by Night* that moves from the number of marriages, births, and deaths to reveal the number of police in New York City who deal with more than a murder per day. From that Mann provides the graphic details.

From the blonde victim floating in the East River and Drummon's strangled body to the grisly killing of Harriet,

violence is a potent expressive component in this film. The matter-of-fact tone of Paul Kelly's narration is reinforced by the casual manner in which the police and the coroner review the forensics of the first case, both of which deeply contrast with Norson's and presumably the viewer's more emotional reaction to a deadly crime. The impotence of Norson's situation, an ordinary man caught up in a situation he cannot control, his Army photo on the front pages of the newspapers, is self-evident. Mann does use some of the same lighting techniques as in the pictures with cinematographer John Alton, but just as often the framing and staging in actual location exteriors are more neutral and let performance alone define character emotions. Even the highly stylized ending in which extreme high-angle shots reveal the cab and police cruisers driving through the concrete canyons of the almost empty city are of necessity flatly lit. Nonetheless the visual analogy with an animal struggling through a maze is obvious. While Norson survives, a half-dozen others perish in a time span far brisker than one per day. **AS**

SINGAPORE (1947)

Director: John Brahm. **Screenplay**: Seton I. Miller and Robert Thoeren. **Producer**: Jerry Bresler. **Director of Photography**: Maury Gertsman. **Art Directors**: Bernard Herzbrun, Gabriel Scognamillo. **Music**: Daniele Amfitheatrof. **Editor**: William Hornbeck. **Cast**: Fred MacMurray (Matt Gordon), Ava Gardner (Linda Grahame/Ann Van Leyden), Roland Culver (Michael Van Leyden), Richard Haydn (Deputy Commissioner Hewitt), Thomas Gomez (Mr. Mauribus), Spring Byington (Mrs. Bellows), Porter Hall (Mr. Bellows), Maylia (Ming Ling), George Lloyd (Sascha). **Released**: Universal International, August 13. 79 minutes.

After World War II, Matt Gordon returns to Singapore to retrieve a fortune in smuggled pearls. While there he reminisces in flashback about his pre-war fiancée, Linda Grahame, and her supposed death during the Japanese attack. But now Linda resurfaces with amnesia and married to a rich planter Van Leyden. Meanwhile, sinister fence Mauribus schemes to get Gordon's pearls while Deputy Commissioner Hewitt keeps an eye on both Gordon and Mauribus. Gradually Linda, under the influence of Gordon's prodding, begins to regain her memory of their affair. Hoping to escape with Linda after taking back the pearls, Gordon's plans are sidetracked by Mauribus who kidnaps Linda. Gordon rescues Linda and turns the criminals over to Hewitt. Linda returns to him as he is leaving Singapore and the lovers are finally reunited.

John Brahm's *Singapore* draws inspiration from both *Casablanca* and *Double Indemnity* in its tale of amnesia, smuggling, and obsessive love. Brahm excels in this filmic exercise, as in his other noirs (*The Lodger*, *The Brasher Doubloon*, etc.), as a visual stylist rooted, like the other émigrés in the noir movement, in European aestheticism. However unlike Wilder or Siodmak, Brahm showed very little interest in script doctoring or in the performance of his actors. Consequently, noir regulars Fred MacMurray and Ava Gardner are at their weakest. MacMurray as the cynical pearl smuggler Gordon does again project the image (as he would in a number of noirs into the 1950s) which Wilder created for him in *Double Indemnity*—the oversized, flabby "chump" with a weak moral center—but seems far more wooden under Brahm's direction. Gardener as Linda Grahame is as radiant as usual in her role as a sultry femme fatale of circumstance (she only betrays her lover Gordon and marries Van Leyden because she suffers from amnesia) but often fails to modulate her performance, as opposed to her portrayal of Kitty in Siodmak's *The Killers* the year before.

The situations in the movie, however, are still affectingly noir. Gordon's flashback to the lovers' whirlwind love affair and his despair over Linda's supposed death during a Japanese bombing hits the right noir tone. Brahm's fetishization of Gardner also nicely enhances her role as a femme fatale: whether dressed in black silk in an overheated tropical hotel room, appearing on the dance floor of a nightclub as if out of Gordon's wet dream, or lying comatose in her veiled bed as both her lover and her husband hover about the object of their own particular obsessions. Even the "happy" ending works as a transgressive affirmation of love beyond the bounds of society's rules as the cuckolded husband delivers his wife to the arms of her lover at the airport (a witty reversal of the ending of *Casablanca*). **JU**

SLEEP, MY LOVE (1948)

Director: Douglas Sirk. **Screenplay**: St. Clair McKelway, Leo Rosten, Cy Enfield, Decla Dunning from the novel by Leo Rosten. **Producers**: Charles Buddy Rogers, Ralph Cohn. **Director of Photography**: Joseph Valentine. **Music**: Rudy Schrager. **Art Director**: William Ferrari. **Editor**: Lynn Harrison. **Cast**: Claudette Colbert (Alison Courtland), Robert Cummings (Bruce Elcott), Don Ameche (Richard Courtland), Rita Johnson (Barby), George Coulouris (Charles Vernay), Hazel Brooks (Daphne), Queenie Smith (Mrs. Tomlinson), Keye Luke (Jimmie), Fred Nurney (Haskins), Raymond Burr (Lt. Strake), Lillian Bronson (Helen), Ralph Morgan (Dr. Rhinehart). **Completed**: August 1, 1947. **Released**: United Artists, February 18. 96 minutes.

Alison Courtland is startled when she wakes up aboard a night train to Boston, as she has no recollection of leaving her home in New York City. Assisted by matronly Mrs. Tomlinson, she contacts her husband Richard, who purposefully allows the police to overhear their conversation, as Alison does not remember that she threatened Richard with a gun. On the plane home, Alison meets a charming friend of a friend, Bruce Elcott, who falls in love with her. Richard convinces his wife to undergo psychiatric treatment at her home with Dr. Rhinehart, who intimidates her and then mysteriously disappears. Richard excuses himself for a business meeting, but he keeps a rendezvous with Daphne; and it is revealed that the illicit couple have conspired with a photographer, Charles Vernay, to pose as Dr. Rhinehart and drive Alison to suicide so that Dick can inherit his wife's fortune. When Bruce finds Alison sleepwalking and about to jump off a balcony, he becomes suspicious of Richard's activities and investigates. Discovering Vernay's photography studio and claiming to need a passport picture, Bruce finds evidence that links Vernay as the man who posed as Dr. Rhinehart. Meanwhile, Richard believes he has drugged Alison and hypnotically suggests that she must kill Dr. Rhinehart to protect herself. But Vernay has realized he is being double-crossed and shocks Alison out of her stupor.

Sleep, My Love: *Bruce Eliot (Robert Cummings), Charles Vernay (George Coulouris), and Daphne (Hazel Brooks).*

Richard kills Vernay and prepares to shoot his wife, but Alison is saved by Bruce's arrival.

Sleep, My Love adds the noir elements of drugs, hypnosis, nightmares, and seemingly innocent but dangerous circumstance to its melodramatic plot of adultery and wife murder. Additionally, the climactic confrontation between Richard, Vemay, Alison, and Bruce derives noir impact because the scene develops in a way none of the characters intended and ensnares them all in revolving positions of helplessness. Alison, only half-drugged as she only half believes her husband capable of deceiving her, is urged by Richard to shoot Vernay's indistinct shadow, which appears through a frosted glass door. But the shadow looms forward and opens the door, and Vernay quickly relates to Alison the vicious truth about her recent neurosis. Richard drops all of his civilized pretensions and savagely shoots Vemay who falls back through the glass, literally shattering all of Alison's illusions about her husband. As Richard turns on her and affirms Vemay's revelations, Alison cowers in a corner, moaning "No. No, no," and the shadow of the stairway's railing figuratively imprisons her. Surprisingly, a figure emerges from behind Richard and kills him. Bruce Elcott's belated arrival undercuts his character's confident control over all situations and initially deludes the audience, who believes that Vernay has struggled to his feet to avenge his betrayal.

This final scene of *Sleep, My Love* overrides the lighthearted and bland characterizations provided by Claudette Colbert as the wife who is afraid but not horrified or alienated by her fear, and Robert Cummings as the sincere, brash hero, Bruce, who never doubts that his instincts are correct. The antagonists are more fully developed as noir characters: Don Ameche's cloying portrayal of the husband with schizophrenic desires; Daphne's icy sensuality; and especially George Coulouris' multifaceted Vernay highlight the motion picture. The scene with these latter three in the photography studio plotting their psychological crime is heightened by the illusory nature of Vernay's profession, photography, and the superficiality of Daphne's skill as a model, someone who bitterly understands that she can only sit in the studio wearing expensive clothes and will never be allowed to actually live a normal life clothed in them. **EW**

THE SLEEPING CITY (1950)

Director: George Sherman. **Screenplay**: Jo Eisinger. **Producer**: Leonard Goldstein. **Director of Photography**: William Miller. **Music**: Frank Skinner. **Art Directors**: Bernard Herzbrun, Emrich Nicholson. **Editor**: Frank Gross. **Cast**: Richard Conte (Fred Rowan), Coleen Gray (Ann Sebastian), Peggy Dow (Kathy Hall), John Alexander (Inspector Gordon), Alex Nicol (Dr. Bob Anderson), Richard Taber (Pop Ware), James J. Van Dyk (Dr. Sharpley), Hugh Reilly (Dr. Foster), Michael Strong (Dr. Connell), Frank M. Thomas (Lt. Lally), Richard Kendrick (Dr. Druta), Henry Hart (Dr. Nester). **Completed**: December 10, 1949. **Released**: Universal, September 20. 85 minutes.

An intern at a metropolitan hospital is murdered and police inspector Gordon assigns an undercover agent, Fred Rowan, to pose as a new intern to discover what is behind the death. His investigation exposes the victim's tormented roommate; a mysteriously criminal nurse, Ann; and an elderly elevator operator, Pop Ware, who extorts the hospital staff to obtain drugs for the black market.

The Sleeping City is an especially disturbing film noir because its plot concerns corruption within a hospital and involves depriving patients of needed drugs. The interns and nurses upon which the story focuses are shown as depressed and neurotic individuals, bitter and desperate people with little chance for a good future, rather than the noble crusaders usually associated with medical stories. The noir heroine of Ann Sebastian, played by Coleen Gray, is a nurse who abuses her patients for the sake of aiding a sick child who is not her own. The ending of the film is very similar to that of The Maltese Falcon but divides audience sympathy between the nurse and the undercover agent who now loves her. The agent watches her being arrested with a regret that suggests that he has not condemned her; and her bleak view of life has been reinforced by the film's images to the point that it has left a stronger emotional impression upon him than his devotion to duty, regardless of his final compliance with that duty. George Sherman directed The Sleeping City with an imaginative visual interpretation, as in the tracking shot preceding the murder at the film's opening; and he guided interesting performances, notably the representatives of the law who—excepting the hero—are unusually hard and cynical. **BL**

SLIGHTLY SCARLET (1956)

Director: Allan Dwan. **Screenplay**: Robert Blees from the novel Love's Lovely Counterfeit by James M. Cain. **Producer**: Benedict Bogeaus (Filmcrest Productions). **Director of Photography**: John Alton. **Music**: Louis Forbes. **Art Director**: Van Nest Polglase. **Editor**: James Leicester. **Cast**: John Payne (Ben Grace), Arlene Dahl (Dorothy Lyons), Rhonda Fleming (June Lyons), Kent Taylor (Jansen), Ted de Corsia (Sol Caspar), Lance Fuller (Gauss), Buddy Baer (Lenhardt), Frank Gerstle (Dietz), Ellen Corby (Martha). **Completed**: August 6, 1955. **Released**: RKO, February 29. 99 minutes.

Ben Grace is a petty criminal working for Sol Caspar, criminal boss of a metropolis. When an honest man runs for mayor, Ben receives information concerning the politician's lovely secretary, June Lyons, and the prison record of her sister Dorothy. Romancing June, Ben gives her incriminating material on Caspar, causing the violent boss to kill an important newspaperman. Caspar must flee the city and Ben takes over, leading an ambiguous existence as a dishonest gang boss with some good instincts while also being genuinely in love with June. Meanwhile, June is apprehensive as Dorothy is attracted to Ben. When Caspar returns to avenge himself, Ben suffers being shot with bullet after bullet so that Caspar may be caught by the police with a gun in his hand. A severely wounded Ben is taken away as Dorothy and June follow.

This rendering of James M. Cain's Love's Lovely Counterfeit considerably alters the story, in which Dorothy enters late in the narrative and becomes Ben's lover, ennobling both of them. In the film, Ben is faithful to June; but Dorothy, although her presence is less motivated from a narrative standpoint, becomes the most interesting character: neurotic, unpredictable, and captivatingly immoral. It may be that Allan Dwan, with his passion for symmetry, introduced Dorothy at the beginning of the story to utilize Rhonda Fleming and Arlene Dahl as complementary redheaded visual objects throughout the film. In any event, the film does succeed visually as a stylistic representation of a triangle, in spite of the fact that the relationship of Ben, Dorothy, and June does not really support it. In the last shot, equal distances separate the three as they exit, with June presented as a figure caught in space between the man whom she loves and the sister whom she obsessively protects.

Slightly Scarlet is one of a series of seven films produced over a two-year period by Benedict Bogeaus and released by RKO which Allan Dwan directed, John Alton photographed, and Van Nest Polglase art directed. Although made with extremely modest budgets, these films are among the most richly colored and decorated of the period and confirm that Alton's imagination in lighting is as distinctive in color as it is in black and white. Slightly Scarlet is the only film noir in this Dwan-Alton series and the most interesting photographically as a Technicolor noir akin to the Leon Shamroy-photographed Leave Her to Heaven. Alton continues to utilize extensive shadows and large black areas, while also accentuating a garish array of pinks, greens, and oranges, producing a startling effect in many scenes. **BL**

The Sniper: *At center Sgt. Ferris (Gerald Mohr) watches Lt. Kafka (Adolphe Menjou).*

THE SNIPER (1952)

Director: Edward Dmytryk. **Screenplay**: Harry Brown based on a story by Edward and Edna Anhalt. **Executive Producer**: Stanley Kramer. **Director of Photography**: Burnett Guffey. **Music**: George Antheil. **Production Designer**: Rudolph Sternad. **Editors**: Aaron Stell, Harry Gerstad. **Cast**: Adolphe Menjou (Lt. Kafka), Arthur Franz (Eddie Miller), Gerald Mohr (Sgt. Ferris), Marie Windsor (Jean Darr), Frank Faylen (Inspector Anderson), Richard Kiley (Dr. James G. Kent), Mabel Paige (Landlady), Marlo Dwyer (May Nelson), Geraldine Carr (Checker), Jay Novello (Pete), Ralph Peters (Police Interlocutor), Max Palmer (Chadwick), **Completed**: October 20, 1951. **Released**: Columbia, May 9. 87 minutes.

A mentally disturbed young man, Eddie Miller, feels compelled to kill. His attempts to find help are met with lack of interest and apathy. Breaking down, he shoots men from rooftops throughout the city. A scruffy and initially unsympathetic policeman, Lt. Kafka, is assigned to capture the sniper. As his investigation zeros in on the imbalanced killer, Kafka realizes that this killing spree is inspired not out of criminal lust but rather from deep psychological problems. Finally tracking the sniper to a cheap hotel room, the police close in. They break in and find their suspect surrounded by a small arsenal of weapons, but he offers no resistance.

The Sniper possesses a visual force reminiscent of director Dmytryk's earlier noir efforts, including *Murder, My Sweet, Crossfire,* and *Cornered.* However, the noir tone and ambience merely serves as a vehicle for the film's indictment of contemporary society for failure to deal with mental problems and urban alienation. But significantly, the film's verdict is lost amid the impact of ritualized violence and the thrill of the police manhunt. Consequently, society's status quo is maintained. The characters found in *The Sniper* exist in a netherworld that permits humanitarian speculation to surface through scenes of humiliation and angst. Although Dmytryk, along with such directors as Nicholas Ray and Elia Kazan, blended social awareness with a noir sensibility, *The Sniper* remains closer to the central noir vision than films like *Knock on Any Door* or *Boomerang.* **CM**

SO DARK THE NIGHT (1946)

Director: Joseph H. Lewis. **Screenplay**: Martin Berkeley and Dwight Babcock from an unpublished story by Aubrey Wisberg. **Producer**: Ted Richmond. **Director of Photography**: Burnett Guffey. **Music**: Morris W. Stoloff, Hugo Friedhofer. **Art Director**: Carl Anderson. **Editor**: Jerome Thoms. **Cast**: Steven Geray (Henri Cassin), Micheline Cheirel (Nanette Michaud), Eugene Borden (M. Michaud), Ann Codee (Mama Michaud), Egon Brecher (Dr. Boncourt), Helen Freeman (Widow Bridelle), Theodore Gottlieb (Georges), Gregory Gay (Commissioner Grande), Jean Del Val (Dr. Manet), Paul Marion (Leon Achard), Emil Ramu (Pere Cortot), Louis Mercier (Jean Duval). **Completed**: December 12, 1945. **Released**: Columbia, October 10. 70 minutes.

Henri Cassin, the top detective of the Paris Sûreté, takes his first vacation in eleven years at the Michaud family inn in the quiet country village of St. Margot and is immediately attracted to pretty, young Nanette Michaud. Mama Michaud does her best to promote her daughter's new romance despite Nanette's engagement to a young local farmer, Leon Archard, since marriage to Henri is an opportunity to enhance her status and live in Paris. While Leon is out of town, Nanette encourages the polite but middle-aged Henri and soon they announce their engagement. Leon accuses Mme. Michaud of "arranging things," and tells Henri that if he marries Nanette, Leon will pursue her and she will never be truly Henri's. Leon leaves and is followed by Nanette, who does not return. Henri is disconsolate, refusing to eat or sleep. When her body is found in the river, Henri discovers that she has been strangled. Leon's body is found at his farm and he has also been strangled. The only clue is the killer's footprint in the wet dirt beneath his body. Agreeing to help the local police, Henri swears to find the killer of his beloved Nanette. Then he receives a note stating, "There will be another murder," and soon the body of Mme. Michaud is discovered. Henri returns to Paris to consult with his superior, Commissioner Grande, and gives the Sûreté artist the killer's physical description as deduced from the footprint. The artist remarks that it resembles Henri. Suspecting himself, Henri writes a murder note with his left hand. It conforms to the original and Henri insists he be put under custody. The police doctor explains it is possible for Henri to have a split personality. Henri relapses and escapes back to the Michaud inn. Poised to kill M. Michaud, the police arrive and shoot Henri through the window.

So Dark the Night demonstrates what Joseph H. Lewis can do with a small budget, a no-name cast, a rather contrived plot and the judicious use of Hollywood studio and ranch facilities. In some ways it is superior to *My Name Is Julia Ross,* his first entry in the cycle. Here Lewis elaborates upon a visual style he discovered in that earlier film, one fully consistent with those "traits" we have come to associate with film noir (and, it would seem, pushing Guffey further in an expressionistic direction). What is surprising is not so much that Lewis was able to evoke much of the charm of a pastoral French setting with limited means but that he was able to infuse it with so many noir elements.

Though obscure, *So Dark the Night* remains the epitome of those film noirs dealing with a detective who has fallen from grace. For Henri Cassin is a master of observation and concentration, like Dupin and Holmes before him. Yet it is those very qualities, especially his ability to cut himself off from the rest of the world, that leads to his fall. A vacation intended to help him recover from the pressures of his job instead involves him in an amour fou and this unhappy affair precipitates the final personality split which divorces his highly rational self from the romantic side that leads him to murder. Lewis' penchant for shooting through windows (from exterior to interior and visa versa) is given full rein and, as in Hitchcock, opens us up to certain theoretical considerations too complex to explore here. What is interesting in this film is that this motif is grounded firmly in the film's structure. This becomes quite obvious in the film's final scene where Henri, dying of a bullet wound and forced to accept both sides of his personality, again looks out the window of the inn only to see himself as he was on the day of his arrival. Then, next to that image of a smiling detective on vacation is an image of him as he is on the night of his death—a serial killer. Recognizing his split personality for perhaps the first time, Henri smashes both "reflections" and exclaims: "Henri Cassin is no more. I have caught him and killed him." **BP**

SO EVIL MY LOVE (1948)

Director: Lewis Allen. **Screenplay**: Ronald Miller, Joseph Shearing and Leonard Spigelgass based on the novel by Joseph Shearing. **Producer**: Hal Wallis. **Director of Photography**: Max Greene. **Music**: William Alwyn and Victor Young. **Art Director**: Thomas N. Morahan. **Editor**: Vera Campbell and Leonard Trumm. **Cast**: Ray Milland (Mark Bellis), Ann Todd (Olivia Harwood), Geraldine Fitzgerald (Susan Courtney), Leo G. Carroll (Jarvis), Raymond Huntley (Henry Courtney), Raymond Lovell (Edgar Bellamy), Martita Hunt (Mrs. Courtney), Moira Lister (Kitty Feathers), Roderick Lovell (Sir John Curle), Muriel Aked (Miss Shoebridge), Finlay Currie (Dr. Krylie). **Released**: Paramount, July 21. 112 minutes.

On a voyage from Jamaica to England, Olivia, a prim and proper widow of a missionary, meets Mark, a smooth-talking jack-of-all-crimes. She takes him in as a boarder and falls in love with him. She believes Mark loves her, too. In fact, his heart is ice, and he has a girlfriend, Kitty, for amusement. Desperate for money, he insists Olivia carry out a blackmail scheme. Olivia's only friend, Susan, is in a miserable marriage to Henry. He is as odious as wealthy. Olivia has scandalous letters from Susan, for which she expects Henry will pay dearly. But Henry turns the tables and shows her a detailed report about Mark's criminal record that he is going to send the police. Olivia lunges at him, and he has a heart seizure. After substituting poison for his medicine, Olivia has Susan give Henry the fatal dose. Susan is convicted of murder. Mark finally admits to himself that he loves Olivia. Just before they sail to America and leave Susan to her fate, Olivia runs into Kitty, who reveals her affair with Mark. For his betrayal, Olivia stabs Mark. Then she goes to a police station to confess.

Since *So Evil My Love* has too much running time and too little noir style, what is there to recommend it? First, from the three actors whose names are above the title (Milland, Todd and Fitzgerald) to the other twenty listed afterward, all performances are strong. Second, the characters they play inhabit a noir world that is one of the most chilling in the

So Evil My Love: *Mark Bellis (Ray Milland) and Kitty Feathers (Moira Lister).*

classic period. Mark is out to get money by any crime necessary, including murder. He is smug that he's not able to love. Effortlessly, he keeps Kitty on a string as his back street girl and makes Olivia believe they are sharing a magical romance. Henry, another *homme fatale*, would rather Susan suffer thinking she is barren than tell her he may be impotent. His desperation to sire a son has made him ill. His mother, who cruelly told Susan that her failure to produce an heir is the cause of Henry's sickness, agrees with him that Susan shouldn't know the truth. One of the doctors Susan consulted about her fertility suggested that sherry might have "a tonic effect." As she has not gotten pregnant, she has increased her drinking. Alone all the time, except for her sneering husband and domineering mother-in-law, Susan becomes alcoholic and mentally unstable.

It is Susan's best friend, Olivia, who is her worst enemy. Olivia starts out simply enjoying how she deceives Susan, such as by cheating Susan out of her bonds, which Mark cashes. Breaking her promise to destroy Susan's confidential letters, Olivia is euphoric to have "the whip hand" and be "utterly in command" in blackmailing Henry for the letters. After Henry's seizure, she rapidly figures out how to poison him and have Susan take the blame. When Olivia visits Susan at a prison hospital, Susan's given up on life. She'd vehemently opposed Henry's intention to place her in a sanatorium. Now she thinks he was right. While Olivia holds her hand, Susan wishes for her execution to come soon. At first, Olivia is deeply troubled by Susan's plight and considers admitting to Henry's murder. However, Mark clears her conscience by predicting Susan won't be hanged but institutionalized. If Susan is fortunate, Olivia may accomplish what Henry didn't. Of course, Olivia well knows Susan isn't insane. Yet at least she can leave England with the prospect that Susan won't die because of her, just waste away. Her coldness toward Susan is exceeded by her attitude towards Mark. As they ride in a hansom cab, he tells her how much he loves her and begs her forgiveness for the things he's done. It's too late. His heart of ice may have melted for her, but Olivia's has frozen for him. Although his affair with Kitty is over, the former missionary has lost the ability to forgive. **DMH**

SOMEWHERE IN THE NIGHT (1946)

Director: Joseph L. Mankiewicz. **Screenplay**: Howard Dimsdale and Joseph L. Mankiewicz adapted by Lee Strasberg from a story by Marvin Borowsky. **Producer**: Anderson Lawler. **Director of Photography**: Norbert Brodine. **Music**: David Buttolph. **Art Directors**: James Basevi, Maurice Ransford. **Editor**: James B. Clark. **Cast**: John Hodiak (George Taylor/Larry Cravat), Nancy Guild (Christy Smith), Lloyd Nolan (Detective Lt. Kendall), Richard Conte (Mel Phillips), Josephine Hutchinson (Elizabeth Conroy), Fritz Kortner (Anzelmo), Margo Woode (Phyllis), Sheldon Leonard (Sam), Lou Nova (Hubert), Charles Arnt (Little Man), Whit Bissell (Bartender). **Completed**: April 5, 1946. **Released**: 20th Century-Fox, June 12. 110 minutes.

George Taylor is a marine whose wartime injury has left him with amnesia, a condition he hides from his superiors. He is discharged from the naval hospital with only two clues to his identity: a bitter letter from a former girlfriend and his last known residence, a hotel in downtown LA. To retrieve his past, he goes to the hotel where he stumbles upon a briefcase containing a gun and a letter from a "friend," Larry Cravat, describing a bank account that Cravat had set up for him. His search for Cravat leads him to a nightclub where he is successively pursued by two thugs in the employ of an opportunistic fortune teller named Anzelmo who has him beaten to get information on Cravat; beguiled by a seductive woman named Phyllis; befriended by nightclub singer Christy Smith, who lets him use her apartment as a sanctuary; and followed by an odd, cigar-smoking little man. Infatuated by Taylor, Christy arranges for him to meet her boss, nightclub owner Mel Phillips, who she feels can help him. Phillips in turn introduces him to Lt. Kendall, who informs Taylor that Cravat, a private detective, and a suitcase filled with $2 million of Nazi loot, disappeared just about the time Taylor had enlisted, and that Cravat, together with another man, are both suspects for the murder of the conveyor of the suitcase. The only witness, Conroy, is unfortunately in an insane asylum. Taylor breaks into the asylum and finds Conroy mortally wounded, but before he dies he tells Taylor that he had hidden the money amidst the pilings of a waterfront dock. Taylor and Christy find the suitcase filled with money and Cravat's overcoat with a label that reads "W. George, Tailor," at which point Taylor realizes that he is Cravat. Despite Christy's entreaties, Taylor suspects that he himself is the murderer and doesn't put up a fight when Anzelmo's thugs bring the couple to Anzelmo who demands the suitcase. Phillips, however, rescues them and brings them back to his club for a nightcap. Once there, Taylor realizes that Phillips is the mysterious third man and the real killer, not Cravat. Using the money as a lure, Taylor gets Phillips to bring Christy and himself to the dock where Kendall shows up in time to shoot Phillips before he can harm the couple. Preferring to start a new life with Christy, Taylor/Cravat rejects the notion of returning to work as a private eye.

Somewhere in the Night might well be a quintessential film noir, not because of its style, structure or performances but because it has a protagonist who meets so many noir criteria: an amnesiac, a war-wounded veteran and a private eye all rolled into one character. The fact that John Hodiak does little more than a credible job portraying him; that his job is not made easier by Nancy Guild's lifeless performance as his love interest (contrast this to Margo Woode's much better job as the ineffectual femme fatale); that the tangled plot fails to further the action and Mankiewicz's direction fails to sustain suspense—despite all this the Fox noir style is enough to carry this film, abetted as it is by a host of noir icons: Richard Conte, Lloyd Nolan, Sheldon Leonard, Charles Arnt and Whit Bissell.

These actors, in turn, are complemented by the presence of Fritz Kortner, a veteran of both Reinhardt's theater and German Expressionist film. Cinematographer Brodine does well with several low-key scenes and even better when he is allowed to roam beyond the confines of the Fox studio to such LA locales as Bunker Hill and Chinatown (prelude to his later work in *Boomerang* and *Kiss of Death*). The effect of WWII on the noir cycle is quite evident here but its essential themes are embedded in the character of Taylor/Cravat. Though the persona of the somewhat shady, calloused private detective has been displaced by the more sensitive and humane Taylor, even he is not beyond exploiting a spinster's loneliness to get information. Yet when Elizabeth Conroy confesses to Taylor that she only pretended to know him in the hope that his company might relieve her of the monotony of her daily existence, he embraces her and, moved by her tears, says, "I know a little bit about being lonely." It is a scene such as this that makes *Somewhere in the Night* worthwhile and, in its understated way, speaks volumes about what noir critics term existential angst. **BP**

SORRY, WRONG NUMBER (1948)

Director: Anatole Litvak. **Screenplay**: Lucille Fletcher from her radio play. **Producers**: Hal B. Wallis, Anatole Litvak. **Director of Photography**: Sol Polito. **Music**: Gene Merritt, Walter Oberst. **Art Directors**: Hans Dreier, Earl Hedrick. **Editor**: Warren Low. **Cast**: Barbara Stanwyck (Leona Cotterell Stevenson), Burt Lancaster (Henry Stevenson), Ann Richards (Sally Hunt Lord), Wendell Corey (Dr. Alexander), Harold Vermilyea (Waldo Evans), Ed Begley (James Cotterell), Leif Erickson (Fred Lord), William Conrad (Morano), John Bromfield (Joe, Detective), Jimmy Hunt (Peter Lord), Dorothy Neumann (Miss Jennings), Paul Fierro (Harpootlian). **Completed**: March 12, 1948. **Released**: Paramount, September 1. 89 minutes.

Sorry, Wrong Number: *Henry Stevenson (Burt Lancaster) and his wife Leona (Barbara Stanwyck).*

Leona Stevenson, an invalid heiress, is alone in her New York apartment one evening when, because of crossed telephone wires, she overhears two men planning to kill a woman. When the police can't investigate on her sketchy information, she makes phone calls to learn more about the murder and discovers that the intended victim is herself. Previously stubborn and self-indulgent, Leona has developed a psychosomatic cardiac condition. Her henpecked husband, Henry, has been blackmailed by a sinister fence named Morano, who, together with chemist Waldo Evans, were part of Henry's scheme of stealing pharmaceuticals from Leona's father's company. Crossed by Henry, Morano demands $200,000 to right things, and suggests that Henry get the money from his wife's insurance since she is ostensibly on the verge of death. When Henry learns that Leona's condition is psychosomatic, Henry tries to call off the plan. Morano refuses to wait and forces Henry to leave town so that Morano can arrange for Leona's death to appear as the result of a robbery attempt. Changing heart, Henry telephones a warning to Leona on his way to Boston. She answers the phone but is unable to leave her bed and get to the window as Henry advises. She screams and drops the phone as her killer approaches. When Henry rings back, a male voice responds "Sorry, wrong number" and hangs up. As Henry starts to leave the phone booth he is picked up by some special investigators who have discovered his plot.

Sorry, Wrong Number was originally a 22-minute radio script written by Lucille Fletcher, starring Agnes Moorehead and broadcast eight times between 1943 and 1947. Because of the huge success of this radio drama, producer Wallis approached Lucille Fletcher with the idea of "fleshing out" her play, which was virtually a monologue, into a feature film. Usually such expansion weakens the action but in retrospect it was fortunate that the film was made at the height of the noir cycle, for it works quite well as a film noir.

By providing Leona with a husband who is trapped in a dead-end marriage with a sick, manipulative wife and her powerful but doting father; by leading Henry slowly down the primrose path in an effort to extricate himself until he destroys both himself and Leona; by creating subsidiary characters both appealing (Sally Lord, Waldo Evans) and menacing (Fred Lord, Morano)—in short, by opening up the action without dissipating the tension, the blueprint for a major film noir was present. It needed only execution and for that Wallis chose Anatole Litvak, veteran of the German and French cinemas of the 1920s and 1930s, who was teamed here with one of his favorite photographers, the talented Sol Polito (they had worked together on *City for Conquest* and *The Long Night*). Litvak's experience with expressionistic *mise en scène* and Polito's fluid camera do nothing but enhance Leona's isolation and entrapment so that when the denouement arrives, it unfolds with a dark inevitability. The entire cast does a fine job but Burt Lancaster, sweating in a darkened phone booth, and Barbara Stanwyck (in an acting tour de force), moving from petulance to abject fear, each represents the apotheosis of the noir protagonist. **BP**

SOUTHSIDE 1-1000 (1950)

Director: Boris Ingster. **Screenplay**: Leo Townsend and Boris Ingster from an unpublished story by Milton Raison and Bert Brown. **Producers**: Maurice and Frank King. **Director of Photography**: Russell Harlan. **Music**: Paul Sawtell. **Production Designer**: Edward S. Haworth. **Editor**: Christian Nyby. **Cast**: Don DeFore (John Riggs/Nick Starns), Andrea King (Nora Craig), George Tobias (Reggie), Barry Kelley (Evans), Morris Ankrum (Eugene Deane), Robert Osterloh (Albert), Charles Cane (Harris), Kippee Valez (Singer). **Location**: San Quentin Prison and Los Angeles, California. **Completed**: June 30, 1950. **Released**: Allied Artists, November 16. 73 minutes.

Master counterfeit engraver Eugene Deane has grown old and sick serving a life sentence in prison. His major solace appears to be religion and he is always reading his Bible, which conceals the counterfeit plates that he works on in his cell. The plates are sneaked out of the prison in a minister's valise and are later picked up by Reggie, a member of a gang headed by Nora Craig, who is ostensibly the respected manager of a Los Angeles hotel but is actually Deane's daughter. Alerted, Treasury agent John Riggs finds evidence of the counterfeit plates in Deane's cell. Tracing the bogus money to Nora's hotel, Riggs assumes the identity of Nick Starns, a gambler wanted by the FBI. He strikes up a romance with Nora who arranges for him to buy some of the counterfeit bills. But she finds a sketch drawn by her father titled "Agent Riggs" and realizes Nick is a T-man. She locks him in the gang's house, which is then set afire. The police and federal men show up to capture all of the gang except Nora. They free Riggs, who pursues Nora through the darkened downtown area and into the freight yards, where he finally catches her. She tries to throw him off a narrow ledge but falls to her death on the tracks below instead.

Although not so fully realized as *T-Men, Southside 1-1000* is significant because it was written and directed by Boris Ingster, who also directed what may be the first film noir, *Stranger on the Third Floor*. Unlike that earlier studio effort, this film is in the style of the pseudo-documentary, but with much chiaroscuro and location work. *T-Men*, to its credit, avoids the super-patriotic narration of this film which, with great lapses of logic, links counterfeiting with the spread of Communism and even the Korean War! But *Southside 1-1000* is worth viewing if for nothing more than the last sequence in which the self-righteous agent Riggs pursues his former lover across a trestle bridge. After a moment in which they are locked in a passionate embrace of love and hate, the chase culminates with her Freudian leap into the darkness below. Don DeFore's soft vulnerability plays well in his few noir roles (*Ramrod*, *Too Late for Tears*, *Dark City*) as it does here. But it is Andrea King, a "bitch-goddess" if there ever was one, who dominates here in a role similar to hers in *Ride the Pink Horse*, where she is described by Gagin, at his most misogynistic, as "a dead fish with perfume on the outside." **BP**

SPELLBOUND (1945)

Director: Alfred Hitchcock. **Screenplay**: Ben Hecht and Angus MacPhail based on the novel Th*e House of Dr. Edwardes* by Francis Beeding. **Producer**: David O. Selznick. **Director of Photography**: George Barnes. **Music**: Miklós Rózsa. **Production Designer**: James Basevi. **Editors**: Hal C. Kern, William Ziegler. **Cast**: Ingrid Bergman (Dr. Constance Peterson), Gregory Peck (John "J.B." Ballantine/Dr. Anthony Edwardes), Michael Chekhov (Dr. Alexander Brulov), Leo G. Carroll (Dr. Murchison), Rhonda Fleming (Mary Carmichael), Norman Lloyd (Garmes), John Emery (Dr. Fleurot), Bill Goodwin (House Detective), Steven Geray (Dr. Graff), Donald Curtis (Harry), Wallace Ford (Man in Hotel Lobby), Art Baker (Lt. Cooley), Regis Toomey (Det. Gillespie). **Released**: Selznick/United Artists, October 31. 111 minutes.

When Dr. Anthony Edwardes arrives at Green Manors mental hospital to replace head psychiatrist Dr. Murchison, there is an immediate attraction between him and female staffer Dr. Peterson. After it becomes clear that Edwardes is disturbed, paranoid and possibly an amnesiac impostor, Murchinson summons the authorities. Edwardes disappears mysteriously followed by a smitten Peterson, who tracks him to New York City and tells him forcefully: "I'm going to do what I want to do: take care of you, cure you." After consulting her mentor, Dr. Brulov, Peterson takes Edwardes to an upstate ski resort where he remembers that he is actually John Ballantine and relives two events: the accidental death of his young brother and the real Dr. Edwardes' death. Ballantine is arrested for Edwardes' murder, and Peterson returns to Green Manors to confront Murchison, who confesses to killing his replacement before he shoots himself.

Spellbound is the bellwether for psychological melodrama in the noir cycle, as it contains the central motif which would inform so many noir films: psychological persecution. The film also epitomizes Hollywood's burgeoning fascination with Freudianism. Dream sequences provide blatant and often simplistic clues not only to Peck's neuroses but also to the mystery of the film. The narrative posits Ballantine, a traumatized and "neurotic" individual, being unhinged by Murchison, a power-hungry psychiatrist who uses childhood guilt to create a "fall guy" for a murder he has committed. In this regard, *Spellbound* uses psychological manipulation as a plot context like *The Scarf*, *Shock*, or *Whirlpool*. However, in *Spellbound* the noir protagonist is a woman, Dr. Peterson, who is described by her colleagues as a "human glacier" and a "smug" professional. When Peterson is first seen, she is behind her desk at the mental institution in a lab coat with her hair up in a bun and wear-

Spellbound: *John Ballantine (Gregory Peck) and Constance Peterson (Ingrid Bergman).*

ing thick glasses—all markers of a repressed woman in traditional Hollywood films including noir. To underscore the contrast Peterson's next patient is the disturbed femme fatale Mary Carmichael who wears low cut blouses, flirts with the attendants, and scratches one of them out of sexual excitement. And although Peterson's ultimate "transformation" into a sexual being is keyed to her infatuation with the handsome Dr. Edwardes, her attraction initially is based on his mysterious psychological disorder.

The film has often been criticized for its simplistic presentation of psychoanalysis as a wonder cure and this criticism is apt. In less than two days Chekhov and Constance manage to not only analyze his fairly complex nightmares—brilliantly visualized by surrealist artist Salvador Dali—but also return to him his memory and the primal moment of his childhood when he believed he caused the death of his brother, thereby "curing" him instantly and permanently. However, the film is also focused on the curative power of love, a theme in many Nicholas Ray noirs including *They Live by Night* and *Party Girl*. Peterson not only transforms her lover back into a "normal" man but she transforms herself as well. As the physically and emotionally altered Peterson—with her hair down and her glasses gone—tells Ballantine in their "honeymoon" room in Brulov's lodge: "It is I who have changed." **JU & AS**

THE SPIRAL STAIRCASE (1945)

Director: Robert Siodmak. **Screenplay**: Ethel Lina White, Mel Dinelli based on the novel *Some Must Watch* by Ethel Lina White. **Producer**: Dore Schary. **Director of Photography**: Nicholas Musuraca. **Music**: Roy Webb. **Art Directors**: Albert S. D'Agostino, Jack Okey. **Editors**: Harry W. Gerstad, Harry Marker. **Cast**: Dorothy McGuire (Helen Capel), George Brent (Professor Albert Warren), Ethel Barrymore (Mrs. Warren), Kent Smith (Dr. Parry), Rhonda Fleming (Blanche), Gordon Oliver (Steve Warren), Elsa Lanchester (Mrs. Oates), Sara Allgood (Nurse Barker), Rhys Williams (Mr. Oates), James Bell (Constable). **Released**: RKO, December 12. 83 minutes.

Young women with an "affliction" are being murdered in a New England town in the early twentieth century. While

The Spiral Staircase: *Mrs. Warren (Ethel Barrymore) and Helen Capel (Dorothy McGuire)*.

Helen watches a silent movie at the town hotel, a lame woman is strangled upstairs. Helen hurries home, where she is a servant to the bedridden matriarch, Mrs. Warren. It's the quintessential old dark house, and it's a stormy night. Helen is in mortal danger because she is mute and the killer lives in the mansion. Dr. Parry, who loves her, is called away from treating Mrs. Warren to see another patient. Blanche, having first left Albert for his younger half-brother, Steve, breaks up with Steve. When Helen discovers Blanche is dead, she thinks Steve is the killer and locks him up in the basement. The real killer, Albert, starts stalking Helen. She desperately tries to telephone Dr. Parry, but she can't make herself speak. She goes down the backstairs to free Steve, but Albert is waiting for her. He chases her up the spiral staircase. Mrs. Warren has managed to leave her bed and is at the top of the stairs holding a pistol. When Albert is in sight, she shoots, and Helen screams. Her voice recovered, Helen completes the phone call to Dr. Parry.

The Spiral Staircase is a notable example of the kind of film noir that challenges traditional studies of film noir. For decades, some terms and concepts that have been among the most frequently used to define film noir have not been applicable, in fact, to many movies that are considered film noir. As a rule, the film noirs that have gotten short shrift are "women's pictures," which are likely to take place in a home and deal with a romantic crisis (so-called "tear-jerkers," "three hankies" or "weepies"). However, during the classic years of film noir, especially in the 1940s (less so in the 1950s), many women's pictures are crime movies that have the characteristics of the noir visual style. What has prevented women's film noirs from getting proper recognition is that both mass media and academic descriptions of film noir are devoted to "hardboiled." As a result, film noir is reduced to these kinds of essentials: the protagonist is male (e.g., an investigator, a criminal, a victim of circumstance); the literary source is hardboiled crime fiction; there is brutal violence (by fists and guns); the time and place is a contemporary U.S. city (e.g., not Victorian London or a family's home). This approach ignores the numerous published stories, novels and plays (or original screenplays) primarily addressing a female audience that were adapted into film

noirs. It lavishes attention on the femme fatale and ignores the woman-in-distress, despite the latter's equally strong presence in film noir. Because the quantity and quality of women's film noirs favorably compare to "hardboiled" ("men's") film noirs, until women's film noirs are properly recognized, a comprehensive history and balanced analysis of film noir will be, by definition, impossible.

The noir style is repeatedly arresting in *The Spiral Staircase*. To take one example, after they kiss and Helen stands in profile at the front door watching Dr. Parry go into the rainstorm, the wall behind her is well lit. She shuts the door and the light fades away, leaving her framed in blackness. The image suggests the presence of danger. Also, by removing the natural background, her environment is re-made into one that is psychological, which superbly establishes the transition to her daydream of her wedding. (In the marriage ceremony, Albert is subtly revealed as the killer.) Helen's "affliction," like Albert's psychosis, is the result of trauma in childhood. Helen hasn't been able to speak since she saw her parents perish in a fire. Albert's father despised his sons as weaklings. Albert tells Helen that he, for one, has changed. "Steven is weak, as I once was. What a pity my father didn't live to see me become strong." Albert's (foster) mother, Mrs. Warren, isn't the kind of mother vilified by Philip Wylie in his *Generation of Vipers*. That is, *The Spiral Staircase* is not aimed at "Momism." At the start of the film, Albert kills a lame woman. Her inability to walk "normally" recalls the late president, FDR (Franklin Delano Roosevelt), who was a paralytic. In different ways, both Albert and his father recall the other President Roosevelt, TR. Although sickly in his youth, Theodore Roosevelt made himself strong, as Albert wishes to do. Like Albert's father, Roosevelt was a big-game hunter. (The portrait of Albert's father, in hunting gear, which hangs above an elephant-tusk in Mrs. Warren's bedroom, resembles Roosevelt.) What links all three—TR, Albert's father and Albert—is eugenics. Theodore Roosevelt was a major proponent of it. Albert violently practices it. In a monstrous way, Albert, too, is a hunter. Albert believes his father would have admired him for disposing of people his father detested, "the weak and imperfects." **DMH**

SPLIT SECOND (1953)

Director: Dick Powell. **Screenplay**: William Bowers, Irving Wallace from a story by Chester Erskine and Irving Wallace. **Producer**: Edmund Grainger. **Director of Photography**: Nicholas Musuraca. **Music**: Roy Webb. **Art Directors**: Albert S. D'Agostino, Jack Okey. **Editor**: Robert Ford. **Cast**: Stephen McNally (Sam Hurley), Alexis Smith (Kay Garven), Jan Sterling (Dorothy "Dottie" Vale), Keith Andes (Larry Fleming), Arthur Hunnicutt (Old Miner), Richard Egan (Dr. Neal Garven), Paul Kelly (Bart Moore), Robert Paige (Arthur Ashton), Frank DeKova (Dummy). **Released**: RKO, May 2. 85 minutes.

Convict Hurley, on the lam with wounded Moore and henchman Dummy, carjacks newly-divorced Kay returning from Reno with boyfriend Arthur. When the car runs out of gas, Hurley keeps them hostage, then carjacks reporter Fleming and bargirl Dorothy. Hurley discovers that divorcee Kay's ex-husband Neal is a doctor, so phones him, threatening to kill Kay unless Neal meets them to patch up Moore. Hurley aims for a ghost town on an A-bomb test site, knowing nobody will look for them there. They just have to be gone by the time of the blast. But the car barely makes it since the radiator has sprung a leak. Later, an old miner becomes another captive. There are verbal sparring sessions between Hurley and his prisoners while they wait. Kay plays up to Hurley after he kills Arthur, however Hurley is even more interested in Dorothy. Neal arrives, patches up Moore, and then announces Moore cannot be moved. Suddenly the bomb alert siren goes off early—the military has decided to move up the test. Hurley absconds with Moore and Kay in Neal's car, but, in their rush, they head towards the bomb. The miner leads the others to a deserted excavation, and they reach shelter seconds before the explosion.

As an actor, crooner star Dick Powell was famous for re-inventing his career as a tough guy in such films as *Murder, My Sweet*, *Cornered*, *Pitfall*, *Cry Danger* and *The Tall Target*. So he had certifiable noir credentials. It is not surprising that his first (and best) project as director was this hardboiled, though very melodramatic, noir thriller. And, like the later *Kiss Me Deadly*, it was one of the few noirs to deal with nuclear paranoia. The evocative title sequence with credits rolling over silhouettes fleeing across cracked, sun-baked mud flats sets the stark tone for the rest of the picture. The film is admirably cast, with an ensemble feel that remains consistent throughout. A good thing, as the narrative flags occasionally, often just marking time once the characters are ensconced in the ghost town saloon-set for almost the entire middle hour of the film. Actor McNally devoted nearly his whole career to playing hard-as-nails tough guys, from straight-arrow cops in such pictures as *Criss Cross* to sadistic hoods in such titles as this and the later *Violent Saturday*. He has rarely been more memorable, chewing scenery like there is no tomorrow. But it is a fitting approach to the bigger-than-life Hurley, a decorated WW II veteran killing machine unable to tame his violent misanthropy once returned stateside.

Scriptwriters Bowers and Wallace make him recognizably human with his one soft spot for his elder comrade, the gut-shot Moore (the great Paul Kelly). Moore had once had an opportunity to do less time if he had testified against Hurley but had refused, thus engendering Hurley's undying loyalty. Sterling is a standout with her perfectly modulated perform-ance as B-girl Dorothy, a brave girl from the wrong side of the tracks. Hunnicutt waltzes through his role as the talkative miner, basically playing himself as he did in countless films from *The Big Sky* and *The Lusty Men* to *El Dorado*. However, despite the good cast, individuals emerge as little more than ciphers with skimpy attention paid to character detail. Exceptions are the divorced, hauntingly tragic noir couple por-trayed by Egan and Alexis Smith. Both do a lot with very little. Egan ably conveys the decent doctor still in love with his wife but resigned to her self-destructiveness. As Kay, Alexis Smith has perhaps her best role, a woman ruled by self-interest, frighteningly unable to conquer her demons, someone who has no character and will do almost anything to survive. Not faring quite as well is Andes' annoyingly glib reporter Fleming and Paige's suicidally stupid Arthur. Despite the film's faults, it is remarkably entertaining, with one of the most over-the-top cli-maxes from the early 1950s. The sequence where Hurley, Kay and Moore flee, only to round a hill to spot the looming bomb tower, then, panic-stricken, try to extricate their car from a rut, is milked by Powell for every last ounce of suspense. Once the bomb goes off, the excellent miniatures and visual effects by Harold E. Wellman are scarily convincing. **CD**

STORM FEAR (1956)

Director/Producer: Cornel Wilde (Theodora Productions). **Screenplay**: Horton Foote from the novel by Clinton Seeley. **Director of Photography**: Joseph La Shelle. **Music**: Elmer Bernstein. **Production Designer**: Rudi Feld. **Editor**: Otto Ludwig. **Cast**: Cornel Wilde (Charlie), Jean Wallace (Elizabeth), Dan Duryea (Fred), Lee Grant (Edna), David Stollery (David), Dennis Weaver (Hank), Steven Hill (Benjie), Keith Britton (Doctor). **Completed**: May 18, 1955. **Released**: United Artists, February 1. 88 minutes.

After a bank heist, Charlie and two of his gang, Benjie and Edna, seek refuge in his older brother Fred's New England farmhouse. There Charlie nurses a gunshot wound in his leg and plans to elude police roadblocks by going on foot over nearby mountains. Charlie also attempts a reconciliation with his brother's wife Elizabeth with whom he previously had an affair and whose son David is also Charlie's. When Hank, Fred's hired hand, escapes from the farm to alert the police, the criminals hastily prepare to leave. Charlie con-vinces David to guide them across the snow-covered moun-tain; and when Fred resists this, he is shot by Benjie. As they cross the open country, Edna breaks her ankle and is aban-doned by Charlie, which shocks David who had thought his "uncle" was a basically good man. Nonetheless, when Benjie attempts to overpower Charlie near the summit and escape alone with the loot, David grabs the gun dropped during the criminals' struggle and shoots Benjie. David helps Charlie, whose wound has been reopened, to the summit. But before he can get over, Charlie is shot by the rifle of the pursuing Fred and dies in the local hospital.

Released late in the classic period and shortly after such cynical films as *Kiss Me Deadly* and *The Big Combo*, the lat-ter also starring Cornel Wilde and Jean Wallace, *Storm Fear's* noir characteristics stem less from its violence or any gritty cityscapes—there are none—than from the claustrophobic quality of the fugitives' stay at the farmhouse. Unlike the brief sojourn by the fugitive couple at the end of *Gun Crazy*, an extended time frame allows the illicit past relationship between the criminal and his brother's seemingly normal family to be resurrected and the remembered passion of Charlie and Elizabeth's past affair to be translated into their unspoken contest for the present affections of their son.

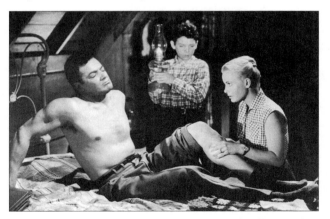

Storm Fear: *Charles (Cornel Wilde), David (David Stollery), and Elizabeth (Jean Wallace).*

As these tensions from the guilty past mingle with the main narrative line of pursued criminals, Wilde adds diverse morbid details: Benjie's sociopathic hatred of all present, Charlie's self-conscious stammer caused by the disapproval of his older brother, and even the cheap dog collar that the family has used to decorate the Christmas tree after their pet's death. The melodrama in *Storm Fear* develops with Ibsen-like pretensions, especially in the hospital epilogue, where Charlie's guilt finally precipitates a rather gratuitous plea for forgiveness. In contrast with his performance under Lewis' direction of *The Big Combo,* Wilde removes any undertones of obsession or surface glamour from his and Jean Wallace's roles in *Storm Fear.* As in *On Dangerous Ground* and the following year's *Nightfall,* the use of winter locations for the flight over the mountain ultimately reduces the diverse interior conflicts to a graphically defined struggle between small, dark figures and a vast, snow-covered landscape. **AS**

THE STRANGE AFFAIR OF UNCLE HARRY
[aka **UNCLE HARRY**] (1945)

Director: Robert Siodmak. **Screenplay**: Stephen Longstreet adapted by Keith Winter from the play by Thomas Job. **Producer**: Joan Harrison. **Director of Photography**: Paul Ivano. **Music**: Hans J. Salter and [uncredited] Mario Castelnuovo-Tedesco, Paul Dessau. **Art Directors**: John Goodman, Eugene Lourie. **Editor**: Arthur Hilton. **Cast**: George Sanders (John "Harry" Quincy), Geraldine Fitzgerald (Lettie Quincy), Ella Raines (Deborah Brown), Sara Allgood (Nona), Moyna MacGill (Hester Quincy), Samuel S. Hinds (Dr. Adams), Harry Von Zell (Ben), Ethel Griffies (Mrs. Nelson), Judy Clark (Helen), Craig Reynolds (John Warren), Will Wright (Mr. Nelson). **Completed**: June 16, 1945. **Released**: Universal, as *The Strange Affair of Uncle Harry,* August 17. 80 minutes.

Note: *Uncle Harry* was previewed in Los Angeles with five different endings for review by the Hays Office. When Universal selected the "dream ending" in order to guarantee receipt of MPAA Seal of Approval, producer Joan Harrison quit.

John Quincy lives a dull life with his domineering sisters, Lettie and Hester, in their family mansion in Corinth, New Hampshire. He meets Deborah Brown, a visiting fashion expert from New York City, at the Quincy mill. Soon their friendship becomes love, and he asks her to marry him. Deborah meets John's family and, although Hester is happy for her brother, Lettie is jealous of Deborah and feigns a heart attack on learning of their engagement. Frustrated and angry at Lettie's attempt to spoil his happiness, John plans to murder her; but Hester drinks the poison intended for Lettie and dies. Lettie is convicted of her sister's murder but does not incriminate John, because she knows that her death will prevent him from marrying Deborah. John wakes up and discovers that the entire situation has been a dream.

The central narrative of *Uncle Harry,* with its portrayal of unnatural, even obsessive, love between a sister and brother and its consequent suggestions of incest, is developed in the same straightforward manner as such other noirs directed by Siodmak that feature mentally imbalanced characters as *Phantom Lady* and *The Dark Mirror.* Geraldine Fitzgerald's interpretation of Lettie, the possessive sister, is punctuated by the same moments of pathological hysteria as Franchot Tone's deranged killer in *Phantom Lady* and Olivia de Havilland's disturbed twin in *The Dark Mirror.*

Lettie's self-destructive failure to exonerate herself as part of a plan to prevent John's marriage makes her monomania one of the most aberrant depicted in film noir. The ending, which discloses that John's plan to murder Lettie and free himself has all been a dream, may seem to take *Uncle Harry* out of the realm of noir melodrama and closer to such black comedies as Siodmak's own *Fly by Night,* a parody of formula thrillers like Hitchcock's *Saboteur.* But *Uncle Harry* is not a parody; and, while the ending may have been selected to mollify the MPAA code administrators, it reveals, like the framing device in Lang's *Woman in the Window,* that ironically the most disturbed psyche in the film may actually have been that of the protagonist. As with Lang's original intention for *Woman in the Window,* it is clear from producer Joan Harrison's reaction that this was not the ending which the filmmakers intended. Nonetheless when the entire narrative becomes a character's dream it invites a reinterpretation of events in terms of the dreamer's hidden fears and desires.

John Quincy's infatuation with Deborah Brown does appear to be threatened in what becomes a dream narrative told from his point of view by Lettie's dominance of his emotions. At the same time both the physical resemblance between Deborah and Lettie and the exaggerated dream portrait of his sister that John renders suggest that John's nightmare could more accurately be a reflection of his own suppressed and socially unacceptable desire than they are of Lettie's. Similarly, his recourse to an elaborate murder scheme rather than a direct, adult confrontation reinforce the likelihood that his reverie is a manifestation not just of deep-rooted psychological dependency on his sister but also of profound guilt over his sexual attraction to her. Like Richard Wanley in *Woman in the Window,* John awakens from an intolerable dream situation with relief but finds himself no less oppressed by reality than he was before. **AS**

STRANGE FASCINATION (1952)

Director: Hugo Haas. **Screenplay**: Hugo Haas. **Producer**: Hugo Haas. **Director of Photography**: Paul Ivano. **Art Direction**: Rudi Feld. **Music**: Vaclav Divina, Jakob Gimpel. **Editor**: Merrill G. White. **Cast**: Hugo Haas (Paul Marvan), Cleo Moore (Margo), Mona Barrie (Diana), Rick Vallin (Carlo), Karen Sharpe (June), Marc Krah (Shiner), Genevieve Aumont (Yvette), Pat Holmes (Walter). **Released**: Columbia, September. 80 minutes.

Paul Marvan is an accomplished European pianist who is discovered by a rich American patron, Diana, and brought to the U.S. While on tour he meets Margo, a young dancer, who falls for Marvan's talent and then moves herself into his apartment, leaving her "abusive" boyfriend and partner Carlo. They marry and soon Marvan is consumed by jealousy. He forces Margo to quit her modeling job and goes into debt trying to support the both of them. Soon Marvan is missing gigs and drinking heavily while Margo complains of his oppressive treatment of her. In order to raise money, the desperate pianist falls into the presses of a publishing company, damaging his insured hands. The insurance company uncovers Marvan's fraud and he gives up any claim to the money and with it any claim to Margo. Marvan ends up playing one-handed piano to a crowd of homeless alcoholics.

The film that most neatly crystallizes the themes and motifs of the Hugo Haas-Cleo Moore series of obsessive noirs is *Strange Fascination*. The film opens on a dialogue-less sequence: a homeless man in an alley behind Carnegie Hall listening to the concert inside. The camera then follows him back to a Salvation Army mission where he begins to play one-handed piano in an empty hall. As the camera moves into a close-up of the man a flashback ensues.

The one-handed homeless man was a world-famous pianist named Paul Marvan who met his own deadly female in the form of the dancer Margo at a club late one night. The oblivious and clumsy Marvan pushed chairs around and talked loudly to the waiter while Margo and her dancing partner/boyfriend tried to perform their act on the dance floor. Enraged at his rudeness ("Clumsy hick . . . eating like a savage"), Margo finds out who he is and decides to harass him at his own concert. Instead she finds his music mesmerizing and turns into a "groupie," telling the delighted Marvan that he has "tamed" her and that she feels like a "schoolgirl" waiting for his autograph backstage. She asks him out, a daring move for a 1950s woman but not for a movie femme fatale, and the nonplussed Marvan agrees. Although it is obvious by her sensual signals and coy dialogue during the date that she wants him to "make a pass," he uses his age as an excuse. She playfully calls him a "coward" for his demurral.

After Marvan returns to New York, Margo turns up again asking him for his "protection" from her abusive boyfriend. She asks to stay with him but again he demurs by bringing up the issue of "appearances." But by the next cut she has moved in, indicating who has the power in this relationship from the very first. With a beautiful woman walking around in nightclothes and towels, Marvan very soon falls under her spell as she had fallen under the spell of his music earlier. And, by implication of course, they become lovers and soon marry, much to the dismay of friends like his agent who calls him an "old fool" and the more subtle disapproval of his "angel" Diana.

Marvan however cannot control his obsession with Margo. He becomes jealous when she flirts with her boss at her modeling job and meets with her ex-boyfriend who wants to put her in a new show. He then refuses to let her work, telling her that he will supply her with whatever she needs. He borrows money from Diana, starts drinking, and then missing performances. They are finally forced to move to a tenement where Margo lies in bed all day like a pampered prisoner and fumes ("I feel like I'm suffocating").

To say the least, this is an imbalanced relationship which goes more off center as the film progresses. While Margo was simply attracted to his talent and prestige, which she hoped would rub off on her, Marvan has raised her up as an icon, a fact Margo cannot understand; "There's nothing so special about me." Marvan's only answer is to weep and tell her in extremely Romantic terms, "It's some sort of strange fascination. It's like a curse, like a heavy veil." Knowing that Margo is on the verge of leaving him, Marvan makes the ultimate sacrifice. He pretends to faint and fall into a music publisher's press, crushing one of his hands (his hands are insured for one hundred thousand dollars). This, however, does not save their relationship as the insurance company discovers the fraud. Margo leaves him and the audience finds him at the end of the film as he was at the beginning, playing piano in a skid row mission. **JU**

STRANGE ILLUSION (1945)

Director: Edgar G. Ulmer. **Screenplay**: Adele Comandini from an original story by Fritz Rotter. **Producer**: Leon Fromkess. **Director of Photography**: Philip Tannura, Eugene Schufftan, Benjamin Kline. **Music**: Leo Erdody. **Art Director**: Paul Palmentola. **Editor**: Carl Pierson. **Cast**: James Lydon (Paul Cartwright), Warren William (Brett Curtis), Sally Eilers (Virginia Cartwright), Regis Toomey (Dr. Vincent), Charles Arnt (Professor Muhlbach), George H. Reed (Benjamin), Jayne Hazard (Dorothy Cartwright). **Completed**: October 16, 1944. **Released**: PRC, March 31. 84 minutes.

Adolescent Paul Cartwright believes that his father's death and his mother's plans for remarriage are not merely coincidental. This suspicion becomes solidified after he receives a letter written by his father before the man was found dead.

Spurred on by this message from beyond the grave, Paul decides to feign insanity in the hopes of catching his mother's suitor off guard and exposing him as his father's murderer. Committed to an asylum by his mother at the prompting of her fiancé, Brett Curtis, the youth is subjected to intense scrutiny by the hospital staff. The plan nearly backfires in the sinister surroundings of the asylum, which drives Paul to the edge of sanity. Finally, the youth gathers enough evidence to convict his mother's lover of his father's murder.

Strange Illusion is another stylish, low-budget feature directed by Edgar G. Ulmer; but unlike his other noir efforts, notably *Detour* and *Ruthless, Strange Illusion* is a relatively actionless production. The most interesting aspect of the film rests in its updating of *Hamlet,* complete with the message from beyond the grave and the faked insanity, into a contemporary thriller. The noir tone of *Strange Illusion* is accentuated by both Warren William's portrayal of the lecherous cad and the claustrophobic atmosphere of the mental hospital. William, who for the previous decade had been one of the Warner's studios matinee idols, adds a naturalistic dimension to the character of the suave, middle-aged gigolo Brett who leers at teenage girls lounging around a private pool. The asylum sequences, on the other hand, are controlled visions of chaos and corruption, a mental hell sardonically defined by Ulmer. **CM**

STRANGE IMPERSONATION (1946)

Director: Anthony Mann. **Screenplay**: Lewis Herman, Mildred [Mindret] Lord, Anne Wigton. **Producer**: W. Lee Wilder (as William Wilder). **Director of Photography**: Robert Pittack. **Music**: Alexander Laszlo. **Production Designer**: Edward C. Jewell (uncredited). **Editor**: John F. Link, Sr. **Cast**: Brenda Marshall (Nora Goodrich), William Gargan (Dr. Stephan Lindstrom), Hillary Brooke (Arline Cole), George Chandler (Jeremiah Wilkins Rinse), Ruth Ford (Jane Karaski), H.B. Warner (Dr. Mansfield), Lyle Talbot (Insp. Malloy), Mary Treen (Nurse), Cay Forrester (Miss Roper), Dick Scott (Detective). **Released**: Republic, March 16. 68 minutes.

Nora Goodrich, a research scientist at a New York chemical company, decides to try her experimental anesthetic on herself with the aid of her lab assistant, Arline Cole. On her way home from work she accidentally backs into a tipsy pedestrian, Jane Karaski. Though Jane appears uninjured, Nora insists on driving her home before she falls into the clutches of J.W. Rinse, a shady ambulance chaser. Entering Jane's rather shabby apartment, Nora makes sure she is safe and leaves her with some money. Shortly after arriving at her own apartment, Nora is visited by her fiancé and co-worker, Dr. Stephan Lindstrom, who wants to marry her without further delay, but she manages to evade the issue so Steve leaves just as Arline arrives. Nora has secretly arranged with Arline to conduct the experiment at her own home where she collects the ingredients, heats the compound over a Bunsen burner and injects herself with the results. Once Nora is asleep, Arline alters the volatile compound and prepares to leave, but Stephan returns just in time to witness the explosion and rescue Nora from the resultant fire. Nora's face is badly disfigured and while she is confined to the hospital, Arline manipulates Nora's doctor so that Stephan is unable to see or even contact Nora. Since Arline is the only channel of information between the two, she arouses distrust in each and the engagement is called off. Nora returns home only to be con-

fronted by Jane Karaski, who, encouraged by Rinse, demands $25,000 from her. Realizing Nora doesn't have that kind of money, Jane pulls a gun on her and takes her jewelry and purse, but Nora manages to get the gun away from her and in the ensuing struggle, the gun goes off and Jane accidentally falls off the balcony to her death. Since Jane was carrying Nora's identification and her face was damaged beyond recognition, her body is mistaken for Nora's. Nora in turn decides to adopt Jane's identity and flies to L.A. where she enlists the aid of a plastic surgeon to repair her face through a series of operations. Naturally, the face she has the surgeon give her is Jane's. When Nora discovers that Stephan has married Arline, she returns to New York and wins a position as his lab assistant. With a troubled marriage, Stephan easily falls in love with "Jane." In a final confrontation with Arline, Nora convinces her of her true identity and her knowledge of Arline's crime, and persuades Arline to leave Stephan. However, Rinse has reappeared and recognizes "Jane" and tips off the police who arrest her for Nora's murder. Unable to convince the police of her innocence, Nora calls upon Arline to confirm her true identity. Arline refuses, and under great stress, Nora passes out, only to wake up in her own apartment with Stephan attending to her. It seems the whole affair was a dream induced by the experimental anesthetic!

Although he would not hit his stride until *Desperate* (1947), this film, and the earlier *The Great Flamarion* (1945), demonstrates Anthony Mann's progression towards being one of the most significant, certainly the most representative, directors of noir films, a strong claim for a director who is known as much for his westerns, perhaps even his epic films, as he is for his film noirs. But the evidence is there: besides directing more traditional "hardboiled" entries like *Railroaded* and *Raw Deal,* Mann introduced the semi-documentary into the cycle (*T-Men*), made period pieces (*The Black Book*) and even historical dramas (*The Tall Target*) in the noir style, and created that blackest of all westerns, *Devil's Doorway*—all within a span of about six years. Directors as renowned as Nicholas Ray have credited Mann with a special gift for heightening cinematic violence without displaying much gore. And his collaborations with photographer John Alton, both at Eagle-Lion and MGM, represent the epitome of the cycle's expressionistic use of light and shadow.

One of his lesser efforts, *Strange Impersonation* was hampered by budgetary and temporal constraints and a plot whose deficiencies strained credulity beyond the breaking point. Yet it remains an important cog in Mann's progression and contains a number of defining motifs of the film noir. Although shot in a rather pedestrian manner, the sequence near the end where Nora is interrogated by the police stands out: Nora is illuminated harshly by an overhead lamp (typical of such interrogation scenes), but camera position alternates obliquely from high angle to low angle in such a way that Nora's sense of oppression and entrapment is enhanced, culminating finally in a montage of accusing faces in extreme close up. The doppelganger theme is given a visual correlative through an abundance of mirror images (a penchant for which Mann would later refine in *T-Men* and *Raw Deal*). Even those sudden, precipitous plot twists leading to a rather weak, preemptive conclusion—"it's all a dream"—is not alien to the film noir (cf. *Woman in the Window*). The film also contains the seeds of two of Borde and Chaumeton's major attributes of the film noir: the *insolite* (unusual) and the *oneiric* (dream-like). **BP**

THE STRANGE LOVE OF MARTHA IVERS (1946)

Director: Lewis Milestone. **Screenplay**: Robert Rossen, Robert Riskin from the story "Love Lies Bleeding" by Jack Patrick. **Producer**: Hal B. Wallis. **Director of Photography**: Victor Milner. **Music**: Miklós Rózsa. **Art Directors**: Hans Dreier, John Meehan. **Editor**: Archie Marshek. **Cast**: Barbara Stanwyck (Martha Ivers), Van Heflin (Sam Masterson), Lizabeth Scott (Toni Marachek), Kirk Douglas (Walter O'Neil), Judith Anderson (Mrs. Ivers), Roman Bohnen (Mr. O'Neil), Darryl Hickman (Sam Masterson, as a boy), Janis Wilson (Martha Ivers, as a girl), Ann Doran (Secretary). **Completed**: December 7, 1945. **Released**: Paramount, July 24. 115 minutes.

An unusual childhood situation results in murder; and young Martha Ivers inherits a large family fortune from her aunt. In the next twenty years, she maintains control of a large industrial plant in a small Midwestern town. An accidental reunion with a childhood friend, Sam Masterson, rekindles old passions and long-forgotten feelings of guilt in Martha. Her weak and alcoholic husband, District Attorney O'Neil, is not pleased when he discovers Masterson's presence and attempts to force him out of town. Masterson quickly realizes that he is being compromised and decides to confront O'Neil but first flatters Martha in order to discover her true motives, discovering that she actually murdered her aunt. He taunts Masterson about his affair with Martha and then falls down the stairs in a drunken rage. Martha urges her supposed lover to murder her husband; but he refuses and leaves Martha alone with O'Neil. The couple realizes that circumstances will force them to reveal the crime they committed long ago. O'Neil retrieves a pistol, and they commit suicide. Masterson leaves with Toni, remarking casually, "I wanted to see if I could be lucky twice."

In the postwar period, Hal Wallis left Warner Bros. to become an independent producer and his predilection for extremely romantic novels and stories placed his noir films in a category of their own. His major characters suffered from psychological obsessions and neuroses but were infrequently criminals from the lower classes. Their presence in a noir film created a lurid appeal. Wallis selected material that enabled veteran directors such as Dieterle, Litvak, and Milestone to have a certain freedom of expression; but patterns of Wallis' authorship occur most frequently in these films, such as the method in which the *mise en scène* is grotesquely overstated at crucial moments to evoke the audience's private romantic fantasies, or the many characters who return to places that hold traumatic associations for them and rekindle suppressed passions.

Miklós Rózsa wrote the music for *The Strange Love of Martha Ivers,* and it illustrates the conventional Holywood leitmotif technique of film scoring. This technique associates a musical theme with each character, setting, or situation, thus heightening the dramatic flux and the audience's unconscious understanding and expectation of the film's story. It should be pointed out that the popular song "Strange Love" represents the sweetness of Toni and the happy ending, not the hardness of Martha. Rózsa overscores to the point that non-musical moments in his films amount to negative emphasis.

The Strange Love of Martha Ivers is filled with noir implications as the characterizations of Martha and the two principal male characters make an absurd love triangle. Dealing in a relationship based on fear, guilt, and cruelty, the noir

characters exhibit an emotional imbalance caused by romantic zeal. Masterson functions as a catalyst. He enters the town and his mere presence is responsible not only for the disruption of normal activities but also the death of the leading citizens. Milestone has created a film that is a testimony to both the affinity between sex and violence and the cruel manipulations of a fatal woman. Kirk Douglas' portrayal of O'Neil reflects the tendency of noir films from this period to cast conventionally strong personalities in a fictional position of impotence. Masterson also has little potency and merely reacts to the manifestations of Martha Ivers' aura of control. The unusual double suicide once again associates film noir with the surrealist concept of amour fou in presenting a love that finds justification only in death. **CM & LS**

THE STRANGE WOMAN (1946)

Director: Edgar G. Ulmer. **Screenplay**: Herb Meadow, Edgar G. Ulmer, Hunt Stromberg based on the novel by Ben Ames Williams. **Producer**: Hedy Lamarr, Hunt Stromberg, Jack Chertok, Eugen Schufftan. **Director of Photography**: Lucien Andriot. **Production Design**: Nicolai Remisoff. **Music**: Carmen Dragon. **Editor**: John Foley, Richard G. Wray. **Cast**: Hedy Lamarr (Jenny Hager), George Sanders (John Evered), Louis Hayward (Ephraim Poster), Gene Lockhart (Isaiah Poster), Hillary Brooke (Meg), Rhys Williams (Deacon Adams), June Storey (Lena), Moroni Olsen (Reverend Thatcher), Alan Napier (Judge Saladine), Olive Blakeney (Mrs. Hollis), Kathleen Lockhart (Mrs. Partridge). **Released**: United Artists, October 25. 100 minutes.

Jenny Hager is a beautiful, willful woman who is intent on gaining power. After escaping her abusive father, she marries the elderly but rich Isaiah Poster. When that life becomes too restrictive, she convinces the enamored Poster son Ephraim to kill his father. He succeeds, almost accidentally, when the canoe he and his father are in overturns and he refuses to help his father. Jenny then rejects him out of disgust for his lack of finesse. She takes over her husband's business and makes his foreman John Evered her lover. In addition to all this she manages to become the primary force behind charity and reform in the town of Bangor. When Evered finds out that she inspired Ephraim to kill his father, he leaves her, at least temporarily. Thinking he has returned to her friend Meg she races to Evered's cabin and is killed as she is thrown from the wagon.

The Strange Woman: *Jenny Hagar (Hedy Lamarr) and John Evered (George Sanders).*

The Strange Woman (like *Leave Her to Heaven*, also based on a novel by Ben Ames Williams) is Edgar G. Ulmer's most impressive example of the "deadly female" subset of noir. Unlike the one-dimensional femme fatale Vera in Ulmer's *Detour*, Jenny Hager in *The Strange Woman* is a finely drawn characterization replete with intriguing contradictions and complex neuroses (undoubtedly part of this is due to the presence of star Hedy Lamarr as producer on the film). When we first see her, as a child, she is already attempting to dominate all those around her, ordering her best friend Meg around and pushing into the water the pusillanimous Ephraim. When her drunken father comes to fetch her, she dawdles by the river, staring at her sultry reflection in the water and stating her very modern post-feminist motto: "Just as soon as I grow up [I'll] have everything . . ."

Jenny does grow up, as we see in the very next sequence, to be a stunning and intelligent beauty who turns the men around her into love slaves with very little effort. Soon she is married to the richest man in town, Isaiah Poster, while romantically linked to his handsome but still weak-willed son Ephraim, from whom she demands "love and obedience," even to the point of murder. And although Ephraim almost bungles the murder in the river, Jenny does obtain what she wants—freedom from control and total power. As a wealthy widow, she takes over her husband's lumbering company, even winning over the men who have qualms about working for a woman, including the stalwart John Evered.

However, as mentioned, Ulmer and his writers insist on presenting Jenny as a multi-dimensional character, who is not just a mass of murder, incest, and manipulation. Early in the film Ulmer shows Jenny being beaten by her father and her initial pleasure at it (hinting at a history of sexual-physical abuse), thereby providing possible motivation for her attempts to control the other men in her life. In addition, she is driven to perform acts of mercy over and over again— pledging money to the church when the men refuse to and then inspiring the other women to do the same; giving the abused Lena a cabin to live in; visiting the sick; becoming a leader in the Temperance League (in reaction one may assume to her father's alcoholism). To the town of Bangor she is nothing less than an "angel of mercy." Even in her final demise is shown with great sympathy. Thrown from a wagon

as she races to what she supposes is the location of a tryst between her lover John and her friend Meg, John runs to her side and declares his love for her, even though she has admitted her complicity in the murder of Poster. As the camera focuses tenderly on her radiant face, she tells him, "I wanted the whole world but it was really only you." **JU**

THE STRANGER (1946)

Director: Orson Welles. **Screenplay**: Anthony Veiller with contributions from [uncredited] John Huston and Welles from a story by Victor Trivas. **Producer**: S. P. Eagle [Sam Spiegel]. **Director of Photography**: Russell Metty. **Musical**: Bronislau Kaper. **Production Designer**: Perry Ferguson. **Editor**: Ernest Nims. **Cast**: Edward G. Robinson (Wilson), Loretta Young (Mary Longstreet), Orson Welles (Franz Kindler/ Professor Charles Rankin), Philip Merivale (Judge Longstreet), Billy House (Mr. Potter), Richard Long (Noah Longstreet), Konstantin Shayne (Konrad Meinike), Martha Wentworth (Sara), Byron Keith (Dr. Lawrence), Pietro Sosso (Mr. Peabody). **Completed**: November 21, 1945. **Released**: RKO, July 21. 95 minutes.

The seemingly peaceful surroundings of a small New England college community are invaded by a fugitive war criminal. His escape was engineered by government agents in the hopes of trailing the zealous Nazi to his superiors. Wilson, the agent sent to follow their human bait, is knocked out before he is able to identify the object of his intense search. Franz Kindler alias Charles Rankin, a supposed college professor, wastes no time in disposing of the unwanted visitor from his Nazi past. He murders his ex-comrade and conceals the body scant hours before he is to wed Mary Longstreet, a prominent young society woman. The small-town atmosphere begins to take on a distinctly morose personality manipulated by Kindler and assaulted by the constant probing of Wilson, the government agent. Ultimately Kindler makes mistakes and his actions betray his deep-rooted Nazi philosophies. Only after exposing Kindler/ Rankin's wife to the atrocities committed by him during the war does the agent begin to tighten the net around the war criminal. Unable to completely believe that the man she loves could be capable of such heinous crimes, Mrs. Rankin confronts her husband for the last time. However Kindler/Rankin has gone over the edge of sanity and attempts to murder her. Cornered by the police and agent Wilson, Kindler falls to his death impaled by a mechanism connected to a huge clock tower.

Probably the most conventional of Orson Welles' films in terms of both its storyline and its production history, *The Stranger* nevertheless is an unusual film noir. Working through a tradition of international intrigue in the mode of writers like Eric Ambler or Graham Greene, Welles and his screenwriters Anthony Veiller and John Huston introduce sensations of irrationality into a small-town environment. Atypical of Welles' work, the images found in *The Stranger* are neither complex nor baroque. Rather the characters tend to be ciphers, mired in cryptic illusions of purpose and rationale. Each of the main characters is a stranger: Franz Kindler, due not only to the fact that he is an alien but also because he masquerades as a completely different person; Wilson, an outsider whose presence upsets the balance of typical routine in the college community; and Mary Longstreet, who never reveals her character until the film's conclusion.

The movie is filled with perverse relationships and equally

The Stranger: *Wilson (Edward G. Robinson), Mary Longstreet (Loretta Young), and Franz Kindler (Orson Welles).*

perverse characterizations. Besides the obvious nature of Kindler's Nazi allegiances, even someone as seemingly harmless as Mr. Potter, the proprietor of the local grocery store, becomes a dark-sided elf, cheating at checkers, overtly suspicious of strangers, and easily convinced of conspiracies. The relationship between Charles Rankin and his wife is surreal in its implications. A viewer may find it implausible that no one, particularly his wife, would be able to see the hidden current of Nazi madness in Rankin/Kindler's personality. The growing relationship in their young marriage is a mild example of mad love as it extends beyond the bounds of normal relationships. Ultimately the mockery of a marriage and the underlying thread of violence found in Kindler's pulpish characterization underscore the noir quality to *The Stranger. The Stranger* exists as an answer to the critics who complained that Welles could not make a "program" picture. He did, and it has found a niche in the canon of the film noir. **CM**

STRANGER ON THE THIRD FLOOR (1940)

Director: Boris Ingster. **Screenplay**: Frank Partos, Nathaniel West (uncredited). **Producer**: Lee Marcus. **Director of Photography**: Nicholas Musuraca. **Music**: Roy Webb. **Art Directors**: Van Nest Polglase, Albert D'Agostino. **Editor**: Harry Marker. **Cast**: Peter Lorre (Stranger), John McGuire (Mike Ward), Margaret Tallichet (Jane), Charles Waldron (District Attorney), Elisha Cook, Jr. (Joe Briggs), Charles Halton (Meng), Ethel Griffies (Mrs. Kane), Cliff Clark (Martin), Oscar O'Shea (Judge), Alec Craig (Attorney), Charles Judels (Nick, the café owner). **Completed**: July 3, 1940. **Released**: RKO, September 1. 64 minutes.

Newspaper reporter Mike Ward is the star witness at the trial of a taxi driver, Briggs, accused of a brutal throat-slashing murder. Although Mike's evidence is circumstantial, it secures a guilty verdict and capital punishment from a rather detached judge and jury. Mike's fiancée, Jane, believes Briggs is innocent and encourages Mike to help prove it. One night on his way into his apartment, he sees a stranger with a white scarf first outdoors and then lurking in the shadows on the stairwell. Subsequently

noticing that he cannot hear the usual snoring of his elderly next-door neighbor, Albert Meng, Mike begins to worry that Meng might be dead but falls asleep in his chair. Mike dreams that he is arrested, tried, and convicted for Meng's murder. Finally strapped into the electric chair, Meng himself, cruelly laughing, enters to witness Mike's execution. Waking from this nightmare, Mike rushes next door, and finds Meng's throat slashed. Suspecting the stranger, Mike reports the murder to the police, who suspect him. Jane scours the neighborhood looking for the stranger and, seeing a bizarre little man wearing a white scarf, she asks to walk with him for protection. She presses him for information and discovers he has escaped from a mental institution. When the stranger realizes Jane has lied about where she lives he suspects she is helping to return him to the institution and begins to act in a threatening manner. Jane escapes his clutches and runs across the street. The stranger gives chase, but he is hit by a truck and, before dying, confesses to the murders. Mike and Jane plan to be married and a smiling Briggs, now free, ushers them into his taxicab for a ride to the courthouse.

Stranger on the Third Floor is the first true film noir, though some critics would place such earlier films as *Blind Alley, Rio* and *Let Us Live* within the cycle. Unlike these earlier films, the unique manner in which it combines elements from a variety of classic Hollywood genres—gangster/crime, detective, horror, even social problem—represents enough of a break with the 1930s to usher in the era of the film noir. If Partos' story betrays its pulp sources in its illogic and incongruities, it owes to them as well in its depiction of an oppressive world filled with fear and paranoia, one that we would come to associate with the fiction of Woolrich and, subsequently, of the noir cycle.

This film certainly displays most of the qualities that Borde and Chaumeton associate with the film noir: the *oneiric* blurring of dream and reality; the *insolite* or the cruelty of a sudden act; the *erotic* (e.g., the scene in which Jane dries off in Mike's apartment and especially the prurient Meng's reaction to it). Latvian-born Ingster suffuses the story with expressionistic touches throughout but it is the dream sequence, a montage bordering on the surreal, that is both impressive and a chilling indictment of the American judicial system. Ingster seems to draw as much as possible from the limited talents of actor McGuire, emphasizing physical gesture over performance in a virtual throw-back to the tenets of German Expressionism (even McGuire's flat

delivery of Mike's interior monologue somehow works). And he derives even more from the brief screen time afforded to the more talented Lorre, whose every gesture and expression confirms his agonized state and whose short-hand ability to evoke sympathy for his character is reminiscent of his performance in *M*. Finally, almost a year before the release of *Citizen Kane* and well before the production of *The Cat People*, the basis of the RKO noir style (Musuraca, Webb, D'Agostino) was established. **BP**

STRANGERS ON A TRAIN (1951)

Director/Producer: Alfred Hitchcock. **Screenplay**: Raymond Chandler and Czenzi Ormonde adapted by Whitfield Cook from the novel by Patricia Highsmith. **Director of Photography**: Robert Burks. **Music**: Dimitri Tiomkin. **Art Director**: Ted Haworth. **Editor**: William H. Ziegler. **Cast**: Farley Granger (Guy Haines), Ruth Roman (Anne Morton), Robert Walker (Bruno Antony), Leo G. Carroll (Senator Morton), Patricia Hitchcock (Barbara Morton), Laura Elliott (Miriam), Marion Lorne (Mrs. Antony), Jonathan Hale (Mr. Antony), Howard St. John (Capt. Turley), John Brown (Professor Collins), Norma Varden (Mrs. Cunningham), Robert Gist (Hennessey), John Doucette (Hammond). **Released**: Warner Bros., June 30. 101 minutes.

While traveling by train, Guy Haines, a champion tennis pro, is approached by Bruno Antony, a professed fan. Armed with an astonishing knowledge of Guy's personal life, Bruno proposes an unusual arrangement: crisscross murders, with Bruno killing Guy's wife, who refuses to give him a divorce so he can remarry, and Guy murdering Bruno's strict father. Appalled, Guy jokingly rejects the proposal; but the psychotic Bruno carries out his part of the plan by strangling Guy's wife in an amusement park. Guy is unable to provide a solid alibi to the police; and they keep him under observation. Bruno demands Guy carry out his part of the so-called bargain. Guy is evasive; but his feelings of guilt cause him to appear increasingly suspicious to the police. Bruno threatens to implicate Guy by planting the tennis pro's lighter at the scene of the crime. Guy must race through a scheduled tennis match in order to catch up with Bruno before he plants the evidence. In the end, Bruno is crushed to death by a runaway merry-go-round, and Guy is cleared of the crime.

Guilt if only by association is a theme that Hitchcock turns to obsessively, often focusing on an entirely innocent man who by some mischance is implicated in a crime he did not commit. In hiring Raymond Chandler to adapt Highsmith's novel, Hitchcock may have wanted to counter-balance the light tone of her prose. Although Chandler's legendary disdain for Hollywood annoyed Hitchcock, particularly when the novelist made the producer/director travel to his home many miles south of Los Angeles for story meetings, the resulting script was an effective conflation of the traditional distinctions between protagonist and antagonist in the noir style. In *Strangers on a Train*, Guy's innocence is a technicality. The character of Guy, incarnated by Farley Granger, is self-serving, opportunistic, and, by his refusal to take Bruno seriously, at least partially responsible for his wife's murder. Guy never disputes Bruno's observations that if he were free Guy could make a politically advantageous marriage. Guy's weak rebuff of Bruno's proposal implies a subconscious assent and his subsequent actions are motivated more by a

Strangers on a Train: *Guy Haines (Farley Granger) and Bruno Antony (Robert Walker)*.

desire to avoid trouble than to bring Bruno to justice.

Bruno, the actual murderer, is an extremely idiosyncratic individual who blithely ignores normal social boundaries. Slyly incarnated by Robert Walker, Bruno is witty, straightforward, and sadly sympathetic. Even after he is seen viciously strangling Guy's wife, Walker portrays Bruno as the betrayed victim when the obnoxious Guy will not hold up his end of the bargain. The world of *Strangers on a Train* depends on a transference between the guilty and the innocent which is both characteristically noir and characteristically Hitchcock. More pointedly that any other filmmaker of the classic period, Hitchcock puts his particular spin on film noir and manipulates the audience into moments of siding with the killer. That sequence in *Strangers on a Train* comes when Bruno is en route to plant Guy's lighter at the scene of the crime but drops the incriminating object down a grate. His struggles to retrieve it, intercut with scenes of Guy feverishly trying finish a tennis match so that he can go after Bruno, create a powerful tension which the viewer wants resolved even if it means hoping that Bruno will succeed. As the audience empathizes with a killer, they are likely aware that he will ultimately fail. Nonetheless in the context of noir, where protagonists sometimes perish, and because of Guy's dissociative guilt, the other possibility is there. **JK**

STREET OF CHANCE (1942)

Director: Jack Hively. **Screenplay**: Garrett Fort from the novel *The Black Curtain* by Cornell Woolrich. **Producer**: Sol Siegel. **Director of Photography**: Theodor Sparkuhl. **Music**: David Buttolph. **Art Directors**: Hans Dreier, Haldane Douglas. **Editor**: Arthur Schmidt. **Cast**: Burgess Meredith (Frank Thompson/Dan Nearing), Claire Trevor (Ruth Dillon), Louise Platt (Virginia Thompson), Sheldon Leonard (Det. Joe Marucci), Frieda Inescort (Alma Diedrich), Jerome Cowan (Bill Diedrich), Adeline de Walt Reynolds (Grandma Diedrich), Arthur Loft (Sheriff Lew Stebbins), Clancy Cooper (Burke). **Completed**: February 19, 1942. **Released**: Paramount, November 18. 74 minutes.

After blacking out when hit by falling rubble, Frank Thompson awakens in an unfamiliar section of New York, carrying a cigarette case and hat marked with the initials "D.N." Returning home, he discovers his wife has moved and traces her to where she lives under her maiden name of Virginia Morrison. Recovering from the initial shock of seeing Frank, Virginia explains that he had disappeared completely over a year ago, but Frank has no memory of what has happened during that time. Fortunately, he is allowed back at his position of accountant; but, upon returning to the office the next day, he notices a sinister individual watching him from outside the building. Leaving work that evening, Frank is aware that the same man has followed him home and is waiting outside his apartment with some other men. Fleeing with his wife via the fire escape, Frank tells Virginia to go to her mother's where he will contact her after he attempts to discover what happened during the missing year of his life. He haunts the area where the accident occurred, and one evening a girl calls to him. Pretending to know her, Frank discovers she knows him as Dan Nearing and that her name is Ruth Dillon. He is shocked to discover from Ruth, who claims to be his fiancée, that as Nearing he is wanted for the murder of Ruth's employer, Harry Diedrich. Persuading Ruth to take him with her to the Diedrich mansion, where she works as a maid, Frank hopes to prove his innocence. He also learns that his sinister pursuer is Detective Joe Marucci. At the mansion, Frank meets Grandma Diedrich, a speechless invalid. Working out an eye code with Grandma, Frank discovers it was Ruth who killed Harry Diedrich. Ruth admits that she stabbed Diedrich when he caught her stealing money, money she had hoped to elope with. Frank in turn confesses that he has no memory of his life as Nearing and plans to return to his wife once he is no longer wanted for murder. Ruth pulls a gun on Frank and in the struggle over the weapon she is shot. Realizing Ruth has only moments to live, Frank affirms her assertion that the amnesia was a lie and that he loves her. Marucci hears Ruth's dying confession and Frank is now free to return to his normal existence.

Although somewhat obscure, *Street of Chance* is an important early entry in the noir cycle for it establishes a number of conventions that later helped to define film noir and set it off from its predecessors. It is the first adaptation of a Cornell Woolrich story in the noir cycle and it authentically captures the atmosphere of Woolrich's universe: the hapless and desperate individual at loose in New York City; a sense of doom and foreboding; and the use of amnesia. Woolrich's greatest weakness is in his plotting, where contrivances, coincidences, and even contradictions impugn the story's coherency.

Yet it is this very weakness which helps develop the black and chaotic world that is unique to Woolrich and makes his narratives compatible with film noir. In this case writer Fort has improved upon the Woolrich original by altering the weak ending so that the killer is no longer a peripheral character but Ruth herself. It is also fortunate that this early adaptation of Woolrich was photographed by Theodor Sparkuhl. Veteran of both German Expressionism and French poetic realism, Sparkuhl had earlier helped to define the noir style in *Among the Living* and this style would soon evolve into a near perfect visual analogue of Woolrich's world. It is a style whose *mise en scène* contrasts markedly with that of similar melodramas produced earlier, especially in its distinctive use of space: rooms with lowered ceilings to enhance a sense of enclosure; the use of forced perspective to allow greater depth staging; areas of white now broken up by patterns of diagonal and vertical lines. Finally, mention should be made also of the contribution of Hans Dreier, another German expatriate, who as head of Paramount's art department was a major architect of that studio's noir style. **BP**

THE STREET WITH NO NAME (1948)

Director: William Keighley. **Screenplay**: Harry Kleiner. **Producer**: Samuel G. Engel. **Director of Photography**: Joe MacDonald. **Music**: Lionel Newman. **Art Directors**: Lyle Wheeler, Chester Gore. **Editor**: William Reynolds. **Cast**: Mark Stevens (Gene Cordell/Joe Manley), Richard Widmark (Alec Stiles), Lloyd Nolan (Inspector Briggs), Barbara Lawrence (Judy Stiles), Ed Begley (Chief Harmatz), Donald Buka (Shivvy), Joseph Pevney (Matty), John McIntire (Cy Gordon), Howard Smith (Commissioner Demory), Walter Greaza (Lt. Staller), Bill Mauch (Mutt), Sam Edwards (Whitey), Don Kohler (FBI Agent Atkins), Roger McGee (Joe), Vincent Donahue (Cholly), Phillip Pine (Monk), Robert Patten (Danker). **Completed**: March 7, 1948. **Released**: 20th Century-Fox, July 14. 91 minutes.

FBI Inspector Briggs discovers that the primary suspect in a nightclub holdup in Center City, Ed Danker, was framed, arrested then released on bail and mysteriously killed. Suspecting this is part of a crime wave perpetrated by a well-organized gang, Briggs and his assistant, Cy Gordon, bring in agent Gene Cordell to go undercover with the identity of Joe Manley, a drifter with a police record. Cordell arrives in Center City and quickly impresses fight promoter Alec Stiles who is the prime suspect. Cordell gives Gordon the details of the gang's next caper, but Stiles is warned by his informant, Commissioner Demory. After Cordell obtains a spent bullet from Stiles' luger to compare with evidence from a past robbery, Stiles realizes his gun has been used and has Demory check the fingerprints which reveal Cordell as an undercover agent. Stiles then plans to set up Cordell during a robbery so that he will be killed by the police. But Briggs and his associates discover that Demory was the gangster's informant in time to thwart the plot. Wounded, Stiles tries to shoot Cordell but Cordell kills Stiles instead. Chief Harmatz arrives in time to arrest Demory for his complicity.

Street with No Name was one of several semi-documentary thrillers produced at Fox beginning with *House on 92nd Street* (from which the character of Insp. Briggs, played by Lloyd

The Street with No Name: *Alec Stiles (Richard Widmark) and Gene Cordell (Mark Stevens).*

Nolan, is carried over into this film). There is an inherent tension between the semi-documentary and the film noir in terms of both style (the "realism" of those portions depicting police procedures—usually high key and flat lighting—vs. the expressionism of the noir portions) and content (the stereotyping of government agents to portray them in the best light vs. the moral ambiguity of the noir universe). Push too far in one direction and we have the *film policier* (*House on 92nd Street, Walk East on Beacon*) or even something akin to propaganda (*I Was a Communist for the FBI*).

Film policier becomes film noir when the moral authority of the agent is impugned and his life hangs by a thread because he has gone undercover; or when the figure of the "heavy," because of his idiosyncrasies, displaces police procedures as the center of interest. So the potential of the semi-documentary as film noir owes more to Anthony Mann (*T-Men, He Walked By Night*) than to Louis De Rochemont (*House on 92nd Street*). It owes as well to the Fox noir style (beginning with *I Wake Up Screaming*) where photographers like Joe MacDonald were given the tools (and the liberty) to leave an expressionistic fingerprint on film noirs ranging from private eye (*The Dark Corner*) to semi-documentary (*Call Northside 777*) to period piece (*Moss Rose*). Or where directors like Henry Hathaway could take his experience with *House* to the streets of New York to make a fine film noir like *Kiss Of Death*. Of course some mention should be made of this film's two leads. Mark Stevens' small stature, no asset in an adventure film, plays well in the film noir because it lends iconic value to his vulnerability, whether he is a private detective or a government agent. As for Richard Widmark, this talented actor is arguably the quintessential noir protagonist. He has slightly muted the hysteria of his performance as Tommy Udo (*Kiss of Death*) here but enough of that persona remains so that Stiles' misogyny (he brutally beats his wife) and his affectations (use of nasal inhaler, fear of germs) are given real impact—helped by just a suggestion of Udo's crazy cackle. **BP**

THE STRIP (1951)

Director: Leslie Kardos. **Screenplay**: Allen Rivkin. **Producer**: Joe Pasternak. **Director of Photography**: Robert Surtees. **Music**: Georgie Stoll. **Art Directors**: Cedric Gibbons, Leonid Vasian. **Editor**: Albert Akst. **Cast**: Mickey Rooney (Stanley Maxton), Sally Forrest (Jane Tafford), William Demarest (Fluff), James Craig (Delwyn "Sonny" Johnson), Kay Brown (Edna), Louis Armstrong and Band (Themselves), Tommy Rettig (Artie Ardrey), Tom Powers (Lt. Bonnabel), Jonathan Cott (Behr), Tommy Farrell (Boynton), Myrna Dell (Paulette Ardrey), Jacqueline Fontaine (Frieda), Vic Damone, Monica Lewis (Singers). **Completed**: February 9, 1951. **Released**: MGM, August 15. 84 minutes.

An aspiring actress, Jane Tafford, is dying of a gunshot wound and her lover, Sonny Johnson, is dead. The police arrest jazz drummer Stan Maxton, Jane's ex-boyfriend, on suspicion of murder. He tells the police that he is a Korean War veteran who came to Los Angeles to resume his career as a drummer but initially got involved in Sonny Johnson's bookmaking racket. Later, Stan met Jane, an aspiring actress, who worked as a cigarette girl and dancer at a jazz bistro on the Sunset Strip. Jane, in turn, introduced him to the club's owner, Fluff, and, since Stan had fallen for her, easily persuaded him to go to work for Fluff, playing drums. Jane and Sonny become romantically involved and Stan, realizing that Sonny is just using Jane, warns Sonny off by threatening to expose his bookmaking operation. A couple of Sonny's thugs beat Stan up and proceed to take him for a ride out of town or worse. But Stan escapes, reveals Sonny's background to Jane, and warns her to get out of town just as he is about to do. Jane, however, believes she can get Sonny to leave Stan alone. As Stan is finishing his story Lt. Bonnabel gets a phone call from the hospital and intimates that Jane has recovered sufficiently to sign a confession. To protect Jane Stan confesses to shooting both Sonny and Jane but the police eventually secure a deathbed confession from Jane exonerating Stan.

The Strip is one of a series of minor noir films that Mickey Rooney starred in during the 1950s (*Quicksand, Drive A Crooked Road*) when his career was flagging. Typically, he portrayed a sincere little guy subjected to the vicissitudes of life and, more often than not, victimized by an opportunistic woman. This film, however, was produced at MGM and, while not as noir as it might have been (especially in its visual style), contains some fine jazz interludes. Indeed, if there were such a category as the noir musical, this film could well be included. Like Albert Dekker, James Craig plays Sonny Johnson with just the right flair, covering his penchant for ruthlessness with the suave manner of an aesthete (an amateur horticulturist, at one point Johnson fusses over the flowers he is sending to the funeral of a rival he has eliminated). And as the once-brash persona of Mickey Rooney is being displaced by that of the loser, he settles easily into the role of the drummer who retreats to his music to avoid life's pain—much as Charles Aznavour would later in *Shoot the Piano Player*. **BP**

SUDDEN FEAR (1952)

Director: David Miller. **Screenplay**: Lenore Coffee and Robert Smith from the novel by Edna Sherry. **Producer**: Joseph Kaufman. **Director of Photography**: Charles Lang, Jr. **Music**: Elmer Bernstein. **Art Director**: Boris Leven. **Editor**: Leon Barsha. **Cast**: Joan Crawford (Myra Hudson), Jack Palance (Lester Blaine), Gloria Grahame (Irene Neves), Bruce Bennett (Steve Kearney), Virginia Huston (Ann), Touch [Mike] Connors (Junior Kearney). **Released**: RKO, August 7. 110 minutes.

Myra Hudson, a successful playwright and San Francisco heiress, is in New York to help cast her new play. During the auditions she vetoes actor Lester Blaine because he doesn't look like a romantic lead. Meeting her again on the train to San Francisco, Lester romances Myra, and they soon marry and settle in the Hudson mansion in San Francisco. Lester meets with Irene Neves, his flashy ex-girlfriend, and makes it clear that he married for reasons other than love; but he warns Irene against attempting to break up his marriage. Lester uses Irene's friendship with Junior Kearney, whose brother Steve is Myra's attorney, to find out about his wife's finances. He discovers that Myra plans to donate her father's estate to a heart foundation and live solely on her income as a playwright. Secretly meeting in Myra's study, Lester and Irene find a new will leaving Lester $10,000 per year until he remarries. This will was devised by Myra's lawyer without Myra's consent and Lester is unaware that his wife has already dictated a new, more generous will. Irene informs Lester the will cannot become valid until after the weekend and urges Lester to arrange for Myra to have a fatal

accident soon. By chance, Myra had left her dictating machine running, inadvertently recording the lovers' conversation. Listening to the machine, Myra realizes Lester's intentions. She goes to bed that evening terrified and stays awake the whole night devising a plan to kill Lester. The next day she secretly enters Irene's apartment, where she finds some poison and a gun which she steals. By means of a forged note, Myra arranges for Lester to meet Irene in her apartment late Sunday night so that Myra can kill Lester there with Irene's gun. She also forges a note from Lester instructing Irene to meet him in a nearby garage at the same time, thus insuring that Irene will be held for Lester's murder. When he arrives at the apartment, Myra finds she is incapable of firing the gun. Dropping the weapon, she runs from the apartment but Lester pursues her in his car. When Lester fails to keep his rendezvous, Irene begins to walk back to her apartment. Since she is dressed in a fur coat and white scarf similar to Myra's, Lester mistakes Irene for Myra and starts to run her down. As she screams, he recognizes Irene and attempts to swerve the car, killing both of them.

Sudden Fear reworks the theme of a wife's suspicion of her husband, a noir staple since *Suspicion*, in a rather effective manner despite some melodramatic plot contrivances and a first half that moves rather slowly. In many ways this film stands at the juncture between the "traditional" film noirs of the 1940s and the more "aberrant" entries of the late 1950s and it shows it. Certainly Joan Crawford draws upon previous roles which made her an icon of the noir cycle as a strong-willed woman who, betrayed by love, stands in fear of her life while maintaining the pretense of a devoted wife (and a fine job she does too).

Jack Palance, not yet the icon he would become after *Shane*, evokes a more modern "method" of acting in skillfully blending the sinister with the romantic. Elmer Bernstein's musical score and the use of locations also pull the film in a more modern direction. Yet the talents of Charles Lang and his associates keep the film well within a recognizable RKO noir style. The Academy aspect ratio sets the proper frame for the profusion of noir mannerisms showcased here: oblique angles; depth of field; lowered ceilings and chiaroscuro lighting from the very beginning. Indeed, Miller's and Lang's use of San Francisco's hills, stairwells, alleys and apartment courts at the film's suspenseful conclusion set a noir standard that would not be exceeded until *Kiss Me Deadly*. **BP**

SUDDENLY (1954)

Director: Lewis Allen. **Screenplay**: Richard Sale. **Producer**: Robert Bassler (Libra Productions). **Director of Photography**: Charles Clarke. **Music**: David Raksin. **Art Director**: Frank Sylos. **Editor**: John F. Schreyer. **Cast**: Frank Sinatra (John Baron), Sterling Hayden (Tod Shaw), James Gleason (Pop Benson), Nancy Gates (Ellen Benson), Kim Charney (Pidge), Paul Frees (Benny Conklin), Christopher Dark (Bart Wheeler), Willis Bouchey (Dan Carney), Paul Wexler (Slim Adams), Jim Lilbum (Jud Hobson), Charles Smith (Bebop), Ken Dibbs (Wilson), Clark Howatt (Haggerty). **Completed**: May 1, 1954. **Released**: United Artists, October 7. 77 minutes.

The peaceful surroundings of a small California town are quietly invaded by a trio of hired assassins who intend to kill the President of the United States. Forcing their way into a house that overlooks a train depot where the President is secretly scheduled to transfer to a private motorcar, the gunmen hold the Benson family and the local policeman, Tod Shaw, hostage as they await the train's arrival. John Baron is in charge of this operation and seizes every opportunity to frighten, humiliate, and bully his hostages. After what seems like an endless period of psychopathic threats, the assassination plan is put into effect. Shaw finds a way to escape and subdues the would-be killers only moments before the train pulls into the station.

Just as its title implies, *Suddenly* is a taut, fast-paced thriller that emphasizes the vicious sadism of the key conspirator, John Baron. His boastful, Machiavellian attitude links *Suddenly* with the more brutal noir films of the 1950s such as *The Big Night* and *Kiss Me Deadly*. Beyond this preoccupation with violence, the sense of claustrophobia and despair unleashed by the assassins in *Suddenly* is completely amoral, and totally opposite the style of harassment found in such socially redemptive films as *The Desperate Hours*. The criminals in *Suddenly* have a purpose that director Lewis

Allen and writer Richard Sale exploit only as action; they exclude any significant level of social protest or criticism. There are no reasons given, or asked for, regarding the assassination—the entire incident functions as a nightmare, a very real nightmare that invades the serenity of a small town. At the end of the film it is apparent that the Benson family will never be the same, suddenly scarred by people out of nowhere who irrevocably disrupt their middle-class tranquility. **CM**

SUNSET BOULEVARD (1950)

Director: Billy Wilder. **Screenplay**: Charles Brackett, Billy Wilder, and D. M. Marshman, Jr. **Producer**: Charles Brackett. **Director of Photography**: John F. Seitz. **Music**: Franz Waxman. **Art Director**: Hans Dreier, John Meehan. **Editors**: Arthur Schmidt, Doane Harrison. **Cast**: William Holden (Joe Gillis), Gloria Swanson (Norma Desmond), Erich von Stroheim (Max Von Mayerling), Nancy Olson (Betty Schaefer), Fred Clark (Sheldrake), Lloyd Gough (Morino), Jack Webb (Artie Green), Cecil B. DeMille, Hedda Hopper, Buster Keaton, Anna Q. Nilsson, H.B. Warner (themselves, the Waxworks). **Completed**: June 18, 1949. **Released**: Paramount, August 10. 115 minutes.

Pursued by creditors who want to confiscate his car, down-and-out screenwriter Joe Gillis turns into a Sunset Boulevard driveway and finds shelter in a crumbling garage flanked by a massive, faded mansion. The half-ruined estate is occupied only by Norma Desmond, a long-forgotten silent film star, and her faithful butler, Max, who was once her husband and a famous director. Attracted to Joe, Norma offers him a job helping her prepare the script of her comeback film, *Salome*. Because he is broke, Joe accepts and moves into a room over the garage at Norma's insistence. The spineless writer soon becomes Norma's kept man. Bored and fed up with Norma's world of past glories, Joe escapes one evening to a local hangout, where he meets Betty Schaefer, a young studio reader. Together they try to write a screenplay. Soon falling in love with Betty, Joe tries to make a clean break with Norma but is pulled back into her orbit when she attempts suicide. Joe finally summons up enough courage to walk out, but as he does so, the hysterical Norma kills him.

It is the rare film that declares itself as immediately as does *Sunset Boulevard*. Opening with the sardonic narration of a dead man commenting mordantly on the circumstances of his own murder, this highly unusual work announces itself as a bleak but irresistibly sardonic motion picture, a trenchant observation of Hollywood's most bizarre human artifacts. One can only imagine the effect of the film's original opening, which was shot but discarded; it featured the dead Joe Gillis sitting up on his slab in the morgue and telling his story to a captive audience of corpses.

The fusion of writer-director Billy Wilder's biting humor and the classic elements of film noir make for a strange kind of black comedy, as well as a strange kind of film noir. There are no belly laughs here, but there are certainly strangled giggles: at the pet chimp's midnight funeral; at Joe's discomfited acquiescence to the role of gigolo at Norma's Mack Sennett-style "entertainments" for her uneasy lover; and at the ritualized solemnity of Norma's "waxworks" card parties, which feature such former lumi-

Sunset Boulevard: *Above, Joe Gillis (William Holden) and Betty Schaefer (Nancy Olson). Below, Joe with Norma Demond (Gloria Swanson).*

naries as Buster Keaton as Norma's has-been cronies. It should be noted that, although much of *Sunset Boulevard's* peculiar brand of humor derives from the strange circumstances of Norma's life, very little, if any, of that humor is actually at Norma's expense. The real anti-hero of the piece is the weak, wavering Joe, played with highly appropriate, slack-jawed prettiness by William Holden. Norma herself, as portrayed by Gloria Swanson, is a tragic figure, imbued by Wilder with powerful romantic presence. A woman obsessed, she clings to her vision with a tenacity that must ultimately be granted a grudging admiration, and she is the only character in the film, with the possible exception of Erich von Stroheim's fanatically loyal Max, who inspires genuine sympathy. Watching herself on screen in an old movie, she leaps into the projector's blast of light and cries, "They don't make faces like that anymore!" It is difficult for the viewer to favor Joe's cynicism over her fervor, however misguided or self-centered it may be. **JK**

THE SUSPECT (1944)

Director: Robert Siodmak. **Screenplay**: Arthur T. Horman, Bertram Millhauser based on the novel *This Way Out* by James Ronald. **Producer**: Islin Auster. **Director of Photography**: Paul Ivano.

Music: Frank Skinner. **Art Directors**: John B. Goodman, Martin Obzina. **Editor**: Arthur Hilton. **Cast**: Charles Laughton (Philip Marshall), Ella Raines (Mary Gray), Molly Lamont (Edith Simmons), Stanley C. Ridges (Insp. Huxley), Henry Daniell (Gilbert Simmons), Rosalind Ivan (Cora Marshall), Dean Harens (John Marshall), Raymond Severn (Merridew), Eve Amber (Sybil Packer), Maude Ebune (Mrs. Packer), Clifford Brooke (Mr. Packer). **Released**: Universal, December. 85 minutes.

Philip's wife, Cora, drives their son, John, out of their home. Without further need to keep up marital pretences, Philip moves into John's bedroom, infuriating Cora. Philip meets Mary and starts taking her out to restaurants and shows. Philip asks Cora for a divorce, but she refuses. Cora finds out about Mary and threatens to ruin Philip and Mary's lives. Making it look like an accident, Philip kills Cora. After the funeral Huxley shows Philip how Cora's death could have been murder. Mary and Philip get married. It's all going well until Huxley talks to Gilbert, Philip's malevolent and penniless next-door neighbor. Gilbert tries to exploit Huxley's suspicions. He tells Philip he'll say he heard him kill Cora unless Philip gives him money, for the rest of his life. Instead, Philip poisons Gilbert and prepares to move to Canada with Mary and John. Just before they sail, Huxley goes on board and tells Philip that Gilbert's wife is going to be charged with murder. Huxley believes the story will force Philip to come back on shore and give himself up because of his "sense of decency."

The strength of *The Suspect* is in the performances. One key weakness is the lack of suspense. Every scene that suggests suspense may be built up promptly goes flat. Philip hears someone following him on a foggy street. He steps into a doorway and watches Cora walk by. John's girlfriend shrieks when she feels something under the sofa (where Gilbert's corpse is hidden). John reaches down and pulls out a cat. As soon as Huxley says Philip's not going to leave the ship and turn himself in, Philip steps into view. The other chief weakness is the lack of noir style. There's one strong but brief expressionist shot of Philip moving toward the sofa to get rid of Gilbert's body. Huxley's re-enactment of Cora's murder lasts a couple of minutes and is a tour de force. The style in the rest of *The Suspect* is not on a par with other Siodmak noirs. **DMH**

SUSPENSE (1946)

Director: Frank Tuttle. **Producer**: Maurice and Frank King. **Screenplay**: Philip Yordan. **Director of Photography**: Karl Struss. **Music**: Daniele Amfitheatrof. **Art Director**: F. Paul Sylos. **Editors**: Dick Heermance, Otho Lovering. **Cast**: Belita (Roberta Elba), Barry Sullivan (Joe Morgan), Albert Dekker (Frank Leonard), Eugene Pallette (Harry), Bonita Granville (Ronnie), Edith Angold (Nora), George Stone (Max). **Completed**: December 7, 1945. **Released**: Monogram, June 15. 101 minutes.

Joe Morgan, a former nightclub manager now on the skids, gets a job selling peanuts with Frank Leonard's Los Angeles ice show. After devising a dangerous "hoop" of swords through which his boss's wife, skating star Roberta Elba, will jump, Joe is promoted to the show's ringmaster and takes over as manager while Frank is out of town. A romance begins between Roberta and Joe, and the suspicious Frank persuades his wife to vacation with him at his mountain lodge. Joe is accosted by Ronnie, an ex-girlfriend from Chicago, who wishes to rekindle their romance but Joe refuses. He goes up to Frank's lodge on a pretext of business and is invited to stay. After pretending to retire early, Frank observes his wife embrace Joe. The next day Joe is watching Roberta perform some turns on the frozen lake when someone shoots at Joe with a rifle but misses and causes an avalanche. Discovering both Frank and a rifle missing from the lodge, the couple believe Frank fired the shot and was buried in the avalanche. Joe takes over administration of the ice show and their romance continues although the memory of Frank haunts them and telltale signs of his presence keep showing up. One night Frank appears in Joe's office with a gun, the two scuffle and Frank is killed. Roberta ultimately realizes that Joe killed Frank and stuffed his body in the roll top desk that he later burned. When Roberta refuses to agree with his plans and encourages Joe to give himself up, Joe decides to kill her by loosening one of the swords in her act. But seconds before she is to jump, he stops the act and fixes the sword. Explaining that the ringmaster's hat never fit him anyway, Joe walks out of the show and into the night. However, Ronnie has not gotten over being jilted and kills him just as he approaches the street.

Suspense is the first of Monogram's higher budget films, to be followed shortly by *The Gangster* which re-teamed Barry Sullivan and Belita. And while *The Gangster* is self-consciously "arty" it is a more cohesive film than this one. Yet by all counts *Suspense* should have been a little gem of a film noir for it combined the talents of so many veterans of the cycle—writer Yordan; art director Sylos; composer Amfitheatrof—and even director Frank Tuttle. Tuttle, while not a household name to noir fans, again shows a penchant for combining authentic locales (here LA's Pan Pacific Auditorium) with studio work, just as he had earlier in *This Gun for Hire*. Here he is abetted by the rich, darkly expressive photography of the brilliant Karl Struss. Unfortunately, *Suspense* is weighed down by its musical production numbers (except for the sword-hoop sequences performed against the surreal backdrop of a skull through which Belita enters the ice) and fails to generate tension until it is two-thirds over. To a degree, it is rescued by the performance of the ever-reliable Barry Sullivan, even more so by the presence of Albert Dekker, although his screen time is too short and the final confrontation between Frank and Joe disappointingly off camera. Dekker's cool, slightly aberrant persona was a real gift to the film noir and would reach its fruition in *Kiss Me Deadly*. **BP**

SUSPICION (1941)

Director: Alfred Hitchcock. **Screenplay**: Samson Raphaelson, Joan Harrison, Alma Reville based on the novel *Before the Fact* by Francis Iles. **Producer**: Harry E. Edington [Uncredited]. **Director of Photography**: Harry Stradling. **Music**: Franz Waxman. **Art Director**: Van Nest Polglase. **Editor**: William Hamilton. **Cast**: Cary Grant (Johnnie), Joan Fontaine (Lina), Sir Cedric Hardwicke (General McLaidlaw), Nigel Bruce (Beaky), Dame May Whitty (Mrs. McLaidlaw), Isabel Jeans (Mrs. Newsham), Heather Angel (Ethel), Auriol Lee (Isobel Sedbusk), Reginald Sheffield (Reggie Wetherby), Leo G. Carroll (Captain George Melbeck). **Completed**: May 16, 1941. **Released**: RKO, November 14. 99 minutes.

Shy, bookish Lina meets and marries charming, handsome, carefree Johnnie, who turns out to be an irresponsible rogue planning to live off of her inheritance. Her dad gets him a job, but he doesn't show up, embezzles funds, gambles away all her money and even sells her heirloom chairs. After a spending spree and lavishing the household with gifts, he seems to have reformed, but Lina suspects all is not right as Johnnie becomes moody, distant, volatile and cold. When his friend and business partner, Beaky, mysteriously dies, and Johnnie becomes fascinated with methods of murder at a dinner party, Lina fears he will murder her. Paranoia ensues when it appears he has brought her a poisoned glass of milk and nearly drives her off a cliff, but in the end, it is all in her mind and Johnnie wants to make good.

Based on the British roman noir novel, *Before the Fact*, about a dubious man plotting to murder his wife, Hitchcock's female gothic thriller *Suspicion* (working title *Before the Fact*), was a follow-up to his Hollywood directorial debut, *Rebecca*, the year before. Originally intended as a low-budget project in the mid-1930s, RKO upped the budget when Hitchcock became interested. On the heels of *Rebecca*, Fontaine pleaded for the chance to work with Hitchcock again and play the lead. RKO paid a hefty fee to borrow the actress and director from producer David O. Selznick (after Selznick chastised Fontaine for begging Hitchcock for the role), and eventually Fontaine earned a Best Actress Oscar. Produced by out-going RKO Vice President in charge of production (and star Grant's former agent) Edington, *Suspicion* cost over $1 million, more than the studio's other productions; yet, it grossed over $2 million, the highest grossing RKO picture that year.

RKO promoted the film as recasting former screwball comedy star Grant against type (as a "reckless gambling adventurer") in a darker dramatic role. An influential early noir prelude, Hitchcock builds suspense to cast doubt on the shady antihero as the film becomes a psychological study in paranoia, casting the distraught heroine's suspicions of her husband as mere imaginings—an illusion in her head, the product of female hysteria—providing subjective point of view to replace the book's murder scheme. While most of the picture is not very dark in terms of noir visual style, the

Suspicion: *Johnnie (Cary Grant) and Lina (Joan Fontaine).*

shadowy pitch-black climactic scene of Grant climbing the stairs with a "poison" glass of milk for his spouse was the stuff noir was made of. Hitchcock lit the inside of the glass so the drink glowed in the dark as a shrouded Grant carried the milk up to Fontaine's bedside (the paranoid wife is poisoned in the book).

The film was shot in spring 1941 and after lukewarm audience previews in June, additional scenes were shot for a revised ending in late July-August 1941. An earlier ending had Grant leave to join the RAF, but in the final version the couple makes up after their suspicious misunderstanding and drive off together to start over. While a few preview viewers thought Grant should have stuck to comedy, several thought he should have followed through and actually killed Fontaine, and one viewer called it the "finest pseudo-mystery" they'd ever seen. Hitchcock's study in gender distress was a huge success for RKO. **SCB**

SWEET SMELL OF SUCCESS (1957)

Director: Alexander Mackendrick. **Screenplay**: Clifford Odets, Alexander Mackendrick, adapted by Ernest Lehman from his short story "Tell Me about It Tomorrow." **Producer**: James Hill (Norma-Curtleigh Production). **Director of Photography**: James Wong Howe. **Music**: Elmer Bernstein. **Art Director**: Edward Carrere. **Editor**: Alan Crosland, Jr. **Cast**: Burt Lancaster (J.J. Hunsecker), Tony Curtis (Sidney Falco), Susan Harrison (Susan Hunsecker), Martin Milner (Steve Dallas), Sam Levene (Frank D'Angelo), Barbara Nichols (Rita), Jeff Donnell (Sally), Joseph Leon (Robard), Edith Atwater (Mary), Emile Meyer (Harry Kello), Joe Frisco (Herbie Temple), David White (Otis Elwell), Lawrence Dobkin (Leo Bartha), Lurene Tuttle (Mrs. Bartha), Queenie Smith (Mildred Tam). **Completed**: May, 1957. **Released**: United Artists, June 27. 96 minutes.

Low-rent Broadway publicist Sidney Falco is supposed to do a favor for the monomaniacal columnist J.J. Hunsecker: break up a romance between Hunsecker's sister Susan and musician Steve Dallas. Falco attempts blackmail and then pimps a would-be singer to a columnist to get an item published that smears Dallas as a marijuana user and possible Communist. Hunsecker then pretends to be sympathetic, gets Dallas his job back, but demands a token of gratitude. Dallas refuses and asks Susan to choose between them. When a wavering Susan commits to Dallas again, Hunsecker offers Falco a three-month guest editorship of his column if he plants marijuana on Dallas and uses Hunsecker's pet cop Fallon to make the arrest. Falco is celebrating when he is called to Hunsecker's apartment and finds a disheveled Susan about to commit suicide. Hunsecker enters and assumes that Falco has sexually assaulted his sister. Falco leaves as Hunsecker calls Fallon to arrest Falco for framing Dallas. Susan packs a small suitcase and announces that she is leaving her brother's home for good. As Susan crosses the street in front of the apartment building, Falco is beaten by Fallon and taken into custody.

Noir films about the entertainment industry often center on its "parasites" who are not creative themselves but prey off the artistic talents of others. The sycophantic press agent epitomized by Sidney Falco and described as "the man with the ice cream face . . . who has the scruples of a guinea hen and the morals of a gangster" most closely resembles Smiley Coy in *The Big Knife* who willingly commits manslaughter to ingratiate himself with an actor or the character of Harry Fabian in Dassin's *Night and the City*. What makes these characters noir protagonists is their desperate, misguided ambition, and their delusion that they are important people about to achieve greatness when actually they are cruelly manipulated by almost everyone around them. Lacking self-awareness, these men commit crimes or actions that hopelessly ensnare them. Falco, Coy, and Fabian are expendable pawns to their respective kingpins: Hunsecker, studio-chief Hoff, and wrestling-promoter Kristo respectively. They become sympathetic characters because they seem to be pitifully ignorant and because their selfish actions are less disgusting as those of their manipulators.

In fact, both Coy and Fabian understand how low they are. The difference in Falco's case is that he actually rationalizes his callousness into indignation and even self-righteousness. What Falco cannot confront is his own insignificance. Hunsecker believes himself to be Broadway's avenging angel and millions of Americans do read his opinions each morning over breakfast. Subliminally realizing that this faith is dependent upon illusion, Hunsecker wants the mocking musician destroyed to prove his omnipotence. Hunsecker's arrogance recalls the superior attitude of Clifton Webb as Waldo Lydecker in *Laura* or Hardy Cathcart in *The Dark Corner*. The difference, of course, is that Hunsecker is portrayed by Burt Lancaster playing against his iconic status as a classic period protagonist in *The Killers* and *Criss Cross* but still a polar opposite from Clifton Webb. Coming as it does near the end of the classic period, *Sweet Smell of Success* is better able to play with viewer expectations for dramatic effect. Lancaster, in glasses and business suits, looks more intellectual and less physically threatening than in earlier roles, but he still manages to use his physicality to reinforce Hunsecker's psycholog-

Sweet Smell of Success: *Sidney Falco (Tony Curtis) curries favor with J.J. Hunsecker (Burt Lancaster).*

ical dominance of all those around him. Unlike either *Dark Corner* or *Laura* or most of noir of a decade earlier, *Sweet Smell of Success* does not need murder or detection as plot elements to express entrapment and alienation. Using unusual variants on obsession and with an undertone of violence and exploitation, *Sweet Smell of Success* is mostly an expressionistic character study.

The character of Susan shares many traits with the earlier classic period women who are deceived and manipulated by powerful men. Although she must stand on the brink and contemplate suicide, she is the only character freed from the alienating forces of the noir underworld as she literally crosses over to the sunny side of the street to start a new life with Dallas. After the opening montage of newspapers being distributed at dawn, very little of *Sweet Smell of Success* is day lit. Tellingly the only other time Susan is seen in daylight is when she leaves the shadowy arena of the theater where Hunsecker is doing his radio broadcast to walk and talk with Dallas by the river's edge. While Susan asserts that their love can never work, he is able to convince her that she can break free of her brother and the nocturnal cycle of dependency. After that Susan becomes an unintended femme fatale, who brings down both her brother and, by manipulating him, Falco, and in the process rescues her lover Dallas. While waiting to tell her brother the truth and betraying Falco are in isolation ignoble acts, Susan's empowerment is the ironic closure on the typical arc in which men are brought down. Steve Dallas does not arrive to rescue her; she doesn't even mention him as she leaves her brother's apartment and so is not portrayed as running from one man's dominion to another's. This type of transformation is what distinguishes later noir where the consequences of using others can be dire and where only those who can empower themselves against their oppressors may survive but not forget. **EW**

T-MEN (1948)

Director: Anthony Mann. **Screenplay**: John C. Higgins from an unpublished story by Virginia Kellogg based upon the files of the U.S. Treasury Department. **Producer**. Aubrey Schenck. **Executive Producer**: Edward Small (Reliance Pictures). **Director of Photography**: John Alton. **Music**: Paul Sawtell. **Art Director**: Edward C. Jewell. **Editor**: Fred Allen. **Cast**: Dennis O'Keefe (Dennis O'Brien), Alfred Ryder (Tony Genaro), Mary Meade (Evangeline), Wallace Ford (Schemer), June Lockhart (Tony's Wife), Charles McGraw (Moxie), Jane Randolph (Diana), Art Smith (Gregg), Herbert Heyes (Chief Carson), Jack Overman (Brownie), John Wengraf (Shiv), Jim Bannon (Undsay), William Malten (Paul Miller). **Completed**: September, 1947. **Released**: Eagle-Lion Films, January 22. 92 minutes.

Two Treasury agents, O'Brien and Genaro, are brought into a counterfeiting case. Assuming the identities of small-time hoods, they begin their undercover work by joining the Vantucci mob in Detroit. A man named Schemer in Los Angeles is involved, and O'Brien goes there to pursue the case. Introduced into the counterfeiting ring, O'Brien produces a phony bill for which he claims to have the plates and sends for his partner. O'Brien bargains with the ring for a deal on the plates while they investigate. They room with Schemer who is frightened that he is going to be killed by the ring. One day, in the market, Schemer and Genaro run into the agent's wife; they pretend not to know each other, but Schemer is suspicious and bargains with his potential killer, Moxie, by giving him this information. Genaro finds the key that will lead to Schemer's coded information just as the gang, with O'Brien among them, comes to kill him. O'Brien watches helplessly as Moxie shoots Genaro. One member of the ring, Paul Miller, knows O'Brien's plates are the work of a counterfeiter currently in prison. O'Brien is exposed and shot. A wounded O'Brien avenges Genaro by killing Moxie, as the other T-Men arrive and break up the counterfeiting ring.

T-Men established the reputations of its director, Anthony Mann, and its photographer, John Alton. Within a year, both were hired by MGM on the strength of this Eagle-Lion sleeper. The realization of this film creates its true subject, which is not the heroic accomplishments of Treasury agents but rather the perversity and unreality of life as an undercover agent. At the outset of the film it is explained that the story is a composite case from Treasury files; but the very first shot, opening on a night scene, in which mysterious figures shoot it out, staged in strange perspectives, contradicts the matter-of-fact introduction. As a stolid narrative voice continues to trace the activities of the two agents, the *mise en scène* and the manner in which the agents behave as criminals directs our attention to a level of meaning denied by the narration. O'Brien and Genaro are consumed by their roles. Their placement in the compositions emphasizes their ease in the criminal milieu. The pull of the story itself is such as to make them schizophrenic: narratively they are stalwart heroes, visually they are brutal hoods. Mann emphasizes the poignancy of this dichotomy in close-ups of the two men. Genaro is ostentatiously displaced from the background in a close-up when he looks at his wife. Similarly, O'Brien reacts to Genaro's death with an involuntary twitching of his face and slight lowering of the head, while shots are heard over his close-up.

Many of Mann's films feature interesting villains; but although Wallace Ford's Schemer is an arresting characterization, it is the two T-Men who dominate this film. Dennis O'Keefe and Alfred Ryder, as O'Brien and Genaro, blend like chameleons into the noir atmosphere as if to deny their existence as human beings independent of their jobs. In fact, the film does not explore their "real" personalities. They come alive in the moment when they step into the expensive clothes they will wear in their criminal identities and introduce themselves to each other. All that is divulged of their personal life is that Genaro has been married only a few months. The bravery and resourcefulness of both men is secondary in the film's realization to the mystery surrounding their true natures.

Alton's photography is a primary dramatic force in the film. The placement of characters at opposite ends of the frame in deep focus on a diagonal plane illustrates how the photography complements the direction. Examples are the nightclub scene in which O'Brien watches Schemer; the strange shot in the market in which Genaro and Schemer are reflected in one window while reflected from another window at a double remove; and the eerie lighting of the steam room sequence in which Schemer is killed and the black screen is filled with flourishes of light. Each sequence, with its distortions of space and unpredictable, dissonant lighting, forces an awareness of the visual narrative so that the jingoism of the Treasury Department may be ignored and a vision of the noir underworld may emerge. **BL**

TALK ABOUT A STRANGER (1952)

Director: David Bradley. **Screenplay**: Margaret Fitts from the short story "The Enemy" by Charlotte Armstrong. **Producer**: Richard Goldstone. **Director of Photography**: John Alton. **Music**: David Buttolph. **Art Directors**: Cedric Gibbons, Eddie Imazu. **Editor**: Newell P. Kimlin. **Cast**: George Murphy (Robert Fontaine, Sr.), Nancy Davis (Marge Fontaine), Billy Gray (Robert Fontaine, Jr.), Lewis Stone (Mr. Wardlaw), Kurt Kasznar (Matlock), Anna Glomb (Camille), Katharine Warren (Dr. Dorothy Langley), Teddy Infuhr (Gregory). **Released**: MGM, April 18. 65 minutes.

Bobby, the young son of citrus rancher Robert Fontaine, encounters Matlock, an unfriendly stranger in the supposedly empty house next door. Bobby thinks that this is an enemy. When the boy finds his dog dead, he believes that Matlock poisoned it. Mr. Wardlaw, the editor of the local newspaper, listens to Bobby's story but gently cautions him to get evidence before making accusations. The boy gathers evidence that he believes will prove that Matlock has murdered a human being as well as the dog. For revenge Bobby unplugs Matlock's oil tank which depletes the local ranchers' supply of vital fuel for smudge pots needed during a freezing spell. The mystery is solved when the newspaper editor discovers that Matlock is a doctor who retreated from the world after his son's death. Bobby's dog was accidentally poisoned by someone else. As a friendly gesture, the doctor gives Bobby a new pet and the citrus crop is saved when oil trucks arrive with more fuel.

The most disturbing aspect of *Talk About a Stranger* is its central character: a paranoid and destructive juvenile with whom the viewer is led to identify throughout most of the film. The effective use of John Alton's location photography in the opening scenes around the orange groves, the family ranch house, and the dusty streets of a Southern California farm town economically establish a realistic milieu of which Bobby Fontaine seems a normal part. The death of Bobby's dog and the genuinely dour aspect of the new neighbor Matlock further support the credibility of Bobby's assumption that the man has malignant intentions. At this point, the audience might be directed to shift its identification to Bobby's father or to the newspaper editor who offers him counsel; but neither of these characters is developed in a manner that would encourage this. Instead, as Bobby searches for hard evidence on the editor's advice, the film shifts from daylit scenes to a series of night sequences. As darkness falls and the orange groves become menacing tangles of light and shadow—an appropriate, nightmare landscape in which Bobby can situate his fantasies—the boy's mania leads him to tamper with Matlock's oil tank. The wide-angle, low-key shot as Matlock looms over the boy by a

pool of escaping oil is the Wellesian climax to a succession of strikingly Gothic compositions.

Director David Bradley was perhaps the most unusual of the new talents brought to MGM under the unofficial discovery program initiated when Dore Schary came to MGM, where Robert Aldrich also got his first opportunity to direct a feature. Having made ultra-low-budget adaptations of *Peer Gynt* and *Julius Caesar* starring an undiscovered Charlton Heston, Bradley had a strong Wellesian connection and had been considered a prodigy at the Todd School which he attended shortly after Welles. Bradley's direction of Billy Gray made him act like an adult noir protagonist. Although the plot reversed the formula of *The Window*, that unlike Tommy in the latter film Bobby's suspicions are proved untrue, the expressionistic lighting in moments as when Kurt Kasznar as Matlock looms up over the young boy in the citrus fields underscores the adult's malevolent aspect. It is only when the viewer learns that Bobby's accusations have been unfounded and his actions criminally unjust, that these images acquire a different psychological as well as decorative value. By causing the viewer to participate in the visual and narrative point of view of the disturbed child, David Bradley ultimately reveals that his expressionistic *mise en scène* was not merely directorial flourish but a subjective visualization aptly keyed to Bobby's confusion and fear. **AS**

THE TATTERED DRESS (1957)

Director: Jack Arnold. **Screenplay**: George Zuckerman. **Producer**: Albert Zugsmith. **Director of Photography**: Carl E. Guthrie. **Music**: Frank Skinner. **Art Directors**: Alexander Golitzen, Bill Newberry. **Editor**: Edward Curtiss. **Cast**: Jeff Chandler (James Gordon Blane), Jeanne Crain (Diane Blane), Jack Carson (Nick Hoak), Gail Russell (Carol Morrow), Elaine Stewart (Charleen Reston), George Tobias (Billy Giles), Edward Andrews (Lester Rawlings), Philip Reed (Michael Reston), Edward C. Platt (Ralph Adams), Paul Birch (Frank Mitchell), Alexander Lockwood (Paul Vernon). **Completed**: September 14, 1956. **Released**: Universal, March 14. 93 minutes.

A brilliant and amoral lawyer James Gordon Blane comes to a resortlike desert town in California to defend a rich misfit, Michael Reston, in a murder case. Reston is accused of the

murder of a man who, he claims, assaulted his provocative wife Charleen. The dead man was popular in the region, and Blane makes no friends by defending his killer, especially as Charleen Reston is considered a "tramp." But Blane wins the case, partly by undermining the testimony of the local sheriff, Nick Hoak. Afterward, however, the vengeful sheriff produces charges of bribing a juror, and Blane must defend himself. His estranged wife Diane comes to his side; and the two are reconciled as Blane realizes that his reputation is based on clever courtroom tactics that mock justice. Although most of his clients have been guilty, Blane is innocent and fights passionately for his acquittal. He wins and is further vindicated when Carol Morrow, the woman juror who made the bribery charge, is revealed as Hoak's mistress. As Blane goes free, Carol shoots and kills Hoak on the courthouse steps.

Although *The Tattered Dress* is a modest thriller, it has several noir elements. The hero only becomes sympathetic because of the trouble his own arrogance brings him; and the critical tone toward his morality is reserved until the final reels. As a tarnished lawyer, he is a forerunner of the hero of Nicholas Ray's *Party Girl,* although Blane's crisis does not have the emotional complexity found in Ray's film. The character of Nick Hoak is perhaps more singularly interesting, and provokes ambivalent feelings of sympathy and distaste reminiscent of the antagonists of many film noir. Hoak is portrayed by Jack Carson, who excelled in a number of offbeat characterizations in this period of his career, such as those he played in *A Star Is Born* and *The Tarnished Angels.* The main interest of the film, however, is the visual style of Jack Arnold. The desert setting recalls certain of his science fiction films, such as *It Came from Outer Space* and *Tarantula;* and it reveals that in this wasteland he finds a certain beauty that is very modern and strangely affecting. It is cleverly contrasted to the contemporary decors in which the characters exist and expresses a moral as well as physical desert. **BL**

TENSION (1950)

Director: John Berry. **Screenplay**: Allen Rivkin from an unpublished story by John Klorer. **Producer**: Robert Sisk. **Director of Photography**: Harry Stradling, Sr. **Music**: André Previn. **Art Directors**: Cedric Gibbons, Leonid Vasian. **Editor**: Albert Akst. **Cast**: Richard Basehart (Warren Quimby/Paul Sothern), Audrey Totter (Claire Quimby), Cyd Charisse (Mary Chandler), Barry Sullivan (Lt. Collier Bonnabel), Lloyd Gough (Barney Deager), Tom D'Andrea (Freddie), William Conrad (Lt. Edgar Gonsales), Tito Renaldo (Narco), Philip Van Zandt (Lt. Schiavone). **Completed**: June 22, 1949. **Released**: MGM, January 11. 95 minutes.

Pharmacist Warren Quimby is working nights and saving to buy a home. His wife Claire, whom he met while in the Navy, leaves him for a wealthier Barney Deager, who roughs Warren up when he goes to confront him. A chance remark from Freddie the soda jerk gives him an idea: he will create a second identity and that person with kill Deager. After renting an apartment as "Paul Sothern," he meets and is attracted to Mary Chandler. He goes to Deager's but abandons his plan. To his surprise, Claire returns the next morning with news that Deager is dead. On her heels are Dets. Bonnabel and Gonsales. Although Bonnabel gives the lie to Claire's claim that she only went to Deager's to swim, Deager was shot with his own gun which is missing. After Mary files a missing per-

sons report, the detective discovers that Warren is Paul Sothern. However, he can't break their stories even after he arranges a chance meeting between Warren and Mary at the drug store. Simultaneously Bonnabel takes Claire out several times and tricks her into retrieving and planting the gun at "Sothern's" apartment, whereupon he arrests her.

Tension features an odd mix of narrative viewpoints. A protagonist, who creates a new identity to kill the man who has lured away his unfaithful wife, meets and falls for a new woman. Before any of this happens, before the movie's titles, the audience is addressed directly by Lt. Collier Bonnabel portrayed by Barry Sullivan. In that prologue, Bonnabel stands outside the door to a police office and explains how he likes to solve cases by creating stressful situations. He stretches a rubber band to show how it works, pulling on his suspects until they too snap under the strain. The movie proper unfolds as an informal flashback, with Bonnabel continues to address the viewer as an unseen narrator who speculates about Warren Quimby's emotional condition. Director John Berry had acted with the Orson Welles/John Houseman Mercury Theater group and had shadowed Billy Wilder on *Double Indemnity* but he only made two noir films, this and *He Ran All the Way* with John Garfield. That's because after he did some documentary work about the Hollywood Ten, he joined them on the blacklist. Like Dassin, Losey, and Enfield, Berry went to Europe and left film noir behind. Perhaps what is most remarkable in *Tension,* even more than a relatively inexperienced director such as Berry getting caught in the grip of the noir style, is how cinematographer Harry Stradling lit the movie. Harry Stradling had just shot four Technicolor musicals at MGM including *Easter Parade* and *The Pirate* but his work in *Tension* could rival that of MGM colleague John Alton. Using a docu-noir style in some practical locations, Stradling reserves the most stylized moments for selected night exteriors and emotionally charged scenes such as Quimby hesitating and abandoning his plan to kill Deager at the latter's Malibu house or Bonnabel's interrogation of Quimby in a holding cell lit like an inquisition chamber.

Unlike Robert Montgomery in *Lady in the Lake,* Berry had not dabbled with long takes or sequence shots at MGM or anywhere else in the past. Nonetheless there is a remarkable one created by Berry and Stradling in *Tension.* Shortly after

Bonnabel has finally appeared in the narrative as a character, he and his partner Gonsales go to a boxing auditorium to question Deager's former housebuy Narco about the nature of Claire's relationship to Deager and the telephone threats made by Paul Sothern. As the sequence shot begins, the audience only knows that Quimby is not the murderer. The contemporary viewer would be unlikely to suspect Narco. Nonetheless Berry and Stradling use the staging and lighting to mimic Bonnabel's methodology: having now followed the detective team for a few scenes, this sequence shot comes at a fulcrum point and the visual tension it adds for a brief period mirrors the title and the emotions of the suspects. **AS**

TERROR STREET [aka 36 HOURS] (1953)

Director: Montgomery Tully. **Screenplay**: Steve Fisher based on his story. **Producer**: Anthony Hinds. **Director of Photography**: Walter J. Harvey. **Music**: Ivor Slaney. **Art Director**: J. Elder Wills. **Editor**: James Needs. **Cast**: Dan Duryea (Major Bill Rogers), Elsy Albiin (Katherine Rogers), Ann Gudrun (Jenny Miller), Eric Pohlmann (Slauson), John Chandos (Orville Hart), Kenneth Griffith (Henry Slauson), Harold Lang (Harry Cross), Jane Carr (Soup Kitchen Supervisor), Michael Golden (Inspector), Marianne Stone (Pam Palmer). **Released**: Lippert, December 4. 85 minutes.

An American officer, Major Rogers, flies into London on a military plane, which he must return on in 36 hours, to find his wife who has dropped out of contact. When he finds her new flat a man knocks him out, kills her with Rogers' gun and places it in his hand while he remains unconscious. Rogers tracks down the people his wife had been associating with since he left with the aid of social worker Jenny, who initially hid him from the police. He uncovers a smuggling ring that had duped his wife into aiding them, amongst whom is the killer.

Unlike *Night and the City*, the gold standard for London noir hybrids like this, the production values of *Terror Street* typify the modestly-budgeted British thrillers of the era. Its most intriguing feature is the reversal of gender allocation for the traditional noir downwards spiral into criminality, where one small transgression grows into an irreversible trap. This happens to two women, and for each their decline flows directly from a destabilizing encounter with Major Rogers. The recurrent nature of this suggests that he may be an *homme fatale*. But unlike Dennis O'Keefe's Joe in *Raw Deal*, a perfect inversion of the spiderwoman archetype, here Rogers is merely a catalyst for their descent, his biggest sin being nothing more than unthinking selfishness that leaves trouble in its wake. Memory and the determinism of the past are strong imperatives aligning *Terror Street* with classic noir. "I remember—everything . . ." says Rogers' interior monologue before a trite expository recall of his romance. Unfortunately memory is a double-edged sword here, because the white surfaces and geometric spaces in this flat recall a younger Duryea moving through Kitty's apartment in *Scarlet Street*. It's an invidious comparison, both because the two movies are of unequal stature and the actor aged to a surprising degree in less than a decade.

A number of promising hares are set running throughout the plot of *Terror Street*, including a *Citizen Kane*-style inquisition, public and private strands of detection, racing against the clock and American versus British differences. However none are grasped effectively and all sputter out to nothing. Relief from *Terror Street*'s flat direction and general ordinariness come in two sequences which benefit from noir's visual strategies. Taking flight in social worker Jenny's home, the interiors mix light, darkness and two-shots according to Rogers' fugitive status and her deepening complicity. Even better, the film's final sequence draws on the suggestiveness of Orientalism, using shadowy Buddha figurines in a sustained display of moody, allusive atmosphere. Isolated noir visuals throughout the narrative also help, especially a door's cracked mirror framing a fistfight. But we are reminded of this film's inescapable Britishness when one of its heroines' lapse into a flashback requires the extra step of a letter being read to generate her cinematic detour into events of the past. **RSW**

THEM! (1954)

Director: Gordon Douglas. **Screenplay**: Ted Sherdeman from an adaptation by Russell S. Hughes of a story by George Worthing Yates. **Producer**: David Weisbart. **Music**: Bronislau Kaper. **Director of Photography**: Sid Hickox. **Art Director**: Stanley Fleischer. **Editor**: Thomas Reilly. **Cast**: James Whitmore (New Mexico State Police Sgt. Ben Peterson), Edmund Gwenn (Dr. Harold Medford), Joan Weldon (Dr. Patricia Medford), James Arness (FBI Agent Robert Graham), Onslow Stevens (Gen. Robert O'Brien), Sean McClory (Maj. Kibbee), Chris Drake (Trooper Ed Blackburn), Sandy Descher (Ellinson girl), Mary Alan Hokanson (Mrs. Lodge), Don Shelton (Capt. Fred Edwards), Fess Parker (Alan Crotty), Olin Howland (Jensen), John Beradino (LAPD Officer Ryan). **Released**: Warner Bros., June 16. 94 minutes.

New Mexico State Policemen Peterson and Blackburn find a young girl wandering in the desert near White Sands, New Mexico. Determining that she came from a trailer that was torn apart, they also find a nearby store owner's mutilated body. Blackburn stays at the scene and is attacked. Because the missing father is an FBI agent, Robert Graham joins the investigation and sends a cast of an odd footprint to the FBI lab in Washington. Shortly after, two scientists, Harold Medford and his daughter Pat, arrive. In the desert with Graham and Peterson they encounter the first giant ant, a mutation caused by atomic tests. Accompanied by two Army officers, O'Brien and Kibbee, they find and destroy a giant ant hill but discover that two queen ants have left. In strictest

WARNER BROS. AMAZING NEW SENSATION!
"THEM!" starring JAMES WHITMORE · EDMUND GWENN · JOAN WELDON · JAMES ARNESS

secrecy and on a tip from a hapless pilot named Crotty, who reports ant-shaped UFOs, one queen is found and destroyed on a freighter at sea. A search for missing boys leads to sewers connected to the Los Angeles River, and the Army goes in. Peterson is killed rescuing the boys, but the rest of the ants, presuming there are no other mutations, are destroyed.

"Everything seems to indicate a homicidal maniac." So says State Police Sergeant Ben Peterson to his captain about whoever has killed the storekeeper and abducted or killed his partner and an FBI agent and his wife. Since the only survivor is speechless, there is no reason for Peterson to imagine that the killer or killers who destroy without obvious purpose and leave money and valuables behind might not be human. While it is reasonable to assume that all but a few of the mid-1950s audience for *Them!* knew from trailers, posters, or other promotional materials that this was science fiction story about giant ants, the filmmakers maintain a subjective approach in the early scenes in that the viewer only sees and hears what the characters do. The puzzling crime scenes resemble those in a standard police procedural noir. The film even shifts to an ironic mode when the sounds of the killers are heard and that sparks a reaction from the little girl that none of the characters notice. The attack on Blackburn in the wrecked store uses the lighting conventions of noir. After he reacts to the sounds and draws his weapon, the dark-uniformed trooper walks towards the door turning off the lights hanging down from the ceiling so that he won't make a backlit target. As he pauses a source from somewhere outside the shot rim lights his features. A pan takes him in profile to the door, and he is last seen passing a window before shots and screams are heard.

Although they are soon seen face to face, throughout the movie the menace of the giant insects is often first detected by sound or shadow. Four years after *Kiss Tomorrow Goodbye* director Gordon Douglas could still stage many scenes in the noir style. In the central portion of the story, the agents of law enforcement, scientists, and Army officers are sworn to secrecy, and the "scientific" elements are preeminent. When the locale shifts from New Mexico to Los Angeles, *Them!* reacquires aspects of docu-noir. As Graham and Peterson investigate and interrogate, the secrecy requirements compel them to behave as if they were seeking a homicidal maniac, as if the giants ants were like the elusive Roy Martin in *He Walked by Night*. Ironically both Martin and the ants meet their end in Los Angeles sewers. A final noir aspect of *Them!* is the death of Peterson, portrayed by the top-billed James Whitmore, crushed by enormous mandibles. Like many classic period protagonists in standard thrillers, fate directs him onto a path of destruction where his struggle to survive ends in failure. **AS**

THEY LIVE BY NIGHT
[aka **THE TWISTED ROAD**] (1948)

Director: Nicholas Ray. **Screenplay**: Charles Schnee, adapted by Nicholas Ray from the novel *Thieves Like Us* by Edward Anderson. **Producer**: John Houseman. **Director of Photography**: George E. Diskant. **Music**: Leigh Harline. **Art Directors**: Albert S. D'Agostino, Al Herman. **Editor**: Sherman Todd. **Cast**: Cathy O'Donnell (Keechie), Farley Granger (Bowie), Howard Da Silva (Chickamaw), Jay C. Flippen (T-Dub), Helen Craig (Mattie), Will Wright (Mobley), Marie Bryant (Singer), Ian Wolfe (Hawkins), William Phipps (Young

Farmer), Harry Harvey (Hagenheimer). **Completed**: August 16, 1947. **Released**: RKO, June 28 as *The Twisted Road;* re-released November 4, 1949, as *They Live By Night*. 95 minutes.

Two hardened criminals, Chickamaw and T-Dub, are joined in a prison break by a naive youth, Bowie. Together the three rob a bank. Subsequently, Bowie is hurt in an auto accident caused by Chickamaw and nursed back to health by Keechie, the daughter of a man who helped in the prison escape. Bowie and Keechie fall in love and marry, trying to forget the past as they live on his share of the holdup money; but Chickamaw and T-Dub force Bowie into another robbery. T-Dub is killed; and Chickamaw and Bowie quarrel in the getaway car and part company. Later, Chickamaw is killed by the police. T-Dub's sister, Mattie, negotiates to have her own husband released from prison. She turns Bowie in to the police as he is about to go on the run again, leaving the pregnant Keechie alone until he finds a new home. Bowie is shot down and Keechie is desolate; but his love is confirmed when she finds a letter he wrote to her moments before being killed.

The pre-credit shot shows the lovers deep in the warmth of their affection, even as this warmth is frozen by the writing on the screen, which seals their doom: "This boy and this girl were never properly introduced to the world we live in." The following credit sequence cuts to an overhead of a swiftly moving car full of men destined for violence. Nicholas Ray, as director, establishes visual and emotional contrasts that pervade the entire treatment. His romanticism is punctuated by unexpected moments of unusual violence, as in the moment in which Chickamaw clumsily breaks a Christmas tree ornament—symbolically destroying the possibilities of a normal life for the fugitive lovers. Violence is a trap that consumes some, such as Chickamaw, and renders it impossible for others, such as Bowie and Keechie, to tighten their tenuous hold on their dream. The self-destruction of Chickamaw and the destruction of Bowie by Mattie harshly indicate that the lovers can neither escape nor forget the dark world into which fortune has cast them.

For his first film, Nicholas Ray followed the pattern set by Fritz Lang and Raoul Walsh with their respective classics *You Only Live Once* and *High Sierra* and dealt with the theme of lovers on the run. However, the youth and vulnerability of Bowie and Keechie set them apart from their prototypes in *You Only Live Once* and *High Sierra;* and the gentleness and warmth of Keechie particularly contrasts with her contemporary counterpart, Annie Laurie Starr in Lewis' *Gun Crazy.* Keechie is anything but the customary black widow, being more akin to a madonna, adding a quasi-religious tone to the film. Additionally, the concept of fate is modified in *They Live by Night* by pauses in the thrust of the action in which the lovers' doomed course is forgotten as Ray lingers on their momentary intimacy. This subtle modification makes the predictable denouement uncommonly tragic.

Counterpointing their relationship to a hostile world is the relation of the lovers to each other. Initially mistrustful, they regard each other uneasily in the long scene in which Keechie tends to Bowie's wounds and their tentative attraction is inarticulately expressed. After their marriage, Bowie gains an adult sense of responsibility, tending to his pregnant wife, searching for a refuge where they can be safe. When he is finally betrayed and killed, Keechie walks away with her back to the camera as she reads Bowie's letter, and then turns toward the camera to echo the final words of "I love you," at the film's end. In this fade-out, Ray underlines the inevitability of the desolation that accompanies fugitive love and suggests that their happiness, illustrated in the opening image, could provide only a fleeting, existential moment in the face of eternity. **BL**

THEY MADE ME A KILLER (1946)

Director: William C. Douglas. **Screenplay**: Daniel Mainwaring (as Geoffrey Homes), Winston Miller, and Kae Salkow from a story by Owen Franes. **Producers**: William H. Pine, William C. Thomas (Pine-Thomas Productions). **Director of Photography**: Fred Jackman, Jr. **Music**: Alexander Laszlo. **Art Director**: Frank Paul Sylos. **Editor**: Henry Adams. **Cast**: Robert Lowery (Tom Durling), Barbara Britton (June Reynolds), Lola Lane (Betty Ford), Frank Albertson (Al Wilson), Elizabeth Risdon (Ma Conley), Byron Barr (Steve Reynolds), Edmund MacDonald (Jack Conley aka Chance), Ralph Sanford (Roach), James Bush (Frank Conley), Paul Harvey (Dist. Attny. Booth), John Harmon (Joe Lafferty). **Released**: Metropolis Productions, May 3. 64 minutes.

Tom Durling quits his job as a car mechanic after his brother is killed in an accident "in a souped-up jalopy" and heads for California. He picks up Betty Ford, attractive standard noir femme fatale, who claims to want to buy his car. He is suckered into a bank raid organized by the Conley brothers. Steve Reynolds, a bank clerk staying at the same guest house as Betty, is fatally wounded during the robbery. After a high-speed chase, the car crashes and Durling is knocked unconscious; the robbers escape, leaving him to be arrested and charged with murder. After Reynolds dies without supplying an alibi, Durling escapes, teams up with Reynolds' sister June, and attempts to prove their innocence. They trace Betty and the gang to a roadside diner where they are hiding in the basement. June gets a job as a waitress while Durling joins the gang. An elaborate trick involving a recording of a confession and a jukebox proves their innocence, the gang are shot by police, and Durling and June ride off into the sunset together.

What might have been no more than B-movie melodrama is turned into an interesting, classic noir narrative, through some intelligent writing and strong performances from all the leads.

None of the cast enjoyed particularly successful careers: Robert Lowery (Durling) was always busy (*They Made Me a Killer* was one of six movies in which he featured to be released during 1946), and later credits included Batman/Bruce Wayne in the 1949 version of the story, and Sheriff Pat Garrett in *I Shot Billy the Kid* (1950). Barbara Britton (June) found some kind of fame as the "Revlon Girl" in a long-running series of commercials. But none secured the roles their performances here suggested they might, especially Edmund MacDonald whose Frank Conley is in the Raft/Cagney/Bogart tradition of hard-bitten, wise-cracking gangsters.

Durling is a classic noir hero, an innocent sucked into a mystery he doesn't understand (a plot device favored above all by Hitchcock), and the narrative centers on his attempts to prove his innocence. But along the way, he demonstrates the weakness in all of us that blurs the boundaries between the honest and the criminal when he is tempted to take for himself the proceeds of the bank robbery in which he was inadvertently involved. At one point he refers to Diogenes' doubts about being able to find an honest man. The moral explorations within the movie are emphasized by both lighting and cinematography: the movie begins and ends in bright sunlight, but from the moment of the robbery until the denouement that proves Durling's innocence, the film is shot either at night or in dingily lit interiors. The credibility is almost derailed by an implausible trick in which Durling entices the gang to confess for a recording he makes to be played back by local cops on the diner's jukebox. But that and the instantly happy ending do not seriously mar a tight, well-constructed thriller. **GF**

THEY WON'T BELIEVE ME (1947)

Director: Irving Pichel. **Screenplay**: Jonathan Latimer from an unpublished story by Gordon McDonell. **Producer**: Joan Harrison. **Director of Photography**: Harry J. Wild. **Music**: Roy Webb. **Art Directors**: Albert S. D'Agostino, Robert Boyle. **Editor**: Elmo Williams. **Cast**: Robert Young (Larry Ballentine), Susan Hayward (Verna Carlson), Jane Greer (Janice Bell), Rita Johnson (Greta Ballentine), Tom Powers (Trenton), George Tyne (Lt. Carr), Don Beddoe (Thomason), Frank Ferguson (Cahill), Harry Harvey (Judge Fletcher). **Completed**: October 12, 1946. **Released**: RKO, July 16. 95 minutes.

FAST RIDE TO RUIN— on a one-way track of terror!

SUSAN HAYWARD
ROBERT YOUNG
JANE GREER

They Won't Believe Me!

with RITA JOHNSON

Larry Ballentine, on trial for the murder of his girlfriend, Verna Carlson, is described by his lawyer Cahill as a man of "many derelictions but not murder." Then Ballentine takes the stand and tells his story. Ballentine married his wife Greta only for money and social position. While they lived in New York, Ballentine had an affair with Janice Bell and planned to leave his wife. Greta persuaded Ballentine to move with her to Los Angeles, where she purchased him a stock brokerage firm. He agreed, but soon began a liaison with a young secretary, Verna Carlson. Greta found out about the second affair and moved with Ballentine to a remote ranch. Larry could not endure life there and ran off with Verna to Reno, where he planned a quick divorce and remarriage. On the way, they had an auto accident and Verna burned to death. Ballentine allowed the police to believe that it was his wife who died and, after a short stay in the hospital, returned home to find that Greta had committed suicide. To cover up his lies, he dragged her body into a nearby lake. Trenton, Larry's former partner and an admirer of Verna's, became suspicious of her disappearance and had the police investigate, leading to the discovery of Greta's body. After Ballentine finishes his story, the jury leaves to deliberate. Convinced that the jury would never believe his story, Larry bolts for the courtroom window in an act of desperation and is shot and killed by a marshal. Ironically, the jury renders a verdict of not guilty.

When this film was released some critics suggested disparagingly that it had been heavily influenced by James Cain's fiction and the success of films like *Double Indemnity*. True, no doubt, but from the standpoint of today's noir buffs that can only be a positive influence. What is questionable is the wisdom of the reverse casting of Robert Young in the role of the philanderer. For when Ballentine tells his story to the jury, we, the film audience, can only believe him because of the moral authority Robert Young possesses as icon. Perhaps if an actor with a more morally ambiguous connotation (Mitchum, Ryan, or Bogart, etc.) had played Ballentine, we would have doubted the sincerity of his assertion that the thought of killing his wife had never entered his mind. Certainly the suicidal "escape" attempt at the film's conclusion would have taken on extra layers of ambiguity in the persona of an actor like Robert Mitchum (see *The Locket*). In any case, *They Won't Believe Me* benefits from the RKO noir style, though director Irving Pichel is an unlikely candidate for a film noir. The same can't be said for producer Joan Harrison. **BP**

THE THIEF (1952)

Director: Russell Rouse. **Screenplay**: Clarence Greene and Russell Rouse. **Producer**: Clarence Greene. **Executive Producer**: Harry M. Popkin. **Director of Photography**: Sam Leavitt. **Music**: Herschel Burke Gilbert. **Art Director**: Joseph St. Amand. **Editor**: Chester Schaeffer. **Cast**: Ray Milland (Allan Fields), Martin Gabel (Mr. Bleek), Rita Gam (The Girl), Harry Bronson (Harris), John McKutcheon (Dr. Linstrum), Rita Vale (Miss Philips), Rex O'Malley (Beal), Joe Conlin (Walters). **Location**: Washington, D.C.; New York City. **Completed**: June 13. **Released**: United Artists, October 15. 85 minutes.

The story of Dr. Allan Fields, a scientist at the Atomic Energy Commission in Washington who sells classified secrets to the Communists, unfolds without benefit of any dialogue.

Through an ingenious use of phone-ring codes Fields is able to communicate with his contact, Mr. Bleek, without speaking. His purpose is to pass on strategic information in the form of microfilms of important documents he takes secretly while at work. The microfilms then make their way to New York City, where they will travel by plane to the Middle East. But one of the couriers is killed in New York with the microfilm still in his hand, and the FBI is called in to investigate. In the process of tracing the leak, all AEC employees are investigated. Fields receives a telegram warning him that he must leave the country. The FBI has a record of the telegram but soon discover that the name and address of the sender are fictitious. After driving to New York City, Fields abandons his car and takes the subway to a locker in Grand Central, where he finds a note, a suitcase, and a key to a cheap tenement room. Alone in the room, Fields reads additional instructions to meet a woman atop the Empire State Building who will have the tickets and paperwork for him to ship out of the country. On a given phone signal Fields departs for his rendezvous but the woman is followed by an FBI agent. Fields receives his paperwork but the agent traps him on the observation tower. As the agent is climbing up the tower's exterior stairs, Fields manages to stomp on his hand from above and the agent falls to his death below. Fields is able to exit the building safely but is visibly shaken by the sight of the corpse on the sidewalk. Returning to his room, he breaks down and cries. That night, with tickets in hand, he goes to embark on the ship that will take him out of the country. But at the last moment he throws the phony passport away and, at dawn, waits outside the FBI building to give himself up.

With a major star and budget and a gimmick (first Hollywood film since *Modern Times* without dialogue), *The Thief* was the most publicized of the anti-Communist films produced in the early 1950s. In many respects the script, which relies solely on visuals and sound effects, is ingenious but after a while the silence, as much a part of a spy's world as it may be, becomes tedious and contrived. Yet *The Thief* is superior to most other propaganda films of this ilk—the loss of dialogue in itself is an asset in toning down didacticism—and director Russell Rouse (who, as writer and/or director, had teamed with producer Popkin on a number of other entries, most notably *D.O.A.*) imbues this film with the necessary elements of fear, persecution, alienation, and loneliness.

As is true with most film noirs, photographer Leavitt maintains a consistent, dark visual style that gives the film a cohesiveness it might otherwise lack given the amount of location work. Ray Milland was evidently unhampered by the lack of dialogue and his performance is full of understated tension—as he nervously awaits the ring of the tenement's public telephone, eyed by an exotic woman who is waiting for the same phone to ring; as he desperately searches for a hidden microphone (in a scene similar to his alcoholic frenzy in *The Lost Weekend*); or as he smokes alone in the dark with only the blinking neon signs for illumination. It is a moment of catharsis, for both audience and character, when, overcome with guilt and grief at the agent's death, he breaks down in tears near the film's conclusion. Since the reason for Field's treason is never revealed, he remains a cipher to the end. **BP**

THIEVES' HIGHWAY (1949)

Director: Jules Dassin. **Screenplay**: A.I. Bezzerides from his novel *Thieves' Market*. **Producer**: Robert Bassler. **Director of Photography**: Norbert Brodine. **Music**: Alfred Newman. **Art Directors**: Lyle Wheeler, Chester Gore. **Editor**: Nick De Maggio. **Cast**: Richard Conte (Nick Garcos), Valentina Cortesa (Rica), Lee J. Cobb (Figlia), Barbara Lawrence (Polly), Jack Oakie (Slob), Millard Mitchell (Ed), Joseph Pevney (Pete), Morris Camovsky (Yanko), Tamara Shayne (Parthena Garcos), Kasia Orzazewski (Mrs. Polansky), Norbert Schiller (Polansky), Hope Emerson (Midge), George Tyne (Charles), Edwin Max (Dave), David Clarke (Mitch), Walter Baldwin (Riley), David Opatoshu (Frenchy). **Location**: San Francisco, Oakland, Highway 99, Sebastopol, Calistoga, Santa Rosa, Hueneme, and Oxnard, California. **Completed**: January 6, 1949. **Released**: 20th Century-Fox, September 23. 94 minutes.

Nick Garcos comes home from merchant marine service to find that his father has been crippled in a suspicious truck accident. Delaying his plans to marry Polly, Nick invests his savings in a surplus troop truck and partners with Ed, a local driver. Followed by Ed's former associates Pete and Slob, the men leave with two truckloads of apples for the produce market in San Francisco where an angry Nick plans to confront wholesaler Mike Figlia who exploited his father. Arriving exhausted, Nick parks in front of Figlia's to wait for Ed. Figlia pays a refugee named Rica to entice Nick to her apartment and then sells his produce. In the meantime, Ed's brakes fail and he is killed in a crash. His goods gone, Nick takes Figlia's money and then is robbed by two of Figlia's henchmen. When Pete and Slob arrive with this news of Ed, Nick follows them to a roadhouse, where he beats Figlia savagely until the police, alerted by Rica, arrive. Nick returns to San Francisco to reconcile with Rica.

More than any other major studio Fox embraced the concept of location shooting and "documentary-style." Director Jules Dassin came to Fox from Universal where he had collaborated with producer Mark Hellinger on two pictures that embraced the docu-noir style: *Brute Force* and *The Naked City*. *Thieves' Highway* evokes the style of earlier Dassin and Fox noirs. Bezzerides' novel and screenplay were based on his own experiences as a truck driver. While not as unabashedly political as many classic American proletarian novels, Bezzerides' novel and script hammer on the common-man theme. Nick is a sailor returned from the sea. Bezzerides' settings are the rich farmlands of central California and the warehouse district of San Francisco. Besides San Francisco, the location work was done in Sebastopol, California, a town in Sonoma County north of the San Francisco bay. Sebastopol and its environs stand in for Fresno and central California.

The narrative organization of *Thieves' Highway* spans elements which at are once mythic and everyday. Nick Garcos' return home after several years at sea to find his father disfigured, which awakens a desire for revenge, is telling. Dassin's visual choices underscore the narrative themes: the conflict of obligation versus opportunity, fair dealing versus greed, family values and traditional relationships versus post-war men and women liberated from the pre-war mores by the broad social changes of global conflict. Added to the mythic and proletarian aspects of the original is the fact that this noir protagonist is returning from the war. While Nick is initially motivated not by the disruptive experience of war but the desire to exact revenge for his father, at some level he understands that, had he not been away, his father might not have been duped. Many of the other characters in *Thieves' Highway* appear to be persons affected by the realities of post-war economy. As a refugee from Europe, Rica is much more: a displaced person.

From the earliest scenes, Dassin's staging, from long takes with dolly moves to odd-angled cuts, is also keyed to Nick, to that character's emotional responses. In the first sequence of Nick rejoining his parents and his fiancée, Dassin doesn't use many different shots but maintains a subtle visual tension throughout. Throughout *Thieves' Highway,* the visualization supports this concept of a journey into a hostile or chaotic universe. The images in the Garcos home—with the exception of the odd-angled shot when Nick first realizes his father has lost his legs—are composed at eye level and full-lit, as are those of Ed and Nick loading their trucks at the orchard. As

Nick moves along the highway, the framing becomes more constricted; traffic moving past and, at night, headlights flashing through the cab undercut the static compositions.

By the time of Nick's mishap with the tire, night has fallen, so that strongly side-lit low angle and overhead shots are justified and continue to appear after Nick reaches his destination and begins his confrontation with Figlia. Appropriately, of all the locations in the city, only Rica's apartment is photographed with some measure of normality: more fill light, medium two-shots, and balanced close-ups of Nick and Rica predominate. This visual treatment reinforces the narrative suggestion against type that Rica, despite her foreignness, explicit sexuality, and questionable morality, is worthier of Nick's attention than the blond, Waspish Polly. Throughout the people whom Nick will meet, his temporary partners and his antagonists, will compel Nick to confront his own moral flaws. In all of his noir pictures from *Brute Force* through *Night and the City* and as is typical of the noir movement as a whole, the concepts of trust and betrayal are keys to performance for Dassin. He uses actors as different as Richard Conte as Nick, Lee J. Cobb as Mike Figlia, and Valentina Cortese as Rica to create a realistic narrative which he binds together with a fluid visual style. **AS**

THE 13TH LETTER (1951)

Director/Producer: Otto Preminger. **Screenplay**: Howard Koch from the story and screenplay *Le Corbeau* by Louis Chavance. **Director of Photography**: Joseph LaShelle. **Music**: Alex North. **Art Directors**: Lyle Wheeler, Maurice Ransford. **Editor**: Louis Loeffler. **Cast**: Linda Darnell (Denise Turner), Charles Boyer (Dr. Laurent), Michael Rennie (Dr. Pearson), Constance Smith (Cora Laurent), Françoise Rosay (Mrs. Gautier), Judith Evelyn (Sister Marie), Guy Sorel (Robert Helier), June Hedin (Rochelle Turner). **Locations**: St. Hyacinthe, St. Denis, St. Charles, St. Hilaire, and St. Marc, Quebec, Canada. **Completed**: October 20, 1950. **Released**: 20th Century-Fox, February 21. 85 minutes.

Dr. Pearson is a young, highly talented doctor working in a French-Canadian village hospital. He had abandoned a great career in London after his unfaithful wife committed suicide. Trying to forget the past, he leads a solitary life with only his clock collection as a diversion. His solitude is shattered when Cora Laurent, the pretty young wife of the older, revered Dr. Paul Laurent, receives a poison pen letter accusing her of having an affair with Dr. Pearson. The letters begin to appear elsewhere and all are signed only by the mysterious name of "The Raven." A number of townspeople are suspected as the letters' author: Dr. Pearson himself; Denise, a clubfooted patient of Pearson's who has been trying unsuccessfully to seduce him; Cora's older sister, Marie, a nurse who had previously accused Cora of enticing other men; and a woman whose son, a paranoid veteran, is being treated by Dr. Pearson. The veteran receives a letter from "The Raven," which falsely informs him that he has incurable cancer and he commits suicide. When another poison pen letter drops out of the choir loft onto the church congregation, Dr. Laurent assumes control of the investigation. Despite comparing the handwriting of all eighteen choir members, Laurent fails to establish the author's identity. Dr. Pearson finally discovers the truth. Cora Laurent, attracted to the

aloof Pearson, wrote the first letter in a moment of weakness. When her husband discovered this, he forced her to continue writing the letters to demonstrate his theory of "an insanity of two"—that is, that one person's mad act can inspire cooperation in another. The veteran's mother avenges her son's death by slitting Dr. Laurent's throat just as he is writing a confessional letter. Meanwhile his wife is being committed to an institution.

Since *The 13th Letter* lacks the misanthropic bite (and the surrounding controversy) of Clouzot's *Le Corbeau*, it is generally considered to be a pale imitation of the original and unworthy of a position of status in the pantheon of Preminger's films. No *Laura* (or even *Fallen Angel*), this film works quite nicely as a film noir and in 1950 Preminger still had the advantage of the Fox noir style to rely on. More importantly, perhaps, it represents a good example of how easily the so-called French "film noirs" could be transformed on American soil (especially by directors of a Germanic persuasion). Other examples would be *Human Desire* (*La Bête Humaine*), *The Long Night* (*Le Jour Se Leve*), and *Scarlet Street* (*La Chienne*). In virtually every instance the sexual content of the French originals was bowdlerized because of the restrictions of Hollywood's Production Code. Still, it is a tribute to the ingenuity of the directors and writers working in Hollywood throughout the 1940s and 1950s (when the Code was at is most restrictive) that they were able to continue to push the boundaries of the Code and to tease out of an "approved" script so much sexual content, usually by means of verbal and visual innuendo.

This boundary-pushing was nowhere more apparent that in the noir cycle. Preminger himself readily admitted that he took great pride in leading the charge against Hollywood's Puritanism. Despite Code limitations, Preminger here was able to draw a good deal of suspense out of the plot and an excellent subdued performance from Michael Rennie as Dr. Pearson, a man of guarded sensibilities who has been severely damaged by life. His alienation from others is nowhere better revealed than in the 360° subjective pan around Pearson's clock filled room. Wisely descending into a character role here, Charles Boyer ably captures the perversity behind Dr. Laurent's kindly façade (drawing a bit, perhaps, upon his performance in *Gaslight*). Preminger was wise, as well, in deftly stealing a scene from the original in which Dr.

Laurent's face moves in out of the light cast by a swinging lamp while he proclaims to Pearson: "Good and evil can change places like light and shadow." Something of a credo for denizens of the noir world. **BP**

THIS GUN FOR HIRE (1942)

Director: Frank Tuttle. **Screenplay**: Albert Maltz and W.R. Burnett from the novel *A Gun For Sale* by Graham Greene. **Producer**: Richard M. Blumenthal. **Director of Photography**: John Seitz. **Music**: Frank Loesser and Jacques Press. **Art Directors**: Hans Dreier, Robert Usher. **Editor**: Archie Marshek. **Cast**: Alan Ladd (Phillip Raven), Veronica Lake (Ellen Graham), Robert Preston (Michael Crane), Laird Cregar (Willard Gates), Tully Marshall (Alvin Brewster), Marc Lawrence (Tommy), Pamela Blake (Annie), Frank Ferguson (Albert Baker). **Released**: Paramount, May 13. 80 minutes.

Phillip Raven, a psychologically disturbed young assassin, is hired in San Francisco by Willard Gates to commit murder. Gates, an overweight, unctuous epicure, is an employee of Alvin Brewster, the elderly and crippled head of a large, Los Angeles-based chemical firm. Brewster is making millions selling chemical formulas to the Japanese, and the target is a blackmailing, potential government informant. Raven completes the job successfully and is paid off by Gates. But Gates has given him hot money, and a San Francisco police detail headed by Lt. Detective Michael Crane of Los Angeles (where the money was "stolen" from Brewster's firm) is soon pursuing Raven. He escapes and heads for Los Angeles in an attempt to get even with Gates and his mysterious boss for setting him up. On the train there, he accidentally becomes involved with Ellen Graham, Crane's fiancée, who has been secretly engaged by federal authorities to try and uncover fifth column activity. With this in mind, she has used her charms to get a job as a singer-entertainer at Gates' LA nightclub. Raven initially uses Ellen as a cover to escape the police cordon waiting for him at the LA train station. He is prepared to kill her to keep her from revealing his whereabouts but when he discovers Ellen's connection to Gates he decides to use her to get to Gates. He even rescues her from the clutches of Tommy, Gates' chauffer-henchman, who has been ordered to dispose of her by Gates, now aware of her connection to the police. Ellen begins to empathize with Raven once he discloses to her something of his abusive upbringing. They strike up a bargain: if she helps him escape the police he will attempt to get a signed statement from Gates and his boss, who they now know to be Brewster, regarding their activities. Using a disguise, Raven is able to get into Brewster's virtually impregnable skyscraper office. With the aid of Brewster's disgusted man-servant, Raven isolates himself with Brewster, Gates, and the servant as the police attempt to cut through the heavy metal office door. Brewster grudgingly signs a confession just before dying of a heart attack. Gates signs but Raven then kills Gates just as Lt. Crane, lowered to an outside window on a painter's scaffold, shoots Raven. Raven reconciles with Ellen as he dies.

French cineastes consider *This Gun For Hire* to be one of the essential early film noirs, not only because of its connection to the British thriller via Greene's novel but, more importantly, because of Alan Ladd's role as the hired killer. This certainly was the film that established the trench-

coated figure as a major icon, for good or evil, of the noir cycle. And Ladd's stoic performance would set a hardboiled standard that descends even into today's cinema. Such a reputation, however, can lead a first-time viewer to expect too much from this film. Its wartime propaganda dates badly and the musical interludes (which, unfortunately, became an all-too-familiar "pause" in many film noirs) slow the action. Finally, Veronica Lake's role as a combination chanteuse, government agent, confidante and love interest (for her ostensible co-star, Robert Preston) is complicated and confusing. Stripped of its veneer, Ellen Graham's character is little more than a positive version of the femme fatale, since her success in seducing Raven into helping her, and a government he cares little about, weakens his iron will and ultimately leads to his demise.

Still, *This Gun For Hire* has in its favor the fact that it helped to establish many noir conventions. John Seitz, with director Tuttle's encouragement, skillfully blends studio work with some authentic locales (e.g., Southern Pacific's depot and rail yards in Los Angeles), a visual motif that would become a hallmark of the film noir. Indeed, the nocturnal chase sequence in the "gasworks" near downtown LA looks forward to similar scenes in *D.O.A.* and *White Heat*, just as the presence of Tully Marshall as the wizened Brewster looks backward to the silent era and the Mabuse films. Of course, this film is enhanced by Laird Cregar, whose short film career was so closely tied to the noir cycle. Here his silken voice, suave charm and apparent abhorrence of violence mask a darker personality—a persona that Cregar himself would soon exploit and one that would be mined by actors as diverse as Raymond Burr and Clifton Webb. In the final analysis, however, this film belongs to Alan Ladd, whose Raven represents a distinct break with the gangsters of an earlier era, given his Freudian basis and his lack of emotions. We can read in his face only two fleeting instances of feeling—when his eyes become moist as he relates the events of his childhood and in his enigmatic smile as he lies dying (reinforcing

an earlier scene in which he tells Ellen that he would like to join a cat he is forced to kill in endless sleep). With the exception of his role in *The Glass Key*, Ladd would never again capture so well the essence of the hardboiled protagonist. **BP**

THIS SIDE OF THE LAW (1950)

Director: Richard L. Bare. **Screenplay**: Russell S. Hughes based on a story by Richard Sale. **Producer**: Saul Elkins. **Director of Photography**: Carl Guthrie. **Art Director**: Hugh Reticker. **Music**: William Lava. **Editor**: Frank Magee. **Cast**: Viveca Lindfors (Evelyn Taylor), Kent Smith (David Cummins), Janis Paige (Nadine Taylor), Robert Douglas (Philip Cagle), John Alvin (Calder Taylor), Monte Blue (Sheriff), Nita Talbot (Miss Goff), Frances Morris (Miss Roberts). **Released**: Warner Bros. June 17. 74 minutes.

The story is told by David Cummins in flashback from the inside of a cistern, where he has been thrown. Cummins, a vagrant, is bailed out of jail by lawyer Cagle, who hires him to impersonate a missing millionaire for whom he is a dead ringer. The hitch is that the missing man's estate needs protecting before the man is declared legally dead. Cummins moves into the millionaire's mansion and soon regrets his acquiescence after finding that the missing man's wife, Evelyn, and brother both hate him and his sister-in-law, Nadine, wants to seduce him. When Cagle, who has been plundering the estate, gets everything in place, he shoves Cummins into the cistern to die, as he did the missing millionaire. Cagle plots to arrange the deaths of the other principals to cover his financial misdeeds, but Cummins manages to escape from this prison and save Evelyn, who is about to be done in by Cagle. Cagle tries to get away but is driven into the cistern by the family police dog and captured by the police.

Exemplifying a common noir theme, that of the doppelganger-impersonator who, because of his masquerade, finds himself embroiled in circumstances he did not foresee, *This Side of the Law* manages some measure of suspense and some decent performances from an able cast. The tricky beginning, in which the trapped Cummins relates how he got into this predicament, is handled well. The film as a whole, however, is hampered by a hokey script and perhaps demonstrates Warner Bros.' half-hearted interest in producing B fare. The fact that the Big Four—Warner, Fox, MGM, and Paramount—produced not only fewer B noirs but fewer notable B movies in general seems to reflect the view of the majors' moguls that Bs were strictly to fill the bottom half of the theater bill and had little merit on their own. The author of the original story for *This Side of the Law*, Richard Sale, became a noted writer-director who went on to do the screenplay for the superior Frank Sinatra B noir *Suddenly* and collaborated on such big-budget screenplays as *Around the World in 80 Days*. He also authored several novels blasting the Hollywood studio system, such as *Lazarus #7* and *The Oscar*. The studio execs immortalized Sale's view of them when they made an absolutely abominable movie of the latter in 1966. **AL**

THE THREAT (1949)

Director: Felix Feist. **Screenplay**: Hugh King, Dick Irving Hyland. **Story**: Hugh King. **Producer**: Hugh King. **Director of Photography**: Harry J. Wild. **Music**: Paul Sawtell. **Art Directors**: Albert S.

D'Agostino, Charles F. Pyke. **Editor**: Samuel E. Beetley. **Cast**: Michael O'Shea (Detective Ray Williams), Virginia Grey (Carol), Charles McGraw (Arnold Kluger), Julie Bishop (Ann Williams), Frank Conroy (District Attorney Barker McDonald), Robert Shayne (Inspector Murphy), Anthony Caruso (Nick Damon), Don McGuire (Joe Turner), Frank Richards (Lefty), Michael McHale (Detective Jensen). **Released**: RKO, December 1. 66 minutes.

When Arnold Kluger escapes from prison, a chain of telephone calls and telegraph messages relays the news. Kluger had vowed to kill the two men most responsible for his imprisonment: District Attorney Barker McDonald and Detective Ray Williams. With a crew of henchmen at his call, Kluger's revenge plan immediately goes into motion, and with remarkable speed he abducts both McDonald and Williams, as well as an ex-girlfriend/burlesque girl whom he blames for turning informant. Kluger and his henchmen escape through roadblocks thanks to a commandeered moving van—with their victims in tow. They hole up in an abandoned shack in the desert, waiting for Kluger's partner, Tony, to arrive from Mexico. Together, Kluger and Tony will then enact their revenge. Meanwhile, Inspector Murphy attempts to snare Kluger and save McDonald and Williams.

The Threat is a taut and economical crime drama. From its earliest moments—Kluger's escape takes place as the opening credits roll—*The Threat* surges forward at breakneck pace, showing the amazing speed in which Kluger's revenge plans fall into place. Before ten minutes of screen time have passed, Kluger has captured D.A. McDonald, Det. Williams, and ex-girlfriend Carol. As a result, much of the running time is devoted to Kluger's efforts to avoid the police after he has captured his victims—and then to the rising tensions within Kluger's gang as they wait in a desert shack for Kluger's partner to arrive. Much of the movie's first half utilizes classic film noir stylistics, with many scenes taking place at night, including the prison escape, Det. Williams' abduction, Carol's abduction, and the trip out of town in a moving van. In the movie's latter half, the movie eschews the environs of typical film noir, opting for the bright light and wide-open spaces of the desert. Even then, the characters are largely confined to a shack where squabbles develop within Kluger's gang and tension runs high. The movie remains almost claustrophobic; we get establishing shots of the shack, but afterwards the camera typically stays trapped inside with the characters.

Throughout much of the movie, McDonald and Williams have little to do: they're tied up and gagged. However, the movie supplies Williams with a key background story. His wife is pregnant. In one of the movie's first scenes, Ray and Ann stencil animal shapes on the wall of their nursery and discuss possible child names. "Dexter?" says Ray incredulously. "Before I buy Dexter there will have to be a gun at my back." Seemingly a throwaway bit of dialogue, this exchange takes on much greater value later in the movie when Kluger forces Williams to call the police station and pretend he's on the job. But Ray slips in a message about his child, Dexter, and when the message is forwarded to his wife, she understands (not immediately but eventually) something is amiss and informs the police, who jump to action.

The impact of family/home life on the threat supplied by the crime element softens the movie's noir sensibilities. This is a movie about surviving the threat supplied by noir. There is no sense of spiraling despair for the protagonists, who clearly represent good forces. As such, the protagonists are a bit bland. Faring much better is the moving van driver Joe Turner, who gets roped into Kluger's schemes. He keeps thinking his duties are done so he says he's going to leave. In one of the movie's best scenes, Kluger calmly lets Joe talk about leaving. Joe walks across the room, opens the door, and begins to step out. Kluger says one word, "Joe?" And Joe turns, knowing Kluger will never allow him to leave. His frustration erupts. He slams the door, breaking its glass. Meanwhile, Virginia Grey gives a sensitive, frightened performance as Kluger's ex-girlfriend Carol. She's terrified that Williams will say something that might indicate she had turned informant on Kluger. Much of the movie's focus rests on the shoulders of the durable character actor Charles McGraw as Kluger, but McGraw's one-note gruffness quickly becomes an irritant. He's all bulldog without any of the shadings that might allow him to escape from the conventional and the formulaic. **GJ**

TIMETABLE (1956)

Director: Mark Stevens. **Screenplay**: Aben Kandel based on a story by Robert Angus. **Producer**: Mark Stevens. **Director of Photography**: Charles Van Enger. **Art Director**: William H. Tuntke. **Music**: Walter Scharf. **Editor**: Kenneth Crane. **Cast**: Mark Stevens (Charlie Norman), King Calder (Joe Armstrong), Felicia Farr (Linda Brucker), Marianne Stewart (Ruth Norman), Wesley Addy (Dr. Paul Brucker), Alan Reed (Al Wolfe), Rodolfo Hoyos, Jr. (Lt. Castro), Jack Klugman (Frankie Page), John Marley (Bobik). **Released**: United Artists, February 8. 79 minutes.

A train is robbed of $500,000 through an elaborate plan involving a fake doctor, a sick polio victim, and his wife. The crime seems to have been perfect, based precisely on the train's timetable. Charlie Norman, who is about to go on vacation in Mexico with his wife, is called onto the case as the insurance company's top investigator. He and his partner, Joe Armstrong, manage to track down a stolen ambulance and a helicopter that were used as part of the plot. The strain of solving the crime seemingly starts to take its toll on Norman's relationship with his wife, but the reality is that Norman, fed up with his low-paying job and his devoted wife, masterminded the robbery and is involved in a relationship with Linda Brucker, one of the robbers. She also happens to be married to the fake doctor Brucker. The perfect crime starts to fall apart when one of the gang members is accidentally killed, preventing all from escaping to Mexico, and Norman is forced to murder the owner of the stolen helicopter to prevent the man from turning state's evidence. Brucker and Linda try to evade the police and escape across the border but Brucker is shot to death trying to cross the border at Tijuana. Linda manages to get away but Norman and Armstrong are sent to Tijuana to ferret her out. Norman tracks down Linda through underworld connections and arranges to leave the country with her, but things go wrong and he is forced to kill a gangster to acquire false passports for himself and Linda. In an attempt to escape, Linda is shot to death and Norman's partner is forced to kill him. Norman dies saying, "This wasn't on the timetable, either."

This is a neatly done, tight little film with Stevens nicely juggling two noir themes—the straight-arrow insurance agent gone wrong and the man fed up with the cozy emptiness of this middle-class existence—without getting heavy-handed. The other actors handle their parts with similar restraint, giving this sleeper a feeling of stark realism absent from many 1950s noirs. Stevens is notable both as a noir actor, playing leading roles in such seminal films as *The Dark Corner* and *The Street with No Name*, and as a director-actor in later B noirs such as *Timetable* and *Cry Vengeance*. **AL**

DEADLY MINUTES! MURDEROUS SECONDS!

and then the Screen Explodes!

He had everything planned to the last split-second in this thrill-o-minute crime... then Fate came a few minutes too late.

MARK STEVENS IN "**TIMETABLE**"

with KING CALDER · FELICIA FARR · MARIANNE STEWART

Story by Robert Angus · Screenplay by Aben Kandel · Produced and Directed by Mark Stevens
Released thru United Artists

Tomorrow Is Another Day: *Bill Clark (Steve Cochran) and Catherine Higgins (Ruth Roman).*

TOMORROW IS ANOTHER DAY (1951)

Director: Felix E. Feist. **Screenplay**: Felix Feist, Art Cohn, Guy Endore from his story. **Producer**: Henry Blanke. **Director of Photography**: Robert Burks. **Music**: Daniele Amfitheatrof. **Editor**: Alan Crosland, Jr. **Art Director**: Charles H. Clarke. **Cast**: Ruth Roman (Catherine "Kay" Higgins), Steve Cochran (Bill Clark/Mike Lewis), Lurene Tuttle (Mrs. Dawson), Ray Teal (Mr. Dawson), Morris Ankrum (Hugh Wagner), John Kellogg (Monroe), Lee Patrick (Janet Higgins), Hugh Sanders (Lt. Conover), Stuart Randall (Frank Higgins), Bobby Hyatt (Johnny Dawson), Harry Antrim (Warden), Walter Sande (Sheriff). **Released**: Warner Bros., August 8. 90 minutes.

Bill Clark is released from prison, where he was sent as a youth for murdering his abusive father and where he has grown into a young man without any normal experiences. While concealing his past he tries to start a new life and goes to a dime-a-dance hall to learn how to act with women. He naively falls for the sultry Kay, who is having an affair with a local cop. Believing that he has killed the man to save her from his abuse, Bill and Kay go on the run. In the course of their flight, Bill insists on marrying Kay. While working as pickers in the California farmlands, they are discovered and arrested. Expecting the worst, the couple discovers that their "victim" is still not dead and he exonerates them.

Like the Douglas Sirk/Sam Fuller *Shockproof*, *Tomorrow Is Another Day* (directed by Felix Feist, the scenarist/director of the manic *The Devil Thumbs A Ride* four years earlier) is a more "upbeat" example of the fugitive couple plot than the proto-noir *You Only Live Once* or its near contemporary *Gun Crazy*. The lovers of *Shockproof* and *Tomorrow Is Another Day* survive, but the noir sensibility of these pictures is sustained through a narrative that underscores the sense of amour fou. Both feature protagonists who have already been convicted of a crime when the narrative opens. While *Shockproof* adds the element of the "rogue cop" in the parole officer whose obsessive love drives him to flee with a women parolee

accused of murder, *Tomorrow Is Another Day* goes even farther. The prospective couple is a bizarre admixture of innocence and depravity. The man, Bill, has grown up in prison convicted for a murder committed under the influence of an uncontrollable temper while still a youth. Paroled as an adult, he is sexually inexperienced. As portrayed by Cochran, better known for such supporting roles as the gangster who cuckolds Cagney's Cody Jarrett in *White Heat*, Bill has a physical maturity that belies his stunted emotional growth. The woman, Catherine, who becomes the object of Bill's obsessive love, is a taxi dancer/prostitute. Again the element of the rogue cop is introduced, this time when a detective, who is himself in love with the woman, sexually assaults her and is killed. Like many predecessor fugitive couples, from Eddie and Jo in *You Only Live Once* to Bowie and Keechie in *They Live by Night*, the lovers of *Tomorrow Is Another Day* are proletarian. While the couple in *Shockproof* finds work in an oil field, Bill and Catherine seek refuge in the anonymity of migrant farming.

In the end, the subtlest irony of both *Shockproof* and *Tomorrow Is Another Day* is that neither of these couples can take charge of their own destiny and create their own salvation. Rather they survive because they are both exonerated by their victims. For many fugitive couples, particularly in the context of film noir, the emotional sustenance which may be derived from any hope of escape or the kindness of strangers is secondary to their own obsessive love. When amour fou is as Buñuel suggested an all-consuming passion, every action—hiding out, stealing money, killing interlopers—is a desperate attempt to remain at large where that passion may be sustained. **LB & AS**

TOO LATE FOR TEARS (1949)

Director: Byron Haskin. **Screenplay**: Roy Huggins from the *Saturday Evening Post* serialization of his novel. **Producer**: Hunt Stromberg. **Director of Photography**: William Mellor. **Music**: Dale Butts. **Art Director**: James Sullivan. **Editor**: Harry Keller. **Cast**: Lizabeth Scott (Jane Palmer), Don DeFore (Don Blake), Dan Duryea (Danny Fuller), Arthur Kennedy (Alan Palmer), Kristine Miller (Kathy Palmer), Barry Kelley (Lt. Breach). **Completed**: October 15, 1948. **Released**: United Artists, August 14. 98 minutes.

Alan Palmer and his wife, Jane, are driving to a party one night and have an argument which causes their car to swerve off the road and blink its lights. Another car mistakes this for a signal, and a bag containing $60,000 is thrown into the Palmers' convertible as the two cars pass. Alan would like to turn the money over to the police, but Jane persuades him to keep it and check it at Union Station the next day. A man, identifying himself as private detective Danny Fuller, calls on Jane at home one day and claims the money. They haggle and he finally agrees to split the loot with her. Realizing her husband will never consent to keeping any of the money, Jane hides the claim check and, with Fuller's reluctant help, she kills Alan one evening while the two are boating in Westlake Park. Jane's charms are sufficient to hold Fuller at bay while Jane reports Alan's disappearance to the police and to his sister Kathy, intimating that her husband had run off to Mexico with a girlfriend. Some time later a stranger named Don

Blake arrives at Jane's house and explains that he is Alan's old army buddy. Blake is actually the brother of Jane's first husband, a suicide victim whom he suspects she murdered. Meeting Kathy, Blake confides his true identity and Kathy reveals her suspicions about Alan's disappearance. She had discovered a baggage claim ticket in Alan's bureau drawer where he usually kept his gun and gives the ticket to Blake. Jane, however, is aware of Kathy's surveillance and, again with Fuller's reluctant help, makes plans to poison her. But before she can she discovers the truth about Blake and must retrieve the claim ticket from him and Kathy at gunpoint. She picks up the money bag and joins Fuller at his motel. After hiding out briefly with Fuller, she poisons him and departs for Mexico City. Blake follows her there and calls the police. As she hurries to elude them, Jane falls from the balcony to her death and the money flutters down after her.

As in *Manhandled*, Dan Duryea again portrays a corrupt private eye, one who in this instance, however, has more than met his match. For Danny Fuller's toughness is little more than a pretense and he proves it when he gets himself drunk in order to find the false courage to buy the poison with which Jane intends to kill Kathy. Instead of grabbing a share of the money and running, Danny allows himself to be seduced and manipulated, to the point where he even acquiesces in his own murder, victim of the very poison he had purchased for Jane.

Jane Palmer, on the other hand, is, like Phyllis Dietrichson in *Double Indemnity*, "rotten to the core," although Lizabeth Scott portrays her with somewhat less verve than Barbara Stanwyck. Jane is an extreme example of middle class malaise, which, in a moment of real self-pity, she uses to justify her actions: "We were white collar poor. Middle class poor. The kind of people who can't quite keep up with the Joneses and die a little every day because they can't." Yet the desire to leave the ranks of the middle class is hardly justification for three murders. No, more likely Jane is just another in a long line of noir femmes fatales who take a perverse pleasure in what they do. It is also important to note that the screenwriter Roy Huggins would take a noir sensibility developed in films like this one to television and noir the small screen's landscape with influential series like *The Fugitive*. **BP**

TOUCH OF EVIL (1958)

Director: Orson Welles. **Screenplay**: Welles based on the novel *Badge of Evil* by Whit Masterson. **Producer**: Albert Zugsmith. **Director of Photography**: Russell Metty. **Music**: Henry Mancini. **Art Directors**: Alexander Golitzen, Robert Clatworthy. **Editors**: Virgil M. Vogel, Aaron Stell. **Cast**: Charlton Heston (Ramon Miguel "Mike" Vargas), Janet Leigh (Susan Vargas), Orson Welles (Hank Quinlan), Joseph Calleia (Pete Menzies), Akim Tamiroff (Uncle Joe Grandi), Joanna Moore (Marcia Linnekar), Marlene Dietrich (Tanya), Ray Collins (Adair), Dennis Weaver (Motel Manager), Victor Millan (Manolo Sanchez), Lalo Rios (Risto), Valentin de Vargas (Pancho), Mort Mills (Schwartz), Mercedes McCambridge (Hoodlum), Michael Sargent (Pretty Boy), Zsa Zsa Gabor (Owner of Nightclub), Keenan Wynn (Man), Joseph Cotten (Detective), Phil Harvey (Blaine), Joi Lansing (Blonde). **Completed**: April 1, 1957. **Released**: Universal, May 21. 95 minutes.

Note: After Welles turned in a cut, Universal had Harry Keller shoot additional scenes and reedited the film for the original release. In 1975 a 108-minute "preview" print without Keller's scenes and with some of Welles' deleted scenes was discovered in the UCLA Film and Television. In 1998 Universal created a 111-minute "restored" version using a lengthy memo written by Welles in 1957 as a guide.

Near the Mexican border, a millionaire is blown up along with his blond companion by a bomb planted in his car. At odds in the investigation are Mike Vargas, a Mexican narcotics investigator on his honeymoon with his American wife, Susan, and Hank Quinlan, a shrewd stateside detective. Quinlan believes that a young Mexican, Sanchez, is guilty of the murder and plants evidence to frame him. Discovering this, Vargas tries to expose Quinlan. The outraged Quinlan retaliates by enlisting the help of racketeer Uncle Joe Grandi who sends a gang of punks to a desert motel where Susan Vargas is staying to set her up as an apparent drug addict. To cover his tracks, Quinlan kills Grandi in the hotel room to which Susan has been brought, but Quinlan's devoted partner, Menzies, discovers Quinlan's cane in the room and is pressured by Vargas to expose Quinlan. Menzies gets Quinlan's confession, which is surreptitiously recorded by Vargas. Quinlan discovers the betrayal and shoots Menzies,

Touch of Evil: *Hank Quinlan (Orson Welles), Susan Vargas (Janet Leigh), and Uncle Joe Grandi (Akim Tamiroff).*

who in turn shoots him. The two men die as news arrives that Sanchez has confessed to the initial bomb murder.

Initially underrated by all but a few, *Touch of Evil* is now perhaps a bit overrated, at least in relation to some less widely known but equally impressive noir films. Of course, Orson Welles is a substantial presence off and on the screen; still it must be admitted that there is more subtle artistry in *On Dangerous Ground, White Heat, Criss Cross, Angel Face,* and *The Big Heat,* to name only a few; nevertheless, those films cannot tarnish Welles' vivid creation of a Mexican nightmare out of the strange decor of Venice, California, or his realization of a host of characters who are colorful and resonant. Welles utilizes his bravura style so effectively that it cannot always be discerned which moments create the dramatic thrust of the film and which are simply full of sound and fury.

The opening shot, lasting over three minutes, displays Welles' propensity for the moving camera and the long take, and immediately establishes the premise around which the narrative is structured. The camera begins on a close-up of a time bomb and then cranes up to reveal the bomb being planted in a car. Linnekar and his girlfriend emerge out of the background darkness and, as they enter the car and begin to drive away, the high craned camera travels up and back, moving with them along the streets toward the border. Slowly, the camera descends as Vargas and Susan cross the street at a traffic light where Linnekar is stopped. Tracking alongside and in front of the couple, the camera then cranes up again as the car moves past them and onward to the customs station. The camera continues moving with Vargas and Susan when suddenly there is a blinding explosion as the bomb goes off in the car. The shot is completed with a close-up of the car engulfed in flames, followed by a reverse zoom away from the wreck. The uninterrupted fluidity of this opening shot works in direct opposition to the violence of the imagery, and the suspense which the visual style engenders is heightened by the fact that only the spectator is aware of the bomb's presence. This cinematic fluidity is continued throughout *Touch of Evil* and not only creates tension as a visual device but is also appropriate to the shadowy characters and their complex and rapid comings and goings across the border. Russell Metty's camerawork exhibits film noir lighting at its peak and the matching of studio shots with Venice locations is especially effective. The scene in the hotel room where Quinlan murders Grandi is particualrly memorable. The sometimes clichéd device of an exterior neon light flashing into a room is powerfully expressive as Quinlan and Grandi move in and out of the darkness within a restricted space. Welles varies the tempo in the similarly lit sequence of Sanchez's interrogation, which is dominated by a long take that is remarkable for its constantly varying composition.

In the character of Hank Quinlan, Welles gives one of his most persuasive performances. Visually, his vast paunch, his limp, his half-closed eyes, and his fondness for cigars and candy bars, all contribute to the seediness of the character he portrays. And yet, Welles creates a sympathetic antagonist who exhibits a human, almost wistful quality when speaking of the wife he lost years before. Through such characters as the fortune telling Tanya and police assistant Menzies, Quinlan demonstrates that he is capable of inspiring devotion. Equally essential in creating an atmosphere of lurking evil are the secondary characters of the obscene and vulgar Grandi, with his hair slicked down and popping eyes; his

sadistic gang, which includes a lesbian hoodlum; and the ineffectual night man at the motel, whose nervousness and incoherent, mumbling speech becomes more exaggerated as he is confronted by Vargas. Ultimately Welles makes Hank Quinlan into an imposing and driven figure whose face reflects the ancient but still intense anguish of his wife's ambiguous murder and the fatal corruption that will destroy him. The sight of Quinlan staggering down an embankment of the Venice canals to die in a river of garbage is a moment at once grotesque and tragic, underscored by Tanya's understated epitaph that "He was some kind of man." **BL & TT**

TRAPPED (1949)

Director: Richard Fleischer. **Screenplay**: Earl Felton and George Zuckerman based on their story. **Producer**: Bryan Foy. **Director of Photography**: Guy Roe. **Music**: Sol Kaplan. **Art Director**: Frank Durlauf. **Editor**: Alfred DeGaetano. **Cast**: Lloyd Bridges (Tris Stewart), Barbara Payton (Meg Dixon, alias Laurie Fredericks), John Hoyt (Agent John Downey, alias Johnny Hackett), James Todd (Jack Sylvester), Russ Conway (Chief Agent Gunby), Robert Karnes (Agent Fred Foreman). **Released**: Eagle Lion, October 1. 78 minutes.

Tris is in prison for counterfeiting money. He used plates that almost perfectly duplicate U.S. bills. After he promises Treasury Department agents to help them get the plates, they stage his escape. They also let him think he's double-crossed them and given them the slip to get back to his girlfriend, Meg. She's a cigarette girl at a nightclub, where agent John Downey, pretending to be a well-heeled grifter, is keeping an eye on her. Jack Sylvester, who now has the plates, offers Tris $250,000 counterfeit for $25,000 real money. John cons Tris into asking him to put up the $25,000. The sting operation is spoiled, however, when Meg overhears a man at the club say John is a government agent. Tris tries to kill John and steal the real money, but he fails and is sent back to prison. John goes with Sylvester to a trolley car shack, where Sylvester has the counterfeit money and the plates. Meg tries to warn Sylvester that John is a T-Man, but Sylvester doesn't trust her. Sylvester turns and shoots Meg, giving John a chance to get away. The police arrive and chase Sylvester among the trolley cars, until he touches a live wire.

Trapped is notable for several reasons. First, it features the star-crossed blonde bombshell Barbara Payton (whose ghost-written autobiography *I Am Not Ashamed* traced her personal descent into her own noir nightmare) in a sympathetic role as a put-upon "bad girl" who tries to remain faithful to her criminal lover Tris but ends up dead for her trouble. She will bring the same weary sexuality evidenced in this role to her more notable performance as James Cagney's abused moll in *Kiss Tomorrow Goodbye*, the following year. It also show-cases several noir-inflected action sequences shot on actual locations in Los Angeles, most notably, the robbery of a small market on Franklin Avenue in West Hollywood and a chase through the Los Angeles trolley car yard which ends in the accidental electrification of the criminal Sylvester. **JU**

TRY AND GET ME
[aka THE SOUND OF FURY] (1950)

Try and Get Me: *Howard Tyler (Frank Lovejoy) and Sheriff Demig (Cliff Clark).*

Director: Cyril Endfield. **Screenplay**: Cy Endfield, Jo Pagano from his novel *The Condemned.* **Executive Producer**: Robert Stillman. **Director of Photography**: Guy Roe. **Music**: Hugo Friedhofer. **Art Director**: Perry Ferguson. **Editor**: George Amy. **Cast**: Frank Lovejoy (Howard Tyler), Kathleen Ryan (Judy Tyler), Richard Carlson (Gil Stanton), Lloyd Bridges (Jerry Slocum), Katherine Locke (Hazel), Adele Jergens (Velma), Art Smith (Hal Clendenning), Renzo Cesana (Dr. Simone), Irene Vernon (Helen Stanton), Lynn Gray (Vi Clendenning), Cliff Clark (Sheriff Demig), Dabbs Greer (Mike), Mack Williams (Professor Martin), Jane Easton (Barbara Colson), John Pelletti (Herb Colson), Mary Lawrence (Kathy), Donald Smelick (Tommy Tyler). **Completed**: August 28, 1950. **Released**: United Artists, as *The Sound of Fury* on December 12; as *Try and Get Me* on March 26, 1951 while the film was still in general release. 90 minutes.

A down-on-his-luck veteran, Howard Tyler, finds that after returning from the service he is unable to provide his family with such material goods as television sets, clothes, and entertainment, which he feels they want. Out of desperation he teams up with a casual acquaintance, Jerry Slocum, in order to pull off a series of robberies. The robberies evolve into a kidnapping plot that quickly results in the unnecessary death of the victim. Howard's marriage slowly crumbles as he becomes moody and irrational. In a drunken haze, Harry confessess to a casual acquaintance and the two are finally indentified and apprehended. Fueled by the sensationalist press, the local citizens burst into the jail, savagely beat the two men, and drag them off to be lynched.

Utilizing the structural device of a voice of reason (the left-ist Italian intellectual Dr. Simone) in order to smooth over the brutal and naturalistic vision of society shown by the filmmak-ers, *Try and Get Me* functions both as a docu-noir exposing social inequity as well as a disturbing example of existentialist film noir. With its dark vision of American society (the story is based on a true incident which took place in 1933 in San Jose—although the film is shot in Phoenix, Arizona), it is little wonder that Cy Enfield's American film career was destroyed by the Blacklist within a few years of this film (Enfield returned to his native England and in 1964 made the impres-sive anti-colonialist film *Zulu.*). The film chronicles the destruction of a man, Howard Tyler, hopelessly lost in his own

society. Returning from war, like so many noir protagonists, he cannot adjust either to his family life or the pressures of earn-ing a living in this new post-war order of the nuclear family where the burden falls on the husband to support the unit. Joining forces with the psychopathic Jerry, Howard becomes the getaway man in a series of robberies. Given new hope by a little cash in his pocket, Howard immediately begins partic-ipating in the consumer ethic so promoted by business and government in the 1950s—taking his wife and son out to buy new outfits and promising them a television.

Trying desperately to continue to perform his middle class "husbandly" duty, Tyler goes aganst his instincts and agrees to participate in the kidnapping of a rich man's son. The kidnapping goes awry when Jerry kills the boy. After this, Tyler sinks deeper and deeper into alcoholism and paranoia, including auditory and visual hallucinations. Enfield and screenwriter Jo Pagano further stack the deck in favor of Tyler by portraying the press as yellow journalists (the parallels with Billy Wilder's *Ace in the Hole* are striking), intent on selling newspapers as they whip the towns-people into a frenzy. We first see the journalist Stanton, who eventually writes these inflamatory articles, sumptuously enter-taining guests in his luxurious home directly following a scene with Tyler and his family in their run-down, lower middle class house where the family struggles to afford ham and eggs. This visual dialectic more than any dialogue establishes the inequities in society which Dr. Simone hints at and which may be the cause of crime in his view. The attack on the jail cell at the end of the movie and the subsequent lynching is harrowing, shot in an almost newsreel style and using real people from the town as extras. The huge crowd completely overrunning the police and then dragging the two prisoners from their jail and the sound of their roars in the distance as the hangings take place are unfor-gettable moments in the history of noir filmmaking. **JU**

THE TURNING POINT (1952)

Director: William Dieterle. **Screenplay**: Warren Duff from the story *Storm in the City* by Horace McCoy. **Producer**: Irving Asher. **Director of Photography**: Lionel Lindon. **Music**: Irvin Talbot; stock music by Victor Young & Miklós Rózsa (uncredited). **Art Directors**: Hal Pereira, Joseph McMillan Johnson. **Editor**: George

Tomasini. **Cast**: William Holden (Jerry McKibbon), Edmond O'Brien (John Conroy), Alexis Smith (Amanda Waycross), Tom Tully (Matt Conroy), Ed Begley (Neil Eichelberger), Dan Dayton (Ackerman), Adele Longmire (Carmelina), Ray Teal (Capt. Clint), Ted De Corsia (Harrigan), Don Porter (Joe Silbray), Howard Freeman (Fogel), Neville Brand (Red). **Completed**: November 6, 1951. **Released**: Paramount, November 14. 85 minutes.

John Conroy, an honest lawyer and politician, is head of a special committee investigating organized crime in a large mid-Western city. His boyhood friend, cynical investigative reporter Jerry McKibbon, is shocked to discover that Conroy's father, Matt, was once a policeman on the syndicate payroll. McKibbon decides not to tell Conroy about his father and instead gets Matt to work with him in trying to get evidence against the syndicate. As the committee puts pressure on the syndicate chieftain, Eichelberger, the gangsters decide that Matt Conroy must be killed. They arrange for a hit that makes it appear as if Matt was killed trying to prevent a service station robbery. John Conroy redoubles his efforts to indict the syndicate, while McKibbon writes newspaper exposés with information gleaned from underworld contacts. The committee subpoenas incriminating records from Eichelberger which could mean the end of his empire. The files are stored in a downtown tenement building which Eichelberger has burned down, killing many of the people who live there. Ultimately, the wife of the hit man who killed Matt reveals herself to the committee when she realizes her husband had also been set up. Meanwhile, McKibbon walks into a trap set by Eichelberger by attending a prizefight where a hired assassin awaits him. Conroy learns of the plot, but McKibbon is shot and killed before the police can arrive.

The Turning Point is another film noir inspired by the work of the Keufauver Committee with less emphasis on the semi-documentary approach of films like *Captive City* and far less ominous overtones than films like *711 Ocean Drive* or *New York Confidential*, where a national crime syndicate remains entrenched at the film's conclusion. Corruption is also less pervasive here than it is in other film noirs, being restricted to one city in the Midwest (though there is a good deal of location footage of LA standing in for the fictional city) and being directed by one man, Neil Eichelberger. But in Ed Begley's capable hands, Eichelberger becomes the very objective correlative of evil: he calmly drinks a glass of water while deciding to burn down the tenement building, his utter inhumanity revealed in his sweaty face and his gleaming, beady eyes.

Finally, the nocturnal sequence of the tenement fire, with men, women and children screaming in the midst of the conflagration and scores of charred bodies littering the landscape, must surely be among one of the most startling scenes in the annals of film noir. **BP**

THE TWO MRS. CARROLLS (1947)

Director: Peter Godfrey. **Screenplay**: Thomas Job based on a play by Martin Vale. **Producer**: Mark Hellinger. **Director of Photography**: Peverell Marley. **Music**: Franz Waxman. **Art Director**: Anton Grot. **Editor**: Frederick Richards. **Cast**: Humphrey Bogart (Geoffrey Carroll), Barbara Stanwyck (Sally Morton Carroll), Alexis Smith (Cecily Latham), Nigel Bruce (Dr. Tuttle), Isobel Elsom Mrs. Latham), Ann Carter (Beatrice Carroll), Patrick O'Moore (Charles Pennington), Anita Bolster (Christine), Barry Bernard (Horace Blagdon). **Completed**: 1945. **Released**: Warner Bros., March 4. 99 minutes.

Geoffrey Carroll is a disturbed American painter living in England who meets an heiress, Sally Morton, while on vacation in Scotland. They fall in love, but when Sally discovers Geoffrey is married she breaks off the relationship. Back home, Geoffrey buys an unidentified substance from a local pharmacist, which he signs for using a false name and poisons his wife. After his wife's death he marries Sally and takes up residence in her luxurious home in the country. Now his career as a painter takes off and as a result Cecily Latham, the beautiful, spoiled daughter of a wealthy neighbor, insists that he paint her portrait, but he puts her off. However the pharmacist, Horace Blagdon, has recognized him and blackmails Geoffrey for his silence regarding the drug purchase. In order to secure more money, he takes the portrait assignment and in the process of painting Cecily he succumbs to her seduction. Geoffrey follows the same regimen with Sally as with his first wife but Sally becomes suspicious as her health declines. Meanwhile Geoffrey, pressured by Cecily to run off with her to South America and by Blagdon for more money, begins to lose control. He clubs Blagdon to death in his pharmacy late one night and makes it appear as a robbery. Geoffrey attempts to hasten Sally's death but when he discovers she has disposed of the milk he had given her, he attempts to strangle her with a drape tie. Sally's former suitor arrives to save her.

The Two Mrs. Carrolls is quite derivative of other thrillers

The Two Mrs. Carrolls: *Sally Carroll (Barbara Stanwyck) and her husband Geoffrey (Humphrey Bogart).*

(cf. *Suspicion*, *Gaslight*) in its mixture of the Gothic with the noir and as a whole is less successful, perhaps because of its staginess and Bogart's obvious discomfort at playing the demented artist. His iconic value in film noir was not fully realized in 1945 (when this film was completed) though he had mastered the gesture of staring at his hands—a sign of the unbalanced artist which descends from Expressionism (*The Hands of Orlac*) through the Gothic (*Mad Love*) and into the noir cycle (*Phantom Lady*). It was only later, in a film like *In a Lonely Place*, that Bogart would walk the fine line between the normal and the abnormal, between the loving and the violent, with ease. And as far as the threatened wife on the throes of hysteria is concerned, Stanwyck as well would perfect that later in *Sorry, Wrong Number*. Still, it is left to Bogart to deliver the film's best line: when Sally informs Cecily that Geoffrey must have an idea before he can paint and Cecily asks him if she does not give him an idea, Geoffrey responds, "Yes, but nothing I would care to paint." **BP**

TWO O'CLOCK COURAGE (1945)

Director: Anthony Mann. **Screenplay**: Gelett Burgess. **Producer**: Ben Stoloff. **Director of Photography**: Jack MacKenzie. **Music**: Roy Webb. **Art Directors**: L.O. Croxton and Albert S. D'Agostino. **Editor**: Philip Martin, Jr. **Cast**: Tom Conway (The Man, Ted Allison), Ann Rutherford (Patty Mitchell), Richard Lane (Al Haley), Lester Mathews (Mark Evans), Roland Drew (Steve Maitland), Emory Parnell (Insp. Bill Brenner), Jean Brooks (Barbara Borden). **Released**: RKO, April 13. 68 minutes.

At the end of *Two O'Clock Courage*, Ted and Patty are married. Ted, who was the prime suspect, has been cleared of suspicion of murdering Robert, a theater producer. Barbara is the killer. Robert threatened to show the letters she had written him to Steve, her jealous boyfriend. Barbara and Steve are starring in a play that Mark has falsely taken credit for writing. Robert, who is producing the play, knows Mark is a plagiarist and has made Mark share the royalties with him. Ted knows the real author was Larry, who has been mysteriously murdered. Just after Ted tells Robert that all the royalties belong to Larry's mother, Barbara kills Robert and knocks Ted out. At the start of the film, Ted has come to, but he has amnesia. He meets Patty, a taxi driver. She helps him find out his identity, and they fall in love. (It is never revealed who killed Larry. Presumably, Mark killed him to collect the royalties.)

Two O'Clock Courage has the same array of plot elements that are in several other early film noirs, from 1940 to 1944. These elements are not representative of postwar film noir. The following six plot elements are characteristic, in part or en toto, of wartime film noir. Examples are taken from *Two O'Clock Courage*. First, crimes are about "personal" property, not "public" property. Bank-robbing or racketeering is public. What is intimately associated with a person—his or her own life or money—is personal. Royalties for Larry's play are personal. During the war years, there is almost no film noir with a public property crime. However, it is pervasive in postwar film noir. Second, the police fail to catch the criminal, or they are absent from the story. Thanks to Ted and Patty, the investigation succeeds. The city police are comic. Postwar law enforcement—which is usually state or federal, not local—consistently catches the criminal. Furthermore, several post-

war film noirs, like Anthony Mann's *T-Men*, are depictions of the competency of federal law enforcement agencies. Third, unless there is espionage, the murder is committed out of passion (anger or jealousy), like Barbara's motive for killing Richard. Fourth, along with a murder from passion, there is a whodunit, like who killed Richard. In postwar film noir, there is rarely a "puzzle" because it is known who is guilty. In fact, the story is often about someone who is guilty. Fifth, the leading man, who is falsely jailed or hunted by the police, has to prove he's innocent of murder, like Ted. As a rule in postwar film noir, the accused criminal is guilty, whatever the crime. Sixth, a woman helps crack the mystery. She has both a job and a brain, like Patty. In postwar film noir, women are less often a man's crime-solving "ally." Instead, they're likely to be a woman-in-distress, a femme fatale or a homemaker. Some examples of early film noirs with this "formula" are: *Stranger on the Third Floor*, *I Wake Up Screaming*, *Saboteur*, *Street of Chance*, *Phantom Lady*. Other early film noirs may not have the complete array, but they will have at least some of these plot elements. All six plot elements in combination, which comprise the "war noir" formula, don't similarly combine in postwar film noirs. For example, in two of Mann's later film noirs, *Desperate* and *Side Street*, a woman merely accompanies a man. *Two O'Clock Courage* marks the final hour for the working-class woman who has wits and moxie and actively tries to clear a man.

Two O'Clock Courage shows little of the noir style. It opens strongly, with Ted wandering on a foggy street (in a studio, not on location). Nothing else is visually interesting, except when Ted searches Robert's dark house with a flashlight. The film also lacks the startling kind of violence that typically occurs in Mann's later film noirs and westerns. **DMH**

UNDER THE GUN (1951)

Director: Ted Tetzlaff. **Screenplay**: George Zuckerman from a story by Daniel B. Ullman. **Producer**: Ralph Dietrich. **Directors of Photography**: Henry Freulich, John L. Herman. **Music**: Milton Rosen using excerpts from scores by Lloyd Akridge, Miklós Rózsa, Hans J. Salter, Paul Sawtell, Frank Skinner, Leith Stevens. **Art Directors**: Bernard Herzbrun, Edward Ilou. **Editor**: Virgil Vogel. **Cast**: Richard Conte (Bert Galvin), Audrey Totter (Ruth Williams), Sam Jaffe (Samuel Gower), John McIntire (Sheriff Bill Langley), Shepperd Strudwick (Milo Bragg), Gregg Martell (Nero), Phillip Pine (Gandy), Donald Randolph (Arthur Sherbourne, district attorney), Royal Dano (Sam Nugent, trustee-gunner), Richard Taber (Five Shot), Dabbs Greer (Stoner). **Released**: Universal, February 22. 83 minutes.

Small-time mobster Bert Galvin tries to combine business with pleasure. As he drives back to New York with Miami nightclub diva Ruth Williams, he also takes care of an overdue hit. Despite her desires, Williams finds she cannot commit perjury—"You just weren't worth the lies," she later tells Galvin—so he pulls a twenty-year sentence at a prison farm in the deep South, where the concept of parole is unknown. However, as his bunkmate Sam Gower explains, trustees who foil escapes earn their release. Rather than bribe Nugent to let him escape, Galvin encourages another inmate to make a run for it. Nugent shoots him, gets out, and Galvin takes his place. Impatient to get even with Williams, Galvin makes Gower an offer: try to escape and your family will be well taken care of.

Under the Gun finds noir icon Audrey Totter a long way from the blonde and sultry conniver in *Tension* and the blonde and long-suffering Adrienne Fromsett of *Lady in the Lake*. Richard Conte on the other hand was in the midst of

Under the Gun: *Richard Conte, right.*

a string of roles that would alter the prototype of the noir cycle's anti-heroes. Trapped in the prison farm, Conte makes Galvin less of a caged animal and more of a ferret desperate for survival, as Machiavellian as he is ruthless. When he coaxes a simple-minded inmate into testing Nugent's reflexes he used the deadly charm that would carry *The Big Combo*'s Mr. Brown to the top of the syndicate hierarchy.

Ted Tetzlaff, the director, handles the ironies and ambiguities in the plot adroitly. A former cinematographer, his work in and around the noir cycle was sometimes routine, as in *A Dangerous Profession* and *Gambling House*, but occasionally exceptional, as in *Riffraff* and *The Window*. *Under The Gun* is somewhat hobbled by a pedestrian ending which not even performers like Conte and Totter can redeem. **BMV & AS**

THE UNDERCOVER MAN (1949)

Director: Joseph H. Lewis. **Screenplay**: Sydney Boehm with additional dialogue by Malvin Wald, based on a screen story by Jack Rubin from an article "Undercover Man: He Trapped Capone" by Frank J. Wilson. **Producer**: Robert Rossen. **Director of Photography**: Burnett Guffey. **Music**: George Duning. **Art Director**: Walter Holscher. **Editor**: Al Clark. **Cast**: Glenn Ford (Frank Warren), James Whitmore (George Pappas), Barry Kelley (Edward O'Rourke), David Wolfe (Stanley Weinburg), Frank Tweddell (Inspector Herzog), Howard St. John (Joseph S. Horan), John F. Hamilton (Sergeant Shannon), Leo Penn (Sidney Gordon), Joan Lazer (Rosa Rocco), Angela Clarke (Theresa Rocco), Anthony Caruso (Salvatore Rocco), Robert Osterloh (Manny Zanger), Kay Medford (Gladys LaVeme). **Completed**: April 20, 1948. **Released**: Columbia, April 20. 85 minutes.

A group of undercover agents working for the Internal Revenue Service attempt to discover information that would prove a top mobster guilty of tax evasion. Frank Warren, an extremely dedicated family man, and his partner, George Pappas, begin questioning people who had access to the bookkeeping records. Their first contact is shot down by unknown assassins. The tedious, painstaking job of locating another individual willing to jeopardize his life in order to see the mob leader behind bars takes Warren and Pappas into a strange twilight world of intense paranoia. After a second witness is savagely murdered in broad daylight, the entire scheme seems doomed to failure. The agents finally get the information from the murdered bookkeeper's wife. Indictments are handed down.

Another in a cycle of noir films made during the late 1940s that approach the subject of organized crime through the conventions of supposed documentary technique, *The Undercover Man* emphasizes the ability of the noir film to suspend disbelief. The nature of the unresolved murders in the film coupled with Joseph H. Lewis' eclectic direction gives the film a very

The Undercover Man: *Glenn Ford as Agent Frank Warren.*

episodic quality. Lewis draws heavily from a base of pure romanticism, embellished with stylistic touches of American expressionism and his own natural flare for the surreal. The convention of this type of film, much in the same manner as *T-Men, Naked City,* or even *House on 92nd Street,* plays on the ability to relate a great deal of the action with newsreel style film footage. The grotesqueness of the characters and the unorthodox nature of much of the action allows these films to become noir while maintaining their documentary flavor. **CM**

UNDERCURRENT (1946)

Director: Vincente Minnelli. **Screenplay**: Edward Chodorov, with contributions from Marguerite Roberts and George Oppenheimer from the novel *You Were There* by Thelma Strabel. **Producer**: Pandro S. Berman. **Director of Photography**: Karl Freund. **Music**: Herbert Stothart, Mario Castelnuovo-Tedesco. **Art Directors**: Cedric Gibbons, Randall Duell. **Editor**: Ferris Webster. **Cast**: Katharine Hepburn (Ann Hamilton), Robert Taylor (Alan Garroway), Robert Mitchum (Michael Garroway), Edmund Gwenn (Professor Dink Hamilton), Marjorie Main (Lucy), Clinton Sundberg (Mr. Warmsley), Dan Tobin (Professor Herbert Bangs). **Completed**: April 27, 1946. **Released**: MGM, November 28. 114 minutes.

Ann Hamilton leads a sheltered life with her father, a gentle professor, until she meets handsome and charming Alan Garroway, an airplane manufacturer. They fall in love and are married but Alan is emotionally disturbed and obsessed with hatred for his long-missing brother, Michael. Alan claims that Michael cheated him in business and then disappeared. Ann gradually discovers the truth from other sources, and a new portrait of Michael emerges, that of a gentle and sensitive man who may be missing because Alan has killed him. Curious, Ann visits Michael's ranch where she meets a man she assumes is the caretaker but who is actually Michael. Later, Michael confronts Alan because he is concerned that his brother will ruin Ann's life. Alan persuades Michael not to interfere by claiming that he loves Ann. However, realizing that Ann no longer loves him, Alan attempts to kill her but is killed himself by Michael's horse.

Film noir encompasses much of the most imaginative work of great directors, as illustrated by the works of Lang, Ray, Preminger, and Mann. Unfortunately, the lone contribution to the cycle by Minnelli is a confusing and convoluted work, not without interesting qualities but ultimately lacking in power. This is regrettable because the premise is characteristic of Minnelli's best work: a character discovers the reality of the world outside his/her sheltered niche to be a nightmare. In this case, the nightmare is personified by her husband Alan from whom she finds refuge by falling in love with a dream personified by Michael. Katharine Hepburn gives one of her most controlled performances in this role but that tone is not supported by Minnelli's indulgence of the obvious symbolism of Michael's horse or the motif of the flickering fireplaces in each key setting.

Although Minnelli is customarily more precise in his characteristic visual usages, certain sequences manifest an awareness of the noir style: the confrontation between Michael and Alan, for instance, is dramatically heightened by the swinging lamp in the stable where they talk. The most memorable moment occurs when Ann is alone on a train at night; and, as she is unable to sleep, her face reflects waking nightmares both real and imagined. Curiously, Minnelli, who has painted profound portraits of madness in such films as *Madame Bovary, Cobweb,* and *Lust for Life,* seems ill at ease with the character of Alan, perhaps because his illness is a melodramatic contrivance of the story rather than a subjective state the director understands and with which he feels some kinship. Yet the inferiority and persecuted hysteria suffered by Alan is very characteristic of film noir. **BL & EW**

UNDERTOW (1949)

Director: William Castle. **Screenplay**: Lee Loeb, Arthur T. Horman from his story. **Producer**: Ralph Dietrich. **Director of Photography**: Irving Glassberg. **Music**: Milton Schwarzwald. **Art Directors**: Bernard Herzbrun, Nathan Juran. **Editor**: Ralph Dawson. **Cast**: Scott Brady (Tony Reagan), Peggy Dow (Ann McKnight), Bruce Bennett (Det. Charles Reckling), Dorothy Hart (Sally Lee), John Russell (Danny Morgan), Dan Ferniel (Gene), Thomas Browne Henry (Capt. Kerrigan), Charles Sherlock (Det. Cooper), Gregg Martell (Frost), Robert Anderson (Stoner), Rock Hudson (Detective), Robert Easton (Fisher). **Released**: Universal, December 1. 71 minutes.

Veteran and former gambler Tony Reagan plans on a new start by buying and operating a mountain lodge. In Reno, he bumps into an old pal from mobbed-up Chicago, Danny Morgan, and they compare the diamond rings purchased for their respective fiancées. Although engaged, on the flight home Reagan flirts with Ann McNight whom he met in a casino. When he is framed for the murder of local crime boss Big Jim, who happens to be the uncle of his fiancée Sally, Reagan goes on the lam to try and clear himself. He enlists Ann's help and soon stumbles onto the fact that his Sally is also engaged to Morgan who is likely the one who framed him.

Undertow is one of a handful of noirs that William Castle directed before turning his attention to horror films. While none of them is so good as his first—*When Strangers Marry* with young Robert Mitchum and Kim Hunter—*Undertow* is a solid noir: pure story competently executed if devoid of any memorable moments or stylistic touches. In his lead role, Scott Brady reveals why he never escaped from his brother Lawrence Tierney's imposing shadow, as he never gives Reagan the edginess that was Tierney's trademark. He is particularly weak when paired against femme fatale Sally, portrayed by Dorothy Hart, whose handful of credits starting with *Naked City* are mostly noir. **BMcV**

THE UNDERWORLD STORY (1950)

Director: Cyril Endfield. **Screenplay**: Cy Endfield, Henry Blankfort based on the story by Craig Rice. **Producer**: Hal E. Chester. **Director of Photography**: Stanley Cortez. **Music**: David Rose. **Art Director**: Gordon Wiles. **Editor**: Richard Heermance. **Cast**: Dan Duryea (Mike Reese), Herbert Marshall (E.J. Stanton), Gale Storm (Cathy Harris), Howard Da Silva (Carl Durham), Michael O'Shea (the District Attorney), Mary Anderson (Molly Rankin), Gar Moore (Clark Stanton), Melville Cooper (Major Redford), Frieda Inescort (Mrs. Eldridge), Harry Shannon ("Parky," the printer) Roland Winters (Stanley Becker, the lawyer). **Released**: United Artists, July 26. 94 minutes.

Mike Reese is fired from his paper, owned by magnate E.J. Stanton, for printing a story enabling gangster Carl Durham to murder a key witness. Reese exploits this to ask Durham for money so that he can buy into a small-town newspaper. His cynicism antagonizes co-owner Cathy Harris but when Stanton's daughter-in-law is murdered and a young African-American, Molly Rankin, a friend of Cathy's, is accused, Reese and Cathy mount a campaign to raise funds to defend her. The murderer is Stanton's son Clark and father and son exploit Reese's moral ambiguity to turn the town against him and Molly. However, a witness turns up who can prove Molly has been telling the truth and Stanton's son, in desperation, gets Durham to lean on Reese. When this fails, Durham resorts to strong-arm tactics, in exchange for the Stanton newspapers' silence over his activities. Stanton himself, increasingly disgusted with himself for turning his back on his principles and unable to condone Clark's readiness to kill Reese, shoots his son down. Durham is arrested by the District Attorney, tipped off by Cathy about the plot to kill Reese.

The cynical journalist with a heart of gold, the idealistic young newspaper proprietor, the elderly magnate who rediscovers his principles just in time, the rotten son, the sadistic gangster. *The Underworld Story* seems to accumulate the clichés of the genre, with actor Howard Da Silva's laugh a nod in the direction of Widmark in *Kiss of Death*. In reality, the script is dense and subtle and the film expertly directed by Endfield. The opening sequence where the witness is gunned down, the character of Durham (Da Silva), and the

use of lighting and iconography to suggest corruption and betrayal are integral to film noir.

Apart from its considerable cinematic qualities, the film's interest lies elsewhere: as an extended metaphor for witch-hunting in the aftermath of the HUAC Hollywood Hearings of 1947 ("I'm blacklisted," says Reese after being fired and forced to leave town). Molly's very name—Rankin—is a reference to the bigoted Dixiecrat who surfed on HUAC, but the film casts its net far wider. The action takes place in New England and Stanton's son, who knows that nobody will "take the word of a nigger against ours" is a product of a very different social environment: that of the Republican Right. The retired Major refers disparagingly to Molly as the sort of person expecting a helping hand and resenting it when refused, a clear reference to opposition by Republicans and Dixiecrats to Roosevelt's welfare programs. The liberal Mrs. Eldridge considers the Major as someone who sees anyone as an interloper if their ancestors were not among the town's witch burners (a reference less to Salem than to the lynching of African-Americans in the South), but quickly abandons the Committee formed to defend Molly when Stanton, the Major and other upper-class citizens start smearing Reese. This can doubtless be interpreted as a reference to Bogart ditching the Committee for the First Amendment but more generally to the way liberals shed their principles in favor of the anti-Communist crusade under way by the late 1940s.

Other elements of the film are less obvious. One paper demands "a finger-print law for employees," surely a reference to Truman's loyalty oath, in 1950 the site of a major confrontation within the Screen Directors' Guild. Molly's unprincipled lawyer states: "If you want to live, you have to plead guilty," an uncanny anticipation of the "naming of names" that became the order of the day in 1951. *The Underworld Story* (a genre title having little to do with the movie's real concerns) was balefully prophetic: within a year Blankfort, Endfield and Da Silva were blacklisted. That the film finishes positively, with the District Attorney coming to the rescue, indicates that the Left had not abandoned all hope. Within months Endfield's last Hollywood movie, *The Sound of Fury*, an attack on the lynch mentality on the verge of engulfing the US in general and Hollywood in particular, suggested that the Left no longer entertained any illusions. **RH**

UNDERWORLD U.S.A. (1961)

Director/ Producer: Samuel Fuller (Globe Enterprises). **Screenplay**: Samuel Fuller from the *Saturday Evening Post* articles by Joseph F. Dinneen. **Director of Photography**: Hal Mohr. **Music**: Harry Sukman. **Art Director**: Robert Peterson. **Editor**: Jerome Thoms. **Cast**: Cliff Robertson (Tolly Devlin), Dolores Dorn (Cuddles), Beatrice Kay (Sandy), Paul Dubov (Gela), Robert Emhardt (Conners), Larry Gates (Driscoll), Richard Rust (Gus), Gerald Milton (Gunther), Allan Gruener (Smith), David Kent (Tolly at twelve), Tina Rome (Woman), Sally Mills (Connie), Robert P. Lieb (Officer), Neyle Morrow (Barney), Henry Norell (Prison Doctor). **Completed**: August 8, 1960. **Released**: Columbia, May 13. 99 minutes.

After witnessing the New Year's Eve murder of his hoodlum father, twelve-year-old Tolly Devlin swears vengeance. As an imprisoned adult, Tolly recognizes inmate Vic Farrar as one of his father's killers. Before dying Vic tells Tolly the names of the other three who are all crime syndicate leaders: Gela,

Underworld USA: *Tolly Devlin (Cliff Robertson) and Cuddles (Dolores Dorn)*.

Smith, and Gunther. After his release Tolly visits his father's girlfriend Sandy, whose bar has been taken over by Gela. When Tolly helps one of Gela's girls, Cuddles, he is hired by the mobster. Tolly persuades Cuddles to give information to Driscoll a government agent investigating the syndicate. Smith is arrested. Assigned by mob-boss Conners to raid Driscoll's files, Tolly arranges instead to provide phony files incriminating Gela and Gunther as government witnesses, so that Conners will have them killed. His father avenged, Tolly refuses to help Driscoll further. From Gus, one of Conners' hit men, Tolly learns that Cuddles is to be killed also. When he confronts Conners, Tolly is mortally wounded. Cuddles is determined to avenge his death by testifying against the mob.

Like Nicholas Ray, Robert Aldrich, or Don Siegel, postwar director Samuel Fuller made war films, Westerns, and many non-noir features. Perhaps more than his American contemporaries or any other filmmaker of the classic period, Fuller put a very particular spin on the noir style. For *Underworld U.S.A.* Fuller imbues his characters with the same attitude as figures in his war films from *Steel Helmet* to *The Big Red One*. The conflict between the F.B.I. and the crime syndicate is described in militaristic terms. Like many combatants Tolly Devlin finds himself with a personal agenda to push during a larger conflict. As an orphan who desires revenge he is almost like a refugee. At a certain level his fate is collateral damage. Like one inured to war's horrors and shut off to any consideration other than personal survival, Tolly is incapable of human response unless it relates to his vindictive goals. His relationship with Cuddles is less about love or sex than about his need for information about his enemies. Once his mission is accomplished, Tolly's intervention on Cuddles' behalf is as much or more about guilt over than about his tender feelings for her.

Fuller often exploits brutal violence for visual impact. Both Tolly's and Cuddles' faces are marred by vivid bruises and large bandages throughout much of the film; and their visages passively reflect the fundamental and pervasive influence that violence exerts on their lives. Under that influence Tolly is unrelentingly and mechanistically devoted to his personal battle-plan, and Fuller's staging and composition constantly underscore his position in opposition to both criminal and legal forces. In this self-centered position, Tolly resembles Skip McCoy in Fuller's *Pickup on South Street*. Unlike McCoy, Tolly Devlin is not saved by the influence of Cuddles and Sandy as McCoy was by the similar characters of Candy and Moe in the earlier film. Perhaps because Devlin's overriding motivation is revenge rather than simple avarice, perhaps because the efforts of Cuddles and Sandy in his behalf are not as selfless as those of Candy and Moe for McCoy, Devlin does not survive. Like an exhausted warrior, Tolly is literally and figuratively finished when his revenge is complete; and he dies, alone, in the same alley where his father perished to the ironic strains of "Auld Lang Syne." **MB & AS**

THE UNFAITHFUL (1947)

Director: Vincent Sherman. **Screenplay**: David Goodis, James Gunn based on the novel by W. Somerset Maugham (uncredited). **Producer**: Jerry Wald. **Director of Photography**: Ernest Haller. **Music**: Max Steiner. **Art Director**: Leo K. Kuter. **Editor**: Alan Crosland, Jr. **Cast**: Ann Sheridan (Chris Hunter), Lew Ayres (Larry Hannaford), Zachary Scott (Bob Hunter), Eve Arden (Paula), Jerome Cowan (Prosecuting Attorney), Steven Geray (Martin Barrow), John Hoyt (Det. Lt. Reynolds), Peggy Knudsen (Claire), Marta Mitrovich (Mrs. Tanner), Douglas Kennedy (Roger), Claire Meade (Martha), Frances Morris (Agnes), Jane Harker (Joan). **Locations**: Angel's Flight Railway, Bunker Hill, Downtown, Los Angeles, California, USA. **Released**: Warner Bros., June 5. 109 minutes.

The night before Bob returns from a business trip, Chris is attacked at home by an intruder, Tanner, and she stabs him to death. The next day she tells Hannaford (a friend who is a divorce lawyer), the police and Bob that she had never seen the man before. Hannaford learns she's lying when Barrow, a small-time art dealer, tries to sell for $10,000 a sculpture of Chris' head, signed by Tanner. Hannaford turns Barrow down and tells Chris. She wants to pay the blackmailer because she doesn't want Bob to find out she had an affair with Tanner during the war. Chris and Hannaford expect Barrow to call her. Instead, Barrow takes the sculpture to Mrs. Tanner and

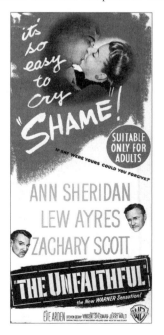

they show it to Bob. Angry at Chris for betraying him, Bob tells her he wants a divorce. Mrs. Tanner wants Chris imprisoned, so she takes the sculpture to the police. Chris is charged with Tanner's murder. At the trial Hannaford argues to the jury that, although Chris is guilty of infidelity, she killed Tanner in self-defense. Chris is acquitted. Just before she moves out, Hannaford convinces Bob to hang on to his marriage with her.

The woman-in-distress in *The Unfaithful* is unique in film noir. She is not threatened with losing her sanity (like *Gaslight*, *Possessed* and *Whirlpool*) or her life (like *Notorious, Sorry, Wrong Number* and *Sleep, My Love*). But she may lose her husband. During the 1940s, the U.S. divorce rate increased modestly from 2.0 per 1000 to 2.6, much lower than the growth rates after 1970. However, *The Unfaithful* suggests that stable marriage in postwar America is in jeopardy. When the movie begins, a voice-over intones, "The problem with which it deals belongs not to any one city, town or country but is of our times." Women casually (and comically) parade through Hannaford's law office to file for divorce, not necessarily their first one. Paula, a divorcee and Bob's cousin, says, "If there's one person in this town you can trust, it's Chris." After Chris' affair is exposed, the implication is that there are no exceptions. However, the association of the "unfaithful" with Everywoman is challenged later on. Multiple scenes deal with the social and sexual pressures experienced by women who were married but alone for the duration. Chris tries to get Bob to understand what her long loneliness was like. At the trial, Hannaford says without the war there would have been no affair. Most interestingly, Paula tells Bob he's not blameless because he rushed Chris into marriage after knowing her just two weeks before he shipped out. "You didn't want anyone making time with her while you were away, so you hung up a 'No Trespassing sign,' like you'd stake a gold claim." The film ends with Chris' infidelity contextualized and forgiven, but this "problem . . . of our times" continues. **DMH**

UNION STATION (1950)

Director: Rudolph Maté. **Screenplay**: Sydney Boehm from an unpublished story by Thomas Walsh. **Producer**: Jules Schermer. **Director of Photography**: Daniel L Fapp. **Music**: Irvin Talbot. **Art Directors**: Hans Dreier, Earl Hedrick. **Editor**: Ellsworth Hoagland. **Cast**: William Holden (Lt. William Calhoun), Nancy Olson (Joyce Willecombe), Barry Fitzgerald (Inspector Donnelly), Lyle Bettger (Joe Beacom), Jan Sterling (Marge Wrighter), Herbert Heyes (Henry Murcall), Don Dunning (Gus Hadder), Fred Graff (Vince Marley), James Seay (Detective Shattuck). **Completed**: March 7, 1950. **Released**: Paramount, October 4. 80 minutes.

A tense situation develops at Chicago's Union Station when a grotesque loser, Joe Beacom, kidnaps a blind girl. The head of depot security, Lt. Calhoun, must contend with the crisis without causing a panic in the busy train terminal. The police, headed by Inspector Donnelly, are called in when the kidnapper escapes with the child and a concentrated search turns up two of Beacom's accomplices. The police arrive at Beacom's hideout only to find the kidnapper and his victim gone. Beacom's mistress tells the police of his plans to murder the girl after he receives the ransom money, and she is shot by Beacom for her treachery. A frantic chase takes place, ending up in an underground tunnel laced with high-tension wires. In a desperate shootout in the electrified tunnel Calhoun kills Beacom.

The dehumanization of Joe Beacom, an average man turned into a vile kidnapper, is a characteristic symptom of the sense of helplessness inherent in noir films. There is a cynical outlook that moves beyond the simple apprehension of the criminals. Even the actions of the police, in forcing the suspected kidnapper to talk under the threat of death, suggest an acceptance of their unnecessarily brutal tactics as normal police procedure. The cheapness of life and the level of destructive irony needed to restore order betray a definite noir outlook, despite the routine plot development in *Union Station*. The characters explored in this film exist in a twilight world in which freedom of choice is unknown and temptations fostered by an ill-defined fate lead men through a moral maze as figuratively constricting as the tunnels through which Beacom is pursued and in which he perishes. **CM**

THE UNKNOWN MAN (1951)

Director: Richard Thorpe. **Screenplay**: Ronald Millar and George Froeschel. **Producer**: Robert Thomsen. **Director of Photography**: William Mellor. **Music**: Conrad Salinger. **Art Directors**: Cedric Gibbons, Randall Duell. **Editor**: Ben Lewis. **Cast**: Walter Pidgeon (Dwight Bradley Mason), Ann Harding (Stella Mason), Barry Sullivan (D.A. Joe Buckner and Narrator), Keefe Brasselle (Rudi Wolchek), Lewis Stone (Judge Hulbrook), Eduard Franz (Andrew Jason Layford), Richard Anderson (Bob Mason), Dawn Addams (Ellie Fansworth), Phil Ober (Wayne Kellwin), Mari Blanchard (Sally Tever), Konstantin Shayne (Peter Hulderman). **Completed**: February 2, 1951. **Released**: MGM, November 16. 86 minutes.

Brad Mason, a highly respected civil attorney with a keen moral sense, has a great respect for the law and a strong belief of the role justice plays therein. His father was a judge and his son Bob is preparing to join his firm once he passes the bar. One day a classmate from his days in law school, Wayne Kellwin, calls on Brad and asks him to take over the pro bono defense of one of his clients, Rudi Wolchek, who, Kellwin asserts, has been wrongfully accused of murder. Though a bit awkward at first, Brad demonstrates that D.A. Buckner's key witness, locksmith Peter Hulderman, father of the victim, could not have identified Wolchek as the killer without his glasses as Hulderman insists. Wolcheck is acquitted but when Brad discovers that Wolcheck is much more affluent than he had been led to believe, his suspicions are aroused. He interviews Hulderman in his store and Hulderman confesses that his son was killed because

Hulderman refused to ante up to some protection racketeers but was afraid to say anything at the trial for fear of his own life. He recognized Rudi as the killer because he had changed the locks on Wolchek's apartment shortly before the murder. Hulderman gives Brad a duplicate key to the apartment and when Hulderman is killed in a hit and run accident Brad decides to pay an impromptu visit to Wolchek. He enters the empty apartment and, with a bit of searching, discovers the murder weapon, a knife hidden in the handle of Rudi's walking cane. Disconsolate at the thought of helping a guilty man escape the law, Brad suddenly decides to pay a visit to his friend, Andrew Layford, head of a local crime commission even though it is rather late at night. When Layford gets another noctural caller, Brad realizes the caller is Rudi and then begins to suspect that it is Layford himself who is the city's crime boss. When Brad places his suspicions on the table, Layford makes veiled threats, intimating that if he were such a figure he would be able to crush anyone who tried to bring him to justice. With that, Brad loses control and stabs Layford with Rudi's knife, which he had pocketed. Wolchek is arrested for Layford's murder but Brad again defends him, proving in court that there was an "unknown man" at Layford's house at the same time as Rudi, almost admitting his own guilt during the trial. Rudi, however, is convicted and though Brad confesses to Buckner, Buckner refuses to do anything, feeling that justice has already been served. Brad persuades Buckner to allow him to visit Rudi in his cell. He tells Rudi all of the circumstances surrounding Layford's murder and then leaves the knife, which he has stolen from Buckner's office, next to Rudi on his bunk. Turning his back on Rudi, Brad begins to read from the prison bible and Rudi, of course, takes the opportunity to kill Brad. Substituting for Brad as the keynote speaker at his son's graduating class, Buckner extols Brad for his sense of justice.

The French might call *The Unknown Man* a *film gris* rather than a film noir because there is nothing really very noir about its visual style and its production values are typical of MGM. As one might expect the acting generally is quite good which helps carry us through a plot that strains credulity, in particular Brad's sudden conversion from stalwart citizen to thief and then murderer. What makes it noir is the way in which the underworld is beginning to displace the overworld in terms of respectability, so that a figure like Andrew Layford can masquerade as a upright citizen while simultaneously controlling a large city's rackets and maintaining enough power to sway politicians and other civic officials. Noir as well is the way in which a well-to-do lawyer like Brad Mason can himself be trapped in a world of corruption so that, it appears, his only recourse is to kill the man in control. Once having done so, it is quite fitting that Brad give Rudi the opportunity to kill him because only in this way can he expiate for his sins. And while Joe Buckner might laud Brad in front of the graduating class, if we take that speech as part of the story Buckner has been telling us as well as the new lawyers (actor Sullivan, in character, has been narrating virtually the whole film), then Brad's victory is a Pyrrhic one since his own reputation, and that of his family, has been forever compromised. **BP**

THE UNSUSPECTED (1947)

Director: Michael Curtiz. **Screenplay**: Ranald MacDougall, from the adaptation by Bess Meredyth of the novel by Charlotte Armstrong.

Producer: Charles Hoffman. **Director of Photography**: Woody Bredell. **Music**: Franz Waxman. **Art Director**: Anton Grot. **Editor**: Frederick Richards. **Cast**: Joan Caulfield (Matilda Frazier), Claude Rains (Alexander Grandison), Audrey Totter (Althea Keane), Constance Bennett (Jane Moynihan), Hurd Hatfield (Oliver Keane), Michael North (Steven Francis Howard), Fred Clark (Richard Donovan), Harry Lewis (Max), Jack Lambert (Mr. Press). **Completed**: March 15, 1947. **Released**: Warner Bros., October 3. 103 minutes.

A young woman is murdered by her employer, Alexander Grandison, a noted radio personality, who makes the slaying appear as a suicide. His appetite for death and deception is fed by his radio mystery programs, which detail murder and brutality with shocking accuracy. His well-constructed web of intellectual evil is disturbed when the mysterious Steven Howard returns from the war and attempts to avenge his dead fiancée, Grandison's murdered secretary. Howard uses a number of unsavory methods, including impersonation, to force Grandison to confess to the murder. Finding that the only way to maintain control of the family fortune and keep young Howard from exposing him as a murderer is to strike first, Grandison contacts a fugitive that he is blackmailing and forces him to dispose of the troublesome Howard. Meanwhile, Grandison fails in an attempt to poison Matilda and make it look like a suicide. Howard is saved from death; and Grandison is made to pay for his crimes.

The Unsuspected is a self-conscious film noir which repeatedly emphasizes style over content. Charlotte Armstrong's story serves merely as a framework for Michael Curtiz to construct a visual portrait of a decadent murderer trapped in a world of his own machinations. The use of expressionist lighting and threatening shadows epitomize the noir pattern. The imaginative direction, highlighted by Woody Bredell's chiaroscuro cinematography, links the upper class world of Grandison with that of the unsavory underworld. There is one particular sequence in *The Unsuspected* that crystallizes the quality of paranoia and claustrophobia so often found in noir films. Jack Lambert as the blackmailed killer lies in bed smoking. The radio is on and Alexander Grandison is detailing the story of his particular crime. The only source of illumination in this dingy hotel room comes from a partially obscured flashing neon sign. The letters that are visible through the window seem to echo the thoughts of the uncomfortable murderer as they keep blinking "KILL . . . KILL . . . KILL." **CM**

THE VERDICT (1946)

Director: Don Siegel. **Screenplay**: Peter Milne based on the novel *The Big Bow Mystery* by Israel Zangwill. **Producer**: William Jacobs. **Executive Producer**: Jack L. Warner. **Directors of Photography**: Ernest Haller, Robert Burks [uncredited]. **Music**: Frederick Hollander. **Art Director**: Ted Smith. **Editor**: Thomas Reilly. **Cast**: Sydney Greenstreet (Supt. George Edward Grodman), Peter Lorre (Victor Emmric), Joan Lorring (Lottie Rawson), George Coulouris (Supt. John R. Buckley), Rosalind Ivan (Mrs. Vicky Benson), Paul Cavanagh (Clive Russell), Arthur Shields (Rev. Holbrook), Morton Lowry (Arthur Kendall), Holmes Herbert (Sir William Dawson), Art Foster (Warren), Clyde Cook (Barney Cole). **Released**: Warner Bros., November 23. 86 minutes.

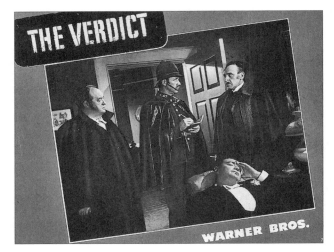

Immediately after a man is hanged for killing Kendall's aunt, Grodman, who was responsible for the man's conviction, learns the man was innocent. Grodman is forced to resign from Scotland Yard and is replaced by Buckley. Grodman and Buckley detest one another. But Kendall, a mine-owner, and Russell, a champion of Kendall's mine workers, hate each other even more. One night, Kendall and Russell exchange death threats in front of their friends, Emmric and Grodman, as well as Kendall's mistress, Rawson; and Grodman and Emmric witness Rawson threaten to have Kendall killed. The next morning, Kendall's landlady gets no response when she knocks on his door. She gets Grodman to break it down. Kendall's murdered. Based on incriminating but circumstantial evidence, Buckley arrests Russell, who is tried and sentenced to death. After searching for a witness who can clear Russell, Grodman learns she's died. Left with no alternative to saving Russell's life, Grodman tells Buckley that Kendall murdered his aunt then he killed Kendall. Since Buckley failed to solve the mystery, Grodman revels in Buckley's "humiliation and defeat."

Among the so-called "gaslight melodramas" that are considered U.S. film noirs, *The Verdict* is special in several ways. First, although the movie has gaslight, it isn't *per se* a melodrama. If it were, women and romance would be central, both to the crimes and the conclusion of the story. However, neither Lottie Rawson nor Mrs. Benson is critical to the plot; and two other women, Arthur Kendall's aunt and Clive Russell's aristocratic married lover, are mentioned but never shown. The three characters who dominate the film are men (Grodman, Emmric and Buckley). Furthermore, nothing in the story hinges on romance. For example, neither murder is committed because of love or jealousy. Second, it is one of the best gaslight melodramas in terms of the noir style. At one extreme is *The Suspect*, in which the style is present for a few minutes total. At the

other extreme is *The Verdict*, which is nearly suffused in it. A third way *The Verdict* is atypical is that it has a lot of light comedy. Comic scenes with Mrs. Benson, as well as Barney Cole, the burglar, and Robertson, the undertaker, interrupt an otherwise strong noir story and visual style. Interestingly, Israel Zangwill, the author the book on which *The Verdict* is based, later regretted how he subverted the mood of this locked room mystery. He said, "[T]he humor is too abundant. Mysteries should be sedate and sober. There should be a pervasive atmosphere of horror and awe such as Poe manages to create. Humor is out of tone; it would be more artistic to preserve a somber note throughout." Alfred Hitchcock may often play up humor, but Don Siegel would have benefited by toning it down.

The Verdict was the first feature film Siegel directed. Considering the accusations leveled at him later in his career for being a misogynist, some might see *The Verdict* as early evidence. Other gaslight melodramas feature at least one important female character, for example, "strong" (but evil) like a femme fatale or "weak" (and too virtuous) like a woman-in-distress. In *The Verdict*, as noted above, women hardly count. Since each of these three ways of presenting women is open to criticism, the treatment of women in *The Verdict* doesn't necessarily prefigure Siegel's later work. But the character of Superintendent George Edward Grodman does. Grodman is unswervingly committed to bringing criminals to justice—to rendering the verdict—by any means necessary. He's contemptuous of his superiors at the department. If he has to, he conducts his investigations outside official channels. He's both an agent of law enforcement and an avenger. Grodman boasts, "It'll be quite a job to fill [my britches]!" Indeed, it took a quarter of a century before Siegel had someone who could, Inspector Harry Francis Callahan—Dirty Harry. **DMH**

VERTIGO (1958)

Director: Alfred Hitchcock. **Screenplay**: Alec Coppel, Samuel A. Taylor, Maxwell Anderson [uncredited0 based on the novel *D'Entre Lews Morts* by Pierre Boileau and Thomas Narcejac. **Producer**: Alfred Hitchcock. **Director of Photography**: Robert Burks. **Art Director**: Hal Pereira, Henry Bumstead. **Music**: Bernard Herrmann. **Editor**: George Tomasini. **Cast**: James Stewart (Scottie Ferguson), Kim Novak (Madeleine/Judy), Barbara Bel Geddes (Midge Wood), Tom Helmore (Elster), Henry Jones (Coroner), Raymond Bailey (Doctor), Ellen Corby (Hotel Manager). **Released**: Paramount, May 9. 128 minutes.

A San Francisco detective, Scottie Ferguson, has left the force after a near death experience caused by his formerly undiagnosed acrophobia (fear of heights). An old friend Elster lures Scottie out of retirement to shadow his wife Madeleine whom he believes is possibly delusional as well as suicidal. Scottie eventually agrees but during the investigation falls deeply in love with Madeleine. Scottie tries to save his troubled love by convincing her that this obsession with the past and a woman—Carlotta—who committed suicide is but an illusion. But ultimately he fails and she throws herself from the tower of a Spanish mission. Scottie slips into deep depression after the suicide. After a stint in a mental institution he returns to "normal" life but the image of Madeleine continues to haunt him. One day he sees a woman, Judy, who resembles Madeleine walking in front of some storefronts. Scottie courts Judy, gradually turning her into a duplicate of Madeleine in dress, hair, and make-up. Seeing her wearing a necklace that was linked with Madeleine, he suspects her of tricking him. He takes her to the scene of Madeleine's "suicide" and learns from her that she played Elster's wife for money and that Elster actually murdered his wife that day. Scottie takes her up to the tower and frightened by a nun in the darkness she falls to her death.

Alfred Hitchcock's *Vertigo* is a clever reworking of the Pygmalion myth in a noir mystery context. Here a clinically depressed detective Scottie decides to turn a woman he meets on the street—Judy—into a duplicate of the image he has of an "ideal" love—Madeleine. He bribes and cajoles her into changing her hair, her clothes, her make-up so that she finally matches the dead Madeleine (Judy: "What good will it do?" Scottie: "I don't know.") But he does know. For it is only when Judy emerges from the bathroom, bathed in an ethereal green light from the neon outside her window and attired and made up like Madeleine, that Scottie can finally love her. They kiss passionately as the camera circles them and the backgrounds morph into the mission stables where he last kissed Madeleine as Hitchcock strikes the noir motif of amour fou.

In a remarkably daring move typical of Hitchcock, the director now turns the tables on the viewer and reveals that it is not Scottie who is pulling the strings in this noir melodrama. Rather it is Scottie who is the puppet (a point Tanya Modleski supports in her book *The Women Who Knew Too Much*). Judy has revealed to the audience through an interior monologue right after she first meets Scottie on the

Vertigo: *Judy (Kim Novak) and Scottie Ferguson (James Stewart).*

street that she *is* in fact Madeleine, that Elster had hired her to pretend to be his wife so that when he threw his wife from the tower at the mission the blame would fall on Scottie (who is unable to climb the stairs of the tower due to his vertigo) and so he would act as a witness to the suicidal proclivities of the dead Madeleine. The wrinkle is that Judy has fallen in love with Scottie and so sees this chance meeting as a way of starting again. She is the puppet master, not him.

Ultimately Scottie figures out the scam and drags her back to the scene of the crime: the tower at the mission. Although Judy admits the ruse, she pleads with him to forgive her and reaffirms her love for him. But Scottie is too obsessive-compulsive to live with that. He must recreate the whole event again and in some way punish her. He drags her up the stairs, at times mixing her up with the ideal by calling her "Madeleine." At the top of the tower, a nun emerges from the darkness, like an avenging angel, and Judy falls to her death. Scottie watches on helpless, once again. Slowly, the camera cranes back as Scottie stands at the edge of the tower, freed finally of his acrophobia but left desolate and alone. He has lost his love twice and found no real redemption, the goal of so many noir protagonists. **JU**

VICKI (1953)

Director: Harry Horner. **Screenplay**: Dwight Taylor with additional dialogue by Harold Greene and Leo Townsend from the novel *I Wake Up Screaming* by Steve Fisher. **Producer**: Leonard Goldstein. **Director of Photography**: Milton Krasner. **Music**: Leigh Harline. **Art Directors**: Lyle Wheeler, Richard Irvine. **Editor**: Dorothy Spencer. **Cast**: Jeanne Crain (Jill), Jean Peters (Vicki Lynn), Elliott Reid (Steve Christopher), Richard Boone (Lt. Ed Cornell), Casey Adams (Larry Evans), Alex D'Arcy (Robin Ray), Carl Betz (McDonald), Aaron Spelling (Harry Williams). **Completed**: April 4, 1953. **Released**: 20th Century-Fox, September 7. 85 minutes.

Detective Lt. Ed Cornell cuts short his vacation to take over the investigation of popular New York model Vicki Lynn's

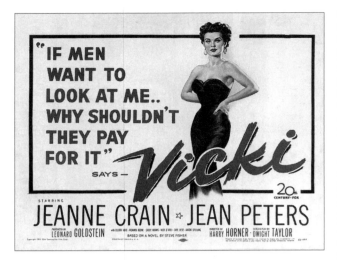

"IF MEN
WANT TO
LOOK AT ME..
WHY SHOULDN'T
THEY PAY
FOR IT"

SAYS —

Vicki

20. CENTURY-FOX

STARRING

JEANNE CRAIN ✧ JEAN PETERS

PRODUCED BY LEONARD GOLDSTEIN

DIRECTED BY HARRY HORNER · DWIGHT TAYLOR

BASED ON A NOVEL BY STEVE FISHER

murder. Steve Christopher, Vicki's publicist, is the first suspect interrogated at length. A flashback reveals his discovery of Vicki waitressing in a café. Cornell's partner questions Vicki's sister Jill who suggests the police search for a man that watched Vicki at the café. She is astonished when Cornell enters, since he is that very man. Cornell accuses Jill being infatuated with Christopher, and she admits that she found Christopher alone with her sister's body. Without evidence, Christopher is released, but Cornell follows him to a rendezvous with Jill and overhears her admit to concealing an incriminatory note. When Cornell tries to arrest Christopher, Jill knocks out the detective. Christopher goes to the detective's partner and they get a confession from hotel night clerk Harry Williams, who also says that Cornell knew of his guilt. When the group goes to confront Cornell, they find a shrine to Vicki in his apartment. Cornell admits his own love for Vicki and his envy of Christopher for taking her away.

Vicki uses a complex flashback structure to unmask the self-serving motivations of virtually all its characters. *Vicki* is not just the second adaptation of Steve Fisher's *I Wake Up Screaming* at Fox but also follows the studio's more successful adaptation of the similarly themed *Laura.* In this context, the viewer expectations for *Vicki* are also more complex than with either precedent movie. While the audience may not have expected Vicki Lynn's sudden reanimation in the manner of Laura Hunt, the figure of Cornell could be colored by aspects of Laird Cregar's performance in the original version and also Dana Andrew's as Mark McPherson in *Laura.* Certainly Richard Boone's portrayal of Cornell and his dogged persecution of his prime suspect recalls McPherson's insistent probing of Laura's fiancé Shelby Carpenter in *Laura.* However, much of McPherson's distaste for Carpenter, Lydecker, and the others in Laura's circle was from a class-conscious. McPherson's sudden immersion into a world of snobbish sophistication suggests that part of his fascination with Laura through her portrait was also a yearning for this life style.

Cornell's obsession in *Vicki* as the ending reveals is with the title character as she was, with the waitress, not with a minor celebrity on the rise. As the pre-credit night sequence of Vicki's body being carried from her hotel suggests and the flashbacks confirm, this dead woman had a far different life than Laura. The small cramped apartments in which this story unfolds are also far different milieus than the richly furnished apartments of Laura and Lydecker. Vicki has a fundamentally proletarian background and in that background Cornell found her and fantasized her into a love object. The photos and objects which Cornell uses to create Vicki's shrine and in front of which he places votive candles celebrate Vicki as he knew her, as a proletarian goddess.

This revelation of Cornell's incipient madness is only one aspect of *Vicki's* noir structure. Unlike Laura Hunt, the flashbacks reveal Vicki Lynn as an exploitive and ruthlessly ambitious person with little regard for those who have helped her. Unlike McPherson's investigation, in this context Cornell's obsessesive inquiry lacks any underlying audience empathy. Not that Christopher or Jill are sympathetic figures either. Although the publicist is technically not guilty of Vicki's murder, his motives for promoting her are suspect and his emotional exploitation of Vicki and her sister are venal. There is a three-way character parallel between Cornell, Christopher, and Williams that relies on the sort of transference of guilt with which film noir audiences were familiar. Like Kristo's pursuit of Fabian rather than the Strangler after his father's death in *Night and the City*, in his disturbed psyche Cornell readily exonerates the man who physically killed the woman he loved in order to bring down the man who took her from him and is emotionally arguably responsible for her death. Certainly Cornell's belief that Christopher has casually corrupted Vicki and indirectly caused her death by taking her from the proletarian environment in which she was safe from harm is not entirely illogical. As the moral failings of all its protagonists are gradually revealed, *Vicki's* story of murder and fixation acquires a darker aspect as noir and as social commentary. Although Cornell is crushed and Christopher and Jill are free to continue their romantic relationship, the opening sequence with Vicki's corpse being removed is ironically mirrored as the camera's focus moves from the couple to a billboard outside where Vicki's likeness is being replaced by that of another. **AS**

A VOICE IN THE WIND (1944)

Director: Arthur Ripley. **Screenplay**: Friedrich Torberg based on a story by Ripley. **Producer**: Rudolph Monter, Arthur Ripley. **Director of Photography**: Richard Fryer. **Music**: Michel Michelet. **Music**: Bedrich Smetana. **Production Designer**: Rudi Feld. **Editor**: Holbrook N. Todd. **Cast**: Francis Lederer (Jan Volny), Sigrid Gurie (Marya), J. Edward Bromberg (Dr. Hoffman), J. Carrol Naish (Luigi), Alexander Granach (Angelo), David Cota (Marco), Olga Fabian (Anna), Howard Johnson (Capt. von Neubach), Hans Schumm (Piesecke). **Released**: United Artists, March 3. 85 minutes.

Jan and Marya Volny are star-crossed lovers living in Nazi-occupied Prague in 1939. Together with their friends, Dr. and Anna Hoffman, they intend to flee to America via Paris. Jan is a pianist and plans one last concert before they leave. The Nazis have given him permission to perform, but have forbidden him to play Smetana's *The*

Moldau because of its political ramifications. The night of the concert Volny succumbs to the audience's behest and plays the piece. He is arrested and the Nazi interrogator strikes him on the head, causing him to lose his memory and perhaps his sanity. Overpowering his captors, Volny manages to stow aboard a ship owned by two nefarious brothers, Angelo and Luigi, and he ends up on the French island of Guadalupe. There he is known only as "El Hombre," a mad sailor who sometimes works for the two brothers and is usually found in a waterfront bar, playing classical music on the piano for drinks. The brothers are using their ship to con money from helpless refugees whom they leave stranded, or worse, instead of getting them to America. When their ship is destroyed by fire, Luigi, the younger and decidedly more evil of the two, believes that "El Hombre" was behind the fire. Luigi plans to kill Volny but Angelo, who has an almost fraternal love for "El Hombre" precisely because he is crazy, prevents him. Unknown to Volny, the Hoffmans and Marya have also ended up on Guadalupe where Marya lies bedridden with pneumonia in a hotel room near the bar. When she hears his piano playing, she is attracted by the music and attempts to make her way unaided to the bar, but collapses on the darkened street. Volny finds her and while her face fails to bring back his memory, the sight of the cross she wears begins to have an effect. He returns to his room to dig a rosary out of a box of trinkets but just as he begins to regain his memory, Luigi enters and shoots him. Angelo enters on the heels of this and while he is grieving over Volny, Luigi stabs him. But Angelo survives to kill his evil brother. Meanwhile, Volny, memory and sanity now fully intact, has mustered enough strength to get to Marya's hotel room where he collapses over the body of his dead wife.

Voice In The Wind is a strange little film, filled with romantic angst and closer in spirit to nineteenth century opera than to film noir. Yet by any reckoning it is one of the darkest films of the cycle, lacking even one daylight scene (the fact that the film was purportedly shot in 12 days on a shoestring budget may also have something to do with this). It is certainly a rarity: the only film produced at PRC to have been nominated for not one but two academy awards (sound and music). Others have criticized it for being "arty" rather than artful, having the texture but not the substance of a for-

eign film. Yet these weaknesses do not demean its place in any study of classic American film noir, a cycle of films whose very lifeblood depended on the production of these low-budget "thrillers" despite their deficiencies. And the fact that it was directed by Arthur Ripley, a "cult" director of some renown, does nothing to lessen its appeal.

If we dwell on these weaknesses a bit more, we can tease from them two important antecedents of American film noir: German expressionism and French poetic realism. For the sets here are nothing if not distorted (and artificial) and the presence of Francis Lederer as Volny, whose decline harkens back to Lederer's portrayal of the hapless Alwa Schoen in *Pandora's Box*, provides the requisite link. One need but compare the shot of Volny descending the staircase leading to Marya's hotel room to a similar shot of Alwa descending the stairwell leading to Lulu's room in Pabst's film. And the story of doomed lovers set in a fog-bound waterfront where every action is punctuated by the forlorn sound of the foghorn can't help but evoke memories of films like *Quai des Brumes* (whose co-star, Michele Morgan, also co-starred in Ripley's *The Chase*). Finally, this film is "dated" not so much by its reliance on these foreign antecedents as by the presence of a wartime patriotism that sought to elevate the Americas as a sanctuary for all who wish to escape Nazism. **BP**

WALK SOFTLY, STRANGER (1950)

Director: Robert Stevenson. **Screenplay**: Frank Fenton based on a story by Manuel Seff, Paul Yawitz. **Producer**: Robert Sparks. **Executive Producer**: Dore Schary. **Director of Photography**: Harry J. Wild. **Music**: Frederick Hollander. **Art Directors**: Albert S. D'Agostino, Alfred Herman. **Editor**: Frederick Knudtson. **Cast**: Joseph Cotten (Chris Hale aka Steve), Alida Valli (Elaine Corelli), Spring Byington (Mrs. Brentman), Paul Stewart (Whitey Lake), Jack Paar (Ray Healy), Jeff Donnell (Gwen), John McIntire (Morgan), Howard Petrie (Bowen), Frank Puglia (A.J. Corelli), Esther Dale (Miss Thompson), Marlo Dwyer (Mabel), Robert Ellis (Skating Boy). **Released**: RKO, October 14. 81 minutes.

Good things happen to Chris after he comes to Ashton, Ohio. The kindly Mrs. Brentman invites him to board in her house, where he says he grew up, and she gets him a job in a shoe factory. He also meets Elaine, the daughter of the factory owner, and falls in love. Whether or not Ashton is his hometown (evidence goes both ways), he is building a new life to have after he commits a robbery. He flies to a big city and meets an accomplice, Whitey. They steal $100,000 in cash from Bowen, the head of a gambling house. When they split the money, Chris tells Whitey to get a new identity so that Bowen can't find him. Because Elaine is confined to a wheelchair, she's vulnerable to thinking that love with Chris won't work. She leaves town but can't stay away. Their romance is put on hold when Whitey shows up, broke and scared. Chris tries to hide Whitey. He plans to give his share of the money back to Bowen. Instead, Bowen finds Whitey and the money, and takes Chris for a ride. Chris lives and when he gets out of prison, Elaine promises to "belong" to him.

In *A Place in the Sun* the dichotomy between romantic melodrama and noir is represented by two characters, Angela and Alice, as well as by two visual styles, classic and noir. In *Walk Softly, Stranger*, it's based on geography. The romantic world is fictitious Ashton, where, as a brochure says, people can "enjoy healthful, happy living." The noir world is located far away, in places reached by airplanes, where Chris has been "a gambler, a card shark, a dice hustler [and] a thief," and his name is "Steve." Epitomized by Mrs. Brentman, friendliness and generosity prevail in Ashton, and social distinctions do not matter. The stakes in card games played by different classes are about the same, just friendly wagers, without heavy betting as in the noir world. When Corelli factory workers play poker at home, the pots are no more than a few dollars. At the Ashton Country Club, Elaine's father is delighted to be up sixty-five cents in gin rummy. At the country club and a working class nightclub, couples dance to identical music. Ashton is also associated with romanticized geography through the film's title. The lines "Walk softly, stranger. You stand on holy ground," come from a tribute written during WW II to the "beauty [and] wonder that is America."

A man Chris has beaten at cards criticizes him: "You can't let yourself lose. You can't help it, can you?" From their first meeting Elaine is attracted to Chris. When he takes her to a nightclub, they have fun until she bets him that he can't get a woman he stood up for a date to dance with him. Winning the bet isn't enough; he dances closely with the woman right in front of Elaine. It is not being paralyzed from a skiing accident that makes Elaine embittered. Chris is at fault. She thinks he could not really love her because he would be "tied down to a cripple." Her dark past is inside—feeling "dead" because she can't "walk and dance and live" as before. However, despite his mistakes from character flaws, Chris does not give up trying to win her love. He is like the male intruder-redeemer in later 1950s melodramas, such as *Young at Heart* and *Picnic*. Before Chris takes a ride with Bowen, Elaine says her love for him is "real and alive and whole." He has helped her see that even if her body isn't whole, she can be alive, not dead. His dark past is outside—Bowen. Elaine also says, "Be lucky, Chris." Indeed! As Chris holds a blanket over the driver's head so he can't steer Bowen's car, Bowen shoots Chris three times at point-blank range. The car runs off the road and bursts through a billboard, which shows an airplane and reads, "Next Time Go By Air." In places where planes fly, the noir world, the bullets and the crash would most likely kill Chris. But since he belongs to the charmed community of Ashton, governed by romantic melodrama, the gangsters die, and he survives to have Elaine. **DMH**

WHEN STRANGERS MARRY (1944)

Director: William Castle. **Screenplay**: Philip Yordan and Dennis J. Cooper from a story by George V. Moscov and W.K. Howard. **Producers**: Franklin King, Herman King, Maurice King. **Director of Photography**: Ira Morgan. **Music**: Dimitri Tiomkin. **Art Director**: Paul Sylos. **Editor**: Martin G. Cohn. **Cast**: Dean Jagger (Paul Baxter), Kim Hunter (Millie Baxter), Robert Mitchum (Fred Graham), Neil Hamilton (Lt. Blake), Lou Lubin (Houser), Milt Kibbee (Charlie). **Completed**: August 7, 1944. **Released**: Monogram, August 21. 67 minutes

Sam Prescott, attending a Lions Club convention at the Philadelphia Hotel, is drunk in the hotel bar and foolishly reveals he is carrying a large sum of money. A man he meets in the bar has no hotel room so Prescott offers to share his. The next morning Prescott is found strangled with a woman's silk stocking and his money gone. The next day Millie Baxter checks into the New York hotel where she is to be reunited with her new husband, Paul. In the lobby she happens to meet her old boyfriend, Fred Graham, who is surprised to learn she is married but offers her best wishes anyway. Paul fails to arrive and Millie spends a lonely night in the hotel room. The next day, Fred urges her to report Paul's disappearance to the police but in the process homicide detective Lt. Blake begins to suspect her husband of the Philadelphia strangling. Later, Paul telephones her and asks her to meet him secretly. His subsequent behavior causes Millie to fear he is involved in the Prescott killing which she has learned about through Fred. As they elude the police together, Paul confesses to Millie that he was the stranger in the bar. Although tempted, Paul claims that he did not take the money, and that when he left Prescott's room the man was alive. The newlyweds manage to elude the police but eventually they trace them to their boarding house sanctuary and arrest Paul. New evidence leads Millie to suspect Fred of the murder and she tells Lt. Blake of her suspicions. A search of Graham's hotel room proves fruitless but the clever Blake manages to unhinge the normally phlegmatic Graham just as he drops the money in the hotel mail slot in an envelope addressed to himself in another city.

When Strangers Marry is a low-budget quickie (purportedly shot in 7 days) that manages to deliver, primarily by throwing in as many Woolrich-like plot devices as possible and embellishing them with a good deal of expressive studio photography. In this early effort, director Castle has already proven himself to be an avid student of both Hitchcock and Lewton in his ability to overcome plot contrivances by milking a scene of its suspense. In what was fast becoming a major idiom of the film noir (as opposed to a distinct studio style), the film makers here (including, certainly, Paul Sylos) create on studio lot a fear-provoking N.Y.C.—filled with blinking neon signs, dark, wet streets, cacophonous sounds and menacing jazz joints. The tension inherent in Millie's nighttime forays through the city are enhanced by the fragility of actress Kim Stanley. The fear written in the face of actor Lou Lubin as the bartender who agonizes, under threat of death, to recall the markings on a suspect's luggage contains the essence of the human as monad in the city of darkness. Dean Jagger strikes the proper note of ambiguity in his portrayal of Paul (one that is barely resolved at the film's conclu-

sion). Robert Mitchum, of course, impresses in his first major role—from today's perspective it is hard to accept him as the villain of the piece once he dons hat and trench coat. Even harder to accept is the rapidity with which he loses his characteristic cool when badgered by the police detective at the end. **BP**

WHERE DANGER LIVES (1950)

Director: John Farrow. **Screenplay**: Charles Bennett from an unpublished story by Leo Rosten. **Producers**: Irving Cummings, Jr., Irwin Allen. **Director of Photography**: Nicholas Musuraca. **Music**: Roy Webb. **Art Directors**: Albert S. D'Agostino, Ralph Berger. **Editor**: Eda Warren. **Cast**: Robert Mitchum (Jeff Cameron), Faith Domergue (Margo Lannington), Claude Rains (Frederick Lannington), Maureen O'Sullivan (Julie), Charles Kemper (Police Chief), Ralph Dumke (Klauber, the tout), Billy House (Mr. Bogardus), Harry Shannon (Dr. Maynard), Philip Van Zandt (Milo DeLong), Jack Kelly (Dr. Mullenbach), Lillian West (Mrs. Bogardus). **Completed**: February 22, 1950. **Released**: RKO, July 14. 82 minutes.

After attempting suicide, Margo Lannington is treated by a doctor, Jeff Cameron, who is attracted to her. Led to believe by Margo that wealthy Frederick Lannington is her abusive father not her husband, Cameron breaks up with his girlfriend, Julie. After drinking heavily Cameron goes to confront Lannington. He learns the truth but is heedless of her husband's warnings about Margo's mental state. After Lannington hits him with a poker, Cameron knocks the older man out. When a dazed Cameron staggers to the bathroom, unknown to him (or the viewer) Margo smothers Lannington with a pillow. Believing he has killed Lannington, Cameron agrees that he and Margo must flee. Fearing police at the airport are there for them they change plans and drive south towards Mexico. As his condition deteriorates Cameron lets Margo take control. They buy passage across the border, but as they wait in a hotel, Margo lets slip the truth and Cameron realizes the depth of her psychosis. As Cameron follows to the border, she shoots him and is subsequently shot by the police. Refusing to be pitied, Margo confesses to sole responsibility for Lannington's murder before dying. Jeff recovers and is reunited with Julie.

Where Danger Lives: *Fugitive couple Jeff Cameron (Robert Mitchum) and Margo Lannington (Faith Domergue).*

WHERE DANGER LIVES

In this first of three sequence-shots, once the visual anomaly of the grossly overweight burlesque performer has been absorbed and sensing that the end of the movie must be near, the viewer waits to see where the fugitive couple portrayed by Robert Mitchum and Faith Domergue are lurking. But the performer takes her time as she moves to the back of the small auditorium, interacting with a man in the front row and swinging her oversized purse as she sashays past the patrons. Finally the pair is revealed in the last row, but there is still no cut. Mitchum's character, Jeff Cameron, has an injured arm and fidgets with downcast eyes. Domergue's Margo Lannington pouts and casts a disapprov-

ing glance at him. Then a man appears behind them and taps Cameron on the shoulder. The camera pulls back as Jeff and Margo stand and holds them for a moment in a rim light two shot then follows them through a curtained doorway to the right, which reveals another set. The camera hangs back as they cross towards a pebbled glass door being held open for them and captures Cameron's last glance behind him, as if he were wishing for the simpler, more detached position of a moment ago, sitting and watching a fat exotic dancer in a dimly lit auditorium.

The angle inside, with a new character (Milo DeLong) in the right foreground, matches precisely: Margo is intently moving forward while Cameron looks back for one instant longer. In this second sequence shot, as they haggle over their condition and the price of passage to Mexico, Mitchum's figure initially dominates this shot at frame center and the bright spot on the ceiling hovers behind his head like a mock halo, ironically recalling that he started this movie as a respected physician and was first seen in a pediatric ward tending to a young girl in an iron lung. But even as the audience may want Cameron to discover the truth before it's too late, seeing him trapped inside this sequence shot with a femme fatale and a very shady character like DeLong, leaves the typical viewer as frustrated as he is. As Cameron's expression changes from semi-attentive to glazed over, DeLong walks around them and the shot re-forms with a pan left so that Margo is at the center. DeLong's innocuous chit-chat continues for a bit longer, even turning to the accordion on the desk in the foreground. "You two are hot," he says to the disheveled and sweating Cameron; but he emphasizes what sense of the word he means to deflect Cameron's feeble protest about just being a tourist. DeLong pours himself a beer and doubles the price. The camera rises slightly before Cameron asks, "What kind of a shakedown is this?" Then the unseen voice of the owner, Klauber, answers and the camera counters that figure's move forward. DeLong disappears outside the left edge of the frame, as the camera resettles into a tighter three-shot with Klauber at the center. This literally divides the couple in a more constricted frame, restating the emotional positions and stripping away the options. With his cheap cigar pointed at Cameron's face Klauber asks, "How are things back how in San Francisco?" As his criminal notoriety has spread, the noir underworld has engulfed Mitchum's Jeff Cameron as completely as it did his Jeff Bailey in *Out of the Past.* The source music of burlesque riffs heard through the open office door has played throughout the sequence and relentlessly mocked Cameron's plight. Off Margo's frown, the next scene dissolves in.

As this third and longest sequence shot begins, Margo steps in front of a mirror, takes a last drag, then stubs out her cigarette. Roy Webb's underscore returns and its ominous measures will continue till the end of the scene. The mirror and its second face is a metaphor both for Margo's hypocrisy and her paranoid schizophrenia. In many earlier scenes, Farrow has seldom shown the couple in an embrace or other intimate pose but more frequently positioned and framed them so that they are not looking at each. The camera pulls back as Margo crosses to glance out a window. The initial staging here is fairly straightforward. Some lamp outside is flashing and intermittently puts Margo in rim light. The anxious Margo woman paces back and forth like a trapped animal. The light keeps pulsing behind her. She snaps at the seated Cameron, recriminating because "his idea" has gotten them here, whereas her plan to walk across the border in daylight out in the desert "might have worked." Then she softens, apologizes, even checks her lip-stick. As a self-pitying Cameron is anchored to a chair in the foreground, the soft focus on his features is appropriate to his clouded mental state. As Margo's agitation intensifies, he seems on the brink of unconsciousness, then the sound of vehicles is heard outside like a *deus ex machina* and draws Margo back to the window.

A push-in follows Cameron as he tries to rise and cross to see out but must slump back down on a bed. The camera then pans and moves rights to end in a two-shot, when Margo comes over to sit behind him. Cameron is still soft but Margo is sharper now, the perspiration glistening off her skin as she smirks and reveals her secret bank account waiting in Mexico. Hearing this compels Cameron towards a full realization of the depth of her paranoia and duplicity. The most significant "sub-text" of any sequence shot is the frustration of audience expectation, which derives from the subconscious understanding on the part of the viewer that Hollywood movies normally cut from one angle to another within a scene. Although new angles and framing can be achieved within a sequence shot, the viewer also understands that the recording device must be moved to accommodate this and that this is much more difficult than a simple cut.

The next reset takes the figures to the window, the camera precipitously "leaping" over the bed after the unsteady Cameron as he lurches towards it. While Margo remains shadowed on the right, the source of the flashing is now visible: a neon sign for the café across the alley. Now Cameron's face is hit by it, an analog for the emotional realizations that are throbbing through him, and he tells Margo she must go on alone. Not merely is he too weak to escape, but he reads the name on the sign, *Rosa Blanca* or *White Rose,* and is gripped by the irony. It taunts him by recollecting the alternate course he could have followed as the film began. Instead he stopped giving white roses to the nurse who was his fiancée and started sending red flowers to Margo, who lets the curtain slip back so the lettering is obscured. Here the viewer might expect balanced close-ups between the characters, revealing their reactions more closely. Instead the sequence shot continues.

As Margo pries Cameron's hand from the window sill to lead him towards the door, the camera slides left. It captures an abrupt and awkward moment: Margo pushes Cameron, and he crumples to the floor. There she laments his weakness and looms over him. Cameron's slurred speech recalls another bad decision: had he not gotten drunk before going to confront Margo and her husband, a man she had told him was her controlling father, violence might have been avoided. When he refers to her as a patient, an annoyed Margo moves away and sits on the bed. Now she is in softer focus in the foreground; and as he grasps his position more clearly, Cameron is sharper in the rear ground. With his figure mostly hidden behind the bed, hemmed in by a much larger Margo in the two dimensions on the frame on the left, Cameron is physically and emotionally helpless as Margo reveals her history of mental illness for the first time. Again Farrow's actors do not face each other. Even when he calls her calls her "a pathological liar" and imagines the web of deceit into which she has drawn him, Margo does not turn back, not even to remark, "Don't you have any feeling?" She does, however, pointedly look down at him when saying, "Do you think you're the only man who ever found me attractive?" and again when he says he pities her.

As the tissue of lies dissolves, as the dialogue makes it clear that the rupture between these fugitive lovers can never to be repaired, as they continue to hold their unnatural positions and talk about pathology, suicide, a whole catalogue of mischances and misunderstandings in an almost off-handed way, the perspectives of audience and characters coalesce further. Both are held in the confines of the sequence shot and unable to escape. Cameron's last attempt to assert dominance over Margo is to grab her wrist and literally twist her arm to force a confession from her. A wild-eyed Margo waits for her moment, then her answer to his insistence on learning "how" she killed her husband is to throw Cameron to the floor and to reenact what the viewer already knows: she suffocated her husband with a pillow and now does the same to her lover.

What is the audience to imagine or expect at this point? While moviegoers who watched film noir in 1950, were as unlikely to know the term as the filmmakers, just as the filmmakers knew what they were doing, the audience knew what it was watching. Could the lead actor die? However enfeebled, could Robert Mitchum perish at the hands of a deranged woman? Hadn't Jeff Bailey succumbed because of a lying femme fatale in *Out of the Past?* So it was possible. As if to underscore this, the camera tilts up so that Cameron is no longer even visible, erased from the sequence shot as he might well be erased from the movie. At the bottom left of the frame, Margo is a small hunched figure, shuddering occasionally from the effort of pressing the pillow into his face. Seen from this perspective and out of context, Margo's action could be confused for an attempt to resuscitate Cameron. Instead it's a grotesque parody of saving a life.

Having elevated the viewer's desire for a glimpse of Cameron, dead or alive, to the highest possible degree, Farrow dollies and pans with Margo as she carries her appliquéd murder weapon back to the window and whispers "I'm coming" to an unseen truck driver. As she drops the pillow and takes her handbag, the camera pans with her: she moves towards the door of the room for the first time, but even as she steps gingerly past Cameron's body and moves in and out of the light, her eyes remain fixed on that spot on the floor where her victim must be lying. She even changes the hand with which she holds the knob, so that she can keep staring at him right up until the instant the door closes. Farrow refuses to use a cutaway to her point of view, or to any shot that would break the visual tension.

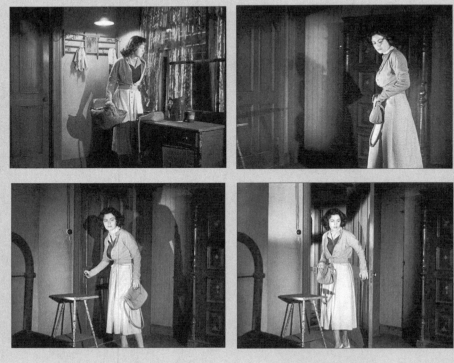

Roy Webb is finally permitted a musical crescendo, as if to announce the end of the scene; but it's not over yet. Instead the camera pans, not quickly to be sure, into the room, across the top of the bed, still staying far enough back to prevent the viewer from peering over its edge and seeing the spot on the floor where Cameron was killed. All the tension built up over nearly seven minutes of unbroken shot—and yes that's how long this take lasts—is focused on one thing. Of course, Cameron isn't dead. The bed spread moves. His hand appears at its edge then grips it. He pulls himself up. Did Margo lack the resolution to finish the job? It doesn't matter how he survived. He's not dead . . . yet. The movie's not over. He can't run after Margo, but he can somehow stagger to his feet, fall, get up again and reach the door. The odd angle as he lifts up and plunges palpably captures and conveys Cameron's profound mental and physical disequilibrium to the viewer. It takes him five full seconds from when he grips the knob to wrestle it open, but finally he limps out of the room to follow Margo, and after seven minutes and fifteen seconds, the shot and the sequence are finally done. **AS**

In *Where Danger Lives,* his first noir picture at Howard Hughes' RKO, John Farrow creates a femme fatale unusual even for noir. Most of the cycle's "spider women" are heartless schemers empowered by a deadly eroticism, often deadly for themselves as well as their male victims. Margo, however, is an out-of-control schizophrenic, who seems truly to believe in the fantasies she has concocted to ensnare her hapless lover, Dr. Jeff Cameron. In this she is unlike such classic femme fatales as the cold and cunning Phyllis Dietrichson of *Double Indemnity,* but anticipates a later, more conflicted heroine such as Diane Tremayne of Otto Preminger's 1953 *Angel Face.*

The viewer's first close-up glimpse of Margo is from Cameron's point of view as he bends over her supine body and questions her regarding her attempted suicide. Her naked shoulders peek out seductively from beneath the hospital sheets. Her black hair frames her softly focused face like a demonic halo. His attraction is immediate as he sees in her both sexual object and damsel in distress. By the time she asks rhetorically, "Why should I live?" Cameron has already supplied an answer. Margo is driven by a hysterical intensity which in turn drives all around her, including the submissive hero, into violence. Cameron's confrontation with Margo's husband (who she originally tells him is her father) is particularly illustrative. The scene is staged largely in three-shots which reify the triangular conflict of Margo, her husband Lannington, and Cameron. When the fatal fight between Cameron and Lannington finally breaks out, it is instigated by another of Margo's hysterical fits.

In his injured state, Cameron is sucked into the back draft created by Margo's frenetic energy. As a consequence Cameron is among the most masochistic in a long line of pained noir protagonists. Even though it violates his medical oath, his code of morality, and common sense, Margo's sexual magnetism and willful control drag Cameron into a becoming half of a fugitive couple on the run to Mexico with a woman any trained doctor could plainly see is suffering from acute schizophrenia. The appeal this neurotic woman holds for him is two-fold: she is a dangerous and exciting object of desire that stimulates him from the first shots of her bare shoulders and sultry expressions. But more importantly, especially considering his profession, he sees her as a fulfillment of his messiah complex. Or as Lannington says when they first meet, ". . . a clinging vine brings out your protective side." Lannington's words are visually complemented by a two-shot a few minutes later in which Margo clutches him desperately and whispers in his ear, "How much I need you now."

As Margo alternates between loving partner and ruthless exploiter, Cameron grows weaker and weaker, bodily and mentally. His physical decline is an externalization of his psychic or spiritual wound. As his strength diminishes, hers grows. Like a dominatrix or an emotional vampire, the femme fatale feeds off the weakness of her victim. Margo hectors him constantly to keep moving towards "freedom" and the Mexican border by saying, "If you love me, you'll make it," even though she realizes his paralysis and possible death is imminent. In a seedy hotel near the border, a neon sign flashes into the dimly lit room and in a seven-minute-long take the camera locks onto Margo at her most frenetic, pacing the room as a pained Cameron slumps on a bed in the foreground while she gradually reveals the truth about herself, that she

was under psychiatric care, that she actually murdered her husband. While it could be argued that the demented Margo only half-heartedly attempts to smother Cameron as she did her husband, it is that momentary hesitation or weakness on the part of the femme fatale that spares him.

At RKO, Farrow and his collaborators were permitted more exteriors, particularly at night, than at Paramount. As with Bunker Hill in *Night Has a Thousand Eyes,* the dingy border town in *Where Danger Lives* provides a graphic context for the protagonist's fall: from manors to shacks, from doctor to transient on the lam. As a limping Cameron pursues Margo through that environment, Farrow's staging underscores the twisted relationship between the two. The injured Cameron staggers along a line of posts, clinging to them as he pursues the source of his pain. An extreme low-angle frames Margo as she slips from the truck and holds her in a medium close shot as she pulls out a pistol. Even after she shoots him, the masochistic Cameron keeps coming. In a final reversal, she clears Cameron of the murder of her husband. While clinging to the chain-link fence, she defiantly delivers her own epitaph: "Nobody pities me." **JU, AS & BP**

WHERE THE SIDEWALK ENDS (1950)

Director/Producer: Otto Preminger. **Screenplay**: Ben Hecht adapted by Victor Trivas, Frank P. Rosenberg and Robert E. Kent from the novel *Night Cry* by William L. Stuart. **Director of Photography**: Joseph LaShelle. **Music**: Cyril Mockridge. **Art Directors**: Lyle Wheeler, J. Russell Spencer. **Editor**: Louis Loeffler. **Cast**: Dana Andrews (Mark Dixon), Gene Tierney (Morgan Taylor), Gary Merrill (Scalise), Bert Freed (Klein), Tom Tully (Jiggs Taylor), Karl Malden (Lt. Thomas), Ruth Donnelly (Martha), Craig Stevens (Ken Paine), Robert Simon (Inspector Foley), Harry von Zell (Ted Morrison), Don Appell (Willie), Neville Brand (Steve), Grace Mills (Mrs. Tribaum), Lou Krugman (Mike Williams), David McMahon (Harrington), David Wolfe (Sid Kramer), Steve Roberts (Gilruth). **Released**: 20th Century-Fox, July 7. 95 minutes.

A police officer with a history of unnecessary brutality, Dixon, inadvertently kills a suspect while trying to get some information out of him. He camouflages the accidental slaying by making the whole incident appear to be a gangland murder. However, the circumstantial evidence leads to Jiggs Taylor, a cab driver whose daughter, Morgan, is married to the murdered man. Through the course of the investigation, Morgan falls in love with Dixon. In an attempt to swing the evidence away from Morgan's father and into the lap of Scalise, an important underworld figure, Dixon comes face to face with the mobster and his henchmen. After Dixon is wounded, the police arrive and arrest the mob. In a final moment of moral reassessment, Dixon confesses to the original killing and goes to jail satisfied in the knowledge that Morgan will be waiting for him when he gets out.

Co-written by Ben Hecht and directed by Otto Preminger, *Where the Sidewalk Ends* concerns itself with a hero of questionable virtue and limited potency trying to react to a society of confused moral values. The character of Mark Dixon is plagued by the shadow of his father, a onetime mobster. His brutal treatment of criminal suspects gives a strangely distorted and easily corruptible quality to the image of authority he portrays; and this brand of corruption, linked with the potential

Where the Sidewalk Ends: *Morgan Taylor (Gene Tierney) and Mark Dixon (Dana Andrews)*.

for violence lurking below the veneer of urban society, is an important noir motif. The writers take this situation one step further by presenting the police, in the guise of Dixon, as violent and unstable. It is this lack of control, and the eventual nightmare it produces, which forms the central noir statement of the film. In attempting to come to grips with the obvious incongruities of his position, Dixon becomes an archetypical noir hero, a man both existentially adrift and trapped by circumstance, whose redemption—but not salvation—is made possible by his own ironic sense of justice.

Hecht's film scripts in the late 1940s replaced such grotesque figures as Tony Camonte in *Scarface,* and Anthony Mallare in *The Scoundrel,* with such noir everymen as Mark Dixon in *Where the Sidewalk Ends* and Gagan in *Ride the Pink Horse.* There is a common feeling of alienation and loneliness that molds these characters of Hecht's imagination. Not only do the heroes of Hecht's screenplays change drastically, but the underworld he created has been transformed into a realistic backdrop, ideal for the criminal acts and capers of dark personalities. It is a vision of the urban jungle far removed from the stylized settings of *Underworld* and *Scarface.* Although *Where the Sidewalk Ends* reunites many of the elements of Preminger's earlier noir film *Laura,* under Hecht's influence, the decadent world of the corrupted upper class explored in *Laura* has been replaced by a gritty, naturalistic milieu. Both *Laura* and *Where the Sidewalk Ends* do demonstrate Preminger's precise visual style. But one film remains noir due mainly to its exposure of corruption on a high social level; the other becomes noir through detailing the exploits of a less-than-powerful hero involved in a deeply corrupted society. **CM**

WHILE THE CITY SLEEPS (1956)

Director: Fritz Lang. **Screenplay**: Casey Robinson from the novel *The Bloody Spur* by Charles Einstein. **Producer**: Bert Friedlob. **Director of Photography**: Ernest Laszlo. **Music**: Herschel Burke Gilbert. **Art Director**: Carroll Clark. **Editor**: Gene Fowler, Jr. **Cast**: Dana Andrews (Edward Mobley), Rhonda Fleming (Dorothy Kyne), George Sanders (Mark Loving), Howard Duff (Lt. Burt Kaufman), Thomas Mitchell (John Day Griffith), Vincent Price (Walter Kyne, Jr.), Sally Forrest (Nancy Liggett), John Barrymore, Jr. (Robert Manners), James Craig (Harry Kritzer), Ida Lupino (Mildred Donner), Robert Warwick (Amos Kyne), Ralph Peters (Meade), Vladimir Sokoloff (George Pilski), Mae Marsh (Mrs. Manners), Sandy White (Judith Fenton). **Released**: RKO, May 16. 99 minutes.

A series of brutal murders by the "lipstick killer" is terrifying the city. Immediately after his father's death, dilettante Walter Kyne, Jr. announces a competition among his staff: the one who unmasks the killer will be the paper's new editor in chief. Griffith, the city editor, enlists the aid of prize-winning reporter turned television commentator Edward Mobley, who knows lead investigator Det. Kaufman. Debonair Mark Loving, the wire service editor, uses attractive "women's writer" Mildred Donner. Photo editor Harry Kritzer is having an affair with Kyne's wife Dorothy. Mobley attacks the megalomaniacal killer on the air and permits his girlfriend Nancy Liggett to act as "bait" for the killer, mother's boy Robert Manners. Unable to get at Liggett, Manners attacks Dorothy in her love nest across the hall. She beats him off with a heavy ashtray, as Mobley and the police arrive and capture the fleeing Manners in the subway. All the competitors are promoted, while Mobley marries Nancy and is named managing editor of the paper.

This film is a multifaceted drama, in which two equally interesting threads—the lipstick killings and the competition for the newspaper's editorship—are woven together. The pitiful murderer, given to outbursts of bitterness and rage against his overly protective mother, emerges as a vivid and fully realized character in his own right despite the narrative emphasis on the newspaper people. They are admittedly an interesting and realistic ensemble, especially as played by Dana Andrews, Ida Lupino, and George Sanders. Since the killer cannot help himself and is even compulsively given to writing "Catch me before I kill again," there is an unusual reversal in which he is more sympathetic than the newspaper people, who will do anything to get ahead (even Mobley's participation is initially due to financial considerations). Indeed, the fact that three men in this story willingly use their girlfriends as "bait" of one kind or another does not speak well for their fundamental humanity.

Fritz Lang's style had become very refined by the time of this film, one of his last in the United States; and it is revealing of how an effective film noir can be created without

recourse to a great deal of the stylistic mannerisms, without mood lighting or odd camera angles. Lang remained subtly expressionistic in his use of decor as illustrated by Kyne's apartment, which is reminiscent of the silent "Dr. Mabuse" films; but the simple formal elements of *While the City Sleeps* testify to Lang's sometime disdain for affectation. Presented with a highly melodramatic script, Lang tackles it straighforwardly without any artifice which would undermine the lucidity of its presentation. Lang effectively undercuts viewer expectations on many levels, including the intrusions of the killer and the motives of the characters.

Affinities of composition and judicious editing integrate the killer into the world through which the "normal" people move; and in the climax both killer and reporter run through the darkness of the subway tunnels that lie beneath the city streets. The true suspense of the film is manifest in the narrative probing of the critical relationship between society's illnesses and its normality; and the formal precision of each scene reasserts the existence of this relationship. One of the central values implicit in film noir is that there is no separation between the disturbed depths of a society (its noir underworld) and the acceptable modes of living within that society. The venality of almost all of its protagonists, each of whom excepting Nancy and Kaufman but including Mobley relentlessly pursues his or her own agenda, is constantly underscored. Mobley's smug and somewhat self-righteous broadcasts, a pulpit to which he rose because of his accomplishments as a print reporter, infuriate Manners but ring hollow. Lang also exposes Mobley's alcoholism (Dana Andrews plays the reporter from drunk to slightly intoxicated but almost never appears entirely sober) as well as the moral and emotional failings of all the other law-abiding characters. In this context, Lang's staging of the last scene, in a honeymoon hotel in which Nancy reads the litany of new jobs from the newspaper ending with Mobley's appointment, is darkly ironic in that the ill-fated Manners and his victims are reduced to sacrifices on the altar of their self-serving success. **BL**

WHIRLPOOL (1949)

Director: Otto Preminger. **Screenplay**: Ben Hecht, Andrew Solt from the novel *Methinks the Lady* by Guy Endore. **Producer**: Otto Preminger. **Director of Photography**: Arthur Miller. **Production Designer**: Leland Fuller, Lyle Wheeler. **Music**: David Raksin. **Editor**: Louis Loeffler. **Cast**: Gene Tierney (Ann Sutton), Richard Conte (Dr. Bill Sutton), José Ferrer (David Korvo), Charles Bickford (Lt. James Colton), Barbara O'Neil (Theresa Randolph), Eduard Franz (Martin Avery). **Released**: 20th Century-Fox, November 28. 98 minutes.

Los Angeles. Ann, kleptomaniac and wife of psychoanalyst William, is caught shoplifting in a department store. Korvo, a suave astrologer and hypnotist, convinces the store owner to release her. While William intuits nothing of Ann's problems, Korvo convinces her to be his patient. He cures her insomnia through hypnotic suggestion, but also secretly directs her to steal William's disc recording of sessions with Korvo's ex-patient Theresa, then to hide them in Theresa's apartment. Police, entering at this point, find Theresa strangled to death and arrest Ann. Due to evidence planted by Korvo, Ann's guilt comes to seem incontrovertible, and she

Whirlpool: *Ann Sutton (Gene Tierney) and David Corvo (José Ferrer).*

wonders whether she is insane. William, with policeman Colton, investigates Korvo's shady financial dealing with Theresa; however, his alibi is solid—he was undergoing surgery on the murder night. Ann delves into traumatic memories of her rich father. William's hypothesis that Korvo uses self-hypnosis is demonstrated when the latter leaves the hospital bed and arrives at Theresa's apartment to seize the hidden disc. Ann, William and Colton suddenly arrive; Korvo hides, while William leads Ann to a new self-awareness. Korvo, gun in hand, compels Ann to distract the men, but she relents. Already profusely bleeding, Korvo falls down the stairs and dies.

It is almost 35 minutes into *Whirlpool* before recognizably noir elements appear in force: the classic sequence in which a sleepwalking Ann, dressed in black, walks calmly through surreally opening doors and, acting on hypnotic suggestion, goes to an apartment to hide incriminating evidence. Until then, and indeed for much of the rest of the film, Preminger prefers the disquieting, frequently public spaces of daylight: outdoor lunches, well-lit department stores. This personal adaptation of noir style and iconography goes hand in hand with a very particular presentation of psychoanalysis and psychotherapy.

Although clearly in the tradition of *Spellbound* and many other Freudian-Gothic tales of repressed memory, Preminger offers a startlingly prescient depiction of the rise of pop psychology in everyday American life. For Preminger (unlike Lang in *Secret Beyond the Door* or Renoir in *The Woman on the Beach*) is not terribly interested in dreams, or the deep, liberating interpretation of unconscious traces. Rather, the diagnosis of symptoms becomes a daily power game—Ann is constantly labelled and defined, by all characters, as one kind of person or another—and, on this level, there is scarcely any difference between William's "certified" practice and Korvo's more vulgar techniques of astrology and hypnosis. Preminger views the social world (and this is enduring throughout his career) as a constant courtroom trial: what matters is what you can make someone believe or accept, what you can render "manifest" (even via sleight-of-hand), not what is necessarily real or true. And, in this light, what could be a better instance of Foucault's notion that social rituals rest upon a "work on the self" than Korvo's self-hypnosis, so crazy and yet so undeniably effective?

Whirlpool, which is in many respects a companion piece to Preminger's better-known classic *Laura*, is based on a delicious, even perverse irony: as Jacques Lourcelles has suggested, whereas William's "blind love" misrecognizes his wife's situation, it is the sinister manipulator Korvo who, in fact, sees the absolute truth of Ann's place in the world: being a privileged wife has transformed her into a neurotic mess, a condition indelibly captured by Tierney. Preminger's powerful and masterfully controlled *mise en scène* reaches a zenith here: his camera movements and fluid staging are not conventionally "lyrical," but instead trace the fundamental tension between an open world in which surprises lurk everywhere (sudden entries into the frame frequently change the course of the plot), and a more Langian vision in which a cruel destiny is exposed lying in wait at the end of every trajectory (as in the revelation of Theresa's dead body that concludes Ann's hynotized stroll). Ultimately, as Gérard Legrand has remarked, the fascination of Preminger's work—and especially *Whirlpool*—derives from the dialectic at its heart: on the one hand, the brittle world of social games, and on the other, a dark, subterranean unconscious that forbids facile "decipherment," but drives people mysteriously, as if through "still but dangerous waters" presented with the "hard clarity of an aquarium" (Lourcelles). **AM**

WHISPERING CITY (1947)

Director: Fedor Ozep [Fyodor Otsep]. **Screenplay**: Rian James, Leonard Lee from a story by Michael Lennox and George Zuckerman with additional dialogue by Hugh Kemp, Sydney Banks, Gina Kaus. **Producer**: George Marton. **Directors of Photography**: Charles Quick, Guy Roe. **Music**: Morris C. Davis. **Art Director**: William Koessler. **Editors**: Leonard Anderson, Douglas Bagier, Richard J. Jarvis. **Cast**: Paul Lukas (Albert Frédéric), Mary Anderson (Mary Roberts), Helmut Dantine (Michel Lacoste), John Pratt (Edward Durant, editor), George Alexander (Insp. Renaud), Joy Lafleur (Blanche Lacoste), Mimi D'Estée (Renée Brancourt), Arthur Lefebvre (Sleigh Driver), Lucie Poitras (Hospital Room Sister), J. Léo Gagnon (Frederic's Butler). **Released**: Eagle-Lion, November 20. 98 minutes.

The death of a long-retired actress in an auto accident spurs crime reporter Mary Roberts to work up a feature story: the woman was sent to a sanitarium years before for insisting that her fiancé's death was actually murder. Pursuing a lead, Anderson interviews prosperous benefactor of the arts Albert Frédéric, who seems curiously bothered by the visit. Frédéric is the patron of an impoverished young pianist/composer Michel Lacoste, who is working on something called The Quebec Concerto. When Lacoste's disturbed shrewish wife commits suicide, which is made to look like murder, it leads to a blackmail scheme to engineer another murder and a faked death to look like still another murder.

Despite an extremely complicated narrative—Eagle-Lion was not known for the elegant simplicity of its plots—*Whispering City* effectively evokes the noir mood. That is partly due to the telling use of locale: Quebec City, that odd European fortress set high over the St. Lawrence River,

which comes to life as fully here as it would for Alfred Hitchcock in *I Confess* a few years later.

As Roberts, Mary Anderson combines aspects of earlier noir turns by Teresa Wright and Bonita Granville, while she sleuthes around in a jaunty tam like Nancy Drew. Russian-born director Fyodor Otsep had kicked around Europe and was just managing to revive his war-derailed career with what would turn out to be his last movie and only noir. In fact, he made two versions of this movie, this one and in the manner of early talkies another with French-speaking actors substituting in all the lead roles. **BMV**

WHISPERING FOOTSTEPS (1943)

Director: Howard Bretherton. **Screenplay**: Gertrude Walker and Dane Lussier, based on the story by Gertrude Walker. **Producer**: George Blair. **Director of Photography**: Jack Marta. **Music**: Morton Scott. **Art Director**: Russell Kimball. **Editor**: Ralph Dixon. **Cast**: John Hubbard (Marcus Borne), Rita Quigley (Brook Hammond), Joan Blair (Helene LaSalle), Charles Halton (Harry Hammond), Cy Kendall (Brad Doland), Juanita Quigley (Rose Murphy), Mary Gordon (Ma Murphy), Billy Benedict (Jerry Murphy), Matt McHugh (Cy Walsh), Marie Blake (Sally Lukens). **Released**: Republic, December 30. 54 minutes.

Marcus, an Ohio man, hears a radio bulletin linking female strangling victims in Indiana and Michigan to a suspect whose description matches his exactly, a resemblance remarked upon by the other tenants in his boarding house, as they note his return from a vacation in Indiana. Outside the bank where he works a cop follows him, driving Marcus to escape into the adjacent library where he picks up the nearest book, *Psychology of a Homicidal*. At the police station the strangler's identikit shows a remarkable likeness to Marcus but the police chief alibis him. Marcus reunites with his boss's daughter, Brook, who requests a late night rendezvous in the park where, alone, she sees an unidentifiable man in the distance who causes her to flee. As more murders follow increasingly close to town, Marcus' neighbors become increasingly suspicious. After a woman is found murdered next door and Brook alibis him falsely, Marcus confronts Brook's father before the alibi can be challenged, an encounter which convinces him to leave town. As he departs, staring down his fellow tenants, a radio report exonerates him completely as the real killer is caught.

By focussing on one of noir's central thematic elements and eschewing most others, this little film gains in power. That element is society's pettiness and duplicity which hinder and imperil the solitary noir protagonist. Agnes Moorhead's sneakily prying neighbor in *Dark Passage* is one prominent example while another, the mendacious marriage registrar in *They Live By Night*, indicates that corruption is as pervasive in society's institutions as in its ordinary townsfolk. Here we see both, with Marcus' boss at the bank a philanderer and his boarding house neighbors a small-minded Greek chorus of notably dull lives, and no aspirations to transcend them for anything better.

The script of *Whispering Footsteps* works overtime to show its audience circumstantial evidence which these townspeople can't see, suggesting if not Marcus' guilt then at least an amnesiac Jekyll and Hyde duality. Yet all they or we need to exonerate him is described early in an airtight alibi provided by the local police chief (notwithstanding that he undercuts his credibility by citing his wife as the real authority on important police matters). Marcus is established as different ("I never remember jokes," he tells a co-worker) from the norms of this white picket fence town, whose syrupy soundtrack is rebuked in a concise exchange when the local store mistakes the music of Tchaikovsky for Beethoven. If these lives aren't corrupt like the adulterous bank manager then they're empty, and both Marcus and his love interest Brook explicitly bemoan the gossip that fills the gap for these people. But many of these residents have something to hide, enabling red herrings to proliferate, especially in the enigmatic businesswoman Ms. LaSalle who tells Marcus she "used to know [a murderer]." A brief, chiaroscuro montage of "Chinese whispers" among the residents underlines the film's title, which is referenced explicitly later.

The incipient paranoia becomes pervasive through the omnipresence of a suspicious cop, a special investigator shadowing Marcus, whose girth adds to his oppressiveness; Marcus by contrast strongly resembles a svelte Ray Milland. As the circumstantial evidence grows, even casting suspicion on an alternate suspect, the townspeople underline their impoverished worldview by referencing the devices of pulp fiction and B-movies to implicate Marcus. In classic noir fashion he is on a steady downward spiral and selective lighting shows him to be a marked man. As the entire town turns against him, a tracking shot down a sidewalk evokes comparisons with the communal tide turning in Frtiz Lang's *M*. But this is 1943 America, and even if the President's portrait is juxtaposed against shadowy war bonds posters, it's still FDR, whose trademark aspiration for Americans, "freedom from fear," is explicitly reiterated by Marcus in his climactic speech. Transcendence *is* possible as Marcus shows when he drops the mask of politeness and stops pandering to his soon-to-be-ex-neighbors and, having learned a valuable lesson, abandons them and sets out to answer his own rhetorical question: "Is there a place where there aren't any people?" **RSW**

WHISTLE STOP (1946)

Director: Léonide Moguy. **Screenplay**: Philip Yordan based on the novel by Maritta M. Wolff. **Producer**: Seymour Nebenzal. **Director of Photography**: Russell Metty. **Music**: Dimitri Tiomkin. **Art Director**: Rudi Field. **Editor**: Gregg Tallas. **Cast**: George Raft (Kenny Veech), Ava Gardner (Mary), Victor McLaglen (Gitlo), Tom Conway (Lew Lentz), Jorja Curtright (Fran), Jane Nigh (Josie Veech), Florence Bates (Molly Veech), Charles Drake (Ernie), Charles Judels (Sam Veech), Carmel Myers (Estelle), Jimmy Conlin (Al, the Barber), Mack Gray (Bartender). **Released**: United Artists, January 25. 85 minutes.

After two years in Chicago, Mary returns to Ashbury to get back together with Kenny, but his jealousy spoils it for them. She starts seeing Lew, who owns a small nightclub and hates Kenny. At the town's annual fair Lew makes a lot of money, which he takes by train to deposit in Detroit. Kenny and a friend, Gitlo, plan to kill Lew at the station, steal the money and hide his body so it will look like he never came back from Detroit. After Kenny promises Mary he is going to take her away, they resume dating. The night of the robbery Mary

suspects Kenny is up to no good, and she prevents him from getting to the station. When she discovers he has a gun, she is heartbroken. She goes back to Lew, but it doesn't work out, and she reconciles with Kenny. For revenge, Lew tries to frame Gitlo and Kenny for murder. Kenny is wounded by the police, but he and Gitlo make it to another town. Gitlo comes back to tell Mary where Kenny is. He goes after Lew, and they kill each other. Knowing Kenny is innocent, Mary brings him home.

Although there are important ways *Whistle Stop* is bifurcated, it consistently sticks to the social world of the Ashbury working class. The townspeople are shown at a barbershop, pool hall, beer joint, and the fair. The story's characters and the crimes some of them commit, photographed without the glossiness of an A-picture budget, could be in a pulp magazine. However, the film also tells of love that is lost, unrequited, regained, rejected, and, ultimately, triumphant. Kenny and Mary's on-again, off-again passion for each other, which forms the heart of the film, could be in a romantic potboiler. The mix between the two kinds of storylines, hardboiled and melodramatic, follows the film's source, *Whistle Stop*, the first novel by 22-year old Maritta M. Wolff. Published in 1941, it was a best seller, titillating both sexes. However, the Hollywood version bowdlerizes the original, in which, for example, Mary is Kenny's sister and incest is suggested.

As in melodrama, there are other love interests for the principals. Fran, a waitress at Lew's club, is devoted to Kenny. Lew is a heel Mary takes up with when Kenny won't make the changes she wants. As in hardboiled fiction, a bad influence, Gitlo, has a scheme to get Kenny what he wants—money and Mary. The melodramatic solution for Fran is accidental death. The hardboiled method for getting rid of Gitlo and Lew is violent death. Indeed, each of them dies the appropriate way. Meanwhile, Kenny and Mary learn melodrama's lesson for staying together, which is, as Kenny puts it, "You get what you give." Mary had urged Kenny to move with her to Chicago, but he refused because he didn't want to wind up digging ditches. Instead, he stayed in Ashbury and continued "boozing, loafing and playing cards." After she returns to the town, she repeatedly fails to get him to change. But when she decides to "love him the way he is," he immediately takes a job laying railroad track. The work isn't too different from ditch-digging, but he is doing it on his terms. Kenny must compromise, too. More than once Mary makes the first move to give their relationship another chance. Then she breaks up with him because he treats her commitment as his due and he won't give an inch on changing. When he stops trying to have his cake as well as eat it, he gets her for keeps.

Whistle Stop is almost entirely shot at an angle that is slightly upwards, which creates an affirmative viewpoint of the working class characters. Only in a couple of instances is there a point-of-view looking downwards, mainly when Lew faces Mary and later Gitlo seated below him in his office. The mixture of melodrama and hardboiled storylines is replicated in the *mise en scène*. On the one hand, the Veech's house, especially Mary's bedroom, is brightly lit. On the other, an impressive noir style is used for the locations associated with crime—the whistle stop and Lew's office. **DMH**

WHITE HEAT (1949)

Director: Raoul Walsh. **Screenplay**: Ivan Goff and Ben Roberts based on a story by Virginia Kellogg. **Producer**: Lou Edelman. **Director of Photography**: Sid Hickox. **Music**: Max Steiner. **Art Director**: Edward Carrere. **Editor**: Owen Marks. **Cast**: James Cagney (Cody Jarrett), Virginia Mayo (Verna Jarrett), Edmond O'Brien (Hank Fallon/Vic Pardo), Margaret Wycherly (Ma Jarrett), Steve Cochran (Big Ed Somers), John Archer (Phillip Evans), Wally Cassell (Cotton Valetti), Fred Clark (The Trader), Ford Rainey (Zuckie Hommell), Fred Coby (Happy Taylor), G. Pat Collins (The Reader), Mickey Knox (Het Kohler), Paul Guilfoyle (Roy Parker). **Released**: Warner Bros., September 2. 114 minutes.

After robbing a train, Cody Jarrett and his gang, including his mother, take refuge in a mountain cabin. Cody suffers from blinding headaches relieved only by the attentions of Ma Jarrett, while one gang member, Big Ed, covets both the gang's leadership and Cody's wife, Verna. Cody confesses to a lesser crime in order to avoid implication in the murder of a railroad man. In prison, he is befriended by Vic Pardo, who is actually Hank Fallon, an undercover police detective. Cody learns that Big Ed and Verna have murdered Ma and he breaks down hysterically in the prison dining hall. With Fallon's help Cody escapes and kills Big Ed, but Verna persuades him that she is innocent of Ma's murder. Cody then plans a payroll robbery, which is frustrated by Fallon and results in the deaths of all of the gang members. Mortally wounded, Cody shoots it out from the top of a huge tank of explosive gas, which finally blows up as he shouts to his dead mother that he is on "top of the world."

White Heat's Cody Jarrett is one of film noir's most crippled and maladjusted protagonists. Nevertheless, on the strength of James Cagney's interpretation of the role and Walsh's direction, Cody is a believable figure whose violent nature and desire for a perverse kind of glory prevent the character from becoming a caricature. In contrast, the ostensible hero of the film, Fallon, has a monotonous and impersonal normality and seems more a betrayer than an agent of justice, especially in view of the psychological methods he uses to gain Cody's trust. *White Heat* is not notable for expressionistic lighting or oppressive doom-laden camera

White Heat: *James Cagney as gangster Cody Janett.*

angles. But it is a film noir, with a visual character appropriate to the cycle. In place of the more common characteristics, Walsh employs arresting moves of the camera, which build tension by virtue of their economy. The introduction of Verna in close-up and the following of her movements as she gets out of bed in this shot as well as the sudden move back from Cody as he has his first headache and slumps to the floor in agony are effective moments of *mise en scène*.

Other shots establish the fatal links between characters, such as the one in which Big Ed and Verna kiss while chewing gum and the camera pans rapidly to Ma observing them from a window. The energy of Walsh's camera style in the prison dining room sequence, which combines high angles and dynamic tracking shots, complements the celebrated playing of this scene by Cagney. The presence of conventional sequences and characters in the law enforcement episodes sets off the darker scenes, which focus on Cody, Verna, Big Ed, and Ma and which are the core of the narrative. The tone of individual scenes is alternately stark, humorous, violent, brooding, and, finally, powerful. Further, while the myth of the heroic outlaw is time-honored, the strategy of inducing the audience to accept a psychotic protagonist as representative of this myth is intuitively modern. In keeping with this approach, Walsh subtly modifies his traditional style without sacrificing it. A tragic grandeur, often elusive in the postwar cinema, is achieved through this style and culminates in Cody's delirious and explosive self-immolation atop a metallic pyre. **BL**

WICKED WOMAN (1953)

Director: Russell Rouse. **Screenplay**: Clarence Greene, Russell Rouse. **Producer**: Clarence Greene (Edward Small Productions). **Director of Photography**: Eddie Fitzgerald. **Music**: Buddy Baker. **Production Designer**: Joseph St. Amand. **Editor**: Chester W. Schaeffer. **Cast**: Beverly Michaels (Billie Nash), Richard Egan (Matt Bannister), Percy Helton (Charlie Borg), Evelyn Scott (Dora Bannister), Robert Osterloh (Larry Lowry), William "Bill" Phipps (Gus), Frank Ferguson (Bill Porter), Bernadene Hayes (Mrs. Walters), Tristram Coffin (Mr. Cutler). **Released**: United Artists, December 9. 77 minutes.

Billie Nash arrives in town with only two small suitcases. Taking a cheap rented room, she uses vague promises of a date to borrow money from her unpleasant neighbor Charlie Borg. Billie talks saloon owner Dora Bannister into a waitress job, and is a success with the patrons. She soon begins an affair with Dora's husband Matt, the bartender. Matt admits that he's lost respect for his wife because of her heavy drinking. Billie urges Matt to sell the bar and run away with her to Mexico. Afraid to lose Billie, Matt has her pose as Dora to sign the bill of sale, discovering only afterwards that they must wait several days for escrow to close. Charlie has eavesdropped on the scheming pair and blackmails Billie into spending her free time with him. Matt becomes suspicious and discovers Billie and Charlie in a compromising clinch. He rejects her and confesses all to Dora. Taking the first bus out of town, Billie immediately attracts another man.

The 1950s saw an upsurge of independent productions exploiting themes avoided by the major studios. The Greene-Rouse creative team had previously made the well received *D.O.A.* and *The Thief* with producer Leo Popkin. Flirting with the production code, *Wicked Woman* confects a sordid pulp fiction tale concerned more with sex than crime. One tracking shot reveals the sultry Billie Nash sprawled in her rented room, neatly evoking the girls on the covers of cheap paperbacks.

Wicked Woman encourages us to ogle its bleached-blonde heroine, an unprincipled "looker" who turns heads and incites trouble. Billie callously uses her neighbor Charlie, but only after he reveals himself as a bothersome sneak. Reckless and impatient, Billie is soon disrupting an already troubled marriage. Wife Dora is too inebriated to realize that Billie is slipping her drinks to keep her out of the way. The handsome Matt turns out to be a moral weakling, committing fraud like a foolish amateur. Dora reclaims control of the wayward Matt, while Billie rages in frustration that her cheap tricks have once again failed. Ironically, Billie's dreams of romance and easy living culminate in a humiliating mauling by the "runt" Charlie, a man who turns her stomach.

With its moralistic framework, *Wicked Woman* has only its convincing depiction of a tawdry life of "rat-hole" hotel rooms and cheap bars to suggest a noir ambience. The TV-scaled and flat-lit production allows little room for suggestive visuals or expressionistic touches. The acting of the statuesque leading lady Beverly Michaels is striking, frequently verging on unintentional self-parody. **GE**

THE WINDOW (1949)

Director: Ted Tetzlaff. **Screenplay**: Mel Dinelli from the novella *The Boy Cried Murder* by Cornell Woolrich. **Producers**: Frederic Ullman Jr., Dore Schary. **Director of Photography**: William Steiner, Robert De Grasse. **Music**: Roy Webb. **Art Directors**: Walter E. Keller, Sam Corso, Albert D'Agostino. **Editor**: Frederic Knudtson. **Cast**: Barbara Hale (Mrs. Woodry), Bobby Driscoll (Tommy), Arthur Kennedy (Mr. Woodry), Paul Stewart (Joe Kellerson), Ruth Roman (Jean Kellerson), Anthony Ross (Ross), Richard Benedict (Drunken Seaman). **Location**: N.Y.C. **Completed**: January 6, 1948. **Released**: RKO, August 6. 73 minutes.

Tommy Woodry often tells innocent lies that embarrass his working-class mother and father. One hot summer night,

The Window: *Bobby Driscoll as Tommy.*

Tommy goes out onto the tenement fire escape to sleep and climbs up one floor to cool off. Through a window he sees the Kellersons robbing and killing a drunken seaman. Tommy runs back to his apartment, but his parents don't believe him. So the next day he sneaks out and tells the police, who send an investigator posing as a building inspector. He finds nothing, but Mrs. Woodry learns that Tommy spoke to the police and forces him to apologize to Mrs. Kellerson. When Mrs. Woodry leaves to care for her sister, Tommy plans to run away but is interrupted by his father who locks Tommy in so he can go to his night job. Joe Kellerson enters the Woodry apartment with a passkey and abducts Tommy. He plans for the boy to die in an "accidental" fall. But Mrs. Kellerson vacillates allowing Tommy to escape to a condemned building next door. When Mr. Woodry returns to find Tommy gone, he alerts the police. The Kellersons pursue Tommy into the derelict building, forcing Tommy to climb out onto a bare rafter. Mr. Kellerson tries to follow but falls to his death. The police arrive and direct Tommy to jump into a safety net. When Tommy tells the police that Mrs. Kellerson and the body of the murdered man are still inside the abandoned building, he is vindicated in the eyes of both the police and his parents.

The Window, one of the most financially successful thrillers of 1949, exploits the ironies of the childhood fear of adults. Director Tetzlaff uses experience gained as the cinematographer of Hitchcock's *Notorious* and benefits from a well constructed script by Mel Dinelli (*Spiral Staircase*) to transpose Woolrich's darkly oppressive vision of N.Y.C. onto the studio settings of *The Window*. The photographers, aided by a well-developed RKO noir style, seamlessly join actual exteriors to studio interiors where cramped quarters and deteriorating buildings authentically capture New York's tenement district. Unlike *The Naked City*, location work here creates an urban landscape that seems almost infernal with its decaying tenement buildings baking in the hot sun while laundry, hanging on clotheslines outside, provides the only glimpse of cleanliness. The neighborhood's disreputable streets are enclosed by the elevated train and parallel the quality of the inhabitants' lives. Such a world represents the inverse of the American dream of freedom, and it is not surprising that when his mother tells him not to go out of the apartment, Tommy replies ingenuously that "There's no place for me to go." In one of life's strange ironies, two children discovered the body of Bobby Driscoll in an abandoned tenement building in 1968, victim of a drug overdose. **BP**

WITHOUT WARNING (1952)

Director: Arnold Laven. **Screenplay**: William Raynor. **Producer**: Arthur Gardner, Jules V. Levy. **Director of Photography**: Joseph Biroc. **Production Designer**: Ted Haworth. **Music**: Herschel B. Gilbert. **Editor**: Arthur H. Nadel. **Cast**: Adam Williams (Carl Martin), Meg Randall (Jane Saunders), Ed Binns (Lt. Pete Hamilton), Harlan Warde (Detective Sgt. Don Warde), John Maxwell (Fred Saunder), Angela Stevens (Blonde), Byron Kane (Police Chemist Wilkins), Connie Vera (Carmelita), Robert Shayne (Dr. Werner). **Released**: United Artists, May 8. 75 minutes.

Carl Martin is a deranged serial killer whose blonde wife ran out on him. To exact revenge on her, he picks up look-alikes in bars and stabs them to death with garden shears. Detectives Hamilton and Warde use blonde undercover policewomen in an attempt to catch the killer, but he does not fall for the bait. Martin is finally undone by forensic evidence left at a crime scene and is captured by the police.

Done in semi-documentary style, *Without Warning* was one of the first noirs to deal with a serial killer, a theme all too common on the screen and in today's newspapers. Although the film suffers in comparison to Stanley Kramer and Edward Dmytryk's *The Sniper*, a film noir with a similar theme released the same year, it is a taut little film with good performances; an understated script; good photography by Joseph Biroc, a veteran of many B films noirs; and tight editing by Arthur Nadel. Presumably for all those reasons, Sol Lesser, who in the early 1940s had been production head at RKO (he broke away to form his own production company, which became best known for cranking out the Tarzan series), acquired an interest in the film and made arrangements with United Artists for its release. **AL**

WITNESS TO MURDER (1954)

Director: Roy Rowland. **Screenplay**: Chester Erskine, [uncredited] Nunnally Johnson. **Producer**: Chester Erskine. **Director of Photography**: John Alton. **Music**: Herschel Burke Gilbert. **Art Director**: William Ferrari. **Editor**: Robert Swink. **Cast**: Barbara Stanwyck (Cheryl Draper), George Sanders (Albert Richter), Gary Merrill (Lt. Lawrence Mathews), Jesse White (Sgt. Eddie Vincent), Harry Shannon (Capt. Donnelly), Claire Carleton (Mae, the Blond), Lewis Martin (Psychiatrist), Dick Elliott (Apartment Manager). **Completed**: December 7, 1953. **Released**: United Artists, April 15. 83 minutes.

While closing her window against the wind Cheryl Draper witnesses a murder: in the apartment directly across the way writer Albert Richter kills his mistress to protect his engagement to a wealthy woman. Richter hides the body in a nearby vacant apartment, so that the police, summoned by

Cheryl, conclude that she was mistaken. Richter visits Cheryl and tampers with her lock, so that he can enter her apartment later to write and mail a series of threatening letters to himself on her typewriter. He then shows them to police as proof that she is mentally disturbed and harassing him. Cheryl is committed for observation and breaks down under the strain. By the time she is released, the victim's body has been discovered in Griffith Park. Once Cheryl figures out how Richter framed her, she confronts him and, since the two are alone, Richter reveals a Nietschean belief that the dead woman's life was insignificant compared to the importance of his future—which, he believes, includes nothing less than the creation of a fourth reich! He plans to forge a suicide note and murder Cheryl, but she escapes. Pursued by Richter, she runs into a building under construction and climbs up onto the wooden scaffolding. The police arrive and in the ensuing scuffle Richter falls to his death. Cheryl, however, is saved by Lt. Mathews seconds before the scaffolding collapses.

When *Witness to Murder* was released in 1954 it was promoted as "topping the thrills of *Double Indemnity* and *Sorry, Wrong Number.*" Although an ably constructed and suspenseful film, *Witness to Murder* is compromised by its position late in the noir cycle, at which time most of its formal devices—an innocent witness to murder, a hysterical victim to whom the city is indifferent, even a woman trapped in a psycho ward—had become stereotyped. Sequences of Cheryl in the mental ward, whether repulsed by the other patients or interviewed by a psychiatrist, include shots from exceedingly high angles where oblique shadows heighten the feeling of delirium and entrapment in a manner reminiscent of *The Snake Pit* and *The Lost Weekend*. As the victimized Cheryl, Barbara Stanwyck effectively constructs what is for her a composite of many past roles. The same is true of George Sanders' performance but the concept of a cryptofascist murdering like Leopold and Loeb was somewhat dated by 1954.

John Alton's photography is, as always, evocative of the noir style, particularly in the opening shot of the hot, nocturnal wind rippling through an awning outside one of those typical West Los Angeles apartments. The use of the wind and the constricted framing add a deterministic undertone as the figure of Cheryl rises and walks to the window to become a witness to murder. Unlike his police dramas, *Scene of the Crime* and *Rogue Cop,* director Rowland does not organize the elements of *Witness to Murder* in such a way as to suggest a surrounding noir milieu of explosive instability. Richter's threat to Cheryl is much more personal and physical than the vague, criminal underworld that thwarts and menaces the characters in those other films. In fact, the central irony of *Witness to Murder* is that Richter is able to recruit the agencies of social stability to persecute the hapless Cheryl. Cheryl's fortuitous survival undercuts to some degree the noir statement of the film and reduces the symbolic value of Richter's character to that of a cliché. **BP & AS**

WOMAN IN HIDING (1950)

Director: Michael Gordon. **Screenplay**: Roy Huggins, Oscar Saul based on the novel by James Webb. **Producer**: Michael Kraike. **Director of Photography**: William Daniels. **Music**: Frank Skinner. **Art Director**: Robert Clatworthy and Bernard Herzbrun. **Editor**: Milton Carruth. **Cast**: Ida Lupino (Deborah Chandler/Anne Clark), Stephen McNally (Selden Clark), Howard Duff (Keith Ramsey), Peggy Dow (Patricia Monahan), John Litel (John Chandler), Taylor Holmes (Lucius Maury), Irv Bacon (Pops Link), Don Beddoe (Drunk Conventioneer), Joe Besser (Conventioneer with drum). **Released**: Universal, February 22. 92 minutes.

Deborah Chandler marries Selden Clark, the manager of her lumber mill, unaware that he has arranged the "accidental" death of her father John in order to gain control of the mill. He has confessed his plans to his mistress, Patricia Monahan, and when Deborah learns of them on her wedding night she escapes their honeymoon cabin in her car. Selden, however, has fixed the brakes but Deborah manages to leap from the car before it falls into the river. She is presumed dead but, with bleached hair and under an assumed name, has gone to Raleigh to locate Patricia who she hopes will back up her story. Seldon, however, is unsure of her death and puts out a $5,000 reward for her. Deborah is befriended by Keith Ramsey, a Korean war vet, but when he sees her picture in the paper he uses a ploy to return her to her husband. Selden tells her he is going to have her committed but when the two are on a train together she hits him over the head and escapes. She is picked up by Keith, who now believes her story, and the two decide to have Deborah get Patricia to back her up. Pat, however, is back with Selden and, under the pretense of helping, manages to get Deborah to the mill at night where Selden has arranged for another "accident" by removing a portion of the guard railing. Pat gets lost in the dark factory and, because she is dressed in an outfit similar to Deborah's, Selden mistakenly pushes her off the landing. Meanwhile, Keith has broken into the factory and gets into a fight with Selden. Believing Deborah to be dead, Selden is frightened by her sudden appearance in the dark and accidentally falls off the landing himself. Deborah and Keith are now free to be married and head for a special place on the California coast that Keith knows of.

Woman In Hiding, true to noir form, opens with the sepulchral voice-over narration of Ida Lupino as we watch the wreck of a car that has plummeted over a bridge in North Carolina: "That's my body they're looking for." And while only the beginning of the action is told from the standpoint

Woman in Hiding: *Keith Ramsey (Howard Duff) and Selden Clark (Stephen McNally).*

of a woman fleeing for her life, it sets the tone for the rest of the film. The mood of this film and the efforts of a superior cast help elevate it from the run-of-the-mill woman-in-distress picture. And the final sequence in the dark factory, a setting whose grotesquerie is enchanced by Daniel's brilliant photography and the unsettling sounds of the whirring machinery, is well worth waiting for. *Woman In Hiding* also anticipates the later *Sudden Fear* in its story of a wife trying to fend off a homicidal husband who has a bad girl on the side. **BMV & BP**

THE WOMAN IN THE WINDOW (1945)

Director: Fritz Lang. **Producer/Screenplay**: Nunnally Johnson from the novel *Once Off Guard* by J. H. Wallis. **Director of Photography**: Milton Krasner. **Music**: Arthur Lange. **Art Director**: Duncan Cramer. **Editors**: Marjorie Johnson, Gene Fowler Jr., Paul Weatherwax. **Cast**: Edward G. Robinson (Richard Wanley), Joan Bennett (Alice Reed), Raymond Massey (Frank Lalor), Edmond Breon (Dr. Barkstane), Dan Duryea (Heidt/the Doorman), Thomas E. Jackson (Inspector Jackson), Arthur Loft (Mazard/Howard/Charlie), Dorothy Peterson (Mrs. Wanley), Frank Dawson (Steward), Carol Cameron (Elsie), Robert Blake (Dickie Wanley). **Completed**: June 3, 1944. **Released**: RKO, January 26. 99 minutes.

On his way home from his club Professor Richard Wanley passes an art gallery with a painting of a beautiful woman in the window and is startled when the model Alice Reed suddenly appears next to him. He sees her home to her apartment, where her boyfriend arrives in a jealous rage and attacks Wanley. Alice hands Wanley a pair of scissors, and he kills the boyfriend. Wanley dumps the body behind a deserted fence in the woods. When the body is discovered, because the police inspector is a close friend, Wanley must listen politely to details of the unsolved murder. Alice tells Wanley that Heidt, the dead man's bodyguard, is blackmailing her. He decides they should turn themselves in. Unable to face the disgrace, Wanley prepares to swallow poison. Heidt is killed in a gun battle with police, who

The Woman in the Window: *Alice Reed (Joan Bennett) and Richard Wanley (Edward G. Robinson)*.

suspect him of the murder. Alice calls to tell Wanley they are saved; but he has apparently taken the poison and cannot hear the phone. When the camera pulls back from Wanley slumped in an armchair, it is revealed that he has fallen asleep at his club and had a nightmare. On his way home, a woman approaches him as he passes the same gallery but he hurries away.

The central motif of *Woman in the Window* is the doppelgänger which implies a good and evil universe. Wanley himself is the key to this double system. On the one hand he is a middle-class family man, sober, responsible, and just a little bored. On the other, Wanley is an impulsive adventurer, whose one flirtation leads to murder and suicide. The clear dividing line is the family, and it is not until Wanley's family leaves town for the summer that his desires and interests as an individual can express themselves. The family from whom Wanley parts at the train station are the epitome of a bourgeois unit: the children are engrossed in their comic books and the husband and wife say farewell without so much as a perfunctory embrace. While Wanley may not be really in full flight from this de-eroticized relationship, he does allow his mind to wander over the possibilities, couching it all in wistful joking and male camaraderie with his friends at the club. He is permitted to imagine and fantasize a sexual identity as long as the object of his dreams remains safely abstracted in a painting. The sudden appearance of the real woman, both in reflection and in the flesh, opens the door to the other world, where desires are gratified instead of repressed.

The inevitability of sordidness, crime, and disaster may seem as unjustified in *Woman in the Window* as it does in Lang's subsequent and parallel film *Scarlet Street*, which also stars Edward G. Robinson, Joan Bennett, and Dan Duryea. In the context of a world at war and of film noir, even the slightest transgression of bourgeois morality may be severely punished, whether the sinner is escaping from a horrible shrewish wife or whether he is an innocent merely daydreaming about adultery. Indeed, Wanley desires to be dis-

covered and punished, while at the same time he struggles desperately to conceal the evidence of his crime. Since its release some commentators have criticized the filmmakers for the "happy" ending in which the fatal narrative is revealed as a dream. Lang himself sometimes defended the ending and at other times disparaged it as a ploy to make the film more fiscally successful. Certainly Lang's credentials as creator of bleak and deterministic stories were well established before he left Germany and reaffirmed powerfully in the fugitive couple drama *You Only Live Once* and would find later evocation in *Scarlet Street*, *Rancho Notorioius*, *The Big Heat*, and *Human Desire*.

From the first, *Woman in the Window* is set up as a dream reflection, a pointed conflict between id and superego of middle-class rectitude. Wanley's lectures and comments—such as the quote from Raymond Chandler's "Simple Art of Murder" that "the streets were dark with something more than night"—are pointedly self-conscious. Alice's appearance outside the painting is a mythic invocation while Wanley links his sexual arousal directly to the phallic murder of Alice's boyfriend. Finally there is dream reversal when he constantly suggests to the district attorney that all the evidence could point to him, an inconsequential little professor, as the arch-villain of this scenario. From his initial lecture on Freud and the criminal mind to his final self-punishment, Wanley's nightmare vision is consistent with an attempt to reconcile his internal emotional conflicts. He scripts, directs, and even set decorates around them as he incorporates scores of mirrors and window reflections throughout the film/dream, reinforcing the Freudian implications of doppelgänger in the characters and situations. Wanley is permitted this glance over the edge of the abyss as a learning experience; and the object of the lesson is demonstrated to be effective when Wanley refuses to give even a match to a passing streetwalker and runs chastened back to his safely circumscribed life. **EM & AS**

WOMAN ON PIER 13
[aka I MARRIED A COMMUNIST] (1949)

Director: Robert Stevenson. **Screenplay**: Charles Grayson and Robert Hardy Andrews. **Producer**: Jack J. Gross. **Executive Producer**: Sid Rogell. **Director of Photography**: Nicholas Musuraca. **Music**: Leigh Harline. **Art Directors**: Albert D'Agostino, Walter Keller. **Editor**: Roland Gross. **Cast**: Laraine Day (Nan Collins), Robert Ryan (Brad Collins), John Agar (Don Lowry), Thomas Gomez (Vanning), Janis Carter (Christine Norman), Richard Rober (Jim Travis), William Talman (Bailey), Harry Cheshire (Mr. Cornwall). **Released**: RKO, October 8. 72 minutes.

Brad Collins, a former stevedore trusted by both bosses and unionists, heads a commission into labor relations on the San Francisco waterfront. Christine Norman, with whom he had an affair when both were members of the Communist Party in the 1930s, fails to win him back to the Party line and he is contacted by Vanning, the local CP leader, who holds compromising documents on his past. Collins is forced to sabotage the discussions, which provokes the incredulity of his friend, an anti-Communist unionist named Travis. Meanwhile Christine has won Collins' young brother-in-law Don over to radical politics but he rejects her when he learns

she is a Communist. Vanning hires a hit-man, Bailey, to kill him and make it seem an accident, then pushes Christine from her top-floor apartment as her love for Don makes her a liability. But she has already told the truth to Nan Collins who decides to use her charms to trap Bailey. Tipped off, he kidnaps her and takes her to Vanning's office in a warehouse on the waterfront. Guessing where she is, Collins shoots it out with Vanning and Bailey. All three men are killed, with Collins dying in Nan's arms.

The first Hollywood movie (with *The Red Menace* the same year) to take the CPUSA as its target, *Woman on Pier 13* is a dishonest but revealing combination of film noir and propaganda. The villains are immediately recognizable. Vanning is fat, sneers and browbeats his interlocutors verbally and physically, Bailey is a gaudily-dressed, slimy womanizer, Christine shifts from nymphomania to melodramatics according to the sex and function of the person she's with, intellectuals have upper-class accents and wear spectacles. Close-ups of Collins have him narrowing his eyes and grimacing to indicate his ambiguities and doubts.

That Reds are really gangsters masquerading as honest citizens was Hollywood's new doxa, enabling studios to smite the enemy and turn out genre movies. But the femme fatale is cold rather than sexy and her well-paid job as fashion editor plus her diamond earrings (insisted on in a huge close-up when she kisses Don!) make her the signifier of well-heeled Hollywood Reds, with a plush apartment standing in for the swimming pool. Less obvious is the implication that Travis is the anti-Communist Hollywood unionist Roy Brewer and that the intellectual at Christine's party represents Hollywood's Reds (blacklisted writers John Howard Lawson and Dalton Trumbo combined, perhaps). Most interesting of all is the fact that the film is obliged to explain why Collins became a Communist—the Depression and unemployment—and, especially, that Travis comes across at the outset as a unionist determined to defend the workers against greedy bosses. Significantly, given the film's basic line that only Reds are anxious to tie up the water-

front, it is he who considers that such a situation is inevitable because of the attitude of the bosses, although his remark about "hot heads on both sides" allows the script to displace all the blame onto Reds: soon Travis is a good anti-Communist.

The film is careful not to present any arguments for either bosses or labor, just in case audiences should still identify with working-class militancy as in 1945-46. The discussions where Don defends such options—much to the embarrassment of Travis and the satisfaction of a CP unionist—are filmed without dialogue, thus enabling the film's makers to hedge their bets the better to influence the audience, just as they have recourse elsewhere to iconography, cliché, innuendo, distortion, and prejudice. The film opened in Los Angeles in October 1949 but only in June 1950 in New York. Was Hollywood unsure of its reception outside of a community committed to blacklisting and propaganda? Was its original title, *I Married a Communist*, too un-commercial? (The anti-Nazi *The Man I Married* had formerly been titled *I Married a Nazi*.) They needn't have worried: McCarthy came to their rescue in February 1950. Smear tactics and the Big Lie became official policy, with Hollywood nominating the vile *I Was a Communist for the FBI* for an Oscar as best documentary (!) in 1951. **RH**

THE WOMAN ON THE BEACH (1947)

Director: Jean Renoir. **Screenplay**: Frank Davis, Jean Renoir, J.R. Michael Hogan from the novel *None So Blind* by Mitchell Wilson. **Producer**: Jack J. Gross. **Director of Photography**: Leo Tover, Harry Wild. **Production Designers**: Albert S. D'Agostino, Walter E. Keller. **Music**: Hanns Eisler. **Editors**: Lyle Boyer, Roland Gross. **Cast**: Joan Bennett (Peggy), Robert Ryan (Scott), Charles Bickford (Tod), Nan Leslie (Eve), Walter Sande (Otto Wernecke), Irene Ryan (Mrs. Wernecke). **Released**: RKO, June 2. 71 minutes.

Scott, a Coast Guard officer, is wracked by nightmares after his traumatic war experience. These dreams are also prophetic of people and events about to enter his life. Awaiting his military discharge so that he can marry Eve, his fiancée, Scott meets the "woman on the beach" he imagined. She is Peggy, the wife of a tormented, blind ex-painter, Tod; the couple live in an isolated, somewhat Gothic seaside

house. Scott and Peggy begin a clandestine relationship, and he begins to believe that she is an abuse victim at her husband's hands. Burnett also suspects that Tod is only feigning his affliction, so he takes the painter out to a dangerous cliff edge, from which he falls and miraculously survives. Determined now to end the affair, Scott tries to repair his relationship with Eve. However, a frantic phone call from Peggy summons him to the site of a catastrophe: Tod has decided to destroy, in a fire, both his art and his house. Peggy rescues her husband; they, like Scott, depart to construct whatever future is possible.

In other directorial hands, *The Woman on the Beach* could have been a familiar, conventional film noir of the 1940s: Bennett as the duplicitous, manipulative femme fatale she played immortally for Fritz Lang in *Scarlet Street* and *The Woman in the Window*; Ryan as the traumatised war hero reaching moral and psychological equilibrium via a purgative act of violence; a suspicious, disapproving light cast upon sinisterly motivated artist-intellectuals; and the decorative presence of elaborately surreal dream sequences filled with portentous symbolism. But, under Renoir's vigilance, everything quickly attains a more mysterious state of ambiguity and complexity. He spoke of the film as being based on "purely physical attractions," but the subterranean psychological intrigue is intense and knotty: guilt, emotional sado-masochism, passive-aggressive relations, a pointed reversal of gender roles (feminized men and masculinized women), and erotic perversity form the paradoxical basis for the film's strange and haunting lyricism. Perhaps, as André Bazin once suggested, the film is poetic precisely because the psychology is not truly individualized: its sensuality "goes from one character to another like a mysterious ball of fire," and the atmosphere of the dream sequences more than spills over into the story's real world. The film is also remarkable, for today's viewers, for the subtle way it evokes and probes the legacy of war trauma in Scott's character—and, by extension, in an entire social fabric convulsing with a symptomatic hysteria, its once-held certainties (especially in the sphere of intimate life) swiftly unravelling.

The Woman on the Beach can be fruitfully approached as an opportune, risky melding of genres, similar in this respect to *The Secret Beyond the Door*: it has the oneiric atmosphere of a Val Lewton supernatural mystery (Lewton was originally to be its producer); the emotional sophistication of a European melodrama; and the scattered, rather pulverized plot elements of a noir thriller. But it was not conceived so schematically: Renoir declared that he had "never shot a film with so little written scenario and so much improvisation," and the disastrous preview of the first cut led to reshoots and drastic shortening of the running time. However, what might have seemed at the time as a missed opportunity for Renoir, today looks exceptionally potent, and has received a welcome re-evaluation by such contemporary scholars as Janet Bergstrom: in its intense brevity and its mysterious ellipses, in the disarming simplicity and directness of its *mise en scène*, *The Woman on the Beach* indeed achieves the psychic condensation of a feverish dream, and registers, as Bazin speculated, as a "very personal" work of its director. **AM**

A FIDELITY PICTURES PRODUCTION · A UNIVERSAL INTERNATIONAL RELEASE

WOMAN ON THE RUN (1950)

Director: Norman Foster. **Screenplay**: Alan Campbell and Norman Foster from a magazine story by Sylvia Tate. **Producer**. Howard Welsch (Fidelity Pictures). **Director of Photography**: Hal Mohr. **Music**: Emil Newman, Arthur Lange. **Art Director**: Boris Leven. **Editor**: Otto Ludwig. **Cast**: Ann Sheridan (Eleanor Johnson), Dennis O'Keefe (Danny Leggett), Robert Keith (Inspector Ferris), Frank Jenks (Detective Shaw), Ross Elliott (Frank Johnson), John Qualen (Mailbus), J. Farrell McDonald (Sea Captain), Thomas P. Dillon (Joe Gordon). **Location**: San Francisco. **Completed**: August 1, 1950. **Released**: Universal, November 29. 77 minutes.

When failed artist Frank Johnson innocently witnesses a murder while walking his dog at night, he hides out of fear that the murderer will try to kill him too. Police Inspector Ferris asks Johnson's wife Eleanor to help find him. Her marriage to Frank is shaky and she resists helping the police but once she realizes the extent of Frank's danger she decides to try and locate him on her own. She is aided in this effort by tabloid reporter Danny Leggett, who promises to give Frank $1,000 to blow town if Frank gives him an exclusive. Eleanor agrees and they set out to find Frank from a cryptic clue in a letter he sent her via the department store where Frank worked as a window dresser. This takes the two on a San Francisco tour where they manage to stay a few steps ahead of the police. It culminates in a nighttime rendevous with Frank at a waterfront amusement park. Leggett persuades Eleanor to join him on the roller-coaster to avoid their police trail and to remain on the coaster while he meets Frank alone underneath the ride's scaffolding. But a casual remark tips Eleanor off to the fact that Leggett is the killer. Stuck on the coaster, she attempts to yell down to warn her hapless husband but her screams are lost amidst those of the other riders and the screeches of the arcade's giant mannequin. Aware of Frank's cardiac condition, Leggett attempts to initiate a heart attack by pummeling him but Inspector Ferris, acting on a tip, arrives in time to shoot and kill Leggett before he succeeds. With Leggett lying face down in the water, Frank and Eleanor find each other's arms amidst the cacophony of the arcade and the ongoing squeals of the mannequin.

Woman on the Run was directed and co-written by Norman Foster, long-time member of Welles' Mercury Theater, and someone sufficiently infused with Wellesian pyrotechnics to co-direct *Journey Into Fear* and, later, direct *Kiss the Blood Off My Hands*. He and photographer Mohr do a nice job exploiting the San Francisco locales (though not quite up to par with those in *Sudden Fear*), hitting their stride in the final segment where they capitalize on the grotesqueries and noise of the amusement park to heighten tension. Tension is further heightened by the fact that the audience is let on to the identity of the killer long before the other characters (when Leggett tells Eleanor that his nickname is "Danny Boy," the appellation used by the victim addressing the faceless killer in the opening sequence).

Surprisingly, this film has some of the best dialogue in the noir cycle outside of *Double Indemnity*. Ann Sheridan, an actress whose roles never failed to capitalize on her ability to deliver a sarcastic remark, is allowed here to skewer anyone who comes within her range. Her repartee with Dennis O'Keefe (a noir icon known for his fast-paced delivery) especially sparkles, as Leggett, increasingly smitten with Eleanor, fends off her best with aplomb. Actually, *Woman on the Run* is one of those forgotten noirs that deserves lengthier treatment than can be afforded here. Suffice it to say that it touches upon many forward-looking issues (e.g., the role of communication in marital estrangement) and creates a quite complex iconic structure (e.g. the "severe" mannequin Frank creates resembling his wife vs. the grotesque giant mannequin in the arcade). Perhaps the best moment in the film is when Leggett shows Eleanor the dark, remote spot under the scaffolding where he is to meet with Frank, informing her that this was where he used to take a young lady for a romantic tryst when he was a youngster. When she retorts that the place is more frightening than romantic, he counters: "That's the way love is when you're young and life is when you're older." Welcome to the noir world! **BP**

WORLD FOR RANSOM (1954)

Director: Robert Aldrich. **Producers**: Aldrich, Bernard Tabakin. **Screenplay**: Lindsay Hardy and [uncredited] Hugo Butler. **Director of Photography**: Joseph Biroc. **Music**: Frank DeVol. **Art Director**: William Glasgow. **Editor**: Michael Luciano. **Cast**: Dan Duryea (Mike Callahan), Gene Lockhart (Alexis Pederas), Patric Knowles (Julian March), Reginald Denny (Major Bone), Nigel Bruce (Governor Coutts), Marian Carr (Frennessey March), Douglas Dumbrille (Inspector McCollum), Keye Luke (Wong), Clarence Lung (Chan), Lou Nova (Guzik), Arthur Shields (Sean O'Connor). **Completed**: September 1, 1953. **Released**: Allied Artists, January 27. 82 minutes.

Mike Callahan is a war veteran working as a private investigator in Singapore. When he visits his sometime lover Frennessey, she confides that her husband Julian may be engaged in some illegal activities and asks Callahan to disentangle him. Black marketeer Alexis Pederas kidnaps nuclear physicist Sean O'Connor and sends a message to authorities that he is offering the scientist to the highest bidder, whether Russian, Chinese, or Western. An informant of Callahan's implicates March, who alerts Pederas. He has the man killed and incriminating material planted in Callahan's room. Forced to escape from the police,

World for Ransom: *Frennessey March (Marian Carr) and Mike Callahan (Dan Duryea).*

Callahan stays at Frennessey's and plans to visit a deserted jungle village where O'Connor may be hidden. Major Bone of British Intelligence spots Callahan and decides to follow at a distance. In a confrontation with March in a bunker, Callahan uses two grenades to kill the kidnappers and then frees O'Connor. Callahan returns to Frennessey who rejects him violently and explains that her platonic relatiohship with March was because men are physically repellent to her. Callahan leaves and returns to the streets of Singapore.

"You shouldn't play Galahad. You're way out of character." By saying that the detective is not Galahad, March ironically confirms that Callahan is precisely the Galahad type—the disillusioned idealist turned hardboiled hero. This portrait of Callahan is additionally colored by the element of locale: "Singapore" stenciled over the first black-and-white frame triggers associations with mystery and exoticism, with opium rings and knife-wielding assassins bringing sudden death. From this typical film noir background of sleazy bars and wet, shiny streets, the thin, white-suited figure of Mike Callahan detaches itself. The opening conflict contained within this first sequence and first frame is a profoundly archetypal one: East (milieu) versus West (hero), Galahad (white-suited purity) versus the forces of darkness (the shadowy, low-key aspect of the city).

Like most heroes of noir fiction, Callahan is caught in a struggle to survive, which for director Robert Aldrich motivates an expressive exploration of the confining structures that entrap Callahan. As with many noir in the 1950s, such an exploration reveals an underlying determinism. From the establishing long shot of the street banked with flashing neon the cut-in is to a medium close shot of the woman Mai Ling selling fortunes. The tout is to "take a chance"; but the talk of inherited luck, of a hereditary fate, seems to contradict the notion of chance. The ambiguity of the fortune teller's line is really a formula of words chosen for their come-on value and uttered by rote. The audience can appreciate, after these introductory shots, that the preoccupied Callahan must and will "take a chance"; but their understanding of Callahan's position remains nonspecific. They sense that some conflict is present but do not know the details. A clarifying medium shot follows, isolating Callahan against a dark building as he turns up an alleyway. Visually, the conflict has now been fully stated: high angle of the entire street (milieu), emergence of a figure from a background (hero), and finally situation of the hero in graphic opposition to milieu. As Callahan moves up the alley, goes through a doorway, and starts up a flight of stairs, the camera as if under the power of a predestined pull travels in behind him. As the angle narrows, the wedges of light on each side of the doorway disappear from the frame. The blank diagonal walls siding the stairwell focus the converging lines of perspective on a corridor at the top of the stairs. A figure steps out into the vanishing point. For a moment, the perspectives of Callahan and the viewer merge as they share the sudden perception of a dark form at the top of the steps. A reverse angle looking down at Callahan reveals another figure blocking the doorway to the alley. A trap has, literally, closed on him, a trap that the components of the shot imply hold him in its grasp halfway between top and bottom, between polarities.

Callahan is, of course, within the traditional noir conception of the private eye. The character's mocking self-appraisal ("Mike Callahan . . . [shaking his head] . . . Private Eye") or insistent idealization of Frennessey March, the woman who rejects him ("You were the only one that was way out there on that hill . . . the only one that was straight from beginning to end"), are not without irony or precedent and anticipate the position of neo-noir anachronisms in *Hickey & Boggs* or *The Long Goodbye*. What most gives dimension to Callahan as a classic period noir figure are the scenes with Frennessey. The sequence-shot encounter between them on the eve of the pursuit and combat in the jungle provides the best illustration of this effect. A low angle captures Callahan reclining on a divan with a small table fan behind to his right in frame center—a possible extension of an earlier fan motif, which can serve as metaphor for turmoil at the emotional center of the film itself. Frennessey is again "frenetic," walking nervously back and forth on the left, an action that continues as they discuss the coming day's endeavors. As she tries to bring Callahan around to her way of thinking, the camera cranes up, coming in close behind her and tilting down at him, visually underscoring her attempt to assume a dominant position. The scene ends in much the same way as the earlier sequence in her dressing room: Callahan stands up and the pent-up energy of the sustained take is concentrated into a close two-shot. With Frennessey's preeminence of the shot reduced and Callahan's delivery of the line about her being "Way up there on that hill," the viewer may expect the tension built up in the staging to be released in a kiss; and it is.

The dissolve from this moment to the jungle exterior is not just a time-lapse short hand for physical consummation of their attraction but also a final, possibly fatal enmeshment of the protagonist seen in visual overlay. The ultimate noir statement of *World for Ransom* derives from the narrative revelation that Frennessey has indeed been lying. Callahan survives the real world, specifically the combat in the jungle, by physically defeating March and his associates, but that fails to insulate him against emotional destruction when he is cursed and viciously slapped by

Frennessey. How well he survives is an unanswered question, tinged with fallen idealism. All that Callahan is offered by way of consolation are a repetition of Mai Ling's words: "Take a chance, Mr. Callahan. Love is a white bird; yet you cannot buy her." **AS**

THE WRONG MAN (1956)

Director/Producer: Alfred Hitchcock. **Screenplay**: Maxwell Anderson and Angus MacPhail from "The True Story of Christopher Emmanuel Balestrero" by Maxwell Anderson. **Director of Photography**: Robert Burks. **Music**: Bernard Herrmann. **Art Directors**: Paul Sylbert, William L Kuehl. **Editor**: George Tomasini. **Cast**: Henry Fonda (Manny Balestrero), Vera Miles (Rose Balestrero), Anthony Quayle (O'Connor), Harold J. Stone (Lt. Bowers), Esther Minciotti (Manny's Mother), Charles Cooper (Detective Matthews), Nehemiah Persoff (Gene Conforti), Laurinda Barrett (Constance Willis), Norma Connolly (Betty Todd). **Completed**: June 8, 1956. **Released**: Warner Bros., December 23. 105 minutes.

Christopher Emmanuel Balestrero, a New York bass player, works nights at the Stork Club and comes home to his wife Rose and family in the early morning. Manny, as he is called, goes to turn in his wife's insurance policy for extra money and is wrongly recognized as a holdup man by one of the cashiers. Returning home, he is picked up by detectives who take him in for questioning and ask him to write a note like that used by the holdup man. The anxious Manny accidentally misspells a word in the same way as the note and soon, identified by employees of the insurance company, he is

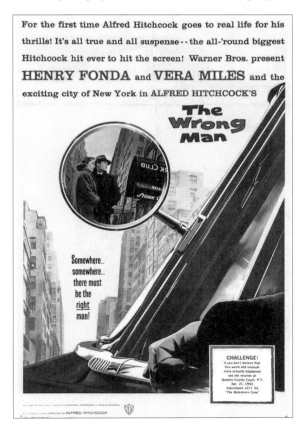

Warner Bros. Presents **HENRY FONDA** and **VERA MILES** in ALFRED HITCHCOCK'S **The Wrong Man**

spending the night in jail. In the morning, he is freed on bail and retains a lawyer, O'Connor, who believes in his innocence. Manny and Rose attempt to establish his alibi; but they find that the witnesses are either missing or dead. Rose has a nervous breakdown and is placed in a mental hospital. The saddened Manny proceeds to trial; but a mistrial is declared, and he is faced with the prospect of going through the entire process again. The actual criminal attempts another robbery but is subdued by his would-be victims. One of the detectives who arrested Manny notices the resemblance, and Manny is cleared.

Other directors make noir films that are often highly individualized manifestations of personal feelings, but Alfred Hitchcock, whose work is diverse in range and tone, makes films that seem as if they would exist independently of the traditions offered by any genre. His technique, remaining supple over the years, is simply a refinement of classical practices employed with unceasing resourcefulness. *The Wrong Man* betrays no cynicism and makes no recourse to facile melodramatics. This film's story of the near destruction of a man through a merciless quirk of fate, which becomes the actual destruction of his more fragile wife, describes a cruel and uncaring universe. Here the characters do not choose to suffer like the crippled beings of other films in the noir cycle but are enmeshed against their will and because their limitations are turned against them by the caprices of circumstance. The quiet Manny journeys through his modern hell with a childlike awe, and this same innocence prevents him from ever knowing the inner hell of his wife who suffers a nervous breakdown as a result of this ironic twist of fate.

Hitchcock's presentation uses subjective techniques for Manny; and the audience is encouraged to be disturbed as each shot darkens his nightmare. But the camera does not encourage identification with Rose, and the audience is as surprised as Manny is when he learns that as a result of psychological transference, his wife has wrongly assumed the burden of his guilt. Hitchcock's choices when determining the nature of each shot, visual and psychological, result in the possibility of feeling genuine compassion. He makes the film appear detached and restrained, even while touching the audience's fears, until the final subdued meeting of the broken-hearted Manny and the disturbed Rose, which brings forth the feeling of catharsis that Hitchcock has held in suspense. **BL**

APPENDIX

◇

Chronology of Classic Period Film Noir

1940

City for Conquest (Warner Bros.)

The Stranger on the Third Floor (RKO)

1941

Among the Living (Paramount)

High Sierra (Warner Bros.)

Maltese Falcon (Warner Bros.)

The Shanghai Gesture (United Artists)

1942

The Glass Key (Paramount)

I Wake Up Screaming (20th Century-Fox)

Johnny Eager (MGM)

Street of Chance (Paramount)

This Gun for Hire (Paramount)

1943

Calling Dr. Death (Universal)

The Fallen Sparrow (RKO)

Journey into Fear (RKO)

Night without Sleep (20th Century-Fox)

The Ox-Bow Incident (20th Century-Fox)

Shadow of a Doubt (Universal)

Whispering Footsteps (Republic)

1944

Bluebeard (PRC)

Christmas Holiday (Universal)

Dangerous Passage (Paramount)

Double Indemnity (Paramount)

Gambling House (RKO)

Guest in the House (United Artists)

Laura (20th Century-Fox)

The Lodger (20th Century-Fox)

The Mask of Dimitrios (Warner Bros.)

Murder, My Sweet (RKO)

Phantom Lady (Universal)

The Suspect (Universal)

A Voice in the Wind (United Artists)

When Strangers Marry (Monogram)

1945

Apology for Murder (PRC)

Bewitched (MGM)

Conflict (Warner Bros.)

Cornered (RKO)

Danger Signal (Warner Bros.)

Detour (PRC)

Escape in the Fog (Columbia)

The Glass Wall (Columbia)

Hangover Square (20th Century-Fox)

House on 92nd Street (20th Century-Fox)

Johnny Angel (RKO)

The Lady Confesses (PRC)

Lady on a Train (Universal)

Leave Her to Heaven (20th Century-Fox)

Mildred Pierce (Warner Bros.)

Ministry of Fear (Paramount)

My Name Is Julia Ross (Columbia)

Scarlet Street (Universal)

Spellbound (United Artists)

The Spiral Staircase (RKO)

The Strange Affair of Uncle Harry [aka *Uncle Harry*] (Universal)

Strange Illusion (PRC)

Two O'Clock Courage (RKO)

The Woman in the Window (RKO)

1946

The Big Sleep (Warner Bros.)

Black Angel (Universal)

The Blue Dahlia (Paramount)

The Chase (United Artists)

Crack-Up (RKO)

The Dark Corner (20th Century-Fox)

The Dark Mirror (Universal)

Deadline at Dawn (RKO)

Decoy (Monogram)

Duel in the Sun (Selznick Releasing)

Fallen Angel (20th Century-Fox)

Fear (Monogram)

Gilda (Columbia)

The Killers (Universal)

Mysterious Intruder (Columbia)

Night Editor (Columbia)

Nobody Lives Forever (Warner Bros.)

Nocturne (RKO)

Notorious (RKO)

The Postman Always Rings Twice (MGM)

Shock (20th Century-Fox)

So Dark the Night (Columbia)

Somewhere in the Night (20th Century-Fox)

Strange Impersonation (Republic)

The Strange Love of Martha Ivers (Paramount)

The Strange Woman (United Artists)

The Stranger (RKO)

Suspense (Monogram)

They Made Me a Killer (Metropolis)

Undercurrent (MGM)

The Verdict (Warner Bros.)

Whistle Stop (United Artists)

1947

Backlash (20th Century-Fox)

Blackmail (Republic)

Blind Spot (Columbia)

Body and Soul (United Artists)

Born to Kill (RKO)

The Brasher Doubloon (20th Century-Fox)

Brute Force (Universal)

Calcutta (Paramount)

Crossfire (RKO)

Dark Passage (Warner Bros.)

Dead Reckoning (Columbia)

Desperate (RKO)

The Devil Thumbs a Ride (RKO)

Fall Guy (Monogram)

Fear (Monogram)

Fear in the Night (Paramount)

Framed (Columbia)

The Gangster (Allied Artists)

The Guilty (Monogram)

High Tide (Monogram)

The High Wall (MGM)

Impact (United Artists)

Ivy (Universal)

Johnny O'Clock (Columbia)

Kiss of Death (20th Century-Fox)

Lady in the Lake (MGM)

The Locket (RKO)

The Long Night (RKO)

The Man I Love (Warner Bros.)

Moss Rose (20th Century-Fox)

Nightmare Alley (20th Century-Fox)

Nora Prentiss (Warner Bros.)

Out of the Past (RKO)

Possessed (Warner Bros.)

The Pretender (Republic)

Pursued (Warner Bros.)

Railroaded (PRC)

Ramrod (United Artists)

Ride the Pink Horse (Universal)

The Red House (Thalia)

Repeat Performance (Eagle-Lion)

Shoot to Kill (Lippert)

Singapore (Universal)

They Won't Believe Me (RKO)

The Two Mrs. Carrolls (Warner Bros.)

The Unfaithful (Warner Bros.)

The Unsuspected (Warner Bros.)

Whispering City (Eagle-Lion)

The Woman on the Beach (RKO)

1948

Behind Locked Doors (Eagle-Lion)

Berlin Express (RKO)

The Big Clock (Paramount)

Blonde Ice (Film Classics)

Blood on the Moon (RKO)

Bodyguard (RKO)

Call Northside 777 (20th Century-Fox)

Canon City (Eagle-Lion)

Cry of the City (20th Century-Fox)

The Dark Past (Columbia)

A Double Life (Universal)

Force of Evil (MGM)

Hollow Triumph (Eagle-Lion)

The Hunted (Allied Artists)

I Walk Alone (Paramount)

I Wouldn't Be in Your Shoes (Monogram)

Inner Sanctum (Film Classics)

Key Largo (Warner Bros.)

Kiss the Blood Off My Hands (Universal)

The Lady from Shanghai (Columbia)

The Naked City (Mark Hellinger)

Night Has a Thousand Eyes (Paramount)

The Pitfall (United Artists)

Raw Deal (Eagle-Lion)

Return of the Whistler (Columbia)

Road House (20th Century-Fox)

Secret Beyond the Door (Universal)

Sleep, My Love (United Artists)

So Evil My Love (Paramount)

Sorry, Wrong Number (Paramount)

The Street with No Name (20th Century-Fox)

They Live By Night (RKO)

T-Men (Eagle-Lion)

1949

Abandoned (Universal)

The Accused (Paramount)

Act of Violence (MGM)

Beyond the Forest (Warner Bros.)

The Big Steal (RKO)

Border Incident (MGM)

The Bribe (MGM)

Caught (MGM-Enterprise)

Champion (United Artists)

Chicago Deadline (Paramount)

Criss Cross (Universal)

The Crooked Way (United Artists)

Follow Me Quietly (RKO)

He Walked by Night (Paramount)

House of Strangers (20th Century-Fox)

I Shot Jesse James (Film Classics)

Johnny Stool Pigeon (Universal)

Knock on Any Door (Columbia)

Manhandled (Paramount)

Moonrise (Republic)

Port of New York (Eagle-Lion)

The Reckless Moment (Columbia)

Reign of Terror [aka *The Black Book*] (Eagle-Lion)

Scene of the Crime (MGM)

The Set-Up (RKO)

Shockproof (Columbia)

Thieves' Highway (20th Century-Fox)

Too Late for Tears (United Artists)

The Threat (RKO)

Trapped (Eagle-Lion)

The Undercover Man (Columbia)

Undertow (Universal)

Whirlpool (20th Century-Fox)

White Heat (Warner Bros.)

The Window (RKO)

Woman on Pier 13 (RKO)

1950

Armored Car Robbery (RKO)

The Asphalt Jungle (MGM)

Backfire (Warner Bros.)

Between Midnight and Dawn (Columbia)

The Breaking Point (Warner Bros.)

Caged (Warner Bros.)

The Clay Pigeon (RKO)

Convicted (Columbia)

D.O.A. (United Artists)

The Damned Don't Cry (Warner Bros.)

Dark City (Paramount)

The Day the Earth Stood Still (20th Century-Fox)

Destination Murder (RKO)

Devil's Doorway (MGM)

Edge of Doom (RKO)

The File on Thelma Jordon (Paramount)

Guilty Bystander (Film Classics)

Gun Crazy (United Artists)

In a Lonely Place (Columbia)

Kiss Tomorrow Goodbye (Warner Bros.)

A Lady without Passport (MGM)

Mystery Street (MGM)

Night and the City (20th Century-Fox)

No Man of her Own (Paramount)

One Way Street (Universal)

Panic in the Streets (20th Century-Fox)

Quicksand (United Artists)

The Secret Fury (RKO)

711 Ocean Drive (Columbia)

Shakedown (Universal)

Side Street (MGM)

The Sleeping City (Universal)

Southside 1-1000 (Allied Artists)

Sunset Boulevard (Paramount)

The Tattooed Stranger (RKO)

Tension (MGM)

This Side of the Law (Warner Bros.)

Try and Get me (United Artists)

The Underworld Story (United Artists)

Union Station (Paramount)

Walk Softly, Stranger (RKO)

Where Danger Lives (RKO)

Where the Sidewalk Ends (20th Century-Fox)

Woman in Hiding (Universal)

Woman on the Run (Universal)

1951

Appointment with Danger (Paramount)

Ace in the Hole [aka *The Big Carnival*] (Paramount)

The Big Night (United Artists)'

Cause for Alarm (MGM)

Cry Danger (RKO)

Detective Story (Paramount)

The Enforcer (Warner Bros.)

Gambling House (RKO)

He Ran All the Way (United Artists)

His Kind of Woman (RKO)

The Hollywood Story (Universal)

House on Telegraph Hill (20th Century-Fox)

I Was a Communist for the F.B.I. (Warner Bros.)

The Killer That Stalked New York (Columbia)

M (Columbia)

The Man Who Cheated Himself (20th Century-Fox)

Man with My Face (United Artists)

The Mob (Columbia)

No Questions Asked (MGM)

The People Against O'Hara (MGM)

Pickup (Columbia)

A Place in the Sun (Paramount)

The Prowler (United Artists)

The Racket (RKO)

The Raging Tide (Universal)

Rawhide (20th Century-Fox)

Red Light (United Artists)

Roadblock (RKO)

The Second Woman (United Artists)

The Scarf (United Artists)

Strangers on a Train (Warner Bros.)

The Strip (MGM)

The 13th Letter (20th Century-Fox)

Tomorrow is Another Day (Warner Bros.)

Under the Gun (Universal)

The Unknown Man (MGM)

1952

Affair in Trinidad (Columbia)

Beware, My Lovely (RKO)

The Captive City (United Artists)

Clash by Night (RKO)

Hoodlum Empire (Republic)

Kansas City Confidential (United Artists)

The Las Vegas Story (RKO)

Loan Shark (Lippert)

Macao (RKO)

The Narrow Margin (RKO)

On Dangerous Ground (RKO)

Rancho Notorious (RKO)

Scandal Sheet (Columbia)

The Sniper (Columbia)

Strange Fascination (Columbia)

Sudden Fear (RKO)

Talk About a Stranger (MGM)

The Thief (United Artists)

The Turning Point (Paramount)

Without Warning (United Artists)

1953

Angel Face (RKO)

The Big Heat (Columbia)

The Bigamist (Filmakers Releasing)

The Blue Gardenia (Warner Bros.)

The City That Never Sleeps (Republic)

Cry of the Hunted (MGM)

The Hitch-Hiker (RKO)

I Confess (Warner Bros.)

I, the Jury (United Artists)

Invaders from Mars (20th Century-Fox)

Jeopardy (MGM)

Man in the Attic (20th Century-Fox)

Man in the Dark (Columbia)

The Naked Spur (MGM)

Niagara (20th Century-Fox)

99 River Street (United Artists)

Pickup on South Street (20th Century-Fox)

Second Chance (RKO)

Split Second (RKO)

Terror Street (Lippert)

Vicki (20th Century-Fox)

Wicked Woman (United Artists)

1954

Crime Wave (Warner Bros.)

Cry Vengeance (Allied Artists)

Drive a Crooked Road (Columbia)

Hell's Half Acre (Republic)

Highway Dragnet (Allied Artists)

Human Desire (Columbia)

Johnny Guitar (Republic)

The Long Wait (United Artists)

Loophole (Allied Artists)

Make Haste to Live (Republic)

Naked Alibi (Universal)

The Other Woman (20th Century-Fox)

Private Hell 36 (Filmakers)

Pushover (Columbia)

Riot in Cell Block 11 (Allied Artists)

Rogue Cop (MGM)

Shield for Murder (United Artists)

Suddenly (United Artists)

Them! (Warner Bros.)

Witness to Murder (United Artists)

World for Ransom (Allied Artists)

1955

The Big Combo (Allied Artists)

The Big Knife (United Artists)

The Brothers Rico (Columbia)

The Desperate Hours (Paramount)

Female Jungle (Kaiser)

Hell's Island (Paramount)

House of Bamboo (20th Century-Fox)

I Died a Thousand Times (Warner Bros.)

Illegal (Warner Bros.)

Killer's Kiss (United Artists)

Kiss Me Deadly (United Artists)

Mr. Arkadin (M & A/Alexander)

Murder Is My Beat (Allied Artists)

New York Confidential (Warner Bros.)

Night of the Hunter (United Artists)

The Night Holds Terror (Columbia)

The Phenix City Story (Allied Artists)

1956

Beyond a Reasonable Doubt (RKO)

A Cry in the Night (Warner Bros.)

The Harder They Fall (Columbia)

Invasion of the Body Snatchers (Allied Artists)

The Killer Is Loose (United Artists)

The Killing (United Artists)

A Kiss Before Dying (United Artists)

Nightmare (United Artists)

Please Murder Me (DCA)

Slightly Scarlet (RKO)

Storm Fear (United Artists)

Timetable (United Artists)

While the City Sleeps (RKO)

The Wrong Man (Warner Bros.)

1957

Affair in Havana (Allied Artists)

The Brothers Rico (Columbia)

The Burglar (Columbia)

Crime of Passion (United Artists)

The Garment Jungle (Columbia)

Hit and Run (United Artists)

The Hollywood Story (Universal)

The Night Runner (Universal)

Nightfall (Columbia)

Plunder Road (20th Century-Fox)

Short Cut to Hell
(Paramount)
Sweet Smell of Success
(United Artists)
The Tattered Dress
(Universal)

1958
The Lineup (Columbia)

Murder by Contract
(Columbia)
Party Girl (MGM)
Screaming Mimi (Columbia)
Touch of Evil (Universal)
Vertigo (Paramount)

1959
The Beat Generation
(MGM)

City of Fear (Columbia)
The Crimson Kimono
(Columbia)
Odds Against Tomorrow
(United Artists)

1960
Five Minutes to Live [aka
Door-to-Door Maniac]
(Sutton/AIP)

Key Witness (MGM)

1961
Blast of Silence (Universal)
Underworld U.S.A.
(Columbia)

1962
Cape Fear (Universal)

Experiment in Terror
(Columbia)

1963
Johnny Cool (United
Artists)

1964
The Naked Kiss (Allied
Artists)

Classic Period Film Noir by Studio
(two or more releases)

Allied Artists
Affair in Havana (1957)
The Big Combo (1955)
Cry Vengeance (1954)
The Gangster (1947)
Highway Dragnet (1954)
The Hunted (1948)
*Invasion of the Body
Snatchers* (1956)
Loophole (1954)
Murder Is My Beat (1955)
The Naked Kiss (1964)
The Phenix City Story
(1955)
Riot in Cell Block 11 (1954)
Southside 1-1000 (1950)
World for Ransom (1954)

Columbia
Affair in Trinidad (1952)
*Between Midnight and
Dawn* (1950)
The Big Heat (1953)
Blind Spot (1947)
The Brothers Rico (1955)
The Burglar (1957)
City of Fear (1959)
Convicted (1950)
The Crimson Kimono
(1959)
The Dark Past (1948)
Dead Reckoning (1947)
Drive a Crooked Road
(1954)
Escape in the Fog (1945)
Experiment in Terror
(1962)
Framed (1947)
The Garment Jungle (1957)
Gilda (1946)
The Glass Wall (1953)
The Harder They Fall (1956)
Human Desire (1954)
In a Lonely Place (1950)
Johnny O'Clock (1946)
*The Killer That Stalked New
York* (1951)
Knock on Any Door (1949)

The Lady from Shanghai
(1948)
The Line-Up (1958)
M (1952)
Man in the Dark (1953)
The Mob (1951)
My Name Is Julia Ross
(1945)
Murder by Contract (1958)
Mysterious Intruder (1946)
Night Editor (1946)
The Night Holds Terror
(1955)
Nightfall (1957)
Pickup (1951)
Pushover (1954)
The Reckless Moment (1949)
Return of the Whistler
(1948)
Scandal Sheet (1952)
Screaming Mimi (1958)
711 Ocean Drive (1950)
Shockproof (1949)
The Sniper (1952)
So Dark the Night (1956)
Strange Fascination (1952)
The Undercover Man (1949)
Underworld U.S.A. (1961)

Eagle-Lion
Behind Locked Doors (1948)
Canon City (1948)
Hollow Triumph (1948)
Port of New York (1949)
Raw Deal (1948)
Reign of Terror [aka *The
Black Book*] (1949)
Repeat Performance (1947)
T-Men (1948)
Trapped (1949)
Whispering City (1947)

Film Classics
Blonde Ice (1948)
Guilty Bystander (1950)
I Shot Jesse James (1949)
Inner Sanctum (1948)

Lippert
Loan Shark (1952)
Shoot to Kill (1947)
Terror Street (1953)

**Metro-Goldwyn-Mayer
[MGM]**
Act of Violence (1949)
The Asphalt Jungle (1950)
The Beat Generation (1959)
Bewitched (1945)
Border Incident (1949)
The Bribe (1949)
Caught (1949)
Cause for Alarm (1951)
Cry of the Hunted (1953)
Devil's Doorway (1950)
Force of Evil (1948)
Gaslight (1944)
The High Wall (1947)
House of Numbers (1957)
Jeopardy (1953)
Johnny Eager (1942)
Key Witness (1960)
Lady in the Lake (1947)
A Lady without Passport
(1950)
Mystery Street (1950)
The Naked Spur (1953)
No Questions Asked (1951)
Party Girl (1958)
The People Against O'Hara
(1951)
Rogue Cop (1954)
Scene of the Crime (1949)
Side Street (1949)
The Strip (1951)
Talk About a Stranger (1952)
Tension (1950)
The Undercover Man (1951)
Undercurrent (1946)
The Unknown Man (1951)

Monogram
Decoy (1946)
Fall Guy (1947)
Fear (1946)

The Guilty (1947)
High Tide (1947)
I Wouldn't Be in Your Shoes
(1948)
Suspense (1946)
When Strangers Marry
(1944)

Paramount
The Accused (1949)
Among the Living (1941)
Appointment with Danger
(1951)
The Big Carnival (1951)
The Big Clock (1948)
The Blue Dahlia (1946)
Calcutta (1947)
Chicago Deadline (1949)
Dangerous Passage (1944)
Dark City (1950)
The Desperate Hours (1955)
Detective Story (1951)
Double Indemnity (1944)
Fear in the Night (1947)
The File on Thelma Jordon
(1950)
The Glass Key (1942)
He Walked by Night (1949)
Hell's Island (1955)
I Walk Alone (1948)
Manhandled (1949)
Ministry of Fear (1945)
Night Has a Thousand Eyes
(1948)
No Man of her Own (1950)
A Place in the Sun (1951)
Short Cut to Hell (1957)
So Evil My Love (1948)
Sorry, Wrong Number
(1948)
*The Strange Love of Martha
Ivers* (1946)
Street of Chance (1942)
Sunset Boulevard (1950)
This Gun for Hire (1942)
The Turning Point (1952)
Union Station (1950)
Vertigo (1958)

**Producers Releasing
Corporation (PRC)**
Bluebeard (1944)
Detour (1945)
The Lady Confesses (1945)
Railroaded (1947)
Strange Illusion (1945)

**Radio-Keith-Orpheum
[RKO]**
Angel Face (1953)
Armored Car Robbery (1950)
Berlin Express (1948)
Beware, My Lovely (1952)
Beyond a Reasonable Doubt
(1956)
The Big Steal (1949)
Blood on the Moon (1948)
Bodyguard (1948)
Born to Kill (1947)
Clash by Night (1952)
The Clay Pigeon (1949)
Cornered (1945)
Crack-Up (1946)
Crossfire (1947)
Cry Danger (1951)
Deadline at Dawn (1946)
Desperate (1947)
Destination Murder (1950)
The Devil Thumbs a Ride
(1947)
Edge of Doom (1950)
The Fallen Sparrow (1943)
Follow Me Quietly (1949)
Gambling house (1951)
His Kind of Woman (1951)
The Hitch-Hiker (1953)
Johnny Angel (1945)
Journey into Fear (1943)
The Las Vegas Story (1952)
The Locket (1947)
The Long Night (1947)
Macao (1952)
Murder, My Sweet (1944)
The Narrow Margin (1952)
Nocturne (1946)
Notorious (1946)

On Dangerous Ground (1952)

Out of the Past (1947)

The Racket (1951)

Rancho Notorious (1952)

Roadblock (1951)

Second Chance (1953)

The Secret Fury (1950)

The Set-Up (1949)

Slightly Scarlet (1956)

The Spiral Staircase (1945)

Split Second (1953)

The Stranger (1946)

Stranger on the Third Floor (1940)

Sudden Fear (1952)

The Tattooed Stranger (1950)

They Live by Night (1949)

They Won't Believe Me (1947)

The Threat (1949)

Two O'Clock Courage (1945)

Walk Softly, Stranger (1950)

Where Danger Lives (1951)

While the City Sleeps (1956)

The Window (1949)

The Woman in the Window (1945)

Woman on Pier 13 (1949)

The Woman on the Beach (1947)

Republic

City That Never Sleeps (1953)

Moonrise (1949)

The Pretender (1947)

Blackmail (1947)

Hell's Half Acre (1954)

Hoodlum Empire (1952)

Johnny Guitar (1954)

Make Haste to Live (1954)

The Great Flamarion (1945)

Strange Impersonation (1946)

Whispering Footsteps (1943)

20th Century-Fox

Backlash (1947)

The Brasher Doubloon (1947)

Call Northside 777 (1948)

Cry of the City (1948)

The Dark Corner (1945)

The Day the Earth Stood Still (1951)

Fallen Angel (1946)

Hangover Square (1945)

House of Bamboo (1955)

House of Strangers (1949)

House on 92nd Street (1945)

House on Telegraph Hill (1951)

I Wake Up Screaming (1942)

Invaders from Mars (1953)

Kiss of Death (1947)

Laura (1944)

Leave Her to Heaven (1945)

The Lodger (1944)

Man in the Attic (1953)

The Man Who Cheated Himself (1951)

Moss Rose (1947)

Niagara (1953)

Night and the City (1950)

Night without Sleep (1943)

Nightmare Alley (1947)

The Other Woman (1954)

The Ox-Bow Incident (1943)

Panic in the Streets (1950)

Pickup on South Street (1953)

Plunder Road (1957)

Rawhide (1951)

Road House (1948)

Shock (1946)

Somewhere in the Night (1946)

The Street with No Name (1948)

Thieves' Highway (1949)

The 13th Letter (1951)

Vicki (1953)

Where the Sidewalk Ends (1950)

Whirlpool (1949)

United Artists

Baby Face Nelson (1957)

The Big Knife (1955)

The Big Night (1951)

Body and Soul (1947)

The Captive City (1952)

Champion (1949)

The Scarf (1951)

The Chase (1946)

Crime of Passion (1957)

The Crooked Way (1949)

D.O.A. (1949)

Guest in the House (1944)

Gun Crazy (1950)

He Ran All the Way (1951)

Hit and Run (1957)

I, the Jury (1953)

Impact (1947)

Johnny Cool (1963)

Kansas City Confidential (1952)

The Killer Is Loose (1956)

Killer's Kiss (1955)

The Killing (1956)

A Kiss Before Dying (1956)

Kiss Me Deadly (1955)

The Long Wait (1954)

Man with My Face (1951)

Night of the Hunter (1955)

Nightmare (1956)

99 River Street (1953)

Odds Against Tomorrow (1959)

Pitfall (1948)

The Prowler (1951)

Quicksand (1950)

Ramrod (1947)

Red Light (1950)

The Second Woman (1951)

The Shanghai Gesture (1941)

The Shield for Murder (1954)

Sleep, My Love (1948)

Spellbound (1945)

Storm Fear (1956)

The Strange Woman (1946)

Suddenly (1954)

Sweet Smell of Success (1957)

The Thief (1952)

Timetable (1956)

Too Late for Tears (1949)

Try and Get Me (1950)

The Underworld Story (1950)

A Voice in the Wind (1944)

Whistle Stop (1946)

Wicked Woman (1953)

Without Warning (1952)

Witness to Murder (1954)

Universal

Abandoned (1949)

Black Angel (1946)

Blast of Silence (1961)

Brute Force (1947)

Calling Dr. Death (1943)

Cape Fear (1962)

Christmas Holiday (1944)

Criss Cross (1949)

The Dark Mirror (1946)

A Double Life (1948)

The Hollywood Story (1951)

Ivy (1947)

Johnny Stool Pigeon (1949)

The Killers (1946)

Kiss the Blood Off My Hands (1948)

Lady on a Train (1945)

Naked Alibi (1954)

The Naked City (1948)

The Night Runner (1957)

One Way Street (1950)

Phantom Lady (1944)

The Raging Tide (1951)

Ride the Pink Horse (1947)

Scarlet Street (1945)

Secret Beyond the Door (1948)

Shadow of a Doubt (1943)

Shakedown (1950)

Singapore (1947)

The Sleeping City (1950)

The Strange Affair of Uncle Harry [aka Uncle Harry] (1945)

The Suspect (1944)

The Tattered Dress (1957)

Touch of Evil (1958)

Under the Gun (1951)

Undertow (1949)

Woman in Hiding (1950)

Woman on the Run (1950)

Warner Bros.

Backfire (1950)

Beyond the Forest (1949)

The Big Sleep (1946)

The Blue Gardenia (1953)

The Breaking Point (1950)

Caged (1950)

City for Conquest (1940)

Conflict (1945)

Crime Wave (1954)

A Cry in the Night (1956)

The Damned Don't Cry (1950)

Danger Signal (1945)

Dark Passage (1947)

The Enforcer (1951)

High Sierra (1941)

I Confess (1953)

I Died a Thousand Times (1955)

I Was a Communist for the F.B.I. (1951)

Illegal (1955)

Key Largo (1948)

Kiss Tomorrow Goodbye (1950)

The Letter (1940)

The Maltese Falcon (1941)

The Man I Love (1947)

The Mask of Dimitrios (1944)

Mildred Pierce (1945)

Mr. Arkadin [aka Confidential Report] (1955)

New York Confidential (1955)

Nobody Lives Forever (1946)

Nora Prentiss (1947)

Possessed (1947)

Pursued (1947)

Strangers on a Train (1951)

Them! (1954)

This Side of the Law (1950)

Tomorrow is Another Day (1951)

The Two Mrs. Carrolls (1947)

The Unfaithful (1947)

The Unsuspected (1947)

The Verdict (1946)

White Heat (1949)

The Wrong Man (1956)

PART TWO

◇

Neo-Noir

INTRODUCTION: NEO-NOIR

◇

To realize the power of light and what it can do to the mind of the audience, visualize the following little scene: The room is dark. A strong streak of light sneaks in from the hall under the door. The sound of steps is heard. The shadows of two feet divide the light streak. A brief silence follows. There is suspense in the air. Who is it? What is going to happen? Is he going to ring the bell? Or just insert a key and try to come in? Another heavier shadow appears and blocks the light entirely. A dim hissing sound is heard, and as the shadow leaves, we see in the dim light a paper slip onto the carpet. The steps are heard again . . . This time they leave. A strong light appears once more and illuminates the note on the floor. We read it as the steps fade out in the distance. "It is ten o'clock. Please turn off your radio. The Manager."
—JOHN ALTON, *Painting with Light*

What is film noir? Not a genre. Producers and consumers both recognize a genre as a distinct entity; nobody set out to make or see a film noir in the sense that people deliberately chose to make a Western, a comedy, or a musical. Is film noir then a style? Critics have not succeeded in defining specifically noir visual techniques . . . or narrative structure. The problem resembles one in art history, that of defining "non-classical" styles.
—DAVID BORDWELL, *The Classical Hollywood Cinema*

DAVID BORDWELL'S COMMENTS APPEARED IN A GENERAL reference work published in 1985 within in a sub-section called "The case of film noir." At first glance there seems to be little to dispute, no direct refutation of Paul Schrader's seminal assertion in 1972 that

> Film noir is not a genre. It is not defined, as are the western and gangster genres, by conventions of setting and conflict, but rather by the more subtle qualities of tone and mood. . . . The fundamental reason for film noir's neglect, however, is the fact that it depends more on choreography than sociology, and American critics have always been slow on the uptake when it comes to visual style. Like its protagonists, film noir is more interested in style than theme, whereas American critics have been traditionally more interested in theme than style.

Neglected no more, whether it is called a series, style, genre, movement, cycle, or all of the above, every commentator must certainly agree that film noir is an observable phenomenon. While not conforming in every detail—and when have critics ever done that?—film historians have now discussed the movement, its start and end points, its visual techniques and narrative structures, the system of production and social events coincident to its time, in scores of books and hundreds of articles. Despite this some commentators have asserted—and still assert—that the concept of film noir was invented after the fact, that it is the creation of observers and not filmmakers. (For more on this see also my

Introduction in *Film Noir Reader*.) Granted, it was Jean-Pierre Chartier (or someone lost to film history) who invented the term. However, Impressionism was also first used by a critic, in that case as a derisive moniker for that cabal led by Monet, Degas, and Renoir. The painters didn't care that the man who dubbed them Impressionists also said he found their work less appealing than wallpaper; and absent something better, the term became widespread. Like the people who made film noir from the beginning of the 1940s till the end of the 1950s, the Impressionists produced a body of work for two decades before an observer gave them a name. One wonders then why some film scholars continue to confuse lack of term for lack of intent.

Of course, film and its questions of style are not those of painting or theater or music or literature or any combination of these; and the problems of art history have limited relevance. The solution to the case of film noir, if one must be had, will never be found in hardboiled fiction, German Expressionism, or postwar paranoia. The investigator must first look, as always, at the heart of the matter, at the films themselves. Any commentator who asserts or merely implies that filmmakers were unaware of working in a style, of being part of a movement, of utilizing an iconography, should look again at the work itself. John Alton called a sub-section of his extraordinary 1949 text on cinematography "The Power of Light." What better demonstration could there be of his conscious understanding of that power than his work on *T-Men* or *The Big Combo* or the B-unit programmer *Mystery Street* or the period drama *Reign of Terror* or a score of other classic period noir? Whether they had a name for it or not, whether they called their pictures thrillers or mysteries, actioners or mellers, the pictures themselves affirm that the filmmakers of the noir cycle were well aware of what type of movie they were making. Very few of the people who created film noir knew of, let alone immediately embraced, the term when it became "official"

with Borde and Chaumeton's book in 1955. But some did. If you doubt that take a look at the picture of Robert Aldrich standing on the set of *Attack!* in 1956 and displaying a copy of *Panorama du Film Noir Américain*.

As noted in the introduction to Part 1, while the noir cycle never formally concluded, the attempts to sustain its viewpoint were few in the 1960s and 1970s. The 1980s, however, brought a significant resurgence of interest in the themes and protagonists that typified classic film noir. The next two decades have added scores more. The significant difference between then and now is, of course, what motivates the creation of the films.

At the height of the original movement individual noir films transcended any personal or stylistic outlooks to reflect something larger, or as Schrader put it, "auteur criticism is interested in how directors are different; film noir criticism is concerned with what they have in common." Very shortly after the end of the classic period, a "Neo-Noir" era began. Most of these movies that have attempted to recreate the noir mood, whether in remakes or new narratives, have been undertaken by filmmakers cognizant of the stylistic heritage from noir's classic period and intent on placing their own interpretation on it. As the various interviews conducted by Todd Erickson and reproduced in his thesis affirm, many of these filmmakers approach neo-noir with a conscious, expressive intent. David Mamet put it most succinctly regarding *House of Games*: "I am very well acquainted with [noir], both in print and on film, and I love it. I tried to be true." If neo-noir is to some extent like its antecedent America's stylized vision of itself, one might expect a cynicism made even harsher by over fifty years of wars, cold and hot, by pervasive fiscal uncertainties, by technological and cultural revolutions unimaginable to the filmmakers of the classic period. While a narrative or iconic emphasis may have shifted in recent years reflecting a parallel shift in social realities, the outpouring of neo-noir films has continued.

One aspect of film noir which many neo-noir filmmakers have chosen to underscore is its forlorn romanticism, the need to find love and honor in a new society that venerates only sex and money, beginning with the perverse code of conduct manifest by one of its earliest anti-heroes Walker in *Point Blank*. In neo-noir titles again tell the tale: the words "kill" or "dead" or "black" appear in scores of them. Characters are deceived, shattered, fatally attracted and sleeping with the enemy, presumably with one eye open. Well beyond the limits of the genre, the impersonal aspect of urban sprawl established in the title sequences of such classic period movies as *He Walked by Night* and *The Naked City* are also a key visual motif in the openings of neo-noir from *New Jack City* to *Sin City*. Echoes of the classic period, from its undercurrent of despair to its dark visual style, continue to manifest themselves in other types of films, in corruption exposes—whether retro (*True Confessions*, *L.A. Confidential*) or contemporary (*The Border*, *Witness*)—in the surreal *Fight Club* or *Mulholland Drive*, the quasi-docudramas *Rush* or *Murder in the First*, or the big-budget, comic book series about a *Batman* seeking revenge or *Spiderman*'s existential anguish.

While the late 1980s and early 1990s may have seen the broadest resurgence of interest in the themes and styles of film noir, the body of neo-noir continues to expand in the 21st century. In terms of those themes and styles, many of these motion pictures, but not all, would have met the criteria in our original selection process for the main body of this book. If film noir is no longer *the* American style, certainly no other movement has emerged to replace it. And, unless filmmakers discover another mirror to hold up to American society, none ever will. **AS**

Sin City

A new generation of expressive cinematographers such as Juan Ruiz Anchia (Liebestraum, At CLose Range, House of Games) and Jordan Cronenweth (Blade Runner, State of Grace, The Nickel Ride) brought a lighting style as striking as John Alton's to neo-noir.

AFTER DARK, MY SWEET (1990)

Director: James Foley. **Screenplay**: Robert Redlin, James Foley based on the novel by Jim Thompson. **Producers**: Robert Redlin, Ric Kidney. **Director of Photography**: Mark Plummer. **Production Designer**: David Brisbin. **Music**: Maurice Jarre. **Editor**: Howard Smith. **Cast**: Jason Patric (Collie), Rachel Ward (Fay), Rocky Giordani (Bert), Bruce Dern (Uncle Bud), Thomas Wagner (Counterman), George Dickerson (Doc Goldman). **Locations**: Indio, California. **Released**: Avenue Pictures, August 24. 114 minutes.

Collie, a punch-drunk prize fighter, is homeless after some time spent in an institution. His violent self-defense in a desert bar impresses another patron, Fay, who offers room and board if he will help her repair a house inherited from her ex-husband. She begins a sexual liaison with Collie. Fay's Uncle Bud, who is a local grafter, recruits both of them into a scheme to kidnap the son of a wealthy local resident. When the plan goes awry, Collie realizes he has been used by his criminal partners and precipitates a deadly final confrontation.

Jim Thompson's personages are often trapped in what he saw as their personal hells. Often they are also people whose business is deception, but others are the victims of physical or emotional turmoil such as "Collie" in *After Dark, My Sweet*. For Thompson and many of the filmmakers who have adapted his work, point of view is crucial. The credit sequence is an expressionistic rendering of the prize fight in which Collie kills his opponent. Midway through the titles, a sound-buffered jump cut takes the viewer to a tight close-up of him as he now is. *After Dark, My Sweet* is a first-person film on several levels, from the voiceover narration to the optical and sound effects which intermittently externalize his troubled mental state. Employing these stylistic elements typical of the classic period permits all the narrative tensions to be effectively laid out within the first few minutes. A cut back from the close-up reveals the protagonist in a desert landscape coming out of an escarpment of large stones. As he shuffles across the highway, the narration rambles over the shot: "I wonder where I'll be tomorrow . . ." The key phrase is, "I couldn't walk away." As he enters the town, the sound of a train is heard and a sudden, sidewise camera move swings past him but holds the figure in a 180 degree arc, fixes his body in the sun-bleached highway. It prevents him from walking out of the shot, figuratively holding him as firmly as his troubled memories grip his mind.

Like all Thompson's characters, Collie is slowly dying in this personal hell. When Fay, a femme fatale in sandals and a straw hat, picks him up, she treats him like a stray puppy, patting the car seat and saying, "Come on, now, there's a good boy" to entice him in. Her directness—she wants to call him Collie because he reminds her of a shaggy dog—is what makes her ambiguous,

After Dark, My Sweet: *Collie (Jason Patric) and Fay (Rachel Ward).*

what sets her apart in a Thompson-esque milieu of con men and petty crooks. The desert itself with its clean, brightly-lit vistas is in constant contrast to the emotional darkness within. But it is through Patric's performance, full of tics, stumbling, and false starts, that *After Dark, My Sweet* evokes the hopelessness of both Thompson and film noir more forcefully than *The Grifters*. **AS**

AGAINST ALL ODDS (1984)

Director: Taylor Hackford. **Screenplay**: Eric Hughes based on the screenplay for *Out of the Past* by Daniel Mainwaring. **Producers**: Taylor Hackford, William S. Gilmore (Columbia-Delphi). **Director of Photography**: Donald Thorin. **Music**: Larry Carlton, Michel Colombier. **Editors**: Fredric Steinkamp, William Steinkamp. **Cast**: Rachel Ward (Jessie Wyler), Jeff Bridges (Terry Brogan), James Woods (Jake Wise), Alex Karras (Hank Sully), Jane Greer (Mrs. Wyler), Richard Widmark (Ben Caxton), Dorian Harwood (Tommy), Swoosie Kurtz (Edie), Saul Rubinek (Steve Kirsch). **Released**: Columbia-EMI-Warner, March 2. 121 minutes.

Terry Brogan, a former Outlaws-team footballer, is hired by his bookmaker friend, Jake Wise, to help locate his girlfriend, heiress Jessie Wyler, who has absconded to Mexico with a large sum of money. Jessie's mother, a powerful businesswoman and owner of the Outlaws club, and her associate, Ben Caxton, who wish to keep Wise away from Jessie, also approach Brogan. Brogan locates Jessie on a remote island, and though she is initially cautious, the two soon become lovers. Wise sends Outlaws coach, Sully, in search of the couple and in a struggle Sully is fatally shot. Jesse returns to Los Angeles and resumes her relationship with Wise. Persuaded by Wise to retrieve business files from the office of his former manager Steve Kirsch, Brogan finds Kirsch murdered. With the help of Kirsch's secretary, Edie, Brogan discovers that

Caxton is behind a fraudulent betting system involving Wise, Sully and Kirsch. Brogan manages to set up a rendezvous with Caxton and Wise, during which the latter is shot dead by Jessie. Wise is made scapegoat, Jessie returns to Mrs. Wyler, and Brogan visits Jessie in the hope they might be reunited.

Against All Odds is a transformed remake of *Out of the Past*, the paradigmatic noir directed by Jacques Tourneur and adapted by Daniel Mainwaring from his 1946 novel, *Build My Gallows High* (penned under the pseudonym Geoffrey Holmes). Taking the barest narrative outline from *Out of the Past*—one man is dispatched by another to Mexico to locate a beautiful, missing woman—*Against All Odds* reinvents the classic noir as a romantic thriller for the 1980s. Rather than directly evoke its precursor, *Against All Odds* trades on the popular success of Taylor Hackford's previous feature, *An Officer and a Gentleman* (1982), and the profiles of its upcoming stars: Jeff Bridges, Rachel Ward and James Woods.

Along with its scenic locations, sweat-drenched sex scenes and the music video promotion of Phil Collins' song, "Against All Odds (Take a Look at Me Now)," this transforms the source material into high concept, "California-noir" of the type found in contemporaneous noir remakes such as *The Morning After* (also starring Bridges). Thrust reluctantly into the role of detective—first to locate spoiled heiress Jessie Wyler, and later to expose corrupt gambling and real estate operations—the ex-footballer Terry Brogan, as lazily played by Bridges, at once recalls the Philip Marlowe of Robert Altman's *The Long Goodbye*, and anticipates Bridges' own Chandler-esque role as "The Dude" in *The Big Lebowski* (1998). Additionally, the theme of patriarchal immorality (in the socio-economic context of 1980s America), not only recalls the father figures of earlier neo-noirs, such as *Chinatown* and *Body Heat*, but a similar struggle to expose the rich and powerful in another Bridges' vehicle, *Cutter and Bone* (1981). At the end of the film, it is Jessie's wealthy mother—played by Jane Greer from *Out of the Past*—and the ruthless patriarch Ben Caxton (another noir icon, Richard Widmark) who triumph. This leaves the leads—Brogan and Jessie—alive, but uncertain of any future together. **CV**

AT CLOSE RANGE (1986)

Director: James Foley. **Screenplay**: Nicholas Kazan. **Producers**: Don Guest, Elliot Lewitt. **Executive Producers**: John Daly, Derek Gibson. **Director of Photography**: Juan Ruiz Anchía. **Production Designer**: Peter Jamison. **Music**: Patrick Leonard. **Editor**: Howard Smith. **Cast**: Sean Penn (Brad Whitewood, Jr.), Christopher Walken (Brad Whitewood, Sr.), Mary Stuart Masterson (Terry), Christopher Penn (Tommy Whitewood), Millie Perkins (Julie), Eileen Ryan (Grandma), Jake Dengel (Lester), Crispin Glover (Lucas). **Released**: Hemdale Film Corporation, 18 April. 111 minutes.

In Pennsylvania, Brad, Jr. lives with his brother Tommy, mother Julie and grandmother. A tough but deeply feeling teenager, he begins a tender relationship with local girl Terry. After clashing with Julie's boyfriend, Brad, Jr. leaves home and seeks out his alluring criminal father, Brad, Sr., who leads a gang of family members and associates. Alternately paternal and dismissive, Brad, Sr. draws in and manipulates Brad, Jr. and Tommy, gradually initiating them into the code of his world. The teens form their own group in order to prove they are able thieves. As Brad, Jr.'s bond with Terry grows, her presence disturbs Brad, Sr.'s

At Close Range: *Sean Penn as Brad Whitewood, Jr.*

gang. Increasingly paranoiac, Brad, Sr. kills Lester, a former associate he suspects of informing to the police. Brad, Jr. is arrested during a theft. While he is in jail, Brad, Sr. rapes Terry. The disintegration of the gang continues with Brad, Sr.'s killing (by his own or another's hand) of Tommy and Terry, and his attempted murder of Brad, Jr. Surviving this attack, Brad, Jr. confronts his father and then turns him over to the police. He testifies against Brad, Sr. and his surviving associates in court.

The 1980s are usually painted as a return to conventional and ideologically reassuring narrative formats within American cinema, after the freewheeling, politically aware experiments of the 1970s. But the legacy of Robert Altman and others survived in an unexpected place: the "teen movie" genre, upon which *At Close Range* is an especially dramatic, even Gothic variation (the true-life story from the mid-1970s on which the film is quite closely based was described by *Time* magazine as "Pennsylvania Gothic"). Many actors familiar from the teen comedies and romances of the early 1980s (the Penns, Masterson, Glover, Kiefer Sutherland) appear, albeit in a starkly realist low life context; Foley himself had previously made the classic teen rebel story *Reckless* (1984).

Although *At Close Range* builds an impressive noir atmosphere of escalating (frequently nocturnal) dread, Foley's primary concern is scarcely to tell a tight, driving story: it is well over an hour before the first major violent incident occurs. Rather, the film focuses on creating a mood (alternately languorous and elliptical), describing a milieu, and exploring the theme of a malignant family unit where otherwise admirable codes of honor, loyalty, and closeness have become evil and ultimately self-destructive over time. As Foley remarked during production, the material of the true story was so bleak that it proved difficult to fix on anything positive or redemptive in it: the one spark of hope of integrity is provided by Brad, Jr. and his final rejection of his father's control, and to this role Penn brings a poignant mix of brutishness and sensitivity. Richly textured, *At Close Range* is, in retrospect, a remarkably daring film in style as in content—harking back to the severe narrative experiments of Monte Hellman (a tribute signalled by the presence of Millie Perkins), and anticipating the 1990s work of Larry Clark in the US, as well as Claire Denis in France. Although overlooked in its day (partly due to the collapse of Hemdale, which also produced the similarly dark and moody teen drama *River's Edge* [1986]), *At Close Range* now rates as Foley's finest work. **AM**

BAD INFLUENCE (1990)

Director: Curtis Hanson. **Screenplay**: David Koepp. **Producer**: Steve Tisch. **Executive Producers**: Richard Becker, Morrie Eisenman (Epic Productions). **Director of Photography**: Robert Elswit. **Music**: Trevor Jones. **Editor**: Bonnie Koehler. **Cast**: Rob Lowe (Alex), James Spader (Michael Boll), Lisa Zane (Claire), Marcia Cross (Ruth Fielding), Rosalyn Landor (Britt), Tony Maggio (Patterson), Kathleen Wilhoite (Leslie), Christian Clemenso (Pismo). **Released**: Triumph Releasing Corporation, March 9. 99 minutes.

Michael Boll is a mild-mannered junior analyst on track for promotion at a Los Angeles investment firm, but there's one obstacle in his way—a conniving colleague named Patterson who is vying for the same promotion. Late one afternoon as he unwinds at a local bar, Michael is roughed up by a jealous boyfriend. A stranger steps in to protect him, and then disappears. Michael runs into the stranger later that night while jogging on a pier near his condo. The stranger introduces himself as Alex, and encourages Michael to join him exploring the underground club scene. Alex dominates the relationship, and within a few days turns Michael's entire life upside down in a drunken crime spree that includes armed robberies of a liquor store and a hamburger stand, and a violent assault on his colleague, Patterson. Michael orders Alex out of his life, but Alex ups the ante and murders Claire in Michael's apartment. Realizing he's been framed, Michael confesses everything to his brother, Pismo, and the two dispose of the body. Then they devise a plan to trap Alex and get him to unwittingly admit to the murder on videotape.

Bad Influence is perhaps the most deliberate attempt to explore the doppelganger theme in the post-classic film noir period. Alex is a demonic sociopath focused on transforming the wimpy Michael into his evil twin. Their meeting is a chance encounter, but everything Alex does to manipulate Michael's life thereafter is calculated and prescient. The use of names is particularly revealing as the narrative unfolds. Alex easily slips into different personalities and corresponding names as his opportunity to wreak havoc unfolds. He uses an accent and goes by the name of "Franco" in the underground club scene when he picks up Claire for Michael. Later than night, he changes Michael's name to "Mick." Michael's transformation to Mick is swift. When Alex wants him to go to the race track, he declines, but then heads back to work and after instructing his secretary to call him "Mick," makes an extremely risky business decision that could have cost him his job. Doppelgangers thrive on the chaos they create for their victim's family and friends, and in the sequence where Michael arrives at his fiancée's home for a black tie dinner party, he is startled to find Alex there posing as "François," a French business colleague. After charming the hosts and their guests, Alex/François whisks Michael away from the gathering, leaving behind a shocked assemblage

and a shattered wedding engagement as a video of Michael and Claire writhing in sexual intercourse plays on the TV.

Curtis Hanson paints a cinematic canvas that is convincingly noir, from the opening credits where Alex pilfers items from his lover's bedroom in the darkness of early morning to the interior shots of Michael's condo where ever present window blind shadows depict his psychological captivity. Exterior night locations, including the seaside piers or the shiny, wet streets and alleyways of Los Angeles at night render similar insights about the protagonist's descent into darkness. David Koepp's dialogue gives an early key to Alex's true nature when he coaxes Michael to "tell me what you want more than anything else in the world." Leaning in and out of the shadows while he preens Michael's ego, it's as if the Devil and his quarry were discussing a deal at the veritable Crossroads. Alex's boastful instruction to Michael, "Confess to one lie, but continue another—nothing like it to confuse people," is equally a feigned confession and arrogant self-praise. Because his very existence is predicated on deception, Claire's ability to see through him prefigures her horrible fate. Michael's older brother Pismo also sees Alex for who he really is, and serves as Michael's conscience after he falls under Alex's influence. When Michael can't see any way out of his dilemma other than to kill Alex, Pismo warns "now you're thinking like him." **TE**

BAD LIEUTENANT (1992)

Director: Abel Ferrara. **Screenplay**: Victor Argo, Paul Calderon, Abel Ferrara, Zoe Tamerlis-Lund. **Executive Producers**: Ronna B. Wallace, Patrick Wachsberger. **Director of Photography**: Ken Kelsch. **Music**: Joe Delia. **Production Designer**: Charles Lagola. **Editor**: Anthony Redman. **Cast**: Harvey Keitel (The Lieutenant), Zoe Tamerlis-Lund (Zoe), Anthony Ruggiero (Lite), Victoria Bastel

(Bowtay), Eddie Daniels (Jersey Girl Driver), Bianca Bakija (Jersey Girl, passenger), Robin Burrows (Ariane), Victor Argo (Beat Cop). **Released**: Aries Films, November 20. 96 minutes.

It's the National League playoffs and a miracle is happening in the City of the Angels: the New York Mets are bouncing back from a 0-3 deficit to defeat the Los Angeles Dodgers, a dramatic comeback that has never happened before in a pennant race. Meanwhile, back in New York, a corrupt police Lieutenant is on a losing streak, and as the Mets continue their ascent he sinks further into drugs, debt and desperation. While taking bets from fellow police officers and keeping his own bookie at bay, the Lieutenant does whatever it takes to snort, smoke and shoot himself into oblivion. Initially cynical when a nun is brutally raped by two teenage hoods, the woman's decision to forgive her assailants (and thus refusal to identify them) awakens in the Lieutenant his long repressed religious past. The latter is manifested in a hallucinatory scene where Christ appears to him. Filled with remorse and a need for redemption, the Lieutenant discovers where the rapists are hiding and holds them until the seventh game of the series ends. With the Mets victorious but his own fate sealed, he puts the teenagers on a bus before being gunned down.

Brilliantly written and shot, with a tour-de-force performance by Harvey Keitel, *Bad Lieutenant* is Abel Ferrara's dark character study of corruption and redemption. Ferrara plunges the corrupt cop of classic noir into a cesspool of vice and criminality, creating a character whose badness is so extreme as to verge on parody. Yet this Lieutenant is "bad" on both secular and cosmic levels. Abusing his authority to uphold the law of the land through a range of criminal activities, he has also forsaken his Catholic upbringing, and has thus failed as "God's lieutenant" on earth. For this jaded believer adrift in a fallen world, the Church has become just one "racket" among others, and his own life is now devoted to filling his inner emptiness with alcohol, narcotics and sex. That his search for ecstasy is ultimately self-destructive does not deter him from his mission. "Vampires are lucky, they can feed on others," observes the Lieutenant's junkie girlfriend, Zoe (played by actress-writer Zoe Tamerlis-Lund of Ferrara's earlier film *Ms. 45*). "We gotta eat away at ourselves until there's nothing left but appetite."

Abel Ferrara's films have often been compared to those of Martin Scorsese, but with *Bad Lieutenant* references to *Mean Streets* are simply unavoidable. Both deal with the issues of crime, morality, and religion, both are set in the rougher locales of New York City, and both feature Keitel in the lead role. Yet in Ferrara's film it's as if the once devout character of Scorsese's young Charlie has been twisted over two decades to resemble the reckless gambler Johnny Boy, but without completely destroying his moral center. A beacon in the utter darkness of his world, the Nun's selfless gesture strengthens the Lieutenant's desire to do something good and perhaps save his soul. At first he behaves like Satan by promising the Nun that he can "beat the system and do justice, real justice" if she would only name her attackers. After an anguished confrontation with the silent Jesus, the Lieutenant resolves to follow the Nun's example of Christ-like submission. He thus sacrifices himself for two fellow sinners who might seem to deserve far less, pressing on them a cigar box filled with $30,000 of drug money that, along with the $50,000 reward he would have

earned for catching these rapists, might have saved him. In such a corrupt and hopeless world, the Lieutenant's final act of forgiveness will make no sense to anyone except him. The end of the film reveals how prescient were Zoe's earlier statements during her "sermon" on appetite: "No one will ever understand why, why you did it. They'll just forget about you tomorrow, but you gotta do it." **CF**

BADLANDS (1973)

Producer, Screenplay, Director: Terrence Malick. **Executive Producer**: Edward R. Pressman. **Directors of Photography**: Tak Fujimoto, Stevan Larner, Brian Probyn. **Art Director**: Jack Fisk. **Music**: Erik Satie, Carl Orff. **Editor**: Robert Estrin. **Cast**: Martin Sheen (Kit Carruthers), Sissy Spacek (Holly Sargis), Warren Oates (Holly's Father), Ramon Bieri (Cato), Alan Vint (Deputy), Gary Littlejohn (Sheriff). **Released**: Warner Bros., October 15. 95 minutes.

Shortly after being fired from his job as a garbage collector Kit Carruthers meets 15-year-old Holly Spargis. Holly's widower father tries to prevent a relationship; but she and Kit meet in secret and ultimately Kit walks into their house and casually shoots Mr. Spargis to death, then drags his body to the basement, and sets fire to the house. After a few idyllic days in the nearby woods, Kit and Holly flee towards Canada, leaving a path of murder and destruction (inspired by the true story of fugitive couple Charles Starkweather and Caril Ann Fugate whose 1958 killing spree left 11 people dead). Hemmed in and without Holly, Kit makes a desperate cross-country dash for the border but is apprehended.

Part homage to the 1950s, part naive noir, the first person narrative of *Badlands* is straight out of Holly's movie mags, which she reads to her personal James Dean as they travel the back roads of the Dakotas. The landscape of this film, framed by her dark narrative, is spectacular; but at the same time she is detached, as if recalling another lifetime. *Badlands* skirts the dark corners of classic noir. Its horizontal aspect created by the meeting of land and sky is closest to the few examples of open landscapes of the classic period such as *Nightfall* or *Ace in the Hole*. The fateful quality of the first meeting of the soon-to-be fugitive couple is both reinforced and mocked by Holly's voiceover as she explains that it was "better to spend a week with one who loved me for what I was than years of

loneliness." Her pointedly rural accent and meticulous inflection create an unrelenting and dark tension in her narration. While the voiceover tradition is deeply imbedded in noir, classic femme fatales rarely address the viewer directly. Terence Mallick's script infuses both voiceover and dialogue with a banality that contrasts chillingly with the violence.

As the Spargis home burns, both Holly's dollhouse and the family's household possessions are outlined in flames. Visually this suggests that, in Holly's adolescent perception, both are the same: the dollhouse and real house; the young rebels in her movie magazines and Kit; fact and fiction intermixed inextricably. While he may show a few odd moments of conscience later in the film, Kit is mostly lost in his own fugitive-couple, desperate-character fantasy. The self-image he constructs requires him to play the gallant and, after he stage manages his own capture, to take full responsibility for the killing spree. For Kit being part of a fugitive couple is the existential self-expression of the unhappy garbage collector. Holly is less love object than decoration: he would "love" her or anyone else that had been in her place. Their dance to Mickey and Silvia's "Love is Strange" is one the most darkly comic moments of neo-noir. As the couple sways languidly, eyes closed, Holly barefoot, Kit in his cowboy boots, the music and the cluttered aspect of their wooded hideaway are a long way from the young love of Bowie and Keechie in *They Live by Night*. Still twenty years before the excesses of *Natural Born Killers*, *Badlands'* mix of ingenuous angst and sudden death make Kit and Holly ring truer than Oliver Stone's twisted fugitives in a post-modernist context. **LB**

BASIC INSTINCT (1992)

Director: Paul Verhoeven. **Screenplay**: Joe Eszterhaz. **Producer**: Alan Marshall. **Director of Photography**: Jan de Bont. **Production Designer**: Terence Marsh. **Music**: Jerry Goldsmith. **Editor**: Frank Urioste. **Cast**: Sharon Stone (Catherine Tramell), Michael Douglas (Det. Nick Curran), George Dzundza (Gus Moran), Jeanne Tripplehorn (Dr. Beth Garner), Denis Arndt (Lt. Philip Walker), Leilani Sarelle (Roxy), Bruce A. Young (Andrews), Dorothy Malone (Hazel Dobkins), Daniel von Bargen (Lt. Nilsen), Wayne Knight (John Correli), Chelcie Ross (Capt. Talcott). **Released**: TriStar/Carolco, March 20. 127 minutes.

Former rock star Johnny Boz is brutally killed during sex, and the case is assigned to Detective Nick Curran. During the investigation, Nick meets Catherine Tramell, a crime novelist who was Boz's girlfriend when he died. Catherine proves to be a very clever and manipulative woman, and though Nick is more or less convinced that she murdered Boz, he is unable to find any evidence. Instead he finds himself obsessed with her sexually and romantically. Later, when Nick's rival in the police department is killed, Nick suspects Catherine. After Nick's partner is murdered as well as Catherine's lesbian lover, Nick falls into confusion about Catherine and his own sanity. In the end it is revealed that the psychologist and former lover of both Nick and Catherine, Beth Garner, is the murderer, as a blonde wig (obviously used to disguise herself as Tramell) as well as an ice pick is found at her apartment after Nick shoots her. Nick and Catherine become lovers again in a rather ambiguous ending.

Basic Instinct is in some ways a post-modern version of

Basic Instinct: *Nick Curan (Michael Douglas) and Catherine Tramell (Sharon Stone).*

Hitchcock's *Vertigo*. Like the earlier film, a San Francisco detective becomes obsessed with a cool, complex, and blonde "ice princess" and in his attempt to understand/possess/save her he becomes unhinged physically as well as mentally. Nick is a recovering addict who is nicknamed "the shooter" for a series of rogue cop incidents which culminated when he shot several innocent bystanders. Although he was reinstated, he remains under the care of his ex-lover and psychiatrist Beth. While investigating a sex murder in which a blonde ties her lover to the headboard of his bed and then kills him with an ice pick during climax (a scene which opens the movie), the evidence leads Nick to the San Francisco mansion of their prime suspect Catherine Tramell (Sharon Stone in a role that catapulted her into stardom).

Catherine is a novelist who first perplexes Nick with her cool, noirish repartee:

NICK: How long were you dating him [the murder victim]?

CATHERINE: I wasn't dating him. I was fucking him.

GUS: What are you a pro?

CATHERINE: No, I'm an amateur.

and then completely unsettles him in the controversial crotch-flash scene in the interrogation room at police headquarters. In this scene, as well as numerous ones to follow, director Paul Verhoeven ironically turns the tables on the visual dynamic inherent in movies of this genre where the woman is the passive if knowing object of the male gaze (e.g. *Gilda*, *Vertigo*, etc.). Catherine instead uses her keen intelligence (she is a writer) as well as her overt sexuality to lead the group of leering male cops where she wants them to go, refusing to put out her cigarette, answering their questions the way she prefers.

In fact, Catherine is in many ways the metaphorical writer of the movie. She controls the narration and action through her novels. As Nick becomes more obsessed with her, especially after their first sexual encounter in which she ties him to the bed like the murdered man in the first scene, she directs him where to go and how to act, e.g. inserting his character into her newest novel; luring him to the disco where he becomes inflamed when he sees her having sex with her lesbian lover Roxy in the stall of the bathroom; writing scenes for the novel which work themselves out in reality, like the murder of his partner; and even solving the crime, in theory, by revealing that Beth is a stalker who loved Catherine in college.

In the final analysis, Nick is a man out of his depth, pulled by women who control him in various ways—his wife who committed suicide; Beth who can break his career with a negative report; and Catherine to whom he is addicted. Even though he manages to maintain the thin façade of trying to somehow understand and even redeem her by convincing her to give up her criminal and perverse friends (the lesbian Roxy, the convicted murderer Hazel) and settle down and raise "rug rats" with him (Catherine: "I hate rug rats"), it is patently obvious in the final frames that he has been engulfed by her. As they return to their lovemaking, the camera pans down below the bed to reveal an ice pick like the one found in the body at the beginning of the movie. Is Catherine the murderer? It is obvious that the man on the bed above no longer cares. **JU**

THE BEDROOM WINDOW (1987)

Director: Curtis Hanson. **Screenplay**: Curtis Hanson based on the novel *The Witnesses* by Anne Holden. **Producers**: Robert Towne, Martha De Laurentiis (Schumaker). **Director of Photography**: Gilbert Taylor. **Music**: Patrick Gleeson, Michael Shrieve. **Production Designer**: Ron Foreman. **Editor**: Scott Conrad. **Cast**: Steve Guttenberg (Terry Lambert), Elizabeth McGovern (Denise), Isabelle Huppert (Sylvia Wentworth), Paul Shenar (Collin Wentworth), Carl Lumbly (Detective Quirke), Wallace Shawn (Henderson's attorney), Frederick Coffin (Detective Jessup), Brad Greenquist (Carl Henderson). **Released**: DEG, January 16. 112 minutes.

After having perhaps one drink too many, Terry Lambert finds himself taking his boss's wife Sylvia back to his apartment for a nightcap that soon turns into a passionate sexual encounter. Later that night when Terry is in the bathroom, Sylvia hears a commotion outside and becomes the unwitting witness to the attempted murder of Denise by the distinctively red-haired Henderson, who sees Sylvia as much as she sees him. Learning that this man succeeded in murdering another victim the same night, the pair decides to go to the police. But Sylvia, fearing exposure, cannot, so she tells Terry what she knows. At a police line-up, Terry fails to identify Henderson positively as does Denise. Convinced that he is the killer, however, Terry decides to trail Henderson, eventually casting suspicion on himself. Brought to trial, Henderson is acquitted when the defense lawyer tears Terry's story to shreds. Upon his release, Henderson tracks down and murders Sylvia, and the circumstances of her killing throw further suspicion on Terry, who is now forced to find some way to prove that Henderson is the killer. He achieves this by persuading Denise, with whom he has begun a romantic relationship, to disguise herself as a gum-chewing, if sluttily attractive, barfly. Though Denise is put in terrible danger and Terry is somewhat ineffectual in tracking her movements, the trap works and Terry is vindicated, presumably to continue his relationship with Denise.

The Bedroom Window is less noir than Hitchcockian, with a palpable homage as well to Brian De Palma's *Blow Out*. The innocent protagonist embroiled by circumstances in a plot that eventually threatens his very life is straight out of *The 39 Steps* and *North by Northwest*, while the remaking of

Denise to trap Henderson recalls Scotty's reconstitution of the "real" Madeline in *Vertigo*. As Terry's double (a deadlier exploiter of women than his more conventional counterpart), Henderson is trapped into repeating his actions (with Denise playing herself in disguise) just as Bruno falls into a similar trap laid by Guy in *Strangers on a Train*. Like Farley Granger, Steve Guttenberg makes an excellent foil to the physically strong and resourceful Henderson; he is weak, easily manipulated, but just barely able to exculpate himself and thereby eliminate the continuing threat Henderson poses to Denise. The focus of the film is squarely on him, as there is no doubt about the identity or motives of the murderer he is tracking.

Director Curtis Hanson manages to give the film's Baltimore locations a convincing noir stylization—every exterior shot seems to emphasize dark, hidden spots from which danger might emerge at any turn. And even the city's more public, upscale spots promise no safety—Sylvia is murdered during a performance at the Stevens Center for Performing Arts, in a chilling sequence. Denise's performance as a down-market version of a noir femme fatale is convincing and effective as, in a gesture toward classic noir, she draws her victim, intent on murder, into self-destruction. **RBP**

BEST SELLER (1987)

Director: John Flynn. **Screenplay**: Larry Cohen. **Producer**: Carter DeHaven. **Executive Producers**: John Daly, Derek Gibson (Hemdale Film Corporation). **Director of Photography**: Fred Murphy. **Music**: Jay Ferguson. **Editor**: David Rosenbloom. **Cast**: James Woods (Cleve), Brian Dennehy (Dennis Meechum), Victoria Tennant (Roberta Gillian), Allison Balson (Holly Meechum), Paul Shenar (David Madlock), George Coe (Graham), Ann Pitoniak (Mrs. Foster), Mary Carver (Cleve's mother), Sully Boyar (Monks), Kathleen Lloyd (Annie). **Locations**: Los Angeles; New York, NY; El Paso, TX; Oregon. **Released**: Orion Pictures, September 25. 110 minutes.

Dennis Meechum is a detective who gained a measure of celebrity as an author with his first book about an infamous unsolved case in which he was seriously wounded. Following his wife's premature death, Meechum experiences interminable writer's block. His next book is due and the publisher is hounding him. Wanting both respect and revenge, a professional hit man named Cleve seeks out Meechum and offers to disclose the details about how his killings created a corporate empire if Meechum will write a book about it. Quick trips to New York and El Paso leave a trail of dead witnesses—all victims of the corporation's new hit men who are tailing Cleve and Meechum. Meechum is finally convinced to write the book when he realizes that Cleve is one of the crooks from the unsolved case, and that all of his crimes are linked to the corporation. When David Madlock, the corporate founder, learns that he cannot buy off the author, he kidnaps his daughter. While Meechum and Madlock negotiate inside the latter's oceanside estate, Cleve systematically eliminates all of Madlock's security personnel and then willingly gives up his life to save Meechum and the new book.

The opening sequence of *Best Seller* is shot from a subjective point of view in a vehicle driving through a dark and desolate underground garage. Four successive dissolves lead us from the tunnel-like garage to street level brightness where the frame totally overexposes and the film's title wipes on the

Best Seller: *Dennis Meechum (Brian Dennehy) and Cleve (James Woods).*

screen. This opening sequence is a metaphor for the world encountered in *Best Seller*. Darkness vs. light—a good cop/author who must confront and make sense of a criminal's murderous past. The emphasis on the past is an obvious noir motif, as is the notion of a fractured family structure, which helps to undercut any sense of character stability, especially in the noir protagonist. Meechum is widowed and struggling to raise a teenage daughter. Coupled with his police work, it makes for an unbalanced home life; an environment that Cleve is able to easily penetrate and parlay into gaining Meechum's acceptance to document his criminal story. As their relationship develops and they talk about personal issues, Cleve accurately surmises that Meechum's wife "was the clean part of your life. I'm the dirty part—the criminal."

John Flynn's affinity for noir storytelling is best illustrated in the scene at the old, abandoned boat dock where Cleve and Meechum encounter each other for the first time. As Meechum arrives in his car, the characteristic shiny, wet pavement is lit by a solitary street lamp. When he tells Cleve it's crazy to even suggest writing such a preposterous story, the nemesis responds from the shadows in droll, noir fashion, "Well, it's a crazy world." Moments later, a section of the decaying pier caves in under Meechum's weight and Cleve leaps to save him from what certainly could have been a fatal accident. A subjective insert shot of where Meechum would have fallen rests on the screen just long enough for the viewer to perceive the message that there is no sure footing in the noir world.

As a veteran of several crime films including *Night Moves*, *The Onion Field*, *Fast Walkin'*, *Against All Odds*, *Cop*, and *True Believer*, to name a few, Woods is a certifiable neo-noir icon of the contemporary American cinema. Playing the role of Cleve to snaky perfection, he provides the film's evil equivalent to Meechum's honest cop, where the two characters wage battle on a metaphysical level. Anxious to gain absolution for his crimes, Cleve tries to get Meechum to justify his actions: "You and I know things other people don't, don't we? How it feels to kill a man, for instance. Cop; Killer. Two sides of the same coin. We have a natural bond, you and I. This unlikely bond almost becomes a transference of darkness, when in his weakest moment, Meechum barely avoids pulling the trigger on the unarmed Madlock. The dying Cleve then concedes the spiritual battle to Meechum and with his last bit of strength, utters a cynical endnote: "Always the good cop." **TE**

BEYOND A REASONABLE DOUBT #2 (2009)

Director/Director of Photography: Peter Hyams. **Screenplay**: Hyams based on the original screenplay by Douglas Morrow. **Producers**: Limor Diamant, Mark Damon, Ted Hartley (RKO). **Production Designer**: James Gelarden. **Music**: David Shire. **Editor**: Jeff Gullo. **Cast**: Jesse Metcalfe (C.J. Nicholas), Amber Tamblyn (Ella Crystal), Michael Douglas (Mark Hunter), Joel Moore (Corey Finley), Orlando Jones (Det. Nickerson), Laurence Beron (Det. Merchant). **Location**: Shreveport, Louisiana. **Released**: Autonomous, September 11. 105 minutes.

After producing a prize-winning documentary in upstate New York, television reporter C.J. Nicholas is hired by a station in Shreveport but mostly assigned innocuous pieces. He suspects that local prosecutor and probable gubernatorial candidate Mark Hunter is manipulating DNA to get convictions. Although he obtains possibly incriminating material from his new girlfriend Ella Crystal, an assistant district attorney, his editor will not authorize further investigation. Then he convinces his colleague Corey Finley to help in an outlandish scheme: document the planting of circumstantial evidence so that Nicholas will be arrested and tried for murder then reveal the ruse after Hunter "fixes" the case. All goes as planned until Finley is killed by Hunter's police accomplice Merchant. Nicholas is convicted. Although uncertain of his innocence, Crystal finds proof that Hunter has doctored an earlier crime-scene photo. After Hunter is arrested and Nicholas conditionally released from death row, she discovers that the murder victim was the supposedly dead subject of Nicholas' documentary and realizes he actually is the killer. She calls the police who rearrest him.

Released 53 years almost to the day after Fritz Lang's last film noir, the key narrative change is the substitution of exposing prosecutorial corruption for the simpler anti-death penalty motive of the original. Unlike Lang's work, which filtered events through a distorted perspective focused on distracting detail and reduced nuance in performances, the remake's style seems mostly inspired by contemporary television dramas produced by Jerry Bruckheimer or Dick Wolf that focus on police and legal procedures. Both movies rely on the audience's empathy with the false killer and the presumption from the actor's past roles that the character has naïvely exposed himself to a horrendous turn of events but is innocent. Just as Dana Andrews had portrayed obsesssive

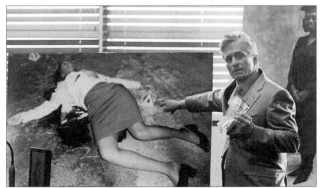

Beyond A Reasonable Doubt: *D.A. Mark Hunter (Michael Douglas) presents doctored evidence to a jury..*

and violent cops in *Laura* and *Where the Sidewalk Ends*, former teen star Jesse Metcalfe has already grown up on *Desperate Housewives* and crossed the line in *Loaded* (2008). The nervous energy and self-deprecating humor in his courtship of Crystal does contrast with Andrews' mature and measured portrayal of novelist Tom Garrett. While the film-makers presume that few in the contemporary audience will know the 1956 production, the plot enhancement of official corruption raises the stakes and distracts the viewer from the possibility that Nicholas is actually guilty.

Whereas Lang filmed Morrow's script as if he were Otto Preminger, filtered through a morass of details and character eccentricities, Hyams substitutes his usual visual style (he is also the director of photography on his last dozen features):" foreground clutter, shadowy frames, and an occasional unmotivated camera move. Unlike his prior neo-noir remake —*Narrow Margin* almost twenty years ago—which was effectively anchored by Gene Hackman mirroring the performance of Charles McGraw in the classic period, despite the conspiracy, fatal car chase and assault in a parking garage, despite the new dialogue and younger, ostensibly hipper characters, this *Beyond A Reasonable Doubt* never recreates the sense of noir underworld that lingered with subtle malaise in the original. **AS**

THE BLACK DAHLIA (2006)

Director: Brian De Palma. **Screenplay**: Josh Friedman from the novel *The Black Dahlia* by James Ellroy. **Producers**: Rudy Cohen, Moshe Diamant, Avi Lerner, Art Linson (Millennium Films/Equity Pictures/Nu Image Entertainment/Signature Pictures). **Director of Photography**: Vilmos Zsigmond. **Production Designer**: Dante Ferretti. **Music**: Mark Isham. **Editor**: Bill Pankow. **Cast**: Josh Hartnett (Dwight "Bucky" Bleichert), Scarlett Johansson (Kay Lake), Aaron Eckhart (Lee Blanchard), Hilary Swank (Madeleine Linscott), Mike Starr (Russ Millard), Mia Kirshner (Elizabeth Short), Fiona Shaw (Ramona Linscott), John Kavanagh (Emmett Linscott), Rachel Miner (Martha Linscott), Richard Brake (Bobby DeWitt), Bill Finley (George Tilden). **Released**: Universal Pictures, September 15. 121 minutes.

Los Angeles. Policemen Dwight and Lee meet during the 1943 "Zoot Suit" riot. Dwight and Lee are sent on a stake out; in a shootout, Lee saves Dwight's life, and Fitch, another criminal, dies. Simultaneously, in the grass behind the building, the mutilated corpse of "Black Dahlia" Short is discovered. Dwight realizes that Lee's girlfriend, Kay, was once a prostitute for DeWitt, Lee's nemesis. Dwight and an increasingly agitated Lee investigate Short's history, including her involvement with pornographic films and the lesbian underground. Dwight is led to Madeleine and her rich, eccentric father Emmett and mother Ramona; Dwight and Madeleine begin an affair. Dwight tracks DeWitt, and witnesses Lee's murder. Kay and Dwight begin a relationship. Dwight discovers Lee's money taken from DeWitt and Fitch, and realizes that Lee murdered both. Dwight grasps the connection between Emmett's real estate dealings and the porno featuring Short. Confronting Emmett and Madeleine, Dwight learns that Emmett's associate George is Madeleine's true father, that Emmet had procured Short for George, and that Ramona in a jealous rage killed and disfigured her. Dwight confronts

The Black Dahlia: *Josh Harnett as Det. Dwight "Bucky" Bleichert.*

Madeleine with his realization that she and George killed Lee. Dwight kills Madeleine, and returns to Kay.

Through the coincidence of *Femme Fatale* and *The Black Dahlia* as consecutive films in his career, De Palma has become indelibly associated with neo-noir. But where *Femme Fatale* vigorously takes a central feminine archetype of the genre and spins a postmodern fantasia around it, *The Black Dahlia*, at least on its glossy surface, has more in common with nostalgic 1970s revisitations/remakes like *Farewell, My Lovely*. Although De Palma touted it during production as the "ultimate film noir," its evocation of the genre is mainly iconographic and stylistic: settings such as diners, boxing halls, and police offices; shadows cast upon faces by Venetian blinds; classic glamour outfits for a rather wooden Johansson.

Narratively the borrowing is even more diffuse: the femme fatale role is split between sexy victim Kay and perverse manipulator Madeleine; and Dwight (with his voice-over narration) frequently finds himself overwhelmed by the complex mechanism of a conspiracy plot that is several steps ahead of him. Particular aspects of this condensed, somewhat awkward adaptation of Ellroy's popular novel are congenial to De Palma, resulting in several striking set-pieces: the secret coincidence of two plots (Lee's murder of Fitch and the discovery of Short's corpse) viewed in a single, elaborate crane shot; the enigmatic murder of Lee, as viewed from Dwight's distant, impotent position. But other aspects—the moral dilemmas of loyalty and acquiescence for Dwight, Ellroy's panoramic interest in LA's social and political history—are conveyed in a rather flat, purely expositional way. Predictably, on its release, the film was heavily criticized in comparison with Hanson's *L.A. Confidential*—the reviewers' mantra being that the characters are uninvolving, and the narrative impossible to follow.

But *The Black Dahlia* becomes more intriguing if we focus upon its gorily horrific, exaggeratedly grotesque, and classically Expressionist elements (cued by clips from Paul Leni's 1928 *The Man Who Laughs*). It as if De Palma began from the image of Short's corpse, and followed the "figural contagion" that results from it—rendering all living characters somewhat less than human, more brute bodies (frequently bleeding, maimed, cut, and dismembered) than three-dimensional people. It is in this light that the psychosexual dimension of the piece (Dwight's perverse, indirect desire to "fuck a corpse," as both Madeleine and Kay claim) truly emerges: Dwight's viewings of Short's audition reels and porno films are presented as his virtual mental fantasy-projections. This is why, at the end, no happy ending is possible: the image of the corpse returns, heralded by the sight and sound of suitably Expressionist crows. **AM**

BLACK RAIN (1989)

Director: Ridley Scott. **Screenplay**: Craig Bolotin and Warren Lewis. **Producers**: Stanley R. Jaffe and Sherry Lansing. **Director of Photography**: Jan de Bont. **Music**: Hans Zimmer. **Art Directors**: John Jay Moore and Herman F. Zimmerman. **Editor**: Tom Rolf. **Cast**: Michael Douglas (Nick Conklin), Andy Garcia (Charlie Vincent), Ken Takakura (Masahiro Matsumoto), Kate Capshaw (Joyce Kingsley), Yusaku Matsuda (Sato), Shigeru Koyama (Ohashi), John Spencer (Oliver), Guts Ishimatsu (Katayama), Yuya Uchida (Nashida), Tomisaburo Wakayama (Sugai), Luis Guzman (Frankie). **Released**: Paramount Pictures, September 22. 125 minutes.

While under investigation for bribery, New York detective Nick Conklin receives an assignment to escort Japanese gangster Sato back to Tokyo. Although Nick is accompanied by his partner Charlie Vincent, Sato's gang helps him escape at the airport. Although they are supposed to work with Japanese Inspector Masahiro, Conklin and Vincent behave as free agents until Sato murders Charlie. A chastened Conklin realizes he must follow Masahiro's lead in dealing with Japanese yakuza. After witnessing a violent confrontation of rival gangs over counterfeit plates, Conklin chases and captures Sato on a motorcyle which makes it possible for Masahiro to regain "face" with his colleagues. Conklin leaves Tokyo to face sanctions back in New York.

Black Rain was released at the height of the 1980s Japanese economic groundswell that threatened American global financial hegemony. Ridley Scott's film both displays the contemporary Reaganite xenophobic mood that characterized many films of that era and exhibits that specifically American cultural discourse concerning fears of alternative cultures that pockmark Hollywood cinema. It is not surprising that *Black Rain* reproduces many of its predecessors' visual motifs with the opening scenes of New York representing the urban decline of the earlier noir films. *Black Rain*'s main character is an unpleasant, divorced, financially burdened macho cop whom the film later reveals is actually "on the take." After confronting the violent technology represented by Sato in a restaurant meeting between Mafia and yakuza leaders, Nick and his partner Charlie escort the more affluent gangster back to Japan with its high power technological world contrasting with America's urban decay. Ironically, before Sato's murder of senior yakuza associates, the background music plays Bobby Darin's version of "Beyond the Sea." Once in Tokyo, overwhelmed by the culture's technological affluence and different customs, Nick and Charlie behave like ugly Americans abroad until Charlie dies in a motorcycle attack led by Sato. The Americans become little better than vulnerable animals in a bullfight dominated by sinister bike-riding yakuza in a neo-noir representation of the yellow peril's threat to American masculinity. Nick and Charlie now experience the dark side of a culture making American fascination with Honda motor cycles possible as well as threatening the home market with a more advanced technological import.

As well as continuing Scott's visual innovations within the context of contemporary American neo-noir in *Blade Runner* and *Someone To Watch over* Me (1987), *Black Rain* also interrogates (from a Western perspective) the changing world of Japanese yakuza culture that Kinji Fukasaku had significantly treated in his *Yakuza Papers* (*Battles without Honor and Humanity*) films a decade earlier. As in American films such as *The Rise and Fall of Legs Diamond*, a battle exists between different generations of the gangster fraternity. Despite his violent nature, older *oyabun* Sugai still believes in those traditional codes of honor and loyalty represented by Takakura Ken in his *giri-ninjo* (duty/humanity) roles in the classical *yakuza-eiga* films of the 1950s and 1960s. *Black Rain* now significantly places him on the right side of the law and it is he who teaches the ugly American character of Charlie virtues of honor and loyalty to the group.

No matter how much American ideology may deny it, Sato is both an American *and* monstrous Japanese creation. In one of the most memorable lines in the film, Tomisaburu Wakayama—best-known to Western audiences for his association with the 1972-74 *Lone Wolf and Cub* series—as Sugai explains the significance of "black rain," a title which appears enigmatic for most American audiences. *Black Rain* is the English translation of the famous post-Hiroshima Japanese novel by Masuji Ibuse. Sugai later tells Nick that his former lieutenant Sato "might as well be an American" since his disloyal and disrespectful behavior is solely orientated towards money. By contrast, Sugai wishes to destroy the American economy in revenge for the bombing of Hiroshima. "You made our rain black. We forgot who we were. You created Sato and thousands like him. I'm paying you back."

Even Takakura's Masahiro articulates Japanese feelings for revenge on their old enemy who has drastically changed their culture. "All America is good for is the movies. We made the machines. We won the peace." Traditional and modern machine imagery dominates the film both in the technological cityscape and the hellish regions of the steel smelting factor where Sato and Sugai hold their first meeting. Yet despite contemporary ideological currents of "Jap-bashing" fears that do motivate this film, the film also yearns for those former codes of loyalty and honor that not only motivated the old-fashioned yakuza genre but also contain the seeds for a future rapprochement between Eastern and Western cultures that still have much to learn from each other. As Joyce states in her farewell to Nick, "A love-hate relationship can last a very long time." At the end of the film Nick decides not to take advantage of the

Black Rain: *Mike Douglas as Conklin (left) and Andy Garcia as Charlie.*

counterfeit plates that would solve his economic problems but instead returns them to Masahiro. By this gesture, he redeems not only himself by saving face but also saves the honor of Masahiro, the Japanese police department, and the memory of his deceased partner Charlie. **TW**

BLACK WIDOW (1987)

Director: Bob Rafelson. **Screenplay**: Ronald Bass. **Producer**: Harold Schneider. **Executive Producer**: Laurence Mark. **Director of Photography**: Conrad L. Hall. **Music**: Michael Small. **Production Designer**: Gene Callahan. **Editor**: John Bloom. **Cast**: Debra Winger (Alexandra), Theresa Russell (Catharine), Sami Frey (Paul), Dennis Hopper (Ben), Nicol Williamson (William), Terry O'Quinn (Bruce), James Hong (Shin), Diane Ladd (Etta), Lois Smith (Sara), Leo Rossi (Ricci), Danny Kamekona (Detective), David Mamet (Herb). **Released**: 20th Century-Fox, February 6. 101 minutes.

Black Widow: *Alexandra (Debra Winger) and Catharine (Theresa Russell)*.

Alexandra is a data analyst with the U.S. Department of Justice Investigative Task Force when she becomes obsessed with both a femme fatale and a "black widow" murder case. Catharine, an attractive serial killer, is the object of Alex's pursuit. The film reveals methods that Catharine employs to kill Texas toy maker Ben and Seattle Museum curator William. Alex intuits the murderer's identity, insists to her older, love-struck boss Bruce that she will catch this criminal with or without his blessing, and quits her job to prove it. When she fails to save William but comes very close to catching Catharine in Seattle, Catharine flees to Hawaii and Alex pursues undercover. Alex befriends Catharine during a scuba diving lesson, meets and is attracted to the next mark, Paul, and makes love to him with Catharine's blessing, because the playboy is seduced by Catharine's refusal to consummate. Catharine ultimately conquers Paul in a late-night nude swimming pool scene and her charms speed up their marriage plans. Alex attends the wedding ceremony, then Catharine temporarily leaves the island, and Alex solves the case by setting an elaborate trap where Paul plays a murder victim and Alex is charged as a spurned lover. Catharine, upon jail-cell provocation from Alex, confesses her criminality, is surprised by Paul's entrance, and is busted.

Black Widow is the second of a series of interesting neo-noirs directed by Bob Rafelson that also includes the remake of *The Postman Always Rings Twice* (1981), *Blood and Wine* (1997), and *No Good Deed* (2002). *Black Widow* is perhaps best remembered as the first woman-centered neo-noir film where the detective and the criminal are both female. Comparison and contrast between the two women is illustrated in montage as each woman sips wine and concentrates on the task at hand. Alex builds a case by studying files, photo slides, and evidence while Catharine stays up late examining totem poles, coins, and films about tribal life in order to seduce her next victim. Catharine is the stunning femme fatale with long blonde hair, a voluptuous body, and attractive clothes. Conrad Hall often lights her cunningly, with a mysterious, dark shadow across her heavily made-up eyes. Alex begins the film with baggy pants, blouses, unkempt hair, and no make-up and is treated as "one of the guys," but ends the film with stylish hair, a Hawaiian tan, and in a feminine, tight, blue dress with white flowers.

Marina Heung in *Film Quarterly* argues that Alex studies the femme fatale and "is turned back into an awareness of what she herself lacks." *Black Widow* is also unusual in that its setting is chiefly outdoors in sunlight, rather than in the customary noir spaces of bars, nightclubs, and warehouses. Still, there are noir moments as when, after the wedding ceremony, Alex gifts Catharine with a black widow pin. Catharine responds to the cat and mouse challenge with: "She mates and she kills. Your question is does she love? It's impossible to answer that unless you live in her world." After both women make it clear that the pursuit is not over, Catharine grabs Alex by the back of the neck, jerks her forward, and kisses her in challenge. Alex's additional bravery with men like Bruce, whose sexual harassment she rebuffs, Ricci the smarmy cop who does not help her on the case, Shin who is a lazy, inefficient, junkie detective, and Paul who is an expert seducer of women helps to invent a new, strong female investigator who is better and harder working than her male counterparts. Winger's tough, loner investigator role is further expanded upon with other actresses in *Blue Steel* (1989), *Impulse* (1990), *Deceived* (1991), or *Love Crimes* (1992), and continues in films such as *In the Cut* (2003), *Twisted* (2004), and *Taking Lives* (2004). **WC**

BLADE RUNNER (1982)

Director: Ridley Scott. **Screenplay**: Hampton Fancher and David Peoples based on the novel *Do Androids Dream of Electric Sheep?* by Philip K. Dick. **Producer**: Michael Deeley. **Director of Photography**: Jordan Cronenweth. **Music**: Vangelis. **Production Designer**: Lawrence G. Paull, Peter J. Hampton. **Editor**: Marsha Nakashima. **Cast**: Harrison Ford (Rick Deckard), Rutger Hauer (Roy Batty), Sean Young (Rachael), Edward James Olmos (Gaff), M. Emmet Walsh (Bryant), Daryl Hannah (Pris), William Sanderson (J.F. Sebastian), Brion James (Leon Kowalski), Joe Turkel (Eldon Tyrell), Joanna Cassidy (Zhora), James Hong (Hannibal Chew). **Completed**: June 30, 1981. **Released**: Warner Bros., June 25. 117 minutes. **Note**: There are several versions now available on DVD of the movie with varying endings, with and without Deckard's narration.

The opening crawl recounts a mutiny by NEXUS-6 replicants—androids of superior strength—used as slave labor "off-world" from Earth. Special squads called "Blade Runner Units" were created to police and/or "retire" (i.e. assassinate) renegade replicants. In Los Angeles, November 2019, at the headquarters of Tyrell Corporation, Blade Runner Dave Holden interrogates Leon Kowalski who blasts Holden into an adjoining room. In a deluge of rain, P.I. Rick Deckard's meal is interrupted by Gaff who arrests and brings him to police Captain Bryant. Bryant wants Deckard to find and destroy four Nexus-6 "skin jobs" that murdered 23 people and commandeered a shuttle to Earth, where they are trying to infiltrate the Tyrell Corporation. Deckard is coerced into accepting a reactivation of his police status. At the Tyrell Corporation, Deckard verifies the reliability of a Voight-Kampff test for Nexus-6 units and inadvertently exposes the replicant status of Tyrell's assistant Rachael who is unwilling to believe she is not human. After she gains his trust by saving him from Leon, Deckard finds himself falling for a "skin job." One by one Deckard tracks down and retires three replicants and discovers their true reason for returning to earth was to extend their genetically programmed four-year lifespan by finding their programmer Tyrell and, failing that, exact revenge on him. When he faces the replicant leader Roy Batty, Deckard is defeated but spared.

Los Angeles is a bleak, overpopulated and sunless city of the future with towering skyscraping monstrosities and fire-breathing processing plants, all veiled under a constant rain and gritty fog. The claustrophobic packed streets are congested with hoards of lethargic people concealed in protective clothing and clinging to the last remnants of "normal" life on earth. Above these human beings there drones a slow moving zeppelin which advertises a chance at a better life "off-world" but only for those few who can escape. Stylistically director Scott uses iconic markers of classic noir in his future setting: Deckard in a trench coat and Rachael in a tailored suit and 1940s hair style harkening back to femme fatales like Barbara Stanwyck in *Double Indemnity*; unfiltered cigarettes and classic noir locales such as the Bradbury building of *D.O.A.* or Losey's *M*. In addition, as in the noir of the classic period, ever present flashing neon adds a barrage of texture and color, bombarding the viewer with so much visual information that one might get more absorbed in the *mise en scène* than the story.

Also like many of their noir antecedents, the participants are trapped in a claustrophobic, seedy environment. However, as the bounty-hunting task unfolds through Deckard's narration, he is struck by an eerie connection with the replicants he is tracking. Although there is resonance of characters such as the sardonic Mike Hammer stalking the streets of downtown L.A. in *Kiss Me Deadly*, director Ridley Scott sets up Rick Deckard more as a modern Dixon Steele from *In a Lonely Place*, a closed-off hero of once high standing that is past his peak and now questioning his self-worth and the meaning of existence. In addition, after being saved from the clutches of Leon's hands by Rachael, Deckard becomes indebted to her and finds himself falling for the synthetic life. This exacerbates Deckard's existential angst all the more. Parallel to this is Roy Batty, the antagonist leader of the Nexus-6 rebellion, who also seeks existential resolution by returning to his metaphoric father Eldon Tyrell, ostensibly to deactivate his preprogrammed expiration but also to force Tyrell to face the mental anguish he has caused in his own creations. The somber conclusion of the movie and final encounter between Deckard and Batty on top of a rusty and dilapidated rooftop in the rain is a pyrrhic victory for the blade runner. Rather than becoming the triumphant hero he is rescued from death by Batty.

Blade Runner: *Deckard (Harrison Ford) and Roy Batty (Rutger Hauer)*

While outwardly delivering a highly stylized approach with hardboiled elements and the chiaroscuro imagery of classic noir intact, *Blade Runner* refocuses the movement's complexity of form. Its visual cacophony of dissident technological turbulence mirrors the psychological exploration of what constitutes human feeling. Philip K. Dick distilled the question into his original title, *Do Androids Dream of Electric Sheep*. Beyond visual style or purple prose or sci-fi clichés, the ultimate philosophical dilemma is not the terminal condition of rebelling Nexus-6 mechanisms but Deckard's realization, as the protagonist bearing the filmmakers' message, that humanity is not about what's under the skin but rather about living fully whatever time we are allotted. **PAD**

BLINK (1994)

Director: Michael Apted. **Screenplay**: Dana Stevens. **Producer**: David Blocker. **Executive Producers**: Robert Shaye and Sara Risher. **Director of Photography**: Dante Spinotti. **Music Supervisor**: Brad Fiedel. **Production Designer**: Dan Bishop. **Editor**: Rick Shaine. **Cast**: Madeleine Stowe (Emma Brody), Aidan Quinn (Detective John Hallstrom), James Remar (Thomas Ridgely), Peter Friedman (Dr. Ryan Pierce), Bruce A. Young (Lieutenant Mitchell), Laurie Metcalf (Candice), Matt Roth (Crowe), Paul Dillon (Neal Booker), Marilyn Dodds Frank (Emma's mother). **Released**: New Line Cinema, January 26. 106 minutes.

Emma Brody is an attractive, blind fiddler in a local Irish folk/punk band, The Drovers. John Hallstrom is a hardboiled Chicago detective. Ophthalmologist Dr. Pierce locates a cornea donor and performs an immediate operation, allowing Emma to see for the first time since she was eight years old. Emma notices problems explained as a perceptual delay, where an image is out of focus at first but later abruptly jumps into focus when her brain catches up. One night crashing noises awaken Emma from a drunken sleep. At her door she sees, out of focus, a man going down the stairs. Hallstrom officially meets Emma the next day, informing her that she witnessed the second murder of a serial killer. Hallstrom has sex and becomes obsessed with Emma, until reminded of his job with a third victim's manifestation. Hallstrom discovers a pattern connecting each crime to an unstable hospital employee, Neal

Booker, obsessed with an organ donor named Leslie Davison. Booker stalks and traps Emma as the lone witness to his second murder, kills Crowe, the cop who is supposed to protect her, and terrorizes Emma in an abandoned warehouse until she shoots him. The next morning John returns Emma's wounded guide dog and they walk off to have breakfast together.

Blink might have been a typical woman-in-peril film but director Apted is careful to make Emma strong-willed, mentally tough, and sexually liberated. For example, while trapped in a garage with serial killer Neal Booker and after missing him badly with three shots from Crowe's handgun, Booker taunts Emma by whistling "Three Blind Mice." Emma refuses to be a victim and survives by using her hearing skills to empty the final three bullets into the criminal. In a nice contrast, Apted makes the physically able rivals, the cop and the medical doctor, men who are emotionally disabled. Hallstrom may be good at his job, but he is also a lonely man who drinks too much and uses his rugged good looks to pick-up various women for one-night stands. John drags his detective buddies to a local Irish bar to drink and "share with you the music of my people" but, once he sees Emma performing, he promises his pals that "I'm going to get to know that girl" and he crudely strips off his clothes and dances in front of her nearly naked, without realizing she is blind.

Coming in at a distant fifth to more common locations like L.A., New York, San Francisco and the state of Florida, the various Chicago locations are effective in creating an urban noir atmosphere. The film imitates stylistic devices from the classic noir period in its use of Venetian blinds and darkness for chiaroscuro effects (Emma leaves the lights off in her apartment because the glare bothers her eyes), mirror shots reflecting psychological questions of identity (Emma's memories of her evil mother), and other scenes set either in clubs where the Drovers perform, or inside the grungy confines of the police department. Yet, the movie develops into a love story. John first confronts Emma with the doomed romance aspect of their relationship: "You think we have some kind of future together? Some kind of suburban bullshit? You're the type of woman who needs a man you can control. Well, guess what, I'm not that man." Emma leaves John but, immediately following this harsh scene, John admits out loud to himself that he has lied and the audience knows the couple will soon be reunited, privileging the love story over the gritty criminal narrative. The emphases on physical disability and ethnic pride in *Blink*, recalls aspects of Michael Apted's other neo-noirs: *Thunderheart* (1992) which concerns Native American pride and *Enough* (2002) about a woman's battle to re-build her ego after surviving as a battered spouse. As much as they are crime stories, Apted's neo-noirs are also genre hybrids, often focused upon particular melodramatic and sociopolitical issues. **WC**

BLOOD SIMPLE (1985)

Director: Joel Coen. **Screenplay**: Joel Coen and Ethan Coen. **Producer**: Ethan Coen. **Executive Producer**: Daniel F. Bacaner (Foxton Entertainment). **Director of Photography**: Barry Sonnenfeld. **Music**: Carter Burwell. **Editors**: Joel and Ethan Coen [as Roderick Jaynes], Don Wiegmann. **Cast**: John Getz (Ray), Frances McDormand (Abby), Dan Hedaya (Julian Marty), M. Emmett Walsh (Loren Visser), Samm-Art Williams (Meurice). **Released**: Circle Films, January 18. 99 minutes.

Marty owns a two-bit honky tonk bar in Nowheresville, Texas, and he hires Visser, an unscrupulous private dick, to spy on his wife, Abby. Visser produces photographic evidence that Abby is having an affair with Ray, one of Marty's bartenders. Marty hires Visser to kill Abby and Ray. Visser produces for Ray a photo of the couple retouched to appear that they were dead, and then shoots him with Abby's revolver to set the frame. Ray goes to the bar to get his last paycheck and finds Marty dead in his office, along with Abby's gun. Convinced that Abby killed her husband, he drives Marty's body out to some freshly ploughed farmland in the middle of the night and struggles to bury him. Abby tries to persuade Ray she didn't murder Marty, but he has to find out the hard way with a bullet from Visser in his back. Visser then stalks Abby in her new apartment but suffers a violent fate himself.

A complex, suspenseful plot with twists and double-crosses, where anything that can go wrong does. Check. Paranoia, jealousy, and bizarre, random violence. Check. A classic love triangle with a woman nobody can trust. Check. Lonely, deserted roads at night with a mysterious car tailing the protagonists. Check. All the ingredients that would meet James M. Cain's approval are in place in this low budget production that put the Coen Brothers on the moviemaking map and helped fuel the development of the modern noir genre in the 1980s. The title of the film is a term taken from Dashiell Hammett's novel *Red Harvest* and refers to the fearful psychological state a person can descend into after exposure to intense, violent situations. You won't find many more hair-raising moments in the contemporary noir cinema than you will in *Blood Simple* with Abby fighting off Visser in her apartment, or Ray trying to dispose of the half-dead Marty. The tension that builds up in the burial scene, followed by Ray's fear, suspicion, and remorse is bone chilling and palpable. He's a lost soul without any visible redeeming values, but he's the character most easy to identify with. **TE**

BODY HEAT (1981)

Director/Screenplay: Lawrence Kasdan. **Producer**: Fred T. Gallo (Ladd Company). **Director of Photography**: Richard H. Kline. **Production Designer**: Bill Kenney. **Music**: John Barry. **Editor**: Carol Littleton. **Cast**: William Hurt (Ned Racine), Kathleen Turner (Matty Walker), Richard Crenna (Edmund Walker), Ted Danson (Peter Lowenstein), J.A. Preston (Oscar Grace), Mickey Rourke (Teddy Lewis), Kim Zimmer (Mary Ann Simpson), Jane Hallaren (Stella). **Released**: Warner Bros, August 28. 118 minutes.

Blood Simple: *Frances McDormand as Abby.*

A simple boy-meets-new-girl beginning: small-time defense attorney Ned Racine meets sultry but married Matty Walker outside a bar. After a series of intense sexual encounters, the couple decides to kill her rich but nasty husband Edmund. After careful planning and the actual murder, Racine uses a fire bomb from Teddy Lewis, an arsonist client, to cover traces of foul play. Unfortunately, soon after the deed is done Racine learns of a suspicious last-minute change in Edmund's will, superseding a pre-nup and cutting out Matty's sister-in-law Roz. What's more Edmund's eye-glasses have somehow fallen into the hands of a housekeeper with blackmail in mind. Finally Teddy tells Racine that he sold Matty an incendiary device of her very own. Despite knowing that both his D.A. friend Peter Lowenstein and homicide detective Oscar Grace have doubts about the accidental death and may have him or his paramour under surveillance, Racine goes to confront Matty, who apparently dies when her boathouse explodes. Racine is arrested and faces certain conviction. In prison, he realizes that Matty has pulled a switch. Her high school yearbook confirms that she is actually Mary Ann Simpson, and the charred body of the real Matty must be the one retrieved from the boathouse. Indeed, Matty/Mary Ann is sunning herself on a South American beach and enjoying the proceeds of her successful scheme.

As many commentators have noted, *Body Heat* is *Double Indemnity* for the post-Code era, a conspicuous reworking of the Cain novel as adapted by Chandler and Wilder without being an official remake or even acknowledging its source. While Lawrence Kasdan's screenplay necessarily alters quite a few details, the Florida setting is another sunny clime (where murder can still smell like honey suckles), the protagonist is another semi-sleazy hustler (more intent on ambulance chasing than on actuarial tables), and the Barton Keyes part is split between the two acquaintances, a canny detective and an even sharper assistant district attorney, both of whom the protagonist knows must be deceived when he concocts a murder scheme for love and money. Of course, while Neff is a top agent with Pacific All Risk, Ned Racine is a low-rent mouthpiece, who a judge remarks is sorely in need of a better class of client. While the plot to kill the husband involves a will rather than an insurance policy, the most important twist—and subsequently most imitated in neo-noir—is that the murdering couple does not ride the streetcar to the end of the line together. Instead the femme fatale gets away with it by finding a corpse to stand in for her.

Body Heat also offers the neo-noir viewer what an audience in 1944 could only imagine. When Walter Neff dug his fingers into Phyllis Dietrichson's sweater and said, "I'm crazy about you, baby," the scene ended. Whether by cut, dissolve or fade out, sex between the murderous couple in *Double Indemnity* was the unseen event in a Production Code-mandated ellipsis. *Body Heat* opens with a naked, sexually sated Racine staring out a window at a distant fire, wondering if a client of his is responsible. One quickly loses count of the number of subsequent sexual scenes, not to mention the variety of props and positions, between Racine and Matty, which certainly contributed to both the notoriety and the popularity of the film that grossed the 1981 equivalent of $100 million in its initial release. Matty tells Ned, in one of the many bits of dialogue that mirror the slightly more oblique double entendres in *Double Indemnity*, that her "engine runs a little hotter than

Body Heat: *Ned Racine (William Hurt).*

normal" and then proves it to him and the viewer: she leads him to her home, provokes a 1940s style metaphor for sex by having him break a glass door to get in, and finally surrenders to him on the carpet with unabashed concupiscence. As with Neff and Dietrichson, this reckless passion for each other makes it difficult for them to stay apart after the murder of her husband. But unlike Neff who forces Phyllis to meet him guardedly in a local market and despite the fact that Edmund's niece is staying in the house, Ned rushes over in the throes of uncontainable desire for Matty to fellate him—all this as if to demonstrate the truth of Matty's early remark: "You're not too smart, are you? I like that in a man."

Although the complications which ensue continue to mirror *Double Indemnity*—like Neff, he suspects that Matty may be setting him up as the investigators become more suspicious of the accidental nature of the death, they naturally focus on the wife—Racine never manages to give the lie to Matty's assessment of his intelligence. The final mirror between the adulterous killers is their last fateful and fatal meeting. By the boathouse, Matty again confesses her love for Racine, even though she no longer thinks he believes her. Whereas, having lured Neff into her darkened parlor, Phyllis' inability to shoot again and finish him off unexpectedly confirms her emotional attachment to him, Matty is a blacker widow. While Neff can look back, accept that he killed for money and a woman, and ruefully conclude "I didn't get the money, and I didn't get the woman. Pretty isn't it?" the imprisoned Racine continues to delude himself that his purposes were somehow purer than Matty's, that she was and is a woman "who could do what was necessary. Whatever was necessary." The coda that reveals Matty on the beach, as a young stud serves her drinks, evidences a new post-feminist point of view on the part of the filmmakers. In the classic noir, a female criminal, no matter how appealing or wronged, like Debby March in *The Big Heat,* had to suffer and die for her mistakes. In neo-noir, a criminal woman's sheer force of will may permit her survival. But there is a possible caveat. As Matty stares out at the beach before her, she looks genuinely melancholy and wistful. She pays little attention to her companion. Is it possible that, like Phyllis, Matty did love Ned? Did doing what was necessary to survive include giving up a man she loved? Is this really the implication in Kathleen Turner's performance—or just a desperate patriarchal grasp for a morsel of residual potency?

More than twenty-five years after its release, *Body Heat* remains the earliest and perhaps best example of neo-noir films that directly confront the love/sex, honor/money dichotomies. Certainly Kasdan's script has as many twists and turns as the most complicated classic period narrative, but his male protagonist is emotionally closer to Steve Thompson in *Criss Cross* than to Walter Huff in Cain's *Double Indemnity* or Neff in *Double Indemnity* the movie. That leaves him vulnerable to the ultimate double-cross by a 1980s-style femme fatale not only more cunning and ruthless than Phyllis Dietrichson but than just about any of her antecedents or her successors. **AS & JU**

THE BORDER (1982)

Director: Tony Richardson. **Screenplay**: David Freeman, Walon Green, Deric Washburn. **Producer**: Edgar Bronfman, Jr. **Director of Photography**: Ric Waite. **Production Designer**: Toby Carr Rafelson. **Music**: Ry Cooder, Domingo Samudio. **Editor**: Robert K. Lambert. **Cast**: Jack Nicholson (Charlie Smith), Elpidia Carrillo (Maria), Harvey Keitel (Cat), Warren Oates (Red), Shannon Wilcox (Savannah), Valerie Perrine (Marcy), Manuel Viescas (Juan), Jeff Morris (J.J.), Mike Gomez (Manuel), Dirk Blocker (Beef), Lonny Chapman (Andy). **Released**: Universal/RKO, January 31. 108 minutes.

Charlie Smith is an INS border agent in Texas. In order to keep his wife Marcy happy and support his middle-class lifestyle, he becomes involved with border agents Cat and Red in an illegal alien smuggling racket. When he begins to suspect that Cat has murdered a competing smuggler, Charlie tries to back out but is framed for the death of two illegals. He falls back in line but finds himself drawn more and more across the border to Mexico where he follows the struggles of a young woman, Maria, to find work in the U.S. and to keep her family together. When her baby is stolen to be sold to an Anglo family, Charlie resolves to help her. In the process he is pursued by Cat and Red, who die in a shoot out in the desert with Charlie. Charlie rescues the baby and returns him to his mother in Mexico.

British New Wave director Tony Richardson (*The Loneliness of the Long Distance Runner, Tom Jones*, etc.) constructs a dialectical meditation on borders of various kinds in his unjustly ignored neo-noir *The Border*, starring Jack Nicholson. The film is constructed with crosscutting between its male protagonist—a Texas border agent Charlie Smith in his anguished struggle to attain the middle-class American dream of tract house, pool, and neighborhood barbecues—and its female protagonist—Maria (played with an almost mute delicacy by Elpidia Carrillo) in her own struggle to keep what is left of her family intact by finding work across the border in Texas. The cutting back and forth across the border between the United States and Mexico works on several levels. Physically, it is the arbitrary division between two countries across which the poor like Maria must cross in order to find work to support their families (her husband has died in an earthquake and she must support her baby as well as her brother). But it also represents, as conceived by Richardson, as a division between the artificial and the authentic—between the middle-class American life of consumerism, debt, and corruption and the genuine struggle of the Mexican impoverished to support their families under the most difficult conditions, natural and man-made.

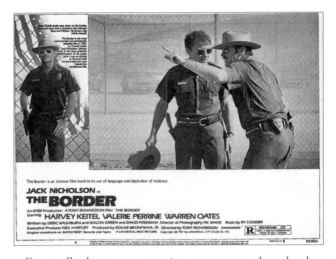

The Border is an intense film both in its use of language and depiction of violence.

JACK NICHOLSON as
THE BORDER
An EFER Production A TONY RICHARDSON Film "THE BORDER"
starring HARVEY KEITEL VALERIE PERRINE WARREN OATES
Written by DERIC WASHBURN and WALON GREEN and DAVID FREEMAN Director of Photography RIC WAITE Music by RY COODER
Executive Producer NEIL HARTLEY Produced by EDGAR BRONFMAN, JR. Directed by TONY RICHARDSON PANAVISION®
Original soundtrack on BACKSTREET Records and Tapes. A UNIVERSAL-RKO PICTURE Copyright © 1981 by UNIVERSAL CITY STUDIOS, INC.

Eventually the two protagonists meet across these borders and the conflicted and corrupted Charlie finds himself drawn to this young woman's genuineness, especially blatant when placed against his own wife's Barbie-like vapidness (in the first scenes with Marcy a Barbie doll shares the frame with her). Maria inspires Charlie, who has become part of the illegal alien smuggling ring in order to support his middle-class lifestyle, to become a "better man" or as he says himself, "I wanna feel good about something . . ." And so he draws his own border in the sand and tells Cat, the border agent who first introduced him to the smuggling racket, "You see this line . . . this line I do not cross." In a violent climax Charlie is true to his word and redeems himself by saving Maria's baby and returning it to her as they both stand in the Rio Grande, across the border that had divided them and their cultures for most of the movie. **JU**

BOUND (1996)

Directors/Screenplay: Andy and Larry Wachowski. **Producers**: Stuart Boros, Andrew Lazar, Jeffrey Sudzin. **Director of Photography**: Bill Pope. **Production Designer**: Eve Cauley. **Music**: Don Davis. **Editor**: Zach Staenberg. **Cast**: Jennifer Tilly (Violet), Gina Gershon (Corky), Joe Pantoliano (Caesar), John P. Ryan (Micky Malnato), Christopher Meloni (Johnnie), Richard C. Sarafian (Gino Marzzone), Mary Mara (Bartender), Susie Bright (Jesse). **Released**: Spelling/De Laurentiis, October 4. 108 minutes.

Corky, an ex-con, takes a job as a handywoman for a mob boss. While fixing up an apartment, she meets Violet, the girlfriend of mob "launderer" Caesar. Violet seduces the wary and cynical Corky and then proposes a scheme to escape Caesar and steal over two million dollars from the mob. The plan goes awry, causing the mob to pursue Caesar. When Caesar discovers that Corky and Violet are the perpetrators, he threatens them both. But before he can act on his threats, Violet shoots him. They then dispose of the body, convincing mob boss Micky that Caesar has absconded with the loot.

The Wachowski Brothers (who brought their noir sensibilities to their epic multi-part sci-fi film *The Matrix* three years later) repackage a number of themes, archetypes, and motifs from classic noir heist films like *Criss Cross* and *The Asphalt Jungle* in their premiere neo-noir movie *Bound*. Trust, betrayal, corruption, and amour fou, all noir staples,

NEO-NOIR/RETRO-NOIR

Classic film noir—black-and-white Hollywood crime films made in the 1940s and 1950s, roughly post-gangster and pre-color, or just pre-World War II to just after the Korean War—exists in a discrete historical moment. Post-classic noir designates films made after that, movies which reflect narratively, visually, and/or thematically the classic period. It seems useful to separate post-classic noir into two strands, retro-noir and neo-noir. Retro-noir designates films made after the classic period which use the 1940s and 1950s as a setting including, for example, *Mulholland Falls* (1996), *L.A. Confidential* (1997), *The Man Who Wasn't There* (2001), and *Black Dahlia* (2006). Neo-noir films are made after the classic period but produced and set in a contemporary time frame such as *The Long Goodbye* (1974), *Body Heat* (1981), *Jackie Brown* (1997), *Twilight* (1998), *Collateral* (2004), and *Brick* (2005).

L.A. Confidential

Retro-noirs provide the myriad pleasures of seeing a cultural moment recreated. In the case of film noir, the moment may be more cinematic than realistic, but it remains vibrant in the popular imagination, a time when trench-coated, fedora wearing doomed men were tough-talking and hard-boiled; when deadly women were slinky, gorgeous, grasping, and equally doomed; when dark and empty urban streets were slashed with the light of a lone street light and slicked with recent rain. Hollywood often tells and retells the same stories; retro-noir allows the rescreening of an enduring and distinctly American style. Along with those pleasures, retro-noirs often provide ideologically reactionary tales, especially with regard to men and women. The intriguing gender disruptions of classic noir, perhaps reflecting the discomfort of men returning from war to find women thriving without them, dissipate in retro-noir. Men are less vulnerable and doomed, more muscular and masculine, as in *Mulholland Falls*. The women of classic noir, the femmes fatales who determined the outcome of the narrative, become pastiches: they look like dangerous dames but have no real agency. Examples include Lynn (Kim Basinger) in *L.A. Confidential* and Kay (Scarlett Johansson) in *Black Dahlia*. The result is a series of films that look like but do not work like classic film noir. Instead of infusing the mostly working-class protagonists with angst and alienation that crosses gender lines, retro-noir focuses on stable masculinity, relying on men, not women to drive the action forward.

Collateral

Black Dahlia

Neo-noirs, with their contemporaneous setting, are not as locked into the reactionary ideological project as many retro-noirs. Instead, the gender disruptions and dislocations of the late twentieth and early twenty-first century receive screen time. Here, the post-feminist femme fatale gets away with the cash while the men that mess with her wind up dead or in jail, as in *Body Heat*, *The Last Seduction* (1994), or *Bound* (1996), where the butch femme and femme fatale drive off into the sunset together. She may not kill every man she uses—Max survives *Jackie Brown*— but femininity in neo-noir remains powerful. The Production Code once insisted that the femme fatale of classic noir pay for her anti-social desires; neo-noir offers her the chance not just to survive, but to thrive. Retro-noir and neo-noir differ, in setting, characters, and storyline, providing spectators with substantially different visual and narrative pleasures. **JBW**

Evelyn Mulwray, one of the earliest retro femme fatales, fixes much less vulnerable or doomed P.I. Jake Gittes a highball in Chinatown.

inform this tale of a criminal couple in love who decide to steal mob money and live happily ever after. The significant difference, however, between this heist film and its predecessors is simply that the couple consists of two women in what may be the first mainstream lesbian noir.

Corky, as played with a brooding intensity by Gina Gershon, is a traditional noir protagonist—a cynical ex-con who against her better judgment falls for a slinky, goth Violet (Jennifer Tilly delivers another performance laced with kink and sexuality), the "moll" of mob launderer Caesar. Like most noir heist films, the primary theme is trust and its constant companion betrayal. Corky has been burned before, by a former girlfriend, and so is gun shy when Violet turns on the femme fatale sex appeal to seduce and then involve Corky in her plan to free herself from the bondage (hence the title) imposed by Caesar. Like Violet, Corky too has endured her own bondage—five years in prison for theft, the same amount of time Violet has spent with Caesar, linking them even further.

In order to further objectify this theme of bondage, the filmmakers have Caesar tie up both women towards the end of the film and verbally abuse them by calling them "dykes" (in fact, Caesar seems more outraged by the fact that they are lovers than the reality that they have stolen mob money and made him their patsy). Symbolically, it is crucial that the women free themselves from the ropes as they free themselves of Caesar's oppression. It is Violet who takes the lead, demonstrating her fidelity to Corky by shooting Caesar to death. In the last sequence, as Tom Jones sings on the soundtrack "She's a lady," Corky and Violet climb into their new truck and join hands as they take off for their "happy ever after" resolution. **JU**

BREATHLESS (1983)

Director: Jim McBride. **Screenplay**: L. M. Kit Carson, Jim McBride based on the screenplay for *A bout de souffle* by Jean-Luc Godard and story by François Truffaut. **Producer**: Martin Erlichman (Breathless Associates). **Director of Photography**: Richard H. Kline. **Music**: Jack Nitzsche. **Editor**: Robert Estrin. **Cast**: Richard Gere (Jesse Lujack), Valerie Kaprisky (Monica Poiccard), William Tepper (Paul), John P. Ryan (Lieutenant Parmentel), Art Metrano (Birnbaum), Robert Dunn (Sergeant Enright), Garry Goodrow (Tony Berrutti), Waldemar Kalinowski (Tolmatchoff), Lisa Persky (Salesgirl). **Released**: Orion Pictures, May 13. 101 minutes.

Driving from Las Vegas across the Mojave Desert in a stolen car, hustler and small time criminal Jesse Lujack accidentally shoots and kills a highway patrolman. Fleeing to Los Angeles, Jesse seeks out Monica Poiccard, a French architecture student, with whom he has had a brief relationship in Las Vegas. While waiting for money from his friend Tolmatchoff, Jesse tries to persuade the reluctant Monica to flee with him across the border to Mexico. The couple resume their relationship, Monica at once drawn to, and cautious of, Jesse's reckless outlook. Led by Lieutenant Parmentel, the LA police trace Jesse's involvement with Monica, but with her assistance Jesse manages to temporarily evade the law. Knowing that she is pregnant, Monica joins Jesse but realizing the hopelessness of their situation she notifies the police in the hope that he will leave her and save himself. Rather than flee, Jesse stays to face the law and certain death.

Breathless is a remake of Jean-Luc Godard's 1959 *nouvelle vague* landmark, *A bout de souffle*. Godard's film had already reworked the conventions—in particular, the motifs of pursuit and entrapment—of the quintessential American film noir, and included references to such films as *The Harder They Fall, Ten Seconds to Hell* and *Whirlpool*. McBride and co-writer "Kit" Carson described *Breathless* as a "double-remake," a film that would revisit *A bout de souffle* and some of its key intertexts. McBride's *Breathless* generally embraces Godard's enthusiasm for American pop-cultural iconography to include, for instance, extended quotations from Marvel Comics' *The Silver Surfer*. The Surfer—"a space-lost freak, looking for love"—reflects Jesse's outlaw character, and the situation of The Surfer and his girlfriend, "trapped in two different galaxies," reflects the film's central theme of *l'amour fou*. In another example, Godard's enthusiasm for American B-movies is acknowledged through the direct quotation of *A bout de souffle* prototype, *Gun Crazy*. Above all, *Breathless* strives to capture the vitality—the movement and energy—of American *film noir* through its stylistic innovation.

As in *Gun Crazy*, this energy is expressed in vehicular terms, specifically in the sequence in which Jesse picks up Monica in a classic Ford Thunderbird convertible. The camera assumes a position just outside the driver's-side door to take in a close-up shot of Monica and Jesse, and then scribe a 180-degree arc across the bonnet of the car and then back again. Accompanied by the driving surf-guitar of Link Wray's "Jack the Ripper," there follows a sequence in which Jesse reverses the T-bird half way down the street, before turning it in the opposite direction and taking it at high speed up and over a crest in the road. The movement of the car literally flying over the hill, renders in action the film's breathless-style, and literalizes Monica's earlier comment to Jesse: "you're like one of those rides at Disneyland . . . Wow, you make me dizzy." Monica's words point not only to Jesse's "breathless" character, but also to Richard Gere's remarkable somatic performance. Gere runs, pumps and hustles his way through the entire film. This nervous energy begins outside a Las Vegas casino with Jesse stealing a Porsche, which he drives out across the Mojave Desert, singing and wildly gesticulating to the sounds of Jerry Lee Lewis' recording of "Breathless." And it culminates in the film's closing sequence when, having refused to flee, Jesse finds himself caught between Monica and the cops. At this point Jesse performs one last wild rendition of "Breathless," singing and dancing, pumping his arms defiantly at the police, reaching out longingly to Monica. She screams out his name and runs toward him. Jesse reaches down, picks up the gun, and turns to face the police. The image freezes at the moment of his (inevitable) death, and to the sounds of X's punk, cover-version of "Breathless." **CV**

CAPE FEAR (1991)

Director: Martin Scorsese. **Screenplay**: James R. Webb, Wesley Strick based on the novel *The Executioners* by John D. MacDonald. **Producers**: Robert De Niro, Barbara De Fina. **Director of Photography**: Freddie Francis. **Music**: Bernard Herrmann. **Production Designer**: Harry Bumstead. **Editor**: Thelma Schoonmaker. **Cast**: Robert De Niro (Max Cady), Nick Nolte (Sam Bowden), Jessica Lange (Leigh Bowden), Juliette Lewis (Danielle Bowden), Joe Don Baker (Claude Kersek), Robert Mitchum (Lt. Elgart), Gregory Peck (Lee Heller), Martin Balsam (Judge), Illeana Douglas (Lori Davis). **Released**: Universal, November 13. 128 minutes.

A former Atlanta public defender, Sam Bowden has moved his wife and teenage daughter to the quiet town of New Essex, NC, where he now practices corporate law. Just released from prison after serving a long sentence for rape, Max Cady comes to New Essex looking for revenge. He knows that Bowden withheld information that might have reduced his sentence. Careful to stay within the law, Cady harasses and then terrorizes Bowden and his family, who finally flee up the Cape Fear river to a secluded hideaway where Bowden intends to trap and kill his persecutor. After an epic battle, Cady is killed and the Bowdens emerge relatively unscathed but deeply shaken.

Like most neo-noir remakes, Scorsese's *Cape Fear* features more violence and explicit sex than its original, themes that are enhanced by Scorsese's often obtrusive and shocking stylizations, including solarized photography, alternating forms of film stock, canted framings, anti-realist acting (De Niro's per-

formance especially), and jarring editing patterns. At the same time, the film is a profound homage to the J. Lee Thompson original, with three prominent performers (Peck, Balsam, and Mitchum) featured in minor roles, and Bernard Herrmann's pounding score effectively recycled. If the original treats the unexpected danger that awaits even the most innocent and normal (with the lawyer father guilty of no crime but bearing witness to what he saw Cady do), Scorsese's version foregrounds the power of vengeance, as the family's superficial happiness is deconstructed to reveal both repressed malfeasance and discontent. The Bowdens' marriage is troubled by his infidelity and has turned violent, while their sexually naive daughter, because she rightly feels ignored and abandoned, finds herself easily seduced by Cady's smarmy appeal and his canny knowledge of how to manipulate and use others. **RBP**

CHARLEY VARRICK (1973)

Director: Don Siegel. **Screenplay**: Dean Riesner, Howard Rodman based on the novel *The Looters* by John Reese. **Producer**: Don Siegel. **Director of Photography**: Michael Butler. **Music**: Lalo Schifrin. **Art Director**: Fernando Carrere. **Editor**: Frank Morriss. **Cast**: Walter Matthau (Charley Varrick), Joe Don Baker (Molly), Felicia Farr (Sybil Fort), Andrew Robinson (Harman Sullivan), Sheree North (Jewell Everett), Norman Fell (Mr. Garfinkle), Benson Fong (Honest John), William Schallert (Sheriff Bill Horton), Jacqueline Scott (Nadine), John Vernon (Maynard Boyle). **Locations**: Mustang, Nevada; Boulder Dam, Nevada; Carson City, Nevada; Dayton, Nevada. **Released**: Universal Pictures, October 19. 111 minutes.

Charley Varrick is a small-time crook who robs a bank in Tres Cruces, New Mexico. The take is some three quarters of a million dollars. Varrick, a quick study, realizes that the small branch bank is in reality a drop site for Mafia money on its way out of the country for laundering. The mob sends a hit man, Molly, to retrieve the money. Molly tracks down and kills Sullivan, Varrick's accomplice in the robbery, but the money remains in Varrick's possession. He knows he will never be free unless the mob thinks he is dead. He uses Molly's suspicion that the robbery was an inside job to set up Boyle, the president of the corporation that owns the branch. Varrick tells Boyle he wants to return the money, but only if Boyle will call off Molly. At the site of the return, Varrick makes it appear to Molly, who is observing from a distance, that Boyle was the inside man. Molly kills Boyle and is himself killed in a car bomb explosion rigged by Varrick, who has faked his own death by switching his dental records with Sullivan's and placing the dead man's body in the car's trunk.

Charley Varrick, a confluence of skillful construction, felicitous casting, and irony, offers a good look at director

Don Siegel's distinctive neo-noir approach. Here Siegel takes film noir out of the night and the city into the bright Southwest. Charley Varrick, a crop duster when he is not robbing banks, is a type found in the Harry Callahan character (*Dirty Harry*) and elsewhere in Siegel's work, a self-described "last of the independents." Under Siegel's direction, the wide-open spaces of the film's Nevada locations portend freedom for Varrick while the enclosed, claustrophobic interiors—the small bank lobby, the basement office where the Mafia boss does business, the dark, tightly-packed trailer house where Sullivan is beaten to death, the sordid Mustang Ranch brothel where Molly spends the night—symbolize the cramped moral lives and dead-end destinies of nearly everyone else in the film. The film's well cast characters suggest a neo-noir world of warped lives, deception, and betrayal in which no one can be trusted, where everyone is looking for an angle in order to settle a score or turn a fast buck, and the last man standing will be the most manipulative if not the most ruthless.

Siegel puts film noir veteran Tom Tully to good use in a bit part as the gun shop owner who sells Varrick out. When Molly shoves the wheelchair bound Tully crashing backwards into a wall, one is inevitably reminded of the famous scene in *Kiss of Death* where Richard Widmark's sadistic killer Tommy Udo gleefully pushes Ma Rizzo down a flight of stairs in a wheelchair. Siegel makes the scene work at the most fundamental visceral level by showing the off-handed way the psychopathic Molly practices his trade. Matthau's loose, gum-chewing Varrick is reminiscent of his character in *The Taking of Pelham One Two Three* (Joseph Sargent, 1974), a man who keeps his cool and cracks wise while everyone around him has reached their boiling point. Beneath the calm exterior lies a savvy manipulator. He cons Boyle, the president of the ironically named "Western Fidelity" bank corporation that owns the branch, into meeting him for the putative give-back at a deserted airstrip, but this is only to lure him into a trap. He greets Boyle as if the two of them have succeeded in ripping off the Mafia. Molly, already suspicious that Boyle is the inside man, runs him over and charges full speed at Varrick's small plane, preventing him from taking off. Utilizing skills he developed during his barnstorming days as a biplane-flying stunt pilot, Varrick fakes a crash in which he overturns his plane. He leads Molly to his death by inducing him to open up the trunk of a bomb-rigged auto where Molly thinks Varrick has hidden the haul from the bank. As if to signal Varrick's absorption into anonymity, a craned camera travels up and back as Varrick gets into his car with the Mafia's money and heads toward the highway and freedom. **SMS**

CHINA MOON (1994)

Director: John Bailey. **Screenplay**: Roy Carlson. **Producer**: Barrie M. Osborne. **Director of Photography**: Willy Kurant. **Music**: George Fenton. **Production Designer**: Conrad Agone. **Editors**: Carol Littleton and Jill Savitt. **Cast**: Madeline Stowe (Rachel Munro), Ed Harris (Detective Kyle Bodine), Benicio Del Toro (Lamar Dickey), Charles Dance (Rupert Munro), Patricia Healy (Adele), Tim Powell (Fraker), Robb Edward Morris (Pinola), Theresa Bean (Felicity Turner). **Released**: Metro-Goldwyn-Mayer, March 4. 100 minutes.
Kyle Bodine is the best homicide detective in Brayton,

Florida. Rachel is unhappily married to a philandering banker named Rupert Munro. When Rachel and detective Dickey rebel, Rachel hires Dickey to shadow and photograph her husband's indiscretions while Lamar plots with Rachel to get Rupert's twelve million dollars. An unaware Kyle meets Rachel in J.J.'s Blues Lounge and, despite her initial rebuffs, repeatedly requests time alone with Rachel which is granted late at night, on a small boat, under a "china moon," culminating in skinny-dipping and sex. Soon after, Rachel commits "justified homicide" by shooting her abusive husband and Kyle covers up the crime, disposing of the body. Yet Lamar quickly uncovers clues by discovering Munro's missing car, body, and bullets that match those of Kyle's gun, even though another gun had been used in the murder. Back at J.J.'s Lounge, the partners meet, Kyle figures out that Lamar knows too much, and pins the set-up on him. Lamar continues to dupe his senior partner, getting Kyle killed by the local police, but Rachel ends the crime spree, murdering Lamar point blank.

Following a narrative pattern begun in classic noirs *Double Indemnity* (1944) or *The Postman Always Rings Twice* (1946) and continued in the neo-noir *Body Heat* (1981), *China Moon* is another Cain-inspired love triangle where a younger male first steals a young woman from her nasty, older husband, then is led by sexual obsession into crime and deception that ends with dire consequences. The first conversation between Kyle and Rachel is classic noir: Mind some company?/Am I safe talking to you?/ We live in dangerous times./And we meet in dangerous places./I've had too much to drink in this one. The twist in *China Moon* is that the femme fatale is actually lovesick and the true criminal is the main character's cop partner. Thus, an ironic situation is put into place when Lamar promises that one day his detective work may surprise Kyle and Kyle claims, "I might be incapable of surprise. Could be, in this lifetime, I'm all surprised out." Despite Kyle's hardboiled cynicism, Lamar's double crosses shock the complacency right out of him as Kyle fruitlessly fights to clear his name.

Director John Bailey is best known as a cinematographer for such films as *American Gigolo* (1980), *The Big Chill* (1983), and *Groundhog Day* (1993). As director of *China Moon*, he includes some beautiful sets such as shots of rain-soaked streets, mysterious indoor and outdoor moonlighting, and various night scenes by the lake. Stowe looks stunning in her white, femme fatale dresses, or re-arranging her long hair so as to illuminate an exposed neckline or facial expression. But the narrative adds little that has not been dramatized in previous films. The twist of *China Moon* is that the woman ends up the only main character still alive. This becomes a common pattern in contemporary neo-noirs and Linda Williams calls such dramas part of a "sexualized noir form in which the man is a function of the woman's story" (*The Erotic Thriller in Contemporary Cinema*). The viewer is left to wonder whether Rachel lost her true love with Kyle's death, or, with Rupert, Kyle, and Lamar dead, she will live happily on her ex-husband's wealth. **WC**

CHINATOWN (1974)

Director: Roman Polanski. **Screenplay**: Robert Towne. **Producer**: Robert Evans (Penthouse/The Long Road Productions). **Director of Photography**: John A. Alonzo. **Music**: Jerry Goldsmith. **Production Designer**: Richard Sylbert. **Editor**: Sam O'Steen. **Cast**: Jack Nicholson (J.J. Gittes), Faye Dunaway (Evelyn Mulwray), John

Chinatown: *Jake Gittes (Jack Nicholson) and Evelyn Mulwray (Faye Dunaway); Right, Orange Grove: Jack Nicholson.*

Huston (Noah Cross), Perry Lopez (Escobar), John Hillerman (Yelburton), Darrell Zwerling (Hollis Mulwray), Diane Ladd (Ida Sessions), Roy Jenson (Mulvihill), Roman Polanski (Man with Knife), Dick Bakalyan (Loach), Joe Mantell (Walsh), Bruce Glover (Duffy), Nandu Hinds (Sophie), James O'Reare (Lawyer), James Hong (Evelyn's Butler), Beaulah Quo (Maid), Jerry Fujikawa (Gardener). **Released**: Paramount, June 21. 130 minutes.

Los Angeles in 1937 is suffering through a drought. J.J. Gittes, an ex-cop and private detective specializing in divorce work, is hired by a woman claiming to be Evelyn Mulwray to discover whether her husband, the water commissioner, is faithful. Gittes spies on Hollis Mulwray and sees him with a young girl. The story makes front-page headlines and Gittes learns he has been duped in a plot to discredit the commissioner, who opposes construction of a water reservoir in the San Fernando Valley farmlands near Los Angeles. The authentic Mrs. Mulwray, who is the daughter of powerful magnate Noah Cross, threatens to sue Gittes. But when her husband is found murdered, she asks Gittes to find the criminal. The detective uncovers a crooked land deal, whereby acreage in the San Fernando Valley is being purchased cheaply by Noah Cross and his associates under false names for speculation pending the reservoir's construction. Gittes is aided and hindered by the anguished Evelyn Mulwray. He learns that the young girl spotted with Hollis Mulwray is Evelyn's daughter and sister, Kathryn, the offspring of Noah's rape of Evelyn when she was fifteen years old. Gittes falls in love with Evelyn and agrees to help her smuggle Kathryn out of the country. However, the police follow his trail to Chinatown where Evelyn and Kathryn await Gittes. Noah Cross arrives also, and Evelyn wounds her father while attempting to flee with Kathryn. Handcuffed, Gittes is powerless to help and must watch while Evelyn is fatally shot by the police and Cross comforts his granddaughter, who is also his daughter.

Screenwriter Robert Towne has devised a metaphor in *Chinatown* that is easily applicable to film noir in general. Many noir characters have shadowy pasts and are plagued by subconscious fears. Gittes' worries stem from "Chinatown": a state of mind and a spiritual landscape where monstrous deeds are performed in the name of progress and eyes are quickly averted. If 1937 Los Angeles, as viewed in this film, has a definable personality, then Chinatown is its id. It does not appear as a location until the end of the story, but its ambience permeates the film. The mere mention of it causes people to respond in the manner that children react to the "bogeyman." J.J. Gittes referred to it obliquely. "You may think you know what you're dealing with but believe me, you don't," and "Talking about the past bothers everyone who works in Chinatown because you can't always tell what's going on . . ."

Based on an incident in Los Angeles history, Towne's script clothes its symbols with the trappings of a hardboiled pulp detective yarn. It is structured in the conventional private-eye style in which a straightforward investigation proves to be just the tip of the iceberg. Importantly, however, *Chinatown*'s protagonist is no Philip Marlowe who prides himself on the fact that he *doesn't* do divorce work. It is J.J. Gittes' specialty, and he is a tasteless little gumshoe with pretensions to class. Traditionally, the private eye is a man with a code, who functions like a wandering knight. He is outside the law, which is usually either corrupt or ineffectual. Gittes is as unlikely a Sir Galahad as Mike Hammer was in *Kiss Me Deadly*. Like Hammner, his main concern is "what's in it for me," getting paid. It is hinted, however, that while patrolling Chinatown he tried to prevent something terrible from happening to a woman he cared for, but his interference only hastened the calamity, and he quit the force. He continually clashes with his former colleagues, even though they are bound together in unspoken ways. When Gittes attempts to save Evelyn Mulwray, he literally gets into deep water and finds his personal history foredoomed to repeat itself.

Water is one of the many ingenious symbols used in the film. Los Angeles has been utilized effectively many times for its symbolic resonances. It is the city of eternal sunshine where prayers are answered, but it is also the dead end of the continent. When there are no more mountains to cross, the lemmings run into the sea. In *The Day of the Locust*, Nathanael West saw it as the place people come to die; Horace McCoy staged his marathon dance of death in *They Shoot Horses, Don't They?* in a squalid ballroom on the Santa Monica pier jutting into the Pacific Ocean. In *Chinatown* Los Angeles is in the midst of a drought, a parched community desperately in need of both water and spiritual relief, and the film chronicles the chicanery behind the building of a reservoir in the San Fernando Valley. The chief villain ironically named Noah is a craggy old robber baron whose incestuous rape of his daughter is paralleled by his violation of the land. The daughter, Evelyn Mulwray, is a traditional noir heroine. A genuine black widow, she ensnares the detective in a web of opposing allegiances and motives. As a professional snoop, "sticking his nose in other people's business," Gittes has his nostril slashed with a knife, brandished by director Roman Polanski as one of the villain's minions. It becomes his scarlet letter, and he sports it like a badge of courage.

Roman Polanski and Robert Towne clashed over the ending, as Towne had written that Mrs. Mulwray murders her father and Gittes spirits her daughter/sister across the Mexican border. Polanski prevailed and the finale is despairing; but more consistent with all that has preceded it. The mordant tone is in accord with Polanski's chilly temperament. Shots are composed in a constricting fashion, giving the impression that things of importance are happening just beyond the frame, on the fringes of our perception. This gives the film an airless, suffocating feeling that befits the dusty, hot climate. In collaboration with his gifted cinematographer, John Alonzo, Polanski chose elemental colors to enhance this desert-like aura, using earthy browns and sun-drenched yellows; *Chinatown* is a melancholy and savage film. Robert Towne may have set the plan in motion, but it is Polanski who wields the knife. **JB**

COLLATERAL (2004)

Director: Michael Mann. **Screenplay**: Stuart Beattie. **Producers**: Michael Mann, Julie Richardson (Dream Works, Paramount). **Directors of Photography**: Dion Beebe, Paul Cameron. **Music**: James Newton Howard. **Editors**: Jim Miller, Paul Rubell. **Cast**: Tom Cruise (Vincent), Jamie Foxx (Max Durocher), Jada Pinkett Smith (Annie Farrell), Mark Ruffalo (Fanning), Peter Berg (Richard Weidner), Bruce McGill (Pedrosa), Irma P. Hall (Ira), Barry Shabaka Henley (Daniel), Javier Barden (Felix). **Released**: United International Pictures, August 6. 120 minutes.

Cab driver, Max Durocher, picks up federal prosecutor, Annie Farrell, and the two develop a rapport before he drops her at the Los Angeles courthouse. There he picks up his next passenger, Vincent, who hires Max to drive him to five addresses across the evening. At the first, Max discovers that Vincent is a professional killer. Stowing the body of the first victim in the trunk, Vincent and Max drive to the next destination, where a second man is killed. Vincent has Max drive to a jazz club where the owner is the third victim. Max destroys Vincent's list of remaining targets, so Vincent forces Max to masquerade as himself to retrieve a new list from his employer, Felix. At a nightclub, Max finds his fourth target, but a police team, led by detective Fanning, also makes its way to the club. Max and Vincent escape the ensuing shootout but on route to the final destination Max overturns the cab and escapes. Realising that Annie is the final target, Max races to the courthouse, and helps her escape to the subway. Vincent pursues them there until he is shot dead by Max.

Collateral: *Tom Cruise (left) as Vincent and Jamie Foxx as Max Durocher..*

With *Collateral*, Michael Mann extends the professional codes, noir themes and expressive stylization—established in his earlier features, notably *Thief* and *Heat*—to tell the story of gentle Los Angeles cabbie, Max, caught in the trap of steely hit man, Vincent. Max's profession, and the dense blacks and bright neon of *Collateral*'s electrified, after-hours cityscape make the transitional noir of *Taxi Driver* (1976) a key point of reference. The film's sense of fate and coincidence is established early as Max hesitates just long enough to ensure that prosecution attorney, Annie Farrell, is his next fare. In a dreamy set-up, the two establish an instant connection as Max's light-streaked cab—a "lifeboat," as Mann describes it—makes its journey through the moody, urban glow to the Los Angeles law courts.

Max's next passenger, Vincent—the clinical professional and existentialist ruminator—proceeds to enlist the hapless driver as his unwilling accomplice in an evening of pre-assigned killings that eventually leads Max back to Annie, Vincent's final target. An unlikely but well matched team, Vincent and Max exchange tales and anecdotes—and, at one point, even identities—before Max slips out of the ever-tightening noose by spectacularly crashing his cab. Along the way there are highlights, such as jazz club owner Daniel's reminiscences about the night Miles Davis came to his joint and crime boss Javier's quietly menacing story of Santa Claus' helper, Black Pedro. At the end, *Collateral* settles into its climatic pursuit, first through a downtown Los Angeles skyscraper and next into the anonymity of the new Los Angeles subway network where the fatally wounded Vincent recounts—now enacts—the presage of his earlier joke: "Hey Max, a guy gets on the MTA here in LA, dies. Think anybody will notice?" **CV**

THE CONVERSATION (1974)

Producer, Screenplay, Director: Francis Ford Coppola. **Co-producer**: Fred Roos. **Director of Photography**: Bill Butler. **Production Designer**: Dean Tavoularis. **Music**: David Shire. **Editors**: Walter Murch, Richard Chew. **Cast**: Gene Hackman (Harry Caul), John Cazale (Stan), Allen Garfield (Bernie Moran), Frederick Forrest (Mark), Cindy Williams (Ann), Teri Garr (Amy), Harrison Ford (Martin Stett), Michael Higgins (Paul). **Released**: Paramount, April 7. 113 minutes.

Harry Caul is a technical legend and a loner who guards his privacy with a paranoiac fervor. Caul takes satisfaction in being the best but is troubled by the current job eavesdropping on a couple as they walk in a crowded square. As he dubs, augments and patches pieces of their conversation together, Caul cannot help but think that the couple may somehow be in danger. When a rival tells a story at a party of how Caul once bugged a crooked union official, who assumed his accountant had betrayed him and had his family murdered, Caul realizes that he "can't let it happen again." After his master tapes are stolen, Caul decides to try and warn the couple.

Coppola's visualization is keyed to technology. The spaces of the loft which house Caul's operation are compartmentalized by grilled enclosures, so that even at the party characters are constantly framed against electronic equipment and metal. Caul's bus ride back from his girlfriend's apartment, which he leaves abruptly because she asks too many personal questions, is a long side angle close-up with his silhouette framed against the studded white-painted wall and dark window of the bus, his face thus isolated against stark manufactured forms. It is only in his traditionally furnished apartment, playing his saxophone, that Caul lets down his guard and reveals his humanity.

Unlike Paul Magwood's *Chandler* (1971) where the riffling piano underscore contributed another layer of heavy nostalgia, David Shire's clean, jazzy measures are a contrast, an element of irregular, non-mechanized expression. It is in the final sequence, when Caul discovers that things were the opposite of what they seemed, that his insular world collapses. The closing panning shot as he sits playing the sax after tearing up the wall and floors of his apartment searching for a bug create a disturbing metaphor. For in divulging the industrial underpinnings behind the walls and under the floors, Caul himself has created an apparition of technical ruin that undermines his belief system. Like for many characters in neo-noir, success creates questions, questions create fear, and fear creates havoc inside an existential hell. **AS**

Harry Caul is
an invader of privacy.
The best in the business.
He can record
any conversation
between two people
anywhere.

So far,
three people are dead
because of him.

The Directors Company presents
GENE HACKMAN
in
"THE CONVERSATION"

COP (1988)

Director: James B. Harris. **Screenplay**: James B. Harris based on the novel *Blood on the Moon* by James Ellroy. **Producers**: James B. Harris and James Woods (Harris-Woods Productions). **Executive Producers**: Thomas Coleman, Michael Rosenblatt. **Director of Photography**: Steve Dubin. **Music**: Michel Colombier. **Editor**: Anthony Spano. **Cast**: James Woods (Lloyd Hopkins), Lesley Ann Warren (Kathleen McCarthy), Charles Durning (Dutch Peltz), Charles Haid (Delbert "Whitey" Haines), Raymond J. Barry (Captain Fred Gaffney), Randi Brooks (Joanie Pratt), Steven Lambert (Bobby Franco). **Released**: Atlantic Entertainment Group, February 5. 110 minutes.

Lloyd Hopkins is an LAPD detective obsessed with finding a serial killer while his personal life crumbles around him. His only friend is Dutch Peltz, a former partner who helps him out with special departmental requests from time to time. Hopkins discovers two key leads in Delbert Haines, a West Hollywood deputy sheriff, and Kathleen McCarthy, a feminist poet/bookstore owner. He breaks into Haines' home and identifies a link between Haines and "Birdman" Henderson, a street punk who helps Haines pinch the local drug and prostitution traffic. Hopkins scuffles and kills Haines on a return visit to his home and then Henderson is killed before he can be located. Hopkins breaks into McCarthy's home and finds a box of poems from an anonymous person with dates coinciding with the serial murders. Hopkins is suspended from the force, and when McCarthy realizes that one of the suspects is a boy she liked in high school, she warns him about the police. Hopkins intervenes and manages to arrange a meeting with the suspect at the local high school gymnasium. Packing a sawed-off shotgun, Hopkins outmaneuvers the serial killer and enforces his own brand of justice.

As Hopkins works his way back into the past to unravel the identity of the serial killer, a curious narrative pattern between illicit sex and deadly violence begins to emerge. When Hopkins arrives at the scene of the first crime, which an anonymous 911 caller has described as "something out of a Peckinpah movie," he finds the mutilated body of a young woman hanging by her feet from the bedroom ceiling. Sitting at her desk, Hopkins picks through the woman's belongings and finds classified ads from two newspapers that read: "Your place or mine? Let's get together and rap. Any and all sexually liberated people are invited to write me at . . ." With a heavy sigh, Hopkins lights a cigarette and sits back pensively, the corpse silhouetted behind him in the background. The cause and effect is obvious, underscoring a common obsession in 1980s neo-noir cinema of people being brutally punished for their sexual desires. The rest of the narrative plots out a series of similar incidents. When a robbery suspect is found in his car with a prostitute and pulls a gun on Dutch, Hopkins empties all six chambers of his .38 handgun into the man. Delbert Haines, the sleazy cop who not only raped Kathleen McCarthy back in high school, but also skimmed money from the local gay prostitution ring, meets a similar fate when Hopkins guns him down. Birdman Henderson, another McCarthy rapist and a partner in the prostitution ring, dies at the hands of the serial killer. And finally, Joanie Pratt, the hooker, is mutilated by the serial killer. James B. Harris demonstrates his consciousness of the genre's preoccupation with sex and violence, winking at the audience in the scene when Hopkins is engaged in foreplay with Joanie Pratt. Their embrace is emphasized by one of her bare legs dangling provocatively across the gun in Hopkins' hip holster.

Harris' lean cinematic landscape satisfies generic expectations. Even interiors shot in broad daylight, such as the first murder victim's apartment or Haines' residence, are filled with murky shadows, veiled further by cigarette smoke. As Hopkins pauses to take a drag from a cancer stick in front of the apartment building where the first murder occurred, squad car strobes flash across the frame and a police radio emits the call of a "211 in progress," punctuating the reality of the city's non-stop criminal activity. In the background we see shadows of the homicide crew taking the victim's body down from the ceiling. The same melancholy noir mood is evoked when Hopkins sits curled up behind the door in Haines' residence awaiting his arrival. A saxophone moans a bluesy line while the detective, fatigued from the psychological pressure of matching wits with the serial killer, reflects on his estranged family and recent suspension from the force. True to Jack Shadaoin's premise, "If the nature of the hero can be said to determine the nature of the film," then *Cop*, "is a dark film indeed." **TE**

CRIMINAL LAW (1989)

Director: Martin Campbell. **Screenplay**: Mark Kasdan. **Producers**: Robert Maclean, Hilary Heath, Ken Cord Hemdale. **Director of Photography**: Philip Meheux. **Production Designer**: Curtis Schnell. **Music**: Jerry Goldsmith. **Editor**: Chris Wimble. **Cast**: Gary Oldman (Ben Chase), Kevin Bacon (Martin Thiel), Karen Young (Ellen Faulkner), Joe Don Baker (Detective Mesel), Tess Harper (Detective Stillwell). **Released**: TriStar, April 28. 117 minutes.

Ben Chase, an aggressive attorney, successfully defends Martin Thiel, a client who is accused of a brutal rape and murder. After the not guilty verdict, Chase learns that Thiel actually committed the crime. When Thiel is arrested for another, Chase agrees to defend him again but plans to betray his client, cooperate with investigators and get him convicted. When Thiel realizes what Chase is doing, he threatens him and forces Chase to confront moral and ethical conflicts he had ignored throughout his career.

Criminal Law incorporates diverse elements without having recourse to extensive narrative complication. The premise is direct and echoes the conflicted position of Father Logan in *I Confess*. The character motivations are also direct. Not only must the attorney blame himself for leaving a dangerous psychopath at large, but he would still be ethically compromised if he used information acquired within the context of attorney/client privilege against him. A version of the same dilemma confronts the assistant district attorney in *Presumed Innocent* (1990), for as he investigates the murder of a colleague with whom he had an affair, he finds that much of the physical evidence could incriminate him. In this picture and the earlier *Frantic* (1988), Harrison Ford's portrayals capture the edge between panic at confronting circumstances beyond one's control and resilience in fighting to regain it. In *Criminal Law* Gary Oldman's portrayal of Chase is much edgier. Only when he begins to feel threatened himself does Chase finally empathize with the victims of the criminals he has so vigorously represented.

What separates the moral problem of this attorney, initially at least, from those in *True Believer* or *Suspect*, from courtroom drama, is the profundity of his error. The defense attorneys in *True Believer* and *Suspect* are idealists at heart, whose discovery of corruption within the system does imperil them, but whose faith in that same system is ultimately redemptive, particularly in *True Believer*. The protagonist of *Criminal Law* ends up resembling *D.O.A.*'s Frank Bigelow in his determined resolve to put things right. When his client threatens another woman with whom the attorney is emotionally involved, the web of circumstances closes and creates a quandary as dark as Vanning's in *Nightfall*. Like other neo-noir victims caught in such a web, thrashing about is futile. Only those able to seek and find assistance manage to survive. **AS**

D.O.A. (1988)

Directors: Rocky Morton, Annabel Jankel. **Screenplay**: Charles Edward Pogue based on the screenplay for *D.O.A.* by Russell Rouse, Clarence Greene. **Producers**: Ian Sander, Laura Ziskin (Touchstone Pictures). **Director of Photography**: Yuri Neyman. **Music**: Chaz Jankel. **Editors**: Michael R. Miller, Raja Gosnell. **Cast**: Dennis Quaid (Dexter Cornell), Meg Ryan (Sydney Fuller), Charlotte Rampling (Mrs. Fitzwaring), Daniel Stern (Hal Petersham), Jane Kaczmarek (Gail Cornell), Christopher Neame (Bernard), Robin Johnson (Cookie Fitzwaring), Rob Knepper (Nicholas Lang), Jay Patterson (Graham Corey), Brion James (Detective Ulmer). **Released**: Warner Bros, March 18. 97 minutes.

English professor Dexter Cornell enters a police station to report his own murder, and proceeds to tell his story. Cornell's student, Nick Lang, who is awaiting feedback on his first novel, commits suicide. Cornell gets drunk and is helped from a club by a student, Sydney. The next day, Dexter discovers that he has been poisoned and has only a day or two to live. Dexter's wife Gail is found dead, and the police, believing that she and Nick were lovers, suspect Cornell. Remembering that wealthy Mrs Fitzwaring was putting Nick through college, Cornell investigates. Fitzwaring's daughter, Cookie, accuses her of killing Nick because they were in love. Cornell sees Cookie accidentally killed and then survives an assault by Fitzwaring's bodyguard, who falls to his death. Fitzwaring explains that Nick was actually her son, and commits suicide. Confused, Cornell finally secures a confession from his colleague, Petersham, who admits to having murdered Nick to steal his manuscript, and to poisoning Cornell and killing Gail because he thought they had read it. In a struggle with Cornell, Petersham falls to his death.

D.O.A. extends the remaking strategies of earlier 1980s neo-noirs—*Against All Odds*, *The Morning After*, *No Way Out*—and consolidates film noir as a commercial genre for the 1990s. Rudolph Maté's 1950 film *D.O.A.* was previously remade in Australia as *Color Me Dead* (1970). This little known version of *D.O.A.* closely follows the dialogue and plot of Maté's film and is notable for its opening, an atmospheric night-sequence filmed through the windscreen of a car on the Sydney Harbour Bridge. By contrast, the 1988 update might be described as a *non*-remake, the Rocky Morton and Annabel Jankel version retaining the original title, but transforming the earlier property beyond recognition.

The basic narrative line becomes, in this remake, little more than a high concept story pitch for initializing the project and then marketing the product to the public: "Someone poisoned Dexter Cornell. He's got to find out why. He's got

Dark City: *Richard O'Brien as Mr. Hand.*

to find out now. In twenty-fours hours he'll be Dead On Arrival." In a similar way, the title—*D.O.A.*—functions as a saleable generic marker of, and literal shorthand for, neo-noir and a readily identifiable and transferable logo for the promotion of the film. Following the trajectory signalled by the *Body Heat* revision of *Double Indemnity*, *D.O.A.* announces itself as a high-tech noir, complete with a four minute, black-and-white prologue—brimming with shadows and tilted compositions—in which college professor Cornell staggers into a police station to report that a murder has been committed and that Cornell *himself* is the victim. The remake takes this basic set-up from the original and then spins it into a convoluted trail of bigamy and murder, infidelity and suicide. The MTV credentials of directors Morton and Jankel led to the identification of *D.O.A.* as a pop-promo revision of noir motifs, and in this way it anticipates a 1990s interest in classic film noir as a readily adaptable stylistic and narrative source not only for contemporary filmmakers, but also television programmers and advertisers. **CV**

DARK CITY (1998)

Director: Alex Proyas. **Screenplay**: Alex Proyas, Lem Dobbs, David S. Goyer. **Producers**: Alex Proyas, Andrew Mason. **Director of Photography**: Dariusz Wolski. **Production Designer**: George Liddle, Patrick Tatopoulos. **Music**: Trevor Jones. **Editor**: Dov Hoenig. **Cast**: Rufus Sewell (John Murdoch), William Hurt (Inspector Frank Bumstead), Jennifer Connelly (Emma/Anna), Kiefer Sutherland (Dr. Daniel Schreber), Richard O'Brien (Mr. Hand), Ian Richardson (Mr. Book), Bruce Spence (Mr. Wall), Colin Friels (Detective Eddie Walenski), John Bluthal (Karl Harris), Melissa George (May). **Released**: New Line, February 27. 100 minutes.

John Murdoch wakes in a hotel bathtub, having suffered amnesia. He is contacted by Dr. Daniel Schreber, who urges him to flee the hotel from a group of men called "The Strangers." Murdoch escapes, eventually uncovers his real name, and tracks down his supposed wife Emma. He is also sought for a series of murders, which he cannot remember, by police inspector Frank Bumstead. Murdoch stays on the move in the city, which experiences never-ending night. He sees people fall comatose at the stroke of midnight, and he is pursued by The Strangers. In the chase, he discovers that he has psychokinetic powers like The Strangers and uses it to escape them. Eventually, after being captured, he realizes that the humans are all guinea pigs on an alien satellite and their memories are implanted as part of an experiment in immortality. Murdoch uses his powers to destroy the underground machinery and then rebuild the city above to his liking—a sunny seaside resort where he once again meets Emma, who has been implanted with yet another identity.

Dark City brings us back to one of the chief sources of noir—German expressionism. Alex Proyas, who also directed the Gothic *Crow*, constructs a world owing much to German expressionism and, of course, Fritz Lang's *Metropolis*. On a satellite in the sky, a race of dying aliens are conducting a massive lab experiment, seeking there a "cure for mortality," as their human accomplice Dr. Schreber puts it. Each night, from their underground headquarters, the aliens, through an ability called "tuning," destroy and then rebuild parts of the city above, as well as change the identities of the inhabitants in that section of the metropolis. The viewer does not witness this amazing transformation until mid-way through the film as this city, in which there is never any day, comes to a halt—cars stopping dead on city silent streets, individuals falling asleep in mid-sentence. And as they sleep, new buildings arise resembling the city in the first shots of *Metropolis*. As in Lang's classic, the city is imposing, stylized, angular, almost Gothic. But in a departure from its model, Proyas, in direct homage to the classic period of film noir, has given his dark city a 1940s patina through costuming and set dressing. While the city sleeps, aliens, who resemble Nosferatu with their long black coats, sharp teeth, bent posture, and bald heads, glide through the streets and hallways, accompanied by the Judas-like Dr. Schreber who implants new memories in the guinea pigs' brains, while the aliens spread new artifacts throughout the humans' abodes.

The film proposes a supremely existential dilemma. On an allegorical level the inhabitants of this city stand for all humanity caught in the web of a seemingly absurd and meaningless existence over which they have no control. The solution to their cosmic dilemma is the one put forth by existential writers like Sartre and Camus—consciousness of the absurdity followed by action. The protagonist Murdoch experiences such an epiphany when in close-up he suddenly awakes in his bath to find blood on his forehead from an aborted injection and a dead woman in his apartment.

The remainder of the film tracks Murdoch in his search for his real identity. For the partial injection has erased much of his former memories, leaving him unsure of himself or anyone else, including his own "wife" Emma or his "beloved" Uncle Karl—who both turn out to be but two more guinea pigs with implanted memories.

Pursued by a melancholy detective, looking much like the classic noir sleuths in trench coat, fedora and suit, who also begins to doubt the reality of his own identity, Murdoch finds he has assimilated some of the powers of the aliens, most notably their ability to transform reality by "tuning." And so the final battle in this Maya-like universe comes down to a contest of wills. Murdoch wins, defeating the aliens at their own game by destroying the underground machinery which operates the city above—recalling a similar destruction by the workers in *Metropolis*. With his victory in hand, Murdoch accepts the unreality of his life and so decides to create a new one. Much like Deckard in *Blade Runner*, Murdoch is haunted by a vision, a dream, possibly even a memory, in this case of a place called Shell Beach where the sun always shines and the colors are vibrant. Utilizing his newly found powers, he decides to construct this beach, flooding the city and then causing the ground to thrust up and create a land's end. In the final scenes he walks down a pier to his waiting "wife" who has now become Anna through yet another memory implant. Together they walk off to Shell Beach, a land of illusion but at least a benign one. **JU**

DARK COUNTRY (2009)

Director: Thomas Jane. **Screenplay**: Tab Murphy. **Producers**: Ashok Amritraj, Patrick Aiello. **Director of Photography**: Geoff Boyle. **Art Department Head**: Billy W. Ray. **Music**: Eric Lewis. **Editor**: Robert K. Lambert, John Lafferty. **Cast**: Thomas Jane (Richard), Lauren German (Gina), Ron Perlman (Deputy), Chris Browning (Stranger in the Diner). **Location**: New Mexico. **Released**: Sony, October 16. 105 minutes.

Newlyweds Richard and Gina leave their desert motel at sunset, drive off, and get lost. After dark a distracted Richard almost hits an injured Man, whose face is bloodied beyond recognition and whose wrecked car is nearby. They are out of cell phone range and uncertain of where to find the nearest help. The Man regains consciousness, becomes extremely agitated then attacks Richard, who defends himself by fracturing his skull with a rock. The panicked couple decides to bury the body in the desert. At a roadside rest stop, Richard notices his watch is missing then confronts Gina about a gun in her purse and his suspicion that she knew the Man. They argue and reconcile, then Richard leaves a fearful Gina behind with the gun, drives back for the watch but finds the grave empty. Distant gunshots send him racing to the rest stop. Gina is gone, and he now sees that all the other parked cars are dusty from disuse. He flags down a deputy sheriff, who is diverted to a crime scene by a radio call. The dusty vehicles from the rest stop are there and also the body of a woman. Richard starts one of the vehicles and speeds off. He evades the pursuing police but flips the car, staggers out onto the highway and collapses. He comes to in the back seat of another car and realizes that Richard and Gina are in the front.

There is an explicit irony in the opening narration of *Dark Country* and a conscious evocation of classic period style. The visual treatment of the first scenes is certainly ominous, starting with a pan and 90-degree tilt down and away from a motel sign and into the window of a room. Inside, cut by seemingly endless shadows from Venetian blinds, Richard awakens, recaps his situation by talking to himself—newly married to a woman he has just met in Las Vegas ("You don't even know how to spell her name")—and suggests a flashback structure that will never be confirmed...or denied. Richard is a man who quit his job, cleaned out his bank account and hit the road for reasons

unknown. He tells his new wife the somewhat incongruous and plaintive story of a girl he saw on a train when he was 16 but never approached. Now married to a relative stranger, the dialogue as he recalls the girl creates an immediate counter-tone to his earlier questions: "If you knew then what you know now would it make any difference? Do you think you could save her? Do you think you could save yourself?"

Does Richard know he is locked in a nightmare? The dichotomy between the narrative set-up, including an odd interaction with a stranger in the diner, creates an appropriate suspense that points towards the elaborate effects shot of the car disappearing into the horizon. Although props and decor from the drink machine, styrofoam cups, and the price of gasoline indicate that the film is contemporary, the use of a vintage Dodge Phoenix as the couple's car, inside of which much of the narrative time will be spent, sets a graphic foundation for a sense of amorphous time. The speedometer displays, push-button transmission, old style AM-FM radio are all vintage high tech, which underscore the aura of time displacement. In the metaphysics of the ending the possibility of a dark past for either Gina or Richard is left unresolved. The various comments by the personnel at the crime scene are appropriately undercut by the focus on Richard trapped in the back seat of the police cruiser. As with other surreal neo-noir, such as David Lynch's *Lost Highway* or *Mulholland Drive,* beginning with of the dusty cars at the rest stop, the illogical aspects of the situation are secondary to the protagonist's ever expanding existential anguish. The pay off comes with the POV shots from the injured Richard's helpless position in the back seat, where this new perspective reveals to the viewer in its second iteration the true horror of his long, agonizing scream of "No!" **AS**

DEATH WISH (1974)

Director: Michael Winner. **Screenplay**: Brian Garfield and Wendell Mayes based on the novel *Death Wish* by Garfield. **Producers**: Hal Landers, Bobby Roberts, Dino De Laurentiis [uncredited]. **Director of Photography**: Arthur J. Ornitz. **Music**: Herbie Hancock. **Production Designer**: Robert Grundlach. **Editor**: Bernard Gribble. **Cast**: Charles Bronson (Paul Kersey), Hope Lange (Joanna Kersey), Vincent Gardenia (Frank Ochoa), Steven Keats (Jack Toby), William Redfield (Sam Kreutzer), Stuart Margolin (Ames Jainchill), Stephen Elliott (Police Commissioner), Kathleen Tolan (Carol Toby), Jack Wallace (Hank), Fred J. Scollay (District Attorney), Chris Gampel (Ives), Robert Kya-Hill (Joe Charles), Ed Grover (Lt. Briggs), Jeff Goldblum (Freak #1). **Locations**: Brooklyn, New York; Manhattan, New York; Tucson, Arizona; Chicago, Illinois. **Released**: De Laurentiis/ RKO, July 24. 93 minutes.

Paul Kersey and his wife Joanna return to New York after their holiday in Hawaii. When Paul goes back to work, hoodlums invade his apartment, murder Joanna, and rape their daughter Carol, who lapses into a semi-comatose state. Angered at the inability of law enforcement officials to find the criminals, Kersey himself fends off a mugger with an improvised weapon. When the former pacifist is sent to Tucson by his firm, he witnesses a re-enactment of a Western gunfight and is given a gun by his client Ames Jainchill. Back in New York, Kersey walks the streets inviting attack and kills several assailants. The media coverage of the man they dub the vigilante irritates the police. After one of Kersey's battles go wrong, a detective under orders from the district attorney tells him to leave town. The film ends with Kersey's arrival in Chicago, and a suggestion that he will continue his activities there.

Closely based on Brian Garfield's novel (with the exception of one passage revealing Paul experiencing orgasm following one nightly excursion), *Death Wish* is a film that reunites those Western and urban gangster traditions influencing American cultural representations of violence documented within Richard Slotkin's *Gunfighter Nation: The Myth of the Frontier in Twentieth Century America* (1992). Several critics have noted that the gangster film and noir represent the twentieth century successor to the classical western. What *Death Wish* does is realign those two diverse traditions within an urban context according to the ideas later outlined by Slotkin where the urban underclass represents a dangerous threat to the normal American citizen.

Like Robert Montgomery Bird's Nathan Slaughter in *Nick of the Woods* (1837), Kersey's pacifism results in the death of his family by hostile external forces. He then becomes another dark version of the hunter figure from the Puritan Captivity Mythology that influenced both American literature and cinema. Like Lt. DeBuin in Robert Aldrich's *Ulzana's Raid* (1972), Kersey changes from pacifist to Herman Melville's vengeful Indian hater of *The Confidence Man*. But, unlike Ethan Edwards in *The Searchers* (1956), Kersey cannot eventually find rest by killing his "Scar." Instead, by a perverse re-working of Horace Greeley's statement, "Go West, Young Man" Kersey will move to another urban frontier and continue his work. *Death Wish* reworks the violent traditions of American culture within a new context.

Its several action-packed and hyper-violent sequels lead many to overlook the quiet psychological dimensions of this noirish crime drama. While the attack on Kersey's family is very brutal, and the film later shows several shootings, the larger focus is on Kersey's transformation. He is a self-described "bleeding-heart" liberal who was a conscientious objector during the Korean War, so his transition to death-dealing vigilante must be portrayed carefully, lest it be unbelievable. Thanks to Winner's direction, and Bronson's underrated performance, however, the viewer really sees how Kersey could change the way he does. Stuart Margolin is also very effective in a small but crucial role. The gritty, all-location photography in 1970s Manhattan, mostly at night, lends dark realism to the tense story, as does Herbie Hancock's unsettling score.

The film raises significant questions about the ethics of vigilantism. All the people Kersey shoots are in the process of using deadly force to attack him, and as the killings get more publicity, other inhabitants of the city begin to defend themselves, and the mugging rate drops dramatically. Kersey seems to find a renewed sense of meaning in his life as he helps rid the city of crime. Nevertheless, it might make the city *more* dangerous if everyone were to act as Kersey does, so the viewer is left to deliberate the moral issues. Like *Dirty Harry* (1971), *Death Wish* is often accused of promoting a "fascist" agenda, on the grounds that punishment is dispensed in the absence of legal formalities, but both films are better understood as meditations on crime and morality rather than as unambiguous political manifestoes. To its credit, *Death Wish* does not move towards the convenient resolution of Kersey finding the killers of his family: he accidentally passes them one night with neither party recognizing each other. Instead, the chain of violence will continue with no hope of resolution. Despite *Death Wish*'s notorious repudiation and the increasingly mediocre levels of its successors, the film is an important cultural document—no matter how much it offends liberal sensibilities. **TW & AJS**

DECEIVER (1997)

Director: Jonas Pate, Josh Pate. **Screenplay**: Jonas Pate, Josh Pate. **Producers**: Peter Glatzer, Don Winston. **Executive Producer**: Mark Damon. **Director of Photography**: Bill Butler. **Music**: Harry Gregson-Williams. **Production Designer**: John D. Kretschmer. **Editor**: Dan Lebental. **Cast**: Chris Penn (Det. Phillip Braxton), Ellen Burstyn (Mook), Tim Roth (James Walter Wayland), Renée Zellweger, (Elizabeth), Michael Rooker (Det. Edward Kennesaw), Rosanna Arquette (Mrs. Kennesaw), Don Winston (Warren), Michael Parks (Dr. Banyard), Mark Damon (Wayland's father), J.C. Quinn (Priest), Jody Wilhelm (Mrs. Wayland). **Released**: MGM, January 30. 101 minutes.

The body of Elizabeth, a prostitute, is found cut in two, and James Wayland, textile company heir and Princeton psychology graduate, is the only suspect. Detectives Kennesaw and Braxton investigate the murder, principally through extended interviews using a polygraph. However, Wayland's intellect (and powerful contacts) enables him to uncover the deceptions in the two detectives' lives. Braxton has serious gambling debts and Kennesaw was also seeing Elizabeth. Although much in the film's complex plot remains ambiguous, Wayland confronts Kennesaw about the cop's role in Elizabeth's murder, the policeman shoots him, and Wayland is taken away in a body-bag. However in the final scene (one year later), Wayland reappears, picking up another girl in the park.

"Deception" is at the heart of the movie, and not just through the inventions of Tim Roth's mendacious Wayland: the lives of the two investigating cops are wrapped up in deception as well. But above all, "deceiver" refers to the director/screenwriters too, as the movie is built around surprise, distractions and red herrings, its non-linear plot designed to sustain the deceptions worked on the audience: even the lie detector cannot be relied upon. (The Pates are twins, and the movie is indeed a family affair: Mark Damon, the executive producer, appears as

Wayland's father, one of the producers has a small role as a cop, and the director of photography's children are also featured.) It's not quite as demanding as Lynch's *Mulholland Drive* (2001) but heading in that direction.

Roth is genuinely scary as the narcissistic suspect, and there are strong performances from Chris Penn and Michael Rooker, assisted by some stylish dialogue. The narrative is developed almost entirely in the interrogation room, the lie detector interviews interspersed with flashbacks and the development of the subplots that link the lives of the three main characters. These sequences, often photographed with a fixed camera from the suspect's point of view, are dark and claustrophobic. Wayland's superior intellect enables him to win out in the mind games between interrogators and suspect, and the shift of control as accused becomes accuser is well handled. "Are you trying to put one over on us, Wayland?" asks Penn, to which he replies "That's the point of the game isn't it?" The narrative is convoluted, at times serpentine, maybe trying to be too clever. Critics were divided over whether the twist at the end is predictable or out of the blue, but it may depend on how closely they were paying attention. Despite the over-complication, powerful performances (from Zellweger and Burstyn as well as the three male leads) and strong scripting make the movie highly watchable. **GF**

DECEPTION (2008)

Director: Marcel Langenegger. **Screenplay**: Mark Bomback. **Producers**: Arnold Rifkin, Robbie Brenner, David L. Bushell, Christopher Eberts, Hugh Jackman, John Palermo. **Director of Photography**: Dante Spinotti. **Music**: Ramin Djawadi. **Production Designer**: Patrizia von Brandenstein. **Editors**: Douglas Crise, Christian Wagner. **Cast**: Ewan McGregor (Jonathan McQuarry), Hugh Jackman (Wyatt Bose), Michelle Williams (S), Natasha Henstridge (Simone Wilkinson), Charlotte Rampling (Wall Street Belle), Lisa Gay Hamilton (Detective Russo), Bruce Altman, Andrew Ginsburg (Lawyers). **Released**: 20th Century-Fox, April 25. 107 minutes.

Corporate accountant Jonathan McQuarry is a working alone one night in a deserted office when a stranger, Wyatt Bose, enters. Claiming to be an attorney with the firm, Wyatt befriends Jonathan. He introduces Jonathan to posh tennis

Deception: *"S" (Michelle Williams) and Wyatt Bose (Hugh Jackman).*

clubs and high-roller night spots where beautiful if high-maintenance women hang out. After they "mistakenly" swap cell phones just before Wyatt leaves on an overseas trip, Jonathan starts getting phones calls asking "Are you free tonight?" The calls are from horny, executive women who need a quick sexual fix. Jonathan obliges them, starts to make calls to "The List" on his own, and falls for one of the women, "S." When Wyatt returns, he kidnaps "S" and, as ransom, demands that Jonathan use his special access to one of his corporate clients to transfer $20 million into an account in Madrid. Jonathan complies, and Wyatt believes he has killed him only to discover that Jonathan is alive and in Madrid. Wyatt can't access the account without Jonathan's co-signature. Jonathan has discovered the truth: "S" was conspiring with Wyatt and the kidnapping was faked. Jonathan and Wyatt get the money from the bank, and when Wyatt tries to again to kill Jonathan, "S" shoots Wyatt in the back. Jonathan and "S" go off together. [Note: In the director's alternative ending, which is on the DVD, the three characters are alive at the end, each going his/her own separate ways.]

The elegiac opening shot of *Deception*—carefully composed and lit in a deep-focus that captures glaring contrasts, by renowned cinematographer Dante Spinotti—reveals Jonathan alone at night at the end of a large conference table in a deserted office suite. The lighting and his posture, hunched over his computer while "audit managing" the company's books, give the viewer an immediate sense of his personality: emotionally isolated and consumed by his work. Then brief long lens shots from Jonathan's POV of two janitors, one male and one female, in an adjacent office, capture the woman leading the man into the unisex bathroom for some sexual contact. This establishes the film's primary emotional arc, Jonathan's sexual longing and frustration. The set-up is a familiar one from classic period noir.

Seemingly out of nowhere, Wyatt Bose, a figure of corporate confidence and sexual prowess, bursts into Jonathan's isolated world. When an unlikely friendship is struck between these opposite types and Bose reveals the sexual opportunities available to those who want the "good life," Jonathan is more than merely intrigued. As he is drawn into this world, shots of beautiful women from Jonathan's POV become a visual motif throughout the film.

"Are you free tonight?" The calls are for Wyatt, but the sexually timid Jonathan answers them at the other end. While he does consent to sexual encounters, Jonathan remains timid and compliant at first. Then he starts calling women on "The List" himself. Jonathan's sexual and emotional fixation with "S" is another character link to classic noir, and one that viewers may well expect to be perilous. In a reversal that is more typical of neo-noir, what neither Wyatt nor the viewer expects is that Jonathan's growing personal confidence will not only embolden him but also make him suspicious of Wyatt. When Jonathan investigates and discovers Wyatt's real identity, it becomes apparent that the intended entrapment has actually liberated Jonathan. In one small but revealing sequence, Jonathan passes a newsstand where one of the women whom Jonathan has met and had sex with from "The List" has her face blazoned on the front cover of a national magazine as a typical "Woman Executive." Jonathan's broad smirk as he stares at the picture, reveals the depth of his transformation.

Unlike the figures portrayed by Mickey Rooney or Elisha

Cook Jr. in the classic period, also unlike *Double Indemnity*'s Walter Neff, who kills his co-conspirator before she can do that to him, even unlike the sexually obsessed and betrayed characters of early neo-noir like Ned Racine in *Body Heat* or Mike Swale in *The Last Seduction*, Jonathan's loss of "innocence" does not doom him. Noir males seduced by scheming femme fatales seldom find their strength to break free, and certainly never to break free through growing confidence gained through sexual experience with other women. It is the notion that male identity and male confidence are established through sexual experience—a notion seldom found in the more Puritanical American cinema—that gives this film a so-far unique place in neo-noir. **RA**

DEEP COVER (1992)

Director: Bill Duke. **Screenplay**: Michael Tolkin, Henry Bean. **Producers**: Henry Bean, Pierre David. **Executive Producers**: David Streit, Ron Stacker Thompson. **Director of Photography**: Bojan Bazelli. **Production Designer**: Pam Warner. **Music**: Michel Colombier. **Editor**: John Carter. **Cast**: Laurence Fishburne (John Hull), Jeff Goldblum (David Jason), Victoria Dillard (Betty McCutcheon), Charles Martin Smith (Gerald Carver), Sydney Lassick (Gopher), Clarence Williams III (Taft), Gregory Sierra (Felix Barbosa), Arthur Mendoza (Anton Gallegos), René Assa (Hector Guzman). **Released**: New Line Productions, 15 April. 107 minutes.

Los Angeles. As a child, John witnessed the violent death of his drug-addicted father, and swore to become a cop. Judging his hate-filled adult personality an asset, Carver sends John undercover to gain evidence on a drug ring whose chain of command runs from Guzman down through Gallegos and Barbosa. John kills a low-level dealer to gain entry into this underworld. Arrested during a drug transaction, John maintains his secret identity. In jail, he is confronted by fervent anti-drugs campaigner Reverend Taft. In court, John is cleared by the crooked lawyer David, who becomes his partner in the drug business and dreams of pioneering new designer drugs. John begins a relationship with money-laundering art dealer Betty. Increasingly megalomaniacal, David kills Barbosa, instantly putting himself and John in contact with higher echelons. Frustrated by Carver's contradictory instructions—which follow an ever-shifting government agenda—John murders Gallegos, then secretly records

Deep Cover: *Betty McCutcheon (Victoria Dillard) and John Hull (Laurence Fishburne).*

Guzman during a confrontation in which David kills Taft and John kills David. John subverts Carver's gag order by releasing this tape in court. Left with Betty and eleven million in stolen drug money, John ponders his options: to keep this "reward," give it to police, or use it to make a positive social change.

From its first moments, *Deep Cover* is an unusual and compelling film. Its superbly crafted voice-over narration delivered by Fishburne has the cadence and literary flourishes of contemporary spoken word poetry. The plot's sometimes outrageous air of limitless possibility and digression includes a psychotic lawyer who talks in philosophical maxims ("in dreams begin responsibilities"), a diminutive police agent who likes to refer to himself as "God," a money-launderer who runs a gallery for African art, and an earnest Reverend who presses prayer books onto criminals.

The film is brave, too, in its anti-government critique, its refusal to tie up its dilemmas too neatly, and, in its final line, the explicit posing of a moral-political question to the viewer ("What would you do?"). When Duke (well-known as an actor) made *Deep Cover*, he was coming off the success of the stylish gangster piece *A Rage in Harlem* (1991). Although he has subsequently directed other features (including *Hoodlum*, 1997) with an African-American focus, his career has mainly proceeded in television. *Deep Cover* remains his finest work. Clearer today than at the moment of its release is its enormous debt to Ferrara's *King of New York* (also shot by Bazelli, and featuring Fishburne in a radically different part); it overlaps uncannily, too, with *Bad Lieutenant* (1992), released around the same time. Like Ferrara, Duke expertly uses experimental techniques (such as step-printing frames, and jump-cutting to hip hop beats), and the violent action scenes have a startling, kinetic force.

Writers Tolkin (*The Player*, 1992) and Bean (*Internal Affairs*, 1990) take a narrative staple of noir—the anti-hero in a spiral of trouble, unable to escape without making a bold move beyond the law—and build upon it a complex meditation on morality and amorality: as in Ferrara's work, it is not good (or law) which vanquishes evil, but the intensification of evil itself, a transgressive identification with the power of evil. The film mixes noir elements with a popular contemporary plot device: the undercover cop who gradually loses his identity, as in *Cruising* (1980), *Donnie Brasco* (1997), and *The Departed* (2006). As equally fascinating, ultimately, as the central character's dark journey is the arc that takes a wonderfully inventive Goldblum from being a meek lawyer—similar to the Sean Penn character in De Palma's *Carlito's Way* (1993)—to the heights of Nietzschean delirium: chanting "I want my cake and eat it too," challenging gangsters to knuckle fights, and quoting (complete with Cuban accent) the motto from *Scarface* (1983), "my balls and my word," at the height of a tense negotiation. **AM**

THE DEEP END (2001)

Director: Scott McGehee, David Siegel. **Screenplay**: Scott McGehee, David Siegel based on the story by Elisabeth Sanxay Holding. **Producers**: Laura Greenlee, David Siegel, Scott McGehee. **Director of Photography**: Giles Nuttgens. **Production Designers**: Kelly McGehee, Chris Tandon. **Music**: Peter Nashel. **Editor**: Lauren Zuckerman. **Cast**: Tilda Swinton (Margaret Hall), Goran Visnjic (Al Spera), Jonathan Tucker (Beau Hall), Peter Donat (Jack Hall), Josh Lucas (Darby), Raymond Barry (Nagle), Tamara Hope (Paige Hall), Jordon Dorrance (Dylan Hall). **Released**: 20th Century Fox, October 17. 101 minutes.

Margaret Hall, an upper middle class housewife living in Lake Tahoe, finds the body of her older son's lover on the shore. He has fallen to his death after fighting with her son. Margaret takes the body out to the center of the lake and sinks it. Two blackmailers find a tape of her son having sex with the dead man and demand $50,000 from Margaret. One of the blackmailers, Al, finds himself drawn to Margaret in her struggle to protect her family and tries to cut a deal with his more vicious partner. The partner attacks Margaret and Al kills him. In order to further shield Margaret from the police, the wounded Al transports the body but dies in a car accident on the mountain road.

The Deep End is a remake of Max Ophuls' *The Reckless Moment* (the films use the same story by Elisabeth Sanxay Holding as their source). Both films explore a common noir theme: the unpredictable moment in which a reckless act can allow the dark underworld of violence, desire, and corruption into the upper world of middle class normalcy (most pointedly developed in Andre De Toth's *Pitfall*). The filmmakers (David Siegel and Scott McGehee) carefully establish the milieu of Margaret Hall: her spacious lakeside home isolated from the congested city of Reno; her life of carpools, jogging, and errands; her loneliness as she tries to contact her absent husband (he is in the Navy). Margaret is in fact a model housewife, juggling her children's schedules, taking out the trash, keeping her home immaculate.

So it is not such a stretch to believe that when the underworld, represented by her son's hustler boyfriend (Darby), invades this world and the boyfriend falls to his death, she takes care of the sticky situation with as much efficiency as she runs her home: sinking his body with an anchor in the lake, driving his car back into the city, cleaning up blood and fingerprints while hardly missing a beat. The problem in noir is of course once you have touched that world it is hard to disentangle yourself from it (the filmmakers use the motif of water to convey the feeling of losing control, of being overwhelmed).

Margaret's relationship with the compassionate blackmailer Al becomes the core of the remainder of the film. In the world of noir brief encounters can easily turn into erotic fixations and even full-blown obsessions. And that is the case here. To Margaret, Al is a man who cares for her (she begins dressing up for their clandestine meetings), who listens patiently to her problems even when she is berating him, who even saves her life, unlike her distant husband. In addition Al is handsome, dangerous, very much like the man her son fell for.

For Al, Margaret represents a world which we must infer he has had little contact with, conveyed as he wanders through her house, sadly touching photos of her families, caressing the furniture. His final sacrifice, dying for her on the road (as she tries to save him their faces touch like lovers briefly) while sending her back to her family, has several layers of bittersweet irony. In the final shot, Margaret lies on her bed weeping as the camera tracks slowly into her face. As she opens her eyes wide, we see a look of despair and grief. She is now back to her insular home, safe from the underworld. But at what price? Is this even a world she wants anymore, a world of routine, a world bereft of passion and excitement, a "safe" world? In noir it is hard to return to normalcy after you have survived in the "deep end." **JU**

DELUSION (1991)

Director: Carl Colpaert. **Screenplay**: Colpaert, Kurt Voss. **Producer**: Daniel Hassid (Cineville). **Director of Photography**: Geza Sinkovics. **Production Designer**: Ildiko Toth. **Music**: Barry Adamson. **Editor**: Mark Allan Kaplan. **Cast**: Jim Metzler (George O'Brien), Jennifer Rubin (Patti), Kyle Secor (Chevy), Jerry Orbach (Larry). **Released**: I.R.S. Releasing, June 7. 100 minutes.

Embittered over his long-time employer's sale of the company, George O'Brien has embezzled a million dollars and is driving to Las Vegas with the cash in his trunk. He stops to help a young couple, Patti and Chevy, in a car that has swerved off the road, and they abduct him. O'Brien does not realize that the young tough does not know about the money, and has not been planning to kill him until Chevy kills someone else. Now O'Brien is a witness; and they dump him in the desert. He survives; but by the time he tracks them down, Patti has found the money and is preparing to go off on her own.

Delusion is derivative of Al Robert's "mysterious force" in *Detour*. Stylistically both of these films benefit from the isolated or seedy locales, which permit a spare and stark visualization in the manner of *Border Incident* or *On Dangerous Ground*. As in *After Dark, My Sweet* or *Kill Me Again*, the desert locations in *Delusion* permit an arrangement of figures in a landscape that create a sense of otherworldliness or "mirage" (which was the film's original title). Al Roberts' sense of acting out a bad dream is reenacted without having recourse to optical effects or mood lighting. Whether at the trailer site of Chevy's intended victim, which is by the side of the road in the middle of some badlands, or at a rundown motel at the aptly named Death Valley Junction, the isolated environment underscores the narrative tension in the classic noir manner. The last shot literally drives away from O'Brien: he stands looking off from the wounded Chevy lying in the dusty driveway and the shot continues down the road for the entirety of the end credits. When that shot cedes to Patti, back to working as a showgirl and singing "These Boots are Made for Walking," the final note is both sardonic and deterministic. **AS**

Delusion: *Jennifer Rubin as Patti.*

Devil in a Blue Dress: *Jennifer Beals as Daphne Monet.*

DEVIL IN A BLUE DRESS (1995)

Director: Carl Franklin. **Screenplay**: Carl Franklin based on the novel by Walter Mosley. **Producers**: Jesse Beaton, Gary Goetzman. **Director of Photography**: Tak Fujimoto. **Production Designer**: Gary Frutkoff. **Music**: Elmer Bernstein. **Editor**: Carole Kravetz. **Cast**: Denzel Washington ("Easy" Rawlins), Jennifer Beals (Daphne Monet), Tom Sizemore (Albright), Don Cheadle ("Mouse" Alexander), Maury Chaykin (Matthew Terell), Terry Kinney (Todd Carter), Mel Winkler (Joppy), Lisa Nicole Carson (Coretta James), Albert Hall (Degan). **Released**: TriStar, September 29. 102 minutes.

"Easy" Rawlins, an African-American factory worker who has been recently laid off, needs money to pay his mortgage. His friend Joppy introduces Easy to Albright who is looking for someone to help him find a missing "white" woman, Daphne Monet, assumed to be hiding somewhere in the Black community. Easy eventually accepts. Monet is known to spend time in the Black jazz clubs in South Central Los Angeles and she is the girlfriend of wealthy Todd Carter, who is the favorite in the Los Angeles mayoral race. Easy enlists the help of his trigger-happy friend "Mouse." Soon, Easy becomes implicated in two murders, including a female friend he had spent the night with. Daphne has also revealed to him that she has hidden her mixed race background. Eventually he discovers that Albright is working for Carter's political opponent Terell who wants Daphne because she has incriminating photos of Terell with children. Easy rescues Daphne from the clutches of Albright. He returns her to Carter but Carter does not have the courage to marry her, fearing her mixed race background will lose him the mayoral prize.

Devil in a Blue Dress is based on a novel by one of the best-known neo-hardboiled noir novelists, Walter Mosley. It is one of the few noir films to deal directly with the unmitigated racism in Los Angeles in 1940s and 1950s. The film opens near Central and 24th Street with a detailed recreation of the mood and style of the place and time: murals, movie theaters, bars, jazz riffs emanating from radios, and middle-class African-Americans hanging out. "Easy" Rawlins has been recently laid off from his manufacturing job and is desperate to make his mortgage payments. The noirish plot engages as a thug named Albright approaches the desperate Rawlins and offers him work as a "detective," a job Rawlins rejects at first. Eventually his need for funds compels him to accept. The thug then sends him on a quest for Daphne Monet (played with delicate and sultry beauty by Jennifer Beals), the missing fiancée of mayoral candidate Todd Carter.

To find Daphne, Rawlins must venture into all-White areas. On the Westside at the Malibu Pier, White punks from the Midwest harass him. At the prestigious Ambassador Hotel he must enter through the servants' entrance. It is at this swank L.A. landmark that Rawlins finds the mysterious Daphne, dressed in her signature blue. Like Marlowe's Mrs. Grayle or Hammer's "great whatsit" or Spade's "stuff that dreams are made of," many are seeking Daphne. Carter wants her back because he is in love with her. Albright wants her for Carter's political rival, Matthew Terell. And Rawlins wants her to pay his mortgage. In the process Rawlins is beaten by racist L.A.P.D. cops and almost murdered by Albright. But the most significant element in the metaphoric nature of Daphne is her revelation to Rawlins that she is half-Black. While not a shocking as the revelation of incest in *Chinatown,* the overt symbolism of someone who is neither one nor the other underscores the artifice of rampant racism as does her final rejection by Carter who does not have the courage of his convictions, refusing to risk his political future to marry her. **JU**

DIARY OF A HITMAN (1992)

Director: Roy London. **Screenplay**: Kenneth Pressman based on his play *Insider's Price*. **Producer**: Amin Q. Chaudhri. **Executive Producer**: Mark Damon. **Director of Photography**: Yuri Sokol. **Art Director**: Rusty Smith. **Music**: Michel Colombier. **Editor**: Brian Smedley-Ashton. **Cast**: Forest Whitaker (Dekker), Sherilyn Fenn (Jain), Seymour Cassel (Koenig), Lewis Smith (Al Zidzyk), John Bedford-Lloyd (Dr. Jamison), Sharon Stone (Kiki), James Belushi (Shandy), Lois Chiles (Sheila), Wayne Crawford (Wallace), Jimmy Butler (Eddie). **Released**: Vision, May 29. 91 minutes.

Dekker, a low-profile hitman, is a burnt-out case seeing a psychoanalyst and planning to quit after one last job. His last assignment is particularly unsavory: mob boss Al Zidzyk wants someone to kill both his wife Jain and her baby and to bring back a body part as proof of death. While casing the job Dekker meets Jain; and after a quirky encounter the professional can no longer bring himself to fulfill his contract. Realizing that a second killer will soon be dispatched, Dekker decides to defend his former target.

Like *Reservoir Dogs* made in the same year, *Diary of a Hitman* is a modestly-budgeted picture that confronts the issue of criminal "professionalism" most directly. Although he is a killer for hire, the African-American title character of *Diary of a Hitman* more closely resembles John Hull in *Deep Cover* than the dozens of analogs in other neo-noir films. Unlike *Deep Cover*, the real irony of *Diary of a Hitman* may be unconscious in casting an African-American actor in a part not necessarily written for one. Also unlike Larry Fishburne in *Deep Cover*, Forest Whitaker does not bring an iconic signature to *Hitman*, does not suggest (there's no other way to put it) a "black" noir persona. His character, Dekker, is a throwback and the film's narrative style follows suit.

Because the story unfolds as a flashback, a message which Dekker is leaving on his "booking agent's" answering machine, his voiceover narration is used heavily throughout. While not as cynical or ironic as the second-person narration in the low-budget hitman piece of classic period's *Blast of Silence,* the narration does add a dimension of existential reflection not present in the equally low-budget *Murder by Contract*, which *Diary of a Hitman* mirrors closely in the key plot point of male killer-for-hire thrown off his game when assigned a young female victim. Early on, Dekker confesses to being troubled by his work and maintaining the illusion that "it's not personal." He even consults a psychiatrist, to whom he confesses the killings as "bad dreams." Because *Hitman* ultimately becomes a performance piece for Whitaker and Sherilyn Fenn as his last victim, Jain, most of these echoes of classic noir are left unexplored. Dekker's key comment is "I was a pro. A pro is a pro, right?" In the more direct world of neo-noir, one possible answer comes from Mr. Pink in *Reservoir Dogs*: "A psychopath ain't a professional." **AS**

THE DRIVER (1978)

Screenplay, Director: Walter Hill. **Producer**: Lawrence Gordon (EMI). **Director of Photography**: Philip Lathrop. **Production Designer**: Harry Horner. **Music**: Michael Small. **Editors**: Tina Hirsch, Robert K. Lambert. **Cast**: Ryan O'Neal (The Driver), Bruce Dern (The Detective), Isabelle Adjani (The Player), Ronee Blakely (The Connection), Matt Clark (Red Plainclothesman), Felice Orlandi (Gold Plainclothesman), Joseph Walsh (Glasses), Rudy Ramos (Teeth). **Released**: 20th Century-Fox, July 28. 91 minutes.

The Driver is a specialist. The Connection markets his particular talent behind the wheel of a getaway car to robbers who will pay his fee. Laconic and secretive, the Driver lives by his own set of rules and leaves no evidence for the police to use against him. A frustrated robbery-homicide Detective is willing to bend the law to arrest "the cowboy that's never been caught." The Detective uses the bank robber Glasses to set up a sting for the Driver. Suspicious, the Driver uses the Player to find out what's going on but still ends up enmeshed in the Detective's trap.

One of the earliest and most stylized examples of conscious neo-noir is *The Driver* (1978). Walter Hill's main characters are so explicitly archetypal that they do not even have names. They are simply the Driver, the Detective, and the Player. The narrative is spare, alternating balletic interludes of high-speed chases down dark, wet streets or in claustrophobic parking structures with terse, expository scenes. The Detective is so obsessed with catching the Driver that he blackmails another criminal into setting him up. The woman known as the Player is so obsessed with gambling that she is unable to give the Driver any emotional support. While *their* motivations are reasonably clear, the Driver's never is. Being the "best wheel man in town" leaves him in the grip of some quasi-existential anguish. Like many classic noir figures, wandering through dark rooms, silhouetted or in sidelight, the Driver lives on the edge of an ill-defined underworld. Like the title figure in Melville's *Le Samourai* (1967) he lives by an unwritten code, but it seems mostly to burden him as relentlessly as Sisyphus' stone. When he finally violates its basic tenet ("Never carry a gun") in what could be either a liberating act or a hollow

The Driver: *Ryan O'Neal is the Driver.*

triumph, it merely completes the Driver's transformation into a cipher.

The viewer can accept a noir protagonist without a name but one without an identity is a hard sell. Both as a film and as a character, *The Driver* takes the concept of action as being, creates dramatic conflict, then leaves it unresolved in a sort of existential limbo. The two seemingly antithetical characters thrown together by circumstances—a rumpled, alienated detective and a glib well-dressed criminal—create the strongest irony in *The Driver*. As in the Hill-scripted *Hickey and Boggs*, where one of the title characters observes that "It's not about anything anymore," the alcoholic detective in Hills' *48 Hrs*. has to wrestle with his lost idealism more conspicuously than the rule-obsessed title character or his cop antagonist in *The Driver*. **AS**

THE DROWNING POOL (1975)

Director: Stuart Rosenberg. **Screenplay**: Walter Hill, Tracy Keenan Wynn, Lorenzo Semple, Jr., Eric Roth based on the novel by Ross Macdonald. **Producers**: David Foster, Lawrence Turman. **Director of Photography**: Gordon Willis. **Production Designer**: Paul Sylbert. **Editor**: John C. Howard. **Cast**: Paul Newman (Lew Harper), Joanne Woodward (Iris Devereaux), Anthony Franciosa (Chief Broussard), Murray Hamilton (Kilbourne), Gail Strickland (Mavis Kilbourne), Melanie Griffith (Schuyler Devereaux), Linda Haynes (Gretchen), Richard Jaeckel (Lt. Franks), Coral Browne (Olivia Devereaux). **Released**: Warner Bros., July. 108 minutes.

Called away from his seedy Los Angeles practice, private eye Lew Harper travels to Louisiana to work for Iris Devereaux, who is the wife of an oil tycoon, to deal with a blackmail letter she has received. If she does not pay up, the blackmailer will tell her husband James, who, it turns out, is a homosexual, of an affair she claims never happened. It does come out, however, that Iris had an affair with Harper many years before. Iris' mother-in-law Olivia is soon found murdered, and Harper begins to realize that the simple blackmail case is connected to shady dealings in real estate and oil, with a healthy dose of police corruption stirring the pot (here the morally ambiguous figure of Lieutenant Broussard plays a key role). A blackmailing chauffeur briefly

becomes the focus of the investigation, only to be found dead as well. Harper eventually realizes that the villain of the piece is oil baron Kilbourne, but not before a series of near-romantic and almost deadly encounters with others, including Iris' daughter Schuyler, Mavis Kilbourne, and Gretchen, who is very eager for the kind of male companionship Harper might provide even though she is a hooker. The film's set piece features the detective and erstwhile female companion escaping from a locked room (from which, it seems, they will soon be taken out and killed) by contriving to flood it. The plan is on the verge of failure when one of Kilbourne's henchmen accidentally opens it and winds up drowning himself. Having saved Iris' millions from Kilbourne, Harper returns to L.A.

A kind of sequel to the somewhat darker *Harper*, whose main character it recycles, *The Drowning Pool* is likewise adapted from a Ross Macdonald novel that studiously copies its structure and themes from the more famous fiction of Raymond Chandler. *The Drowning Pool*, in fact, offers an interesting recycling of both Chandler's *Farewell, My Lovely* (filmed initially as *Murder, My Sweet*) and, more centrally, *The Big Sleep*. Like Philip Marlowe, Harper is a world-weary cynic, uncomplainingly accepting of a pervasive criminality and venality that he is nonetheless dedicated to identifying and uprooting. Attractive to women, Harper proves immune to their charms; he dispatches their flirtatious advances with dry wit and a palpable sense of ennui. Not given to violence, he proves nonetheless extremely capable of defending himself and, when necessary, absorbing punishment without complaint.

Like that of the two Chandler novels mentioned above, the plot of *The Drowning Pool* (true to the spirit of the novel though divergent in some important details) kicks open an anthill of corruption, tracing the particular crime with which it begins (the blackmail) to a larger scheme involving much larger rewards, even as it reveals more generally an intriguing gallery of social types, from the criminal to the upper classes, all of whom are involved in a desperate struggle for material gain and personal advancement. Harper, as in so much else, remains immune to such desires, and his apartness and alienation from the corrupt world in which he moves evidences key traditional elements of the noir protagonist. **RBP**

8 MILLION WAYS TO DIE (1986)

Director: Hal Ashby. **Screenplay**: Oliver Stone and David Lee Henry based on the novels *A Stab in the Dark* and *Eight Million Ways to Die* by Lawrence Block. **Producer**: Steve Roth. **Co-Producer**: Charles Mulvehill. **Director of Photography**: Stephen H. Burum. **Music**: James Newton Howard. **Production Designer**: Michael Haller. **Editor**: Stuart Pappé and Robert Lawrence. **Cast**: Jeff Bridges (Matthew J. Scudder), Rosanna Arquette (Sarah), Alexandra Paul (Sunny), Andy Garcia (Angel Maldonado), Randy Brooks (Willie "Chance" Walker), Tom "Tiny" Lister, Jr. (Nose Guard), Lisa Sloan (Linda Scudder), Christa Denton (Laurie Scudder), Wilfredo Hernández (Hector Lopez), Vyto Ruginis (Joe Durkin), William Marquez (Tio). **Released**: Tri-Star/Producers Sales Organization, April 25. 115 minutes.

After killing a small-time dealer named Hector in front of his family, alcoholic Matt Scudder drinks away occupational traumas. Matt misses taking his daughter horseback riding for her birthday and, although paid to protect a prostitute named Sunny, he fails and instead watches her be killed. Before her death and his leave of absence from the force, Sunny invites Matt to a party where he is reacquainted with ex-criminal Chance, now a businessman and owner of a neighborhood supermarket. Chance traffics in high priced hookers, gambling, and Sarah, Chance's love interest and call-girl "playing manager," who is attracted to and repulsed by Matt. At Chance's party, Matt also meets Angel, a cocaine dealing "scumbag" trying to convince Chance to let him deal drugs out of Chance's market. From a gym bag that Sunny leaves behind, Scudder locates evidence that shows Angel killed Sunny because of her knowledge about his illegal cocaine activities. The movie's action concludes with Matt's police sting at an abandoned San Pedro warehouse. Instead of a smooth exchange of Angel's cocaine for the kidnapped Sarah, machismo-fueled tempers escalate into a shootout where Angel is wounded and everyone else except Matt and Sarah is killed. Matt later kills Angel back at Chance's house. The film concludes with Matt telling an AA meeting he has gone five months without a drink and is in love with Sarah.

Hal Ashby's auteur status was established in the 1970s with important films like *Harold and Maude* (1971), *The Last Detail* (1973), *Shampoo* (1975), and *Coming Home* (1978) but his final film, *8 Million Ways to Die*, is merely a minor neo-noir. Detective Sergeant Matthew J. Scudder begins the narrative in a voiceover that tips its hat to old noir. Talking to his partner, Joe, in an aerial shot above Los Angeles, says: "Yeah, there are eight million stories in the naked city. Remember that old TV show? Yep. What we got in this town? We got eight million ways to die. Alright, let's cut the crap and do what we get paid for." Despite his allusion to a noir classic, Matt is too troubled

by his job to be either hardboiled or cynical. *8 Million Ways to Die* is an existential detective film, shot in bright California sunlight, focusing on the rehabilitation of a damaged man.

The film employs few noir stylistic devices other than its opening voiceover, its two shady femme fatales, and its basic mystery narrative. Even with greased back ponytail, explicit violence, and dialogue sprinkled with curse words that could not be spoken in earlier noirs, Andy Garcia falls far short, for example, of Al Pacino's menacing gangster in *Scarface* (1983). Bridges plausibly underplays the most fully-developed character in this existential narrative that fulfills Robert Porfirio's definition by beginning "with a disoriented individual facing a confused world that he cannot accept." Scudder quits the police force and his family life because of his inability to save damaged petty criminals like Hector and Sunny and he must also quit his alcohol addiction to gain enlightenment.

The emotionally-damaged Sarah, who is looking for a father-figure to replace the real father she lost to alcoholism, is terrorized after being taken hostage by Angel and must watch her previous lover Chance murdered in the warehouse fiasco. She becomes both a replacement wife (for Lisa) and daughter surrogate (for Laurie). Matt admits as much in the film's final dialogue: "I live in a world I didn't make. I know that now. I had to be beaten into that reasonableness . . . I wake up. I don't come to. I'm in love. What can I say? It's a great feeling." The film ends in a romantic montage of Sarah and Matt walking and kissing on an L.A. beach, and is one of the "happy" noir endings that will become more prevalent throughout the 1980s and 1990s. **WC**

F

FAREWELL, MY LOVELY (1975)

Director: Dick Richards. **Screenplay**: David Zelag Goodman based on the novel by Raymond Chandler. **Producers**: George Pappas, Jerry Bruckheimer. **Director of Photography**: John A. Alonzo. **Music**: David Shire. **Production Designer**: Dean Tavoularis. **Editors**: Walter Thompson, Joel Cox. **Cast**: Robert Mitchum (Philip Marlowe), Charlotte Rampling (Mrs. Grayle), John Ireland (Nulty), Sylvia Miles (Mrs. Florian), Anthony Zerbe (Brunette), Harry Dean Stanton (Billy Rolfe), Jack O'Halloran (Moose Malloy), Joe Spinell (Nick), Sylvester Stallone (Jonnie), Kate Murtagh (Frances Amthor), John (O'Leary (Marriott), Walter McGinn (Tommy Ray), Burton Gilliam (Cowboy), Jim Thompson (Mr. Grayle). **Completed**: April 21, 1975. **Released**: Avco Embassy, August 20. 97 minutes.

Private detective Philip Marlowe is hired by a hulking ex-con, Moose Malloy, to find his missing girlfriend, Velma. At the same time, a somewhat peculiar gentleman hires Marlowe to help him buy back a stolen necklace for a mysterious Mrs. Grayle. Working simultaneously on both cases, Marlowe becomes involved with murder: he is drugged and almost murdered himself at a brothel run by a sadistic madam, Frances Amthor, and finds himself attracted to the seductive Mrs. Grayle. When he finds Mrs. Grayle has connections with a sharpster named Brunette who runs an exclusive high-stakes gambling ship, Marlowe surreptitiously boards the vessel and confronts Brunette. Unknown to Marlowe, he is followed by Moose. Mrs. Grayle is also present; and it becomes apparent that she is Moose's faithless Velma. Moose is shot, but he manages to kill Velma before Marlowe can stop him; and the ineffectual detective is left with only his baseball hero, Joe DiMaggio, to believe in.

Robert Mitchum is an icon of the cinema noir films of the 1940s and 1950s; and it is his presence, nothing short of mythic, that lends force to *Farewell, My Lovely*. The result is a film more atmospherically faithful to the ethos of Chandler's novel than *Murder, My Sweet*, the 1944 version, which starred a hardboiled Dick Powell. Mitchum's shell may be as tough as Powell's but within he is a turmoil of unspoken passions and lost dreams. The hooded eyes in the life-creased face may seem remote at first glance; but they are fastened on idealistic dreams and veil a hidden vulnerability.

A slow, neon-lit pan first reveals Mitchum's physiognomy, while in voice-over, he speaks in his familiar, unemotional tones about the winter creeping into his bones and heart. Like Mitchum, this is a tough-shelled film with a soft core of sentimentality; but it never, amazingly, descends into the maudlin. The period production design by Dean Tavoularis utilizes the Los Angeles locations with clarity and respect. Moody color cinematography by John Alonzo and a jazz-ori-

Farewell, My Lovely: *Philip Marlowe (Robert Mitchum) and Moose Malloy (Jack O'Halloran).*

ented score by David Shire balance the performances and compensate for an occasionally confusing script. But the main element is Mitchum as Marlowe, moving with disillusioned but steady tread, taken with Joe DiMaggio, love-struck thugs, and wise-eyed women, all of whom will disappoint him, but all of whom he will go on loving anyway, in his weary fashion. **JK**

FATAL ATTRACTION (1987)

Director: Adrian Lyne. **Screenplay**: James Dearden, Nicholas Meyer [uncredited]. **Producers**: Stanley Jaffe, Sherry Lansing. **Director of Photography**: Howard Atherton. **Production Designer**: Mel Bourne. **Music**: Maurice Jarre. **Editors**: Michael Kahn, Peter Berger. **Cast**: Michael Douglas (Dan Gallagher), Glenn Close (Alex Forrest), Anne Archer (Beth), Ellen Hamilton Latzen (Ellen), Stuart Pankin (Jimmy), Ellen Foley (Hildy), Fred Gwynne (Arthur). **Released**: Orion, September 11. 119 minutes.

Married attorney Dan Gallagher meets and is attracted to Alex Forrest, a book editor. While his wife and daughter are away for the weekend, Gallagher indulges in a sexual liaison with Forrest. Slightly disturbed by Forrest's possessive behavior as the weekend winds down, Gallagher explains that he plans to go home to his family and that the affair is done. Forrest persists: calling him, stalking him and even pretending to be pregnant. Realizing that he cannot continue to keep the situation secret from his wife Beth, Gallagher confesses, and the family moves from a Manhattan co-op to a suburban home. Forrest finds them, and after first killing a pet rabbit returns to murder Beth. With considerable difficulty, his wife kills her instead.

Fatal Attraction: *Dan Gallagher (Michael Douglas) and Alex Forrest (Glenn Close)*.

The popular success of a picture such as *Fatal Attraction* is heavily dependent on the noir formula. In its very title it uses the same "boldface" anticipation of a menacing situation as many classic period films. Despite this explicit invocation preceding the movie itself, *Fatal Attraction* still manages to manipulate viewer expectations. More significantly, it manipulates them by drawing the viewer into the protagonist's point of view. Even presuming that most viewers knew from previews or other promotional methods what the "fatal attraction" would be, the audience may still fail to discern the latent psychoses of Alex Forrest, fail to read any real menace in her slight lack of focus or an occasional nervous gesture, because Dan Gallagher does not see it. Alex Forrest is no femme fatale, luring the unwary hero down a deadly path of criminal activity or other degradation. Like Nancy Blair, the disturbed fiancée in *The Locket*, the veneer of normality is enhanced by Alex's sexual vulnerability. From the protagonist's, and audience's, frame of reference, her behavior is more disturbing for its unexpectedness. Like many noir figures before him, Gallagher's inability to anticipate or respond is the real source of peril. Like Sam Bowden in *Cape Fear*, he finds that the authorities cannot help him, that the very social order which he thought would protect him only makes him and his family easier to assail. Even more significantly, in terms of noir antecedents, like insurance executive John Forbes in *Pitfall*, Gallagher sees his comfortable family life completely imperiled by a reckless impulse that seemed free of consequences.

Beginning with *Play Misty for Me*, neo-noir has fatal men as well as women, although the cultural prejudices which helped create the femme fatale are still in play even after she becomes a sexual obsessed stalker. Tim Whelan, the protagonist of *Masquerade* (1988), is a gigolo intent on seducing an heiress. As with the classic period character Nick Blake in *Nobody Lives Forever*, the victim's naiveté gives Whelan pause; but in the typical schematic of neo-noir, nothing can prevent his destruction. *Fatal Attraction* atypically promises more than a mere schematic when it uses the sexual allure and fatality that surrounds both Forrest and Gallagher but soon deviates into crass and predictable events. In its much imitated conclusion, Alex Forrest is transformed from merely a mad (in more than one sense of the word) woman into an elemental, destructive harpy whose destruction seems impossible to accomplish. Many of the figures in neo-noir become victims of circumstance because of an ill-advised proclivity for love with an improper stranger. While resembling Forbes' fate, outside the classic period context Gallagher's comeuppance seems entirely deserved and Forrest's madness and death entirely excessive. **AS**

FEAR (1996)

Director: James Foley. **Screenplay**: Christopher Crowe. **Producers**: Brian Grazer, Ric Kidney, Karen Snow (Imagine Entertainment). **Executive Producer**: Karen Kehela. **Director of Photography**: Thomas Kloss. **Production Designer**: Alex McDowell. **Music**: Carter Burwell. **Editor**: David Brenner. **Cast**: Mark Wahlberg (David McCall), Reese Witherspoon (Nicole Walker), William Petersen (Steve Walker), Amy Brenneman (Laura Walker), Alyssa Milano (Margo Masse), Christopher Gray (Toby Walker), Tracy Fraim (Logan). **Released**: Universal Pictures, 12 April. 97 minutes.

Nicole is a bright teenager living in an upper-middle-class Seattle household that is troubled by signs of malaise: strains in the marital relationship of anxious Laura and over-protective Steve; hints that the traditional division between parents and children has broken down. Visiting a working-class bar with Margo, her best friend, Nicole's curiosity fixes on the James Dean-like David. The morning after their first tryst (where Nicole loses her virginity), David begins revealing his psychoses (expressed, for instance, in his brutal jealousy of Nicole's male friends)—but Nicole, blind to this, over-trustingly gives him her home's security code. Margo is drawn into an abusive three-way relationship with David and his best friend Logan, and is initially rejected afterwards by the disbelieving Nicole. Steve, increasingly disturbed by David's violent and provocative behavior, uncovers his criminal past. Steve's intervention in ending the teenage romance triggers a series of confrontations that culminate in a prolonged siege of the family home by David and his companions. In the ensuing struggle, Nicole stabs David in the back and Steve hurls him out of a first-floor window, killing him and reuniting the family.

A wave of films emerged in the early 1990s, especially in the US, comprising a sub-genre known as the *intimacy thriller*: stories in which the menace of the "other" comes from someone initially reassuring, protective, with privileged access to the domestic sphere: cops, babysitters, landlords, architects, family friends. A pronounced class consciousness is evident in many of these films, like Scorsese's *Cape Fear* remake (1991): the monster figure (for the intimacy thriller invariably marries film noir and horror elements) is often a disgruntled, resentful member of the proletariat who seeks revenge on the professional class for some social wrong done to him or her. Foley and screenwriter Crowe (who directed the notable *Whispers in the Dark*, 1992) fully and vividly dramatize in *Fear* the ambivalence and ambiguity at the heart of the intimacy thriller. David is certainly portrayed as the ultimate "white trash" villain: he does not attend school, cannot spell properly, drinks beer, shoots pool, spray-paints his abode, and even keeps a *Child's Play* Chucky doll in his room. But, no matter how psychotic or evil he becomes (and the film moves relentlessly towards "erasing" him so that the status quo can prevail), it is still impossible not to feel some sympathy for him. He consistently exposes, with biting accuracy, the malaise in the Walker family: the father's overly-intense interest in his children, the mother's willingness to stray, the daughter's eagerness to walk on the wild side. On this level, *Fear* is a clear descendant of Hitchcock's noir/family melodrama classic *Shadow of a Doubt*, updated with a spectacular home-siege finale reminiscent of Peckinpah's *Straw Dogs* (1972).

Although dismissed by some reviewers on its release as a sensationalist, hysterical, formulaic piece, *Fear* has improved with age. Foley is a minor master at wielding what critic Raymond Durgnat once described as the "energy realism" of contemporary American cinema: as in his feature debut *Reckless* (1984)—a lyrical teen movie that shares some key elements with *Fear*—the narrative accelerations, dramatic crescendos, and visceral combinations of image and music are particularly effective. Foley, too, as he has often proved, gets the best out of his actors: Witherspoon and Wahlberg, in early roles, are more impressive here than was evident to others at the time. And the splendid scene in which David masturbates Nicole as they ride a Big Dipper, a cover version of The Rolling Stones' "Wild Horses" filling the soundtrack, is an immortal ode to transgressive teen eroticism. **AM**

FEAR CITY (1985)

Director: Abel Ferrara. **Screenplay**: Nicholas St. John. **Executive Producers**: Stanley R. Zupnick, Tom Curtis. **Director of Photography**: James Lemmo. **Music**: Dick Halligan. **Production Designer**: Vincent Cresciman. **Editor**: Jack W. Holmes, Anthony Redman. **Cast**: Tom Berenger (Matt Rossi), Billy Dee Williams (Detective Al Wheeler), Jack Scalia (Nicky Parzeno), Melanie Griffith (Loretta), Rossano Brazzi (Carmine), Rae Dawn Chong (Leila), Joe Santos (Frank), Michael V. Gazzo (Mike), Jan Murray (Goldstein), Janet Julian (Ruby), Daniel Feraldo (Sanchez), Maria Conchita Alonso (Silver), Ola Ray (Honey), Cihangir Gaffari (Pazzo), Emilia Crow (Bibi), Juan Fernandez (Jorge). **Released**: 20th Century-Fox, February 16. 96 minutes.

Someone is assaulting strippers in New York City, and seems to be targeting women represented by talent agents Matt Rossi and Jacky Scalia. Detective Al Wheeler suspects that mob tensions play some role in these attacks, and takes a special interest in the case. For ex-boxer Rossi this violence dredges up memories of his own past, where he quit the ring after fatally wounding his opponent, Kid Rico, and of his broken relationship with the stripper and ex-junkie Loretta. Deeming these attacks "bad for business," rival mob factions decide to work together to flush out the killer, who adheres to a samurai-style code of purity and has been keeping a record of his deeds in a book entitled "Fear City." After beating a man mistaken for the killer, Rossi is arrested for assault and brutally interrogated by Wheeler, who preaches about the "power of the law." When his partner Scalia is hospitalized by the killer, Rossi, now out on bail, rents a hotel room, honing his fighting skills by day while searching for the killer at night. Meanwhile Loretta, who has begun using again, encounters the killer while trying to buy drugs, but Rossi rescues her and kills the man.

Neon lights and rain-slicked streets provide the impressive visual content of Abel Ferrara's noirish exploration of sex and violence, though these are not enough to overcome the film's derivative script and stilted dialogue. Repeating themes central to classic film noir, *Fear City* depicts a world in which all are corrupt or corruptible and the forces of law and order are impotent. "No one is innocent!" fumes Detective Wheeler, especially when one is faced with a "city full of suspects." The main tensions of *Fear City* revolve around Rossi, Wheeler and the slasher-killer, each of whom mirrors the other in various ways. An ex-vice cop now working for homicide, Wheeler is so personally invested in the law that he resembles Jim Wilson from *On Dangerous Ground* (1952), but without any of his depth. Matt Rossi, by contrast, is more complex. Afraid of his own violent potential, Rossi cannot decide how to deal with these assaults on his livelihood and reflects upon his fatal bout for answers. Chastised by his manager for having taken pity on the battered Kid Rico in an earlier round, Rossi was told to do "his job"—"You get out there and you kill him." Other flashbacks remind him of how he witnessed a mob hit while working as a shoeshine boy, more evidence of how the "job" is done in this tough business.

Wheeler insists that the police represent the only line between criminals and innocent people, and claims that the cuffs that bind Rossi's hands during his interrogation "represent the power of the law." However, Rossi's view of the law has been jaded by his experience in the ring, where the referee (effectively the policeman of boxing) failed to stop the fight before the fatal blow was dealt. In this respect the law fails to protect people; its enforcers cannot do their "job" properly. Yet what really bothers Rossi is his inability to curb his own violence. His rage mounts with each new killing, as do flashbacks to his own history of violence. While the killer may be mad, he is nevertheless disciplined and methodical, basing his violence on principles of purity and dispensing it in a cold and calculated way. In this sense, the killer has more in common with Wheeler, who is equally obsessed with cleaning up the city but conspicuously unable to get results. Intercutting scenes of Rossi and the killer practicing their fighting techniques effectively conveys how much Rossi has "learned" from his enemy; yet in the final confrontation the former boxer once again pummels his opponent to death, revealing that an "unlawful" loss of control may be a useful thing when the law itself is powerless. Like the referee who failed to stop Kid Rico from getting killed, Wheeler too fails to save the slasher killer from Rossi's wrath, but more or less endorses his methods at the end of the film: "You think you're a hero, Rossi? . . . Maybe you are." **CF**

FEMME FATALE (2002)

Director: Brian De Palma. **Screenplay**: Brian De Palma. **Producers**: Tarak Ben Ammar, Marina Gefter (Epsilon Motion Pictures, Quinta Communications). **Executive Producers**: Mark Lombardo, Chris Soldo. **Director of Photography**: Thierry Arbogast. **Production Designer**: Anne Pritchard. **Music**: Ryuichi Sakamoto. **Editor**: Bill Pankow. **Cast**: Rebecca Romjin-Stamos (Laure/Lily), Antonio Banderas (Nicolas Bardo), Peter Coyote (Watts), Eriq Ebouaney (Black Tie), Edouard Montoute (Racine), Rie Rasmussen (Veronica). **Released**: Warner Bros. Pictures, November 6. 114 minutes.

A heist at the Cannes Film Festival: after seducing Veronica and stealing her jewelry, Laure double-crosses her accomplices Racine and Black Tie. Racine tracks Laure down and

Femme Fatale: *Laure/Lily (Rebecca Romijn-Stamos) and Nicolas Bardo (Antonio Banderas).*

throws her off a hotel balcony. Surviving the fall, Laure is rescued by a couple who mistake her for their daughter Lily. While Laure bathes, Lily enters and kills herself. Laure takes Lily's identity and plane ticket to America; she meets Ambassador Watts, whom she marries. Seven years later: returning to France, Laure's photo is snapped by paparazzo-artist Nicolas. Black Tie and Racine revive their pursuit of Laure, after throwing her girlfriend into an oncoming truck. Laure uses Nicolas in a plan to blackmail Watts. After receiving the money, Laure kills both him and Nicolas—but her accomplices appear and throw her off a bridge. Laure re-awakens in the bath: she has dreamt everything from that point. Events re-begin exactly as before, except that Laure stops Lily from suiciding and persuades her to take the plane. Seven years later: Laure is receiving the heist proceedings from her girlfriend, revealed as Veronica; when Black Tie and Racine appear, it is they rather than Veronica who are killed. Nicolas introduces himself to Laure.

Beginning with a clip of Stanwyck shooting MacMurray in *Double Indemnity* (an action which is duly reprised, much later, between Laure and Nicolas), *Femme Fatale* takes the noir figure of a ruthless, manipulative, scheming, highly sexualized woman and places it within a novel context: a great deal of the plot, as we eventually learn, is only Laure's dream. If there is such a thing as post-modern noir, *Femme Fatale* surely fits the bill. With inspired ingenuity, De Palma found the perfect way to respond to two recurrent critiques of his work: that his heroines tend to be victims of patriarchy; and that his plotting has a cartoonish, risible quality. Here, Laure becomes an extravagantly shape-shifting, omniscient, almost superhuman character; and every bizarre, highly coincidental or illogical thing that occurs to and around her finds its retroactive motivation in the dream-state.

Freed in this way from conventional realism, De Palma delivers his most extravagant, delirious, yet most purely formalist work: motifs swirl from scene to scene in dreamlike reprises (all clocks are fixed at 3:33 PM, water flows everywhere, posters on Paris streets endlessly mirror or comment upon proceedings), and a large repertoire of stylistic devices (including slow motion, split screen, and the insistent counterpoint of Sakamoto's superb score) are used in lively permutation, resulting in several impressive set-pieces. De Palma succeeds here

(as few filmmakers have done) in making a highly self-conscious, flagrantly contrived and artificial film which is at once ironic (to the point of camp self-parody) and compelling—both a narrative illusion and the auto-analysis of that illusion. Ultimately, the film's merrily baroque contortions (it frequently seems like an anthology of great De Palma moments) serve a pleasingly coherent theme: like so many recent movies with supernatural premises (in genres ranging from the romantic comedy of *Sliding Doors* [1998] to the art-film metaphysical puzzle of *The Double Life of Veronique* [1991]), *Femme Fatale* is a meditation on multiple lives, changing identities, and second chances. But where the dream-and-reality structure of Lynch's *Mulholland Drive* (2001) arrives at a bleak, nihilistic conclusion, *Femme Fatale* is among this director's few truly upbeat, optimistic works. Even the familiar, cynical end-point of many De Palma films—the absorption of the characters and their private deeds into an indifferent, omnivorous, public media spectacle—receives a light-hearted tweak, as Nicolas' wall-sized David Hockney-style photo-collage (devised by the director's brother Bart) receives its final image from the surreal life going on just beyond the artist's balcony. **AM**

FIGHT CLUB (1999)

Director: David Fincher. **Screenplay**: Jim Uhls based on the novel *Fight Club* by Chuck Palahniuk. **Producers**: Art Linson, Ceán Chaffin, Ross Grayson Bell. **Executive Producer**: Arnon Milchan. **Director of Photography**: Jeff Cronenweth. **Music**: The Dust Brothers, Michael Simpson, John King. **Production Designer**: Alex McDowell. **Editor**: Jim Haygood. **Cast**: Brad Pitt (Tyler Durden), Edward Norton (Narrator), Helena Bonham Carter (Marla Singer), Meat Loaf (Bob Paulson), Sach Grenier (Richard Chesler, boss), Richmond Arquette (Intern), David Andrews (Thomas), George Maguire (Group Leader), Eugenie Bondurant (Weeping Woman), Christina Cabot (Group Leader), Sydney "Big Dawg" Colston (Speaker), Rachel Singer (Chloe). **Released**: 20th Century-Fox, October 15. 139 minutes.

A sleep-deprived, cubicle-dwelling narrator finds relief from his ennui by attending support groups for people with fatal illnesses or other major health problems. The delicate balance he has achieved in his unhappy life is upset by the arrival of another tourist at the sessions, and especially at the testicular cancer group, the cigarette smoking pseudo-femme fatale Marla. The trouble with Marla breathes life into Tyler Durden, an anarchic stud who appears to be everything the narrator is not. The narrator and Tyler set up housekeeping in a decaying mansion and start Fight Club, where men indulge in their animal maleness by beating each other bloody. Tyler initiates a rough, orgiastic sexual relationship with Marla and then dumps her. Tyler and the narrator franchise Fight Club which morphs into Project Mayhem, an anti-capitalist terrorist group bent on wiping out credit card debt with Tyler as the group's absolute commander. The dénouement of the film reveals the narrator's psychosis: the narrator and Tyler are the same person. In the final sequence, after he (the Norton character) has managed to eliminate Tyler or become Tyler, he and Marla watch as the city crumbles around them. Project Mayhem has come to fruition.

With its voice-over male narration, erotic triangle, female object of desire who is both like the narrator and dangerous to him, and male antagonist who is both like the narrator

Fight Club: *Edward Norton as the unnamed Narrator.*

and dangerous to him, *Fight Club* mirrors many classic noirs, even as it revels in and satirizes many of the culturally current issues of the late 1990s. Although a costly, successful, and highly profitable Hollywood film, *Fight Club* advances a critique of late-market capitalism, of the enforced feminization of males in consumption-driven postmodern culture, and finally of the dangerous, misogynist, conformist, and racist potential of cults of white masculinity. The final sequence even serves as an eerie forecast of the momentous event that definitively ended the twentieth century: the collapse of the World Trade Center towers in September, 2001.

In addition to narrative surprise and witty repartee, the film offers gorgeous visual spectacles: molecule-eye views of energy flowing through conduit; a floating live-action IKEA catalog; evocative, dripping, low-light *mise en scène*; half-clad, sweating, muscular men; and various imperceptible splices of an erect penis (mirroring the actions of super-stud Tyler within the story). The discernable focus on masculinity makes *Fight Club* a dick flick, a hard-on reaction against romantic comedies which glorify marriage, home, lawn mowers, and curtain choices: everything that the film seeks to denigrate. *Mr. and Mrs. Smith* (2005) offers a similar assessment of capitalism and domestic bliss, without putting the blame on women. Classic noir often provided a muted critique of heterosexual domesticity by portraying it as a gray, dull, safe alternative to the exciting but frequently deadly life of the male protagonist and femme fatale. Perhaps because it is so much a product of the culture it seeks to critique, the ideological project of *Fight Club* comes up empty-handed, managing primarily to appeal to appetites it promises to interrogate. **JBW**

FRIENDS OF EDDIE COYLE (1973)

Director: Peter Yates. **Producer and Screenplay**: Paul Monash based on the novel by George V. Higgins. **Director of Photography**: Victor J. Kemper. **Music**: Dave Grusin. **Production Designer**: Gene Callahan. **Editor**: Pat Jaffe. **Cast**: Robert Mitchum (Eddie Coyle), Peter Boyle (Dillon), Richard Jordan (Dave Foley), Steven Keats (Jackie), Alex Rocco (Scalise), Joe Santos (Artie Van), Mitchell Ryan (Waters), Peter MacLean (Partridge), Marvin Lichterman (Vernon), Carolyn Pickman (Nancy), James Tolkan (Contact Man), Margaret Ladd (Andrea). **Completed**: December 1972. **Released**: Paramount, June 27. 102 minutes.

Realizing that an upcoming trial might force him to live the rest of his life behind bars, a middle-aged, three-time-loser Eddie Coyle is out on bail. He decides to become a police informant and engage in plea bargaining with treasury agent Dave Foley. But Coyle also continues to transport illegal goods across state lines for the mob. While the police pressure Eddie for information without any intention of shortening his probable jail sentence, the mob also manipulates him. Coyle's underworld contact and friend, Dillon, is hired by the mob to kill the apparent informer. Finding out that the contract is for Eddie, Dillon is still determined to go through with the assassination. Like a pig fattened up before the slaughter, Coyle is treated to a last fling by his eventual murderer. After a hockey game and several drinks, Eddie Coyle is driven to a lonely spot, killed, and left in an abandoned car.

Adapted from a novel by George V. Higgins, *The Friends of Eddie Coyle* comes closer to capturing the feeling and mood of the noir films of the late 1940s than many neo-noirs. Many of the elements that define the noir bias are present in the film. Not only is there an overwhelming mood of corruption complicated by an ethos of hopelessness and fatalism, but there is equally a sharp sense of alienation and fear. *The Friends of Eddie Coyle* deals with a contemporary world still confined by the goals and situations of the noir environment. There even remains a ritualization of violence, as indicated by the elongated execution of Eddie Coyle, that recalls the best work of Anthony Mann and Jules Dassin. Robert Mitchum provides a physical link to the 1940s noir film because, by the time of *Eddie Coyle,* his well-established persona developed in such noir films as *Out of The Past* and *Crossfire* had decomposed into the aged portrait of a man faced with the reality of no real escape. The cynical nature of the police and the young punks with whom Coyle comes in contact merely reinforce the noir ambience present in the film. The downbeat ending and ultimate grotesqueness of the portrayals by Peter Boyle and the assorted young hoods, along with the other more debasing characteristics of the film, place *The Friends of Eddie Coyle* closer to the sensibility of the classic period than the homages offered by such films as *Chinatown* and *Farewell, My Lovely.* **CM**

Friends of Eddie Coyle: *Robert Mitchum as Eddie Coyle.*

THE GAME (1997)

Director: David Fincher. **Screenplay**: John Brancato, Michael Ferris. **Producers**: John Brancato, Michael Ferris, Steve Golin, Ceán Chaffin. **Director of Photography**: Harris Savides. **Music**: Howard Shore. **Production Designer**: Jeffrey Beecroft. **Editor**: James Haygood. **Cast**: Michael Douglas (Nicholas Van Orton), Sean Penn (Conrad Van Orton), Deborah Kara Unger (Christine), James Rebhorn (Jim Feingold), Peter Donat (Samuel Sutherland), Carroll Baker (Ilsa), Anna Katarina (Elizabeth), Armin Mueller-Stahl (Anson Baer). **Released**: Polygram, September 12. 128 minutes.

On his forty-eighth birthday emotionally detached but highly successful New York businessman Nicholas Van Orton meets his wastrel brother Conrad, from whom he is somewhat estranged, for lunch and receives an unusual present: participation in a game that Conrad assures him will change his life. Curious yet dubious, Nicholas presents himself at Consumer Recreation Services (whose offices are artfully concealed within another building) and discovers that a physical exam has disqualified him from participation. Soon, however, he learns that the game has begun after experiencing a series of assaults on his dignity and, soon thereafter, on his safety. Nicholas is reminded by "the game" that his own father committed suicide by jumping off a building at exactly the same age. Aided by Christine, an erstwhile employee of CRS, Nicholas makes a series of desperate escapes from the company's armed attackers, but is eventually captured, flown to Mexico, and deposited without resources in a shabby town. As Nicholas attempts to reconstruct his life, he learns that all his assets have been stolen. Returning to New York, where he takes a revolver from his apartment, he breaks into the CRS offices in a skyscraper, and takes one of the employees hostage, who tells him that the company has replaced all the shells in his guns with blanks. At this moment, Nicholas is surprised by a door opening, and in reflex he fires, apparently hitting his brother Conrad, who holds a celebratory bottle of champagne. Overcome with guilt, Nicholas re-enacts his father's suicide, jumping off the building. But his fall is broken by a judiciously placed airbag. He meets up with Conrad, who tells him that the gun actually did contain only blanks. "The Game" was only a game designed to make Nicholas appreciate what he has and take joy in life again. As the film ends, Nicholas re-unites with Christine.

The Game draws on a number of obvious literary and cinematic sources for its dramatization of a hypothetical "other path" for its protagonist; these include Dickens' *A Christmas Carol* (Nicholas is something of a modern day Scrooge) and *It's A Wonderful Life* (which also, in a notable sequence, traces the paranoid horrors of a life lived in absence of one's identity). The idea of a shadow corporation, all-knowing and seemingly all-powerful, devoted to the dubious joys of personal transformation, and located mysteriously in the interstices of an urban business district is lifted from John Frankenheimer's *Seconds*.

The Game also shares much in common with the paranoid thriller of an earlier era, *The Conversation*, *The Parallax View*, *Three Days of the Condor*, and, more recently, such films as *Enemy of the State* and *The Pelican Brief*. With its notion of virtual reality gaming, however, *The Game* also connects to those of the current younger generation interested in live action role-playing. In some respects, *The Game*, of course, is quintessentially noir, particularly in its depiction of the protagonist's economic descent from the pinnacle of success (a fancy home complete with servants) to absolute penury (his abandonment in a dusty, impoverished hovel south of the border). The film engages with one of noir's classic themes—the inevitably paranoid experience of identity loss and the desperate struggle to regain one's "self" (as in *Somewhere in the Night*). Unsympathetic, hard-edged, but physically and emotionally resourceful, Nicholas Van Orton traces his lineage to many a classic noir protagonist, even if he enjoys a happy ending denied to many of them. **RBP**

GATTACA (1997)

Director: Andrew Niccol. **Screenplay**: Andrew Niccol. **Producers**: Danny DeVito, Gail Lyon, Michael Shamberg, Stacey Sher. **Director of Photography**: Slawomir Idziak. **Production Designer**: Jan Roelfs. **Music**: Michael Nyman. **Editor**: Lisa Zeno Churgin. **Cast**: Ethan Hawke (Vincent Freeman), Uma Thurman (Irene Cassini), Gore Vidal (Director Josef), Xander Berkeley (Dr. Lamar), Elias Koteas (Antonio Freeman), Jayne Brook (Marie Freeman), Jude Law (Jerome Eugene Morrow), Alan Arkin (Detective Hugo), Loren Dean (Anton Freeman), Ernest Borgnine (Caesar), Tony Shalhoub (German). **Released**: Columbia, October 24. 101 minutes.

In a "not too distant" future, where genetic engineering of humans is common and DNA plays the primary role in determining social class, Vincent is conceived and born without the aid of this technology. Suffering from the physical dysfunctions of nearsightedness and a congenital heart defect, Vincent faces discrimination as an "in-valid." The only way he can achieve his life-long dream of becoming an astronaut is to impersonate someone else. He assumes the identity of swimming star Jerome Morrow who became paraplegic as a result of a botched suicide attempt. Vincent

Gattaca: *Vincent Freeman (Ethan Hawke) precedes Irene Cassini (Uma Thurman) through a checkpoint.*

uses "valid" DNA and tissue samples provided by Jerome, and gains admittance to the Gattaca Aerospace Corporation, the most prestigious space-flight conglomerate of the day. The plan works perfectly until, a week before Vincent is scheduled to leave for Titan, the mission director is murdered and evidence of Vincent's own DNA is found at the crime scene. Vincent must evade ever-increasing security as his mission launch date approaches and he pursues a relationship with his co-worker Irene Cassini. The police, led by his valid brother Anton, discover the real murderer, one of the directors of Gattaca, Josef. While Jerome commits suicide, Vincent flies to Titan as planned.

Gattaca creates a dystopia which in design owes more to the Bauhaus style than German expressionism. It is an immaculate, orderly universe—sleek, modern, symmetrical, yet somehow still sinister. The scenes at night are tinted eerily red, blue, or green—disorienting the viewer's color expectations. The day scenes are blazingly bright with rockets flying like meteors over the Gattaca headquarters at regular intervals. The Gattaca offices are modern, minimalist, with rows of dark-suited employees marching automaton-like through turnstiles, in a clear homage to *Metropolis*. The central conflict of the film revolves around identity. This "brave new world" will genetically engineer children for the right price, thereby producing a two-tiered society of "valids" and "in-valids." "Valids" occupy the upper echelon positions while "in-valids" perform the menial jobs. As a result the society is obsessed with keeping track of its citizens' identities through the use of methods like electronic scanning and periodic blood-urine testing.

Vincent is an in-valid, "conceived in love," who narrates the film in traditional noir style. His brother Anton, however, was genetically engineered. Vincent's greatest ambition is to travel in space, even though his father tells him, "The only way you'll see the inside of a spaceship is cleaning it." Although handicapped, he is determined to live out his dream. And so he illegally exchanges his identity with a valid ex-athlete, Jerome. In order to maintain this facade, Vincent/Jerome must painfully scrub away his identity every morning—seen in the first shots of the film in a series of close-ups as Vincent washes away every dead cell and follicle he can find. Although he is scheduled to travel to Titan,

he lives in a state of constant fear of being discovered, particularly since a murder has occurred at Gattaca which brings in the police.

Three key scenes in this movie are the swimming contests between Vincent and Anton at various ages. These scenes not only crystallize the conflict between the brothers, as well as the class conflict in their society, but it also serves to demonstrate Vincent's perseverance in the face of pain and fear. Although, as he tells the viewer through his narration, he always lost the contests as a boy to his genetically superior brother, as a teen things change and Vincent wins. The spectator sees him outdistance his brother and in fact rescue him from the deep waters. This contest is repeated for a last time, towards the end of the film. It is night and the boys are adults. Vincent finally confirms for his doubting brother the superiority of will over genetics as he again beats his brother, rescuing him from the sea once more. As he pulls Anton's spent body back, Vincent stares up at the stars he so longs to visit.

In the final scene of the movie, the filmmakers construct a powerful montage based on the film's themes of identity and Nietzschean "will to power." The film intercuts between Vincent/Jerome walking through tunnels and boarding the spaceship to Titan while the original Jerome, who has become a second brother to Vincent, prepares to immolate himself in a furnace, thereby giving up completely his identity to Vincent. The rocket rises. Flames spew forth from the boosters as the fire of the furnace devours Jerome who holds his Olympic medal in a final moment of pride for past accomplishments. The film then cuts to a close-up of Vincent, tears in his eyes, "Every atom in our body was once part of a star . . . Maybe I'm going home." Noir melancholy and existential doubt color his final victory as it does the entire film. **JU**

THE GETAWAY (1972)

Director: Sam Peckinpah. **Screenplay**: Walter Hill based on the novel by Jim Thompson. **Producers**: Mitchell Brower, David Foster. **Director of Photography**: Lucien Ballard. **Art Directors**: Angelo P. Graham, Ted Haworth. **Music**: Quincy Jones. **Editor**: Robert Wolfe. **Cast**: Steve McQueen (Carter "Doc" McCoy), Ali MacGraw (Carol

The Getaway: *"Doc" McCoy (Steve McQueen) and his wife Carol (Ali McGraw).*

McCoy), Ben Johnson (Jack Beynon), Sally Struthers (Fran Clinton), Al Lettieri (Rudy Butler), Slim Pickens (Cowboy), Richard Bright (Thief at railway station), Jack Dodson (Harold Clinton), Dub Taylor (Laughlin), Bo Hopkins (Frank Jackson), Roy Jenson (Cully). **Released**: Warner Bros., December 13. 122 minutes.

In order to get "Doc" McCoy released from prison, his wife Carol makes a proposition to Jack Beynon: if he will arrange for McCoy's parole, the robber will reward him with most of the proceeds from a lucrative bank job. To seal the deal, Carol must submit to Beynon's sexual advances. After the job erupts in violence, Doc realizes he has been set up to be killed by his accomplice Rudy Butler. Although that is foiled and Butler left for dead, soon after Carol confesses to Doc what she had to do to free him. Although on the run from the law, Beynon's henchmen, and even the wounded Butler, who kidnaps a veterinarian and his wife to help him chase them, the McCoys manage to get to a border-town hotel. After a final gun fight, the couple cross the border in the car of a gregarious old cowboy who admires their apparent devotion to one another.

In the various adapters' hands, Jim Thompson's usual assumptions about the sordidness of crime and its corrupting influence on the criminal's will are transformed into a tale of betrayal and redemption, of self-righteous violence and paranoiac romance. In these terms and as a fugitive-couple narrative, the 1972 version of *The Getaway* provides an expressive link to the films of the classic period of film noir. The opening focuses on "Doc" in prison. Carol is first seen in the form of two snapshots taped to the wall of his cell. Moreover Peckinpah unabashedly puts forth his typical naturalistic metaphors. The first shot is of a kneeling doe, followed by a stag. From this, there is a pan up to reveal a prison watchtower. Finally a long shot of sheep zooms back to reveal rows of cell blocks. Noise from the prison textile mill fades in. The isolated male and female animals prefigure Doc's overwhelming sense of sexual repression. The machine noise; Doc upsetting chess pieces and his opponent's remark, "Oh, man, it's just a game;" the destruction of the match stick bridge—all this overt symbolism establishes a deterministic undertow; and even though the machine noise stops with marked abruptness when Doc is released, this undertow will grip Peckinpah's fugitive couple unrelentingly.

Throughout the film, other elements, from Lucien Ballard's flat lighting scheme to the clipped dialogue adapted by scenarist Hill from novelist Thompson, reinforce the realism. In the escape from the bank robbery, a crossing guard stops Doc and Carol's car. The red, handheld "Stop" sign which she holds up for them to see is a typical expression of noir fatalism always threatening to capsize a scheme that goes back to the grind of the starter motor in *Double Indemnity*. For Wilder and Chandler adapting Cain, the engine finally starts. For Peckinpah and Hill interpreting Thompson, the delay creates a moment of chaos and violence, which the characters must stoically endure. The supporting players are nasty, garrulous, and otherwise unattractive in line with Peckinpah's naturalist bent and they are, of course, given to offhanded and extreme violence. His car chases are full of odd angles and cut points. The sound effects complement the lighting,

they are muted and hollow. For Peckinpah, violent action is a transcendent activity. The slow motion and other stylistic manipulations create a distorted perspective for the viewer that is meant to be roughly equivalent to the temporal and sensory distortions which real violence imposes on its participants. **AS**

THE GETAWAY (1994)

Director: Roger Donaldson. **Screenplay**: Walter Hill and Amy Jones based on the novel by Jim Thompson. **Producers**: David Foster, John Alan Simon, Lawrence Turman. **Director of Photography**: Peter Menzies, Jr. **Production Designer**: Joseph Nemec III. **Music**: Mark Isham. **Editor**: Conrad Buff. **Cast**: Alec Baldwin (Carter "Doc" McCoy), Kim Basinger (Carol McCoy), Michael Madsen (Rudy Travis), James Woods (Jack Benyon), David Morse (Jim Deer Jackson), Jennifer Tilly (Fran Carvey), James Stephens (Harold Carvey, DVM), Richard Farnsworth (Slim), Philip Seymour Hoffman (Frank Hansen), Burton Gilliam (Gollie). **Released**: Universal, February 11. 115 minutes.

The story opens with Doc's abandonment by his partners, which reinforces the irony of having to work on the job for Benyon with one of his betrayers. In other respects, the essential plot is the same as the earlier version.

While the narrative events of both versions of *The Getaway* are closely aligned—not surprising given that Walter Hill's adaptation of Thompson's book is the starting point for each—the subversive undertone of Peckinpah's version is severely restricted in the remake. Roger Donaldson, the director of the 1994 *The Getaway*, stages and edits the same action sequences in a more standard way. Although the viewer/camera rides along in the careening vehicles with the fugitive couple, the mechanics of the editing scheme have a depersonalizing effect.

Although the screen personas of both Carols, Ali MacGraw in 1972 and Kim Basinger in 1994, "glamorize" the character, perhaps the greatest shift in emphasis between the versions is between the proto-feminist portrayal by MacGraw and the more explicitly liberated posture of Basinger. While Doc's reaction when he learns of Carol's infidelity remains understandable in a patriarchal context, the 1994 Carol challenges his perspective more emphatically when she asks "You'd do the same for me, wouldn't you, Doc? You'd humiliate yourself for me?" As a "1990's woman," Bassinger's Carol not only wants the biggest gun, she wants to control her own destiny. MacGraw's Carol winces when she shoots people; but she does shoot them. When Bassinger expertly plays the dumb decoy or runs interference for her husband's scam from the driver's seat, it belies her ability to drive, shoot, and even throw a punch like a man. In this sense, she is closer to Annie Laurie Starr. The title sequence of the later version exemplifies this.

Compared to the introduction of the MacGraw Carol as she visits Doc/McQueen in prison, the Basinger Carol is first seen at target practice. A slow motion, extreme close-up of a finger pulling a trigger injects a note of genre awareness that verges on parody. The actors' names are superimposed as the frame widens via a zoom back to reveal the muzzle flash and recoil of the shots and a cutaway reveals tin cans jumping as they are hit. Doc and Carol are first seen in a two shot. She wears a sleeveless turtleneck under a black halter top, the lines of which mirror his shoulder holster. The first shot of her alone is as she fires a smaller caliber handgun. She wants the .45, but a smiling Doc asserts that "It's mine." Her answer—"but I want it"—effectively summarizes the dynamics of their relationship. The associations of gunplay and sexplay develop naturally from the staging and statements ("We go together . . . like guns and ammunition . . .") of more than forty years earlier in *Gun Crazy*. **LB**

THE GRIFTERS (1990)

Director: Stephen Frears. **Screenplay**: Donald E. Westlake based on the novel *The Grifters* by Jim Thompson. **Producers**: Robert A. Harris, Martin Scorsese, Jim Painter. **Director of Photography**: Oliver Stapleton. **Music**: Elmer Bernstein. **Editor**: Mick Audsley. **Cast**: Angelica Huston (Lilly Dillon), John Cusack (Roy Dillon), Annette Bening (Myra Langtree), Pat Hingle (Bobo Justus), Michael Laskin (Irv), Eddie Jones (Mintz), Gailard Sartain (Joe), Noelle Harling (Nurse Carol Flynn), J.T. Walsh (Cole). **Released**: Miramax Films, December 5. 119 minutes.

Roy Dillon is a 25-year-old, small-time, short-con artist living in Los Angeles. He doesn't know his new girlfriend, Myra Langtree, is a long-con roper from Texas, turning tricks to make ends meet in LA. When Roy's mother, Lilly, is ordered by her mob boss to travel from New Mexico to Southern California to play back the odds at the La Jolla racetrack, she decides to make a detour and see her son. It's their first reunion in years, and Lilly immediately sends Roy to the hospital for a serious injury he suffered grifting in a local bar. Myra and Lilly dislike each other from the start. Myra spies on Lilly at the race track. When she learns Lilly is skimming from the cash, Myra rats to the mob to flush her out on the open road. She tails Lilly to a two-bit motel in Arizona, and goes for the kill, but Lilly survives and heads back to LA to get runaway money from Roy. He's not the dutiful son type, so Lilly is forced to use every wile in her book to claim Roy's cash stash for herself.

The opening credits fade in and out against a montage of black and white photographs that depict contemporary Los Angeles architecture existing side by side with structures from the classic noir period. It's a nice touch that acknowledges the film's literary and cinematic antecedent. There's a pale amber wash to Oliver Stapleton's cinematography that brings to mind Edward Hopper paintings in exterior shots like the Bryson Hotel where Roy lives, or interiors like the diner where Lilly elbows the drunken businessman. Westlake's script lifts plenty of snappy dialogue from Thompson's novel—a wise decision that maintains characters who are slightly caricatured yet believable. They've got one foot in the post-World War II era and one in the modern world. For example, Roy's rejection of Myra when she pushes him to team together sounds like Walter Neff right out of *Double Indemnity*: "You scare the hell out of me. I have seen women like you before, baby. You're double tough and you're sharp as a razor, and you get what you want or else. But you don't make it work forever. Sooner or later, the lightning hits and I'm not gonna be around when it hits you."

The Grifters: *John Cusack as Roy Dillon.*

Flashbacks contrast Roy's indoctrination to the short-con business from an old time grifter who plied his trade twenty bucks at a time against Myra's greenback lust that stemmed from her involvement in a successful and sophisticated scheme that bilked oil tycoons for six-figure scores. These glimpses into each character's past foreshadow how disconnected they are outside the bedroom, culminating with Roy's violent smack-down that sends Myra scurrying for the exit. Pat Hingle and J.T. Walsh are perfectly cast as Lilly's boss, Bobo Justus, and Myra's former long-con partner, Cole Langley, respectively. Bobo's sly, brutal nature and Cole's severe psychological wipeout inform the greedy motivations the dueling vixens bring to their deadly triangle with Roy. It all adds up to a satisfying, combustible mixture of self-conscious neo-noir cinema. **TE**

GUNCRAZY (1993)

Director: Tamra Davis. **Screenplay**: Matthew Bright. **Producers**: Zane W. Levitt and Diane Firestone (Zeta Entertainment). **Director of Photography**: Lisa Rinzler. **Music**: Ed Tomney. **Editor**: Kevin Tent. **Cast**: Drew Barrymore (Anita), James Legros (Howard), Ione Skye (Joy), Michael Ironisde (Kincaid), Joe Dallesandro (Rooney), Billy Drago (Hank), Rodney Harvey (Tom), Jeremy Davies (Bill), Tracey Walter (Elton). **Released**: Overseas Filmgroup, January 20. 96 minutes.

Anita is a high-school student who lives in a trailer and is sexually abused by her mother's boyfriend Rooney. Derided by her classmates, Anita starts to exchange letters with Howard, who is imprisoned, awaiting parole and fascinated with firearms. Eventually Anita obtains a pistol and after Rooney rapes her again, she kills him and conceals the body. When Howard is paroled, Anita attempts to seduce him but discovers that he is impotent. Nonetheless they begin a liaison that revolves around guns. When his parole officer Kincaid attempts to reincarcerate Howard, the couple escapes and become fugitives. They take over a home and consummate their relationship. When they are tracked down, before he is shot by authorities, Howard tells Anita to say that he kidnapped her

Guncrazy: *Drew Barrymore as Anita.*

Gun Crazy (1950): *Annie Laurie holding pistols over her head.*

They go together like guns and ammunition.

Guncrazy is not a remake of the Joseph H. Lewis movie but a mixture of the fugitive couple and kid noir concepts. The script posits a high-school girl alone in a trailer with an abusive adult while her mom turns tricks in Fresno. The concept of becoming pen pals with and eventually marrying a young ex-con with a fascination for handguns mirrors aspects of the original *Gun Crazy*. The film further echoes that classic period title with visual imagery such as the scene of the couple locked in a parody of embrace while they shoot at cans and bottles. It also uses ingenuous dialogue in the manner of Nicholas Ray's *They Live by Night*. Howard and Anita themselves are much more like Ray's Bowie and Keechie than those in Robert Altman's aimless adaptation of the same novel, *Thieves Like Us.*

Director Tamra Davis' couple naively romanticize their sordid dilemma, epitomized when they break into a house and dress up for a candle-lit dinner. Their inadvertent, grisly killing spree often becomes darkly comic. In a sense, perhaps the strongest allusion and the blackest joke is in the implicit parallel to *Tomorrow Is Another Day* as the mocking Freudianism of Howard's high-caliber impotence and idealization of Anita despite her numerous sexual experiences are the 1990s equivalent of Steve Cochran's character having gone through puberty in prison and fixating on a taxi dancer. When Anita fulfills her promise to Howard, who purposely walks into a hail of police gunfire, and glances up from his body to flatly intone, "He made me do it," the emotional transaction is much closer to *They Live by Night* than the quirky neo-realism of Altman's remake. There is, in fact, a different kind of transference at work, more akin to the love of kidnapper and victim in Robert Aldrich's bleak period picture, *The Grissom Gang* (1971), based on the celebrated novel *No Orchids for Miss Blandish.* In a sequence such as when Howard and Anita bury their first victims, the high school boys who have tormented her, shot in one take with the camera looking up from inside a shallow grave at their silhouettes against the sky and ending as the last shovel full of dirt covers the lens, both the narrative and the grimly humorous style most closely recall the tone of Terrence Malick's *Badlands.* **AS**

HAMMETT (1982)

Director: Wim Wenders. **Screenplay**: Dennis O'Flaherty, Thomas Pope, Ross Thomas from the novel by Joe Gores. **Producers**: Don Guest, Fred Roos, Ronald Colby, Francis Ford Coppola. **Director of Photography**: Joseph Biroc. **Music**: John Barry. **Production Designer**: Dean Tavoularis. **Editors**: Janice Hampton, Marc Laub, Robert Q. Lovett, Randy Roberts. **Cast**: Frederic Forrest (Hammett), Peter Boyle (Jimmy Ryan), Marilu Henner (Kit Conger/Sue Alabama), Roy Kinnear (English Eddie Hagedorn), Elisha Cook, Jr. (Eli), Lydia Lei (Crystal Ling), R.G. Armstrong (Lt. O'Mara), Richard Bradford (Detective Bradford), Michael Chow (Fong Wei Tau), David Patrick Kelly (The Punk), Sylvia Sidney (Donaldina Cameron), Jack Nance (Gary Salt), Elmer Kline (Doc Fallon), Royal Dano (Pops), Samuel Fuller (Old Man in Pool Hall). **Released**: Warner Bros., September 17. 97 minutes.

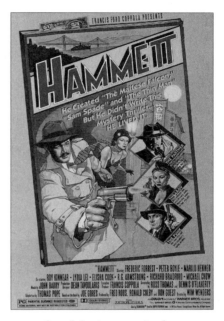

Retired from detective work and writing mystery stories for *Black Mask* magazine, Hammett is surprised when his old mentor in detection Jimmy Ryan solicits his help in finding Crystal Ling, a prostitute on the run from Chinatown gangster Fong Wei Tau. When Ryan disappears, crooked cops Lt. O'Mara and Detective Bradford tell Hammett to go back to his writing. Hammett presses on, linking Crystal to the suicide of a prominent San Francisco citizen. Stalked by English Eddie's "The Punk" and distracted by pornographer Gary Salt, Hammett makes contact with Crystal, but she's murdered the next day. As it turns out, Crystal is alive and plotting with Ryan to shake down a number of millionaires photographed having sex in Gary Salt's stag movie studio. Hammett makes the pay-off backed by his old cabbie buddy Eli and an amorous, trusted neighbor, librarian Kit Conger. Crystal gives Hammett the compromising negatives but murders Ryan and escapes. Hammett returns to his typewriter, reworking his adventure into something more suitable for pulp fiction.

This somewhat whimsical look at author Dashiell Hammett imagines that his life was as colorful as the detective adventures he bangs out on his typewriter, casting friends and acquaintances as key players. In a fantasy sequence illustrating his tale *Caught in the Middle,* Hammett's beautiful neighbor Kit Conger becomes the deadly adventuress Sue Alabama. Familiar types from *The Maltese Falcon*—a conniving dame, a corpulent, effete villain—appear as idealized, almost comforting types. Unlike Hammett's originals, the reassuring hunt to find a missing damsel and a kidnapped partner is preempted by more prosaic forms of corruption. Hammett retains his dignity but ends up another cog in the machinery that covers up the misdeeds of rich men.

Director Wenders pays homage to noir's hardboiled literary roots while Joseph Biroc's candy-colored images envision San Francisco as a fanciful playground of steep streets and Chinatown mysteries; the proto-noir world prior to the Golden Gate Bridge hasn't yet faded to a regretful B&W. A partnership still means something, even if Hammett's old pal has gone crooked. The cops are on the take and the cheap hoods have spirit, if not much style. Psychosis and alienation have yet to become the norm. Hammett loses the only copy of his latest story but happily retreats to his typewriter to write it again, recasting the colorful characters he's encountered in new roles. Re-imagined through a haze of nostalgia, *Hammett* is an affectionate homage that doesn't embarrass its origin. **GE**

HARDCORE (1979)

Director: Paul Schrader. **Screenplay**: Paul Schrader. **Producers**: Buzz Feitshans, John Milius. **Director of Photography**: Michael Chapman. **Music**: Jack Nitzsche. **Production Designer**: Paul Sylbert. **Editor**: Tom Rolf. **Cast**: George C. Scott (Jake VanDorn), Peter Boyle (Andy Mast), Season Hubley (Niki), Dick Sargent (Wes DeJong), Leonard Gaines (Bill Ramada), David Nichols (Kurt), Gary Rand Graham (Tod), Larry Block (Detective Burrows), Marc Alaimo (Ratan), Ilah Davis (Kristen VanDorn). **Released**: Columbia, February 9. 109 minutes.

When his daughter Kristen disappears on a church trip to Disneyland, Iowa furniture manufacturer Jake VanDorn leaves his rigid Dutch Reformed Calvinist community and travels to Los Angeles. Jake's square appearance guarantees non-cooperation from the underworld, so he hires detective Andy Mast, a sleazy operative. Mast returns with horrifying information: Kristen is performing in porn films. Mortified, Jake resolves to recover his daughter even if it means immersing himself in the "Sodom" of the Hollywood vice industries. Keeping Mast on payroll, he poses as an investor interested in triple-X rated movies. Jake also befriends peep show parlor girl and sometime prostitute Niki. Jake is thoroughly demoralized by his experience but manages the beginnings of a communication with Niki. Mast finds out that Kristen is under the influence of notorious porn filmmaker Ratan, who may be planning to murder her on camera in a snuff film. Jake rushes headlong into Ratan's skid row den and rescues his daughter. Kristen at first violently rejects her father, but Jake tearfully begs her to forgive and trust him.

One of several early Paul Schrader screenplays inspired by John Ford's *The Searchers,* the harsh neo-noir *Hardcore* constructs an uncomfortable clash of incompatible lifestyles. The uptight Jake VanDorn seemingly risks his own soul by descending into the "Hell" of the L.A.-based porn industry to recover his lost daughter. His Midwestern Calvinist community is slow to forgive and quick to forget those that stray from the fold.

Classic noirs often allude to a chaotic underworld of perverted human values, whether represented by shady criminal organizations or the morally compromised environments of carnivals, show business, etc. *Hardcore* is set in the real world of adult bookstores, peepshows and massage parlor brothels. Behind them is the porn industry, dominated by shady operators and financed by middle-aged men looking for sex with young women. Mast explains that Kristen's porn film is a phantom product: "Nobody makes it. Nobody shows it. Nobody sees it. It's like it doesn't even exist." Working out a personal conflict that sees true Christianity as incompatible with the real world (or, the venal real world unfit for Christianity), Schrader takes his theme a step further into horror territory by asserting the existence of a circle of porn Hell beneath the norm, where fiendish snuff filmmakers actually kill their performers for the gratification of specially screened viewers.

Commercial considerations limit *Hardcore's* ability to follow through on its premise, and Schrader's nightmarish scripted conclusion was significantly softened during production. But Jake's degrading experience is lightened by his relationship with Niki, a hooker who thinks they might reach an understanding on the subject of sex. Jake and Niki both believe that sex is unimportant but take absurdly opposite reactions. Jake abstains fastidiously while Niki's instinct is to be completely promiscuous.

This character development abruptly ceases when Jake transforms into a stalwart revenging hero. Losing his self-doubt, Jakes uses brute force to rescue his daughter from the clutches of the demonized Ratan. Despite Kristen's initial rejection of her father, the compromised happy ending undercuts the film's implied descent toward a revelatory horror climax.

Hardcore simulates clandestine porn shoots and films actual prostitution and peepshow haunts in Hollywood and Los Angeles. The San Francisco setting is stylized in the direction of classic horror, especially when the venal Ratan is cornered in a brothel. Jake smashes through walls into different-colored but otherwise identical assignation rooms, a visual motif seemingly patterned from Prince Prospero's color-coded chambers in Roger Corman's film version of *Masque of the Red Death*, another tale about a descent into Evil. **GE**

HARPER (1966)

Director: Jack Smight. **Producers**: Jerry Gershwin and Elliott Kastner. **Screenplay**: William Goldman based on the Lew Archer novel *The Moving Target* by Ross Macdonald. **Director of Photography**: Conrad Hall. **Music**: Johnny Mandel, Andre Previn, Dory Previn. **Art Director**: Alfred Sweeney. **Cast**: Paul Newman (Lew Harper), Lauren Bacall (Mrs. Sampson), Julie Harris (Betty Fraley), Arthur Hill (Albert Graves), Janet Leigh (Susan Harper), Pamela Tiffin (Miranda Sampson), Robert Wagner (Alan Taggert), Robert Webber (Dwight Troy), Shelley Winters (Fay Estabrook), Harold Gould (Sheriff Spanner), Roy Jensen (Puddler), Strother Martin (Claude). **Released**: Columbia, February 23. 121 minutes.

Detective Lew Harper, on the recommendation of old friend Albert Graves, is hired by Mrs. Sampson to find her missing husband, a rich businessman. She assumes that he has run off with a young woman. Harper's investigation takes him into a demi-monde of drunks, junkies, menacing heavies, cultists, and an illegal smuggling ring. On his journey, he discovers that Ralph Sampson was kidnapped and that the Sampsons' chauffeur, Alan Taggert, organized the crime. After a showdown with Taggert, Harper tracks down Taggert's accomplice Betty Fraley. She's being tortured by Dwight Troy in a beach house. Harper rescues her and finds out that Sampson is alive and housed in an abandoned oil tanker. However, before he can free Sampson from the tanker's depths, Harper is sapped. He awakes to find Sampson dead. In a long car ride, Harper confronts Graves. He killed Sampson. "When it came to cruelty, he could be incredibly versatile," Graves says as way of defense.

Visually, *Harper*, with its sun-drenched landscapes, lacks the neon glamour and dark-lit ambience of Raymond Chandler's Los Angeles. Lew Harper (the filmmakers changed the name of Macdonald's hardboiled detective Lew Archer) isn't a tarnished angel (he is far more cynical) and his Los Angeles mean streets are in this film shot in day for night. But Ross Macdonald's Archer novels do have a dark mood of dislocation. Whereas Chandler's Marlowe often tries to find the girl or navigate various blackmail schemes, Macdonald's hero is trapped in family dysfunction (a theme in many of Ross Macdonald's noir novels). Mrs. Sampson, in her safe gated community, doesn't really love her husband. "I only want to outlive him," she says. She and her step daughter (Miranda) don't like each other. Miranda calls her "frigid," and Mrs. Sampson, upon hearing of her husband's death, purrs with sing-song irritation: "Miranda. Mommy has something to tell you." Even Miranda doesn't love her father. When told of her father's death, she snaps, "I don't give a damn about my father. Never did. He's a terrible man and whatever he gets he deserves."

While navigating through this dysfunction, Harper has his own alienation to deal with. The film opens with him waking up on a couch in his office. Rack focus blurs a portrait of his wife. There are no coffee grounds and he has to reach into the trash and recycle yesterday's. Director Jack Smight's choices show a man who lacks the amenities of home and later in a lawyer's office Harper's alienation is confirmed. Susan, his soon to be ex, shouts at him through her lawyer: "Tell the man he is not loved." This lack of familial harmony gives *Harper* its noir ethos, as does Newman's performance. Unlike the witty zingers Humphrey Bogart tosses off in *The Big Sleep*, Newman's Harper is world weary and defeated, his comments caustic. "You can be very cruel, you know that?" Taggert says, tears in his eyes, after hearing Harper refer to the woman Taggert loves as a "freak show," a "pig," and "a piece of fungus." Harper plays on people's weaknesses to get information. But like the Marlow of *Heart of Darkness* he does have a redemptive moment, lying to Betty Fraley, telling her that Taggert died "saying your name." In the end, despite his success in "solving" the mystery, Harper is ineffectual. He rescues Betty, only to have her hot wire his car and die in a wreck. He locates Sampson, but before he can free him, Harper is sapped and Sampson killed. By contrast, in Robert Altman's *The Long Goodbye*, Marlowe takes action against his ineffectualness. Upon meeting up with Terry in Mexico and discovering how he double-crossed him, Marlowe executes him. In *Harper*, the detective discovers his friend's duplicity but neither man can act. "Ah, hell," Graves says, as his gun trained on Harper's back now drops to his side. "Ah, hell," Harper echoes, holding up his arms and Smight freeze frames on Newman, creating a sense of stasis. Indecision resonates. **GT**

HEAT (1995)

Director: Michael Mann. **Screenplay**: Michael Mann. **Producers**: Art Linson, Michael Mann. **Director of Photography**: Dante Spinotti. **Music**: Elliot Goldenthal. **Editors**: Pasquale Buba, William Goldenberg, Dov Hoenig, Tom Rolf. **Cast**: Al Pacino (Lt. Vincent Hanna), Robert DeNiro (Neil McCauley), Val Kilmer (Chris Shiherlis), Jon Voight (Nate), Tom Sizemore (Michael Cheritto), Diane Venora (Justine Hanna), Amy Brenneman (Eady), Ashley Judd (Charlene Shiherlis), Mykelti Williamson (Sgt. Drucker), Danny Trejo (Trejo). **Released**: Warner Bros. Pictures, December 15. 171 minutes.

Neil McCauley is a professional thief with a small, close-knit crew that specializes in elaborate seven-figure heists. A successful armored car hold-up is soured when Waingro, a last minute addition to McCauley's crew, gets trigger happy, forcing them to kill all three guards. This puts LAPD detective Vincent Hanna hot on their trail. Neil tries to kill Waingro, but he escapes. Eventually, Hanna and his team are able to track Neil and his crew, foiling one of their heists, and setting off a frantic game of cat-and-mouse. Neil strikes up a relationship with Eady, a younger woman he meets at a restaurant, and begins planning one last score —a $12 million bank robbery. Meanwhile, Waingro now works for Roger Van Zant, a Malibu-based money launderer, whose offshore bonds were the prize of the armored car heist. Waingro tortures Trejo for information about the bank robbery, and then tips off the LAPD. A furious gun battle ensues outside the bank. Cheritto is killed, but Neil and Chris escape. Neil kills Van Zant and then leaves Eady behind to take out Waingro. Hanna hunts down

Heat: *Al Pacino as Lt. Vincent Hanna.*

Neil before he can get back to Eady and their private getaway jet.

Michael Mann's extensive research and penchant for relative realism renders a Los Angeles that crackles with noirish verisimilitude in *Heat*. The narrative's heightened yet peculiar determinism emphasizes singular moments of choice and how it affects individual fates. Donald Breedan chooses to leave his parole-arranged restaurant job on the spur of the moment and drive for Neil's bank heist. Cherrito elects to turn down Neil's suggestion to sit out the bank heist. Even Neil turns down Nate's suggestion to pass on scoring the bank. The pinnacle scene where Vincent Hanna and Neil McCauley size up each other over coffee underscores the knife's edge of crime both men cling to for their livelihood. Hanna is the predator and McCauley the prey in LA's vast urban hunting ground.

The film is populated with fractured relationships, collapsing under the pressure of constant exposure to crime or the criminal element. Chris Shiherlis is a compulsive gambler married to a former prostitute, Charlene, and their child becomes a pawn when the cops pinch her to finger Chris after the bank robbery shootout. Neil tells Eady that his parents are both deceased and that he never really had much of a relationship with his father. Donald Breedan is an ex-con who can't fathom how his wife can still care for him. Hanna's third marriage "is on the down-slope" with a wife who gets by each day on Prozac and pot. His stepdaughter is neglected by her biological father and ends up as an attempted suicide statistic. He admits to McCauley, "My life's a disaster zone." Hanna's wife, Justine, is a bit more descriptive, telling him "You don't live with me, you live among the remains of dead people. You sift through the detritus, you read the terrain, you search for signs of passing, for the scent of your prey, and then you hunt them down. That's the only thing you're committed to. The rest is the mess you leave as you pass through." Michael Cheritto seemingly has the most stable home life of all the characters, which Neil urges him to consider before committing to participate in the bank robbery, but for Cheritto, "the action is the juice." His addiction, like Neil's obsession with gaining vengeance, proves just as deadly as the other criminal proclivities portrayed in *Heat*. **TE**

HEIST (2001)

Director: David Mamet. **Screenplay**: David Mamet. **Producers**: Art Linson, Elie Samaha, Andrew Stevens. **Director of Photography**: Robert Elswit. **Music**: Theodore Shapiro. **Editor**: Barbara Tulliver. **Cast**: Gene Hackman (Joe Moore), Danny DeVito (Mickey Bergman), Rebecca Pidgeon (Fran Moore), Delroy Lindo (Bobby "Bob" Blane), Sam Rockwell (Jimmy Silk), Ricky Jay (Don "Pinky" Pincus), Patti LuPone (Betty Croft). **Released**: Warner Bros. Pictures, November 9. 109 minutes.

Joe Moore and his partners (wife Fran, Bobby and Pinky) pull off a high stakes jewelry heist for Mickey Bergman. Security cameras record Joe during the robbery, so he needs to split town. Mickey won't pay him until he does one more heist—an airport shipment of Swiss gold bars. Mickey aggravates Joe further by insisting his nephew Jimmy Silk joins the crew. Joe and company pull off the heist. As anticipated, Jimmy double-crosses Joe, but Joe is prepared with his own double-cross. Joe and Bobby secretly melt down the gold and reshape it using metal molds from Joe's sailboat repair business. Mickey has Pinky killed when he won't sell out Joe. Fran meets Joe at a designated dock, presumably to sail to South America, but Pinky and his henchmen are there, too, having used Fran as bait. Fran drives off with Jimmy. Bobby appears from hiding in the nick of time to help Joe battle Mickey and four henchmen. After Joe arranges to wire Bobby his cut, Jimmy and Fran confront him at the sailboat repair shop. Prepared with yet another deception, Joe lets the couple drive off with fool's gold.

In typical David Mamet fashion, the dialogue in *Heist* is crisp and clipped in throwback noir form and function, and the ending is slyly ambiguous. Did Fran really betray Joe, or was she still helping him play out his final deception? Despite their familiar chitchat in the presence of Jimmy Silk, which mimicked previous verbal tip-offs between themselves, it's doubtful that Fran is still aligned with Joe for his grand finale. Taking Mamet at face value, that big grin we see on Joe's mug in the concluding shot must stem from the satisfaction of knowing that the "little vixen" who flew the coop didn't take the keys to the chicken shack with her. Yes, she's a bad girl of the noir variety. Not your prototypical bitch goddess, mind you, but after willingly accepting an assignment to tug on Jimmy Silk's zipper, we certainly don't expect her to become a champion of fidelity with Joe in the future. From Joe's perspective, Fran becomes a disposable commodity when Mickey raises the stakes and withholds payment for the jewelry store robbery. If she happens to survive the double crosses around the next bend, fine. If not, well, that's fine, too, because despite being Joe's wife, she isn't a member of his inner-inner circle.

Heist marks the third time in Mamet's filmography (the first two being *House of Games* and *The Spanish Prisoner*) where he explores the Freudian psychological phenomenon of personality transference. While Joe is clearly the ringleader, Pinky and Bobby are one and the same with Joe on several levels. They think alike, act alike, and they don't trust anyone except each other. The cliché "honor among thieves" truly describes their partnership. Pinky chooses death rather than reveal Joe's location to Mickey's thugs, and Bobby trusts Joe implicitly to wire him his cut of the Swiss gold bar heist

Heist: *Joe Moore (Gene Hackman), Mickey Bergman (Danny DeVito) and Jimmy Silk (Sam Rockwell, at rear).*

after he relocates outside the continental U.S. The partners share the uncanny ability to talk their way out of any tense situation, and they are unequalled in their meticulous preparation, execution, and contingency planning (that is, always ready to trump the double-cross with a triple play of their own). Fran craves the supernatural bond of personality that Bobby and Pinky have with Joe and she works hard to please, but her vamp nature pulls her down a different path in the end. It's a path that the older, wiser Joe is savvy enough to avoid, unlike most other noir protagonists. **TE**

HELL UP IN HARLEM (1973)

Director: Larry Cohen. **Screenplay**: Larry Cohen. **Producer**: Larry Cohen. **Director of Photography**: Fenton Hamilton. **Music**: Fonce Mizell. **Production Designer**: Larry Lurin. **Editors**: Franco Guerri and Peter Honess. **Cast**: Fred Williamson (Tommy Gibbs), Julius Harris (Papa Gibbs), Gloria Hendry (Helen), Margaret Avery (Sister Helen), D'Urville Martin (Reverend Rufus), Tony King (Zack), Gerald Gordon (Di Angelo), Bobby Ramsen (Joe Frankfurter), James Dixon (Irish). **Released**: American International, December 3. 98 minutes.

When he is eriously wounded following an assassination attempt, Tommy Gibbs' gang rushes him to Harlem Hospital. After Tommy recovers, he manages to escape and obtains a Grand Jury acquittal for his former crimes following a deal with corrupt District Attorney Di Angelo. Tommy soon involves his father in gangster activities and rejects his wife for her earlier betrayal and takes away her children. When she is killed, Tommy blames his father and not his ambitious henchman Zack, who is responsible for the crime. Tommy moves to California and leaves his father in charge of New York operations. Zack eventually murders Mr. Gibbs and makes a deal with Di Angelo. Once Tommy finds out, he pursues Zack from New York to Los Angeles in an airplane chase and kills his rival on the luggage retrieval carousel. When Di Angelo kidnaps his son, Tommy sets out in pursuit and lynches him. Reunited with his son, Tommy disappears from society.

Responding to demands for a sequel to *Black Caesar*, Larry Cohen shot *Hell Up in Harlem* in New York and California on weekends following his weekday filming of *It's Alive*. This resulted in a rushed production with too many

ideas crammed into the screenplay for appropriate development. Although it is one of two films Cohen directed that he expresses dissatisfaction with, *Hell Up in Harlem* has interesting links with those former Monogram and Poverty Row classical noir productions whose ambitious and flawed nature made them more interesting than big budget productions. Cohen raises his hero from the dead to continue his gangster activities thus reversing Robert Warshow's classic definition of the gangster hero's rise and fall by showing that Tommy can also rise again after he falls.

Hell Up in Harlem also continues *Black Caesar's* assault on the hero's arrogance and his destruction of the family as well as emphasizing undeveloped ideas in classical gangster films such as *Little Caesar* (1931), *The Public Enemy* (1931), and *Scarface* (1932) involving certain dysfunctional family influences that may explain the big timer's psychopathological behavior. Like Ann Blyth in *Mildred Pierce* (1945) and Zachary Scott in *Ruthless* (1948), Tommy is a monster nurtured within the American family. He aligns himself with the worst aspects of predatory capitalism to the detriment of those closest to him. Indirectly responsible for the deaths of his father and former wife, he ironically tells his son at the end of the film, "I'm going to love you like I loved my Pa." Despite its problematic structure and rushed schedule, *Hell Up in Harlem* is a film by a director who knows his classical American cinema very well and reworks its premises in radical and subversive ways. **TW**

HICKEY & BOGGS (1972)

Director: Robert Culp. **Screenplay**: Walter Hill. **Producer**: Fouad Said. **Director of Photography**: Wilmer Butler. **Music**: Ted Ashford. **Editor**: David Berlatsky. **Cast**: Bill Cosby (Al Hickey), Robert Culp (Frank Boggs), Rosalind Cash (Nyona), Sheila Sullivan (Edith Boggs), Isabel Sanford (Nyona's Mother), Ta-Ronce Allen (Nyona's Daughter), Lou Frizzell (Lawyer), Nancy Howard (Apartment Manager's Wife), Bernard Nedell (Used Car Salesman), Carmen [Moreno] (Mary Jane), Robert Mandan (Mr. Brill), Louis Moreno (Quemando). **Completed**: October 1, 1971. **Released**: United Artists, October 4. 111 minutes.

Low-rent private detectives Al Hickey and Frank Boggs are hired for $200 a day by a lawyer named Rice to locate his "girlfriend," Mary Jane. After several people on Rice's contact list are killed, the police become suspicious of Hickey and Boggs, who have discovered that Mary Jane is married to Quemando, an imprisoned Chicano radical, and has the $400,000 proceeds from a bank heist designed by Mr. Brill, a syndicate chieftain. Hickey and Boggs decide to retrieve the stolen money and collect the syndicate reward. They interrupt a meeting between Mary Jane and potential buyers at the Los Angeles Coliseum but she escapes with the money. Despite warnings from Rice, who actually works for Leroy, a Black Panther type, the police, and the mob, Hickey and Boggs need the money. When Hickey's estranged wife is brutally murdered by Brill's henchmen, their attitude changes into a desire for vengeance. Ultimately, they confront the recently released Quemando at a beach where he and Mary Jane have set up Leroy for the syndicate. Brill and his mobsters arrive in a helicopter and battle fiercely with Leroy's guerrilla organization. Hickey and Boggs are the sole survivors.

Film noir has often used the character of the male private investigator to illustrate the alienated and paranoid nature of men in postwar America. As detectives these men become involved in dangerous situations that they feel compelled to control and change while attempting to re-establish morality in a world that appears to ignore it. After the classic period of film noir, the private detective still remained an occasional protagonist in a traditional mystery film. Only a few times in the early neo-noir, which followed close on the heels of the classic period in the 1960s and 1970s, did filmmakers evoke the noir sensibility through the "P.I." The two most prominent examples from the early 1970s, *Hickey & Boggs* and *The Long Goodbye*, share a self-consciousness of the history of film noir and an underlying irony in that the classic P.I. is a human anachronism.

The writer of *Hickey & Boggs*, Walter Hill (who has gone on to write and direct many other neo-noir films), has two protagonists and a convoluted plot line that recalls elements of the caper film and the gangster genre. The co-stars of *Hickey & Boggs,* Bill Cosby and Robert Culp (who also directed), play against the personas established in the *I Spy* television series. While the detectives of *Hickey & Boggs* share the independent spirit of their earlier counterparts in classic noir, they differ in the extent to which they can control their situation. Ten years after the tail end of the classic

Hickey & Boggs: *Al Hickey (Bill Cosby) and Frank Bobbs (Robert Cupp).*

Hickey & Boggs: *Robert Culp as Frank Boggs.*

period, the neo-noir protagonist has lost any ability to effect change in a modern world, and this increasing powerlessness is a correlative of diminishing social morality. This powerlessness is sardonically expressed by Frank Boggs when he says, "I gotta get a bigger gun. I can't hit anything." His revolvers, small and large, are trademarks of his profession, icons that recall the "gats" and "roscoes" of a more colorful era. As symbols of both his personal power and genre identity, they are nothing compared to the modern arsenal of weapons possessed by the gangsters and the political guerrillas, who annihilate each other with carbines and high-caliber automatic rifles at the film's climax. Hickey and Boggs are too small, too unimportant, to control anything.

Even the film's plot only marginally involves them. The cache of stolen money hidden by Quemando and his wife Mary Jane is the real cause of the film's action. Rice hires the private detectives as unwitting decoys. When the trio of syndicate "soldiers" on the trail of the money murder Hickey's wife it is more of a professional than personal act. In this sense Hickey and Boggs are the film's protagonists by default. They are after all the title characters and because the film's events are seen and/or evaluated mostly from the point of view of these down-at-the-heels detectives for hire, the film *Hickey & Boggs* is more a character study than a narrative thriller. In the beginning, the behavior of the syndicate killers is mechanical and psychopathic; but in certain ways their peculiar code is a counterpart to Hickey and Boggs' fallen romanticism. By the end, the last survivor, the feeble-minded strong-arm man, enraged at the killing of his partners, attacks Hickey for emotional reasons. Hickey and Boggs themselves seem to alternate in their desire for money and revenge. At the end Hickey is forced to the realization that vengeance is futile. He had previously complained that "there's nothing left of this profession, it's all over. It's not about anything." But Boggs, the dissolute believer in a bygone heroism, seemed to understand their existential dependence on this profession and insists it is important to "try and even it up, make it right." As the smoke clears over the carnage and destruction of the final scene, Hickey again asserts, "Nobody came, nobody cares. It's still not about anything." Boggs wearily replies, "Yeah, you told me."

As if to epitomize the underlying disorder of the modern society, all of the sequences involving the search for the missing money in *Hickey & Boggs* take place during broad daylight. It is events in the private lives of the detectives that take place at night. Contrary to any heroic iconic archetype, even that of the hardboiled P.I., these men are not strikingly handsome or romanticized loners but weary, displaced persons. Hickey's nighttime arrival at the home of his estranged wife scares and angers her. Her off-handed complaint that she is not running a boarding house captures the transitory nature of Hickey's lifestyle. Boggs is an alcoholic, who spends his off hours in bars, where he watches television commercials and broods about his ex-wife. His fixation on her leads him to frequent the sleazy nightclub where she works as a strip teaser. Her mockery psychologically castrates him. This is a severe statement about the place of men in the world that is as a dismal as any from the classic period of film noir.

Both of these men are adrift, alienated from their environment and their families, clearly out of any mainstream lifestyle. They are superfluous figures, wandering through the urban landscape. Instead of the anonymity provided in many film noir by crowded city streets, much of the action of *Hickey & Boggs* occurs in large areas of unoccupied public space. The violence that takes place in a deserted stadium, ball park, neighborhood park, and coastal beach underscore the sense of decay of social strictures. It sets the same tone as many classic film noir by suggesting that society has lost control of the subversive and antagonistic forces within it. The sheer firepower of the final shoot-out verges on satire as the gangsters' helicopter gunship shoots a Rolls Royce full of holes. The absurdity of the gangsters and Panther clones slaughtering each other in this sequence also recalls a similarly extravagant moment as the unstable "great whatsit" explodes at the end of *Kiss Me Deadly*. In a closing, sardonic variant of the old-fashioned happy ending the detectives walk off into the sunset, together but not side-by-side. Hickey and Boggs are the only survivors; but they have survived only because they are unimportant. **EW**

HOMICIDE (1991)

Director/Screenwriter: David Mamet. **Producers**: Michael Hausman, Edward R. Pressman. **Executive Producer**: Ron Rotholz. **Director of Photography**: Roger Deakins. **Music**: Alaric Jans. **Production Designer**: Michael Merritt. **Art Direction**: Susan Kaufman. **Editor**: Barbara Tulliver. **Cast**: Joe Mantegna (Bobby Gold), William H. Macy (Tim Sullivan), Ving Rhames (Randolph), J.S. Block (Dr. Klein), Rebecca Pidgeon (Miss Klein), Natalia Nogulich (Chava), Vincent Guastaferro (Lt. Senna). **Released**: Triumph, October 9. 102 minutes.

On one case, the apprehension of drug dealer Randolph, Detective Gold is assigned to another, the murder of an elderly Jewish shopkeeper. Initially skeptical about her family's view that the murder was racial, Gold, much to his partner Sullivan's irritation, becomes increasingly preoccupied with the case. His encounters with a group of "heavy hitters" from the Jewish community provoke an identity crisis in Gold regarding his own Jewishness to the extent that he becomes involved in the bombing of an anti-semitic organization. The "heavy hitters" then attempt to blackmail him to suppress evidence of the elderly shopkeeper's former Zionist activities. Sidetracked, Gold misses a rendezvous with Sullivan at which he was to play a pivotal role in apprehending Randolph as a result of which Sullivan is killed and Gold severely wounded. Limping into the precinct station some weeks later, Gold is met with embarrassed silences and the news that he is "off Homicide." The old lady, it is revealed, had been murdered by local kids for "the treasure in her cellar."

Homicide is a largely unrecognized masterpiece. As extensively populated with characters and narratively as dense (if less self-consciously stylish) as *Miller's Crossing* or *Road to Perdition*, its profound morality exposes the superficial darkness of many neo-noirs. Delivering, as they do, all the forensic detail of the best *policiers*, the investigations into Randolph and the dead shopkeeper are, on the other hand, the McGuffins which provide the linear narrative tapestry into which the film weaves its bleak morality tale: Gold's self-betrayal through the seduction of ethnic identity.

Like all Mamet's work, *Homicide* is beautifully paced. The fact of Gold's Jewishness is raised at the outset when he is racially abused by a Black official from the mayor's office. But the film constantly demonstrates that there need be no issue of identity for Gold: his identity lies in what he does. This is particularly true of his relationship with Sullivan. Their duologues are pearls of Mametian verbal non-sequiturs, but the level of emphatic communication between them is intense. A resonant exchange has Gold say, "You're like my family" and Sullivan reply, "I *am* your family." It is Gold's encounters with the Zionists around the dead woman's family which precipitates his moral collapse. Constantly challenged about his identity as a Jew, he ends up placing the bomb while his *real* family, Sullivan, is being murdered. Mamet is too sophisticated to lay the blame solely on the Zionists, shabby and heartless as they are revealed to be. In a conversation with Chava, Gold speaks of the attractions of "a country of your own" and of how he has had to overcome the stereotype of the Jew as weak and "feminine" by always being first through the door to confront armed suspects.

While the movie does not carry an ounce of excess weight, everything connects up and resonates with what has gone before. It displays the structural quality Robert Towne achieved (and has spoken so eloquently about) in *Chinatown* whereby it knows exactly how to place information for maximum dramatic and moral effect. One of the "clues" which make Gold take the racial angle on the shopkeeper's death more seriously is a piece of paper bearing the word "Grofaz." Informed that this is an alias for Hitler, Gold asks a subordinate to trace the paper's origin. It is only at the end of the film, when the full moral horror of his situation is sinking in, that the subordinate casually informs him that the piece of paper is a torn fragment from a bag of pigeon feed called Grofazt. The film's sophistication is evident in the motivation of the shopkeeper's killers. If it demonstrates that ethnic identity is a lure and a trap, it also recognizes that ethnic stereotyping can get you killed. However, in many ways the moral tour de force of the film lies in the strategic return of a minor character, a crazed arrestee who has murdered his entire family and who has earlier offered to tell Gold "the meaning of evil." Led past the desolate Gold, he turns and looks wistfully at him as though saying, "Now you know, my friend." **CMcA**

THE HOT SPOT (1990)

Director: Dennis Hopper. **Screenplay**: Nona Tyson and Charles Williams, based on the novel *Hell Hath No Fury* by Charles Williams. **Producer**: Paul Lewis (Film Now). **Director of Photography**: Ueli Steiger. **Production Designer**: Cary White. **Music**: Jack Nitzsche. **Editor**: Wende Phifer Mate. **Cast**: Don Johnson (Harry Madox), Virginia Madsen (Dolly Harshaw), Jennifer Connelly (Gloria Harper), Charles Martin Smith (Lon Gulik), William Sadler (Frank Sutton), Jerry Hardin (George Harshaw). **Released**: Orion, October 12. 128 minutes.

Newly arrived in a small town outside Austin, grifter Harry Madox finds work selling used cars for a local dealership. When the local bank is left open and unstaffed during a nearby fire, Harry realizes that it would be easy pickings and a ticket out of this hick town. Unable to extricate himself from a loveless sexual affair with Dolly, the wife of his boss, Harry simultaneously becomes involved with the dealership's young accountant Gloria who he discovers is being blackmailed for an indiscretion with another woman. Harry's affairs eventually entangle him in violence that leads to murder and seem likely to trap him in Hicksville forever.

The Hot Spot is a reciprocal of *Strange Love of Martha Ivers* or what might have happened if Martha Ivers had accomplished her aims. The film's fatal woman, Dolly Harshaw, does manage to kill her husband and trap the protagonist in her black widow's web. Of course, Harry Madox, *The Hot Spot*'s protagonist, is a con-man, bank robber, and killer, who in the film's final words accepts his fate: "I found my level, and I'm living it." *The Hot Spot* is fully as self-conscious of the noir tradition as *The Driver* or *Body Heat*. It differs by embracing a directness that verges on parody. From the opening titles, revealing its "hero" among sand dunes under a blistering sky as a hawk screeches on the soundtrack, director Dennis Hopper uses the shorthand of iconic indicators like a wry commentary.

The robbery, the extortions, the seductions are secondary elements in a plot hinged on an allegorical triangle that

The Hot Spot: *Harry Madfox (Don Johnson) and Dolly Harshaw (Virginia Madsen).*

seems descended from those of David Goodis. On the one hand is the lascivious, animalistic Dolly, repeatedly posed with her legs parted or covered with shaving cream, linked in fatalistic side moves of the camera with a rearing polar bear, or, in the penultimate sequence, crawling on the floor counterposed with a stuffed cougar. On the other hand is Gloria, demure, virginal, blackmailed by Frank Sutton who has photographs of her in an apparently lesbian interlude. "That little gal's got you all stoked up," Sutton correctly observes to Harry; and what really has Harry stoked up is the hint of sordidness in Gloria. It is the sights and sounds of the milieu where the buzz of a fly on Sutton's hand is like the stench of corruption or where Madox's black-finned Studebaker swoops down on Sutton's place like a bird of prey that truly situate *The Hot Spot* in the depths of the noir tradition, depths in which Harry Madox is enclosed in a personal hell as fiery as any of Jim Thompson's. **AS**

HOUSE OF GAMES (1987)

Screenplay, **Director**: David Mamet. **Producer**: Michael Hausman (Filmhaus). **Director of Photography**: Juan Ruiz Anchia. **Production Designer**: Michael Merritt. **Music**: Alaric Jans. **Editor**: Trudy Ship. **Cast**: Lindsay Crouse (Margaret Ford), Joe Mantegna (Mike), Mike Nussbaum (Joey), Lilia Skala (Dr. Littauer), J.T. Walsh (Businessman), Willo Hausman (Girl with Book), Steven Goldstein (Billy Hahn), Jack Wallace (Bartender), Scott Zigler (Western Union Clerk), William H. Macy (Sgt. Moran). **Released**: Orion, October 11. 101 minutes.

Dr. Margaret Ford is a successful psychiatrist and best-selling author of self-help books. After her depressed patient Billy Hahn threatens suicide, Ford learns that he is despondent over a large gambling debt. She goes to the "House of Games," a bar where Mike, the man with Billy's marker, plays poker in a back room. Mike claims Billy's debt is quite small and offers to forgive it, if Ford helps him spot a "tell" from another player. Although the request is shortly revealed to be a set-up, Ford is drawn by Mike's charm and his willingness to reveal trade secrets and is eventually enmeshed in a high-stake con which ends in violence. Ford discovers that this too was a con of which Billy was a part that has bilked her out of thousands of dollars. Although she can afford the loss, Ford takes a gun and goes to the airport to confront Mike.

For the grifters and con artists in *House of Games* or the remake of *Night and the City* redemption is not an issue. In *House of Games* the con itself is the ritual. Margaret Ford, the female psychiatrist and best-selling author who believes she has accidentally stumbled into their world, finds out the hard way that the con men are like the like the scorpion in Arkadin's parable: they cannot help but sting because it's their nature. The lack of perception by Dr. Ford, an expert who has studied and written about compulsive behavior, may lack verisimilitude, but since the viewer is drawn into the plot in subjective mode, that is, through Ford's point of view, that condition is only apparent when Ford and the viewer simultaneously discover the truth. In the enclosed world of marks and cheats delineated by writer/director David Mamet, misdirection is the key to making a buck and creating a plot twist. Getting caught up in that illicit milieu and its freedom from responsibility is a giddy experience for Dr.

Ford. As the ostensible protagonist, her outrage at betrayal is both the fury of a woman scorned and of a child deprived of her secret playground. Her need for revenge is quite different from the typical neo-noir figure, such as Frank in *Thief*. Her real crime, committed after being drawn into a false crime, turns the film's conclusion into a ritual reversal. It is a full and final initiation into the noir underworld which fascinates her and makes the premise of her new book, *Forgive Yourself*, disturbingly ironic. **AS**

HUSTLE (1975)

Director/Producer: Robert Aldrich. **Screenplay**: Steve Shagan. **Executive Producer**: Burt Reynolds. **Director of Photography**: Joseph Biroc. **Music**: Frank DeVol. **Art Director**: Hilyard Brown. **Editor**: Michael Luciano. **Cast**: Burt Reynolds (Lt. Phil Gaines), Catherine Deneuve (Nicole Britton), Ben Johnson (Marty Hollinger), Paul Winfield (Sgt. Louis Belgrave), Eileen Brennan (Paula Hollinger), Eddie Albert (Leo Sellars), Ernest Borgnine (Santoro), Jack Carter (Herbie Dalitz), Sharon Kelly (Gloria Hollinger), Don "Red" Barry (Airport Bartender), Dave Willock (Liquor Store Clerk). **Completed**: February 11, 1975. **Released**: Paramount, December 25. 120 minutes.

Police Lt. Phil Gaines' morning off is interrupted when a young woman's body is found. Leaving the home he shares with Nicole, a French-born prostitute, Gaines joins his partner, Sgt. Belgrave. When told that the woman, Gloria Hollinger, probably died of a self-induced drug overdose, her father accuses the police of covering up a murder because his family are "nobodies." Although convinced the death is a suicide, Gaines agrees to investigate a photograph found in Gloria's possession. Discovering that the man in Gloria's photograph is Leo Sellars, a prominent but corrupt attorney who is responsible for bringing Nicole to the United States, Gaines confronts him about Gloria. He admits knowing her but not to being involved in her death. Meanwhile, Hollinger investigates on his own and is brutally beaten by bouncers at a club where Gloria worked. Despite Gaines' warnings Hollinger eventually tracks down Leo Sellars. Learning this Gaines and Belgrave rush to protect the attorney but arrive just after Hollinger has killed him. Gaines tampers with the evidence to make it appear Hollinger acted in self-defense. On his

Hustle: *Marty Hollinger (Ben Johnson) and Leo Sellars (Eddie Albert).*

Hustle: *Phil Gaines (Burt Reynolds) and Nicole Britton (Catherine Deneuve).*

way to meet Nicole for a weekend out of town, Gaines happens on a liquor store burglary and is killed.

In counterpart to the fatigued private detectives in *Hickey & Boggs,* Phil Gaines represents the alienated cop in early neo-noir. Like Hickey and Boggs, Gaines is something of a relic, a contemporary character whose "old-fashioned" beliefs are rooted in the classic era of film noir. Like many later self-conscious neo-noir figures, he is fundamentally disillusioned with the course of his life's work and the system that supports it. "Don't you know what country you live in?" Gaines asks; "Can't you smell the bananas? You live in Guatemala with color television." While Gaines tries to detach himself emotionally from both his job and his lover, the high-priced call girl, Nicole, he understands how impossible that is. His jealousy over Nicole's profession and his outrage over the fact that "everybody hustles" are manifestations of a companion neo-existential despair over loss of influence or control.

As much or more as in any of his classic period noirs, Aldrich keys the *mise en scène* to the protagonist's alienated point of view. The initial sequence in Gaines and Nicole's home is remarkably diffracted. It begins with an aerial shot that swoops in on the exterior, then there are two cuts which pull back, and finally another cut into a close-up of Nicole's face. The color and details of the setting are attenuated by the high contrast and hard edge in the lighting. The dialogue between the couple is mostly in close shots, which isolate them visually from each other. When two shots are used, they are framed tightly, so constricted that they cut off the foreheads. Gaines' expensive home is made to seem unattractive and claustrophobic, even as he is visually distanced from the woman with whom he lives. The first shots of Gaines' office, after he has been knocked down by the distraught Hollinger in the morgue, reveal an even less appealing locus: dark, grimy cubicles separated by cracked partitions of frosted glass and illuminated by a few traces of filtered sunlight which cannot dispel the pervasive shadows.

While "Dirty Harry" Callahan may take to the streets in search of confrontation and catharsis, Gaines retreats from

oppressive realities into himself. He is openly nostalgic: "I like the 30s, Cole Porter, Dizzy Dean," which suggests the same fallen romanticism of another Callahan, Aldrich's character in *World for Ransom*. Gaines is not inured to the violence of the world, not even when he administers a coup de grace to a homicidal mental patient, so that the man will never be allowed to go free again. Gaines adopts metaphors for this violence, his favorite being the movie version of *Moby Dick*. If Gaines does see himself as Ahab, driven mad by his own moral outrage, he must also see himself reflected in the felons and psychopaths who wage their own war against society and the system. For a street cop in the context of neo-noir, there may be an emotional equation between self and other; each action against the social outcasts may reflectively become an action against the underpinnings of his own persona. By the time Nicole comes home to find him watching *Moby Dick* on television and crouched in the shadows like Charlie Castle in Aldrich's *The Big Knife*, the myths have begun to lose their therapeutic value for Gaines. He begins a noir transference with the pitiful Marty Hollinger.

Hollinger, the Korean War vet still afflicted by shell shock, has already been identified with Gaines in visual and narrative terms. The balanced framing between the two men as they stand beside the body of Hollinger's daughter in the morgue is carried over into matching shots of them from a low angle with side light in their respective homes. The memories of an ostensibly happier past for both are incorporated into the film as brief flashbacks. Gaines' lover routinely "betrays" him with other men, and he knows that Hollinger's wife has betrayed him as well. Finally, both men share a hatred of smooth syndicate attorney Leo Sellars. Gaines' hatred stems from the belief that Sellars corrupted Nicole. Hollinger holds Sellars responsible for his daughter's involvement in syndicated-controlled pornographic film production, which led to her death. While Hollinger's hatred of Sellars is purely vindictive, Gaines also regards the attorney as a symbol of the same "darkness and corruption" that surrounded Hammer in *Kiss Me Deadly*. When Sellars asks him, "Why single me out?" Gaines replies simply, "I can't get everyone."

Through his surrogate, Hollinger, Gaines does get Sellars; but the death of his antagonist cannot be without moral consequence. When Gaines and his partner make it seem as if Hollinger killed in self-defense, the transference of responsibility is complete. Gaines carries that into the liquor store where he happens to interrupt a robbery. The anonymity of Gaines' killer is central to the neo-irony of *Hustle*. Like so many noir protagonists from the classic period, Gaines perishes in an existential affirmation of his despair. Unlike Harry Callahan, Gaines cannot dismiss the consequences of his actions. In killing Sellars, he destroys the last vestige of his own faith in the system which employs him to enforce its laws. Whether or not Gaines has a moment of realization before dying about the causes of his destruction is less significant than the event itself. The decisions to cover up Sellars' killing and to confront the armed robber are simultaneously actions which affirm his existence and which cause him to perish. **AS**

I, THE JURY (1982)

Director: Richard T. Heffron, Larry Cohen (uncredited). **Screenplay**: Larry Cohen based on the novel *I, The Jury* by Mickey Spillane. **Producer**: Robert H. Solo. **Director of Photography**: Andrew Laszlo. **Music**: Bill Conti. **Production Designer**: Robert Gundlach. **Editor**: Garth Craven. **Cast**: Armand Assante (Mike Hammer), Barbara Carrera (Dr. Charlotte Bennett), Laurene Landon (Velda), Alan King (Charles Kalecki), Geoffrey Lewis (Joe Butler), Paul Sorvino (Detective Pat Chambers), Judson Scott (Charles Kendricks), Barry Snider (Romero), Julia Barr (Norma Childs), Jessica James (Hilda Kendricks). **Released**: American Cinema Productions, April 22. 111 minutes.

Alcoholic Vietnam veteran and private eye Mike Hammer grieves over the murder of his friend Jack Williams. After meeting Jack's psychiatrist Dr. Charlotte Bennett, Mike goes on the vengeance trail but finds out he is a minor pawn in a corrupt game organized by his own government. Fellow Vietnam veteran Joe Butler tells Mike that Jack discovered a CIA mind control operation first begun in Vietnam and now operating in America by former Green Beret Captain Romero who uses the same techniques for political assassinations in America disguised as sex crimes by disturbed killer Kendricks. The CIA use both Mike and Pat Chambers for their own ends. Eventually Mike defeats his adversaries and discovers that Charlotte was responsible for Jack's death. Like in Spillane's original novel and the earlier 1953 film version, Mike avenges his friend's death by shooting Charlotte and taking gratuitous satisfaction from the act.

Fired after a week of directing, Larry Cohen's name remained on the credits of the film as scenarist. But his work was drastically altered by American Cinema and replacement director Richard T. Heffron. Cohen's original screenplay updated the original Mickey Spillane novel to include the post-Vietnam era, CIA black operations, and aspects of perverse sexuality that the 1953 version could not depict. Cohen intended to depict Hammer as a mass of psychologically complex and contradictory features. Rather than Spillane's macho original, Hammer is a repressed homosexual taking out his frustrations in violence and devastated on learning that his deceased friend had unwholesome desires for him. Certain critics have seen similar contradictions affecting the Hammer character in Robert Aldrich's *Kiss Me Deadly* (1955) that Cohen and others regard as the best film version of a Spillane novel. So expectations of a similar subversive treatment arose when Cohen was originally announced as the film's director.

Unfortunately, these expectations were dashed when American Cinema fired Cohen. The radical connotations of Cohen's screenplay became diluted. It now became a mediocre action-centered narrative of incoherent proportions that failed to develop satisfactorily Cohen's iconoclastic attack on violent masculinity and explicit revelation of government involvement in murder and sexual programming that would have made it a worthy successor to *The Private Files of J. Edgar Hoover* (1977). Although elements from the original screenplay still appear in the released film, they are diminished by hasty direction and drastic rewriting by other hands. Like Aldrich and A.I. Bezzerides in *Kiss Me Deadly*, Cohen understood that the best way to direct a Mike Hammer film lay in undermining the right-wing tendencies behind the original novels and attacking its main character. **TW**

IMPULSE (1990)

Director: Sondra Locke: **Screenplay**: John DeMarco, Leigh Chapman. **Producers**: Andre Morgan, Albert S. Ruddy. **Director of Photography**: Dean Semler. **Production Designer**: William A. Elliott. **Music**: Michel Colombier. **Editor**: John W. Wheeler. **Cast**: Theresa Russell (Detective Lottie Mason), Jeff Fahey (Stan), George Dzundza (Lt. Joe Morgan), Alan Rosenberg (Charley Katz), Nicholas Mele (Rossi), Eli Danker (Dimarjian), Shawn Elliott (Tony Peron), Lynne Thigpen (Dr. Gardner), Charles McCaughan (Frank Munoff), Angelo Tiffe (Luke). **Released**: Warner Bros., April 6. 109 minutes.

In Hollywood, Detective Lottie Mason works undercover as a prostitute with the vice-squad led by the corrupt Lt. Joe Morgan. She is having sessions with a police psychologist for evaluation, has troubled relationships with men, and heavy debts. When she works with a lawyer in the district attorney's office, Stan, they feel attracted to each other and have an affair. After an assignment, she goes to a bar to kill time while her car is fixed. Completely upset, she meets the charming criminal Tony Peron, the object of Stan's drug investigation. While in his mansion, she witnesses the execution of Tony, and she anonymously calls the police. In the house, she finds a key to a locker where there is a bag with one million dollars that Tony stole from drug dealers. Lottie is tempted to keep the money and leave Los Angeles, especially since she is now stalked by an obsessive and suspicious Morgan. But at the airport she has second thoughts and turns the money over to Stan.

Impulse, directed by actress Sondra Locke, opens with one of the most telling images of the decay of Hollywood. It is night. The streets are wet in classic noir style, reflecting the neon signs of the cheap motels that lined Sunset Boulevard and Las Palmas during that period. Most of them cater to hookers and drug addicts. On the deserted street the viewer

Impulse: *Theresa Russell as Det. Lottie Mason.*

sees the lone figure of a prostitute. She is dressed in a skin tight, vinyl mini-dress, stiletto heels, and a tawdry wig. She is approached by a "john" who wants a "date." She agrees to the transaction and leads him to a motel. Once they are near the booked room, the "john" begins to rough the hooker up as part of his sex play. But before he can gratify his sadistic desires in the isolation of the motel room, the vice squad breaks in and arrests him. This opening sequence is much grimmer than any vision of Wilder or Chandler. There are no old Hollywood landmarks, no decaying mansions, no "smell of honey suckle." It's all drug dealing, violence, and sex for sale.

Within a few minutes it is revealed that the prostitute is actually undercover vice cop Lottie Mason whose job it is to seduce men and then call in reinforcements after they commit a bookable offense. Lottie is a typical neo-noir protagonist: broke, desperate, and bitter about her work in the urban jungle. However, she is also atypical as she is a female protagonist, not an antagonistic femme fatale (a part Theresa Russell, who plays Lottie, had limned formerly in films like *Bad Timing* and *Black Widow*). And although Unlike the secretary-turned-detective "Kansas" in *Phantom Lady*, Lottie never becomes a Marlowe or Sam Spade in designer hats and heels, she holds her own in the male-dominated police force of the 1980s.

But with all her snappy repartee and bravado, despite her deftness with her oversized gun and muscle car (both phallic symbols that she co-opts from the male world), she is, in some ways, still a victim of the system. Lottie personifies noir's class/gender-conscious view of society. Painfully and gradually she has discovered that it is still men who have the power, the money, and the influence. She plays a prostitute who caters to men and is so convincing that at one point she begins to identify with the role. She is sexually harassed by a stalker cop. Her relationships with men are transitory and messy; even the sensitive lawyer Jeff ends up beating her when she withholds information from his investigation. Ultimately, she tries to find comfort and safety in the drug

money she steals in order to leave the urban jungle, but even that fails her as she sits in LAX in the final scene, agreeing to return the money to the authorities, as trapped as ever in a decaying Hollywood of the 1980s. **JU**

IN THE CUT (2003)

Director: Jane Campion. **Screenplay**: Jane Campion, Susanna Moore, Stavros Kazantzidis based on the novel by Moore. **Producers**: Nicole Kidman, Laurie Parker. **Director of Photography**: Dion Beebe. **Music**: Hilmar Orn Hilmarsson. **Production Designer**: David Brisbin. **Editor**: Alexandre de Franceschi. **Cast**: Meg Ryan (Frannie), Jennifer Jason Leigh (Pauline), Sharrieff Pugh (Cornelius), Nick Damici (Detective Rodriguez), Mark Ruffalo (Detective Malloy). **Released**: Screen Gems, October 31. 119 minutes.

Frannie is an English teacher, of somewhat prim manner, who is looking for erotic, preferably kinky, adventure; frequenting a shady bar, she gets turned on looking at a woman performing oral sex on her date in a secluded corner, a key to her psychology as important as the scraps and bits of poetry she pastes all over her bedroom walls. A committed feminist (one project is collecting bits and pieces of misogynist language for a linguistic study of the phenomenon), Frannie is not alone in her sexual dissatisfaction, though at first she seems content with the safety of masturbatory fantasy. She is encouraged to live out these imaginings by her half-sister Pauline, who is more completely given to erotic, sleazy abandon as she lives over a strip club and makes a habit out of having "zipless" sex with married doctors. Frannie's interest in the wild side of urban living is apparent to the men in her life, including a neurotic ex-boyfriend and her student Cornelius, who, with Frannie's help, is writing a paper devoted to serial killer John Wayne Gacy. Someone in the neighborhood is living out that same fantasy, as the "disarticulated" corpse of a woman, who turns out to be the one Frannie observed in the bar, is found beneath her window. When the police come to investigate, Frannie hooks up with detective James Malloy, and the two quickly determine to devote themselves to passionate, unrestrained sexual indulgence. Her sister Pauline is killed and beheaded, and Frannie comes to suspect Malloy, misinterpreting evidence she finds on him. But the real killer, it turns out, is Malloy's partner Rodriguez, who was the man Frannie saw in the bar, and with whom she

In the Cut: *Frannie (Meg Ryan) and Det. Malloy (Mark Ruffalo).*

meets up after leaving Malloy behind. Recognizing at last the danger she is in, she kills Rodriguez with a gun she had found in Malloy's jacket.

An interesting body of neo-noir films like *In the Cut* engages with the difficulties and discontents of single women in a post-feminist world. Most of these erotic thrillers link sexual pleasure and indulgence to male anger; their plots often center around the appearance of male avenger figures eager to kill and mutilate women, apparently in revenge for the very loosening of taboos that would seem to be to their advantage. Rodriguez exemplifies the type, murdering the very woman who had just provided him with sexual pleasure (and dismembering her body in an apparent act of debasement). The film engages deeply with misogyny and sexual violence; as his desire for power over the woman's body is revealed, he becomes a plausible serial killer.

In Frannie, the film dramatizes a woman's deep discontent with the limitations that traditional moral strictures have placed on her sexual expression. Hollywood had a problem with Campion's intentions as well, with Code and Ratings Administration requiring severe cuts at points, though much that is somewhat shocking remains, giving the film an almost early 1970s feel. That it displays "nice girl" Meg Ryan masturbating and, with Malloy, thoroughly enjoying cunnilingus makes manifest director Campion's desire to destroy the very stereotype on which the actress had constructed a flourishing career. Intensely confused and dissatisfied, Frannie moves through a noirish cityscape as if she is sleepwalking, unable to decide where to go and what to do next. Her always ambivalent desire to be the subject of desire is constantly thwarted by a culture that relentlessly and almost fatally turns her into an object. Only when she seizs Malloy's gun (in a moment whose Freudian implications should not be neglected) does she regain power over herself. **RBP**

INSOMNIA (2002)

Director: Christopher Nolan. **Screenplay**: Hillary Seitz based on the screenplay by Nikolaj Frobenius and Erik Skjoldbjaerg. **Producers**: Broderick Johnson, Paul Junger Witt, Andrew A. Kosove, Edward McDonnell, Emma Thomas. **Director of Photography**: Wally Pfister. **Production Designer**: Nathan Crowley. **Music**: David Julyan. **Editor**: Dody Dorn. **Cast**: Al Pacino (Detective Will Dormer), Martin Donovan (Detective Hap Eckhart), Robin Williams (Walter Finch), Hilary Swank (Detective Ellie Burr), Paul Dooley (Chief Charlie Nyback), Nicky Catt (Fred Dugar), Katharine Isabelle (Tanya), Jonathan Jackson (Randy Stetz), Maura Tierney (Rachel Clement), Ole Zemen (Pilot). **Released**: Warner Bros., May 3. 118 minutes.

Sent from the city to investigate the murder of a teenage girl in a small Alaska town, burnt-out police detective Will Dormer accidentally shoots his own partner Hap while trying to apprehend a suspect. The detective is given an unexpected alibi by the girl's killer, Walter Finch, a writer who identifies with Dormer. He also still has a murder to solve, in addition to the blackmail and framing of an innocent bystander being orchestrated by Finch. In addition, a local detective and fan of Dormer, Detective Ellie Burr, is con-

Insomnia: *Walter Finch (Robin Williams) and Det. Will Dormer (Al Pacino).*

ducting her own personal investigation of his partner's death. When Finch tries to involve Ellie, Dormer rushes to Finch's cabin where Finch is holding Ellie captive. A gun battle ensues and the two men kill each other.

Christopher Nolan's *Insomnia* is a remake of a compelling Scandinavian neo-noir of the same name made in 1997 and starring the remarkable Swedish actor Stellan Skarsgard. Both films trace the disintegration of a personality under pressure from guilt, stress, and sleepless nights. Like Graham Greene's protagonist in his novel *A Burnt-Out Case*, Detective Will Dormer, in Nolan's version, has been sent to Alaska during a series of "white nights" (a series of weeks during the summer solstice in higher latitudes during which darkness is never complete) partially to evade an internal affairs investigation, partially to aid the local police in finding a murderer. Al Pacino, like Skarsgard, projects a "weariness to the bones" in manner, speech, and tone. After shooting his partner in the fog during a chase, a partner who was going to give evidence to internal affairs, Dormer's disintegration accelerates. He begins to hallucinate (seeing glimpses of his partner, of the murdered girl; hearing normal sounds amplified, etc.). He begins to speak almost in a whisper. And even after boarding up the windows with furniture in his hotel room, he still can only see the burning sun, a symbol for his guilt as well as his rapidly dissolving psyche.

The only person who can understand Dormer is, ironically, the killer himself, Walter Finch, played creepily by Robin Williams. Nolan underlines the doppelganger quality of these two men, much as he will later in his 2006 film about two rival magicians—*The Prestige*. They are both guilty of crimes which were, at least on a conscious level, accidental. They both are unable to sleep. And they are both clever puzzle solvers—Dolmer solves real-life crimes; Finch writes mystery novels. Nolan further reinforces their duality by framing them visually in matched frame halves. And when they shoot each other in the climax of the movie, the scene plays out symbolically as an attempt by each man to rid himself of his demonic double. After this act of exorcism, both men can finally sleep: Finch floating in the lake he has fallen into; Dormer, finally at rest, dead on the wharf. **JU**

JACKIE BROWN (1997)

Director: Quentin Tarantino. **Screenplay**: Quentin Tarantino based on the novel *Rum Punch* by Elmore Leonard. **Producers**: Lawrence Bender and Paul Hellerman. **Director of Photography**: Guillermo Navarro. **Production Designer**: David Wasco. **Editor**: Sally Menke. **Cast**: Pam Grier (Jackie Brown), Samuel L. Jackson (Ordell), Robert Forster (Max Cherry), Robert De Niro (Louis Gara), Michael Keaton (Ray Nicolette), Michael Bowen (Det. Dargus), Bridget Fonda (Melanie). **Locations**: Carson, CA; Compton, CA; Del Amo Fashion Center, Torrence, CA; Hawthorne, CA; Sams' Hofbrau Strip Club, Los Angeles; Del Amo Mall, Torrance, CA. **Released**: Miramax Films, December 25. 154 minutes.

Jackie Brown is a middle-aged flight attendant who is arrested for smuggling money into the country for her associate, gun dealer Ordell Robbie, who is greedy and violent. The officers making the arrest, ATF Agent Ray Nicolette and LA Detective Mark Dargus, are really after Ordell, and so they attempt to pressure Jackie into acting as witness against him. Jackie devises a plan to smuggle Ordell's half a million dollars into the country and keep it for herself. She tells Ordell that she's going to lead Nicolette and Dargus into thinking that she is in fact working with them in order to catch Ordell with his ill-gotten money, when in fact she'll be allowing Ordell to get away clean with his cash. However, with the help of her bail bondsman and new friend, Max Cherry, Jackie executes her plan and successfully double-crosses Ordell, keeping his money. When Ordell realizes what's happened and threatens Jackie in order to retrieve his cash, she lures him to Max's office where Nicolette and Dargus are waiting, and they shoot him dead. Jackie gets away with the money.

Jackie Brown is one of Tarantino's lesser films. However, in comparison with *Reservoir Dogs* and *Pulp Fiction* most films would fare poorly. And so *Jackie Brown*, while not quite measuring up to Tarantino's best work, is still a solid piece of entertainment. Elmore Leonard is a master noir story-teller, and Tarantino's script stays largely faithful to the twists and turns of his narrative, while it updates and relocates the story. Tarantino's love of the history of cinema is evident here, especially his fondness for trashy 70s films, in this case blaxploitation movies. We see this influence, for example, in his use of Pam Grier in the title role and in a number of his soundtrack choices.

The performances in the film are all solid. Robert Forster is a particularly strong presence as Max Cherry, and Samuel L. Jackson is a delight as the pony-tailed gun runner, Ordell. Michael Keaton and Michael Bowen are solid as the zealous cops out to bust Ordell. It's a treat to see Pam Grier in a

Jackie Brown: *Jackie Brown (Pam Grier) and Max Cherry (Robert Forster)*.

meaty, leading role like this, and she's appropriately gutsy in her performance. We see Tarantino's brilliance as a filmmaker here, for example, in the series of shots of the same climactic sequence of events, shown from different characters' perspectives. His writing contains much of the sharp and clever dialogue we've come to expect from him, though some critics criticized the film for Ordell's overly frequent use of the unforgivable "N-word." At two and a half hours, the film feels a little long, since it doesn't sustain its energy in nearly the way *Pulp Fiction* does, for example. Still, *Jackie Brown* is a satisfying, if not brilliant, neo-noir. **MTC**

JAGGED EDGE (1985)

Director: Richard Marquand. **Screenplay**: Joe Eszterhas. **Producer**: Martin Ransohoff. **Director of Photography**: Matthew F. Leonetti. **Music**: John Barry. **Production Designer**: Gene Callahan. **Editor**: Sean Barton, Conrad Buff. **Cast**: Glenn Close (Teddy Barnes), Maria Mayenzet (Page Forrester), Jeff Bridges (Jack Forrester), Peter Coyote (Thomas Krasny), Lance Henriksen (Frank Martin), William Allen Young (Greg Arnold), Dave Austin (Policeman). **Released**: Columbia, October 4. 108 minutes.

When a San Francisco heiress is murdered and mutilated at her remote beach house, the killing initially seems the work of a homicidal maniac. But her ostensibly shocked husband Jack soon falls under suspicion. Brought to trial, the charming, handsome man is defended by Teddy Barnes who is soon not only convinced of Jack's innocence, but also falls desperately in love with him. Though Jack is successful in manipulating her emotions, evidence soon accumulates of his guilt, though it is possible that prosecutor Krasny has engineered a frame-up. As the courtroom drama ebbs and flows, Barnes continues to believe, though with increasing uncertainty, in his innocence, eventually wining his acquittal. But the verdict does not end her suspicions, and Jack attempts to murder her in the same savage way he murdered his wife in order to establish his innocence and rid himself of a pesky doubter. Smart enough to have taken precautions, however, Barnes manages to shoot him dead.

The charming but murderous *homme fatal* character is not unknown in classic noir (as in *Shadow of a Doubt*, *The Stranger*, and *A Kiss Before Dying*), but second stage feminism provides an interesting twist in this film, as Jack becomes dependent on the good will, lawyerly skill, and trust of a career woman, who nonetheless almost dies because she is smitten enough by his charms to subject herself (though not conclusively) to his violent impulses. If weak on plot (the ending sequences, with no real twists, are entirely predictable), *Jagged Edge* is nonetheless an interesting study in gender politics, with its ostensibly liberated surface (a focus on a strong single mother professional who can do without a man in her life) revealing a culturally conservative interior. Barnes only barely saves herself from an exploitative male, whose ostensible kindness, gentility, and grief are only a pose, perhaps confirming the "woman's lib" point that "all men are pigs." **RBP**

JOHNNY HANDSOME (1989)

Director: Walter Hill. **Screenplay**: Ken Friedman based on the novel by John Godey. **Producer**: Charles Roven (Carolco). **Director of Photography**: Matthew F. Leonetti. **Production Designer**: Gene Rudolf. **Music**: Ry Cooder. **Editors**: Freeman Davies, Carmel Davies, Donn Aron. **Cast**: Mickey Rourke (John Sedley/Johnny Mitchell), Ellen Barkin (Sunny Boyd), Elizabeth McGovern (Donna McCarty), Forest Whitaker (Dr. Steven Resher), Lance Henriksen (Rafe Garrett), Morgan Freeman (Lt. A.Z. Drones), Scott Wilson (Mikey Chalmette). **Released**: TriStar, September 29. 94 minutes.

"Johnny Handsome" is the sardonic moniker slapped on deformed grifter John Sedley by his criminal associates, principally Rafe Garrett. After being apprehended during a robbery and imprisoned, Sedley is attacked by fellow cons at the behest of Garrett. Thinking that plastic surgery might help rehabilitate Sedley, prison doctor Steven Resher gives him a new face. Once paroled, Sedley becomes Johnny Mitchell and begins an affair with Donna McCarty. At the same time, Mitchell "meets" Garrett and Sunny Boyd, who do not recognize him as the former Johnny Handsome. Using the suspicions of Lt. Drones to his advantage, Sedley/Mitchell sets in motion a plan for revenge with predictably fatal results.

In turning on the plot point of an identity change via plastic surgery, *Johnny Handsome* harks back to *Dark Passage* and *The Hollow Triumph*; but the theme here is revenge. In the jewelry store robbery sequence, director Walter Hill immediately inserts the violent action, which typifies his work from *The Warriors* (1979) and *Streets of Fire* (1984). But the other thrust is towards the mood of noir. The seamier *quartiers* of New Orleans, the setting of Hill's first picture, the period piece *Hard Times* (1975), provide the dark, wet streets that are the stereotypical noir locus. But unlike *Hard Times* or

Johhny Handsome: *Michey Rourke as Johnny Handsome. Below: Rafe (Lance Henriksen) and Sonny (Ellen Barkin).*

The Warriors, where Hill successfully merged genre expectations and a dark visual style to create set pieces more reminiscent of the samurai film than noir, *Johnny Handsome* has a neo-noir narrative core.

In some ways, Charles Bronson's character in *Hard Times* is more effectively a noir-cum-samurai protagonist than Mickey Rourke in *Johnny Handsome*. Certainly if there is a contemporary actor who could typify the neo-noir angst, Rourke seems a likely candidate; yet the portrayal here alternates between undercurrents of sensitivity and psychoses that remain ambiguous. As revenge ends in self-destruction, the potentially powerful irony is slightly undercut by the commentary of Lt. Drones, the detective who has dogged Johnny's trail. From his earliest work scripting *Hickey & Boggs* and adapting *The Getaway* to his second feature as director *The Driver*, Hill has been as or more conscious of the workings of genre expectations and the noir tradition than any other writer or director. Neo-noir *Johnny Handsome* does resonate iconically with the classic period, while the irony of Johnny's ersatz attractiveness belongs to some other tradition of transformation more akin to *Now, Voyager* (1942) or *Charly* (1968). The ultimate irony, as with so many classic period precursors, is that while Johnny might have survived in an unhandsome condition, he is undone by what he mistakes for good fortune. **AS**

KILL ME AGAIN (1989)

Director: John Dahl. **Screenplay**: John Dahl and David W. Warfield. **Producers**: Steve Golin, Sigurjon Sighvatsson and David W. Warfield (Propaganda Films). **Executive Producers**: Michael Kuhn and Nigel Sinclair. **Director of Photography**: Jacques Steyn. **Music**: William Olvis. **Art Directors**: Michelle Minch. **Editor**: Eric L. Beason, Frank E. Jimenez and Jonathan P. Shaw. **Cast**: Val Kilmer (Jack Andrews), Joanne Whalley-Kilmer (Fay Forrester), Michael Madsen (Vince Miller), Pat Mulligan (Sammy), Nick Dimitri (Marty), Jim Boeke (Javonovitch), Jonathan Gries (Alan Swayzie), Michael Greene (Lt. Hendrix), Lee Wilkof (Big Jim), Joseph Carberry (Jonesy). **Released**: MGM, October 27. 94 minutes.

Fay Forrester sees an opportunity to escape from her violent and jealous gangster boyfriend, Vince, and double-crosses him while picking up money for him. She hires Jack Andrews, an oily private detective, to fake her death so she can restart her life with a new identity and the money she stole from Vince. Jack, who has financial problems of his own, decides to hook up with Fay. Vince, however, discovers that Fay is still alive, and immediately goes on the pursuit. Fay asks Jack to fake her death again, but now Jack is disenchanted and decides to double-cross Fay for her money.

Kill Me Again updates the setting and period but remains true to the dark heart of film noir, creating believable characters and plots without unnecessary stylization. Like a great deal of classic noir, *Kill Me Again* appears to take its primary influence from American crime literature, in this case Jim Thompson. Thompson's dialogue, his gift for plot twists and his cynical approach to women characters all translate brilliantly into writer/director John Dahl's screenplay. Though it's unclear how consciously influenced Dahl was by Thompson (Dahl denies any influence), this film, along with *Romeo is Bleeding*, is one of the most successful adaptations of the Jim Thompson style, if not his actual work. The acting is crisp and sharp all around with only Madsen going a bit overboard. **JEB**

KILLER (1995)

Director: Mark Malone. **Screenplay**: Gordon Melbourne, story by Mark Malone. **Producers**: Robert Vince and William Vince (Keystone Film Company). **Director of Photography**: Tobias A. Schliessler. **Music**: Graeme Coleman. **Art Director**: Eric McNab. **Editor**: Robin Russell. **Cast**: Anthony LaPaglia (Mick), Mimi Rogers (Fiona), Matt Craven (Archie), Peter Boyle (George), Monika Schnarre (Laura), Joseph Maher (Dr. Alstricht), Mark Acheson (Hellbig), Phil Hayes (FBI Agent). **Released**: Republic Pictures, March 31. 95 minutes.

Kill Me Again: *Pay Forrester (Joanne Whalley-Kilmer) and Vince Miller (Michael Madsen).*

Mick is a smooth-as-silk hit-man coming off a job botched by his friend, Archie. Having only just finished cleaning up that job, Mick is questioning his profession and his sanity. Mick is then hired by an acquaintance, George, for a last-minute hit: a society woman named Fiona who owes 1.3 million in overdue debts. Even after he's told Fiona is expecting him, Mick accepts the job. On arriving at her apartment, Mick is seduced by Fiona and in short order he's unaccountably head-over-heels in love. He soon discovers that Fiona may have actually hired her own killer because of an incurable psychiatric condition. He resolves not to kill her but his friend Archie, seeing an opportunity to prove himself to Mick, kills her himself.

Killer appears to have more in common with a certain type of theatrical melodrama than film noir, with its existential meanderings, overly convoluted plot, and unsuccessful shifts in tone. The film is not quite sure whether it would like to be Godot, Melville or Tati. Whichever, though, *Killer* manages to fail, unexceptionally. By virtue of its pretensions, the film chooses to expound rather than portray, and, as is typical with pretension, it betrays its ambitions only to expose its lack of substance and subtext. Peter Boyle is minimalist and direct, Mimi Rogers is perhaps too convincing in portraying a psychologically damaged vamp, while Anthony LaPaglia, shifting constantly into and out of his Australian accent, is, as always, a ham and poor Craven is, at best, inept. **JB**

The Killers: *Charlie Strom (Lee Marvin), Sheila Farr (Angie Dickinson), and Lee (Clu Gulager).*

THE KILLERS (1964)

Director: Don Siegel. **Producer**: Don Siegel. **Screenplay**: Gene L. Coon based on the Ernest Hemingway short story "The Killers." **Director of Photography**: Richard L. Rawlings. **Music**: Stanley Wilson, Johnny Williams, Don Raye, Henry Mancini. **Art Directors**: Frank Arrigo and George Chan. **Cast**: Lee Marvin (Charlie Strom), Angie Dickinson (Sheila Farr), John Cassavetes (Jerry Nichols/Johnny North), Ronald Reagan (Browning), Clu Gulager (Lee), Claude Akins (Earl Sylvester), Norman Fell (Mickey), Virginia Christine (Miss Watson), Don Haggerty (Mail-truck driver), Robert Phillips (George). **Completed**: January, 1964. **Release Date**: July 7. 95 minutes.

Two hit men, Charlie Strom and Lee, arrive at a school for the blind and find their target, Johnny North. "He just stood there and took it," Charlie says, wondering why North didn't run or plead for his life before being executed. He also wonders why they were so overpaid for a simple hit and what happened to the million dollars with which North allegedly absconded. Charlie convinces Lee to find out who hired them for the contract and to track down the missing money. Together they intimidate and menace a series of witnesses and cohorts: Earl Sylvester, a mechanic, Mickey, a low-level gangster, and Sheila, a femme fatale. They trace the money back to Jack Browning, now a legitimate businessman—a land developer. But before they can get to Browning, he strikes first, killing Lee with a high-powered rifle. Mortally wounded and running out of time, Charlie drives to Browning's house where he kills Browning and his wife Sheila. He then stumbles from the home, a cache of money under his arm, but he never makes it to his car. As the police arrive, he falls and money splashes about.

In Ernest Hemingway's classic short story "The Killers," Nick Adams runs to Ole Anderson's apartment and tells him that two men are coming to kill him. Anderson, resigned to death, refuses to save himself and stares at the wall. Nick can't take it and he decides to leave Summit. Writer Gene L. Coon took this basic premise and transformed it, giving it greater shades of darkness. Instead of writing his screenplay through the lens of a youthful, confused kid, his point of view, courtesy of three involved flashbacks, is from the jaundiced eyes of a

pair of killers. Charlie wonders why Johnny North, Coon's re-working of Anderson, is so resigned to death. Hit men as anti-heroes gives Coon's film an edginess. By contrast, Robert Siodmak's 1946 *The Killers* followed an intrepid, insurance investigator. Here, in Don Siegel's vision, we're in the black and blood-red world of two vicious men. Charlie and Lee strong-arm and intimidate everyone they meet, including holding Sheila outside a high hotel window.

Lee is narcissistic: he does wrist-strengthening exercises, push-ups, and often catches his look in mirrors and sunglasses. Charlie is sadistic, enjoying mayhem and the threat of death. But their greedy quest for a million seals their doom. Together they allude to the fleeting quality of their lives. "Lady, we don't have the time," Charlie says because an aura of fatalism surrounds them. In searching for the man who gave them their contract, they break the professional code, and in a way are rushing toward their own deaths. Moreover, the back story that unfolds is full of all kinds of noir elements. Sheila is the femme fatale. With her bright eyes and glamour, she cozies up to Johnny, a racer, to help her and Jack with a caper. She pretends that she loves Johnny, but she and Jack are using him. Jack, Ronald Reagan in his last screen performance, is the jaded kingpin of the outfit. He's the respected businessman, but he oozes *ennui,* his left eyebrow raised by his wife's antics, his mouth in a perpetual smirk. And Johnny, the racer, is a loser in love. He didn't run from the hit men, Charlie finally discovers, because "the only man who's not afraid to die is the one who is dead already . . . and," he tells Sheila, "you killed him four years ago." **GT**

THE KILLING OF A CHINESE BOOKIE (1976)

Director: John Cassavetes. **Screenplay**: John Cassavetes. **Producer**: Al Ruban. **Director of Photography**: Mitch Breit, Al Ruban. **Production Designer**: Sam Shaw. **Music**: Bo Harwood. **Editor**: Tom Cornwell. **Cast**: Ben Gazzara (Cosmo Vitelli), Timothy Carey (Flo), Seymour Cassel (Mort Weil), Robert Phillips (Phil), Morgan Woodward (John), Al Ruban (Marty), John Kullers (Eddie Red), Azizi Johari (Rachel), Virginia Carrington (Rachel's Mother), Meade Roberts (Mr. Sophistication), Haji (Haji). **Released**: Faces, February 15. 135 minutes.

The Killing of a Chinese Bookie: *John the Boss (Morgan Woodward) and Cosmo Vitelli (Ben Gazzara).*

Cosmo Vitelli owes money to the mob which demands that he do a "favor" for them in order to repay his debt. He must kill a troublesome Chinese bookie. Reluctantly, Vitelli agrees and performs the hit, only to find that he has been betrayed by the mob. In a gun battle with mob hit men, he is shot in the stomach. He returns to his club and gives a final speech to the crowd.

The Killing of a Chinese Bookie, directed by the father of the modern independent American film, John Cassavetes, documents the West Hollywood Sunset Strip in transition. The days of glamorous nightclubs like The Trocadero and the Garden of Allah have disappeared and the energy of the counterculture's 1960s has dissipated as well. Clubs like Gazzarri's, the actual location for the strip joint run by the protagonist (Cosmo Vitelli) in the film, were desperately trying to stay afloat. Cassavetes evokes this mood for the audience early in the film as Cosmo stands outside his club, surveying the half-empty streets, waiting for potential customers to tout. To Cosmo, his club is his life, a fantasy life but a life. In order to buffer himself from the reality outside, Cosmo surrounds himself with beautiful strippers, one of whom is his lover. He pays meticulous attention to all the details of the business, including the tawdry stage show. To preserve his beloved club, Cosmo even borrows money from the mob.

Cosmo's obsession with this club will not even take a backseat to murder. On his way to kill a bookie for the mob in repayment of his debt, he stops to make a phone call in order to check up on how the show is going. Like Mildred Pierce or a score of other noir characters, Cosmo wants desperately to live the American Dream. He travels in a limousine surrounded by his dancers, spends money freely at restaurants and department stores. Cosmo's dream, however, like so many noir protagonists', comes to a bloody end as he is shot by the mob. Bleeding, he returns to supervise the stage show in his club and gives a rambling speech to a drunken crowd. The fantasy dies hard for this two-bit entrepreneur, who, like so many in the world of Los Angeles noir, came for the dream and stayed for the nightmare. **JU**

THE KILL-OFF (1990)

Director: Maggie Greenwald. **Screenplay**: Greenwald, based on the novel by Jim Thompson. **Producer**: Lydia Dean Pilcher. **Director of Photography**: Declan Quinn. **Production Designer**: Pamela Woodbridge. **Music**: Evan Lurie. **Editor**: James Kwei. **Cast**: Loretta Gross (Luane), Jorja Fox (Myra Pavlov), Andrew Lee Barrett (Bobbie), Jackson Sims (Pete Pavlov), Steve Monroe (Ralph), Cathy Haase (Danny Lee), William Russell (Rags). **Released**: Palace/Cabriolet, October 19. 110 minutes.

Luane is a poisonous gossip who interferes in the lives of several characters in a small town. Her words and actions inspire hatred and vows of revenge against her. Bobbie, a drug dealer, has an abusive relationship with Myra, the daughter of the local bar owner. Pete, the bar owner, who has raped his daughter Myra, harasses Luane for $10,000 he believes she cheated him out of. Ralph is Luane's young husband who falls for the stripper/prostitute Danny Lee and plans to murder his wife for the money. Ultimately, it is Peter who ends Luane's life and then kills Bobbie who is trying to rob him of his money and daughter. Myra turns Bobbie's gun on her father and kills him.

Director-writer Maggie Greenwald's low-budget adaptation of *The Kill-Off* manages to capture the brutality and naturalism of the hardest of the hardboiled writers Jim Thompson (*The Grifters*, *After Dark, My Sweet*, etc.). The film opens on shots of the economically depressed, semi-deserted factory town (enhanced by the muted colors and low-key photography) and its corrupt inhabitants, which include drug dealers, prostitutes, vicious gossips, child molesters, and alcoholics. Luane operates as the poisonous center of this corrupt town. As she lies in her invalid's bed, surrounded by cheap jewelry and tattered clothes, spreading gossip about the town's denizens, like some small town Hedda Hopper, the camera pans across the phone lines. On the soundtrack her words are electronically accelerated as they spread her invidious message. We see the first result of her words as a brother and sister accused of incest commit double suicide.

This noir doom which lies in wait for the other characters of the film is further reinforced by the musical "fate motif": the minimalist repetitive chords reminiscent of composer Philip Glass which act as the soundtrack for the film. Probably the most poignant character in the film is Myra (played hauntingly by Jorja Fox—one of the stars of the influential TV noir show *CSI*). With her stooped posture, her face covered by her long hair, she is the ultimate victim. Raped by her father Pete, the bar owner, beaten repeatedly by her drug dealer boyfriend Bobbie, she finds her only release in the heroin her boyfriend supplies her. It is, however, Myra who ultimately survives the "kill-off" of the final scenes of the movie. Pete not only murders Luane, who knows his secret that he raped his own daughter, but then kills Bobbie as he tries to escape with Pete's "property"—his money and his daughter. But before Pete can harm his daughter once again, Myra grabs Bobbie's gun and kills her father, finally seizing control of her own life in an act equal parts desperation and empowerment. **JU**

KING OF NEW YORK (1990)

Director: Abel Ferrara. **Screenplay**: Nicholas St. John. **Producers**: Augusto Caminito, Mary Kane (Reteitalia/Scena International). **Director of Photography**: Bojan Bazelli. **Production Designer**: Alex Tavoularis. **Music**: Joe Delia. **Editor**: Anthony Redman. **Cast**: Christopher Walken (Frank White), David Caruso (Dennis Gilley), Larry Fishburne (Jimmy Jump), Victor Argo (Bishop), Wesley Snipes (Thomas Flanigan), Janet Julian (Jennifer), Joey Chin (Larry Wong), Giancarlo Esposito (Lance), Paul Calderon (Joey Dalesio), Steve Buscemi (Test Tube). **Released**: Seven Arts/Rank, September 28. 103 minutes.

New York. Criminal warlord Frank White leaves prison. His mission is to save the city from corruption and build a children's hospital in Harlem. To accomplish this, Frank—with his gang and legal representatives in tow—sets about eliminating rival gangs (Colombian, Italian, and Chinese) and reclaiming his drug empire. An official ceremony to unveil the hospital plan honors Frank, the new "King of New York." Confronted with this triumph, Bishop, a law-abiding cop, and Dennis, his driven partner, look for any way to end Frank's reign. Across a series of raids and confrontations, White loses key members of his gang. After killing Bishop on a train, Frank bleeds to death in a traffic-jammed Manhattan.

Starting with *Fear City* (1984), the team of director Abel Ferrara and screenwriter Nicholas St. John fashioned a remarkable series of urban dramas about law, crime, political power, multi-racialism and ambiguous heroism: *China Girl* (1987), *Bad Lieutenant* (1992), and *The Funeral* (1996) as well as *King of New York*, a key work of the 1990s. The film works strong variations on what were, by the end of the 1980s, familiar themes and stock situations: Frank's justification of how building a drug empire squares with his benevolent plan for urban restoration; a grand scene with singer Freddy Jackson that encapsulates the *Godfather* trilogy's equation of show business, big business, and criminal business; dazzling set-piece showdowns in the rain, on a train, and in a gridlock of motor vehicles; and (like *New Jack City*, 1991) gangsters' molls who nowadays double as crack-shot bodyguards.

But *King of New York* both is and is not a genre piece. It deliberately obscures or minimizes plot articulations in order to immerse us in a richly atmospheric noir world—the expert use of cool blue tones, for instance, outdoes what Michael Mann had already pioneered in *Manhunter* (1986) and on television (Ferrara had previously directed episodes of *Miami Vice* and *Crime Story* for Mann). What matters more than plot or coherent character psychology here is the striking, expressionistic use of color, rhythm, music (the film blazed a trail in its extensive and sympathetic use of hip hop), and a highly physical mode of acting performance. As Frank, Walken is stunning; he resembles David Bowie's pop persona of the mid 1970s, the Thin White Duke. He is pale, wiry, seemingly transparent, metaphorically "back from the dead" like De Niro in Sergio Leone's *Once Upon a Time in America* (1984). Ferrara even manages to place a clip from Murnau's *Nosferatu* in a Chinese mobster's private cinematheque as visual reinforcement of Frank's image. Although the middlebrow art-houses of 1990 were unresponsive to Ferrara's achieve-

ment, *King of New York* announced a heady, shotgun marriage of the minimalist stylistics of a Bresson or Dreyer with the kinetic, off-beat action dynamics of a Scorsese or John Cassavetes. **AM**

A KISS BEFORE DYING (1991)

Director: James Dearden. **Screenplay**: James Dearden based on the novel by Ira Levin. **Producer**: Robert Lawrence. **Director of Photography**: Mike Southon. **Music**: Howard Shore. **Production Designer**: Jim Clay. **Editor**: Michael Bradsell. **Cast**: Sean Young (Ellen/Dorothy Carlsson), Matt Dillon (Jonathan Corliss), Max von Sydow (Thor Carlsson), Diane Ladd (Mrs. Corliss), James Russo (Dan Corelli). **Released**: Universal, April 26. 94 minutes.

Jonathan Corliss is a poor kid who has made the most of his brains and verve to become a student at the University of Pennsylvania, where he meets and, in secret, woos Dorothy, the daughter of millionaire Thor Carlsson, whose freight cars, bearing the Carlsson company logo, had rumbled past Jonathan's house when he was younger. Jonathan's only interest in Dorothy is the chance it might give him to make it big. But Dorothy turns up pregnant and tells Jonathan that her father will disinherit her. They go to city hall, ostensibly to get married, but Jonathan lures her to the top of the building and pushes her off, making her death look like a suicide. Faking his own death (and deserting his mother in the process), Jonathan moves to Manhattan, where as "Jay" he becomes a social worker and cunningly woos Dorothy's twin sister Ellen. Soon they are married, and within only a short time Jonathan has wormed his way into Carlsson's good graces and is rewarded with a job in the family firm. But questions about Dorothy's death persist. Ellen's insatiable desire to learn the truth leads Jonathan to kill those who might be able to identify him as Dorothy's erstwhile boyfriend. Ellen comes close enough to learning the truth that Jonathan feels forced to plot her death as well, but as he chases her down he is himself killed, ironically enough, by a train.

A remake of the 1956 film of the same title, director Dearden's version of Ira Levin's terrifying novel departs considerably from its source in its picture of Corliss, who is no longer a conflicted if ambitious young man who is led out of desperation to end the life of the woman he has made pregnant. While Jonathan's decision to kill Dorothy comes early in the 1991 film, reflecting his untroubled sociopathy, in the 1956 version his counterpart tries desperately to extricate himself otherwise from the entrapments of a shotgun wedding. Eager for the glitter and "bling" of life among the wealthy in 1980s America given to excess, Matt Dillon's Jonathan projects the spiritual emptiness of a later generation, too narcissistic and forward-looking to even give the horrifying murder of an innocent more than a moment's thought.

Blinded by Jonathan's good looks and deceived by his pretense to be interested in social work, Ellen does eventually prove smart enough to see through the charade. As a *homme fatal* (a character not unknown in classic noir), Jonathan uses sexual allure and his considerable charms to climb the social ladder, but in Dillon's effective performance Jonathan is made to seem all surface and no depth, the perfect reflection of an era given over absolutely to greed and self-indulgence. *A Kiss Before Dying* suggests not the existence of an underworld scarcely concealed by the official respectability of the modern city (as in classic noir), but rather a pervasive anomie that problematizes the passing down of wealth from the generation of rough and ready capitalists like Carlsson to slick, amoral operators like Corliss, who live out a nightmare version of the American dream. **RBP**

KISS OF DEATH (1995)

Director: Barbet Schroeder. **Screenplay**: Richard Price from a screenplay by Ben Hecht and Charles Lederer. **Producers**: Susan Hoffman, Barbet Schroeder. **Director of Photography**: Luciano Tovoli. **Production Designer**: Mel Bourne. **Music**: Trevor Jones. **Editor**: Lee Percy. **Cast**: David Caruso (Jimmy Kilmartin), Samuel L. Jackson (Calvin Hart), Nicolas Cage (Little Junior Brown), Helen Hunt (Bev Kilmartin), Kathryn Erbe (Rosie Kilmartin), Stanley Tucci (Frank Zioli), Michael Rapaport (Ronnie Gannon), Ving Rhames (Omar), Philip Baker Hall (Big Junior Brown). **Released**: Twentieth Century-Fox, April 21. 101 minutes.

New York. Jimmy and Bev are trying to go straight and raise their daughter—he is an ex-criminal, she is a recovering alcoholic. Jimmy's cousin Ronnie pressures him to do one last job, transporting stolen cars for Little Junior, son of underworld boss Big Junior. The police interrupt the job and arrest Jimmy; in the ensuing mêlée, policeman Hart is wounded. In jail, Prosecutor Zioli urges Jimmy to give up his colleagues, but he protects Ronnie who, in the meantime, has hired Bev to work at his car yard. As a result of Jimmy's advances, Bev dies in a car accident; when Jimmy realizes this, he contrives a way to inform on the underworld. Little Junior kills Ronnie. In order to see his daughter, Jimmy (who has developed a tentative relationship with Rosie) agrees to infiltrate Little Junior's operations wearing a wire, under the brutal supervision of Hart. Once Junior is arrested and Jimmy's cover is blown, his family comes under threat. A power game shifts between police, lawyers and the ambitious Zioli to decide Junior's fate, especially after the death of undercover agent Omar. The situation is resolved only after Jimmy secretly tapes Junior confessing.

Barbet Schroeder's films, whatever part of the world they may be set in, have always trained a keen, quasi-ethnographic gaze on diverse sectors of society: from sadomasochists to alcoholics, professional criminals to the filthy rich. His remake of the 1947 noir classic *Kiss of Death* takes us into an underworld based on a commerce in cars: stolen, transported, swapped, disguised, and taken apart in seconds. Just as Hathaway's *Kiss of Death*, in its time, signalled a step forward in screen realism, Schroeder embeds his version in the nitty-gritty, everyday detail of this strange, parallel world of crime, with its gaudy clubs ("Baby Cakes"), and out-of-the-way rendezvous points. The general mythic thrust of the tale, however, is classic noir: "a man trapped and fighting to get on top," as Schroeder put it. The script, elegantly constructed by Price, borrows only a few scenes and plot premises from the original, while cleverly expanding its central theme: the paradoxes and problems of being (and staying) "honorable" ("Are you a man of honor?" Jimmy repeatedly asks the shifty Zioli). Honor among thieves, it transpires, no longer exists;

and the clandestine arrangements between lawmen and criminals willing or eager to squeal guarantee just as little protection. In this story of perpetual, ubiquitous vulnerability to harm and violation, Price and Schroeder hone in on the small but decisive shifts in the balance of power between the players in this game.

Schroeder's storytelling style, somewhat surprisingly and paradoxically (given his artistic background), owes more to the classical American B-film than to the French New Wave. A keen student of films from the 1940s and 1950s, he reinvents, in his own way, the prime lesson of that era: every scene should simultaneously advance plot, theme, and character. His brisk scenes (complete with clever transitions in and out) concentrate on physical action: encounters and gestures encapsulate the clash of moral positions. At the same time, Price and Schroeder tweak the given, over-familiar elements of the genre by consistently employing ellipsis, indirection, and unusual points of view (as when, for instance, we do not see Jimmy receive the news of his wife's death, but only hear his cries as the camera stays outside in the corridor). A striking contemporary example of what Manny Farber once baptized as "termite art"—films that use familiar generic structures in order to work, ingeniously, on the fine details—*Kiss of Death* is particularly impressive in the casting and direction of its ensemble of actors (some, like Caruso and Hunt, mainly associated with television). Each character has his or her own enjoyable (and often frankly infantile) "tic," like Jackson forever dabbing his injured, weeping eye with a handkerchief, or Rhames' superstitious fear of the color red, or Cage (wildly larger than life) using his girlfriend as an exercise barbell, doing a violent pogo to assuage grief over his father's death, or explaining his new age theory of the personal, positive acronym, such as his own "BAD—Balls, Attitude, and Direction." **AM**

KLUTE (1971)

Director: Alan J. Pakula. **Screenplay**: Andy Lewis and Dave Lewis. **Producer**: Alan J. Pakula. **Director of Photography**: Gordon Willis. **Music**: Michael Small. **Art Director**: George Jenkins. **Editor**: Carl Lerner. **Cast**: Jane Fonda (Bree Daniels), Donald Sutherland (John Klute), Charles Cioffi (Peter Cable), Roy Scheider (Frank Ligourin), Dorothy Tristan (Arlyn Page), Rita Gam (Trina), Nathan George

Klute: *Jane Fonda as Bree Daniel.*

(Trask), Vivian Nathan (Psychiatrist), Morris Strassberg (Mr. Goldfarb), Barry Snider (Berger), Betty Murray (Holly Gruneman), Jane White (Janie Dale), Shirley Stoler (Momma Rose), Robert Mill (Tom Gruneman), Maureen Stapleton (Goldfarb's Secretary). **Released**: Warner Bros., June 23. 114 minutes.

Leaving law enforcement to become a private detective, John Klute moves from Pennsylvania and goes to New York to search for his friend Tom Gruneman who has disappeared during the last six months. While there he contacts prostitute Bree Daniels for information, believing that Tom was one of her clients. Klute and Bree begin an antagonistic relationship but become close when the detective penetrates her defensive barriers. Unknown to them, the real killer, Tom's boss and CEO Charles Cable, obsessively spies on their activities. He has murdered Tom, who witnessed one of his sadistic encounters with a prostitute, and now seeks to eliminate Bree and her drug-addicted former associate Arlyn Page. Torn between Klute and a profession which seems to offer her control over men despite submission to the controlling powers of her pimp Frank Ligourin, Bree eventually faces Cable in a deserted garment factory after he has murdered Arlyn. Before Cable can kill her in a berserk rage, Klute eventually arrives to save her and Cable commits suicide by jumping through a window. Although Bree's final voice-over monologue expresses fear of commitment to her psychiatrist, the final scene of the film shows her leaving her apartment with Klute.

Alan Pakula's *Klute* represents an important example of contemporary advances in American cinematography. New developments in visual style significantly complement those darker and more sinister levels of meaning originating within classical film noir. *Klute* facilitated the rise of an initial movement within neo-noir that reached its artistic heights in works such as *Chinatown* (1974) and *Hustle* (1975). This phase did not sacrifice serious explorations of character to gratuitous displays of visual style as in the next decade's MTV-influenced examples such as *D.O.A.* (1988). *Klute* also became the site of contesting feminist interpretations by critics comparing it with representations of women in traditional film noir. Pakula's *Klute* visually reproduces those classical features of noir style defined by J.A. Peterson and Janey Place in their innovative essay in a highly sophisticated manner. The film now has the added advantage of innovative contrasting variations in color film stock to depict in contemporary stylistic terms those essential scenic features of an alienating urban landscape and accompanying paranoia associated with the genre's classical roots.

Like certain examples of traditional film noir, *Klute* contrasts country and city. But, unlike *Out of the Past* (1947) where Jeff Bailey's idyllic rural landscape is fully represented, *Klute* never reveals the Pennsylvania countryside but chooses instead to open with claustrophobically framed interior shots of a family meal by daylight suggesting hidden conflicts within a supposedly happy communal gathering. Close-shots of a loving husband and wife alternate with a right-to-left tracking shot of the entire group. Klute and Cable also appear at the table, two key players in the following drama. Ironically, a tape recorder frames this opening scene that concludes with credits appearing over the same tape recorder that now plays the voice of Bree Daniels advising her unseen audience to "let it all hang out." Before a hand switches off the recorder, her final world is "fuck." Bree's voice appears to represent aurally the femme fatale of film noir who will disrupt the documentary-like "realistic" depiction of family and friends at the table with a four letter word that "dared not speak its name" in the classical phase of film noir.

Since the following scene shows the stark disruption of the opening sequence by filming it at night with only four people present, including a policeman, and those present before such as Cable, Mrs. Gruneman, and Klute in police uniform, noirish overtones fully dominate the interior. An obscene letter, supposedly written by the missing husband to Bree Daniels, suggests the other side of a loving husband, whose solitary photo appears to the right of another showing his wife and child. From its carefully constructed opening scenes, *Klute* introduces a duality common to classical film noir that it will explore in its own significant way. Like Sam Spade in *The Maltese Falcon,* Klute investigates a devious woman, and tries to establish her guilt to do justice to a friend he has known for many years. However, the path towards this goal is now much more complex. This is not just due to sophisticated developments affecting generic themes over the past thirty years. They also result from a more ambiguous treatment of duality in which nothing is ever simple or even satisfactorily resolved at the climax.

As Diane Giddis noted in her 1973 essay "The Divided Woman: Bree Daniels in *Klute*," the film actually centers upon a female dilemma involving Bree Daniels and not the title character. She fears losing autonomy and independence in her involvement with the well-meaning character of Donald Sutherland's Klute. Giddis sees Cable as another dual projection of what Bree fears and also what she would like to be, namely in terms of becoming emotionally numb and maintaining a form of control that would make her a true professional as a "working woman." Contradictions exist between what Bree says in her final words to a psychiatrist concerning a relationship she feels will not work and what viewers see in the final shot of the film where she leaves her empty apartment to go to "Cabbageville" with Klute.

In the first edition of the 1978 anthology *Women in Film Noir*, Christine Gledhill interrogates the film in more rigorous terms, seeing it as indebted to its noir background in which the centrality of the discourse of the woman that Giddis sees is actually more restricted. Bree is not a free agent but rather "the object in a struggle between two different male constructions on female sexuality." Like Giddis, Gledhill sees visual parallels between Cable and Klute. Both men spy on Bree and seek to control her in different ways. Gledhill notes that two sides of the 1940s stereotypical attitude to fallen women appear in the film: romantic idealization and embittered disgust. "Whereas Cable seeks to punish and destroy, representing the nineteenth century, Victorian ethic, Klute, a modern humanitarian spirit, seeks to save." Despite representing the female voice, Gledhill sees the film as falling within the confines of traditional male control within classical noir.

However, despite this reading, it is also possible to see the film as much more ambivalent. The "moral, existential alienation of the psyche" that Gledhill sees as detrimental to a more materialist reading of the film is actually a key element. It occurs in film noir as well as the influence of the work of Edward Hopper that Abraham Polonsky "quotes" in his introductory "Third Avenue" shot in *Force of Evil* (1949). Edward Hopper's *Nighthawks* (1943), depicting alienated men and women against a dominating urban landscape, also influences a film made at a time when noir can now appropriately match the colors in the artist's original painting. *Klute's* urban environment creates a devastating emotional landscape allowing not just for personal alienation in the case of Bree but also generating the expression of dark tendencies within Cable and Klute as well as the Chicago businessman client Bree entertains after her unsuccessful audition. That setting revealed her dominated by three alienating modernist female heads representing her status as an object within the urban landscape. The heads also evoke those fears of modern art endemic to classical noir films such as *Phantom Lady* (1944) and *Strangers on a Train* (1951) as well as Bree's own fears of female castration within a male world she seeks to control with decapitation symbolizing the defeat of feminine control evoked by the fate of Medusa in classical mythology.

But rather than represent the total victory of male discourse on its antagonistic female opposite in *Klute's* concluding

Klute: *Donald Sutherland as John Klute.*

scene, contrasting levels of image and sound actually evoke classical devices of those ambivalent challenging closures within traditional film noir that studio-imposed "happy endings" did not entirely overcome. Bree's voice-over doubts occur in the final scene where she supposedly succumbs to the silent control of Klute (whose presence duplicates the silent repressed control evoked by Cable in earlier scenes and her capitulation to Frank after being shocked by Arlyn's drug-addicted co-dependence status). This contradictory conjuncture of image and sound may actually represent deliberate ambivalence rather than an attempt to privilege one technique over another as traditional theories concerning the priority of visual elements over acoustic features argue. When Klute rescues Bree in the garment factory, Cable crashes through a window. His final image resembles an abstracted art animated figure. Mirror imagery and framing through windows also signify Cable's ominous presence during the film. Both men gaze at Bree. The camera frames both men. Although Klute rescues Bree at the end, there is no guarantee that Cable has finally disappeared. Pakula's sophisticated neo-noir treatment of classical film noir themes in *Klute* suggests that anything is possible. **TW**

L.A. Confidental: *Russell Crowe as "Bud" White.*

L.A. CONFIDENTIAL (1997)

Director: Curtis Hanson. **Screenplay**: Brian Helgeland, Curtis Hanson from the novel by James Ellroy. **Producers**: Curtis Hanson, Arnon Milchan, Michael Nathanson. **Director of Photography**: Dante Spinotti. **Music**: Jerry Goldsmith. **Production Designer**: Jeannine Claudia Oppewall. **Editor**: Peter Honess. **Cast**: Kevin Spacey (Det. Sgt. Jack Vincennes), Russell Crowe (Officer Wendell "Bud" White), Guy Pearce (Det. Lt. Edmund Jennings "Ed" Exley), James Cromwell (Capt. Dudley Liam Smith), Kim Basinger (Lynn Bracken), David Strathairn (Pierce Morehouse Patchett), Danny DeVito (Sid Hudgens), Graham Beckel (Det. Sgt. Dick Stensland), Ron Rifkin (Dist. Atty. Ellis Loew), Matt McCoy (Brett Chase), Darrell Sandeen (Leland "Buzz" Meeks), Simon Baker Denny (Matt Reynolds), Gwenda Deacon (Mrs Lefferts), Paolo Seganti (Johnny Stompanato). **Released**: Warner Bros., September 19. 138 minutes.

A racially motivated Christmas Eve brawl at a police precinct results in the dismissal of several cops, including tough but chivalrous Officer Bud White. Shifty "hipster" Det. Jack Vincennes is forced to name names to keep his coveted advisory job on a pro-police TV program, while Officer Ed Exley cooperates with the investigation in exchange for a promotion. Captain Dudley Smith quietly reinstates Bud and assigns him to rough duty in his secret anti-mobster unit. Bud, Jack and Ed converge separately on Smith's ambitious plan to become the ringleader of L.A.'s narcotics and vice trade, which involves murdering gangland figures and framing small-time black thugs. Bud learns more from Lynn Bracken, an expensive call girl for elitist procurer Pierce Patchett, who, along with the corrupt D.A. Ellis Loew, is prominent in civic affairs. Despondent over his passive involvement in a sex killing, Jack Vincennes is murdered by Dudley Smith but manages to sneak a final word clue to Ed Exley, who teams up with Bud White to oppose Smith's renegade police hit men. Dudley is killed and the injured Bud retires to Arizona with Lynn. Ed Exley blackmails his superiors into making him the face of the future for the L.A.P.D.

The police procedural of the 1950s succumbs to urban sprawl, taking in organized crime, civic corruption, sleazy snoop magazines and exotic prostitution rackets. The American Dream has sold out and everyone seems to be on the take. A notorious elite police squad created to combat organized crime (cleaned up and dubbed The Hat Squad in 1995's *Mulholland Falls*) is here envisioned as a secret conspiracy to take over the vice rackets. L.A.'s growing race divide is highlighted when renegade cops scapegoat Mexican- and African-Americans to deflect suspicion from their criminal schemes.

James Ellroy's ambitious multi-story framework charts the progress of three ambitious policemen. Bud White is little more than a thug for Dudley Smith's secret torture sessions and yearns for the opportunity to do real police work. Jack Vincennes takes payola to entrap luckless actor hopefuls for muckraking *Hush-Hush* publisher Sid Hudgens, and feeds his ego on glamorous consultant work on *Badge of Honor*, a *Dragnet*-like TV show. And cop's son Ed Exley is a hotshot political player willing to risk his life to gain publicity and rise in the department.

James Ellroy's source novel makes the story's heroes active participants in the general corruption. All three are actively or passively complicit in murders and cover-ups, and are duped into helping execute the black rapists framed by Dudley Smith's ruthless two-man hit teams. The trio's eventual bonding to defeat the Smith conspiracy changes very little in the department; like *Chinatown*, *L.A. Confidential* shows how an openly corrupt institution morphed into a modern monolith more adept at hiding its still-substantial flaws.

Hollywood glamour is a major part of a soured nostalgia evoked by period music, Sid Hudgen's tattletale scandal magazine and brushes with shady celebrities like Lana Turner and Johnny Stompanato. Film noir history is further referenced by dream girl Lynn Bracken's masquerade as Veronica Lake from *This Gun for Hire*, and Mrs. Lefferts' agonized identification of her daughter's body replays *The Naked City*. That L.A.'s future is being decided by media-savvy vice lords is made clear when Pierce Patchett presides over a groundbreaking for the Santa Monica Freeway. The unlikely conclusion resembles one of the forced happy endings imposed on old noirs like *Kiss of Death*: Bud White's survival seems yet another compromise in a city that corrupts everyone from bit players to civic leaders. **GE**

THE LAST SEDUCTION (1994)

Director: John Dahl. **Screenplay**: Steve Barancik. **Producers**: Jonathan Shestack, Nancy Rae Stone. **Director of Photography**: Jeff Jur. **Production Designer**: Linda Pearl. **Music**: Joseph Vitarelli. **Editor**: Eric Beason. **Cast**: Linda Fiorentino (Bridget/Wendy), Peter Berg (Mike Swale), Bill Pullman (Clay Gregory), Brien Varady (Chris), Dean Norris (Shep), Bill Nunn (Harlan), J.T. Walsh (Frank), Herb Mitchell (Bob), Serena (Trish Swale). **Released**: ITC, October 26. 110 minutes.

Bridget is a "femme fatale" who steals her criminal husband's money and heads for a small town. There she meets Mike, who falls in love with her. But Mike has no idea about Bridget's past and her plans to use him to get rid of her husband who is still pursuing her, eager to retrieve his drug money. Mike finds it difficult to keep up with the twists and turns in Bridget's moods as well her schemes. Finally he reluctantly agrees to kill her husband but botches the job, leaving Bridget with no choice but to finish the job herself. Disappointed in Mike, she plants evidence which connects him to the murder, leaving her free to escape with the cash and find a new life.

Bridget Gregory aka Wendy Kroy of *The Last Seduction* is a post-modern femme fatale much like Matty in *Body Heat* (in fact both films draw on *Double Indemnity* for plot points and direct references). She is a manipulative, sexually aggressive, and smart female who makes her own rules, refusing to live by those of others. She leaves her drug-dealing husband and steals his "take" after he strikes her; she plans his murder as a form of revenge after he stalks her. Like many third wave feminists she has co-opted negative male language and made it her own: Mike: "I'm trying to figure out whether you are a total fucking bitch or not." Bridget: "I am a total fucking bitch." Like a man she peppers obscenities throughout her speech, uses her new lover Mike like a "sex object," and disdains "sharing" feelings.

In counterweight to Bridget is the masochistic Mike who is drawn to her the first time she walks into the bar and, after being ignored, yells, "Who do I have to suck off to get a drink around here?" When his friend asks what he sees in her, he replies, "Maybe a new set of balls." Hers, probably. For the power dynamic of this couple rests on a reversal of traditional gender roles. Mike complains about her "zipless fucks" (to use writer Erica Jong's term): "[You] treat me like a 4H experiment" and misses the tenderness and emotional connection: "I'm having more and more trouble with this, Wendy." He is also by implication bisexual as the audience and Bridget find out later when she tracks down his hidden transvestite wife.

As much as Mike complains, however, he cannot leave her. Even when Bridget lets him in on her plan to murder her husband, he only balks initially and then agrees to it in order to placate her. For as Bridget tells him, he has to prove his "unconditional love" to be with her. But Mike botches that job too and so Bridget must come in to finish off her husband. In order to shift the blame from herself to Mike, she sets him up with incriminating evidence and he is jailed for the murder. He has failed her test and so he must suffer for it, much like Ned in *Body Heat*.

In the final shots of the movie, Bridget drives away in a limousine. Like Matty on her tropical island, the post-modern femme fatale is allowed to enjoy the fruits of her

The Last Seduction: *Mike (Peter Berg) and Bridget (Linda Fiorentino).*

crimes. She is, in a way, rewarded for being clever enough to upset the corrupt rules of the patriarchy and for being strong enough to defy all authority. **JU**

LIEBESTRAUM (1991)

Screenplay, Director: Mike Figgis. **Producer**: Eric Fellner. **Director of Photography**: Juan Ruiz Anchía. **Production Designer**: Waldemar Kalinowski. **Music**: Mike Figgis; Franz Liszt ("Liebestraum"). **Editor**: Martin Hunter. **Cast**: Kevin Anderson (Nick Kaminsky), Pamela Gidley (Jane Kessler), Bill Pullman (Paul Kessler), Kim Novak (Lillian), Graham Beckel (Sherff Ricker), Zach Grenier (Barnard Ralston), Thomas Kopache (Dr. Parker), Max Perlich (Orderly), Catherine Hicks (Mary Parker), Taina Elg (Mother Ralston). **Released**: MGM, September 13. 112 minutes.

Celebrated young architect Nick Kaminsky returns to his birthplace in Illinois where Lillian, the mother who had given him up for adoption, is dying of cancer. A friend from college, Paul Kessler, is tearing down a local department store, the scene of a murder-suicide three decades earlier. Nick gets permission to study the wrought-iron interiors and meets Paul's wife, Jane, who is a photographer. Nick uses the building as an escape from the emotional context of his mother's hospital room and begins an affair with Jane, while he searches for details about his own early life.

Liebestraum takes its name from a Liszt piece and its dreamlike style is as insistently imposed as the droning underscore. As in *At Close Range* cinematographer Juan Ruiz Anchia's hard light knifes though the images, both real and dreamed, to create a tangible fatality. The plot turn which brings Nick to the town where he was born expands to encompass a deadly lovers' tryst in a 1950s-style department store. That scene is staged or remembered—the first of many narrative uncertainties—in the movie's opening sequence. Because the point of view may be either omniscient or subjective, whether the events of the scenes are actual or imagined is always in question. It is in the protagonist's flashbacks, where shafts of light seem to pierce passing hopper cars, that the style and sensation of the first sequence most impinge on the present; but its tone hangs over the entire film and welcomes the viewer to his nightmare.

As Nick begins the affair with Jane, the lines between dream and reality, past and present are further blurred. The audience can fully empathize with the chance remark of the cab driver who takes the architect to Paul's party: "You mind if I ask you a question? I feel like I know you. You on TV or what?" Squirming inexplicably in the back seat as patches of white and red light cut in and out of the frame, the architect's reply can only be an ambiguous "What." Because the entire film is suffused with an hallucinatory languor, seeming at times to move in slow motion, it not only tests the limits of photographic reality but of what the viewer will tolerate. By the time the end credits arrive and a young girl plays "Liebestraum" on the piano in an unlikely homage to *Guest in the House*, some points have been clarified, but most have not. This leaves *Liebestraum* as much a neo-Jungian, plastic-fantastic voyage as neo-noir. **AS**

THE LIMEY (1999)

Director: Steven Soderbergh. **Screenplay**: Lem Dobbs. **Producers**: John Hardy, Scott Kramer. **Director of Photography**: Edward Lachman. **Production Designer**: Gary Frutkoff. **Music**: Cliff Martinez. **Editor**: Sarah Flack. **Cast**: Terence Stamp (Wilson), Lesley Ann Warren (Elaine), Luis Guzman (Eduardo Roel), Barry Newman (Avery), Joe Dallesandro (Uncle John), Nicky Katt (Stacy), Peter Fonda (Terry Valentine), Amelia Heinle (Adhara), Melissa George (Jenny), Bill Duke (DEA agent), Carol White (Wilson's Wife). **Released**: Artisan, October 8. 89 minutes.

A professional criminal, Wilson, from London comes to Los Angeles to investigate the mysterious death of his estranged daughter Jenny. Finding her friends there—a drama coach Elaine and an ex-con Eduardo—he begins to accumulate clues which lead him to her last boyfriend—record producer and drug money launderer Terry Valentine. Valentine's security chief, Avery, sends two thugs after Wilson but they are arrested by DEA agents who give Wilson tacit permission to go after Valentine. Valentine flees to his cabin in Big Sur with his bodyguards and newest girlfriend. Wilson pursues him and during a gun battle in the night, Wilson chases Valentine to the beach and learns from the terrified Valentine how he accidentally killed Wilson's daughter who was threatening to turn him into the police. Wilson refrains from killing Valentine and returns to London.

In *The Limey* Steven Soderbergh takes a fairly common noir plot (a man seeks revenge for the death of a family member—*The Big Heat*, *Cry Vengeance*, etc.) and gives it his unique ironic, post-modern treatment. The story is fractured much like the mind of the career criminal Wilson (played with a combination of world-weary humor and suppressed grief by Terence Stamp) who is beset by feelings of guilt and rage over what he believes is the murder of his estranged daughter Jenny. Lines and shots are repeated, conveying their emotional weight in his mind. Images from the past wash over him constantly—his daughter, phone in hand, threatening to turn him in if he commits another crime; her smiling face as she frolics at the beach; his relationship with her mother (here Soderbergh cleverly inserts shots from Ken Loach's 1967 film *Poor Cow* which starred a young Terence Stamp). This subjectification of the movie draws the viewer even further into the mind of this man who rarely shows his

emotions to the world, playing instead the limey street tough.

The casting of 1960s icon Peter Fonda as the venal record producer Terry Valentine also helps create the irony inherent in the film. His shallowness (we see him rhapsodizing incoherently about the "sixties" to his newest nubile girlfriend—the one who replaced the dead Jenny—while flossing his newly capped teeth) and lack of courage (he runs away from all problems as when he accidentally kills Jenny and leaves his "right hand man" Avery to clean up the mess and fake a car accident) contrast with the gritty combativeness of Wilson. Wilson, however, finds his redemption via Valentine, on a beach not unlike the one his daughter loved. About to kill Valentine, he remembers the image of his daughter holding the phone and threatening to turn him in if he committed another crime. And so out of love for her, he refrains from eliminating her murderer and walks away, returning to London to find a little peace. **JU**

THE LONG GOODBYE (1973)

Director: Robert Altman. **Screenplay**: Leigh Brackett from the novel by Raymond Chandler. **Producer**: Jerry Bick. **Director of Photography**: Vilmos Zsigmond. **Music**: John Williams. **Editor**: Lou Lombardo. **Cast**: Elliott Gould (Philip Marlowe), Nina van Pallandt (Eileen Wade), Sterling Hayden (Roger Wade), Mark Rydell (Marty Augustine), Henry Gibson (Dr. Verringer), David Arkin (Harry), Jim Bouton (Terry Lennox), Warren Berlinger (Morgan), Jo Ann Brody (Jo Ann Eggenweiler), Jack Knight (Hood), Pepe Callahan (Pepe), Vince Palmieri, Arnold Strong (Hoods). **Released**: United Artists, March 7, 1973 in Los Angeles, Philadelphia, and Chicago. Re-released with new advertising campaign in New York on October 28, 1973. 113 minutes.

Terry Lennox asks his friend Philip Marlowe to drive him to the Mexican border. When Marlowe returns to Los Angeles, he is interrogated by police investigating the brutal murder of Terry's wife Sylvia. Three days later, when they learn of Terry's suicide and confession in Mexico, the cops free Marlowe, who is determined to find out the truth. At the same time Lennox's neighbor Eileen Wade hires him to find her alcoholic husband Roger, whom Marlowe rescues from sanitorium operated by Verringer. A goodbye note from Terry Lennox with $5,000 enclosed arrives in Marlowe's mail and shortly he is visited by gangster Marty Augustine who thinks Marlowe knows where the money Lennox stole from him is. After the detective confronts Eileen about Lennox, Roger Wade commits suicide by drowning. Eileen admits that her husband may have killed Sylvia Lennox, who was his mistress. When the police refuse to reopen the Lennox case, Marlowe goes back to the Mexican village, bribes the local officials and finds Lennox luxuriating by a pool. Realizing Lennox and Eileen Wade have conspired to dupe him, he kills his manipulative friend. As Marlowe leaves Lennox's hideout, he passes the arriving Eileen Wade.

The Long Goodbye was the second neo-noir incarnation of Chandler's universally recognized private investigator Philip Marlowe. In using Elliott Gould as his Marlowe, Altman cast strongly against type. As noted about *Hickey & Boggs*, a 1970s neo-noir P.I. with classic period proclivities was an anomaly. Also like *Hickey & Boggs*, *The Long Goodbye* is as much about friendship and betrayal as it is about violence and murder. P.I. Marlowe's primary purpose is to clear his friend's name and to help a woman find her disturbed husband, whom he believes she loves very much. Where Hickey and Boggs confronted

The Long Goodbye: *Eileen Wade (Nina van Pallandt) and Philip Marlowe (Elliott Gould).*

ruthless syndicate soldiers, Marlowe must deal with his own vicious gangster, Marty Augustine, who is looking for the person who took his money. The mystery that ensnares the characters is something that Philip Marlowe stumbles upon. At some level, he doesn't really want to unravel it but cannot help doing so. The 1970s Marlowe is a man lost in a world he does not understand. Rather than facing the fact that his profession is "not about anything anymore," Marlowe constantly attempts to convince himself that each antagonizing incident is "O.K. with me"; but obviously it is not.

All of the film Marlowes carry the baggage of Chandler's literary urban knight, a man who lives by a code as rigorous as that of chivalry. For such a man, nothing is as it seems and nothing is right. As Chandler himself wrote in his oft-quoted essay, "The Simple Art of Murder": "But down these mean streets a man must go who is not himself mean, who is neither tarnished nor afraid. . . . The detective in this kind of story must be such a man. He is the hero; he is everything. . . . The story is this man's adventure in search of a hidden truth." Because he is such a man, Marlowe can ignore the whacked-out girls next door or the rude market clerk, but he cannot ignore what he supposes is a convenient frame-up of his friend and, finally, he cannot be indifferent to his friend's exploitation of his trust. When Terry Lennox tells him, "But that's you, Marlowe . . . you'll never learn, you're a born loser," Marlowe righteously kills him, because Terry is wrong. Marlowe is a loner but not a loser. He lives in a world of other values, "neither tarnished nor afraid." Walter Hill played with this concept in his original script to *Hickey & Boggs.* Twenty-five years after she worked on Hawk's & of *The Big Sleep* screenwriter Leigh Brackett does the same in this movie.

Given Chandler's chivalric attitude towards women, there is further irony in that *The Long Goodbye* depicts a considerable amount of violence towards them. Women, too, are murderously beaten like Sylvia Lennox, casually struck like Eileen Wade, and even willfully disfigured like Augustine's girlfriend. For Marlowe this is the ultimate in savagery. The first thing Marlowe notices about Eileen Wade is the bruise which she tries to hide with her long blond hair. When Marlowe touches it gently, she politely ignores his concern. He admires her stoicism and, correspondingly, she admires the loyal friendship

he has shown Lennox. Marlowe and Eileen Wade greatly resemble each other, which is a considerable departure from Chandler's novel, where Eileen is a femme fatale and murderess. In the film she, like Marlowe, tries to hide her alienation. But her method is to hide behind a facade of cheerfulness and beauty. She attempts to conceal her bruised face, a symbol of her internal suffering. She also conceals her belief that her husband murdered Sylvia Lennox. She knows Roger Wade is capable of extreme violence when drunk, for she bears the mark of it; but she cannot betray him. Conversely, she shares Marlowe's inaccurate conviction that Terry Lennox is incapable of murder. Marlowe and Eileen work at cross purposes to achieve the same goal, neither realizing that the goal is worthless. From the endistanced perspective of the disaffected 1970s, this is the additional irony that filmmakers Altman and Brackett have imposed on Chandler's character.

Even in a neo-noir context, *The Long Goodbye* evokes the emotions of a mainstream classic period noir. The powerlessness of its independent protagonists, Marlowe and Eileen Wade, to untangle a moral dilemma in a modern, corrupt world makes them prototypically noir. While Marlowe may not verbalize his sense of anachronistic despair as directly as Hickey or Boggs, he shares their ability to endure physical and emotional punishment. As a P.I. Marlowe is expected from genre convention to understand and discern a solution to this puzzle; but even the police know more than he does. Unlike the attitudes of the police conveyed in film noir of the classic period, the "modern" corruption of the police in *The Long Goodbye* is not caused by individual ambition and greed but by overload and burn-out. All the police want is their paperwork completed, a murder confessed, and a suicide certified by the proper official. They crave simple solutions regardless of conflicting facts because they lack energy and time to explore alternative answers. While Chandler's novels use the police as identifiable personalities and antagonists, Altman makes the police relatively anonymous and surly, interchangeable and unimportant. A policeman's face is never lingered upon in the film without a distracting element occurring simultaneously. When Marlowe is interrogated at the station, he is the center of the frame while the police circle about him like gnats firing questions. All the while Marlowe plays with the inky smears left by the fingerprinting

The Long Goodbye: *Marty Augustine (Mark Rydell) and Marlowe (Elliott Gould).*

procedure. He does this while looking at his reflection in a two-way mirror, as if to demonstrate his contempt for the police authorities he knows are watching on the other side of the glass. Later, when he confronts the police face to face at the scene of Wade's suicide, Marlowe drunkenly waves a wine glass in their faces while they exhibit little expression.

Altman uses glass throughout the film as a fragile and reflective prop to express the illusory nature of clarity and appearances. Just as the plot will reveal that Lennox has deceived everyone and that Roger Wade, for all his rowdiness, directed his murderous violence inward, even simple textural details are not as they seem. The Wades' beach house is made almost entirely of glass. While Roger and Eileen stand inside and watch Marlowe out on the beach, Roger condemns the detective as an ignorant slob. A few minutes later, Marlowe watches the couple argue fiercely; and his image is placed between the two of them in the window's reflection, suggesting that he brought them back together and that he may have to protect each one from the other. Marlowe's quizzical look indicates that he isn't sure what to do. Later, Marlowe and Eileen argue over dinner inside, while outside, visible through a window, Roger commits suicide; but their plain view of his action does not make them able to help him. Marlowe again watches through the window while the gangster Augustine intimidates Eileen; but he is unable to make a clear connection between the two until he sees her leave Augustine's building. The undraped picture windows in the gangster's office do not hinder Augustine's attempt to get at the truth and would not hold him back from killing Marlowe, even though literally anyone passing by could watch the crime. But the city is silent and indifferent. As Augustine's girlfriend is carried out screaming and bleeding profusely, the neighboring girls are too self-engrossed to notice her plight. Malibu neighbors crowd around the scene of Roger's suicide with the tinkling wine glasses they have carried from their parties. In *The Long Goodbye*, Altman adds society's conscious indifference to the long list of alienating elements that comprise film noir.

This social indifference is at the heart of the neo-noir films of the 1970s. It is the reason that the profession of Marlowe and of Hickey and Boggs is "not about anything anymore." In a world where no one cares, men with a code are out of place. Hickey and Boggs come to admire Quemando and Mary Jane for trying to beat the odds. The shot of their bodies lying peacefully in the sand reflects that sentiment. It is that same sentiment which compelled Marlowe to suffer brutalization and almost be killed rather than betray his friend Terry. In the end it is that same sentiment which makes Marlowe react so violently to Terry's perfidiousness. For Marlowe his act is not about revenge. Like Boggs, he acts out of a motive that is "about making it right." **EW**

LOST HIGHWAY (1997)

Director: David Lynch. **Screenplay**: David Lynch, Barry Gifford. **Producers**: Deepak Nayar, Mary Sweeney, Tom Sternberg. **Director of Photography**: Peter Deming. **Music**: Angelo Badalamenti. **Editor**: Mary Sweeney. **Cast**: Bill Pullman (Fred Madison), Patricia Arquette (Renee/Alice), Balthazar Getty (Peter Dayton), Robert Blake (Mystery Man), Natasha Gregson Wagner (Sheila), Richard Pryor (Arnie), Robert Loggia (Mr.Eddy/Dick Laurent), Gary Busey (William Dayton), Scott Coffey (Teddy), Lucy Butler (Candace Dayton), Michael Massee (Andy). **Released**: October Films, February 21. 135 minutes.

Lost Highway: *Bill Pulllman as Fred Madison.*

Fred Madison is a saxophonist who is undergoing a psychotic breakdown. He murders his wife and is sentenced to death. While on death row he "imagines" he has entered the body of Peter Dayton, a young mechanic. As Dayton, he falls for a mobster's girlfriend, Alice, a double for his own dead wife Renee. Alice convinces Dayton to help her escape the grip of her mobster lover. In the process they accidentally murder another of Alice's lovers. They steal some jewelry from him and head for the desert to meet a "fence." In the desert while making love, Madison re-emerges from the body of Dayton. Alice leaves him but with the help of the "fence," Madison kidnaps and murders mobster Laurent. In the final scene he is pursued down the highway by the police who have been tailing him.

Like his later neo-noir *Mulholland Drive*, David Lynch in *Lost Highway* takes the audience into the mind of a psychotic, blending fantasy and reality in often overlapping folds. The film opens in a homage to Robert Aldrich's *Kiss Me Deadly*, with titles superimposed over a highway at night and David Bowie singing "I'm Deranged" on the soundtrack. The movie then moves into the moderne Hollywood Hills house of saxophonist Fred Madison and his wife Renee. Renee, as played with femme fatale style by Patricia Arquette, is, with her auburn wig and 1940s-style clothes, a cross between Rita Hayworth in *Gilda* (Lynch also uses Hayworth as his model for the amnesiac "Rita" character in *Mulholland Drive*) and Barbara Stanwyck in *Double Indemnity*. Madison can never quite read his wife who keeps a cool distance from him and is mysterious about her shady past. As his jealousy grows, so does his psychosis, best objectified by the presence of the demonic "Mystery Man" (played frighteningly with pasty face and dyed black hair by Robert Blake) who seems to have privileged access to not only Madison's house but his mind as well (he also turns out to be the "fence" in the final scenes who helps him murder the mobster Laurent).

After Madison is convicted of murdering his wife, his psychosis moves into overdrive and he "reincarnates" himself in the body of the young mechanic Dayton. In this alternate universe, his wife is also "reincarnated," this time in the form of Alice (also played by Arquette with a blonde wig a la Stanwyck in *Double Indemnity*), a far more sexually liberated doppelganger (multiple identities are a staple of noir) of his wife who keeps multiple lovers, including himself, and presses him into service in her liberation from her mobster boyfriend. The scene where Dayton and Alice make love in the Mojave desert, as the red sands around them swirl and the lights of the car overexpose their bodies, is the climactic moment for Madison as he again tries to possess his wife who tells him in no uncertain terms that he can never really have her. Without her, there is nothing left for Madison, now in his original body, and so he once again sinks into his mind, visualized in the final scene by his screaming face altered digitally to resemble Munch's painting *The Scream* as he races down the highway, police in pursuit. **JU**

LOVE CRIMES (1992)

Director: Lizzie Borden. **Screenplay**: Allan Moyle and Laurie Frank based on a story by Moyle. **Producers**: Lizzie Borden, Randy Langlais (Miramax/Sovereign). **Director of Photography**: Jack N. Green. **Production Designer**: Armin Ganz. **Music**: Graeme Revell. **Editors**: Nicholas C. Smith, Mike Jackson. **Cast**: Sean Young (Dana Greenway), Patrick Bergin ("David Hanover"), Arnetia Walker (Lt. Maria Johnson), James Read (Stanton Gray), Ron Orbach (Tully), Fern Dorsey (Colleen Dells), Tina Hightower (Anne Winslow), Donna Biscoe (Hanna). **Released**: Millimeter, January 24. 85 minutes.

Fresh from a sting operation in which an undercover female office posed as a prostitute to ferret out corrupt vice cops, District Attorney Dana Greenway becomes involved in the case of a serial sexual predator, a charlatan who by posing as famous photographer "David Hanover" can seduce and abandon women who refuse to press charges against him. After flashbacks reveal a troubled past involving family abuse, Greenway goes undercover herself and plans to become Hanover's latest "victim," in order to be able to prosecute him. Once caught up in Hanover's emotional web, Greenway must face her own "dark past" in order to extricate herself.

The troubled production history of *Love Crimes*, with scenes re-shot and performances altered in post-production, make for an aesthetic result that is uneven at best. Nonetheless *Love Crimes* is arguably the most iconoclastic statement from a woman filmmaker using elements of neo-noir. In pop-critical jargon, Lizzie Borden takes a cinematic ax and gives her audience forty whacks. From the first scene, which frames the narrative and in which Johnson—an African-American female police lieutenant—makes a statement about a woman prosecutor, the point is that things would have gone differently "if she wasn't a woman." The androgyny of the prosecutor Dana Greenway, from her name to her hairstyle, is both subtler and more significant than in the "female cop" drama *Blue Steel* (1990). As in *Impulse*, the first scene involves an undercover officer posing as a prostitute; but in this case the police preying on hookers are the targets.

Although the narrative is encumbered with numerous complications, most notably from the flashback-within-flashbacks to Greenway's apparent abuse by a father who killed her mother, the clear focus of *Love Crimes* on one level is the transference relationship between Greenway and the sexual predator she is pursuing. The revelations in flash-cuts that he resembles her abusive father who locked her in a closet as a child are timed to create visual irony but blur the issue of women fighting male stereotypes. It is that stereotyping which on another level

the two female protagonists are actually confronting and which in the end they can only overcome by behaving unethically and destroying evidence.

The narrative ironies are multiform. When Greenway changes her hair and her clothes and abandons her masculine style to "go undercover" posing as a schoolteacher on vacation, she is falling back on those stereotypes, perhaps more consciously than the protagonists of *Blue Steel* or *Impulse* but entrapped by them nonetheless. When "David Hanover" (whose real name is never revealed) holds her hostage, his mind game is to convince Greenway that he can set her free of her inhibitions. When circumstances impugn her behavior, even police lieutenant Johnson assumes that she may have succumbed to the strange allure of her antagonist. The sexual dynamics may differ but the issues become much the same as in *Manhunter* or *Point Break* (1991): law enforcers encountering the surprisingly complex criminal mind and misled by the charm of the sociopath. The final irony—that it is Greenway's surprising resistance to that charm of his which traps "Hanover"—makes him unable to return to seducing others until he has settled his score with her. In the climactic scene, the flashes of his camera strobe violate her more profoundly that any physical assault, triggering more flashbacks and pulsing through the frame like an externalization of her psychic spasms. It is that strobe, which keeps going even after he is struck down and drops the camera, which is isolated in a final close-up, and which triggers a white optical that blots out the frame, that is the mechanistic metaphor for the social strictures that hinder Greenway, Johnson, and all the other women "victims." In that context, Greenway's burning the Polaroids that "Hanover" had taken while he held her hostage becomes less an act of destruction than one of liberation from her dark pasts, both distant and immediate. **AS**

Love Crimes: *Dana Greenway (Sean Young) and "Dan Hanover" (Patrick Bergin).*

MADIGAN (1968)

Director: Don Siegel. **Screenplay**: Henri Simoun and Abraham Polonsky from the novel *The Commissioner* by Richard Dougherty. **Producer**: Frank P. Rosenberg. **Director of Photography**: Russell Metty. **Music**: Don Costa. **Art Directors**: George C. Webb, Alex Golitzen. **Editor**: Milton Shifman. **Cast**: Richard Widmark (Daniel Madigan), Henry Fonda (Commissioner Russell), Inger Stevens (Julia Madigan), Harry Guardino (Rocco Bonaro), James Whitmore (Chief Inspector Charles Kane), Susan Clark (Tricia), Michael Dunn (Castiglioni), Steve Ihnat (Barney Benesch), Sheree North (Jonesy), Don Stroud (Hughie), Warren Stevens (Capt. Ben Williams), Raymond St. Jacques (Dr. Johnston), Bert Freed (Chief-of-Detectives Lynch), Harry Bellaver (Mickey Dunn). **Completed**: June 23, 1967. **Released**: Universal, March 29. 101 minutes.

New York detectives Dan Madigan and Rocco Bonaro break into a tenement room to bring in a small-time hood, Barney Benesch. Distracted by the naked woman whom Benesch pushes out of his bed, the policemen let Benesch get the drop on them and permit him to escape. Only later do they learn that Benesch is wanted for murder. The police commissioner Russell threatens Madigan and Bonaro with suspension unless the suspect is captured within 72 hours. The pair begins an intense and illegal on-and-off-duty search. They terrorize a woman to find out the whereabouts of a bookie with a grudge against Benesch, deal with him for the name of a man who provides Benesch with women, and through this man set a trap. It fails; but Benesch is pursued through Spanish Harlem and cornered in an apartment house. As the police surround the building, Madigan and Bonaro impatiently charge in. Benesch is killed; but Madigan is mortally wounded and dies in a nearby hospital.

From its opening shots of the deserted New York City streets at daybreak, *Madigan* evokes the ambience of two decades earlier and the Hellinger/Dassin *Naked City*. One of the few directors to have multiple classic period and neo-noirs to his credit, Siegel knew the Hellinger approach. In fact, he had been strongly considered as a directorial candidate by Hellinger for the original version of *The Killers* which Siegel remade three years before *Madigan*. Siegel tackles the complex narrative in a constricted time frame head on by intercutting freely between the political "damage control" of Commissioner Russell over departmental integrity and the personally significant efforts of Madigan and Bonaro to correct their blunder. These frequent cutaways could be interpreted as gratuitous moralizing or even filler for the time gaps in the two detectives' search, but, while the conflicts that Siegel defines may be simplistic, they are not isolated or unrevealing, similar in many ways to co-screenwriter Abraham Polonsky's classic noir *Force of Evil*.

If Russell regards Madigan as a poor example of a policeman, the commissioner's sexual estrangement, like that of Madigan's wife, betrays an unrealistic view of human nature. Madigan is not troubled by contradiction. His own alienation in the classic noir tradition is more narrowly focused and more purely existential. Although he is neither a rogue cop nor an embezzler as in Siegel's *Private Hell 36*, Madigan does use the meager perks of his job. Being stripped of his gun by a felon should not be read in Freudian terms as a castration but in the noir context as a threat to his lifestyle and by extension his being. From this perspective, Madigan's casual attitude towards violence and corruption, whether overturning a secretary's desk, menacing a suspect or blackmailing Benesch's part-time pimp, is part of the easiest response a noir protagonist can make to an oppressive quirk of fate. Madigan perishes then not in expiation for being unscrupulous (if anything the scenes with Russell establish Madigan's relative honesty) or immoral (he is too tired to indulge in the sexual transgressions that plague Russell and tempt Madigan's wife) but in a final assertion of personal identity that is as fleeting and explosive as the bursts from his gun. **AS**

MAN ON FIRE (2004)

Director: Tony Scott. **Screenplay**: Brian Helgeland based on the novel by A.J. Quinnell. **Producers**: Lucas Foster, Tony Scott. **Director of Photography**: Paul Cameron. **Music**: Harry Gregson-Williams. **Production Designers**: Benjamín Fernandez, Chris

Seagers. **Editor**: Christian Wagner. **Cast**: Denzel Washington (Creasy), Dakota Fanning (Pita), Marc Anthony (Samuel), Radha Mitchell (Lisa), Christopher Walken (Rayburn), Giancarlo Giannini (Manzano), Rachel Ticotin (Mariana), Jesús Ochoa (Fuentes), Mickey Rourke (Jordan), Angelina Peláez (Sister Anna), Gustavo Sánchez Parra (Daniel Sanchez), Gero Camilo (Aurelio Sanchez), Rosa María Hernández (Maria). **Released**: 20th Century-Fox, April 21. 146 minutes.

John Creasy is an out-of-work former "special ops," a counter-terrorism intelligence agent who has been wandering around South America and now made his way to Mexico to visit an old comrade-in-arms, Rayburn. Through Rayburn, Creasy is hired by the wealthy Ramos family—Samuel, his Anglo wife Lisa and their only child/daughter, Pita—as a bodyguard for the girl. Despite Creasy's heroic efforts—he is shot repeatedly—Pita is eventually kidnapped. When the drop-off of the ransom money is botched by Mexico's special anti-kidnapping police agents, she is murdered. After Creasy recovers from his wounds, he initiates a vendetta against everyone who he believes is responsible for Pita's death. Ultimately Creasy discovers that Pita is still alive but that, in order to return her to her parents, he must put himself in the hands of the kidnappers.

A written prologue and a visual prologue underneath the credits establish how common and how brutal kidnapping is in Mexico. The first sight of John Creasy is in a cab entering Mexico from the United States. The visuals capture the natural landscape that Creasy sees from the window of the vehicle and that are similar to the landscapes that Creasy will see from the window of the car in which he dies at the end of the film. This does not mean that the narrative structure of the film is elliptical, but it does suggest that Creasy's "life journey" is always a kind of return, which interacts with the fatalistic tone of the entire film. After he rescues Pita from the kidnappers by sacrificing his own life, the idea of return is explicitly reinforced: Pita tells Creasy that she is now going home and he answers that he is going home too.

Man on Fire is first and foremost a film about redemptive action, about Creasy's need for redemption and about how he accomplishes it. But this redemption is on two levels and requires two different, even diametrically opposed, responses in terms of both physical action as well as emotional involvement. First, Creasy needs/seeks redemption from his present psychological/emotional predicament: He is an emotionally detached, depressed alcoholic with suicidal tendencies. His redemption from this state comes through his relationship with Pita, not simply as her bodyguard, but also as her friend and substitute father. He is also something of a born-again Christian. His rejection of the "bottle" and the softening of his gruff personality are concurrent with the development of a bond with Pita. At one poignant moment in the film, Pita tells Creasy that she has noticed him, finally, smiling. Not quite ready to admit to his softened persona, Creasy jokingly remarks that it was a "smirk" not a "smile." The first half of the film is focused on the Creasy/Pita relationship and the amelioration of his alcoholism, his suicidal depression and his emotional detachment from those around him.

Creasy also needs and seeks another kind of redemption, not so much from his present psychological state but from his past deeds. The two, of course, are linked, but for Creasy they require different courses of action. In the beginning of

Man on Fire: *Pita (Dakota Fanning) runs to the fallen Creasy (Denzel Washington)*.

the film, Creasy asks Rayburn if he thinks that God will ever forgive them for what they have done. "No," replies Rayburn. "Me either," says Creasy. When Manzano, the Mexican Federal Agent tracking Creasy and the kidnappers, asks Rayburn what can be expected of Creasy, Rayburn replies that everyone is an artist and "Creasy's art is Death. He's about to paint his masterpiece." So begins the second half of the film and the second level path of Creasy's redemption.

The fatalistic and pessimistic tone of the film comes not just from the way that the characters and organizations betray one another. Jordan Kalfus, the Ramos attorney, hatches the kidnapping plan and betrays the family. Samuel Ramos eventually kills Kalfus, but Ramos himself betrays his wife and child. The anti-kidnapping agents betray the family and so on. This chain of betrayal affects the way director Tony Scott visionalizes the Mexican urban landscape: it is less a picture of a troubled social milieu than it is a portrait of Hell. The over-saturated images of the city with the jittery camerawork, the reverse processing, the step-printing, the jump-cuts, the rejection of any "classical" editing, the momentary shifts between normal and slow-motion, the juxtaposition of black-and white images with color—all give the sense of a world that is completely unstable and lacking in any consistency. There is no normal social order to protect, no "civil" society to make better. Creasy is not motivated by any loyalty to a social order, as there is none, or desire to make society a better place; his motivation is purely personal.

Furthermore while Creasy does receive some help from his friend Rayburn and the crusading reporter, Mariana, he is otherwise isolated. Forced to do whatever he does alone, Creasy becomes a purely existential anti-hero. His personal revenge is informed not only by the quest to avenge Pita's death but also by an unconscious need to atone for his past killings. Like so many protagonists of both classic period and neo-noir, Creasy's revenge/redemption takes him on a suicidal mission of extreme violence (including torture of one of his victims), destruction and death that leads to his own end in the back seat of a car driven by murderous kidnappers and assassins. He clutches the medallion of St. Jude, a gift from Pita. She had explained it featured "the patron saint of lost causes" who in this instance is more like the patron saint of lost souls.

The evocative power of *Man on Fire* derives as fully from what it does not depict (or accede to) as what it does. There is no Hollywood ending, no final Resolution via a grand shoot-out where a hero assaults a citadel of power as in *The Bourne Identity* (2002) or *The Shooter* (2007) to confront and annihilate the leader of the evil group. In the neo-noir context, what is depicted in *Man on Fire* is the dispersion of "evil" across all layers of society. There is no locus of evil here to confront because it pervades the milieu. It is in this sense that Creasy's final act has a connotation of gratuitousness, unless it is understood as an act of total and personal sacrifice and redemption. This core of this power is certainly Denzel Washington's performance. As perhaps the most significant actor/star of his generation, he has created a persona through his competence, his range, his depth and his willingness to accept the roles of unsavory characters (*Training Day*), and has become the most accomplished actor of the post-World War II American cinema, on a par with James Stewart and Marlon Brando in his ability to bring complex characters to cinematic life. Combined with Scott's uncompromising direction of Brian Helgeland's adapted screenplay and Paul Cameron's stunning cinematography, the outstanding performances of Washington and the other members of the cast establish *Man on Fire* as one of the most important neo-noirs. **RA**

MANHUNTER (1986)

Director: Michael Mann. **Screenplay**: Michael Mann based on the novel *Red Dragon* by Thomas Harris. **Producers**: Dino De Laurentiis and Richard Roth. **Director of Photography**: Dante Spinotti. **Music**: Michel Rubini. **Art Direction**: Jack Blackman. **Editor**: Dov Hoenig. **Cast**: William Petersen (Will Graham), Kim Griest (Molly Graham), Joan Allen (Reba McClaine), Brian Cox (Dr. Hannibal Lecktor), Dennis Farina (Jack Crawford), Tom Noonan (Francis Dollarhyde), Stephen Lang (Freddy Lounds), David Seaman (Kevin Graham), Benjamin Hendrickson (Dr. Frederick Chilton), Michael Talbott (Geehan), Dan Butler (Jimmy Price). **Released**: De Laurentiis Entertainment Group, August 15. 120 minutes (Director's cut, 124 minutes).

Retired from the FBI and now living in Florida, Will Graham reluctantly returns to his old profession of tracking serial killers, largely due to pressure by former boss Jack Crawford. Tracing the murder of two families to an unknown figure nicknamed the "Tooth Fairy" by the popular press, Graham enlists the help of Dr. Hannibal Lecktor. Confined to an insane asylum after Graham's successful detection of his crimes several years before, Lecktor plays mind games with his former victim whom he had attacked before his arrest leaving deep physical and psychological scars. As well as aiding Graham, Lecktor attempts to set him up by revealing his home address to the "Tooth Fairy." Graham also sets up journalist Freddie Lounds who stalks him and preys on his psychological insecurities. Lounds later undergoes a gruesome fate at the hands of serial killer Francis Dollarhyde. Sending his family away, Graham attempts to enter the mind of Dollarhyde who has now fallen for blind co-worker Reba. Believing that she has betrayed him, Dollarhyde kidnaps her. Before Dollarhyde slaughters her as his next sacrificial victim Graham breaks into his house. He faces his adversary for the first and last time before killing him. In Mann's original version, the penultimate scene shows

Manhunter: *William Petersen as Will Graham.*

Graham visiting Dollarhyde's future intended victim Mrs. Sherman to reassure her that all is well before finally returning to his own family in Florida.

Manhunter represents one of the most stylistically accomplished examples of neo-noir cinematography. Visualized according to Michael Mann's personal style of modernist alienation and expertly photographed by Dante Spinotti, who employs green, purple, and magenta to emphasize dark emotional moods, *Manhunter* significantly employs the duality inherent within classical American film noir in its own creative manner. Retiring from the FBI after suffering a murderous attack by a dangerous serial killer and suffering from a psychological aftermath equivalent to the contaminating bite of a vampire, Graham has to reawaken certain disturbing symbiotic powers that he fears makes him identical to those he pursues. Like a classical film noir hero, influenced by a dark alter ego, Graham has to explore his own psyche before he enters the dark world of Francis Dollarhyde to face possible loss of his own fragile identity. Will Graham represents a neo-noir version of Victor Mature's Nick Bianco from *Kiss of Death*, forced by an authoritarian figure to descend into a world he seeks escape from and become bonded with his violent alter ego Tommy Udo. *Manhunter's* Jack Crawford is a neo-noir version of Brian Donlevy's District Attorney D'Angelo in the earlier film with Dollarhyde as a more dangerous version of Tommy Udo. By indirectly causing the death of Freddie Lounds, Graham also reveals his dark affinities with both Lecktor (who indirectly attempts to cause the deaths of Graham and his family) and Dollarhyde himself.

Like David Fincher's *Seven* (1995), *Manhunter* develops the neo-noir style not only for its affinities with the American Gothic tradition but also to explore further this dark symbiotic relationship between detective and the serial killer. In his 2001 book, *The Gates of Janus: Serial Killing and Its Analysis*, British Moors Murderer serial killer Ian Brady describes such affinities in the following manner: "The serial killer and the detective, to a significant extent, necessarily share many characteristics, including a common unorthodox philosophy in tandem with solitary dedication and commitment. Both protagonists must be ruthless in purpose, astute in deceit, clear in strategy; temper self-confidence with caution; cultivate doubt where there is certainty and certainty where there is doubt; feign incompetence to provoke overconfidence; nourish arrogance by fake humility; deny, affirm and divert with dexterity as tactics dictate; incite anger to obtain the unguarded response and sow confusion; exude synthetic sympathy for trust whilst doubting everyone; regard all individuals as essentially corrupt and guided by self-interest; live and breathe moral and legal relativism whilst projecting moral and legal rectitude; and above all, as already postulated, believe and act in the certainty that the end always justifies the means."

Graham, has much in common with Dollarhyde and Lecktor. By setting up Freddy Lounds he is Dollarhyde's accomplice in all but name. When Graham eventually sees the slaughtered Mrs. Leeds through the eyes of his quarry, he stands at the threshold of succumbing to his darkest desires by identifying too closely with a serial killer fascinated by a family world he is alienated from. In profiling this killer, Graham ultimately puts his own family in jeopardy. Dollarhyde initially feels safe by finding love in the arms of a blind woman whose dead eyes cannot reflect his own perverse fantasies. But when he misrecognizes a harmless farewell outside her door, he captures her, intending another dark performance of his chosen role as William Blake's powerful Red Dragon dominating the female clothed by the rays of the sun. Unlike his alter ego, Graham manages to break out of a dark fantasy world and total identification with his blood brothers Lecktor and Dollarhyde. He destroys a glass window whose fragments duplicate those mirror shards used by Dollarhyde to reflect the perverse acceptance he so desperately needs. Like Ethan Edwards in *The Searchers*, Graham manages to destroy his Scar. He manages to destroy his demons, both internal and external, and can return safely to his family in Florida. **TW**

MEMENTO (2000)

Director: Christopher Nolan. **Screenplay**: Christopher Nolan based on the story "Memento Mori" by Jonathan Nolan. **Producers**: Jennifer Todd and Suzanne Todd (Team Todd). **Director of Photography**: Wally Pfister. **Music**: David Julyan. **Art Director**: Patti Podesta. **Editor**: Dody Dorn. **Cast**: Guy Pearce (Leonard), Carrie-Anne Moss (Natalie), Joe Pantoliano (Teddy Gammell), Mark Boone Junior (Burt), Russ Fega (Waiter), Jorja Fox (Leonard's Wife), Stephen Tobolowsky (Sammy), Harriet Sansom Harris (Mrs. Jankis), Thomas Lennon (Doctor), Callum Keith Rennie (Dodd), Kimberly Campbell (Blonde), Marianne Muellerleile (Tattooist), Larry Holden (Jimmy). **Released**: Newmarket Films, October 11. 113 minutes.

[*Note*: Memento is told almost entirely in backward chronological sequence. For simplicity's sake the following summary is told chronologically.]

Leonard Shelby wakes up in a strange hotel room disoriented and wondering where he is. The phone rings and he tells the unseen caller how two men broke into his home, and raped and murdered his wife. Leonard managed to shoot one intruder but was then attacked by the second man. From the injuries to his head, he developed a form of amnesia that keeps him from being able to form new memories. He cannot remember anything after this incident for more than several minutes and systematically compensates for his faulty memory by writing himself notes, taking Polaroids, and tattooing important facts on his body. Leonard is now obsessed with locating and killing the second intruder to avenge his wife's death. One of his few clues is a tattoo of the killer's name, "John G." Teddy, the caller on the phone, tells Leonard he is a police officer who took pity on him and helped him track down and kill the real John G. more than a year before, but Leonard forgot he had completed his revenge and continued his search for John G. Leonard, frustrated and angry at these revelations, attempts to manipulate himself into killing Teddy. Before he can forget, he quickly writes down Teddy's license plate number and calls it John G.'s. After meeting a woman named Natalie, he tells her about his condition and she tracks down the license number, leading Leonard back to Teddy. Leonard concludes that Teddy is John G. and takes him to an abandoned building and shoots him.

Memento belongs in the tradition of noirs, like *Lady in the Lake* and *Dark Passage*, which attempt to recruit the viewer into sympathizing with the main character by creating a subjective conceit. Where the latter films both used a first person camera, so that the viewer is seeing what the main character sees, *Memento* attempts a more psychologically based effect, disorienting the viewer by telling the story backwards, forcing the viewer into a persistent state of confusion much like the constant confusion of the main character, Leonard. Like him, we must decode, decipher and detect, and though we are not always in step with him, we're almost always as disoriented. The brilliance of the film lies in its adoption and subversion of many of the tropes of classic film noir. The non-linear storytelling recalls *The Killing*, Leonard's profession recalls *Double Indemnity* and of course his "condition" recalls any number of films with amnesia as its primary plot device. The film's central twist, however, with Leonard cast as both manipulator and the manipulated, both detective and killer, elevates the film well beyond pastiche. And though the audience is itself manipulated, one is hard-pressed not to feel anything but sympathy for Leonard and his tragic quest, as he is doomed to repeat not just his revenge but his grief. **JEB**

MIAMI BLUES (1990)

Director: George Armitage. **Screenplay**: George Armitage from the novel by Charles Willeford. **Producers**: Jonathan Demme, Gary Goetzman, Edward Saxon, Kenneth Utt, Fred Ward. **Director of**

Photography: Tak Fujimoto. **Music**: Gary Chang. **Production Designer**: Maher Ahmad. **Editor**: Craig McKay. **Cast**: Alec Baldwin (Frederick J. Fringer, Jr.), Fred Ward (Sgt. Hoke Moseley), Jennifer Jason Leigh (Susie Waggoner), Charles Napier (Sgt. Bill Henderson), Nora Dunn (Ellita Sanchez), Paul Gleason (Sgt. Frank Lackley), Shirley Stoler (Edie Wulgemuth). **Released**: Orion Pictures, April 20. 97 minutes.

Ex-con and psychotic thief "Junior" Fringer arrives in Miami, steals a woman's suitcase and breaks the finger of an airport Hare Krishna out of pure malice. The Krishna dies of shock and Detective Hoke Moseley is put on the case. Fringer cons hotel hooker Susie Waggoner into believing that he's madly in love with her, and then uses her as cover for his daily business of robbing petty street thieves. Moseley shows up at their apartment and jokingly provokes Fringer, but loses his sense of humor when Junior beats him severely and steals his gun, I.D. and false teeth. Using Hoke's badge, Fringer robs bookie joints and drug dealers. Hoke locates Susie and undermines her confidence in Junior, who has become so enamored of playing cop that he is injured while preventing a convenience store holdup. Susie determines on her own that her boyfriend has indeed been lying to her. Junior robs pawnshop owner Edie Wulgemuth but she hacks off four of his fingers before he can escape. After a street battle, Hoke follows Junior home and shoots him dead. Hoke asks social worker Ellita Sanchez not to prosecute the gullible Susie.

An eccentric and frequently funny exercise in the hard-boiled cop tradition, *Miami Blues* centers on Junior Fringer's enthusiastic misuse of Detective Moseley's police identity. In almost a parody of *Stray Dog*, the chameleon-like Fringer's impersonations falter when he becomes genuinely confused as to his own identity, announcing himself to unsuspecting marks with the gusto of a fake TV character. [Note: in an excised scene, Fringer lapses briefly into a psychotic confusion, unable to decide if he's a cop or a crook.]

Miami Blues' emphasis on grisly humor and lowlife realities is nothing like the stylized *Miami Vice*. Hero Hoke Moseley lives in a seedy flop house, bums money from his associates and must scramble to replace his stolen teeth. Even though co-worker Ellita Sanchez seems interested, Moseley lacks the temperament, and the hygiene, for romance. The brutal but personable Fringer finds the perfect clueless confederate in Susie, a naïve prostitute easily charmed with visions of bliss behind a white picket fence. Ironically, Junior's demise comes about from his betrayal of Susie's domestic dreams, and she unmasks his empty promises. Moseley must improvise to hunt down Fringer, borrowing an antiquated six-gun rather than face the humiliation of asking his superiors for a replacement. The film's twisting of crime show conventions reaches its apex in the climactic shoot-out, when both criminal and cop shout, almost in unison, "Freeze, police!" **GE**

MIAMI VICE (2006)

Director: Michael Mann. **Screenplay**: Michael Mann based on the television series *Miami Vice* by Anthony Yerkovich. **Producer**: Pieter Jan Brugge. **Director of Photography**: Dion Beebe. **Music**: John Murphy. **Art Director**: Carlos Menendez. **Editors**: William Goldenberg, Paul Rubell. **Cast**: Colin Farrell (Det. James "Sonny" Crockett), Jamie Foxx (Det. Ricardo Tubbs), Gong Li (Isabella),

Miami Vice: *Sonny Crockett (Colin Farrell) and Ricardo Tubbs (Jamie Foxx).*

Naomie Harris (Det. Trudy Joplin), John Ortiz (Jose Yero), Luis Tosar (Arcangel de Jesus Montoya), Elizabeth Rodriguez (Det. Gina Calabrese), Justin Theroux (Det. Larry Zito), Domenick Lombardozzi (Det. Stan Switek), Ciaran Hinds (FBI Agent Fujima), Barry Shabaka Henley (Lt. Martin Castillo). **Locations**: Miami, Florida; Canelones, Uruguay; Barranquilla, Colombia; Ciudad del Este, Paraguay; Santo Domingo, Dominican Republic. **Released**: Universal Pictures, July 28. 134 minutes. **Notes**: A director's cut DVD was released December 12, 2006. 139 minutes.

Vice detectives Crockett and Tubbs must infiltrate an international drug trafficking organization to find out who leaked the identities of some murdered undercover FBI agents. This leads them to Yero, a middle manager in the organization who is charged with screening the pair, posing as drug transportation specialists, before they meet the top man, Montoya, a ruthless kingpin who hires them to transport some drugs from South America to Miami. Crockett begins an affair with Montoya's banker and lover, Isabella. But Yero observes Crockett and Isabella together and tells Montoya they are romantically involved. Isabella tells Montoya she is prepared to kill Crockett if their business with him does not go smoothly, and much of the film dwells on how this relationship, with its attendant peril for Crockett, plays out. Eventually, Montoya abandons Isabella and Yero brings her to a meet putatively where drugs and money are to be exchanged, but in reality where Crockett and Tubbs have been set up to be killed. During the ensuing shoot-out, Yero and his men are killed. Knowing their love is doomed, Crockett spirits Isabella away from the scene and puts her on a boat to her home in Cuba.

Michael Mann brings narratives with psychological edge and an existentialist's awareness of the vicissitudes of life to his films as well as to the television series he executive produced in the mid-1980s, *Miami Vice* and *Crime Story*. The theatrical film *Miami Vice* has bravura moments where state of the art cinematography is put in the service of style. Mann creates inventive aerial shots and exhilarating powerboat racing sequences in the Atlantic Ocean off Miami Beach that display Miami at its bedizened best. His well known command of detail and ability to choreograph action sequences with precision and verve are on full view here, though perhaps none achieve the emotional intensity of the shoot-outs that climax *Thief* (1981) and *Heat* (1995), two of Mann's most accomplished efforts.

Thematically, much of Mann's work concerns the problematic nature of living authentically, a thread that runs throughout neo-noir from *Point Blank* to *Memento* and gives *Miami Vice* its neo-noir edge. Crockett and Tubbs' quest for the source of the leak that has led to the death of two undercover FBI agents is essentially an inconsequential plot device Mann uses for setting the film's action in motion and giving Crockett and Tubbs something to do. At this point, *Miami Vice* becomes a film not only about a particular mission, but also one about undercover police work in its most risky and terrifying entirety.

Mann's engagement with the patterns of contingency in which undercover work is inevitably enmeshed shows how variegated these can be, and this, too, is an indication of his neo-noir sensibility at work. By tracing the steps Crockett and Tubbs must take to infiltrate a multi-billion dollar drug trafficking operation, Mann adds drama to the inherently ambiguous situation they face when they try to internalize their fabricated identities and somehow recover their authentic selves once the assignment is over. When Crockett begins an affair with Isabella (played by Chinese femme fatale actress Gong Li), a target of his investigation, he finds it increasingly difficult to draw the line between his fabricated and true identity. It is as if he is in flight from his authentic self. He must make an existential choice, and in putting her out of harm's way he gives up any hope of a future with her. *Miami Vice* shows the risk of being trapped inside the role dictated by one's undercover masquerade as well as the psychological cost that comes with the need to perpetually suppress and recover one's true identity. Unfortunately, the depiction of searing moments of self-disclosure between Crockett and Tubbs, so prominent in the television series, is not substantially developed here. Ultimately, we are left to question whether Crockett and Tubbs are reducible to what they do, or whether each has an inexpressible and perhaps inexplicable self. **SMS**

MIKE'S MURDER (1984)

Director, Screenplay, Producer: James Bridges. **Director of Photography**: Reynaldo Villalobos. **Original Music**: Joe Jackson. **Production Designer**: Peter Jamison. **Editor**: Dede Allen. **Cast**: Debra Winger (Betty Parrish), Mark Keyloun (Mike Chuhutsky), Darrell Larson (Pete), Paul Winfield (Phillip), Brooke Alderson (Patty), Robert Crosson (Sam). **Released**: The Ladd Group/Warner Bros., March 9. 109 minutes.

Betty Parish is a love struck bank teller desiring another date with Mike Chuhutsky, a handsome but unreliable southern California tennis coach, petty thief, and cocaine dealer. After an opening flashback montage where Betty dreams of their previous lovemaking, the film flashes forward three months to Mike narrowly escaping a drug deal gone wrong. He hides out at photographer buddy Sam's house and then bums a ride with Betty to wealthy record producer Phillip's mansion, promising he will take her on another date. Betty discusses her frustrations with friend Patty while Mike gets deeper into trouble, stealing a portion of the cocaine he and his partner

Pete deliver to powerful L.A. dealers. Pete drops him off outside his apartment complex, where Mike is escorted upstairs and brutally murdered. Sam calls Betty, telling her the news, and after viewing photos Sam has taken of Mike and Betty playing tennis, she decides to investigate Mike's murder. Betty meets gay producer Phillip who confirms that he fell in love with Mike during Mike's unsuccessful bisexuality experiment. Pete, realizing Mike is dead, goes on the lam, eventually trapping Betty in her home, until hired killers track and kill him, just before he can fatally harm Betty. Betty ends the film alone, with black and white photos of herself and Mike, playing the scales on her newly tuned piano.

Mike's Murder is a minor neo-noir. Despite a talented director and pop/jazz music by Joe Jackson that creates a noir mood, *Mike's Murder* is merely a partially successful genre hybrid of love story, detective film, film noir, and woman-in-peril thriller. The film imitates stylistic devices from the classic noir period in its use of Dutch angles, Venetian blinds for chiaroscuro effects, mirror shots reflecting psychological questions of identity, and heavy shadows within numerous night shots. Yet, once Mike is murdered, the film focuses on Pete, who is too unstable for some of his noir dialogue to be effective. Pete offers social class analysis to justify his crimes against the dealers he has ripped off: "Do you know how much they have? How well they live? Do you know how much I have? How I live?" He is self-aware enough to realize that everyone believes "he's not good enough" but craftily intuits that "the good are guilty too." Yet the audience is so alienated by his sweaty, unpredictable, and sleazy behavior that his insightful dialogue is easily dismissed.

Paul Winfield and Debra Winger might also have had more screen time together as their scenes convey power through both high quality acting and more fully embodied characters who each have been betrayed by their romantic beliefs in love and Mike's charisma. The ultimate success of this film is that it introduces the first of many hardboiled roles for Debra Winger who finished the 1980s with similar roles in *Black Widow* (1987), *Betrayed* (1988), and *Everybody Wins* (1990). Despite Linda Mizejewski's claim that Winger is a "lower-voltage Jodie Foster" (*Hardboiled and High Heeled*), Winger's tough, loner investigator is the model that so many others imitate in this now popular character role from within female-centered neo-noir filmmaking. **WC**

THE MONEY TRAP (1965)

Director: Burt Kennedy. **Screenplay**: Walter Bernstein from a book by Lionel White. **Producers**: David Karr, Max E. Youngstein. **Director of Photography**: Paul Vogel. **Music**: Hal Schaefer. **Art Directors**: Carl Anderson, George W. Davis. **Editor**: John McSweeney, Jr. **Cast**: Glenn Ford (Joe Baron), Elke Sommer (Lisa Baron), Rita Hayworth (Rosalie Kelly), Joseph Cotten (Dr. Horace Van Tilden), Ricardo Montalban (Pete Delanos), Tom Reese (Matthews), James Mitchum (Detective Wolski), Argentina Brunetti (Aunt), Fred Essler (Mr. Klein). **Locations**: Hancock Park, Mount Olympus and Angel's Flight, Los Angeles. **Released**: MGM, February 2. 91 minutes.

L.A. detective Joe Baron fears that his wife Lisa will leave him if he cannot maintain their Hollywood Hills lifestyle, now that her father's estate is no longer paying dividends.

The Money Trap: *Glenn Ford as Joe Baron.*

Joe and his partner Pete Delanos are barely consulted when the wealthy Dr. Van Tilden is presumed innocent in the death of Phil Kenny, a burglar shot while robbing an empty safe. Before Phil dies, he tells Joe about a missing half of a million dollars. Kenny's widow turns out to be Rosalie, Joe's old girlfriend fallen on hard times. Pete now reveals that he's been following Joe and wants to partner with him to rob Van Tilden. They conclude that Dr. Van Tilden has mob connections and that Phil was secretly working for him. Rosalie dies after being pushed from the roof of a building. Pete and Joe blow Van Tilden's safe but a shootout leaves Pete badly wounded. Half of the loot is in heroin, which Joe trades to Van Tilden for medical attention for Pete. Pete dies anyway; Joe shoots Van Tilden and his murderous associate Matthews. Wounded, Joe leaves the doctor in the street with the heroin, returns home and asks Lisa to call an ambulance.

In *The Money Trap* writer Walter Bernstein sums up the concerns of 1950s thrillers and adds a bitter, unsubtle criticism of American values. As in Joseph Losey's *The Prowler,* a middle class cop compromises everything to secure the California dream: a trophy wife, and a ranch house with a pool. One of the last of the B&W studio films, this relatively inexpensive production employs an all-star cast of faded noir notables, reuniting Ford and Hayworth twenty years after their pairing in *Gilda.*

Director Burt Kennedy gives the film a standard noir look lacking in visual stylization, leaving Glenn Ford on his own to express Joe Baron's disillusion. Rich crooks like Dr. Van Tilden get a free ride through the justice system while Joe and Pete must track down a poor man who murdered his wife because she turned to prostitution to keep her family together. Similarly, Joe surrenders his principles when he chooses becoming a rogue cop over losing his upscale lifestyle. Hayworth's Rosalie reminds Joe of romantic roads not taken, while he worries that his wife is attracted to other men. Allied with the greedy Pete Delanos, Joe quickly falls into a trap of his own devising. Like robber Johnny Clay watching the money blow away in *The Killing,* also from a source novel by Lionel White, Joe can only return home and wait for the police to arrive, contemplating the petty luxuries he threw his life away to keep. **GE**

THE MORNING AFTER (1986)

Director: Sidney Lumet. **Screenplay**: James Cresson (as James Hicks). **Producers**: Bruce Gilbert, Louis Bonfiglio, Wolfgang Glattes (American Filmworks, Lorimar Productions). **Director of Photography**: Andrzej Bartkowiak. **Music**: Paul Chihara. **Art Director**: Kandy Stern. **Editor**: Joel Goodman. **Cast**: Jane Fonda (Alex Sternberg), Jeff Bridges (Turner Kendall), Raul Julia (Joaquin Romero), Diane Salinger (Isabel Harding), Richard Foronjy (Sgt. Greenbaum), Geoffrey Scott (Bobby Korschak), James Haake (Frankie), Kathleen Wilhoite (Red), Don Hood (Hurley), Michael Prince (Judge Harding), Frances Bergen (Mrs. Harding). **Released**: 20th Century-Fox, December 25. 103 minutes.

Alex Sternberg, a failed actress and drunk, wakes up with a hangover to discover she is in bed next to a dead man with a knife in his chest. She flees in panic, fails to get a flight as it's Thanksgiving, returning instead (thanks to a lift from Turner Kendall, an ex-cop) to clean up the loft where the stabbing took place. That night (after Turner has cooked her a makeshift Thanksgiving dinner) the corpse turns up in her apartment. She is now identified as the prime suspect, because of a record of violence when drunk, so she hides out in Turner's apartment, but her estranged husband Joaquin persuades Alex that it is the ex-cop who is trying to set her up. Actually, it's Joaquin himself, covering for his WASP bride-to-be Isabel, who was being blackmailed by the dead man. However when the police arrive Isabel accuses Joaquin and as she is the daughter of a judge, he is arrested.

Sydney Lumet has a distinguished record (four Best Director Oscar nominations) but *The Morning After* is not one of his best movies. He describes it in the commentary on the DVD as a "melodrama," and apparently only made the movie since Fonda brought him the script and he had worked extensively with her father. The plot is implausible with some key twists not fully explained, and the writing variable: Fonda is given some wisecrack lines that don't work well in the context, and at times she overacts extravagantly (though not enough to prevent an Oscar Best Actress nomination). Jeff Bridges shuffles amiably and laconically through the piece. But there are some interesting subtexts that are only hinted at.

Set in Los Angeles, the city itself becomes a protagonist: in his commentary Lumet talks of the light and color that characterize LA, and the movie flouts noir convention with its intense lighting and primary colors. It touches on Hollywood itself (Fonda's washed-up actress has hints of "Baby Jane," and at one point she says "I could have been a contender . . ."), and it is surely no accident that both Fonda and Bridges come from Hollywood dynasties. There's also an undercurrent reflecting LA's ethnic and cultural diversity, which demonstrates the limits on minorities' capacity to reach the top. Turner constantly offers pithy, vaguely racist analyses of the city's ethnic groups ("What are you, a Klan anthropologist?" Alex asks him). Joaquin confesses that he only wants to marry Isabel to gain access to the clout that comes from a WASP family of impeccable "early American" breeding. It's Joaquin's word against Isabel's about who is guilty, and as Turner says, "Who do you think they're gonna believe: her or a guy named Joaquin Romero?" Perhaps inevitably the movie confirms Hollywood's insatiable desire for happy endings. **GF**

MS. 45 (1981)

Director: Abel Ferrara. **Screenplay**: Nicholas St. John. **Producer**: Rochelle Weisberg. **Director of Photography**: James Lemmo [as James Momel]. **Art Director**: Ruben Masters. **Music**: Joe Delia. **Editor**: Christopher Andrews. **Cast**: Zoe Tamerlis-Lund (Thana), Albert Sinkys (Albert, the Boss), Darlene Stuto (Laurie), Helen McGara (Carol), Nike Zachmanoglou (Pamela), Abel Ferrara as Jimmie Laine (First Rapist), Peter Yellen (The Burglar), Editta Sherman (Landlady), S. Edward Singer (The Photographer), Stanley Timms (The Pimp). **Released**: Navaron/Rochelle, April 24. 80 minutes.

Thana is an introverted, mute seamstress who works for a garment district designer. While walking home one night, Thana is raped by a masked assailant and then when returning to her apartment she is again attacked, this time by a burglar. During the attempted rape, she grabs a glass paperweight and smashes the burglar in the head with it. Disposing of the burglar's body, she keeps his gun. These two events change Thana. She becomes more aggressive and outgoing in her manner and dress. She takes to the streets with gun in hand and begins eliminating men she considers abusive. In the final scene, she attends a party given by her boss who tries to molest her. His actions trigger her murderous impulses once again and she initiates a shooting rampage until she is stabbed by one of her co-workers—Laurie.

Ms. 45 (1981), directed by independent neo-noir filmmaker Abel Ferrara, traces the character trajectory of a young mute seamstress who after two brutal attacks transforms herself from submissive victim to avenging angel (one of the film's aliases is *Angel of Vengeance*). Thana is played by writer-actress Zoe Tamerlis-Lund (who collaborated with Ferrara on several scripts, including *Bad Lieutenant*) with a sultry vulnerability. She is, at least initially, submissive to her boss, dedicated to her tedious work, and emotionally isolated from her co-workers, even when they try to be solicitous towards her. She lives alone in small Eastside apartment, observed closely by a nosy landlady. Thana's appearance and facial expression connote "victim," e.g., her large, vulnerable eyes; her habitual expression of fear and anxiety; her frumpy clothes. And although her inability to speak is never explained, there are brief visual and audio references to a childhood event, traumatic enough to have caused a form of hysterical muteness.

It is ironically the two initial acts of violence against Thana, as brutal as they are, which become the sources of empowerment for this alienated, conflicted woman. After the shock of the events wears off, Thana the warrior bursts forth from her cocoon. At work she begins to rebel against her boss in a very passive-aggressive manner. She also begins going out with her female co-workers with whom she forms a bond, no matter how delicate.

Visually Ferrara externalizes Thana's newly found sense of control and power by her clothes and make-up. She begins to dress more colorfully, favoring black and reds. She wears boots, berets, trench coats. She paints her lips deep red and her eyeliner is black, much to the dismay of her interfering landlady. Alongside this physical makeover comes a psychological one as Thana begins to haunt the streets for abusive males to eliminate with the gun she has taken from the dead burglar who attacked her.

Ferrara portrays the men in this film as almost universally abusive and deceptive. They are double-dealing photographers who seduce women through the use of their cameras; they are pimps who beat their sex workers; they are local hoods who surround and then rape lone women in the park. Thana "takes back the night" for all the women who are too afraid to walk the streets. She executes the wrongdoers and then returns to her home, filled with a sense of accomplishment.

Ultimately, of course, this path of violence exacts its psychological toll on Thana as she begins to form an erotic attachment to the act itself. Before the climactic Halloween party Thana puts together a costume right out of fetish magazines, a dominatrix nun with black boots and stockings who conceals a pistol in her thigh highs. She sits before the mirror in her room, posing with the gun, in an obvious homage to Scorsese's *Taxi Driver*. At the party her boss falls at her feet and licks her boots as she pulls out her gun and begins to eliminate all the men in the room, including him. She seems unstoppable, lost in an orgasmic fury of violence. But she *is* stopped. As Ferrara points out in interviews, politically only a woman could and should "bring her down." As one of her co-workers, Laurie, takes a knife and stabs Thana, she turns to her like a lost child and, refusing to fire her gun, she falls to the bloodied floor in slow motion. **JU**

MULHOLLAND DRIVE (2001)

Director: David Lynch. **Screenplay**: David Lynch. **Producers**: Neal Edelstein, Joyce Eliason, Tony Krantz, Michael Polaire, Alain Sarde, Mary Sweeney, John Wentworth. **Director of Photography**: Peter Deming. **Production Designer**: Jack Fisk. **Music**: Angelo Badalamenti. **Editor**: Mary Sweeney. **Cast**: Naomi Watts (Diane Selwyn/Betty Elms), Laura Harring (Camilla/Rita), Ann Miller (Coco), Dan Hedaya (Vincenzo Castigliane), Justin Theroux (Adam Kesher), Robert Forster (Detective Harry McKnight), Katharine Towne (Cynthia Jenzen), Lee Grant (Louise Bonner), Billy Ray Cyrus (Gene), Chad Everett (Jimmy Katz). **Released**: Asymmetrical/Alain Sarde/Canal +, October 12. 145 minutes.

Mulholland Drive tells two stories simultaneously—one real, one a dream. In both the protagonist is Diane Selwyn (Betty in the dream) who is a struggling actress from the Mid-West in love with femme fatale Camilla (Rita in the dream).

Mulholland Drive: *Camilla/Rita (Laura Harring) and Diane Selwyn/Betty Elms (Naomi Watts).*

Camilla betrays Diane with the director Adam Kesher who is having trouble financing his new film. In revenge Diane hires a hit man to murder Camilla. In her dream state, Diane as Betty arrives in Hollywood to stay in her aunt's apartment. There she meets an amnesiac femme fatale—Camilla as Rita. Rita had stumbled into the apartment after an accident on Mulholland Drive. Becoming lovers, Betty and Rita try to put together clues to Rita's identity which, ultimately, lead them to Diane Selwyn and her dead body.

Mulholland Drive is present-day Hollywood in the final stages of decay. It is the most caustic attack on the ethos of Hollywood since Nathaniel West's bitter narrative *The Day of the Locust*. As in West's novel, director David Lynch turns Hollywood into a surreal nightmare of greed, lust, betrayal, jealousy, and hypocrisy, and of course noir dystopia.

The film is the story of struggling actress Diane Selwyn who, like the protagonists in other Lynch films such as *Lost Highway*, leads a schizophrenic life: half-real, half-dream. In the early part of the movie the audience sees Diane (in her dream form "Betty") arriving at LAX from the "heartland." She is full of middle-American aspirations and naiveté ("Of course I'd rather be known as a great actress than a movie star. But, you know, sometimes people end up being both. So that is, I guess you'd say, sort of why I came here").

Staying in her aunt's Spanish stucco apartment, "Betty" becomes involved with a classic femme fatale—"Rita," who has been in an accident on Mulholland Drive and wandered in a daze into the courtyard apartment of "Betty's" aunt. "Rita" is clearly the reincarnation of Rita Hayworth in *Gilda*, a poster for which she sees before assuming the name of "Rita" (she suffers from amnesia). Her sultry looks and voluptuous figure are irresistible to the innocent "Betty," and they become lovers. In the dream form of this relationship the love is as tender as in any pulp romantic novel. "Betty" then takes the lead as she assists her amnesiac lover in her search for her true identity.

But when the film relocates from dream life to Diane's real life in the last part of the movie, the audience realizes that "Rita," whose real name is Camilla, is the actually the dominant one. Camilla taunts her ex-lover Diane with her new fiancé, the director Adam Kesher, as well as other female lovers, at a party. Diane retreats again into her dream world, which is much more comforting, as the two lovers, like girlfriends in a Nancy Drew mystery, go hunting for the "key," literally and figuratively in this case, to the crime seen at the beginning of the movie, and in the process become inseparable.

Diane has created her own neo-noir movie in her head, not much worse or much better than the average Hollywood fare: filled with suspense, a mysterious and beautiful love object, and unexplained plot points. When, *Alice in Wonderland*-like, the insertion of an enigmatic blue key drives Diane back into reality, her final sexual encounter with Camilla has none of the tenderness of her dream sex scenes. Instead it is filled with anger and frustration as she claws at her lover, almost raping her, before Camilla forces her to stop.

The ever-creative Diane then concocts another bit of Hollywood drama by hiring a hit man to eliminate Camilla, but it is too late. Her loss and guilt results in a figurative self-immolation and the inevitable headlines which proclaim a "true" Hollywood story: "Starlet found dead in quaint historical Hollywood apartment." Lynch returns to the opening image of the movie—the decaying body of a woman, Diane herself—and adds a layer of irony by superimposing overexposed shots of "Betty" and "Rita" laughing and smiling, blissfully happy in Diane's own personal Hollywood movie. **JU**

MULHOLLAND FALLS (1996)

Director: Lee Tamahori. **Screenplay**: Peter Dexter based on a story by Peter Dexter, Floyd Mutrux. **Producers**: Richard D. Zanuck, Lili Fini Zanuck. **Director of Photography**: Haskell Wexler. **Music**: Dave Grusin. **Production Designer**: Richard Sylbert. **Editor**: Sally Menke. **Cast**: Nick Nolte (Max Hoover), Melanie Griffith (Katherine Hoover), Chazz Palminteri (Elleroy Coolidge), Michael Madsen (Eddie Hall), Chris Penn (Arthur Relyea), Treat Williams (Col. Nathan Fitzgerald), Jennifer Connelly (Allison Pond), Daniel Baldwin (McCafferty), Andrew McCarthy (Jimmy Fields), John Malkovich (Gen. Thomas Timms). **Locations**: Desert Hot Springs, Los Angeles, Malibu, California; Wendover, Utah. **Released**: MGM, April 26. 107 minutes.

After an opening sequence that appears to be home movies of a social get-together, a military base, and then a sexual tryst between Allison and Timms, Allison's body turns up at an L.A. construction site. Max and his partners, Elleroy, Eddie, and Arthur, detectives in a well-dressed, brutal, elite pre-Miranda police squad, investigate the murder. Max also had an affair with Allison. The investigation leads to her best friend Jimmy, and then to Timms, the head of the nascent Atomic Energy Commission. Allison discovered, and filmed on a home movie camera, a hospital housing radiation-sick men while visiting Timms. Max and Elleroy realize that an overzealous military man (Fitzgerald) pushed her out of a plane, viewing her as a national security risk. In an ensuing mid-air battle, Fitzgerald is pushed out of the plane, Elleroy and the pilot are shot, and the plane crashes. Although a nuclear bomb test is imminent, the film ends not with an explosion but with the funeral of Elleroy and with Katherine, Max's wife, leaving him, having discovered the affair between Max and Allison.

Nuclear noir has a venerable tradition, including *The House on 92nd Street* (1945), *D.O.A.* (1949), and the much praised and analyzed *Kiss Me Deadly* (1955). All these films imbue the secrecy surrounding nuclear research and weaponry with fear and dread. *Mulholland Falls*, a retro-noir set in the 1950s, has been maligned as "numbskull noir" and even "Chinatown for chowder heads." While it also centers on a nuclear mystery, it fails to live up to its predecessors. Directed by New Zealander Tamahori, who also directed *Once Were Warriors* (1994), featuring gorgeous cinematography and painstakingly recreated 1950s locales and costuming, starring capable actors, and drawing on a rich noir canon, it still falls flat.

Like many classic noirs, it features a wife, Katherine, and a dangerous dame. As usual, the wife survives, and the dangerous dame, Allison, is murdered, ostensibly for the minor act of taking home movies of a military hospital. After solving her murder and thereby exposing the deadly secret, Max ignores it, in no way acknowledging that the larger crime, the hundreds of soldiers sick and dying because of nuclear testing, remains an issue. Max's home life has been destroyed by his affair with Allison, but his professional life remains relatively unscathed, although his squad disbands after the death of Elleroy. As Timms explains to Max, both men are connected by an ethos that suggests certain people are allowed, even expected, to subvert the law in search of a greater good. Timms parallels his murder and maiming of soldiers in nuclear experiments with Max's lawless brand of justice. He establishes his moral right to do what he does and insists Max exercises the same right; Max, and the narrative itself, tacitly accepts Timms' assessment. Two white men both feel justified in their abuse of humanity. Max's power lies in his physical strength and muscularity as well as his position as the right hand of law and order. Timms' strength lies in his knowledge of the ultimate form of muscularity, the destructive potential of nuclear weapons, and in his position as the right hand of military might. Allison's death—the death of a beautiful, pliable sexual toy—at least arouses remorse in both men, but the nuclear secret barely arouses anything. **JBW**

MURDER IN THE FIRST (1995)

Director: Marc Rocco. **Screenplay**: Dan Gordon. **Director of Photography**: Fred Murphy. **Music**: Christopher Young. **Editor**: Fred Livingstone. **Art Director**: Michael Rizzo. **Cast**: Christian Slater (James Stamphill), Kevin Bacon (Henri Young), Gary Oldman (Associate Warden Milton Glenn), Embeth Davidtz (Mary McCasslin), William H. Macy (D.A. William McNeil), Stephen Tobolowsky (Mr. Henkin), Brad Dourif (Byron Stamphill), R. Lee Ermey (Judge Clawson), Mia Kirshner (adult Rosetta Young), Ben Slack (Jerry Hoolihan), Stefan Gierasch (Warden James Humson), Kyra Sedgwick (Blanche), David Sterling (Rufus "Ray" McCain). **Released**: Warner Bros Pictures, January 20. 122 minutes.

In 1941 freshman lawyer James Stamphill is handed the case of Henri Young, who killed a fellow inmate at the infamous Alcatraz prison. As Stamphill learns more about what everyone tells him is an unwinnable case, he discovers the truth about the appalling conditions in the penitentiary. Sent to Alcatraz in 1938 for stealing $5 to feed his starving sister, Young took part in an unsuccessful escape attempt. Betrayed by another escapee who tipped off the associate warden in exchange for leniency, Young spends three years in solitary confinement. After his release Young immediately kills the inmate who betrayed him. Stamphill argues that the Alcatraz prison officials facilitated Young's act through the inhumane treatment to which them subjected him, and thus must be considered co-conspirators to the crime. In this highly publicized case, Stamphill faces the challenges of a political system ill-inclined to tarnish the reputation of Alcatraz and a nearly catatonic defendant who has lost all hope of justice. The jury finds Young not guilty of first-degree murder, and submits a petition to investigate "crimes against humanity" committed at Alcatraz. As the prison becomes the target of an official inquiry, Henri Young is found dead in his cell.

Murder in the First: *James Stamphill (Christian Slater) and Henri Young (Kevin Bacon).*

Based on a true story, *Murder in the First* was one of several prison films to appear during the mid-1990s, though somewhat overshadowed by higher-profile releases like *The Shawshank Redemption* (1994) and *Dead Man Walking* (1995). Amalgamating a long cinematic tradition probing corruption in the penal system, *Murder in the First* presents a Depression-era story inflected with several key noir motifs, notably alienation, corruption, cruelty and revenge. Jules Dassin's *Brute Force* (1947) is perhaps the most obvious noir reference for this film, with the brutality of Associate Warden Glenn reminiscent of the fascistic sadism of *Brute Force*'s Captain Munsey. While the prisoners in Dassin's film know why they are there, Young's petty crime and subsequent escape attempt seem trivial compared to the wrath that rains down upon him in Alcatraz. Yet it is the utter neglect of Warden Humson, who was rarely on the premises and thus unaware of what was happening in his own prison, which renders Young's case an example of more systemic abuse. Young's alienation is graphically conveyed in an almost Kafkaesque manner through the dark, wet and claustrophobic scenes in the "dungeons" of Alcatraz, where the disoriented prisoner struggles to keep track of time while the guards ignore his pleas to tell him how long he's been there. All of this underscores the pervasive hypocrisy of social institutions that preach religion while torturing inmates, speak of family values while neglecting those in their care, and celebrate the virtues of "the American way" while behaving like the very Nazis the country is about to fight. **CF**

NARROW MARGIN (1990)

Director: Peter Hyams. **Screenplay**: Peter Hyams based on the screenplay by Earl Felton. **Producers**: Jerry Offsay, Jonathan Zimbert. **Director of Photography**: Peter Hyams. **Music**: Bruce Broughton. **Production Designer**: Joel Schiller. **Editors**: Beau Barthel, James Mitchell. **Cast**: Gene Hackman (Robert Caulfield), Anne Archer (Carol Hunnicut), James Sikking (Nelson), J.T. Walsh (Michael Tarlow), M. Emmet Walsh (Sergeant Benti), Susan Hogan (Kathryn Weller), Nigel Bennett (Jack Wooton). **Released**: TriStar, September 21. 97 minutes.

Out on a blind date in Los Angeles, Carol reluctantly agrees to go to Tarlow's hotel room before heading off for dinner. While she is in the bathroom, he is visited by mob boss Watts, whom he has cheated. Carol witnesses Tarlow shot dead and, although she returns home, she immediately flees, hoping to evade any resulting police investigation. But she tells her roommate. Deputy District Attorney Caulfield suspects that Tarlow was killed by Watts, whom he is out to convict, and, when he discovers evidence suggesting the presence of a witness in the man's apartment, quickly discovers the woman's identity and the location of the cabin which is her remote wilderness hiding place. Arriving there with his partner, Sgt. Benti, Caulfield tries to persuade Carol to return to L.A.; their discussion is interrupted by the arrival of a helicopter full of mob hit men who riddle the cabin with bullets, killing Benti. Carol and Caulfield escape by SUV down the mountain road, pursued by the helicopter, and board a passenger train, along with, as it turns out, the killers. The remainder of the film's action takes place on the train as the two killers play a deadly game of cat and mouse with Caulfield in an attempt to eliminate Carol, whom they have never seen clearly and therefore cannot identify easily. The climactic sequence takes place on the roof of the car when the remaining killer is decapitated as the train enters a tunnel. Carol is delivered to the authorities, the traitor within Caulfield's office is identified, and in the trial scene coda Watts is convicted and sent to prison.

Unlike the Richard Fleischer 1952 original, from which it draws its basic premise (a mental but minimally physical battle waged in the narrow confines of a passenger train), Peter Hyams' film is a heart-stopping actioner with several elaborately staged and edited violent sequences. Unlike her model in the original (a gangster's moll), Carol is a respectable woman, reluctant to perform her civic duty only because she comes to suspect, and with good reason, that the police cannot protect her from Watts. As the protagonist, Hackman provides the film with its passion and energy. Somewhat world-weary, like his counterpart in the Fleischer version (played by Charles McGraw), Caulfield carefully negotiates his way through the dangers posed by deceptive

appearances. He cannot be sure if his fellow passengers are simply ordinary folk or Watt's hirelings. Caulfield meets one woman who seems merely desperately lonely, but turns out to be one of the killers. That he is betrayed, though not fatally, by someone in his own office evokes the persistent difficulty in the noir universe of telling the difference between those who are on your side and those who intend you harm. **RBP**

NEW JACK CITY (1991)

Director: Mario Van Peebles. **Screenplay**: Thomas Lee Wright and Barry Michael Cooper based on a story by Thomas Lee Wright. **Producers**: George Jackson, Doug McHenry, Preston L. Holmes (co-producer). **Director of Photography**: Francis Kenny. **Music**: Vassal Benford, Michel Colombier. **Production Designer**: Charles C. Bennett. **Editor**: Steven Kemper. **Cast**: Wesley Snipes (Nino Brown), Ice-T (Scotty Appleton), Allen Payne (Gee Money), Chris Rock (Pookie), Mario Van Peebles (Stone), Michael Michele (Selina), Bill Nunn (Duh Duh Duh Man), Russell Wong (Park), Bill Cobbs (Old Man), Christopher Williams (Kareem Akbar), Judd Nelson (Nick Peretti), Vanessa Williams (Keisha), Tracy Camilla Johns (Uniqua), Anthony DeSando (Frankie Needles), Nick Ashford (Reverend Oates), Phyllis Yvonne Stickney (Prosecuting Attorney Hawkins). **Released**: Warner Bros., March 6. 93 minutes.

Nino Brown presides over the rise of a crack empire in late-1980s New York City. With ordinary police efforts stymied, Stone recruits Appleton and Peretti to lead a special task force to bring down Nino and the Cash Money Brothers. Part of their plan includes placing recovering addict Pookie inside the CMB organization to gather evidence. But when Pookie has a relapse and is discovered, he is killed and the task force is shut down. Appleton and Peretti then go under-

New Jack City: *Detectives Nick Paretti (Judd Nelson) and Scotty Appleton (Ice-T).*

cover themselves in an attempt to bring Nino to justice. When Nino is finally arrested and brought to trial, he attempts to implicate another member of the CMB as the real leader, so the district attorney makes him a deal for a reduced sentence in exchange for his testimony. Leaving the courtroom, Nino is shot dead by an old man from the neighborhood where the CMB first exercised its corruption.

The "dark world" here is not so much about police corruption, but about the corruption of entire neighborhoods by the allure of easy money offered by crack dealers. Indeed, one might be surprised that the corruption of law enforcement doesn't figure in this at all. But the story is gripping and dark, with well-executed action sequences, realistic "gangsta" dialogue, surprising plot twists, and extreme use of noir's trademark unusual and unsettling photography. It updates the 1930s-era gangster movie to the late 1980s, but with knowing references to its ancestors, both in the filmmaking and within the narrative: Nino and Appleton reflect on George Raft, Nino and Gee Money watch *Scarface* repeatedly.

Some critics dismissed *New Jack City* as an updated "blaxploitation" film, but this criticism is superficial. The multiracial task force, and their observation that crack doesn't discriminate, undermines this to some extent, but more importantly, the mere presence of African-Americans in several leading roles doesn't make it "blaxploitation." Besides being unfairly dismissive of some very powerful performances, including a surprisingly good dramatic turn by comic Chris Rock, this criticism neglects the truly disturbing camera work and successful updating of the classic gangster drama to a modern setting. Nino's final betrayal of Gee Money is moving without being manipulative, and the twist murder of Nino is simultaneously satisfying and troubling. On the other hand, revealing Nino to be the one who, years earlier, had murdered Appleton's mother, is an extra which might be considered a little bit over the top. But all in all, Mario Van Peeples' directorial debut is an excellent crime drama. **AJS**

THE NICKEL RIDE (1975)

Director/Producer: Robert Mulligan. **Screenplay**: Eric Roth. **Executive Producers**: David Foster, Lawrence Turman. **Director of Photography**: Jordan Cronenweth. **Music**: Dave Grusin. **Art Director**: Larry Paull. **Editor**: O. Nicholas Brown. **Cast**: Jason Miller (Cooper), Linda Haynes (Sarah), Victor French (Paddie), John Hillerman (Carl), Bo Hopkins (Turner), Richard Evans (Bobby), Brendan Burns (Larry), Lou Frizzell (Paulie), Jeanne Lange (Jeannie), Bart Burns (Elias), Harvey Gold (Chester), Mark Gordon (Tonozzi). **Released**: 20th Century-Fox, November 15. 114 minutes.

Cooper is a low-level, "old school" gangster whose style the new syndicate higher-ups disdain. Presently these bosses are annoyed that Cooper has not closed a deal for an abandoned warehouse where the mob can cache stolen goods. They assign Turner to keep an eye on Cooper. When the warehouse deal falls through, Cooper has vivid fantasies in which he imagines murderous assaults by Turner. Cooper sends his girlfriend Sarah away and confronts his immediate superior, who denies any plan to rub him out. That evening Turner walks in and shoots Cooper, who nonetheless manages to strangle Turner. The next morning Cooper's body is found sitting on a bench. His huge ring of keys falls from his hand to the pavement.

The Nickel Ride is an early neo-noir portrait of a criminal who has outlived his time and is no longer in tune with his "corporation." Like many classic period figures or the characters adapted from "Richard Stark" novels in *Point Blank* and *The Outfit*, Cooper is a throwback, a man whose sense of self and whose existential angst ebb and flow with the respect he commands from others. Although the people on his home turf still support and even admire him, some of them have heard that "Coop" is on his way out. This murkiness of Cooper's troubles, his bewilderment and growing paranoia because he knows how "these things" can be arranged, follow a direct line from a classic period personality like Shubunka in *The Gangster*. Jason Miller's portrayal of the local capo is typically brooding yet contemplative. Given a character who has always been able to hold his life together by the sheer force of his personality, Miller plays him as a man who is perceptive enough to sense change but possibly potent enough to resist. Of course, like Shubunka, he is not that powerful.

Unlike John Boorman in *Point Blank,* director Robert Mulligan eschews any fractured narrative in favor of performance. Cinematographer Jordan Cronenweth's scheme for the color photography in the city sequences is grainy and nearly colorless and aptly types Cooper's neighborhood as a small and inconsequential part of a large city. It is obvious that the territory was never a prime location and, like him, it has grown old without prospering. The fantasy sequences of paranoia and violence are shot in the same style and integrated into the film as if they were actual plot developments. So until they are over, the viewer co-experiences the same shaken relief and yet continuing terror of a man who is losing his grip on his destiny. **EM & AS**

NIGHT AND THE CITY (1992)

Director: Irwin Winkler. **Screenplay**: Richard Price based on the novel by Gerald Kersh. **Producers**: Jane Rosenthal and Winkler. **Executive Producers**: Harry and Mary Jane Ufland (Penta Entertainment). **Director of Photography**: Tak Fujimoto. **Production Designer**: Peter Larkin. **Music**: James Newton Howard. **Editor**: David Brenner. **Cast**: Robert De Niro (Harry Fabian), Jessica Lange (Helen Nasseros), Cliff Gorman (Phil Nasseros), Jack Warden (Al Grossman), Alan King (Ira "Boom Boom" Grossman) Eli Wallach (Peck), Barry Primus (Tommy Tessler). **Released**: 20th Century-Fox, October 11. 105 minutes.

This neo-Harry Fabian is a cheap-talking ambulance chaser, specializing in large complaints and small settlements. Like her predecessor, the neo-Helen Nasseros is hoping to escape a loveless marriage and pays Fabian with sex to help get the needed licenses for her own place. In this adaptation of Kersh's novel, Grossman, the sports promoter on whose territory Fabian attempts to encroach, controls low-end boxing, not wrestling, but most of the plot mechanics are the same: despite being sternly warned Fabian recruits Grossman's brother, who dies unexpectedly and leaves Fabian in deadly peril.

Superficially *Night and the City* is a straightforward remake moved from postwar London to contemporary New York. Its protagonist, Harry Fabian, is still a cheap hustler, still trying to muscle in on the fight game and conning money from Helen Nasseros with a forged liquor license. The changes, the missing characters, the rougher language, are relatively minor; but the tone is different. Widmark's Harry Fabian never was more than a hustler, an American in a strange country trying to turn a buck. De Niro's Fabian is an attorney who admits to chasing ambulances in his own neighborhood: "I never been out of New York practically. One time I was gonna move to L.A. I wanted to be a talent scout, but . . ." Where Widmark's character seemed trapped by circumstances of time and place and driven by a need to score big, De Niro's seems to be where he is by his own choice looking for an easy buck because it's easy. Both Fabians make the same play and appear to meet the same fate—except, of course, that this later Fabian is more like *Kiss of Death* in that he manages to survive. Dassin's last noir was made during his transition into blacklisted exile, and its brutality and violence were appropriate reflections on the underworld of noir and the over world of politics; but in this remake, the ironies, like the scams, are mostly off the mark. **AS**

NIGHT MOVES (1975)

Director: Arthur Penn. **Screenplay**: Alan Sharp. **Producer**: Robert M. Sherman. **Director of Photography**: Bruce Surtees. **Music**: Michael Small. **Production Designer**: George Jenkins. **Editor**: Dede Allen. **Cast**: Gene Hackman (Harry Moseby), Susan Clark (Ellen), Edward Binns (Ziegler), Harris Yulin (Marty Heller), Kenneth Mars (Nick), Janet Ward (Arlene Iverson), James Woods (Quentin), Anthony Costello (Marv Ellman), John Crawford (Tom Iverson), Melanie Grfffith (Delly Grastner), Jennifer Warren (Paula). **Released**: Warner Bros., July 2. 99 minutes.

Harry Moseby is a small-time private detective with an obsession for "finding out" things. He searched for his father for years, only to refuse at the last moment to see or speak to a man he neither knew nor loved. Harry is shattered when he discovers his wife is having an affair. Against this backdrop of his unhappy life, Harry is hired by an aging film star, Arlene, to find her runaway daughter, Delly. The actress only wants the girl back so she can continue to control her daughter's trust fund; and she suggests that a stepfather, Tom Iverson, has lured Delly to Florida. Harry first traces the wild and promiscuous Delly to a film location in the Southwest where she supposedly is living with a stunt pilot; but the girl is gone. Harry finds her at Tom Iverson's fishing cabin in the Florida Keys and Delly refuses to leave. Harry is attracted to Paula, Tom's mistress, and they begin an affair. Delly discovers the sunken, crashed plane of her stuntman lover while swimming and, horrified, agrees to return to her mother. Harry returns to his wife and takes Delly back to her Los Angeles home. The next day Delly is killed while filming a movie stunt. Harry watches the footage repeatedly and is convinced that she was murdered. Returning to Florida, he discovers that Iverson and Paula have committed several murders to cover up their smuggling of pre-Columbian art into the United States. After a fight, a chase, and a plane crash that kills the smugglers, a wounded Harry is left stranded and helpless in a motorboat, which runs in ever-widening circles.

The chief motivation behind the narrative structure of *Night Moves* is Harry Moseby's compulsive "need to know." But whereas this curiosity, combined with emotional detachment, was Philip Marlowe's strength, it is Harry's fatal flaw. The traditional detective derived his power not just from the ability to track one clue to the next but from the insight that enabled him to see the larger picture, to justify the sordidness of his

search by creating meaning out of mystery. In this sense, Harry is impotent. Times have changed since Marlowe and the Continental Op. Harry stands under the light of modern psychologizing; and what was once investigation is now recognized as cheap spying and a vicarious emotional life. Far from giving him power over the people he deals with, his aloofness leaves him weak, abandoned, and lonely. Harry resembles Delly; both suffer the same adolescent dilemma of being smart but not smart enough. The illusion that each can control his or her life, make choices, and impose meaning on other people's choices, obscures the one truth of their universe: that there is no truth and no amassing of evidence will make any difference. Knowledge is no longer power; the final image of the man trapped in a boat that travels in concentric circles around the site of a disaster caps the futility of Harry's life. **EM**

NO COUNTRY FOR OLD MEN (2007)

Directors/Producers: Ethan and Joel Coen. **Screenplay**: Coens based on the novel by Cormac McCarthy. **Producer**: Scott Rudin. **Director of Photography**: Roger Deakins. **Music**: Carter Burwell. **Production Designer**: Jess Gonchor. **Editors**: Joel and Ethan Coen [as Roderick Jaynes]. **Cast**: Josh Brolin (Llewelyn Moss), Tommy Lee Jones (Ed Tom Bell), Javier Bardem (Anton Chigurh), Woody Harrelson (Carson Wells), Kelly Macdonald (Carla Jean Moss), Garret Dillahunt (Wendell), Tess Harper (Loretta Bell), Barry Corbin (Ellis), Stephen Root (Wells' employer), Rodger Boyce (El Paso Sheriff), Beth Grant (Carla Jean's Mother), Ana Reeder (Woman by the pool). **Locations**: Marfa, Texas; Albuquerque, Santa Fe, Las Vegas, New Mexico. **Released**: Paramount Vantage, Novrember 9. 122 minutes.

Anton Chigurh kills a deputy and then a local motorist whose car he steals. Somewhere nearby, hunter Llewelyn Moss happens upon a group of corpses and cars. In one truck are a wounded man and a mass of heroin. In a satchel is a mass of money. After he initially abandons the man, Moss returns to find him dead and himself hunted. As he flees with his wife Carla, Moss doesn't realize there is an electronic device in the satchel that permits Chigurh and others to track him. Moss sends his wife to her mother's and holes up in a motel. He narrowly escapes a group of pursuers who are slaughtered by Chigurh. At a border hotel, Moss discovers the transponder moments before Chigurh arrives at his door. Both men are wounded in a gunfight, but Moss escapes to Mexico. In a hospital, another hired killer named Wells offers to spare

No Country for Old Men: *Javier Bardem as Anton Chigurh.*

Moss in exchange for the money. Back at the hotel, Chigurh is waiting for Wells, kills him, and takes a phone call from Moss, who rejects the killer's offer to spare Carla if he gets the money. Moss flees and without the transponder Chigurh cannot track the money. At Carla's request, Sheriff Bell goes to intercept Moss in El Paso but is too late: other drug dealers have killed him. Chigurh tracks Carla to her home and offers to let her call a coin flip to determine whether or not he will kill her. She refuses. When Chigurh leaves he is in a car accident. He buys a bicycle from a young passer-by and rides away before the police arrive.

Since their debut film *Blood Simple* the Coen brothers have maintained an on-going if somewhat tortuous relationship with noir. There are traces of it in their gangster pastiche *Miller's Crossing* (1990), *faux* Hollywood gothic *Barton Fink* (1991), and grisly crime comedies *Raising Arizona* (1987) and the break-through *Fargo* (1996). Even *The Big Lebowski* with its narrative core of mistaken identity throws a dark cloak around its humorously ill-fated protagonist. In terms of conscious nods to the classic period, few neo-noir efforts could claim to surpass *The Man Who Wasn't There* (2001), the Coens' unwieldy black-and-white mélange of Cain, Woolrich, and a hardboiled kitchen sink.

While it may not be far in terms of discordant monikers from Nirdlinger—the named lifted directly from Cain's *Double Indemnity* that adorns the department store in the *Man Who Wasn't There*—to the pitiless Anton Chigurh, the characters in *No Country for Old Men* are physically and figuratively in another world. Certainly it was helpful for admirers of Peckinpah, as the Coens profess to be, to have McCarthy's novel as a neo-noir template. Reverential in their adaptation, the Coens extracted the Jim Thompson-esque essence from the novel and, more than thirty-five years after *The Getaway*, used a book's narrative violence to choreograph deadly encounters in the Peckinpah style. While there are many parallels between *The Getaway* and *No Country for Old Men*, from their simple satchels of money to deadly encounters in Texas hotels near the Mexican border, while McCarthy's characters are often trying to escape across that border and can be as nasty, garrulous, and otherwise unattractive as any of Thompson's or Peckinpah's, as given to offhanded and extreme violence, the focus of *No Country for Old Men*, novel and film, is on a more sympathetic if hapless character. Llewellyn Moss is not cut from quite the same cloth as Lou Ford (from Thompson's *The Killer inside Me*), even though Chigurh could be taken as the killer inside the contemplative Sheriff Bell. Whereas Thompson's Doc McCoy in *The Getaway* was a post-romantic criminal trying to reconcile the fact that his wife's sacrifice for him required her infidelity, Moss is just a man trying to get away to a better life with his faithful wife.

Nor is Moss a typical character for the Coens. While there may be resonances to a figure like McDunnogh in *Raising Arizona*, there is none of the quirkiness that is the *sine qua non* of their oeuvre. The intricate and ultimately imprudent murder schemes of Joe Wilmot, the small time projectionist in Thompson's *Nothing More than Murder*, and Ed Crane, the seemingly mild-manned barber in the Coens' original screenplay for *The Man Who Wasn't There*, are both about cheating wives, anger at the world's indifference, and the killer that can be inside almost anyone. Whereas Thompson's naturalism was a perfect fit for Peckinpah, the Coens' vision of ordinary

No Country for Old Men: *Josh Brolin as Llewelyn Moss.*

people confronting twisted killers has tended towards grim irony and little more. *Blood Simple* was just that, while being stylistically akin to the classic period and Hitchcock's essay on how hard it is to kill in *Torn Curtain*. In a new millennium and in a semi-retro-noir set in 1980 West Texas, or just a few years and a few miles removed from the Thompson/Walter Hill/Peckinpah *The Getaway,* the Coens have let McCarthy's characters override their typical inclinations. In doing so, they have resurrected their neo-noir credentials and created a tableau of darkness deep in the heart of Texas that captures the vision Thompson and McCarthy share. **AS**

NO WAY OUT (1987)

Director: Roger Donaldson. **Screenplay**: Robert Garland based on the novel *The Big Clock* by Kenneth Fearing. **Producers**: Robert Garland, Laura Ziskin (Orion). **Director of Photography**: John Alcott, Alun Bollinger. **Music**: Maurice Jarre. **Editor**: Neil Travis. **Cast**: Kevin Costner (Tom Farrell), Gene Hackman (David Brice), Sean Young (Susan Atwell), Will Patton (Scott Pritchard), Howard Duff (Senator Duvall), George Dzundza (Sam Hesselman), Jason Bernard (Major Donovan), Iman (Nina Beka), Fred Dalton Thompson (Marshall). **Released**: Rank, August 14. 115 minutes.

Interrogated by two agents, naval intelligence officer Tom Farrell tells his story, beginning six months earlier. Farrell is invited by his friend Scott Pritchard to a Washington reception where he meets Secretary of Defense, David Brice. Farrell also meets Brice's mistress, Susan Atwell, and they begin a torrid affair. Later, Farrell joins Brice's staff at the Pentagon where his former colleague Hesselman is in charge of operations. Brice suspects Susan has taken another lover, and in a confrontation she is accidentally killed. Fearing that Susan's lover has recognized him, Brice confides in Pritchard and together they devise a plan to find him. Announcing that Susan's lover-murderer is one and the same as a rumored KGB mole in the Pentagon, they put Farrell in charge of an internal investigation to find his own self. Taking Hesselman into his confidence, Farrell persuades him to delay a computer drawing that will reveal his identity. Hesselman finds evidence of Brice's connection to Susan and is murdered by Pritchard. Farrell finally confronts Brice, Pritchard kills himself, and Brice is discredited. Farrell, who turns out to be the undercover Russian agent, disappears.

No Way Out is a transformed remake of *The Big Clock*, taking only the basic narrative framework from the original—a man conducts a murder investigation, *on himself*—and relocating the action from a bustling, 1940s New York media empire to a preglasnost, 1980s Washington Department of Defense. Whereas John Farrow's stylishly filmed version of *The Big Clock* streamlines the unusual narrative structure of Kenneth Fearing's novel, *No Way Out* convolutes the source material, introducing the sub-plot of a phantom submarine project and a final twist which reveals that naval intelligence officer Tom Farrell is in fact rumored Soviet agent, Yuri. While this seems a highly improbable dénouement—especially with Kevin Costner, fresh from his much-publicized success in *The Untouchables* (1987), in the role of Farrell—it does explain his growing anxiety during the top-security enquiry he is forced to conduct.

Following lighter (in tone and style) scenes that depict Farrell's passionate affair with Susan Atwell, the suspenseful countdown of the latter part of *No Way Out* takes place mainly in the hermetic world of the Pentagon. Farrell races the clock to uncover Susan's true murderer while a computer simulation program—a clever updating of Elsa Lanchester's abstract painting of the suspected murderer from *The Big Clock*—gradually renders his facial details from the remnant of a Polaroid photo found at Susan's apartment. While it is the case that *No Way Out* mostly eschews overtly noir *mise en scène* to embrace instead noir thematic elements—fate, deceit, entrapment—and the generic conventions of the 1980s Hollywood thriller, the staging of the murder investigation in the labyrinthine corridors of the Pentagon does communicate the protagonist's desperate feeling that there is, indeed, no way out. **CV**

THE NUMBER 23 (2007)

Director: Joel Schumacher. **Screenplay**: Fernley Phillips. **Producers**: Beau Flynn, Tripp Vinson. **Director of Photography**: Matthew Libatique. **Music**: Harry Gregson-Williams. **Production Designer**: Andrew Laws. **Editor**: Mark Stevens. **Cast**: Jim Carrey (Walter Sparrow/Fingerling), Virginia Madsen (Agatha Sparrow/Fabrizia), Logan Lerman (Robin Sparrow/Young Fingerling), Danny Huston (Isaac French/Dr. Miles Phoenix), Rhona Mitra (Laura Tollins), Michelle Arthur (Sybil), Patricia Belcher (Dr. Alice Mortimer), Lynn Collins (Suicide Blonde/Mrs. Dobkins). **Released**: New Line, February 23. 97 minutes.

Obsessed by a novel, *The Number 23*, animal control officer Walter Sparrow tries to fill in gaps in his own past. The novel is a gift from his wife Agatha, and its anonymous narrator Fingerling mirrors certain aspects of Sparrow's life. As aspects of the book disturb him, Sparrow is compelled to probe the number 23. Discovering aspects of the number permeating his life, he believes he is doomed to follow in Fingerling's murderous footsteps. As he imagines his wife having an affair with his friend, psychologist Isaac French, Sparrow does find another doctor who knows something about his past. Ultimately, Sparrow discovers that he did murder his unfaithful girlfriend, conceal her body, and attempt suicide; but he lost all memory of those events—and the book he wrote during the height of his mania—despite treatment in a mental facility. A doctor stole his manuscript and published it under a pseudonym. Freed of his demons, Sparrow turns himself into the police.

While there are many stylistic references to the classic

The Number 23: *Jim Carrey as Walter Sparrow.*

period—the visualized excerpts from the novel are shot to resemble a noir comic book in such high-contrast that they seem monochromatic—the invocation and oblique narrative line of *The Number 23* is its strongest link to traditional noir. Like Neff in *Double Indemnity* or Steve Thompson in *Criss Cross*, Sparrow's voiceover narration runs throughout the film. His opening comments about the quirk of fate which led him to his own novel about which he has no memory are rueful: "I'd like two words on my tombstone—what if?" The visualization is heavily manipulated as layered flashbacks reveal mundane events that set the narrative in motion: a Christmas party, his wife's cold, a cake in the shape of a dog, and the spurned advances of a drunken radio dispatcher. This same dispatcher now sends him on a call which makes him late. "Destiny. Maybe that's too big a word for it . . . I was late and that's all it took." Because while she waits, his wife Agatha walks by the book store, A Novel Fate, located next to her cake shop. Cross-traveling shots moving towards Agatha standing transfixed and into a book with a bright orange cover hammer home the sense of predetermination with a vigor that is very over the top.

If there is an echo of Steve Thompson's angst—"It was in the cards or it was fate or a jinx or whatever you want to call it"—the recitation itself works against the sense of mischance. Part of the expressive failure is a performance issue in that Jim Carrey's wide-eyed and wheezing self-pity as Walter Sparrow is a far cry from Burt Lancaster's doomed and desperate Thompson. As Walter's go, the character ends up closer to Mitty than to Neff. The other part is the self-consciousness which the filmmakers bring to the recitation of Sparrow's "novel fate," a relentless ironic overstatement that moves from pastiche to parody to meta-comment, as Sparrow asks when Agatha gives him the book, why "have some writer fill my head with nonsense. I'll wait for the movie." At the end when the presence of his son compels the suicidal Sparrow to step out of the way of a bus—No. 23 route, of course—he feebly concludes that "there's no such thing as destiny, there are only different choices." For the filmmakers, the choices are mostly off the mark. The presence of Carrey as protagonist and the extreme skewing of décor, lighting, and angle are burdensome stylistic overlays. While the idea may have been to recall the predicament of Gregory Peck's amnesiac character in *Spellbound*, Carrey in *Number 23* is too often closer to Bob Hope in *My Favorite Blonde*. **AS**

ONE FALSE MOVE (1992)

Director: Carl Franklin. **Screenplay**: Billy Bob Thornton and Tom Epperson. **Producers**: Jesse Beaton and Ben Myron. **Executive Producers**: Miles A. Copeland III, Paul Colichman and Harold Welb. **Director of Photography**: James L. Carter. **Music**: Peter Haycock and Derek Holt. **Production Designer**: Gary T. New. **Editor**: Carole Kravetz. **Cast**: Bill Paxton (Dale "Hurricane" Carter), Cynda Williams (Fantasia/Lila Walker), Billy Bob Thornton (Ray Malcolm), Michael Beach (Pluto), Jim Meltzer (Detective Dud Cole), Earl Hollings (Detective John McFeely), Natalie Canerday (Cheryl Ann Dixon), Kevin Hunter (Ronnie Walker), Roger Anthony Bell (Byron Walker), Robert Ginnaven (Charlie), Jesse Dabson (Beaver). **Released**: I.R.S. Media, May 8. 106 minutes.

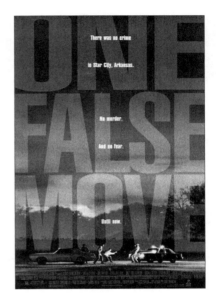

Three criminals on the run for murder travel from L.A. to Arkansas in *One False Move*. Ray is a Southern, white, short-tempered thief willing to do anything to get money and cocaine. Pluto is a Black, college educated ex-con from Chicago, adept with a knife. Fantasia/Lila, Ray's girlfriend, is an actress. After an urban crime spree where Ray and Pluto kill small-time crooks and Lila saves a young Black boy's life, the three criminals leave L.A., pointed toward both Houston to unload the drugs and Star City, Arkansas so Lila can see her family. Dud, a white L.A. detective, and John, his Black partner, travel by airplane to meet Dale "Hurricane" Dixon, the white local sheriff of Star City, Arkansas, to ambush these three criminals. Dale is happily married and has an eight-year-old daughter with Cheryl Ann. Because of a slight by the L.A. cops, Dale stakes out alone and discovers Lila's hideout when Ronnie, Lila's brother, takes Byron to visit his mother. When Ronnie leaves, Dale enters the hideout with Lila and he kills both male criminals once they arrive, but not before first being stabbed in the stomach by Pluto and shot in the shoulder by Ray. Detectives Cole and McFeely arrive after the bloodbath, discovering three dead bodies, and a dying Dale.

One False Move, inexpensively made and structured like a classic Hollywood couples on the run film, travels from L.A. to Star City, Arkansas and employs the theme of fate to reach its satisfying conclusion. The film also imitates stylistic devices from the classic noir period in its use of Dutch angles, rain, cigarettes, night shots, shadows, and guns in handbags. The film still resonates because of its art cinema parallels to films like Bertrand Tavernier's *Coup de Torchon* (1981) and Roman Polanski's *Chinatown* (1973), especially their cultural lessons. This film, not satisfied with the genre pastiche and hybrid techniques of most 1970s and 1980s American neo-noirs, invites the viewer to analyze such issues as miscegenation, cultural guilt, and white privilege. These three ideas may be summed up most succinctly in the scene where Lila confronts Dale about their past: "Me and my brother's Daddy's white, did you know that? Of course we never knew him. He had another family. That's why I kinda look white 'cuz my Daddy was white. I guess you figure 'cuz I kinda look white you can fuck me, what the hell. Because I was kinda black, you could drop me, what the hell."

Most of the film takes place in rural Arkansas, revealing the big city cops as amused by Dale's excitement, or charmed by the town's food and people. African-American detective John eats comfortably ("food like my Mama used to make") in the town diner without recognizing he is getting special treatment because he's an out-of-town cop working with Dale. All the other African-Americans seen in this film live harshly on the outskirts of town, running bait shops, drive-ins, gas stations, or populating "N-town." Race privilege is further present when Cheryl Ann apologizes to Dud (rather than John) for Dale's racist slur at dinner and in Dale's offer to provide money to help Lila raise Byron, rather than accept his paternal responsibilities.

Lila is a femme fatale but the movie illustrates that she steals the drug money from Ray for a moral reason, financial security for a son who will otherwise be abandoned. Dale moves toward redemption in the powerful final scene where he invites Byron to "come back here and stay with me," rather than letting the boy wander away and discover the dead body of his mother. The film fades out, leaving the audience wondering whether Dale will survive his injury, confess his sexual misdeed, and accept Byron into his family. The film raises

One False Move: *Cynda Williams as Fantasia and Billy Bob Thornton as Ray.*

Original Sin: *Julia/Bonnie (Angelina Jolie) and Luis Vargas (Antonio Banderas).*

more questions than it answers but, as Richard Martin posits when discussing this film among others, "they reflect all that is immoral and perverse in American society, cataloging a history of injustice, criminality, violence, and corruption" (*Mean Streets and Raging Bulls*). *One False Move* influenced subsequent message-oriented Black neo-noir films like *The Glass Shield* (1995), *Clockers* (1995) and *Inside Man* (2006). **WC**

ORIGINAL SIN (2001)

Director: Michael Cristofer. **Screenplay**: Michael Cristofer based on *Waltz into Darkness* by Cornell Woolrich. **Producers**: Denise Di Novi, Kate Guinzburg, Carol Lees, Edward McDonnell. **Director of Photography**: Rodrigo Prieto. **Production Designer**: David J. Bomba. **Music**: Terence Blanchard. **Editor**: Eric A. Sears. **Cast**: Angelina Jolie (Julia/Bonnie), Antonio Banderas (Luis Vargas), Thomas Jane (Walter/Billy), Jack Thompson (Alan Jordan), Gregory Itzin (Colonel Worth), Allison Mackie (Augusta Jordan), Joan Pringle (Sara), Cordelia Richards (Emily Russell), Pedro Armendariz, Jr. (Jorge Cortes), Mario Ivan Martinez (Priest), Harry Porter (Stage Manager). **Released**: MGM, July 31. 118 minutes.

When Luis Vargas selects a mail order bride, he is surprised to see the beauty Julia who appears before him. She alleges that she sent false photos to him to assure that he would love her for what she is and not for her beauty. However, she turns out to be a con artist and actress named Bonnie, who teams with a fellow actor and lover Walter/Billy to steal money from men. Luis hunts Bonnie down and confronts her but instead of killing her he joins her as her accomplice and lover. Pursued by a determined detective and harassed by her former lover, they seek refuge. Luis still suspects Bonnie's motives but is willing to kill for her as well as swallow the poison she gives him under pressure from Billy. Bonnie kills Billy and is incarcerated but escapes with the help of a young priest. She returns to Luis.

In 2001 writer/director Michael Christofer reunited with star Angelina Jolie, whom he had collaborated on in the award-winning biopic *Gia,* to film noir novelist Cornell Woolrich's *Waltz into Darkness* (adapted by Francois Truffaut earlier under the title *Mississippi Mermaid*). *Original Sin*

adhered closely to Woolrich's concept of the perversity and sexual power of the femme fatale but also, in a typically post-feminist move, gave her control of the narrative.

The Julia/Bonnie of *Original Sin* is, like her predecessor in the novel, a sexually charged, cigar-chomping seductress who delights in her power over men (enhanced by the presence of Jolie who has developed that image off and on screen). To the Colonel who is courting her in the second half of the film, she is a dominatrix who makes him beg outside her door and dismisses him with a threatening wave of her cane. With her lover and criminal accomplice Billy, she indulges her sadomasochistic urges which include blood-drinking, cutting, and rough sex. And to her duped husband Luis, she is "the death" of him, someone he "can't live without."

The film opens on Bonnie's close-up in prison (this framing device and the twist ending are two major changes made to the novel) as she narrates the story: "This is not a love story. This is a story of love and the power it has over life . . . the power to heal or to destroy." When she arrives in Cuba to marry her coffee magnate, she initially takes on the more demure façade of the real Julia but soon discards that and reveals the sexually insatiable woman beneath.

After her theft of Luis' money, Bonnie returns to the life of a courtesan and card shark. When Luis tracks her down, after losing himself in the flesh of prostitutes who resembled her, she easily turns him back into her lover by placing the barrel of his gun against her partially revealed breasts. Luis collapses emotionally and physically, unable to resist her appeal: "Don't you see I can't live without you."

From that point on Luis demonstrates his willingness to love her unconditionally, although often intermingled with great angst: "If I ever lost you, there would be nothing left for me." He murders (or thinks he does), cheats at cards, evades the law, and even submits to her cuckolding of him with her ex-lover Billy (again an element resurrected by the filmmakers from Woolrich's novel). Like Louis in Truffaut's film he too gladly accepts death at her hands and drinks the poison: "No matter the price you cannot walk away from love."

Again like Truffaut, the filmmakers of *Original Sin* do take mercy on their fugitive couple, as opposed to Woolrich in his original story. Bonnie is sentenced to death for the murder of

Billy. She escapes by seducing an innocent monk to whom she tells her story (the framing device of the movie). In the final scene she is radiant again, draped in an expensive gown and sporting brilliant jewelry. She walks around a table of gamblers, pouring them drinks as she signals to Luis, using a code to indicate the hands of the other men. In a final close-up she smiles and runs her finger across her throat, signaling on one level a dangerous card hand while at the same time expressing to the audience the danger of her character and the price one must pay to be with such a woman. **JU**

OUT OF TIME (2003)

Director: Carl Franklin. **Writer**: Dave Collard. **Producers**: Neil H. Moritz and Jesse Beaton. **Executive Producers**: Kevin Reidy, Damien Saccani, Jon Berg, and Alex Gartner. **Director of Photography**: Theo Van de Sande. **Music**: Graeme Revell. **Production Designer**: Paul Peters. **Editor**: Carole Kravetz Aykanian. **Cast**: Denzel Washington (Matt Lee Whitlock), Eva Mendes (Alex Diaz Whitlock), Sanaa Lathan (Ann Merai Harrison), Dean Cain (Chris Harrison), John Billingsley (Chae), Robert Baker (Tony Dalton), Alex Carter (Cabot), Antoni Corone (Deputy Baste), Terry Loughlin (Agent Stark), Nora Dunn (Dr. Donovan), James Murtaugh (Dr. Frieland). **Released**: Original Film Monarch Pictures/Metro-Goldwyn-Mayer, October 3. 105 minutes.

Matt Whitlock has an affair with Ann Merai who is married to a physically abusive ex-pro football player named Chris Harrison. Matt loses his detective wife Alex to this philandering. Matt is buddies with Chae, a local medical examiner who hopes to partner with Matt on a Costa Rican charter boat business. Suddenly, Ann tells Matt that she has terminal cancer, only six months left to live, and a one million dollar life insurance policy with Matt as beneficiary. Hoping to get Ann experimental cancer treatment, or the ability to buy a "living gift" insurance policy, Matt temporarily steals 485,000 dollars he holds in a police safe from a drug bust. Once Ann accepts this money, things go wrong. Her house burns down, two bodies are found inside (assumed to be Chris and Ann), yet the fire investigator easily discovers arson. Agent Stark of the DEA calls Matt and demands the drug money immediately

Out of Time: *Denzel Washington as Sheriff Whitlock.*

because they need the serial numbers, and Whitlock spends the rest of the film trying to apprehend Ann and Chris, retrieve the money for the DEA, and convince his estranged wife to return home. Through various action scenes, Ann kills Chris, shoots Matt in the right thigh, and then Alex kills Ann just before Ann can murder Matt. In the end, Matt returns the stolen money, keeps his job, and Alex comes home.

Carl Franklin makes the theme of his film obvious in the bravura opening shot of *Out of Time*. With a crane shot that starts high near a "Temptation Restaurant" sign, the camera dollies slowly down to street level and Banyon Key Florida police chief Mathias Whitlock as he checks to make sure all the doors are locked for the evening in his small town's businesses. The rest of the film is a romantic thriller about how sex, money, and job temptations lead basically good people to do bad things. Franklin employs Cuban music, good-looking actors sweating in the Florida sun, and various symbolic uses of weather, including heat lightning and rainy evenings, to build a small-town noir aura. Because of deadlines, various last-minute rescues, and assorted action scenes Matt demonstrates heroics and also parallels Chae's sarcastic quotation about human nature where he claims, "what tangled webs we weave."

Matt learns his lesson by film's end, stating, "Sometime people, you know, do stupid things, especially when they're still in love" and warns his friend Chae, "Just never leave your wife. That's what happened to me." The film ends with Alex's inquiry of Matt, "Are you going to behave?" *Out of Time* is a morality tale about avoiding greed and accepting and appreciating what you already have. Franklin has directed a series of neo-noirs like *One False Move* (1992), *Devil in a Blue Dress* (1995) and *High Crimes* (2002), each more interesting than this project. Denzel Washington previously starred as Easy Rawlins for Franklin in *Devil in a Blue Dress* (1995), won an Oscar in 2002 for his role as a neo-noir anti-hero in *Training Day* (2001), and consistently shines as a leading man. *Out of Time* gives him much less of a narrative to work with and is merely a stylish thriller and minor entry in the neo-noir canon. **WC**

Out of Time: *Ann (Sanaa Lathan) and Sheriff Whitlock (Denzel Washington).*

The Outfit: *Earl Macklin (Robert Duvall) and Cody (Joe Don Baker).*

THE OUTFIT (1973)

Director/Screenplay: John Flynn from the novel by Richard Stark [Donald E. Westlake]. **Producer**: Carter De Haven. **Director of Photography**: Bruce Surtees. **Music**: Jerry Fielding. **Art Director**: Tambi Larsen. **Editor**: Ralph E. Winters. **Cast**: Robert Duvall (Earl Macklin), Karen Black (Bett Jarrow), Joe Don Baker (Cody), Robert Ryan (Mailer), Timothy Carey (Jake Menner), Sheree North (Buck's wife), Marie Windsor (Madge Coyle), Jane Greer (Alma), Henry Jones (Doctor), Joanna Cassidy (Rita). **Released**: MGM, September 2. 103 minutes.

A professional thief named, Earl Macklin, is released from prison and learns that his brother has been murdered by syndicate gunmen. Macklin's girlfriend, Bett, confesses that she has been forced to set him up by Jake Menner, a syndicate underling commissioned to eliminate Macklin, his brother, and their partner Cody for inadvertently robbing a syndicate bank. Macklin intercepts Menner's hit man, beats him, then recruits Cody in a scheme to get even with the mob. They stage a succession of raids on syndicate gambling rooms and bookie joints. Mailer, the local syndicate chief, summons Menner and issues an ultimatum: kill Macklin or forfeit his own life. After an ambush on a country road misfires, Menner and his cohorts are killed by Macklin and Cody, but Bett also dies in the exchange of gunfire. Macklin decides to strike at Mailer himself. After penetrating Mailer's mansion and setting a bomb to cover their retreat, Macklin finds Mailer and mercilessly shoots him. Cody is wounded; but they steal an ambulance and escape in the confusion of fire trucks and police responding to the explosion. [**Note**: The television version of the film ends with Macklin and Cody ostensibly trapped in a back room as the police and fire trucks arrive.]

The Outfit is loosely adapted from one of the sequels to Richard Stark's first "Parker" novel, *The Hunter,* which became *Point Blank.* As in the previous book, the central figure is a free-lance robber who finds himself suddenly under attack from organized crime and decides that his best chance of survival lies in active retaliation. The adaptors of *The Outfit* confront a central narrative that suggests an exis-

tential set piece in which a loner salves his alienation through murderous violence. It is also a mock epic in which the "little man" defeats the dehumanized, organizational machine. The closing shot of *The Outfit*—a freeze-frame of Macklin and Cody smiling in exhilaration at their victory— would seem to fall into the latter category, particularly in contrast to the ambiguous conclusion of *Point Blank.* However, this ending is a single moment and does not controvert the fundamentally noir vision of the film, which situates itself wholly in an underworld where the uncertainty of surface appearances undermines the very concepts of victory or defeat. That uncertainty is present in the film's prologue in which men who appear to be a priest and a cab driver murder Macklin's brother. It is elaborated on in a later sequence when Macklin is shown a souped-up car that looks like a Volkswagen but, as the mechanic laments, "I just can't make her sound like a Volkswagen." In the face of these masquerades, Macklin realizes that he cannot take the advice of his brother's common-law wife who asks, "What do you want it [money] for? You got a woman; you got time." In Macklin's perception of how things stand or fall, money and time are both symbolic values, both keys to survival.

Macklin's position in these early scenes—recently released from prison, hiding out in a dingy motel room, betrayed by Bett—recalls classic period motifs. Macklin's response to his situation, accentuated by Robert Duvall's laconic performance reminiscent of Robert Montgomery's in *Ride the Pink Horse,* resembles similar noir figures, all mindful of their own possible destruction but compelled to even the score. More than most of those precursors Macklin has the tools to accomplish this. He has the ruthlessness of Hammer in *Kiss Me Deadly* without his egocentricity, the inside knowledge of Kelvaney in *Rogue Cop* without his indecision, and the sheer killing ability of Callahan in *Dirty Harry* without any pretense of abiding by the law. Macklin can forgive Bett's potentially deadly betrayal; or he can with equal dispassion release a man sent to kill him with the offhand remark, "Die someplace else."

If Macklin appears to move through the array of noir cons arrayed against him—from Robert Ryan and the maniacal Timothy Carey as the syndicate man to such bit players as Elisha Cook, Jr., Marie Windsor, and Emile Meyer—it may be because they evoke, like the old car parked outside Macklin's first heist, an antique vision of the noir underworld. Unlike Dancer in *The Line-Up,* infuriated by his exasperating inability to reconcile the syndicate boss to his honest mistake, Macklin understands from the start that he will never be able to do that, that the unwritten rules which are the only element of stability in the noir underworld have condemned him. By systematically disrupting that literal and figurative underworld, Macklin almost becomes a cipher for that system turning destructively against itself. The protest of Mailer's wife against hiding in the safety of his mansion— "How long are we going to stay cooped up in this mausoleum?"—betrays the true nature of the cardboard killers who Bett remarks "act like they own the world" and whom Macklin easily defeats. Having metaphorically lost faith, as their own institutions become mausoleums, they are noir artifacts who are brought down as much by their own anachronism as they are by the free-lancers. **AS**

PAYBACK (1999)

Director: Brian Helgeland. **Screenplay**: Helgeland, Terry Hayes, based on the novel *The Hunter* by Richard Stark [Donald E. Westlake]. **Producer**: Bruce Davey. **Director of Photography**: Ericson Core. **Production Designer**: Richard Hoover. **Music**: Chris Boardman. **Editor**: Kevin Stitt. **Cast**: Mel Gibson (Porter), Gregg Henry (Val Resnick), Maria Bello (Rosie), David Paymer (Arthur Stegman), Bill Duke (Det. Hicks), Deborah Kara Unger (Mrs. Lynn Porter), William Devane (Carter), James Coburn (Fairfax), Lucy Liu (Pearl), Jack Conley (Det. Leary), Kris Kristofferson (Bronson), John Glover (Phil). **Released**: Paramount, February 5. 100 minutes.

Five months after being betrayed by his wife Lynn and partner-in-crime, Val Resnick, Porter returns in search of emotional and fiscal payback. He lifts a wallet and its cash and credit cards to outfit himself. Shortly after he finds his wife, she dies of a heroin overdose and Porter viciously interrogates the delivery boy which leads him to petty dealer Arthur Stegman and corrupt cops Hicks and Leary and the knowledge that Resnick has used the money to restore his "made-man" status and lives in a mob hotel. With the help of Rosie, a high-end prostitute for whom Porter was once bodyguard, Porter kills Resnick then shoots his way up the hierarchy. He murders Carter, terrorizes Fairfax, and kidnaps the son of top man Bronson demanding only the $70,000 stolen by Resnick. Although captured and tortured by Bronson's thugs, Porter manages a final reversal: he watches as Bronson is immolated in his own booby-trap and drives off with Rosie and his money.

The central concept of Donald Westlake's novel, *The Hunter*, is the monomaniacal small-mindedness of its protagonist. In its first movie adaptation, *Point Blank*, the "hunter" is called Walker and portrayed by Lee Marvin, whose character unveils dark layers of a criminal underworld lurking beneath the surface of the contemporary world, killers passing for ordinary citizens in clean, well-lit homes by the beach. In this adaptation, de facto executive producer and star Mel Gibson preserves the small mindedness and opts as well for a minimalist performance of a well-dressed man moving through a world of back rooms and petty mobsters who mostly wear their occupations on their sleeves. As part of this transformation, the anti-social violence becomes a much grimmer, anti-personal violence in a movie whose central axiom is, as the title suggests, that "payback is a bitch." With his quest for revenge being as dogged as a samurai's, at times Porter evokes that ancient ethos as when a small-time hoodlum he is questioning near a playground asks, "Are you going to kill me?" and Porter answers simply that he would not do that in front of children. While Walker discovered that betrayal was a reflex, in writer/director Helgeland's would-be post-modernist approach, treachery is replaced by honor and code, an almost military adherence to chain of command but all of it among thieves. Certainly there are "parody" elements, most notably the Asian-American dominatrix Pearl who is paid to inflict sexual pain, the ultimate expression of which is her comment when she and her cohorts drive up expecting to kill Porter: "Hubba, hubba."

The desaturated colors and vaguely period (set in the Nixon era) ambience, in which suits are retro rather than costume and cars are classic rather than antique, create a mood that is at times nightmarish but mostly bring to mind a graphic novel or just plain comic book. The aspect of *Payback* which most heavily evokes the classic period of noir is its narration. Porter's observations reverberate laconically over the soundtrack from the first scene: lying on a table in some grimy background as an overweight, inebriated "doctor" pulls bullets out of his body and blood streams down his distorted features, Porter notes that in the over world medical institutions must report gunshot wounds which they call GSWs, as if that would insulate them from the material world of real violence and death. **AS**

PLAY MISTY FOR ME (1971)

Director: Clint Eastwood. **Screenplay**: Jo Heims and Dean Riesner. **Producers**: Robert Daley, Jennings Lang [uncredited]. **Director of Photography**: Bruce Surtees. **Music**: Dee Barton. **Art Director**: Alexander Golitzen. **Editor**: Carl Pingitore. **Cast**: Clint Eastwood (Dave Garland), Jessica Walter (Evelyn Draper), Donna Mills (Tobie Williams), John Larch (Sergeant McCallum), Jack Ging (Dr. Frank Dewan), Irene Hervey (Madge Brenner), James McEachin (Al Monte), Clarice Taylor (Birdie), Don Siegel (Murphy the bartender), Duke Everts (Jay Jay), George Fargo (Man), Mervin W. Frates (Locksmith). **Location**: Monterey Peninsula, California. **Released**: Universal, November 3. 102 minutes.

In Carmel, California Dave Garland is a late-night DJ whose show specializes in music and poetry "to be very, very nice to each other by." At a bar he meets and is seduced by Evelyn Draper, who confesses that she is the caller who frequently requests that he "play 'Misty' for me." When Garland makes it clear he has no interest beyond a one-night stand, Draper refuses to be dumped. She calls him at work, stalks him at a business lunch, breaks in and trashes his home, and finally threatens to kill his former girlfriend Tobie, who is newly returned to Carmel. Concerned about the effect it might have on his career Garland initially does not report Draper's verbal and physical assaults to the authorities. Ultimately the unhinged Draper falls to her death while planning to attack Tobie, who is then free to resume her idyllic romance with Garland.

Clint Eastwood's directorial debut is obviously influenced by his participation as an actor in *Dirty Harry*—whose director Don Siegel plays a minor role in *Play Misty for Me*—but he casts himself in a far different role than Harry Callahan. Although a local celebrity, Garland has never made the connection in his own mind between his social role and his personal life. His attitude about sex and love is hip and contemporary in an "I'm-okay-you're-okay" world. Like many figures in classic period noir, that attitude and lack of self-awareness underscore the irony when his complacent world is shattered by a violent eruption of seemingly irrational forces. While Draper is more of a force than a fully realized character—the back story of her mental illness is never recounted—there is a certain amount of sympathy generated for her. In contrast to the somewhat superficial relationship between Garland and Tobie and Garland's own liberated lifestyle, Draper has palpable emotional substance: fears, anxieties, passions, a turmoil of impulses that create her obsession.

As in Hitchcock's work, the atmosphere of anxiety is not created by the depth with which the film probes surface reality, by "psychological truth," but by the realization that the surface is all there is for a character like Garland. Beneath this surface, there is no revelation of a heroic protagonist. The easy way in which he goes back to normal life and Garland's inability to recognize his own guilt in creating an atmosphere that unleashes Draper's demons instill the ending of the film with a profound sense of pessimism. In fact, Draper is part of the atmosphere of possible menace, of people out there in the dark, that he has helped to create. After Draper attacks his housekeeper, a local cop asks Garland, "This Evelyn Draper, where does she come from?" His reply, with its hint of existential malaise, is one of the most telling neo-noir moments of the film: "I don't know. She just listens to my show." As "Misty" fills the soundtrack over an image of waves surging against the rocks where Draper's body is sprawled, the viewer knows there will be more like her in the future. **RA**

POINT BLANK (1967)

Director: John Boorman. **Screenplay**: Alexander Jacobs, David Newhouse, and Rafe Newhouse from the novel *The Hunter* by Richard Stark [Donald E. Westlake]. **Producers**: Judd Bernard, Robert Chartoff. **Director of Photography**: Philip H. Lathrop. **Music**: Johnny Mandel. **Art Directors**: George W. Davis, Albert Brenner. **Editor**: Henry Berman. **Cast**: Lee Marvin (Walker), Angie Dickinson (Chris), Keenan Wynn (Yost), Carroll O'Connor

(Brewster), Lloyd Bochner (Frederick Carter), Michael Strong (Stegman), John Vernon (Mal Reese), Sharon Acker (Lynne), James Sikking (Hired Gun), Sandra Warner (Waitress), Roberta Haynes (Mrs. Carter). **Completed**: April 27, 1967. **Released**: MGM, September 18. 92 minutes.

A man, Walker, is shot point-blank in a cell on deserted Alcatraz prison island by his friend Reese, with whom he has been hijacking a crime syndicate's money. Walker's wife, Lynne, is also present and, as he becomes unconscious, it is clear that Lynne has been unfaithful and helped Reese betray him. But somehow, Walker survives. Later, he meets a mysterious man, Yost, who offers Walker support in a plan for revenge and recovery of the $93,000 taken by Reese and Lynne. Walker goes to Los Angeles, shooting Lynne's bed full of holes but unable to kill her. She later dies of an overdose of sleeping pills. Walker finds he must not only revenge himself on Reese but also collect his money from the top members of the syndicate, who are Carter, Brewster, and Fairfax. He uses Lynne's friend, Chris, to set up Reese by seducing him. Walker enters the security penthouse but Reese is so frightened by Walker that he accidentally falls from the roof. Walker attempts to get his money from Carter, who plans to have him shot. At the designated place, the sniper shoots at long range and kills Carter instead. Taking Chris with him, Walker goes to Brewster's house to wait. When Brewster arrives, he tells Walker that they have to go to Alcatraz for the money, but this is to lure Walker into a trap. Yost, who is in fact Fairfax, is also at Alcatraz and has Brewster killed by the same sniper who killed Carter. As Fairfax shouts at Walker to come and get his money, Walker withdraws into the shadows.

Point Blank is not a literal narrative. The shooting of Walker at point-blank range realistically suggests that he is dead from the first few moments of the film. His inexplicable survival and subsequent reserve dominates even violent moments, and his face is a mask, permanently registering the emotions of the exact moment when he comprehended his betrayal. The technical complexity of the film, which at times is powerfully expressive, supports the view that the film actually tells a story that is in Walker's mind. He considers the possibilities of revenge open to him *if* he had lived and, at last, determines that they lead nowhere.

This fascinating premise is influenced by the films of Alain Resnais, manifesting a profound concern with the ambiguities of time and space. In addition, *Point Blank* brings film noir into a contemporary world of cold glass and steel, of gray suits and modish decor. Telephoto lenses and unbalanced compositions, emphasizing Walker's total alienation, enhance the presentation of Walker as a noir hero situated in a world where women take tranquilizers and gangsters have no personality. John Boorman's attention to every aspect of the work is remarkable, and his direction of Lee Marvin as Walker and Angie Dickinson as Chris results in unusual and notable performances. Although the extroverted role of Carroll O'Connor as the gangster, Brewster, is disruptive to the film, the first few reels are hypnotic, especially the sequence of Walker's walk through the Los Angeles airport intercut with shots of Lynne in her apartment, which combine the loud reverberation of his footsteps over each image. **BL**

POINT OF NO RETURN (1993)

Director: John Badham. **Screenplay**: Robert Getchell, Alexandra Seros based on the film *Nikita* by Luc Besson. **Producer**: Art Linson. **Director of Photography**: Michael Watkins. **Music**: Hans Zimmer. **Editor**: Frank Morriss. **Cast**: Bridget Fonda (Maggie Hayward), Gabriel Byrne (Bob), Dermot Mulroney (J.P.), Miguel Ferrer (Kaufman), Anne Bancroft (Amanda), Olivia D'Abo (Angela), Richard Romanus (Fahd Bahktiar), Harvey Keitel (Victor the Cleaner). **Released**: Warner Bros, March 19. 108 minutes.

A young junkie, Maggie, takes part in a raid on a pharmacy, and in the ensuing shoot-out kills a police officer. She is sentenced to death by lethal injection but wakes to find herself alive in a government facility. A trainer, Bob, gives her a choice of working to become a professional assassin or returning to death row. Although initially uncooperative, Maggie is gradually won over by Bob and a graceful woman, Amanda, who trains her in social etiquette. After completing her final test—the assassination of a dignitary in an expensive restaurant—Maggie is released into the community under the name of Claudia, where she carries out occasional missions and falls in love with J.P., a young artist. Maggie asks Bob to release her and he agrees provided that she completes one last operation. The mission goes wrong, and it is only with the assistance of Victor the Cleaner that Maggie accomplishes it. Fearing that she has now become a target, Maggie disposes of Victor and disappears. Bob glimpses her on the street but reports that she has been killed.

Point of No Return (also known as *The Assassin*) is a remake of Luc Besson's glossy 1990 French-Italian production, *Nikita*. A fine example of the high-tech visual style of 1980s French *cinéma du look*, *Nikita* draws upon the conventions of American film noir and Hong Kong action cinema to tell a Pygmalion-type story of a young drug addict, Nikita, who is reprieved from a death sentence to be made over as an undercover government assassin. Immediately remade in Hong Kong as *Black Cat* (1991) and later the source of the television series, "La Femme Nikita" (1997–2001), Besson's film is most closely shadowed by John Badham's almost scene-by-scene remake, *Point of No Return*.

Relocating the action to Washington and (later) Venice Beach, Badham's version intensifies—through the casting of

Point of No Return: *Bridget Fonda as Maggie Hayward.*

Bridget Fonda in the lead role of Maggie and Gabriel Byrne as her mentor, Bob—the father-daughter relationship and the subsequent Oedipal sparring between Bob and Maggie's artist-boyfriend, J.P. Maggie's character is informed not only by the active sexuality of the neo-noir femme fatale (her initial seduction of J.P., for instance), but also the strong-woman of contemporary Hollywood action cinema. The latter is most evident in the film's faithful recreation of Besson's centerpiece, the spectacular restaurant-kitchen shootout (and the heroine's diving escape down a laundry chute ahead of a huge fireball) that follows the dispatch of Maggie's first target. Finally, in the film's most substantial departure from the original, Bob falsely reports Maggie's death to his superiors, effectively setting her free to begin a new life with J.P. **CV**

THE POSTMAN ALWAYS RINGS TWICE (1981)

Director: Bob Rafelson. **Screenplay**: David Mamet based on the novel by James M. Cain. **Producers**: Rafelson and Charles Mulvehill. **Director of Photography**: Sven Nykvist. **Production Designer**: George Jenkins. **Music**: Michael Small. **Editor**: Graeme Clifford. **Cast**: Jack Nicholson (Frank Chambers), Jessica Lang (Cora Papadakis), John Colicos (Nick Papadakis), Michael Lerner (Katz), John P. Ryan (Kennedy), Anjelica Huston (Madge), Christopher Lloyd (Salesman). **Released**: Paramount, March 20. 125 minutes.

Frank Chambers, a man like so many displaced by the Great Depression, stops in a country café and is hired as a handyman by owner Nick Papadakis. Soon Frank begins an affair with Nick's younger wife Cora. Unwilling to abandon the business she has helped to build, Cora convinces Frank that they should stage an accident that results in Nick's death. Although a suspicious prosecutor probes the event and initially alienates the couple from each other, they reconcile and are married. Disaffected by Cora's relentless ambition to get more profit from the café, Frank leaves for a while and even has an affair; but eventually returns. Ironically as the prospect of "normal" domesticity seems within reach, Cora dies in a car accident and Frank is convicted of her murder.

In this adaptation, Cain's café somewhere "near Glendale" is relocated in a bucolic countryside with a "highway" that winds through meadowland and "mountains" that are soft, green, and bathed in mist.

The Postman Always Rings Twice: *Frank Chambers (Jack Nicholson) and Cora Papadakis (Jessica Lange)*.

Cain's bloody details and even the ironic undertone of the final sequence are eliminated as the auto accident is staged against the warm, golden hues of the afternoon sun. Compared to the original, staged at night so that its disquieting stillness could be a counter-point to the car wreck, and centered emotionally on the lipstick that rolls out of the dead Cora's hand, a fetish which brings together Cora's feminine mystique and Frank's fatal obsession, the remake is quite pallid.

But such visual disparities are less problematic than the iconology, beginning with the casting of Jack Nicholson. It is not that something is "wrong" with this actor's performance here; in fact it's remarkably subdued. The trouble lies rather in the economy of means which casts Nicholson in a role that draws upon a portion of his pre-established "star" qualities; the viewer perceives Frank from the first as too devious and cunning. The Frank of Cain's novel is hardly "cool" by traditional hardboiled standards. He is more the passionate man whose emotions sometimes betray him and whose toughness is defined by the immediacy of his actions and his resignation to their consequences.

By having Frank Chambers tell his sordid story, Cain compelled an acceptance of Frank's point of view and permitted a potentially unpleasant character to engage reader emotions. From the first, iconographic elements associated with Jack Nicholson mitigate against creating sympathy for his character. This more recent *The Postman Always Rings Twice* compounds this distancing effect with an expository narrative that favors an objective visual style. John Garfield's narration in the MGM film shades our apprehension of the story, providing a running commentary on the action, explaining emotions, creating an aural POV which reinforces its subjective camera POV's in a manner that is missing from the later version. Of equal importance, it fosters a sympathetic response by deepening our involvement with his character. Garfield captures more of Cain's Frank than Nicholson does because he can convey a sensibility that might well say: "I kissed her. Her eyes were shining up at me like two blue stars. It was like being in church." Such words voiced by Jack Nicholson could only sound disingenuous. **BP**

PRETTY POISON (1968)

Director: Noel Black. **Screenplay**: Lorenzo Semple, Jr. based on the novel *She Let Him Continue* by Stephen Geller. **Producers**: Marshal

Backlar, Noel Black. **Director of Photography**: David Quaid. **Music**: Johnny Mandel. **Art Directors**: Jack Martin Smith, Harold Michelson. **Editor**: William Ziegler. **Cast**: Anthony Perkins (Dennis Pitt), Tuesday Weld (Sue Ann Stepanek), Beverly Garland (Mrs. Stepanek), John Randolph (Morton Azenauer), Dick O'Neill (Bud Munsch), Clarice Bronson (Mrs. Bronson), Ken Kercheval (Harry Jackson), Don Fellows (detective). **Locations**: Great Barrington and North Adams, Massachusetts. **Released**: 20th Century-Fox, October 23. 89 minutes.

Dennis Pitt has been confined to a state facility for disturbed juveniles for an act of arson that killed his aunt. Once released, Pitt makes his way to a small western Massachusetts town where he induces a pretty blond high school majorette, Sue Ann Stepanek, to join in his plan to sabotage the chemical plant where he works. Sue Ann needs help with a plan of her own to escape from a slatternly, domineering mother. Pitt's plan goes awry when he is caught by the night watchman. Sue Ann knocks him unconscious and rolls his body into the river at the plant's edge. By this time, Pitt's case worker, Azenauer, has tracked him down and threatens to take him back to the facility for violating the terms of his release. Pitt and Sue Ann plan to flee to Mexico but when they encounter her mother, Sue Ann shoots her four times, laughing after the deed is done. On his way to dispose of the body, Pitt, wracked with guilt, phones the police. But Sue Ann has already called them and implicated him in the murder, for which he is convicted and sentenced to prison.

The theme of the femme fatale in whom seductiveness goes hand in hand with treachery is prominent in neo-noir from *Body Heat* to *The Last Seduction*. *Pretty Poison* makes reference to this theme and gives it a neo-noir twist all its own by depicting the innocent looking Sue Ann as the amoral killer who, we are led to surmise, will eventually go too far and expose the depravity beneath her surface beauty. *Pretty Poison* is faithful to noir in other respects as well, most conspicuously in its disoriented, isolated protagonist, portrayed by a post-*Psycho* Anthony Perkins. Perkins' strong performance as Sue Ann's victim engages audience sympathy with his performance as a disturbed young man who cannot escape his past and whose passivity reflects the inertia that leads him to his fate. Director Noel Black gives his debut film some nice stylistic flourishes, as when he shoots Pitt from a low angle through the magnifying screen he uses to inspect bottles of chemicals on an assembly line, exaggerating his features and rendering them surreal.

Pretty Poison enacts the kind of noir anxiety that accompanies Pitt's realization that he has succumbed to a life of fantasy-adventure. This life suddenly breaks apart when he becomes aware that Sue Ann embodies forces far more lethal than any he can find in himself. He realizes how precarious is his hold has been on reality, and this realization immobilizes him as he slips into catastrophe. All this is expressed in the film's signature scene, when Azenauer visits Pitt in prison, a year after the murders. Pitt tells the caseworker, who knows he is no murderer, a parable that is meant to explain his curious passivity in the face of Sue Ann's crimes: "There was some poison once, but no one recognized it. In fact, that poison was quite pretty looking." So the problem was what to do about the poison, and Pitt explains that he eventually came to realize he could do nothing, because no one would listen to him, an unstable person with a questionable past. "But if that poison just stayed

Pretty Poison: *Dennis Pitt (Anthony Perkins) and Sue Ann Stepanek (Tuesday Weld).*

there," he remarks, "getting worse and worse like poison always does, spreading until even the blindest man could see, until he had to see. . . ." At the film's end, Azenauer is observing from a distance as Sue Ann lures another victim into her web at the hot dog stand across the stream from the chemical plant. **SMS**

THE PUBLIC EYE (1992)

Screenplay, Director: Howard Franklin. **Producer**: Sue Baden-Powell. **Director of Photography**: Peter Suschitzky. **Production Designer**: Marcia Hinds-Johnson. **Music**: Mark Isham. **Editor**: Evan A. Lottman. **Cast**: Joe Pesci (Leon Bernstein), Barbara Hershey (Kay Levitz), Stanley Tucci (Sal), Jerry Adler (Arthur Nabler), Richard Schiff (Thompson Street Photographer), Dominic Chianese (Spoleto), Richard Riehle (Officer O'Brien), Laura Cerón (Puerto Rican Woman), Jack Denbo (Photo Editor), Bob Gunton (Older Agent), Richard Foronjy (Frank Farinell). **Released**: Universal, October 14. 99 minutes.

In the 1940s Leon "Bernzy" Bernstein prowls the night chasing pictures of "true crime" in the manner of celebrated shutterbug, "Weegee the Famous," a "character" created by photographer Arthur Fellig. Kay Levitz asks Bernzy for help with the mobsters who are trying to muscle in on her late husband's club. He accepts and inevitably is drawn into a mostly unrequited infatuation with Kay. While working to get incriminating information, Bernzy collects photographs of Kay's club and its patrons for a book he hopes someday to publish. When Bernzy discovers that Sal, his informant, has been killed, he also realizes that Kay has been bought and knows that their complicated relationship cannot continue. Having been willing to sacrifice his life for art or love, Bernzy is liberated, free to return to his relentless stalking of gruesome images for the tabloids of the era.

The opening of this movie features some of Weegee's most famous photos as they appear in the developing tray of "Bernzy" Bernstein. When Bernzy rises at 2:00 PM and grimaces at his own reflection in the mirror, he is the daylit equivalent of the images he stalks at night: worn yet resilient, ugly yet beautiful. Like Weegee, this character is at home with cops and crooks as well as New York's hoi polloi. It is this fine line that Joe Pesci as Bernstein walks in *The Public Eye* when he has foreknowledge of a murder which he chooses to photograph rather than to stop. Bernzy's photo book in progress is central to *The Public Eye*'s neo-noir evocation of mainstay emotions from the classic period: alienation and obsession. Rejected by mainstream publishers, Bernzy's work is more than obsession, it is his existential affirmation, a noir icon both in theme and in content. Unlike most classic period femme fatales, Kay is genuinely drawn to Bernzy because of his talent and by the raw emotion contained in his photographs, especially by his juxtaposition of one photo of her captioned "Beauty" with a battered prizefighter labeled "Beast."

In *The Public Eye*, the quest for recognition as an artist runs parallel to the quest for love. Bernzy points his camera at a sailor kissing a girlfriend good-bye and lurks in the shadows of unfulfilled longing. Artie, a newspaper columnist who has broken through on Broadway, tells him bluntly, "No woman could love a shabby little guy who sleeps in his clothes, eats out of cans and cozies up to corpses so much that he begins to stink like one." The short, unattractive Bernzy is a classic noir outsider reminiscent of Mickey Rooney's noir portrayals in *Drive a Crooked Road* and *Quicksand*. Professionally, Bernzy can sustain his pose of self-assurance, even cockiness, even if grilled by cops or slapped by mobsters. But the rush of human feeling can only come to him filtered through the lens of his camera. Fame, recognition, and simple respect are what drive Bernzy to point his camera directly at a loaded gun during the restaurant massacre. When the gunman spots him under the table, Bernzy is ready to die. He has half expected that his specially-rigged camera on wheels might capture the moment of his own death. But as fate would have it, Bernzy's number isn't up and a stray bullet brings down his would-be killer. As both Artie and his noir antecedents have predicted, Bernzy does not get the girl. Instead he ends up with respect and admission to the Stork Club; but he is alone and obsessed, unable to shut off the police radio that blares non-stop inside his car and inside his fevered brain. **LB**

The Public Eye: *Joe Pesci as Leon "Bernzy" Bernstein.*

A RAGE IN HARLEM (1991)

Director: Bill Duke. **Screenplay**: Bobby Crawford, John Toles-Bey based on the novel by Chester Himes. **Producers**: Kerry Rock, Forest Whitaker, Stephen Woolley. **Director of Photography**: Toyomichi Kurita. **Music**: Elmer Bernstein, Jeff Vincent. **Production Designer**: Steven Legler. **Editor**: Curtiss Clayton. **Cast**: Forest Whitaker (Jackson), Gregory Hines (Goldy), Robin Givens (Imabelle), Zakes Mokae (Big Kathy), Danny Glover (Easy Money), Badja Djola (Slim), John Toles-Bey (Jodie), Stack Pierce (Coffin Ed), George Wallace (Gravedigger), Tyler Collins (Teena). **Released**: Miramax, May 3. 115 minutes.

Imabelle is a gangster's moll, who after a bloody shoot-out flees to Harlem with a trunk load of gold. She later finds herself involved with the shy, religious Jackson who falls immediately under this femme fatale's spell. Soon Imabelle's gangster boyfriend comes to town looking for her and the gold. Imabelle takes off with Slim and Jackson pursues her with the help of his hustler brother Goldy. After a demonstration of heroics, Jackson saves Imabelle and retrieves the gold.

African-American writer Chester Himes is one of the most neglected noir writers of the last five decades. His series of books set in Harlem and featuring his two ribald and hardboiled detectives Coffin Ed and Gravedigger Jones evoke not only the ambience of Harlem in the 1950s and 60s but also combine urban Black humor, social commentary, and a fatalism very much in keeping with the noir ethos. In 1970 actor Ossie Davis wrote and directed the first adaptation of Himes' work with *Cotton Comes to Harlem* starring comedian Godfrey Cambridge and Raymond St. Jacques as the iconoclastic duo.

In 1991, another African-American actor/director, Bill Duke (*Deep Cover*), freely adapted Himes' *A Rage in Harlem*, bringing to the fore a minor character in the novel—the shy, religious Jackson (played with a humorous awkwardness by Forest Whitaker)—and building the script around him and his awakening under the ministrations of a classic femme fatale—Imabelle. As played by Robin Givens, Imabelle is a force of nature who uses her curvaceous body and childlike pout to entangle all the men around her, including her criminal boyfriend, a local mob boss, and, of course, the naïve Jackson. Whether seducing the virginal Jackson by running her naked foot across his mouth or plying the mobster with honeyed words, she ranks with the best of neo-noir femme fatales whose energy and sexuality force the neo-noir protagonist (in this case, Jackson) to the heights and depths of experience. **JU**

RED ROCK WEST (1992)

Director: John Dahl. **Screenplay**: John Dahl, Rick Dahl. **Producers**: Steve Golin, Sigurjon Sighvatsson. **Director of Photography**: Marc Reshovsky. **Music**: William Olvis. **Production Designer**: Robert Pearson. **Editor**: Scott Chestnut. **Cast**: Nicolas Cage (Michael Williams), Dennis Hopper (Lyle), Lara Flynn Boyle (Suzanne Brown/Ann McCord), Dwight Yoakam (Trucker), J.T. Walsh (Wayne Brown/Kevin McCord), Michael Rudd (Bartender), Craig Reay (Jim), Vance Johnson (Mr. Johnson), Robert Apel (Howard). **Locations**: Wilcox, Arizona. **Released**: PolyGram/Propaganda, April 8, 1994. 98 minutes. **Note**: Shot for theatrical release in 1992 but sold to HBO then played to limited engagements almost two years later.

Former marine Michael Williams journeys from Texas to Wyoming in search of a job in the oil fields. The after effects of a wound prevent him from being hired and he moves on down the road to Red Rock, where Wayne Brown presumes him to be the hit man he has contacted about killing his wife. Learning that Brown is ready to pay $10,000 for his wife's murder, he accepts the deal. After Brown's wife Suzanne offers Williams twice as much, he leaves town with the money after writing a letter to the sheriff. In a storm Williams has an accident and discovers that Brown is the sheriff, who soon drives Williams out of town to kill him. Williams escapes and gets a ride back into town with a trucker. At the door, he meets Lyle whom he realizes is the actual hit man. Much potentially deadly skirmishing, involving all four principals, then ensues, before they all end up in a cemetery where Wayne has buried the proceeds of a robbery he and Suzanne committed elsewhere and earlier. Wayne and Lyle are killed in a confrontation over the loot, Michael and Suzanne hop a passing freight train, taking the money with them. But disgusted by the events in which he has accidentally become involved, Michael tosses the woman off the train and most of the money blows away. He, however, retains one packet of cash—a sort of tip for his troubles—and the train chugs off into the night, bearing him toward his unknown fate.

Nightmares don't usually come equipped with signposts. But every time Michael Williams, the penniless drifter, either escapes or returns to the eponymous western town his passage is recorded from a vantage point that includes the sign, "Welcome to Red Rock." It is very much a signal of the deadpan humor of John Dahl's ingeniously plotted, flavorsomely realized, western noir.

For some reason, *Red Rock West* had a checkered history. Completed in 1992, it went straight to TV before a successful run in a San Francisco theater encouraged a reluctant and limited release two years later. That's possibly because of the film's ambiguous tonality, its lack of any figure we can whole-heartedly root for. Michael, for example, is both shrewd and stupid—in his way a classic noir protagonist—but hardly a conventional movie hero (the film was made in a period when Nicolas Cage had not yet settled for action hero mediocrity). The husband and wife who each hire him to kill the other are as affectless and cold as a pair of vipers, their essential mean-ness and overwhelming cupidity stirred by a clueless intrud-er, their malice expressed in flat voices and blank stares. You half expect them to start hissing their malice. And that says nothing about the real hit man, Lyle from Dallas, who's played by Dennis Hopper with his patented blend of noisy good cheer and psychopathic menace. When he belatedly turns up, his business in this movie is to raise its stakes, to twist its dark logic toward full-scale madness.

What's best about the movie (which Dahl wrote with his brother Rick) is its non-committal attitude. Classic noir films—think *They Live By Night* or *Side Street*—often muster a certain sympathy for young folks who make one little mis-take and innocently get caught up in evil's complex machi-nations. But there's nothing like that in *Red Rock West*. Michael is, possibly, a dimly decent guy when he's not involved in a desperate struggle to escape with his life and few bucks for his troubles. But he's scarcely a romantic and he's hardly a man besotted by moral principle. He's just improvising his way through the morass he's stumbled upon. And Dahl coolly watches him squirm his way to a survival that is by no means triumphant or instructive. The director's mode isn't tragic, satiric or ironic; it is post-ironic —purely objective.

Putting it mildly, this is not a stance that encourages a lot of mass audience enthusiasm. *Red Rock West* was, and will remain, an acquired, minority taste. But in its brisk, no-non-sense story telling, its minimal, but sharply-etched, charac-terizations, its bleakly handsome *mise en scène,* it is a trea-surably amoral assault on bourgeois values, on the pre-dictable moves and business-as-usual attitude of the crime thriller as we've grown accustomed to encountering it. **RS**

RESERVOIR DOGS (1992)

Screenplay, Director: Quentin Tarantino. **Producer**: Lawrence Bender. **Director of Photography**: Andrzej Sekula. **Production Designer**: David Wasco. **Music Supervisor**: Karyn Rachtman. **Editor**: Sally Menke. **Cast**: Harvey Keitel (Mr. White), Tim Roth (Mr. Orange/Freddy), Michael Madsen (Mr. Blonde/Vic), Chris Penn (Nice Guy Eddie), Steve Buscemi (Mr. Pink), Lawrence Tierney (Joe Cabot), Eddie Bunker (Mr. Blue), Quentin Tarantino (Mr. Brown), Randy Brooks (Holdaway), Kirk Baltz (Marvin Nash). **Released**: Miramax, October 8. 99 minutes.

Joe Cabot, an old-school mobster, puts together a six-man crew for a diamond heist. The group includes brains, mus-cle, neophytes and sociopaths. When the job goes awry, the anonymously named robbers rendezvous in a warehouse and pick through the events together. Flashbacks provide hap-hazard details of the recruitment, planning, disagreements over tactics, etc. When it becomes apparent to the five sur-vivors, including a seriously wounded Mr. Orange, that they were most likely foiled by the presence of an informer, the

Reservoir Dogs: *Mr. Blonde (Michael Madsen), Mr. White (Harvey Keitel), and Joe Cabot (Lawrence Tierney).*

wary men cross-examine each other to discover the truth before the police can track them down.

From the perspective of the classic noir style and narra-tive, *Reservoir Dogs* is pointedly aware of a relationship to that tradition, starting with the casting of classic period B-budget icon Lawrence Tierney as Cabot. As is evident from its plot *Reservoir Dogs* derives from the caper film. As in *The Asphalt Jungle* an organizer recruits a group of otherwise unrelated criminals for one job and in this iteration keeps their true identities from each other with "colorful" names. The botched robbery itself is never seen, only its aftermath as the survivors come to the meeting place and bicker over what happened and what to do now.

The flashbacks within flashbacks create narrative layers that are both "traditionally" noir and endistance the modern viewer from identification with the criminal protagonists. Equally endistancing are slow motion optical effects and moments of grisly, self-conscious humor. The psychopathic Mr. Blonde might well be alluding to *Point Blank* when he confesses to being "a big Lee Marvin fan"; but his character grimly transcends the violence of that type of picture when he cuts off the ear of a police hostage and talks to it. In the end, *Reservoir Dogs* is also about self-immolation, but not just because the characters shoot each other in an absurd, quasi-parody of a Mexican standoff. There is an also existen-tial justice in the fact that what may be Mr. White's one redemptive quality, his sense of loyalty to the severely wounded Mr. Orange, is also his undoing. That personal connection to a cohort who is actually an undercover cop is both human and, in the noir scheme of things, appropri-ately deadly. **AS**

ROMEO IS BLEEDING (1994)

Director: Peter Medak. **Screenplay**: Hilary Henkin. **Producers**: Hilary Henkin, Paul Webster, Michael Flynn. **Director of Photography**: Dariusz Wolski. **Production Designer**: Stuart Wurtzel. **Music**: Mark Isham. **Editor**: Walter Murch. **Cast**: Gary Oldman (Jack Grimaldi), Lena Olin (Mona Demarkov), Annabella Sciorra (Natalie Grimaldi), Juliette Lewis (Sheri), Roy Scheider (Don Falcone), David Proval (Scully), Will Patton (Martie), Larry Joshua (Joey), James Cromwell (Cage), Michael Wincott (Sal),

Romeo is Bleeding: *Jack Grimaldi (Gary Oldman) and Mona Demarkov (Lena Olin).*

William Duff-Griffin (Paddy), Tony Sirico (Malacci). **Released**: Polygram, February 4. 100 minutes.

Jack Grimaldi is a corrupt cop and womanizer. He takes bribes from the mob for various services and information. He neglects his wife Natalie and exploits his mistress Sheri. All this changes when the Russian hit woman Mona comes on the scene. Hired by mob boss Don Falcone to eliminate her or face the consequences, Jack pursues her but is stymied at every turn—seduced, beaten, and outwitted. Eventually Mona convinces him to join her in her plot to kill and bury Don Falcone himself. He agrees. After the deed is done, Mona betrays him. Arrested for his crimes, Jack confronts Mona in the courthouse, steals a gun, and shoots her. The Feds reward him by giving him a new identity and housing him in a diner, the one he had asked his wife to meet him at when he sent her away in order to protect her. At the end of the film he continues to wait for his wife to return.

Writer-producer Hilary Henkin's *Romeo Is Bleeding* traces the downfall of a weak, venal cop named Jack Grimaldi, who narrates the story with typically neo-noir irony from his desert exile in a small Arizona diner where he waits for the "true love" of his life, his long-suffering wife Natalie, to return to him. Jack is a womanizer who, as he admits, can only make "the hole" in his yard, into which he "feeds" his bribes from the mob, "happy" (the use of the term "hole" is not accidental; for it is the way Jack sees women). His wife suffers quietly with only momentary outbursts as when she turns her husband's gun on him and then laughs. His mistress is a cocktail waitress who performs various fantasies for Jack and whom he ends up murdering by mistake.

The only woman who stands up to Jack and maintains the upper hand, until she too is shot by him, is the truly intimidating Russian hit woman Mona, played by Lena Olin as part dominatrix, part monster, part sexual predator, part cyborg. Mona acts as the avenger for all the "normal" women Jack has betrayed. She handcuffs him to her bed, unstraps her leather harness which holds a prosthetic arm, and sexually assaults Jack with a savage fury. Dressing Jack's mistress as herself, she tricks him into shooting her. While handcuffed in the backseat of his car, she chokes him with her powerful legs and then escapes his custody by kicking free through the front windshield. In the end she betrays him and delivers him to the cops.

After all this suffering and punishment, Jack does make one final stab at redemption. He gives his bribe money to his wife and helps her escape before the mob disfigures her. He declares his love and asks her to go to a diner in the desert and wait for him every May 1 and December 1. After Jack is tricked into shooting Mona by the Feds, he is given a new identity and relocated to that same diner. And there he waits, haunted by the ghosts of the women he harmed, including Mona, but never losing hope that Natalie will return one day to rescue him from his isolation and guilt. **JU**

RUSH (1991)

Director: Lili Fini Zanuck. **Screenplay**: Peter Dexter based on the novel by Kim Wozencraft. **Producer**: Richard D. Zanuck (The Zanuck Company). **Director of Photography**: Kenneth MacMillan. **Music**: Eric Clapton. **Art Director**: Paul Sylbert. **Editor**: Mark Warner. **Cast**: Jason Patric (Jim Raynor), Jennifer Jason Leigh (Kristen Cates), Sam Elliott (Dodd), Max Perlich (Walker), Gregg Allman (Gaines), Tony Frank (Nettle), William Sadler (Monroe), Special K. McCray (Willie Red), Dennis Letts (Senior District Attorney). **Released**: MGM, December 22. 120 minutes.

Undercover narcotics officer Jim Raynor chooses a new and inexperienced partner for his next assignment, the tough Kristen Cates. Together, they must find hard evidence against the elusive drug dealer Gaines. But as they get deeper undercover, they fall in love and become addicted to the same drugs they've been charged with keeping off the street, further complicating matters. Finally, lacking any real evidence, but reasoning that Gaines must be put away, they manufacture evidence in order to get a conviction. Ultimately, as her conscience gets the better of her, Kristen reverses herself and Gaines is released.

Enjoyably gritty in a 1970's John Schlesinger or Sidney Lumet sort of way, *Rush* is a bleakly stylish police drama based on a true story of a Texan drug sting. What makes *Rush* noir is its insistent but subtle assertion that corruption is seductive and, in certain situations, mandatory. And though its tale of compromised cops is common in noir, perhaps one of the few true parallels it has amongst classic noir, in tone and theme, if not plot, is the similarly melancholy *Touch of Evil. Rush* is at its best when it's describing the slow descent into corruption and addiction, asserting its position of moral ambiguity and further blurring the line between crime and law enforcement. It also successfully refuses to demonize the drug dealers, placing the drama and conflict firmly within the protagonists' own conscience. **JEB**

THE SALTON SEA (2002)

Director: D.J. Caruso. **Screenplay**: Tony Gayton. **Producers**: Ken Aguado, Jim Behnke, Eriq La Salle and Butch Robinson. **Director of Photography**: Amir M. Mokri. **Music**: Thomas Newman. **Production Designer**: Tom Southwell. **Editor**: Jim Page. **Cast**: Val Kilmer (Danny Parker/Tom Van Allen), Vincent D'Onofrio (Pooh-Bear), Adam Goldberg (Kujo), Luis Guzmán (Quincy), Doug Hutchison (Gus Morgan), Anthony LaPaglia (Al Garcetti), Glenn Plummer (Bobby), Peter Sarsgaard (Jimmy the Finn), Deborah Kara Unger (Colette), Chandra West (Liz). **Released**: Warner Bros., April 23. 103 minutes.

The audience gets a quick history of the world of methamphetamine and are brought into the narrator's psyche, deep in the throes of addiction. Tom Van Allen, trumpet player and devoted husband, has been self-transformed into Danny Parker, speed freak and police informant. Working with narcotics officers Gus Morgan and Al Garcetti, Danny becomes their lead snitch in the underworld of meth and becomes a marked man by a local drug dealer, Domingo. In a supposed deal of a lifetime to get $25,000 and implicate Domingo, Danny settles a score with the infamous meth maker "Pooh-Bear." The FBI is brought in after Danny reveals that his narcotic officers are corrupt. Along the way, Danny befriends a battered woman who lives across the hall from him. He confides in her regarding the murder of his wife, and the two injured souls console each other as lovers. As the final deal with Pooh-Bear gets set, we discover that the men responsible for his wife's death are, in fact, the corrupt Morgan and Garcetti, and that Tom Van Allen's transformation into Danny is actually a set-up to avenge his wife's murder by killing the two officers responsible.

Despite the desert locale of its title, *Salton Sea*'s highly stylized neo-noir tale of vengeance and redemption is mainly set in the seedy meth-infused industrial streets of Los Angeles. Mired in this carefree world of fast-talking yet directionless groups of young people, protagonist Danny Parker leads the viewer through mind-numbing detective work, aided by his amazing photographic memory, while he teeters on a fine line, often falling victim to the foggy world engulfing him. Like Frank Bigelow in *D.O.A.*, Danny is a walking dead man, if only in his heart and soul. He is forced into doing his own detective work because there is no other help in sight. Plunged deeper into hopelessness, the only grip he has on sanity is to rummage through an old suitcase cradling his trumpet and to connect to his past as a reminder of his true identity and as a reason to stay alive.

As in Orson Welles' *A Touch of Evil*, the audience is deposited into a world of colorfully dangerous people, all motivated by a desire to maintain their small piece of the power pie. As director D.J. Caruso pushes deeper into Danny's pain-filled past, he creates a fever dream populated by characters from that classic noir underworld full of paranoia and moral ambiguity. At first Danny seems to be using everyone to untangle the true identities of the masked men who murdered his wife. Gradually Danny's true position is revealed as an anti-hero on the edge, uncertain of who he is, what he is doing or how to carry out his plan. Despite cravenly witnessing his wife's death, Danny becomes a sympathetic character by default. Riding along with a sociopath who is, like a ticking bomb in a Hitchcock narrative, ready to explode at any moment, the viewer is immersed in a twisted journey with a voyager who wreaks havoc on all he encounters, yet at the end expresses hope that in the midst of extreme tragedy may lie the possibility of salvation. **PAD**

The Salton Sea: *Val Kilmer as Tom Van Allen/Danny Parker.*

SEA OF LOVE (1989)

Director: Harold Becker. **Screenplay**: Richard Price. **Producers**: Martin Bregman, Michael Bregman, Louis A. Stoller. **Director of Photography**: Ronnie Taylor. **Music**: Trevor Jones. **Production Designer**: John Jay Moore. **Editor**: David Bretherton. **Cast**: Al Pacino (Det. Frank Keller), Ellen Barkin (Helen Kruger), John Goodman (Det. Sherman), Michael Rooker (Terry), William Hickey (Frank Keller), Richard Jenkins (Gruber), Paul Calderon (Serafino), Gene Canfield (Struk), Larry Joshua (Dargan), John Spencer (Lieutenant), Christine Estabrook (Gina Gallagher), Barbara Baxley (Miss Allen), (Harry), Marlo Dwyer (Miss Lewis). **Released**: Universal, September 15. 113 minutes.

Frank Keller celebrates twenty years as a Manhattan detective the day a man is found shot, naked on a bed, with "Sea

of Love" playing. He teams up with Detective Sherman, investigating a similar murder in Queens. Both victims subscribed to a lonely-hearts column, through messages in doggerel, so the police assume therefore that the perpetrator is female. A third murder with the same MO enables them to persuade Frank's chief that they should place a similar message, and go undercover to investigate the women who respond. Frank embarks on a tempestuous affair with Helen, a separated single mother who replies to the advertisement. He is aware that it's unprofessional, and that the case could be jeopardized. As the affair develops, a wealth of evidence points to Helen, especially as she had dated all three victims. Frank concludes she is the perpetrator, but that his involvement with her means the case cannot get to court. Meanwhile, he is being stalked, and is attacked in his apartment by Helen's ex-husband, driven by jealousy to track and kill the men she dates. After a struggle Frank's attacker falls to his death from one of the apartment windows.

Sea of Love could have been little more than a classy but predictable police procedural: Frank Keller, cynical and world-weary cop after twenty years on the street (and inevitably unorthodox) takes on a serial killer who leaves a trail of distinctive clues. Along the way Frank develops a classic cop-partner relationship with Sherman, alongside his tempestuous affair with Helen, which includes torrid, erotic and at times graphic sex. But the movie is transformed, first by some intelligent and often funny writing, offering Pacino crackling dialogue through which to develop his relationships, especially with Goodman. Secondly, Becker uses the script to coax superb performances from the three leads. *Sea of Love* was Pacino's first film in four years (he made seven in the next four), and his previous movies (*Revolution*, *Scarface*, *Author Author*) had been poorly received by the critics. But his performance here is intelligent, edgy and sympathetic and earned him a Golden Globe nomination.

Thirdly, the movie rises above a routine serial killer chase because of the way it explores the relationship between Pacino and Barkin which underpins the narrative. The tensions within the affair arise ostensibly from the fact that Frank's lover could be (and as the movie develops probably is) a serial killer. A similar idea had been pursued earlier in *Jagged Edge* (1985), and would be a little later with *Basic Instinct* (1992). *Sea of Love* handles the implications of the relationship better than either however since it uses the premise to explore more gen-

erally the dangers (for anyone) of opening up to another in an intense affair, especially when both parties have been damaged by previous relationships turned sour. Helen is at first wary of Frank since she is used to being deceived and used by men, hence her devastation at discovering that Frank too has used her, albeit in the cause of law enforcement. And the film explores at times brutally and erotically how sexual attraction can overcome reason, potentially becoming fatal. The movie's implausibly happy ending strikes a slightly discordant note, but nevertheless *Sea of Love* is a powerful and satisfying contribution to the neo-noir canon. **GF**

SEVEN (1995)

Director: David Fincher. **Screenplay**: Andrew Kevin Walker. **Producers**: Phyllis Carlyle, Arnold Kopelson, Stephen Brown (co-producer), Nana Greenwald (co-producer), Sanford Panitch (co-producer). **Director of Photography**: Darius Khondji. **Music**: Howard Shore. **Production Designer**: Arthur Max. **Editor**: Richard Francis-Bruce. **Cast**: Brad Pitt (Detective David Mills), Morgan Freeman (Detective Lt. William Somerset), Gwyneth Paltrow (Tracy Mills), R. Lee Ermey (Police Captain), Andrew Kevin Walker (Dead Man), Daniel Zacapa (Detective Taylor), John Cassini (Officer Davis), Bob Mack (Gluttony Victim), Peter Crombie (Dr. O'Neill). **Released**: New Line, September 22. 127 minutes.

Just a few days short of retirement, Detective Somerset finds himself reluctantly drawn into both a partnership with young hotshot Detective Mills, and a case involving a sadistic and ingenious serial killer whose murders are based on the Seven Deadly Sins. Each crime scene—gluttony, sloth, lust—offers clues which suggest the killer is testing the detectives' skills. As they begin to unravel the secrets which will lead them to the identity of the killer, whom they only know as John Doe, John Doe comes to discover things about the detectives. Ultimately, John Doe murders Mills' wife, and turns himself in. John Doe explains that the murder of Mills' wife represented John Doe's envy, and he describes the murder so that Mills himself will commit the sin of wrath, avenging his wife's murder but destroying his career.

Seven is jarring and unnerving right from the shaky opening credits. The gruesome crime scenes are scary, to be sure, but the whole city seems unwelcoming. The way it is shot, it is simultaneously crowded and empty, busy but lonely. By the time the closing credits roll (backwards), the viewer has been thoroughly shocked, not in the cheap-scare sense, but in the sense of having been forced to contemplate evil. Part of what makes the John Doe character so disturbing is that his rationale, even if sociopathic, has a grain of truth to it: "We see a deadly sin on every street corner, in every home, and we tolerate it. We tolerate it because it's common, it's trivial. We tolerate it morning, noon, and night." He sees himself as setting a new pattern for ridding the world of sin. Yet his methods are diabolical, cruel, and ingenious.

The viewer finds it hard to accept this solution, yet it is true that we tolerate sin and regard it as banal. But the viewer's moral unease is exacerbated by Mills' torment at learning of his innocent wife's murder, and his killing of John Doe echoes Greek tragedy in its inevitability and self-destruction. Somerset's existential despair seems all too validated by his encounter with John Doe and his inability to prevent Mills

from executing John Doe's final plan. Although the crime scenes are gory, the body count is relatively low, and the film's greatest tensions are psychological, as we watch the detectives try to make sense out of madness. The dark world they inhabit is partly in the mind of John Doe, but it is partly the real world, as Somerset already knows and as Mills comes to discover. **AJS**

SHARKY'S MACHINE (1981)

Director: Burt Reynolds. **Screenplay**: Gerald Di Pego based on the novel of the same name by William Diehl. **Producer**: Hank Moonjean. **Director of Photography**: William A. Fraker. **Production Design**: Walter Scott Herndon. **Editors**: William D. Gordean and Dennis Virkler. **Cast**: Burt Reynolds (Sgt. Tom Sharky), Vittorio Gassman (Victor), Brian Keith (Papa), Charles Durning (Friscoe), Earl Holliman (Hotchkins), Bernie Casey (Arch), Henry Silva (Billy Score), Richard Libertini (Nosh), Darryl Hickman (Smiley), Rachel Ward (Dominoe), Joseph Mascolo (Joe Tipps), Carol Locatell (Mabel). **Released**: Warner Bros., December 18. 122 minutes.

Detective Tom Sharky is forced into unorthodox tactics after a botched set-up of a local drug lord, during which Sharky's methods inadvertently get a civilian wounded in crossfire. He is subsequently demoted and transferred from narcotics to the dingy basement rabble of vice. There Sharky stumbles onto a connection between a mysterious well-connected kingpin who has his fingers in high-class prostitution and police bribery, and a candidate for governor. Sharky quickly assembles his washed-up vice detectives ("the machine") to begin an ad-hoc investigation, Sharky's way. Upon discovering that the machine is surveying his prize prostitute Dominoe for information, the Italian boss Victor orders her murder to silence the leak. Unfortunately, his cocaine-addicted assassin brother Billy kills the wrong girl. When Victor realizes the mistake, he turns to wiping out the entire vice squad. Sharky and Dominoe go into hiding, where they promptly fall for each other. Meanwhile, Victor's psychotic brother, in a drug-induced delirium, pays back his brother's arrogance by riddling Victor with lead. Sharky and crew take on the stealthy assassin high on the upper floors of a sky-scraper. In the final standoff between Billy and Sharky, the last cog in his own ill-fated "machine," Sharky discharges his weapon into the killer, propelling him through a window to his violent demise.

Sharky's Machine, which was actor Burt Reynolds' third outing as a feature director, is a gritty, street-wise blend of hardboiled detective work and gut wrenching violence. The ending is almost supernatural, an annihilation of practically all involved with only love surviving, reminiscent of the resolution of *Kiss Me Deadly*. *Sharky's Machine*'s subtext is the convoluted delusion of modern life and the redemptive power of love in a dreary world. Sharky is an emotionally stagnant man who dreams of a normal, wholesome life while existing in a seedy city of sin. His closest friend languishes in the real American dream which evades Sharky. Instead, he secretly purchases his childhood home, a distant memory of the only family life he's known, in a bright sunny neighborhood where children's laughter drifts into his open windows. He doodles designs, wood-carves flowers, and works relentlessly in restoring his home for a future, idealized family.

However, as Sharky's real world deteriorates from a highly decorated detective's to that of a vice-cop misfit, he uses a group of "sad cases" like himself and constructs a working family to fulfill his inner need for connection. This is taken even further while doing surveillance on the prostitute Dominoe. Sharky pays little heed to the fact that Dominoe is a deeply disturbed woman, abused and traumatized in childhood. Instead, like the homicide detective in *Laura* obsessed with the portrait of a dead murder victim, Sharky transforms Dominoe into an ideal love candidate to share in his fantasy of family. Being at her core of the same romantic mindset, Dominoe rejects the reality of her abduction and sexual training at age twelve and mentally transforms herself into a housewife-in-waiting. Whenever questioned about her profession, she boldly claims that she is a dancer despite the comments from her instructor ("Get off your fat ass"). Her true skill is as sexual object for hire, who entrances men like the governor-to-be.

Given the bleak reality of their respective situations, Sharky and Dominoe embrace the chance to become who in their repressed psychological desires they wish to be. Once they are thrown together in hiding, a synergistic dynamic between their fantasies is unleashed, superseding the sordid real world with their fictitious one. Dominoe is immediately entranced by the make-believe house Sharky is creating, which forebodes an inevitable clash between the internalized transformation of their desire for familial connection and that darker world of perversion, apathy and detachment in which they are both mired. Burt Reynolds' ability to bring together a well-crafted ensemble of actors that riff and handle hardboiled banter easily creates a base of tightly connected relationships. This adds an element of shock and dismay to their fates. In the end, with everyone else viciously rubbed out, the image of Sharky and Dominoe happily playing on a swing in the backyard, lost in fully actualized fantasy, is both highly ironic and disturbingly off-key in its denial of their past. **PAD**

The Silence of the Lambs: Anthony Hopkins as Dr. Hannibal Lecter.

THE SILENCE OF THE LAMBS (1991)

Director: Jonathan Demme. **Screenplay**: Ted Tally based on the novel by Thomas Harris. **Producers**: Ron Bozman, Edward Saxon and Kenneth Utt (Strong Heart/Demme Production). **Director of Photography**: Tak Fujimoto. **Music**: Howard Shore. **Art Directors**: Kristi Zea and Tim Galvin. **Editor**: Craig McKay. **Cast**: Jodie Foster (Clarice Starling), Anthony Hopkins (Dr. Hannibal Lecter), Scott Glenn (Jack Crawford), Anthony Heald (Dr. Frederick Chilton), Ted Levine (Jame "Buffalo Bill" Gumb), Frankie Faison (Barney Matthews), Kasi Lemmons (Ardelia Mapp), Brooke Smith (Catherine Martin). **Released**: Orion Pictures, February 14. 118 minutes.

The FBI, desperate to find a serial killer called "Buffalo Bill," enlists a promising FBI cadet, Clarice Starling, to interview a notorious psychiatrist turned killer, Hannibal Lecter, in an asylum. Lecter resists, but ultimately gives her information leading to an early as yet undiscovered victim of Buffalo Bill's. Lecter then makes a deal with Starling. If she gets him transferred to a more attractive prison, he will profile Buffalo Bill for the FBI. Using clues Lecter provides, Starling investigates in the hometown of Buffalo Bill's first victim, a seamstress. While the FBI follows independent, but misleading, information, Starling goes to a house where the first victim once worked. The door is answered by a man claiming his name is "Jack Gordon," but Starling sees clues in the house that lead her to believe that Gordon is actually Buffalo Bill. After a terrifying chase through his house, Starling manages to kill Buffalo Bill and saves his latest victim.

The lasting influence of *Silence of the Lambs'* reinvention of the crime procedural cannot be overstated. From film to television, the prevalence of its effect is ubiquitous. *Silence of the Lambs* does more than update the police-perspective style of films like *T-Men, He Walked by Night, Naked City* and many others. The film, from top to bottom, re-conceptualizes the motivations and effects of such hackneyed devices as the voice-of-god narration, and the faux-documentary style, replacing them with simple, naturalistic devices that serve the same effect, but less obtrusively. Like classic noir, it continues to borrow from documentary film style, using updated devices such as the in-scene time and location stamps, but now with

an intent to submerge the viewer rather than as an attempt to be an all-seeing narrator. Though the film teeters into grand guignol on occasion, the overall effect is still one of documenting a methodical and systematic investigation, much as in the earlier films. The performances are all excellent, if not exactly subtle, but one of the film's most appreciated parallels with classic noir is its willingness to entertain. **JEB**

SIMPATICO (1999)

Director: Matthew Warchus. **Screenplay**: Warchus and David Nicholls based on the play by Sam Shepard. **Producers**: Jean-François Fonlupt, Dan Lupovitz, Timm Oberwelland. **Director of Photography**: John Toll. **Music**: Stewart Copeland. **Production Designer**: Amy B. Ancona. **Editors**: Pasquale Buba, Seth Flaum. **Cast**: Nick Nolte (Vincent Webb), Jeff Bridges (Lyle Carter), Sharon Stone (Rosie Carter), Catherine Keener (Cecilia), Albert Finney (Simms/Ryan Ames), Shawn Hatosy (Young Vinnie Webb), Kimberly Williams (Young Rosie), Liam Waite (Young Lyle Carter), Whit Crawford (Jean), Bob Harter (Louis). **Released**: Fine Line, December 15. 106 minutes.

As teenagers Lyle, Vinnie and Rosie are in a *Jules et Jim*-style ménage that tests the limits of both friendship and love. They plot to "beat the races" and succeed in their fraud by winning large amounts of money on long shots. Whe a racetrack official discovers the scheme they blackmail him into silence. In their naiveté they do not realize that committing these crimes makes them criminals. Although they get off scot-free with the money, all of them soil their lives irrevocably and only later realize that cheating and blackmailing others means they have cheated and betrayed each other. The consequences come many years later, when Vinnie has fallen on hard times and learns that Lyle and Rosie are selling their racehorse Simpatico. For a while Vinnie manages to swap places with Lyle before he ultimately realizes that you cannot reinvent your life.

Simpatico is a neo-noir uninhibited by classification. It stretches the urban noir boundaries, as it explores the actions of three teenage friends who grew up outside of Los Angeles, in the last idyllic countryside of Azusa, which legend was dubbed thus by its founders because it "has everything in the USA from A to Z." When ordinary people decide to delve into crime just one time but then are forever trapped into guilt and shame, they define the core existentialism of noir. Many years after their crime, Vinnie, Lyle and Rosie continue to wallow in separate lonely pits of despairing guilt and resentment. Lyle and Vinnie's unconscious identity switch almost parodies classic noir plotting. Meanwhile Rosie attempts redemption by refusing to allow Simpatico, their famous but now-sterile race-horse, to be part of her husband's big-score breeding fraud.

However, this story is not so clear-cut as this explanation. "Simpatico" is the Spanish noun for not just "friendship" but also a deep asexual soul-connection between people. Thus this story is actually about the changing nature of all the characters' essential relations to each other as they play out the plot's convoluted and unlikely actions. The symbol of their connection is a valuable horse, which fluctuates between being adored as a living being and treated as a mere totem that represents their greed.

Adapted from Sam Shepard's 1994 play the film *Simpatico* can alternate between wide vista and claustrophobic interiors, a visual fluctuation that externalizes the emotional ups-and-downs of the characters. The visual "confusion" mounts as the characters undergo a shift in identity and the story's conflict turns the personas of Lyle and Vinnie inside-out. After opening credits of fluttering snapshots and someone's huge hands struggling to tape a flimsy box, the principal male characters are introduced briefly in barest outline: Vinnie is destitute and telephones polished businessman Lyle. While Vinnie whines about his problem incoherently, Lyle postures stiffly; but it turns when Vinnie gives hints of blackmail. From this context, flashbacks filmed by Vinnie with his super-8 camera fill in tantalizing fractions of back story. When a lovely young, Rosie, is introduced, it is difficult to tell which young man she favors as the trio frolics outdoors at horse tracks and nearby pastures and ride on motorcycles and in convertible gas-guzzlers. As details are filled in the viewer can piece together how childish foolishness initiated fatal consequences.

This neo-noir alternately uses grainy and saturated color to accentuate the contrast between innocent, pastoral nature and contemporary consumer-civilization's greed. By utilizing saturated and stylized color expertly, the film expresses golden youthful days followed by scenes of sex-crimes committed at night in dark confusion under a steely downpour. The blackmail also requires disguises and spying behind false mirrors. The film's finale uses a palette of vivid blue-green grass under dark gray cloudy skies while Rosie wears a shining blood-red satin gown and thunders across the pastures of her Kentucky estate, taking a farewell ride upon her fabled but sterile black stallion. The epilogue is shot in bright travel-channel style. Two "marks" keep their rendezvous at the Kentucky Derby and beam happily while they enjoy being guilt-free survivors amongst the derby crowd. And in neo-noir, of course, protagonists need not suffer retribution for their criminal pasts. **EW**

A SIMPLE PLAN (1998)

Director: Sam Raimi. **Screenplay**: Scott B. Smith based on his novel. **Producers**: James Jacks, Adam Schroeder, Michael Polaire [co-producer]. **Director of Photography**: Alar Kivilo. **Music**: Danny Elfman. **Production Designer**: Patrizia von Brandenstein. **Editor**: Eric L. Beason, Arthur Coburn. **Cast**: Bill Paxton (Hank Mitchell), Bridget Fonda (Sarah Mitchell), Billy Bob Thornton (Jacob Mitchell), Brent Briscoe (Lou Chambers), Jack Walsh (Tom Butler), Chelcie Ross (Sheriff Carl Jenkins), Becky Ann Baker (Nancy Chambers), Gary Cole (Neil Baxter), Bob Davis (FBI Agent Renkins), Peter Syvertsen (FBI Agent Freemont), Tom Carey (Dwight Stephanson), John Paxton (Mr. Schmitt), Marie Mathay (News Reporter). **Locations**: Ashland, Wisconsin; Delano, St. Paul, Minnesota. **Released**: Paramount, December 11. 121 minutes.

Hank, his brother Jacob, and their friend Lou stumble upon a crashed plane in the forest, and recover a gym bag filled with millions of dollars. They surmise it is a drug dealer's money, and decide to keep it. The "simple plan" is to refrain from spending it for a few months, and then if no one shows up looking for the money, they can spend it. But they grow impatient, and then careless, and then distrustful of each other. The drug dealers do come around looking for the money. The web of lies grows bigger, resulting in several deaths and shattered lives.

A Simple Plan uses many noir conventions, but is not self-consciously positioning itself as a throwback. The unsettling camera angles and long shots that suggest isolation achieve their effect in an original way, transposing the usual noir scene to a rural area. The femme fatale character is present, but with a twist: she is Hank's pregnant wife. Voice-over narration is used, but sparingly. It has twists that evoke classic noir but yet are not predictable. The suspense lies largely in seeing how the plan unravels, but the film also offers a compelling portrait of moral corruption. By showing an otherwise good man driven to lie, steal, and commit murder, the film demonstrates the self-destructive effects of moral corruption. Even the femme fatale character is shown rapidly descending from virtue to vice: early on, Sarah Mitchell is the voice of reason and righteousness, but by the end of the film, she seems to be cut from the same mold as Brigid O'Shaughnessy of *The Maltese Falcon*. Bill Paxton's performance as a man presiding over his own downfall is very engaging. One of the film's strengths is the way it builds the violent scenes upon the psychological transformation of the characters. The story is tense and exciting even at the surface level, but beneath that lies an exploration of one of the most enduring moral questions: why bother being moral? As with *The Postman Always Rings Twice*, the viewer is left contemplating that very issue. **AJS**

SIN CITY (2005)

Directors: Frank Miller, Robert Rodriguez, Quentin Tarantino. **Screenplay**: Frank Miller based on his graphic novels *Sin City*. **Producers**: Elizabeth Avellan, Bob Weinstein, Harvey Weinstein. **Director of Photography**: Robert Rodriguez. **Art Director**: Jeanette Scott, Steve Joyner. **Music**: John Debney, Graeme Revell, Robert Rodriguez. **Editor**: Robert Rodriguez. **Cast**: Jessica Alba (Nancy Callahan), Devon Aoki (Miho), Alexis Bledel (Becky), Powers Boothe (Senator Roark), Rosario Dawson (Gail), Benicio Del Toro (Jackie Boy), Carla Cugino (Lucille), Jaime King (Goldie/Wendy), Michael Madsen (Bob), Frank Miller (Priest), Brittany Murphy (Shellie), Clive Owen (Dwight), Mickey Rourke (Marv), Nick Stahl (Junior),

Sin City: *Nancy Callahan (Jessica Alba) and Hartigan (Bruce Willis)*.

Sin City: *Dwight (Clive Owen) and Jackie Boy (Benicio del Toro).*

Bruce Willis (Hartigan), Elijah Wood (Kevin), Rutger Hauer (Cardinal Roark). **Released**: Troublemaker/Miramax/Dimension, March 28. 124 minutes; 147 minutes (director's cut).

Sin City tells four stories. "The Customer Is Always Right" is about a hired killer who puts victims out of their misery upon request. In "That Yellow Bastard" Hartigan, a cop, saves a young girl, Nancy, from a pedophile (Junior), castrating him in the process. Junior is the son of the powerful Senator Roark so Hartigan is imprisoned and tortured for the act. When released after confessing to the crime of molestation, he returns to Nancy who is now working as a stripper. She is again kidnapped by Junior. Hartigan rescues her but kills himself in order to protect Nancy who will be pursued by the Senator unless he is dead. In "The Big, Fat Kill" Dwight becomes involved with his ex-lover, dominatrix Gail, the head of a self-sufficient group of warrior prostitutes. They hold off an invasion of hoods who wish to take over the prostitute's territory. In "The Hard Goodbye" Marv, a psychotic, falls for a prostitute Goldie who spends one night with him and then is murdered. He pursues her killer (Kevin) and finds not only him but his powerful patron, Cardinal Roark. Both routinely kill and cannibalize prostitutes. Marv kills them and is executed for his deeds.

Sin City, based on the graphic novels of Frank Miller (the man responsible for "noiring" the image of the comic book hero in the eighties), who co-directs with Robert Rodriguez and Quentin Tarantino, interweaves four stories in a complex visual recreation of the noir world of the classic period. Using CGI techniques the film resembles an animated version of Miller's comic books, with chiaroscuro slashes of light and dark interrupted periodically by splashes of color. The four stories themselves ("The Customer Is Always Right," used only as framing device, "That Yellow Bastard," "The Big, Fat Kill," and "The Hard Goodbye"), which overlap in time and space, recycle for a new generation many of the themes and motifs from the classic period. Obsession, femme fatales, existential "chumps," and corruption abound.

In "The Big, Fat Kill" Dwight is fixated on his ex-lover, the bi-sexual dominatrix Gail, played by Rosario Dawson, who leads the gang of warrior prostitutes who have established sovereignty over a part of Basin City called "Old Town." He returns to help them out when a rogue cop and the mob invade their territory but soon learns that these femme fatales are able to defend themselves. Dressed in fetish outfits and sporting swords, knives, and automatic weapons these femme fatales are "Valkyrie" right out of 1970s warrior women exploitation movies. In "The Hard Goodbye" (the name of course references Chandler's novel), Marv, as played by Mickey Rourke whose own world-weary face requires the minimum amount of prosthetics, is a brute-like "maniac" who even prostitutes will not touch. After one luminous "goddess" (his words) takes pity on him and spends one night with him in a heart-shaped bed and then is murdered in the morning, he tears apart the town to find her murderer. When he is executed for his "crimes," the camera zooms into his eye to reveal his last thoughts—Goldie making love to him on that red, heart-shaped bed.

The most classically noir of the pieces is "That Yellow Bastard." Bruce Willis plays an aging cop named Hartigan who has a "bad heart" as well as a strong sense of chivalry. As with the other pieces, he narrates the tale in traditional noir fashion, calling himself "old man" and putting himself through masochistic situation after masochistic situation in order to protect Nancy, the stripper he saved as a child from a child molester. Their relationship is typical of the perverse couplings in much of noir. Nancy has written him every week while he served time on a trumped up charge. When he goes to find her she is on stage, dressed as a cowgirl. As he is deciding to leave, sensing he is being followed, Nancy, who in the person of Jessica Alba is a Lolita wet dream, ropes her "bull" before he can leave, jumping from the stage and crushing him in her embrace. Hartigan, who tells her he is old enough to be her "grandfather," tries to resist her aggressive advances but finds himself too drawn to this "granddaughter-lover." In the final scene, Hartigan performs the ultimate act of devotion and chivalry, killing himself in order to save Nancy from the political powers that are bent on his destruction. As he sinks into the snow, he pronounces his own epitaph with an existential fatalism common to noir protagonists, "An old man dies, a young woman lives, fair trade." **JU**

SLAM DANCE (1987)

Director: Wayne Wang. **Screenplay**: Don Opper. **Producers**: Rupert Harvey, Barry Opper, Don Keith Opper. **Director of Photography**: Amir Mokri. **Production Designer**: Eugenio Zanetti. **Music**: Mitchell Froom. **Editor**: Lee Percy, Sandy Nervig. **Cast**: Tom Hulce (Drood), Virginia Madsen (Yolanda Caldwell/Nancy Barron), Mary Elizabeth Mastrantonio (Helen Drood), Adam Ant (Jim), Judith Barsi (Bean Drood), Rosalind Chao (Mrs. Bell), Don Opper (Buddy), John Doe (Gilbert), Harry Dean Stanton (Smiley), Millie Perkins (Bobby Nye), Robert Beltran (Frank). **Released**: Island, November 6. 100 minutes.

Drood, a punk cartoonist, has an affair with a mysterious call girl named Yolanda. When she is found dead, he is pursued by the police as well as by a hit man on the payroll of Yolanda's ex-lover, the wealthy Bobby Nye. The police detective Gilbert tries to frame Drood for Yolanda's murder but Drood stumbles into several clues which lead him to the real "murderers," Bobby Nye and Buddy, the hit man. Buddy takes Drood to the Hollywood sign to execute him but instead kills himself out of guilt for causing Yolanda's death. Smiley, an honest cop, saves Drood from Gilbert and Drood escapes. In order to misdirect the police, he burns up Buddy's body, leaving evidence that will lead authorities to think it is his body. In the final scene he drives his wife and child away from his own funeral.

Wayne Wang's *Slam Dance* invokes Hollywood of the 1980s. From its decaying sign atop Mt. Lee (some of the letters are burnt out and the rear is filled with graffiti) through its punk culture (John Doe of the groundbreaking punk band *X* plays Gilbert, a cop on the take; music from artists like Stan Ridgway and the Fibonaccis punctuate the sound track; a punk club acts as a central metaphor in the film) to its greedy upper classes (referencing the redistribution of wealth beginning in the Reagan years) Wang carefully establishes a neo-noir atmosphere of corruption and decay.

Drood, the protagonist of the film, is an alienated and anarchic cartoonist who does not allow himself to connect with anyone. His irresponsibility and infidelity has alienated his wife Helen, causing their separation. When he is in trouble he still turns to her like a lost child (in fact he seems only comfortable in the presence of his children—his young daughter included) but her patience is wearing thin. As the hit man sent to kill him (played by the writer of the film Don Opper) tells him, "The lights are on but nobody's home." Drood's solution to this alienation he feels is casual sex and drunken slam dancing (a Dionysian punk dance form in which the participants smash into each other as they move to the music). Even when he meets the gorgeous and sensual femme fatale Yolanda (played by Virginia Madsen with the same aggressive sexuality she demonstrated in *The Hot Spot*), he cannot let go. She angrily decries his inability to commit to her—"You're so guarded"—implying that he will lose her like he has lost his wife. And when her dead body is discovered by the police, her unspoken prophecy comes true.

Pursued by corrupt cops, thugs hired by Yolanda's rich lover Bobby Nye (played majestically by Millie Perkins), and his own sense of despair, Drood finally performs his first forward-thinking act of the film—staging his own death to evade his pursuers and then escaping with his wife and daughter in tow. **JU**

SLEEPING WITH THE ENEMY (1991)

Director: Joseph Ruben. **Screenplay**: Ronald Bass based on the novel by Nancy Price. **Producers**: Leonard Goldberg, Joel Chernoff. **Director of Photography**: John Lindley. **Music**: Jerry Goldsmith. **Production Designer**: Doug Kraner. **Editor**: George Bowers. **Cast**: Julia Roberts (Laura Burney), Patrick Bergin (Martin Burney), Kevin Anderson (Ben Woodward), Elizabeth Lawrence (Chloe Williams). **Released**: 20th Century-Fox, February 28. 94 minutes.

Living on Cape Cod with her abusive investment counselor husband, Martin, Laura fakes her drowning death, moves to small-town Cedar Falls and builds a new identity. Though suspicious and watchful, she finds herself forming a relationship with drama teacher Ben. Learning that, far from being unable to swim, Laura had been attending swimming classes, Martin ransacks his Cape Cod house and finds her discarded wedding ring. He also discovers that Laura's mother had not, as he had been told, died, but had been moved from her care home by Laura several months earlier. Employing a pri-

Sleeping with the Enemy: *Sara/Laura (Julia Roberts) and Martin (Patrick Bergin).*

vate detective, Martin tracks down the mother and, through her, Laura. Threatening to kill her if she will not return to him, Martin is shot dead by Laura.

The pleasures of *Sleeping with the Enemy* are manifold, not least the star quality of Roberts and Bergin's chilling Martin. Also, despite the overall linear lucidity of the plot, the film is astute in its giving and withholding of information. For instance, Laura's "drowning" is initially played "straight," the audience learning only after the fact that she has faked it. This gives an intriguing quality to several of her early, otherwise inexplicable, actions like her smashing of the floodlight on the beach, the absence of which will guide her to the shore. In addition, apart from the somewhat predatory sex scene between Martin and Laura—in which he falls on her like an animal on its prey—his physical abuse of her is confined to one short scene. Infinitely more terrifying are the objective correlatives the film constructs for Martin's obsessive control of Laura: the lining-up of the patterns on the bathroom towels and the careful stacking of the tins in the larder (for an altogether more demented version of this same theme see Rainer Werner Fassbinder's *Martha*). The film cleverly reprises these images to signal Martin's re-entry to Laura's life.

One of the reasons the film is so easily readable is that it draws on a series of ideological oppositions deeply sedimented in American culture, associating Ben with the positive side of these oppositions and Martin with the negative. The oppositions are:

(Europe)	(America)
Boston/Cape Cod	Cedar Falls
concrete/steel/glass	wood
investment counseling	humanities teaching
haute cuisine	apple pie
Berlioz	Van Morrison
moustache	beard
tailored suit	jeans
etc.	etc.

Clearly, the set of oppositions is helped by Anderson being American and Bergin European, although in order to play Martin the latter had to completely suppress his "Irishness." The film displays one of the key features of the neo-noir, the tendency to genre crossover, in this case the thriller and the horror movie. His black coat swirling, Martin evokes the figure of Dracula. Also, the film at one point forgets which genre(s) it is working within and—in a "dressing-up" sequence to Van Morrison's *Brown-Eyed Girl*—attempts to reprise the Rodeo Drive shopping sequence in *Pretty Woman*, proof that star image as much as genre can write a movie. **CMcA**

THE SPLIT (1968)

Director: Gordon Flemyng. **Screenplay**: Robert Sabaroff from the novel *The Seventh* by Richard Stark [Donald Westlake]. **Producers**: Irwin Winkler and Robert Chartoff (Spectrum Productions). **Director of Photography**: Burnett Guffey. **Music**: Quincy Jones. **Art Directors**: Urie McCleary, George W. Davis. **Editor**: Rita Roland. **Cast**: Jim Brown (McClain), Diahann Carroll (Ellie), Julie Harris (Gladys), Ernest Borgnine (Bert Clinger), Gene Hackman (Lt. Walter Brill), Jack Klugman (Harry Kifka), Warren Oates (Marty Gough), James Whitmore (Herb Sutro), Donald Sutherland (Dave Negli), Jackie Joseph (Jackie). **Completed**: April 17, 1968. **Released**: MGM, October 14. 91 minutes.

McClain and Gladys recruit a gang for a plan to steal receipts from a sold-out football game. Each prospective member of the group is tested, as McClain picks a fight with strong-arm man Bert Clinger, duels with shootist Dave Negli, and races with driver Harry Kifka. This planning brings positive results and the $500,000 in proceeds is hidden with McClain's estranged wife Ellie. McClain wants to retire from crime and reconcile with Ellie. However, she is raped and killed by her landlord Herb Sutro who also finds and takes the money. As Lt. Brill investigates the murder and ties it to the robbery, the gang members presume McClain has double-crossed them. Although McClain proposes a deal to him, when Brill apprehends the killer he can take the $500,000. McClain demands and gets a cut from Brill, but the gang ambushes them. Victorious in a shoot-out, Brill becomes a police hero. Although permitted to escape with a share of the money, McClain is haunted by the memory of Ellie.

Like *Point Blank, The Split* is an early neo-noir adaptation of a Richard Stark novel. These books have no heroes, as the distinctions between criminal and cop are blurred and roles reversed. In the wake of such classic period caper films as *The Asphalt Jungle* and *The Killing*, the ritualization of violence, the aura of corruption, the dual emotions of hopelessness and alienation infuse *The Split* with a noir tone. Here, as in *Point Blank* and the later adaptation *The Outfit*, traditional noir attitudes and objectives are reformed and restated by a neo-noir filmmakers.

Stylistically *The Split* is filled with low-key images and tight claustrophobic settings. Although these settings are contemporary and the movie shot in Metrocolor and wide-screen Panavision, the classic-period veteran cinematographer Burnett Guffey easily creates a retro look. The risky casting of former athlete Jim Brown as a desperate character may not recall similar portrayals by Robert Mitchum or Sterling Hayden but nonetheless succeeds because of Brown's physical presence and dour mien as McClain. Although the extensive narrative set-up tests the limits of Brown's abilities as an actor, the undertone of racial prejudice against a powerful African-American is subtly present in his confrontations with others portrayed by Ernest Borgnine, Warren Oates, Jack Klugman and Donald Sutherland. Of course, Brown's interactions with a hard-bitten, sneering Gene Hackman as the overweaning Detective Brill are key. While less than a decade removed from a movie like *Odds Against Tomorrow*, in a neo-noir context *The Split* has a its own style of social consciousness, in which there is no retribution for or even mitigation of a racist rogue cop's triumph while a black protagonist is left emotionally shattered. **CM & AS**

STATE OF GRACE (1990)

Director: Phil Joanou. **Screenplay**: Dennis McIntyre. **Producers**: Ned Dowd, Randy Ostrow, Ron Rotholz (Cinehaus). **Director of Photography**: Jordan Cronenweth. **Production Designers**: Patrizia Von Brandenstein, Doug Kraner. **Music**: Ennio Morricone. **Editor**: Claire Simpson. **Cast**: Sean Penn (Terry Noonan), Ed Harris (Frankie Flannery), Gary Oldman (Jackie Flannery), Robin Wright (Kathleen Flannery), John Turturro (Nick), John C. Reilly (Stevie), R.D. Call (Nicholson), Burgess Meredith (Finn). **Released**: Orion, September 14. 134 minutes.

Terry Noonan returns to Hell's Kitchen after a decade away. While his apparent reason for revisiting the old neighborhood is purely nostalgic, he is actually an undercover NYPD office sent to gather information on petty Irish-American mobster Frankie Flannery. He starts the process of infiltration with his childhood friend, Frankie's brother Jackie, who is now a thuggish enforcer. He also discovers that their sister Kathleen is still living there and unattached. His affair with her exacerbates his already difficult emotional position of deceiving old friends in order to bring them to justice.

As with many other edgy neo-noirs *State of Grace* unflinchingly questions many of the values in the standard cops-and-robbers or good-guys-versus-bad approach of so many law enforcers of the classic period. While he is neither a rogue in the manner of Jim Wilson in *On Dangerous Ground* nor on a vendetta like Jim Bannion in *The Big Heat*, undercover cop Terry Noonan in *State of Grace* is sent back to his old neighborhood to bring down the friends of his childhood and finds himself in a position akin to that of Candella in *Cry of the City*. What most distinguishes Noonan's situation from that

State of Grace: *Frankie Flannery (Ed Harris), Kathleen Flannery (Robin Wright), Nicholson (R.D. Call) and Terry Noonan (Sean Penn).*

of Lt. Candella is that, as the distinctions between good and evil are increasingly blurred, the warring factions do not merely murder in the cold-blooded tradition of the 1930s gangster film but rationalize it as well, like the hospital-endowing drug lord of *King of the City* who remarks about his victims, "I never killed anybody that didn't deserve it."

As in *Deep Cover* and *Homicide*, ethnic prejudice is also a key issue in *State of Grace*. While the guilt-ridden Noonan may try to achieve catharsis by confronting his antagonists and opening fire, most neo-noir protagonists in that situation have no method to expiate their convoluted betrayals. Jordan Cronenweth was certainly one of the most remarkable of contemporary American cinematographers whose style stressed source light and naturalistic effects. Again and again his camera captures Noonan framed in hard light, vacillating between loyalties to kin and to job. The frustration and confusion which Noonan experiences are not only disquieting but they short-circuit the kind of Hawksian professionalism in which he thought he had found an identity. The film's ending, in which he is blackmailed by those he took to be his new brothers and loses his partner as a consequence of his personal failure, is a descent into self-loathing from which redemption may or may not be possible. **AS**

SUTURE (1994)

Director: Scott McGehee, David Siegel. **Screenplay**: Scott McGehee, David Siegel. **Producers**: Alison Brantley, Buddy Enright, David Siegel, Michele Petin, Scott McGehee. **Director of Photography**: Greg Gardiner. **Music**: Cary Berger. **Production Designer**: Kelly McGehee. **Editor**: Lauren Zuckerman. **Cast**: Dennis Haysbert (Clay Arlington), Mel Harris (Dr. Renée Descartes), Sab Shimono (Dr. Shinoda), Dina Merrill (Alice Jameson), Michael Harris (Vincent Towers), David Graf (Lt. Weismann), Fran Ryan (Mrs. Lucerne), John Ingle (Sidney Callahan), Sanford Gibbons (Dr. Fuller), Mark DeMichele (Detective Joe). **Released**: Samuel Goldwyn Company, January 1994. 105 minutes.

Millionaire Vincent Towers has murdered his father, but has no intention of going to prison. In an attempt to fake his own death and avoid prosecution, Vincent maneuvers his nearly-identical but economically disadvantaged half-brother, Clay Arlington, into switching places with him. Yet the car bomb that should have killed Clay has only left him maimed and suffering from amnesia. As his face is reconstructed with the help of Dr. Renée Descartes, Clay undergoes psychoanalysis in order to regain his memory. This poses problems for police Lt. Weismann, whose only witness to the murder cannot pick the physically altered suspect from a line-up. While in recovery Clay has a number of memory flashbacks to his previous life and his initial encounters with Vincent. When Vincent returns to kill Clay, his face (and identity) is blown away by a shotgun blast. With Vincent out of the way and his memories fully restored, Clay decides to retain his new identity. The film ends with snapshots of Clay and Renée's appar-

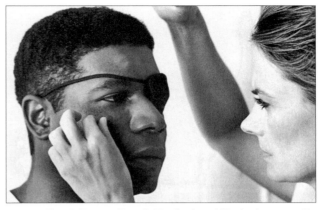

Suture: *Clay Arlington (Dennis Haysbert) and his plastic surgeon Dr. René Descartes (Mel Harris).*

ently happy married life, while a disapproving voiceover predicts that only false happiness can come from denying one's true identity: "He has lost all that makes life worth living."

Heavily inflected by contemporary film theory and European art cinema, *Suture* plays with many conventions of the classic noir film, but in many respects is more successful as an intellectual exercise than as an engaging thriller. Black and white contrasts structure the film's visual and thematic content, but these distinctions are in many ways blurred and reversed, partly through the film's oneiric qualities and implicit racial themes. From the outset the problem of identity, both physical and psychological, is posited as a central theme ("How is it that we know who we are?" asks the stentorian psychoanalytic voiceover), and enacted through Clay's subsequent amnesia and surgical reconstruction, thus referencing classic noirs like *Somewhere in the Night* (1946) and *The Dark Passage* (1947). Vincent himself is almost a caricature of the noir criminal millionaire: cold, sinister and effete, his staging of his own death pays an obvious homage to *Gilda* (1946).

The psychoanalytic framework that informs many classic noirs is here given a distinctly postmodern twist. While "suture" suggests the literal suturing of Clay's face via surgery, it is also the French psychoanalyst Jacques Lacan's term for the "conjunction of the imaginary and the symbolic" that offers a sense of personal wholeness, and the process of de-suturing is when unsavory aspects of reality disrupt the illusion of individual coherence. Informed by Lacanian theory, suture is finally a film theory term for "viewer positioning" that makes us forget that it is the camera that does the looking. The blurring of dream and reality that de-suturing brings about renders the problem of identity more complex in this film, especially for the viewer: Clay, supposedly a dead ringer for Vincent, is played by an African-American actor who bears no resemblance to the other actor. As no one in the film is aware of this racial marking, *Suture* thus comments on race as an invisible yet glaringly obvious issue that disrupts the viewer's sense of continuity and closure. **CF**

TAXI DRIVER (1976)

Director: Martin Scorsese. **Screenplay**: Paul Schrader. **Producers**: Michael and Julia Phillips. **Director of Photography**: Michael Chapman. **Music**: Bernard Herrmann. **Art Director**: Charles Rosen. **Editors**: Tom Rolf, Melvin Shapiro, Marcia Lucas. **Cast**: Robert De Niro (Travis Bickle), Jodie Foster (Iris), Albert Brooks (Tom), Peter Boyle (Wizard), Cybill Shepherd (Betsy), Leonard Harris (Senator Palantine), Harvey Keitel (Sport), Murray Mosten (Timekeeper), Richard Higgs (Secret Service Agent), Vic Argo (Melio, Delicatessen Owner), Steven Prince (Gun Salesman), Martin Scorsese (Weird Passenger). **Released**: Columbia, February, 1976. 113 minutes.

Travis Bickle, an ex-Marine and lonely drifter in New York City, takes a job as a cab driver on the night shift. He can find neither rest nor peace and considers the city filthy. Meeting Betsy, an attractive campaign worker for presidential candidate Senator Charles Palantine, Travis arranges a date; but Betsy is disgusted when he takes her to a pornographic film and leaves him. Travis's depression increases and he buys guns and puts himself through a series of rigid physical exercises. He meets Iris, a twelve-year-old prostitute, and buys time with her from her pimp, Sport, to persuade her to return to school. Now sure of his "mission," Travis goes fully armed to a Palantine rally at Columbus Circle. Chased away by Secret Service men, he goes to Iris's place instead and shoots Sport, his crony, and Iris' customer. After being treated as a hero by the press, Travis acts coolly toward Betsy when she rides in his cab.

By the 1950s the two types of noir hero had merged into a basically good man who had been psychologically scarred and became obsessed with attaining a goal. His obsession usually leads to a violent act, which he later regrets, as exemplified by Barney Nolan in *Shield for Murder* and Howard Tyler in *Try and Get Me*. Travis Bickle of *Taxi Driver* is that kind of protagonist. In addition, Bickle also resembles Raymond Chandler's protagonists because he is a man who moves through the city at night and whose frustrated and repressed emotions focus on "angelic" blonds. Like many noir protagonists of the 1950s Travis is obsessed with attaining the admiration of these women and saving them from what he considers to be a malevolent society. Importantly, however, Travis does not regret his violence; instead he receives praise and gains self-confidence, rejecting the woman he once desired. Travis' alienation and loneliness have not dispersed, and he may again reach a boiling point where he explodes into violence.

Taxi Driver's visual style also derives from the classic period of film noir. From the opening shot of a hazy, neon New York as seen by Travis' blurring vision, the city is presented as a hard,

Taxi Driver: *Betsy (Cybill Shepherd) and Travis Bickle (Robert De Niro).*

elusive, cold, and corrupt enemy. Bernard Herrmann's score movingly states the alternating themes of alienation and self-terror that Travis feels. Paul Schrader, who has written at length on film noir, provides a spare, Bressonian script style that director Martin Scorsese's firsthand knowledge of the New York streets makes into a film that owes much to Hollywood's past, yet reflects the self-destructive urges and the craze for vengeance that preoccupied the American screen in the 1970s. **JC**

THIEF (1981)

Director: Michael Mann. **Screenplay**: Michael Mann based on the novel *The Home Invaders* by Frank Hohimer. **Producers**: Jerry Bruckheimer, Ronnie Caan. **Director of Photography**: Donald Thorin. **Music**: Tangerine Dream (Christopher Franke, Edgar Froese, Johannes Schmölling). **Editor**: Dov Hoenig. **Cast**: James Caan (Frank), Tuesday Weld (Jessie), Willie Nelson (Okla), James Belushi (Barry), Robert Proskey (Leo), Tom Signorelli (Attaglia), Dennis Farina (Carl), W.R. Brown (Mitch), Nick Nickeas (Nick), Norm Tobin (Guido), John Santucci (Urizzi), Gavin MacFadyen (Boreckso). **Released**: United Artists, March 27. 122 minutes.

Frank is a tough ex-con who learned to crack safes from his prison buddy, David Okla. After losing an associate and $185,000 to the mob, he plays tough with the gangsters and recoups his money. Leo, the mob boss, is impressed with Frank's skill and asks him to work for the mob. Frank loathes working for someone else, but is lured by the offer to make over a million dollars in a few big heists. Leo even buys Frank and his wife a home and helps them adopt a baby.

Meanwhile, the cops have been tailing Frank and try to pinch him for a piece of the action. After the first heist, Frank decides to take his cut and retire. When Leo hands him $90,000 and tells him the rest was invested in future heists, Frank demands the money and threatens Leo. Leo retaliates by killing Frank's closest associate, Barry. Seeing no way out, Frank sends his wife away and systematically destroys the home Leo bought for him and the cocktail lounge he owned in the city. He then sets fire to Leo's car lot, and finally breaks into his home, gunning down Leo and his henchmen.

Like many of its noir predecessors, *Thief* is a film about entrapment and survival in a modern society where "honor among thieves" is an outmoded code. Writer-director Michael Mann creates an authentic noir environment in part through economic, hardboiled dialogue and Donald Thorin's dark, expressive photography. The opening sequence takes place at night in a light, but steady, rainfall. A luxury sedan turns its headlights on and drives down a deserted street, where rows of streetlights from both sides converge into an inky blackness. The rain-slicked pavement reflects the smeared red from the automobile's tail lights. The next shot slowly tilts downward, following an intricate maze of emergency escape steps that zigzag in descent to the alleyway below. Moving inside the car, we notice the serious expression on the driver's face, and then the police band radio with its blinking red indicator lights and crisp, static-staccato intercourse of police reports. The expressionistic photography in this sequence coupled with an incessant electronic score serves to create and sustain a pessimistic mood that permeates the rest of the film.

The faces that occupy *Thief's* screen space are among the most authentic street types in the neo-noir cinema, many of whom were real life criminals that Mann cast to provide a "neo-realistic quality" to the film. When Frank visits his buddy, David Okla, in prison, Okla describes how bad the criminal element in society has become: "You wouldn't believe the quality of people they're putting in here these days. Ten or fifteen years ago they'd have dumped 'em in a funny farm somewhere." Frank's relationship with Okla is tantamount to his budding relationship with Jessie, and an integral piece of the puzzle that he desperately wants to piece together. When Okla asks him what he's going to do now that he's divorced, Frank simply replies, "I'm gonna put it back together." "It" is Frank's idealistic vision a good life. This ideal is so important to him that he carries a miniature collage in his wallet featuring photos of Okla, a woman, a car, and some children. When Frank shows the collage to Jessie the night he proposes to her, he says emphatically, "That is my life. Nothing, nobody can stop me from making that happen."

However, Frank is a noir protagonist, and he makes a characteristic and costly mistake that prevents him from attaining the freedom he desires. By teaming up with the mob, Frank brings upon himself an imprisonment that is every bit as tangible as the prison sentence that kept him locked up for eleven years of his life. Forced to revert to the meaningless, existential plateau he had attained in prison where "nothing means nothing," Frank sends his wife and child away and sets off to exact revenge upon his captors. The final sequence is significant in its dream-like depiction of violence and death, the only ending that can bring Frank any semblance of freedom in his world. **TE**

Thief: *Attaglia (Tom Signorelli) is menaced by Frank (James Caan).*

THINGS TO DO IN DENVER WHEN YOU'RE DEAD (1995)

Director: Gary Fleder. **Screenplay**: Scott Rosenberg. **Producer**: Cary Woods. **Director of Photography**: Elliot Davis. **Music**: Michael Convertino. **Art Director**: Burton Rencher. **Editor**: Richard Marks. **Cast**: Andy Garcia (Jimmy "The Saint" Tosnia), Christopher Lloyd (Pieces), William Forsythe (Franchise), Bill Nunn (Easy Wind), Treat Williams (Critical Bill), Jack Warden (Joe Heff), Steve Buscemi (Mister Shhh), Fairuza Balk (Lucinda), Gabrielle Anwar (Dagney), Christopher Walken (The Man with the Plan), Michael Nicolosi (Bernard), Bill Cobbs (Malt), Marshall Bell (Lt. Atwater), Glenn Plummer (Baby Sinister). **Released**: Miramax Films, December 1. 115 minutes.

Jimmy "The Saint" Tosnia has a failing business videotaping the terminally-ill, so they can leave "Afterlife Advice" to their survivors. Jimmy is forced to turn to loan-sharks to prop up his business, along with his taste for the good life. A local crime boss buys his debt then demands a favor of Jimmy in exchange for the interest. Jimmy agrees to put a scare into a small-time crook by roughing him up. Unfortunately, the operation goes awry and Jimmy and all his crew wind up with contracts on their heads.

Things To Do in Denver When You're Dead was part of the unfortunate first wave of Quentin Tarantino wannabe films that predictably were unable to match either his style, wit or substance, such as it was. That said, the film is not without its pleasures and fits in nicely with classic noir misfits-on-a-heist films like *Asphalt Jungle* and *The Killing*. As in those films, a feeling of inevitable doom pervades the proceedings. However, as much as the film would like to recruit us to cheer for the criminals, its preening artificiality keeps us from actually feeling any sympathy. The arch, sometimes painful, dialogue is supposed to be all too clever, but comes across as all too cute, though it did get Rosenberg questionable jobs penning *Con-Air* and *Armageddon*. At least he must be pleased that there's now an entire generation of moviegoers who may forever mistake "smart ass" for smart. The underrated Andy Garcia elevates every scene he's in and he manages to make the dialogue sound passable, if not quite natural, as does the exotic Fairuza Balk as the troubled Lucinda. **JEB**

TO LIVE AND DIE IN L.A. (1985)

Director: William Friedkin. **Screenplay**: Gerald Petievich and William Friedkin based on the novel *To Live and Die in L.A.* by Gerald Petievich. **Producer**: Irving H. Levin. **Director of Photography**: Robby Müller. **Music**: Wang Chung. **Editor**: M. Scott Smith. **Cast**: William Petersen (Richard Chance), Willem Dafoe (Eric "Rick" Masters), John Pankow (John Vukovich), Debra Feuer (Bianca Torres), John Turturro (Carl Cody), Darlanne Fluegel (Ruth Lanier), Dean Stockwell (Bob Grimes), Steve James (Jeff Rice), Robert Downey Sr. (Thomas Bateman), Michael Green (Jim Hart). **Released**: MGM/UA Distribution Company, November 1. 116 minutes.

Treasury Agent Richard Chance's partner is murdered by Eric Masters, a ruthless counterfeiter, and Chance vows to get revenge. Chance and new partner, Vukovich, get a tip that helps them arrest one of Masters' money men, Carl Cody. Masters visits Cody in prison and learns that another money man had set Cody up, stealing $600,000 in the process. Masters and girlfriend, Bianca, retrieve the loot and kill the traitor. Masters then hires Jeff Rice to kill Cody so he can't testify, but the assassination fails and Masters has to kill Rice. Posing as offshore bankers, Chance and Vukovich arrange to buy a million dollars of Masters' counterfeit bills. They need cash to make the deal, but their supervisor won't approve the amount, so they act on a tip from Chance's girlfriend/informant, and rob a Chinese businessman instead. Unaware the businessman is an undercover FBI agent, Chance and Vukovich barely escape death at the hands of the FBI's backup marksmen. The two agents hatch their sting operation, but Masters is forewarned and kills Chance in a shootout. Vukovich tracks Masters to his warehouse where he is setting fire to the evidence. After a brief struggle, he guns down Masters.

To Live and Die in L.A. is a gritty, realistic glimpse into undercover law enforcement. The Los Angeles we are shown festers with crime and corruption. It's a hellhole where only warehouses, loading docks, taverns and strip joints seem to exist. The claustrophobic sense of entrapment is emphasized by the frequent use of telephoto lenses, especially in the freeway chase scenes. The story covers a time frame from December 20th to January 30th and the lack of any visual or verbal mention of the holiday season underscores the premise that there is little reason to celebrate life in the neo-noir city. Reinforced by a relentless, catchy rock soundtrack and the periodic flash of the date and military time on the screen, the viewer is propelled through the narrative with an almost real-life perspective excerpted from the protagonist's diary. We are consumed, as is Chance, with the obsession to hunt Masters down like an animal and kill him. The level of co-experience is so palpable after Chance's death, that we willingly squeeze the trigger along with Vukovich and vicariously unload every bullet into the sinister Eric Masters.

Willem Dafoe portrays Masters, an ex-con who also happens to be an artist. Dafoe's physical features immediately bring to mind Dan Duryea, a classic noir period actor known for his bad guy roles. Masters is an intensely disturbed psychotic who has no respect for human life, so there's little surprise when we see him setting fire to his agonizing, expressionistic self-portrait. William Petersen, now an icon of neo-noir television with his quirky performance as forensics scientist Gil Grissom on the influential *CSI* series, renders subtly the

To Live and Die in L.A.: *Thomas Ling (Michael Chong) is threatened by Agents Vukovich (John Pankow) and Chance (William Petersen).*

alienation and obsessive nature of the classic noir detective.

William Friedkin and director of photography Robby Müller deftly emphasize the tortured inner state of their noir protagonists through color and composition in the scene where Chance and Vukovich argue in the stairwell after learning that the Chinese businessman whose death they were responsible for was actually an undercover FBI agent. Vukovich is livid but Chance is flippant. The light source in the stairwell is a red ceiling bulb which bathes everything in an eerie, reddish tone. The shadows of the stairway banister knife downward in the frame to the bottom of the stairs. This visual text accentuates the anxiety the men feel toward each other, one of the tangible aspects of their spiritual descent into corruption. In the denouement, Vukovich goes to Chance's home, where he finds Ruth, Chance's girlfriend, packing her belongings. "You're working for me now," he declares. The close-up of Ruth's face emits a painful hopelessness, the Long Beach Bridge looming slightly out of focus in the background. The music score winces in subdued resignation, and we understand there is no escaping the clutches of the city. Roles are merely perpetuated, and as the noir code of ethics dictates, the law of survival remains the only law that really matters. **TE**

TRUE CONFESSIONS (1981)

Director: Ulu Grosbard. **Screenplay**: Joan Didion, John Gregory Dunne, Gary S. Hall [uncredited] from the novel *True Confessions* by John Gregory Dunne. **Producers**: Irwin Winkler, Robert Chartoff (Chartoff-Winkler Productions). **Director of Photography**: Owen Roizman. **Music**: Georges Delerue. **Production Designer**: Stephen Grimes. **Editor**: Lynzee Klingman. **Cast**: Robert De Niro (Des Spellacy), Robert Duvall, (Thomas Spellacy), Charles Durning (Jack Amsterdam), Kenneth McMillan (Frank Crotty), Ed Flanders (Dan T. Campion), Cyril Cusack (Cardinal Danaher), Burgess Meredith (Seamus Fargo), Rose Gregorio (Brenda Samuels), Dan Hedaya (Howard Terke), Gwen Van Dam (Mrs. Fazenda), Thomas Hill (Mr. Fazenda), Jeanette Nolan (Mrs. Spellacy), Louisa Moritz (Whore). **Released**: United Artists, September 25. 108 minutes.

Police detective Tom Spellacy visits Des, his terminally ill priest brother, who has a micro-parish in an early 1960s desert community. The story flashes back to late 1940s Los Angeles. Tom and partner Frank are called to a downtown whorehouse where a priest trick has had a fatal heart attack. Tom—who had briefly been a mob bagman—and the cynical madam, Brenda, had a relationship years before that had been torn apart by scandal. Tom was only demoted, but Brenda had received jail time. It is another reason why Tom has such antipathy for one of Des' prize parishioners, Jack Amsterdam, a building contractor and former pimp. Des is Cardinal Danaher's golden boy monsignor leading the archdiocese to unprecedented prosperity. But things unravel when a Black Dahlia-style murder occurs. It's on Tom's watch, and he learns that not only Amsterdam and Amsterdam's friend knew the victim, but that the unwitting Des also had a nodding acquaintance with the girl. Tom deduces that a porno film producer was undoubtedly the killer, but decides to bring down Amsterdam anyway, knowing the scandal may ruin Des' career. Back in the present, Des tells Tom that what he did actually saved, not ruined, him, pulling him away from too materialistic a path.

Perhaps the most intriguing thing about *True Confessions* is how it emerges as not only an effective paean to innocence lost and the evaporation of once-cherished values, but also a harrowing trek through the toxicity of big city secular life, from law enforcement to the business side of organized religion. Bitter cop Tom does not consciously link his own crooked past with brother Des' spiritually compromised-for-expedience present. Nevertheless, through his own history dealing with small-time corruption, Tom's hatred of hypocrisy has grown to the point it can no longer be stifled, especially when he sees it flowering unchecked in Des' own backyard. The grisly Black Dahlia-style murder serves as not only a catalyst for Tom's burgeoning crisis of conscience and sometimes insufferable self-righteousness but a metaphor for the pathetically fragile, transient nature of human life as well. Director Grosbard, who helmed the excellent neo-noir *Straight Time*, and screenwriters Dunne and Didion do not hit us over the head with pretentious symbolism. As with their films *Panic in Needle Park* (1971) and *Play It As It Lays* (1972), both of which also had simpatico directors, Dunne and Didion emerge as much auteurs here as Grosbard, and it is a tribute to all three of them that they blend the plot and character elements so well.

True Confessions is a certifiable neo-noir, but it is also a kind of anti-thriller. All suspense grows from the advent of seemingly unstoppable doom and whether individual characters will be able to overcome their personality flaws to achieve some kind of redemption. There are never any artificial thriller constructs. Miraculously, Hollywood studio higher-ups did not seem to interfere with the project. Perhaps the fact that it turned out to be an intensely personal character study about the frailty of human values rather than a conventional mystery thriller is why the picture was damned with faint praise on its first release. It deserves far more recognition that it has so far seen. There are some staggeringly powerful scenes in the film, and two, in particular, stand out. One is when Tom is called to the morgue and ends up having to identify former flame Brenda after she has gassed herself in despair. Duvall underplays Tom's emotions beautifully—his regret, remorse and repressed affection for the woman show through in his tender gestures. Likewise, when Tom finally locates the abandoned porno film set where murder victim,

Louise Fazenda, was butchered, the building of emotion quietly reaches an unbearable crescendo. The camera follows Tom as he wanders through the warehouse, at last finding a blood trail, which leads him to the bathroom and gory tub where the girl was bisected. Delerue's elegiac score has been swelling imperceptibly, and it complements the range of feelings we see pass across Duvall's hardened but mortified face. It is one of the most painful yet sensitive portraits ever put on film of the lonely hell many cops must traverse, touring the blackest depths to which mankind can sink. **CD**

TRUE ROMANCE (1993)

Director: Tony Scott. **Screenplay**: Quentin Tarantino and Roger Avery (uncredited). **Producers**: Gary Barber, Samuel Hadida, Steve Perry, Bill Unger. **Director of Photography**: Jeffrey L. Kimball. **Music**: Hans Zimmer. **Production Designer**: Benjamin Fernandez. **Editor**: Michael Tronick and Christian Wagner. **Cast**: Christian Slater (Clarence), Patricia Arquette (Alabama), Michael Rapaport (Dick), Val Kilmer (Elvis), Bronson Pinchot (Elliot), Gary Oldman (Drexl), Dennis Hopper (Clifford Worley), Christopher Walken (Vincenzo Coccotti), Saul Rubinek (Lee Doniwitz), James Gandolfini (Virgil), Tom Sizemore (Cody Nicholson), Chris Penn (Nicky Dimes), Brad Pitt (Floyd), Samuel L. Jackson (Big Don). **Locations**: Ambassador Hotel, Los Angeles; Detroit; Rae's Restaurant, Santa Monica, CA; Safari Inn, Burbank, CA; California Institute of Technology, Pasadena, CA. **Released**: Warner Bros., September 10. 120 minutes.

Clarence is a comic book store clerk who takes advice from an imagined Elvis. He unexpectedly meets a young woman, Alabama, at the movies on his birthday, and the two have a night of romance. Afterwards, she reveals to him that she's a hooker paid by his boss to show him a good time, but also says that she loves him. He responds that he loves her and then seeks out her pimp, Drexl, to free her from his grasp. Things turn violent, and Clarence kills Drexl. He retrieves a suitcase, which he believes contains Alabama's things, but which actually holds a large shipment of mob cocaine. Newly married, Clarence and Alabama head to California, in hopes of selling the cocaine to a movie producer friend of Clarence's friend, Dick. The producer's assistant, Elliot, is arrested with some of the cocaine and makes a deal with the police by informing them of the drug buy. In addition, the mobsters have tracked their cocaine to California. The mobsters and police shoot it out at the drug buy, and Clarence and Alabama escape with the producer's money, a little worse for the wear and tear.

The real shame about *True Romance* is that Quentin Tarantino, who wrote the script, didn't direct it. The story and dialogue are pure Tarantino, and if the movie lacks in certain ways, the fault surely belongs to Tony Scott, who at that point was known for films like *Top Gun* and *Beverly Hills Cop II*, rather than for neo-noirs. The story has great energy, and the script contains memorable flourishes, such as Clarence's discussions with his imaginary Elvis. The casting is good, and the performances are solid, some of them excellent. The chameleon Gary Oldman is over the top as the pimp Drexl, Tom Sizemore and Chris Penn are great as the cops pursuing Lee Doniwitz, and Brad Pitt is hilarious as the stoner Floyd. Patricia Arquette is sensual and strong as Alabama, and Christian Slater is, for the most part, convincing as Clarence. His killing of Drexl seems slightly out of tune with the thoughtfulness and sweetness with which Slater portrays the character, however. Dennis Hopper and Christopher Walken give peak performances in a classic and unforgettable scene in which Clarence's father attempts to withhold the knowledge of his son's whereabouts from the gangster Coccotti, who's determined to do what he has to in order to get that information. Another intense and gritty scene with real energy pits a beaten and bloody Alabama against the gangster sent to kill her, played with cheek by James Gandolfini. *True Romance* is a solid neo-noir. **MTC**

TWILIGHT (1998)

Director: Robert Benton. **Screenplay**: Robert Benton, Richard Russo. **Producers**: Arlene Donovan, Scott Rudin. **Director of Photography**: Piotr Sobocinski. **Music**: Elmer Bernstein. **Production Designer**: David Gropman. **Editor**: Carol Littleton. **Cast**: Paul Newman (Harry Ross), Susan Sarandon (Catherine Ames), Gene Hackman (Jack Ames), Reese Witherspoon (Mel Ames), Stockard Channing (Verna Hollander), James Gardner (Raymond Hope), Giancarlo Esposito (Reuben Escobar), Liev Schreiber (Jeff), Margo Martindale (Gloria), M. Emmet Walsh (Lester), John Spencer (Capt. Phil Egan). **Locations**: Cedric Gibbons/Delores Del Rio house, Santa Monica, CA; LAPD Hollywood Station, L.A., CA; unfinished Frank Lloyd Wright project, Malibu, CA; John Lautner house, L.A., CA. **Released**: Paramount, March 6. 94 minutes.

Harry, a former cop, retrieves the daughter of his employers from a tryst in Mexico and winds up shot in the groin. Two years later, his voice-over narration begins in an L.A. police station. His employers, a famous but aging Hollywood couple, Catherine and Jack, have a secret hidden in their past. Twenty years earlier, Catherine's first husband confronted her lover Jack and wound up dead and buried at Jack's unfinished beach house. Raymond, a studio guard and former

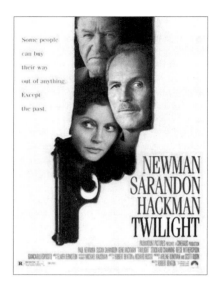

cop, helped the couple "clean things up." Raymond, also a friend of Harry's, sets him up with the Mexico job, after which Harry lives above the garage at the couple's palatial home. Other violent deaths soon occur. Blackmailers seek to reawaken the past Catherine prefers be left alone, especially since Jack is dying of cancer. Harry's attempts to investigate lead police detective Verna, his former partner, right to the star couple and the mysterious disappearance of Catherine's husband years earlier. Raymond, still working for Catherine, actually committed all the recent murders, and also murdered Catherine's first husband, who was injured but not dead after confronting Jack. Harry's rekindled investigative skills lead him to Raymond, and Harry kills him.

Like many classic noirs, *Twilight* features the voice-over narration of the male protagonist, an erotic triangle, the revival of an old crime, and moody low-light cinematography that takes advantage of mirrors, sunsets, and darkened streets. It also incorporates classic California architecture in strategic location shooting: run-down bungalows, a vintage Hollywood mansion, a John Lautner house, and an unfinished Frank Lloyd Wright project. Unlike most classic noirs, however, the protagonists themselves are in the twilight of their lives. Newman, Hackman, and Garner were all in their late 60s or early 70s in 1998, causing critics to label the film "geriatric," or (less fondly) "geezer noir" by virtue of the male protagonists alone. Yet these mature actors, with well- documented public and star personas, bring depth to the characters. The film's femme fatale Catherine is an actress who had starred in such films as *The Last Rebel* and *The End of Desire* and seems as though she might have almost as impressive a filmography as Sarandon, who imbues Catherine with many of the qualities spectators associate with the actress herself. Traces of Newman's roles reside in Harry. Garner's roles, especially as television's Jim Rockford in *The Rockford Files*, give Raymond a past. One of Hackman's films actually stands in for one of Jack's movies. The interplay of filmic, star, and public personas within the characters developed in *Twilight* provide a postmodern depth to the neo-noir narrative.

A fictional Hollywood mystery serves as the motivation for the narrative of *Twilight*, which along the way finds time to sympathize with the white low-life blackmailers, Jeff and

Gloria, who will die at Raymond's hand. While Harry's working-class Latino partner Reuben remains an unfortunate stereotype, Jeff and Gloria are humanized, resembling many of the desperate couples in classic noir: Roy (Humphrey Bogart) and Marie (Ida Lupino) in *High Sierra*, and Davy (Jamie Smith) and Gloria (Irene Kane) in *Killer's Kiss*. Classic noir frequently portrayed its lower-class protagonists' overwhelming desire for economic success sympathetically, despite the constraints of the Production Code, which allowed no crime to go unpunished. Gloria and Jeff die, but Harry does not feel good about it, recognizing they have more in common with him than with his famous employers. With no Production Code to ensure her punishment Catherine, who is directly responsible for multiple murders, survives. Harry's conscience won't let Raymond, who actually did the killing, go unpunished; he ends up shooting his friend. After many sunsets, killings, and regrets, Harry survives, walking off into the morning sunlight with Verna, supposedly to rekindle a past affair. After all that immanent mortality, the sunny ending offers an unbelievable respite. **JBW**

THE TWO JAKES (1990)

Director: Jack Nicholson. **Screenplay**: Robert Towne. **Producers**: Robert Evans, Harold Schneider, and Jack Nicholson (uncredited). **Director of Photography**: Vilmos Zsigmond. **Music**: Van Dyke Parks. **Art Director**: Richard Schreiber. **Editor**: Anne Goursaud. **Cast**: Jack Nicholson (J.J. "Jake" Gittes), Harvey Keitel (Julius "Jake" Berman), Meg Tilly (Kitty Berman), Madeleine Stowe (Lillian Bodine), Eli Wallach (Cotton Weinberger), Ruben Blades (Michael "Mickey Nice" Weisskopf), Frederic Forrest (Chuck Newley), David Keith (Det. Lt. Loach), Richard Farnsworth (Earl Rawley), Tracey Walter (Tyrone Otley), Joe Mantell (Lawrence Walsh), James Hong (Kahn), Perry Lopez (Captain Lou Escobar), Jeff Morris (Ralph Tilton), Rebecca Brousard (Gladys). **Released**: Paramount, August 10. 138 minutes.

Ten years after witnessing the traumatic death of Evelyn Mulwray in Chinatown, private detective Gittes has survived World War II and now concentrates on divorce cases. After one of his set-ups misfires with the murder of businessman Mark Bodine at the hands of his partner Julius Berman, Jake finds himself re-experiencing a past he can never forget when it appears that Evelyn's daughter is somehow involved in a scheme involving oil rights in the developing post-war Los Angeles economy. Facing attempts by Bodine's widow Lillian and gangster "Mickey Nice" to retrieve a recording documenting incriminating conversations occurring in the last moment before Berman's entry into the hotel room where his wife and Bodine conducted an adulterous liaison, Jake eventually discovers that Evelyn's daughter Kitty is now Berman's wife and that the guilty husband actually intervened to prevent a blackmail attempt and the revelation of her past. After doctoring the tape for a court hearing to remove incriminating evidence, Jake visits Julius for the last time. Dying of cancer, Julius commits suicide after oil appears on his property that will allow his widow to live in comfort and security for the rest of her life. Tempted to relive the past by succumbing to Kitty's romantic yearnings, Jake sends her away from his office.

Like all plot synopses, the above cannot do justice to one of the richest films to have emerged from the American neonoir tradition. *The Two Jakes* represents a late flowering of this movement that had begun with great promise during the early 1970s before substance became sacrificed to style a decade later. Intended as a sequel to the critically and commercially successful *Chinatown*, the film received a cool response and still awaits a DVD release. Designed to feature Jack Nicholson in a reprise of his acclaimed role in Polanski's earlier film (with its producer Robert Evans in the role eventually played by Harvey Keitel), *The Two Jakes* deliberately disappointed audiences by not delivering what a sequel usually promised in the *Star Wars* era, namely an entertaining recapitulation of themes associated with the earlier film in an unchallenging manner. Instead Jack Nicholson directed an entirely different film having much in common with the independent and iconoclastic nature of his brief ventures into the director's chair such as *Drive He Said* (1971) and *Goin' South* (1978) that all attempted the subversion of audience generic expectations. *The Two Jakes* is a film of morbid visual moods and haunted characterization calling upon its viewers not only to *not* expect another *Chinatown* but also to actively work towards reading its entirely different perspective. The film opens with a sepia-tinted image of the Paramount logo. But its nostalgia is double-edged. *The Two Jakes* is no period recreation. It is a film haunted by a past realm of American personal and political corruption also relevant to the present.

Jake Gittes is a man haunted by the past whose nature differs from that of the earlier film. Unlike the traditional postwar classical film noir protagonist Jake is less haunted by the

From 1937 to 1947—or 1974 to 1990—Jack Nicholson as Jake Gittes many have morphed in Noah Cross. His changing face: with Noah Cross (John Houston) left, in Chinatown *and Jake Berman (Harvey Keitel) right, in* The Two Jakes.

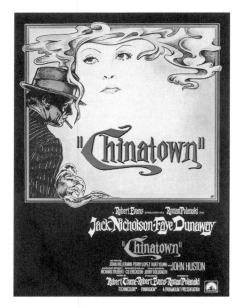

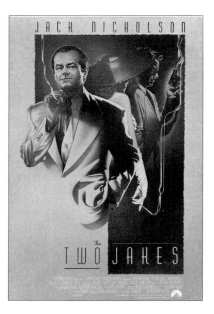

recent war he has participated in and more by the memory of a traumatic past involving the death of Evelyn Mulwray. He is as much a "walking wounded" character as Captain Escobar who has lost a leg in the war. Jake's scars are more emotional than physical. He has masochistic desires to punish himself for failing to save Evelyn by concentrating on sordid divorce cases, increasing his weight (so he no longer physically resembles his earlier self in *Chinatown*), and becoming engaged to women who resemble his lost love like a Edgar Allan Poe character seeking for "his lost Lenore."

Kahn recognizes this morbid hold of the past when Jake asks him about Evelyn's daughter, "You are a prisoner of the past. You would do more harm than good." Zsigmond's cinematography and the haunted form of acting in this film evoke overtones of a neo-noir version of Marcel Proust's *Remembrance of Times Past* with the noted difference that these memories are totally masochistic and painful. *The Two Jakes* re-employs elements from the classical film noir tradition such as voice-overs and dualities, the latter seen in the title relationship between Gittes and Berman. These two older men fall into the trap of being unconscious father figures who may cause Evelyn's daughter further psychological damage as much as Noah Cross did after the conclusion of *Chinatown*. In fact, Jake's 1947 bodily appearance makes him resemble a younger version of Noah Cross.

Both Julius "Jake" Berman and his alter-ego "Jake" Gittes may believe they have good intentions towards Evelyn's orphaned daughter but darker feelings also dominate their psyches making them potential heirs to Noah Cross. Gittes narrowly avoids this fate at the end of the film. His tortured confession to Kitty that the past "never goes away" in the concluding shot is one of the finest and most poignant moments in American cinema involving the realization of masculine maturity, responsibility, and implicit self-revelation of the dark psychological pitfall threatening to devour him. After Jake's door closes showing the significant sign, "Private 308," the viewer knows that he will continue to suffer the torments of the damned.

The Two Jakes is a neo-noir reworking of American literature's Gothic tradition with particular reference to Edgar Allan

Poe's quasi-incestuous explorations in *The Fall of the House of Usher*, *Morella*, and *Ligeia*. Katherine Mulwray's fate echoes that of her mother, Evelyn, who speaks to Jake beyond the grave in one scene via a voice-over as he reads her last letter to him. Sexually exploited by her grandfather, she is vulnerable to the charms of older men such as Jake Berman and his more devious partner Mark Bodine. Berman sees Kitty as a fragile child while Bodine sexually exploits her. Jake Gittes realizes that he, too, could become another link in an incestuous eternal triangle that has blighted the lives of the Mulwray women. But he steps back from the brink before it is too late.

The tragic dimension of *The Two Jakes* is not only personal but also political. Like the pre-war water rights in *Chinatown*, the post-war economy now moves in another direction. "The name of the game is oil." The Mulwray vineyards of *Chinatown* are now a desert wasteland ready for exploitation in the post-war suburban housing boom. Urban capitalism makes the Frontier redundant as seen in brief shots of cowboys herding cattle prior to Jake's visit to magnate Earl Rawley whose oil derricks now dominate the Pacific landscape of the Californian coastline. Ironically, gangster "Mickey Nice" owns a gay nightclub while class and racial discriminations still rule Los Angeles. Jake has recently gained admission to the Wilshire Country Club which excludes Jews. So also do the new suburban housing developments he promotes to W.A.S.P. veterans and couples, as he tells a visiting couple. By contrast, Berman can invite Jake to his golf club with Black caddies prominently in the background watching the game.

The Two Jakes is a major achievement, deserving urgent re-evaluation. It is not just an outstanding example of what neo-noir can achieve but also emphasizes those darker elements in American culture and literature often denied proper representation in film. As an accomplished cinematic version of elements contained within literary studies such as Leslie A. Fiedler's *Love and Death in the American Novel*, *The Two Jakes* is not just a major example of what this *Encyclopedia* in all its editions defines as a particular "American style." It also contains a rich subversive content operating in the best alternative and progressive dimensions of film noir itself. **TW**

THE UNDERNEATH (1995)

Director: Steven Soderbergh. **Screenplay**: Steven Soderbergh as Sam Lowry and Daniel Fuchs based on the novel *Criss Cross* by Don Tracy. **Producer**: John Hardy. **Director of Photography**: Eliot Davis. **Production Designer**: Howard Cummings. **Music**: Cliff Martinez. **Editor**: Stan Salfas. **Cast**: Peter Gallagher (Michael Chambers), Alison Elliott (Rachel), William Fichtner (Tommy Dundee), Adam Trese (David Chambers), Joe Don Baker (Clay Hinkle), Paul Dooley (Ed Dutton), Shelley Duvall (Nurse), Elisabeth Shue (Susan), Anjanette Comer (Mrs. Chambers). **Released**: Populist/Gramercy, April 28. 99 minutes.

Michael is a ne'er-do-well who gambles away money and ignores his wife Rachel's pleas for responsibility on his part. Finally he deserts her without warning to escape creditors and she divorces him. When Michael finally returns to town Rachel has left him for the mobster Dundee. In order to win her back he joins Dundee in the heist of an armored car company Michael works for. Rachel betrays both Dundee and Michael, absconding with the heist money and leaving the wounded to Michael to take the rap.

Steven Soderbergh's remake of *Criss Cross*, *The Underneath*, follows the basic plot line of the original film but with some significant changes which mark it as a post-feminist film. Soderbergh delves into the married life of the noir couple (here named Michael and Rachel) in an attempt to shift the sympathy away from the male protagonist onto the female protagonist while humanizing the character of the femme fatale.

Although Rachel does, like Anna, love money and sex (in one scene we see her happily manipulating both her lover's penis as well as a bag of illicit money with her naked foot), she is also a wronged woman. She attempts to establish a solid relationship with her husband Michael, a scalawag with a gambling addiction, but he refuses to accept responsibility: using her ticket money for an audition in Los Angeles to buy a car and a large screen television ("You never do what you say you're going to do") and keeping her at a distance even during their lovemaking (Rachel: "I'd like to be close"). The final straw is of course when he deserts her and his friends as he skips town after accumulating too many gambling debts.

Michael only realizes the depth of his love once he has lost Rachel. Returning to town he finds her engaged to a local hood, Tommy Dundee. Now that she is technically unobtainable he pursues her with an overwhelming, masochistic passion: watching her with glazed eyes as she dances to a rock band; seeing her image when he is making love to a one-night stand; even coming up with the heist plan to win her back (Rachel: "You know I like money"). But her bitterness

The Underneath: *Michael Chambers (Peter Gallagher) and his ex-wife Rachel (Alison Ellliott).*
Below: Less "cool" and certainly more volatile than their post-feminist counterparts, the original doomed couple Anna (Yvonne DeCarlo) and Steve (Burt Lancaster) in Criss Cross.

towards him remains palpable as she reproaches him repeatedly for his betrayal of her. Even though they unite to perform the heist, the viewer is never convinced of Rachel's commitment to him. And in the final scene not only does she betray him but leaves him to take the rap for the death of Dundee. Like another post-feminist femme fatale, Matty in *Body Heat*, Rachel is allowed to escape ("Now I understand the power of just walking away"), although in this case there lingers a suggestion that she may be pursued by the rest of Dundee's heist mob. **JU**

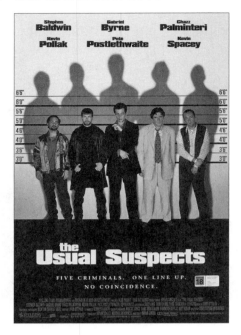

The Usual Suspects: *Kevin Spacy as Roger Kint and perhaps Keyser Söze.*

THE USUAL SUSPECTS (1995)

Director: Bryan Singer. **Screenplay**: Christopher McQuarrie. **Producers**: Michael McDonnell and Bryan Singer (Polygram). **Director of Photography**: Newton Thomas Sigel. **Music**: John Ottman. **Art Director**: David Lazan. **Editor**: John Ottman. **Cast**: Stephen Baldwin (Michael McManus), Gabriel Byrne (Dean Keaton), Benicio Del Toro (Fred Fenster), Kevin Pollak (Todd Hockney), Kevin Spacey (Roger "Verbal" Kint), Chazz Palminteri (Dave Kujan), Pete Postlethwaite (Kobayashi), Giancarlo Esposito (Jack Baer), Suzy Amis (Edie Finneran), Dan Hedaya (Sgt. Jeffrey). **Released**: Gramercy Pictures, August 16. 106 minutes.

Police investigating an exploded boat on a San Pedro pier discover 27 bodies and $91 million worth of drug money. The only survivors are a severely burned and terrified Hungarian and Verbal Kint, a club-footed con-man. Kint is arrested and pressured into explaining what happened on the boat. His story begins six weeks earlier in a New York City holding cell with five criminals, suspected of hijacking a truck. While they're together, the men plan an intricate heist, which they complete on their release, and which brings them to the attention of the legendary crime boss Keyser Söze, a figure of possibly mythological proportions, who forces them into taking on a suicidally dangerous job. The job goes awry, but it appears the gang was set up, as the purpose of the job turns out to be protecting Keyser Söze's identity. Verbal Kint, who in retrospect has been mixing truth and fiction, is released by the police, just before they discover that he may in fact be Keyser Söze.

Taking its title from the most famously borderline noir of all near-noir films, *Casablanca*, *The Usual Suspects* uses all the props and vernacular of the crime film to its own purposes, marking it as less of a true noir than it seems on the surface. Because of its focus on storytelling and mythology, *The Usual Suspects* has more in common with horror/noir hybrids like Tourneur's *Cat People*, than with other classic heist films, albeit in a roundabout way. The film expends its subtext on a story well told, rather than on the morality of the various goings on. However, despite its ultimate admission of manipulation, the film is almost unremittingly entertaining. The performances, from a large and varied cast, are all top notch, the dialogue is highly enjoyable, and Verbal Kint's story is myth-making at its best. **JEB**

WARNING SHOT (1967)

Director: Buzz Kulik. **Screenplay**: Mann Rubin based on the novel *711 – Officer Needs Help* by Whit Masterson. **Producer**: Buzz Kulik (Bob Banner Associates). **Director of Photography**: Joseph F. Biroc. **Music**: Jerry Goldsmith. **Art Directors**: Roland Anderson, Hal Pereira. **Editor**: Archie Marshek. **Cast**: David Janssen (Sgt. Tom Valens), Ed Begley (Capt. Roy Klodin), Keenan Wynn (Sgt. Ed Musso), Sam Wanamaker (Frank Sanderman), Lillian Gish (Alice Willows), Stefanie Powers (Liz Thayer), Eleanor Parker (Doris Ruston), George Grizzard (Walt Cody), George Sanders (Calvin York), Steve Allen (Perry Knowland), Carroll O'Connor (Judge Paul Jerez), Joan Collins (Joanie Valens), Walter Pidgeon (Orville Ames). **Released**: Paramount, January 18, 1967. 100 minutes.

Still recovering from being shot in the line of duty and now going through a painful divorce, veteran LA police sergeant Tom Valens shoots and kills a man in self-defense while on a stake-out for a serial killer outside the Seascape Apartments. However, the man's gun is not found and the victim turns out to be the respected doctor and philanthropist, Dr. James Ruston. Valens becomes the target of a police inquiry and an escalating media circus. Unemployed, vilified by the press and abandoned by his friends, Valens' only hope of clearing his name is to uncover why Ruston acted so suspiciously that night and to locate the missing gun. The only sympathy he receives comes from a playboy airline pilot, Walt Cody, who also lives at the Seascape and is surprisingly eager to assist. Valens' inquiries into Ruston's finances reveal that he had been dealing drugs on the side, and had been coming to the Seascape to meet his contact, who turns out to be Cody. Discovering that Ruston's drug-filled toy gun has been buried in a dog's casket, Valens shoots Cody with a real gun in self-defense.

Like many classic films noirs, *Warning Shot* takes an almost sadistic pleasure in the persecution of its male protagonist. Unlike *The Big Heat* (1953), where Detective Bannion's stubborn commitment to justice is paid for by the women he encounters, in *Warning Shot* Valens bears the full brunt of what the world throws at him. In addition to being pilloried in the media, he is beaten up by hoodlums, mysteriously gassed in his home, and subjected to emotional blackmail by his wife. Valens is thus a cop who can take it, but just barely. Emotionally and physically wounded after being shot a year earlier, Valens is not a model of hardboiled manhood. His constant and conspicuous imbibing of buttermilk, hardly the draft of heroes, symbolizes his vulnerable state as much as it soothes his wounded stomach. Weakness like this is what sets the vultures circling.

All who condemn Valens seem motivated by superficial political agendas or base personal motives. Anti-war protestors rallying with Civil Rights activists denounce Valens as a symptom of a corrupt system while the district attorney goes out of his way to nail Valens on manslaughter charges, largely out of a personal vendetta against past police injustice. Even those who profess to support him are either doing so cynically (television personality Perry Knowland) or to conceal their own guilt (Walt Cody). Sensing that Valens' new vulnerability might allow them to save their marriage, his soon-to-be ex-wife lends him apparent support, but on the condition that he admit having been mistaken (thus giving her the upper hand in their relationship). *Warning Shot* thus faithfully presents a noir universe in which a single honest man confronts social and political institutions that seem hopelessly self-serving. That he is proven right in the end only underscores that corruption. **CF**

WHO'LL STOP THE RAIN (1978)

Director: Karel Reisz. **Screenplay**: Judith Rascoe, Robert Stone from the novel *Dog Soldiers* by Robert Stone. **Producers**: Herb Jaffe, Gabriel Katzka (Katza-Jaffe). **Director of Photography**: Richard H. Kline. **Music**: Laurence Rosenthal. **Production Designer**: Dale Hennesy. **Editor**: John Bloom. **Cast**: Nick Nolte (Ray Hicks), Tuesday Weld (Marge Converse), Michael Moriarty (John Converse), Anthony Zerbe (Antheil), Richard Masur (Danskin), Ray Sharkey (Smitty), Gail Strickland (Charmian), Charles Haid (Eddie Peace), David Opatoshu (Bender), Joaquin Martinez (Angel). **Released**: United Artists, August. 126 minutes.

Vietnam war correspondent John Converse, disillusioned at the senseless carnage he has seen, cynically decides to buy heroin to sell, and he convinces a friend, merchant seaman Ray Hicks, to smuggle it into the United States. When Hicks arrives stateside in Berkeley, he finds Converse's tranquilizer-popping wife, Marge, knows nothing about it. He also discovers that corrupt DEA agent Antheil is aware of the parcel and has sent sociopathic goons Danskin and Smitty to retrieve it. Hicks takes Marge with him, and the two stay one step ahead of their pursuers, finally ending up at one of Hicks' old haunts, a deserted, rural New Mexico commune. When Converse returns home, Anthiel and company hold him hostage. They follow Hicks and Marge's trail and threaten to kill Converse unless the pair gives up the package. Hicks plays for time, finally turning the tables, saving Converse and Marge and causing the killers to self-destruct. But he himself is mortally wounded in the process.

It could be argued that on some level protagonist Ray Hicks' mission to deliver an illicit parcel for a friend is analogous to the United States' involvement in the Vietnam War. Like the US government, Hicks is a mass of contradictions—altruistic, yet selfish and mercenary; honorable, yet blindly unprincipled in key areas. He goes on a fool's errand that he thinks will be relatively quick and easy, but suddenly finds himself caught fast in a quagmire of deceit and violence. To director Reisz's credit, if the analogy was intended, it's handled in a fairly subtle manner.

Certainly co-screenwriter Stone had much to say about the Vietnam war and alienation in the 1960's in his original novel, *Dog Soldiers*. This remains the most faithful film of Stone's work (the one other Stone adaptation, *WUSA*, 1970, from his excellent novel *Hall of Mirrors*, is flawed, but nevertheless underrated and unjustly forgotten). Reisz, veteran of gritty, touchstone British New Wave cinema like *Saturday Night and Sunday Morning* (1960), directs with a ferocious naturalism that keeps this neo-noir firing on all cylinders. Weld is spot-on as the weak, vulnerable and addicted Marge, who nevertheless emerges as a pillar of strength when the chips are down. Moriarty skillfully walks a tightrope as her husband, the smugly cynical Converse, an obnoxious meathead who attains some small bit of wisdom by the film's end, though it comes at a horrendous price—his own humiliating torture and his best friend's death. Richard Masur and Ray Sharkey are simultaneously scary and scathingly funny—Masur as Danskin, a bitterly sadistic Jewish hippie with an inferiority complex and Sharkey as Smitty, a moronic, Vietnam vet jailbird with delusions of eventually "working for the agency."

But ultimately the film is about self-educated loner Hicks, and the character is actor Nolte's shining hour. He expertly brings off his strangely conflicted personality: a former Marine with borderline fascist tendencies who studies Nietzsche but who also practices Tai Chi and reads the I-Ching; someone who is reluctant to smuggle heroin as it is "bad karma," but not above nearly overdosing a naïve rich couple just to teach former associate, drug dealer Eddie Peace, a harsh lesson. In the final analysis, Nolte's Hicks proves Converse's and Marge's savior, a humbly chivalrous warrior who is willing to sacrifice everything for his friends. The scene where Converse and Marge find his lifeless corpse on the railroad tracks in the desert—where he has bled to death waiting for them—is a moving denouement to the saga. The film's one failing is that the producers seemed to have pinched pennies in licensing appropriate 1960s and 1970s tunes for ambient background music—although I am a Creedence Clearwater fan, the couple of Creedence songs that are used are repeated ad nauseam, and, by the time the title composition plays all the way through as the end credits roll, it has worn out its welcome long before. **CD**

WITNESS (1985)

Director: Peter Weir. **Screenplay**: Earl W. Wallace and William Kelley based on a story by William Kelley, Pamela Wallace and Earl W. Wallace. **Producer**: Edward S. Feldman. **Director of Photography**: John Seale. **Music**: Maurice Jarre. **Editor**: Thom Noble. **Cast**: Harrison Ford (Detective Capt. John Book), Kelly McGillis (Rachel Lapp), Josef Sommer (Chief Paul Schaeffer), Lukas Haas (Samuel Lapp), Jan Rubes (Eli Lapp), Alexander Gudonov (Daniel Hochleitner), Danny Glover (Detective Lt. James McFee), Brent Jennings (Detective Sgt. Elden Carter), Patti LuPone (Elaine), Angus MacInnes (Detective Fergie), Frederick

Witness: *Rachel (Kelly McGillis), Samuel (Lukas Hass), Eli Lapp (Jan Rubes), and Det. Capt. John Book (Harrison Ford).*

Rolf (Stoltzfus), Viggo Mortensen (Moses Hochleitner). **Released**: Paramount Pictures, February 8. 112 minutes.

Rachel Lapp, a young Amish widow, and her son, Samuel, are traveling to visit relatives in Baltimore. While waiting for their train in Philadelphia, the boy witnesses a brutal, throat-slashing murder in the men's restroom. Detective John Book is assigned to the case and the next morning, Samuel identifies another detective as the killer. Book informs his superior, Paul Schaeffer, who tells him to keep it confidential. That night, Book is attacked by McFee, the suspect detective. Realizing there is a conspiracy, Book frantically gathers Rachel and Samuel and drives them back to their home in Lancaster County. Moments after arriving, Book collapses from his gunshot wound. Rachel nurtures him back to health and Book begins to appreciate a pace of life within the idyllic Amish community far different from his own. He is shocked back to reality when he learns his partner was killed by Schaeffer and McFee. Book bids a romantic farewell to Rachel, but as he is leaving the next morning, his corrupt associates descend on the Lapp farm. He manages to kill McFee and another detective, but Schaeffer takes Rachel hostage. However, dozens of unarmed Amish community members gather around Schaeffer and he finally surrenders.

The pleasant, open compositions of pastoral Pennsylvania grain fields waving in the breeze to the soothing strains of Maurice Jarre's title track create a dreamlike atmosphere. It is a dream in contrast to the nightmare that exists outside this world. When Rachel Lapp and her son Samuel venture away from the confines of their Amish community, they are subject to the irrational laws that govern life in the noir city. Peter Weir visually emphasizes the implications of the city by closing down the frame space to claustrophobic dimensions. The most expansive shots Weir shows of the city are masked by night photography in a light, but steady rain. The rain, combined with the saturated, murky brown tones of Weir's palette, draw attention to the colorful pulsing strobes of police vehicles and iconic neon signs of urban nightlife. The subplot of forbidden love between John Book and Rachel Lapp adds contrast to the two environments. It's easy to understand why Book is attracted to the sensitive, nurturing Rachel. After all, the only women the noir city has to offer are the suspicious, neurotic type, like Book's sister. In fact, one early version of the script contrasted the two women more extensively, showing Book's sister become extremely defensive about her homemaking skills after Rachel exerts considerable effort to help clean her hostess' home.

The character of Eli, Rachel's father-in-law, serves as an interpretive device to cut through the moral complexities the "man from the city" has brought to their simple existence. When he finds Samuel examining Book's handgun, Eli teaches his grandson the concept of pacifism with a maxim that serves as one of the film's themes: "What you take into your hands, you take into your heart." The incompatibility of the two cultures propels the story headlong into a violent climax. Unable to restrain his aggressive nature in the face of humiliation, Book pummels a smart-aleck city punk, thus alerting his pursuers to his whereabouts. Book's use of violence to combat injustice is a familiar noir protagonist trait, and one he appears incapable of overcoming. In the final confrontation sequence, Weir composes the corrupt detectives descending from a hill overlooking the Lapp farm to appear as if they were biblical angels of destruction. Although Book ultimately dispatches the invaders from the city, the nightmare has not ended—at least for him. Eli points this out to Rachel, saying "He's going back to his world, where he belongs. He knows it, and you know it, too." *Witness* posits a powerful contrast similar to what Jacques Tourneur offered in *Out of the Past* (1947) when Robert Mitchum's character, Jeff, is compelled to leave the sylvan environment of his new life to confront the dark questions of his past. As much as Rachel and her environment beckon to John Book with hope of relief from his world-weary duties, he accepts his fate. Like other noir protagonists, he cannot escape the city and the shadow it has cast over his existence. **TE**

THE ZODIAC (2006)

Director: Alexander Bulkley. **Screenplay**: Kelly Bulkley and Alexander Bulkley. **Producer**: Corey Campodonico. **Director of Photography**: Denis Maloney. **Music**: Michael Suby. **Production Designer**: Jack Taylor. **Editor**: Gregory Tillman. **Cast**: Justin Chambers (Matt Parish), Robin Tunney (Laura Parish), Rory Culkin (Johnny Parish), Philip Baker Hall (Frank Perkins), Brad Henke (Bill Gregory), William Mapother (Dale Coverling), Rex Linn (Jim Martinez), Marty Lindsey (Zodiac), Brian Bloom (Voice of Zodiac), Molly Mulholland (Waitress), Luis Zaguar (Karzoso). **Released**: Think, March 17. 92 minutes.

The Zodiac follows the investigation of Detective Parish (whose jurisdiction seems to be the town of Vallejo) on the five known murders in four attacks from December 1968 through October 1969. Parish is frustrated at the media hype, particularly after the first letters arrive at the *Vallejo Tribune* (and two San Francisco newspapers) in August 1969. His marriage strained by his long hours and heavy drinking, Parish is unaware that his 11-year-old son is doing his own investigating, seeking connections in astronomical occurrences. An interview with the waitress friend of one victim leads Parish to focus on a man named Karzoso. Despite the admonition of his superior Perkins, Parish raids Karzoso's home only to discover he is not the Zodiac. *The Zodiac* ends

with Parish demoted back to uniformed officer and reduced to following his son's school bus in his patrol car.

Although they portray many of the same events, the differences between the $1-million budgeted *The Zodiac* and just plain *Zodiac*, the project funded by two major studios at nearly 100 times that cost, are more about fundamental approaches to neo-noir than about production cost. While its script and performances often betray its limited resources, *The Zodiac* more distinctly echoes the classic period. The unrelenting, amped-up Parish recalls figures as varied as Culloran in *Beat Generation* and Capt. McQuigg in *The Racket*. While Justin Chambers' iconic status is a far cry from Robert Mitchum's or even Steve Cochran's, the alternate narrative points of view from Parish's wife and son, a wistful young man whose single expression suggests extreme emotional repression, create the same undercurrent of chaos lurking in the shadows that was common in classic period productions. There are repeated visual links between the lurking Zodiac, whose face is never seen, and Johnny Parish that simultaneously suggest a dark menace and a mirror, as if the Zodiac were watching a flashback to his own dysfunctional childhood. The Zodiac hates his mother, suggests a glib psychiatrist whom the detectives consult. While young Johnny may not hate her, he runs away from his mother when she plans to leave Parish and their home.

Like the main titles and stock footage of the moon landing, some of the exterior daylight scenes are staged in a documentary style. Like the clips from *The Most Dangerous Game,* which appear in a screening attended by the killer and in a montage flashback, the use the car beams and flashlights in the night sequences and a low-key and semi-monochrome scheme saturated in yellow and green inside the Parish house play against any sense of documentary reality. During the attacks and other scenes, there are also shots from the Zodiac's point of view. Some are straightforward depictions of the killer's eye-line during the violence. Others, as in a brief encounter with a waitress in a diner, are fractured and overlaid, a severe disruption of realistic perspective that is easily read as the killer's emotional point of view, severely distorted and dissociative. While one actor portrays the killer on screen, another gives voice to the letters. The fact that this voice is measured and slightly over-modulated, reminiscent of HAL in *2001*, is subtle and disturbing, running against viewer expectations even as it invokes an aural

Zodiac: *Marty Lindsey as the Zodiac.*

archetype for a dysfunctional machine. The explicit ironies at the end of *The Zodiac* also work at different levels somewhat counter to normal. Parish's demotion permits a tenuous reconciliation with his son and his wife who has repeatedly accused him of ignoring his family and a possible threat to them. The voice of the Zodiac has the last words taken from his final letter: "I am waiting for a good movie about me. Who will play me?" **AS**

ZODIAC (2007)

Director: David Fincher. **Screenplay**: James Vanderbilt based on the books *Zodiac* and *Zodiac Unmasked* by Robert Graysmith. **Producers**: James Vanderbilt, Mike Medavoy, Bradley Fischer, Arnold Messer, Cean Chaffin. **Director of Photography**: Harris Savides. **Music**: David Shire. **Production Designer**: Donald Graham Burt. **Editor**: Angus Wall. **Cast**: Mark Ruffalo (Inspector Dave Toschi), Jake Gyllenhaal (Robert Graysmith), Robert Downey, Jr. (Paul Avery), Anthony Edwards (Inspector William Armstrong), Brian Cox (Melvin Belli), Chloe Sevigny (Melanie), John Carroll Lynch (Arthur Leigh Allen), Philip Baker Hall (Sherwood Morrill), Elias Koteas (Sergeant Jack Mulanax), Dermot Mulroney (Captain Marty Lee), Ione Skye (Kathleen Johns), Charles Fleisher (Bob Vaughan). **Released**: Warner Bros./Paramount, March 2. 158 minutes.

The events from *The Zodiac* make up the first half of the narrative of *Zodiac*. Parallel investigative stories involving San Francisco Detective Inspectors Toschi and Armstrong and newspapermen Avery and Graysmith move into high gear after receipt of letters by the *San Francisco Chronicle*. Unlike the ten month span of *The Zodiac*, the narrative of *Zodiac* covers over twenty years and several other killings and contacts which have never been certainly linked to the serial killer. The last portion revolves around Graysmith's disintegrating marriage as he obsessively completes the research for his book, in the process often revealing facts to police officials from various jurisdictions that their counterparts had kept from them. As does the fictional Parish in *The Zodiac*, Graysmith focuses on a possible acquaintance of the second woman killed. He runs down one false lead and then discovers that Arthur Leigh Allen, the likeliest suspect of detectives Toschi and Armstrong, also knew the woman. After a survivor of the second attack identifies Allen, the ending titles disclose that he died of natural causes before he could be arrested.

The first neo-noir to feature the serial killer who dubbed himself the Zodiac was *Dirty Harry*. Renamed "Scorpio," that fictional figure did what the Zodiac merely threatened and attacked a school bus. The fictionalization in *Dirty Harry* permits the killer to have a face and a personality. From the first, *Zodiac* implies that it will strictly adhere to the facts. Using graphics that repeatedly set date, time, and location,

Zodiac: *Robert Graysmith (Jake Gyllenhaal) and Melanie (Chloe Sevigny).*

the first half of *Zodiac* is a more detailed and dispassionate reenactment than *The Zodiac*. One hundred minutes into the movie, there is a narrative fulcrum in *Zodiac* when handwriting analysis seems to clear the perfect suspect: after Detective Toschi confesses that he can no longer tell whether he is disappointed because he strongly believed the man was guilty or strongly wanted the case to end, his captain suggests that he take some time off. It is nothing like the scathing lecture that Parish receives in *The Zodiac*, and Toschi is not demoted back to uniformed patrolman. But in terms of dramatic arc, the movie could end here.

Instead the film continues for another hour, as the shared perspective refocuses predominantly on the writer Graysmith. Near the end, after Graysmith's wife has left him and taken his children because she fears his monomania will destroy them all, there is an extended sequence when Graysmith visits retired theater owner Bob Vaughan and learns that his handwriting, a possible match for the Zodiac's, is on the posters. With forced creepiness, Graysmith is compelled to follow Vaughan into his basement and when his fearful departure is stopped by a locked door, creates pointless suspense. The encounter leads nowhere and does little except to underscore Graysmith's social and emotional dyslexia. Certainly that "dyslexia" could be taken as a parallel for whatever drives the actual killer. But as Jake Gyllenhaal's performance turns on this detachment, the audience no longer has the easy identification it made with Mark Ruffalo and Anthony Edwards as partners Toschi and Armstrong. It doesn't even have a character like Parish who is melodramatically coming apart. Without that *Zodiac* trudges with hollow footsteps to its necessarily enigmatic conclusion. In doing so, it demonstrates again that the most effective evocations of the noir sensibility are not about A-budgets and extraordinary resources. **AS**

BIBLIOGRAPHY

◇

OTHER BOOKS ABOUT FILM NOIR BY THE EDITORS

Porfirio, Robert. *The Dark Age of American Film: A Study of American Film Noir (1940-1960)*. Unpublished Doctoral Dissertation, Yale University, 1979.

Porfirio, Robert, Alain Silver, and James Ursini, editors. *Film Noir Reader 3*. New York: Limelight Editions, 2001. [Original Interviews with Andre De Toth, Edward Dymytrk, Samuel Fuller, Fritz Lang, Joseph H. Lewis, Otto Preminger, Robert Wise, Billy Wilder, James Wong Howe, Daniel Mainwaring, Miklós Rózsa, Dore Schary, Elisabeth Scott, John F. Seitz, and Claire Trevor]

Silver, Alain and James Ursini. *The Noir Style*. New York: Overlook, 1999.

_____. *Film Noir*. London and Cologne: Taschen, 2004.

_____. *Film Noir Graphics: Where Danger Lives*. Santa Monica: Pendrgon Books, 2010.

_____. *L.A. Noir: The City as Character*. Santa Monica: Santa Monica Press, 2005.

Silver, Alain and James Ursini, editors. *Film Noir Reader*. New York: Limelight Editions, 1994.

_____. *Film Noir Reader 2*. New York: Limelight Editions, 1999.

_____. *Film Noir Reader 4*. New York: Limelight Editions, 2004.

_____.*Gangster Film Reader*. New York: Limelight Editions, 2007.

Ursini, James and Dominique Mainon. *Femm Fatale*, New York: Limelight Editions, 2009

Ward, Elizabeth and Alain Silver. *Raymond Chandler's Los Angeles*. Overlook, 1987.

OTHER BOOKS ABOUT FILM NOIR BY CONTRIBUTORS

Biesen, Sheri Chinen. *Blackout: World War II and the Origins of Film Noir*. Baltimore: Johns Hopkins University Press, 2005.

Conard, Mark T., editor. *The Philosophy of Film Noir*. Foreword by Robert Porfirio. Lexington: University Press of Kentucky, 2006.

Covey, William B. *Compromising Positions: Theorizing American Neo-Noir Film*. Unpublished Doctoral Dissertation, Purdue University of Illinois, 1996.

Erickson, Todd R. *Evidence of Film Noir in the Contemporary American Cinema*. Unpublished Master's Thesis, Brigham Young University, 1990.

Lyons, Arthur. *Death on the Cheap: the Lost B Movies of Film Noir*. New York: Da Capo Press, 2000.

McArthur, Colin. *Underworld USA*. Cinema One, No. 20. New York: Viking, 1972.

Palmer, R. Barton. *Hollywood's Dark Cinema: the American Film Noir*. New York: Twayne Publishers, 1994.

_____. editor. *Perspectives on Film Noir*. New York: G.K. Hall; London: Prentice Hall International, 1996.

Schickel, Richard. *Double Indemnity*. London: BFI Publishing, 1992.

Wager, Jans B. *Dangerous Dames: Women and Representation in the Weimar Street Film and Film Noir*. Athens: Ohio University Press, 1999.

_____. *Dames in the Driver's Seat: Rereading Film Noir*. Austin: University of Texas Press, 2005.

BOOKS

Abbott, Megan E. *The Street was Mine: White Masculinity in Hardboiled Fiction and Film Noir*. New York: Palgrave Macmillan, 2002.

Alloway, Lawrence. *Violent America: The Movies 1946-1964*. New York: Museum of Modern Art, 1971.

Ballinger, Alex and Danny Graydon. *The Rough Guide to Film Noir*. London: Rough Guides, 2007.

Bassoff, Lawrence. *Crime Scenes: Movie Poster Art of the Film Noir: The Classic Period, 1941-1959*. Beverly Hills, CA: L. Bassoff Collection, 1997.

Borde, Raymonde, and Étienne Chaumeton. *Panorama du Film Noir Américain (1941-1953)*. Paris: Editions de Minuit, 1955.

_____. *A Panorama of American Film Noir* (translated by Paul Hammond). San Francisco: City Lights, 2002.

Broe, Dennis. *Film Noir, American Workers, and Postwar Hollywood*. Gainsville, Florida: University Press of Florida, 2009.

Butler, David. *Jazz Noir: Listening to Music from* Phantom Lady *to* The Last Seduction. Westport: Praeger, 2002.

Bould, Mark. *Film noir: from* Berlin *to* Sin City. London and New York: Wallflower, 2005.

Cameron, Ian. *A Pictorial History of Crime Films*. London: Hamlyn, 1975.

Cameron, Ian, editor. *The Book of Film Noir*. New York: Continuum, 1993.

Cauliez, Armand-Jean. *Le Film Criminal et le Film Policier*. Paris: Editions du Cerf, 1956.

Chopra-Gant, Mike. *Hollywood genres and postwar America: masculinity, family and nation in popular movies and film noir*. London & New York: Tauris, 2006.

Christopher, Nicholas. *Somewhere in the Night: Film Noir and the American City*. New York: Free Press, 1997.

Clarens, Carlos. *Crime Movies*. New York: W.W. Norton, 1980.

Conard, Mark T., editor. *The Philosophy of Neo-Noir*. Lexington: University of Kentucky, 2006.

Conoley, Gillian. *Woman Speaking Inside Film Noir*. Spokane: Lynx House, 1984.

Copjec, Joan, editor. *Shades of Noir: A Reader*. London and New York: Verso, 1993.

Crowther, Bruce. *Film Noir: Reflections in a Dark Mirror*. New York: Continuum, 1989.

Deming, Barbara. *Running Away from Myself: A Dream Portrait of America Drawn the Films of the Forties*. N.Y.: Grossman Publishers, 1969.

Derry, Charles. *The Suspense Thriller*. Jefferson, North Carolina: McFarland, 1988.

Dickos, Andrew. *Street with No Name: A History of the Classic American Film Noir*. Lexington: University Press of Kentucky, 2002.

Dimendberg, Edward. *Film Noir and the Spaces of Modernity*. Cambridge, Mass.: Harvard University Press, 2004.

Dixon, Wheeler Winston. *Film Noir and the Cinema of Paranoia*. Edinburgh: Edinburgh University Press, 2009.

Dumont, Herve. *Robert Siodmak: le maître du film noir*. Lausanne: Editions l'Age d'homme, 1981.

Duncan, Paul. *Film Noir: Films of Trust and Betrayal*, 2nd ed. London: Oldcastle, 2006.

Flory, Dan. *Philosophy. Black Film, Film Noir*, University Park: Penn State University Press, 2008.

Gifford, Barry. *The Devil Thumbs A Ride & Other Unforgettable Films*. New York: Grove Press, 1988.

_____. *Out of the Past: Adventures in Film Noir*. Jackson, Mississippi: University Press of Mississippi, 2001.

Guerif, Francois. *Le Film Noir Américain*. Paris: Henri Veyrier, 1979.

Hannsberry, Karen Burroughs. *Femme Noir: Bad Girls of Film*. Jefferson, North Carolina: McFarland, 1998.

Hanson, Helen. *Hollywood Heroines: Women in Film Noir and the Female Gothic Film*. London & New York: Tauris, 2007

Hanson, Helen and Catherine O'Rawe, editors. *The Femme Fatale: Images, Histories, Contexts*. New York: Palgrave Macmillan, 2010

Hare, William. *Early Film Noir: Greed, Lust and Murder Hollywood Style*. Jefferson, North Carolina: McFarland, 2003.

_____. *L.A. Noir: Nine Dark Visions of the City of Angels*. Jefferson, North Carolina: McFarland, 2004.

Hirsch, Foster. *The Dark Side of the Screen: Film Noir*. New York: A.S. Barnes, 1981.

_____. *Detours and Lost Highways: A Map of Neo-Noir*. New York: Limelight, 2004.

Hollinger, Karen Wallis. *Embattled Voices: the Narrator and the Woman in Film Noir and Women's Films*. Unpublished Doctoral Dissertation, University of Illinois, Chicago, 1990.

Irwin, John T. *Unless the Threat of Death is Behind Them: hard-boiled Fiction and Film Noir*. Baltimore: Johns Hopkins University Press, 2006.

Kaplan, E. Ann, editor. *Women in Film Noir*. London: British Film Institute, 1998 (Revised edition).

Karimi, Amir M. *Toward a Definition of the American Film Noir (1941-1949)*. New York: Arno Press, 1976.

Keaney, Michael F. *Film Noir Guide: 1940-1959*. Jefferson, North Carolina: McFarland, 2003.

Kitses, Jim. *Gun Crazy*. London: BFI Publishing, 1996.

Krutnik, Frank. *In A Lonely Street, Film Noir, Genre, Masculinity*. London and New York: Routledge, 1991.

Langman, Larry and Daniel Finn. *A Guide to American Crime Films of the Forties and Fifties*. Westport, Connecticut: Greenwood Press, 1995.

Martin, Richard. *Mean Streets and Raging Bulls: The Legacy of Film Noir in Contemporary American Cinema*. Lanham, Maryland: Scarecrow Press, 1997.

Mayer, Geoff and Brian McDonnell. *Encyclopedia of Film Noir*. Westport, Connecticut: Greenwood Press, 2007.

McCarthy, Todd, and Charles Flynn, editors. *Kings of the B's: Working within the Hollywood System*. New York: E. 7P. Dutton, 1975.

Meyer, David N. *A Girl and a Gun: The Complete Guide to Film Noir on Video*. New York: Avon, 1998.

Muller, Eddie. *Dark City: The Lost World of Film Noir*. New York: St. Martin's Griffin, 1998.

_____. *Dark City Dames: The Wicked Women of Film Noir*. New York: Regan Books, 2001.

_____. *The Art of Noir: The Posters and Graphics from the Classic Era of Film Noir*. Woodstock: Overlook Press, 2002.

Naremore, James. *More Than Night: Film Noir in its Contexts*. Berkeley: University of California Press, 1998.

Oliver, Kelly and Benigno Trigo. *Noir Anxiety*. Minneapolis: University of Minnesota Press, 2003.

Ottoson, Robert. *A Reference Guide to the American Film Noir*. Metuchen, New Jersey: The Scarecrow Press, 1981.

Phillips, Gene D. *Creatures of Darkness: Raymond Chandler, Detective Fiction, and Film Noir*. Lexington: University Press of Kentucky, 2000.

Richardson, Carl. *Autopsy: An Element of Realism in American Film Noir*. Metuchen, New Jersey: The Scarecrow Press, 1992.

Robson, Eddie. *Film Noir*. London: Virgin, 2005.

Rosow, Eugene. *Born to Lose, The Gangster Film in America*. New York: Oxford University Press, 1978.

Sarris, Andrew. "The Film Noir" in *"You Ain't Heard Nothin' Yet": the American Talking Film, History & Memory, 1927-1949*. New York: Oxford University Press, 1998.

Schwartz, Ronald. *Neo-noir: the New Film Noir Style from* Psycho *to* Collateral. Lanham, Maryland: Scarecrow Press, 2005.

_____. *Noir, Now and Then: Film Noir Originals and Remakes, (1944-1999)*. Westport, Connecticut: Greenwood Press, 2001.

Selby, Spencer. *Dark City, the Film Noir*. Jefferson, North Carolina: McFarland, 1984.

Server, Lee, Martin H. Greenberg and Ed Gorman. editors. *The Big Book of Noir*. New York: Carroll & Graf, 1998.

Shadoian, Jack. *Dreams and Dead Ends, The American Gangster/Crime Film*, Cambridge. Massachusetts: MIT Press, 1977.

Siclier, Jacques. *Le Mythe de la Femme dans la Cinema Américain*. Paris: Editions du Cerf, 7eme Art series, 1956.

Spicer, Andrew. *Film noir*. New York: Longmans/Pearson, 2002.

Stephens, Michael L. *Film Noir: A Comprehensive, Illustrated Reference to Movies, Terms, and Persons*. Jefferson, North Carolina: McFarland, 1995.

Straw, William O. *Problems in the Historiography of Cinema: the Case of Film Noir*. Unpublished Master's Thesis, McGill University, 1980.

Telotte, J.P. *Voices in the Dark, The Narrative Patterns of Film Noir*. Urbana, IL: University of Illinois Press, 1989.

Thompson, Peggy and Saeko Usukawa. *Hard-boiled: Great Lines From Classic Noir Films*. San Francisco: Chronicle Books, 1995.

Tuska, Jon. *Dark Cinema: American Film Noir in Cultural Perspective*. Westport, CT: Greenwood Press, 1984.

Werner, Paul. *Film Noir: Die Schattenspiele der "Schwarzen Serie."* Frankfurt: Fischer-Taschenbach, 1985.

West, Ann Adele. *Comedie Noire Thrillers of Alfred Hitchcock: Genres, Psychoanalysis, and Woman's Image*. Unpublished Doctoral Dissertation, University of California, Berkeley, 1982.

ARTICLES and ESSAYS

[NOTE: Many of the seminal articles on film noir have been reprinted in *Film Noir Reader* and *Film Noir Reader 2*. For these, the original publication information is included below, but instead of page numbers the reprint volume is indicated.]

Appel, Alfred. "Fritz Lang's American Nightmare." *Film Comment* 10, No. 6 (1974), pp. 12-17.

Armstrong, Stephen B. "*Touch of Evil* and the End of the Noir Cycle," in *Film Noir Reader 4*.

Arnett, Robert. "Eighties noir: the dissenting voice in Reagan's America, *Journal of Popular Film and Television* 34, No. 3 (Fall 2006).

Arthur, Paul. "Film noir as Primal Scene." *Film Comment* (September-October, 1996).

_____. "The Gun in the Briefcase: Or, the Inscription of Class in Film Noir" in *The Hidden Foundation: Cinema and the Question of Class*. Minneapolis: University of Minnesota Press, 1996, pp. 90-113.

_____. "Murder's Tongue: Identity, Death, and the City in Film Noir" in *Violence and American cinema*. New York: Routledge, 2001, pp. 153-75.

Baxter, John. "Something More Than Night." *Film Journal* 2, No. 4.

Belton, John. "Film Noir's Knights of the Road." *Bright Lights*, No. 54 (November, 2006).

Biesen, Sheri Chinen. "Bogart, Bacall, Howard Hawks and Wartime Film Noir at Warner Bros.: *To Have and HaveNot* and *The Big Sleep*." *Popular Culture Review* (January, 2002).

_____. "Joan Harrison, Virginia Van Upp and Women Behind-the-Scenes in Wartime Film Noir." *Quarterly Review of Film and Video* (April-June, 2003).

_____. "Manufacturing Heroines: Gothic Victims and Working Women in Classic Noir Films," in *Film Noir Reader 4*.

Boozer, Jack. "The Lethal Femme Fatale in the Noir Tradition." *Journal of film and video*. 51, No. 3-4, (Fall 1999): 20.

Borde, Raymonde, and Étienne Chaumeton. "A Propos du Film Noir Américain." *Positif* 19 (1956), pp. 52-57.

_____. "Vingt Ans Apres, Le Film Noir des Années 70." *Écran* 32, January, 1975, p. 5.

_____. "Towards a Definition of Film Noir" (translated by Alain Silver), in *Film Noir Reader*.

Bregent-Heald, Dominique. "Dark Limbo: Film noir and the North American borders." Journal of American Culture 29, No. 2 (June, 2006).

Bronfen, Elisabeth. "Femme Fatale: Negotiations of Tragic Desire." *New Literary History: A Journal of Theory and Interpretation* (Winter, 2004).

Brookover, Linda. "*Blanc et Noir*. Crime as Art" in *Film Noir Reader*.

Brookover, Linda and Alain Silver. "What is this Thing Called Noir?" in *Film Noir Reader*.

_____. "Mad Love is Strange: More Neo-noir Fugitives" in *Film Noir Reader 2*.

Butler, Jeremy G. "'Miami Vice' The Legacy of Film Noir." *Journal of Popular Film*, 13, No. 3 (Autumn, 1985) reprinted in *Film Noir Reader*.

Carter, Beverley. "The Way of the Sexes: Men in Film Noir and *D.O.A.*" in *Film Noir Reader 4*.

Chabrol, Claude. "Evolution du Film Policier." *Cahiers du Cinéma* 54 (1955) reprinted in *Film Noir Reader 2* (translated by Alain Silver and Christiane Silver).

Chartier, Jean-Pierre. "Les Americains Aussi Font des Films Noirs." *Revue du Cinéma* 2 (1946), reprinted in *Film Noir Reader 2* (translated by Alain Silver).

Cieutat, Michel. "La Ville dans le Film Policier Americain." *Positif* 171-172 (1975), pp. 26-38.

Cohen, Mitchell S. "Villains and Victims." *Film Comment* 10 No. 6 (1974), pp. 27-29.

Conley, Tom. "Decoding film noir: *The Killers, High Sierra*, and *White Heat*" in *Film Hieroglyphs: Ruptures in Classical Cinema*. Minneapolis: University of Minnesota Press, 1991.

Covey, William. "The Genre Don't Know Where It Came From: African American Neo-Noir Since the 1960s" *Journal of Film and Video*, 55 No. 2/3 (Summer-Fall, 2003), p. 59-72

_____. "Girl Power: Female Centered Neo-Noir" in *Film Noir Reader*.

Damico, James. "Film Noir: A Modest Proposal." *Film Reader 3* (1978), reprinted in *Film Noir Reader*.

Dargis, Manohla. "N for Noir." *Sight and Sound*, 7, No. 7 (July, 1997), pp: 28-31.

Desser, David. "The Wartime Films of John Huston: Film Noir and the Emergence of the Therapeutic" in *Reflections in a male eye: John Huston and the American experience*, Washington: Smithsonian Institution Press, 1993.

Dick, B.F. "Columbia's Dark Ladies and the Femmes-Fatales of Film Noir." *Literature-Film Quarterly*, 23, No. 3.

Doremieux, Alain. "Le Film Policier." *Cinématographie Française* 30.1 (1965), pp. 10-15, 18-22.

Dorfman, Richard. "Conspiracy City." *Journal of Popular Film and Television*, 7 No. 4 (1980), pp. 434-456.

_____. "D.O.A. and the Notion of Noir." *Movietone News* 48 (February, 1976), pp. 11-16.

Durgnat, Raymond. "Paint It Black: The Family Tree of Film Noir." *Cinema* (U.K) 6/7 (1970), pp. 49-56.

_____. "The Family Tree of Film Noir." [Revised text and graph] *Film Comment* 10 No. 6 (1974), reprinted in *Film Noir Reader*.

Dyer, Richard. "Homosexuality and film noir," in *The Matter of Images: Essays on Representation*, London: Routledge, 2002.

Erickson, Glenn. "Expressionist Doom in *Night and the City*" in *Film Noir Reader*.

_____. "Fate Seeks the Loser: Edgar G. Ulmer's *Detour*" in *Film Noir Reader 4*.

_____. "White Heat" in *Gangster Film Reader*.

Erickson, Todd. "Kill Me Again: Movement becomes Genre" in *Film Noir Reader*.

Everson, William K. "British Film Noir." *Films in Review*, 38, No. 5 (May, 1987).

_____. "British Film Noir II." *Films in Review*, 38, Nos. 6/7 (June-July, 1987).

Ewing, Dale E., Jr. "Film Noir: Style and Content." *Journal of Popular Film and Television*, 16, No. 2 (Summer, 1988), reprinted in *Film Noir Reader 2*.

Farber, Stephen. "Violence and the Bitch Goddess." *Film Comment* 10, No. 6 (1974), reprinted in *Film Noir Reader 2*.

Ferrini, F. "Generi Classici del Cinema Americano." *Bianco & Nero* 35 (1974), pp. 32-39.

Fischer, Hans. "Amerikas Schwarze Serie: Entstehung und Geschichte." *Filmstudio* 42 (1964), pp. 36~15.

Flinn, Tom. "The Big Heat and The Big Combo: Rogue Cops and Mink Coated Girls." *The Velvet Light Trap* 11 (1974), pp. 23-28.

_____. "Three Faces of Film Noir." *The Velvet Light Trap* 5 (1972), reprinted in *Film Noir Reader 2*.

Frank, Nino. "Un Nouveau Genre 'Policier': L'Adventure Criminelle." *L'Écran Française* 61, No. 28.8 (1946), reprinted in *Film Noir Reader 2* (translated by Alain Silver).

Gaines, Philip. "Noir 101" in *Film Noir Reader 2*.

Gregory, Charles. "Living Life Sideways." *Journal of Popular Film*, Vol. V, No. 3-4 (1976), pp. 289-311.

Gross, Larry. "Film Apres Noir." *Film Comment* 12, No. 4 (1976), pp. 44~9.

Grost, Michael. "*Kiss Me Deadly*: Composition and Meaning" in *Film Noir Reader 4*.

Guibert, Pierre. "Film Noir: Ou Film Policier." *Cahiers du Cinéma* 20 (Summer, 1976), pp. 38-45.

Hagopian, Kevin. "'How You Fixed for Red Points?': Anecdote and the World War II Homefront in *The Big Sleep*" in *Film Noir Reader 4*.

Henry, Clayton R., Jr. "Crime Films and Social Criticism." *Films in Review* 2, No. 5 (1951), pp. 31-34.

Higham, Charles and Joel Greenberg. "Noir Cinema" [from *Hollywood in the Forties*] in *Film Noir Reader*.

Hillis, Ken. "Film Noir and the American Dream: the Dark Side of Enlightenment." *Velvet Light Trap* (Spring, 2005).

Hodges, Daniel M. "The Rise and Fall of the War Noir" in *Film Noir Reader 4*.

Hollinger, Karen. "Film Noir, Voiceover, and the Femme Fatale" in *Film Noir Reader*

Horsley, Lee and Katharine Horsley. "Meres Fatales: Maternal Guilt in the Noir Crime Novel." *Modern Fiction Studies*, 45, No. 2 (Summer, 1999), pp. 369-402

House, Rebecca R. "Night of the Soul: American Film Noir." *Studies in Popular Culture*, 9, No. 1.

Houston, Penelope. "The Private Eye." *Sight and Sound* 26 No. 1 (1956), pp. 22-23, 55.

Humphries, Reynold. "The politics of crime and the crime of politics. Post-war noir, the liberal consensus and the Hollywood Left" in *Film Noir Reader 4*.

Jameson, Richard T. "Son of Noir." *Film Comment* 10 No. (1974), reprinted in *Film Noir Reader*.

Jenkins, Stephen. "James M. Cain and Film Noir." *Screen* No. 23, (1982), pp. 80-82.

Jensen, Paul. "Raymond Chandler and the World You Live In." *Film Comment* 10, No. 6 (1974), pp. 18-26.

_____. "The Return of Dr. Caligari: Paranoia in Hollywood." *Film Comment* 7, No. 4 (1971), pp. 36-45.

Johnson, Gary. "*Gun Crazy*," in *Film Noir Reader 4*.

Kearns, Cimberli. "The Homme Fatal: Living and Dying for Style." *Cinefocus*, 3.

Kerr, Paul. "Out of What Past? Notes on the B film noir." *Screen Education*, Nos. 32-33 (Autumn/Winter, 1979-80), reprinted in *Film Noir Reader*.

Krohn, Bill. "Le Film Noir: Aventures et Mesaventures d'un Genre." *Cahiers du Cinéma*, No. 524 (May, 1998).

Krutnik, Frank. "Desire, Transgression, and James M. Cain." *Screen* No. 23 (1982), pp. 31-44.

Legrand, Gerard. "Elixirs des Navets et Philtres sans Etignette." *L'Age du Cinéma* 4/5 (1951), pp. 17-20.

_____. "Reflections in a Dark Eye: Sur la 'Saga' des 'Prive.'" *Positif* 171/172 (1975), pp. 19-25.

Levy, Emanuel. "The Resurrection of Noir" in *Cinema of Outsiders: the Rise of American Independent Film*. New York: New York University Press, 1999.

Lippe, Richard. "At the Margins of Film Noir: Preminger's *Angel*

Face," *CineAction*, Nos. 13-14, Summer, 1988, reprinted in *Film Noir Reader*.

Lott, Eric. "The Whiteness of Film Noir." in *National Imaginaries, American Identities: the Cultural Work of American Iconography*. Princeton, New Jersey: Princeton University Press, 2000.

Lyons, Barry. "Fritz Lang and the Film Noir." *Mise-En-Scène* 1 (1972), pp. 11-15.

Madden, David. "James M. Cain and the Movies of the Thirties and Forties." *Film Heritage* 2 No. 4 (1972), pp. 925.

Maltby, Richard. "Film Noir: the Politics of the Maladjusted Text." *Journal of American Studies*, 18 No. 1 (1984), pp. 49-71.

Martin, Adrian. "Violently Happy: *Gun Crazy*," in *Film Noir Reader 4*.

Miller, Don. "Films on TV." [Film Noir on Television.] *Films In Review* 12 No. 8 (1961) pp. 495-497, and 12 No. 9 (1961), pp.561-563.

_____. "Private Eyes: from Sam Spade to J. J. Gittes." *Focus On Film* 22 (1975), pp. 15-35.

Minturn, Kent. "Peinture Noire: Abstract Expressionism and Film Noir" in *Film Noir Reader 2*.

Munby, Jonathan. "The Un-American Film Art: Robert Siodmak, Fritz Lang, and the Significance of Film Noir's German Connection" in *Public Enemies, Public Heroes: Screening the Gangster from* Little Caesar *to* Touch of Evil. Chicago: University of Chicago Press, 1999.

Nachbar, Jack. "Film Noir" in *Film Genres*, Wes D. Gehring, ed. Westport, CT: Greenwood Press, 1988, pp. 64-84.

Naremore, James. "American Film Noir: The History of an Idea." *Film Quarterly*, 49, No. 2 (Winter, 1995).

_____. "Hitchcock at the Margins of Noir" in *Alfred Hitchcock: Centenary*, pp. 263-77, London: British Film Institute, 1999.

O'Brien, Geoffrey. "The Return of Film Noir!" *New York Review of Books*, 38, No. 14 (August 15, 1991).

Orr, Christopher. "Genre Theory in the Context of the Noir and Post-noir Film" *Film Criticism*, 22, No. 1 (Fall, 1997).

Palmer, R. Barton. "Lounge Time" Reconsidered: Spatial Discontinuity and Temporal Contingency in *Out of the Past*" in *Film Noir Reader 4*.

_____. "Moral Man and the Dark City: Film Noir, the Postwar Religious Revival and *The Accused*" in *The Philosophy of Film Noir*, pp. 187-205.

_____. "The Sociological Turn of Adaptation Studies: the Example of Film Noir." in *A Companion to Literature and Film*, edited by Robert Stam, Alessandra Raengo, Oxford: Blackwell Pub., 2004.

Paris, James. "'Murder can sometimes smell like honeysuckle': Billy Wilder's *Double Indemnity*" in *Film Noir Reader 4*.

Pettengell, Michael. "The Expanding Darkness: Naturalistic Motifs in Hard-Boiled Detective Fiction and the Film Noir," *Clues*, 12, No. 1 (Spring-Summer, 1991).

Place, Janey. A. and Lowell S. Peterson. "Some Visual Motifs of Film Noir." *Film Comment* 10, No. 1 (1974), reprinted in *Film Noir Reader*.

Polan, Dana. "Film Noir." *Journal of Film & Video* (Spring, 1985), pp. 75-83.

Porfirio, Robert G. "Dark Jazz: Music in the Film Noir," in *Film Noir Reader 2*.

_____. *The Killers*: Expressiveness of Sound and Image in Film Noir" in *Film Noir Reader*.

_____. "No Way Out: Existential Motifs in the Film Noir." *Sight and Sound* 45 No. 4 (1976), reprinted in *Film Noir Reader*.

_____. "The Noir Title Sequence" in *Film Noir Reader 4*.

_____. "*The Unsuspected* and the Noir Sequence: Realism, Expressionism, Style" in *Film Noir Reader 4*.

_____. "Whatever Happened to the Film Noir: The Postman Always Rings Twice, (1946-1981)," *Literature/Film Quarterly* (No. 2, 1985), reprinted in *Film Noir Reader*.

Renov, Michael. "*Raw Deal*: the Woman in the Text." *Wide Angle*, 6 No. 2 (1984), pp. 18-22.

Saada, Nicholas. "The Noir Style," in *Film Noir Reader 4*.

Schickel, Richard. "Rerunning film noir," *The Wilson Quarterly*, 31, No. 3 (Summer, 2007).

Schiff, Stephen. "Collector's Choice: Film Noir, a dozen gloomy movies on cassette that shine in a darkened living room." *American Film* (May, 1983), pp. 21-23.

_____. "Film noir,"*American Film* (May, 1983).

Schrader, Paul, "Notes On Film Noir." *Film Comment* 8 No. 1 (1972) reprinted in *Film Noir Reader*.

Schwartz, Ginny. "It's Déjà vu All Over Again: *Double Indemnity* Resonates with Generation X," in *Film Noir Reader 4*.

Shearer, Lloyd. "Crime Certainly Pay on Screen," *New York Times Magazine*, August 5, 1945 reprinted in *Film Noir Reader 2*.

Silver, Alain. "Kiss Me Deadly: Evidence of a Style." *Film Comment* 11 No. 2 (1975) reprinted in *Film Noir Reader*.

_____. "Fragments of the Mirror: Hitchcock's Noir Landscape," *Wide Angle*, Volume 1, No. 3 (1976) in *Film Noir Reader 2*.

_____. "The Gangster and Film Noir: Themes and Styles," in *Gangster Film Reader*.

_____. "*Ride the Pink Horse*: Money, Mischance, Murder, and the Monads of Film Noir" in *The Philosophy of Film Noir*, pp. 223-237.

_____. "Son of Noir: the Emergence of the Neo-Film Noir and the Neo-B Picture," *The DGA Magazine*, 17 No. 3 (June-July, 1992) reprinted in *Film Noir Reader*.

Silver, Alain and James Ursini. "Crime and the Mass Media," *Blackwell Companion to Crime Fiction*, Chapter 4, edited by Charles Rzepka, Lee Horsley, Oxford: Blackwell, 2010.

_____. "John Farrow: Anonymous Noir" in *Film Noir Reader*.

Simsolo, Noel. "Notes sur Le Film Noir." *Cinéma* (Paris), 223 (July, 1977), pp. 23-30.

Sobchack, Vivian. "Lounge Time: Postwar Crises and the Chronotope of Film Noir" in *Refiguring American Film Genres: History and Theory*, edited by Nick Browne, Berkeley: University of California Press, 1998, pp. 129-70.

Somer, Eric. "The Noir Horror of *Cat People*," in *Film Noir Reader 4*.

Tabrizian, Mitra. "Correct Distance: Photo Texts on Film Noir." *Screen* No. 25 (1984), pp. 157-163.

Tasker, Yvonne. "'New Hollywood', New Film Noir, and the Femme Fatale." in *Working girls: Gender and Sexuality in Popular Cinema.* New York: Routledge, 1998.

Telotte, J.P. "The Call of Desire and the Film Noir." *Literature-Film Quarterly* , 17, No. 1 (Jan, 1989).

_____. "Fatal Capers: Strategy and Enigma in Film Noir" *Journal of Popular Film and Television* (Winter, 1996).

_____. "Film Noir at Columbia: Fashion and Innovation" in *Columbia Pictures: Portrait of a Studio,* Lexington: University Press of Kentucky, 1992.

_____. "Siodmak's Phantom Woman and Noir Narrative." *Film Criticism,* 11, No. 3 (Spring, 1987).

_____. "Talk and Trouble, *Kiss Me Deadly's* Deadly Discourse," *Journal of Popular Film* (No. 2, 1985), pp. 69-79.

_____. "Voices from the Deep: Film Noir and Psychodrama," in *Film Noir Reader 4.*

_____. "The woman in the door: framing presence in film noir" in *The Eye of the Beholder: Critical Perspectives in Popular Film and Television.* Bowling Green: Bowling Green State University Popular Press, 1997.

Tracey, Grant. Covert Narrative Strategies to Contain and Punish Women in *The Big Heat* and *The Big Combo*," in *Film Noir Reader 4.*

_____. "Film Noir and Samuel Fuller's Tabloid Cinema: Red (Action), White (Action), and Blue (Romance)," in *Film Noir Reader 2.*

Ursini, James. "Angst at Sixty Fields per Second," in *Film Noir Reader.*

_____. "Noir Science," in *Film Noir Reader 2.*

_____. "Noir Westerns," in *Film Noir Reader 4.*

Van Wert, William. "Philip Marlowe: Hardboiled to Soft-boiled to Poached." *Jump Cut* 3 (1974), pp. 10-13.

Verevis, Constantine. "Through the Past Darkly: Noir Remakes in the 1980's" in *Film Noir Reader 4.*

Vernet, Marc. "The Filmic Transition: on the Openings of Films Noirs." *Velvet Light Trap* 20 (Summer, 1983), reprinted in *Film Noir Reader 2.*

Vesselo, Arthur. "Crime Over the World." *Sight and Sound,* 6, No. 23 (1937), pp. 135-137.

Wager, Jans B. "Jazz and cocktails: reassessing the white and black mix in film noir." *Literature-Film Quarterly,* 35, No. 3 (July, 2007).

Ward, Elizabeth. "The Post-Noir P.I.: *The Long Goodbye* and *Hickey and Boggs*," in *Film Noir Reader.*

_____. "The Unintended Femme Fatale: *The File on Thelma Jordon* and *Pushover*," in *Film Noir Reader 2.*

Wegner, Hart. "From Expressionism to Film Noir: Otto Preminger's *Where the Sidewalk Ends*." *Journal of Popular Film and Television,* 13, No. 2 (Summer, 1985), pp. 59-65.

Wead, George. "Towards a Definition of Filmnoia." *The Velvet Light Trap,* No. 13.

Whalen, Tom. "Film Noir: Killer Style." *Literature-Film Quarterly,* 23, No. 1 (Jan, 1995).

Whitehall, Richard. "Crime Inc.: A Three Part Dossier on the American Gangster Film." *Films and Filming,* 10, No. 4, pp. 7-12.

Whitehall, Richard. "Some Thoughts on Fifties Gangster Films." *The Velvet Light Trap* 11 (1974), pp. 17-19.

Whitney, J. S. "A Filmography of Film Noir." *Journal of Popular Film,* 5, Nos. 3-4, pp. 321-371.

Williams, Tony. "*The Big Night*: a Naturalist *Bildungsroman*" in *Film Noir Reader 4.*

_____. "British Film Noir," in *Film Noir Reader2.*

_____. "*Phantom Lady*, Cornell Woolrich, and the Masochistic Aesthetic," *CineAction!,* Nos. 13-14, Summer, 1988, reprinted in *Film Noir Reader.*

Wilson, Richard. "Hoodlums: Or the Reality." *Films and Filming,* 5, No. 9, p. 10.

Wood, Robin. "Creativity and Evaluation: Two Film Noirs of the Fifties," *CineAction!,* Nos. 21-22 (Summer-Fall, 1990), reprinted in *Film Noir Reader 2.*

_____. "*Rancho Notorious*: A Noir Western in Color," in *Film Noir Reader 4.*

DVD COMMENTARIES BY THE EDITORS

Boomerang (20th Century-Fox, Alain Silver & James Ursini)

Brute Force (Universal, Criterion Collection, Alain Silver & James Ursini)

Call Northside 777 (20th Century-Fox, Alain Silver & James Ursini)

Crossfire (RKO, Warner Bros. DVD, Alain Silver & James Ursini)

The Dark Corner (20th Century-Fox, Alain Silver & James Ursini)

House of Bamboo (20th Century-Fox, Alain Silver & James Ursini)

Kiss of Death (20th Century-Fox, Alain Silver & James Ursini)

Lady in the Lake (MGM, Warner Bros. DVD, Alain Silver & James Ursini)

The Lodger (20th Century-Fox, Alain Silver & James Ursini)

Murder My Sweet (RKO, Warner Bros. DVD, Alain Silver)

Mystery Street (MGM, Warner Bros. DVD, Alain Silver & Elizabeth Ward)

Nightmare Alley (20th Century-Fox, Alain Silver & James Ursini)

Out of the Past (RKO, Warner Bros. DVD, James Ursini)

Panic in the Streets (20th Century-Fox, Alain Silver & James Ursini)

The Street with No Name (20th Century-Fox, Alain Silver & James Ursini)

Tension (MGM, Warner Bros. DVD, Alain Silver & Elizabeth Ward)

Thieves Highway (20th Century-Fox, Criterion Collection, Alain Silver)

Where Danger Lives (RKO, Warner Bros. DVD, Alain Silver & James Ursini)

INDEX

◇

Both films and novels appear in italics. Novels are identified as such parenthetically. However, novels of which the film adaptations use the same title are no longer indexed separately. Production years appear only where needed to distinguish between films with the same title, for example: *The Glass Key* (1935) and *The Glass Key* (1942). For individuals with the same name, occupations appear in parentheses in order to distinguish them. Page numbers in italics indicate illustrations. Alternate titles appear in italics and are cross-indexed to the release titles. Pseudonyms are cross-indexed to actual names. Although the individual filmographies may use variant on-screen credits, the preeminent spellings are used in the index. Neither the Chronologies in the Appendix to the Classic Period nor the Bibliography are indexed.

A Bout de Soufle, 366
Aaker, Lee, 154
Abandoned, 20, 23
Abandoned Woman see
    Abandoned
Abbot, Anthony see Oursler,
    Fulton
Abrams, Ron, 8, 376-77, 420,
    439-40
Accused, The, 20, 23-24, *24*
Ace in the Hole, 24-25, *25*
Acheson, Mark, 407
Acker, Sharon, 440
Acosta, Rudolfo, 219
Act of Violence, 17, 25-26, *26*
Adams, Casey, 203, 317
Adams, Dorothy, 177
Adams, Gerald Drayson, 30,
    47, 92, 133
Adams, Henry, 86, 297
Adams, Julie, 136
Adams, Warren, 231
Adamson, Barry, 379
Adamson, Harold
Addams, Dawn, 314
Addy, Wesley, 40, 115, 167,
    303
Adjani, Isabelle, 380
Adler, Bob, 57
Adler, Buddy, 89, 138
Adler, Jay, 39, 75, 80, 166,
    211
Adler, Jerry, 443
Adler, Luther, 74, 84, 137,
    139, 171, 184
An Affair of the Heart see *Body
    and Soul*
Affair in Havana, 26-27

Affair in Trinidad, 27, *27*
After Dark, My Sweet, 351,
    351
Against All Odds, 351-52
Agar, John, 264, 337
Agee, James, 207
Agonei, Conrad, 368
Aiello, Patrick, 374
Ahern, Lloyd, 57, 81
Aherne, Brian, 143, 180
Ahmad, Maher, 424
Ahn, Philip, 128, 149, 185
Ainley, Lynn, 189
Akins, Claude, 264, 408
Akst, Albert, 156, 286, 294
Alba, Jessica, 451-52, *451*
Albert, Arnold, 186
Albert, Eddie, 400, *400*
Albertson, Frank, 209, 297,
    336
Albertson, Jack, 126
Albiin, Elsie, 295
Albright, Lola, 67, 162
Alcaide, Chris, 40
Alcott, John, 433
Alda, Robert, 186, 215
Alderson, Brooke, 425
Aldrich, Robert, 40, 44, 115-
    16, 167-70, 340, 350,
    350, 400-01
Alexander, George, 331
Alexander, Jeff, 224, 243
Alexander, John, 270
All Through the Night (novel),
    80
Allan, Richard, 203
Allen, Corey, 161, 224
Allen, Dede, 217, 425, 432

Allen, Fred, 71, 104, 128,
    135, 185, 247, 292
Allen, Irwin, 321
Allen, Joan, 422
Allen, Lester, 88, 119
Allen, Lewis, 29, 68, 148,
    272, 287-88
Allen, Steve, 465
Allen, Ta-Ronce, 397
Allgood, Sara, 23, 153, 181,
    181, 275, 278
Allman, Gregg, 446
Alonso, Maria Conchita, 385
Alonzo, John A., 368, 383
Alper, Murray, 186
Alperson, Edward, 150
Altman, Robert (director), 46,
    392, 416-418
Altman, Robert (writer), 54
Alton, John, 39, 55-56, 64,
    78, 98-99, 127-28, 135,
    145, 198, 225, 234, 244,
    247-48, 270, 292-93,
    335, 349

Alvarado, Don, 47
Alwin, William, 272
Amber, Eve, 289
Ambler, Eric, 159, 190
Ameche, Don, 269
American Tragedy, An (novel),
    229
Ames, Jimmy, 67
Ames, Leon, 28, 174, 233, 256
Ames, Preston, 174
Ames. Ramsay, 63
Amphitheatrof, Daniele, 32,
    40, 84, 98, 139, 141,
    153, 156, 268, 289, 304
Amitraj, Ashok, 374
Amy, George, 71, 307
Among the Living, 27-28, *28*
Anchia, Juan Ruiz, 350, 352,
    400, 415
Ancona, Amy B., 450
Anders, Glenn, 174, 184
Anders, Merry, 207
Anderson, Judith, 177, 236,
    246, 281

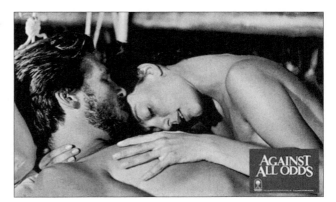

At Close Range

Anderson, Carl, 73, 266, 271, 425
Anderson, Edward, 226, 296
Anderson, Kevin, 415, 453
Anderson, Leonard, 331
Anderson, Mary, 145, 312, 331
Anderson, Maxwell, 160-161, 317, 341
Anderson, Richard, 66, 155, 213, 225, 314
Anderson, Robert, 207, 311
Anderson, Roland, 38, 267, 465
Anderson, U.S., 132
Anderson, Warner, 132, 179
Andes, Keith, 71
Andrews, Christopher, 427
Andrews, Dana, *14*, 36, *37*, 55, 104, 107-08, *107*, 177, *177*, 221, 328-29, *329*
Andrews, David, 386
Andrews, Edward, 126, 293
Andrews, Robert Hardy, 337
Andriot, Lucien, 281
Angel Face, 20, 28-29, *28*, 164, 328
Angel, Heather, 290
Angus, Robert, 303
Anhalt, Edna, 223, 271
Anhalt, Edward, 223, 271
Ankrum, Morris, 85, 132, 145, 149, 151, 174, 233, 274, 304
Ant, Adam, 452
Antheil, George, 138, 149, 172, 248, 271
Anthony, Marc, 421
Antrim, Harry, 25, 29, 110, 212, 267, 304
Anwar, Gabrielle, 457
Aoki, Devon, 451
Apology for Murder, 29

Appointment with Danger, 29-30, *29*
Apted, Michael, 361-62
Arbogast, Thierry, 385
Archer, Anne, 383, 430
Archer, John, 70, 333
Archibald, William, 143
Arden, Eve, 191, 313
Arden, Robert, 192
Argo, Victor, 353, 409, 456
Arkin, Alan, 388
Arkin, David, 416
Armendariz, Pedro, Jr., 436
Armitage, George, 423-24
Armored Car Robbery, 30
Armstrong, Arnold B., 244
Armstrong, Charlotte, 293, 315
Armstrong, Louis, 33, 286
Armstrong, R.G., 393
Armstrong, Robert, 93, 107
Arndt, Denis, 355
Arness, James, 225, 295
Arnold, Edward, 71, 156
Arnold, Jack, 293-94
Arnsten, Stefan, 134
Arnt, Charles, 86, 107, 132, 189, 273, 279
Arquette, Patricia, 418, 459-60
Arquette, Richmond, 386
Arquette, Rosanna, 376, 382
Art of Murder, The see *Double Life, A*
Arthur, Michelle, 434
Arthur, Robert, 24, 40
Arrigo, Frank, 49, 137, 408
Ashby, Hal, 382
Asher, Irving, 307
Asher, William, 155
Ashford, Nick, 430
Ashford, Ted, 397
Ashley, Audrey, 244
Ashley, Edward, 214

Aslan, Gregoire, 192
Asphalt Jungle, The, 30-31, *30-31*, 445
Asphalt Jungle, The (novel), 30
Assante, Armend, 402
Asther, Nils, 53
Astor, Mary 25, 166, 186
At Close Range, 350, *350*, 352, *352*
Atherton, Howard, 383
Atlas, Dorothy, 93
Atlas, Leopold, 244
Atwater, Barry, 210
Atwater, Gladys, 199
Aubert, Lenore, 249
Audsley, Mick, 391
Auer, John H., 71, 128
Auer, Mischa, 192
Aumont, Genevieve, 279
Auster, Islin, 288
Austin, Dave, 405
Austin, J. W., 125
Austin, William, 107
Avery, Margaret, 396
Avery, Roger, 459
Avil, Gordon, 264
Ayres, Lew, 88, 313
Aznavour, Charles, 286

Babcock, Dwight, 183, 271
Bacall, Lauren, 45-47, 88, 160-161, *161*, 394
Bachelin, Franz, 61, 68, 87, 146, 205
Bachelor, Stephanie, 49
Bacher, William A., 178
Backfire, 32
Backlar, Marshall, 442
Backlash, 32-33
Backus, Georgia, 66
Backus, Jim, 28, 133, 136, 155, 184
Bacon, Irving, 66, 193
Bacon, Kevin, 372, 429, *429*
Badalamenti, Angelo, 418, 427
Badham, John, 441
Bad Influence, 353
Bad Lieutenant, 353-54, *353*, 378, 410
Baden-Powell, Sue, 443
Badge of Evil (novel), 305
Badlands, 354-55, *354*, 392
Baer, Buddy, 270
Baer, Max, Sr., 126
Baer, Richard L., 302
Baggett, Lynn, 84
Bagier, Douglas, 331

Bagier, W.L., 50, 227
Bailey, John, 368
Bailey, Raymond, 179, 317
Bainter, Fay, 90, *90*
Bair, David, 245
Bait, 220
Bakaleinikoff, Constantin, 98, 134, 240, 260
Bakaleinikoff, Mischa, 50, 179, 196-97, 249, 257
Bakalyan, Richard (Dick), 369
Baker, Art, 66, 149
Baker, Becky Ann, 451
Baker, Buddy, 333
Baker, Carroll, 388
Baker, Graham, 85, 242
Baker, Joby, 161
Baker, Joe Don, 368, 372, 438, *438*, 463
Baker, Robert, 437
Baker, Roy Ward, 208
Bakija, Bianca, 354
Balderston, John L., 116
Baldwin, Alec, 390, 424
Baldwin, Daniel, 428
Baldwin, Stephen, 464
Baldwin, Walter, 299
Balk, Fairuza, 457
Ball, Lucille, 87
Ballard, Lucien, 34, 70, 141, 162, 166, 181, 194, 208, 389-90
Ballinger, William S., 238
Balsam, Martin, 64, 367
Balson, Allison, 356
Bancroft, Anne, 202, 209, 441
Bancroft, George, 41, *41*
Banderas, Antonio, 385, *386*, 436, *436*
Banks, Joan, 80
Banks, Lionel, 193, 242
Banks, Sidney, 331
Banning, Leslie, 133
Bannon, Jim, 113
Baragrey, John, 266
Barancik, Steve, 415
Barclay, Steve, 119
Bardem, Javier, 370, 432, *432*
Bardette, Trevor, 122, 137
Bari, Lynn, 214, *215*, 265-66
Barker, Jess, 255
Barker, Lex, 79
Barkin, Ellen, 406, *406*, 447-48
Barkley, Lucille, 220
Barnes, George, 110, 112, 275
Barnes, Mae, 217
Barnett, Griff, 77

Barnett, Vince, 163, 266
Baron, Allen, 49-50
Barr, Byron, 99, 228, 297
Barrett, Andrew Lee, 409
Barrett, Laurinda, 341
Barrie, Mona, 279
Barron, Jerry, 7, 149, 407, 423, 446, 450, 457, 464
Barry, Gene, 199
Barry, Donald "Red," 247, 400
Barry, John, 362, 393, 405
Barrymore, Drew, 391, *392*
Barrymore, Ethel, 193, 275, *276*
Barrymore, John (Drew), Jr., *19*, 44, *44*
Barrymore, Lionel, 103, 160
Barsi, Judith, 452
Barsche, Leon, 286
Barthell, Beau, 430
Bartlett, Sy, 64
Barton, Dee, 439
Barton, James, 254
Barton, Sean, 405
Bartkowiak, Andrzej, 426
Basehart, Richard, 127, 141, 247-48, 294
Basevi, James, 57, 87, 181, 221, 225, 273, 275
Basic Instinct, 355-56, *355*, 448
Basinger, Kim, *365*, 390, 414
Bass, Ronald, 360, 453
Basserman, Albert, 263
Bassler, Robert, 57, 125, 141, 181, 208, 287, 299
Bassman, George, 233
Bates, Barbara, 239
Bates, Charles, 266
Bates, Florence, 57, 258, 332
Bates, Harry, 91
Batista, Henry, 50, 195
Batman, 350
Baum, Vicki, 119
Bavier, Frances, 188
Baxley, Barbara, 447
Baxter, Alan, 260
Baxter, Anne, 52, *52*, 120, 143
Bazelli, Bojan, 377, 409
Be Still, My Love (novel), 23
Beach, Michael, 435
Beat Generation, The, 33-34, *33*, 467
Beal, John, 68
Beals, Jennifer, 379, *379*
Bean, Henry, 377-78
Beason, Eric, 415, 451
Beaton, Jesse, 379, 435, 437

Beattie, Stuart, 370
Beaumont, Hugh, 29, 52, 107, 173, 208, 241
Beckell, Graham, 415
Becker, Harold, 447
Beddoe, Don, 104, 183, 202, 207, 297
Bedford-Lloyd, John, 380
Bedoya, Alfonso, 56
Bedroom Window, The, 356
Beebe, Dion, 370, 403, 424
Beecroft, Jeefrey, 388
Beeding, Francis, 275
Beetley, Samuel E., 47, 51, 72, 185, 220, 302
Beeson, Eric L., 407
Before I Die, 174
Before the Fact (novel), 290
Begley, Ed, 32, 55, 73, 87, 217-18, 273, 285, 307-08, 465
Behind Locked Doors, 34
Behind the Law see *Unknown Man, The*
Behind This Mask see *In a Lonely Place*
Bel Geddes, Barbara, 51, 65, *65*, 181, *182*, 223, 317
Belafonte, Harry, 217, *217*
Belcher, Patricia, 434
Belding, Dale , 150
Belita, 114, *115*, 142, 289
Bell, James, 50, 76, 92
Bellah, Ross, 179, 209
Bellamy, Ralph, 120
Bellaver, Harry, 59
Bellem, Robert, 49
Bello, Maria, 439
Belloc-Lowndes, Marie, 153, 181, 188
Beltran, Robert, 452
Belushi, James, 380, 456
Ben Ammar, Tarak, 385
Benair, Jonathan, 7, 106, 166, 223-24, 368-70
Bender, Lawrence, 405, 445
Bendix, William, 47, 52, 61, 87, 96, 114, 118, 185
Benedek, Laslo, 25, 232
Benedict, Billy, 331
Benedict, Richard, 24, *25*, 32, 256, 334
Benford, Vassal, 430
Bengal, Ben, 74
Benjamin, Richard, 76
Bennett, Bruce, 85, 88, 187, *187*, 191, 198, 215, 263, 286, 311

Bennett, Charles, 153, 321, 430
Bennett, Constance, 315
Bennett, Dorothy, 57
Bennett, Joan, 132-33, 135, 245, *245*, 255, *255*, 259-60, 336-39, *337*
Bennett, Marjorie, 189
Bennett, Nigel, 430
Bennett, Ray, 64
Bening, Annette, 391
Benson, James, 102
Benson, Sally, 212, 262
Benton, Robert, 460
Beranger, George, 252
Bercovici, Leonardo, 87, 171
Berenger, Tom, 385
Berg, Peter, 370, 415, *415*
Bergen, Polly, 64, 82
Berger, Peter, 383
Berger, Cary, 455
Berger, Ralph, 30, 47, 185, 218, 321
Bergin, Patrick, 419, *419*, 453, *453*
Bergman, Ingrid, 116, 216, *216*, 275, *275*
Berke, William A., 86, 266
Berkeley, Martin, 265, 271
Berkeley, Xander, 388
Berkes, John, 24
Berkman, Ted, 267
Berlatsky, David, 397
Berlin Express, 34-35, *34*
Berlinger Warren, 416
Berman, Henry, 440
Berman, Pandro S., 58, 311
Bernardi, Herschel, 194
Bernhard, Jack, 50, 93, 142
Bernhardt, Curtis, 72-73, 132, 232-33
Bernie, Jason, 50, 93
Bernstein, Elmer, 185, 277, 286-87, 290, 379, 391, 444, 460

Bernstein, Walter, 171, 425-26
Beron, Laurence, 357
Berry, John, 65, 127, 294
Besser, Joe, 336
Besson, Luc, 441
Best, Roy, 64
Best Seller, 356-57, *357*
Best Years of Our Lives, The, 87
Bête Humaine, La (novel), 141-42
Betrayal see *Manhandled*
Bettger, Lyle, 212, 314
Bettis, Valerie, 27
Between Midnight and Dawn, 35
Betz, Carl, 317
Beware My Lovely, 35-35, *35*
Bewitched, 36
Beyond a Reasonable Doubt (1956), 36-37, *37*
Beyond a Reasonable Doubt (2009), 357, 58, *357*
Beyond the Forest, 37-38, *38*
Bezzerides, A.I., 167-68, 218, 299
Biberman, Abner, 207
Bice, Robert (Bob), 127
Bick, Jerry, 416
Bickford, Charles, 59, 103, 107, 241, 330, 338
Biddell, Sidney, 92
Bieri, Ramon, 354
Biesen, Sheri, Chinen, 9, 27, 116-17, 262-63, 290
Big Bow Mystery (novel), 316
Big Carnival, The see *Ace in the Hole*
Big Clock, The, 18, 22, 38-39, *38*, 433-34
Big Clock, The (novel), 433
Big Combo, The, *13*, 19, 39, *39*, 349
Big Heat, The, 19, 40, *40*, 454

Big Knife, The, 40, 44, *44*, 401

Big Night, The, 19, *19*, 44-45, *45*

Big Sleep, The (1946), 30, 45-47, *46*

Big Steal, The, 47, *47*

Big Tree, Chief John, 98

Bigamist, The, 47-48, *48*

Bigger Than Life, 229

Billingsley, John, 437

Binns, Edward, 36, 335, 432

Birch, Paul, 293

Biroc, Joseph F., 80, 115, 119, 162-63, 179, 209, 335, 340, 393, 400, 465

Bischoff, Samuel, 226, 228

Bishop, Dan, 361

Bishop, Joey, 155

Bishop, Julie, 131, 302

Bishop, William, 182, 267

Bissell, Whit, 39, 59, *59*, 64, 94, 101, 127, 162, 251, 267, 273

Black Angel, 47-48

Black Book, The see *The Reign of Terror*

Black Curtain, The (novel), 284

Black Dahlia, 358-59, *358*, 365, *365*

Black, Karen, 438

Black, Noel, 442

Black Path of Fear (novel), 66

Black Rain, 359-60, *359*

Black Widow, 360, *360*, 403

Blackboard Jungle, The

Blackmail, 49

Blackman, Jack, 422

Blackmer; Sidney, 36, *37*

Blade Runner, 350, *350*, 360-61, *361*

Blades, Ruben, 461

Blair, Betsy, 198

Blair, George, 331

Blair, Joan, 331

Blair, Patricia, 70

Blake, Arthur, 232

Blake, Bobby (Robert), 336, 418

Blake, Larry, 32, 142

Blake, Madge, 235

Blake, Oliver, 121

Blake, Pamela, 197, 301

Blake, Richard, 150

Blakely, Ronee, 380

Blanchard, Mari, 314

Blanchard, Terence, 436

Blangsted, Folmer, 147

"Blank Wall, The" (story), 245

Blanke, Henry, 37, 190, 304

Blankfort, Henry, 312

Blankfort, Michael, 89

Blast of Silence, 49-50

Blau, Raphael, 267

Blaustein, Julian, 91

Bledel, Alexis, 451

Blees, Robert, 257, 270

Blind Alley, The see *Dark Past, The*

Blind Alley, The (novel), 89

Blind Spot, 50

Blink, 361-62

Bliss, Lela, 88

Block, J.S., 398

Block, Lawrence, 382

Block, Larry, 393

Block, Libbie, 65

Blocker, David, 361

Blocker, Dirk, 364

Blonde Ice, 50-51, *50*

Blondell, Joan, 210

Blood on the Moon, 51, *51*

Blood on the Moon (novel), 371

Blood Simple, 362, 433

Bloody Spur, The (novel), 329

Bloom, Brian, 467

Bloom, Harold Jack, 201

Bloom, John, 360, 465

Blore, Eric, 263-64

Blue Dahlia, The, 30, 52, *52*

Blue Gardenia, 52-53, *52*

Blue, Monte, 32, 160, 302

Bluebeard, 53

Blumenthal, Richard M., 301

Blyth, Ann, 56, 191, *191*

Blythe, Betty, 136

Boardman, Chris, 439

Bochner, Lloyd, 440

Bock, Edward, 249

Body and Soul, 54, *54*

Body Heat, 362-64, *363*, 365, *365*, 377, 399

Bodyguard, 54-55

Boehm, Sydney, 40, 132, 198, 253, 258, 267-68, 310, 314

Boemler, George, 30

Boetticher, Oscar (Budd), Jr., 34, 105, 162

Bogart, Humphrey, 45-47, *46*, 72-73, *73*, 89, 92, 94, 104-05, *105*, 126-27, *126*, 130, 149, *149*, 160-61, *161*, 172, 186, *186*, 308-09, *308*

Bogeaus, Benedict, 78, 90, 270

Bogert, Vin, 189

Boggs, Haskell B., 267

Bohem, Endre, 205

Bohnen, Roman, 59, 205, 281, 304

Bois, Curt, 65

Boileau, Pierre, 317

Boland, Mary, 122

Boles, Jim, 189

Bollinger, Alun, 433

Bolotin, Craig, 359

Bolster, Anita, 197

Bolton, Muriel Roy, 196

Bomba, David J., 436

Bomback, Mark, 376

Bonanova, Fortunio, 99, 167, 258

Bond, Lilian, 188

Bond, Rudy, 209

Bond, Ward, 156, 171, 186, 218, *218*

Book, Leslie, 50-51

Boomerang, 55

Boone, Richard, 40, 115, 317-18

Boorman, John, 440

Booth, Charles G., 140, 154

Boothe, Powers, 451

Borde, Raymond and Chaumeton, Etienne, 170

Borden, Eugene, 271

Border, The, 350, 364, *364*

Border Incident, 55-56, *56*

Borden, Lizzie, 419

Border Patrol see *Border Incident*

Borgnine, Ernest, 156, 388, 400, 454

Born to Kill, 56-57, *56*

Boros, Stuart, 364

Borowsky, Marvin, 114, 273

Borzage, Frank, 193

Botkin, Perry, 194

Bottome, Phyllis, 85

Bouchey, Willis, 40, 115, 207, 228, 287

Bound, 364-66, *366*

Bourgoin, Jean, 192

Bourne, Mel, 383, 410

Boumeuf, Philip, 36, 44

Bousel, Morris, 165

Bouton, Jim, 416

Bowen, Michael, 405

Bowers, George, 453

Bowers, William, 73, 80, 276-77

Bowman, Lee, 138

Boy Cried Murder, The (novel), 334

Boyce, Rodger, 432

Boyer, Charles, 116, *116*, 300

Boyer, Lyle, 338

Boyle, Geoff, 373

Boyle, Lara Flynn, 444

Boyle, Peter, 387, 393, 407, 456

Boyle, Robert, 59, 64, 76, 207, 214, 249, 262, 297

Bozeman, Ron, 450

Brackett, Charles, 104, 203, 288

Brackett, Leigh, 45, 416

Bradford, Richard, 393

Bradley, David, 293

Bradley, Deputy Chief, 127

Bradley Meson Story, The see *Unknown Man, The*

Bradley, Truman, 62

Bradsell, Michael, 410

Brady, Fred, 136

Brady, Leo, 104
Brady, Ruth, 65
Brady, Scott, 64, 127, 156, 232, 311-12
Brahm, John, 57, 120, 125-26, 180-81, 268-69
Brancato, John D., 388
Brand, Neville, 84, *84*, 160, 171, 251, 308, 328
Brando, Jocelyn, 40, 209
Brandon, Henry, 64
Brasher Doubloon, The, 57, *57*
Brasselle, Keefe, 229, 241, 314
Brazzi, Rossano, 385
Breaking Point, The, 57-58
Breathless, 366
Brecher, Egon, 271
Bredell, Elwood (Woody), 68, 109, 163, 225-26, 315
Breen, Richard, 29-30, 203
Bregman, Martin, 448
Bregman, Michael, 448
Bremer, Lucille, 34
Bren, J. Robert, 199
Brennan, Eileen, 400
Brennan, Walter, 51, 213
Brenneman, Amy, 384, 395
Brenner, Albert, 440
Brenner, Alfred, 181
Brenner, David, 384, 431
Brent, Eve, 110
Brent, George, 275
Brent, Romney, 257
Breon, Edmond, 188, 336
Bresler, Jerry, 23, 36, 73, 268
Bresson, Robert, 456
Bretherton, David, 447
Bretherton, Howard, 331
Brett, Mitch, 408
Brian, David, 37, 84
Bribe, The, 58, *58*
Brick, 365
Brick Foxhole, The (novel), 79
Bricker, George, 83, 183, 188, 251
Bridges, James, 425
Bridges, Jeff, 351-52, 382, 405, 426, 450
Bridges, Lloyd, 193, 242, 306-07
Bright, John, 146
Bright, Matthew, 391
Bright, Richard, 390
Bright, Susie, 364
Brisbin, David, 351, 403
Briscoe, Brent, 451
Briskin, Mort, 239, 258
Brissac, Virginia, 36, 225

Britton, Pamela, 84, 297
Brodie, Steve, 30, 54, 79, 93, 184, 220
Brodine, Norbert, 55, 140, 170, 273, 299
Brody, Jo Ann, 416
Brody, Meredith, 8, 104-05, 145-46, 185, 193, 263-64, 312-13
Brody, Merrill, 49
Brolin, Josh, 432, *432*
Bromberg, J. Edward, 122, 144, 318
Bronfman, Edgar, 364
Bronner, Robert, 224
Bronson, Betty, 200
Bronson, Charles, 76, 375
Bronson, Clarice, 442
Brorison, Harry, 78, 298
Brook, Jayne, 388
Brooke, Hillary, 151, 280-81
Brookover, Linda, 8, 41-43, 304, 354-55, 390-91, 443
Brooks, Albert, 456
Brooks, Arthur, 266
Brooks, Geraldine, 232, 245
Brooks, George, 35, 249
Brooks, Hazel, 54, *54*, 269, *269*
Brooks, Jean, 309
Brooks, Leslie, 135
Brooks, Phyllis, 86, 253
Brooks, Randy, 382
Brooks, Richard, 59-60, 79, 160, 163, 198
Brothers Rico, The, 58-59
Broughton, Bruce, 430
Browe, Otto, 103
Brower, Mitchell, 389
Brown, Charles D., 29, 45, 112, 147, 163, 205, 241
Brown, Fredric, 74, 257
Brown, Harry, 171, 229, 271
Brown, Harry Joe, 257
Brown, Hilyard (Hildyard), 207, 241, 400
Brown, James S., Jr., 119
Brown, Jim, 454
Brown, John, 284
Brown, Kay, 286
Brown, Malcolm, 36, 55, 81, 161, 201
Brown, O. Nicholas, 431
Brown, Rowland, 160, 214
Brown, W.R., 456
Brown, Wally, 216
Browne, Coral, 381

Browning, Chris, 374
Bruce, David, 63, 68
Bruce, George, 160
Bruce, Nigel, 290, 308, 340
Bruce, Sally Jane, 207
Bruce, Virginia, 205
Bruckheimer, Jerry, 383, 456
Brugge, Pieter Jan, 424
Brun, Joseph, 217
Brunetti, Argentina, 59
Brute Force, 59-60, *59*
Bryant, Marie, 296
Brynner, Yul, 232
Buba, Pasquale, 395, 450
Bubbico, Joe, 49
Buchanan, Edgar, 98, 113, 141, 185, 244
Buchinsky, Charles see Bronson, Charles
Buckner, Robert, 213
Buff, Conrad, 390, 405
Build My Gallows High see *Out of the Past*
Build My Gallows High (novel), 220
Buka, Donald, 35, 285
Bulkley, Alexander, 467
Bulkley, Kelly, 467
Bullock, Walter, 248
Bumstead, Henry, 212, 317, 367
Bunker, Eddie, 445
Burdick, Hal, 205
Burem, Stephen, 382
Burgess, Gelett, 309
Burgess, Grover, 199
Burglar, The, 60, *60*
Burke, James, 27, 186, 210
Burke, Walter, 15, 87, 184
Burks, Robert, 37, 104-05, 143, 284, 304, 316-17, 341

Burnett, W. R, 30-31, 130, 143-44, 148, 213-14, 240, 267, 301
Burns, Bart, 431
Burns, Brendan, 431
Burns, Paul L., 205
Burr, Raymond, 23, 26-27, 52, 75-76, 93, 133, 184, 228-31, *228*, 244, 247, 269
Burstyn, Ellen, 376
Burt, Donald Graham, 468
Burton, Bernard W., 80
Burton, Robert, 40
Burwell, Carter, 362, 384, 432
Buscemi, Steve, 409, 445, 457
Busch, Niven, 103, 193, 233, 236
Busey, Gary, 418
Bushman, Francis X., 136
Butler, Bill (Wilmer), 370, 376, 397
Butler, Gerald, 171, 218
Butler, Hugo, 127, 235, 340
Butler, Michael, 367
Butterfield, Herbert, 264
Buttolph, David, 55, 57, 76, 104, 140, 143, 170, 193, 273, 284, 293
Butts, R. Dale, 71, 128, 304
Byington, Spring, 98, 268, 320
Byrne, Gabriel, 441, 464
Byrnes, Harold, 227
Byrd, Ralph, 64
Bystander, The see *Angel Face*

Caan, James, 456, *457*
Cabot, Bruce, 107
Cabot, Susan, 104
Cady, Frank, 24, 73
Cady, Jerome, 62, 80

FILMED WITH THE NAKED FURY OF FACT!

CANON CITY

WHERE IT ACTUALLY HAPPENED... WITH THE PEOPLE IT HAPPENED TO!

introducing SCOTT BRADY ... JEFF COREY WHIT BISSELL
STANLEY CLEMENTS · CHARLES RUSSELL · DeFOREST KELLEY

Cage, Nicolas, 411, 444-45
Caged, 61, *61*
Cagney, James, 69-70, 171-72, 267, 333, *333*
Cagney Jeanne, 239
Cagney, William, 171
Cahn, Edward L., 95
Cahn, Phillip, 95
Cailliet, Lucien, 206
Cain, Dean, 437
Cain, James M., 99-101, 191-92, 220, 233, 270, 363-64, 441-42
Calcutta, 61-62, *62*
Calder, King, 303
Calderon, Paul, 353, 447
Caldwell, Dwight, 197, 249
Calhern, Louis, 30, *31*, 98, 216
Calhoun, Rory, 246
Calker, Darrell, 32, 190
Call Northside 777, 62-63, *62*
Call, R.D., *454*
Callahan, Gene, 360, 387, 405
Callahan, George, 247
Callahan, Pepe, 416
Callaway, Cheryl, 83
Calleia, Joseph, 92, 117-18, 305
Calling Dr. Death, 63-64, *63*
Calvert, Phyllis, 29
Camden, Joan, 65
Cameron, Paul, 370, 420
Caminito, Augusto, 409
Campbell, Alan, 339
Campbell, Beverly, 84
Campbell, Martin, 372
Campbell, Vera, 272
Campbell, William, 57, 225
Campion, Jane, 403-04
Campodonico, Corey, 467

Camus, Albert, 20
Cane, Charles, 92, 274
Canerday, Natalie, 435
Canfield, Gene, 447
Canon City, 64, *64*
Cape Fear (1962), 64-65, *64*, 384
Cape Fear (1991), 367, *367*
Capell, Peter, 60
Caplan, Jodie, 121
Capps, McClure, 246
Captive City, The, 65
Capshaw, Kate, 359
Card, Kathryn, 90
Cardwell, James (Jimmy), 109, 127, 249
Carey, Harry, 27, *28*
Carey, Harry, Jr., 138, 193, 236
Carey, Macdonald, 262
Carey, Olive, 144, 253
Carey, Philip, 147, 238, 257
Carey, Timothy, 76, 139, 166, 408, 438
Carey, Tom, 351
Carfagno, Edward, 176
Carillo, Elpedia, 364
Carleton, Claire, 335
Carlson, Richard, 34, 307
Carlson, Roy, 368
Carlton, Larry, 351
Carlton, Rex, 122
Carlyle, Phyllis, 448
Carmen Jones, 28
Carmichael, Hoagy, 154, 176
Came, Sturges, 174
Carney, Alan, 234
Carnovsky, Morris, 74, 92, 122, 258, 299
Carr, Jane, 295
Carr, Marian, 98, 168, 210, 340, *340*

Carradine, John, 53, 107, 109-10, *110*, 156
Carras, Nicholas, 109
Carrera, Barbara, 402
Carrere, Edward, 57, 143, 290, 333
Carrere, Fernando, 202, 367
Carrey, Jim, 434, *434*
Carroll, Diahann, 454
Carroll, Leo G., 140, 272, 275, 284, 290
Carruth, Milton, 171, 219, 262-63, 336
Carson, Jack, 191, 293-94
Carson, L.M. "Kit," 366
Carter, Alex, 437
Carter, Ann, 308
Carter, Helena, 151, 171
Carter, Helena Bonham, 386
Carter, Jack, 400
Carter, Janis, 113, 205, 337
Carter, James L., 435
Carter, John, 377
Carter, Lynn, 232
Caruso, D.J., 447
Caruso, David, 409, 411
Caruso, Anthony, 15, 30, 205, 256, 302, 310
Casablanca, 127
Case, Kathleen, 141
Case of Lena Smith, 41
Casey, Bernie, 449
Cash, Johnny, 111
Cash, Rosaland, 397
Caspary, Vera, 52, 177
Cassavetes, John, 26-27, 206, 408-09
Cassel, Seymour, 380, 408
Cassell, Wally, 71, 121, 234, 239, 33
Cassidy, Joanna, 360, 438
Cassini, Don, 448
Castillo, Gloria, 207
Castle, Don, 121, *121*, 131, 147
Castle, Peggie, 145, 182, 211
Castle, William, 136, 158, 197, 311, 321
Castle, Walter H., 33
Castlenuova-Tedesco, Mario, 105, 182, 205, 278, 311
Cathcart, Daniel B., 267
Catt, Nicky, 404
Caught, 65-66, *65*
Cavanaugh, Hobart, 48
Cavanagh, Paul, 316
Cauley, Eve, 364
Caulfield, Joan, 315

Cause for Alarm, 66, *66*
Cazale, John, 370
Celli, Teresa, 56
Cesana, Renzo, 307
Cerf, Norman, 63
Cerón, Laura, 443
Chaffin, Céan, 388, 468
Chair for Martin Rome, The see *Cry of the City*
Chair for Martin Rome, The (novel), 81
Challee, William, 93
Chamberlin, George Agnew, 246
Chamberlain, Howland, 44, 59, 104, 112, 227
Chambers, Justin, 467
Chambers, Phil, 238
Chambers, Wheaton, 235
Chambers, Whitman, 50, 190
Champion, 66-67, *67*
Chan, George, 408
Chandler, George, 92, 280
Chandler, Jeff, 23, 293
Chandler, Lane, 242
Chandler, Mack, 76
Chandler, Raymond, 45-47, 52, 57, 99-101, 174-76, 195-96, 250, 284, 337, 352, 363-64, 380, 383, 403, 416-18
Chandos, John, 295
Chaney, Lon, Jr., 63, 144
Chang, Gary, 423
Channing, Stockard, 460
Chanslor, Roy, 48
Chapin, Billy, 199, 207
Chapin, Michael, 205
Chaplin, Charles Jr., 33
Chapman, Leigh, 402
Chapman, Michael, 393, 456
Charise, Cyd, 224, *224*, 294
Charles, Zachary, 114
Charney, Jack, 231
Charney, Kim, 287
Chanslor, Roy, 156
Chantler, David C., 230
Chao, Rosalind, 452
Charley Varrick, 367-68
Chartier, Jean-Pierre, 239
Chartoff, Robert, 440, 454, 458
Chase, The, 67-68, *67*, 319
Chase, Barrie, 64
Chase, Ilka, 40
Chaudhri, Amin Q., 380
Chavance, Louis, 300
Chaykin, Maury, 379

Cheadle, Don, 379
Cheirel, Micheline, 74, 271
Chekhov, Michael, 275
Cherney, Linda, 257
Chernoff, Joel, 453
Chester, Hal, 312
Chestnut, Scott, 444
Chew, Richard, 370
Chianese, Dominic, 443
Chicago Deadline, 68, *68*
Chienne, La, 255
Chienne, La (novel), 255
Chihara, Paul, 426
Chin, Joey, 409
China Moon, 368
Chinatown, *347*, 365, *365*,
    368-70, *369*, 380, 412
Chodorov, Edward, 252, 311
Chong, Michael, *458*
Chong, Rae Dawn, 385
Chooluck, Leon, 79, 194, 231
Christine, Virginia, 162, 210,
    408
Christmas Holiday, 68-69, *69*
Churgin, Lisa Zeno, 388
Ciannelli, Eduardo (Edward),
    190, 225
Cioffi, Charles, 411
Citizen Kane, 18
City for Conquest, 69-70, *69*
City of the Angels see *Hustle*
City of Fear, 70-71, *70*
City That Never Sleeps, 71, *71*
Clapton, Eric, 446
Clark, Al, 73, 158, 179, 199,
    310
Clark, Asa Boyd, 234
Clark, Carroll, 28, 36, 71, 74,
    195, 216, 258, 260, 329
Clark, Cliff, 307, *307*
Clark, Dane, 32, 193, *193*
Clark, Fred, *22*, 81, 136, 229,
    249, 288, 315, 33
Clark, Gage, 210
Clark, James B., 138, 178,
    193, 252, 273
Clark, Judy, 278
Clark, Matt, 380
Clark, Roger, 97
Clark, Susan, 420, 432
Clark, Walter Van Tilburg, 221
Clarke, Charles H., 61, 89,
    104, 287, 304
Clarke, David, 202, 299
Clarke, Patricia, 45
Clash by Night, 71-72, *71*
Clatworthy, Robert, 68, 225,
    263, 305, 336

Claxton, William F., 32
Clay Pigeon, 72, *72*
Clay, Jim, 410
Clayton, Curtiss, 444
Clayworth, June, 54
Clean Break, The (novel), 166
Clements, Stanley, 64, 95
Clifford, Graeme, 441
Clift, Montgomery, 143, *143*,
    229, *229*
Close, Glenn, 383, *384*, 405
Clume, Peter, 49
Clurman, Harold, 92
Cobb, Lee J., 55, 62, 90, 115,
    115, 158, 189, *189*, 224,
    299-300
Cobbs, Bill, 430, 457
Coburn, Arthur, 451
Coburn, Charles, 149, *149*,
    182, 438
Coby, Fred, 333
"Cocaine" (story), 107
Cochran, Steve, 33, 67, 84,
    235, *235*, 304, *304*, 333
Cockrell, Frank, 90
Cockrell, Marion, 90
Codee, Ann, 271
Coe, George, 356
Coen, Ethan, 362, 432-33
Coen, Joel, 362, 432-33
Coffee, Lenore, 37, 286
Coffin for Dimitrios, A (novel),
    190
Cohen, Albert J., 207
Cohen, Herman, 75
Cohen, Joan, 7, 54, 62-63,
    96-97, 127, 160-161,
    205-06, 456
Cohen, Larry, 356, 396-97,
    402
Cohen, Rudy, 358
Cohn, Art, 260, 304
Cohn, Martin G., 320
Cohn, Ralph, 269
Cohn, Robert, 162
Colbert, Claudette, 260, 269
Colbert, Norman, 34, 232
Colby, Anita, 59
Cole, Gary, 451
Cole, Lester, 27, 132
Cole, Nat "King" 52-53
Cole, Royal K., 49
Coleman, Graeme, 407
Colicos, John, 441
Collard, Dave, 437
Collateral, 365, *365*, 370, *370*
Collier, Constance, 87
Collinge, Patricia, 262

Collins, Anthony, 185
Collins, Frank J., 148
Collins, Joan, 465
Collins, Ray, 74, 94, 101, 178,
    240, 305
Collins, Richard, 151, 159,
    251
Collins, Russell, 266
Colman, Ronald, 101-02
Colombier Michel, 351, 371,
    377, 380, 402, 430
Colpaert, Carl, 379
Colton, John, 263
Comandini, Adele, 85, 279
Comfort, Madi, 167
Comer, Anjanette, 463
Comi, Paul, 64
Comingore, Dorothy, 44
Commissioner, The (novel),
    420
Compton, Joyce, 85
Conard, Mark T., 8, 405,
    459-60
Conde, Rita, 249
Condemned, The (novel),
    307
Confidential Report see
    Mr. Arkadin
Confidential Squad see
    Sleeping City, The
Conflict, 72-73, *73*
Conley, Jack, 439
Conlin, Jimmy, 172, 332
Conlin, Joe, 298
Connelly, Jennifer, 373, 399,
    428
Connolly, Norma, 341
Connors, Chuck, 199
Connors, Touch (Michael),
    286
Conrad, Karen, 200

Conrad, William, 54, 80, 82,
    163, *165*, 219, 240, 273,
    294
Conrad, Scott, 356
Conroy, Frank, 221, 302
Considine, Bob, 137
Considine, John W., Jr., 156
Conte, Richard, 39, 52, 59,
    62, 81, *81*, 132-33, 136,
    139-40, 202-203, 241,
    270, 273, 299-300, 310,
    310, 330
Conti, Bill, 402
Contino, Dick, 33
Conversation, The, 370-71,
    371, 388
Converse, Peggy, 241
Convertino, Michael, 457
Convicted, 73-74, *73*
Conway, Curt, 244
Conway, Russ, 147, 306
Conway, Tom, 248, 309, 332
Cornwell, Tom, 408
Corone, Antoni, 437
Cooder, Ry, 364, 406
Coogan, Jackie, 33
Cook, Elisha Jr., 45, 56, 90,
    107, 114, 145-46, 153,
    166, *166*, 181, 186, *186*,
    225-26, 231, 283, 377,
    393, 438
Cook, Tommy, 81, 223
Cookson, Peter, 109
Coon, Gene L., 408
Cooper, Barry Michael, 430
Cooper, Charles, 341
Cooper, Clancy, 241, 284
Cooper, Dennis J., 109, 320
Cooper, George, 79
Cooper, Jeanne, 231
Cooper, Maxine, 167, *168*

Cooper, Melville, 312
Coote, Robert, 34
Cop, 371-72
Copeland, Stewart, 450
Coppel, Alec, 317
Coppola, Francis Ford, 370-71, 393
Corbeau, Le, 300
Corbett, Glen, 76, *76*
Corbin, Barry, 432
Corby, Ellen, 61, 90, 270, 317
Core, Ericson, 439
Corey, Jeff, 59, 64, 112, 244
Corey, Jonathan, 110
Corey, Wendell, 23, 40, 110, *111*, 128-29, 146, 162, *162*, 273
Corman, Roger 132-33
Cornered, 74, *74*
Cornfield, Hubert, 231
Corrigan, Lloyd, 67
Corso, Sam, 334
Cortese, Valentina, 299-300
Cortez, Ricardo, 49, 180
Cortez, Stanley, 200, 207, 259, 312
Cosby, Bill, 397, *397*
Cost of Living, The see *The Prowler*
Cost of Loving, The see *The Prowler*
Costa, Don, 420
Costello, Anthony, 432
Costner, Kevin, 433-34
Cota, David, 318
Cotten, Joseph, 37, 103, 116, 159, 162, 203, 262, *263*, 305, 320, 425
Coulouris, George, 213, 269, *269*, 316
Covey, William, 9, 360-62, 368, 382, 425, 435-36\7

Cowan, Jerome, 69, 92, 186, 205, 284, 313
Cowl, Jane, 212, 260
Cowling, Bruce, 66, 176
Cox, Brian, 422, 468
Cox, Joel, 383
Coyote, Peter, 385, 405
Crack-Up, 74-75
Craig, Catherine, 234
Craig, Helen, 296
Craig, James, 176, 267, 286, 329
Crain, Jeanne, 178, 293, 317
Cramer, Duncan, 84, 88, 336
Crane, Kenneth, 303
Craven, Garth, 402
Craven, Matt, 407
Crawford, Robert, 444
Crawford, Broderick, 48, 73, 141, 202-203, 254, *254*
Crawford, Joan, 84-85, 156, *157*, 191, *191*, 232-33, *233*, 286-87
Creasap, Charles, 49
Creber, Lewis H., 131, 140, 190
Cregar, Laird, 125-26, *125*, 181, *181*, 301, 318
Crenna, Richard, 362
Cresciman, Vincent, 385
Cresson, James, 426
Crime and Punishment (novel), 109
Crime of Laura Saurelle, 193
Crime of Passion, 75-76, *75*
Crime Wave, 76, *76*
"Criminal Code" (play), 73
Criminal Law, 372
Crimson Kimono, The, 76-77, *76*
Crise, Douglas, 376
Crisp, Donald, 69, 242
Criss Cross, 17, 20-21, 77-78,

77, 434, 463
Criss Cross (novel), 463
Cristofer, Michael, 436
Cromwell, James, 414, 445
Cromwell, John, 61, 92, 240
Conenweth, Jeff, 386
Cronenweth, Jordan, 350, 360, 431, 454-55
Cronjager, Edward J., 138, 145-46
Cronyn, Hume, 233, 262
Crooked Way, The, 78-79, *79*
Crosby, Cathy, 33
Crosby, Floyd, 188
Crosland, Alan, Jr., 290, 304, 313
Cross, David, 206
Cross, Dennis, 75
Cross, Marsha, 353
Crossfire, 79-80, *80*
Crossland, Marjorie, 65
Crosstown see *River Street*
Crouse, Lindsay, 400
Crowe, Christopher, 384
Crowe, Russell, *365*, 414, *414*
Crowley, Kathleen, 109
Crowley, Nathan, 404
Crowley, Pat, 161
Crozton, L.O., 309
Cruise, Tom, *365*, 370, *370*
Cruz, Celia, 26
Cry Danger, 80, *80*
Cry in the Night, A, 80-81, *81*
Cry of the City, 81-82, *81*, 454
Cry of the Hunted, 82-32, *82*
Cry Vengeance, 83, *83*
Cugino, Carla, 451
Cukor, George, 101-02, 116-17
Culkin, Rory, 467
Culp, Robert, 397, *397-98*
Culver, Roland, 268
Cummings, Howard, 463
Cummings, Irving, Jr., 321
Cummings, Robert, 23, 67, 247, 269, *269*
Cummins, Peggy, 122, *123-4*, 193, *193*, 392
Cunningham, Robert, 145
Curtis, Alan, 130, 225
Curtis, Donald, 275
Curtis, Tony, 158-59, 290, *290*
Curtiss, Edward, 23, 59, 293
Curtiz, Michael, 57, 191, 315

Curtright, Jorja, 332
Cusack, Cyril, 458
Cusack, John, 391, *391*
Cutner, Sidney, 105
Cyrus, Billy Ray, 427

D, Chris, 7, 155-56, 219, 276-77, 458-59, 465-66
da Silva, Howard, 52, 56, 184, 296, 312
D'Abo, Olivia, 441
Dafoe, Willem, 458
D'Agostino, Albert S., 28, 30, 34-35, 51, 54, 56, 71-72, 74, 79, 93, 98, 112, 114, 133-34, 154-55, 159, 176, 180, 185, 195, 201, 214, 216, 218, 220, 240, 251, 258, 260, 275-76, 283, 296-97, 302, 309, 320-21, 334, 337-38
Dahl, Arlene, 213, 247, 256, 270
Dahl, John, 407, 415, 444-45
Dahl, Rick, 444
Dale, Virginia, 107
Dalio, Marcel, 263-64
Daley, John, 356
Daley, Robert, 439
Dali, Salvador, 275
Dall, John, 122, *123-4*, 164, 189
Dallesandro, Joe, 391, 416
Damici, Nick, 403
Damned Don't Cry, The, 84-85, *85*
Damon, Mark, 357, 376, 380
Dana, Mike, 165
Dance, Charles, 368
D'Andrea, Tom, 89, 294
Dane, Patricia, 156
Danger Signal, 85-86, *86*
Dangerous Passage, 86
Daniell, Henry, 289
Daniels, Eddie, 354
Daniels, Harold, 251-52
Daniels, Henry H., Jr., 36
Daniels, William, 23, 59, 199-200, 336
Danker, Eli, 402
Dann, Roger, 143
Dano, Royal, 75, 310, 393
Danson, Ted, 362
Dante, Michael, 200
Dantine, Helmut, 331
Danton, Ray, 33, 207-08
D'Arcy, Alex, 317

Dark City (1950), 87, *87*
Dark City (1998), 373-74, *373*
Dark Corner, The, 87-88, *87*
Dark Country, 374-75, *374*
Dark Highway see *On Dangerous Ground*
Dark Mirror, The, 19, 88, *88*
Dark Page, The see *Scandal Sheet*
Dark Page, The (novel), 254
Dark Passage, 89, *89*
Dark Past, The, 19, 89-90, *89*
Dark Tower, The see *Night Moves*
Dark Waters see *Crime Wave*
Dark Waters, 90-91, *90*
Darnell, Linda, 107, *107*, 125, 208, 258, 300
Darren, James, 59
Darrin, Sonia, 45, 65
Darwell, Jane, 47, 61, 221
Dassin, Jules, 59-60, 199-200, 204-205, 299-300
Daves, Delmer, 88, 246-47
Davey, Bruce, 439
David, Pierre, 377
Davidtz, Ambeth, 429
Davies, Carmel, 406
Davies, Freeman, 406
Davies, Jeremy, 391
Davis, Bette, 37, *38*
Davis, Bob, 451
Davis, Don, 364
Davis, Elliot, 457, 463
Davis, Frank, 338
Davis, George W., 139, 161, 244, 425, 440, 454
David, Morris C., 331
Davis, Nancy, 293
Davis, Sammy, Jr., 155
Davis, Tamra, 391-92
Davis, William, 30
Dawson, Hal K., 65
Dawson, Ralph, 153, 249, 311
Dawson, Rosario, 451-52
Day, Laraine, 180, 337
Day of the Locust (novel), 369
Day of the Outlaw, 76
Day, Richard, 55, 80, 104, 112, 145, 193, 221
Day the Earth Stood Still, The, 91-92, *91*
Day without End see *Beware, My Lovely*
Dayton, Dan, 308
de Bergh, Joanne, 62
De Bont, Jan, 355, 359

DeCamp, Rosemary, 85, 215, 254
De Carlo, Yvonne, 59, 77, *77*, *463*
de Corsia, Ted, 39, 76, 104-05, 166, 174, 188, 199, 270, 308
De Fina, Barbara, 367
de Franceschi, Alexandre, 403
De Grasse, Robert, 54, 56, 72, 74, 112, 334
De Haven, Carter, Jr., 356, 438
De Haven, Gloria, 256
de Havilland, Olivia, 88, *88*
de la Fouchardiere, Georges, 255
De Laurentiis, Dino, 375, 422
De Laurentiis, Martha, 356
De Niro, Robert, 367, 395, 405, 410, 431-32, 456, *456*, 458-59
De Palma, Brian, 358, 385-86
De Rochemont, Louis, 55, 140-41, 286
de Toth, André, 76, 90, 120, 228, 242
de Toth, William, 228
de Vargas, Valentin, 305
De Wit, Jacqueline, 85
Dead Reckoning, 92, *92*
Deadlier Than the Male see *Born to Kill*
Deadlier Than the Male (novel), 57
Deadline at Dawn, 92-93, *93*
Deadly Is the Female see *Gun Crazy*
Deakins, Roger, 398, 432
Dearden, James, 383, 410
Death Wish, 375-76
Debney, John, 451
Deceiver, 376
Deception, 376-77, *376*
Decoy, 92
DeCuir, John F., 59, 141, 199
Deeley, Michael, 360
Deep Cover, 377-78, *378*
Deep End, The, 378
Deering, Olive, 61
Defore, Don, 242, 274-75, 304
DeGaetano, Alfred, 127, 241, 244, 248, 306
Dehner, John, 95
Dein, Edward, 63
Dekker, Albert, 27, *28*, 95, 148, 163, 167, 234, 289-90

DeKova, Frank, 276
Del Rio, Dolores, 159
Del Rio, Jack, 35
Del Ruth, Roy, 247
Del Toro, Benicio, 368, 451, *452*, 464
Del Val, Jean, 135, 271
Del Valle, Jaime, 179
DeLacy, Ralph M., 63
DeLaire, Diane, 141
Delerue, Georges, 458
Delia, Joe, 353, 409, 427
Dell, Myrna, 214
Delusion, 379, *379*
DeMaggio, Nick, 141, 204, 208, 227, 299
DeMarco, John, 402
Demarest, William, 205, 286
DeMille, Cecil B., 288
Deming, Peter, 418, 427
Demme, Jonathan, 423, 450
DeMond, Albert, 49, 265
Dempster, Austin, 204
D'Entre Les Morts (novel), 317
Deneuve, Catherine, 400, *401*
Denisson, Jo-Carroll, 227
Dennehy, Brian, 356, *357*
Denner, John, 230
Denning, Richard, 118, 212
Dennis, Nick, 40, 167, 188
Denny, Reginald, 180, 340
DePrato, Bill, 49
Derek, John, 172, *172*, 254, *254*
Dern, Bruce, 351, 380
Dervin, Joseph, 213
DeSando, Anthony, 430
Descher, Sandy, 295
Desperate, 20, 93-94, *94*
Desperate Hours, The, 94-95, *95*
Dessau, Paul, 215, 234, 278
D'Estée, Mimi, 331
Destination Murder, 95-96

Detective Story, 96-97, *96*
Detour, 20, 97-98, *97*
Deutsch, Adolph, 85, 130, 186, 190, 213, 242
Deutsch, Helen, 266
Devane, William, 439
Devereux, Marie, 200
Devil in a Blue Dress, 379-80, *379*, 437
Devil Thumbs A Ride, The, 98
Devil's Doorway, The, 18, 98-99
DeVito, Danny, 388, 396, *396*, 414
Devlin, Joe, 54
DeVol, Frank, 40, 340, 400
Dexter, Alan, 238
Dexter, Brad, 138, 176, 185, 211
Dexter, Peter, 428, 446
Di Novi, Denise, 436
Di Pego, Gerald, 449
Diamond, David, 226
Diamont, Limor, 357
Diamont, Moshe, 358
Diary of a Hitman, 380
Dick, Douglas, 23
Dick, Philip K., 360-61
Dickerson, George, 351
Dickinson, Angie, 408, *408*, 440-41
Didion, Joan, 458-59
Diehl, William, 449
Dieterle, William, 23, 87, 103, 307
Dietrich, Marlene, 242-43, 305
Dietrich, Ralph, 310-11
Dillahunt, Garret, 432
Dillard, Victoria, 377 *377*
Dillon, Matt, 410
Dillon, Robert, 70
Dimaggio, Ross, 102, 188
Dimitri, Nick, 407
Dimsdale, Howard, 176, 273

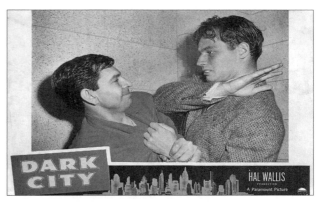

Dinelli Mel, 35, 66, 138, 154, 245, 275, 334
Dinneen, Joseph, 312
Dirty Harry, 376
Diskant, George E., 35, 47, 93, 160, 201-02, 218-29, 232, 240, 296
Divina, Vaclav, 279
Dix, Richard, 197-98
Dixon, Joan, 251
Dixon, Ralph, 331
Djawadi, Ramin, 376
Djola, Badja, 444
Dmytryk, Edward, 74, 79, 195-96, 271
D.O.A. (1950), 20, 84, *84*, 361, 373
D.O.A. (1988), 373
Do Androids Dream of Electric Sheep? (novel), 360
Dobbs, Lem, 373, 416
Docks of New York, The, 41
Doe, John, 452-43
Dog Soldiers (novel), 465
Domergue, Faith, 321-22, *321-27*
Dominguez, Frances, 24
Donaldson, Roger, 390, 433
Donat, Peter, 378, 388
Donlevy, Brian, 39, 118, 137, 149, 170, *170*, 263
Donnell, Jeff, 52, 149, 205, 290, 320
Donnelly, Ruth, 328
D'Onofrio, Vincent, 447
Donovan, King, 104-05, 151, 219
Donovan, Martin, 404
Dooley, Paul, 404, 463
Doran, Ann, 109, 114, 228
Dorn, Dody, 404, 423
Dorn, Dolores, 312, *313*
D'Orsay, Fifi, 114

Dorsey, Fern, 419
Dortort, David, 71
Dostoevski, Fyodor, 109
Double Indemnity, 16, 19, 21, 99-101, *99-101*, 154, 170, 305, 328, 363-64, 377, 386, 434
Double Life, A., 101-02, *102*
Doucette, John, 73, 77-78, 83, 138, 242
Dougherty, Richard, 420
Douglas, Diana, 139
Douglas, Don, 195
Douglas, Gordon, 34, 147, 171, 295-96
Douglas, Haldane, 27, 118, 284
Douglas, Kirk, 24-25, *25*, 66, *67*, 96, 146, *146*, 220, *220*, 281
Douglas, Michael, 355, *355*, 357, *357*, 359, *359*, 383, *384*, 388
Douglas, Paul, 71, 223
Douglas, Robert, 302
Douglas, William C., 297
Douglas, Warren, 83, 183
Dourif, Brad, 429
Dow, Peggy, 263, 270, 311, 336
Dowd, Ned, 454
Dowling, Constance, 48, 50
Dowling, Doris, 52
Downey, Robert, Jr., 468
Downey, Robert, Sr., 458
Downs, Cathy, 87
Dragnet, The, 41
Drago, Billy, 391
Dragon, Carmen, 151, 171, 225, 281
Drake, Betsy, 258-59, *259*
Drake, Charles, 73, 234, 332
Drake, Chris, 295

Drake, Claudia, 97, 173
Drake, Dona, 37, 160
Dratler, Jay, 62, 87, 149, 176-77, 228
Dreadful Summit (novel), 44
Dream Street, 41
Dreier, Hans, 23, 29, 38, 51, 61, 68, 87, 110, 118, 205, 212, 229, 273, 281, 284-85, 288, 301, 314
Dreiser, Theodore, 229
Drew, Ellen, 78, 158
Drew, Roland, 309
Driscoll, Bobby, 334-35, *334*
Drive a Crooked Road, 102-03, *102*
Driver, The, 380-81, *381*
Drowning Pool, The, 381, *381*
Dru, Joanne, 261
Duane, Michael, 249
Dubin, Steve(n), 371
Dubov, Paul, 312
Duel in the Sun, 103, *103*
Duell, Randall, 30, 224, 233, 311, 314
Duff, Howard, 59, 158-59, 199, 235, 263, 329, 336, *336*, 433
Duff, Warren, 29, 68, 108, 114, 185, 220, 307
Duffy, Albert, 89
Duguay, Yvette, 225
Duke, Bill, 377-78, 416, 439, 444
Dumbrille, Douglas, 340
Dumke, Ralph, 57, 151, 321
Dunaway, Faye, *347, 365*, 368, *369*
Duning, George, 35, 58, 73, 89, 158, 209, 254, 266, 310
Dunlap, Paul, 75, 80, 83, 183, 200, 264
Dunlap, Scott R., 142
Dunn, James, 27, 313
Dunn, Nora, 424
Dunn, Ralph, 177
Dunn, Rex, 159
Dunn, Robert, 366
Dunne, John Gregory, 458-59
Dunne, Stephen, 90, 265
Dunning, Decla, 269
Dunning, Don, 314
Dunnock, Mildred, 170
DuPar, Edwin, 147
Dupont, E.A., 230, 254-55
Duprez, June, 61

Durazzo, Paolo, 8, 360-61, 447, 449
Durbin, Deanna, 68, *69*
Durlauf, Frank, 64, 135, 306
Durning, Charles, 371, 449, 458
Duryea, Dan, 48, 60, 77, 119, 158, 190, 219, 255, *255*, 277, 295, 304-05, 312, 336-37, 340, *340*
DuSoe, Robert C., 98
Duvall, Robert, 438, *438*, 458-59
Duvall, Shelley, 463
Dvorak, Ann, 181
Dwan, Allan, 41, 270
Dwyer, Marlo, 271
Dyne, Aminta, 171
Dzundza, George, 355, 402, 43

Eagle, S.P. see Spiegel, Sam
Earle, Edward, 249
East Side Story see *House of Strangers*
Eastwood, Clint, 439-40
Ebouaney, Eriq, 385
Eckhart, Aaron, 358
Edelman, Lou, 333
Edeson, Arthur, 186, 190, 213
Edge of Doom, 104, *104*
Edwards, Anthony, 468
Edwards, Blake, 102, 106
Edwards, Bruce, 107
Edwards, James, 260
Edwards, Vince, 70, 134, 166, 194, 206, 253
Egan, Richard, 85, 136, 276, 333
Eggers, Fred, 132
8 Million Ways to Die, 382, *382*
Eight Million Ways to Die (novel), 382
Eilers, Sally, 279
Einstein, Charles, 329
Eisen, Robert S., 39, 151, 220
Eisinger, Jo, 75, 117, 204, 270
Eisler, Hanns, 92, 338
Eisley, Anthony, 200
Ekberg, Anita, 257
Elam, Jack, 160, 168, 242, 244-45
Eldredge, John, 32, 86
Elfman, Danny, 451
Elg, Taina, 415
Elkins, Saul, 302
Ellen see *The Second Woman*

Ellenstein, Robert, 148, 253
Ellroy, James, 358, 371, 414
Ellin, Stanley, 44
Elliott, Alison, 463, *463*
Elliot, Biff, 138, 145
Elliott, Laura, 110, 284
Elliott, Ross, 339
Elliott, Sam, 446
Elliott, Shawn, 402
Elliott, Stephen, 375
Elliott, William A., 402
Ellsworth, James, 111
Elman, Irving, 32
Elsom, Isobel, 308
Elswit, Robert, 353, 396
Emerson, Faye, 85, 122, 190, *190*
Emerson, Hope, 61, 81, 139, 299
Emery, John, 275
Emery, Katherine, 180
Emhardt, Robert, 312
Endfield, Cyril, 269, 307, 312
Endore, Guy, 127, 304, 330
"Enemy, The" (story), 293
Enforcer, The, 104-105, *105*
Engel, Samuel G., 204, 244, 285
English, Maria, 264
English, Richard, 261
Epperson, Tom, 435
Epstein, Philip, 45
Erbe, Kathryn, 411
Erdman, Richard, 52, 80, 85
Erdody, Leo, 29, 53, 97, 279
Erickson, Glenn, 7, 34, 143, 150-53, 207, 226-27, 333-34, 393-94, 414, 423-26
Erickson, Leif, 114, 151, 273
Erickson, Todd R., 9, 353, 356-57, 362, 371-72, 390, 395-96, 456-58, 466-67
Erlichinan, Martin, 366
Ermey, R. Lee, 429, 448
Erskine, Chester, 276, 335
Escape in the Fog, 105-06, *105*
Esposito, Giancarlo, 409, 460, 464
Essex, Harry, 54, 93, 127, 145, 160, 162, 176
Estrin, Rob(ert), 354, 366
Eszterhaus, Joe, 355, 405
Ettlinger, Don, 122
Eunson, Dale, 120
Evans, Charles, 78, 88
Evans, Gene, 23, 30, 182

Evans, Joan, 104
Evans, Rex, 263
Evans, Richard, 431
Evans, Robert, 368, 461
Evelyn, Judith, 300
Everest, Barbara, 116
Everett, Chad, 427
Ewing, John, 181
Executioners, The (novel), 64, 367
Experiment in Terror, 106, *106*
Eyer, Richard, 94
Eythe, William, 140, *140*, 221

Fahey, Jeff, 402
Falkenberg, Paul, 184
Fall Guy, 107
Fallen Angel, 28, 107-08, *107*
Fallen Sparrow The, 108-09, *108*
Fancher, Hampton, 360
Fanning, Dakota, 421, *421*
Fantl, Richard, 113, 205
Fapp, Daniel L., 212, 314
Farewell, My Lovely, 382, *383*
Farewell, My Lovely (novel), 195-96
Fargo, 433
Farina, DennIs, 422, 456
Farmer, Frances, 27
Farnsworth, Richard, 390, 461
Farr, Felicia, 303, 367
Farrell, Charles, 204
Farrell, Colin, 424, *424*
Farrell, Glenda, 156
Farrington, Betty, 99
Farrow, John, 38, 61, 133-34, 205-06, 321, 324, 326, 328, 434
Fatal Attraction, 383-84, *384*
Faulkner, William, 45, 191
Faure, John, 103
Fay, Marston, 93
Faye, Alice, 107
Faye, Herbie, 126
Faylen, Frank, 51-52, 73, 96, 211, 251, 271
Fear (1946), 109
Fear (1996), 384-85
Fear City, 385
Fear in the Night, 109
Fearing, Kenneth, 38, 433
Fega, Russ, 423
Fehr, Rudi, 37, 84, 160, 213, 232
Feindel, Jockey A., 53
Feist, Felix E., 98, 189, 302, 304

Feitshans, Buzz, 393
Feitshans, Fred R., Jr., 150, 194
Feld, Rudi, 39, 134, 220, 227, 277, 279, 318, 332
Feldman, Edward, 466
Fell, Norman, 367
Fellner, Eric, 415
Fellows, Don, 442
Fellows, Robert, 29, 68, 107, 257
Felton, Earl, 30, 133, 176, 201, 306, 430
Female Jungle, 109-110, *110*
Femme Fatale, 385-85, *386*
Femme Nikita, La, 441
Fenn, Sherilyn, 380
Fenton, Frank, 54, 72, 133, 214, 220, 320
Fenton, George, 368
Ferguson, Frank, 65, 112, 142, 242, 333
Ferguson, Jay, 356
Ferguson, Perry, 261, 282, 307
Fernandez, Benjamin, 420, 459
Ferrara, Abel, 353-54, 378, 385, 409-10, 427
Ferrari, William, 150, 153, 269, 335
Ferrer, Jose, 260, 330, *330*
Ferrer, Mel, 240, 242, 260
Ferrer, Miguel, 441
Ferretti, Dante, 358
Ferris, Michael, 388
Feuer, Debra, 458
Fichtner, William, 463
Fieberling, Hal, 260
Field, Martin, 194
Field, Virginia, 248
Fielding, Jerry, 438
Fielding, Sol Baer, 154
Figgis, Mike, 415

Fight Club, 350, 386-87, *387*
File on Thelma Jordon, The, 110-11, *111*
Fillmore, Clyde, 177
Fincher, David, 386, 388, 448, 468
Finney, Albert, 450
Finney, Jack, 139, 151
Finston, Nat, 258
Fiorentino, Linda, 415, *415*
Firestone, Diane, 391
Fischer, Bradley, 468
Fischer, Laurence (Larry), 377-78, *377*, 409
Fisher, Steve, 71, 92, 128, 142, 145-46, 147-48, 154-55, 174, 251-52, 295, 317-18
Fisk, Jack, 354, 427
Fitts, Margaret, 293
Fitzgerald, Barry, 199, *200*, 314
Fitzgerald, Eddie (Edward), 202, 220, 33
Fitzgerald, Geraldine, 213, 272, 278
Five Minutes to Live, 111
Fix, Paul, 156
Flack, ben, 429
Flack, Sarah, 416
Flanders, Ed, 458
Flannery, William E., 76, 126
Flaum, Seth, 450
Flavin, James, 30, 45, 73, 95, 177, 210, 213
Flavin, Martin, 73
Fleder, Gary, 457
Fleischer, Richard, 30, 54-55, 72, 112, 133, 201-02, 306
Fleischer, Stanley, 76, 85, 148, 186, 226, 296
Fleisher, Charles, 468

Fatal Attraction

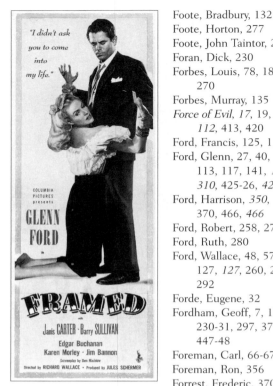

"I didn't ask you to come into my life."

COLUMBIA PICTURES presents

GLENN FORD in

FRAMED

Janis CARTER · Barry SULLIVAN

Edgar Buchanan
Karen Morley · Jim Bannon

Directed by RICHARD WALLACE · Produced by JULES SCHERMER

Fleming, Rhonda, 80, 162, 220, 270, 275, 329
Flemying, Gordon, 454
Fletcher, Lucille, 273-74
Flippen, Jay C., 59, 166, 176, 225, 296
Flores, Iris, 249
Florey, Robert, 78-79, 85-86
Flotow, Rudolph, 197
Fluegel, Darlanne, 458
Fly by Night, 278
Flynn, Beau, 434
Flynn, John, 356-57, 438
Foch, Nina, 89, 105-06, 148, 158, 196, *196*
Foley, Ellen, 383
Foley, James, 351-52, 384-85
Foley, John, 281
Follow Me Quietly, 112, *112*
Folsey, George J., 139
Fonda, Bridget, 405, 441, *441*, 451
Fonda, Henry, 43, *43*, 181, *182*, 221, *222*, 341, 420
Fonda, Jane, 411, *412*, 426
Fonda, Peter, 416
Fong, Benson, 61, 367
Fonlupt, Jean-Francois, 450
Fontaine, Joan, 36, *37*, 47, 153, 171, *171*, 290, *290*

Foote, Bradbury, 132
Foote, Horton, 277
Foote, John Taintor, 216
Foran, Dick, 230
Forbes, Louis, 78, 189, 228, 270
Forbes, Murray, 135
Force of Evil, *17*, 19, 112-13, *112*, 413, 420
Ford, Francis, 125, 131, 221
Ford, Glenn, 27, 40, 73, 106, 113, 117, 141, *142*, 310, *310*, 425-26, *426*
Ford, Harrison, *350*, 360, *361*, 370, 466, *466*
Ford, Robert, 258, 276
Ford, Ruth, 280
Ford, Wallace, 48, 57, 74, 92, 127, *127*, 260, 262, 275, 292
Forde, Eugene, 32
Fordham, Geoff, 7, 188, 230-31, 297, 376, 426, 447-48
Foreman, Carl, 66-67, 72
Foreman, Ron, 356
Forrest, Frederic, 370, 393, 461
Forrest, Robert, 238
Forrest, Sally, 198, 286, 329
Forrest, Steve, 253
Forrester, Cay, 84, 111
Forster, Robert, 405, *405*, 427
Forsythe, William, 457
Forsythe, John, 65
Fort, Garrett, 27, 284
Forth, Christopher E., 7, 353-54, 385, 429, 455, 465
Foronjy, Richard, 426
Foster, David, 381, 389-90, 431
Foster, Dianne, 59, 102
Foster, Jodie, *348*, 450, 456
Foster, Lewis, 190
Foster, Norman, 159, 171, 339-40
Foster, Preston, 44, *142*, 144-45, 160, 242, *242*
Fowler, Gene, Jr., 36, 329, 336
Fowler, Marjorie, 75, 188
Fowley, Douglas, 30, 32, 34, 93, 104, *104*, 107
Fox, Jorja, 409, 423
Fox, Michael, 40, 231
Foxx, Jamie, *365*, 370, *370*, 424, *424*
Foy, Bryan, 76, 135, 147, 306

Fraker, William A., 449
Framed, 18, 20, 113, *113*
Francen, Victor, 190
Franciosa, Anthony, 381
Francis, Anne, 253
Francis, Freddie, 367
Francis, Linda, 200
Francis-Bruce, Richard, 448
Frank, Carl, 174
Frank, Laurie, 419
Frank, Tony, 446
Frank, W.R., 80
Franklin, Carl, 379, 435, 437
Franklin, Howard, 443
Franz, Arthur, 36, 135, 151, 247, 271
Franz, Eduard, 314, 330
Frawley, William, 171, 242
Frazen, Stanley, 119
Frears, Stephen, 390
Frederick, Lee, 94
Freed, Bert, 55, 94, 261, 328, 420
Freeman, David, 364
Freeman, Helen, 271
Freeman, Howard, 52, 181
Freeman, Kathleen, 34
Freeman, Mona, 28, 85
Freeman, Morgan, 406, 448
Fredericks, Ellsworth, 151
Frees, Paul, 251, 287
Fregonese, Hugo, 188, 219
French, Valerie, 115
French Victor, 431
Freres Rico, Les (novel), 58
Freulich, Henry, 310
Freund, Karl, 160, 311
Frey, Sami, 360
Fried, Gerald, 165
Friedhofer, Hugo, 25, 54, 104, 126, 181, 188, 212, 242, 271, 307
Friedkin, William, 458
Friedlob, Bert, 36, 329
Friedman, Ken, 406
Friedman, Irving, 34, 64, 247
Friedman, Josh, 358
Friedman, Peter, 361
Friedman, Seymour, 179
Friends of Eddie Coyle, The, 387, *387*
Frightened Child, The (novel), 141
Frightened City see *Killer that Stalked New York, The*
Frings, Ketti, 23, 87, 110, 120
Frison, Paul, 122
Frizzell, Lou, 397, 431

Frobenius, Nikolaj, 404
Froeschel, George, 314
Fromkess, Leon, 53, 97, 279
Froom, Mitchell, 452
Frutkoff, Gary, 379, 416
Frye, Stuart, 131
Fryer, Richard, 318
Fryman-ZS Inc., 15
Fuchs, Daniel, 77, 114-15, 135, 223, 463
Fuji, 76, *76*
Fujikawa, Jerry, 369
Fujimoto, Tak, 354, 379, 423, 431, 450
Fuller, Lance, 270
Fuller, Leland, 87, 107, 170, 177, 188, 220, 330
Fuller, Sam, 76-77, 138-39, 144, 200, 227-28, 254, 266, 312-13, 393
Furthman, Jules, 41, 45, 193, 210, 263
Fury, 41-42, *42*

Gabel, Martin, 184, 298
Gabor, Zsa Zsa, 305
Gaines, Leonard, 393
Gaines, Richard, 24, 59, 99, 213, 249
Gallaudet, John, 267
Gallagher, Peter, 463, *463*
Gallo, Fred T., 362
Galvin, Tim, 450
Gam, Rita, 298, 411
Gambling House, 114
Game, The, 388
Gamet, Kenneth, 50
Gandolfini, James, 459-60
Gangster, The, 114-15, *115*
"Gangsters in the Dress Business" (article), 115
Gann, Ernest K., 241
Ganz, Armin, 419
Garcia, Andy, 359, *359*, 382, 457
Garde, Bettey, 61-62, 81
Gardenia, Vincent, 375
Gardiner, Greg, 455
Gardner, Arthur, 335
Gardner, Ava, 58, 163, *163*, 268-69, 332
Gardner, Ed, 189
Garfield, Allen, 370
Garfield, Brian, 375
Garfield, John, *16-17*, 54, *54*, 57, 107, *108*, 112-13, *112*, 127, *127*, 213, 233, *234*, 442

Gargan, William, 145, 205, 280
Garland, Beverly, 442
Garland, Robert, 433
Garmes, Lee, 65, 94, 96, 103, 120, 210
Garment Jungle, The, 22, 115-16, *115*
Garner, James, 460
Garnett, Tay, 66, 233-34, 240
Garralaga, Martin, 249
Garrett, Oliver H. P., 92, 103
Garson, Henry, 245
Gaslight, 116-17, *116*
Gassman, Vittorlo, 82, 119, 449
Gattaca, 388-89, *389*
Gates, Larry, 59, 151, 312
Gates, Nancy, 128, 287
Gaudio, Tony, 130
Gay, Gregory, 271
Gaython, Tony, 447
Gazzara, Ben, 408, *408*
Gazzo, Michael, V., 385
Gebert, Gordon, 201
Geer, Will, 73
Gelarden, James, 357
Gelsey, Erwin, 114
Geller, Stephen, 442
Gendron, Pierre, 53
Gent from Frisco, The see *Maltese Falcon, The*
George, George W., 54, 68, 96, 127
George, Gladys, 186
George, Melissa, 373, 416
George, Nathan, 411
Geray, Steven, 27, 50, 74, 90, 92-93, 117, 149, 176, 190, 202, 208, 271, 275, 313
Gere, Richard, 366
German, Lauren, 374
Gershenson, Joseph, 207, 263
Gershon, Gina, 364, 366
Gershwin, Jerry, 394
Gerstad, Harry, 66, 79, 122, 271, 275
Gerstad, Merritt, 72
Gerstle, Frank, 147, 270
Gertsman, Maury, 158, 219, 268
Gertz, Irving, 50, 95, 231
Getaway, The (1972), 389-90, *389*, 433
Getaway, The (1994), 390-91
Getchell, Robert, 441
Getty, Balthazar, 418

Getz, John, 362
Giannini, Giancarlo, 421
Gibbons, Cedric, 25, 30, 36, 55, 58, 66, 82, 98, 116, 132, 154, 156, 174, 176, 198, 201, 213, 225, 233, 253, 256, 267, 286, 293-94, 311, 314
Gibney, Sheridan, 180
Gibson, Henry, 416
Gibson, Mel, 439
Gidding, Nelson, 217
Gidley, Pamela, 415
Gielgud, Irwin, 23
Gierasch, Stefan, 429
Gifford, Barry, 418
Gilbert, Anthony, 196
Gilbert, Bruce, 426
Gilbert, Herschel Burke, 36, 209-10, 251, 254, 298, 329, 335
Gilda, 27, 117-18, *117*, 426, 428
Giler, Berne, 213
Gill, Robert (Bob), 231
Gilliam, Burton, 383
Gillie, Jean, 93
Gilmore, Lowell, 61, 154, 251
Gillmore, Margalo, 66
Gimpel, Jacob, 279
Ging, Jack, 439
Giordani, Rocky, 351
Gish, Lillian, 103, 207, 465
Gist, Robert, 28
Gittens, George, 162, 166, 210
Givens, Robin, 444
Glasgow, William, 40, 167, 266, 340
Glass Key, The (1935), 118
Glass Key, The (1942), 30, 118-19, *118*
Glass, Ned, 106
Glass Wall, The, 119
Glassberg, Irving, 263, 311
Glasser, Albert (Al), 33, 144, 194, 230
Gleason, James, 207, 287
Gleason, Paul, 424
Gleeson, Patrick, 356
Glenn, Scott, 450
Glennon, Bert, 76, 246-47
Glickman, Mort, 49
Glover, Bruce, 369, 466
Glover, Crispin, 352
Glover, Danny, 444
Glover, John, 439
Gluck, Joseph, 254

Godard, Jean-Luc, 366
Godey, John, 406
Godfrey, Peter, 230-31, 308
Goff, Ivan, 32, 333
Goff, Lloyd see Lloyd Gough
Gold, Ernest, 25, 220
Goldbeck, Willis, 143
Goldberg, Adam, 447
Goldberg, Leonard, 453
Goldblum, Jeff, 375, 377
Golden, Robert, 185, 207, 251
Goldenberg, William, 395, 424
Goldenthal, Elliot, 395
Goldin, Pat, 134
Goldman, Harold, 38
Goldman, William, 393
Goldsmith, I.G., 254
Goldsmith, Jerry, 70, 355, 368, 372, 414, 453, 465
Goldsmith, Martin M., 50, 97, 129, 201, 263
Goldstein, Leonard, 136, 219, 270, 317
Goldstein, Steven, 400
Goldstone, Richard, 260, 293
Goldwyn, Samuel, 104
Golitzen, Alexander, 64, 199, 207, 255, 293, 305, 420, 439
Golin, Steve, 388, 407, 444
Gollard, Jerome T., 150
Gombell, Minna, 130
Gomez, Thomas, *17*, 112, 158, 160, 185, 225, *226*, 249, 268, 337
Gonchor, Jess, 432
Gonzalez, Gonzalez, 144
Goodis, David, 60, 89, 209, 313, 400
Goodkind, Saul A., 48
Goodman, David Zelag, 383
Goodman, Joel, 426

Goodman, John (actor), 447
Goodman, John B., 63, 68, 225, 262, 278, 289
Goosson, Stephen, 92, 113, 117, 158, 174
Gorcey, Bernard, 227
Gordean, William D., 449
Gordon, Bernard, 76
Gordon, Dan, 429
Gordon, Gordon, 106, 185
Gordon, Lawrence, 380
Gordon, Leo, 15, 251
Gordon, Mary, 331
Gordon, Michael, 336
Gordon, Mildred, 106, 185
Gordon, Robert, 50
Gordon, Roy, 39, 194
Gordon, Ruth, 101-02
Gore, Chester, 55, 285, 299
Gorman, Cliff, 431
Gosnell, Raja, 373
Gottlieb, Alex, 52, 185
Gottlieb, Theodore, 271
Gough, Lloyd, 54, 254, 288, 294
Gould, Elliott, 416, *417*
Goulding, Edmund, 210
Goursaud, Anne, 461
Goyer, David, S., 373
Grable, Betty, 145-46, *145*
Grady, William, 82
Graf, David, 455
Graff, Fred, 314
Graff, Wilton, 90
Graham, Angelo, 389
Graham, Sheilah, 149
Grahame, Gloria, 40, *40*, 79, 119, 141-42, *142*, 149, *149*, 185, 199, 217, 286
Grainger; Edmund, 240, 276
Granache, Alexander, 318
Granet, Bert, 34, 180
Granger, Farley, 104, 267-68, 284, *284*, 296

The Getaway

Grant, Beth, 432
Grant, Cameron, 233
Grant, Cary, 216, *216*, 275, 290, *290*
Grant, James Edward, 156
Grant, Kathryn, 59, 226, *226*
Grant, Lee, 96, 277, 427
Granville, Bonita, 118, 121, 289
Graves, Peter, 207
Gray, Billy, 91, 293
Gray, Christopher, 384
Gray, Coleen, 160, 166, 170, 210, *211*, 270
Gray, Feild (Field) M., 54, 176, 179
Gray, Hugh, 171
Gray, Lynn, 307
Graysmith, Robert, 468
Grayson, Charles, 337
Grazer, Brian, 384
Great Flamarion, The 119-20, *120*
Great Gatsby, The, 68
Green, Alan, 182
Green, Dorothy, 40
Green, Jack N., 419
Green, Walon, 364
Greene, Clarence, 84, 202, 298, 333-34, 373
Greene, Eve, 56
Greene, Graham, 267, 301
Greene, Harold, 160, 317
Greene, Jaclynne, 76
Greene, Max, 204, 272
Greene, Michael, 407
Greenhalgh, Jack, 29, 109, 173
Greenlee, Laura, 378
Greenstreet, Sydney, 73, 186, 190-91, 316
Greenwald, Maggie, 409

Greer, Dabbs, 15, 307
Greer, Jane, 47, 220-21, *220-21*, 297, 351, 438
Gregg, Virginia, 54
Gregory, James, 209
Gregory, Paul, 207
Gregson-Williams, Harry, 376, 420, 434
Grenier, Zach, 386, 415
Gresham, William Lindsay, 210-11
Grey, Duane, 110
Grey, Virginia, 75, 200, 302
Gribble, Bernard, 375
Grier, Pam, 405, *405*
Gries, Jonathan, 407
Griest, Kim, 422
Griffies, Ethel, 278, 283
Griffim, Robert, 75
Griffith, D.W., 41
Griffith, James, 50
Griffith, Kenneth, 295
Griffith, Melanie, 381, 385, 428, 432
Grifters, The, 390, *391*
Grimes, Stephen, 458
Gropman, David, 460
Grosbard, Ulu, 458-59
Grose, Paul, 213
Gross, Frank, 270
Gross, Jack J., 47, 74, 154, 337-38
Gross, Loretta, 409
Gross, Roland, 92, 114, 218, 260, 337-38
Grost, Michael, 8, 128-29
Grot, Anton, 32, 191, 215, 232, 308, 315
Grubb, David, 207
Gruber, Frank, 154-55, 190
Gruen, Margaret, 252
Gruenberg, Louis, 105, 114, 239
Gruener, Allan, 312
Grundlach, Robert, 375
Grusin, Dave, 387, 428, 431
Guardino, Harry, 420
Gudonov, Alexander, 466
Gudrun, Ann, 295
Guerri, Franco, 396
Guest, Don, 352, 393
Guest in the House, 120-21
Guffey, Burnett, 58, 73, 113, 126, 141, 149, 158, 172, 196-97, 205, 209, 235, 245, 254, 257, 271, 310, 454
Guild, Nancy, 57, 273

Guilfoyle, Paul, 112
Guilty, The, 121, *121*
Guilty Bystander, 122, *122*
Gulager, Clu, 408, *408*
Gullo, Jeff, 357
Gun for Sale, A (novel), 267, 301
Gun, The see *Man Wino Cheated Himself, The*
Gun Crazy, 17, 19, *19,* 82, 122-24, *122-24,* 154, 170, 366, 392
Guncrazy, 391-92, *392*
Gundlach, Robert, 402
Gunmen's Chance (novel), 51
Gunn, James, 56
Gurie, Sigrid, 318
Guthrie, Carl E., 32, 61, 111, 136, 293, 302
Guttenberg, Steve, 356
Guzman, Luis, 416, 447
Gyllenhaal, Jake, 468, *468*
Gwenn, Edmund, 36, 47, 295, 311
Gwynne, Anne, 109
Gwynne, Fred, 383

Haake, James, 426
Haas, Charles, 33, 193
Haas, Dolly, 143
Haas, Hugo, 134, 220, 227, 279
Haas, Lukas, 466, *466*
Haas, Robert, 37, 69, 84, 186
Haase, Cathy, 409
Hackford, Taylor, 351-52
Hackman, Gene, 358, 370, 396, *396* 430, 432-33, 454, 460
Hadley, Reed, 57, 64, 87, 127, 132, 140, 144, 162-63, 178, 265
Hagen, Jean, 30, *31,* 40, 213, 267-68
Hagerman, Richard, 263
Hagerthy, Ron, 147, 185
Haggerty, Don, 30, 66, 83, 114, 183, 199, 408
Haid, Charles, 371, 465
Haight, George, 174
Haines, William, 240
Haji, 408
Hakim, Raymond, 181
Hakim, Robert, 181
Hale, Alan, 236
Hale, Alan, Jr., 162, 253
Hale, Barbara, 72, 334
Hale, Jonathan, 206, 284

Hall, Charles D., 264
Hall, Conrad, 360, 394
Hall, Daniel, 52
Hall, Geraldine, 24, 65
Hall, Irma P., 370
Hall, Philip Baker, 467-68
Hall, Porter, 24, 99, 268
Haller, Ernest, 191, 231, 313, 316
Haller, Michael, 382
Halligan, Dick, 385
Halton, Charles, 283, 331
Hamilton, Fenton, 396
Hamilton, Kim, 217
Hamilton, Margaret, 120
Hamilton, Murray, 381
Hamilton, Neil, 320
Hamilton, Patrick, 116, 125-26
Hamilton, William, 290
Hammett, 393, *393*
Hammett, Dashiell, 118, 186
Hampton, Janice, 393
Hampton, Peter, 360
Hancock, Herbie, 375
Hands of Orlac, The, 226
Hangover Square, 125-126, *125*
Hannah, Daryl, 360
Hannah, Dorothy, 57
Hannemann, Walter, 120, 171
Hanson, Curtis, 353, 356, 414
Hard Bargain see *Thieves'*
Harens, Dean, 74
Hardcore, 393-94
Harder They Fall, The, 126-127, *127*
Hardin, Jerry, 399
Harding, Ann, 314
Hardwicke, Sir Cedric, 153, 181, *181,* 290
Hardy, John, 416, 463
Hardy, Lindsay, 340
Harens, Dean, 68
Harewood, Dorian, 351
Harlan, Russell, 122, 189
Harlin, Russell, 242, 251, 274
Harline, Leigh, 47, 74, 133, 138, 154, 176, 214, 227, 296, 317, 337
Harling, Noelle, 391
Harmon, John, 107
Harolde, Raff, 34, 195
Harper, 394-95
Harper, Tess, 372, 432
Harrelson, Woody, 432
Harring, Laura, 427, *427*
Harrington, Joy, 197

Harris, Ed, 368, 454, *454*
Harris, Harriet Sansom, 423
Harris, James B., 166, 371-72
Harris, Julie, 394, 454
Harris, Julius, 396
Harris, Leonard, 456
Harris, Naomie, 424
Harris, Mel, 455, *455*
Harris, Michael, 455
Harris, Robert A., 391
Harris, Stacy, 29
Harris, Thomas, 422, 450
Harrison, Doane, 24, 99, 288
Harrison, Joan, 90, 214, 249-50, 278, 290, 297
Harrison, Lynn, 269
Harrison, Susan, 161, 290
Hart, Dorothy, 147, 179, 199, 311
Hart, Richard, 247
Hartley, Ted, 357
Hartnett, Josh, 358, *358*
Harvey, John, 189
Harvey, Michael, 34
Harvey, Paul, 130, 267
Harvey, Rodney, 391
Harvey, Walter G., 295
Harwood, Bo, 408
Haskin, Byron, 146, 304
Hasse, O.E., 143, *143*
Hassid, Daniel, 379
Hasso, Signe, 101, 140, 154
Hatfield, Hurd, 95, 315
Hathaway, Henry, 62-63, 87-88, 140-41, 170, 203, 244-45
Hatosy, Shawn, 450
Hauer, Rutger, 360, *361*, 451
Hausman, Michael, 398, 400
Hausmam, Willo, 400
Havlick, Gene, 35, 92, 245, 257, 266
Havoc, June, 68
Hawke, Ethan, 388, *389*
Hawkins, John, 162
Hawkins, Ward, 162
Hawks, Howard, 45-
Haworth, Ted, 151, 274, 284, 335, 389
Hayakawa, Sessue, 138
Haycock, Peter, 435
Haydn, Richard, 268
Hayden, Barbara, 76
Hayden, Harry, *165*
Hayden, Nora, 231
Hayden, Sterling, 30, *31*, 75-76, *76*, 126, 156, *157*, 166, 190, *190*, 199, 287, 416

Hayes, Alfred, 71, 141
Hayes, Bernadene, 65
Hayes, Herbert, 34, 229, 314
Hayes, Joseph, 94
Hayes, Margaret, 118
Hayes, Maggie, 33
Hayes, Sam, 135
Hayes, Terry, 439
Haygood, Jim, 386, 388
Hayne, Ben, 50
Haynes, Linda, 431
Haynes, Robert, 440
Haysbert, Dennis, 455, *455*
Hayton, Lennie, 267
Hayward, Lillie, 51, 112
Hayward, Louis, 138, 248, 281
Hayward, Susan, 27, 92, 139, 244, 297
Hayworth, Rita, *9*, 27, 117, *117*, 173-74, 425-26
Hayworth, Ted, 143
He Ran All the Way, 127, *127*
He Walked by Night, 127-28, 296, 350
Heald, Anthony, 450
Healey, Patricia, 368
Heat, 395, *395*
Heath, Hilary, 372
Heather, Jean, 99
Hecht, Ben, 103-04, 117, 159, 170, 216, 249-50, 275, 328-30, 411
Hecht, Ted, 114, 266
Hedaya, Dan, 362, 427, 458, 464
Hedrick, Earl, 23-24, 96, 110, 273, 314
Heermance, Richard (Dick), 142, 247, 289, 312
Heffron, Richard T., 402
Heflin, Van, 25-26, *26*, 156, 232-33, 235-36, *236*, 271
Hehr, Addison, 33, 91, 138, 166, 208
Heims, Jo, 439
Heindorf, Ray, 57
Heisler, Stuart, 27, 118, 143
Heist, 396, *396*
Helgeland, Brian, 414, 420, 422, 439
Hellerman, Paul, 405
Hellinger, Mark, 59-60, 77-78, 141, 163, 165, 199-200, 204-205, 308
Hell Hath No Fury (novel), 399

Hell Up in Harlem, 396-97, *397*
Hell's Half Acre, 128-29, *128*
Hell's Island, 129, *129*
Helm, Fay, 180, 225
Helmore, Tom, 317
Helseth, Henry Edward, 81
Helton, Percy, *21*, 77-78, 168, 260, 333
Hemingway, Ernest, 57, 163, 408
Henderson, Marsha, 199
Hendrickson, Benjamin, 422
Hendrix, Wanda, 132, 155, 249, *250*
Hendry, Gloria, 396
Henke, Brad, 467
Henkin, Hilary, 445-46
Henner, Marilu, 393
Hennesy, Dale, 465
Henreid, Paul, 135
Henriksen, Lance, 405-06, *406*
Henry, David Lee, 382
Henry, Gloria, 242
Henry, Gregg, 439
Henry, Thomas Browne, 34, 311
Henstridge, Natasha, 376
Hepburn, Katharine, 311
Herczeg, Geza, 263
Here Lies Love see *The Second Woman*
Hereford, Kathryn, 161
Herman, Ace, 107, 132, 183
Herman, Alfred, 34-35, 79, 114, 180, 296 320
Herman, John, L., 310
Herman, Lewis, 280
Herndon, Walter Scott, 449
Herald, Heinz, 119

Hern, Pepe, 185
Hernandez, Juano, 57, 167
Hernandez, Wilfredo, 382
Hero and the Terror, The
Herrmann, Bernard, 64, 91, 125, 218-29, 317, 341, 367, 456
Hershey, Barbara, 443
Hervey, Irene, 68, 190, 439
Herzbrun, Bernard, 23, 59, 77, 136, 158, 171, 219, 241, 249, 263, 268, 270, 310-11, 336
Heston, Charlton, 87, 305
Heydt, Louis Jean, 45, 244, 251
Heyes, Herbert, 171
Heyward, Louis, 138
Hickey, William, 447
Hickey & Boggs, 381, 397-98, *397-87*, 417-18
Hickman, Darryl, 178, 260, 281, 449
Hickox, Sid, 44, 89, 186, 295, 333
Hicks, Catherine, 415
Hicks, James see James Cresson
Hicks, Russell, 29, 142
Higgins, George V., 292, 387
Higgins, John C., 55, 128, 241-42, 244, 264
Higgs, Richard, 456
High Sierra, 130, *130*, 144, 164, 461
High Sierra (novel), 143-44
High Tide, 131-32, *131*
High Wall, The, 132, *132*
High Window, The see *The Brasher Doubloon*
High Window, The (novel), 57

Highsmith, Patricia, 284
Hightower, Tina, 419
Highway Dragnet 132-33, *133*
Hill, Arthur, 394
Hill, Craig, 96
Hill, James, 290
Hill, Steven, 176, 277
Hill, Walter, 380-81, 389-90, 397, 406
Hillerman, John, 369, 431
Hilmarsson, Hilmar Orn, 403
Hilton, Arthur, 138, 163, 225, 255, 259, 278, 289
Himes, Chester, 444
Hinds, Anthony, 295
Hinds, Ciaran, 424
Hinds, Samuel S., 255, 278
Hinds, Nandu, 369
Hinds-Johnson, Marcia, 443
Hines, Gregory, 444
Hingle, Pat, 391
Hirsch, Tina, 380
Hirschfeld, Gerald, 122
His Kind of Woman, 133-34, *133*
Hit and Run, 134
Hitchcock, Alfred, 143, 208, 216, 262-63, 275, 284, 290, 317, 341-42
Hitchcock, Patricia, 284
Hitch-hiker, The, 134-45, *135*
Hively, Jack, 284
Hoagland, Eilsworth, 314
Hobart, Rose, 73
Hodges, Daniel, 7, 53, 90-91, 94-95, 120-21, 131-32, 153, 166-67, 181-82, 193-94, 212-13, 229-230, 258, 265-66, 272, 275-76, 288-89, 309, 313-14, 316-17, 320, 332-33

Hodiak, John, 58, 176, 225, 273
Hoenig, Dov, 373, 395, 422, 456
Hoffenstein, Samuel, 177
Hoffman, Charles, 52, *315*
Hoffman, Leonard, 62
Hoffman, Philip Seymour, 390
Hoffmann, Susan, 411
Hogan, J.R. Michael, 338
Hogan, Susan, 430
Hogsett, Albert, 81
Hohimer, Frank, 456
Holden, Anne, 356
Holden, William, 89, 164, 288, *288*, 308, 314
Holding, Elizabeth Sanxay, 245, 378
Holland, John, 50
Holland, Marty, 107, 100
Hollander, Frederick, 34, 65, 72, 316, 320
Holliman, Earl, 39, 143, 449
Hollings, Earl, 435
Hollow Triumph, 135-36, *135*
Hollywood Story, 136
Holm, Celeste, 252
Holmes, Jack W., 385
Holmes, Milton, 158
Holmes, Taylor, 35, 55, 170, 210, 239, 336
Holscher, Walter, 27, 102, 162, 238, 310
Holt, Derek, 435
Holt, Jack, 67
Holt, Tim, 133
Borne Free see *Hustle*
Homes, Geoffrey see Mainwaring, Daniel
Home Invaders, The see *Desperate Hours*
Home Invaders, The (novel), 456

Homeier, Skip, 83
Homicide, 398-99
Homicide see *Naked City, The*
Honess, Peter, 414
Hong, James, 360-61, 369, 461
Hood, Don, 426
Hoover, Richard, 439
Hoodlum Empire, 137-38, *137*
Hope, Tamara, 378
Hopkins, Anthony, *348*, 450, *450*
Hopkins, Bo, 390, 431
Hopkins, George James
Hopper, Dennis, 156, 161, 360, 399, 444-45, 459-60
Hopper, Jerry, 199
Hopper, Hedda, 288
Horman, Arthur T., 72, 288, 311
Horn, Herta, 60
Hornbeck, William, 229, 268
Hornblow, Arthur Jr., 30, 116
Horner, Harry, 35, 101, 127, 317, 380
Horning, William A., 33, 224
Hot Spot, The, 399-400, *399*
Hot Spot see *I Wake Up Screaming*
Hotaling, Frank, 144, 185
House, Billy, 150, 282, 321
House by the River, 138
House of Bamboo, 138-39, *139*
House of Dr. Edwardes, The (novel), 275
House of Numbers, 139
House of Games, 350, 396, 400
House of Strangers, 139-40, *140*
House on 92nd Street, 140-41, *140*
House on Telegraph Hill, The, 141, *141*
Houseman, John, 52, 218, 296
Houser, Lionel, 260
Howard, Esther, 61, 119, 195
Howard, James Newton, 370, 382, 431
Howard, John, 185
Howard, John C., 381
Howard, Kathleen, 177
Howard, Lisa, 189
Howard, Nancy, 397
Howard, Ron (Ronnie)
Howard, W(illiam) K., 320

Howat, Clark, 135
Howe, James Wong, 54, 69, 85, 127, 215, 236-37, 290
Hoyos, Rodolfo ,Jr., 303
Hoyt, John, 39, 58-59, 179, 306, 313
Hubbard, John, 331
Hubbard, Tom, 132
Hubley, Season, 393
Hudson, Rock, 311
Huggins, Roy, 238, 304-05, 336
Hughes, Dorothy B., 107, 149, 249-50
Hughes, Eric, 351
Hughes, Howard, 176-77, 240, 258, 328
Hughes, Mary Beth, 119-20, 132-33, 150, 173, 183, 221
Hughes, Russell S., 295, 302
Hulett, Otto, 71
Hulce, Tom, 452
Hull, Henry, 130, 136
Human Interest Story, The see *The Big Carnival*
Human Desire, 141-42, *142*
Humberstone, H. Bruce, 145-46
Hume, Cyril, 176
Humphrey, Reynold, 8, 114-15, 312, 337-38
Hunnicutt, Arthur, 56, 276
Hunt, Helen, 411
Hunt, Jimmy, 151, 228, 273
Hunt, J. Roy, 79, 98
Hunt, Marsha, 244
Hunt, Martita, 272
Hunted, The, 142
Hunter, The (novel), 439-40
Hunter, Jeffrey, 161, 166, *167*
Hunter, Kevin, 435
Hunter, Kim, 320
Hunter, Martin, 415
Hunter, Ross, 199
Huntley, Raymond, 272
Huppert, Isabelle, 356
Hurlbut, Gladys, 65
Hurt, William, 362, *362*, 373
Hush, Hush, Sweet Charlotte, 28
Hustle, 170, 400-01, *400-01*
Huston, Anjelica, 391, 441
Huston, Danny, 434
Huston, John, 30-31, 130, 160-161, 163, 186, 282, 368, *461*

Huston, Patricia, 106
Huston, Virginia, 214, 220, 240, 286
Huston, Walter, 103, 263
Hutchinson, Josephine, 273
Hutchison, Doug 447
Hutton, Robert, 240, *240*
Hyams, Peter, 357-58, 430
Hyatt, Bobby, 90, 127
Hyde, Donald, 230
Hyer, Martha, 72, 83
Hyland, Dick Irving, 50, 302

I Confess, 143, *143*
I Died a Thousand Times, 143-44, *144*
I Married a Dead Man, 212
I Shot Jesse James, 144-45
I, the Jury (1953), 145
I, the Jury (1982), 402
I Wake Up Screaming, 145-46, *145*, 318
I Wake Up Screaming (novel), 317-18
I Walk Alone, 20, 146, *146*
I Was a Communist for the FBI, 147, *147*
I Wouldn't Be in Your Shoes, 147-48, *147*
Ice-T, 430, *430*
Idziak, Slawomir, 388
Ihnen, Wiard, 145, 171, 242
I'll Never Go There Again (novel), 139
Iles, Francis, 290
Illegal, 148
Ilou, Edward S., 34, 127, 135, 160, 232, 244, 247, 310
Iman, 433
Imazu, Eddie, 293
Impact, 149, *149*
Impulse, 402-03, *403*
In A Lonely Place, 19-20, 149-50, *149*
In the Cut, 403-04, *403*
Inescort, Frieda, 284, 312
Infuhr, Teddy, 293
Ingram, Rex, 90, 193
Ingster, Boris, 274, 283
Inner Sanctum, 150
Inness, Jean, 207
"Inside Story" (story), 205
Insomnia, 404
Intruder in the Dust, 15
Invaders from Mars, 150, *151*
Invasion of the Body Snatchers, 151-53, *152*

Ireland, John, 114, 144, 224, 241, *241*, 244, 248, 254-55, 383
Irish, William, see Woolrich, Cornell
Iron Kiss, The see *Naked Kiss, The*
Ironside, Michael, 391
Irvine, Richard, 57, 317
Irwin, Coulter, 205
Isham, Mark, 358, 390, 443, 445
Ishimatsu, Guts, 359
Itzin, Gregory, 436
Ivan, Rosalind, 255, 289, 316
Ivano, Paul, 48, 114, 227, 263, 278-79, 288
Ivers, Robert, 267
Ivy, 153

Jackie Brown, 365, 405, *405*
Jackman, Hugh, 376, *376*
Jackman, Fred, Jr, 86, 189, 206, 297
Jacks, James, 451
Jacks, Robert L., 162, 166, 188
Jackson, Felix, 68
Jackson, George, 430
Jackson, Harry, 207
Jackson, Joe, 425
Jackson, Mike, 419
Jackson, Samuel L., 405, 411, 459
Jackson, Selmer, 228
Jackson, Sherry, 57
Jackson, Thomas, 45, 121, 336
Jacobs, Alexander, 440
Jacobs, William, 72, 85, 215, 316
Jacobson, Egon, 184
Jaeckel, Richard, 137, 179, 381
Jaffe, Herb, 465
Jaffe, Pat, 387
Jaffe, Sam, 23, 30, 91, 310
Jaffe, Stanley R., 359, 383
Jagged Edge, 405-06, 448
Jagged Edge, The see *I Died a Thousand Times*
Jagger, Dean, 87, 235-36, 244, 320
James, Brion, 373
James, Rian, 331
James, Steve, 458
Jameson, House, 199
Jamison, Peter, 352, 425

Jane, Thomas, 374-75, 436
Janis, Conrad, 57
Jankel, Annabel, 373
Jankel, Chaz, 373
Jans, Alaric, 398, 400
Jansen, Adolf, 184
Janssen, David, 465
Janssen, Werner, 120
Jarre, Maurice, 351, 383, 433, 466
Jarret, Jerry, 165
Jarrico, Paul, 176-77
Jarvis, Richard J., 331
Jay, Ricky, 396
Jeans, Isabel, 290
Jenkins, George, 411, 432, 441
Jenkins, Richard, 447
Jenks, Frank, 339
Jennings, Brent, 466
Jensen, Roy, 369
Jeopardy, 154
Jergens, Adele, 30, 90, 104, 267, 307
Jessel, George, 210
Jewell, Edward C., 29, 97, 248, 280, 292
Jewell, Isabel, 56, 188
Jimenez, Frank, 407
Joanou, Phil, 454
Job, Thomas, 278, 308
Johansson, Scarlett, 358, *365*
Johari, Azizi, 408
Johnny Angel, 154-55, *155*
Johnny Cool, 155-56, *155*
Johnny Eager, 156, *156*
Johnny Guitar, 156-58, *157*
Johnny Handsome, 406, *406*
Johnny O'Clock, 158, *158*
Johnny Stool Pigeon, 158-59
Johns, Tracy Camilla, 430
Johnson, Ben, 390, 400, *400*

Johnson, Broderick, 404
Johnson, Don, 399, *399*
Johnson, Gary, 7, 98, 302-03
Johnson, Georgann, 267
Johnson, Joseph McMillan, 94, 103, 133, 307
Johnson, Lamont, 59, 230
Johnson, Marjorie, 336
Johnson, Nunnally, 88, 335-36
Johnson, Rita, 38, 269, 297
Johnson, Robin, 373
Johnson, Russell, 180
Johnson, Tor, 34
Johnson, Van, 256
Johnson, Vance, 444
Joiner, Patricia, 104
Jolie, Angelina, 436, *436*
Jones, Amy, 390
Jones, Carolyn, 40, 151, 185, 264
Jones, Eddie, 391
Jones, Gordon, 27
Jones, Harmon, 55, 81, 139, 223, 265
Jones, Henry, 317, 438
Jones, Jennifer, 103, *103*
Jones, Orlando, 357
Jones, Quincy, 389, 454
Jones, Tommy Lee, 432
Jones, Trevor, 353, 373, 410, 447
Jordan, Bert, 261
Jordan, Henry, 158
Jordan, Richard, 387
Joseph, Al(brecht), 179, 207, 258
Joseph, Jackie, 454
Joseph, Robert, 111, 134
Joshua, Larry, 447
Joslyn, Allyn, 145-46, 193
Jour Se Leve, Le, 181-82
Journey into Fear, 20, 159

Johnny Handsome

"Killer's Kiss"

Judd, Ashley, 395
Jugger, The (novel), 454
Julia, Raul, 426
Julian, Janet, 409
Julyan, David, 404, 423
Junior, Mark Boone, 423
Jur, Jeff, 414
Juran, Nathan, 54, 132, 145, 171, 311

Kaczmarek, Jane, 373
Kahn, Michael, 383
Kaiser, Burt, 109-10
Kalinowski, Waldemar, 415
Kamb, Karl, 65, 228
Kandel, Aben, 69, 303
Kane, Irene, 165
Kane, Joseph, 137
Kane, Robert T., 64, 127
Kanin, Garson, 101-02
Kanin, Michael, 101
Kantor, MacKinlay, 122
Kansas City Confidential, 160, *160*
Kaper, Bronislaw, 25, 36, 116, 132, 156, 201, 282, 295
Kaplan, Mark Allan, 379
Kaplan, Sol, 60, 135, 141, 203, 232, 244, 247, 261, 306
Kaprisky, Valerie, 366
Kardos, Leslie, 286
Karlson, Phil, 58-59, 129, 160-62, 211, 226, 254
Karn, Bill, 111
Karnes, Robert, 242
Karr, David, 425
Karras, Alex, 351
Kasdan, Lawrence, 362-64
Kasdan, Mark, 372
Kastner, Elliot, 394

Kasznar, Kurt, 293
Katch, Kurt, 190
Katcher, Leo, 184
Kaufman, Joseph, 286
Kaufman, Millard, 122
Kaufman, Susan, 398
Kaus, Gina, 331
Kay, Beatrice, 312
Kay, Edward J., 93, 107, 132, 142, 147
Kay, Mary Ellen, 182
Kazan, Elia, 55, 69, 223
Kazan, Nicholas, 352
Kazantzidis, Stavros, 403
Keane, Robert Emmett, 109
Keaton, Buster, 288
Keaton, Michael, 405
Keats, Steven, 375, 387
Keefe, Cornelius, 110
Keefer, Don, 251
Keene, Tom, 79
Kenner, Catherine, 450
Keighley, William, 285
Keitel, Harvey, 353-54, 364, 441, 445, *445*, 456, 461, *461*
Keith, Brian, 209, 449
Keith, David, 461
Keith, Ian, 210
Keith, Robert, 55, 104, *104*, 179, 339
Kellaway, Cecil, 233
Keller, Harry, 193, 304-05
Keller, Walter E., 51, 56, 72, 93, 112, 134, 235, 251, 334, 337-38
Kelley, Barry, 30, 110, 162, 172, 261, 274, 304, 310
Kelley, William, 466
Kelley, De Forest, 64, 109, 138, 148

Kellman, Louis W., 60
Kellogg, John, 104, 304
Kellogg, Virginia, 61, 292, 33
Kelly, Claire, 224
Kelly, Ed, 241
Kelly, Gene, 68-69, *69*
Kelly, Jack, 102, 206, 321
Kelly, Patsy, 200
Kelly, Paul, 79, 109-10, 260, 267-68, 276-77
Kelly, Sharon, 400
Kelvaney see *Rogue Cop*
Kelsch, Ken, 353
Kemp, Hugh, 331
Kemper, Charles, 218, 321
Kemper, Steven, 430
Kemper, Victor J., 387
Kendall, Cyrus W., 331
Kennedy, Arthur, 55, 66, 68-69, 94, 130, 242, 304, 334
Kennedy, Burt, 260, 425-26
Kennedy, Douglas, 73, 83, 89, 313
Kennedy, Harold J., 65
Kennedy, Tom, 234
Kenney, Bill, 362
Keneshea, Ellen, 7, 191-92 ,195-95, 233-34
Kenny, Francis, 430
Kent, David, 312
Kent, Robert (actor), 266
Kent, Robert E., 245, 328
Kent, Ted J., 68, 77, 158, 241
Kercheval, Ken, 442
Kern, Hal C., 275
Kern, James V., 258
Kern, Robert J, 256
Kersh, Gerald, 204, 431
Kerz, Leo, 122, 217
Key Largo, 15, 160-161, *161*
Key Witness, 161-62
Keyes, Evelyn, 128, 158, 162, *163*, 211, 235, *236*
Keyloun, Mark, 425
Khondji, Darius, 448
Kidman, Nicole, 403
Kilbride, Percy, 120
Kiley, Richard, 226, *226*, 228, 271
Kilian, Victor, 86
Kill Me Again, 407, *407*
Kill-Off, The, 409
Killer Is Loose, The, 162, *162*
Killer That Stalked New York, The, 162-63, *163*
"Killer Wore A Badge, The" (story), 238

Killers, The (1946), 20, 163-65, *165*
Killers, The, (1964), 408, *408*, 420
Killer's Kiss, 165, *165*, 461
Killian, Victor, 144
Killifer, Jack, 130
Killing The, 166, *166*, 426
Killing of a Chinese Bookie, The, 408-08, *408*
Kilmer, Val, 395, 407, 447, *447*, 459
Kimball, Jeffrey, 459
Kimball, Russell, 331
Kimble, Lawrence, 219
Kimlin, Newell P., 154, 293
King, Alan, 402, 431
King, Andrea, *22*, 186, 249, 274-75
King, Edith, 61
King, Frank, 114, 122, 274, 289, 320
King, Herman, 320
King, Hugh, 302
King, Jamie, 451
King, Maurice, 114, 122, 274, 289, 320
King, Rufus, 259
King, Sherwood, 174
King, Tony, 396
King of New York, 378, 409-10, *410*
Kingdom of Johnny Cool, The (novel), 155
Kingsley, Sidney, 96
Kinnear, Roy, 393
Kinney, Terry, 379
Kirgo, Julie, 6, 24-25, 45-47, 65-66, 71-72, 101-02, 130, 149-50, 177-78, 200-01, 216, 255-56, 262-63, 284, 288, 383
Kirk, Mark-Lee, 62, 193
Kirk, Phyllis, 76
Kirkpatrick, Jess, 84
Kirshner, Mia, 358, 429
Kish, Joseph, 50
Kiss Before Dying, A (1956), 166-67, *167*, 410
Kiss Before Dying, A (1991), 410-11
Kiss Me Deadly, 17, 21-22, *21*, 167-70, *167-69*, 361, 438
Kiss Me, Kill Me see *Killer's Kiss*
Kiss of Death (1947), 22, 170-71, *170*, 245, 411, 414, 422

Kiss of Death (1995), 411
Kiss the Blood Off My Hands, 171, *171*
Kiss Tomorrow Goodbye, } 171-72, 296
Kivilo, Alar, 451
Klatzkin, Leo, 150
Klein, Adelaide, 199
Kleiner, Harry, 107, 115, 138, 285
Kline, Benjamin H., 32, 97, 266, 279
Kline, Richard H., 362, 366, 465
Klingman, Lynzee, 458
Kloss, Thomas, 384
Klugman, Jack, 303, 454
Klute, 411-13, *411-13*
Knife, The see *Unknown Man, The*
Knight, Jack, 416
Knight, Patricia, 266
Knock on Any Door, 172, *172*
Knowles, Patric, 47, 153, 340
Knox, Elyse, 147
Knox, Mickey, 23, 172, 33
Knudsen, Peggy, 313
Knudtson, Frederic, 28, 74, 133, 176, 320, 334
Koch, Howard W., 264, 300
Kodl, James, 110
Koehler, Bonnie, 353
Koessler, William, 331
Kohler, Fred, 170
Kohlmar, Fred, 87, 118
Kohner, Fred, 36
Kolker, Henry, 53
Kolster, Clarence, 143
Konstantin, Madame, 216
Koepp, David, 353
Kopache, Thomas, 415
Kopp, Rudolph G., 81, 198
Kopta, Josef, 227
Kortner, Fritz, 34, 57, 273
Korvin, Charles, 34, 162, *163*
Koschetz, Nina, 67
Koteas, Elias, 388, 468
Koyama, Shigeru, 359
Kraike, Michel, 93
Kramer, Cecile, 242
Kramer, Stanley, 66, 271
Kraner, Doug, 453-54
Krasner, Milton, 23, 88, 101-02, 139, 244-45, 255-56, 260, 317, 336
Kraushaar, Raoul, 52, 150

Kravetz, Carole, 379, 435, 437
Kress, Harold F., 213
Kretschmer, John D., 376
Kreuger, Kurt, 87
Krizman, Serge, 119
Kroeger, Barry, 25, 68, 81, 90
Kruger, Otto, 105, 195, 261-62
Kruschen, Jack, 64, 206
Kubik, Gail, 94
Kubrick, Stanley, 165-66
Kubrick, Ruth, 166
Kulik, Buzz, 465
Kullers, John, 408
Kuluva, Will, 23, 217
Kupferman, Meyer, 49
Kurant, Willy, 368
Kurita, Toyomichi, 444
Kurtz, Swoosie, 351
Kuter, Leo K., 147, 160, 313
Kwei, James, 409

L.A. Confidential, 350, 365, *365*, 414, *414*
Lacca, Yolanda, 67
Lachman, Edward, 416
Ladd, Alan, 29-30, 52, 61-62, 68, 118, 301-02
Ladd, Diane, 360, 369, 410
Lady Confesses, The, 173
Lady from Shanghai, The, 10, 82, 173-74, *174*
Lady in Distress see *Lady on a Train*
Lady in the Lake, 21, 174-76, *175*, 250
Lady Without Passport, A, 176, *176*
Lafferty, John, 374
LaFleur, Joy, 331
Lagennegger, Marcel, 376
Lagola, Charles, 353
Lait, Jack, 202-203
Lake, Veronica, 52, 118, 242, *242*, 301, 414
Lamarr, Hedy, 176, *176*, 281-82, *282*
Lambert, Jack, 168, 211
Lambert, Robert K., 364, 374, 380
Lamont, Molly, 289
Lamour, Dorothy, 190, *190*
Lancaster, Burt, 59, 77-78, *77*, 146, *146*, 163-65, *163-64*, 171, *171*, 273-74, *274*, 290-91, *290, 463*
Lancelot, Sir, 59

Lanchester, Elsa, 38, 128-29, 198
Landau, Richard H., 78, 251
Landers, Harry, 102, 122
Landers, Hal, 375
Landers, Lew, 150, 188
Landis, Carole, 145-46
Landon, Joseph, 155
Landon, Laurene, 402
Landor, Rosalyn, 353
Landres, Paul, 144
Lane, Burton, 25
Lane, Charles, 197
Lane, Lola, 92, 297
Lane, Mike, 126
Lane, Priscilla, 54
Lane, Richard, 249, 309
Lane, Rusty, 126
Lang, Barbara, 139
Lang, Charles B., Jr., 25, 40, 286-87
Lang, Charles, 22
Lang, Fritz, 36-37, 40-43, 52-53, 71-72, 138, 141-42, 242-43, 255-56, 259-60, 329-30, 336-37, 374
Lang, Harold, 295
Lang, Jennings, 439
Lang, Otto, 62
Lang, Stephen, 422
Langan, Glen, 125, 211
Lange, Arthur, 211, 242, 336, 339
Lange, Hope, 375
Lange, Jessica, 367, 431, 441, *442*
Langton, Paul, 40, 194
Lanning, Reggie, 49, 137
Lansbury, Angela, 115, 230-31
Lansing, Joi, 305

Lansing, Sherry, 359, 383
LaPaglia, Anthony, 407, 447
Larch, John, 162, 439
Lardner, Ring, Jr., 66-67, 177
Larkin, Peter, 431
Larner, Stevan, 354
La Roche, Mary, 179
Larsen, Tambi, 438
Larson, Darrell, 425
La Rue, Jack, 74, 86
Las Vegas Story, The, 176-77
LaShelle, Joseph, 75, 107-08, 125, 177, 252, 277, 300, 328
Lassick, Sidney, 377
Last Seduction, The, 365, 377, 415, *415*
Laszlo, Alexander, 86, 119, 280, 297
Laszlo, Andrew, 402
Laszlo, Ernest, 40, 84, 149, 167, 184, 190, 329
Lathan, Sanaa, 437, *437*
Lathrop, Philip, 106, 380, 440
Latimer, Jonathan, 23, 38, 118, 205-06, 214, 297
Latimore, Frank, 265
La Torre, Charles, 101
Latzen, Ellen Hamilton, 383
Laub, Marc, 393
Laughton, Charles, 38-39, *38*, 58, 207, 289
Laura, 14, 20, 177-178, *177*, 291, 329
Laurents, Arthur, 65
Lava, William, 193, 302
Laven, Arnold, 335
Law and Martin Rome, The see *Cry of the City*
Law, Jude, 388
Lawford, Betty, 98

Lawford, Peter, 155
Lawler, Anderson, 273
Lawrence, Barbara, 285, 299
Lawrence, Elizabeth, 453
Lawrence, Marc, 30, 146, 153, 160, 301
Lawrence, Mary, 307
Lawrence, Robert (editor), 70, 382
Lawrence, Robert (producer), 410
Lawrence, Viola, 27, 89, 149, 172, 174, 188
Laws, Andrew, 434
Lawson, Kate, 110
Lawton, Charles, Jr., 102, 174, 266
Lazan, David, 464
Lazar, Andrew, 364
Leachman, Cloris, 167-68
Leave Her to Heaven, 178-79, *178*
Leavitt, Sam, 64, 76, 155, 298
Lebedeff, Ivan, 263
Lebental, Dan, 376
Le Borg, Reginald, 63, 107
Lederer, Charles, 170, 249-50, 411
Lederer, Francis, 318-19
Lederman, D. Ross, 249
Lee, Anna, 76
Lee, Canada, 54
Lee, Gypsy Rose, 257
Lee, Leonard, 331
Lefevre, Arthur, 331
Leeds, Lila, 174
Legler, Steven, 444
Legros, James, 391
Lehman, Ernest, 290
Lehman, Milton, 162

Lei, Lydia, 393
Leiber, Fritz, 98, 150
Leicester, James, 270
Leigh, Janet, 25-26, *26*, 201, *201*, 253, 305, 394
Leigh, Jennifer Jason, 403, 424, 446
Leisen, Mitchell, 212
Leith, Virginia, 84, 166
Lemmo, James, 385, 426
Lemmons, Kasi, 450
Lennon, Thomas, 423
Lennox, Michael, 331
Leon, Joseph, 290
Leonard, Elmore, 405
Leonard, Jack, 82, 129, 133, 188, 201, 260
Leonard, Jim, 60
Leonard, Patrick, 352
Leonard, Queenie, 181, *181*, *196*, 197, 202
Leonard, Robert Z., 58
Leonard, Sheldon, 93, 112, 114, 273, 284
Leone, Sergio, 410
Leonetti, Matthew, 405-06
Lerman, Logan, 434
Lerner, Carl, 411
Lerner, Geraldine, 122
Lerner, Joseph, 122
Lerner, Irving, 70, 194
Lerner, Michael, 441
LeRoy, Mervyn, 156
Leslie, Joan, 130, 248
Leslie, Nan, 98, 338
Leslie, William, 179
Lesser, Sol, 246
Lettieri, Al, 390
Leven, Boris, 77, 95, 138, 182, 239, 258, 263, 265, 286, 339

Levene, Sam, 55, 59, 79, 122, 163, 290
Levin, Henry, 73, 205
Levin, Ira, 166, 410
Levin, Irving H., 458
Levine, Ted, 450
Levitt, Alfred, Lewis, 263
Levitt, Gene, 208
Levitt, Zane W., 391
Levy, Jules, 335
Lewis, Andy, 411
Lewis, Ben, 33, 314
Lewis, Dave, 411
Lewis, Eric, 374
Lewis, Geoffrey, 402
Lewis, Harry, 122, 160
Lewis, John, 217, 271, 278
Lewis, Joseph H., 39, 82, 122-24, 176, 196-97, 310-11
Lewis, Juliette, 367, 445
Lewis, Tom, 66
Lewis, Warren, 359
Lewton, Val, 260-61
Libatique, Matthew, 434
Libertini, Richard, 449
Li, Gong, 424-25
Lichterman, Marvin, 387
Liddle, George, 373
Liebestraum, 350, 415-16
Lightning Strikes Twice see *Beyond the Forest*
Lincoln, Elmo, 105
Linder, Alfred, 57, 64
Lindo, Del Roy, 396
Lindfors, Viveca, 32, 87, 302
Lindley, John W., 453
Lindon, Lionel, 52, 129, 239
Lindsay, Margaret, 255
Link, John F., 119, 234, 280
Lineup, The, 179, *179*
Limey, The, 416
Lindsey, Marty, 467, *467*
Ling, Eugene, 34-35, 232, 254, 265
Linn, Rex, 467
Linson, Art, 386, 395-96, 441
Lippert, Robert, 144
Lipsky, Eleazar, 170, 225
Lipstein, Harold, 82, 213
Lister, Moira, 272, *272*
List, Tom "Tiny," Jr., 382
Litel, John, 121, 171, 228, 336
Little Caesar, 397
Little Giant see *Drive a Crooked Road*
Little, Mickey, 122

Littlejohn, Gary, 354
Littleton, Carol, 362, 368, 460
Littleton, Scott, 205
Litvak, Anatole, 69, 181, 273-74
Liu, Lucy, 439
Livingston, Roy, 147
Livingstone, Fred, 429
Lloyd, Christopher, 441, 457
Lloyd, Doris, 181, 197
Lloyd, Kathleen, 356
Lloyd, Norman, 127, 184, 247, 256, 275
Loan Shark, 179-80, *180*
Loaf, Meat, 386
Locke, Katherine, 307
Locke, Sondra, 402-03
Locked in see *Caged*
Locket, The, 20, 180, *180*, 384
Lockhart, Gene, 137, 140, 178, 247, 281, 340
Lockhart, June, 292
Lockhart, Kathleen, 36, 174
Lodger, The, 181, *181*
Lodato, Carlo, 194
Loeb, Lee, 311
Loeb, Phillip, 101
Loeffler, Louis, 177, 300, 328, 330
Loesser, Frank, 301
Loft, Arthur, 118, 255, 336
Loggia, Robert, 115, 418
Lom, Herbert, 204
Lombardo, Lou, 416
London, Julie, 246
London, Roy, 380
Lonergan, Arthur, 66, 228
Long, Audrey, 56, 73
Long Chance, The see *Murder is My Beat*
Long Goodbye, The, 365, 416-18, *417*
Long Night, The, 181-82, *182*
Long, Richard (Dick), 77, 88, 282
Long Wait, The, 182-83, *182*
Longmire, Adele, 308
Longstreet, Stephen, 278
Loo, Anita, 106
Loo, Richard, 72
Loophole, 183
Looters, The (novel), 367
Lopez, Perry, 143, 369, 461
Lord, Mildred, 280
Lord, Robert, 132, 149, 172
Loring, Teala, 53, 107
Lorne, Marion, 284

Lorre, Peter, *42*, 48, 67, 186, 190-91, 239, 283, 316
Lorring, Joan, 44, 114, 316
Los Angeles Investigator, The see *He Walked By Night*
Losch, Tilly, 103
Losey, Joseph, 44, 184, 235-36
Lost Highway, 375, 418-19, *418*
Lottman, Evan A., 443
Lourie, Eugene, 200, 278
Love Crimes, 419, *419*
Love Is a Weapon see *Hell's Island*
Love Story see *Crime of Passion*
Lovejoy, Frank, 135, 147, 149, 307, *307*
Lovering, Otho, 289
Love's Lovely Counterfeit (novel), 270
Lovett, Robert Q., 393
Low, Warren, 23, 87, 110, 158, 273
Lowe, Rob, 353
Lowell, Robert, 147
Lowery, Robert, 86 297
Luber, Bernard, 179
Lubin, Arthur, 149
Lubin, Lou, 320
Lucas, Blake, 6, 25-26, 48-49, 55-57, 61, 64-65, 76-77, 79-80, 97-103, 107-08, 138-40, 146, 162, 171-72, 179-80, 201-02, 206-07, 211, 218-21, 227-28, 252-53, 270, 292-94, 296-97, 305-06, 311, 329-30, 333, 341-42, 440-41
Lucas, John (Jack) Meredyth, 87
Lucas, Josh, 378
Lucas, Marcia, 456
Luciano, Michael, 40, 167, 340, 400
Lucidi, Renzo, 192
Ludwig, Otto, 155, 242, 277, 339
Luez, Laurette, 84
Lukas, Paul, 34, 92-93, 331
Luke, Keye, 128, 269, 340
Lumet, Sidney, 426
Lund, John, 205, 212, *212*
Lundigan, William, 112, 141
Lupino, Ida, 35, 40, 47-48, 130, 134-35, 187, *187*, 218-29, *218*, 235, *235*, 252, 329, 336

LuPone, Patti, 396, 466
Lurie, Evan, 409
Lurin, Larry, 396
Lussier, Dane, 331
Lydon, James, 279
Lyles, A.C., 267
Lynch, David, 375, 418, 427-28
Lynch, John Carroll, 468
Lynch, Warren E.
Lyndon, Barré, 23, 125, 140, 181, 188, 205-06
Lyne, Adrian, 383
Lynn, Diana, 225
Lynn, Mauri, 44
Lyon, Dana, 140
Lyon, William A., 115, 141, 209
Lyons, Art, 6, 49, 136, 142, 232, 301, 303, 335
Lyons, Francis, 54, 127

M (1931), 41, *42*
M (1951), 17, 184-85, *185*, 361
Macao, 185, *185*
Macaulay, Richard, 56
MacBride, Donald, 130, 163
MacCrorie, Alma, 212
MacDonald, Edmund, 97, 173, 266, 297
MacDonald, J. Farrell, 125, *125*, 154
MacDonald, Joe, 62, 87-88, 138, 193, 203, 223, 227-28, 265, 285-86
MacDonald, John D., 64, 367
MacDonald, Ian, 252
Macdonald, Kelly, 432
MacDonald, Philip, 89, 189, 215
Macdonald, Ross, 381, 394
MacDonald, Wallace, 105, 188, 196
MacDougal, Ranald, 57, 191, 232, 315
Macek, Carl, 6, 30-31, 34-35, 39, 41-43, 52, 57, 59-60, 66, 73-74, 84, 87-90, 92-94, 112-13, 122-24, 140-41, 163, 165, 171-72, 174-76, 182-83, 185, 191-93, 195-96, 199-200, 205, 233-34, 241-42, 244, 264-65, 271, 279-83, 287-88, 310-11, 314-15, 328-29, 387, 454

MacGill, Moyna, 278
MacGraw, Ali, 389, *389*
MacInnes, Angus, 466
MacKendrick, Alexander, 290
MacKenzie, Aeneas, 247
MacKenzie, Jack, 309
MacKenzie, Joyce, 95, 208, 240
MacLane, Barton, 130, 171, 197, 247
MacLean, Peter, 387
Maclean, Robert, 372
MacLiammoir, Michael
Mackay, Phoebe, 60
Mackie, Allison, 436
MacMahon, Aline, 120
MacMillan, Kenneth (cinematographer), 446
MacMurray, Fred, 99-101, *101-2*, 164, 238, *238*, 268
MacPhail, Angus, 275, 341
Macready, George, 38, *38*, 96, 117, 166, 172, 176, *176*, *196*, 197
MacVicar, Bill, 7, 25-26, 32-33, 50, 54-55, 72, 105-06, 139, 147-48, 158-59, 185-86, 189-90, 199, 241, 254-55, 260, 266-67, 310-12, 331, 336
Macy, Jack, 220
Macy, William H., 398, 400, 429
Mad with Much Heart (novel), 218
Maddow, Ben, 30-31, 113, 171, 194
Made in U.S.A., 454
Madigan, 410, *420*
"Madman's Holiday" (story), 74

Madsen, Michael, 390, 407, *407*, 428, 445, *445*, 451-53
Madsen, Virginia, 399, *399*, 434
Magee, Frank, 85, 302
Maggio, Tony, 353
Maguire, George, 386
Maher, Joseph, 407
Mahin, John Lee, 156
Maibaum, Richard, 38, 212
Main, Marjorie, 311
Mainwaring, Daniel, 47, 86, 134-35, 151-53, 220-21, 226, 251-52, 297, 351-52
Make Haste To Live, 185-86
Malden, Karl, 55, 143, 170, 328
Malick, Terence, 354
Malleson, Lucy, 196
Malkames, Don, 60
Malkovich, John, 428
Malone, Dorothy, 44, 73, 162, 183, 235, 238, *238*, 355
Malone, Mark, 407
Maloney, Denis, 467
Maltese Falcon, The (1930), 186
Maltese Falcon, The, (1941) 15, 186-87, *186*
Maltese Falcon, The (novel)
Maltz, Albert, 199-200, 246, 267, 301
Mamet, David, 350, 396, 398-400, 441
"Man, The" (story), 35
Man in the Attic, 188
Man in the Dark, 188-89, *188*
Man in the Saddle, 76
Man I Love, The, 187-88, *187*

Man on Fire

Man on Fire, 420-22, *421*
Man Who Cheated Himself, The, 189, *189*
Man Who Stole a Dream, A see *Manhandled*
Man Who Wasn't There, The, 365
"Man Who Stole a Dream, The" (story), 190
Man with My Face, 189-90
Mancini, Henry, 106, 305, 408
Mandan, Robert, 397
Mandel, Johnny, 440, 442
Mandell, Daniel, 104
Mander, Miles, 195
Manhandled, 190, *190*
Manhunter, 422-23, *422*
Mankiewicz, Don, 139
Mankiewicz, Herman J., 68
Mankiewicz, Joseph L., 139-40, 273
Mann, Anthony, 55-56, 93-94, 98-99, 112, 119-20, 127, 141, 201, 241, 244, 247-48, 267-68, 280, 286, 292, 309
Mann Der Seimen Morder Sucht, Der, 84
Mann, Edward, 44, 52, 67, 184
Mann, Michael, 370, 395, 410, 422, 424-25, 456-57
Manning, Bruce, 137
Mansfield, Jayne, 60, 109-10, 148
Mantegna, Joe, 398, 400
Mantell, Joe, 369, 461
Mapother, William, 467
Mara, Adele, 49
March, Fredric, 94
March of Time (newsreel series), 141
Margolin, Stuart, 375
Marcus, Larry, 32, 66, 87

Marcus, Lee, 283
Marin, Edwin L., 154, 214
Mark, Michael, 119
Marker, Harry, 260, 275, 283
Markey, Enid, 199
Markey, Gene, 193
Marks, Owen, 61, 186, 215, 33
Marks, Richard, 457
Marley, J. Peverell, 148, 171, 308
Marlowe, Faye, 125
Marlowe, Hugh, 91, 148, 204, 244
Marquand, Richard, 405
Marquette, Desmond, 30
Marr, Eddie (Edward), 85, 206
Mars, Kenneth, 432
Marsh, Mae, 208
Marsh, Terence, 355
Marshall, Alan, 355
Marshall, Brenda, 280
Marshall, E. G., 62, 238
Marshall, George, 52
Marshall, Herbert, 28, 74, 132, 153, 312
Marshall, Tully, 301
Marshall, William, 49
Marshek, Archie, 61, 118, 129, 281, 301, 465
Marshman, D. M., Jr., 258, 288
Marta, Jack, 331
Martha (opera), 169
Martin, Adrian, 6, 138, 187-88, 259-60, 330-31, 338-39, 352, 358-59, 377-78, 384-86, 409-11
Martin, Dewey, 94
Martin, Don, 95, 23
Martin, D'Urville, 396
Martin, John Bartlow, 256
Martin, John, J., 132
Martin, Helen, 173

Martin, Lewis, 24, 335
Martin, Lori, 64
Martin, Pete, 147
Martin, Philip, Jr., 309
Martin, Strother, 394
Martindale, Margo, 460
Martinelli, Tony, 49
Martinez, Cliff, 416, 463
Martinez, Joaquin, 465
Marton, George, 331
Marvin, Lee, 40, *40*, 143, 408, *408*, 440-41
Marx, Samuel, 176
Mascolo, Joseph, 449
Mask of Dimitrios, The, 190-91, *191*
Mason, James, 65, *65*, 219, 245-46, *245*
Mason, Pamela, 111
Massey, Raymond, 232, *233*, 336
Masson, Osa, 92
Masters, Ruben, 427
Masterson, Mary Stuart, 352
Masterson, Whit, 305, 465
Mastrantonio, Mary Elizabeth, 452
Masur, Richard, 465-66
Maté, Rudolph, 84, 89, 117, 258, 314
Mather, Aubrey, 181
Matheson, Richard, 33
Mathews, Carole, 189, 212
Matsuda, Yusaku, 359
Matthau, Walter, 367-68
Matthews, Kerwin, 115, *115*
Matthews, Lester, 309
Mature, Victor, 81, *81*, 114, 145-46, *145*, 170, *170*, 176, 193, *193*, 263
Maugham, W. Somerset, 68, 313
Max, Arthur, 448
Max, Edwin, 112, 267
Maxey, Paul, 202
Maxwell, John, 235, 335
Maxwell, Lois, 90
Maxwell, Marilyn, 66, 202
Mayenzet, Maria, 405
Maylia, 268
Mayes, Wendell, 375
Mayo, Virginia, 32, 247, 33
Mazurki, Mike, 23, 87, 146, 195, 197-98, 202, 204, 210, 263-64
McAdo, Ken, 267
McArthur, Colin, 7, 194, 398-99, 453-54

McBride, Jim, 364
McBride, Percy, 107
McBride, Robert, 189
McCalla, Irish, 33
McCallister, Lon, 246
McCambridge, Mercedes, 156, *157* 254-55, 305
McCarthy, Cormac, 432
McCarthy, Kevin, 102, 151, *152*, 209, *210*
McCarthy, Molly, 49
McClaglen, Victor, 332
McCleary, Urie, 454
McClory, Sean, 295
McCluskey, Joyce, 206
McCord, Ted, 57, 84, 143
McCormack, Patrick, 106
McCoy, Horace, 171-72, 307
McCrae, Gordon, 32
McCrea, Joel, 242, *242*
McDonald, J. Farrell, 339
McDonald, Marie, 120
McDormand, Frances, 362, *362*
McDowell, Alex, 384, 386
McEachin, James, 439
McEvoy; Earl, 162
McGann, William, 22
McGara, Helen, 427
McGarry, Eileen, 7, 38-40, 84-85, 89, 170-71, 336-37, 431-32
McGaugh, Wilbur, 76
McGavin, Darren, 109
McGehee, Kelly, 378, 455
McGehee, Scott, 378, 455
McGillis, Kelly, 466, *466*
McGivern, William P., 40, 217, 253, 264
McGovern, Elizabeth, 356, 406
McGraw, Charles, 30, 51, *51*, 56, 114, 133, 142, 163, *165*, 181, 183, 201-02, 247-48, 251-52, 267, 292, 302, 358
McGregor, Ewan, 376
McGuire, Biff, 226
McGuire, Don, 30
McGuire, Dorothy, 185, 275, *276*
McGuire, George, 97
McGuire, John, 283
McHugh, Frank, 69
McIntire, John, 30, 62, 158, 226, 241, 256, 285, 310, 320

McIntyre, Dennis, 454
McKay, Craig, 424, 450
McKay, Scott, 120
McKelway, St. Ciair, 269
McKnight, Tom, 48
McKutcheon, John, 298
McLean, Barbara, 203, 210
McMahon, Horace, 96, 188
McMillan, Kenneth (actor), 458
McNabb, Eric, 407
McNally, Stephen, 36, 77, 185, 241, 276-77, 336, *336*
McNeil, Allen, 221
McPartland, John, 155
McQuarrie, Christopher, 464
McQueen, Butterfly, 103, 191
McQueen, Steve, 389, *389*
McSweeney, John, Jr., 139, 224, 425
McVey, Paul, 112
Meade, Mary, 292
Meadow, Herb, 132, 281
Meadows, Jayne, 174
Medak, Peter, 445
Medavoy, Mike, 468
Medford, Harold, 34, 84, 162
Medlord, Kay, 122
Medina, Patricia, 192-93
Meehan, Canny, 49
Meehan, George, 50, 105, 288
Meehan, John, 188, 28
Meeker, Ralph, *21*, 154, 167-68, *168*, 201
Meheux, Philip, 372
Melbourne, Gordon, 407
Meli, Nicholas, 402
Mellor, Willliam, 201, 229, 304, 314
Meltzer, Jim, 435
Meltzer, Lewis, 33, 58
Memento, 423, *423*
Memonas, Milda, 49
Mendes, Eva, 437
Mendl, Sir Charles, 216
Mendoza, Arthur, 377
Menendez, Carlos, 424
Menjou, Adolphe, 271, *271*
Menke, Sally, 405, 428, 445
Menzies, Jr., Peter, 390
Menzies, William Cameron, 103, 150-51, 153, 247
Meredith, Burgess, 284, 454, 458
Meredyth, Bess, 315
Merivale, Philip, 282
Merrill, Dina, 455

Merrill, Gary, 208-09, 328, 335
Merritt, Gene, 273
Merritt, Michael, 398, 400
Mescall, John, 90
Messer, Arnold, 468
Metcalf, Laurie, 361
Metcalfe, Jesse, 357-58
Methinks the Lady (novel), 330
Metrano, Art, 366
Metropolis, 374
Metty, Russell, 21, 153, 171, 199, 241, 249, 282, 305-06, 332, 420
Metzler, Jim, 379
Meyer, Emile, 44, 179, 251, 264, 290, 438
Meyer, Nicholas, 383
Miami Blues, 423-24
Miami Vice, 424-25, *424*
Michaels, Beverly, 227, 333-34
Michaels, Sidney, 161
Michele, Michael, 430
Michelet, Michel, 67-68, 149, 184, 318
Michelson, Harold, 442
Mlddleton, Charles, 234
Middleton, Robert, 39, 94
Mike's Murder, 425
Milano, Alyssa, 384
Milchan, Arnon, 386, 414
Mildred Pierce, 16, 191-92, *191*, 397
Miles, Sylvia, 383
Miles, Vera, 341
Milestone, Lewis, 120, 281, 314
Milford, Gene, 189
Milius, John, 393
Miljan, John, 163
Millan, VIctor, 305
Milland, Ray, 38, 272, 298-99
Millar, Ronald, 314
Millard, Oscar, 28, 258
Millbrook, Les, 56, 154
Miller, Ann., 427
Miller, Arthur, 55, 221, 235, 330
Miller, Colleen, 207
Miller, David, 286-87
Miller, Doris, 234
Miller, Ernest, 144
Miller, Frank, 451-52
Miller, Jason, 431
Miller, Jim, 370

Miller, Kristine, 146, 304
Miller, Marvin, 57, 92-93, 154
Miller, Michael R., 373
Miller, Ronald, 272
Miller, Seton I., 61, 73, 189, 268
Miller, Virgil, 63
Miller, Wade, 122
Miller, Willlam, 270
Miller, Winston, 297
Miller's Crossing, 433
Millhauser, Betram, 288
Millican, James, 147, 244
Mills, Donna, 439
Mills, Mort, 83, 102
Milne, Peter, 131, 316
Milner, Martin, 65, 290
Milner, Victor, 87, 154, 281
Milton, David (Dave), 83, 93, 107, 109, 132, 147, 183, 251
Minch, Michelle, 407
Minciotti, Esther, 139, 266, 341
Minciotti, Silvio, 72, 168
Minnelli, Vincente, 311
Minotis, Alex(is), 67, 216, 223
Miracle in the Street see *The Scoundrel*
Miranda, Aurora, 225
Mirisch, Walter, 107, 147
Misraki, Paul, 192
Mississippi Mermaid, 436
Mitchell, Cameron, 138
Mitchell, Grant, 73
Mitchell, James (actor), 56, 98
Mitchell, James (editor), 430
Mitchell, Millard, 73, 101, 170, 201, 299
Mitchell, Rahda, 421
Mitchell, Thomas, 88, *88*, 90, 329
Mitchum, James (Jim), 33, 425

Mitchum, Robert, 28, *28*, 47, 51, *51*, 64-65, 79, *79*, 133, *133*, 164, *164*, 180, 185, 207, *207*, 220-21, *220-21*, 236, *237*, 240, 258, 311, 321-22, *321-27*, 326, 367, 383, *383*, 387, *387*
Mitra, Rhona, 434
Mitrovich, Marta, 313
Mizell, Fonce, 396
Mockridge, Cyril, 87, 145, 208, 210, 221, 252, 328
Moffett, Sharyn, 180
Moffitt, Jack, 242
Moguy, Leonide, 332
Mohr, Gerald, 96, 117, 271, *271*
Mohr, Hal, 44, 179, 242, 258-59, 312, 339
Mokae, Zakes, 444
Mokri, Amir, 447, 452
Moll, Elick, 141, 208
Monash, Paul, 387
Money Trap, The, 425-26, *426*
Monks, John, Jr., 140, 172, 225
Monroe, Marilyn, 30, *31*, 71, *71*, 203
Monroe, Robert, 78
Monroe, Steve, 409
Montagne, Edward, 189-90
Montalban, Carlos, 126
Montalban, Ricardo, 56, 198, 425
Montgomery, Elizabeth, 155
Montgomery, George, 57
Montgomery, Robert, 21-22, *22*, 174-76, 249-50, *250*
Montoute, Edouard, 385
Moody, Ralph, 143
Mooney, Martin, 50
Moonjean, Hank, 449
Moonrise, 193, *193*

Moonrise

New Jack City

Moore, Cleo, 114, 134, 218, 220, 279
Moore, Dickie, 34, 220
Moore, Gar, 312
Moore, Joanna, 305
Moore, Joel, 357
Moore, John J., 359, 447
Moore, Juanita, 27
Moore, Susanna, 403
Moore, Terry, 114
Moorehead, Agnes, 61, 89, 159
Mora, Bradley, 66
Morahan, Thomas N., 272
Morales, Esy, 77
Moran, Dolores, 186
Moreno, Carmen, 397
Moreno, Louis, 397
Morgan, Harry Hays, 197
Morgan, Henry, 29, 38, 87, 114, 193, 221, 247, 254
Morgan, Ira, 320
Morgan, Michele, 67, 319
Mori, Paola, 192
Moriarty, Michael, 465
Moriss, Frank, 441
Morison, Patricia, 63, 107
Moritz, Louisa, 458
Moritz, Neil H., 437
Morley, Karen, 113
Morning After, The, 426
Moross, Jerome, 65
Morricone, Ennio, 454
Morris, Chester, 50
Morris, Wayne, 231
Morrison, Ann, 65
Morriss, Frank, 367
Morross, Richard, 150
Morrow, Douglas, 36, 357
Morrow, Neyle, 76
Morse, David, 390
Mortensen, Viggo, 466
Mortimer, Lee, 202-203
Morton, Arthur, 238

Morton, Rocky, 373
Moscov, George V., 320
Mosley, Walter, 379
Moss, Arnold, 56, 129, 247
Moss, Carrie-Anne, 423
Moss, Jack, 159
Moss, Jimmy, 85
Moss Rose, 193-94, *193*
Moss, William, 109
Mostel, Zero, 104-05, *105*, 23
Mosten, Murray, 456
Motley, Willard, 172
Mouezy-Eon, 255
Mourse, Allen, 238
Moving Target, The (novel), 394
Mowbray,Alan, 145-46
Mowery, Helen, 197
Moyle, Allan, 419
Mr. Angel Comes Aboard (novel), 154
Mr. Arkadin, 19, 192, *192*
Mr. Smith Goes to Washington
Ms. 45, 427
Mudie, Leonard, 197
Muir, Gavin, 68
Mulholland Drive, 350, 375, 386, 427-28
Mulholland Falls, 365, 428-29
Mulholland, Molly, 467
Mullendore, Joseph, 202
Muller, Robby, 458
Mulligan, Pat, 407
Mulligan, Robert, 431
Mulrooney, Dermot, 441, 468
Mulvehill, Charles, 382, 441
Munson, Ona, 246, 263, *264*
Murch, Walter, 370, 445
Murder, The see *Angel Face*
Murder at Harvard see *Mystery Street*
Murder by Contract, 194
Murder in the First, 350, 429, *429*

Murder Is My Beat, 194-95, *195*
Murder, My Sweet, 16, 21, 195-96, *195*
Murphy, Brittany, 451
Murphy, Fred, 356, 429
Murphy, George, 56, 213, 293
Murphy, John, 424
Murphy, Mary, 94, 129, 185
Murphy, Richard, 55, 81, 223
Murphy, Tab, 374
Murray, Ben, 232
Murray, Jan, 385
Murray, Lynn, 44, 235
Murtagh, Kate, 383
Murtaugh, James, 437
Musketeers of Pig Alley, The, 41
Musuraca, Nicholas, 51-53, 71, 92, 107, 134, 154-55, 180, 220-21, 251-52, 275-76, 283, 321, 337
Mutrux, Floyd, 428
My Name is Julia Ross, 196-97, *196*
Myers, Carmel, 332
Mysterious Intruder, 197-98, *197*
Mystery Street, 17, 198, *198*, 349
Myton, Fred, 29

Nadel, Arthur H., 84, 149, 335
Naish, J. Carrol, 63, 71, 202, 318
Nakashima, Marsha, 360
Naked Alibi, 199, *199*
Naked City, The (film), 199-200, *200*, 350
Naked Jungle, The, 146
Naked Kiss, The, 200-01, *200*
Naked Spur, The, 201, *201*
Napier, Alan, 77, 125, 153, 190, 281
Narcejac, Thomas, 317
Narciso, Grazia, 35
Narrow Margin, The (1952), 201-02, *202*, 430
Narrow Margin (1990), 358, 430
Nash, Johnny, 161
Nash, Richard, 215
Nashel, Peter, 378
Nathan, Vivian, 412
Navarro, Guillermo, 405
Navarro, Ramon, 47
Nayar, Deepak, 418

Nayfack, Nicholas, 55, 98, 213, 253
Neal, Patricia, 57, 91
Neal, Tom, 97, *97*
Nealis, Edward G., 158
Neame, Christopher, 373
Nebel, Frederick, 58
Nebenzal, Seymour, 184, 332
Nedell, Bernard, 397
Needs, James, 295
Neff, Hildegarde, 208
Negulesco, Jean, 190, 213-14, 252
Neill, Roy William, 48
Nelson, Bany, 156, 189
Nelson, Charles, 40, 59, 117
Nelson, Gene, 76, *76*
Nelson, Judd, 430, *430*
Nelson, Lori, 143
Nelson, Willie, 456
Nemec, Joseph, 390
Nervig, Conrad A., 25, 56, 81, 98, 132, 267
Nervig, Sandy, 452
Neufeld, Sam, 29
Neumann, Alfred, 72
Neumann, Harry, 142, 226
New, Gary T., 435
New Jack City, 350, 430-31, *430*
New York Confidential, 202-203, *202*
Newberry, Bill, 293
Newcom, James E., 66, 120, 253
Newhouse, David, 440
Newhouse, Rafe, 440
Newfield, Sam, 29, 173
Newman, Alfred, 62, 81, 178, 208, 223, 299
Newman, Barry, 416
Newman, Emil, 80, 211, 242, 265, 339
Newman, Joseph M., 23, 261
Newman, Lionel, 162, 166, 285
Newman, Paul, 381, 394-95, 460
Newman, Thomas, (actor), 64
Newman, Thomas (composer), 447
Newman, Walter, 24
News Is Made at Night see *While the City Sleeps*
Newton, Robert, 171
Ney, Richard, 153
Neyman, Yuri, 373
Niagara, 203-04, *203*
Niblo, Fred, Jr., 54, 73

Niccol, Andrew, 388
Nicholls, David, 450
Nichols, Barbara, 36, 290
Nichols, Dudley, 244, 255
Nicholson, Emrich, 158, 270
Nicholson, Jack, 364, *365*, 368, *369*, 441-42, *442*, 461, *461*
Nickel Ride, The, 431
Nicol, Alex, 241, 270
Nigh, Jane, 332
Nigh, William, 147
Night and the City (1950), 17, 22, 170, 204-205, *204*, 431-32
Night and the City (1992), 431-32
Night Cry see *Where the Sidewalk Ends*
Night Cry (novel), 328
Night Editor, 205
Night Has a Thousand Eyes, 205-07, *206*, 328
Night Holds Terror, The, 206-07
Night Moves, 432
Night of the Hunter, 207, *207*
Night Runner, The, 19, 207-08
Night Shift (novel), 186
Night Watch, The (novel), 238
Night without Sleep, 208-09, *208*
Nightfall, 17, 209, *209*
Nightmare, 209-10, *210*
Nightmare Alley, 19, *19*, 210-11, *211*
Niles, Ken, 220
Niles, Wendell, 135
Nilsson, Anna Q., 288
Nims, Ernest, 88, 282
99 River Street, 211
Nitzsche, Jack, 366, 393, 399
Nixon, Allan, 227
"No Blade Too Sharp" (story), 78
No Down Payment, 229
No Escape see *Dark City*
"No Exit" (play), 59
Noble, Thom, 466
Nobody Lives Forever, 20, 213-14, *214*
Nocturne, 214-15, *215*
Nolan, Christopher, 404, 423
Nolan, Jeanette, 23, 40, 458
Nolan, Jonathan, 423
Nolan, Lloyd, 140, 174, 273, 285

Nolte, Nick, 367, 428, 450, 465
No Country for Old Men, 432-33, *432-33*
No Man of Her Own, 212-13, *212*
No Questions Asked, 213, *213*
No Way Out, 433-34
Noonan, Tom, 422
Noonan, Tommy, 144
Nora Prentiss, 215-16, *215*
Noriega, Eduardo, 129
Noriega, Joseph, 74, 195
Norman, C. P., 204
Norris, Dean, 415
Norris, Edward, 93
North, Alex, 300
North by Northwest, 216
North, Edmund H., 91, 149
North, Sheree, 367, 420, 438
North, Ted, 98
Norton, Edward, 386, *387*
None So Blind (novel), 338
Notorious, 216, *216*
Nova, Lou, 340
Novak, Jane, 110
Novak, Kim, 238, *238*, 317, *317*, 415
Novello, Jay, 76, 171, 271
Now It Can Be Told see *House on 92nd Street*
Nozaki, Albert, 29, 38
Nugent, Frank, 28
Number 23, The, 434, *434*
Numbers Racket, The see *Force of Evil*
Nunez, A. Robert, 132
Nunn, Bill, 415, 430, 457
Nussbaum, Mike, 400
Nuttgenn, Gilles, 378
Nyby, Christian, 45, 236, 274
Nykvist, Sven, 441
Nyman, Michael, 388

Oakie, Jack, 299
Oates, Warren, 354, 364, 454
Ober, Philip, 260
Oberon, Merle, 34, *34*, 90, *90*, 181, *181*
Oberst, Walter, 273
O'Brien, Edmond, 32, 35, 47-48, 84, *84*, 101, 135, 163, 261-62, 264-65, 308, 33
O'Brien, Pat, 74, 225
O'Brien, Richard, 373, *373*
Obzina, Martin, 48, 163, 184, 289

Oboler, Arch, 36
Ochoa, Jesus, 421
O'Connell, L. William, 93, 248
O'Connor, Carroll, 440, 465
O'Connor, Una, 153
O'Curran, Charles, 19
Odds Against Tomorrow, 217-18, *218*
O'Dea, Dennis, 203
O'Dea, John, 107
Odell, Cary (Carey), 50, 89, 158, 245, 257
Odets, Clifford, 40, 71, 92, 216, 290
Odlum, Jerome, 132
O'Donnell, Cathy, 96, 267-68, 296
O'Driscoll, Martha, 107
Off the Record see *Loophole*
Offsay, Jerry, 430
O'Flaherty, Dennis, 393
O'Halloran, Jack, 383, *383*
O'Hanlon, James, 260
O'Hara, Maureen, 107
Okamura, George, 76
Okazaki, Robert, 76
O'Keefe, Dennis, 23, 164, *164*, 244, 292, 339-40
Okey, Jack, 74, 92, 154, 201, 220, 240, 260, 275-76
Oldman, Gary, 429, 445, *446*, 454, 459-60
Olds, Charles, 90
Olin, Lena, 445-46, *446*
Olmos, Edward James, 360
Olsen, Moroni, 62, 118, 132, 181, 191, 213, 216, 232, 281
Olson, Nancy, 288, *288*, 314
Olvis, William, 407, 444

O'Moore, Patrick, 73, 308
O'Morrison, Kenny, 260
Once off Guard (novel), 336
Once to Often (novel), 50
On Dangerous Ground, 20, 218-29, *218*
O'Neal, Ryan, 380, *381*
One False Move see *Beware, My Lovely*
One False Move (1992), 435-37, *435-36*
One Man's Secret (novel), 232
One Man's Secret see *Possessed, The*
One Way Out see *Convicted*
One Way Street, 219
One Woman see *Chicago Deadline*
One Woman (novel), 68
O'Neil, Barbara, 28, 259, 330
O'Neill, Dick, 442
O'Neill, Henry, 73, 212, 245, 254, 258, *259*
On the Waterfront see *The Harder They Fall*
Opatoshu, David, 224, 299, 465
Operation Terror (novel), 106
Ophuls, Max, 65-66, 245-46
Oppenheimer, George, 311
Oppewall, Jeannine Claudia, 414
Opper, Barry, 452
Opper, Don (Keith), 452-43
O'Quinn, Terry, 360
Orbach, Ron, 419
Orbach, Jerry, 379
Orff, Carl, 354
Original Sin, 436-47, *436*
Orlandi, Felice, 126, 165, 380
Ornitz, Arthur J., 375

Ortiz, John, 424
Orzazewski, Kasia, 62
Osborne, Frances, 145
O'Shea, Michael, 302, 312
O'Steen, Sam, 368
Osterloh, Robert, 90, 156, 176, 251, 261, 274, 310, 333
Ostrow, Randy, 454
O'Sullivan, Maureen, 38, 321
Oswald, Gerd, 166, 257
Other Woman, The, 220
Otterson, Jack, 48, 163
Ottman, John, 464
Oursler, Fulton, 55
Ouspenakaya, Maria, 263-64
Out of the Dark, 220-21, *220-21*
Out of the Night see *Strange Illusion*
Out of the Past, 17-18, 164, *164*, 170, 323, 326, 351-52, 412, 467
Out of Time, 437, *437*
Outbreak see *Panic in the Streets*
Outfit, The, 438, *438*
Outside the Wall, 64
Overman, Jack, 57, 59, 292
Owen, Clive, 451, *452*
Owen, Garry, 88
Ox-Bow Incident, The, 221-22, *221-22*
Oyama, Aya, 76
Ozep (Otsep), Fedor (Fyodor), 331

Paar, Jack, 320
Pacino, Al, 395, *395*, 404, *404*, 447-48
Packer, Netta, 121
Pagano, Jo, 187, 307

Page, Jim, 447
Paget, Debra, 81, 139
Paige, Janis, 302
Paige, Mabel, 104, 135, 271
Paiva, Nestor, 109, 112, 266
Pakula, Alan J., 411-13
Palahniuk, Chuck, 386
Palance, (Walter) Jack, 40, *44*, 139, 143, 164, *164*, 188, 223, 258, 286-87
Pall, Gloria, 76
Pallette, Eugene, 289
Palmentola, Paul, 53, 173, 279
Palmer, R. Barton, 8, 66, 251, 356, 367, 381, 388, 403-06, 410-11, 430
Palmer, Byron, 188
Palmer, Lilli, 54
Palmieri, Vince, 416
Palminteri, Chazz, 428, 464
Paltrow, Gwyneth, 448
Panic in the Streets, 223-24, *223*
Pankin, Stuart, 383
Pankow, Bill, 358, 385
Pankow, John, 458, *458*
Pantoliano, Joe, 264, 423
Pappas, George, 383
Pappé, Stuart, 382
Paris, James, 8, 45-47, 119
Paris, Jerry, 102
"Parker" novels, 438
Parker, Eleanor, 61, *61*, 96, 465
Parker, Fess, 295
Parker, Jean, 53
Parker, Max, 259
Parks, Hildy, 206
Parks, Michael, 376
Parks, Van Dyke, 461
Parnell, Emory, 50

Parra, Gustavo Sanchez, 421
Parrish, Robert, 54, 65, 80, 101
Parsonnet, Marion, 117
Parsons, Harriet, 71
Parsons, Lindsley, 83, 107, 183
Partos, Frank, 141, 208, 283
Party Girl, 19, 224-25, *224*
Passage to Marseilles, 180
Pasternak, Joe, 224, 286
Pate, Jonas and Josh, 376
Pate, Michael, 162
Patric, Jason, 351, *351*, 446
Patrick, Dorothy, 112, 132, 261
Patrick, George, 227
Patrick, Jack, 113, 281
Patrick, Lee, 61, 69, 150, 186, 191, 304
Patterson, Robert, 59
Patterson, Shirley, 182
Patton, Will, 433, 445
Paul, Alexandra, 382
Paull, Lawrence (Larry) G., 360, 431
Paxinou, Katlna, 192
Paxton, Bill, 435, 451
Paxton, John, 74, 79, 195-96
Payback, 439
Payne, Allen, 430
Payne, John, 78, *79*, 129, 160, 211, 270
Paymer, David, 439
Payton, Barbara, 171, 194, 306-07
Pearce, Guy, 414, 423
Pearl, Linda, 415
Pearson, Beatrice, 112
Pearson, Robert, 444
Peck, Gregory, 64, 103, *103*, 275, *275*, 367
Peckinpah, Sam, 389-90, 433
Pedi, Tom, 77, 199
Peeples, David, 360
Pembroke, George, 53
Penn, Arthur, 432
Penn, Christopher, 352, 376, 428, 445, 459-60
Penn, Clifford, 107
Penn, Leo, 310
Penn, Sean, 352, *352*, 388, 454, *454*
Pentacle, The see *Conflict*
People Against O'Hara, The, 225
Pereira, Hal, 24, 96, 99, 129, 267, 307, 317, 465

Pereira, William, 23
Percy, Lee, 411, 452
Perfect Crime, The, 41
Perkins, Anthony, 442, *442*
Perkins, Millie, 352, 452-43
Perlich, Max, 415, 446
Perlman, Ron, 374
Perreau, Janine, 151, *184*
Perrine, Valerie, 364
Perry, Barbara, 200
Perry, Ben, 58
Perry, Sara, 85
Perry, Susan, 172
Persky, Lisa (Jane), 366
Pesci, Joe, 443, *443*
Persoff, Nehemiah, 126, *126*, 341
Persuader, The see *Hitch-Hiker, The*
Peters, Hans, 25, 55, 253
Peters, Jean, 203, 227, *227*, 317
Peters, Paul, 437
Petersen, William, 384, 422, *422*, 458, *458*
Peterson, Dorothy, 336
Peterson, Lenka, 226
Peterson, Robert, 32, 40, 106, 115, 141, 149, 172, 205, 254, 312
Petrie, Howard, 166
Petievich, Gerald, 458
Pevney, Joseph, 54, 214, 263, 285, 299
Pfister, Wally, 404, 423
Phantom Lady, 2, 225-26, *226*, 402, 413
Phenix City Story, The, 226-27, *226*
Phifer, Wende, 399
Philips, Arnold, 227
Phillips, Fenley, 434
Phillips, Jean, 27
Phillips, Julia, 456
Phillips, Mary, 178
Phillips, Michael, 456
Phillips, Robert, 408
Phillips, Wendell, 60
Phipps, William, 79, *79*, 180, 296, 333
Pierce, Bruce B., 251
Pierlot, Francie, 109
Picerni, Paul, 59, 102, 129, 147
Pichel, Irving, 239, 297-98
Pickens, Slim, 390
Pickman, Carolyn, 387
Pickup, 227

Pickup on South Street, 227-28, *227*

Picture of Dorian Gray, The

Pidgeon, Walter, 314, 465

Pidgeon, Rebecca, 396, 398

Pierson, Carl, 279

Pilcher, Lyndia Dean, 409

Pinchot, Bronson, 459

Pine, Phillip, 194

Pine, William H., 86, 109, 129, 190, 209, 297

Pingitore, Carl, 109, 439

Pitfall, 18, 228-29, *229*

Pitoniak, Ann, 356

Pitt, Brad, 386, 448, 459-60

Pittack, Robert, 280

Pivar, Ben, 63

Place in the Sun, A, 229-230, *229*

Planer, Franz F., 66-68, 77, 182, 211, 254, 261

Platt, Edward, 64, 139, 148, 293

Platt, Louise, 284

Play Misty for Me, 384, 439-40, *439*

Please Murder Me, 230-31, *230*

Plummer, Glenn, 457

Plummer, Mark, 350

Plunder Road, 231-32, *231*

Podesta, Patti, 423

Poe, James, 40, 254

Pogue, Charles Edward, 373

Pohlmann, Eric, 295

Point Blank, 440-41, *440*, 445

Point of No Return, 441, *441*

Poitras, Lucie, 331

Polanski, Roman, 368-70

Polglase, Van Nest, 78, 107, 117, 189, 270, 283, 290

Polito, Sol, 69, 181, 273-74

Pollak, Kevin, 464

Polonsky, Abraham, 54, 112-13, 217, 420

Poole, Roy, 106

Pope, Bill, 364

Pope, Thomas, 393

Popkin, Harry M., 84, 149, 258-59, 298

Popkin, Leo C., 84, 149

Poplin, Jack, 70, 194

Porfirio, Robert, 6, 23-24, 27-28, 29-30, 35-36, 50, 52-58, 61-62, 64-65, 67-69, 72-76, 78-79, 81-82, 85-86, 91-93, 95-96, 104, 107, 109,
113-14, 118-19, 121-22, 126-28, 132, 134-36, 141-42, 144-45, 147, 147-48, 154-55, 162-63, 179-80, 183-85, 189-90, 194-98, 202-203, 209-10, 213, 215-18, 220, 225-26, 228-29, 231-37, 244-49, 251-52, 256, 258-59, 261-63, 265-66, 271-75, 280, 283-87, 289-90, 297-302, 304-05, 307-09, 314-15, 318-19, 321, 328, 334-36, 339-40, 441-42

Port of New York, 232, *232*

Porter, Don(ald), 240, 261, 308

Porter, Jean, 80

Possessed, 232-33, *233*

Posteltwaite, Peter, 464

Postman Always Rings Twice, The (1946), 16, 233-34, *233-34*, 442

Postman Always Rings Twice, The (1981), 441-42, *442*

Powell, Dick, *16*, 74, 80, *158*, 195-96, *195*, 228-29, *228*, 276-77

Powell, Tim, 368

Power, Tyrone, *19*, 210, *211*, 244

Powers, Mala, 71

Powers, Richard, 34

Powers, Stefanie (Stephanie), 106, 465

Powers, Tom, 52, 68, 286, 297

Pozner Vladimir, 88

Prager, Stanley, 112

Praskins, Leonard, 57

Pratt, John, 331

Preminger, Otto, 28, 107-08, 177, 300, 328-31

Presnell, Robert, Sr., 121, 131, 258

Press, Jacques, 301

Pressburger, Arnold, 263

Pressman, Edward R., 398

Pressman, Kenneth, 380

Preston, J. A., 362

Preston, Robert, 51, *51*, 301

Pretender, The, 17, 234-35

Pretty Poison, 442-43, *443*

Previn, André, 55, 66, 139, 224, 256, 294, 394

Previn, Dory, 394

Price, Nancy, 453

Price, Richard, 411, 431, 447

Price, Vincent, 58, 133, 176, 177-78, 181, 193, 265-66, 329

Prieto, Rodrigo, 436

Primus, Barry, 431

Prince, William, 92

Pringle, Joan, 436

Pritchard, Anne, 385

Private Hell 36, 235, *235*, 420

Probyn, Brian, 354

Proskey, Robert, 456

Prouty, Jed, 122

Proval, David, 445

Prowl Car see *Between Midnight and Dawn*

Prowler, The, 235-36, *236*

Proyas, Alex, 373-74

Pryor, Richard, 418

Public Enemy, The, 397

Public Eye, The, 443, *443*

Pugh, Sharief, 403

Puglia, Frank, 59

Pullman, Bill, 415, 418, *418*

Pulp Fiction, 405

Pursued, 18, 236-37, *237*

Pushover, 238-39, *238*

Pycha, Jerome, Jr., 105, 196

Pyke, Charles F., 98, 302

Pyle, Denver, 230

Quaid, David, 442

Quaid, Dennis, 373

Qualen, John, 47, 90, *90*, 135, 145, 220, 339

Quarry, Robert, 166

Quayle, Anthony, 341

Quick, Charles, 331

Quicksand, 239, *239*

Quigley, Juanita, 331

Quigley, Rita, 331

Quine, Richard, 72, 102, 238

Quinn, Aidan, 361

Quinn, Anthony, 69, 182, 221

Quinn, Declan, 409

Quinnell, A.J., 420

Raab, Leonid, 112, 127

Rachmil, Lewis J., 141

Racket, The, 240-41, *240*, 467

Rackin, Martin, 93, 104, 179

Radons, Hans, 197

Rafelson, Bob, 360, 441

Rafelson, Toby, 364

Rafferty (novel), 238

Rafferty, Thomas, 45

Raft, George, 154-55, *155*, 179-80, 214-15, *215*, 247, 253, *253*, 332, 431

Rage in Harlem, 444

Ragged Edge, The see *Beware, My Lovely*

Raging Tide, The, 241

Railroaded, 20, 241-42, *241*

Raimi, Sam, 451

Raine, Norman Reilly, 184

Raines, Ella, 59, *59*, 149, 225-26, *226*, 278, 289

Rainey, Ford, 333

Rains, Claude, 216, *216*, 315, 321

Raising Arizona, 433

Raksin, David, 39, 107-08, 112, 176-77, 287, 330

Ralston, Vera, 137

Rambeau, Marjorie, 23

Ramos, Rudy, 380

Rampling, Charlotte, 373, 376, 383

Ramrod, 242, *242*

Rancho Notorious, 242-44, *243*

Randall, Meg, 23, 77, 335

Randolph, Donald, 208
Randolph, Jane, 241, 292
Randolph, John, 442
Ransford, Maurice, 125, 178, 203, 223, 252, 273, 300
Ransohoff, Martin, 405
Rapf, Harry, 256
Raphaelson, Samson, 290
Rapaport, Michael, 411, 459
Rascoe, Judith, 465
Rascoe, Stephanie
Rasmussen, Rie, 385
Ratoff, Gregory, 193
Raw Deal, 164, *164*, 244, *244*
Rawhide, 244-45
Rawlings, Richard, 408
Ray, Aldo, 209
Ray, Billy W., 374
Ray, Nicholas, 149-50, 156-58, 172, 185, 218-29, 224, 240, 296-97
Ray, Ola, 385
Raymond, Gene, 180, 231
Raymond, Paula, 71, 98
Raymond, Robin, 36, 119
Raynor, William, 335
Read, James, 419
Rebhorn, James, 388
Rebel Without a Cause, 172, 224

Reckless, 385
Reckless Moment, The, 245-46, *245*
Red Dragon (novel), 422
Red House, The, 246-47, *246*
Red Light, 247
Red Menace, The, 147
Redgrave, Michael, 192, 259
Red Rock West, 444-45
Redfield, William, 375
Redlin, Robert, 351
Redman, Anthony, 353, 385, 409
Reed, Alan, 94, 145, 233, 303
Reed, Dolores, 134
Reed, Donna, 68, 254
Reed, Marshall, 179
Reed, Philip, 54, 190
Reed, Tom, 193
Reed, Walter, 129
Reese, John, 367
Reese, Tom, 425
Reeves, George, 52, 242
Reeves, Theodore, 146
Regeneration, The, 41
Reid, Carl Benton, 73, 149, 162
Reid, Dorothy, 149
Reid, Elliott, 317
Reign of Terror, 247-48, *248*, 349, *349*
Reilly, Hugh, 270
Reilly, John C., 454
Reilly, Thomas, 32, 76, 148, 295, 316
Reinhardt, Betty, 177
Reinhardt, John, 121, 131
Reinhardt, Wolfgang, 65
Reis, Irving, 74
Reisch, Walter, 116, 203
Reisz, Karel, 465-66
Remar, James, 361
"Remember Me" (poem), 168
Remember That Face see *Mob, The*
Remick, Lee, 106
Remisoff, Nicolai, 120, 230, 281
Remisoff, Nicholas, 44
Rencher, Burton, 457
Rennahan, Ray, 103
Rennie, Michael, 91, 300
Renoir, Jean, 142, 338-39
Repeat Performance, 248-49
Repp, Stafford, 231
Reservoir Dogs, 405, 445, *445*
Reshovsky, Marc, 444
Resnais, Alain, 440

Reticker, Hugh, 213, 302
Rettig, Tommy, 286
Return of the Whistler, 249
Reagan, Ronald, 408
Revell, Graeme, 419, 437, 451
Revere, Anne, 54, 107, 229, 259
Reville, Alma, 262, 290
Reynolds, Burt, 400, *401*, 449
Reynolds, Gene, 211
Reynolds, Harry, 57, 107, 125
Reynolds, Marjorie, 133
Reynolds, Quentin, 62
Reynolds, William, 91, 285
Rhames, Ving, 398, 411
Rhodes, Grandon, 141, 249
Richards, Addison, 36
Richards, Ann, 273
Richards, Cordelia, 436
Richards, Dick, 383
Richards, Frederick, 190, 308, 315
Richards, Robert L., 25, 158
Richards, Sylvia, 232, 242, 259
Richards, Thomas, 186
Richardson, Ian, 373
Richardson, Tony, 364
Richmond, Ted, 50, 205, 209, 263, 271
Ride the Pink Horse, 16, 19, 21-22, *22*, 249-51, *250*
Ridgely (Ridgley), John, 45, 55, 85, 104, *104*, 132, 186, 215, 232
Ridges, Stanley, 110, 232, 289
Riedel, Richard, 153
Riehle, Richard, 443
Riesner, Charles F., 241
Riesner, Dean, 367, 439
Rifkin, Ron, 414
Rigaud, George, 146
Riggins, Kathy
Riley, Elaine, 38
Rinaldo, Tito, 249, 294
Rinzler, Lisa, 391
Rios, Lalo, 305
Riot in Cell Block 11, 251, *251*
Ripley, Arthur, 67-68, 318-19
Risdon, Elisabeth, 132, 260, 297
Riskin, Robert, 281
Ritch, Steven, 70, 231
Ritter, Thelma, 228
Rivkin, Allen, 23, 92, 286, 294
Rizzo, Michael, 429

Road House, 252-53, *253*
Roadblock, 251-52, *252*
Robards, Jason, Sr., 93
Robbins, Gale, 35
Rober, Richard, 32, 110, 232, 337
Roberts, Allene, 172, *172*, 246
Roberts, Arthur, 151
Roberts, Ben, 32, 333
Roberts, Bob, 112, 127
Roberts, Bobby, 375
Roberts, Clete, 226
Roberts, Davis, 110
Roberts, Julia, 453, *453*
Roberts, Marguerite, 58, 311
Roberts, Mead, 408
Roberts, Ralph, 165
Roberts, Randy, 393
Roberts, Roy, 57, 104, *105*, 112, 127, 210, 245, 258
Roberts, Tracey, 194
Roberts, William, 174
Robertson, Cliff, 312, *313*
Robertson, Willard, 221
Robinson, Andrew (Andy), 367
Robinson, Ann, 119
Robinson, Betty, 200
Robinson, Casey, 329
Robinson, Dewey
Robinson, Edward G., 99-101, *100*, 139, *140*, 147, 160-161, 205, *206*, 210, 246, 255, 282, *283*, 336-37, *337*
Robinson, Frances, 32
Robinson, George, 50, 207
Robson, Mark, 66-67, 104, 126, 159
Rocco, Alex, 387
Rocco, Mark, 429
Rock, Chris, 430-31
Rock, Kerry, 444
Rockwell, Sam, 396, *396*
Roderick, Robert William
Rodgers, Gaby, *21*, 167
Rodgers, Gene, 266
Rodman, Howard, 367
Rodney, John, 236
Rodriguez, Elizabeth, 424
Rodriguez, Robert, 451-52
Roe, Guy, 241, 306-07, 331
Roelfs, Jan, 388
Roemheld, Heinz, 174, 179
Rogell, Sid, 54
Rogers, Charles Buddy, 269
Rogers, Jean, 32
Rogers, Mimi, 407

Rogers, Stan, 156
Rogue Cop, 253, *253*
Roizman, Owen, 458
Roland, Rita, 454
Rolf, Tom, 359, 393, 395, 456
Rolfe, E.A., 254
Rolfe, Sam, 201
Roman, Lawrence, 166, 199
Roman, Ruth, 37, 66, 284, 304, *304,*
Rome, Tina, 312
Romeo is Bleeding, 445-46, *446*
Romijn(-Stamos), Rebecca, 385-86, *386*
Ronald, James, 288
Rooker, Michael, 376, 447
Rooney, Mickey, 15, 102-03, 239, 286, 377
Roos, Fred, 370, 393
Root, Stephen, 432
Rosa Moline see *Beyond the Forest*
Rosay, Francoise, 300
Rose, David, 312
Rose, Jackson J., 95, 109
Rose, Sherman A., 242
Roseman, Ben, 109
Rosen, Charles, 49, 456
Rosen, Milton, 310
Rosenberg, Aaron, 158, 241
Rosenberg, Alan, 402
Rosenberg, Frank P., 148, 328, 420
Rosenberg, Scott, 457
Rosenberg, Stuart, 381
Rosenbloom, Maxie, 33
Rosenbloom, David, 356
Rosenthal, Jane, 431
Rosenthal, Laurence, 465
Rosenwald, Francis, 112
Ross, Anthony, 35, 170, 218, 253, 334
Ross, Arthur A., 232
Ross, Chelchi, 451
Ross, Ellen, 174
Ross, Sam, 127
Rossen, Robert, 54, 112-13, 158, 281, 310
Rossetti, Christina, 168
Rossi, Leo, 360
Rosson, Harold, 30, 103, 156
Rosten, Leo, 87, 269, 321
Roth, Eric, 381, 431
Roth, Matt, 361
Roth, Richard, 422
Roth, Steve, 382
Roth, Tim, 376, 445

Rotter, Fritz, 279
Rourke, Mickey, 362, 406, *406*, 421, 451-52
Rouse, Russell, 84, 139, 202, 298, 333-34, 373
Roven, Charles, 406
Rowe, Guy, 30, 34
Rowland, Roy, 253, 256, 335-36
Royle, Selena, 85, 127, 193-94
Rózsa, Miklós, 30, 58-59, 77, 90, 99, 101, 163, 171, 199, 246-47, 259, 275, 281
Ruban, Al, 408
Rubell, Paul, 370, 424
Ruben, Joseph, 453
Rubes, Jan, 466, *466*
Rubin, Jack, 310
Rubin, Jennifer, 379, *379*
Rubin, Mann, 465
Rubin, Stanley, 93, 185, 201
Rubinek, Saul, 459
Rubini, Michel, 422
Ruby Virgin, The see *Hell's Island*
Rudd, Michael, 444
Ruddy, Albert S., 402
Rudin, Scott, 432, 460
Rudley, Herbert, 93, 135
Rudolf, Gene, 406
Ruffalo, Mark, 370, 403, *403*, 468
Ruggiero, Anthony, 353
Ruggiero, Gene, 38, 55, 174, 225
Ruggles, Charles, 242
Rum Punch (novel), 405
Ruman, Sig, 56
Run for Cover, 172
Run the Man Down see *The Split*
Rush, 350, 446
Ruskin, Harry, 233
Russell, Charles, 64, 150
Russell, Connie, 210
Russell, Gail, 61-62, 193, *193*, 205, 293
Russell, Jane, 133, 176-77, 185
Russell, John, 137, 311
Russell, John L., Jr., 71, 128, 185, 193
Russell, Lewis L., 171
Russell, Robin, 407
Russell, Theresa, 360, *360*, 402-03, *403*

Rogue Cop

Russo, Richard, 460
Rust, Richard, 312
Rutherford, Ann, 309
Ruttenberg, Joseph, 58, 66, 116, 267
Ruysdael, Basil, 110, 114, 219, 254
Ryan, Edmond, 57, 267
Ryan, Fran, 455
Ryan, Irene, 338, 352
Ryan, John P., 364, 366, 441
Ryan, Kathleen, 307
Ryan, Meg, 373, 403-04, *403*
Ryan, Mitchell, 387
Ryan, Robert, 25-26, 34-35, *34*, 65, 71-72, 79, 138, 201, 217-19, *218*, 240, 260-71, *261*, 337-39, 438
Ryan, Sheila, 241, *241*
Ryan, Ted, 160
Ryan, Tim, 97, 112
Rydell, Mark, 416, *417*
Ryder, Alfred, 292

Sabaroff, Robert, 454
Sackheim, William, 188
Sackin, Louis H., 64, 241, 248
Sackler, William, 165
Sadler, William, 399, 446
Sahl, Mort, 155
Said, Fouad, 397
St. Amand, Joseph, 298, 333
St. Jacques, Raymond, 420
St. John, Howard, 44, *44*, 144, 261, 266, 284, 310, 409-10
St John, Nicholas, 385, 427
Sakamoto, Ryuichi, 385
Sale, Richard, 287-88, 302
Salerno, Charles, Jr., 36

Salfas, Stan, 463
Salinger, Conrad, 314
Salinger, Diane, 426
Salkow, Kae, 297
Salt, Waldo, 49-50, 184-85
Salter, Hans J., 68, 162, 225, 245, 255, 278
Salton Sea, The, 447, *447*
Samuels, Lesser, 24, 182
Sande, Walter, 50, 52, 214, 240, 304, 338
Sanders, George, 125, 181, 278, 281, *282*, 329, 335, 465
Sanders, Hugh, 85
Sanders, Lee, 8, 281
Sanders, Steven M., 9, 151-53, 367-68, 424-25, 442-43
Sanderson, Ruth, 23
Sanderson, William, 360
Sanford, Erskine, 74, 174, 232
Sanford, Isabel, 397
Sanford, Ralph, 297
Santos, Joe, 385, 387
Santucci, John, 456
Sarafian, Richard, 364
Sarandon, Susan, 460
Sarelle, Leilani, 355
Sargent, Anne, 199
Sargent, Dick, 393
Sarsgaard, Peter, 447
Sartre, Jean-Paul, 59
Satan Met a Lady, 186
Satie, Erik, 354
Saul, Oscar, 27, 89, 252, 336
Savage, Ann, 29, 97, *97*
Savalas, Telly, 64
Savides, Harris, 388, 468
Saville, Victor, 145, 167, 182
Savitt, Jill, 368

Sawtell, Paul, 50, 54, 56, 63, 72, 93, 98, 112, 160, 244, 251, 274, 292, 302
Sawyer, Joe, 92, 101, 117, 166
Saxon, Edward, 450
Scala, Gia, 115
Scalia, Jack, 385
Scandal Sheet, 19, 254, *254*
Scar, The see Hollow Triumph
Scarf, The, 254-55
Scarface, 329, 431
Scarlet Pen, The see Thirteenth Letter, The
Scarlet Street, 20, 255-56, *255*
Scene of the Crime, 256, *256*
Schaefer, Chester, 333
Schaefer, Hal, 425
Schaeffer, Chester W., 298
Schafer, Natalie, 65, 259
Schallert, William, 251, 264, 367
Scharf, Walter, 23, 303
Schary, Dore, 334
Scheider, Roy, 411, 445
Schenck, Aubrey, 232, 248, 264-65, 292
Schermer, Jules, 227, 238
Schickel, Richard, 6, 55, 125-26, 444-45
Schiff, Richard, 443
Schifrin, Lalo, 367
Schiller, Joel, 430
Schillee, Norbert, 299
Schilling, Gus, 174, 218
Schliessler, Tobias, 407
Schlom, Herbert, 98
Schlom, Herman, 30, 56, 72, 112
Schmidt, Arthur 24, 52, 146, 284, 288

Schnee, Charles, 23, 139, 146, 256, 296
Schneider, Harold, 360, 461
Schnell, Curtis, 372
Schoenfeld, Bernard C., 61, 87, 185, 225
Schoonmaker, Thelma, 367
Schrader, Paul, 393-94, 456
Schrager, Rudy, 109, 121, 131, 269
Schreiber, Richard, 461
Schreyer, John F., 264, 287
Schrock, Raymond L., 50
Schroder, Barbet, 411
Schufftan, Eugen, 53, 279, 281
Schumacher, Joel, 43
Schumann, Walter, 207
Schunzel, Reinhold, 34, 216
Schuster, Harold, 183
Schwarzwald, Milton, 158, 311
Sciorra, Annabella, 445
Scognamillo, Gabriel, 25, 198, 268
Scorsese, Martin, 354, 367, 391, 456
Scott, Adrian, 74, 79, 92
Scott, Evelyn, 333
Scott, Geoffrey, 426
Scott, George C., 393
Scott, Jeanette, 451
Scott, Justin, 402
Scott, Kay, 109
Scott, Lizabeth, 87, 92, 146, 228, *228*, 240, *240*, 281, 304-05
Scott, Martha, 94
Scott, Morton, 331
Scott, Nathan, 147
Scott, Ridley, 359-61
Scott, Robert, 117
Scott, Tony, 420, 422, 459-60
Scott, Walter M.
Scott, Zachary, 85, 122, 190-91, *191*, 313
Scourby Alexander, 27, 40
Screaming Mimi, 257, *257*
Sea of Love, 447-48, *448*
Seager, Chris, 421
Seale, John, 466
Sears, Eric A., 436
Second Chance, 258
Second Woman, The, 258-59, *259*
Secor, Kyle, 379
Secret, The see The Possessed
Secret Beyond the Door, The, 259-60, *259*
Secret Fury, The, 260, *260*

Sedgwick, Kyra, 429
Seeley, Clinton, 277
Seid, Art, 112
Seiter, William, 185
Seitz, Hillary, 404
Seitz, John F., 29, 38, 61, 68, 99, 150-51, 205, 253, 288, 301
Seitz, Tani, 145
Sekely, Steve, 135
Sekula, Andrzej, 445
Selander, Lesley, 49
Selby, Sarah, 37
Seltzer, Frank N., 261
Selznick, David O., 103, 275
Semler, Dean, 402
Semple, Lorenzo, Jr., 381, 442
Seros, Alexandra, 441
Sessions, Almira, 109
Set-Up, The, 19, 260-61, *261*
Seven, 448-49, *449*
711 Ocean Drive, 261-62, *261*
711-Officer Needs Help (novel), 465
Seventh, The (novel), 454
Severn, Raymond, 289
Sevigny, Chloe, 468, *468*
Sewell, Rufus, 373
Seymour, Dan, 141, 160, 242, 258
Shadow of a Doubt, 262-63, *263*, 385
Shagan, Steve, 400
Shaine, Rick, 361
Shakedown, 263
Shalhoub, Tony, 388
Shamberg, Michael, 389
Shamroy, Leon, 178
Shane, Maxwell, 109, 119, 129, 209-10
Shane, Robert, 194, 213
Shanghai Gesture, The, 263-64, *264*
Shannon, Harry, 98, 254, 321, 335
Shapiro, Melvin, 456
Shapiro, Theodore, 396
Sharkey, Ray, 465-66
Sharky's Machine, 449
Sharp, Alan, 432
Sharp, Henry, 121, 131
Sharpe, Karen, 279
Shaughnessy, Mickey, 60
Shaw, Anabel, 122, 131, 265
Shaw, Fiona, 358
Shaw, Frank, 68
Shaw, Jonathan, T., 407
Shaw, Sam, 408

Shaw, Victoria, 76
Shawn, Wallace, 356
Shaye, Robert, 361
Shayne, Konstantin, 282
Shayne, Robert, 32, 302, 335
Shayne, Sara, 25
Shayne, Tamara, 299
She Let Him Continue (novel), 442
Shearer, Douglas, 193
Shearing, Joseph, 272
Sheen, Martin, 354
Sheldon, Dean, 49
Sheldon, Sidney, 213
Shenar, Paul, 356
Shepard, Sam, 450-51
Shepherd, Cybill, 456, *456*
Sherdeman, Ted, 254, 295
Sheridan, Ann, 69, 215-16, *215*, 313, 339-40
Sheridan, Margaret, 145
Sherlock, Charles, 311
Sherman, Editta, 427
Sherman, George, 241, 270
Sherman, Harry, 242
Sherman, Robert (actor), 40
Sherman, Robert M., (producer), 432
Sherman, Roger, Jr.
Sherman, Vincent, 27, 32, 84, 115, 215, 313
Shermer, Jules, 113, 314
Sherry, Edna, 286
Shield for Murder, 264-65
Shields, Arthur, 225, 247, 316, 340
Shifman, Milton, 420
Shigeta, James, 76, *76*
Shimono, Sab, 455
Ship, Trudy, 400
Shire, David, 357, 370-71, 383, 468
Shirley, Anne, 195, *195*
Shock, 265-66
Shockproof, 266, *266*
Shoemaker, Ann, 73, 249
Shoot the Piano Player, 286
Shoot To Kill, 266-67, *267*
Shore, Howard, 388, 410, 448, 450
Short, Luke, 51, 242
Shortcut to Hell, 267
Showaltec, Max, 199
Shrader, George, 176
Shrieve, Michael, 356
Shue, Elisabeth, 463
Shumate, Harold, 51
Sickner, William, 83, 183

Side Street, 19, 267-68, *267*

Sidney, Sylvia, *42-3*, 43, 393

Siegel, David, 378, 455

Siegel, Don, 47, 151-53, 179, 235, 251, 316, 367-68, 408, 420, 439-40

Siegel, Sol C., 27, 81, 139, 223, 284

Siegler, Allen, 150

Sigel, Newton Thomas, 464

Sighvatsson, Sigurjon (Joni), 407, 444

Signorelli, Tom, 456, *457*

Sikking, James, 430, 440

Silence of the Lambs, The, *348*, 450, *450*

Silliphant, Sterling, 179, 209

Silva, Henry, 155, 449

Silver, Alain, 6, 23-24, 25-26, 28-29, 33-34, 37-38, 40-47, 49-50, 52, 54, 77-78, 87-88, 99-101, 104-105, 112-13, 115-16, 122-24, 129, 133-35, 138-41, 145-46, 149-50, 156-58, 160, 167-70, 198, 201, 203-05, 207-09, 213-15, 231-32, 235-36, 245-46, 249-51, 253, 256, 263-64, 267-68, 275, 277-78, 293, 295-96, 299-300, 304, 310, 312-13, 317-18, 321-328, 335-37, 340-41, 351, 357-58, 362-64, 370-72, 374-75, 379-81, 383-84, 389-92, 399-401, 406, 415-16, 419-20, 431-34, 438-39, 445, 454-55, 467-78

Silver Heels, Jay, 160

Silvera, Frank, 161, 165

Simcoe, ben, 194

Simenon, Georges, 58

Simmons, Jean, 28, *28*

Simmons, Richard, 174

Simmons, Richard Alan, 264

Simon, John Alan, 390

Simon, Robert F., 253, 328

Simon, Simone, 141

Simoun, Henri, 420

Simpatico, 450-51

Simple Plan, A, 451

Simpson, Claire, 454

Simpson, Robert, 145, 244

Sims, Jackson, 409

Sin City, 350, *350*, 451-52, *451-52*

Singapore, 268-69

Sinatra, Frank, 287

Sinclair, Ronald, 182

Singer, Bryan, 464

Singh, Paul, 61

Sinkovics, Geza, 379

Sinkys, Albert, 427

Siodmak, Curt, 34

Siodmak, Robert, 68-69, 72, 77-78, 81-82, 88, 110, 163, 165, 225-26, 275, 278, 288

Sirk, Douglas, 266, 269

Sisk, Robert, 294

Sistrom, Joseph, 99

Sizemore, Tom, 379, 395, 459-60

Skala, Lilia, 400

Skiles, Marlin, 92, 113

Skinner, Frank, 48, 136, 219, 241, 249, 270, 289, 293, 336

Skirball, Jack H., 260, 262

Skjoldbjaerg, Erik, 404

Skoble, Aeon, 6, 375-76, 430-31, 448-49, 451

Skye, Ione, 391, 368

Slamdance, 452-53

Slaney, Ivor, 295

Slate, Henry, 179, 228

Slater, Christian, 429, *429*, 459-60

Sleep, My Love, 269, *269*

Sleeping City, The, 270, *270*

Sleeping with the Enemy, 453-54, *453*

Slezak, Walter, 56, 74, 107

Slightly Scarlet, 270

Sloan, Lisa, 382

Sloane, Everett, 40, 104-05, 159, 174

Small, Buddy, 160, 211

Small, Edward, 160, 211, 244, 254

Small, Michael, 360, 380, 411, 432, 441

"Smallpox: The Killer that Stalked New York" (article), 162

"Smashing the Bookie Gang Marauders" (story), 256

Smedley-Ashton, Brian, 380

Smetana, Bedrich, 318

Smight, Jack, 394-95

Smiler with a Gun see *His Kind of Woman*

Smith, Alexis, 73, *73*, 276-77, 308

Smith, Art, 54, 59, 65, 149, 162, 190, 239, 249, 292, 307

Smith, Charles Martin, 377, 399

Smith, Constance, 188, 300

Smith, Dean, 90

Smith, Frank T., 155

Smith, Frederick Y., 145, 176

Smith, Hal, 205

Smith, Howard, (actor), 62, 170, 285

Smith, Howard A., (editor), 109, 190

Smith, Howard E., (editor), 351-52

Smith, Jack Martin, 442

Smith, Jada Pinkett, 370

Smith, Jamie, 165

Smith, Kent, 85, 215, 224, 275, 302

Smith, Lewis, 380

Smith, M. Scott, 458

Smith, Nicholas C., 419

Smith, Queenie, 163, 181, 214, 269, 290

Smith, Robert, (Writer), 146, 211, 239, 258, 286

Smith, Rusty, 380

Smith, Scott B., 451

Smith, Shawn, 182

Smith, Ted, 72, 130, 190, 236, 316

Smith, Truman, 226

Snell, David, 174

Sniper, The, 271, *271*

Snipes, Wesley, 409, 430

Snow, Karen, 384

Snyder, William, 36, 258

So Dark the Night, 271-72

So *Evil My Love*, 272, *272*

Sobocinski, Piotr, 460

Sobell, Paul, 215

Soderberg, Robert W., 245

Soderbergh, Steven, 416, 463

Sokol, Yuri, 380

Sokoloff, Vladimir, 185, 255, 329

Solo, Robert, 402

Solt, Andrew; 149, 330

Some Must Watch (novel), 275

Somewhere in the Night, 16, 20, 273, *273*, 388

Sommer, Elke, 425

Sommer, Josef, 466

Sondergaard, Gale, 68

Sonnenfeld, Barry, 362

Sorel, Guy, 300

Sorel, Sonia, 53

Sorry, Wrong Number, 164, 273-74, *274*

Sorvino, Paul, 402

Sothern, Ann, 52, *52*

Sound of Fury, The see *Try and Get Me*

Southon, Mike, 410

Southside 1-1000, 274-75

Southwell, Tom, 447

Spacek, Sissy, 354

Spacey, Kevin, 414, 464, *464*

Spader, James, 353

Spain, Fay, 33

Spanish Prisoner, The, 396

Spano, Anthony, 371

Sparkuhl, Theodore, 27, 118, 284

Sparks, Robert, 133, 320

Speedy Shannon see *The Crooked Road*

Spellbound, 275, *275*, 434

Spelling, Aaron, 317

Spencer, Dorothy, 317

JOHN HODIAK
NANCY GUILD

SOMEWHERE IN THE NIGHT

LLOYD NOLAN RICHARD CONTE

JOSEPHINE HUTCHINSON · FRITZ KORTNER · MARGO WOODE · SHELDON LEONARD · LOU NOVA

20th CENTURY-FOX Directed by JOSEPH L. MANKIEWICZ Produced by ANDERSON LAWLER

Spencer, Douglas, 119
Spencer, J. Russell, 210, 328
Spencer, John, 359, 460
Spencer, Ray, 74
Sperling, Milton, 104, 145, 236
Spiderman, 350
Spiegel, Sam, 235, 282
Spigelgass, Leonard, 23, 198, 272
Spillane, Mickey, 145, 167-68, 182-83, 402
Spinell, Joe, 383
Spinotti, Dante, 361, 376, 395, 414, 422
Spiral Staircase, The, 275-76, *276*
Split, The, 454
Split Second, 276-77
Stab in the Dark, A (novel), 382
Stack, Robert, 138
Staenberg, Zach, 364
Stahl, Nick, 451
Stahl, John M., 178
Stallone, Sylvester, 383
Stamp, Terence, 416
Stanton, Harry Dean, 383, 452
Stanton, Helene, 39
Stanwyck, Barbara, 71-72, 75-76, 99-101, *101*, 110-11, *111*, 153, 212-13, *212*, 273-74, *274*, 281, 308-09, *308*, 335
Stapleton, Maureen, 412
Stapleton, Oliver, 391
Star is Born, A, 293
"Star Sapphire" (story), 133
Stark, Richard see Westlake, Donald E.

State of Grace, 350, 454-55, *454*
Steele, Freddie, 48, 94
Steele, Robert (Bob), 45, *46*, 104
Steiger, Rod, 40, *44*, 126, *126*
Steiger, Ueli, 399
Stein, Herman, 199
Steinberg, Betty, 166
Steiner, Max, 32, 37, 45, 61, 69, 147-48, 160, 186, 191, 236, 313, 333
Steiner, William, 334
Steininger, Franz, 134
Steinkamp, Fredric, 351
Steinkamp, William, 351
Stell, Aaron, 271, 305
Stengler, Mack, 107, 147
Stensvold, Alan, 25, 230
Stephens, James, 390
Stephenson, Henry, 180
Sterling, Jan, 24-25, *25*, 29, 61, 198, 276-77, 314
Sterling, Robert, 156
Stern, Daniel, 373
Stern, Kandy, 426
Sternad, Rudolph, 66, 254, 271
Stevens, Andrew, 396
Stevens, Craig, 328
Stevens, Dana, 361
Stevens, George, 229
Stevens, Inger, 420
Stevens, Leith, 35, 47, 115, 119, 134, 212, 235
Stevens, Mark (actor), 35, 83, *83*, 87-88, 285-86, *285*, 303
Stevens, Mark (editor), 434
Stevens, Onslow, 202, 205, 295

Stevens, Robert, 205
Stevens, Sheila, 61
Stevens, Warren, 420
Stevenson, Houseley, 57
Stevenson, Phil, 165
Stevenson, Robert, 176, 320, 337
Stewart, Douglas, 134
Stewart, Elaine, 293
Stewart, James (actor), 62-63, 201, *201*, 317, *317*
Stewart, Martha, 73, 149
Stewart, Marianne, 303
Stewart, Paul, 66, 104, 156, 167, 179, 320, 334
Steyn, Jacques, 407
Stine, Harold, 19
Stirling, Linda, 234
Stitt, Kevin, 439
Stockwell, Dean, 458
Stoll, Georgie, 286
Stoller, Shirley, 412, 424
Stollery, David, 277, *277*
Stoloff, Ben, 309
Stoloff, Morris W., 27, 117, 271
Stone, Andrew, 206
Stone, Harold J., 115, 126, 139, 341
Stone, LeRoy, 29, 68
Stone, Lewis, 293
Stone, Milburn, 212, 225, 228, 251
Stone, Oliver, 382
Stone, Nancy Rae, 415
Stone, Robert, 465-66
Stone, Sharon, 355, *355*, 380, 450
Stone, Sidney, 204
Stone, Virginia, 206
Storey, June, 81, 281
Storm Fear, 277-78, *277*
Storm, Gale, 23, 35, 312
Storm in the City (novel), 307
Story of Tucker's People, The see *Force* of *Evil*
Stossel, Ludwig, 53
Stothart, Herbert, 311
Stout, Archie, 90
Stowe, Madeleine, 361, 368, 461
Strabel, Thelma, 311
Stradling, Harry, 28, 104, 156, 290, 294
Straithairn, David, 414
Strange Affair of Uncle Harry, The, 278, *278*
Strange Deception see *The Accused*

Strange Fascination, 279, *279*
Strange Illusion, 279-80
Strange Impersonation, 280
Strange Love of Martha Ivers, The, 281, *281*, 399
Strange Woman, The, 281-82, *282*
Stranger, The, 282-83, *283*
Stranger on the Third Floor, 283-84, *283*
Strangers on a Train, 284, *284*, 413
Strasberg, Lee, 273
Strauss, Theodore, 193
Street, David, 193
Street of Chance, 284-85
Street with No Name, The, 285-86, *285*
Street with No Name, The (novel), 138
Strenge, Walter, 134
Strick, Wesley, 368
Strickland, Gail, 381, 465
Strip, The, 286
Stromberg, Hunt, 35, 120, 281, 304
Strong, Arnold, 416
Strong, Leonard, 32, 128
Strong, Michael, 440
Strong, Johnny, 109
Stroud, Don, 420
Strudwick, Sheppard, 36, 68, 229, 245, 310
Struss, Karl, 159, 289
Struthers, Sally, 390
Stuart, William L., 328
Sturges, John, 154, 198, 225
Stutto, Darlene, 427
Suby, Michael, 467
Sudden Fear, 164, *164*, 286-87, *287*
Suddenly, 287-88, *287*
Sukman, Harry, 76, 226, 312
Sullivan, Barry, 66, 82, 113-14, 154, 183, 213, 289, 294, 314-15
Sullivan, Francis L., 129, 204
Sullivan, Frank, 78
Sullivan, James, 47, 71, 156, 194, 304
Sullivan, Sheila, 397
Sunset Boulevard, 288, *288*
Surtees, Bruce, 432, 438-39
Surtees, Robert, 25, 286
Suschitzky, Peter, 443
Suspect, The, 288-89, *289*
Suspense, 289-90, *289*

Suspense (working title) see
Fear
Suspicion, 290, *290*
Sutherland, Donald, 411-12,
413, 454
Sutherland, Kiefer, 373
Sutherland, Victor, 65
Sutton, John, 258
Suture, 455, *455*
Swan, Francis, 261
Swank, Hilary, 358, 404
Swanson, Gloria, 288, *288*
Sweeney, Alfred, 394
Sweeney, Mary, 418, 428
Sweet Smell of Success,
290-91, *291*
Swerling, Jo, 178
Swink, Ralph, 65
Swink, Robert, 94, 96, 98,
181, 201, 335
Swinton, Tilda, 378
Sylbert, Paul, 341, 381, 393,
446
Sylbert, Richard, 368, 428
Sylos, Frank Paul, 65, 86,
109, 114, 119, 142, 209,
211, 234, 247, 287, 289,
297, 320

T-Men, 17, 292-93, *292*, 349
Tabakin, Bernard, 340
Tabori, George, 143
Taber, Richard, 270
Takakura, Ken, 359
Talbot, Irvin, 129, 307, 314
Talbot, Lyle, 70, 280
Talbot, Nita, 302
Talk about a Stranger, 293
Tall Target, The, 202, 277
Tallas, Gregg, 332
Tallichet, Margaret, 283
Tally, Ted, 450
Talman, William, 30, 71, 135,
240, 337
Tamblyn, Amber, 357
Tamblyn, Rusty, 122
Tamehori, Lee, 428
Tamerlis(-Lund), Zoe, 353, 427
Tamiroff, Akim, 114, 192,
305, *305*
Tandon, Chris, 378
Tangerine Dream, 456
Tannura, Philip, 197, 205,
249, 279
Taps, Jonie, 102
Taradash, Daniel, 172, 242
Tarantino, Quentin, 405, 445,
451-52, 459-60

Tarantula, 293
Target, The see *Narrow
Margin, The*
Tarnished Angels, The, 293
Tatapoulos, Patrick, 373
Tattered Dress, The, 293-94,
293
Tattooed Stranger, The
Tavoularis, Alex, 409
Tavoularis, Dean, 370, 383,
393
Taxi Driver, 456, *456*
Tayback, Victor, 111
Taylor, Clarice, 439
Taylor, Don, 199, *200*
Taylor, Dub, 390
Taylor, Dwight, 72, 145, 317
Taylor, Elizabeth, 229
Taylor, Eric, 197
Taylor, Frank E., 198
Taylor, Gil(bert), 356
Taylor, Jack, 467
Taylor, Kent, 270
Taylor, Lawrence, 176
Taylor, Robert, 58, 98, 132,
156, *156*, 224, *224*, 253,
311
Taylor, Ronnie, 447
Taylor, Samuel, 189, 317
Taylor, Vaughn, 179
Taylor-Young, Leigh
Teal, Ray, 24, 59, 65, 94, 304,
308
"Tell Me About It Tomorrow"
(story), 290
Tennant, Victoria, 356
Tension, 294-95, *294*
Tent, Kevin, 391
Tepper, Bill, 366
Terror in the Night see
Night Holds Terror, The
Terror Street, 295
Terry, Philip, 56
Tetzel, Joan, 103
Tetzlaff, Ted, 114, 216, 310,
334
Thatcher, Heather, 116
Thatcher, Torin, 27
Thaxter, Phyllis, 25, 36, 51,
57, 212
Thayer, Tiffany, 68
Them!, 295-96, *295*
Theroux, Justin, 424, 427
They Died with Their Boots on,
130
They Drive by Night, 130
They Live by Night, 17, 172,
296-97, *296*, 355, 392

Taxi Driver

They Made Me a Killer, 297
They Shoot Horses, Don't They,
369
They Walk Alone see *Framed*
They Won't Believe Me,
297-98, *297*
They Won't Forget see *Try and
Get Me*
Thief, 456-57, *457*
Thief, The, 298-99, *298*
Thieves' Highway, 17, 19,
299-300, *299*
Thieves Like Us (novel), 296
Thieves' Market (novel), 299
Thieves' Market see *Thieves'
Highway*
Thigpen, Lynn, 402
Thimig, Helene, 180
Thin Knife, The see *Unknown
Man, The*
*Things To Do in Denver When
You're Dead*, 457
Third Man, The (radio seres),
192
13th Letter, The, 300-01, *300*
36 Hours see *Terror Street*
This Gun for Hire, 301-02,
301, 414
This is Dynamite see *Turning
Point, The*
This Side of the Law, 302
This Way Out (novel), 288
Thoeren, Robert, 235, 268
Thomajan, Guy, 57
Thomas, Leslie, 75, 162
Thomas, Ross, 393
Thomas, William C., 86, 109,
129, 190, 209, 297
Thompson, Dee J., 162, *162*
Thompson, J. Lee, 64
Thompson, Jack, 436

Thompson, Jim, 166, 351, 383,
389-91, 400, 409, 433
Thompson, Marshall, 98, 198
Thompson, Palmer, 111
Thompson, Peter, 101
Thompson, Tracey, 9, 305-06
Thompson, Walter, 112, 115,
228, 239, 258, 383
Thoms, Jerome, 76, 102, 105,
126, 162, 200, 238, 254,
271, 312
Thomsen, Robert, 314
Thorin, Donald, 351, 456-57
Thornton, Billy Bob, 435, *436*,
451
Thorpe, Richard, 314
Threat, The, 302-03, *302*
322 French Street see
Pushover
Thunderbolt, 41
Thurman, Uma, 388, *389*
Ticotin, Rachel, 421
Tierney, Gene, *14*, 177-78,
177-78, 204, *204*,
263-64, *264*, 328, *329*,
330-31, *330*
Tierney, Lawrence, 54, 56-57,
56, 98, 109-10, *110*, 263,
312, 445, *445*
Tierney, Maura, 404
Tiffin, Pamela, 394
Tightrope see *Captive City*
Tillman, Gregory, 467
Tilly, Jennifer, 364, 366, 390
Tilly, Meg, 461
Timetable, 303, *303*
Timms, Stanley, 427
Ting, Eugene, 179
Tiomkin, Dimitri, 28, 66, 84, 88,
103, 122, 143, 154, 181,
247, 262, 284, 320, 332

Tisch, Steve, 353
Tischler, Stanford, 47, 235
To Have and Have Not, 57
To Have and Have Not (novel), 57
To Live and Die in L.A., 458, *458*
Tobey, Kenneth, 28, 47, 164, 171
Tobias, George, 69, 190-91, 213, 244, 260, 274, 293
Tobin, Dan, 38, 311
Tobin, Norm, 456
Tobolowsky, Stephen, 423, 429
Toch, Ernst, 105
Todd, Ann, 272
Todd, Holbrook, 29, 173, 31
Todd, James, 306
Todd, Jennifer, 423
Todd, Suzanne, 423
Todd, Sherman, 34, 240, 296
Tolan, Lawrence, 104
Tolan, Kathleen, 375
Toles-Bey, John, 444
Tolkan, James, 387
Tolkin, Michael, 377-78
Toll, John, 450
Toluboff, Alexander
Tomack, Sid, 50, 112-13, 139
Tomasini, George, 64, 307, 317, 341
Tombes, Andrew, Jr., 98
Tombragel, Maurice, 249
Tomney, Ed, 391
Tomorrow Is Another Day, 304, *304*
Tone, Franchot, 90, 225-26
Too Late for Tears, 304-305, *305*

Toomey, Regis, 37, 45, 80, 121, 131, 147, 197, 225, 244, 275, 279
Torberg, Friedrich, 318
Toren, Marta, 219
Toriel, Caprice, 194
Torn Curtain, 433
Tors, Ivan, 119
Torvay, Jose, 56, 135
Tosar, Luis, 424
Toth, Ildiko, 379
Totter, Audrey, 36, 132, 174, 188, 233, 260, 294, 310, 315
Touch of Evil, 15, 170, 305-06, *305*
Tourneur, Jacques, 34, 209, 220-21, 351-52
Tover, Leo, 91-92, 146, 188, 260, 338
Tovoli, Luciano, 411
Towers, Constance, 200
Towne, Robert, 356, 368-70, 399, 461
Townes, Harry, 257
Townsend, Leo, 232, 274, 317
Tracey, Grant, 7, 36, 69-70, 111, 161-62, 394-95, 408
Tracy, Don, 77, 463
Tracy, Emerson, 235
Tracy, Lee, 131
Tracy, Spencer, 225
Trapped, 306-06, *306*
Travers, Henry, 130, 262
Travis, Merle, 111
Travis, Neil, 433
Travis, Richard, 32
Tree, Dorothy, 30
Trese, Adam, 463
Trevor, Claire, 56, *56*, 74, 154, 160-61, *161*, 195, *195*, 244, 284
Trial, The, 66
Triesault, Ivan, 216
Tripplehorn, Jeanne, 355
Tristan, Dorothy, 411
Trivas, Victor, 282, 328
Tronick, Michael, 459
Trosper, Guy, 98
Trotti, Lamar, 221
True Confessions, 350, 458-59, *459*
True Romance, 459-60
"True Story of Christopher Emmanuel Balestrero, The" (article), 341
Truffaut, Francois, 366, 436

Trumbo, Dalton, 122, 127, 235
Trumm, Leonard, 272
Try and Get Me, 17, 307, *307*
Tucci, Stanley, 411, 443
Tucker, Forrest, 137
Tucker, Jonathan, 378
Tucker, Larry, 49
Tucker's People see *Force of Evil*
Tucker's People (novel), 112
Tufts, Sonny, 78
Tulliver, Barbara, 396, 398
Tully, Montgomery, 295
Tully, Tom, 51, 99, 174, 308, 328, 367-68
Tunney, Robin, 467
Tuntke, William H., 303
Turman, Lawrence, 381, 390, 431
Turner, Kathleen, 362-63
Turner, Lana, *16*, 156, *156*, 233, *234*
Turney, Catherine, 186, 191, 212
Turning Point, The, 307-08, *308*
Turturro, John, 454, 458
Tuttle, Frank, 289, 301
Tuttle, Lurene, 203, 304
Tweddell, Frank, 310
Twelve Miles Out see *The Second Woman*
Twenty-Nine Clues see *He Walked by Nigh*
Twilight, 460-61, *460*
Twisted Road, The see *They Live by Night*
Two Jakes, The, 461-62, *461-62*
"Two Men in a Furnished Room" (story), 121
Two Mrs. Carrolls, The, 308-09, *308*
Two O'Clock Courage, 309, *309*
Tyler, Tom, 144
Tyler, Walter, 52, 229
Tyne, George, 297
Tyson, Nona, 399

Uhls, Jim, 386
Ullman, Frederick, Jr., 334
Ulmer, Edgar, 53, 97, 194-95, 279-80, 281-82
Unafraid, The see *Kiss the Blood off My Hands*
Uncle Harry see *Strange Affair of Uncle Harry, The*

Under the Gun, 310, *310*
Undercover Man, The, 310-11, *311*
"Undercover Man: He Trapped Capone" (article), 310
Undercurrent, 311, *311*
Underneath, The, 463, *463*
Undertow, 311-12
Underworld, 41, *41*
Underworld Story, The, 312
Underworld U.S.A., (film), 312-13, *313*
Unfaithful, The, 313-14, *313*
Unger, Deborah Kara, 388, 439, 447
Union Station, 314, *314*
United States Mail see *Appointment with Danger*
Unknown Man, The, 314-15
Unsuspected, The, 18, 22, 315, *315*
Urecal, Minerva, 241
Urioste, Frank J., 355
Ursini, James, 6, 23, 25-26, 47-48, 50-51, 63-64, 80-81, 83, 98-99, 103, 108-10, 111, 117-20, 132-33, 150, 173-74, 178-79, 181, 210-11, 221-22, 224-25, 235, 239, 242, 246-47, 254, 257, 260-61, 266, 268-69, 275, 279, 281-82, 306-07, 317, 321, 328, 355-56, 362-64, 364, 366, 373-74, 378-80, 389, 402-04, 408-09, 415-16, 418-19, 427-28, 436-47, 444-46, 451-53, 463
Usher, Robert, 67, 301
Usual Suspects, The, 464, *464*

Vacio, Natividad, 135
Vale, Martin, 308
Vale, Nina, 74, 197
Vale, Rita, 298
Valentine, Joseph, 232, 262, 269
Valentine, Paul, 139, *140*, 220
Valli, Alida, 320
Vallin, Rick, 279
Vallone, Raf, 356-57
Vampira, 33
Van Cleef, Lee, 39, 160
van de Sande, Theo, 437
Van Doren, Mamie, 33
Van Druten, John, 116
Van Dyk, James J., 270

Van Enger, Charles, 303
Van Enger, Richard L., 137, 156
Van Eyck, Peter, 192
van Pallandt, Nina, 416, *417*
Van Peebles, Mario, 430
Van Upp, Virginia, 27, 117
Van Zandt, Philip, 35, 38, 39, 93, 133, 294, 321, *323*
Vance, Steve, 9, 176-77
Vance, Vivian, 260
Vanderbilt, James, 468
Vangelis, 360
Varden, Evelyn, 207
Varno, Roland, 197
Vash, Karl, 184
Vasian, Leonid, 98, 132, 256, 286, 294
Veiller, Anthony, 32, 163, 282
Velie, Lester, 115
Venora, Diane, 395
Verdict, The, 316-17, *316*
Verevis, Constantine, 7, 351-52, 366, 370, 373, 433-34, 441
Verhoeven, Paul, 355
Vermilyea, Harold, 38, 68, 104, 190, 273
Vernon, Irene, 307
Vernon, John, 440
Vernon, Richard, 171
Verone, Elmo, 83
Vertigo, 317, *317*
VeSota, Bruno, 109-10, 182
Vickers, Martha, 45, 60, 186
Vickers, Yvette, 267
Vicki, 317-18, *317*
Victor, Charles, 109
Vidal, Gore, 388
Vidor, Charles, 104, 117
Vidor, King, 37-38, 103
Viescas, Manuel, 364
Villalobos, Reynaldo, 425
Vincent, Jeff, 444
Vincent, June, 48, 208
Vincent, Russ, 50
Vinson, Tripp, 434
Vint, Alan, 354
Viot, Jacques, 181
Virgo, Peter, 202
Virkler, Dennis, 449
Visnjic, Goran, 378
Vitarelli, Joseph, 415
Vogan, Emmett, 173
Vogel, Paul C., 132, 174, 176, 256, 425

Vogel, Virgil M., 136, 305, 310
Voice in the Wind, A, 318-19, *319*
Voight, Jon, 395
Voilmoller, Karl, 263
von Brandenstein, Patrizia, 376, 451, 454
von Harbou, Thea, 184
von Sternberg, Josef, 41, 103, 185, 263-64
von Stroheim, Erich, 119-20, *120*, 288
von Stroheim, Erich, Jr.
Von Sydow, Max, 410
Von Zell, Harry, 278, 328
Von Zerneck, Peter, 34
Voriscek, Richard
Voss, Kurt, 379
Vuolo, Tito, 104, 139, 189, 241
Vye, Murvyn, 228, 267

Wacshowski, Andy and Larry, 364, 366
Wade, Russell, 266
Wagers, Jans B., 8, 164, 365, 386-87, 428-29, 460-61
Wagner, Christian, 376, 421, 459
Wagner, Natasha Gregson, 418
Wagner, Robert, 166, *167*, 394
Wagner, Sidney, 233
Wagner, Thomas, 351
Wahlberg, Mark, 384-85
Waite, Liam, 450
Waite, Ric, 364
Walcott, Jersey Joe, 126
Wald, Jerry, 61, 84, 89, 160, 191, 232, 313
Wald, Marvin, 34, 89, 199, 310
Waldon, Edgar E., 227
Waldis, Otto, 34
Waldron, Charles, 44, 283
Walk a Crooked Mile, 141
Walk Softly Stranger, 320, *320*
Walken, Christopher, 352, 409-10, 421, 457, 459-60
Walker, Arnetia, 419
Walker, Andrew Kevin, 448
Walker, Bill, 40
Walker, Gertrude, 84, 241, 331
Walker, Helen, 39, 62, 149, *149*, 210
Walker, Joseph, 27, 89
Walker, Robert, 284, *284*
Wall, Angus, 468
Wall, Geraldine, 110

Wallace, Earl W., 466
Wallace, George, 444
Wallace, Irving, 276-77
Wallace, Jean, 39, *39*, 277-78, *277*
Wallace, Pamela, 466
Wallace, Richard, 108, 113
Wallach, Eli, 179, *179*, 431, 461
Waller, Eddy C., 207, 211
Wallis, Hal B., 23, 69, 87, 110, 146, 186, 272-74, 281
Wallis, J.H., 336
Walsh, J.T., 391, 400, 415, 430, 444
Walsh, Jack, 451
Walsh, Joseph, 380
Walsh, M. Emmet, 360, 362, 430, 460
Walsh, Raoul, 41, 104, 130, 187, 236, 333
Walsh, Thomas, 238, 314
Walter, Jessica, 439
Walters, Luana, 266
Walton, Douglas, 131, 195
Waltz into Darkness (novel), 436
Wanamaker, Sam, 465
Wang Chung, 458
Wang, Wayne, 452-43
Wanger, Walter, 151, 245, 251, 255, 259
Warchus, Matthew, 450
Ward, A.C., 230
Ward, Elizabeth, 6, 24-25, 45-47, 65-66, 84-85, 96-97, 110-11, 156, 174-76, 238-39, 269, 290-91, 311, 397-98, 416-18, 450-51
Ward, Fred, 423

Ward, Janet, 432
Ward, Rachel, 351-52, *351*, 449
Warde, Harlan, 189, 335
Warden, Jack, 189, 431, 457
Ware, Midge, 111
Warfield, David, 407
Warner, H.B., 132, 280, 288
Warner, Jack M., 189
Warner, Jerry, 107
Warner, Mark, 446
Warner, Pam, 377
Warner, Sandra, 440
Warning Shot, 465
Warren, Eda, 38, 133, 205, 321
Warren, Jennifer, 432
Warren, Katherine, 235
Warren, Lesley Ann, 371, 416
Warrick, Ruth, 120, 159
Warth, Theron, 51, 64, 216
Warwick, James, 89
Warwick, Robert, 149
Wasco, David, 405, 445
Washburn, Derick, 364
Washington, Denzell, 379, 421-22, *421*, 437, *437*
Watkin, Pierre, 29, 142
Watkins, Michael, 441
Watling, Jack, 192
Watchman 47 (novel), 227
Watson, Minor, 37, 110
Watts, Naomi, 427, *427*
Watts, William E., 204
Waxman, Franz, 87, 89, 127, 145, 204, 215, 229, 232, 288, 290, 308, 315
Waxman, Philip A., 44
Wayne, David, 184, *184*
Weatherwax, Paul, 35, 199, 235, 336
Weaver, Dennis, 277, 305

The Stars of "The 3rd Man" in a NEW exciting adventure! JOSEPH COTTEN and VALLI in WALK SOFTLY STRANGER

Web of the City see *Sleeping City, The*

Webb, Clifton, 87, 177, 291

Webb, George C., 420

Webb, J. Watson, Jr., 62, 87, 170, 181

Webb, Jack, 29, 87, 127, 288

Webb, James R., 64, 148, 336, 367

Webb, Richard (Dick), 38, 147, 164, 205, 220

Webb, Roy, 30, 51, 71, 74, 79, 107, 114, 159, 180, 195, 216, 220, 258, 260, 275, 276, 283, 297, 309, 321, 324, 327, 334

Webster, Ferris, 198, 311

Webster, Frank, 24

Webster, Paul, 215

Weidman, Jerome, 84, 139

Weidmann, Don, 362

Weil, Richard, 119

Weir, Peter, 466

Weisbart, David, 72, 88, 189, 191, 295

Weisberg, Rochelle, 427

Weinstein, Bob, 451

Weinstein, Harvey, 451

Weld, Tuesday, 442, *442*, 456, 465

Weldon, Joan, 295

Welles, Mel, 40

Welles, Orson, 9, 159, 173-74, 192, *192*, 282-83, *283*, 305-06, *305*

Wellman, Harold, 161, 194

Wellman, William, 221-22

Wells, Alan, 189

Wells, George, 224

Welsch, Howard, 138, 339

Wendell, Howard, 27

Wenders, Wim, 393

Wendkos, Paul, 60

Werker, Alfred, 127, 248, 265

West, Lillian, 321

West, Nathanael, 283

Westcombe, Roger, 8, 70-71, 82-83, 119, 208-09, 295, 331-32

Westcott, Helen, 179

Westlake, Donald E., 390, 438-40, 454

Westrate, Edwin V., 266

Wexlar, Haskell, 428

Wexley, John, 69, 74, 181

Weyl, Carl Jules, 45

Whalley(-Kilmer), Joanne, 407, *407*

Wheeler, John W., 402

Wheeler, Lyle, 62, 81, 91, 107, 125, 138-39, 141, 170, 177-78, 188, 203, 208, 210, 223, 227, 244, 252, 265, 285, 299-300, 317, 328, 330

Whelan, Arleen, 242

Whelan, Michael, 50

When Strangers Marry, 321

Where Danger Lives, 20, 321-28, *321-27*

Where the Sidewalk Ends, 328-39, *329*

While the City Sleeps, 329-30, *329*

Whip Hand, The, 147

Whipper, Leigh, 221, *222*

Whirlpool, 330-31, *330*

Whispering City, 331

Whispering Footsteps, 331-32

Whistle Stop, 332-33, *332*

Whitaker, Forest, 380, 406, 444

White, Cary, 399

White, David, 290

White, Dennis L., 6, 36-37, 143-44, 190-91, 240-41

White, Ethel Lina, 275

White, George, 201, 226, 233

White, Jacqueline, 79, 201

White, Jesse, 128, 335

White Heat, 17, 333, *333*

White, Lester H., 238

White, Lionel, 166, 425-26

White, Merrill, 246, 279

White Rose for Julie see *Where Danger Lives*

White, Sammy, 261

Whitefield, Raoul, 131

Whitehead, O.Z., 35, 252

Whiting, Barbara, 35

Whiting, Napolean, *56*

Whitmore, James, 30, 295-96, 310, 420, 454

Whitney, John, 61

Whitney, Peter, 40

Whittredge, J.R., 180

Whitty, Dame May, 116, 197, 290

Who'll Stop the Rain, 465-66

Whorf, Richard, 68

Whytock, Grant, 202

Wicked Woman, 333-34

Widmark, Richard, 170-71, *170*, 204, *204*, 223, 227, *227*, 245, 252, 285-86, *285*, 351, 368, 420, 432

Wiesenthal, Sam, 80, 258

Wigton, Anne, 119, 280

Wilbur, Crane, 64, 127, 147, 226

Wilcox, Frank, 72-73

Wilcox, Shannon, 364

Wild Calendar (novel), 65

Wild, Harry J., 47, 74, 114, 133, 154, 176, 185, 195, 214, 228, 297, 302, 320, 338

Wilde, Cornel, 39, *39*, 130, 178, 252, 266, 277-78, *277*

Wilde, Hagar, 120

Wilder, Billy, 24-25, 99-101, 288

Wilder, Thornton, 262

Wilder, W. Lee, 119, 234, 280

Wiles, Gordon, 114-15, 122, 312

Wilhelm, Hans, 235

Wilhoite, Kathleen, 426

Willeford, Charles, 423

Willes, Jean, 151

William, Warren, 109

Williams, Adam, 40, 115, 335

Williams, Ben Ames, 178, 281-82

Williams, Bill, 72, 92

Williams, Billy Dee, 385

Williams, Bob, 185

Williams, Cara, 55, 172

Williams, Charles, 399

Williams, Chili, 244

Williams, Christopher, 430

Williams, Cindy, 370

Williams, Clarence, III, 377

Williams, Cynda, 435, *436*

Williams, Elmo, 54, 112, 214, 297

Williams, Emlyn, 254-55

Williams, Frances, 245

Williams, James, 35

Williams, John, 416

Williams, Kimberly, 450

Williams, Mack, 307

Williams, Michelle, 376, *376*

Williams, Rhys, 78, *79*, 98, 156, 171, 188, 193, 210, 275, 281

Williams, Robin, 404, *404*

Williams, Sumner, 218

Williams, Tony, 9, 359-60, 375-76, 396-97, 411-13, 422-23, 461-62

Williams, Treat, 428, 457

Williams, Vanessa, 430

Williams, Warren, 279-80

Williamson, Fred, 396

Williamson, Nicol, 360

Willis, Bruce, 451-52, *451*

Willis, Gordon, 381, 411

Wills, Chill, 71, 178

Wills, J. Elder, 295

Wilson, Carey, 233

Wilson, Don, 67, 203

Wilson, Dooley, 172

Wilson, Frank J., 310

Wilson, Michael, 229

Wilson, Mitchell, 338

Wilson, Scott, 406

Wimble, Chris, 372

Wincott, Michael, 445

Wind Across the Everglades, 224

Window, The, 334-35, *334*

Windsor, Marie, 71, 112, 128, 166, *166*, 201-02, 271, 438

Windust, Bretaigne, 104

Winfield, Paul, 400, 425

Winger, Debra, 360, *360*, 425

Winkle, Irwin, 431, 454, 458

Winkler, Mel, 379

Winner, Michael, 375

Winston, Sam, 263

Winter, Keith, 278

Winters, Ralph E., 116, 438

Winters, Roland, 35, 73, 81

Winters, Shelley, 40, 81, 101, 105, 127, *127*, 143, 158-59, 207, 217, 229, *229*, 241, 393

Wisberg, Aubrey, 105, 194, 271

Wise, Robert, 51, 56-57, 65, 91, 107, 141, 217, 260-61

Wiseman, Joseph, 96, 115

Withers, Googie, 204

Withers, Grant, 49, 137

Withers, Isabel, 232

Witherspoon, Reese, 384-85, 460

Without Warning, 335

Witness, 350, 466-67, *466*

Witness to *Murder*, 335-36, *335*

Witnesses, The (novel), 356

Wilt, Paul Junger, 404

Wolcott, Charles, 161

Wolf, Marion, 82

Wolfe, David, 29, 310

Wolfe, lan, 218, 296

Wolfe, Robert, 389

Wolfurt, Ira, 112

Wolski, Dariusz, 373, 445

Woman in Hiding, 336, *336*

Woman in Red, The (novel), 196

Woman in Red, The see *My Name is Julia Ross*

Woman in the Window, The, 336-37, *337*

Woman on Pier 13, The, 337-38, *338*

Woman on the Beach, The 338-39, *338*

Woman on the Run, 339-40, *339*

Wonacott, Edna Mae, 262

Wong, Anna May, 149

Wong, Russell, 430

Wood, Elijah, 452

Wood, Natalie, 80

Wood, Robin, 8, 242-44

Wood, Sam, 153

Wood, Truman K., 171

Woodbridge, Pamela, 409

Woode, Margo, 273

Woodell, Barbara, 113

Wooden, Christopher

Woods, Donald, 111

Woods, James, 351-52, 356-57, *357*, 371, 390, 432

Woodward, Joanne, 166, *167*, 381

Woodward, Morgan, 408, *408*

Woodworth, Marjorie, St.

Wooley, Sheb, 156

Woolrich, Cornell, 48, 66-67, 92, 107, 109, 121, 147-48, 205-06, 209-10, 212, 225-26, 249, 284-85, 334, 436

World for Ransom, 340-41, *340*

Wormser, Richard, 76

Wozencraft, Kim, 446

Wrather, Jack, 121, 131

Wray, Fay, 75

Wray, Richard G., 281

Wright (Penn), Robin, 454, *454*

Wright, Teresa, 236, *237*, 262

Wright, Thomas Lee, 430

Wright, Will, 25, 156, 161, 176, 203, 278, 296

Wright, William (actor), 105, 149

Wright, William H., 25, 201, 225

Wrong Man, The, 341-42, *341-42*

Wurtzel, Sol M., 32

Wurtzel, Stuart, 445

Wyatt, Jane, 55, 138, 189, *189*, 228-29

Wycherly, Margaret, 154, 33

Wyle; Robert, 96

Wyler, William, 94, 96-97

Wynn, Keenan, 305, 440, 465

Wynn, Tracy Keenan, 381

Wynter, Dana, 151, *152*

Yamaguchi, Shirley, 138

Yates, Herbert J., 71, 128, 137

Yates, Peter, 387

Ybarra, Alfred, 219

Year of the Dragon

Yellen, Peter, 427

Yerge, Oscar, 121

Yerkovich, Anthony, 424

Yirk, Mark-Lee, 159

Yoakam, Dwight, 444

Yordan, Philip, 39, 66, 96-97, 104, 126-27, 139, 156-57, 247, 289, 321, 332

York, Jeff, 109, 233

Yoshinaga, George, 76

You Only Live Once, 20, 42-43, *43*

You Were There (novel), 311

Young, Bruce A., 355, 361

Young, Christopher, 429

Young, Clifton, 89

Young, Collier, 25, 35, 47-48, 134-35, 235

Young, Gig, 71, 94

Young, Jerry S., 231

Young, Karen, 372

Young, Loretta, 23, 66, 282, *283*

Young, Nedrick (Ned), 76, 93, 122, 176

Young, Robert, 79, *79*, 258-59, *259*, 297-98

Young, Sean, *350*, 360, 410, 419, *419*, 433

Young, Victor, 23, 29, 38, 52, 61, 68, 110, 118, 122, 146, 156, 205-06, 272

Young, William Allen, 405

Youngstein, Max E., 425

Your Red Wagon see *They Live by Night*

Yulin, Harris, 432

Zacapa, Daniel, 448

Zachmanoglou, Nike, 427

Zaguar, Luis, 467

Zane, Lisa, 353

Zanetti, Eugenio, 452

Zangwill, Israel, 316

Zanuck, Darryl E., 204-205, 210-11

Zanuck, Lili Fini, 428, 446

Zanuck, Richard D., 428, 446

Zavian, Mary, 82

Zbyszko, Stanislaus, 204

Zea, Kristi, 450

Zeisle Alfred, 109

Zellweger, Renee, 376

Zerbe, Anthony, 383, 465

Ziegler, William, 103, 275, 284, 442

Zigler, Scott, 400

Zimbalist, Efrem Jr., 139

Zimbalist, Sam, 267

Zimm, Maurice, 25

Zimmer, Hans, 359, 441, 459

Zimmer, Kim, 362

Zimmerman, Herman F., 359

Zinneman, Jerry, 168

Zinnemann, Fred, 25-26

Ziskin, Laura, 373, 433

Zodiac, The (2007), 467-68, *467*

Zodiac (2007), 467-68, *468*

Zodiac Unmasked (book), 468

Zola, Emile, 141

Zsigmond, Vilmos, 358, 416, 461-62

Zuberano, Maurice, 65

Zucco, George, 193

Zuckerman, George, 55, 211, 293, 306, 310, 331

Zuckerman, Lauren, 378, 455

Zugsmith, Albert, 33, 293, 305

Zwerling, Darrell, 369

6-11